`D1105864`

McGraw-Hill LearnSmart Student Quick Tips and FAQs

Use this *McGraw-Hill LearnSmart Student Quick Tips and FAQs* to get more out of this learning tool. Remember, LearnSmart is an adaptive learning system designed to help students learn faster, study more efficiently, and retain more knowledge for greater success.

Responding to a LearnSmart Assignment

TIP: Make an honest attempt to assess your confidence level on each probe. Doing so allows LearnSmart to more accurately direct you to the materials you need to study.

1) Click LearnSmart Assignment Title denoted by 🧠 icon.

2) Click on a chapter module.

3) Read the probe & click your level of confidence in knowing the correct answer.

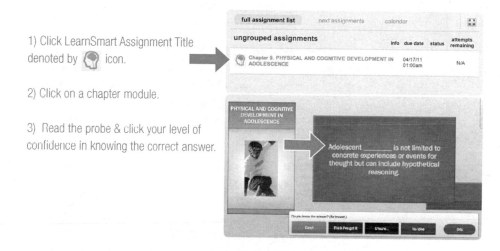

Help Yourself Succeed

TIP: We recommend completing all passive learning activities before you work on LearnSmart – such as reading the chapter, watching animations and videos available in Connect, etc.

Self-Assess

TIP: Before answering each question, click on the most appropriate confidence level to ensure you receive the most efficient learning experience.

Take a Break!

TIP: Use Time-Out! readings to review topics you are struggling to learn.

Refresh Your Memory

TIP: Return to your completed assignments to rework material and refresh your memory before quizzes and tests. Don't be alarmed if you have forgotten some things – it's natural when learning a new subject!

Share Your Feedback

TIP: Click the Challenge Answer button if you feel the content is incorrect or unclear.

Answers to Frequently Asked Questions (FAQs)

How is the percentage for each module calculated?

The percentage indicates the number of correctly answered questions within the module. In other words, the percentage indicates how much of the module you have learned so far. To learn more about your progress and overall status, click the 'Debriefing' button at the top of the screen.

How is my High Score calculated?

The amount of points you earn depends on how you assess your ability to answer a question. For instance, if you click 'Easy' and answer the question correctly, you will get the greatest amount of points. If you answer correctly after selecting one of the other buttons – 'Think I've got it,' 'Unsure,' and 'No idea' – you will also earn points. However, you will receive fewer points for the items you do not believe you know as well. If you select 'Unsure' and get the answer correct, you will get fewer points than if you selected 'Easy' or 'Think I've got it.'

The same applies if you get an answer incorrect. If you do not know the answer after clicking 'Easy,' points will be deducted from your score. Fewer points are deducted if you select 'Think I've got it' or 'Unsure,' and get the answer incorrect. If you click 'Unsure,' points will not be deducted even if you get the question wrong.

Spelling errors, nearly correct answers or partially correct answers also affect your score.

Of course, you can increase your score by going through the same module multiple times, rating your answers as honestly as possible. In essence, the more you learn, the better the score.

Why does the system repeat questions I have already answered?

If you answer a question incorrectly, it will be repeated later in the same session to give you a chance to learn. It might not be the exact same question, but rather a variant that represents the same learning objective. The system will adjust the difficulty of the questions according to your performance. In addition to this, the system will present the same questions the next day to help you remember the material over time. (For more information, see 'Why does it make me start all over on the module when I come back?')

The first day, you might see a 'multiple-choice question about a concept,' and the next day, a 'fill-in-the-blank' for the same concept to make it more difficult. This will assess whether you really know the subject. It closely monitors the exact questions you have been exposed to before, and will vary this in an attempt to match and improve your knowledge level.

Why am I only working on part of a module each day?

Instead of asking you to go through, say, 300 questions in one session, LearnSmart distributes the items and the review of these items over a period of time. Spreading the learning events over multiple sessions increases the likelihood of memory retention. If you are pressed for time, though, you can work ahead and do more questions one day, and LearnSmart will automatically adapt.

Why does it make me start the module again when I come back?

Research tells us frequency increases memory recall. The module seems to start over when logging in the next day in order to frequently assess your mastery of the material. So if you complete 100 flashcards the first day, you can expect about 25 of those to be repeated each of the next four days. If you answer all of these correctly, around 7 will be repeated each session for the next 14 days, and so on. The program automatically calculates the appropriate repetition interval for each student based on your individual 'forget curve' that is tracked in detail. The 'Learning Plan' feature in the LearnSmart Debriefing screen provides a daily estimate of how much you need to do on each module. This plan also adjusts if you skip a day or two or work ahead.

Why is it so strict about spelling?

If you make a small spelling error, the program will accept your answer. If you make a larger mistake, you will be prompted about the same topic again with a chance to improve your score (and your spelling). You might not see the exact same question, but the program allows another opportunity to demonstrate your knowledge.

'Fill-in-the-blank' questions are often the most difficult questions because they rely on active recall, rather than recognition. Once you master the 'fill-in-the-blank' questions, you are really learning!

Why do I need to click the Confidence buttons?

The 'Confidence' buttons are the self-assessment buttons that affect the high score as described above. In addition, rating your confidence also affects the schedule of questions. Simply put, this information is used to determine your awareness of your own knowledge level. It is applied to adjust your learning path. You can use the Metacognitive Skills report in the LearnSmart Debriefing to learn more about this. Click 'Debriefing' at the top of the screen to get access to this information.

Why are there so many questions?

This program is not just a testing system, but a *learning system*. The modules assess most of the material in the book. As you progress through the modules, you will learn most of the material assigned by your instructor for this course. LearnSmart presents the core or most critical material first. If you do not have time to complete the entire module, just work until you are out of time, and you can be assured your have tackled the most important items.

When you return, the system will recall the material for which you have demonstrated mastery and provide opportunities to practice material that still requires review. Again, LearnSmart presents the most important items first, which may include revisiting previous items or new material.

When the deadline has passed, why do I still have to work on the module?

The program prompts you to keep reviewing the same module to ensure recall and true mastery. Use the Learning Plan feature in the LearnSmart Debriefing screen to see the estimated time required for you to retain the information before the deadline approaches. You can also use the 'Status' feature in the 'Debriefing' screen for an estimate of when you are likely to forget what you have learned. If you follow the schedule proposed by the system, the workload for review will be minimal.

How can I change my name in the High Score list?

Just click your name within the list. You can change your name (to an alias) or become anonymous.

Should I continue to practice after my exam?

If you want to commit your new knowledge to long-term memory, we recommend that you keep working the modules even after the deadline. You have the option of setting a new deadline for your own purposes (e.g. 6 months in the future) as a target. The system will continuously monitor what you know and what you tend to forget. It will not prompt you to work on things you most likely remember, minimizing your workload. This will be the optimal way to learn the content and remember it.

What happens when I provide feedback?

We greatly appreciate your feedback. We do read it and use it to improve LearnSmart so that it better serves students like you. In cases where you have questions about the system, we will try to answer them. If you contest an answer or report incorrect markings, we will investigate and update the modules accordingly.

Need More Help with LearnSmart Assignments?

CONTACT US ONLINE:

Visit us at:

www.mhhe.com/learnsmart/support.html

Browse our most up-to-date support materials including tutorial videos and searchable knowledge base. If you cannot find an answer to your question, click on Contact Us to send us an email.

GIVE US A CALL

Call us at:

1-800-331-5094

Our live support is available:
Mon-Thurs:	8 am – 11 pm CT
Friday:	8 am – 6 pm CT
Sunday:	6 pm – 11 pm CT

TENTH EDITION

Essentials of Understanding Psychology

Robert S. Feldman
University of Massachusetts Amherst

Essentials of Understanding Psychology
Customized Edition of Orange Coast College

Mc Graw Hill Education

2 3 4 5 6 7 8 9 10 DIG/DIG 15 14 13

ISBN-13: 978-1-25-911367-3
ISBN-10: 1-25-911367-1

Learning Solutions Consultant: Kimberly Scheyving
Project Manager: Kathy Phelan
Cover Photo Credits: © Julien Tromeur

Dedication

To

Jon, Leigh, Alex, Miles, Josh, Julie,
Sarah, and Kathy

About the Author

ROBERT S. FELDMAN is Professor of Psychology and Dean of the College of Social and Behavioral Sciences at the University of Massachusetts Amherst. A recipient of the College Distinguished Teacher Award, he teaches psychology classes ranging in size from 15 to nearly 500 students. During the course of more than two decades as a college instructor, he has taught undergraduate and graduate courses at Mount Holyoke College, Wesleyan University, and Virginia Commonwealth University in addition to the University of Massachusetts.

Professor Feldman, who initiated the Minority Mentoring Program at the University of Massachusetts, also has served as a Hewlett Teaching Fellow and Senior Online Teaching Fellow. He initiated distance-learning courses in psychology at the University of Massachusetts.

A Fellow of the American Psychological Association and the Association for Psychological Science, Professor Feldman received a BA with High Honors from Wesleyan University and an MS and PhD from the University of Wisconsin-Madison. He is a winner of a Fulbright Senior Research Scholar and Lecturer Award and the Distinguished Alumnus Award from Wesleyan. He is on the Board of the Federation of Associations in Behavioral and Brain Sciences (FABBS) and the president-elect of the FABBS Foundation, which advocates for the field of psychology.

He has written and edited more than 150 books, book chapters, and scientific articles. He has edited *Development of Nonverbal Behavior in Children, Applications of Nonverbal Behavioral Theory and Research, Improving the First Year of College: Research and Practice,* and co-edited *Fundamentals of Nonverbal Behavior.* He is also author of *P.O.W.E.R. Learning: Strategies for Success in College and Life.* His textbooks, which have been used by more than 2 million students around the world, have been translated into Spanish, French, Portuguese, Dutch, German, Italian, Chinese, Korean, and Japanese. His research interests include deception and honesty in everyday life, work that he described in *The Liar in Your Life,* a trade book published in 2009. His research has been supported by grants from the National Institute of Mental Health and the National Institute on Disabilities and Rehabilitation Research.

Professor Feldman loves music, is an enthusiastic pianist, and enjoys cooking and traveling. He has three children and two young grandsons. He and his wife, a psychologist, live in western Massachusetts in a home overlooking the Holyoke mountain range.

Brief Contents

Preface xxiii

CHAPTER 1 Introduction to Psychology 2
MODULE 1   Psychologists at Work 5
MODULE 2   A Science Evolves: The Past, the Present, and the Future 14
MODULE 3   Research in Psychology 26
MODULE 4   Critical Research Issues 40

CHAPTER 2 Neuroscience and Behavior 48
MODULE 5   Neurons: The Basic Elements of Behavior 51
MODULE 6   The Nervous System and the Endocrine System: Communicating Within the Body 60
MODULE 7   The Brain 68

CHAPTER 3 Sensation and Perception 86
MODULE 8   Sensing the World Around Us 89
MODULE 9   Vision: Shedding Light on the Eye 94
MODULE 10   Hearing and the Other Senses 104
MODULE 11   Perceptual Organization: Constructing Our View of the World 116

CHAPTER 4 States of Consciousness 130
MODULE 12   Sleep and Dreams 133
MODULE 14   Drug Use: The Highs and Lows of Consciousness 152

CHAPTER 5

Learning 166

MODULE 15   Classical Conditioning 169

MODULE 16   Operant Conditioning 177

MODULE 17   Cognitive Approaches to Learning 192

CHAPTER 6

Memory 202

MODULE 18   The Foundations of Memory 205

MODULE 19   Recalling Long-Term Memories 218

MODULE 20   Forgetting: When Memory Fails 228

CHAPTER 7

Thinking, Language, and Intelligence 238

MODULE 21   Thinking and Reasoning 241

MODULE 22   Language 257

MODULE 23   Intelligence 266

CHAPTER 8

Motivation and Emotion 286

MODULE 24   Explaining Motivation 289

MODULE 25   Human Needs and Motivation: Eat, Drink, and Be Daring 296

MODULE 26   Understanding Emotional Experiences 313

CHAPTER 9

Development 326

MODULE 27   Nature and Nurture: The Enduring Developmental Issue 329

MODULE 28   Infancy and Childhood 340

MODULE 29   Adolescence: Becoming an Adult 358

MODULE 30   Adulthood 368

CHAPTER 10

Personality 382

MODULE 31   Psychodynamic Approaches to Personality 385

MODULE 32   Trait, Learning, Biological and Evolutionary, and Humanistic Approaches to Personality 395

MODULE 33   Assessing Personality: Determining What Makes Us Distinctive 408

CHAPTER 11 Health Psychology: Stress, Coping, and Well-Being 418

MODULE 34 Stress and Coping 421

MODULE 35 Psychological Aspects of Illness and Well-Being 434

CHAPTER 12 Psychological Disorders 450

MODULE 37 Normal Versus Abnormal: Making the Distinction 453

MODULE 38 The Major Psychological Disorders 463

MODULE 39 Psychological Disorders in Perspective 483

CHAPTER 13 Treatment of Psychological Disorders 492

MODULE 40 Psychotherapy: Psychodynamic, Behavioral, and Cognitive Approaches to Treatment 495

MODULE 41 Psychotherapy: Humanistic, Interpersonal, and Group Approaches to Treatment 507

MODULE 42 Biomedical Therapy: Biological Approaches to Treatment 515

CHAPTER 14 Social Psychology 526

MODULE 43 Attitudes and Social Cognition 529

MODULE 44 Social Influence and Groups 541

MODULE 45 Prejudice and Discrimination 549

MODULE 46 Positive and Negative Social Behavior 555

Glossary G

References R-1

Credits C-1

Name Index I-1

Subject Index I-13

Contents

Preface xxiii
Making the Grade xxxvi

CHAPTER 1

Introduction to Psychology 2

MODULE 1

Psychologists at Work 5

The Subfields of Psychology: Psychology's Family Tree 6
Working at Psychology 9

PSYCHWORK: Licensed Social Worker 10

MODULE 2

A Science Evolves: The Past, the Present, and the Future 14

The Roots of Psychology 14
Today's Perspectives 16

APPLYING PSYCHOLOGY IN THE 21ST CENTURY: Psychology Matters 20
Psychology's Key Issues and Controversies 21

NEUROSCIENCE IN YOUR LIFE: Reading the Movies in Your Mind 23
Psychology's Future 23

MODULE 3

Research in Psychology 26

The Scientific Method 26
Psychological Research 28
Descriptive Research 29
Experimental Research 32

MODULE 4

Critical Research Issues 40

The Ethics of Research 40

EXPLORING DIVERSITY: Choosing Participants Who Represent the Scope of Human Behavior 41

NEUROSCIENCE IN YOUR LIFE: The Importance of Using Representative Participants 42

Should Animals Be Used in Research? 42

Threats to Experimental Validity: Avoiding Experimental Bias 43

BECOMING AN INFORMED CONSUMER OF PSYCHOLOGY: Thinking Critically About Research 44

CHAPTER 2

Neuroscience and Behavior 48

MODULE 5

Neurons: The Basic Elements of Behavior 51

The Structure of the Neuron 51

How Neurons Fire 52

Where Neurons Meet: Bridging the Gap 55

Neurotransmitters: Multitalented Chemical Couriers 56

MODULE 6

The Nervous System and the Endocrine System: Communicating Within the Body 60

The Nervous System: Linking Neurons 60

The Evolutionary Foundations of the Nervous System 63

The Endocrine System: Of Chemicals and Glands 64

MODULE 7

The Brain 68

Studying the Brain's Structure and Functions: Spying on the Brain 68

The Central Core: Our "Old Brain" 70

APPLYING PSYCHOLOGY IN THE 21ST CENTURY: Your Wish Is Its Command: Directing Computers with Your Brain 71

The Limbic System: Beyond the Central Core 72

The Cerebral Cortex: Our "New Brain" 73

PSYCHWORK: Rehabilitation Counselor 75

Neuroplasticity and the Brain 77

NEUROSCIENCE IN YOUR LIFE: The Plastic Brain 78

The Specialization of the Hemispheres: Two Brains or One? 78

EXPLORING DIVERSITY: Human Diversity and the Brain 79

The Split Brain: Exploring the Two Hemispheres 80

BECOMING AN INFORMED CONSUMER OF PSYCHOLOGY: Learning to Control Your Heart—and Mind—Through Biofeedback 81

CHAPTER 3

Sensation and Perception 86

MODULE 8

Sensing the World Around Us 89

Absolute Thresholds: Detecting What's Out There 90
Difference Thresholds: Noticing Distinctions Between Stimuli 91
Sensory Adaptation: Turning Down Our Responses 92

MODULE 9

Vision: Shedding Light on the Eye 94

Illuminating the Structure of the Eye 95

NEUROSCIENCE IN YOUR LIFE: Seeing Vision in the Brain 100
Color Vision and Color Blindness: The 7-Million-Color Spectrum 100

MODULE 10

Hearing and the Other Senses 104

Sensing Sound 104
Smell and Taste 108
The Skin Senses: Touch, Pressure, Temperature, and Pain 110

BECOMING AN INFORMED CONSUMER OF PSYCHOLOGY: Managing Pain 113
How Our Senses Interact 113

MODULE 11

Perceptual Organization: Constructing Our View of the World 116

The Gestalt Laws of Organization 116
Top-Down and Bottom-Up Processing 117
Depth Perception: Translating 2-D to 3-D 119
Perceptual Constancy 120
Motion Perception: As the World Turns 121

APPLYING PSYCHOLOGY IN THE 21ST CENTURY: Do People Have an Internal Sense of Direction? 122
Perceptual Illusions: The Deceptions of Perceptions 122

EXPLORING DIVERSITY: Culture and Perception 124

CHAPTER 4

States of Consciousness 130

MODULE 12

Sleep and Dreams 133

The Stages of Sleep 133
REM Sleep: The Paradox of Sleep 135
Why Do We Sleep, and How Much Sleep Is Necessary? 136
The Function and Meaning of Dreaming 137

APPLYING PSYCHOLOGY IN THE 21ST CENTURY: Dreams of Failure 138

Sleep Disturbances: Slumbering Problems 141

PSYCHWORK: Sleep Technologist 142

Circadian Rhythms: Life Cycles 143

Daydreams: Dreams Without Sleep 144

BECOMING AN INFORMED CONSUMER OF PSYCHOLOGY: Sleeping Better 145

MODULE 14

Drug Use: The Highs and Lows of Consciousness 152

Stimulants: Drug Highs 154

Depressants: Drug Lows 157

Narcotics: Relieving Pain and Anxiety 160

Hallucinogens: Psychedelic Drugs 161

BECOMING AN INFORMED CONSUMER OF PSYCHOLOGY: Identifying Drug and Alcohol Problems 162

CHAPTER 5

Learning 166

MODULE 15

Classical Conditioning 169

The Basics of Classical Conditioning 170

Applying Conditioning Principles to Human Behavior 172

Extinction 173

Generalization and Discrimination 174

Beyond Traditional Classical Conditioning: Challenging Basic Assumptions 174

MODULE 16

Operant Conditioning 177

Thorndike's Law of Effect 177

The Basics of Operant Conditioning 178

APPLYING PSYCHOLOGY IN THE 21ST CENTURY: Using Operant Conditioning Principles to Save Lives 185

PSYCHWORK: Seeing Eye Guide Dog Trainer 186

BECOMING AN INFORMED CONSUMER OF PSYCHOLOGY: Using Behavior Analysis and Behavior Modification 188

MODULE 17

Cognitive Approaches to Learning 192

Latent Learning 192

Observational Learning: Learning Through Imitation 194

NEUROSCIENCE IN YOUR LIFE: Learning Through Imitation 195

EXPLORING DIVERSITY: Does Culture Influence How We Learn? 197

CHAPTER 6

Memory 202

MODULE 18

The Foundations of Memory 205

Sensory Memory 206

Short-Term Memory 207

Working Memory 209

Long-Term Memory 211

NEUROSCIENCE IN YOUR LIFE: Experience, Memory, and the Brain 215

APPLYING PSYCHOLOGY IN THE 21ST CENTURY: Memory from a Bottle 216

MODULE 19

Recalling Long-Term Memories 218

Retrieval Cues 218

Levels of Processing 219

Explicit and Implicit Memory 220

Flashbulb Memories 221

Constructive Processes in Memory: Rebuilding the Past 222

EXPLORING DIVERSITY: Are There Cross-Cultural Differences in Memory? 225

MODULE 20

Forgetting: When Memory Fails 228

Why We Forget 229

Proactive and Retroactive Interference: The Before and After of Forgetting 230

Memory Dysfunctions: Afflictions of Forgetting 232

NEUROSCIENCE IN YOUR LIFE: Alzheimer's Disease and Brain Deterioration 233

BECOMING AN INFORMED CONSUMER OF PSYCHOLOGY: Improving Your Memory 233

CHAPTER 7

Thinking, Language, and Intelligence 238

MODULE 21

Thinking and Reasoning 241

Mental Images: Examining the Mind's Eye 241

Concepts: Categorizing the World 242

Algorithms and Heuristics 243

APPLYING PSYCHOLOGY IN THE 21ST CENTURY: I'll take "Artificial Intelligence" for $1,000, Alex. 224

Solving Problems 245

Creativity and Problem Solving 253

BECOMING AN INFORMED CONSUMER OF PSYCHOLOGY: Thinking Critically and Creatively 255

MODULE 22

Language 257

Grammar: Language's Language 257

Language Development: Developing a Way with Words 258

Understanding Language Acquisition: Identifying the Roots of Language 259

The Influence of Language on Thinking: Do Eskimos Have More Words for Snow Than Texans Do? 261

Do Animals Use Language? 262

EXPLORING DIVERSITY: Teaching with Linguistic Variety: Bilingual Education 263

NEUROSCIENCE IN YOUR LIFE: Bilingualism and the Brain 264

MODULE 23

Intelligence 266

Theories of Intelligence: Are There Different Kinds of Intelligence? 267

Assessing Intelligence 272

Variations in Intellectual Ability 277

PSYCHWORK: Director of Special Education 279

Group Differences in Intelligence: Genetic and Environmental Determinants 280

EXPLORING DIVERSITY: The Relative Influence of Genetics and Environment: Nature, Nurture, and IQ 280

CHAPTER 8

Motivation and Emotion 286

MODULE 24

Explaining Motivation 289

Instinct Approaches: Born to Be Motivated 289

Drive-Reduction Approaches: Satisfying Our Needs 290

Arousal Approaches: Beyond Drive Reduction 291

Incentive Approaches: Motivation's Pull 291

Cognitive Approaches: The Thoughts Behind Motivation 291

Maslow's Hierarchy: Ordering Motivational Needs 293

Applying the Different Approaches to Motivation 294

MODULE 25

Human Needs and Motivation: Eat, Drink, and Be Daring 296

The Motivation Behind Hunger and Eating 296

APPLYING PSYCHOLOGY IN THE 21ST CENTURY: The Rising Stigma of Obesity 298

PSYCHWORK: Nutritionist 300

NEUROSCIENCE IN YOUR LIFE: When Regulation of Eating Behavior Goes Wrong—Bulimia 302

BECOMING AN INFORMED CONSUMER OF PSYCHOLOGY: Dieting and Losing Weight Successfully 303

Sexual Motivation 304

The Needs for Achievement, Affiliation, and Power 309

MODULE 26

Understanding Emotional Experiences 313

The Functions of Emotions 314

Determining the Range of Emotions: Labeling Our Feelings 314

The Roots of Emotions 315

EXPLORING DIVERSITY: Do People in All Cultures Express Emotion Similarly? 320

CHAPTER 9

Development 326

MODULE 27

Nature and Nurture: The Enduring Developmental Issue 329

Determining the Relative Influence of Nature and Nurture 331

Developmental Research Techniques 331

Prenatal Development: Conception to Birth 332

APPLYING PSYCHOLOGY IN THE 21ST CENTURY: Gene Therapy and the Coming Medical Revolution 334

MODULE 28

Infancy and Childhood 340

The Extraordinary Newborn 340

NEUROSCIENCE IN YOUR LIFE: Emotion Recognition in Infancy 343

The Growing Child: Infancy Through Middle Childhood 344

PSYCHWORK: Child Protection Caseworker 350

MODULE 29

Adolescence: Becoming an Adult 358

Physical Development: The Changing Adolescent 358

Moral and Cognitive Development: Distinguishing Right from Wrong 360

Social Development: Finding One's Self in a Social World 362

EXPLORING DIVERSITY: Rites of Passage: Coming of Age Around the World 366

MODULE 30   Adulthood 368

Physical Development: The Peak of Health 369
Social Development: Working at Life 370
Marriage, Children, and Divorce: Family Ties 371
Later Years of Life: Growing Old 373

BECOMING AN INFORMED CONSUMER OF PSYCHOLOGY: Adjusting to Death 377

CHAPTER 10
Personality 382

MODULE 31   Psychodynamic Approaches to Personality 385

Freud's Psychoanalytic Theory: Mapping the Unconscious Mind 385
The Neo-Freudian Psychoanalysts: Building on Freud 391

MODULE 32   Trait, Learning, Biological and Evolutionary, and Humanistic Approaches to Personality 395

Trait Approaches: Placing Labels on Personality 395

APPLYING PSYCHOLOGY IN THE 21ST CENTURY: The Self-Obsessed Generation? 398
Learning Approaches: We Are What We've Learned 398
Biological and Evolutionary Approaches: Are We Born with Personality? 401

NEUROSCIENCE IN YOUR LIFE: Wired to Take Risks—The Biological Underpinnings of Personality 404
Humanistic Approaches: The Uniqueness of You 404
Comparing Approaches to Personality 406

MODULE 33   Assessing Personality: Determining What Makes Us Distinctive 408

EXPLORING DIVERSITY: Should Race and Ethnicity Be Used to Establish Norms? 409
Self-Report Measures of Personality 410
Projective Methods 412
Behavioral Assessment 413

PSYCHWORK: Human Resources Manager 414

BECOMING AN INFORMED CONSUMER OF PSYCHOLOGY: Assessing Personality Assessments 414

CHAPTER 11

Health Psychology: Stress, Coping, and Well-Being 418

MODULE 34

Stress and Coping 421

Stress: Reacting to Threat and Challenge 421
The High Cost of Stress 423
Coping with Stress 428

APPLYING PSYCHOLOGY IN THE 21ST CENTURY: What Doesn't Kill You Really Does Make You Stronger 429

NEUROSCIENCE IN YOUR LIFE: Stress and Social Support 431

BECOMING AN INFORMED CONSUMER OF PSYCHOLOGY: Effective Coping Strategies 432

MODULE 35

Psychological Aspects of Illness and Well-Being 434

The As, Bs, and Ds of Coronary Heart Disease 434
Psychological Aspects of Cancer 435
Smoking 436

NEUROSCIENCE IN YOUR LIFE: The Addictive Pull of Smoking 437

EXPLORING DIVERSITY: Hucksters of Death: Promoting Smoking Throughout the World 439

CHAPTER 12

Psychological Disorders 450

MODULE 37

Normal Versus Abnormal: Making the Distinction 453

Defining Abnormality 453
Perspectives on Abnormality: From Superstition to Science 455
Classifying Abnormal Behavior: The ABCs of *DSM* 458

MODULE 38

The Major Psychological Disorders 463

Anxiety Disorders 463

NEUROSCIENCE IN YOUR LIFE: One Step Closer to Understanding OCD 467
Somatoform Disorders 468

Dissociative Disorders 468

Mood Disorders 470

Schizophrenia 474

NEUROSCIENCE IN YOUR LIFE: Brain Changes with Schizophrenia 477

Personality Disorders 479

Childhood Disorders 480

Other Disorders 481

MODULE 39

Psychological Disorders in Perspective 483

The Social and Cultural Context of Psychological Disorders 484

APPLYING PSYCHOLOGY IN THE 21ST CENTURY: Psychological Problems Are Increasing Among College Students 486

EXPLORING DIVERSITY: *DSM* and Culture—and the Culture of *DSM* 487

BECOMING AN INFORMED CONSUMER OF PSYCHOLOGY: Deciding When You Need Help 488

CHAPTER 13
Treatment of Psychological Disorders 492

MODULE 40

Psychotherapy: Psychodynamic, Behavioral, and Cognitive Approaches to Treatment 495

Psychodynamic Approaches to Therapy 496

Behavioral Approaches to Therapy 498

NEUROSCIENCE IN YOUR LIFE: How Behavioral Therapy Changes Your Brain 502

Cognitive Approaches to Therapy 502

NEUROSCIENCE IN YOUR LIFE: How Cognitive Behavioral Therapy Changes Your Brain 505

MODULE 41

Psychotherapy: Humanistic, Interpersonal, and Group Approaches to Treatment 507

Humanistic Therapy 507

PSYCHWORK: Case Manager and Substance Abuse Counselor 508

Interpersonal Therapy 509

Group Therapies 509

Evaluating Psychotherapy: Does Therapy Work? 510

EXPLORING DIVERSITY: Racial and Ethnic Factors in Treatment: Should Therapists Be Color Blind? 513

MODULE 42 Biomedical Therapy: Biological Approaches to Treatment 515

Drug Therapy 515

APPLYING PSYCHOLOGY IN THE 21ST CENTURY: Taking the Sting Out of Traumatic Memories 518

Electroconvulsive Therapy (ECT) 519

Psychosurgery 519

Biomedical Therapies in Perspective 520

Community Psychology: Focus on Prevention 521

BECOMING AN INFORMED CONSUMER OF PSYCHOLOGY: Choosing the Right Therapist 522

CHAPTER 14

Social Psychology 526

MODULE 43 Attitudes and Social Cognition 529

Persuasion: Changing Attitudes 529

APPLYING PSYCHOLOGY IN THE 21ST CENTURY: Advertising in the Information Age: Aiming at Moving Targets 530

PSYCHWORK: Advertising Agency Creator 532

Social Cognition: Understanding Others 534

EXPLORING DIVERSITY: Attribution Biases in a Cultural Context—How Fundamental Is the Fundamental Attribution Error? 538

MODULE 44 Social Influence and Groups 541

Conformity: Following What Others Do 541

Compliance: Submitting to Direct Social Pressure 544

Obedience: Following Direct Orders 546

MODULE 45 Prejudice and Discrimination 549

The Foundations of Prejudice 550

NEUROSCIENCE IN YOUR LIFE: The Prejudiced Brain 551

Measuring Prejudice and Discrimination: The Implicit Association Test 552

Reducing the Consequences of Prejudice and Discrimination 552

MODULE 46 Positive and Negative Social Behavior 555

Liking and Loving: Interpersonal Attraction and the Development of Relationships 555

NEUROSCIENCE IN YOUR LIFE: The Social Brain 557

Aggression and Prosocial Behavior: Hurting and Helping Others 558

Helping Others: The Brighter Side of Human Nature 561

NEUROSCIENCE IN YOUR LIFE: Moral Decisions and the Brain 563

BECOMING AN INFORMED CONSUMER OF PSYCHOLOGY: Dealing Effectively with Anger 564

Glossary G

References R-1

Credits C-1

Name Index I-1

Subject Index I-13

Preface

Students First.

If I were to use only two words to summarize my goal across the 10 editions of this book, as well as my teaching philosophy, that's what I would say. Students first. I believe that an effective textbook must be oriented to students—informing them, engaging them, and exciting them about the field of psychology and helping them connect it to their worlds.

Re-envisioning and Revolutionizing the Revision Process

Up to now, to achieve my "Students First" goal in each new edition of *Essentials of Understanding Psychology*, the revision process was generally this: Several dozen instructors who used the previous edition of the text provided reviews of that edition. In addition, experts in the field provided reviews that pointed out new material to add, as well as outdated material to remove. Using all these reviews, and feedback from my own students, I revised the text. I also added new topics, citations, and features.

For this edition, however, I had a revolutionary tool that brings this revision to a new level: Systematic and precise feedback from thousands of students. This feedback was anonymously collected from the many students who were using *Connect Psychology's Learn-Smart*, an online adaptive diagnostic program that provides students with an individualized assessment of their own progress. Because virtually every paragraph in the previous edition is tied to several questions that students answered while using *LearnSmart*, I had access to empirical data showing the specific concepts with which students had the most difficulty.

The data I received from *LearnSmart* appeared in the form of a *heat map*, which graphically illustrates "hot spots" in the text that caused students the most difficulty (see Figure 1). Using these hot spots, I then was able to refine the wording to make these areas clearer than before.

Because I had empirically based feedback at the paragraph and even sentence level, I was able to replace educated guesswork and intuition with precise knowledge as I fine-tuned the textbook.

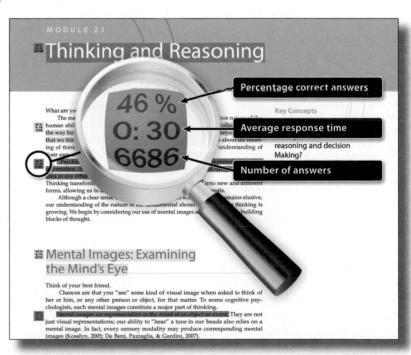

FIGURE 1 For most paragraphs in each chapter, heat maps showed if students had difficulty answering questions in *Connect Psychology's LearnSmart*. The data from these hot spots showed how many students answered the question correctly, how long the average response time was, and how many times the question was answered.

Practically, this means that students reading *Essentials of Understanding Psychology* will have an even greater opportunity to achieve success, and it brings the goal of *Students First* to a new level. This process represents nothing less than a revolution in textbook revision, and I am proud that the new edition of *Essentials of Understanding Psychology* is the first textbook to incorporate this capability.

AND THERE'S MORE . . .

In addition to benefiting from this empirically driven approach to revision, the Tenth Edition of *Essentials of Understanding Psychology* contains a significant amount of new and updated features and content. Specific areas that were updated are advances in neuroscience, the brain and behavior, cognition, emotions, and cultural approaches to psychological phenomenon including social networking technology. In addition, certain chapters were revised more extensively than others, based on expert reviews: Neuroscience and Behavior (Chapter 2), Learning (Chapter 5), Memory (Chapter 6), and Health Psychology (Chapter 11). To keep research current, hundreds of new citations have been added, and most of them refer to articles and books published since 2010.

The following sample of new and revised topics and textual changes provides a good indication of the book's currency:

Chapter 1—Introduction to Psychology
- Social media
- Economic problems, stress, and health
- Consequences of Colorado shooting attack in Batman movie theater
- Reluctance of participants to reveal true behavior in surveys
- Limitations of bystander intervention
- WEIRD acronym for participants in research

Chapter 2—Neuroscience and Behavior
- Moved behavioral genetics material to development chapter
- Updated use of hormone replacement therapy
- Dangers related to steroid use
- Interneuron functions
- Mirror neuron role in speech perception and language
- Electrocorticographic (ECoG) implants
- Sex differences in speed of development of brain
- Communication via thought
- Hemispherectomy

Chapter 3—Sensation and Perception
- Innate sense of direction
- Blindsight
- Brain activation training to reduce experience of pain
- Statistics on chronic pain sufferers
- Human tears and chemosignals
- Technology to aid the blind to see

Chapter 4—States of Consciousness
- Failure dreams
- Gender differences in dreaming
- Link between daydreams and dreams during sleep
- Legalization of marijuana in 13 states
- Medical uses of marijuana
- Insomnia and use of technologies
- Psychological dependence on social networking and e-mail

Chapter 5—Learning
- Operant conditioning approaches to increasing safety
- Behavioral approaches to rewarding drivers
- Positive outcomes of playing prosocial video games
- Social networking and violent video games
- Taste aversion
- Token systems
- Neuroscientific underpinnings of operant conditioning
- Classical conditioning and drug use
- Adaptive learning

Chapter 6—Memory
- Neural communication in Alzheimer's disease
- Hyperthymestic syndrome
- Efficacy and ethics of drugs to enhance memory
- Value of forgetting
- Adaptive nature of constructed memories

- Emotional meaning of experience and recall accuracy
- New example for episodic memory
- Refined definitions for these terms:
  - chunks
  - engram
  - flashbulb memories
  - schemas
  - decay
  - proactive interference
  - retroactive interference
  - retrograde amnesia
- Interference and eyewitness recall
- Memory aided by more extreme font size of material
- Google effect on memory
- Saying names aloud as a means to enhance memory

Chapter 7—Thinking, Language, and Intelligence
- Artificial intelligence and Watson, the computer
- Familiarity heuristic
- Combining divergent and convergent thinking in training creativity
- Linguistic-relativity hypothesis evidence
- Advantages of bilingualism in cognitive development
- Bilingualism and cognitive declines in late adulthood
- Brain processing and bilingualism
- Refined definition for these terms:
  - thinking
  - confirmation bias

- convergent and divergent thinking
- Brain processing and categorization
- Removed language acquisition device
- Refined definition of these terms:
  - fluid intelligence
  - intelligence quotient
- Relationship between use of Internet and intelligence
- New material on savant
- Replaced "mental retardation" with "intellectual disabilities"
- Refined material on heritability
- Adaptive testing criticisms

Chapter 8—Motivation and Emotion
- Self-regulation in people with bulimia
- New definition of drive-reduction theory
- Binge eating in males
- Clarified definition of need for achievement
- Obesity increases and projections
- Weight-loss strategy of getting support of others
- Wireless monitors for weight loss
- Computer facial expression recognition

Chapter 9—Development
- Cloning
- Germline therapy
- Behavioral genetics
- Emotion recognition in infancy
- Refined definition of temperament
- Clarified principle of conservation
- Clarified zone of proximal development
- Use of social media in adolescence

Chapter 10—Personality
- Changes in narcissism trait
- Refined definition and explanation of defense mechanism
- Refined term inferiority complex
- Refined description of learning approaches to personality
- Replaced definition of self-efficacy
- Refined definition of temperament
- Risk-taking behavior

Chapter 11—Health Psychology: Stress, Coping, and Well-Being
- Lingering effects of PTSD/terrorist attacks
- Adolescent smokers' brain activity
- Benefits of adversity on future coping capabilities
- Clarified psychophysiological disorders
- Creative nonadherence refined
- Redefined subjective well-being
- Literacy skills and compliance
- Biological and genetic underpinnings of resilience
- Drug compliance statistics
- Emotional timeline of 9/11
- Witnessing aggression and PTSD
- Resilience and optimism
- Training physicians in communication skills

Chapter 12—Psychological Disorders
- Clarified medical perspective
- Rising incidence of disorders in college student populations
- Refined cognitive perspective
- Clarified sociocultural perspective
- Refined definition of anxiety disorder
- Refined explanation of conversion disorder

- Clarified expressed emotion
- Clarified predisposition model of schizophrenia
- Impulsive Internet use
- Updated universality of *DSM* designations across cultures
- Anorexia in Hong Kong

Chapter 13—Treatment of Psychological Disorders
- Drug treatment to erase anxiety-provoking memories
- Treatment for depression via the web
- Therapy through teleconferencing
- Clarified what an internship is for clinical psychologists
- Redefined repression
- Clarified psychoanalysis
- Redefined dialectical behavior therapy

Chapter 14—Social Psychology
- Communication of social norms through social media
- Accessing attitude change via technology
- Using appropriate language when fighting
- Intervention to increase the social-belonging of minority students
- Refined these terms:
  - central and peripheral route processing
  - cognitive dissonance
  - attribution theory
- Moral decisions and brain activity
- Clarified social pressure
- Clarified definition of diffusion of responsibility

ENGAGING, INFORMING, AND EXCITING STUDENTS ABOUT PSYCHOLOGY

No matter what brings students into the introductory course and regardless of their initial motivation, *Essentials of Understanding Psychology*, Tenth Edition, is designed to draw students into the field and stimulate their thinking. By focusing on *students first* and connecting with them, the text promotes student success by engaging their attention and informing them about the field, which results in students learning the course content and becoming excited about the field of psychology.

Ways of Connecting with Today's Students

Today's students are as different from the learners of the last generation as today's discipline of psychology is different from the field 30 years ago. Students now learn in multiple modalities; rather than sitting down and reading traditional printed chapters in linear fashion from beginning to end, their work preferences tend to be more visual and more interactive, and their reading and study often occur in short bursts. For many students, a traditionally formatted printed textbook is no longer enough when they have instant access to news and information from around the globe.

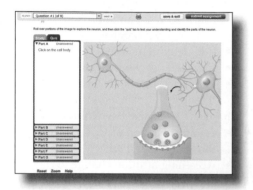

CONNECT PSYCHOLOGY McGraw-Hill's Connect Psychology responds to today's students by offering a wealth of interactive course materials for both instructors and students. Videos, interactive assessments, and simulations invite engagement and add real-world perspective to the introductory psychology course. Detailed reporting helps the student and instructor gauge comprehension and retention—*without adding administrative load.*

LEARNSMART How many students *think* they know what they know but struggle on the first exam? LearnSmart is McGraw-Hill's adaptive learning system. It identifies students' metacognitive abilities and limitations, identifying what they know—and more importantly, what they don't know. Using Bloom's Taxonomy and a sophisticated "smart" algorithm, LearnSmart creates a customized study plan, unique to every student's demonstrated needs. With virtually no administrative overhead, instructors using LearnSmart are reporting an increase in student performance by one letter grade or more.

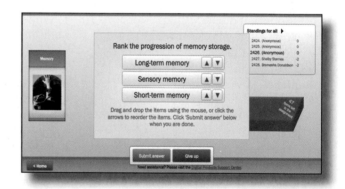

Ways of Engaging Students

PROLOGUE Each chapter starts with an account of a real-life situation that demonstrates the relevance of basic principles and concepts of psychology to pertinent issues and problems. These prologues depict well-known people and events.

LOOKING AHEAD This section ties each prologue to the key themes and issues discussed in the subsequent modules.

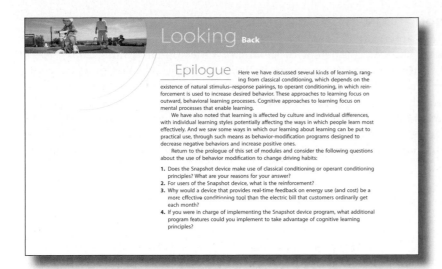

EPILOGUE Found at the end of every set of modules, critical thinking questions in the *Epilogue* relate to the *Prologue* at the opening of the set of modules. These thought-provoking questions illustrate how the concepts addressed in each module apply to the real-world situation described in the *Prologue*.

Ways of Informing Students

COMPREHENSIVE CONTENT COVERAGE *Essentials of Understanding Psychology* provides broad coverage of the field of psychology, including the theories, research, and applications that permeate the discipline. Along with the traditional areas of psychology (neuroscience, sensation and perception, states of consciousness, learning, memory, cognition, human development, personality, abnormal behavior and treatment, and social psychology), the applied topic of health psychology (Chapter 11) receives extensive attention.

MODULAR ORGANIZATION The text is organized into modules in which each of the 14 chapters is divided into three or four manageable, self-contained sections that include learning outcomes and assessment opportunities. Each module ends with questions that assess learning on both an outcome and more conceptual, higher-order level.

Rather than facing a long and potentially daunting chapter, students can study material in smaller chunks, which psychological research long ago found to be the optimal way to learn. Moreover, instructors can customize assignments for their students by asking them to read only those modules that fit their course outline and in the sequence that matches their syllabus. Alternatively, instructors who prefer to assign whole chapters can do so.

CONCEPT CLIPS Created by a team of instructional designers, "Concept Clips" help students comprehend some of the most difficult concepts in introductory psychology. Colorful graphics and stimulating animations break down core concepts in a step-by-step manner, engaging students and aiding in retention. Powered by Connect, "Concept Clips" can be used as a presentational tool for the classroom or can be used for student assessment.

CONNECTION TO APA STUDENT COMPETENCIES Conforming to recommendations of an American Psychological Association (APA) task force report on undergraduate student competencies (Board of Educational Affairs, 2002), *every* component of the text and its package is tied to specific psychological concepts and their application in everyday life. A chart indicating how the features of the textbook directly address the APA student competencies is provided in Figure 2. Equally important, every one of the thousands of test items in the Test Banks available to instructors and all the content in Connect Psychology are keyed to their corresponding APA competencies in a document that is available on the text website.

Book Feature	APA Learning Goals									
	Knowledge Base of Psychology	Research Methods in Psychology	Critical Thinking Skills in Psychology	Application of Psychology	Values in Psychology	Information and Technological Literacy	Communication Skills	Sociocultural and International Awareness	Personal Development	Career Planning and Development
Chapter Content	X	X	X	X	X	X	X	X	X	X
Prologue	X		X	X				X		
Looking Ahead	X	X	X		X					
Learning Outcomes	X		X	X				X		
Applying Psychology in the 21st Century	X	X		X				X	X	X
Exploring Diversity	X				X		X	X	X	
Neuroscience in Your Life	X	X	X	X						
PsychWork	X			X					X	X
PsychTech	X					X				
Running Glossary	X			X		X				
Becoming an Informed Consumer of Psychology	X	X		X	X		X		X	X
Study Alerts	X	X		X						
Recap/Evaluate/Rethink	X		X	X						
Epilogue	X		X	X				X		
Visual Summary	X	X	X	X	X	X	X	X	X	X
LearnSmart	X		X	X		X				

FIGURE 2 This grid shows the relationship between the broad learning goals devised by the American Psychological Association and specific types of content in *Essentials of Understanding Psychology*. In addition, each of the test items in the Test Bank for the book, consisting of nearly 4,000 individual, scorable items, is keyed to specific learning outcomes.

LEARNING OUTCOMES New to this edition, the book includes specific *Learning Outcomes* that are keyed to assessment benchmarks, including the Test Bank and online assessments. *Learning Outcomes* provide a framework for understanding, organizing, and ultimately learning the material, as well as assuring that students have achieved particular learning outcomes.

VISUAL SUMMARIES New to this edition, visual summaries conclude each chapter and tie the chapter concepts together visually. Each of the visual summaries provides a one-page overview of the material in the chapter, offering students a way of rethinking the material in another sensory modality. This innovative new feature will be particularly useful to students who prefer material presented in more graphic form.

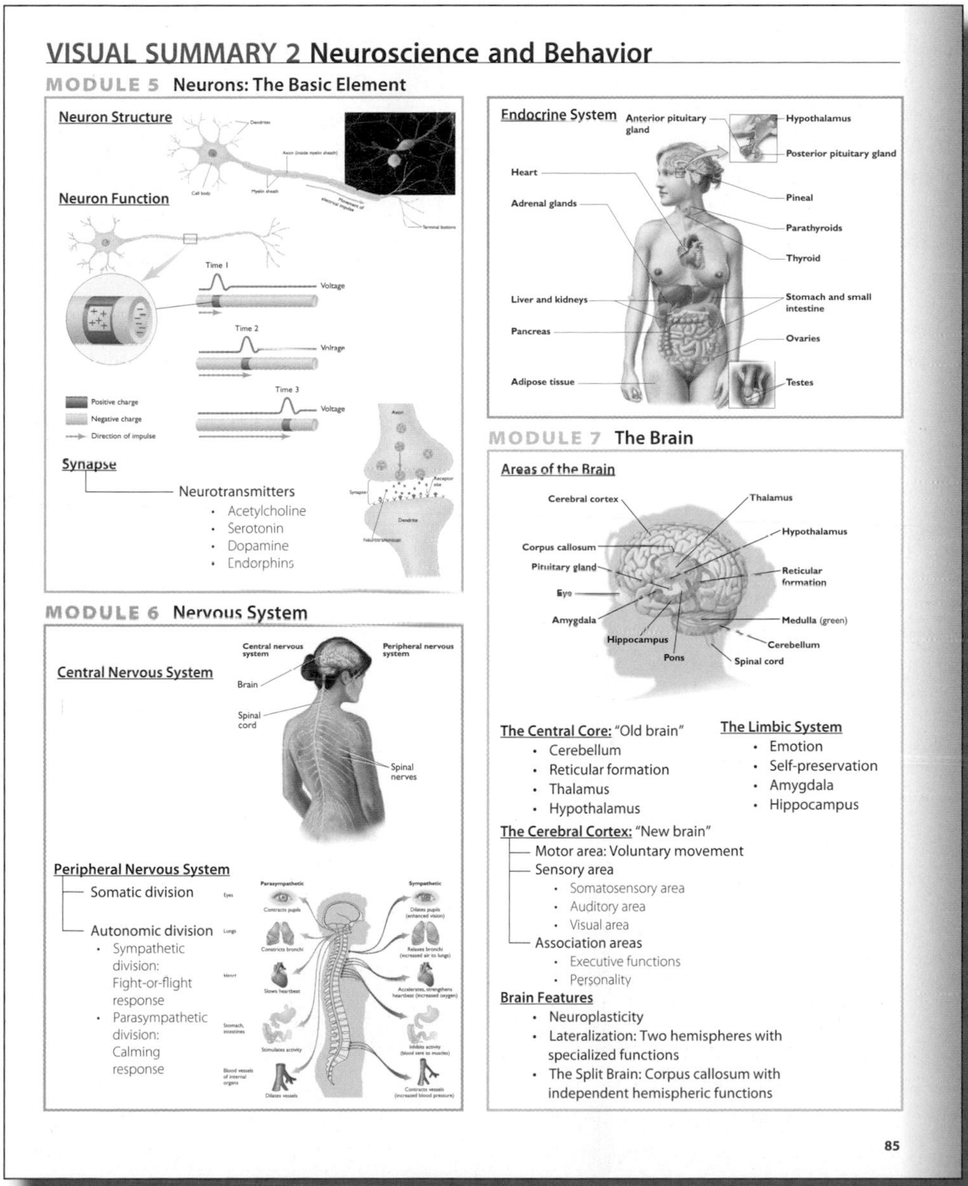
VISUAL SUMMARY 2 Neuroscience and Behavior

MODULE 5 Neurons: The Basic Element

Neuron Structure

Neuron Function

Synapse
- Neurotransmitters
  - Acetylcholine
  - Serotonin
  - Dopamine
  - Endorphins

MODULE 6 Nervous System

Central Nervous System

Peripheral Nervous System
- Somatic division
- Autonomic division
  - Sympathetic division: Fight-or-flight response
  - Parasympathetic division: Calming response

Endocrine System

MODULE 7 The Brain

Areas of the Brain

The Central Core: "Old brain"
- Cerebellum
- Reticular formation
- Thalamus
- Hypothalamus

The Limbic System
- Emotion
- Self-preservation
- Amygdala
- Hippocampus

The Cerebral Cortex: "New brain"
- Motor area: Voluntary movement
- Sensory area
  - Somatosensory area
  - Auditory area
  - Visual area
- Association areas
  - Executive functions
  - Personality

Brain Features
- Neuroplasticity
- Lateralization: Two hemispheres with specialized functions
- The Split Brain: Corpus callosum with independent hemispheric functions

85

Exploring DIVERSITY

Cross-Cultural Routes to Altered States of Consciousness

A group of Native-American Sioux men sit naked in a steaming sweat lodge as a medicine man throws water on sizzling rocks to send billows of scalding steam into the air.

Aztec priests smear themselves with a mixture of crushed poisonous herbs, hairy black worms, scorpions, and lizards. Sometimes they drink the potion.

During the 16th century, a devout Hasidic Jew lies across the tombstone of a celebrated scholar. As he murmurs the name of God repeatedly, he seeks to be possessed by the soul of the dead wise man's spirit. If successful, he will attain a mystical state, and the deceased's words will flow out of his mouth.

Each of these rituals has a common goal: suspension from the bonds of everyday awareness and access to an altered state of consciousness. Although they may seem exotic from the vantage point of many Western cultures, these rituals represent an apparently universal effort to alter consciousness (Bartocci, 2004; Irwin, 2006).

EXPLORING DIVERSITY In addition to substantial coverage of material relevant to diversity throughout the text, every set of modules also includes at least one special section devoted to an aspect of racial, ethnic, gender, or cultural diversity. These sections highlight the way in which psychology informs (and is informed by) issues relating to the increasing multiculturalism of our global society.

STUDY ALERTS Throughout the text, marginal notes point out especially important and difficult concepts and topics. These Study Alerts offer suggestions for learning the material effectively and for studying for tests. In Chapter 4, Module 12, for example, a Study Alert emphasizes the importance of differentiating the five stages of sleep; the feature in Module 13 makes clear the key issue about hypnosis—whether it represents a different state of consciousness or is similar to normal waking consciousness; and in Module 14 it highlights Figure 2 for its clear view of the different ways that drugs produce their effects at a neurological level.

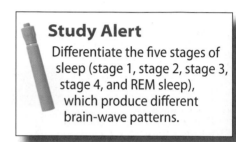

Study Alert

Differentiate the five stages of sleep (stage 1, stage 2, stage 3, stage 4, and REM sleep), which produce different brain-wave patterns.

RECAP/EVALUATE/RETHINK

RECAP

LO 36-1 How do our interactions with physicians affect our health and compliance with medical treatment?

- Although patients would often like physicians to base a diagnosis only on a physical examination, communicating one's problem to the physician is equally important. (p. 442)
- Patients may find it difficult to communicate openly with their physicians because of physicians' high social prestige and the technical nature of medical information. (p. 442)

LO 36-2 How does a sense of well-being develop?

- Subjective well-being, the measure of how happy people are, is highest in people with high self-esteem, a sense of control, optimism, and a supportive network of close relationships. (p. 444)

EVALUATE

1. Health psychologists are most likely to focus on which of the following problems with health care?
   a. Incompetent health-care providers
   b. Rising health-care costs
   c. Ineffective communication between physician and patient
   d. Scarcity of medical research funding

2. If you want people to floss more to prevent gum disease, the best approach is to
   a. Use a negatively framed message
   b. Use a positively framed message
   c. Have a dentist deliver an encouraging message on the pleasures of flossing
   d. Provide people with free dental floss

3. Winning the lottery is likely to
   a. Produce an immediate and long-term increase in the level of well-being
   b. Produce an immediate but not lingering increase in the level of well-being
   c. Produce a decline in well-being over the long run
   d. Lead to an increase in greed over the long run

RETHINK

1. Do you think stress plays a role in making communication between physicians and patients difficult? Why?

2. *From the perspective of a health-care provider:* How would you try to better communicate with your patients? How might your techniques vary depending on the patient's background, gender, age, and culture?

Answers to Evaluate Questions

1-c; 2-b; 3-b

KEY TERMS

subjective well-being   p. 444

RECAP/EVALUATE/RETHINK Each module concludes with a Recap/Evaluate/Rethink section. The *Recap* sections review the concept questions found at the beginning of each module. *Evaluate* sections test recall of the material, assessing the degree of initial learning. The *Rethink* sections provide thought-provoking questions designed to provoke critical thinking about the material.

RUNNING GLOSSARY Key terms are highlighted in boldface type within the text where they are introduced, and definitions are given in the margin of the page, along with pronunciation guides for difficult words. To facilitate study, at the end of each module there is a list of the key terms and concepts introduced in that module. There is also a glossary of all key terms and concepts at the end of the book.

Ways of Exciting Students and Helping Them Relate Psychology to Their World

APPLYING PSYCHOLOGY IN THE 21ST CENTURY These boxes—all new in this edition—highlight the relevance of psychology by presenting current and potential applications of psychological theory and research findings to real-world problems. For example, one box discusses the psychological principles that explain the dangers of texting while driving, whereas another highlights how artificial intelligence researchers are building "smarter" robots that have the potential to transform our daily lives.

Applying Psychology in the 21st Century

Advertising in the Information Age: Aiming at Moving Targets

As a middle-aged man browses a popular sports webpage on his smartphone, more than a dozen cameras monitor his every movement—particularly his eye movements. Other equipment monitors his skin temperature and heart rate, and numerous tiny muscle probes measure every nuance of his changing facial expressions. In a remote room, technicians closely monitor the data his movements produce in real time.

This isn't a scene from a futuristic science-fiction film—it's just an ordinary day at a private research lab owned by the Walt Disney Company. The research technicians are studying the effectiveness of online advertising. While Internet companies have long been investigating the kinds of online ads that successfully entice website users to click through, much less is known about why users *don't* respond. Are the ads failing to capture their attention? If so, what kinds of ads would work better to do that? Is it just a question of creating more vivid visuals, or do users quickly learn to ignore even the most eye-popping banners? Does the structure of the webpage itself make a difference? It's a delicate balance to design online ads that are maximally effective but not so intrusive as

Advertisers are researching how to harness the latest technologies to ensure that they are getting the greatest response for their efforts.

to turn viewers off (Lavrakas, Mane, & Joe, 2010; Hsieh & Chen, 2011).

Advertising companies want to make sure they are getting the most response for their efforts. Rather than leave anything to chance, they are using the latest research methods to ensure that their ads have the intended impact—even going so far as to monitor people's brain activity as they watch televised ads. "You're seeing science move into the marketing sector in a big way," said David Poltrack, chief research officer for CBS. Artie Bulgrin, ESPN's senior vice president of research, concurs: "We see this as a very powerful research and development tool for the entire Disney company. As ideas arise, we want to research them and have the results in the hands of our sales force as fast as possible," he said (Barnes, 2009, p. 6).

The rapid evolution of Internet technology and the ever-changing ways in which people consume online content have far outpaced researchers' attempts to understand people's usage patterns and the most effective ways of introducing advertising into the mix. Private research labs of major stakeholders such as Disney are working frantically to keep up, but much work is yet to be done. For the most part, advertisers are still relying on methods that worked for older technology until newer media forms are better understood (Li & Leckenby, 2007)

RETHINK

- Why do you think it's so difficult to design effective advertisements for online media?
- Why do you think researchers are keenly interested in users' physical responses as they consume online media?

Neuroscience in Your Life: One Step Closer to Understanding OCD

FIGURE 3 People with obsessive-compulsive disorder (OCD) have structural differences in their brains. These images show increased levels of gray matter (i.e., more connections or more neurons) in the thalamus (a) and in the left frontal cortex (b) in people with OCD as compared to people without it. These findings help us to understand the potential causes of OCD and may lead to the development of better treatments for the disorder. (Source: Christian et al., 2008, Figure 1.)

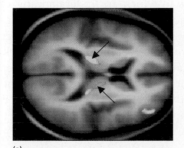
(a)

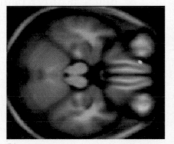
(b)

NEUROSCIENCE IN YOUR LIFE This updated feature, which appears in most chapters, emphasizes the importance of neuroscientific research within the various subfields of the discipline and in students' lives. Compelling brain scans, with both caption and textual explanation, illustrate significant neuroscientific findings that are increasingly influencing the field of psychology. For example, one *Neuroscience in Your Life* feature explains why being sleep deprived may affect us emotionally. Another shows what areas of the brain are affected by taking risks.

BECOMING AN INFORMED CONSUMER OF PSYCHOLOGY Every set of modules includes material designed to make readers more informed consumers of psychological information by giving them the ability to evaluate critically what the field of psychology offers. These discussions also provide sound, useful guidance concerning common problems.

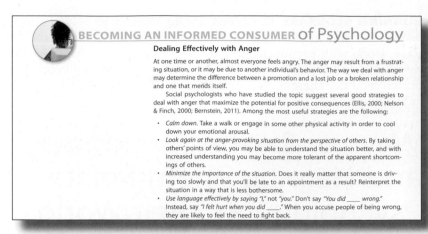

PSYCHINTERACTIVE McGraw-Hill's NEW PsychInteractive allows students the opportunity to experience the scientific method as they learn to observe data, formulate and test a hypothesis, communicate their findings, and apply their understanding of psychology to the world. PsychInteractive is available through Connect.

PSYCHTECH Every chapter now includes new comments in the margin that point out how technology and psychology interact. These comments are designed to speak to today's Net Generation, students who use this technology 24/7.

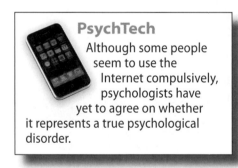

PsychTech

Although some people seem to use the Internet compulsively, psychologists have yet to agree on whether it represents a true psychological disorder.

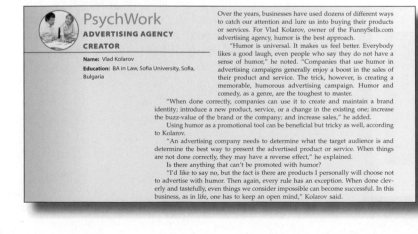

PSYCHWORK *PsychWork* introduces students to different career paths to which an understanding of psychology leads. Each *PsychWork* profile illustrates people in a variety of occupations whose knowledge of psychology informs and enhances their work. Among the individuals profiled are a social worker, a nutritionist, a physical rehabilitation counselor, and an advertising executive, showing that psychology is all around us and important to many occupations.

NEWSFLASH By connecting psychology to students' own lives, concepts become more relevant and understandable. Powered by McGraw-Hill's Connect, "Newsflash" exercises tie current news stories to key psychological principles and learning objectives. After interacting with a contemporary news story, students are assessed on their ability to make the connection between real life and research findings. Many cases are revisited across chapters, encouraging students to consider multiple perspectives.

CUSTOM MODULES The text is now accompanied by a set of four custom modules that can be incorporated into custom versions of the text. These modules are titled *Diversity and Culture, Forensic Psychology, Industrial/Organizational Psychology,* and *Sustainability/Environmental Psychology*.

Integrated Learning System

Resources available for use with this text support both new and veteran instructors, whether they favor traditional text-based instruction or a blend of traditional and electronic media. The Tenth Edition text and support materials provide complementary experiences for instructors and students.

Blackboard Through McGraw-Hill's partnership with Blackboard, *Essentials of Understanding Psychology*, Tenth Edition, offers an ideal integration of content and tools:

- Seamless gradebook between Blackboard and Connect
- Single sign-on providing seamless integration between McGraw-Hill content and Blackboard
- Simplicity in assigning and engaging your students with course materials

Create Craft your teaching resources to match the way you teach. With McGraw-Hill **Create**, www.mcgrawhillcreate.com, you can easily rearrange chapters, combine material from other content sources, and quickly upload content you have written, such as your course syllabus or teaching notes. Find the content you need in Create by searching through thousands of leading McGraw-Hill textbooks. Arrange your book to fit your teaching style. Create even allows you to personalize your book's appearance by selecting the cover and adding your name, school, and course information. Order a Create book and you'll receive a complimentary print review copy in 3 to 5 business days or a complimentary electronic review copy (eComp) via e-mail in about an hour. Go to www.mcgrawhillcreate.com today and register. Experience how McGraw-Hill Create empowers you to teach *your* students *your* way.

Tegrity Campus Tegrity Campus is a service that makes class time available all the time by automatically capturing every lecture in a searchable format for students to review when they study and complete assignments. With a simple one-click start-and-stop process, users capture all computer screens and corresponding audio. Students replay any part of any class with easy-to-use browser-based viewing on a PC or Mac. Educators know that the more students can see, hear, and experience class resources, the better they learn. With Tegrity Campus, students quickly recall key moments by using its unique search feature. This search helps students efficiently find what they need, when they need it, across an entire semester of class recordings. Help turn all your students' study time into learning moments immediately supported by your lectures.

CourseSmart This text is available as an e-textbook at www.CourseSmart.com. At **CourseSmart** your students can take advantage of significant savings off the cost of a print textbook, reduce their impact on the environment, and gain access to powerful web tools for learning. CourseSmart e-textbooks can be viewed online or downloaded to a computer. The e-textbooks allow students to do full-text searches, add highlighting and notes, and share comments with classmates. CourseSmart has the largest selection of e-textbooks available anywhere. Visit www.CourseSmart.com to learn more and to try a sample chapter.

Online Learning Center for Instructors The password-protected instructor side of the Online Learning Center (www.mhhe.com/feldmaness10e) contains the Instructor's Manual, Test Bank files, PowerPoint slides, Image Gallery, and other valuable material to help you design and enhance your course.

Instructor's Manual This comprehensive guide provides all the tools and resources instructors need to present and enhance their introductory psychology course. It contains detailed lecture launchers, learning objectives, interesting lecture and media presentation ideas, student assignments, and handouts. The many tips and activities in this manual can be used with any class, regardless of size or teaching approach.

Test Banks Our new test banks incorporate the new content in *Essentials of Understanding Psychology,* Tenth Edition. Each test bank contains more than 2,000 multiple-choice items, classified by cognitive type and level of difficulty and keyed to the appropriate learning outcome and page in the textbook. Moreover, each of the thousands of test items is keyed to the APA core psychology competencies. All questions are compatible with EZ Test, McGraw-Hill's Computerized Test Bank program.

Image Gallery More than 100 figures from the text can be downloaded from the Image Gallery on the Instructor's Online Learning Center.

PowerPoint Presentations by Cathy Hunt of Pennsylvania State University. These presentations cover the key points of each chapter and include charts and graphs from the text. They can be used as is, or you may modify them to meet your specific needs.

Acknowledgments

One of the central features of *Essentials of Understanding Psychology* is the involvement of both professionals and students in the review process. The Tenth Edition of *Essentials of Understanding Psychology* has relied heavily—and benefited substantially—from the advice of instructors and students from a wide range of backgrounds.

I am extraordinarily grateful to the following reviewers, who provided their time and expertise to help insure that *Essentials of Understanding Psychology,* Tenth Edition, reflects the best that psychology has to offer.

REVIEWERS

Bernice Carson
Virginia State University

Wanda Clark
South Plains College

Lori Heiger
Alamance Community College

Nawshin Hoque
Hunter College

Charles Jerred
Bryant & Stratton College

Matthew Minich
Mount Ida College

Regan Murray
Briar Cliff University

LaTishia Smith
Ivy Tech Community College

In addition, Jane W. Couperus of Hampshire College provided exceptional support in helping identify appropriate neuroscientific research to include in the *Neuroscience in Your Life* features. I thank her for her superb work.

Many teachers along my educational path have shaped my thinking. I was introduced to psychology at Wesleyan University, where several committed and inspiring teachers—and in particular Karl Scheibe—conveyed their sense of excitement about the field and made its relevance clear to me. Karl epitomizes the teacher-scholar combination to which I aspire, and I continue to marvel at my good fortune in having such a role model.

By the time I left Wesleyan I could envision no other career but that of psychologist. Although the nature of the University of Wisconsin, where I did my graduate work, could not have been more different from the much smaller Wesleyan, the excitement and inspiration were similar. Once again, a cadre of excellent teachers—led, especially, by the late Vernon Allen—molded my thinking and taught me to appreciate the beauty and science of the discipline of psychology.

My colleagues and students at the University of Massachusetts, Amherst, provide ongoing intellectual stimulation, and I thank them for making the university a fine place to work. Several people also provided extraordinary research and editorial help. In particular, I am grateful to my superb students, past and present, including Erik Coats, Sara Levine, Jim Tyler, Chris Poirier, and Matt Zimbler. John Bickford, in particular, provided editorial input that has enhanced the book considerably. Finally, I am grateful to John Graiff, whose hard work and dedication helped immeasurably on just about everything involving this book.

I also offer great thanks to the McGraw-Hill editorial team that participated in this edition of the book. Vice President and General Manager Mike Ryan and Director Mike Sugarman created a creative, energetic, and supportive environment, and I am in awe of their enthusiasm, commitment, and never-ending good ideas. I also thank Sue Ewing, Developmental Editor on this edition. Sue, in particular, did a superb job of managing a myriad of details (as well as me). I'm also pleased that Director Krista Bettino worked on this edition (and previous editions) of *Essentials of Understanding Psychology*. She brought motivation, intelligence, and good ideas to the project. Finally, every reader of this book owes a debt to Rhona Robbin and Judith Kromm, developmental editors on earlier editions of *Essentials of Understanding Psychology*. Their relentless pursuit of excellence helped form the core of this book, and they taught me a great deal about the craft and art of writing.

Central to the design, production, and marketing process were Director Krista Bettino, Project Manager Erin Melloy, Buyer Nicole Baumgartner, Designer Preston Thomas, and Photo Editor LouAnn Wilson. I would also like to thank Marketing Managers AJ Laferrera and Ann Helerson for their enthusiasm and commitment to this project. I am proud to be a part of this world-class team.

Finally, I remain completely indebted to my family. My parents, Leah Brochstein and the late Saul D. Feldman, provided a lifetime foundation of love and support, and I continue to see their influence in every corner of my life. I am grateful, too, to the late Harry Brochstein, who enriched my life and thinking in many ways.

My extended family also plays a central role in my life. They include, more or less in order of age, my nieces and nephews, my terrific brother, and my brothers- and sisters-in-law, and the late Ethel Radler. Finally, my mother-in-law, the late Mary Evans Vorwerk, had an important influence on this book, and I remain ever grateful to her.

Ultimately, my children, Jonathan, Joshua, and Sarah; my daughters-in-law Leigh and Julie; my grandsons Alex and Miles; and my wife, Katherine, remain the focal points of my life. I thank them, with immense love, and thank my lucky stars that they are in my life.

Robert S. Feldman
Amherst, Massachusetts

No matter why you are taking introductory psychology, it's a safe bet you're interested in maximizing your understanding of the material and getting a good grade. And you want to accomplish these goals as quickly and efficiently as possible.

Good news: You're taking the right course, and you're learning the right material. Several subfields of psychology have identified a variety of guidelines and techniques that will help you learn and remember material not only related to psychology, but also relevant to every other discipline that you will study. Here's my guarantee to you: If you learn and follow the guidelines in each of these areas, you'll become a better student and get better grades. Always remember that *good students are made, not born.*

Adopt a General Study Strategy

Let's begin with a brief consideration of a general study strategy. Psychologists have devised several excellent (and proven) techniques for improving study skills, two of which are described here: "P.O.W.E.R." or *Prepare, Organize, Work, Evaluate,* and *Rethink;* and "SQ3R," or *Survey, Question, Read, Recite,* and *Review.* By employing one of these two procedures, you can increase your ability to learn and retain information and to think critically.

P.O.W.E.R. The *P.O.W.E.R.* learning strategy systematizes the acquisition of new material by providing a learning framework. It stresses the importance of learning objectives and appropriate preparation before you begin to study as well as the significance of self-evaluation and the incorporation of critical thinking into the learning process. Specifically, use of the P.O.W.E.R. learning system entails the following steps:

- **Prepare.** Before starting any journey, we need to know where we are headed. Academic journeys are no different; we need to know what our goals are. The *Prepare* stage consists of thinking about what we hope to gain from reading a specific section of the text by identifying specific goals that we seek to accomplish. In *Essentials of Understanding Psychology,* Tenth Edition, these goals are called *Learning Outcomes* and are presented as broad questions at the start of each chapter and again at the beginning of each module.

- **Organize.** Once we know what our goals are, we can develop a route to accomplish those goals. The *Organize* stage involves developing a mental roadmap of where we are headed. *Essentials of Understanding Psychology* highlights the organization of each upcoming chapter. Read the outline at the beginning of each chapter to get an idea of what topics are covered and how they are organized.

- **Work.** The key to the P.O.W.E.R. learning system is actually reading and studying the material presented in the book. In some ways *Work* is the easy part because, if you have carried out the steps in the preparation and organization stages, you'll know where you're headed and how you'll get there. Remember, the main text isn't the only material that you need to read and think about. It's also important to read the boxes and the material in the margins in order to gain a full understanding of the material.
- **Evaluate.** The fourth step, *Evaluate*, provides the opportunity to determine how effectively you have mastered the material. In *Essentials of Understanding Psychology*, a series of questions at the end of each module permits a rapid check of your understanding of the material. Quizzes on the book's website provide additional opportunities to test yourself. Evaluating your progress is essential to assessing your degree of mastery of the material.
- **Rethink.** The final step in the *P.O.W.E.R.* learning system requires that you think critically about the content. Critical thinking entails re-analyzing, reviewing, questioning, and challenging assumptions. It affords you the opportunity to consider how the material fits with other information you have already learned. Every major section of *Essentials of Understanding Psychology* ends with a *Rethink* section. Answering its thought-provoking questions will help you understand the material more fully and at a deeper level.

SQ3R. Use of the SQ3R learning system entails the following specific steps:

- **Survey.** The first step of the SQ3R method is to *survey* the material by reading the outlines that open each module, the headings, figure captions, recaps, and Looking Ahead and Looking Back sections, providing yourself with an overview of the major points of the chapter.
- **Question.** The next step—the "Q"—is to *question*. Formulate questions about the material, either aloud or in writing, prior to actually reading a section of text. The questions posed at the beginning of each module and the *Evaluate* and *Rethink* questions that end each part of the chapter are examples.
- **Read.** Read carefully and, even more importantly, read actively and critically. While you are reading, answer the questions you have asked yourself. Critically evaluate material by considering the implications of what you are reading, thinking about possible exceptions and contradictions, and examining underlying assumptions.
- **Recite.** This step involves describing and explaining to yourself (or to a friend) the material you have just read and answering the questions you have posed earlier. Recite aloud; the recitation process helps to

identify your degree of understanding of the material you have just read.

- **Review.** In this final step, review the material, looking it over, reading the Epilogue summaries, the Visual Concept Maps, and answering the in-text review questions.

Manage Your Time

Without looking up from the page, answer this question: What time is it?

Most people are pretty accurate in their answer. And if you don't know for sure, it's very likely that you can find out quickly.

Managing your time as you study is a central aspect of academic success. But remember: The goal of time management is not to schedule every moment so we become pawns of a timetable that governs every waking moment of the day. Instead, the goal is to permit us to make informed choices about how we use our time. Rather than letting the day slip by, largely without our awareness, the time management procedures we'll discuss can make us better able to harness time for our own ends.

Set Your Priorities. To figure out the best use of your time, you need to determine your priorities. *Priorities* are the tasks and activities you need and want to do, rank-ordered from most important to least important. There are no right or wrong priorities; maybe spending time on your studies is most important to you, or maybe your top priority is spending time with your family. Only you can decide. Furthermore, what's important to you now may be less of a priority to you next month, next year, or in 5 years.

The best procedure is to start off by identifying priorities for an entire term. What do you need to accomplish? Don't just choose obvious, general goals, such as "passing all my classes." Instead, think in terms of specific, measurable activities, such as "studying 10 hours before each chemistry exam."

Identify Your Prime Time. Do you enthusiastically bound out of bed in the morning, ready to start the day and take on the world? Or is the alarm clock a hated and unwelcome sound that jars you out of pleasant slumber? Are you zombie-like by 10 at night, or are you a person who is just beginning to rev up at midnight? Each of us has his or her own style based on some inborn body clock. Being aware of the time or times of day when you can do your best work will help you plan and schedule your time most effectively.

Master the Moment. Here's what you'll need to organize your time:

- *A master calendar* that shows all the weeks of the term on one page. It should include every week of the term and seven days per week. Using your class syllabus, on the master calendar note the due date of every assignment and test you will have. Pencil in tentative assignments on the appropriate date. Also include important activities from your personal life, drawn from your list of priorities. And don't forget to schedule some free time for yourself.

- *A weekly timetable,* a master grid with the days of the week across the top and the hours, from 6:00 a.m. to midnight, along the side. Fill in the times of all your fixed, prescheduled activities—the times that your classes meet, when you have to be at work, the times you have to pick up your child at day care, and any other recurring appointments. Add assignment due dates, tests, and any other activities on the appropriate days of the week. Then pencil in blocks of time necessary to prepare for those events.

- *A daily to-do list.* Create your daily to-do list on a small, portable calendar that includes a separate page for each day of the week, or use your smartphone. List all the things that you intend to do during the next day and their priority. Start with the things you know you *must* do and that have fixed times, such as classes, work schedules, and appointments. Then add in the other things that you *should* accomplish, such as an hour of study for an upcoming test, work on research for an upcoming paper, or finishing up a lab report. Finally, list things that are a low priority but enjoyable, like taking in a new movie.

Control Your Time. If you follow the schedules that you've prepared, you've taken the most important steps in time management. However, our lives are filled with surprises: Things always seem to take longer than we've planned. A crisis occurs, buses are late, computers break down, kids get sick.

The difference between effective time management and time management that doesn't work lies in how well you deal with the inevitable surprises. There are several ways to take control of your days and permit yourself to follow your intended schedule:

- **Just say no.** You don't have to agree to every request and every favor that others ask of you.

- **Get away from it all.** Go to the library. Lock yourself in your bedroom. Find an out-of-the-way unused classroom. Adopt a specific spot as your own, such as a corner desk in a secluded nook in the library. If you use it enough, your body and mind will automatically get into study mode as soon as you seat yourself at it.

- **Enjoy the sounds of silence.** Although many students insist they accomplish most while a television, radio, or CD is playing, scientific studies suggest otherwise—we are able to concentrate most when our environment is silent. Experiment and work in silence for a few days. You may find that you get more done in less time than you would in a more distracting environment.

- **Take an e-break.** We may not control when communications arrive, but we can make the messages wait until we are ready to receive them. Take an e-break and shut down your communication sources for some period of time. Phone calls can be stored on voice-mail systems; text messages, IMs, and e-mail can be saved on a phone or computer. They'll wait.
- **Expect the unexpected.** You'll never be able to escape from unexpected interruptions and surprises that require your attention. But by trying to anticipate them in advance and thinking about how you'll react to them, you'll be positioning yourself to react more effectively when they do occur.

Read Your Textbook Effectively

Reading a textbook is different from reading for pleasure. With textbooks, you have specific goals: understanding, learning, and ultimately recalling the information. There are several steps you can take to achieve these goals:

- **Read the front matter.** If you'll be using a text extensively throughout the term, start by reading the preface and/or introduction and scanning the table of contents—what publishers call the *front matter*. It is there that the author has a chance to explain, often more personally than elsewhere in the text, what he or she considers important. Knowing this will give you a sense of what to expect as you read. (Note: You're reading part of the front matter at this very moment!)
- **Identify your personal objectives.** Before you begin an assignment, think about what your specific objectives are. Will you be reading a textbook on which you'll be thoroughly tested? Or, will your reading provide background information for future learning that won't itself be tested? Is the material going to be useful to you personally? Your objectives for reading will help you determine which reading strategy to adopt and how much time you can devote to the reading assignment. You aren't expected to read everything with the same degree of intensity. You may feel comfortable skimming some material. You'll want to put in the maximum effort into other material.
- **Identify and use the advance organizers.** The next step in reading a textbook is to become familiar with the *advance organizers*—outlines, overviews, section objectives, or other clues to the meaning and organization of new material—provided in the material you are reading. Look at the start of every chapter in this book, which includes a chapter outline plus a set of learning outcome questions. You can also create your own advance organizers by skimming material to be read and sketching out the general outline

of the material you'll be reading. These steps can help you recall material better after you've read it.

- **Stay focused as you read.** There are a million and one possible distractions that can invade your thoughts as you read. Your job is to keep distracting thoughts at bay and focus on the material you are supposed to be reading. Here are some things you can do to help yourself stay focused:
  - **Read in small bites.** If you think it is going to take you 4 hours to read an entire chapter, break up the 4 hours into more manageable time periods. Promise yourself that you'll read for 1 hour in the afternoon, another hour in the evening, and the next 2 hours spaced out during the following day.
  - **Take a break.** Actually plan to take several short breaks to reward yourself while you're reading. During your break, do something enjoyable—eat a snack, watch a bit of a ball game on television, play a video game, or the like. Just try not to get drawn into your break activity to the point that it takes over your reading time.
- **Highlight and take notes as you read.** Highlighting and taking notes as you read a textbook are essential activities. Good annotations can help you learn and review the information prior to tests as well as help you to stay focused as you read. There are several things you can do to maximize the effectiveness of your notes:
  - **Rephrase key points.** Make notes to yourself, in your own words, about what the author is trying to get across. Don't just copy what's been said. Think about the material, and rewrite it in words that are your own. The very act of writing engages an additional type of perception that involves the physical sense of moving a pen or pressing a keyboard.
  - **Highlight or underline key points.** Often the first or last sentence in a paragraph, or the first or last paragraph in a section, will present a key point. Before you highlight anything, though, read the whole paragraph through. Then you'll be sure that what you highlight is, in fact, the key information. You should find yourself highlighting only one or two sentences or phrases per page. *In highlighting and underlining, less is more.* One guideline: No more than 10% of the material should be highlighted or underlined.
  - **Use arrows, diagrams, outlines, tables, timelines, charts, and other visuals to help you understand and later recall what you are reading.** If three examples are given for a specific point, number them. If a

sequence of steps is presented, number each step. If a paragraph discusses a situation in which an earlier point does not hold, link the original point to the exception by an arrow. Representing the material graphically will get you thinking about it in new and different ways. The act of creating visual annotations will not only help you to understand the material better, but will also ease its later recall.

- **Look up unfamiliar words.** Even though you may be able to figure out the meaning of an unfamiliar word from its context, look up unfamiliar words in a dictionary or online. You'll also find out what the word sounds like, which will be important if your instructor uses the word in class.

Take Good Notes in Class

Perhaps you know students who manage to write down nearly everything their instructors say in class. And perhaps you have thought to yourself, "If only I took such painstaking notes, I'd do much better in my classes." Contrary to what many students think, however, good notetaking does not mean writing down every word that an instructor utters. With notetaking, less is often more. Let's consider some of the basic principles of notetaking:

- **Identify the instructor's—and your—goals for the course.** On the first day of class, most instructors talk about their objectives for the course. Most review the information on the class syllabus, the written document that explains the assignments for the semester. The information you get during that first session and through the syllabus is critical. In addition to the instructor's goals, you should have your own. What is it you want to learn from the course? How will the information from the course help you to enhance your knowledge, improve yourself as a person, achieve your goals?

- **Complete assignments before coming to class.** Your instructor enthusiastically describes the structure of the neuron, recounting excitedly how electrons flow across neurons, changing their electrical charge. One problem: You have only the vaguest idea what a neuron is. And the reason you don't know is that you haven't read the assignment.

Chances are you have found yourself in this situation at least a few times, so you know firsthand that sinking feeling as you become more and more confused. The moral: Always go to class prepared. Instructors assume that their students have done what the instructors assigned, and their lectures are based on that assumption.

- **Choose a notebook that assists in notetaking.** Loose-leaf notebooks are especially good for taking notes because they permit you to go back later and change the order of the pages or add additional material. Whatever kind of notebook you use, *use only one side of the page for writing; keep one side free of notes.* There may be times that you'll want to spread out your notes in front of you, and it's much easier if no material is written on the back of the pages.

  Walter Pauk devised what is sometimes called the Cornell Method of Notetaking. Using this method, draw a line down the left side of your notebook page, about 2½ inches from the left-hand margin. Keep the notes you write in class to the right of the line. Indent major supporting details beneath each main idea, trying to use no more than one line for each item, and leave space between topics to add information. When it comes time to review your notes later, you'll be able to jot down a keyword, catch phrase, or major idea on the left side of the page (Pauk, 2007).

- **Listen for the key ideas.** Not every sentence in a lecture is equally important. One of the most useful skills you can develop is separating the key ideas from supporting information. Good lecturers strive to make just a few main points. The rest of what they say consists of explanation, examples, and other supportive material that expands upon the key ideas. To distinguish the key ideas from their support, you need to be alert and always searching for the *meta-message* of your instructor's words—that is, the underlying main ideas that a speaker is seeking to convey.

  How can you discern the meta-message? One way is to *listen for key words.* Phrases like "you need to know . . . ," "the most important thing that must be considered . . . ," "there are four problems with this approach . . . ," and—a big one—"this will be on the test . . . " should cause you to sit up and take notice. Also, if an instructor says the same thing in several ways, it's a clear sign that the material being discussed is important.

- **Use short, abbreviated phrases—not full sentences when taking notes.** Forget everything you've ever heard about always writing in full sentences. In fact, it's often useful to take notes in the form of an outline. An outline summarizes ideas in short phrases and indicates the relationship among concepts through the use of indentations.

- **Pay attention to what is written on the board or projected from PowerPoint slides. Remember these tips:**
  - **Listening is more important than seeing.** The information that your instructor projects on screen, while important, ultimately is less critical than what he or she is saying. Pay primary attention to the spoken word and secondary attention to the screen.
  - **Don't copy everything that is on every slide.** Instructors can present far more information on their slides than they would if they were writing on a blackboard. Oftentimes there is so much information that it's impossible to copy it all down. Don't even try. Instead, concentrate on taking down the key points.
  - **Remember that key points on slides are . . . key points.** The key points (often indicated by bullets) often relate to central concepts. Use these points to help organize your studying for tests, and don't be surprised if test questions directly assess the bulleted items on slides.
  - **Check to see if the presentation slides are available online.** Some instructors make their class presentations available to their students on the web, either before or after class time. If they do this before class, print them out and bring them to class. Then you can make notes on your copy, clarifying important points. If they are not available until after a class is over, you can still make good use of them when it comes time to study the material for tests.
  - **Remember that presentation slides are not the same as good notes for a class.** If you miss a class, don't assume that getting a copy of the slides is sufficient. Studying the notes of a classmate who is a good notetaker will be far more beneficial than studying only the slides.

Memorize Efficiently: Use Proven Strategies to Memorize New Materials

Here's a key principle of effective memorization: Memorize what you need to memorize. *Forget about the rest.*

The average textbook chapter has some 20,000 words. But, within those 20,000 words, there may be only 30 to 40 specific concepts that you need to learn. And perhaps there are only 25 key words. *Those* are the pieces of information on which you should focus in your efforts to memorize. By extracting what is important from what is less crucial, you'll be able to limit the amount of the material that you need to recall. You'll be able to focus on what you need to remember.

You have your choice of dozens of techniques of memorization. As we discuss the options, keep in mind that no one strategy works by itself. Also, feel free to devise your own strategies or add those that have worked for you in the past.

Rehearsal. Say it aloud: rehearsal. Think of this word in terms of its three syllables: re—hear—sal. If you're scratching your head about why you should do this, it's to illustrate the point of *rehearsal:* to transfer material that you encounter into long-term memory.

To test if you've succeeded in transferring the word "rehearsal" into your memory, put down this book and go off for a few minutes. Do something entirely unrelated to reading this book. Have a snack, catch up on the latest sports scores on ESPN, or read the front page of a newspaper. If the word "rehearsal" popped into your head when you picked up this book again, you've passed your first memory test—the word "rehearsal" has been transferred into your memory.

Rehearsal is the key strategy in remembering information. If you don't rehearse material, it will never make it into your memory. Repeating the information, summarizing it, associating it with other memories, and above all thinking about it when you first come across it will ensure that rehearsal will be effective in placing the material into your memory.

Mnemonics. This odd word (pronounced with the "m" silent—"neh MON ix") describes formal techniques used to make material more readily remembered. *Mnemonics* are the tricks-of-the-trade that professional memory experts use, and you too can use them to nail down the information you will need to recall for tests.

Among the most common mnemonics are the following:

- **Acronyms.** *Acronyms* are words or phrases formed by the first letters of a series of terms. The word "laser" is an acronym for "light amplification by stimulated emissions of radiation," and "radar" is an acronym for "radio detection and ranging."

  Acronyms can be a big help in remembering things. For example, Roy G. Biv is a favorite of physics students who must remember the colors of the spectrum (red, orange, yellow, green, blue, indigo, and violet). The benefit of acronyms is that they help us to recall a complete list of steps or items.
- **Acrostics.** *Acrostics* are sentences in which the first letters spell out something that needs to be recalled. The benefits—as well as the drawbacks—of acrostics are similar to those of acronyms.
- **Rhymes and jingles.** "Thirty days hath September, April, June, and November." If you know the rest of the rhyme, you're familiar with one of the most commonly used mnemonic jingles in the English language.

Use of Multiple Senses. The more senses you can involve when you're trying to learn new material, the better you'll be able to remember. Here's why: Every time we encounter new information, all of our senses are potentially at work. Each piece of sensory information is stored in a separate location in the brain, and yet all the pieces are linked together in extraordinarily intricate ways.

What this means is that when we seek to remember the details of a specific event, recalling a memory of one of the sensory experiences can trigger recall of the other types of memories. You can make use of the fact that memories are stored in multiple ways by applying the following techniques:

- **When you learn something, use your body.** Don't sit passively at your desk. Instead, move around. Stand up; sit down. Touch the page. Trace figures with your fingers. Talk to yourself. Think out loud. By involving every part of your body, you've increased the number of potential ways to trigger a relevant memory later, when you need to recall it. And when one memory is triggered, other related memories may come tumbling back.

- **Draw and diagram the material.** Structuring written material by graphically grouping and connecting key ideas and themes is a powerful technique. When we draw and diagram material, one of the things we're doing is expanding the modalities in which information can be stored in our minds. Other types of drawing can be useful in aiding later recall. Creating drawings, sketches, and even cartoons can help us remember better.

- **Visualize.** You already know that memory requires three basic steps: the initial recording of information, the storage of that information, and, ultimately, the retrieval of the stored information. *Visualization* is a technique by which images are formed to ensure that material is recalled. Don't stop at visualizing images just in your mind's eye. Actually drawing what you visualize will help you to remember the material even better. Visualization is effective because it serves several purposes. It helps make abstract ideas concrete; it engages multiple senses; it permits us to link different bits of information together; and it provides us with a context for storing information.

- **Overlearning.** Lasting learning doesn't come until you have overlearned the material. *Overlearning* consists of studying and rehearsing material past the point of initial mastery. Through overlearning, recall becomes automatic. Rather than searching for a fact, going through mental contortions until perhaps the information surfaces, overlearning permits us to recall the information without even thinking about it.

Test-Taking Strategies

Preparing for tests is a long-term proposition. It's not a matter of "giving your all" the night *before* the test. Instead, it's a matter of giving your all to every aspect of the course.

Here are some guidelines that can help you do your best on tests:

Know What You Are Preparing For. Determine as much as you can about the test *before* you begin to study for it. The more you know about a test beforehand, the more efficient your studying will be.

To find out about an upcoming test, ask if it is a "test," an "exam," a "quiz," or something else. These names imply different things. Each kind of test question requires a somewhat different style of preparation.

- **Essay questions.** Essay tests focus on the big picture—ways in which the various pieces of information being tested fit together. You'll need to know not just a series of facts, but also the connections between them, and you will have to be able to discuss these ideas in an organized and logical way. The best approach to studying for an essay test involves four steps:

  1. Carefully reread your class notes and any notes you've made on assigned readings that will be covered on the upcoming exam. Also go through the readings themselves, reviewing underlined or highlighted material and marginal notes.

  2. Think of likely exam questions. For example, use the key words, phrases, concepts, and questions that come up in your class notes or in your text. Some instructors give out lists of possible essay topics; if yours does, focus on this list, but don't ignore other possibilities.

  3. Without looking at your notes or your readings, answer each potential essay question—aloud. Don't feel embarrassed about doing this. Talking aloud is often more useful than answering the question in your head. You can also write down the main points that any answer should cover. (Don't write out *complete* answers to the questions unless your instructor tells you in advance exactly what is going to be on the test. Your time is probably better spent learning the material than rehearsing precisely formulated responses.)

  4. After you've answered the questions, check yourself by looking at the notes and readings once again. If you feel confident that you've answered specific questions adequately, check them off. You can go back later for a quick review. But if there are questions that you had trouble with, review that material immediately. Then repeat the third step above, answering the questions again.

- **Multiple-choice, true–false, and matching questions.** While the focus of review for essay questions should be on major issues and controversies, studying for multiple-choice, true–false, and matching questions requires more attention to the details. Almost anything is fair game for multiple-choice, true–false, and matching questions, so you can't afford to overlook anything when studying. It's a good idea to write down important facts on index cards: They're portable and available all the time, and the act of creating them helps drive the material into your memory. Furthermore, you can shuffle them and test yourself repeatedly until you've mastered the material.

- **Short-answer and fill-in questions.** Short-answer and fill-in questions are similar to essays in that they require you to recall key pieces of information rather than finding it on the page in front of you, as is the case with multiple-choice, true–false, and matching questions. However, short-answer and fill-in questions typically don't demand that you integrate or compare different types of information. Consequently, the focus of your study should be on the recall of specific, detailed information.

Test Yourself. Once you feel you've mastered the material, test yourself on it. There are several ways to do this. Often textbooks are accompanied by websites that offer automatically scored practice tests and quizzes. (*Essentials of Understanding Psychology* does: go to www.mhhe.com/feldmaness10e to try one!) You can also create a test for yourself, in writing, making its form as close as possible to what you expect the actual test to be. For instance, if your instructor has told you the classroom test will be primarily made up of short-answer questions, your made-up test should reflect that.

You might also construct a test and administer it to a classmate or a member of your study group. In turn, you could take a test that someone else has constructed. Constructing and taking practice tests are excellent ways of studying the material and cementing it into memory.

Deal with Test Anxiety. What does the anticipation of a test do to you? Do you feel shaky? Is there a knot in your stomach? Do you grit your teeth? *Test anxiety* is a temporary condition characterized by fears and concerns about test-taking. Almost everyone experiences it to some degree, although for some people it's more of a problem than for others. You'll never eliminate test anxiety completely, nor do you want to. A little bit of nervousness can energize us, making us more attentive and vigilant. Like any competitive event, testing can motivate us to do our best.

On the other hand, for some students, anxiety can spiral into the kind of paralyzing fear that makes their minds go blank. There are several ways to keep this from happening to you:

1. *Prepare thoroughly.* The more you prepare, the less test anxiety you'll feel. Good preparation can give you a sense of control and mastery, and it will prevent test anxiety from overwhelming you.
2. *Take a realistic view of the test.* Remember that your future success does not hinge on your performance on any single exam. Think of the big picture: Put the task ahead in context, and remind yourself of all the hurdles you've passed so far.
3. *Learn relaxation techniques.* These techniques are covered in the text's chapter on health psychology, but the basic process is straightforward: Breathe evenly, gently inhaling and exhaling. Focus your mind on a

pleasant, relaxing scene such as a beautiful forest or a peaceful farm or on a restful sound such as that of ocean waves breaking on the beach.

4. *Visualize success.* Think of an image of your instructor handing back your test marked with a big "A." Or imagine your instructor congratulating you on your fine performance the day after the test. Positive visualizations that highlight your potential success can help replace images of failure that may fuel test anxiety.

What if these strategies don't work? If your test anxiety is so great that it's getting in the way of your success, make use of your college's resources. Most provide a learning resource center or a counseling center that can provide you with personalized help.

Form a Study Group. *Study groups* are small, informal groups of students who work together to learn course material and study for a test. Forming such a group can be an excellent way to prepare for any kind of test. Some study groups are formed for particular tests, while others meet consistently throughout the term. The typical study group meets a week or two before a test and plans a strategy for studying. Members share their understanding of what will be on the test, based on what an instructor has said in class and on their review of notes and text material. Together, they develop a list of review questions to guide their individual study. The group then breaks up, and the members study on their own.

A few days before the test, members of the study group meet again. They discuss answers to the review questions, go over the material, and share any new insights they may have about the upcoming test. They may also quiz one another about the material to identify any weaknesses or gaps in their knowledge.

Study groups can be extremely powerful tools because they help accomplish several things:

- They help members organize and structure the material to approach their studying in a systematic and logical way.
- They allow students to share different perspectives on the material.
- They make it more likely that students will not overlook any potentially important information.
- They force members to rethink the course material, explaining it in words that other group members will understand. This helps both understanding and recall of the information when it is needed on the test.
- Finally, they help motivate members to do their best. When you're part of a study group, you're no longer working just for yourself; your studying also benefits the other study group members. Not wanting to let down your classmates in a study group may encourage you to put in your best effort.

Some Final Comments

We have discussed numerous techniques for increasing your study, classroom, and test effectiveness. But you need not feel tied to a specific strategy. You might want to combine other elements to create your own study system. Additional learning tips and strategies for critical thinking are presented throughout *Essentials of Understanding Psychology*.

Whatever learning strategies you use, you will maximize your understanding of the material in this book and master techniques that will help you learn and think critically in all of your academic endeavors. More important, you will optimize your understanding of the field of psychology. It is worth the effort: The excitement, challenges, and promise that psychology holds for you are significant.

Essentials of
Understanding
Psychology

1

Introduction to Psychology

Learning Outcomes for Chapter 1

MODULE 1

LO 1-1 What is the science of psychology?

LO 1-2 What are the major specialties in the field of psychology?

LO 1-3 Where do psychologists work?

Psychologists at Work

The Subfields of Psychology: Psychology's Family Tree

Working at Psychology

PsychWork: Licensed Social Worker

MODULE 2

LO 2-1 What are the origins of psychology?

LO 2-2 What are the major approaches in contemporary psychology?

LO 2-3 What are psychology's key issues and controversies?

LO 2-4 What is the future of psychology likely to hold?

A Science Evolves: The Past, the Present, and the Future

The Roots of Psychology

Today's Perspectives

Applying Psychology in the 21st Century: Psychology Matters

Psychology's Key Issues and Controversies

Neuroscience in Your Life: Reading the Movies in Your Mind

Psychology's Future

MODULE 3

What is the scientific method?

What role do theories and hypotheses play in psychological research?

What research methods do psychologists use?

How do psychologists establish cause-and-effect relationships in research studies?

Research in Psychology

The Scientific Method

Psychological Research

Descriptive Research

Experimental Research

MODULE 4

LO 4-1 What major issues confront psychologists conducting research?

Critical Research Issues

The Ethics of Research

Exploring Diversity: Choosing Participants Who Represent the Scope of Human Behavior

Neuroscience in Your Life: The Importance of Using Representative Participants

Should Animals Be Used in Research?

Threats to Experimental Validity: Avoiding Experimental Bias

Becoming an Informed Consumer of Psychology: Thinking Critically About Research

Prologue *A Dark Night*

For excited moviegoers at the premiere of the Batman film *The Dark Knight Rises,* the sudden appearance of a man armed with several weapons and wearing a ballistics helmet, gas mask, and gloves at first seemed like part of the midnight show festivities. But their amusement turned to horror when he opened fire in the theater, killing a dozen people and injuring 58 others in the largest mass shooting in U.S. history.

At the same time that the killer was showing humanity at its worst, others in the theater demonstrated the most positive aspects of human behavior. At least three people in different parts of the theater gave their lives while protecting the people they were with, and others showed extreme bravery helping strangers escape the killer's rampage.

Looking **Ahead**

The bloody theater massacre gives rise to a host of important psychological issues. For example, consider these questions asked by psychologists following the killing spree:

- What motivated the gunman?
- What biological changes occurred in the bodies of theatergoers who were fleeing for their lives from the theater?
- What memories did people have of the massacre afterward?
- What would be the long-term effects of the killings on the physical and psychological health of the survivors and witnesses?
- What are the most effective ways to help people cope with the sudden and unexpected loss of loved ones?

- Why did several people give up their own lives to save the lives of others?
- What motivated the killer's rampage? Was he psychologically disturbed?
- Could this tragedy have been prevented if the killer had received adequate psychological therapy?

As we'll soon see, psychology addresses questions like these—and many, many more. In this chapter, we begin our examination of psychology, the different types of psychologists, and the various roles that psychologists play.

Psychologists at Work

Psychology is the scientific study of behavior and mental processes. The simplicity of this definition is in some ways deceiving, concealing ongoing debates about how broad the scope of psychology should be. Should psychologists limit themselves to the study of outward, observable behavior? Is it possible to study thinking scientifically? Should the field encompass the study of such diverse topics as physical and mental health, perception, dreaming, and motivation? Is it appropriate to focus solely on human behavior, or should the behavior of other species be included?

Most psychologists would argue that the field should be receptive to a variety of viewpoints and approaches. Consequently, the phrase *behavior and mental processes* in the definition of psychology must be understood to mean many things: It encompasses not just what people do but also their thoughts, emotions, perceptions, reasoning processes, memories, and even the biological activities that maintain bodily functioning.

Psychologists try to describe, predict, and explain human behavior and mental processes, as well as helping to change and improve the lives of people and the world in which they live. They use scientific methods to find answers that are far more valid and legitimate than those resulting from intuition and speculation, which are often inaccurate (see Figure 1).

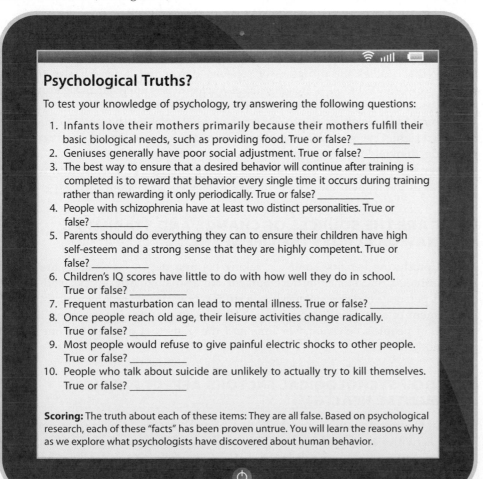

Psychological Truths?

To test your knowledge of psychology, try answering the following questions:

1. Infants love their mothers primarily because their mothers fulfill their basic biological needs, such as providing food. True or false? _____
2. Geniuses generally have poor social adjustment. True or false? _____
3. The best way to ensure that a desired behavior will continue after training is completed is to reward that behavior every single time it occurs during training rather than rewarding it only periodically. True or false? _____
4. People with schizophrenia have at least two distinct personalities. True or false? _____
5. Parents should do everything they can to ensure their children have high self-esteem and a strong sense that they are highly competent. True or false? _____
6. Children's IQ scores have little to do with how well they do in school. True or false? _____
7. Frequent masturbation can lead to mental illness. True or false? _____
8. Once people reach old age, their leisure activities change radically. True or false? _____
9. Most people would refuse to give painful electric shocks to other people. True or false? _____
10. People who talk about suicide are unlikely to actually try to kill themselves. True or false? _____

Scoring: The truth about each of these items: They are all false. Based on psychological research, each of these "facts" has been proven untrue. You will learn the reasons why as we explore what psychologists have discovered about human behavior.

FIGURE 1 The scientific method is the basis of all psychological research and is used to find valid answers. Test your knowledge of psychology by answering these questions. (Source: Adapted from Lamal, 1979.)

The Subfields of Psychology: Psychology's Family Tree

As the study of psychology has grown, it has given rise to a number of subfields (described in Figure 2). The subfields of psychology can be likened to an extended family, with assorted nieces and nephews, aunts and uncles, and cousins who, although they may not interact on a day-to-day basis, are related to one another, because they share a common goal: understanding behavior. One way to identify the key subfields is to look at some of the basic questions about behavior that they address.

WHAT ARE THE BIOLOGICAL FOUNDATIONS OF BEHAVIOR?

In the most fundamental sense, people are biological organisms. *Behavioral neuroscience* is the subfield of psychology that mainly examines how the brain and the nervous system—but other biological processes as well—determine behavior. Thus, neuroscientists consider how our bodies influence our behavior. For example, they may examine the link between specific sites in the brain and the muscular tremors of people affected by Parkinson's disease or attempt to determine how our emotions are related to physical sensations. Behavioral neuroscientists might want to know what physiological changes occurred as movie patrons in the theater where Batman was showing realized they were being shot at.

HOW DO PEOPLE SENSE, PERCEIVE, LEARN, AND THINK ABOUT THE WORLD?

If you have ever wondered why you are susceptible to optical illusions, how your body registers pain, or how to make the most of your study time, an experimental psychologist can answer your questions. *Experimental psychology* is the branch of psychology that studies the processes of sensing, perceiving, learning, and thinking about the world. (The term *experimental psychologist* is somewhat misleading: Psychologists in every specialty area use experimental techniques.)

Several subspecialties of experimental psychology have become specialties in their own right. One is *cognitive psychology*, which focuses on higher mental processes, including thinking, memory, reasoning, problem solving, judging, decision making, and language. For example, a cognitive psychologist might be interested in what the survivors of the Batman theater shooting remembered later about their experience.

WHAT ARE THE SOURCES OF CHANGE AND STABILITY IN BEHAVIOR ACROSS THE LIFE SPAN?

A baby producing her first smile . . . taking his first step . . . saying its first word. These universal milestones in development are also singularly special and unique for each person. *Developmental psychology* studies how people grow and change from the moment of conception through death. *Personality psychology* focuses on the consistency in people's behavior over time and the traits that differentiate one person from another.

HOW DO PSYCHOLOGICAL FACTORS AFFECT PHYSICAL AND MENTAL HEALTH?

Frequent depression, stress, and fears that prevent people from carrying out their normal activities are topics that would interest a health psychologist, a clinical psychologist, and a counseling psychologist. *Health psychology* explores the relationship

Subfield	Description
Behavioral genetics	*Behavioral genetics* studies the inheritance of traits related to behavior.
Behavioral neuroscience	*Behavioral neuroscience* examines the biological basis of behavior.
Clinical psychology	*Clinical psychology* deals with the study, diagnosis, and treatment of psychological disorders.
Clinical neuropsychology	*Clinical neuropsychology* unites the areas of biopsychology and clinical psychology, focusing on the relationship between biological factors and psychological disorders.
Cognitive psychology	*Cognitive psychology* focuses on the study of higher mental processes.
Counseling psychology	*Counseling psychology* focuses primarily on educational, social, and career adjustment problems.
Cross-cultural psychology	*Cross-cultural psychology* investigates the similarities and differences in psychological functioning in and across various cultures and ethnic groups.
Developmental psychology	*Developmental psychology* examines how people grow and change from the moment of conception through death.
Educational psychology	*Educational psychology* is concerned with teaching and learning processes, such as the relationship between motivation and school performance.
Environmental psychology	*Environmental psychology* considers the relationship between people and their physical environment.
Evolutionary psychology	*Evolutionary psychology* considers how behavior is influenced by our genetic inheritance from our ancestors.
Experimental psychology	*Experimental psychology* studies the processes of sensing, perceiving, learning, and thinking about the world.
Forensic psychology	*Forensic psychology* focuses on legal issues, such as determining the accuracy of witness memories.
Health psychology	*Health psychology* explores the relationship between psychological factors and physical ailments or disease.
Industrial/organizational psychology	*Industrial/organizational psychology* is concerned with the psychology of the workplace.
Personality psychology	*Personality psychology* focuses on the consistency in people's behavior over time and the traits that differentiate one person from another.
Program evaluation	*Program evaluation* focuses on assessing large-scale programs, such as the Head Start preschool program, to determine whether they are effective in meeting their goals.
Psychology of women	*Psychology of women* focuses on issues such as discrimination against women and the causes of violence against women.
School psychology	*School psychology* is devoted to counseling children in elementary and secondary schools who have academic or emotional problems.
Social psychology	*Social psychology* is the study of how people's thoughts, feelings, and actions are affected by others.
Sport psychology	*Sport psychology* applies psychology to athletic activity and exercise.

FIGURE 2 The major subfields of psychology.

between psychological factors and physical ailments or disease. For example, health psychologists are interested in assessing how long-term stress (a psychological factor) can affect physical health and in identifying ways to promote behavior that brings about good health (Belar, 2008; Yardley & Moss-Morris, 2009).

Clinical psychology deals with the study, diagnosis, and treatment of psychological disorders. Clinical psychologists are trained to diagnose and treat problems that range from the crises of everyday life, such as unhappiness over the breakup of a relationship, to more extreme conditions, such as profound, lingering depression. Some clinical psychologists also research and investigate issues that vary from identifying the early signs of psychological disturbance to studying the relationship between family communication patterns and psychological disorders.

Like clinical psychologists, counseling psychologists deal with people's psychological problems, but the problems they deal with are more specific. *Counseling psychology* focuses primarily on educational, social, and career adjustment problems. Almost every college has a center staffed with counseling psychologists. This is where students can get advice on the kinds of jobs they might be best suited for, on methods of studying effectively, and on strategies for resolving everyday difficulties, such as problems with roommates and concerns about a specific professor's grading practices. Many large business organizations also employ counseling psychologists to help employees with work-related problems.

HOW DO OUR SOCIAL NETWORKS AFFECT BEHAVIOR?

Our complex networks of social interrelationships are the focus for many subfields of psychology. For example, *social psychology* is the study of how people's thoughts, feelings, and actions are affected by others. Social psychologists concentrate on such diverse topics as human aggression, liking and loving, persuasion, and conformity.

Cross-cultural psychology investigates the similarities and differences in psychological functioning in and across various cultures and ethnic groups. For example, cross-cultural psychologists examine how cultures differ in their use of punishment during child rearing.

EXPANDING PSYCHOLOGY'S FRONTIERS

The boundaries of the science of psychology are constantly growing. Three newer members of the field's family tree—evolutionary psychology, behavioral genetics, and clinical neuropsychology—have sparked particular excitement, and debate, within psychology.

Evolutionary Psychology. *Evolutionary psychology* considers how behavior is influenced by our genetic inheritance from our ancestors. The evolutionary approach suggests that the chemical coding of information in our cells not only determines traits such as hair color and race but also holds the key to understanding a broad variety of behaviors that helped our ancestors survive and reproduce.

Evolutionary psychology stems from Charles Darwin's arguments in his groundbreaking 1859 book, *On the Origin of Species.* Darwin suggested that a process of natural selection leads to the survival of the fittest and the development of traits that enable a species to adapt to its environment.

Evolutionary psychologists take Darwin's arguments a step further. They argue that our genetic inheritance determines not only physical traits such as skin and eye color but certain personality traits and social behaviors as well. For example, evolutionary psychologists suggest that behavior such as shyness, jealousy, and cross-cultural similarities in qualities desired in potential mates are at least partially determined by genetics, presumably because such behavior helped increase the survival rate of humans' ancient relatives (Buss, 2003; Sefcek, Brumbach, & Vasquez, 2007; Ward, Kogan, & Pankove, 2007).

Although they are increasingly popular, evolutionary explanations of behavior have stirred controversy. By suggesting that many significant behaviors unfold automatically, because they are wired into the human species, evolutionary approaches minimize the role of environmental and social forces. Still, the evolutionary approach has stimulated a significant amount of research on how our biological inheritance influences our traits and behaviors (Buss, 2004; Neher, 2006; Mesoudi, 2011).

Behavioral Genetics. Another rapidly growing area in psychology focuses on the biological mechanisms, such as genes and chromosomes, that enable inherited behavior to unfold. *Behavioral genetics* seeks to understand how we might inherit certain behavioral traits and how the environment influences whether we actually display such traits (Bjorklund & Ellis, 2005; Moffitt & Caspi, 2007; Rende, 2007).

Clinical Neuropsychology. *Clinical neuropsychology* unites the areas of neuroscience and clinical psychology: It focuses on the origin of psychological disorders in biological factors. Building on advances in our understanding of the structure and chemistry of the brain, this specialty has already led to promising new treatments for psychological disorders as well as debates over the use of medication to control behavior (Boake, 2008; Holtz, 2011).

Working at Psychology

Help Wanted: Assistant professor at a small liberal arts college. Teach undergraduate courses in introductory psychology and courses in specialty areas of cognitive psychology, perception, and learning. Strong commitment to quality teaching, as well as evidence of scholarship and research productivity, necessary.

Help Wanted: Industrial-organizational consulting psychologist. International firm seeks psychologists for full-time career positions as consultants to management. Candidates must have the ability to establish a rapport with senior business executives and help them find innovative and practical solutions to problems concerning people and organizations.

Help Wanted: Clinical psychologist. PhD, internship experience, and license required. Comprehensive clinic seeks psychologist to work with children and adults providing individual and group therapy, psychological evaluations, crisis intervention, and development of behavior treatment plans on multidisciplinary team.

As these job ads suggest, psychologists are employed in a variety of settings. Many doctoral-level psychologists are employed by institutions of higher learning (universities and colleges) or are self-employed, usually working as private practitioners treating clients (see Figure 3). Other work sites include hospitals, clinics, mental health centers, counseling centers, government human-services organizations, businesses, schools, and even prisons. Psychologists are employed in the military, working with soldiers, veterans, and their families, and they work for the federal government Department of Homeland Security, fighting terrorism (American Psychological Association, 2007; DeAngelis & Monahan, 2008).

Most psychologists, though, work in academic settings, allowing them to combine the three major roles played by psychologists in society: teacher, scientist, and clinical practitioner. Many psychology professors are also actively involved in research or in serving clients. Whatever the particular job site, however, psychologists share a commitment to improving individual lives as well as society in general.

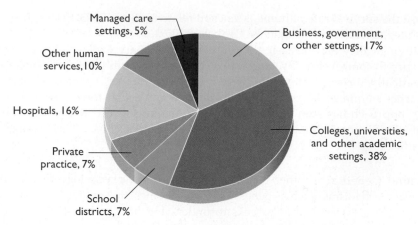

FIGURE 3 The breakdown of where U.S. psychologists (who have a PhD or PsyD degree) work. Why do you think so many psychologists work in college and university settings? (Source: American Psychological Association, 2007.)

Keep in mind that many professionals from a variety of professions use the findings of psychologists. As you can see in each *PsychWork* box here and throughout the text, we focus on how a non-psychologist uses psychology.

PsychWork

LICENSED SOCIAL WORKER

Name: Christin Poirier, LICSW

Education: BA in Psychology, Stonehill College; MA in Social Work, University of New Hampshire

For Christin Poirier, psychology is central to her occupation as a social worker, a field dedicated to enhancing the well-being of individuals, families, groups, and communities. As a social worker, Poirier works at a community mental health center where she helps children and adolescents who are experiencing emotional or behavioral difficulties or both. Says Poirier, "The strategies I employ in counseling sessions are derived from basic psychological concepts and theories. In addition, in order to know what strategies are age-appropriate for a particular client, I need to consider his or her stage of psychological development. Finally, it is necessary to consider how culture and ethnicity affect clients, so I incorporate these aspects into my clients' treatment plans."

PSYCHOLOGISTS: A PORTRAIT

Although there is no "average" psychologist in terms of personal characteristics, we can draw a statistical portrait of the field. There are close to 300,000 psychologists working today in the United States, but they are outnumbered by psychologists in other countries. Europe has more than 290,000 psychologists, and in Brazil alone there are 140,000 licensed psychologists. Although most research is conducted in the United States, psychologists in other countries are increasingly influential in adding to the knowledge base and practices of psychology (Peiro & Lunt, 2002; Stevens & Gielen, 2007; Rees & Seaton, 2011).

In the United States, women outnumber men in the field, a big change from earlier years when women faced bias and were actively discouraged from becoming psychologists. Today, women earn around three-fourths of new psychology doctorate degrees. There is an active debate about whether, and how, to seek balance in the percentage of men and women in the field (Frincke & Pate, 2004; Cynkar, 2007).

The vast majority of psychologists in the United States are white, limiting the diversity of the field. Only 6% of all psychologists are members of racial minority groups. Although the number of minority individuals entering the field is higher than a decade ago—around 20% of new master's degrees and 16% of new doctorate degrees are awarded to people of color—the numbers have not kept up with the dramatic growth of the minority population at large (Hoffer et al., 2005; Maton et al., 2006; Chandler, 2011).

The underrepresentation of racial and ethnic minorities among psychologists is significant for several reasons. First, the field of psychology is diminished by a lack of the diverse perspectives and talents that minority-group members can provide. Furthermore, minority-group psychologists serve as role models for members of minority communities, and their underrepresentation in the profession might deter other minority-group members from entering the field. Finally, because members of minority groups often prefer to receive psychological therapy from treatment providers of their own race or ethnic group, the rarity of minority psychologists can discourage some members of minority groups from seeking treatment (Bernal et al., 2002; Jenkins et al., 2003; Bryant et al., 2005).

THE EDUCATION OF A PSYCHOLOGIST

How do people become psychologists? The most common route is a long one. Most psychologists have a doctorate, either a *PhD* (doctor of philosophy) or, less frequently, a *PsyD* (doctor of psychology). The PhD is a research degree that requires a dissertation based on an original investigation. The PsyD is obtained by psychologists who wish to focus on the treatment of psychological disorders. (Psychologists are distinct from psychiatrists, who have a medical degree and specialize in the diagnosis and treatment of psychological disorders, often using treatments that involve the prescription of drugs.)

Both the PhD and the PsyD typically take four or five years of work past the bachelor's level. Some fields of psychology involve education beyond the doctorate. For instance, doctoral-level clinical psychologists, who deal with people with psychological disorders, typically spend an additional year doing an internship.

About a third of people working in the field of psychology have a master's degree as their highest degree, which they earn after two or three years of graduate work. These psychologists teach, provide therapy, conduct research, or work in specialized programs dealing with drug abuse or crisis intervention. Some work in universities, government, and business, collecting and analyzing data.

CAREERS FOR PSYCHOLOGY MAJORS

Although some psychology majors head for graduate school in psychology or an unrelated field, the majority join the workforce immediately after graduation. Most report that the jobs they take after graduation are related to their psychology background.

An undergraduate major in psychology provides excellent preparation for a variety of occupations. Because undergraduates who specialize in psychology develop good analytical skills, are trained to think critically, and are able to synthesize and evaluate information well, employers in business, industry, and the government value their preparation (Kuther, 2003).

The most common areas of employment for psychology majors are in the social services, including working as an administrator, serving as a counselor, and providing direct care. Some 20% of recipients of bachelor's degrees in psychology work in the social services or in some other form of public affairs. In addition, psychology majors often enter the fields of education or business or work for federal, state, and local governments (see Figure 4; American Psychological Association, 2000; Murray, 2002; Rajecki & Borden, 2011).

Study Alert

Be sure you can differentiate between a PhD (doctor of philosophy) and a PsyD (doctor of psychology), as well as between psychologists and psychiatrists.

Positions Obtained by Psychology Majors

Business Field	Education/ Academic Field	Social Field
Administrative assistant	Administration	Activities coordinator
Advertising trainee	Child-care provider	Behavioral specialist
Affirmative action officer	Child-care worker/ supervisor	Career counselor
Benefits manager		Case worker
Claims specialist	Data management	Child protection worker
Community relations officer	Laboratory assistant	Clinical coordinator
Customer relations	Parent/family education	Community outreach worker
Data management	Preschool teacher	Corrections officer
Employee counselor	Public opinion surveyor	Counselor assistant
Employee recruitment	Research assistant	Crisis intervention counselor
Human resources coordinator/ manager/specialist	Teaching assistant	Employment counselor
Labor relations manager/specialist		Group home attendant
Loan officer		Mental health assistant
Management trainee		Occupational therapist
Marketing		Probation officer
Personnel manager/officer		Program manager
Product and services research		Rehabilitation counselor
Programs/events coordination		Residence counselor
Public relations		Social service assistant
Retail sales management		Social worker
Sales representative		Substance abuse counselor
Special features writing/reporting		Youth counselor
Staff training and development		
Trainer/training office		

FIGURE 4 Although many psychology majors pursue employment in social services, a background in psychology can prepare one for many professions outside the social services field. What is it about the science and art of psychology that makes it such a versatile field? (Source: From Tara L. Kuther, *The Psychology Major's Handbook*, 1st ed., p. 114. © 2003 Wadsworth, a part of Cengage Learning, Inc. Reproduced by permission. www.cengage.com/permissions.)

RECAP/EVALUATE/RETHINK

RECAP

LO 1-1 What is the science of psychology?

- Psychology is the scientific study of behavior and mental processes, encompassing not just what people do but also their biological activities, feelings, perceptions, memory, reasoning, and thoughts. (p. 5)

LO 1-2 What are the major specialties in the field of psychology?

- Behavioral neuroscientists focus on the biological basis of behavior, and experimental psychologists study the processes of sensing, perceiving, learning, and thinking about the world. (p. 6)
- Cognitive psychology, an outgrowth of experimental psychology, studies higher mental processes, including memory, knowing, thinking, reasoning, problem solving, judging, decision making, and language. (p. 6)
- Developmental psychologists study how people grow and change throughout the life span. (p. 6)
- Personality psychologists consider the consistency and change in an individual's behavior, as well as the individual differences that distinguish one person's behavior from another's. (p. 6)
- Health psychologists study psychological factors that affect physical disease, whereas clinical psychologists consider the study, diagnosis, and treatment of abnormal behavior. Counseling psychologists focus on educational, social, and career adjustment problems. (pp. 6, 7)
- Social psychology is the study of how people's thoughts, feelings, and actions are affected by others. (p. 8)

- Cross-cultural psychology examines the similarities and differences in psychological functioning among various cultures. (p. 8)
- Other increasingly important fields are evolutionary psychology, behavioral genetics, and clinical neuropsychology. (pp. 8, 9)

LO 1-3 Where do psychologists work?

- Psychologists are employed in a variety of settings. Although the primary sites of employment are private practice and colleges, many psychologists are found in hospitals, clinics, community mental health centers, and counseling centers. (p. 9)

EVALUATE

Match each subfield of psychology with the issues or questions posed below.

a. behavioral neuroscience
b. experimental psychology
c. cognitive psychology
d. developmental psychology
e. personality psychology
f. health psychology
g. clinical psychology
h. counseling psychology
i. educational psychology
j. school psychology
k. social psychology
l. industrial psychology

1. Joan, a college freshman, is worried about her grades. She needs to learn better organizational skills and study habits to cope with the demands of college.
2. At what age do children generally begin to acquire an emotional attachment to their fathers?
3. It is thought that pornographic films that depict violence against women may prompt aggressive behavior in some men.
4. What chemicals are released in the human body as a result of a stressful event? What are their effects on behavior?
5. Luis is unique in his manner of responding to crisis situations, with an even temperament and a positive outlook.
6. The teachers of 8-year-old Jack are concerned that he has recently begun to withdraw socially and to show little interest in schoolwork.
7. Janetta's job is demanding and stressful. She wonders if her lifestyle is making her more prone to certain illnesses, such as cancer and heart disease.
8. A psychologist is intrigued by the fact that some people are much more sensitive to painful stimuli than others are.
9. A strong fear of crowds leads a young man to seek treatment for his problem.
10. What mental strategies are involved in solving complex word problems?
11. What teaching methods most effectively motivate elementary school students to successfully accomplish academic tasks?
12. Jessica is asked to develop a management strategy that will encourage safer work practices in an assembly plant.

RETHINK

1. Do you think intuition and common sense are sufficient for understanding why people act the way they do? In what ways is a scientific approach appropriate for studying human behavior?
2. *From an educator's perspective:* Suppose you are a teacher who has a 7-year-old child in your class who is having unusual difficulty learning to read. Imagine that you could consult as many psychologists with different specialties as you wanted. What are the different types of psychologists that you might approach to address the problem?

Answers to Evaluate Questions

1. a-4; b-8; c-10; d-2; e-5; f-7; g-9; h-1; i-11; j-6; k-3; l-12

KEY TERM

psychology p. 5

A Science Evolves: The Past, the Present, and the Future

Learning Outcomes

LO 2-1 What are the origins of psychology?

LO 2-2 What are the major approaches in contemporary psychology?

LO 2-3 What are psychology's key issues and controversies?

LO 2-4 What is the future of psychology likely to hold?

William Wundt

structuralism Wundt's approach, which focuses on uncovering the fundamental mental components of consciousness, thinking, and other kinds of mental states and activities.

introspection A procedure used to study the structure of the mind in which subjects are asked to describe in detail what they are experiencing when they are exposed to a stimulus.

Seven thousand years ago, people assumed that psychological problems were caused by evil spirits. To allow those spirits to escape from a person's body, ancient healers chipped a hole in a patient's skull with crude instruments—a procedure called *trephining*.

According to the 17th-century philosopher Descartes, nerves were hollow tubes through which "animal spirits" conducted impulses in the same way that water is transmitted through a pipe. When a person put a finger too close to a fire, heat was transmitted to the brain through the tubes.

Franz Josef Gall, an 18th-century physician, argued that a trained observer could discern intelligence, moral character, and other basic personality characteristics from the shape and number of bumps on a person's skull. His theory gave rise to the field of phrenology, employed by hundreds of practitioners in the 19th century.

Although these explanations might sound far-fetched, in their own times they represented the most advanced thinking about what might be called the psychology of the era. Our understanding of behavior has progressed tremendously since the 18th century, but most of the advances have been recent. As sciences go, psychology is one of the new kids on the block. (For highlights in the development of the field, see Figure 1 on page 16.)

The Roots of Psychology

We can trace psychology's roots back to the ancient Greeks, who considered the mind to be a suitable topic for scholarly contemplation. Later philosophers argued for hundreds of years about some of the questions psychologists grapple with today. For example, the 17th-century British philosopher John Locke believed that children were born into the world with minds like "blank slates" (*tabula rasa* in Latin) and that their experiences determined what kind of adults they would become. His views contrasted with those of Plato and the 17th-century French philosopher René Descartes, who argued that some knowledge was inborn in humans.

However, the formal beginning of psychology as a scientific discipline is generally considered to be in the late 19th century, when Wilhelm Wundt established the first experimental laboratory devoted to psychological phenomena in Leipzig, Germany. At about the same time, William James was setting up his laboratory in Cambridge, Massachusetts.

When Wundt set up his laboratory in 1879, his aim was to study the building blocks of the mind. He considered psychology to be the study of conscious experience. His perspective, which came to be known as **structuralism,** focused on uncovering the fundamental mental components of perception, consciousness, thinking, emotions, and other kinds of mental states and activities.

To determine how basic sensory processes shape our understanding of the world, Wundt and other structuralists used a procedure called **introspection,** in which they presented people with a stimulus—such as a bright green object or a sentence printed on a card—and asked them to describe, in their own words and in as much detail as they could, what they were experiencing. Wundt argued that by analyzing people's reports, psychologists could come to a better understanding of the structure of the mind.

Over time, psychologists challenged Wundt's approach. They became increasingly dissatisfied with the assumption that introspection could reveal the structure of the mind. Introspection was not a truly scientific technique, because there were few ways an outside observer could confirm the accuracy of others' introspections. Moreover, people had difficulty describing some kinds of inner experiences, such as emotional responses. Those drawbacks led to the development of new approaches, which largely replaced structuralism.

The perspective that replaced structuralism is known as functionalism. Rather than focusing on the mind's structure, **functionalism** concentrated on what the mind *does* and how behavior *functions*. Functionalists, whose perspective became prominent in the early 1900s, asked what role behavior plays in allowing people to adapt to their environments. For example, a functionalist might examine the function of the emotion of fear in preparing us to deal with emergency situations.

Led by the American psychologist William James, the functionalists examined how behavior allows people to satisfy their needs and how our "stream of consciousness" permits us to adapt to our environment. The American educator John Dewey drew on functionalism to develop the field of school psychology, proposing ways to best meet students' educational needs.

Another important reaction to structuralism was the development of gestalt psychology in the early 1900s. **Gestalt psychology** emphasizes how perception is organized. Instead of considering the individual parts that make up thinking, gestalt psychologists took the opposite tack, studying how people consider individual elements together as units or wholes. Led by German scientists such as Hermann Ebbinghaus and Max Wertheimer, gestalt psychologists proposed that "The whole is different from the sum of its parts," meaning that our perception, or understanding, of objects is greater and more meaningful than the individual elements that make up our perceptions. Gestalt psychologists have made substantial contributions to our understanding of perception.

functionalism An early approach to psychology that concentrated on what the mind does—the functions of mental activity—and the role of behavior in allowing people to adapt to their environments.

gestalt (geh-SHTALLT) psychology An approach to psychology that focuses on the organization of perception and thinking in a "whole" sense rather than on the individual elements of perception.

WOMEN IN PSYCHOLOGY: FOUNDING MOTHERS

As in many scientific fields, social prejudices hindered women's participation in the early development of psychology. For example, many universities would not even admit women to their graduate psychology programs in the early 1900s.

Despite the hurdles they faced, women made notable contributions to psychology, although their impact on the field was largely overlooked until recently. For example, Margaret Floy Washburn (1871–1939) was the first woman to receive a doctorate in psychology, and she did important work on animal behavior. Leta Stetter Hollingworth (1886–1939) was one of the first psychologists to focus on child development and on women's issues. She collected data to refute the view, popular in the early 1900s, that women's abilities periodically declined during parts of the menstrual cycle (Hollingworth, 1943/1990; Denmark & Fernandez, 1993; Furumoto & Scarborough, 2002).

Mary Calkins (1863–1930), who studied memory in the early part of the 20th century, became the first female president of the American Psychological Association. Karen Horney (pronounced "HORN-eye") (1885–1952) focused on the social and cultural factors behind personality, and June Etta Downey (1875–1932) spearheaded the study of personality traits and became the first woman to head a psychology department at a state university. Anna Freud (1895–1982), the daughter of Sigmund Freud, also made notable contributions to the treatment of abnormal behavior, and Mamie Phipps Clark (1917–1983) carried out pioneering work on how children of color grew to recognize racial differences (Horney, 1937; Stevens & Gardner, 1982; Lal, 2002).

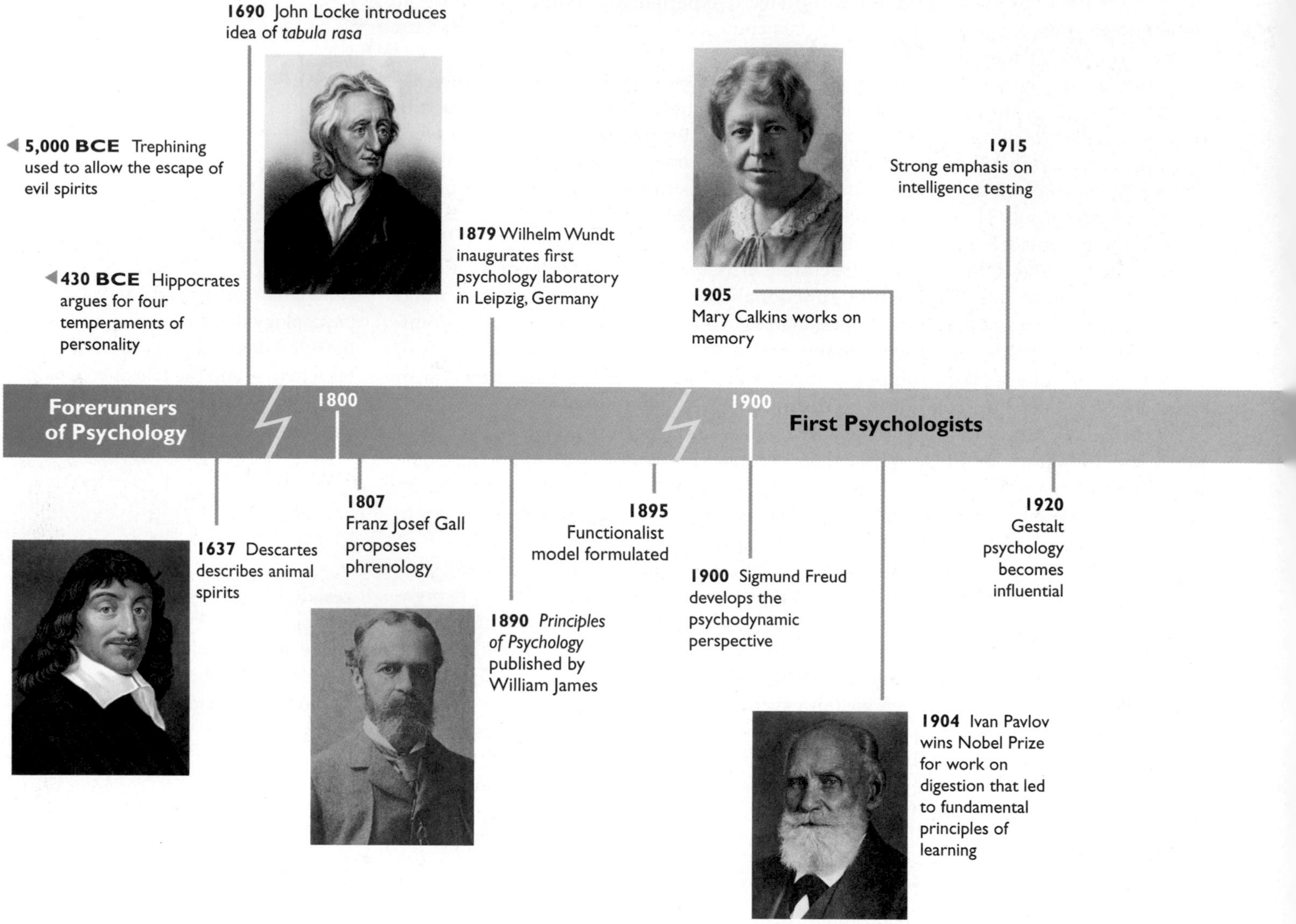

1690 John Locke introduces idea of *tabula rasa*

◀ **5,000 BCE** Trephining used to allow the escape of evil spirits

1879 Wilhelm Wundt inaugurates first psychology laboratory in Leipzig, Germany

1915 Strong emphasis on intelligence testing

◀ **430 BCE** Hippocrates argues for four temperaments of personality

1905 Mary Calkins works on memory

Forerunners of Psychology

1800

1900

First Psychologists

1807 Franz Josef Gall proposes phrenology

1895 Functionalist model formulated

1920 Gestalt psychology becomes influential

1637 Descartes describes animal spirits

1900 Sigmund Freud develops the psychodynamic perspective

1890 *Principles of Psychology* published by William James

1904 Ivan Pavlov wins Nobel Prize for work on digestion that led to fundamental principles of learning

FIGURE 1 This time line illustrates major milestones in the development of psychology.

Today's Perspectives

The men and women who laid the foundations of psychology shared a common goal: to explain and understand behavior using scientific methods. Seeking to achieve the same goal, the tens of thousands of psychologists who followed those early pioneers embraced—and often rejected—a variety of broad perspectives.

The perspectives of psychology offer distinct outlooks and emphasize different factors. Just as we can use more than one map to find our way around a particular region—for instance, a map that shows roads and highways and another map that shows major landmarks—psychologists developed a variety of approaches to understanding behavior. When considered jointly, the different perspectives provide the means to explain behavior in its amazing variety.

Today, the field of psychology includes five major perspectives (summarized in Figure 2 on page 18). These broad perspectives emphasize different aspects of behavior and mental processes, and each takes our understanding of behavior in a somewhat different direction.

Study Alert

Knowing the basic outlines of the history of the field will help you understand how today's major perspectives have evolved.

1924
John B. Watson, an early behaviorist, publishes *Behaviorism*

1951
Carl Rogers publishes *Client-Centered Therapy*, helping to establish the humanistic perspective

1957 Leon Festinger publishes *A Theory of Cognitive Dissonance*, producing a major impact on social psychology

1980
Jean Piaget, an influential developmental psychologist, dies

1990 Greater emphasis on multiculturalism and diversity

2010
New subfields develop such as clinical neuropsychology and evolutionary psychology

Modern Psychology

2000

1928
Leta Stetter Hollingworth publishes work on adolescence

1953
B. F. Skinner publishes *Science and Human Behavior*, advocating the behavioral perspective

1954
Abraham Maslow publishes *Motivation and Personality*, developing the concept of self-actualization

1969
Arguments regarding the genetic basis of IQ fuel lingering controversies

1981 David Hubel and Torsten Wiesel win Nobel Prize for work on vision cells in the brain

1985 Increasing emphasis on cognitive perspective

2000
Elizabeth Loftus does pioneering work on false memory and eyewitness testimony

THE NEUROSCIENCE PERSPECTIVE: BLOOD, SWEAT, AND FEARS

When we get down to the basics, humans are animals made of skin and bones. The **neuroscience perspective** considers how people and nonhumans function biologically: how individual nerve cells are joined together, how the inheritance of certain characteristics from parents and other ancestors influences behavior, how the functioning of the body affects hopes and fears, which behaviors are instinctual, and so forth. Even more complex kinds of behaviors, such as a baby's response to strangers, are viewed as having critical biological components by psychologists who embrace the neuroscience perspective. This perspective includes the study of heredity and evolution, which considers how heredity may influence behavior; and behavioral neuroscience, which examines how the brain and the nervous system affect behavior.

Because every behavior ultimately can be broken down into its biological components, the neuroscience perspective has broad appeal. Psychologists who subscribe to this perspective have made major contributions to the understanding and betterment of human life, ranging from cures for certain types of deafness to drug treatments for people with severe mental disorders. Furthermore, advances in methods for examining the anatomy and functioning of the brain have permitted the neuroscientific

neuroscience perspective The approach that views behavior from the perspective of the brain, the nervous system, and other biological functions.

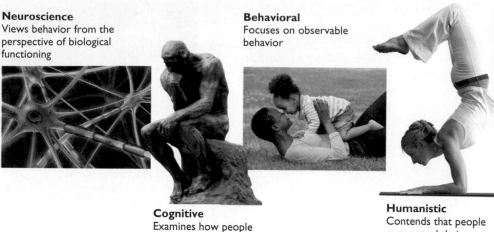

Neuroscience
Views behavior from the perspective of biological functioning

Behavioral
Focuses on observable behavior

Psychodynamic
Believes behavior is motivated by inner, unconscious forces over which a person has little control

Cognitive
Examines how people understand and think about the world

Humanistic
Contends that people can control their behavior and that they naturally try to reach their full potential

FIGURE 2 The major perspectives of psychology.

Study Alert
Use Figure 2 to differentiate the five perspectives, which are important because they provide a foundation for every topic covered throughout the text.

perspective to extend its influence across a broad range of subfields in psychology. (We'll see examples of these methods throughout this book in *Neuroscience in Your Life*.)

THE PSYCHODYNAMIC PERSPECTIVE: UNDERSTANDING THE INNER PERSON

To many people who have never taken a psychology course, psychology begins and ends with the psychodynamic perspective. Proponents of the **psychodynamic perspective** argue that behavior is motivated by inner forces and conflicts about which we have little awareness or control. They view dreams and slips of the tongue as indications of what a person is truly feeling within a seething cauldron of unconscious psychic activity.

The origins of the psychodynamic view are linked to one person: Sigmund Freud. Freud was an Austrian physician in the early 1900s whose ideas about unconscious determinants of behavior had a revolutionary effect on 20th-century thinking, not just in psychology but in related fields as well. Although some of the original Freudian principles have been roundly criticized, the contemporary psychodynamic perspective has provided a means not only to understand and treat some kinds of psychological disorders but also to understand everyday phenomena such as prejudice and aggression.

Sigmund Freud

psychodynamic perspective The approach based on the view that behavior is motivated by unconscious inner forces over which the individual has little control.

behavioral perspective The approach that suggests that observable, measurable behavior should be the focus of study.

THE BEHAVIORAL PERSPECTIVE: OBSERVING THE OUTER PERSON

Whereas the neuroscience and psychodynamic approaches look inside the organism to determine the causes of its behavior, the behavioral perspective takes a very different approach. The **behavioral perspective** grew out of a rejection of psychology's early emphasis on the inner workings of the mind. Instead, behaviorists suggested that the field should focus on observable behavior that can be measured objectively.

John B. Watson was the first major American psychologist to advocate a behavioral approach. Working in the 1920s, Watson was adamant in his view that one could gain a complete understanding of behavior by studying and modifying the environment in which people operate.

In fact, Watson believed rather optimistically that it was possible to elicit any desired type of behavior by controlling a person's environment. This philosophy is clear in his own words: "Give me a dozen healthy infants, well-formed, and my own specified world to bring them up in and I'll guarantee to take any one at random and train him to become any type of specialist I might select—doctor, lawyer, artist, merchant-chief, and yes, even beggar-man and thief, regardless of his talents, penchants, tendencies, abilities, vocations and race of his ancestors" (Watson, 1924).

The behavioral perspective was championed by B. F. Skinner, a pioneer in the field. Much of our understanding of how people learn new behaviors is based on the behavioral perspective. As we will see, the behavioral perspective crops up along every byway of psychology. Along with its influence in the area of learning processes, this perspective has made contributions in such diverse areas as treating mental disorders, curbing aggression, resolving sexual problems, and ending drug addiction (Silverman, Roll, & Higgins, 2008; Schlinger, 2011).

THE COGNITIVE PERSPECTIVE: IDENTIFYING THE ROOTS OF UNDERSTANDING

Efforts to understand behavior lead some psychologists straight into the mind. Evolving in part from structuralism and in part as a reaction to behaviorism, which focused so heavily on observable behavior and the environment, the **cognitive perspective** focuses on how people think, understand, and know about the world. The emphasis is on learning how people comprehend and represent the outside world within themselves and how our ways of thinking about the world influence our behavior.

cognitive perspective The approach that focuses on how people think, understand, and know about the world.

Many psychologists who adhere to the cognitive perspective compare human thinking to the workings of a computer, which takes in information and transforms, stores, and retrieves it. In their view, thinking is *information processing*.

Psychologists who rely on the cognitive perspective ask questions on subjects ranging from how people make decisions to whether a person can watch television and study at the same time. The common elements that link cognitive approaches are an emphasis on how people understand and think about the world and an interest in describing the patterns and irregularities in the operation of our minds.

THE HUMANISTIC PERSPECTIVE: THE UNIQUE QUALITIES OF THE HUMAN SPECIES

Rejecting the view that behavior is determined largely by automatically unfolding biological forces, unconscious processes, or the environment, the **humanistic perspective** instead suggests that all individuals naturally strive to grow, develop, and be in control of their lives and behavior. Humanistic psychologists maintain that each of us has the capacity to seek and reach fulfillment.

humanistic perspective The approach that suggests that all individuals naturally strive to grow, develop, and be in control of their lives and behavior.

According to Carl Rogers and Abraham Maslow, who were central figures in the development of the humanistic perspective, people strive to reach their full potential if they are given the opportunity. The emphasis of the humanistic perspective is on *free will*, the ability to freely make decisions about one's own behavior and life. The notion of free will stands in contrast to *determinism*, which sees behavior as caused, or determined, by things beyond a person's control.

The humanistic perspective assumes that people have the ability to make their own choices about their behavior rather than relying on societal standards. More than any other approach, it stresses the role of psychology in enriching people's lives and helping them achieve self-fulfillment. By reminding psychologists of their commitment to the individual person in society, the humanistic perspective has been an important influence (Dillon, 2008; Robbins, 2008; Nichols, 2011).

Don't let the abstract qualities of the broad approaches we have discussed lull you into thinking that they are purely theoretical: These perspectives underlie ongoing work of a practical nature, as we discuss throughout this book. To start seeing how psychology can improve everyday life, read *Applying Psychology in the 21st Century*.

Psychology Matters

"Investigators search for clues at site of suicide bombing."

"Deepest recession in decades produces huge rates of unemployment."

"Eyewitness to killing proves unable to provide reliable clues."

"Social media like Facebook change how teenagers interact with their friends."

"Childhood obesity rates surge."

A quick review of any day's news headlines reminds us that the world is beset by a variety of stubborn problems that resist easy solutions. At the same time, a considerable number of psychologists are devoting their energies and expertise to addressing these problems and improving the human condition. Let's consider some of the ways in which psychology has addressed and helped work toward solutions of major societal problems:

People all over the world are coping with struggling economic downturns. What can psychologists add to our understanding of the problem?

- **What are the causes of terrorism?** What motivates suicide bombers? Are they psychologically disordered, or can their behavior be seen as a rational response to a particular system of beliefs? As we'll see in Module 39 when we discuss psychological disorders, psychologists are gaining an understanding of the factors that lead people to embrace suicide and to engage in terrorism to further a cause in which they deeply believe (Stroink, 2007; Locicero & Sinclair, 2008; Mintz & Brule 2009; Post et al., 2009).

- **How is the uncertain economic future affecting America's workforce?** Stress, anxiety, depression—all these are unsurprising consequences of hard economic times. But the psychological toll on American workers is making them sick—and that, in turn, has a further harmful effect on the economy. Growing evidence gathered by psychologists shows that in uncertain economic times, people need stability and support to stay healthy and function well (Allen, Hyworon, & Colombi, 2010; Hoare & Machin, 2010).

- **Why do eyewitnesses to crimes often remember the events inaccurately, and how can we increase the precision of eyewitness accounts?** Psychologists' research has come to an important conclusion: Eyewitness testimony in criminal cases is often inaccurate and biased. Memories of crimes are often clouded by emotion, and the questions asked by police investigators often elicit inaccurate responses. Work by psychologists has been used to provide national guidelines for obtaining more accurate memories during criminal investigations (Loftus & Bernstein, 2005; Kassin, 2005; Busey & Loftus, 2007).

- **How are social media changing the way we live?** Social networking media such as Facebook and Twitter are rapidly changing the way people communicate and the way news spreads around the world. How does this new way of communicating affect the way people relate to each other? How does it affect our perceptions of world events? Psychologists are examining the motivations behind social networking, its influence on individuals and social institutions, and possible beneficial applications of the technology (Bergman et al., 2011; Powell, Richmond, & Williams, 2011; Rice, Milburn, & Monro, 2011).

- **What are the roots of obesity, and how can healthier eating and better physical fitness be encouraged?** Why are some people more predisposed to obesity than others are? What social factors might be at play in the rising rate of obesity in childhood? As we discuss in Module 25, obesity is a complex problem with biological, psychological, and social underpinnings. Approaches to treating obesity therefore must take many factors into account in order to be successful. There is no magic bullet providing a quick fix, but psychologists recommend a number of strategies that help make weight-loss goals more achievable (Puhl & Latner, 2007; MacLean et al., 2009; Neumark-Sztainer, 2009).

These topics represent just a few of the issues that psychologists address on a daily basis. To further explore the many ways that psychology has an impact on everyday life, check out the American Psychological Association (APA) website, which features psychological applications in everyday life, at www.apa.org.

RETHINK

- What do *you* think are the major problems affecting society today?
- What are the psychological issues involved in these problems, and how might psychologists help find solutions to them?

Psychology's Key Issues and Controversies

As you consider the many topics and perspectives that make up psychology, ranging from a narrow focus on minute biochemical influences on behavior to a broad focus on social behaviors, you might find yourself thinking that the discipline lacks cohesion. However, the field is more unified than a first glimpse might suggest. For one thing, no matter what topical area a psychologist specializes in, he or she will rely primarily on one of the five major perspectives. For example, a developmental psychologist who specializes in the study of children could make use of the cognitive perspective or the psychodynamic perspective or any of the other major perspectives.

Psychologists also agree on what the key issues of the field are (see Figure 3). Although there are major arguments regarding how best to address and resolve the key issues, psychology is a unified science, because psychologists of all perspectives agree that the issues must be addressed if the field is going to advance. As you contemplate these key issues, try not to think of them in "either/or" terms. Instead, consider the opposing viewpoints on each issue as the opposite ends of a continuum, with the positions of individual psychologists typically falling somewhere between the two ends.

Nature (heredity) versus nurture (environment) is one of the major issues that psychologists address. How much of people's behavior is due to their genetically determined nature (heredity), and how much is due to nurture, the influences of the physical and social environment in which a child is raised? Furthermore, what is the interplay between heredity and environment? These questions have deep philosophical and historical roots, and they are involved in many topics in psychology.

A psychologist's take on this issue depends partly on which major perspective he or she subscribes to. For example, developmental psychologists whose focus is on

Study Alert

Use Figure 3 to learn the key issues that underlie every subfield of psychology.

Issue	Neuroscience	Cognitive	Behavioral	Humanistic	Psychodynamic
Nature (heredity) vs. nurture (environment)	Nature (heredity)	Both	Nurture (environment)	Nurture (environment)	Nature (heredity)
Conscious vs. unconscious determinants of behavior	Unconscious	Both	Conscious	Conscious	Unconscious
Observable behavior vs. internal mental processes	Internal emphasis	Internal emphasis	Observable emphasis	Internal emphasis	Internal emphasis
Free will vs. determinism	Determinism	Free will	Determinism	Free will	Determinism
Individual differences vs. universal principles	Universal emphasis	Individual emphasis	Both	Individual emphasis	Universal emphasis

FIGURE 3 Key issues in psychology and the positions taken by psychologists subscribing to the five major perspectives of psychology.

how people grow and change throughout the course of their lives, may be most interested in learning more about hereditary influences if they follow a neuroscience perspective. In contrast, developmental psychologists who are proponents of the behavioral perspective would be more likely to focus on environment (Rutter, 2002, 2006; Barrett, 2011).

However, every psychologist would agree that neither nature nor nurture alone is the sole determinant of behavior; rather, it is a combination of the two. In a sense, then, the real controversy involves how much of our behavior is caused by heredity and how much is caused by environmental influences.

A second major question addressed by psychologists concerns *conscious versus unconscious causes of behavior.* How much of our behavior is produced by forces of which we are fully aware, and how much is due to unconscious activity—mental processes that are not accessible to the conscious mind? This question represents one of the great controversies in the field of psychology. For example, clinical psychologists adopting a psychodynamic perspective argue that psychological disorders are brought about by unconscious factors, whereas psychologists employing the cognitive perspective suggest that psychological disorders largely are the result of faulty thinking processes.

The next issue is *observable behavior versus internal mental processes.* Should psychology concentrate solely on behavior that can be seen by outside observers, or should it focus on unseen thinking processes? Some psychologists, particularly those relying on the behavioral perspective, contend that the only legitimate source of information for psychologists is behavior that can be observed directly. Other psychologists, building on the cognitive perspective, argue that what goes on inside a person's mind is critical to understanding behavior, and so we must concern ourselves with mental processes.

Free will versus determinism is another key issue. How much of our behavior is a matter of **free will** (choices made freely by an individual), and how much is subject to **determinism,** the notion that behavior is largely produced by factors beyond people's willful control? An issue long debated by philosophers, the free-will/determinism argument is also central to the field of psychology (Dennett, 2003; Cary, 2007; Nichols, 2011).

For example, some psychologists who specialize in psychological disorders argue that people make intentional choices and that those who display so-called abnormal behavior should be considered responsible for their actions. Other psychologists disagree and contend that such individuals are the victims of forces beyond their control. The position psychologists take on this issue has important implications for the way they treat psychological disorders, especially in deciding whether treatment should be forced on people who don't want it.

The last of the key issues concerns *individual differences versus universal principles.* How much of our behavior is a consequence of our unique and special qualities, and how much reflects the culture and society in which we live? How much of our behavior is universally human? Psychologists who rely on the neuroscience perspective tend to look for universal principles of behavior, such as how the nervous system operates or the way certain hormones automatically prime us for sexual activity. Such psychologists concentrate on the similarities in our behavioral destinies despite vast differences in our upbringing. In contrast, psychologists who employ the humanistic perspective focus more on the uniqueness of every individual. They consider every person's behavior a reflection of distinct and special individual qualities.

The question of the degree to which psychologists can identify universal principles that apply to all people has taken on new significance in light of the tremendous demographic changes now occurring in the United States and around the world. As we discuss next, these changes raise new and critical issues for the discipline of psychology in the 21st century.

free will The idea that behavior is caused primarily by choices that are made freely by the individual.

determinism The idea that people's behavior is produced primarily by factors outside of their willful control.

Neuroscience in Your Life:
Reading the Movies in Your Mind

FIGURE 4 Technology is changing at an ever-increasing rate. While once the idea of seeing one's thoughts was found only in the realm of science fiction, today it is becoming a reality— almost. Though researchers expect it will be decades before they can have a good representation of our thoughts, they are starting to see ways in which it might happen. In a recent study researchers asked participants to watch movies while technicians measured the activity of their brain using fMRI (functional Magnetic Resonance Imaging). The researchers used that activity to develop models of how each person's brain activity related to what they were watching. They then were able to create an image that approximated what the participants were watching based on the brain activity. Although the images admittedly are ill-defined, the results do show the possibilities of creating higher-definition images in the future. (Source: Nishimoto et al., 2011.)

Psychology's Future

We have examined psychology's foundations, but what does the future hold for the discipline? Although the course of scientific development is notoriously difficult to predict, several trends seem likely:

- As its knowledge base grows, psychology will become increasingly specialized and new perspectives will evolve. For example, our growing understanding of the brain and the nervous system, combined with scientific advances in genetics and gene therapy, will allow psychologists to focus on *prevention* of psychological disorders rather than only on their treatment (Cuijpers et al., 2008).
- The evolving sophistication of neuroscientific approaches is likely to have an increasing influence over other branches of psychology. For instance, social psychologists already are increasing their understanding of social behaviors such as persuasion by using brain scans as part of an evolving field known as *social neuroscience*. Furthermore, as neuroscientific techniques become more sophisticated, there will be new ways of applying that knowledge, as we discuss in Figure 4 *Neuroscience in Your Life* (Bunge & Wallis, 2008; Cacioppo & Decety, 2009).
- Psychology's influence on issues of public interest also will grow. The major problems of our time—such as violence, terrorism, racial and ethnic

prejudice, poverty, and environmental and technological disasters—have important psychological aspects (Zimbardo, 2004; Hobfoll, Hall, & Canetti-Nisim, 2007; Marshall, Bryant, & Amsel, 2007).

• Finally, as the population becomes more diverse, issues of diversity—embodied in the study of racial, ethnic, linguistic, and cultural factors—will become more important to psychologists providing services and doing research. The result will be a field that can provide an understanding of *human* behavior in its broadest sense (Leong & Blustein, 2000; Chang & Sue, 2005; Quintana et al., 2006).

RECAP/EVALUATE/RETHINK

RECAP

LO 2-1 What are the origins of psychology?

• Wilhelm Wundt laid the foundation of psychology in 1879, when he opened his laboratory in Germany. (p. 14)
• Early perspectives that guided the work of psychologists were structuralism, functionalism, and gestalt theory. (pp. 14, 15)

LO 2-2 What are the major approaches in contemporary psychology?

• The neuroscience approach focuses on the biological components of the behavior of people and animals. (p. 17)
• The psychodynamic perspective suggests that powerful, unconscious inner forces and conflicts about which people have little or no awareness are the primary determinants of behavior. (p. 18)
• The behavioral perspective deemphasizes internal processes and concentrates instead on observable, measurable behavior, suggesting that understanding and control of a person's environment are sufficient to fully explain and modify behavior. (p. 18)
• Cognitive approaches to behavior consider how people know, understand, and think about the world. (p. 19)
• The humanistic perspective emphasizes that people are uniquely inclined toward psychological growth and higher levels of functioning and that they will strive to reach their full potential. (p. 19)

LO 2-3 What are psychology's key issues and controversies?

• Psychology's key issues and controversies center on how much of human behavior is a product of nature or nurture, conscious or unconscious thoughts, observable actions or internal mental processes, free will or determinism, and individual differences or universal principles. (p. 21)

LO 2-4 What is the future of psychology likely to hold?

• Psychology will become increasingly specialized, will pay greater attention to prevention instead of just treatment, will become more and more concerned with the public interest, and will take the growing diversity of the country's population into account more fully. (p. 23)

EVALUATE

1. Wundt described psychology as the study of conscious experience, a perspective he called _____.
2. Early psychologists studied the mind by asking people to describe what they were experiencing when exposed to various stimuli. This procedure was known as _____.
3. The statement "In order to study human behavior, we must consider the whole of perception rather than its component parts" might be made by a person subscribing to which perspective of psychology?
4. Jeanne's therapist asks her to recount a violent dream she recently experienced in order to gain insight into the unconscious forces affecting her behavior. Jeanne's therapist is working from a _____ perspective.
5. "It is behavior that can be observed that should be studied, not the suspected inner workings of the mind." This statement was most likely made by someone with which perspective?
   a. Cognitive perspective
   b. Neuroscience perspective
   c. Humanistic perspective
   d. Behavioral perspective
6. "My therapist is wonderful! He always points out my positive traits. He dwells on my uniqueness and strength as an individual. I feel much more confident about myself—as if I'm really growing and reaching my potential." The therapist being described most likely follows a _____ perspective.
7. In the nature-nurture issue, nature refers to heredity, and nurture refers to the _____.

8. Race is a biological concept, not a psychological one. True or false?

RETHINK

1. Focusing on one of the five major perspectives in use today (that is, neuroscience, psychodynamic, behavioral, cognitive, and humanistic), can you describe the kinds of research questions and studies that researchers using that perspective might pursue?

2. *From a journalist's perspective:* Choose a current major political controversy. What psychological approaches or perspectives can be applied to that issue?

Answers to Evaluate Questions

1. structuralism; 2. introspection; 3. gestalt; 4. psychodynamic; 5. d; 6. humanistic; 7. environment; 8. true

KEY TERMS

structuralism p. 14
introspection p. 14
functionalism p. 15
gestalt (geh-SHTALLT) psychology p. 15

neuroscience perspective p. 17
psychodynamic perspective p. 18

behavioral perspective p. 18
cognitive perspective p. 19

humanistic perspective p. 19
free will p. 22
determinism p. 22

Research in Psychology

Learning Outcomes

LO 3-1 What is the scientific method?

LO 3-2 What role do theories and hypotheses play in psychological research?

LO 3-3 What research methods do psychologists use?

LO 3-4 How do psychologists establish cause-and-effect relationships in research studies?

scientific method The approach through which psychologists systematically acquire knowledge and understanding about behavior and other phenomena of interest.

The Scientific Method

"Birds of a feather flock together". . . or "Opposites attract"? "Two heads are better than one". . . or "If you want a thing done well, do it yourself"? "The more the merrier". . . or "Two's company, three's a crowd"?

If we were to rely on common sense to understand behavior, we'd have considerable difficulty—especially because commonsense views are often contradictory. In fact, one of the major undertakings for the field of psychology is to develop suppositions about behavior and to determine which of those suppositions are accurate.

Psychologists—as well as scientists in other disciplines—meet the challenge of posing appropriate questions and properly answering them by relying on the scientific method. The **scientific method** is the approach used by psychologists to systematically acquire knowledge and understanding about behavior and other phenomena of interest. As illustrated in Figure 1, it consists of four main steps: (1) identifying questions of interest, (2) formulating an explanation, (3) carrying out research designed to support or refute the explanation, and (4) communicating the findings.

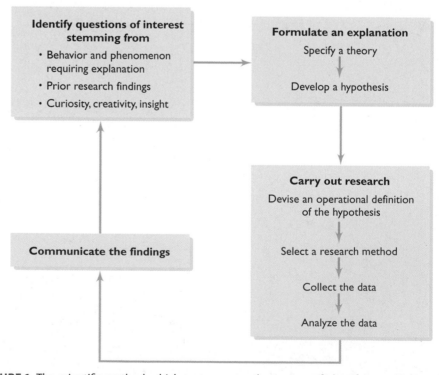

FIGURE 1 The scientific method, which encompasses the process of identifying, asking, and answering questions, is used by psychologists, and by researchers from every other scientific discipline, to come to an understanding about the world. What do you think are the advantages of this method?

Study Alert

Use Figure 1 to remember the four steps of the scientific method (identifying questions, formulating an explanation, carrying out research, and communicating the findings).

THEORIES: SPECIFYING BROAD EXPLANATIONS

In using the scientific method, psychologists start by identifying questions of interest. We have all been curious at some time about our observations of everyday behavior. If you have ever asked yourself why a particular teacher is so easily annoyed, why a friend is always late for appointments, or how your dog understands your commands, you have been formulating questions about behavior.

Psychologists, too, ask questions about the nature and causes of behavior. They may wish to explore explanations for everyday behaviors or for various phenomena. They may also pose questions that build on findings from their previous research or from research carried out by other psychologists. Or they may produce new questions that are based on curiosity, creativity, or insight.

Once a question has been identified, the next step in the scientific method is to develop a theory to explain the observed phenomenon. **Theories** are broad explanations and predictions concerning phenomena of interest. They provide a framework for understanding the relationships among a set of otherwise unorganized facts or principles.

All of us have developed our own informal theories of human behavior, such as "People are basically good" or "People's behavior is usually motivated by self-interest." However, psychologists' theories are more formal and focused. They are established on the basis of a careful study of the psychological literature to identify earlier relevant research and previously formulated theories, as well as psychologists' general knowledge of the field.

Growing out of the diverse approaches employed by psychologists, theories vary both in their breadth and in their level of detail. For example, one theory might seek to explain and predict a phenomenon as broad as emotional experience. A narrower theory might attempt to explain why people display the emotion of fear nonverbally after receiving a threat (Guerrero, La Valley, & Farinelli, 2008; Waller, Cray, & Burrows, 2008; Anker & Feeley, 2011).

Psychologists Bibb Latané and John Darley, responding to the failure of bystanders to intervene when Kitty Genovese was murdered in New York, developed what they

theories Broad explanations and predictions concerning phenomena of interest.

called a theory of *diffusion of responsibility* (Latané & Darley, 1970). According to their theory, the greater the number of bystanders or witnesses to an event that calls for helping behavior, the more the responsibility for helping is perceived to be shared by all the bystanders. Thus, the greater the number of bystanders in an emergency situation, the smaller the share of the responsibility each person feels—and the less likely that any single person will come forward to help.

HYPOTHESES: CRAFTING TESTABLE PREDICTIONS

Although the diffusion of responsibility theory seems to make sense, it represented only the beginning phase of Latané and Darley's investigative process. Their next step was to devise a way to test their theory. To do this, they needed to create a hypothesis. A **hypothesis** is a prediction stated in a way that allows it to be tested. Hypotheses stem from theories; they help test the underlying soundness of theories.

> **hypothesis** A prediction, stemming from a theory, stated in a way that allows it to be tested.

In the same way that we develop our own broad theories about the world, we also construct hypotheses about events and behavior. Those hypotheses can range from trivialities (such as why our English instructor wears those weird shirts) to more meaningful matters (such as what is the best way to study for a test). Although we rarely test these hypotheses systematically, we do try to determine whether they are right. Perhaps we try comparing two strategies: cramming the night before an exam versus spreading out our study over several nights. By assessing which approach yields better test performance, we have created a way to compare the two strategies.

A hypothesis must be restated in a way that will allow it to be tested, which involves creating an operational definition. An **operational definition** is the translation of a hypothesis into specific, testable procedures that can be measured and observed.

> **operational definition** The translation of a hypothesis into specific, testable procedures that can be measured and observed.

There is no single way to go about devising an operational definition for a hypothesis; it depends on logic, the equipment and facilities available, the psychological perspective being employed, and ultimately the creativity of the researcher. For example, one researcher might develop a hypothesis that uses as an operational definition of "fear" an increase in heart rate. In contrast, another psychologist might use as an operational definition of "fear" a written response to the question "How much fear are you experiencing at this moment?"

Latané and Darley's hypothesis was a straightforward prediction from their more general theory of diffusion of responsibility: The more people who witness an emergency situation, the less likely it is that help will be given to a victim. They could, of course, have chosen another hypothesis (try to think of one!), but their initial formulation seemed to offer the most direct test of the theory.

Psychologists rely on formal theories and hypotheses for many reasons. For one thing, theories and hypotheses allow them to make sense of unorganized, separate observations and bits of information by permitting them to place the pieces within a coherent framework. In addition, theories and hypotheses offer psychologists the opportunity to move beyond known facts and make deductions about unexplained phenomena and develop ideas for future investigation (Howitt & Cramer, 2000; Cohen, 2003; Gurin, 2006).

In short, the scientific method, with its emphasis on theories and hypotheses, helps psychologists pose appropriate questions. With properly stated questions in hand, psychologists then can choose from a variety of research methods to find answers.

Study Alert

Remember that a theory is a broad explanation, while a hypothesis is a more narrow prediction.

Psychological Research

Research—systematic inquiry aimed at the discovery of new knowledge—is a central ingredient of the scientific method in psychology. It provides the key to understanding the degree to which hypotheses (and the theories behind them) are accurate.

Just as we can apply different theories and hypotheses to explain the same phenomena, we can use a number of alternative methods to conduct research. As we consider the major tools that psychologists use to conduct research, keep in mind that their relevance extends beyond testing and evaluating hypotheses in psychology. All of us carry out elementary forms of research on our own. For instance, a supervisor might evaluate an employee's performance; a physician might systematically test the effects of different doses of a drug on a patient; a salesperson might compare different persuasive strategies. Each of these situations draws on the research practices we are about to discuss.

Descriptive Research

Let's begin by considering several types of *descriptive research* designed to systematically investigate a person, group, or patterns of behavior. These methods include archival research, naturalistic observation, survey research, and case studies.

ARCHIVAL RESEARCH

Suppose that, like the psychologists Latané and Darley (1970), you were interested in finding out more about emergency situations in which bystanders did not provide help. One of the first places you might turn to would be historical accounts. By searching newspaper records, for example, you might find support for the notion that a decrease in helping behavior historically has accompanied an increase in the number of bystanders.

Using newspaper articles is an example of archival research. In **archival research,** existing data, such as census documents, college records, and newspaper clippings, are examined to test a hypothesis. For example, college records may be used to determine if there are gender differences in academic performance (Sullivan, Riccio, & Reynolds, 2008).

Archival research is a relatively inexpensive means of testing a hypothesis because someone else has already collected the basic data. Of course, the use of existing data has several drawbacks. For one thing, the data may not be in a form that allows the researcher to test a hypothesis fully. The information could be incomplete, or it could have been collected haphazardly (Simonton, 2000; Riniolo et al., 2003; Vega, 2006).

Most attempts at archival research are hampered by the simple fact that records with the necessary information often do not exist. In these instances, researchers often turn to another research method: naturalistic observation.

archival research Research in which existing data, such as census documents, college records, and newspaper clippings, are examined to test a hypothesis.

NATURALISTIC OBSERVATION

In **naturalistic observation,** the investigator observes some naturally occurring behavior and does not make a change in the situation. For example, a researcher investigating helping behavior might observe the kind of help given to victims in a high-crime area of a city. The important point to remember about naturalistic observation is that the researcher simply records what occurs, making no modification in the situation that is being observed (Moore, 2002; Rustin, 2006; Kennison & Bowers, 2011).

Although the advantage of naturalistic observation is obvious—we get a sample of what people do in their "natural habitat"—there is also an important drawback: the inability to control any of the factors of interest. For example, we might find so few naturally occurring instances of helping behavior that we would be unable to draw any conclusions. Because naturalistic observation prevents researchers from making changes in a situation, they must wait until the appropriate conditions occur.

naturalistic observation Research in which an investigator simply observes some naturally occurring behavior and does not make a change in the situation.

Dian Fossey, a pioneer in the study of endangered mountain gorillas in their native habitat, relied on naturalistic observation for her research. What are the advantages of this approach?

survey research Research in which people chosen to represent a larger population are asked a series of questions about their behavior, thoughts, or attitudes.

PsychTech

The most efficient way to conduct surveys is via the web. But web surveys often have sampling problems, as not everyone has easy access to the web, such as people living in poverty. Consequently, web surveys may not be representative of the broader population.

case study An in-depth, intensive investigation of an individual or small group of people.

Furthermore, if people know they are being watched, they may alter their reactions and produce behavior that is not truly representative.

SURVEY RESEARCH

There is no more straightforward way of finding out what people think, feel, and do than asking them directly. For this reason, surveys are an important research method. In **survey research,** a *sample* of people chosen to represent a larger group of interest (a *population*) is asked a series of questions about their behavior, thoughts, or attitudes. Survey methods have become so sophisticated that even with a very small sample researchers are able to infer with great accuracy how a larger group would respond. For instance, a sample of just a few thousand voters is sufficient to predict within one or two percentage points who will win a presidential election—if the representative sample is chosen with care (Sommer & Sommer, 2001; Groves et al., 2004; Igo, 2006).

Researchers investigating helping behavior might conduct a survey by asking people to complete a questionnaire in which they indicate their reluctance for giving aid to someone. Similarly, researchers interested in learning about sexual practices have carried out surveys to learn which practices are common and which are not and to chart changing notions of sexual morality over the last several decades (Reece et al., 2009; Santelli et al., 2009).

However, survey research has several potential pitfalls. For one thing, if the sample of people who are surveyed is not representative of the broader population of interest, the results of the survey will have little meaning. For instance, if a sample of voters in a town includes only Republicans, it would hardly be useful for predicting the results of an election in which both Republicans and Democrats are voting. Consequently, researchers using surveys strive to obtain a *random sample* of the population in question, in which every voter in the town has an equal chance of being included in the sample receiving the survey (Daley et al., 2003; Dale, 2006; Vitak et al., 2011).

In addition, survey respondents may not want to admit to holding socially undesirable attitudes. (Most racists know they are racists and might not want to admit it.) Furthermore, people may not want to admit they engage in behaviors that they feel are somehow abnormal—a problem that plagues surveys of sexual behavior because people are often reluctant to admit what they really do in private. Finally, in some cases, people may not even be consciously aware of what their true attitudes are or why they hold them.

THE CASE STUDY

When they read of a suicide bomber in the Middle East, many people wonder what it is about the terrorist's personality or background that leads to such behavior. To answer this question, psychologists might conduct a case study. In contrast to a survey, in which many people are studied, a **case study** is an in-depth, intensive investigation of a single individual or a small group. Case studies often include *psychological testing,* a procedure in which a carefully designed set of questions is used to gain some insight into the personality of the individual or group (Gass et al., 2000; Addus, Chen, & Khan, 2007).

When case studies are used as a research technique, the goal is often not only to learn about the few individuals being examined but also to use the insights gained from the study to improve our understanding of people in general. Sigmund Freud developed his theories through case studies of individual patients. Similarly, case studies of terrorists might help identify others who are prone to violence.

The drawback to case studies? If the individuals examined are unique in certain ways, it is impossible to make valid generalizations to a larger population. Still, they sometimes lead the way to new theories and treatments for psychological disorders.

CORRELATIONAL RESEARCH

In using the descriptive research methods we have discussed, researchers often wish to determine the relationship between two variables. **Variables** are behaviors, events, or other characteristics that can change, or vary, in some way. For example, in a study to determine whether the amount of studying makes a difference in test scores, the variables would be study time and test scores.

In **correlational research,** two sets of variables are examined to determine whether they are associated, or "correlated." The strength and direction of the relationship between the two variables are represented by a mathematical statistic known as a *correlation* (or, more formally, a *correlation coefficient*), which can range from +1.0 to −1.0.

A *positive correlation* indicates that as the value of one variable increases, we can predict that the value of the other variable will also increase. For example, if we predict that the more time students spend studying for a test, the higher their grades on the test will be, and that the less they study, the lower their test scores will be, we are expecting to find a positive correlation. (Higher values of the variable "amount of study time" would be associated with higher values of the variable "test score," and lower values of "amount of study time" would be associated with lower values of "test score.") The correlation, then, would be indicated by a positive number, and the stronger the association was between studying and test scores, the closer the number would be to +1.0. For example, we might find a correlation of +.85 between test scores and amount of study time, indicating a strong positive association.

In contrast, a *negative correlation* tells us that as the value of one variable increases, the value of the other decreases. For instance, we might predict that as the number of hours spent studying increases, the number of hours spent partying decreases. Here we are expecting a negative correlation, ranging between 0 and −1.0. More studying is associated with less partying, and less studying is associated with more partying. The stronger the association between studying and partying is, the closer the correlation will be to −1.0. For instance, a correlation of −.85 would indicate a strong negative association between partying and studying.

Of course, it's quite possible that little or no relationship exists between two variables. For instance, we would probably not expect to find a relationship between number of study hours and height. Lack of a relationship would be indicated by a correlation close to 0. For example, if we found a correlation of −.02 or +.03, it would indicate that there is virtually no association between the two variables; knowing how much someone studies does not tell us anything about how tall he or she is.

When two variables are strongly correlated with each other, we are tempted to assume that one variable causes the other. For example, if we find that more study time is associated with higher grades, we might guess that more studying *causes* higher grades. Although this is not a bad guess, it remains just a guess—because finding that two variables are correlated does not mean that there is a causal relationship between them. The strong correlation suggests that knowing how much a person studies can help us predict how that person will do on a test, but it does not mean that the studying *causes* the test performance. Instead, for instance, people who are more interested in the subject matter might study more than do those who are less interested, and so the amount of interest, not the number of hours spent studying, would predict test performance. The mere fact that two variables occur together does not mean that one causes the other.

Similarly, suppose you learned that the number of houses of worship in a large sample of cities was positively correlated with the number of people arrested, meaning that the more houses of worship, the more arrests there were in a city. Does this mean that the presence of more houses of worship caused the greater number of arrests? Almost surely not, of course. In this case, the underlying cause is probably the size of the city: In bigger cities, there are both more houses of worship *and* more arrests.

variables Behaviors, events, or other characteristics that can change, or vary, in some way.

correlational research Research in which the relationship between two sets of variables is examined to determine whether they are associated, or "correlated."

Study Alert

The concept that "correlation does not imply causation" is a key principle.

FIGURE 2 If we find that frequent viewing of television programs with aggressive content is associated with high levels of aggressive behavior, we might cite several plausible causes, as suggested in this figure. For example, (a) choosing to watch shows with aggressive content could produce aggression; or (b) being a highly aggressive person might cause one to choose to watch televised aggression; or (c) having a high energy level might cause a person to both choose to watch aggressive shows and to act aggressively. Correlational findings, then, do not permit us to determine causality. Can you think of a way to study the effects of televised aggression on aggressive behavior that is not correlational?

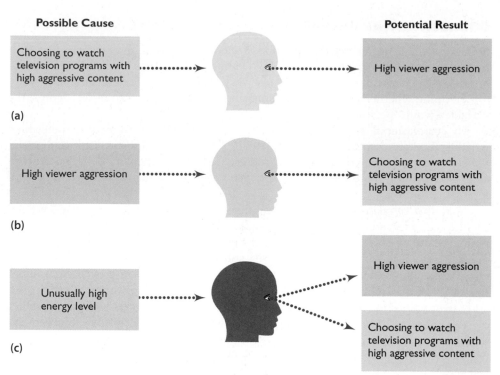

Many studies show that the observation of violence in the media is associated with aggression in viewers. Can we conclude that the observations of violence cause aggression?

experiment The investigation of the relationship between two (or more) variables by deliberately producing a change in one variable in a situation and observing the effects of that change on other aspects of the situation.

experimental manipulation The change that an experimenter deliberately produces in a situation.

One more example illustrates the critical point that correlations tell us nothing about cause and effect but merely provide a measure of the strength of a relationship between two variables. We might find that children who watch a lot of television programs featuring high levels of aggression are likely to demonstrate a relatively high degree of aggressive behavior and that those who watch few television shows that portray aggression are apt to exhibit a relatively low degree of such behavior (see Figure 2). But we cannot say that the aggression is *caused* by the TV viewing, because many other explanations are possible.

For instance, it could be that children who have an unusually high level of energy seek out programs with aggressive content *and* are more aggressive. The children's energy level, then, could be the true cause of the children's higher incidence of aggression. Also, people who are already highly aggressive might choose to watch shows with a high aggressive content *because* they are aggressive. Clearly, then, any number of causal sequences are possible—none of which can be ruled out by correlational research (Feshbach & Tangney, 2008; Grimes & Bergen, 2008).

The inability of correlational research to demonstrate cause-and-effect relationships is a crucial drawback to its use. There is, however, an alternative technique that does establish causality: the experiment.

Experimental Research

The *only* way psychologists can establish cause-and-effect relationships through research is by carrying out an experiment. In a formal **experiment,** the researcher investigates the relationship between two (or more) variables by deliberately changing one variable in a controlled situation and observing the effects of that change on other aspects of the situation. In an experiment, then, the conditions are created and controlled by the researcher, who deliberately makes a change in those conditions in order to observe the effects of that change.

The change that the researcher deliberately makes in an experiment is called the **experimental manipulation.** Experimental manipulations are used to detect relationships between different variables (Staub, 2011).

Several steps are involved in carrying out an experiment, but the process typically begins with the development of one or more hypotheses for the experiment to test. For example, Latané and Darley, in testing their theory of the diffusion of responsibility in bystander behavior, developed this hypothesis: The higher the number of people who witness an emergency situation is, the less likely it is that any of them will help the victim. They then designed an experiment to test this hypothesis.

Their first step was to formulate an operational definition of the hypothesis by conceptualizing it in a way that could be tested. Latané and Darley had to take into account the fundamental principle of experimental research mentioned earlier: Experimenters must manipulate at least one variable in order to observe the effects of the manipulation on another variable while keeping other factors in the situation constant. However, the manipulation cannot be viewed by itself, in isolation; if a cause-and-effect relationship is to be established, the effects of the manipulation must be compared with the effects of no manipulation or a different kind of manipulation.

EXPERIMENTAL GROUPS AND CONTROL GROUPS

Experimental research requires, then, that the responses of at least two groups be compared. One group will receive some special **treatment**—the manipulation implemented by the experimenter—and another group will receive either no treatment or a different treatment. Any group that receives a treatment is called an **experimental group;** a group that receives no treatment is called a **control group.** (In some experiments there are multiple experimental and control groups, each of which is compared with another group.)

By employing both experimental and control groups in an experiment, researchers are able to rule out the possibility that something other than the experimental manipulation produced the results observed in the experiment. Without a control group, we couldn't be sure that some other variable, such as the temperature at the time we were running the experiment, the color of the experimenter's hair, or even the mere passage of time, wasn't causing the changes observed.

For example, consider a medical researcher who thinks he has invented a medicine that cures the common cold. To test his claim, he gives the medicine one day to a group of 20 people who have colds and finds that 10 days later all of them are cured.

Eureka? Not so fast. An observer viewing this flawed study might reasonably argue that the people would have gotten better even without the medicine. What the researcher obviously needed was a control group consisting of people with colds who *don't* get the medicine and whose health is also checked 10 days later. Only if there is a significant difference between experimental and control groups can the effectiveness of the medicine be assessed. Through the use of control groups, then, researchers can isolate specific causes for their findings—and draw cause-and-effect inferences.

Returning to Latané and Darley's experiment, we see that the researchers needed to translate their hypothesis into something testable. To do this, they decided to create a false emergency situation that would appear to require the aid of a bystander. As their experimental manipulation, they decided to vary the number of bystanders present. They could have had just one experimental group with, say, two people present, and a control group for comparison purposes with just one person present. Instead, they settled on a more complex procedure involving the creation of groups of three sizes—consisting of two, three, and six people—that could be compared with one another.

INDEPENDENT AND DEPENDENT VARIABLES

Latané and Darley's experimental design now included an operational definition of what is called the **independent variable.** The independent variable is the condition that is manipulated by an experimenter. (You can think of the independent variable

treatment The manipulation implemented by the experimenter.

experimental group Any group participating in an experiment that receives a treatment.

control group A group participating in an experiment that receives no treatment.

independent variable The variable that is manipulated by an experimenter.

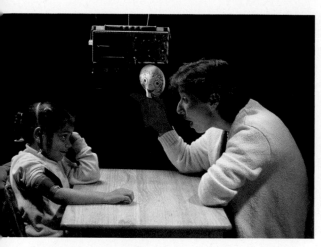

In this experiment, preschoolers' reactions to the puppet are monitored. Can you think of a hypothesis that might be tested in this way?

dependent variable The variable that is measured and is expected to change as a result of changes caused by the experimenter's manipulation of the independent variable.

random assignment to condition A procedure in which participants are assigned to different experimental groups or "conditions" on the basis of chance and chance alone.

as being independent of the actions of those taking part in an experiment; it is controlled by the experimenter.) In the case of the Latané and Darley experiment, the independent variable was the number of people present, which was manipulated by the experimenters.

The next step was to decide how they were going to determine the effect that varying the number of bystanders had on behavior of those in the experiment. Crucial to every experiment is the **dependent variable,** the variable that is measured and is expected to change as a result of changes caused by the experimenter's manipulation of the independent variable. The dependent variable is dependent on the actions of the *participants* or *subjects*—the people taking part in the experiment.

Latané and Darley had several possible choices for their dependent measure. One might have been a simple yes/no measure of the participants' helping behavior. But the investigators also wanted a more precise analysis of helping behavior. Consequently, they also measured the amount of time it took for a participant to provide help.

Latané and Darley now had all the necessary components of an experiment. The independent variable, manipulated by them, was the number of bystanders present in an emergency situation. The dependent variable was the measure of whether bystanders in each of the groups provided help and the amount of time it took them to do so. Consequently, like all experiments, this one had both an independent variable and a dependent variable. *All* true experiments in psychology fit this straightforward model.

RANDOM ASSIGNMENT OF PARTICIPANTS

To make the experiment a valid test of the hypothesis, Latané and Darley needed to add a final step to the design: properly assigning participants to a particular experimental group.

The significance of this step becomes clear when we examine various alternative procedures. For example, the experimenters might have assigned just males to the group with two bystanders, just females to the group with three bystanders, and both males and females to the group with six bystanders. If they had done this, however, any differences they found in helping behavior could not be attributed with any certainty solely to group size, because the differences might just as well have been due to the composition of the group. A more reasonable procedure would be to ensure that each group had the same composition in terms of gender; then the researchers would be able to make comparisons across groups with considerably more accuracy.

Participants in each of the experimental groups ought to be comparable, and it is easy enough to create groups that are similar in terms of gender. The problem becomes a bit more tricky, though, when we consider other participant characteristics. How can we ensure that participants in each experimental group will be equally intelligent, extroverted, cooperative, and so forth, when the list of characteristics—any one of which could be important—is potentially endless?

The solution is a simple but elegant procedure called **random assignment to condition.** Participants are assigned to different experimental groups, or "conditions," on the basis of chance and chance alone. The experimenter might, for instance, flip a coin for each participant and assign a participant to one group when "heads" came up and to the other group when "tails" came up. The advantage of this technique is that there is an equal chance that participant characteristics will be distributed across the various groups. When a researcher uses random assignment—which in practice is usually carried out using computer-generated random numbers—chances are that each of the groups will have approximately the same proportion of intelligent people, cooperative people, extroverted people, males and females, and so on.

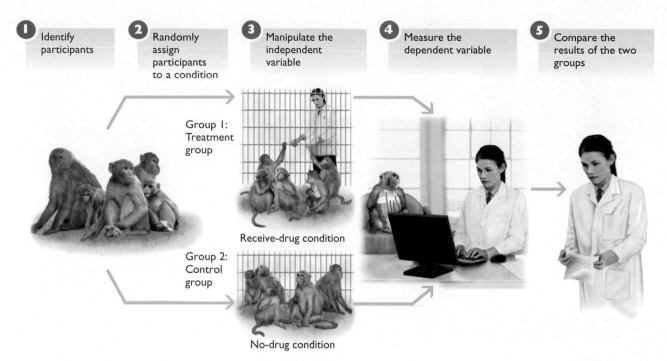

1. Identify participants
2. Randomly assign participants to a condition
3. Manipulate the independent variable
4. Measure the dependent variable
5. Compare the results of the two groups

Group 1: Treatment group

Receive-drug condition

Group 2: Control group

No-drug condition

FIGURE 3 In this depiction of a study investigating the effects of the drug propranolol on heart disease, we can see the basic elements of all true experiments. The participants in the experiment were monkeys who were randomly assigned to one of two groups. Monkeys assigned to the treatment group were given propranolol, hypothesized to prevent heart disease, whereas those in the control group were not given the drug. Administration of the drugs, then, was the independent variable.

All the monkeys were given a high-fat diet that was the human equivalent of two eggs with bacon every morning, and they occasionally were reassigned to different cages to increase their stress. To determine the effects of the drug, the monkeys' heart rates and other measures of heart disease were assessed after 26 months. These measures constituted the dependent variable. The results? As hypothesized, monkeys who received the drug showed lower heart rates and fewer symptoms of heart disease than those who did not. (Source: Based on a study by Kaplan & Manuck, 1989.)

Figure 3 provides another example of an experiment. Like all experiments, it includes the following set of key elements, which you should keep in mind as you consider whether a research study is truly an experiment:

- An independent variable, the variable that is manipulated by the experimenter.
- A dependent variable, the variable that is measured by the experimenter and that is expected to change as a result of the manipulation of the independent variable.
- A procedure that randomly assigns participants to different experimental groups, or "conditions," of the independent variable.
- A hypothesis that predicts the effect the independent variable will have on the dependent variable.

Only if each of these elements is present can a research study be considered a true experiment in which cause-and-effect relationships can be determined. (For a summary of the different types of research that we've discussed, see Figure 4.)

WERE LATANÉ AND DARLEY RIGHT?

To test their hypothesis that increasing the number of bystanders in an emergency situation would lower the degree of helping behavior, Latané and Darley placed the participants in a room and told them that the purpose of the experiment was to talk

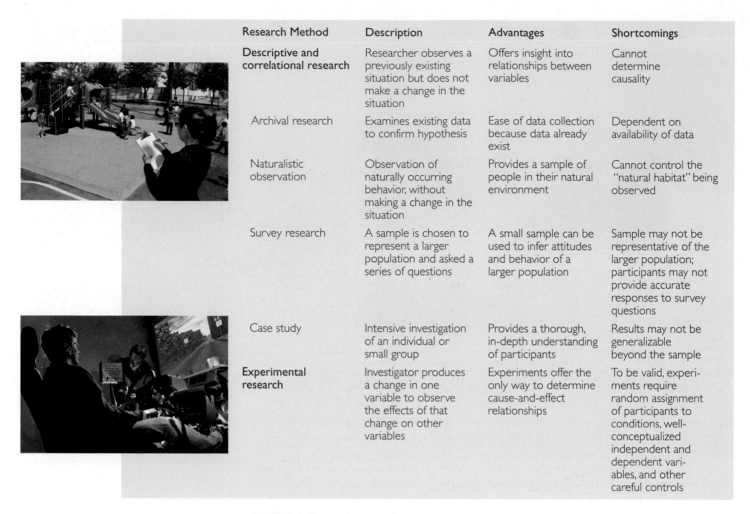

Research Method	Description	Advantages	Shortcomings
Descriptive and correlational research	Researcher observes a previously existing situation but does not make a change in the situation	Offers insight into relationships between variables	Cannot determine causality
Archival research	Examines existing data to confirm hypothesis	Ease of data collection because data already exist	Dependent on availability of data
Naturalistic observation	Observation of naturally occurring behavior, without making a change in the situation	Provides a sample of people in their natural environment	Cannot control the "natural habitat" being observed
Survey research	A sample is chosen to represent a larger population and asked a series of questions	A small sample can be used to infer attitudes and behavior of a larger population	Sample may not be representative of the larger population; participants may not provide accurate responses to survey questions
Case study	Intensive investigation of an individual or small group	Provides a thorough, in-depth understanding of participants	Results may not be generalizable beyond the sample
Experimental research	Investigator produces a change in one variable to observe the effects of that change on other variables	Experiments offer the only way to determine cause-and-effect relationships	To be valid, experiments require random assignment of participants to conditions, well-conceptualized independent and dependent variables, and other careful controls

FIGURE 4 Research strategies.

about personal problems associated with college. The discussion was to be held over an intercom, supposedly to avoid the potential embarrassment of face-to-face contact. Chatting about personal problems was not, of course, the true purpose of the experiment, but telling the participants that it was provided a way of keeping their expectations from biasing their behavior. (Consider how they would have been affected if they had been told that their helping behavior in emergencies was being tested. The experimenters could never have gotten an accurate assessment of what the participants would actually do in an emergency. By definition, emergencies are rarely announced in advance.)

The sizes of the discussion groups were two, three, and six people, which constituted the manipulation of the independent variable of group size. Participants were randomly assigned to these groups upon their arrival at the laboratory. Each group included a trained *confederate*, or employee, of the experimenters. In each two-person group, then, there was only one real "bystander."

As the participants in each group were holding their discussion, they suddenly heard through the intercom one of the other participants—the confederate—having what sounded like an epileptic seizure and then calling for help.

The participants' behavior was now what counted. The dependent variable was the time that elapsed from the start of the "seizure" to the time a participant began trying to help the "victim." If six minutes went by without a participant's offering help, the experiment was ended.

As predicted by the hypothesis, the size of the group had a significant effect on whether a participant provided help. The more people who were present, the

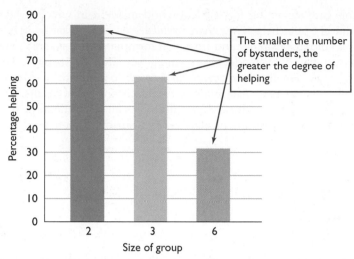

FIGURE 5 The Latané and Darley experiment showed that as the size of the group witnessing an emergency increased, helping behavior decreased. (Source: Darley & Latané, 1968.)

less likely it was that someone would supply help, as you can see in Figure 5 (Latané & Darley, 1970).

Because these results are straightforward, it seems clear that the experiment confirmed the original hypothesis. However, Latané and Darley could not be sure that the results were truly meaningful until they determined whether the results represented a **significant outcome.** Using statistical analysis, researchers can determine whether a numeric difference is a real difference or is due merely to chance. Only when differences between groups are large enough that statistical tests show them to be significant is it possible for researchers to confirm a hypothesis (Cwikel, Behar, & Rabson-Hare, 2000; Cohen, 2002).

significant outcome Meaningful results that make it possible for researchers to feel confident that they have confirmed their hypotheses.

MOVING BEYOND THE STUDY

The Latané and Darley study contains all the elements of an experiment: an independent variable, a dependent variable, random assignment to conditions, and multiple experimental groups. Consequently, we can say with some confidence that group size *caused* changes in the degree of helping behavior.

Of course, one experiment alone does not forever resolve the question of bystander intervention in emergencies. Psychologists—like other scientists—require that findings be **replicated,** or repeated, sometimes using other procedures, in other settings, with other groups of participants, before full confidence can be placed in the results of any single experiment. A procedure called *meta-analysis* permits psychologists to combine the results of many separate studies into one overall conclusion (Tenenbaum & Ruck, 2007; Cooper & Patall, 2009; Liu et al., 2011).

replicated research Research that is repeated, sometimes using other procedures, settings, and groups of participants, to increase confidence in prior findings.

In addition to replicating experimental results, psychologists need to test the limitations of their theories and hypotheses to determine under which specific circumstances they do and do not apply. It seems unlikely, for instance, that increasing the number of bystanders *always* results in less helping. In fact, follow-up research shows that bystander intervention is more likely to occur in situations viewed as clear-cut and dangerous, because bystanders are more likely to perceive that the presence of others will provide resources for helping. In short, it is critical to continue carrying out experiments to understand the conditions in which exceptions to this general rule occur and other circumstances in which the rule holds (Garcia-Palacios, Hoffman, & Carlin, 2002; Fischer et al., 2011).

Before leaving the Latané and Darley study, note that it represents a good illustration of the basic principles of the scientific method we considered earlier (as outlined in Figure 1 of Module 3 on page 26). The two psychologists began with a *question of interest*, in this case stemming from a real-world incident in which bystanders in an emergency did not offer help. They then *formulated an explanation* by specifying a theory of diffusion of responsibility and from that formulated the specific hypothesis that increasing the number of bystanders in an emergency situation would lower the degree of helping behavior. Finally, they *carried out research* to confirm their hypothesis, and they eventually *communicated their findings* by publishing their results. This four-step process embodied in the scientific method underlies all scientific inquiry, allowing us to develop a valid understanding of others'—and our own—behavior.

RECAP/EVALUATE/RETHINK

RECAP

LO 3-1 What is the scientific method?

- The scientific method is the approach psychologists use to understand behavior. It consists of four steps: identifying questions of interest, formulating an explanation, carrying out research that is designed to support or refute the explanation, and communicating the findings. (p. 26)

- To test a hypothesis, researchers must formulate an operational definition, which translates the abstract concepts of the hypothesis into the actual procedures used in the study. (p. 28)

LO 3-2 What role do theories and hypotheses play in psychological research?

- Research in psychology is guided by theories (broad explanations and predictions regarding phenomena of interest) and hypotheses (theory-based predictions stated in a way that allows them to be tested). (pp. 28, 29)

LO 3-3 What research methods do psychologists use?

- Archival research uses existing records, such as old newspapers or other documents, to test a hypothesis. In naturalistic observation, the investigator acts mainly as an observer, making no change in a naturally occurring situation. In survey research, people are asked a series of questions about their behavior, thoughts, or attitudes. The case study is an in-depth interview and examination of one person or group. (pp. 29, 30)

- These descriptive research methods rely on correlational techniques, which describe associations between variables but cannot determine cause-and-effect relationships. (p. 31)

LO 3-4 How do psychologists establish cause-and-effect relationships in research studies?

- In a formal experiment, the relationship between variables is investigated by deliberately producing a change—called the experimental manipulation—in one variable and observing changes in the other variable. (p. 32)

- In an experiment, at least two groups must be compared to assess cause-and-effect relationships. The group receiving the treatment (the special procedure devised by the experimenter) is the experimental group; the second group (which receives no treatment) is the control group. There also may be multiple experimental groups, each of which is subjected to a different procedure and then compared with the others. (p. 33)

- The variable that experimenters manipulate is the independent variable. The variable that they measure and expect to change as a result of manipulation of the independent variable is called the dependent variable. (pp. 33, 34)

- In a formal experiment, participants must be assigned randomly to treatment conditions, so that participant characteristics are distributed evenly across the different conditions. (p. 34)

- Psychologists use statistical tests to determine whether research findings are significant. (p. 37)

EVALUATE

1. An explanation for a phenomenon of interest is known as a _____.
2. To test this explanation, a researcher must state it in terms of a testable question known as a _____.
3. An experimenter is interested in studying the relationship between hunger and aggression. She decides that she will measure aggression by counting the number of times a participant will hit a punching bag. In this case, her _____ definition of aggression is the number of times the participant hits the bag.
4. Match the following forms of research to their definitions:

   1. archival research
   2. naturalistic observation
   3. survey research
   4. case study

   a. directly asking a sample of people questions about their behavior
   b. examining existing records to test a hypothesis
   c. looking at behavior in its true setting without intervening in the setting
   d. doing an in-depth investigation of a person or small group

5. Match each of the following research methods with its primary disadvantage:

1. archival research
2. naturalistic observation
3. survey research
4. case study

a. The researcher may not be able to generalize to the population at large.
b. People's behavior can change if they know they are being watched.
c. The data may not exist or may be unusable.
d. People may lie in order to present a good image.

6. A psychologist wants to study the effect of attractiveness on willingness to help a person with a math problem. Attractiveness would be the _____ variable, and the amount of helping would be the _____ variable.

7. The group in an experiment that receives no treatment is called the _____ group.

RETHINK

1. Starting with the theory that diffusion of responsibility causes responsibility for helping to be shared among bystanders, Latané and Darley derived the hypothesis that the more people who witness an emergency situation, the less likely it is that help will be given to a victim. How many other hypotheses can you think of that are based on the same theory of diffusion of responsibility?

2. *From a lawyer's perspective:* Imagine that you are assigned to a case similar to the one of Kitty Genovese. Your supervisor, who is unfamiliar with psychological research, asks you to provide information about the eyewitnesses to explain why they did not help her. What would you include in your report?

Answers to Evaluate Questions

1. theory; 2. hypothesis; 3. operational; 4. 1-b, 2-c, 3-a, 4-d; 5. 1-c, 2-b, 3-d, 4-a; 6. independent, dependent; 7. control

KEY TERMS

scientific method p. 26
theories p. 27
hypothesis p. 28
operational definition p. 28
archival research p. 29
naturalistic
  observation p. 29

survey research p. 30
case study p. 30
variables p. 31
correlational research p. 31
experiment p. 32
experimental
  manipulation p. 32

treatment p. 33
experimental group p. 33
control group p. 33
independent
  variable p. 33
dependent
  variable p. 34

random assignment to
  condition p. 34
significant
  outcome p. 37
replicated
  research p. 37

Critical Research Issues

You probably realize by now that there are few simple formulas for psychological research. Psychologists must make choices about the type of study to conduct, the measures to take, and the most effective way to analyze the results. Even after they have made these essential decisions, they must still consider several critical issues. We turn first to the most fundamental of these issues: ethics.

The Ethics of Research

Put yourself in the place of one of the participants in the experiment conducted by Latané and Darley to examine the helping behavior of bystanders, in which another "bystander" simulating a seizure turned out to be a confederate of the experimenters (Latané & Darley, 1970). How would you feel when you learned that the supposed victim was in reality a paid accomplice?

Although you might at first experience relief that there had been no real emergency, you might also feel some resentment that you had been deceived by the experimenter. You might also experience concern that you had been placed in an embarrassing or compromising situation—one that might have dealt a blow to your self-esteem, depending on how you had behaved.

Most psychologists argue that deception is sometimes necessary to prevent participants from being influenced by what they think a study's true purpose is. (If you knew that Latané and Darley were actually studying your helping behavior, wouldn't you automatically have been tempted to intervene in the emergency?) To avoid such outcomes, a small proportion of research involves deception.

Nonetheless, because research has the potential to violate the rights of participants, psychologists are expected to adhere to a strict set of ethical guidelines aimed at protecting participants (American Psychological Association, 2002). Those guidelines involve the following safeguards:

- Protection of participants from physical and mental harm.
- The right of participants to privacy regarding their behavior.
- The assurance that participation in research is completely voluntary.
- The necessity of informing participants about the nature of procedures before their participation in the experiment.
- All experiments must be reviewed by an independent panel before being conducted (Fisher et al., 2002; Fisher, 2003; Smith, 2003).

informed consent A document signed by participants affirming that they have been told the basic outlines of the study and are aware of what their participation will involve.

One of psychologists' key ethical principles is **informed consent.** Before participating in an experiment, the participants must sign a document affirming that they have been told the basic outlines of the study and are aware of what their participation will involve, what risks the experiment may hold, and the fact that their participation is purely voluntary and they may terminate it at any time. Furthermore, after participation in a study, they must be given a debriefing in which they receive an explanation of the study and the procedures that were involved. The only time informed consent and a debriefing can be eliminated is in experiments in which the risks are minimal, as in a purely observational study

Although readily available and widely used as research subjects, college students may not represent the population at large. What are some advantages and drawbacks of using college students as subjects?

in a public place (Koocher, Norcross, & Hill, 2005; Fallon, 2006; Barnett, Wise, & Johnson-Greene, 2007; Nagy, 2011).

Exploring DIVERSITY

Choosing Participants Who Represent the Scope of Human Behavior

When Latané and Darley, both college professors, decided who would participate in their experiment, they turned to the people at hand: college students. Using college students as participants has both advantages and drawbacks. The big benefit is that because most research occurs in university settings, college students are readily available. Typically, they cost the researcher very little: They participate for either extra course credit or a relatively small payment.

The problem is that college students may not represent the general population adequately. In fact, undergraduate research participants are typically a special group of people: Relative to the general population, college students tend to be from **W**estern, **e**ducated, **i**ndustrialized, **r**ich, and **d**emocratic cultures. That description forms the acronym WEIRD, which led one researcher to apply the nickname to research participants (Jones, 2010).

It's not that there's anything particularly wrong with WEIRD participants. It's just that they may be different from most other people—those who don't go to college or who didn't grow up in a democratic Western culture, who are less affluent, and so forth. All these characteristics could be psychologically relevant. Yet one review found that most research participants do come from the United States, and about the same proportion of those are psychology majors (Arnett, 2008; Henrich, Heine, & Norenzayan, 2010).

Because psychology is a science whose goal is to explain *all* human behavior generally, its studies must use participants who are fully representative of the general population in terms of gender, age, race, ethnicity, socioeconomic status, and educational level (see Figure 1 *Neuroscience in Your Life*). To encourage a wider range of participants, the National Institute of Mental Health and the National Science Foundation—the primary U.S. funding sources for psychological research—now require that experiments address issues of diverse populations (Carpenter, 2002; Lindley, 2006).

Neuroscience in Your Life:
The Importance of Using Representative Participants

FIGURE 1 We often think of the brain working the same way for everyone. However, our culture, our experiences, and our individual circumstances shape how we react to the world. These brain scans show differences in brain activation between those who perceive themselves to be of different socioeconomic status in responding to the pain of others (i.e., empathy) and in their willingness to donate money subsequently to a worthy cause. The results show the importance of using a wide range of participants in research studies. (Source: Ma , Wang, & Han, 2011.)

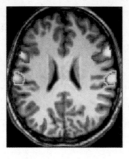
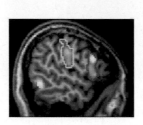
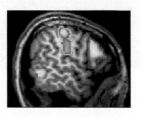

Should Animals Be Used in Research?

Like those who work with humans, researchers who use nonhuman animals in experiments have their own set of exacting guidelines to ensure that the animals do not suffer. Specifically, researchers must make every effort to minimize discomfort, illness, and pain. Procedures that subject animals to distress are permitted only when an alternative procedure is unavailable and when the research is justified by its prospective

Research involving animals is controversial but when conducted within ethical guidelines yields significant benefits for humans.

value. Moreover, researchers strive to avoid causing physical discomfort, but they are also required to promote the *psychological* well-being of some species of research animals, such as primates (Rusche, 2003; Lutz & Novak, 2005; Miller & Williams, 2011).

But why should animals be used for research in the first place? Is it really possible to learn about human behavior from the results of research employing rats, gerbils, and pigeons?

The answer is that psychological research that does employ nonhumans is designed to answer questions different from those posed in research with humans. For example, the shorter life span of animals (rats live an average of 2 years) allows researchers to learn about the effects of aging in a relatively short time frame. It is also possible to provide greater experimental control over nonhumans and to carry out procedures that might not be possible with people. For example, some studies require large numbers of participants that share similar backgrounds or have been exposed to particular environments—conditions that could not practically be met with human beings.

Research with animals has provided psychologists with information that has profoundly benefited humans. For instance, it furnished the keys to detecting eye disorders in children early enough to prevent permanent damage, to communicating more effectively with severely retarded children, and to reducing chronic pain in people. Still, the use of research using nonhumans is controversial, involving complex moral and philosophical concerns. Consequently, all research involving nonhumans must be carefully reviewed beforehand to ensure that it is conducted ethically (Saucier & Cain, 2006; Hackam, 2007; Shankar & Simmons, 2009).

Threats to Experimental Validity: Avoiding Experimental Bias

Even the best-laid experimental plans are susceptible to **experimental bias**—factors that distort the way the independent variable affects the dependent variable in an experiment. One of the most common forms of experimental bias is *experimenter expectations:* An experimenter unintentionally transmits cues to participants about the way they are expected to behave in a given experimental condition. The danger is that those expectations will bring about an "appropriate" behavior—one that otherwise might not have occurred (Rosenthal, 2002, 2003).

A related problem is *participant expectations* about appropriate behavior. If you have ever been a participant in an experiment, you know that you quickly develop guesses about what is expected of you. In fact, it is typical for people to develop their own hypotheses about what the experimenter hopes to learn from the study. If participants form their own hypotheses, it may be the participant's expectations, rather than the experimental manipulation, that produce an effect (Rutherford et al., 2009).

To guard against participant expectations biasing the results of an experiment, the experimenter may try to disguise the true purpose of the experiment. Participants who do not know that helping behavior is being studied, for example, are more apt to act in a "natural" way than they would if they knew.

Sometimes it is impossible to hide the actual purpose of research; when that is the case, other techniques are available to prevent bias. Suppose you were interested in testing the ability of a new drug to alleviate the symptoms of severe depression. If you simply gave the drug to half your participants and not to the other half, the participants who were given the drug might report feeling less depressed, merely because they knew they were getting a drug. Similarly, the participants who got nothing might report feeling no better, because they knew that they were in a no-treatment control group.

experimental bias Factors that distort how the independent variable affects the dependent variable in an experiment.

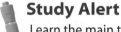

Study Alert

Learn the main types of potential bias in experiments: experimenter expectations, participant expectations, and placebo effects.

placebo A false treatment, such as a pill, "drug," or other substance, without any significant chemical properties or active ingredient.

To solve this problem, psychologists typically use a procedure in which all the participants receive a treatment, but those in the control group receive only a **placebo**—a false treatment, such as a pill, "drug," or other substance that has no significant chemical properties or active ingredient. Because members of both groups are kept in the dark about whether they are getting a real or a false treatment, any differences in outcome can be attributed to the quality of the drug and not to the possible psychological effects of being administered a pill or other substance (Rajagopal, 2006; Crum & Langer, 2007; Justman, 2011).

However, there is one more safeguard that a careful researcher must apply in an experiment such as this one. To overcome the possibility that *experimenter* expectations will affect the participant, the person who administers the drug shouldn't know whether it is actually the true drug or the placebo. By keeping both the participant and the experimenter who interacts with the participant "blind" to the nature of the drug that is being administered, researchers can more accurately assess the effects of the drug. This method is known as the *double-blind procedure*.

BECOMING AN INFORMED CONSUMER of Psychology

Thinking Critically About Research

If you were about to purchase an automobile, you would not likely stop at the nearest car dealership and drive off with the first car a salesperson recommended. Instead, you would probably mull over the purchase, read about automobiles, consider the alternatives, talk to others about their experiences, and ultimately put in a fair amount of thought before you made such a major purchase.

In contrast, many of us are considerably less conscientious when we expend our intellectual, rather than financial, assets. People often jump to conclusions on the basis of incomplete and inaccurate information, and only rarely do they take the time to critically evaluate the research and data to which they are exposed.

Because the field of psychology is based on an accumulated body of research, we must scrutinize thoroughly the methods, results, and claims of researchers. Several basic questions can help us sort through what is valid and what is not. Among the most important questions to ask are these:

- *What was the purpose of the research?* Research studies should evolve from a clearly specified theory. Furthermore, we must take into account the specific hypothesis that is being tested. Unless we know what hypothesis is being examined, we cannot judge how successful a study has been.
- *How well was the study conducted?* Consider who the participants were, how many were involved, what methods were employed, and what problems the researcher encountered in collecting the data. There are important differences, for example, between a case study that reports the anecdotes of a handful of respondents and a survey that collects data from several thousand people.
- *Are the results presented fairly?* Statements must be assessed on the basis of the actual data they reflect and their logic. For instance, when the manufacturer of car X boasts that "no other car has a better safety record than car X," this does not mean that car X is safer than every other car. It just means that no other car has been proved safer, though many other cars could be just as safe as car X. Expressed in the latter fashion, the finding doesn't seem worth bragging about.

These three basic questions can help you assess the validity of research findings you come across—both within and outside the field of psychology. The more you know how to evaluate research in general, the better you will be able to assess what the field of psychology has to offer.

RECAP/EVALUATE/RETHINK

RECAP

LO 4-1 What major issues confront psychologists conducting research?

- One of the key ethical principles followed by psychologists is that of informed consent. Participants must be informed, before participation, about the basic outline of the experiment and the risks and potential benefits of their participation. (p. 40)
- Although the use of college students as participants has the advantage of easy availability, there are drawbacks, too. For instance, students do not necessarily represent the population as a whole. The use of non-human animals as participants may also have costs in terms of the ability to generalize to humans, although the benefits of using animals in research have been profound. (pp. 42, 43)
- Experiments are subject to a number of biases, or threats. Experimenter expectations can produce bias when an experimenter unintentionally transmits cues to participants about her or his expectations regarding their behavior in a given experimental condition. Participant expectations can also bias an experiment. Among the tools experimenters use to help eliminate bias are placebos and double-blind procedures. (p. 43)

EVALUATE

1. Ethical research begins with the concept of informed consent. Before signing up to participate in an experiment, participants should be informed of:
   a. the procedure of the study, stated generally.
   b. the risks that may be involved.
   c. their right to withdraw at any time.
   d. all of these.
2. List three benefits of using animals in psychological research.

3. Deception is one means experimenters can use to try to eliminate participants' expectations. True or false?
4. A false treatment, such as a pill that has no significant chemical properties or active ingredient, is known as a _____.
5. A study has shown that men differ from women in their preference for ice cream flavors. This study was based on a sample of two men and three women. What might be wrong with this study?

RETHINK

1. A researcher strongly believes that college professors tend to show female students less attention and respect in the classroom than they show male students. He sets up an experimental study involving observations of classrooms in different conditions. In explaining the study to the professors and the students who will participate, what steps should the researcher take to eliminate experimental bias based on both experimenter expectations and participant expectations?
2. *From a research analyst's perspective*: You are hired to study people's attitudes toward welfare programs by developing and circulating a questionnaire via the Internet. Is this study likely to accurately reflect the views of the general population? Why or why not?

Answers to Evaluate Questions

1. d; 2. (1) We can study some phenomena in animals more easily than we can in people, because with animal subjects we have greater control over environmental and genetic factors. (2) Large numbers of similar participants can be easily obtained. (3) We can look at generational effects much more easily in animals, because of their shorter life span, than we can with people; 3. true; 4. placebo; 5. There are far too few participants. Without a larger sample, no valid conclusions can be drawn about ice cream preferences based on gender.

KEY TERMS

informed consent p. 40
experimental bias p. 43
placebo p. 44

Looking **Back**

Epilogue

In light of what you've already learned about the field of psychology, reconsider the theater massacre described at the start of the chapter and answer the following questions:

1. If they were using the neuroscience perspective, how might psychologists explain people's fear responses to the shooter?
2. How would a psychologist using the psychodynamic perspective explain the killer's behavior differently from a psychologist using the cognitive perspective?
3. What aspects of the shooting would most interest a clinical psychologist? A social psychologist? A forensic psychologist?
4. What might be some ways in which both nature and nurture could have contributed to the killer's behavior?

VISUAL SUMMARY 1 Introduction to Psychology

MODULE 1 Psychologists at Work

Subfields of Psychology

- **Biological foundations**
  - Behavioral neuroscience
- **Sensing, perceiving, learning, and thinking**
  - Experimental and cognitive psychology
- **Sources of change and stability**
  - Development and personality psychology
- **Physical and mental health**
  - Health, clinical, and counseling psychology
- **Social networks**
  - Social and cross-cultural psychology
- **Expanding frontiers**
  - Evolutionary psychology
  - Behavioral genetics
  - Clinical neuropsychology

Working at Psychology

- Where U.S. psychologists work

Managed care settings, 5%
Other human services, 10%
Hospitals, 16%
Private practice, 7%
School districts, 7%
Business, government, or other settings, 17%
Colleges, universities, and other academic settings, 38%

MODULE 2 A Science Evolves

Roots

- Structuralism
- Functionalism

Today's Perspectives: Five major perspectives

Neuroscience
Views behavior from the perspective of biological functioning

Behavioral
Focuses on observable behavior

Psychodynamic
Believes behavior is motivated by inner, unconscious forces over which a person has little control

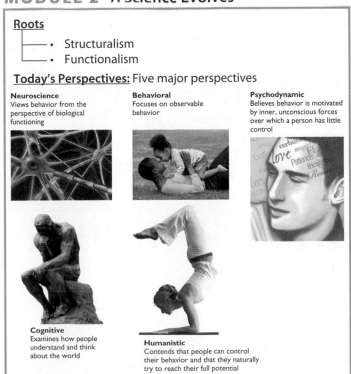

Cognitive
Examines how people understand and think about the world

Humanistic
Contends that people can control their behavior and that they naturally try to reach their full potential

MODULE 3 Research in Psychology

Scientific Method

- Theories: Broad explanations
- Hypotheses: Testable predictions

Descriptive Research: Describes variables and does not explain casuality.

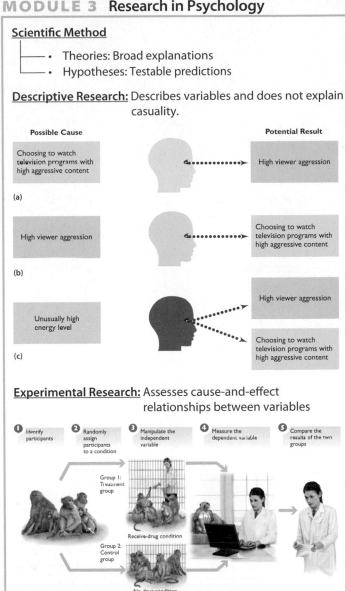

Possible Cause

Potential Result

(a) Choosing to watch television programs with high aggressive content → High viewer aggression

(b) High viewer aggression → Choosing to watch television programs with high aggressive content

(c) Unusually high energy level → High viewer aggression / Choosing to watch television programs with high aggressive content

Experimental Research: Assesses cause-and-effect relationships between variables

1. Identify participants
2. Randomly assign participants to a condition
3. Manipulate the independent variable
4. Measure the dependent variable
5. Compare the results of the two groups

Group 1: Treatment group — Receive-drug condition

Group 2: Control group — No-drug condition

MODULE 4 Critical Research Issues

Ethics of Research

Informed consent

Animal Research

Has significantly benefited humans

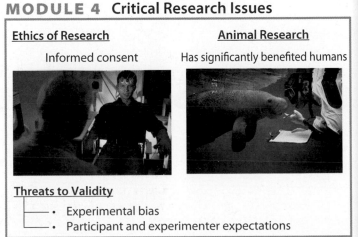

Threats to Validity

- Experimental bias
- Participant and experimenter expectations

2

Neuroscience and Behavior

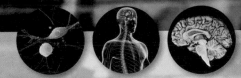

Learning Outcomes for Chapter 2

LO 5-1 Why do psychologists study the brain and the nervous system?

LO 5-2 What are the basic elements of the nervous system?

LO 5-3 How does the nervous system communicate electrical and chemical messages from one part to another?

MODULE 5

Neurons: The Basic Elements of Behavior

The Structure of the Neuron

How Neurons Fire

Where Neurons Meet: Bridging the Gap

Neurotransmitters: Multitalented Chemical Couriers

LO 6-1 How are the structures of the nervous system linked?

LO 6-2 How does the endocrine system affect behavior?

MODULE 6

The Nervous System and the Endocrine System: Communicating Within the Body

The Nervous System: Linking Neurons

The Evolutionary Foundations of the Nervous System

The Endocrine System: Of Chemicals and Glands

LO 7-1 How do researchers identify the major parts and functions of the brain?

LO 7-2 What are the major parts of the brain, and for what behaviors is each part responsible?

LO 7-3 How do the halves of the brain operate interdependently?

LO 7-4 How can an understanding of the nervous system help us find ways to alleviate disease and pain?

MODULE 7

The Brain

Studying the Brain's Structure and Functions: Spying on the Brain

The Central Core: Our "Old Brain"

Applying Psychology in the 21st Century: Your Wish Is Its Command: Directing Computers with Your Brain

The Limbic System: Beyond the Central Core

The Cerebral Cortex: Our "New Brain"

PsychWork: Rehabilitation Counselor

Neuroplasticity and the Brain

Neuroscience in Your Life: The Plastic Brain

The Specialization of the Hemispheres: Two Brains or One?

Exploring Diversity: Human Diversity and the Brain

The Split Brain: Exploring the Two Hemispheres

Becoming an Informed Consumer of Psychology: Learning to Control Your Heart—and Mind—Through Biofeedback

Prologue *Back from the Brink*

ABC News reporter Bob Woodruff nearly lost his life when a roadside bomb blew up in Iraq, causing a severe brain injury. He was in a coma for 36 days, and woke up with extreme memory loss, unable to even recall the names of his two youngest children and struggling to identify everyday objects like scissors.

But several years after the accident, he is busy flying around the world, not only working as a journalist but also bringing attention to the plight of hundreds of others who suffered traumatic brain injury in the long Iraq war.

In many ways, his recovery is nothing short of miraculous. When the shrapnel from the bomb flew into his head, few thought that he could resume normal life, let alone resume his career. Although he doesn't know if he will get his old anchor job back, he is certain of one thing: "I'm going to remain as a journalist" (Dugas, 2010, p. 10D; Pesce, 2011).

Looking Ahead

It's hard to believe that someone can recover from an injury such as Bob Woodruff's at all, much less go on to resume a demanding career within just a few years. But that's just one remarkable capacity of the miraculous brain. An organ roughly half the size of a loaf of bread, the brain controls our behavior through every waking and sleeping moment. Our movements, thoughts, hopes, aspirations, dreams—our very awareness that we are human—all depend on the brain and the nerves that extend throughout the body, constituting the nervous system.

Because of the importance of the nervous system in controlling behavior, and because humans at their most basic level are biological beings, many researchers in psychology and other fields as diverse as computer science, zoology, and medicine have made the biological underpinnings of behavior their specialty. These experts collectively are called *neuroscientists* (Beatty, 2000; Posner & DiGiorlamo, 2000; Gazzaniga, Ivry, & Mangun, 2002; Cartwright, 2006).

Psychologists who specialize in considering the ways in which the biological structures and functions of the body affect behavior are known as **behavioral neuroscientists** (or *biopsychologists*). They seek to answer several key questions: How does the brain control the voluntary and involuntary functioning of the body? How does the brain communicate with other parts of the body? What is the physical structure of the brain, and how does this structure affect behavior? Are psychological disorders caused by biological factors, and how can such disorders be treated?

As you consider the biological processes that we discuss in this chapter, keep in mind the reason why behavioral neuroscience is an essential part of psychology: Our understanding of human behavior requires knowledge of the brain and other parts of the nervous system. Biological factors are central to our sensory experiences, states of consciousness, motivation and emotion, development throughout the life span, and physical and psychological health. Furthermore, advances in behavioral neuroscience have led to the creation of drugs and other treatments for psychological and physical disorders. In short, we cannot understand behavior without understanding our biological makeup (Kosslyn et al., 2002; Plomin, 2003; Compagni & Manderscheid, 2006).

behavioral neuroscientists (or biopsychologists) Psychologists who specialize in considering the ways in which the biological structures and functions of the body affect behavior.

Neurons: The Basic Elements of Behavior

Watching Serena Williams hit a stinging backhand, Dario Vaccaro dance a complex ballet routine, or Derek Jeter swing at a baseball, you may have marveled at the complexity—and wondrous abilities—of the human body. But even the most everyday tasks, such as pouring a cup of coffee or humming a tune, depend on a sophisticated sequence of events in the body that is itself truly impressive.

The nervous system is the pathway for the instructions that permit our bodies to carry out such precise activities. Here we look at the structure and function of neurons, the cells that make up the nervous system, including the brain.

The Structure of the Neuron

Playing the piano, driving a car, or hitting a tennis ball depends, at one level, on exact muscle coordination. But if we consider *how* the muscles can be activated so precisely, we see that more fundamental processes are involved. For the muscles to produce the complex movements that make up any meaningful physical activity, the brain has to provide the right messages to them and coordinate those messages.

Such messages—as well as those that enable us to think, remember, and experience emotion—are passed through specialized cells called neurons. **Neurons,** or nerve cells, are the basic elements of the nervous system. Their quantity is staggering—perhaps as many as 1 *trillion* neurons throughout the body are involved in the control of behavior (Boahen, 2005).

Although there are several types of neurons, they all have a similar structure, as illustrated in Figure 1 on page 52. Like most cells in the body, neurons have a cell body that contains a nucleus. The nucleus incorporates the hereditary material that determines how a cell will function. Neurons are physically held in place by *glial cells.* Glial cells provide nourishment to neurons, insulate them, help repair damage, and generally support neural functioning (Kettenmann & Ransom, 2005; Bassotti et al., 2007; Bassotti & Villanacci, 2011).

In contrast to most other cells, however, neurons have a distinctive feature: the ability to communicate with other cells and transmit information across relatively long distances. Many of the body's neurons receive signals from the environment or relay the nervous system's messages to muscles and other target cells, but the vast majority of neurons communicate only with other neurons in the elaborate information system that regulates behavior.

As shown in Figure 1, a neuron has a cell body with a cluster of fibers called **dendrites** at one end. Those fibers, which look like the twisted branches of a tree, receive messages from other neurons. On the opposite side of the cell body is a long, slim, tube-like extension called an **axon.** The axon carries messages received by the dendrites to other neurons. The axon is considerably longer than the rest of the neuron. Although most axons are several millimeters in length, some are as long as 3 feet. Axons end in small bulges called **terminal buttons,** which send messages to other neurons.

Learning Outcomes

LO 5-1 Why do psychologists study the brain and the nervous system?

LO 5-2 What are the basic elements of the nervous system?

LO 5-3 How does the nervous system communicate electrical and chemical messages from one part to another?

neurons Nerve cells, the basic elements of the nervous system.

dendrite A cluster of fibers at one end of a neuron that receives messages from other neurons.

axon The part of the neuron that carries messages destined for other neurons.

terminal buttons Small bulges at the end of axons that send messages to other neurons.

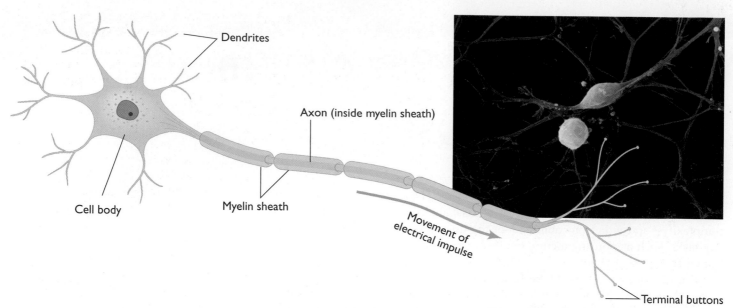

FIGURE 1 The primary components of the neuron, the basic element of the nervous system. A neuron has a cell body and structures that conduct messages: the dendrites, which receive messages from other neurons, and the axon, which carries messages to other neurons or body cells. As with most neurons, this axon is protected by the sausage-like myelin sheath. What advantages does the treelike structure of the neuron provide?

Study Alert

Remember that *d*endrites *d*etect messages from other neurons; *a*xons carry signals *a*way from the cell body.

myelin sheath A protective coat of fat and protein that wraps around the axon.

all-or-none law The rule that neurons are either on or off.

resting state The state in which there is a negative electrical charge of about −70 millivolts within a neuron.

The messages that travel through a neuron are electrical in nature. Although there are exceptions, those electrical messages, or *impulses,* generally move across neurons in one direction only, as if they were traveling on a one-way street. Impulses follow a route that begins with the dendrites, continues into the cell body, and leads ultimately along the tube-like extension, the axon, to adjacent neurons.

To prevent messages from short-circuiting one another, axons must be insulated in some fashion (just as electrical wires must be insulated). Most axons are insulated by a **myelin sheath,** a protective coating of fat and protein that wraps around the axon like the casing on links of sausage.

The myelin sheath also serves to increase the velocity with which electrical impulses travel through axons. Those axons that carry the most important and most urgently required information have the greatest concentrations of myelin. If your hand touches a painfully hot stove, for example, the information regarding the pain is passed through axons in the hand and arm that have a relatively thick coating of myelin, speeding the message of pain to the brain so that you can react instantly.

How Neurons Fire

Like a gun, neurons either fire—that is, transmit an electrical impulse along the axon—or don't fire. There is no in-between stage, just as pulling harder on a gun trigger doesn't make the bullet travel faster. Similarly, neurons follow an **all-or-none law:** They are either on or off, with nothing in between the on state and the off state. Once there is enough force to pull the trigger, a neuron fires.

Before a neuron is triggered—that is, when it is in a **resting state**—it has a negative electrical charge of about −70 millivolts (a millivolt is one $1/1,000$ of a volt). This charge is caused by the presence of more negatively charged ions within the neuron than outside it. (An ion is an atom that is electrically charged.) You might think of the neuron as a miniature battery in which the inside of the neuron represents the negative pole and the outside represents the positive pole.

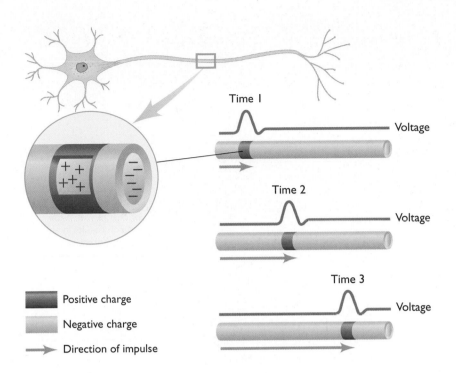

FIGURE 2 Movement of an action potential along an axon. Just before Time 1, positively charged ions enter the cell membrane, changing the charge in the nearby part of the axon from negative to positive and triggering an action potential. The action potential travels along the axon, as illustrated in the changes occurring from Time 1 to Time 3 (from top to bottom in this drawing). Immediately after the action potential has passed through a section of the axon, positive ions are pumped out, restoring the charge in that section to negative. The change in voltage illustrated by the blue line above the axon can be seen in greater detail in Figure 3 on page 54. (Source: Stevens, 1979.)

When a message arrives at a neuron, gates along the cell membrane open briefly to allow positively charged ions to rush in at rates as high as 100 million ions per second. The sudden arrival of these positive ions causes the charge within the nearby part of the cell to change momentarily from negative to positive. When the positive charge reaches a critical level, the "trigger" is pulled, and an electrical impulse, known as an *action potential,* travels along the axon of the neuron (see Figure 2).

The **action potential** moves from one end of the axon to the other like a flame moving along a fuse. As the impulse travels along the axon, the movement of ions causes a change in charge from negative to positive in successive sections of the axon (see Figure 3 on page 54). After the impulse has passed through a particular section of the axon, positive ions are pumped out of that section, and its charge returns to negative while the action potential continues to move along the axon.

Just after an action potential has passed through a section of the axon, the cell membrane in that region cannot admit positive ions again for a few milliseconds, and so a neuron cannot fire again immediately no matter how much stimulation it receives. It is as if the gun has to be reloaded after each shot. There then follows a period in which, though it is possible for the neuron to fire, a stronger stimulus is needed than would be if the neuron had reached its normal resting state. Eventually, though, the neuron is ready to fire once again.

action potential An electric nerve impulse that travels through a neuron's axon when it is set off by a "trigger," changing the neuron's charge from negative to positive.

SPEED OF TRANSMISSION

These complex events can occur at dizzying speeds, although there is great variation among different neurons. The particular speed at which an action potential travels along an axon is determined by the axon's size and the thickness of its myelin sheath. Axons with small diameters carry impulses at about 2 miles per hour; longer and thicker ones can average speeds of more than 225 miles per hour.

Neurons differ not only in terms of how quickly an impulse moves along the axon but also in their potential rate of firing. Some neurons are capable of firing as many as 1,000 times per second; others fire at much slower rates. The intensity of a stimulus determines how much of a neuron's potential firing rate is reached. A strong stimulus, such as a bright light or a loud sound, leads to a higher rate of firing than a less intense stimulus does. Thus, even though all impulses move at the same

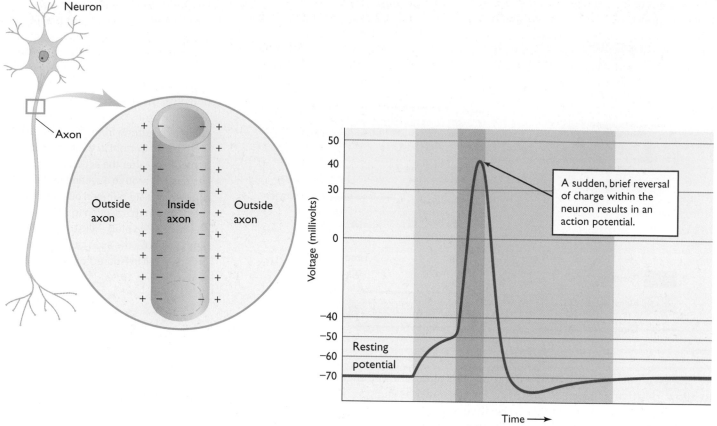

FIGURE 3 Changes in the voltage in a neuron during the passage of an action potential. In its normal resting state, a neuron has a negative charge of about −70 millivolts. When an action potential is triggered, however, the charge becomes positive, increasing from about −70 millivolts to about +40 millivolts. Immediately following the passage of the action potential, the charge becomes even more negative than it is in its typical resting state. After the charge returns to its normal resting state, the neuron will be fully ready to be triggered once again.

strength or speed through a particular axon—because of the all-or-none law—there is variation in the frequency of impulses, providing a mechanism by which we can distinguish the tickle of a feather from the weight of someone standing on our toes.

MIRROR NEURONS

Although all neurons operate through the firing of action potentials, there is significant specialization among different types of neurons. For example, in the last 15 years, neuroscientists have discovered the existence of **mirror neurons,** neurons that fire not only when a person enacts a particular behavior but also when a person simply observes *another* individual carrying out the same behavior (Lepage & Theoret, 2007; Schulte-Ruther et al., 2007; Khalil, 2011).

Mirror neurons may help explain how (and why) humans have the capacity to understand others' intentions. Specifically, mirror neurons may fire when we view someone doing something, helping us to predict what their goals are and what they may do next.

The discovery of mirror neurons suggests that the capacity of even young children to imitate others may be an inborn behavior. Furthermore, mirror neurons may be at the root of empathy—those feelings of concern, compassion, and sympathy for others—and even the development of language in humans (Triesch, Jasso, & Deák, 2007; Iacoboni, 2009; Ramachandra, 2009; Rogalsky et al., 2011).

mirror neurons Specialized neurons that fire not only when a person enacts a particular behavior, but also when a person simply observes *another* individual carrying out the same behavior.

Some researchers suggest an even broader role for mirror neurons. For example, mirror neurons, which respond to sound, appear to be related to speech perception and language comprehension. Furthermore, stimulating the mirror neuron system can help stroke victims as well and may prove to be helpful for those with emotional problems by helping them to develop great empathy (Ehrenfeld, 2011; Gallese et al., 2011).

Where Neurons Meet: Bridging the Gap

If you have looked inside a computer, you've seen that each part is physically connected to another part. In contrast, evolution has produced a neural transmission system that at some points has no need for a structural connection between its components. Instead, a chemical connection bridges the gap, known as a synapse, between two neurons (see Figure 4). The **synapse** is the space between two

synapse The space between two neurons where the axon of a sending neuron communicates with the dendrites of a receiving neuron by using chemical messages.

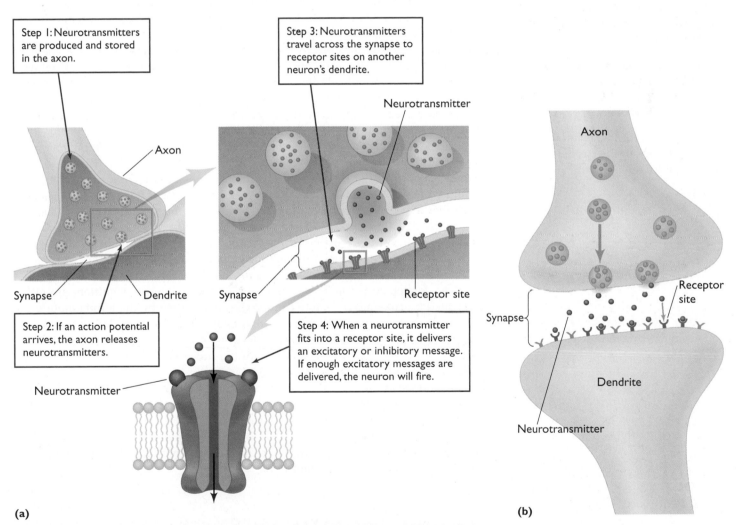

Step 1: Neurotransmitters are produced and stored in the axon.

Step 3: Neurotransmitters travel across the synapse to receptor sites on another neuron's dendrite.

Axon

Neurotransmitter

Synapse

Dendrite

Synapse

Receptor site

Step 2: If an action potential arrives, the axon releases neurotransmitters.

Neurotransmitter

Step 4: When a neurotransmitter fits into a receptor site, it delivers an excitatory or inhibitory message. If enough excitatory messages are delivered, the neuron will fire.

Axon

Receptor site

Synapse

Dendrite

Neurotransmitter

(a)

(b)

FIGURE 4 A synapse is the junction between an axon and a dendrite. Chemical neurotransmitters bridge the synaptic gap between the axon and the dendrite (Mader, 2000). (a) Read Step 1 through Step 4 to follow this chemical process. (b) Just as the pieces of a jigsaw puzzle can fit in only one specific location in a puzzle, each kind of neurotransmitter has a distinctive configuration that allows it to fit into a specific type of receptor cell (Johnson, 2000). Why is it advantageous for axons and dendrites to be linked by temporary chemical bridges rather than by the hard wiring typical of a radio connection or telephone hookup?

neurotransmitters Chemicals that carry messages across the synapse to the dendrite (and sometimes the cell body) of a receiver neuron.

> ## Study Alert
>
> Remember this key fact: Messages inside neurons are transmitted in electrical form, whereas messages traveling between neurons travel via chemical means.

excitatory message A chemical message that makes it more likely that a receiving neuron will fire and an action potential will travel down its axon.

inhibitory message A chemical message that prevents or decreases the likelihood that a receiving neuron will fire.

reuptake The reabsorption of neurotransmitters by a terminal button.

neurons where the axon of a sending neuron communicates with the dendrites of a receiving neuron by using chemical messages (Fanselow & Poulos, 2005; Dean & Dresbach, 2006).

When a nerve impulse comes to the end of the axon and reaches a terminal button, the terminal button releases a chemical courier called a neurotransmitter. **Neurotransmitters** are chemicals that carry messages across the synapse to a dendrite (and sometimes the cell body) of a receiving neuron. Like a boat that ferries passengers across a river, these chemical messengers move toward the shorelines of other neurons. The chemical mode of message transmission that occurs between neurons is strikingly different from the means by which communication occurs inside neurons: Although messages travel in electrical form *within* a neuron, they move *between* neurons through a chemical transmission system.

There are several types of neurotransmitters, and not all neurons are capable of receiving the chemical message carried by a particular neurotransmitter. In the same way that a jigsaw puzzle piece can fit in only one specific location in a puzzle, each kind of neurotransmitter has a distinctive configuration that allows it to fit into a specific type of receptor site on the receiving neuron (see Figure 4b). It is only when a neurotransmitter fits precisely into a receptor site that successful chemical communication is possible.

If a neurotransmitter does fit into a site on the receiving neuron, the chemical message it delivers is basically one of two types: excitatory or inhibitory. **Excitatory messages** make it more likely that a receiving neuron will fire and an action potential will travel down its axon. **Inhibitory messages,** in contrast, do just the opposite; they provide chemical information that prevents or decreases the likelihood that the receiving neuron will fire.

Because the dendrites of a neuron receive both excitatory and inhibitory messages simultaneously, the neuron must integrate the messages by using a kind of chemical calculator. Put simply, if the excitatory messages ("Fire!") outnumber the inhibitory ones ("Don't fire!"), the neuron fires. In contrast, if the inhibitory messages outnumber the excitatory ones, nothing happens, and the neuron remains in its resting state (Mel, 2002; Rapport, 2005; Flavell et al., 2006).

If neurotransmitters remained at the site of the synapse, receiving neurons would be awash in a continual chemical bath, producing constant stimulation or constant inhibition of the receiving neurons—and effective communication across the synapse would no longer be possible. To solve this problem, neurotransmitters are either deactivated by enzymes or—more commonly—reabsorbed by the terminal button in an example of chemical recycling called **reuptake.** Like a vacuum cleaner sucking up dust, neurons reabsorb the neurotransmitters that are now clogging the synapse. All this activity occurs at lightning speed, with the process taking just several milliseconds (Helmuth, 2000; Holt & Jahn, 2004).

Our understanding of the process of reuptake has permitted the development of a number of drugs used in the treatment of psychological disorders. As we discuss later in the book, some antidepressant drugs, called *SSRIs,* or *selective serotonin reuptake inhibitors,* permit certain neurotransmitters to remain active for a longer period at certain synapses in the brain, thereby reducing the symptoms of depression (Montgomery, 2006; Ramos, 2006; Guiard et al., 2011).

Neurotransmitters: Multitalented Chemical Couriers

Neurotransmitters are a particularly important link between the nervous system and behavior. Not only are they important for maintaining vital brain and body functions, a deficiency or an excess of a neurotransmitter can produce severe behavior disorders.

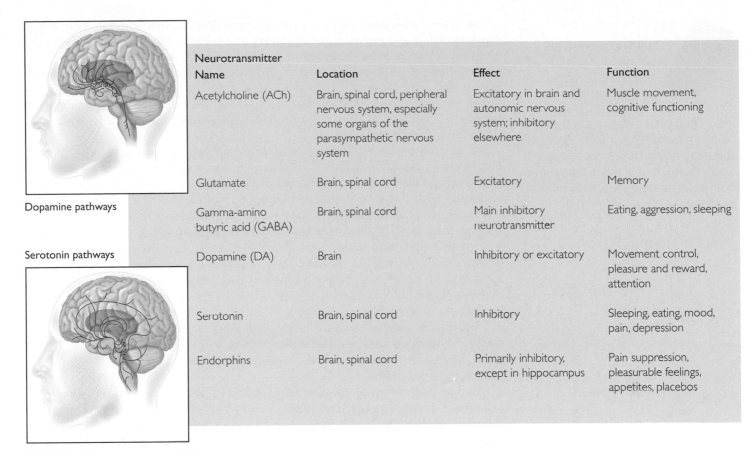

Dopamine pathways

Serotonin pathways

Neurotransmitter Name	Location	Effect	Function
Acetylcholine (ACh)	Brain, spinal cord, peripheral nervous system, especially some organs of the parasympathetic nervous system	Excitatory in brain and autonomic nervous system; inhibitory elsewhere	Muscle movement, cognitive functioning
Glutamate	Brain, spinal cord	Excitatory	Memory
Gamma-amino butyric acid (GABA)	Brain, spinal cord	Main inhibitory neurotransmitter	Eating, aggression, sleeping
Dopamine (DA)	Brain	Inhibitory or excitatory	Movement control, pleasure and reward, attention
Serotonin	Brain, spinal cord	Inhibitory	Sleeping, eating, mood, pain, depression
Endorphins	Brain, spinal cord	Primarily inhibitory, except in hippocampus	Pain suppression, pleasurable feelings, appetites, placebos

FIGURE 5 Major neurotransmitters.

More than a hundred chemicals have been found to act as neurotransmitters, and neuroscientists believe that more may ultimately be identified (Penney, 2000; Schmidt, 2006).

Neurotransmitters vary significantly in terms of how strong their concentration must be to trigger a neuron to fire. Furthermore, the effects of a particular neurotransmitter vary, depending on the area of the nervous system in which it is produced. The same neurotransmitter, then, can act as an excitatory message to a neuron located in one part of the brain and can inhibit firing in neurons located in another part. (The major neurotransmitters and their effects are described in Figure 5.)

One of the most common neurotransmitters is *acetylcholine* (or *ACh*, its chemical symbol), which is found throughout the nervous system. ACh is involved in our every move, because—among other things—it transmits messages relating to our skeletal muscles. ACh is also involved in memory capabilities, and diminished production of ACh may be related to Alzheimer's disease (Mohapel et al., 2005; Bazalakova et al., 2007; Van der Zee, Platt, & Riedel, 2011).

Another common excitatory neurotransmitter, *glutamate,* plays a role in memory. Memories appear to be produced by specific biochemical changes at particular synapses, and glutamate, along with other neurotransmitters, plays an important role in this process (Riedel, Platt, & Micheau, 2003; Winters & Bussey, 2005; Micheau & Marighetto, 2011).

Gamma-amino butyric acid (GABA), which is found in both the brain and the spinal cord, appears to be the nervous system's primary inhibitory neurotransmitter. It moderates a variety of behaviors, ranging from eating to aggression. Several common substances, such as the tranquilizer Valium and alcohol, are effective because they permit GABA to operate more efficiently (Ball, 2004; Criswell et al., 2008; Lobo & Harris, 2008).

Michael J. Fox suffers from Parkinson's disease, and he has become a strong advocate for research into the disorder.

PsychTech

A team of Swedish researchers has discovered a way to stimulate specific neurons via chemical neurotransmitters, rather than using earlier technologies involving electrical signals to stimulate them. This discovery opens a novel path to treat those who suffer from severe psychological disorders produced by brain dysfunction.

Another major neurotransmitter is *dopamine (DA),* which is involved in movement, attention, and learning. The discovery that certain drugs can have a significant effect on dopamine release has led to the development of effective treatments for a wide variety of physical and mental ailments. For instance, Parkinson's disease, from which actor Michael J. Fox suffers among others, is caused by a deficiency of dopamine in the brain. Techniques for increasing the production of dopamine in Parkinson's patients are proving effective (Willis, 2005; Iversen & Iversen, 2007; Antonini & Barone, 2008).

In other instances, *over*production of dopamine produces negative consequences. For example, researchers have hypothesized that schizophrenia and some other severe mental disturbances are affected or perhaps even caused by the presence of unusually high levels of dopamine. Drugs that block the reception of dopamine reduce the symptoms displayed by some people diagnosed with schizophrenia (Murray, Lappin, & Di Forti, 2008; Howes & Kapur, 2009; Seeman, 2011).

Another neurotransmitter, *serotonin,* is associated with the regulation of sleep, eating, mood, and pain. A growing body of research points toward a broader role for serotonin, suggesting its involvement in such diverse behaviors as alcoholism, depression, suicide, impulsivity, aggression, and coping with stress (Murray et al., Popa et al., 2008; Carrillo et al., 2009).

Endorphins, another class of neurotransmitters, are a family of chemicals produced by the brain that are similar in structure to painkilling drugs such as morphine. The production of endorphins reflects the brain's effort to deal with pain as well as to elevate mood.

Endorphins also may produce the euphoric feelings that runners sometimes experience after long runs. The exertion and perhaps the pain involved in a long run may stimulate the production of endorphins, ultimately resulting in what has been called "runner's high" (Kolata, 2002; Pert, 2002; Stanojevic, Mitic, & Vujic, 2007).

Endorphin release might also explain other phenomena that have long puzzled psychologists. For example, the act of taking placebos (pills or other substances that contain no actual drugs but that patients *believe* will make them better) may induce the release of endorphins, leading to the reduction of pain (Wager, 2005; Rajagopal, 2006; Crum & Langer, 2007).

RECAP/EVALUATE/RETHINK

RECAP

LO 5-1 Why do psychologists study the brain and nervous system?

- A full understanding of human behavior requires knowledge of the biological influences underlying that behavior, especially those originating in the nervous system. Psychologists who specialize in studying the effects of biological structures and functions on behavior are known as behavioral neuroscientists. (p. 50)

LO 5-2 What are the basic elements of the nervous system?

- Neurons, the most basic elements of the nervous system, carry nerve impulses from one part of the body to another. Information in a neuron generally follows a route that begins with the dendrites, continues into the cell body, and leads ultimately down the tube-like extension, the axon. (p. 51)

LO 5-3 How does the nervous system communicate electrical and chemical messages from one part to another?

- Most axons are insulated by a coating called the myelin sheath. When a neuron receives a message to fire, it releases an action potential, an electric charge that travels through the axon. Neurons operate according to an all-or-none law: Either they are at rest, or an action potential is moving through them. There is no in-between state. (p. 52)

- Once a neuron fires, nerve impulses are carried to other neurons through the production of chemical substances, neurotransmitters, that actually bridge the gaps—known as synapses—between neurons. Neurotransmitters may be either excitatory, telling other neurons to fire, or inhibitory, preventing or decreasing the likelihood of other neurons firing. (p. 56)

- Endorphins, another type of neurotransmitter, are related to the reduction of pain. Endorphins aid in the production of a natural painkiller and are probably responsible for creating the kind of euphoria that joggers sometimes experience after running. (p. 58)

EVALUATE

1. The _____ is the fundamental element of the nervous system.
2. Neurons receive information through their _____ and send messages through their _____.
3. Just as electrical wires have an outer coating, axons are insulated by a coating called the _____ _____.
4. The gap between two neurons is bridged by a chemical connection called a _____.
5. Endorphins are one kind of _____, the chemical "messengers" between neurons.

RETHINK

1. How might psychologists use drugs that mimic the effects of neurotransmitters to treat psychological disorders?
2. *From the perspective of a health-care provider:* How would you explain the placebo effect and the role of endorphins to patients who wish to try unproven treatment methods that they find on the web?

Answers to Evaluate Questions

1. neuron; 2. dendrites, axons; 3. myelin sheath; 4. synapse; 5. neurotransmitter

KEY TERMS

behavioral neuroscientists (or biopsychologists) p. 50
neurons p. 51
dendrite p. 51
axon p. 51

terminal buttons p. 51
myelin sheath p. 52
all-or-none law p. 52
resting state p. 52

action potential p. 53
mirror neurons p. 54
synapse p. 55
neurotransmitters p. 56

excitatory message p. 56
inhibitory message p. 56
reuptake p. 56

The Nervous System and the Endocrine System: Communicating Within the Body

Learning Outcomes

LO 6-1 How are the structures of the nervous system linked?

LO 6-2 How does the endocrine system affect behavior?

In light of the complexity of individual neurons and the neurotransmission process, it should come as no surprise that the connections and structures formed by the neurons are complicated. Because each neuron can be connected to 80,000 other neurons, the total number of possible connections is astonishing. For instance, estimates of the number of neural connections within the brain fall in the neighborhood of 10 quadrillion—a 1 followed by 16 zeros—and some experts put the number even higher. However, connections among neurons are not the only means of communication within the body; as we'll see, the endocrine system, which secretes chemical messages that circulate through the blood, also communicates messages that influence behavior and many aspects of biological functioning (Kandel, Schwartz, & Jessell, 2000; Forlenza & Baum, 2004; Boahen, 2005).

The Nervous System: Linking Neurons

Whatever the actual number of neural connections, the human nervous system has both logic and elegance. We turn now to a discussion of its basic structures.

CENTRAL AND PERIPHERAL NERVOUS SYSTEMS

As you can see from the schematic representation in Figure 1, the nervous system is divided into two main parts: the central nervous system and the peripheral nervous system. The **central nervous system (CNS)** is composed of the brain and spinal cord. The **spinal cord,** which is about the thickness of a pencil, contains a bundle of neurons that leaves the brain and runs down the length of the back (see Figure 2). As you can see in Figure 2, the spinal cord is the primary means for transmitting messages between the brain and the rest of the body.

However, the spinal cord is not just a communication channel. It also controls some simple behaviors on its own, without any help from the brain. An example is the way the knee jerks forward when it is tapped with a rubber hammer. This behavior is a type of **reflex,** an automatic, involuntary response to an incoming stimulus. A reflex is also at work when you touch a hot stove and immediately withdraw your hand. Although the brain eventually analyzes and reacts to the situation ("Ouch—hot stove—pull away!"), the initial withdrawal is directed only by neurons in the spinal cord.

central nervous system (CNS) The part of the nervous system that includes the brain and spinal cord.

spinal cord A bundle of neurons that leaves the brain and runs down the length of the back and is the main means for transmitting messages between the brain and the body.

reflex An automatic, involuntary response to an incoming stimulus.

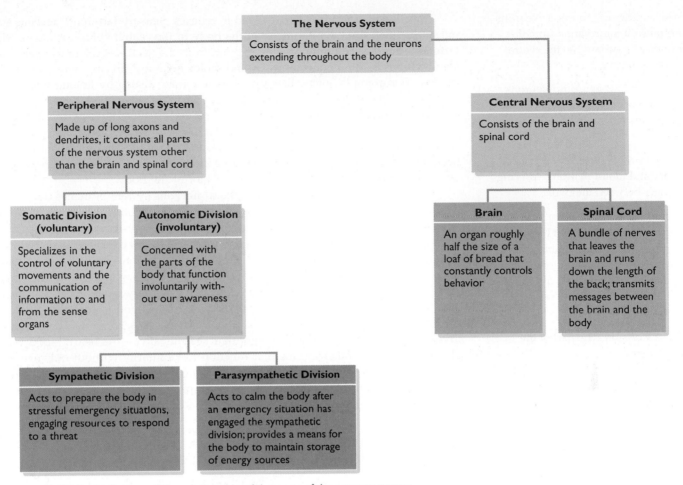

The Nervous System

Consists of the brain and the neurons extending throughout the body

Peripheral Nervous System

Made up of long axons and dendrites, it contains all parts of the nervous system other than the brain and spinal cord

Central Nervous System

Consists of the brain and spinal cord

Somatic Division (voluntary)

Specializes in the control of voluntary movements and the communication of information to and from the sense organs

Autonomic Division (involuntary)

Concerned with the parts of the body that function involuntarily without our awareness

Brain

An organ roughly half the size of a loaf of bread that constantly controls behavior

Spinal Cord

A bundle of nerves that leaves the brain and runs down the length of the back; transmits messages between the brain and the body

Sympathetic Division

Acts to prepare the body in stressful emergency situations, engaging resources to respond to a threat

Parasympathetic Division

Acts to calm the body after an emergency situation has engaged the sympathetic division; provides a means for the body to maintain storage of energy sources

FIGURE 1 A schematic diagram of the relationship of the parts of the nervous system.

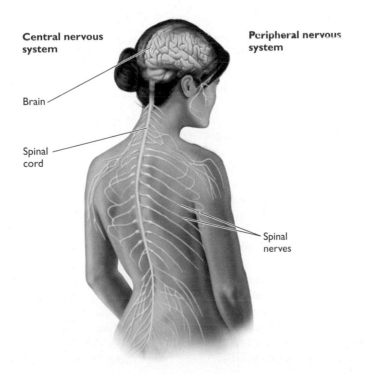

Central nervous system

Brain

Spinal cord

Peripheral nervous system

Spinal nerves

FIGURE 2 The central nervous system consists of the brain and spinal cord, and the peripheral nervous system encompasses the network of nerves connecting the brain and spinal cord to other parts of the body.

Study Alert

Use Figures 1 and 2 to learn the components of the central and peripheral nervous systems.

sensory (afferent) neurons Neurons that transmit information from the perimeter of the body to the central nervous system.

motor (efferent) neurons Neurons that communicate information from the nervous system to muscles and glands.

interneurons Neurons that connect sensory and motor neurons, carrying messages between the two.

peripheral nervous system The part of the nervous system that includes the autonomic and somatic subdivisions; made up of neurons with long axons and dendrites, it branches out from the spinal cord and brain and reaches the extremities of the body.

somatic division The part of the peripheral nervous system that specializes in the control of voluntary movements and the communication of information to and from the sense organs.

autonomic division The part of the peripheral nervous system that controls involuntary movement of the heart, glands, lungs, and other organs.

sympathetic division The part of the autonomic division of the nervous system that acts to prepare the body for action in stressful situations, engaging all the organism's resources to respond to a threat.

parasympathetic division The part of the autonomic division of the nervous system that acts to calm the body after an emergency has ended.

Three kinds of neurons are involved in reflexes. **Sensory (afferent) neurons** transmit information from the perimeter of the body to the central nervous system. **Motor (efferent) neurons** communicate information from the nervous system to muscles and glands. **Interneurons** connect sensory and motor neurons, carrying messages between the two. For example, interneurons help us recognize a song by linking what we are hearing from the auditory senses to the place in the brain where the song is being stored.

The importance of the spinal cord and reflexes is illustrated by the outcome of accidents in which the cord is injured or severed. In some cases, injury results in *quadriplegia*, a condition in which people lose voluntary muscle movement below the neck. In a less severe but still debilitating condition, *paraplegia*, people are unable to voluntarily move any muscles in the lower half of the body.

As suggested by its name, the **peripheral nervous system** branches out from the spinal cord and brain and reaches the extremities of the body. Made up of neurons with long axons and dendrites, the peripheral nervous system encompasses all the parts of the nervous system other than the brain and spinal cord. There are two major divisions—the somatic division and the autonomic division—both of which connect the central nervous system with the sense organs, muscles, glands, and other organs. The **somatic division** specializes in the control of voluntary movements—such as the motion of the eyes to read this sentence or those of the hand to turn this page—and the communication of information to and from the sense organs. The **autonomic division** controls the parts of the body that keep us alive—the heart, blood vessels, glands, lungs, and other organs that function involuntarily without our awareness. As you are reading at this moment, the autonomic division of the peripheral nervous system is pumping blood through your body, pushing your lungs in and out, and overseeing the digestion of your last meal.

ACTIVATING THE DIVISIONS OF THE AUTONOMIC NERVOUS SYSTEM

The autonomic division plays a particularly crucial role during emergencies. Suppose that as you are reading you suddenly sense that a stranger is watching you through the window. As you look up, you see the glint of something that might be a knife. As confusion clouds your mind and fear overcomes your attempts to think rationally, what happens to your body? If you are like most people, you react immediately on a physiological level. Your heart rate increases, you begin to sweat, and you develop goose bumps all over your body.

The physiological changes that occur during a crisis result from the activation of one of the two parts of the autonomic nervous system: the **sympathetic division.** The sympathetic division acts to prepare the body for action in stressful situations by engaging all of the organism's resources to run away or to confront the threat. This is often called the "fight or flight" response.

In contrast, the **parasympathetic division** acts to calm the body after the emergency has ended. When you find, for instance, that the stranger at the window is actually your roommate, who has lost his keys and is climbing in the window to avoid waking you, your parasympathetic division begins to take over, lowering your heart rate, stopping your sweating, and returning your body to the state it was in before you became alarmed. The parasympathetic division also directs the body to store energy for use in emergencies.

The sympathetic and parasympathetic divisions work together to regulate many functions of the body (see Figure 3). For instance, sexual arousal is controlled by the parasympathetic division, but sexual orgasm is a function of the sympathetic division. The sympathetic and parasympathetic divisions also are involved in a number of disorders. For example, one explanation of documented examples of "voodoo death"—in which a person is literally scared to death resulting from a voodoo curse—may be produced by overstimulation of the sympathetic division due to extreme fear (Sternberg, 2002).

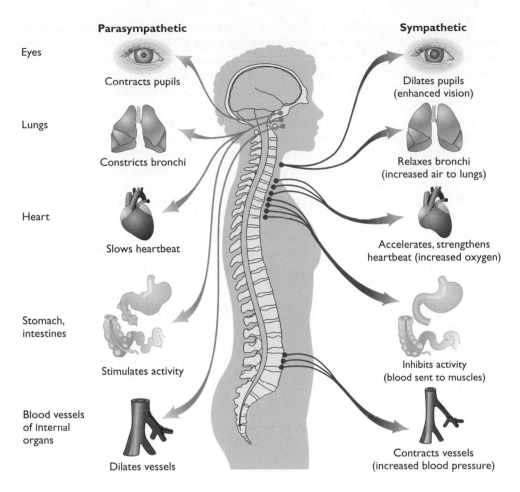

Parasympathetic

Eyes — Contracts pupils

Lungs — Constricts bronchi

Heart — Slows heartbeat

Stomach, intestines — Stimulates activity

Blood vessels of internal organs — Dilates vessels

Sympathetic

Dilates pupils (enhanced vision)

Relaxes bronchi (increased air to lungs)

Accelerates, strengthens heartbeat (increased oxygen)

Inhibits activity (blood sent to muscles)

Contracts vessels (increased blood pressure)

FIGURE 3 The major functions of the autonomic nervous system. The sympathetic division acts to prepare certain organs of the body for stressful situations, and the parasympathetic division acts to calm the body after the emergency has passed. Can you explain why each response of the sympathetic division might be useful in an emergency?

PsychTech
Rob Summers, who was paralyzed when hit by a car at age 20, took his first steps 5 years later after he received an experimental treatment in which electrodes were implanted into his back to stimulate his spinal cord.

The Evolutionary Foundations of the Nervous System

The complexities of the nervous system can be better understood if we take the course of evolution into consideration. The forerunner of the human nervous system is found in the earliest simple organisms to have a spinal cord. Basically, those organisms were simple input-output devices: When the upper side of the spinal cord was stimulated by, for instance, being touched, the organism reacted with a simple response, such as jerking away. Such responses were completely a consequence of the organism's genetic makeup.

Over millions of years, the spinal cord became more specialized, and organisms became capable of distinguishing between different kinds of stimuli and responding appropriately to them. Ultimately, a portion of the spinal cord evolved into what we would consider a primitive brain.

Today, the nervous system is *hierarchically organized*, meaning that relatively newer (from an evolutionary point of view) and more sophisticated regions of the brain regulate the older, and more primitive, parts of the nervous system. As we move up along the spinal cord and continue upward into the brain, then, the functions controlled by the various regions become progressively more advanced.

Why should we care about the evolutionary background of the human nervous system? The answer comes from researchers working in the area of **evolutionary psychology,** the branch of psychology that seeks to identify how behavior is influenced and produced by our genetic inheritance from our ancestors.

evolutionary psychology The branch of psychology that seeks to identify behavior patterns that are a result of our genetic inheritance from our ancestors.

Evolutionary psychologists argue that the course of evolution is reflected in the structure and functioning of the nervous system and that evolutionary factors consequently have a significant influence on our everyday behavior. Their work, in conjunction with the research of scientists studying genetics, biochemistry, and medicine, has led to an understanding of how our behavior is affected by heredity, our genetically determined heritage.

Evolutionary psychologists have spawned a new and increasingly influential field: behavioral genetics. As we will discuss further in the chapter on development, **behavioral genetics** is the study of the effects of heredity on behavior. Consistent with the evolutionary perspective, behavioral genetics researchers are finding increasing evidence that cognitive abilities, personality traits, sexual orientation, and psychological disorders are determined to some extent by genetic factors (Livesley & Jang, 2008; Vernon et al., 2008; Schermer et al., 2011).

behavioral genetics The study of the effects of heredity on behavior.

The Endocrine System: Of Chemicals and Glands

endocrine system A chemical communication network that sends messages throughout the body via the bloodstream.

hormones Chemicals that circulate through the blood and regulate the functioning or growth of the body.

Another of the body's communication systems, the **endocrine system** is a chemical communication network that sends messages throughout the body via the bloodstream. Its job is to secrete **hormones,** chemicals that circulate through the blood and regulate the functioning or growth of the body. It also influences—and is influenced by—the functioning of the nervous system. Although the endocrine system is not part of the brain, it is closely linked to the hypothalamus.

As chemical messengers, hormones are like neurotransmitters, although their speed and mode of transmission are quite different. Whereas neural messages are measured in thousandths of a second, hormonal communications may take minutes to reach their destination. Furthermore, neural messages move through neurons in specific lines (like a signal carried by wires strung along telephone poles), whereas hormones travel throughout the body, similar to the way radio waves are transmitted across the entire landscape. Just as radio waves evoke a response only when a radio is tuned to the correct station, hormones flowing through the bloodstream activate only those cells that are receptive and "tuned" to the appropriate hormonal message.

pituitary gland The major component of the endocrine system, or "master gland," which secretes hormones that control growth and other parts of the endocrine system.

A key component of the endocrine system is the tiny **pituitary gland,** which is found near—and regulated by—the hypothalamus in the brain. The pituitary gland has sometimes been called the "master gland" because it controls the functioning of the rest of the endocrine system. But the pituitary gland is more than just the taskmaster of other glands; it has important functions in its own right. For instance, hormones secreted by the pituitary gland control growth. Extremely short people and unusually tall ones usually have pituitary gland abnormalities. Other endocrine glands, shown in Figure 4, affect emotional reactions, sexual urges, and energy levels.

Despite its designation as the "master gland," the pituitary is actually a servant of the brain, because the brain is ultimately responsible for the endocrine system's functioning. The brain maintains the internal balance of the body through the hypothalamus.

Individual hormones can wear many hats, depending on circumstances. For example, the hormone oxytocin is at the root of many of life's satisfactions and pleasures. In new mothers, oxytocin produces an urge to nurse newborn offspring. The same hormone also seems to stimulate cuddling between species members. And—at least in rats—it encourages sexually active males to seek out females more passionately, and females to be more receptive to males' sexual advances. There's even evidence that oxytocin is related to the development of trust in others, helping to grease

Study Alert

The endocrine system produces hormones, chemicals that circulate through the body via the bloodstream.

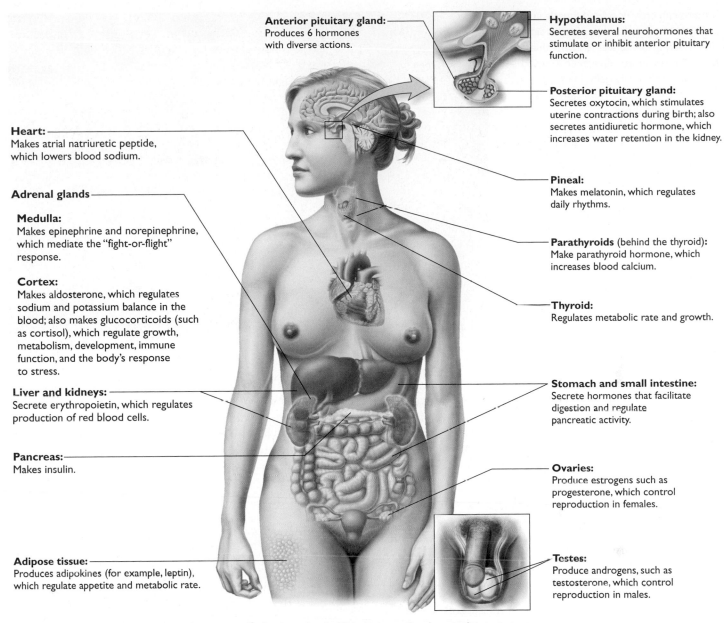

Anterior pituitary gland:
Produces 6 hormones
with diverse actions.

Hypothalamus:
Secretes several neurohormones that
stimulate or inhibit anterior pituitary
function.

Posterior pituitary gland:
Secretes oxytocin, which stimulates
uterine contractions during birth; also
secretes antidiuretic hormone, which
increases water retention in the kidney.

Heart:
Makes atrial natriuretic peptide,
which lowers blood sodium.

Pineal:
Makes melatonin, which regulates
daily rhythms.

Adrenal glands

Medulla:
Makes epinephrine and norepinephrine,
which mediate the "fight-or-flight"
response.

Parathyroids (behind the thyroid):
Make parathyroid hormone, which
increases blood calcium.

Cortex:
Makes aldosterone, which regulates
sodium and potassium balance in the
blood; also makes glucocorticoids (such
as cortisol), which regulate growth,
metabolism, development, immune
function, and the body's response
to stress.

Thyroid:
Regulates metabolic rate and growth.

Stomach and small intestine:
Secrete hormones that facilitate
digestion and regulate
pancreatic activity.

Liver and kidneys:
Secrete erythropoietin, which regulates
production of red blood cells.

Pancreas:
Makes insulin.

Ovaries:
Produce estrogens such as
progesterone, which control
reproduction in females.

Adipose tissue:
Produces adipokines (for example, leptin),
which regulate appetite and metabolic rate.

Testes:
Produce androgens, such as
testosterone, which control
reproduction in males.

FIGURE 4 Location and function of the major endocrine glands. The pituitary gland controls
the functioning of the other endocrine glands and, in turn, is regulated by the hypothalamus.

the wheels of effective social interaction (Meinlschmidt & Heim, 2007; Guastella, Mitchell, & Dadds, 2008; De Dreu et al., 2011).

Although hormones are produced naturally by the endocrine system, the ingestion of artificial hormones has proved to be both beneficial and potentially dangerous. For example, before the early 2000s, physicians frequently prescribed hormone replacement therapy (HRT) to treat symptoms of menopause in older women. However, because recent research suggests that the treatment has potentially dangerous side effects, health experts now warn that in many cases the dangers outweigh the benefits (Herrington & Howard, 2003; Alexandersen, Karsdal, & Christiansen, 2009).

The use of testosterone, a male hormone, and drugs known as *steroids*, which act like testosterone, is increasingly common. For athletes and others who want to bulk up their appearance, steroids provide a way to add muscle weight and increase strength. However, these drugs can lead to stunted growth, shrinking of the testicles,

Steroids can provide added muscle and strength, but they have dangerous side effects. A number of well-known athletes in a variety of sports have been accused of using the drugs illegally. In fact, a number of them have publically said they have used them.

heart attacks, strokes, and cancer, making them extremely dangerous. Furthermore, they can even produce violent behavior. For example, in one tragic case, professional wrestler Chris Benoit strangled his wife, suffocated his son, and later hanged himself—acts that were attributed to his use of steroids (Klötz, Garle, & Granath, 2006; Pagonis, Angelopoulos, & Koukoulis, 2006; Sandomir, 2007).

RECAP/EVALUATE/RETHINK

RECAP

LO 6-1 How are the structures of the nervous system linked?

- The nervous system is made up of the central nervous system (the brain and spinal cord) and the peripheral nervous system. The peripheral nervous system is made up of the somatic division, which controls voluntary movements and the communication of information to and from the sense organs, and the autonomic division, which controls involuntary functions such as those of the heart, blood vessels, and lungs. (p. 60)
- The autonomic division of the peripheral nervous system is further subdivided into the sympathetic and parasympathetic divisions. The sympathetic division prepares the body in emergency situations, and the parasympathetic division helps the body return to its typical resting state. (p. 62)
- Evolutionary psychology, the branch of psychology that seeks to identify behavior patterns that are a result of our genetic inheritance, has led to increased understanding of the evolutionary basis of the structure and organization of the human nervous system. (p. 63)

LO 6-2 How does the endocrine system affect behavior?

- The endocrine system secretes hormones, chemicals that regulate the functioning of the body, via the bloodstream. The pituitary gland secretes growth hormones and influences the release of hormones by other endocrine glands, and in turn is regulated by the hypothalamus. (p. 64)

EVALUATE

1. If you put your hand on a red-hot piece of metal, the immediate response of pulling it away would be an example of a(n) _____.
2. The central nervous system is composed of the _____ and the _____.
3. In the peripheral nervous system, the _____ division controls voluntary movements, whereas the _____ division controls organs that keep us alive and function without our awareness.
4. Maria saw a young boy run into the street and get hit by a car. When she got to the fallen child, she was in a state of

panic. She was sweating, and her heart was racing. Her biological state resulted from the activation of what division of the nervous system?
a. parasympathetic
b. central
c. sympathetic
5. The emerging field of _____ studies ways in which our genetic inheritance predisposes us to behave in certain ways.

1. In what ways is the "fight-or-flight" response helpful to humans in emergency situations?
2. *From the perspective of a medical professional:* How would you explain the risks of using steroids to a teenager who wished to put on weight and muscle to be stronger to play football?

Answers to Evaluate Questions

1. reflex; 2. brain, spinal cord; 3. somatic, autonomic; 4. c. sympathetic; 5. evolutionary psychology

KEY TERMS

central nervous system (CNS) p. 60
spinal cord p. 60
reflex p. 60
sensory (afferent) neurons p. 62

motor (efferent) neurons p. 62
interneurons p. 62
peripheral nervous system p. 62
somatic division p. 62

autonomic division p. 62
sympathetic division p. 62
parasympathetic division p. 62
evolutionary psychology p. 63

behavioral genetics p. 64
endocrine system p. 64
hormones p. 64
pituitary gland p. 64

The Brain

LO 7-1 How do researchers identify the major parts and functions of the brain?

LO 7-2 What are the major parts of the brain, and for what behaviors is each part responsible?

LO 7-3 How do the two halves of the brain operate interdependently?

LO 7-4 How can an understanding of the nervous system help us find ways to alleviate disease and pain?

It is not much to look at. Soft, spongy, mottled, and pinkish-gray in color, it hardly can be said to possess much in the way of physical beauty. Despite its physical appearance, however, it ranks as the greatest natural marvel that we know and has a beauty and sophistication all its own.

The object to which this description applies: the brain. The brain is responsible for our loftiest thoughts—and our most primitive urges. It is the overseer of the intricate workings of the human body. If one were to attempt to design a computer to mimic the range of capabilities of the brain, the task would be nearly impossible; in fact, it has proved difficult even to come close. The sheer quantity of nerve cells in the brain is enough to daunt even the most ambitious computer engineer. Many billions of neurons make up a structure weighing just 3 pounds in the average adult. However, it is not the number of cells that is the most astounding thing about the brain but its ability to allow the human intellect to flourish by guiding our behavior and thoughts.

We turn now to a consideration of the particular structures of the brain and the primary functions to which they are related. However, a caution is in order. Although we'll discuss specific areas of the brain in relation to specific behaviors, this approach is an oversimplification. No straightforward one-to-one correspondence exists between a distinct part of the brain and a particular behavior. Instead, behavior is produced by complex interconnections among sets of neurons in many areas of the brain: Our behavior, emotions, thoughts, hopes, and dreams are produced by a variety of neurons throughout the nervous system working in concert.

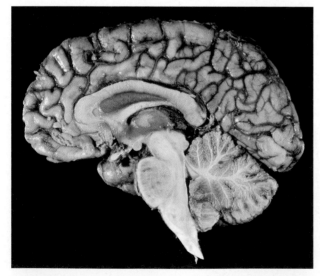

The brain (shown here in cross-section) may not be much to look at, but it represents one of the great marvels of human development. Why do most scientists believe that it will be difficult, if not impossible, to duplicate the brain's abilities?

Studying the Brain's Structure and Functions: Spying on the Brain

The brain has posed a continual challenge to those who would study it. For most of history, its examination was possible only after an individual had died. Only then could the skull be opened and the brain cut into without serious injury. Although informative, this procedure could hardly tell us much about the functioning of the healthy brain.

Today, however, brain-scanning techniques provide a window into the living brain. Using these techniques, investigators can take a "snapshot" of the internal workings of the brain without having to cut open a person's skull. The most important scanning techniques, illustrated in Figure 1, are the electroencephalogram (EEG), positron emission tomography (PET), functional magnetic resonance imaging (fMRI), and transcranial magnetic stimulation imaging (TMS).

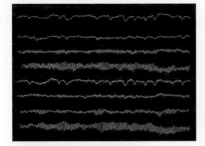

(a) EEG

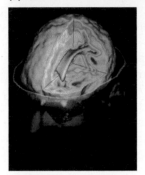

(b) fMRI

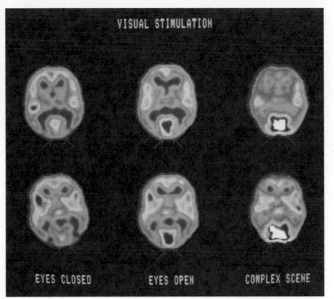

(c) PET scan

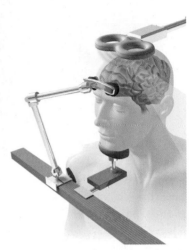

(d) TMS Apparatus

FIGURE 1 Brain scans produced by different techniques. (a) A computer-produced EEG image. (b) The fMRI scan uses a magnetic field to provide a detailed view of brain activity on a moment-by-moment basis. (c) The PET scan displays the functioning of the brain at a given moment. (d) Transcranial magnetic stimulation (TMS), the newest type of scan, produces a momentary disruption in an area of the brain, allowing researchers to see what activities are controlled by that area. TMS also has the potential to treat some psychological disorders.

The *electroencephalogram (EEG)* records electrical activity in the brain through electrodes placed on the outside of the skull. Although traditionally the EEG could produce only a graph of electrical wave patterns, new techniques are now used to transform the brain's electrical activity into a pictorial representation of the brain that allows more precise diagnosis of disorders such as epilepsy and learning disabilities.

Functional magnetic resonance imaging (fMRI) scans provide a detailed, three-dimensional computer-generated image of brain structures and activity by aiming a powerful magnetic field at the body. With fMRI scanning, it is possible to produce vivid, detailed images of the functioning of the brain.

Using fMRI scans, researchers are able to view features of less than a millimeter in size and view changes occurring in intervals of $\frac{1}{10}$ of a second. For example, fMRI scans can show the operation of individual bundles of nerves by tracing the flow of blood, opening the way for improved diagnosis of ailments ranging from chronic back pain to nervous system disorders such as strokes, multiple sclerosis, and Alzheimer's. Scans using fMRI are routinely used in planning brain surgery, because they can help surgeons distinguish areas of the brain involved in normal and disturbed functioning (Quenot et al., 2005; D'Arcy, Bolster, & Ryner, 2007; Loitfelder et al., 2011).

Positron emission tomography (PET) scans show biochemical activity within the brain at a given moment. PET scans begin with the injection of a radioactive (but safe) liquid into the bloodstream, which makes its way to the brain. By locating radiation within the brain, a computer can determine which are the more active regions, providing a striking picture of the brain at work. For example, PET scans may be used in cases of memory problems, seeking to identify the presence of brain tumors (Gronholm et al., 2005; McMurtray et al., 2007).

Transcranial magnetic stimulation (TMS) is one of the newest types of scan. By exposing a tiny region of the brain to a strong magnetic field, TMS causes a momentary

Study Alert

Remember that EEG, fMRI, PET, and TMS differ in terms of whether they examine brain *structures* or brain *functioning*.

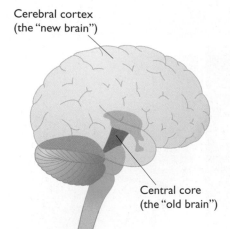

Cerebral cortex
(the "new brain")

Central core
(the "old brain")

FIGURE 2 The major divisions of the brain: the cerebral cortex and the central core. (Source: Seeley, Stephens, & Tate, 2000.)

central core The "old brain," which controls basic functions such as eating and sleeping and is common to all vertebrates.

cerebellum (ser-uh-BELL-um) The part of the brain that controls bodily balance.

reticular formation The part of the brain extending from the medulla through the pons and made up of groups of nerve cells that can immediately activate other parts of the brain to produce general bodily arousal.

interruption of electrical activity. Researchers then are able to note the effects of this interruption on normal brain functioning. The procedure is sometimes called a "virtual lesion," because it produces effects analogous to what would occur if areas of the brain were physically cut. The enormous advantage of TMS, of course, is that the virtual cut is only temporary. In addition to identifying areas of the brain that are responsible for particular functions, TMS has the potential to treat certain kinds of psychological disorders, such as depression and schizophrenia, by shooting brief magnetic pulses through the brain (Fitzgerald & Daskalakis, 2008; Rado, Dowd, & Janicak, 2008; Pallanti & Bernardi, 2009).

Future discoveries may yield even more sophisticated methods of examining the brain. For example, the emerging field of *optogenetics* involves genetic engineering and the use of special types of light to view individual circuits of neurons (Miesenbock, 2008; Gradinaru et al., 2009; Iwai et al., 2011).

Advances in our understanding of the brain also are paving the way for the development of new methods for harnessing the brain's neural signals. We consider some of these intriguing findings in *Applying Psychology in the 21st Century*.

The Central Core: Our "Old Brain"

Although the capabilities of the human brain far exceed those of the brain of any other species, humans share some basic functions, such as breathing, eating, and sleeping, with more primitive animals. Not surprisingly, those activities are directed by a relatively primitive part of the brain. A portion of the brain known as the **central core** (see Figure 2) is quite similar in all vertebrates (species with backbones). The central core is sometimes referred to as the "old brain," because its evolution can be traced back some 500 million years to primitive structures found in nonhuman species.

If we were to move up the spinal cord from the base of the skull to locate the structures of the central core of the brain, the first part we would come to would be the *hindbrain,* which contains the medulla, pons, and cerebellum (see Figure 3 on p. 72). The *medulla* controls a number of critical body functions, the most important of which are breathing and heartbeat. The *pons* is a bridge in the hindbrain. Containing large bundles of nerves, the pons acts as a transmitter of motor information, coordinating muscles and integrating movement between the right and left halves of the body. It is also involved in regulating sleep.

The **cerebellum** extends from the rear of the hindbrain. Without the help of the cerebellum we would be unable to walk a straight line without staggering and lurching forward, for it is the job of the cerebellum to control bodily balance. It constantly monitors feedback from the muscles to coordinate their placement, movement, and tension. In fact, drinking too much alcohol seems to depress the activity of the cerebellum, leading to the unsteady gait and movement characteristic of drunkenness. The cerebellum is also involved in several intellectual functions, ranging from the analysis and coordination of sensory information to problem solving (Paquier & Mariën, 2005; Vandervert, Schimpf, & Liu, 2007; Swain, Kerr, & Thompson, 2011).

The **reticular formation** extends from the medulla through the pons, passing through the middle section of the brain—or *midbrain*—and into the front-most part of the brain, called the *forebrain.* Like an ever-vigilant guard, the reticular formation is made up of groups of nerve cells that can activate other parts of the brain immediately to produce general bodily arousal. If, for example, we are startled by a loud noise, the reticular formation can prompt a heightened state of awareness to determine whether a response is necessary. The reticular formation serves a different function when we are sleeping, seeming to filter out background stimuli to allow us to sleep undisturbed.

Your Wish Is Its Command: Directing Computers with Your Brain

Throw away your computer keyboard. Exterminate your mouse. Get rid of your touch screen. Instead, just think a command that you want your computer to follow, and it will do your bidding.

At least that is the scenario that several research teams hope to see in the not-too-distant future. In their view, computers of the future will be able to respond to people's thoughts. In fact, these predictions are rapidly becoming reality.

Consider, for example, the case of a man in his 20s who has a severe form of epilepsy, a disease that causes seizures. As part of his treatment, surgeons inserted a group of electrodes, called an electrocorticographic (ECoG) implant, on top of the brain's cortex, to help control his seizures. But the ECoG implant did more than alleviate the seizures: research scientists were able to teach the patient to control activities on a computer via the implant in his brain. Remarkably, the patient was able to play the video game "Galaga" using only his thoughts, moving a spaceship on the screen back and forth and shooting at menacing creatures on the screen (Kennedy, 2011; Leuthardt et al., 2011).

Although the ability to play video games mentally may seem like a relatively trivial advance, the accomplishment holds serious implications for future advances. It ultimately may permit people to "speak" using their neurons. For example, eventually we might think of a dog, and immediately see the word "dog" appear on a video screen (Kennedy, 2011).

In another case, a lawyer paralyzed by Lou Gehrig's disease was unable to eat, speak, or even breathe on his own. Although his mind functioned normally,

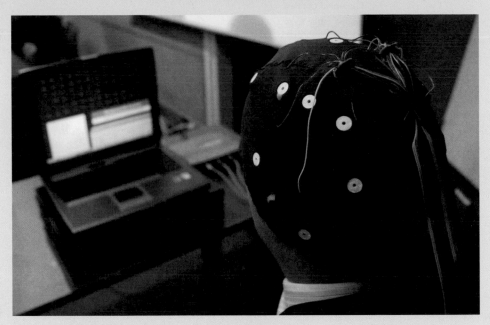

Brain-scanning techniques allow people to communicate via brain waves alone.

he was unable to communicate with the outside world. All that changed after he was fitted with an experimental device that allows brain waves to be translated into written communication. Using EEG scanning techniques that react to the pattern of brain waves originating in the brain, he learned to boost and curtail certain types of brain waves. After hundreds of hours of practice, he was able to select letters that appear on a video screen. By stringing letters together, he could spell out messages. The process, which makes use of brain waves called *slow cortical potentials*, permitted the patient to communicate effectively. Although

the method is slow and tedious, it holds great promise for people with spinal cord injuries and diseases that have left them paralyzed (Neumann & Birbaumer, 2004; Pollack, 2006; Hatsopoulos & Donoghue, 2009).

Neuroscience researchers are making remarkable progress at developing the technology of thought-based interfaces. And ultimately, these advances seem destined to lead to a more startling possibility: communication between two people purely using neuronal and brain activity—that is, mental telepathy. Although we are not close to such a possibility at this point, it is clearly on the horizon.

RETHINK

- What would be required to make brain wave communication two-way instead of only one-way?
- What implications would there be if people gained the ability to communicate with each other in this way?

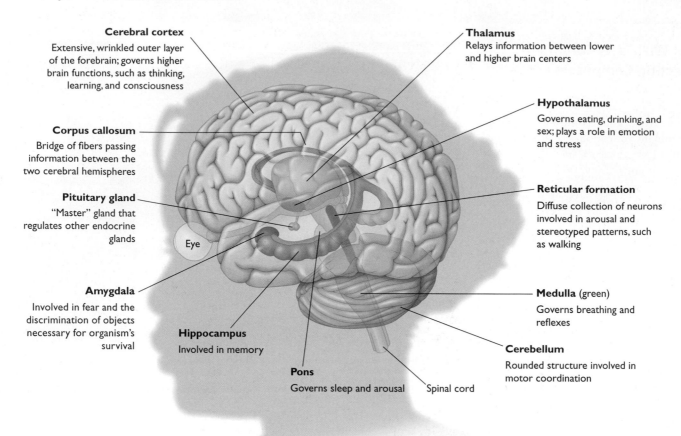

Cerebral cortex
Extensive, wrinkled outer layer
of the forebrain; governs higher
brain functions, such as thinking,
learning, and consciousness

Corpus callosum
Bridge of fibers passing
information between the
two cerebral hemispheres

Pituitary gland
"Master" gland that
regulates other endocrine
glands

Eye

Amygdala
Involved in fear and the
discrimination of objects
necessary for organism's
survival

Hippocampus
Involved in memory

Pons
Governs sleep and arousal

Spinal cord

Thalamus
Relays information between lower
and higher brain centers

Hypothalamus
Governs eating, drinking, and
sex; plays a role in emotion
and stress

Reticular formation
Diffuse collection of neurons
involved in arousal and
stereotyped patterns, such
as walking

Medulla (green)
Governs breathing and
reflexes

Cerebellum
Rounded structure involved in
motor coordination

FIGURE 3 The major structures in the brain. (Source: From *Brain, Mind, and Behavior* by F. Bloom, C. A. Nelson, A. Lazerson. © 2001 by Educational Broadcasting Corporation. Used with permission of Worth Publishers.)

thalamus The part of the brain located in the middle of the central core that acts primarily to relay information about the senses.

hypothalamus A tiny part of the brain, located below the thalamus, that maintains homeostasis and produces and regulates vital behavior, such as eating, drinking, and sexual behavior.

Hidden within the forebrain, the **thalamus** acts primarily as a relay station for information about the senses. Messages from the eyes, ears, and skin travel to the thalamus to be communicated upward to higher parts of the brain. The thalamus also integrates information from higher parts of the brain, sorting it out so that it can be sent to the cerebellum and medulla.

The **hypothalamus** is located just below the thalamus. Although tiny—about the size of a fingertip—the hypothalamus plays an extremely important role. One of its major functions is to maintain *homeostasis*, a steady internal environment for the body. The hypothalamus helps provide a constant body temperature and monitors the amount of nutrients stored in the cells. A second major function is equally important: the hypothalamus produces and regulates behavior that is critical to the basic survival of the species, such as eating, self-protection, and sex.

The Limbic System: Beyond the Central Core

In an eerie view of the future, science fiction writers have suggested that people someday will routinely have electrodes implanted in their brains. Those electrodes will permit them to receive tiny shocks that will produce the sensation of pleasure by stimulating certain centers of the brain. When they feel upset, people will simply activate their electrodes to achieve an immediate high.

Although far-fetched—and ultimately improbable—such a futuristic fantasy is based on fact. The brain does have pleasure centers in several areas, including some in the **limbic system.** Consisting of a series of doughnut-shaped structures that include the *amygdala* and *hippocampus*, the limbic system borders the top of the central core and has connections with the cerebral cortex (see Figure 4).

The structures of the limbic system jointly control a variety of basic functions relating to emotions and self-preservation, such as eating, aggression, and reproduction. Injury to the limbic system can produce striking changes in behavior. For example, injury to the amygdala, which is involved in fear and aggression, can turn animals that are usually docile and tame into belligerent savages. Conversely, animals that are usually wild and uncontrollable may become meek and obedient following injury to the amygdala (Bedard & Persinger, 1995; Gontkovsky, 2005).

Research examining the effects of mild electric shocks to parts of the limbic system and other parts of the brain has produced some thought-provoking findings. In one experiment, rats that pressed a bar received mild electric stimulation through an electrode implanted in their brains, which produced pleasurable feelings. Even starving rats on their way to food would stop to press the bar as many times as they could. Some rats would actually stimulate themselves literally thousands of times an hour—until they collapsed with fatigue (Routtenberg & Lindy, 1965; Olds & Fobes, 1981; Fountas & Smith, 2007).

Some humans have also experienced the extraordinarily pleasurable quality of certain kinds of stimulation: As part of the treatment for certain kinds of brain disorders, some people have received electrical stimulation to certain areas of the limbic system. Although at a loss to describe just what it feels like, these people report the experience to be intensely pleasurable, similar in some respects to sexual orgasm.

The limbic system and hippocampus in particular play an important role in learning and memory, a finding demonstrated in patients with epilepsy. In an attempt to stop their seizures, such patients have had portions of the limbic system removed. One unintended consequence of the surgery is that individuals sometimes have difficulty learning and remembering new information. In one case, a patient who had undergone surgery was unable to remember where he lived, although he had resided at the same address for 8 years. Further, even though the patient was able to carry on animated conversations, he was unable, a few minutes later, to recall what had been discussed (Milner, 1966; Rich & Shapiro, 2007; Grimm, 2011).

The limbic system, then, is involved in several important functions, including self-preservation, learning, memory, and the experience of pleasure. These functions are hardly unique to humans; in fact, the limbic system is sometimes referred to as the "animal brain," because its structures and functions are so similar to those of other mammals. To identify the part of the brain that provides the complex and subtle capabilities that are uniquely human, we need to turn to another structure—the cerebral cortex.

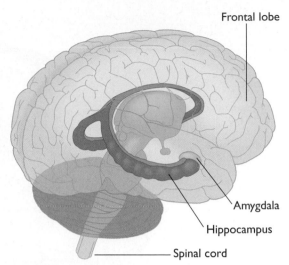

FIGURE 4 The limbic system is involved in self-preservation, learning, memory, and the experience of pleasure.

limbic system The part of the brain that controls eating, aggression, and reproduction.

The Cerebral Cortex: Our "New Brain"

As we have proceeded up the spinal cord and into the brain, our discussion has centered on areas of the brain that control functions similar to those found in less sophisticated organisms. But where, you may be asking, are the portions of the brain that enable humans to do what they do best and that distinguish humans from all other animals? Those unique features of the human brain—indeed, the

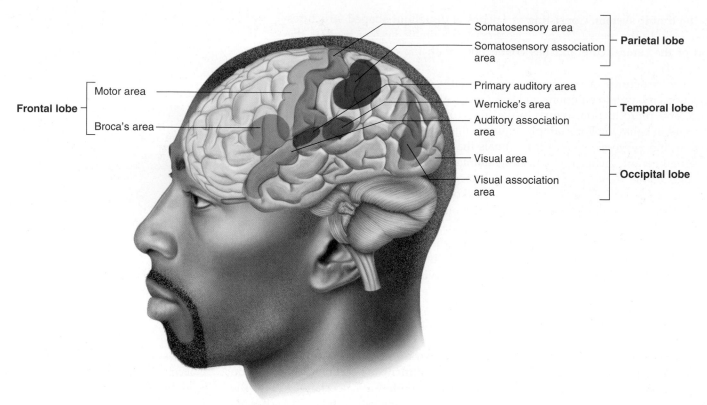

Motor area
Broca's area
Frontal lobe

Somatosensory area
Somatosensory association area
Parietal lobe

Primary auditory area
Wernicke's area
Auditory association area
Temporal lobe

Visual area
Visual association area
Occipital lobe

FIGURE 5 The cerebral cortex of the brain. The major physical structures of the cerebral cortex are called lobes. This figure also illustrates the functions associated with particular areas of the cerebral cortex. Are any areas of the cerebral cortex present in nonhuman animals?

cerebral cortex The "new brain," responsible for the most sophisticated information processing in the brain; contains four lobes.

lobes The four major sections of the cerebral cortex: frontal, parietal, temporal, and occipital.

very capabilities that allow you to come up with such a question in the first place—are embodied in the ability to think, evaluate, and make complex judgments. The principal location of these abilities, along with many others, is the **cerebral cortex.**

The cerebral cortex is referred to as the "new brain" because of its relatively recent evolution. It consists of a mass of deeply folded, rippled, convoluted tissue. Although only about 1/12 of an inch thick, it would, if flattened out, cover an area more than 2 feet square. This configuration allows the surface area of the cortex to be considerably greater than it would be if it were smoother and more uniformly packed into the skull. The uneven shape also permits a high level of integration of neurons, allowing sophisticated information processing.

The cortex has four major sections called **lobes.** If we take a side view of the brain, the *frontal lobes* lie at the front center of the cortex and the *parietal lobes* lie behind them. The *temporal lobes* are found in the lower-center portion of the cortex, with the *occipital lobes* lying behind them. These four sets of lobes are physically separated by deep grooves called *sulci.* Figure 5 shows the four areas.

Another way to describe the brain is in terms of the functions associated with a particular area. Figure 5 also shows the specialized regions within the lobes related to specific functions and areas of the body. Three major areas are known: the motor areas, the sensory areas, and the association areas. Although we will discuss these areas as though they were separate and independent, keep in mind that this is an oversimplification. In most instances, behavior is influenced simultaneously by several structures and areas within the brain, operating interdependently. To give one example, people use different areas of the brain when they create sentences (a verbal task) compared with when they improvise musical tunes. Furthermore, when people suffer brain injury, uninjured portions of the brain can sometimes take over the functions that were previously handled by the damaged area. (Also see *PsychWork.*) In short, the brain is extraordinarily adaptable (Sacks, 2003; Boller, 2004; Brown, Martinez, & Parsons, 2006).

Rehabilitation counselor Monique Tremaine helps individuals who have suffered severe brain injury regain as much normal functioning as possible. She does this by systematically assessing patients' problems, providing psychological and behavioral treatment, and ensuring that the treatment is state-of-the-art and is grounded in evidence gleaned from research.

According to Tremaine, her work requires an understanding of the structure of the brain and nervous system as well as expertise in clinical psychology in order to understand how brain injury affects emotion, function, and behavior.

"Sudden acquired or traumatic brain injury can impact many aspects of an individual's life, including their personality, cognition, sense of physical well-being, family roles, and occupational functioning," she noted. "It is my role to communicate such changes to a multidisciplinary staff, to the patient, and to the family to develop a comprehensive treatment plan."

PsychWork
REHABILITATION COUNSELOR

Name: Monique J. Tremaine

Education: BS in Psychology & Natural Sciences, Ball State University; MA in Clinical Psychology, California School of Professional Psychology; PhD in Clinical Neuropsychology, California School of Professional Psychology

THE MOTOR AREA OF THE CORTEX

If you look at the frontal lobe in Figure 5, you will see a shaded portion labeled **motor area.** This part of the cortex is largely responsible for the body's voluntary movement. Every portion of the motor area corresponds to a specific locale within the body. If we were to insert an electrode into a particular part of the motor area of the cortex and apply mild electrical stimulation, there would be involuntary movement in the corresponding part of the body. If we moved to another part of the motor area and stimulated it, a different part of the body would move.

The motor area is so well mapped that researchers have identified the amount and relative location of cortical tissue used to produce movement in specific parts of the human body. For example, the control of movements that are relatively large scale and require little precision, such as the movement of a knee or a hip, is centered in a very small space in the motor area. In contrast, movements that must be precise and delicate, such as facial expressions and finger movements, are controlled by a considerably larger portion of the motor area (Schwenkreis et al., 2007).

In short, the motor area of the cortex provides a guide to the degree of complexity and the importance of the motor capabilities of specific parts of the body. In fact, it may do even more: Increasing evidence shows that not only does the motor cortex control different parts of the body, but it may also direct body parts into complex postures, such as the stance of a football center just before the ball is snapped to the quarterback or a swimmer standing at the edge of a diving board (Graziano, Taylor, & Moore, 2002; Dessing et al., 2005).

Ultimately, movement, like other behavior, is produced through the coordinated firing of a complex variety of neurons in the nervous system. The neurons that produce movement are linked in elaborate ways and work closely together.

motor area The part of the cortex that is largely responsible for the body's voluntary movement.

THE SENSORY AREA OF THE CORTEX

Given the one-to-one correspondence between the motor area and body location, it is not surprising to find a similar relationship between specific portions of the cortex and the senses. The **sensory area** of the cortex includes three regions: one that corresponds primarily to body sensations (including touch and pressure), one relating to sight, and a third relating to sound. For instance, the *somatosensory area* in the parietal lobe encompasses specific locations associated with the ability to perceive touch and pressure in a particular area of the body. As with the motor area, the amount of brain tissue related to a particular location on the body determines the degree of sensitivity of that location: The greater the area devoted to a

sensory area The site in the brain of the tissue that corresponds to each of the senses, with the degree of sensitivity related to the amount of tissue.

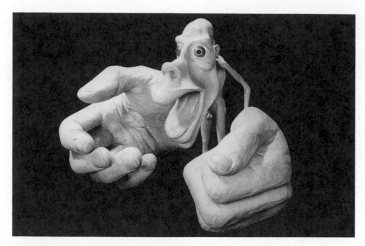

FIGURE 6 The greater the amount of tissue in the somatosensory area of the brain that is related to a specific body part, the more sensitive is that body part. If the size of our body parts reflected the corresponding amount of brain tissue, we would look like this strange creature.

specific area of the body within the cortex, the more sensitive is that area of the body. As you can see from the weird-looking individual in Figure 6, parts such as the fingers are related to a larger portion of the somatosensory area and are the most sensitive.

The senses of sound and sight are also represented in specific areas of the cerebral cortex. An *auditory area* located in the temporal lobe is responsible for the sense of hearing. If the auditory area is stimulated electrically, a person will hear sounds such as clicks or hums. It also appears that particular locations within the auditory area respond to specific pitches (Hudspeth, 2000; Brown & Martinez, 2007; Hyde, Peretz, & Zatorre, 2008; Bizley et al., 2009).

The visual area in the cortex, located in the occipital lobe, responds in the same way to electrical stimulation. Stimulation by electrodes produces the experience of flashes of light or colors, suggesting that the raw sensory input of images from the eyes is received in this area of the brain and transformed into meaningful stimuli. The visual area provides another example of how areas of the brain are intimately related to specific areas of the body: Specific structures in the eye are related to a particular part of the cortex—with, as you might guess, more area of the brain given to the most sensitive portions of the retina (Wurtz & Kandel, 2000; Stenbacka & Vanni, 2007; Libedinsky & Livingstone, 2011).

THE ASSOCIATION AREAS OF THE CORTEX

In a freak accident in 1848, an explosion drove a 3-foot-long iron bar completely through the skull of railroad worker Phineas Gage, where it remained after the accident. Amazingly, Gage survived and, despite the rod lodged through his head, a few minutes later seemed to be fine.

But he wasn't. Before the accident, Gage was hardworking and cautious. Afterward, he became irresponsible, drank heavily, and drifted from one wild scheme to another. In the words of one of his physicians, "he was 'no longer Gage'" (Harlow, 1869, p. 14).

What had happened to the old Gage? Although there is no way of knowing for sure, we can speculate that the accident injured the region of Gage's cerebral cortex known as the **association areas**, which generally are considered to be the site of higher mental processes such as thinking, language, memory, and speech (Rowe et al., 2000).

association areas One of the major regions of the cerebral cortex; the site of the higher mental processes, such as thought, language, memory, and speech.

The association areas make up a large portion of the cerebral cortex and consist of the sections that are not directly involved in either sensory processing or directing movement. The association areas control *executive functions*, which abilities are relating to planning, goal setting, judgment, and impulse control.

Much of our understanding of the association areas comes from patients who, like Phineas Gage, have suffered some type of brain injury. For example, when parts of the association areas are damaged, people undergo personality changes that affect their ability to make moral judgments and process emotions. At the same time, people with damage in those areas can still be capable of reasoning logically, performing calculations, and recalling information (Bechara et al., 1994).

Injuries to the association areas of the brain can produce *aphasia*, problems with language. In *Broca's aphasia*, speech becomes halting, laborious, and often ungrammatical, and a speaker is unable to find the right words. In contrast, *Wernicke's aphasia* produces difficulties both in understanding others' speech and in the production of language. The disorder is characterized by speech that sounds fluent but makes no sense, as in this example from a Wernicke's patient: "Boy, I'm sweating,

I'm awful nervous, you know, once in a while I get caught up, I can't mention the tarripoi, a month ago, quite a little . . ." (Gardner, 1975; Kearns, 2005; Caplan, Waters, & Dede, 2007).

Neuroplasticity and the Brain

Shortly after he was born, Jacob Stark's arms and legs started jerking every 20 minutes. Weeks later he could not focus his eyes on his mother's face. The diagnosis: uncontrollable epileptic seizures involving his entire brain.

His mother, Sally Stark, recalled: "When Jacob was 2½ months old, they said he would never learn to sit up, would never be able to feed himself. . . . They told us to take him home, love him, and find an institution." (Blakeslee, 1992: C3)

Instead, Jacob had brain surgery when he was 5 months old in which physicians removed 20% of his brain. The operation was a complete success. Three years later Jacob seemed normal in every way, with no sign of seizures.

The surgery that helped Jacob was based on the premise that the diseased part of his brain was producing seizures throughout the brain. Surgeons reasoned that if they removed the misfiring portion, the remaining parts of the brain, which appeared intact in PET scans, would take over. They correctly bet that Jacob could still lead a normal life after surgery, particularly because the surgery was being done at so young an age.

The success of Jacob's surgery illustrates that the brain has the ability to shift functions to different locations after injury to a specific area or in cases of surgery. But equally encouraging are some new findings about the *regenerative* powers of the brain and nervous system.

Scientists have learned in recent years that the brain continually reorganizes itself in a process termed **neuroplasticity.** Although for many years conventional wisdom held that no new brain cells are created after childhood, new research finds otherwise. Not only do the interconnections between neurons become more complex throughout life, but it now appears that new neurons are also created in certain areas of the brain during adulthood—a process called **neurogenesis.** Each day, thousands of new neurons are created, especially in areas of the brain related to learning and memory (Poo & Isaacson, 2007; Shors, 2009; Kempermann, 2011).

The ability of neurons to renew themselves during adulthood has significant implications for the potential treatment of disorders of the nervous system (see Figure 7 *Neuroscience in Your Life*). For example, drugs that trigger the development of new neurons might be used to counter such diseases as Alzheimer's, which are produced when neurons die (Tsai, Tsai, & Shen, 2007; Eisch et al., 2008; Waddell & Shors, 2008).

Furthermore, specific experiences can modify the way in which information is processed. For example, if you learn to read Braille, the amount of tissue in your cortex related to sensation in the fingertips will expand. Similarly, if you take up the violin, the area of the brain that receives messages from your fingers will grow—but only relating to the fingers that actually move across the violin's strings (Schwartz & Begley, 2002; Kolb, Gibb, & Robinson, 2003).

The future also holds promise for people who suffer from the tremors and loss of motor control produced by Parkinson's disease, although the research is mired in controversy. Because Parkinson's disease is caused by a gradual loss of cells that stimulate the production of dopamine in the brain, many investigators have reasoned that a procedure that would increase the supply of dopamine might be effective. They seem to be on the right track. When stem cells—immature cells from human fetuses that have the potential to develop into a variety of specialized cell types, depending on where they are implanted—are injected directly into the brains of Parkinson's sufferers, they take root and stimulate dopamine production. Preliminary results have been promising, with some patients showing great improvement (Parish & Arenas, 2007; Newman & Bakay, 2008; Wang et al., 2011).

neuroplasticity Changes in the brain that occur throughout the life span relating to the addition of new neurons, new interconnections between neurons, and the reorganization of information-processing areas.

neurogenesis The creation of new neurons.

Study Alert

Remember that *neuroplasticity* is the reorganization of existing neuronal connections, whereas *neurogenesis* is the creation of new neurons.

Neuroscience in Your Life: The Plastic Brain

FIGURE 7 The brain's ability to reorganize and utilize healthy areas of the brain to perform lost functions is an example of the brain's plasticity. For example, when people survive a stroke—which causes damage to a particular part of the brain—there can be significant changes in brain usage in remaining healthy areas. The left scan in A shows how a stroke patient's right hand was impacted due to a stroke in the left hemisphere, in which subsequently the left hemisphere utilizes areas of the right hemisphere to compensate for damage and to allow for recovery of function of the right hand. In the right scan in A, which is a scan of someone who has not had a stroke, the scan shows that the left hemisphere is mainly used. The scans in B are of hands that were not affected by stroke. Note that the right hemisphere is mainly utilized in both individuals who have had the stroke and healthy individuals. (Source: Grefkes & Fink, 2011.)

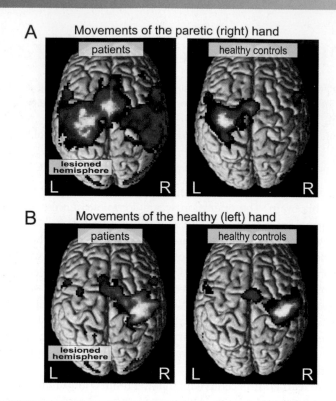

Stem cells thus hold great promise. When a stem cell divides, each newly created cell has the potential to be transformed into more specialized cells that have the potential to repair damaged cells. Because many of the most disabling diseases, ranging from cancer to stroke, result from cell damage, the potential of stem cells to revolutionize medicine is significant.

However, because the source of implanted stem cells typically is aborted fetuses, their use is controversial. Some critics have argued that the use of stem cells in research and treatment should be prohibited, while supporters argue that the potential benefits of the research are so great that stem cell research should be unrestricted. The issue has been politicized, and the question of whether and how stem cell research should be regulated is not clear (Rosen, 2005; Giacomini, Baylis, & Robert, 2007; Holden, 2007).

The Specialization of the Hemispheres: Two Brains or One?

The most recent development, at least in evolutionary terms, in the organization and operation of the human brain probably occurred in the last several million years: a specialization of the functions controlled by the left and right sides of the brain (Hopkins & Cantalupo, 2008; MacNeilage, Rogers, & Vallortigara, 2009; Tommasi, 2009).

The brain is divided into two roughly mirror-image halves. Just as we have two arms, two legs, and two lungs, we have a left brain and a right brain. Because of the way nerves in the brain are connected to the rest of the body, these symmetrical left and right halves, called **hemispheres,** control motion in—and receive sensation from—the side of the body opposite their location. The left hemisphere of the brain, then, generally controls the right side of the body, and the right hemisphere controls the left side of the body. Thus, damage to the right side of the brain is typically indicated by functional difficulties in the left side of the body.

Despite the appearance of similarity between the two hemispheres of the brain, they are somewhat different in the functions they control and in the ways they control them. Certain behaviors are more likely to reflect activity in one hemisphere than in the other, or are **lateralized.**

For example, for most people, language processing occurs more in the left side of the brain. In general, the left hemisphere concentrates more on tasks that require verbal competence, such as speaking, reading, thinking, and reasoning. In addition, the left hemisphere tends to process information sequentially, one bit at a time (Turkewitz, 1993; Banich & Heller, 1998; Hines, 2004).

The right hemisphere has its own strengths, particularly in nonverbal areas such as the understanding of spatial relationships, recognition of patterns and drawings, music, and emotional expression. The right hemisphere tends to process information globally, considering it as a whole (Ansaldo, Arguin, & Roch-Locours, 2002; Holowka & Petitto, 2002).

Keep in mind that the differences in specialization between the hemispheres are not great, and the degree and nature of lateralization vary from one person to another. If, like most people, you are right-handed, the control of language is probably concentrated more in your left hemisphere. By contrast, if you are among the 10% of people who are left-handed or are ambidextrous (you use both hands interchangeably), it is much more likely that the language centers of your brain are located more in the right hemisphere or are divided equally between the left and right hemispheres.

Furthermore, the two hemispheres of the brain function in tandem. It is a mistake to think of particular kinds of information as being processed solely in the right or the left hemisphere. The hemispheres work interdependently in deciphering, interpreting, and reacting to the world.

In addition, people who suffer injury to the left side of the brain and lose linguistic capabilities often recover the ability to speak: The right side of the brain often takes over some of the functions of the left side, especially in young children; the extent of recovery increases the earlier the injury occurs (Gould et al., 1999; Kempermann & Gage, 1999; Johnston, 2004).

Researchers also have unearthed evidence that there may be subtle differences in brain lateralization patterns between males and females and members of different cultures, as we see next.

hemispheres Symmetrical left and right halves of the brain that control the side of the body opposite to their location.

lateralization The dominance of one hemisphere of the brain in specific functions, such as language.

Study Alert

Although the hemispheres of the brain specialize in particular kinds of functions, the degree of specialization is not great, and the two hemispheres work interdependently.

PsychTech

Using a procedure called *hemispherectomy*, in which an entire hemisphere of the brain is removed, surgeons ended Christina Santhouse's seizures, which occurred at the rate of hundreds a day. Despite the removal of the right side of her brain, Christina recently completed a master's degree in speech pathology.

Exploring DIVERSITY

Human Diversity and the Brain

The interplay of biology and environment in behavior is especially clear when we consider evidence suggesting that even in brain structure and function there are both sex and cultural differences. Let's consider sex differences first. Accumulating evidence seems to show intriguing differences in males' and females' brain lateralization and weight (Kosslyn et al., 2002; Boles, 2005; Clements, Rimrodt, & Abel, 2006).

For instance, the two sexes show differences in the speed at which the brain develops. Young girls show earlier development in the frontal lobes, which control aggressiveness and language development. On the other hand, boys' brains develop faster in the visual region that facilitates visual and spatial tasks such as geometry (Giedd et al., 2010; Raznahan et al., 2010).

Furthermore, most males tend to show greater lateralization of language in the left hemisphere. For them, language is clearly relegated largely to the left side of the brain. In contrast, women display less lateralization, with language abilities apt to be more evenly divided between the two hemispheres. Such differences in brain lateralization may account, in part, for the superiority often displayed by females on certain measures of verbal skills, such as the onset and fluency of speech (Frings et al., 2006; Petersson et al., 2007; Mercadillo et al., 2011).

Other research suggests that men's brains are somewhat bigger than women's brains even after taking differences in body size into account. In contrast, part of the *corpus callosum*, a bundle of fibers that connects the hemispheres of the brain, is proportionally larger in women than in men (Cahill, 2005; Luders et al., 2006; Smith et al., 2007).

The meaning of such sex differences is far from clear. Consider one possibility related to differences in the proportional size of the corpus callosum. Its greater size in women may permit stronger connections to develop between the parts of the brain that control speech. In turn, this would explain why speech tends to emerge slightly earlier in girls than in boys.

Before we rush to such a conclusion, though, we must consider an alternative hypothesis: The reason verbal abilities emerge earlier in girls may be that infant girls receive greater encouragement to talk than do infant boys. In turn, this greater early experience may foster the growth of certain parts of the brain. Hence, physical brain differences may be a *reflection* of social and environmental influences rather than a *cause* of the differences in men's and women's behavior. At this point, it is impossible to know which of these alternative hypotheses is correct.

Culture also gives rise to differences in brain lateralization. Native speakers of Japanese seem to process information regarding vowel sounds primarily in the brain's left hemisphere. In contrast, North and South Americans, Europeans, and individuals of Japanese ancestry who learn Japanese later in life handle vowel sounds principally in the right hemisphere. One explanation for this difference is that certain characteristics of the Japanese language, such as the ability to express complex ideas by using only vowel sounds, result in the development of a specific type of brain lateralization in native speakers (Tsunoda, 1985; Kess & Miyamoto, 1994; Lin et al., 2005).

The Split Brain: Exploring the Two Hemispheres

The patient, V. J., had suffered severe seizures. By cutting her corpus callosum, the fibrous portion of the brain that carries messages between the hemispheres, surgeons hoped to create a firebreak to prevent the seizures from spreading. The operation did decrease the frequency and severity of V. J.'s attacks. But V. J. developed an unexpected side effect: She lost the ability to write at will, although she could read and spell words aloud. (Strauss, 1998, p. 287)

People like V. J., whose corpus callosum has been surgically cut to stop seizures and who are called *split-brain patients*, offer a rare opportunity for researchers investigating the independent functioning of the two hemispheres of the brain. For example, psychologist Roger Sperry—who won the Nobel Prize for his work—developed a number of ingenious techniques for studying how each hemisphere operates (Sperry, 1982; Gazzaniga, 1998; Savazzi et al., 2007).

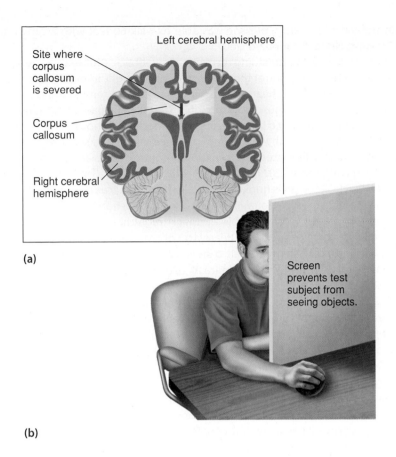

(a)

(b)

FIGURE 8 Hemispheres of the brain. (a) The corpus callosum connects the cerebral hemispheres of the brain as shown in this cross-section. (b) A split-brain patient is tested by touching objects behind a screen. Patients could name the objects they touched with their right hand, but couldn't when they touched them with their left hand. If a split-brain patient with her eyes closed was given a pencil to hold and called it a pencil, what hand was the pencil in? (Source: Brooker et al., 2008, p. 943.)

In one experimental procedure, patients who were prevented from seeing an object by a screen touched the object with their right hand and were asked to name it (see Figure 8). Because the right side of the body corresponds to the language-oriented left side of the brain, split-brain patients were able to name it. However, if patients touched the object with their left hand, they were unable to name it aloud, even though the information had registered in their brains: When the screen was removed, patients could identify the object they had touched. Information can be learned and remembered, then, using only the right side of the brain. (By the way, unless you've had split-brain surgery, this experiment won't work with you, because the bundle of fibers connecting the two hemispheres of a normal brain immediately transfers the information from one hemisphere to the other.)

It is clear from experiments like this one that the right and left hemispheres of the brain specialize in handling different sorts of information. At the same time, it is important to realize that both hemispheres are capable of understanding, knowing, and being aware of the world, in somewhat different ways. The two hemispheres, then, should be regarded as different in terms of the efficiency with which they process certain kinds of information, rather than as two entirely separate brains. The hemispheres work interdependently to allow the full range and richness of thought of which humans are capable.

BECOMING AN INFORMED CONSUMER of Psychology

Learning to Control Your Heart—and Mind—Through Biofeedback

When Tammy DeMichael was involved in a horrific car accident that broke her neck and crushed her spinal cord, experts told her that she was doomed to be a quadriplegic for the rest of her life, unable to move from the neck down. But they were wrong. Not only did

biofeedback A procedure in which a person learns to control through conscious thought internal physiological processes such as blood pressure, heart and respiration rate, skin temperature, sweating, and the constriction of particular muscles.

she regain the use of her arms, but she was able to walk 60 feet with a cane (Morrow & Wolff, 1991; Hess, Houg, & Tammaro, 2007).

The key to DeMichael's astounding recovery: biofeedback. **Biofeedback** is a procedure in which a person learns to control through conscious thought internal physiological processes such as blood pressure, heart and respiration rate, skin temperature, sweating, and the constriction of particular muscles. Although it traditionally had been thought that the heart rate, respiration rate, blood pressure, and other bodily functions are under the control of parts of the brain over which we have no influence, psychologists have discovered that these responses are actually susceptible to voluntary control (Nagai et al., 2004; Cho, Holyoak, & Cannon, 2007; Badke et al., 2011).

In biofeedback, a person is hooked up to electronic devices that provide continuous feedback relating to the physiological response in question. For instance, someone trying to control headaches through biofeedback might have electronic sensors placed on certain muscles on her head and learn to control the constriction and relaxation of those muscles. Later, when she felt a headache starting, she could relax the relevant muscles and abort the pain (Andrasik, 2007; Nestoriuc et al., 2008; Magis & Schoenen, 2011).

DeMichael's treatment was related to a form of biofeedback called *neurofeedback,* in which brain activity is displayed for a patient. Because not all of her nervous system's connections between the brain and her legs were severed, she was able to learn how to send messages to specific muscles, "ordering" them to move. Although it took more than a year, DeMichael was successful in restoring a large degree of her mobility.

Although the control of physiological processes through the use of biofeedback is not easy to learn, it has been employed with success in a variety of ailments, including emotional problems (such as anxiety, depression, phobias, tension headaches, insomnia, and hyperactivity), physical illnesses with a psychological component (such as asthma, high blood pressure, ulcers, muscle spasms, and migraine headaches), and physical problems (such as DeMichael's injuries, strokes, cerebral palsy, and curvature of the spine) (Morone & Greco, 2007; Reiner, 2008; Dias & van Deusen, 2011).

RECAP/EVALUATE/RETHINK

RECAP

LO 7-1 How do researchers identify the major parts and functions of the brain?

- Brain scans take a "snapshot" of the internal workings of the brain without having to cut surgically into a person's skull. Major brain-scanning techniques include the electroencephalogram (EEG), positron emission tomography (PET), functional magnetic resonance imaging (fMRI), and transcranial magnetic stimulation imaging (TMS). (p. 69)

LO 7-2 What are the major parts of the brain, and for what behaviors is each part responsible?

- The central core of the brain is made up of the medulla (which controls functions such as breathing and the heartbeat), the pons (which coordinates the muscles and the two sides of the body), the cerebellum (which controls balance), the reticular formation (which acts to heighten awareness in emergencies), the thalamus (which communicates sensory messages to and from the brain), and the hypothalamus (which maintains homeostasis, or body equilibrium, and regulates

behavior related to basic survival). The functions of the central core structures are similar to those found in other vertebrates. This central core is sometimes referred to as the "old brain." (p. 70)

- The cerebral cortex—the "new brain"—has areas that control voluntary movement (the motor area); the senses (the sensory area); and thinking, reasoning, speech, and memory (the association areas). The limbic system, found on the border of the "old" and "new" brains, is associated with eating, aggression, reproduction, and the experiences of pleasure and pain. (p. 73)

LO 7-3 How do the two halves of the brain operate interdependently?

- The brain is divided into left and right halves, or hemispheres, each of which generally controls the opposite side of the body. Each hemisphere can be thought of as being specialized in the functions it carries out: The left specializes in verbal tasks, such as logical reasoning, speaking, and reading; the right specializes in nonverbal tasks, such as spatial perception, pattern recognition, and emotional expression. (p. 78)

LO 7-4 How can an understanding of the nervous system help us to find ways to alleviate disease and pain?

- Biofeedback is a procedure by which a person learns to control internal physiological processes. By controlling involuntary responses, people are able to relieve anxiety, tension, migraine headaches, and a wide range of other psychological and physical problems. (p. 82)

EVALUATE

1. Match the name of each brain scan with the appropriate description:

   a. EEG
   b. fMRI
   c. PET

   1. By locating radiation within the brain, a computer can provide a striking picture of brain activity.
   2. Electrodes placed around the skull record the electrical signals transmitted through the brain.
   3. This technique provides a three-dimensional view of the brain by aiming a magnetic field at the body.

2. Match the portion of the brain with its function:

   a. medulla
   b. pons
   c. cerebellum
   d. reticular formation

   1. Maintains breathing and heartbeat.
   2. Controls bodily balance.
   3. Coordinates and integrates muscle movements.
   4. Activates other parts of the brain to produce general bodily arousal.

3. A surgeon places an electrode on a portion of your brain and stimulates it. Immediately, your right wrist involuntarily twitches. The doctor has most likely stimulated a portion of the _____ area of your brain.
4. Each hemisphere controls the _____ side of the body.
5. Nonverbal realms, such as emotions and music, are controlled primarily by the _____ hemisphere of the brain, whereas the _____ hemisphere is more responsible for speaking and reading.

RETHINK

1. Before sophisticated brain-scanning techniques were developed, behavioral neuroscientists' understanding of the brain was based largely on the brains of people who had died. What limitations would this pose, and in what areas would you expect the most significant advances once brain-scanning techniques became possible?
2. Could personal differences in people's specialization of right and left hemispheres be related to occupational success? For example, might an architect who relies on spatial skills have a pattern of hemispheric specialization different from that of a writer?
3. *From the perspective of an educator:* How might you use different techniques to teach reading to boys and girls based on the brain evidence?

Answers to Evaluate Questions

1. a-2, b-3, c-1; 2. a-1, b-3, c-2, d-4; 3. motor; 4. opposite; 5. right, left

KEY TERMS

central core p. 70
cerebellum
  (ser-uh-BELL-um) p. 70
reticular formation p. 70
thalamus p. 72

hypothalamus p. 72
limbic system p. 73
cerebral cortex p. 74
lobes p. 74

motor area p. 75
sensory area p. 75
association areas p. 76
neuroplasticity p. 77

neurogenesis p. 77
hemispheres p. 79
lateralization p. 79
biofeedback p. 82

Looking Back

Epilogue

In our examination of neuroscience, we've traced the ways in which biological structures and functions of the body affect behavior. Starting with neurons, we considered each of the components of the nervous system, culminating in an examination of how the brain permits us to think, reason, speak, recall, and experience emotions—the hallmarks of being human.

1. Before proceeding, turn back for a moment to the chapter prologue about Bob Woodruff's remarkable recovery from a severe brain injury. Consider the following questions. What region of the brain would you expect to be least likely to have been injured in a case such as Bob Woodruff's, where the injured person survives and recovers?

2. If you were Bob Woodruff's physician, how would you explain to his family the potential for him to recover from an injury such as the one he suffered?

3. Why do you think Bob Woodruff was able to resume his career as a journalist, but is not yet ready to be a news anchor again?

4. What special challenges might Bob Woodruff be faced with if the shrapnel had damaged his hippocampus? His motor area? His amygdala? His Broca's area?

VISUAL SUMMARY 2 Neuroscience and Behavior

MODULE 5   Neurons: The Basic Element

Neuron Structure

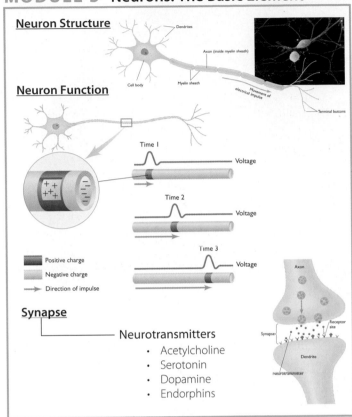

Neuron Function

Synapse

Neurotransmitters
- Acetylcholine
- Serotonin
- Dopamine
- Endorphins

MODULE 6   Nervous System

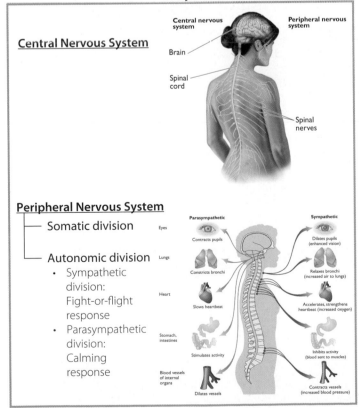

Central Nervous System

Peripheral Nervous System
— Somatic division

— Autonomic division
- Sympathetic division: Fight-or-flight response
- Parasympathetic division: Calming response

Endocrine System

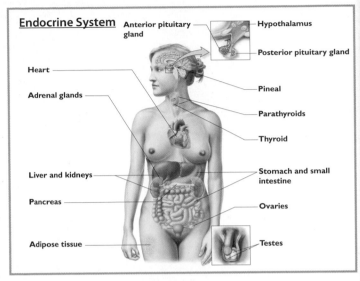

MODULE 7   The Brain

Areas of the Brain

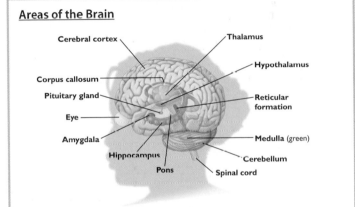

The Central Core: "Old brain"
- Cerebellum
- Reticular formation
- Thalamus
- Hypothalamus

The Cerebral Cortex: "New brain"
— Motor area: Voluntary movement
— Sensory area
- Somatosensory area
- Auditory area
- Visual area
— Association areas
- Executive functions
- Personality

The Limbic System
- Emotion
- Self-preservation
- Amygdala
- Hippocampus

Brain Features
- Neuroplasticity
- Lateralization: Two hemispheres with specialized functions
- The Split Brain: Corpus callosum with independent hemispheric functions

3

Sensation and Perception

Learning Outcomes for Chapter 3

MODULE 8

LO 8-1 What is sensation, and how do psychologists study it?

LO 8-2 What is the relationship between a physical stimulus and the kinds of sensory responses that result from it?

Sensing the World Around Us

Absolute Thresholds: Detecting What's Out There

Difference Thresholds: Noticing Distinctions Between Stimuli

Sensory Adaptation: Turning Down Our Responses

MODULE 9

LO 9-1 What basic processes underlie the sense of vision?

LO 9-2 How do we see colors?

Vision: Shedding Light on the Eye

Illuminating the Structure of the Eye

Neuroscience in Your Life: Seeing Vision in the Brain

Color Vision and Color Blindness: The 7-Million-Color Spectrum

MODULE 10

LO 10-1 What role does the ear play in the senses of sound, motion, and balance?

LO 10-2 How do smell and taste function?

LO 10-3 What are the skin senses, and how do they relate to the experience of pain?

Hearing and the Other Senses

Sensing Sound

Smell and Taste

The Skin Senses: Touch, Pressure, Temperature, and Pain

Becoming an Informed Consumer of Psychology: Managing Pain

How Our Senses Interact

MODULE 11

LO 11-1 What principles underlie our organization of the visual world and allow us to make sense of our environment?

LO 11-2 How are we able to perceive the world in three dimensions when our retinas are capable of sensing only two-dimensional images?

LO 11-3 What clues do visual illusions give us about our understanding of general perceptual mechanisms?

Perceptual Organization: Constructing Our View of the World

The Gestalt Laws of Organization

Top-Down and Bottom-Up Processing

Depth Perception: Translating 2-D to 3-D

Perceptual Constancy

Motion Perception: As the World Turns

Applying Psychology in the 21st Century: Do People Have an Internal Sense of Direction?

Perceptual Illusions: The Deceptions of Perceptions

Exploring Diversity: Culture and Perception

Prologue *The Mystery of Blindsight*

A blind man is making his way down a long corridor strewn with boxes, chairs, and other office paraphernalia. The man, known to the medical world as TN, has no idea the obstacles are there. And yet, he avoids them all, first sidling carefully between a wastepaper basket and the wall, and then going around a camera tripod, all without knowing he has made any special maneuvers (de Gelder, 2010, p. 61).

Looking Ahead

Despite being blind—and he really is unable to see in a traditional sense—TN can navigate quite well. He has what is called *blindsight,* the ability to respond to images that his eyes are detecting without perceiving that he can see.

How can people such as TN visually detect features of their environments without being consciously aware of seeing anything at all? In TN's case, a stroke damaged the primary visual cortex in his brain, robbing him of his sight. Even though his eyes still work perfectly fine, his brain lost the ability to process the incoming visual information—at least consciously. Some neural pathways from the eyes run to areas of the brain other than the visual cortex, and while those areas do not produce conscious vision, they seem to give people with blindsight the uncanny ability to respond to visual information in a non-conscious way.

Conditions such as blindness illustrate how much we depend on our senses to function normally. Our senses offer a window to the world, not only providing us with an awareness, understanding, and appreciation of the world's beauty, but alerting us to its dangers. Our senses enable us to feel the gentlest of breezes, see flickering lights miles away, and hear the soft murmuring of distant songbirds.

In the next four modules, we focus on the field of psychology that is concerned with the ways our bodies take in information through the senses and the ways we interpret that information. We explore both sensation and perception. *Sensation* encompasses the processes by which our sense organs receive information from the environment. *Perception* is the brain's and the sense organs' sorting out, interpretation, analysis, and integration of stimuli.

Although perception clearly represents a step beyond sensation, in practice it is sometimes difficult to find the precise boundary between the two. Indeed, psychologists—and philosophers as well—have argued for years over the distinction. The primary difference is that sensation can be thought of as an organism's first encounter with a raw sensory stimulus, whereas perception is the process by which it interprets, analyzes, and integrates that stimulus with other sensory information.

For example, if we were considering sensation, we might ask about the loudness of a ringing fire alarm. If we were considering perception, we might ask whether someone recognizes the ringing sound as an alarm and identifies its meaning.

To a psychologist interested in understanding the causes of behavior, sensation and perception are fundamental topics, because so much of our behavior is a reflection of how we react to and interpret stimuli from the world around us. The areas of sensation and perception deal with a wide range of questions—among them, how we respond to the characteristics of physical stimuli; what processes enable us to see, hear, and experience pain; why visual illusions fool us; and how we distinguish one person from another. As we explore these issues, we'll see how the senses work together to provide us with an integrated view and understanding of the world.

Sensing the World Around Us

As Isabel sat down to Thanksgiving dinner, her father carried the turkey in on a tray and placed it squarely in the center of the table. The noise level, already high from the talking and laughter of family members, grew louder still. As Isabel picked up her fork, the smell of the turkey reached her and she felt her stomach growl hungrily. The sight and sound of her family around the table, along with the smells and tastes of the holiday meal, made Isabel feel more relaxed than she had since starting school in the fall.

Put yourself in this setting and consider how different it might be if any one of your senses were not functioning. What if you were blind and unable to see the faces of your family members or the welcome shape of the golden-brown turkey? What if you had no sense of hearing and could not listen to the conversations of family members or were unable to feel your stomach growl, smell the dinner, or taste the food? Clearly, you would experience the dinner very differently from someone whose sensory apparatus was intact.

Moreover, the sensations mentioned above barely scratch the surface of sensory experience. Although perhaps you were taught, as I was, that there are just five senses—sight, sound, taste, smell, and touch—that enumeration is too modest. Human sensory capabilities go well beyond the basic five senses. For example, we are sensitive not merely to touch but to a considerably wider set of stimuli—pain, pressure, temperature, and vibration, to name a few. In addition, vision has two subsystems—relating to day and night vision—and the ear is responsive to information that allows us not only to hear but also to keep our balance.

To consider how psychologists understand the senses and, more broadly, sensation and perception, we first need a basic working vocabulary. In formal terms, **sensation** is the activation of the sense organs by a source of physical energy. **Perception** is the sorting out, interpretation, analysis, and integration of stimuli carried out by the sense organs and brain. A **stimulus** is any passing source of physical energy that produces a response in a sense organ.

Stimuli vary in both type and intensity. Different types of stimuli activate different sense organs. For instance, we can differentiate light stimuli (which activate the sense of sight and allow us to see the colors of a tree in autumn) from sound stimuli (which, through the sense of hearing, permit us to hear the sounds of an orchestra). In addition, stimuli differ in intensity, relating to how strong a stimulus needs to be before it can be detected.

Questions of stimulus type and intensity are considered in a branch of psychology known as psychophysics. **Psychophysics** is the study of the relationship between the physical aspects of stimuli and our psychological experience of them. Psychophysics played a central role in the development of the field of psychology. Many of the first psychologists studied issues related to psychophysics, and there is still an active group of psychophysics researchers (Gardner, 2005; Hock & Ploeger, 2006; Bonezzi, Brendl, & De Angelis, 2011).

Learning Outcomes

LO 8-1 What is sensation, and how do psychologists study it?

LO 8-2 What is the relationship between a physical stimulus and the kinds of sensory responses that result from it?

Study Alert

Remember that *sensation* refers to the activation of the sense organs (a physical response), whereas *perception* refers to how stimuli are interpreted (a psychological response).

sensation The activation of the sense organs by a source of physical energy.

perception The sorting out, interpretation, analysis, and integration of stimuli by the sense organs and brain.

stimulus Energy that produces a response in a sense organ.

psychophysics The study of the relationship between the physical aspects of stimuli and our psychological experience of them.

Absolute Thresholds: Detecting What's Out There

absolute threshold The smallest intensity of a stimulus that must be present for the stimulus to be detected.

Just when does a stimulus become strong enough to be detected by our sense organs? The answer to this question requires an understanding of the concept of absolute threshold. An **absolute threshold** is the smallest intensity of a stimulus that must be present for it to be detected (Aazh & Moore, 2007).

Despite the "absolute" in absolute threshold, things are not so cut-and-dried. As the strength of a stimulus increases, the likelihood that it will be detected increases gradually. Technically, then, an absolute threshold is the stimulus intensity that is detected 50% of the time.

It often takes a very small stimulus to produce a response in our senses. For example, the sense of touch is so sensitive that we can feel a bee's wing falling on our cheeks when it is dropped from a distance of 1 centimeter. Test your knowledge of the absolute thresholds of other senses by completing the questionnaire in Figure 1.

In fact, our senses are so fine-tuned that we might have problems if they were any more sensitive. For instance, if our ears were slightly more acute, we would be able to hear the sound of air molecules in our ears knocking into the eardrum—a phenomenon that would surely prove distracting and might even prevent us from hearing sounds outside our bodies.

Of course, the absolute thresholds we have been discussing are measured under ideal conditions. Normally our senses cannot detect stimulation quite as well because of the presence of noise. *Noise*, as defined by psychophysicists, is background stimulation that interferes with the perception of other stimuli. Hence, noise refers not just to auditory stimuli, as the word suggests, but also to unwanted stimuli that interfere with other senses.

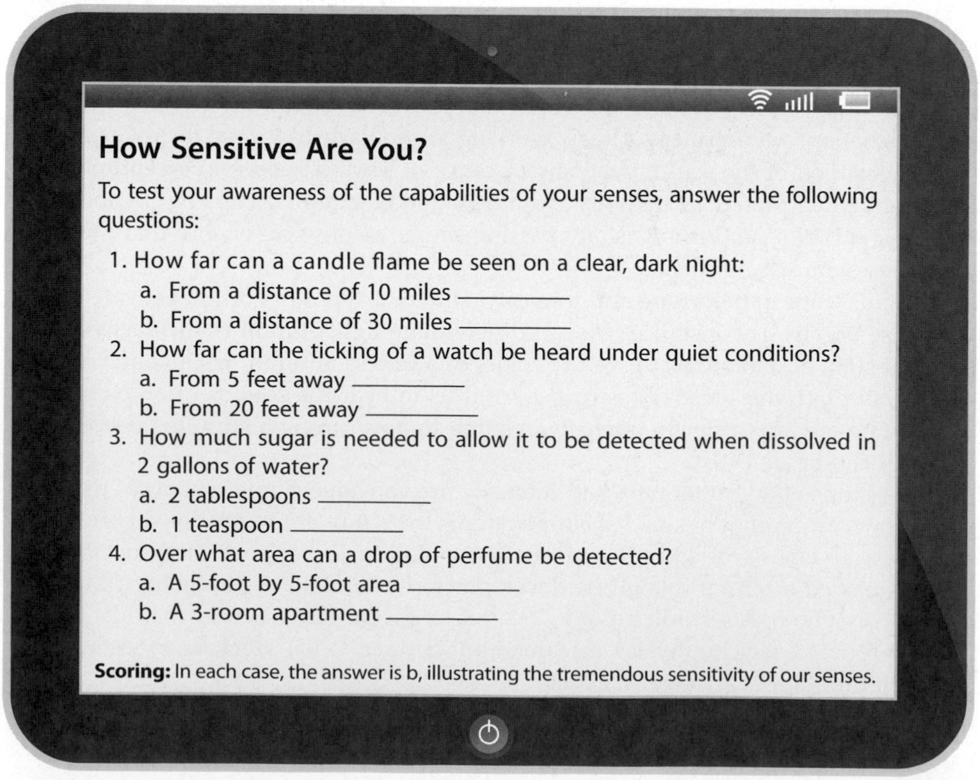

FIGURE 1 This test can shed some light on how sensitive the human senses are. (Source: Galanter, 1962.)

How Sensitive Are You?

To test your awareness of the capabilities of your senses, answer the following questions:

1. How far can a candle flame be seen on a clear, dark night:
   a. From a distance of 10 miles _____
   b. From a distance of 30 miles _____
2. How far can the ticking of a watch be heard under quiet conditions?
   a. From 5 feet away _____
   b. From 20 feet away _____
3. How much sugar is needed to allow it to be detected when dissolved in 2 gallons of water?
   a. 2 tablespoons _____
   b. 1 teaspoon _____
4. Over what area can a drop of perfume be detected?
   a. A 5-foot by 5-foot area _____
   b. A 3-room apartment _____

Scoring: In each case, the answer is b, illustrating the tremendous sensitivity of our senses.

Crowded conditions, sounds, and sights can all be considered as noise that interferes with sensation. Can you think of other examples of noise that is not auditory in nature?

For example, picture a talkative group of people crammed into a small, crowded, room at a party. The din of the crowd makes it hard to hear individual voices. In this case, the crowded conditions would be considered "noise," because it is preventing sensation at more discriminating levels. Similarly, we have limited ability to concentrate on several stimuli simultaneously.

Difference Thresholds: Noticing Distinctions Between Stimuli

Suppose you wanted to choose the six best apples from a supermarket display—the biggest, reddest, and sweetest apples. One approach would be to compare one apple with another systematically until you were left with a few so similar that you could not tell the difference between them. At that point, it wouldn't matter which ones you chose.

Psychologists have discussed this comparison problem in terms of the **difference threshold,** the smallest level of added (or reduced) stimulation required to sense that a *change* in stimulation has occurred. Thus, the difference threshold is the minimum change in stimulation required to detect the difference between two stimuli, and so it also is called a **just noticeable difference** (Nittrouer & Lowenstein, 2007).

The size of a stimulus that constitutes a just noticeable difference depends on the initial intensity of the stimulus. The relationship between changes in the original size of a stimulus and the degree to which a change will be noticed forms one of the basic laws of psychophysics: Weber's law. **Weber's law** (*Weber* is pronounced "VAY-ber") states that a just noticeable difference is a *constant proportion* of the intensity of an initial stimulus (rather than a constant amount).

For example, Weber found that the just noticeable difference for weight is 1:50. Consequently, it takes a 1-ounce increase in a 50-ounce weight to produce a noticeable difference, and it would take a 10-ounce increase to produce a noticeable difference if the initial weight were 500 ounces. In both cases, the same proportional increase is necessary to produce a just noticeable difference—1:5 = 10:500. Similarly, the just noticeable difference distinguishing changes in loudness between sounds is

PsychTech

Our inability to focus on multiple stimuli simultaneously is the reason why texting while driving is so dangerous. One study mounted video cameras inside trucks and found that truckers were 23 times more likely to be in a collision while texting than while not texting.

difference threshold (just noticeable difference) The smallest level of added or reduced stimulation required to sense that a change in stimulation has occurred.

Weber's law A basic law of psychophysics stating that a just noticeable difference is a constant proportion to the intensity of an initial stimulus (rather than a constant amount).

Study Alert

Remember that Weber's law holds for every type of sensory stimuli: vision, sound, taste, and so on.

larger for sounds that are initially loud than it is for sounds that are initially soft, but the *proportional* increase remains the same.

Weber's law helps explain why a person in a quiet room is more startled by the ringing of a telephone than is a person in an already noisy room. To produce the same amount of reaction in a noisy room, a telephone ring might have to approximate the loudness of cathedral bells. Similarly, when the moon is visible during the late afternoon, it appears relatively dim—yet against a dark night sky, it seems quite bright.

Sensory Adaptation: Turning Down Our Responses

You enter a movie theater, and the smell of popcorn is everywhere. A few minutes later, though, you barely notice the smell. The reason you become accustomed to the odor is sensory adaptation. **Adaptation** is an adjustment in sensory capacity after prolonged exposure to unchanging stimuli. Adaptation occurs as people become accustomed to a stimulus and change their frame of reference. In a sense, our brain mentally turns down the volume of the stimulation that it's experiencing (Calin-Jageman & Fischer, 2007; Carbon & Ditye, 2011).

adaptation An adjustment in sensory capacity after prolonged exposure to unchanging stimuli.

One example of adaptation is the decrease in sensitivity that occurs after repeated exposure to a strong stimulus. If you were to hear a loud tone over and over again, eventually it would begin to sound softer. Similarly, although jumping into a cold lake may be temporarily unpleasant, eventually you probably will get used to the temperature.

This apparent decline in sensitivity to sensory stimuli is due to the inability of the sensory nerve receptors to fire off messages to the brain indefinitely. Because these receptor cells are most responsive to *changes* in stimulation, constant stimulation is not effective in producing a sustained reaction (Wark, Lundstrom, & Fairhall, 2007).

Judgments of sensory stimuli are also affected by the context in which the judgments are made. This is the case because judgments are made not in isolation from other stimuli but in terms of preceding sensory experience. You can demonstrate this for yourself by trying a simple experiment:

Take two envelopes, one large and one small, and put 15 nickels in each one. Now lift the large envelope, put it down, and lift the small one. Which seems to weigh more? Most people report that the small one is heavier, although, as you know, the weights are nearly identical. The reason for this misconception is that the visual context of the envelope interferes with the sensory experience of weight. Adaptation to the context of one stimulus (the size of the envelope) alters responses to another stimulus (the weight of the envelope) (Coren, 2004).

RECAP/EVALUATE/RETHINK

RECAP

LO 8-1 What is sensation, and how do psychologists study it?

- Sensation is the activation of the sense organs by any source of physical energy. In contrast, perception is the process by which we sort out, interpret, analyze, and integrate stimuli to which our senses are exposed. (p. 89)

LO 8-2 What is the relationship between a physical stimulus and the kinds of sensory responses that result from it?

- Psychophysics studies the relationship between the physical nature of stimuli and the sensory responses they evoke. (p. 89)
- The absolute threshold is the smallest amount of physical intensity at which a stimulus can be detected. Under ideal conditions absolute thresholds are extraordinarily sensitive, but the presence of noise (background stimuli that interfere with other stimuli) reduces detection capabilities. (p. 90)
- The difference threshold, or just noticeable difference, is the smallest change in the level of stimulation required to sense that a change has occurred. According to Weber's law, a just noticeable difference is a constant proportion of the intensity of an initial stimulus. (p. 91)
- Sensory adaptation occurs when we become accustomed to a constant stimulus and change our evaluation of it. Repeated exposure to a stimulus results in an apparent decline in sensitivity to it. (p. 92)

EVALUATE

1. _____ is the stimulation of the sense organs; _____ is the sorting out, interpretation, analysis, and integration of stimuli by the sense organs and the brain.
2. The term *absolute threshold* refers to the _____ intensity of a stimulus that must be present for the stimulus to be detected.
3. Weber discovered that for a difference between two stimuli to be perceptible, the stimuli must differ by at least a _____ proportion.
4. After completing a very difficult rock climb in the morning, Carmella found the afternoon climb unexpectedly easy. This example illustrates the phenomenon of _____.

RETHINK

1. Do you think it is possible to have sensation without perception? Is it possible to have perception without sensation?
2. *From the perspective of a manufacturer:* How might you need to take psychophysics into account when developing new products or modifying existing ones?

Answers to Evaluate Questions

1. Sensation, perception; 2. smallest; 3. constant; 4. adaptation

KEY TERMS

sensation p. 89
perception p. 89
stimulus p. 89
psychophysics p. 89

absolute threshold p. 90
difference threshold (just
   noticeable difference) p. 91

Weber's law p. 91
adaptation p. 92

Vision: Shedding Light on the Eye

If, as poets say, the eyes provide a window to the soul, they also provide us with a window to the world. Our visual capabilities permit us to admire and to react to scenes ranging from the beauty of a sunset, to the configuration of a lover's face, to the words written on the pages of a book.

Vision starts with light, the physical energy that stimulates the eye. Light is a form of electromagnetic radiation waves, which, as shown in Figure 1, are measured in wavelengths. The sizes of wavelengths correspond to different types of energy. The range of wavelengths that humans are sensitive to—called the *visual spectrum*—is relatively small. Many nonhuman species have different capabilities. For instance, some reptiles and fish sense energies of longer wavelengths than humans do, and certain insects sense energies of shorter wavelengths than humans do. For example, bees are attracted to flowers that reflect ultraviolet rays that humans can't detect.

Light waves coming from some object outside the body (such as the tree in Figure 2) are sensed by the only organ that is capable of responding to the visible spectrum: the eye. Our eyes convert light to a form that can be used by the neurons that serve as messengers to the brain. The neurons themselves take up a relatively small percentage of the total eye. Most of the eye is a mechanical device that is similar in many respects to a nonelectronic camera that uses film, as you can see in Figure 2.

Despite the similarities between the eye and a camera, vision involves processes that are far more complex and sophisticated than those of any camera. Furthermore, once an image reaches the neuronal receptors of the eye, the eye/camera analogy ends, for the processing of the visual image in the brain is more reflective of a computer than it is of a camera.

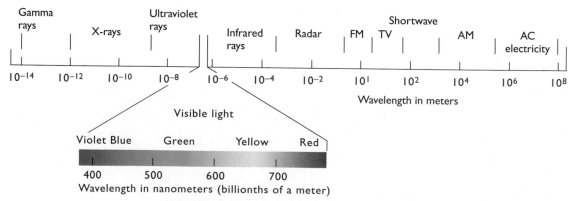

FIGURE 1 The visible spectrum—the range of wavelengths to which people are sensitive—is only a small part of the kinds of wavelengths present in our environment. Is it a benefit or disadvantage to our everyday lives that we aren't more sensitive to a broader range of visual stimuli? Why?

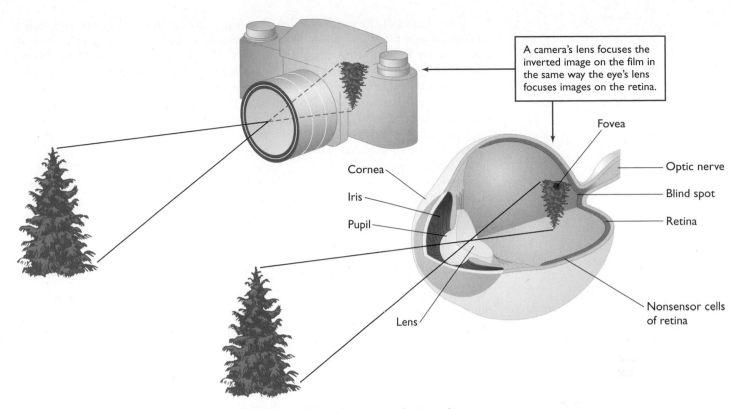

A camera's lens focuses the inverted image on the film in the same way the eye's lens focuses images on the retina.

Fovea

Optic nerve

Blind spot

Retina

Nonsensor cells of retina

Cornea

Iris

Pupil

Lens

FIGURE 2 Although human vision is far more complicated than the most sophisticated camera, in some ways basic visual processes are analogous to those used in photography. Like the automatic lighting system on a traditional, nondigital camera, the human eye dilates to let in more light and contracts to block out light.

Illuminating the Structure of the Eye

The ray of light being reflected off the tree in Figure 2 first travels through the *cornea*, a transparent, protective window. The cornea, because of its curvature, bends (or *refracts*) light as it passes through, playing a primary role in focusing the light more sharply. After moving through the cornea, the light traverses the pupil. The *pupil* is a dark hole in the center of the *iris*, the colored part of the eye, which in humans ranges from a light blue to a dark brown. The size of the pupil opening depends on the amount of light in the environment. The dimmer the surroundings are, the more the pupil opens to allow more light to enter.

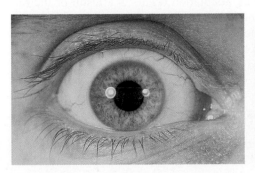

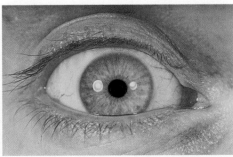

Like the automatic lighting system on a camera, the pupil in the human eye expands to let in more light (left) and contracts to block out light (right). Can humans adjust their ears to let in more or less sound in a similar manner?

Why shouldn't the pupil be open completely all the time, allowing the greatest amount of light into the eye? The answer relates to the basic physics of light. A small pupil greatly increases the range of distances at which objects are in focus. With a wide-open pupil, the range is relatively small, and details are harder to discern. The eye takes advantage of bright light by decreasing the size of the pupil and thereby becoming more discriminating. In dim light the pupil expands to enable us to view the situation better—but at the expense of visual detail. (Perhaps one reason candlelight dinners are thought of as romantic is that the dim light prevents one from seeing a partner's physical flaws.)

Once light passes through the pupil, it enters the *lens,* which is directly behind the pupil. The lens acts to bend the rays of light so that they are properly focused on the rear of the eye. The lens focuses light by changing its own thickness, a process called *accommodation:* It becomes flatter when viewing distant objects and rounder when looking at closer objects.

REACHING THE RETINA

Having traveled through the pupil and lens, the image of the tree finally reaches its ultimate destination in the eye—the **retina.** It is within the retina that the electromagnetic energy of light is converted to electrical impulses for transmission to the brain. Note that, because of the physical properties of light, the image has reversed itself in traveling through the lens, and it reaches the retina upside down (relative to its original position). Although it might seem that this reversal would cause difficulties in understanding and moving about the world, this is not the case. The brain interprets the image in terms of its original position.

The retina consists of a thin layer of nerve cells at the back of the eyeball (see Figure 3). There are two kinds of light-sensitive receptor cells in the retina. The names they have been given describe their shapes: rods and cones. **Rods** are thin, cylindrical receptor cells that are highly sensitive to light. **Cones** are typically cone-shaped, light-sensitive receptor cells that are responsible for sharp focus and color perception, particularly in bright light. The rods and cones are distributed unevenly throughout the retina. Cones are concentrated on the part of the retina called the *fovea.* The fovea is a particularly sensitive region of the retina. If you want to focus on something of particular interest, you will automatically try to center the image on the fovea to see it more sharply.

The rods and cones not only are structurally dissimilar but they also play distinctly different roles in vision. Cones are primarily responsible for the sharply focused perception of color, particularly in brightly lit situations; rods are related to vision in dimly lit situations and are largely insensitive to color and to details as sharp as those the cones are capable of recognizing. The rods play a key role in *peripheral vision*—seeing objects that are outside the main center of focus—and in night vision.

Rods and cones also are involved in *dark adaptation,* the phenomenon of adjusting to dim light after being in brighter light. (Think of the experience of walking into a dark movie theater and groping your way to a seat but a few minutes later seeing the seats quite clearly.) The speed at which dark adaptation occurs is a result of the rate of change in the chemical composition of the rods and cones. Although the cones reach their greatest level of adaptation in just a few minutes, the rods take 20 to 30 minutes to reach the maximum level. The opposite phenomenon—*light adaptation,* or the process of adjusting to bright light after exposure to dim light—occurs much faster, taking only a minute or so.

SENDING THE MESSAGE FROM THE EYE TO THE BRAIN

When light energy strikes the rods and cones, it starts a chain of events that transforms light into neural impulses that can be communicated to the brain. Even before

retina The part of the eye that converts the electromagnetic energy of light to electrical impulses for transmission to the brain.

rods Thin, cylindrical receptor cells in the retina that are highly sensitive to light.

cones Cone-shaped, light-sensitive receptor cells in the retina that are responsible for sharp focus and color perception, particularly in bright light.

Study Alert
Remember that cones relate to color vision.

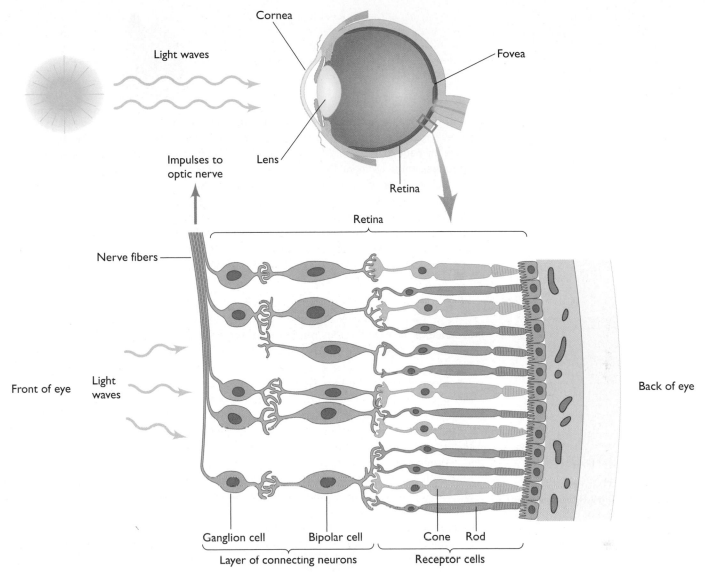

FIGURE 3 The basic cells of the eye. Light entering the eye travels through the ganglion and bipolar cells and strikes the light-sensitive rods and cones located at the back of the eye. The rods and cones then transmit nerve impulses to the brain via the bipolar and ganglion cells. (Source: Shier, Butler, & Lewis, 2000.)

the neural message reaches the brain, however, some initial coding of the visual information takes place.

What happens when light energy strikes the retina depends in part on whether it encounters a rod or a cone. Rods contain *rhodopsin,* a complex reddish-purple substance whose composition changes chemically when energized by light. The substance in cone receptors is different, but the principles are similar. Stimulation of the nerve cells in the eye triggers a neural response that is transmitted to other nerve cells in the retina called *bipolar cells* and *ganglion cells.*

Bipolar cells receive information directly from the rods and cones and communicate that information to the ganglion cells. The ganglion cells collect and summarize visual information, which is then moved out the back of the eyeball and sent to the brain through a bundle of ganglion axons called the **optic nerve.**

Because the opening for the optic nerve passes through the retina, there are no rods or cones in the area, and that creates a blind spot. Normally, however, this

optic nerve A bundle of ganglion axons that carry visual information to the brain.

FIGURE 4 To find your blind spot, close your right eye and look at the haunted house with your left eye. You will see the ghost on the periphery of your vision. Now, while staring at the house, move the page toward you. When the book is about a foot from your eye, the ghost will disappear. At this moment, the image of the ghost is falling on your blind spot.

But also notice how, when the page is at that distance, not only does the ghost seem to disappear, but the line seems to run continuously through the area where the ghost used to be. This simple experiment shows how we automatically compensate for missing information by using nearby material to complete what is unseen. That's the reason you never notice the blind spot. What is missing is replaced by what is seen next to the blind spot. Can you think of any advantages that this tendency to provide missing information gives humans as a species?

PsychTech

New technologies are helping the blind to see. For example, by surgically implanting electrodes into the eyes and using a nose-mounted camera and a video processor strapped to the waist, previously totally blind individuals can differentiate plates from cups and can identify large letters.

absence of nerve cells does not interfere with vision because you automatically compensate for the missing part of your field of vision. (To find your blind spot, see Figure 4.)

Once beyond the eye itself, the neural impulses relating to the image move through the optic nerve. As the optic nerve leaves the eyeball, its path does not take the most direct route to the part of the brain right behind the eye. Instead, the optic nerves from each eye meet at a point roughly between the two eyes—called the *optic chiasm* (pronounced KI-asm)—where each optic nerve then splits.

When the optic nerves split, the nerve impulses coming from the right half of each retina are sent to the right side of the brain, and the impulses arriving from the left half of each retina are sent to the left side of the brain. Because the image on the retinas is reversed and upside down, however, those images coming from the right half of each retina actually originated in the field of vision to the person's left, and the images coming from the left half of each retina originated in the field of vision to the person's right (see Figure 5).

PROCESSING THE VISUAL MESSAGE

By the time a visual message reaches the brain, it has passed through several stages of processing. One of the initial sites is the ganglion cells. Each ganglion cell gathers information from a group of rods and cones in a particular area of the eye and compares the amount of light entering the center of that area with the amount of light in the area around it. Some ganglion cells are activated by light in the center (and darkness in the surrounding area). Other ganglion cells are activated when there is darkness in the center and light in the surrounding areas. The outcome of this process is to maximize the detection of variations in light and darkness. The image that is passed on to the brain, then, is an enhanced version of the actual visual stimulus outside the body (Kubovy, Epstein, & Gepshtein, 2003; Pearson & Clifford, 2005; Lascaratos, Ji, & Wood, 2007; Grünert et al., 2011).

The ultimate processing of visual images takes place in the visual cortex of the brain, and it is here that the most complex kinds of processing occur. Psychologists David Hubel and Torsten Wiesel won the Nobel Prize in 1981 for their discovery that many neurons in the cortex are extraordinarily specialized, being activated only by visual stimuli of a particular shape or pattern—a process known as **feature detection.**

feature detection The activation of neurons in the cortex by visual stimuli of specific shapes or patterns.

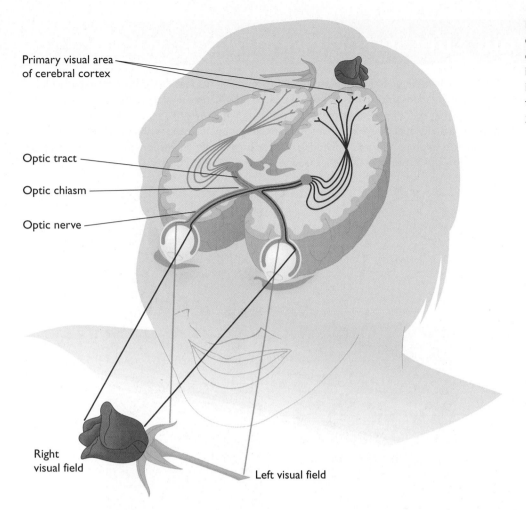

Primary visual area
of cerebral cortex

Optic tract

Optic chiasm

Optic nerve

Right
visual field

Left visual field

FIGURE 5 Because the optic nerve coming from the eye splits at the optic chiasm, the image to a person's right eye is sent to the left side of the brain and the image to the person's left is transmitted to the right side of the brain. (Source: Mader, 2000.)

They found that some cells are activated only by lines of a particular width, shape, or orientation. Other cells are activated only by moving, as opposed to stationary, stimuli (Hubel & Wiesel, 2004; Pelli, Burns, & Farell, 2006; Sebastiani, Castellani, & D'Alessandro, 2011).

More recent work has added to our knowledge of the complex ways in which visual information coming from individual neurons is combined and processed. Different parts of the brain process nerve impulses in several individual systems simultaneously. For instance, one system relates to shapes, one to colors, and others to movement, location, and depth. Furthermore, different parts of the brain are involved in the perception of specific *kinds* of stimuli, showing distinctions, for example, between the perception of human faces, animals, and inanimate stimuli (Winston, O'Doherty, & Kilner, 2006; Werblin & Roska, 2007; Bindemann et al., 2008; Platek & Kemp, 2009).

If separate neural systems exist for processing information about specific aspects of the visual world, how are all these data integrated by the brain? The brain makes use of information regarding the frequency, rhythm, and timing of the firing of particular sets of neural cells. Furthermore, the brain's integration of visual information does not occur in any single step or location in the brain but rather is a process that occurs on several levels simultaneously. The ultimate outcome, though, is indisputable: a vision of the world around us (de Gelder, 2000; Macaluso, Frith, & Driver, 2000; Werner, Pinna, & Spillmann, 2007; also see Figure 6 *Neuroscience in Your Life*).

Neuroscience in Your Life: Seeing Vision in the Brain

FIGURE 6 In addition to having specialized neurons that respond more strongly to particular shapes, orientations, and widths, our brains process information coming from each eye separately, creating what are called ocular dominance columns. With new MRI techniques, researchers can note the activity of each eye more precisely. In these scans we can see the variation in ocular dominance columns for three individuals. The red areas show the response of one eye, and blue areas show the response of the other. (Source: Shmuel et al., 2010.)

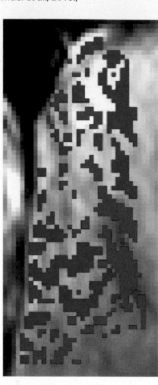

Participant 1   Participant 2   Participant 3

Color Vision and Color Blindness: The 7-Million-Color Spectrum

Although the range of wavelengths to which humans are sensitive is relatively narrow, at least in comparison with the entire electromagnetic spectrum, the portion to which we are capable of responding allows us great flexibility in sensing the world. Nowhere is this clearer than in terms of the number of colors we can discern. A person with normal color vision is capable of distinguishing no less than 7 million different colors (Bruce, Green, & Georgeson, 1997; Rabin, 2004).

Although the variety of colors that people are generally able to distinguish is vast, there are certain individuals whose ability to perceive color is quite limited—the color-blind. Interestingly, the condition of these individuals has provided some of the most important clues to understanding how color vision operates (Neitz, Neitz, & Kainz, 1996; Bonnardel, 2006; Nijboer, te Pas, & van der Smagt, 2011).

(a)   (b)   (c)

FIGURE 7 To someone with normal vision, the hot-air balloon in the foreground appears with regions of very pure red, orange, yellow, green, blue, and violet, as well as off-white; and the balloon in the rear is a bright shade of red-orange. (b) A person with red-green color blindness would see the scene in part (a) like this, in hues of blue and yellow. (c) A person who is blue-yellow blind, conversely, would see it in hues of red and green.

Approximately 7% of men and 0.4% of women are color-blind. For most people with color-blindness, the world looks quite dull (see Figure 7). Red fire engines appear yellow, green grass seems yellow, and the three colors of a traffic light all look yellow. In fact, in the most common form of color-blindness, all red and green objects are seen as yellow. In other forms of color-blindness, people are unable to tell the difference between yellow and blue. In the most extreme cases of color-blindness, which are quite rare, people perceive no color at all. To such individuals, the world looks something like the picture on an old black and white television set.

EXPLAINING COLOR VISION

To understand why some people are color-blind, we need to consider the basics of color vision. Two processes are involved. The first process is explained by the **trichromatic theory of color vision,** which was first proposed by Thomas Young and extended by Hermann von Helmholtz in the first half of the 1800s. This theory suggests that there are three kinds of cones in the retina, each of which responds primarily to a specific range of wavelengths. One is most responsive to blue-violet colors, one to green, and the third to yellow-red (Brown & Wald, 1964). According to trichromatic theory, perception of color is influenced by the relative strength with which each of the three kinds of cones is activated. If we see a blue sky, the blue-violet cones are primarily triggered, and the others show less activity.

However, there are aspects of color vision that the trichromatic theory is less successful at explaining. For example, the theory does not explain what happens after you stare at something like the flag shown in Figure 8 on the next page for about a minute. Try this yourself and then look at a blank white page: You'll see an image of the traditional red, white, and blue U.S. flag. Where there was yellow, you'll see blue, and where there were green and black, you'll see red and white.

trichromatic theory of color vision The theory that there are three kinds of cones in the retina, each of which responds primarily to a specific range of wavelengths.

FIGURE 8 Stare at the dot in this flag for about a minute and then look at a piece of plain white paper. What do you see? Most people see an afterimage that converts the colors in the figure into the traditional red, white, and blue U.S. flag. If you have trouble seeing it the first time, blink once and try again.

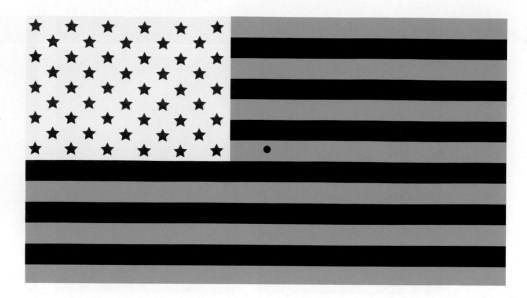

opponent-process theory of color vision The theory that receptor cells for color are linked in pairs, working in opposition to each other.

Study Alert

Keep in mind that there are two explanations for color vision: trichromatic and opponent-process theories.

The phenomenon you have just experienced is called an *afterimage*. It occurs because activity in the retina continues even when you are no longer staring at the original picture. However, it also demonstrates that the trichromatic theory does not explain color vision completely. Why should the colors in the afterimage be different from those in the original?

Because trichromatic processes do not provide a full explanation of color vision, alternative explanations have been proposed. According to the **opponent-process theory of color vision,** first proposed by German physiologist Ewald Hering in the 19th century, receptor cells are linked in pairs, working in opposition to each other. Specifically, there are a blue-yellow pairing, a red-green pairing, and a black-white pairing. If an object reflects light that contains more blue than yellow, it will stimulate the firing of the cells sensitive to blue, simultaneously discouraging or inhibiting the firing of receptor cells sensitive to yellow—and the object will appear blue. If, in contrast, a light contains more yellow than blue, the cells that respond to yellow will be stimulated to fire while the blue ones are inhibited, and the object will appear yellow (D. N. Robinson, 2007).

The opponent-process theory provides a good explanation for afterimages. When we stare at the yellow in the figure, for instance, our receptor cells for the yellow component of the yellow-blue pairing become fatigued and are less able to respond to yellow stimuli. In contrast, the receptor cells for the blue part of the pair are not tired, because they are not being stimulated. When we look at a white surface, the light reflected off it would normally stimulate both the yellow and the blue receptors equally. But the fatigue of the yellow receptors prevents this from happening. They temporarily do not respond to the yellow, which makes the white light appear to be blue. Because the other colors in the figure do the same thing relative to their specific opponents, the afterimage produces the opponent colors—for a while. The afterimage lasts only a short time, because the fatigue of the yellow receptors is soon overcome, and the white light begins to be perceived more accurately.

We now know that both opponent processes and trichromatic mechanisms are at work in producing the perception of color vision, but in different parts of the visual sensing system. Trichromatic processes work within the retina itself, whereas opponent mechanisms operate both in the retina and at later stages of neuronal processing (Gegenfurtner, 2003; Chen, Zhou, & Gong, 2004; Baraas, Foster, & Amano, 2006).

RECAP/EVALUATE/RETHINK

RECAP

LO 9-1 What basic processes underlie the sense of vision?

- Vision depends on sensitivity to light, electromagnetic waves in the visible part of the spectrum that are either reflected off objects or produced by an energy source. The eye shapes the light into an image that is transformed into nerve impulses and interpreted by the brain. (p. 94)
- As light enters the eye, it passes through the cornea, pupil, and lens and ultimately reaches the retina, where the electromagnetic energy of light is converted to nerve impulses for transmission to the brain. These impulses leave the eye via the optic nerve. (p. 95)
- The visual information gathered by the rods and cones is transferred via bipolar and ganglion cells through the optic nerve, which leads to the optic chiasm—the point where the optic nerve splits. (pp. 97, 98)

LO 9-2 How do we see colors?

- Color vision seems to be based on two processes described by the trichromatic theory and the opponent-process theory. (pp. 101, 102)
- The trichromatic theory suggests that there are three kinds of cones in the retina, each of which is responsive to a certain range of colors. The opponent-process theory presumes pairs of different types of cells in the eye that work in opposition to each other. (pp. 101, 102)

EVALUATE

1. Light entering the eye first passes through the _____, a protective window.

2. The structure that converts light into usable neural messages is called the _____.
3. A woman with blue eyes could be described as having blue pigment in her _____.
4. What is the process by which the thickness of the lens is changed in order to focus light properly?
5. The proper sequence of structures that light passes through in the eye is the _____, _____, _____, and _____.
6. Match each type of visual receptor with its function.
   - **a.** rods
   - **b.** cones
     1. used for dim light, largely insensitive to color
     2. detect color, good in bright light
7. _____ theory states that there are three types of cones in the retina, each of which responds primarily to a different color.

RETHINK

1. If the eye had a second lens that "unreversed" the image hitting the retina, do you think there would be changes in the way people perceive the world?
2. *From the perspective of an advertising specialist:* How might you market your products similarly or differently to those who are color-blind versus those who have normal color vision?

Answers to Evaluate Questions

1. cornea; 2. retina; 3. iris; 4. accommodation; 5. cornea, pupil, lens, retina; 6. a-1, b-2; 7. Trichromatic

KEY TERMS

retina p. 96
rods p. 96
cones p. 96

optic nerve p. 97
feature detection p. 98

trichromatic theory of color vision p. 101

opponent-process theory of color vision p. 102

Hearing and the Other Senses

Learning Outcomes

LO 10-1 What role does the ear play in the senses of sound, motion, and balance?

LO 10-2 How do smell and taste function?

LO 10-3 What are the skin senses, and how do they relate to the experience of pain?

The blast-off was easy compared with what the astronaut was experiencing now: space sickness. The constant nausea and vomiting were enough to make him wonder why he had worked so hard to become an astronaut. Even though he had been warned that there was a two-thirds chance that his first experience in space would cause these symptoms, he wasn't prepared for how terribly sick he really felt.

Whether or not the astronaut wishes he could head right back to Earth, his experience, a major problem for space travelers, is related to a basic sensory process: the sense of motion and balance. This sense allows people to navigate their bodies through the world and keep themselves upright without falling. Along with hearing—the process by which sound waves are translated into understandable and meaningful forms—the sense of motion and balance resides in the ear.

Sensing Sound

Although many of us think primarily of the outer ear when we speak of the ear, that structure is only one simple part of the whole. The outer ear acts as a reverse megaphone, designed to collect and bring sounds into the internal portions of the ear (see Figure 1). The location of the outer ears on different sides of the head helps with *sound localization,* the process by which we identify the direction from which a sound is coming. Wave patterns in the air enter each ear at a slightly different time, and the brain uses the discrepancy as a clue to the sound's point of origin. In addition, the two outer ears delay or amplify sounds of particular frequencies to different degrees (Schnupp, Nelken, & King, 2011).

sound The movement of air molecules brought about by a source of vibration.

Sound is the movement of air molecules brought about by a source of vibration. Sounds travel through the air in wave patterns similar in shape to those made in water when a stone is thrown into a still pond. Sounds, arriving at the outer ear in the form of wavelike vibrations, are funneled into the *auditory canal,* a tube-like passage that leads to the eardrum. The **eardrum** is aptly named because it operates as a miniature drum, vibrating when sound waves hit it. The more intense the sound, the more the eardrum vibrates. These vibrations are then transferred into the *middle ear,* a tiny chamber containing three bones (the *hammer,* the *anvil,* and the *stirrup*) that transmit vibrations to the oval window, a thin membrane leading to the inner ear. Because the hammer, anvil, and stirrup act as a set of levers, they not only transmit vibrations but also increase their strength. Moreover, because the opening into the middle ear (the eardrum) is considerably larger than the opening out of it (the *oval window*), the force of sound waves on the oval window becomes amplified. The middle ear, then, acts as a tiny mechanical amplifier.

eardrum The part of the ear that vibrates when sound waves hit it.

The *inner ear* is the portion of the ear that changes the sound vibrations into a form in which they can be transmitted to the brain. (As you will see, it also contains the organs that allow us to locate our position and determine how we are moving through space.) When sound enters the inner ear through the oval window, it moves into the **cochlea,** a coiled tube that looks something like a snail and is filled with fluid that vibrates in response to sound. Inside the cochlea is the **basilar membrane,**

cochlea (KOKE-lee-uh) A coiled tube in the ear filled with fluid that vibrates in response to sound.

basilar membrane A vibrating structure that runs through the center of the cochlea, dividing it into an upper chamber and a lower chamber and containing sense receptors for sound.

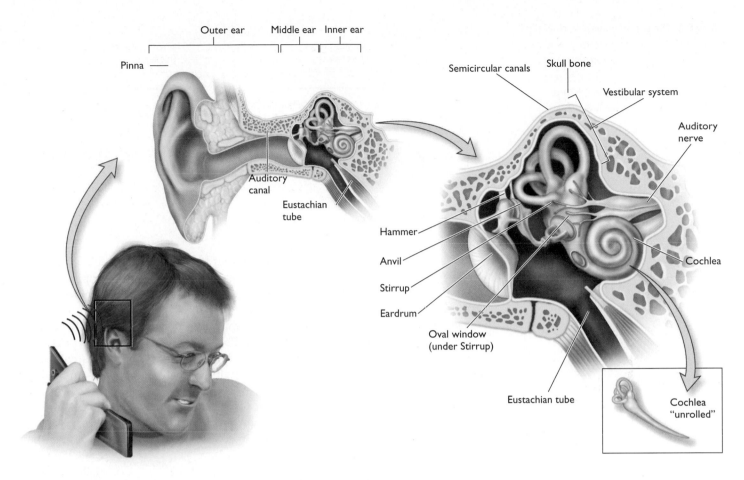

FIGURE 1 The major parts of the ear. (Source: Brooker et al., 2008, Figure 45.6.)

a structure that runs through the center of the cochlea, dividing it into an upper chamber and a lower chamber. The basilar membrane is covered with **hair cells.** When the hair cells are bent by the vibrations entering the cochlea, the cells send a neural message to the brain (Cho, 2000; Zhou, Liu, & Davis, 2005; Møller, 2011).

hair cells Tiny cells covering the basilar membrane that, when bent by vibrations entering the cochlea, transmit neural messages to the brain.

THE PHYSICAL ASPECTS OF SOUND

As we mentioned earlier, what we refer to as sound is actually the physical movement of air molecules in regular, wavelike patterns caused by a vibrating source. Sometimes it is even possible to see these vibrations: If you have ever seen an audio speaker that has no enclosure, you know that, at least when the lowest notes are playing, you can see the speaker moving in and out. Less obvious is what happens next: The speaker pushes air molecules into waves with the same pattern as its movement. Those wave patterns soon reach your ear, although their strength has been weakened considerably during their travels. All other sources that produce sound work in essentially the same fashion, setting off wave patterns that move through the air to the ear. Air—or some other medium, such as water—is necessary to make the vibrations of objects reach us. This explains why there can be no sound in a vacuum.

We are able to see the audio speaker moving when low notes are played because of a primary characteristic of sound called frequency. *Frequency* is the number of wave cycles that occur in a second. At very low frequencies there are relatively few wave cycles per second (see Figure 2 on page 106). These cycles are visible to the naked eye as vibrations in the speaker. Low frequencies are translated into a sound that is very low in pitch. (*Pitch* is the characteristic that makes sound seem "high"

FIGURE 2 The sound waves produced by different stimuli are transmitted—usually through the air—in different patterns, with lower frequencies indicated by fewer peaks and valleys per second. (Source: Seeley, Stephens, & Tate, 2000.)

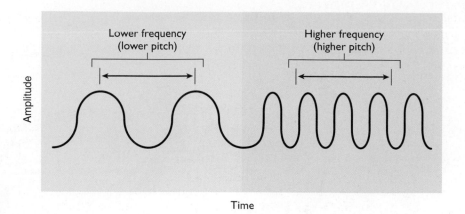

or "low.") For example, the lowest frequency that humans are capable of hearing is 20 cycles per second. Higher frequencies are heard as sounds of higher pitch. At the upper end of the sound spectrum, people can detect sounds with frequencies as high as 20,000 cycles per second.

Amplitude is a feature of wave patterns that allows us to distinguish between loud and soft sounds. Amplitude is the spread between the up-and-down peaks and valleys of air pressure in a sound wave as it travels through the air. Waves with small peaks and valleys produce soft sounds; those with relatively large peaks and valleys produce loud sounds.

We are sensitive to broad variations in sound amplitudes. The strongest sounds we are capable of hearing are over a trillion times as intense as the very weakest sound we can hear. This range is measured in *decibels*. When sounds get higher than 120 decibels, they become painful to the human ear.

Our sensitivity to different frequencies changes as we age. For instance, as we get older, the range of frequencies we can detect declines, particularly for high-pitched sounds. This is why high school students sometimes choose high-pitched ring tones for their cell phones in settings where cell phone use is forbidden: the ringing sound goes undetected by their aging teachers (Vitello, 2006) (see Figure 3).

Sorting Out Theories of Sound. How are our brains able to sort out wavelengths of different frequencies and intensities? One clue comes from studies of the basilar membrane, the area in the cochlea that translates physical vibrations into neural

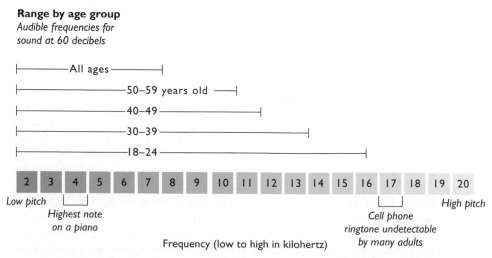

FIGURE 3 Some teenagers set their text-message ring tone to a frequency too high for most adults to hear, allowing them to use cell phones where they are prohibited. (Source: Vitello, 2006.)

impulses. It turns out that sounds affect different areas of the basilar membrane, depending on the frequency of the sound wave. The part of the basilar membrane nearest to the oval window is most sensitive to high-frequency sounds, and the part nearest to the cochlea's inner end is most sensitive to low-frequency sounds. This finding has led to the **place theory of hearing,** which states that different areas of the basilar membrane respond to different frequencies.

However, place theory does not tell the full story of hearing, because very low frequency sounds trigger neurons across such a wide area of the basilar membrane that no single site is involved. Consequently, an additional explanation for hearing has been proposed: frequency theory. The **frequency theory of hearing** suggests that the entire basilar membrane acts as a microphone, vibrating as a whole in response to a sound. According to this explanation, the nerve receptors send out signals that are tied directly to the frequency (the number of wave crests per second) of the sounds to which we are exposed, with the number of nerve impulses being a direct function of a sound's frequency. Thus, the higher the pitch of a sound (and therefore the greater the frequency of its wave crests), the greater the number of nerve impulses that are transmitted up the auditory nerve to the brain.

Neither place theory nor frequency theory provides the full explanation for hearing. Place theory provides a better explanation for the sensing of high-frequency sounds, whereas frequency theory explains what happens when low-frequency sounds are encountered. Medium-frequency sounds incorporate both processes (Hirsh & Watson, 1996; Hudspeth, 2000).

After an auditory message leaves the ear, it is transmitted to the auditory cortex of the brain through a complex series of neural interconnections. As the message is transmitted, it is communicated through neurons that respond to specific types of sounds. Within the auditory cortex itself, there are neurons that respond selectively to very specific sorts of sound features, such as clicks and whistles. Some neurons respond only to a specific pattern of sounds, such as a steady tone but not an intermittent one. Furthermore, specific neurons transfer information about a sound's location through their particular pattern of firing (Middlebrooks et al., 2005; Wang et al., 2005; Alho et al., 2006).

If we were to analyze the configuration of the cells in the auditory cortex, we would find that neighboring cells are responsive to similar frequencies. The auditory cortex, then, provides us with a "map" of sound frequencies, just as the visual cortex furnishes a representation of the visual field. In addition, because of the asymmetry in the two hemispheres of the brain (which we discussed in the last chapter), the left and right ears process sound differently. The right ear reacts more to speech, while the left ear responds more to music (Sininger & Cone-Wesson, 2004, 2006).

Speech perception requires that we make fine discriminations among sounds that are quite similar in terms of their physical properties. Furthermore, not only are we able to understand *what* is being said from speech, we can use vocal cues to determine who is speaking, if they have an accent and where they may be from, and even their emotional state. Such capabilities illustrate the sophistication of our sense of hearing (Fowler & Galantucci, 2008; Massaro & Chen, 2008; Pell et al., 2009; Ross et al., 2011).

Balance: The Ups and Downs of Life. Several structures of the ear are related more to our sense of balance than to our hearing. Collectively, these structures are known as the *vestibular system,* which responds to the pull of gravity and allows us to maintain our balance, even when standing in a bus in stop-and-go traffic.

The main structure of the vestibular system is formed by the **semicircular canals** of the inner ear (refer to Figure 1 on page 105), which consist of three tubes containing fluid that sloshes through them when the head moves, signaling rotational or angular movement to the brain. The pull on our bodies caused by the acceleration of forward, backward, or up-and-down motion, as well as the constant pull of gravity, is sensed by the *otoliths,* tiny, motion-sensitive crystals in the semicircular canals. When we move, these crystals shift as sands do on a windy beach, contacting the

place theory of hearing The theory that different areas of the basilar membrane respond to different frequencies.

frequency theory of hearing The theory that the entire basilar membrane acts like a microphone, vibrating as a whole in response to a sound.

Study Alert
Be sure to understand the differences between the place and frequency theories of hearing.

semicircular canals Three tube-like structures of the inner ear containing fluid that sloshes through them when the head moves, signaling rotational or angular movement to the brain.

The weightlessness of the ear's otoliths produces space sickness in most astronauts.

specialized receptor *hair cells* in the semicircular canals. The brain's inexperience in interpreting messages from the weightless otoliths is the cause of the space sickness commonly experienced by two-thirds of all space travelers, mentioned at the start of this module (Flam, 1991; Stern & Koch, 1996).

Smell and Taste

> Until he bit into a piece of raw cabbage on that February evening . . . , Raymond Fowler had not thought much about the sense of taste. The cabbage, part of a pasta dish he was preparing for his family's dinner, had an odd, burning taste, but he did not pay it much attention. Then a few minutes later, his daughter handed him a glass of cola, and he took a swallow. "It was like sulfuric acid," he said. "It was like the hottest thing you could imagine boring into your mouth." (Goode, 1999, pp. D1–D2)

It was evident that something was very wrong with Fowler's sense of taste. After extensive testing, it became clear that he had damaged the nerves involved in his sense of taste, probably because of a viral infection or a medicine he was taking. (Luckily for him, a few months later his sense of taste returned to normal.)

Even without disruptions in our ability to perceive the world such as those experienced by Fowler, we all know the important roles that taste and smell play. We'll consider these two senses next.

SMELL

More than 1,000 receptor cells, known as olfactory cells, are spread across the nasal cavity. The cells are specialized to react to particular odors. Do you think it is possible to "train" the nose to pick up a greater number of odors?

Although many animals have keener abilities to detect odors than we do, the human sense of smell (*olfaction*) permits us to detect more than 10,000 separate smells. We also have a good memory for smells, and long-forgotten events and memories—good and bad—can be brought back with the mere whiff of an odor associated with a memory (Stevenson & Case, 2005; Willander & Larsson, 2006; Schroers, Prigot, & Fagen, 2007).

Results of "sniff tests" have shown that women generally have a better sense of smell than men do (Engen, 1987). People also have the ability to distinguish males from females on the basis of smell alone. In one experiment, blindfolded students who were asked to sniff the breath of a female or male volunteer who was hidden from view were able to distinguish the sex of the donor at better than chance levels. People can also distinguish happy from sad emotions by sniffing under-arm smells, and women are able to identify their babies solely on the basis of smell just a few hours after birth (Doty et al., 1982; Haviland-Jones & Chen, 1999; Fusari & Ballesteros, 2008; Silva, 2011).

The sense of smell is sparked when the molecules of a substance enter the nasal passages and meet *olfactory cells*, the receptor neurons of the nose, which are spread across the nasal cavity. More than 1,000 separate types of receptors have been identified on those cells so far. Each of these receptors is so specialized that it responds only to a small band of different odors. The responses of the separate olfactory cells are then transmitted to the brain, where they are combined into recognition of a particular smell (Murphy et al., 2004; Marshall, Laing, & Jinks, 2006; Zhou & Buck, 2006).

Smell may also act as a hidden means of communication for humans. It has long been known that nonhumans release *pheromones*, chemicals they secrete into the environment that produce a reaction in other members of the same species, permitting the transmission of messages such as sexual availability. For instance, the vaginal secretions of female monkeys contain pheromones that stimulate the sexual interest of male monkeys (Touhara, 2007; Hawkes & Doty, 2009; Brennan, 2011).

The degree to which pheromones are part of the human experience remains an open question. Some psychologists believe that human pheromones affect emotional responses, although the evidence is inconclusive. For one thing, it is not clear what specific sense organ is receptive to pheromones. In nonhumans, it is the *vomeronasal organ* in the nose, but in humans the organ appears to recede during fetal development (Haviland-Jones & Wilson, 2008; Hummer & McClintock, 2009; Gelstein et al., 2011).

TASTE

The sense of taste (*gustation*) involves receptor cells that respond to four basic stimulus qualities: sweet, sour, salty, and bitter. A fifth category also exists, a flavor called *umami*, although there is controversy about whether it qualifies as a fundamental taste. Umami is a hard-to-translate Japanese word, although the English "meaty" or "savory" comes close. Chemically, umami involves food stimuli that contain amino acids (the substances that make up proteins) (McCabe & Rolls, 2007; Erickson, 2008; Nakamura et al., 2011).

Although the specialization of the receptor cells leads them to respond most strongly to a particular type of taste, they also are capable of responding to other tastes as well. Ultimately, every taste is simply a combination of the basic flavor qualities, in the same way that the primary colors blend into a vast variety of shades and hues (Dilorenzo & Youngentob, 2003; Yeomans, Tepper, & Ritezschel, 2007).

The receptor cells for taste are located in roughly 10,000 *taste buds*, which are distributed across the tongue and other parts of the mouth and throat. The taste buds wear out and are replaced every 10 days or so. That's a good thing, because if our taste buds weren't constantly reproducing, we'd lose the ability to taste after we'd accidentally burned our tongues.

The sense of taste differs significantly from one person to another, largely as a result of genetic factors. Some people, dubbed "supertasters," are highly sensitive to taste; they have twice as many taste receptors as "nontasters," who are relatively insensitive to taste. Supertasters (who, for unknown reasons, are more likely to be female than male) find sweets sweeter, cream creamier, and spicy dishes spicier, and weaker concentrations of flavor are enough to satisfy any cravings they may have. In contrast, because they aren't so sensitive to taste, nontasters may seek out relatively sweeter and fattier foods in order to maximize the taste. As a consequence, they may be prone to obesity (Bartoshuk, 2000; Snyder, Fast, & Bartoshuk, 2004; Pickering & Gordon, 2006).

Are you a supertaster? To find out, complete the questionnaire in Figure 4.

PsychTech

When male participants in a study sniffed women's tears, fMRI brain scans showed reduced activity in the parts of the brain associated with sexual arousal. Apparently, tears contain a chemical signal.

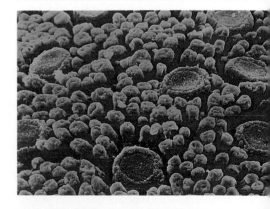

There are 10,000 taste buds on the tongue and other parts of the mouth. Taste buds wear out and are replaced every 10 days. What would happen if taste buds were not regenerated?

FIGURE 4 All tongues are not created equal, according to taste researchers Linda Bartoshuk and Laurie Lucchina. Instead they suggest that the intensity of a flavor experienced by a given person is determined by that person's genetic background. This taste test can help determine if you are a nontaster, average taster, or supertaster. (Source: Bartoshuk & Lucchina, 1997.)

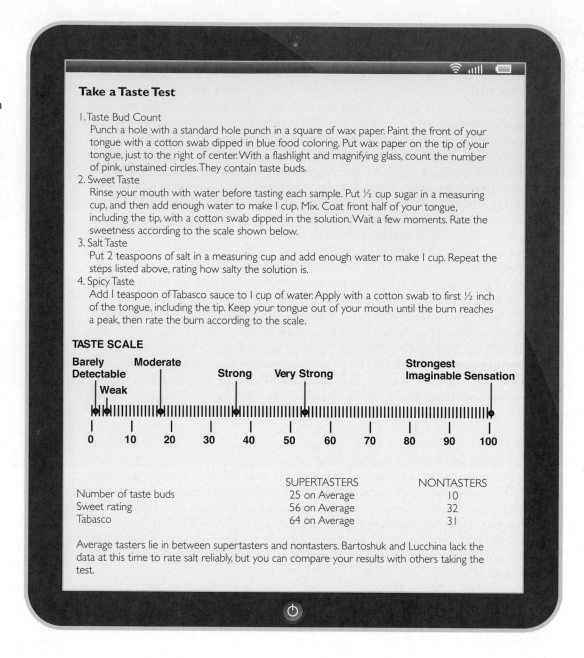

Take a Taste Test

1. Taste Bud Count
   Punch a hole with a standard hole punch in a square of wax paper. Paint the front of your tongue with a cotton swab dipped in blue food coloring. Put wax paper on the tip of your tongue, just to the right of center. With a flashlight and magnifying glass, count the number of pink, unstained circles. They contain taste buds.

2. Sweet Taste
   Rinse your mouth with water before tasting each sample. Put ½ cup sugar in a measuring cup, and then add enough water to make I cup. Mix. Coat front half of your tongue, including the tip, with a cotton swab dipped in the solution. Wait a few moments. Rate the sweetness according to the scale shown below.

3. Salt Taste
   Put 2 teaspoons of salt in a measuring cup and add enough water to make I cup. Repeat the steps listed above, rating how salty the solution is.

4. Spicy Taste
   Add I teaspoon of Tabasco sauce to I cup of water. Apply with a cotton swab to first ½ inch of the tongue, including the tip. Keep your tongue out of your mouth until the burn reaches a peak, then rate the burn according to the scale.

TASTE SCALE

Barely Detectable — Weak — Moderate — Strong — Very Strong — Strongest Imaginable Sensation

0   10   20   30   40   50   60   70   80   90   100

	SUPERTASTERS	NONTASTERS
Number of taste buds	25 on Average	10
Sweet rating	56 on Average	32
Tabasco	64 on Average	31

Average tasters lie in between supertasters and nontasters. Bartoshuk and Lucchina lack the data at this time to rate salt reliably, but you can compare your results with others taking the test.

The Skin Senses: Touch, Pressure, Temperature, and Pain

It started innocently when Jennifer Darling hurt her right wrist during gym class. At first it seemed like a simple sprain. But even though the initial injury healed, the excruciating, burning pain accompanying it did not go away. Instead, it spread to her other arm and then to her legs. The pain, which Jennifer described as similar to "a hot iron on your arm," was unbearable—and never stopped.

The source of Darling's pain turned out to be a rare condition known as *reflex sympathetic dystrophy syndrome*, or RSDS. For a victim of RSDS, a stimulus as mild as a gentle breeze or the touch of a feather can produce agony. Even bright sunlight or a loud noise can trigger intense pain (Coderre, 2011).

Pain such as Darling's can be devastating, yet a lack of pain can be equally bad. If you never experienced pain, for instance, you might not notice that your arm had brushed against a hot pan, and you would suffer a severe burn. Similarly, without the warning sign of abdominal pain that typically accompanies an inflamed appendix, your appendix might eventually rupture, spreading a fatal infection throughout your body.

In fact, all our **skin senses**—touch, pressure, temperature, and pain—play a critical role in survival, making us aware of potential danger to our bodies. Most of these senses operate through nerve receptor cells located at various depths throughout the skin, distributed unevenly throughout the body. For example, some areas, such as the fingertips, have many more receptor cells sensitive to touch and as a consequence are notably more sensitive than other areas of the body (Gardner & Kandel, 2000) (see Figure 5).

Probably the most extensively researched skin sense is pain, and with good reason: People consult physicians and take medication for pain more than any other symptom or condition. Pain costs $100 billion a year in the United States alone (Kalb, 2003; Pesmen, 2006).

Pain is a response to a great variety of different kinds of stimuli. A light that is too bright can produce pain, and sound that is too loud can be painful. One explanation is that pain is an outcome of cell injury; when a cell is damaged, regardless of the source of damage, it releases a chemical called *substance P* that transmits pain messages to the brain.

Some people are more susceptible to pain than others. For example, women experience painful stimuli more intensely than men. These gender differences are associated with the production of hormones related to menstrual cycles. In addition, certain genes are linked to the experience of pain, so that we may inherit our

skin senses The senses of touch, pressure, temperature, and pain.

Study Alert

Remember that there are multiple skin senses, including touch, pressure, temperature, and pain.

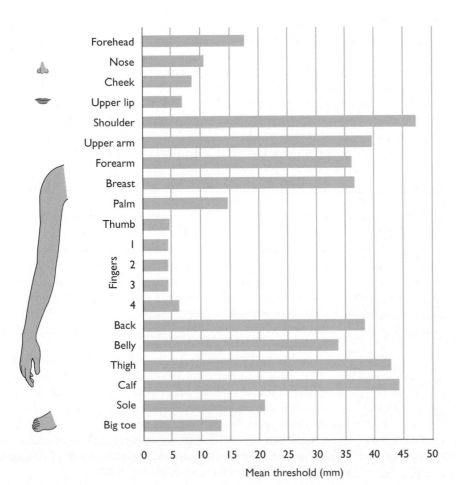

FIGURE 5 Skin sensitivity in various areas of the body. The lower the average threshold is, the more sensitive a body part is. The fingers and thumb, lips, nose, cheeks, and big toe are the most sensitive. Why do you think certain areas are more sensitive than others?

sensitivity to pain (Nielsen et al., 2008; Kim, Clark, & Dionne, 2009; Nielsen, Staud, & Price, 2009).

But the experience of pain is not determined by biological factors alone. For example, women report that the pain experienced in childbirth is moderated to some degree by the joyful nature of the situation. In contrast, even a minor stimulus can produce the perception of strong pain if it is accompanied by anxiety (for example, during a visit to the dentist). Clearly, then, pain is a perceptual response that depends heavily on our emotions and thoughts (Rollman, 2004; Lang, Sorrell, & Rodgers, 2006; Kennedy et al., 2011).

gate-control theory of pain The theory that particular nerve receptors in the spinal cord lead to specific areas of the brain related to pain.

According to the **gate-control theory of pain,** particular nerve receptors in the spinal cord lead to specific areas of the brain related to pain. When these receptors are activated because of an injury or problem with a part of the body, a "gate" to the brain is opened, allowing us to experience the sensation of pain (Melzack & Katz, 2004).

However, another set of neural receptors can, when stimulated, close the "gate" to the brain, thereby reducing the experience of pain. The gate can be shut in two different ways. First, other impulses can overwhelm the nerve pathways relating to pain, which are spread throughout the brain. In this case, nonpainful stimuli compete with and sometimes displace the neural message of pain, thereby shutting off the painful stimulus. This explains why rubbing the skin around an injury (or even listening to distracting music) helps reduce pain. The competing stimuli can overpower the painful ones (Villemure, Slotnick, & Bushnell, 2003; Somers et al., 2011).

PsychTech

Researcher Sean Mackey exposed participants in a study to a painful stimulus while watching an fMRI scan of their brain. Mackey found that the participants could be trained to exert control over the region of the brain activated by the pain, thereby reducing their experience of pain.

Psychological factors account for the second way a gate can be shut. Depending on an individual's current emotions, interpretation of events, and previous experience, the brain can close a gate by sending a message down the spinal cord to an injured area, producing a reduction in or relief from pain. Thus, soldiers who are injured in battle may experience no pain—the surprising situation in more than half of all combat injuries. The lack of pain probably occurs because a soldier experiences such relief at still being alive that the brain sends a signal to the injury site to shut down the pain gate (Turk, 1994; Gatchel & Weisberg, 2000; Pincus & Morley, 2001).

Gate-control theory also may explain cultural differences in the experience of pain. Some of these variations are astounding. For example, in India people who participate in the "hook-swinging" ritual to celebrate the power of the gods have steel hooks embedded under the skin and muscles of their backs. During the ritual, they swing from a pole, suspended by the hooks. What would seem likely to induce excruciating pain instead produces a state of celebration and near euphoria. In fact, when the hooks are later removed, the wounds heal quickly, and after 2 weeks almost no visible marks remain (Kosambi, 1967; Melzack & Katz, 2001).

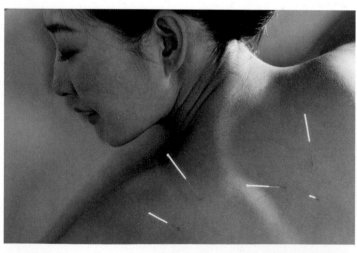

The ancient practice of acupuncture is still used in the 21st century. How does the gate-control theory of pain explain how acupuncture works?

Gate-control theory suggests that the lack of pain is due to a message from the participant's brain, which shuts down the pain pathways. Gate-control theory also may explain the effectiveness of *acupuncture,* an ancient Chinese technique in which sharp needles are inserted into various parts of the body. The sensation from the needles may close the gateway to the brain, reducing the experience of pain. It is also possible that the body's own painkillers—called endorphins—as well as positive and negative emotions, play a role in opening and closing the gate (Fee et al., 2002; Witt, Jena, & Brinkhaus, 2006; Cabioglu, Ergene, & Tan, 2007).

Although the basic ideas behind gate-control theory have been supported by research, other processes are involved in the perception of pain. For instance, it appears that there are multiple neural pathways involved in the experience of pain. Furthermore, it is clear that the suppression of pain can occur through the natural release of endorphins and other compounds that produce a reduction of discomfort and a sense of well-being (Grahek, 2007).

BECOMING AN INFORMED CONSUMER of Psychology

Managing Pain

Are you one of the 76 million people in the United States who suffer from chronic pain? Psychologists and medical specialists have devised several strategies to fight pain. Among the most important approaches are these:

- *Medication.* Painkilling drugs are the most popular treatment in fighting pain. Drugs range from those that directly treat the source of the pain—such as reducing swelling in painful joints—to those that work on the symptoms. Medication can be in the form of pills, patches, injections, or liquids. In a recent innovation, drugs are pumped directly into the spinal cord (Kalb, 2003; Pesmen, 2006; Bagnall, 2010).
- *Nerve and brain stimulation.* Pain can sometimes be relieved when a low-voltage electric current is passed through the specific part of the body that is in pain. For example, in *peripheral-nerve stimulation,* a tiny battery-operated generator is implanted in the low back. In even more severe cases, electrodes can be implanted surgically directly into the brain, or a handheld battery pack can stimulate nerve cells to provide direct relief (Tugay et al., 2007; Landro, 2010; Tan et al., 2011).
- *Light therapy.* One of the newest forms of pain reduction involves exposure to specific wavelengths of red or infrared light. Certain kinds of light increase the production of enzymes that may promote healing (Underwood, 2005; Evcik et al., 2007).
- *Hypnosis.* For people who can be hypnotized, hypnosis can greatly relieve pain (Neron & Stephenson, 2007; Walker, 2008; Accardi & Milling, 2009; Lee & Raja, 2011).
- *Biofeedback and relaxation techniques.* Using *biofeedback*, people learn to control "involuntary" functions such as heartbeat and respiration. If the pain involves muscles, as in tension headaches or back pain, sufferers can be trained to relax their bodies systematically (Nestoriuc & Martin, 2007; Vitiello, Bonello, & Pollard, 2007).
- *Surgery.* In one of the most extreme methods, specific nerve fibers that carry pain messages to the brain can be cut surgically. Still, because of the danger that other bodily functions will be affected, surgery is a treatment of last resort, used most frequently with dying patients (Cullinane, Chu, & Mamelak, 2002; Amid & Chen, 2011).
- *Cognitive restructuring.* Cognitive treatments are effective for people who continually say to themselves, "This pain will never stop," "The pain is ruining my life," or "I can't take it anymore" and are thereby likely to make their pain even worse. By substituting more positive ways of thinking, people can increase their sense of control—and actually reduce the pain they experience (Spanos, Barber, & Lang, 2005; Bogart et al., 2007; Liedl et al., 2011).

How Our Senses Interact

When Matthew Blakeslee shapes hamburger patties with his hands, he experiences a vivid bitter taste in his mouth. Esmerelda Jones (a pseudonym) sees blue when she listens to the note C sharp played on the piano; other notes evoke different hues—so much so that the piano keys are actually color-coded, making it easier for her to remember and play musical scales. (Ramachandran & Hubbard, 2001, p. 53)

The explanation? Both of these people have an unusual condition known as *synesthesia,* in which exposure to one sensation (such as sound) evokes an additional one (such as vision).

The origins of synesthesia are a mystery. It is possible that people with synesthesia have unusually dense neural linkages between the different sensory areas of the brain. Another hypothesis is that they lack neural controls that usually inhibit connections between sensory areas (Pearce, 2007; Kadosh, Henik, & Walsh, 2009).

Whatever the reason for synesthesia, it is a rare condition. (If you'd like to check out this phenomenon, see Figure 6.) Even so, the senses of all of us do interact and

FIGURE 6 (a) Try to pick out the 2s in the display. Most people take several seconds to find them buried among the 5s and to see that the 2s form a triangle. For people with certain forms of synesthesia, however, it's easy, because they perceive the different numbers in contrasting colors as in (b). (Source: From Vilayanur S. Ramachandran and Edward M. Hubbard, "Hearing Colors, Tasting Shapes," *Scientific American* (May 2003). Reproduced with permission. Copyright © 2003 Scientific American, Inc. All rights reserved.)

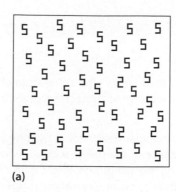

(a)   (b)

integrate in a variety of ways. For example, the taste of food is influenced by its texture and temperature. We perceive food that is warmer as sweeter (think of the sweetness of steamy hot chocolate compared with cold chocolate milk). Spicy foods stimulate some of the same pain receptors that are also stimulated by heat—making the use of "hot" as a synonym for "spicy" quite accurate (Green & George, 2004; Balaban, McBurney, & Affeltranger, 2005; Brang et al., 2011).

It's important, then, to think of our senses as interacting with one another. For instance, brain imaging studies show that the senses work in tandem to build our understanding of the world around us. We engage in *multimodal perception,* in which the brain collects the information from the individual sensory systems and integrates and coordinates it (Macaluso & Driver, 2005; Paulmann, Jessen, & Kotz, 2009).

Moreover, despite the fact that very different sorts of stimuli activate our individual senses, they all react according to the same basic principles that we discussed at the start of this chapter. For example, our responses to visual, auditory, and taste stimuli all follow Weber's law involving our sensitivity to changes in the strength of stimuli.

In short, in some ways our senses are more similar to one another than different. Each of them is designed to pick up information from the environment and translate it into useable information. Furthermore, individually and collectively, our senses help us to understand the complexities of the world around us, allowing us to navigate through the world effectively and intelligently.

RECAP/EVALUATE/RETHINK

RECAP

LO 10-1 What role does the ear play in the senses of sound, motion, and balance?

- Sound, motion, and balance are centered in the ear. Sounds, in the form of vibrating air waves, enter through the outer ear and travel through the auditory canal until they reach the eardrum. (p. 104)
- The vibrations of the eardrum are transmitted into the middle ear, which consists of three bones: the hammer, the anvil, and the stirrup. These bones transmit vibrations to the oval window. (p. 104)
- In the inner ear, vibrations move into the cochlea, which encloses the basilar membrane. Hair cells on the basilar

membrane change the mechanical energy of sound waves into nerve impulses that are transmitted to the brain. The ear is also involved in the sense of balance and motion. (p. 104)

- Sound has a number of physical characteristics, including frequency and amplitude. The place theory of hearing and the frequency theory of hearing explain the processes by which we distinguish sounds of varying frequency and intensity. (p. 105)

LO 10-2 How do smell and taste function?

- Smell depends on olfactory cells (the receptor cells of the nose), and taste is centered in the tongue's taste buds. (p. 109)

LO 10-3 What are the skin senses, and how do they relate to the experience of pain?

- The skin senses are responsible for the experiences of touch, pressure, temperature, and pain. Gate-control theory suggests that particular nerve receptors, when activated, open a "gate" to specific areas of the brain related to pain, and that another set of receptors closes the gate when stimulated. (pp. 111, 112)
- Among the techniques used frequently to alleviate pain are medication, hypnosis, biofeedback, relaxation techniques, surgery, nerve and brain stimulation, and cognitive therapy. (p. 113)

EVALUATE

1. The tube-like passage leading from the outer ear to the eardrum is known as the _____ _____.
2. The purpose of the eardrum is to protect the sensitive nerves underneath it. It serves no purpose in actual hearing. True or false?
3. The three middle ear bones transmit their sound to the _____ _____.
4. The _____ theory of hearing states that the entire basilar membrane responds to a sound, vibrating more or less, depending on the nature of the sound.
5. The three fluid-filled tubes in the inner ear that are responsible for our sense of balance are known as the _____ _____.

6. The _____ _____ theory states that when certain skin receptors are activated as a result of an injury, a "pathway" to the brain is opened, allowing pain to be experienced.

RETHINK

1. Much research is being conducted on repairing faulty sensory organs through devices such as personal guidance systems and eyeglasses, among others. Do you think that researchers should attempt to improve normal sensory capabilities beyond their "natural" range (for example, make human visual or audio capabilities more sensitive than normal)? What benefits might this ability bring? What problems might it cause?
2. *From the perspective of a social worker:* How would you handle the case of a deaf child whose hearing could be restored with a cochlear implant—but different family members have conflicting views on whether the procedure should be done?

Answers to Evaluate Questions

1. auditory canal; 2. false—it vibrates when sound waves hit it, and transmits the sound; 3. oval window; 4. frequency; 5. semicircular canals; 6. gate-control.

KEY TERMS

sound p. 104
eardrum p. 104
cochlea
  (KOKE-lee-uh) p. 104

basilar membrane p. 104
hair cells p. 105
place theory of
  hearing p. 107

frequency theory of
  hearing p. 107
semicircular canals
  p. 107

skin senses p. 111
gate-control theory
  of pain p. 112

Perceptual Organization: Constructing Our View of the World

Learning Outcomes

LO 11-1 What principles underlie our organization of the visual world and allow us to make sense of our environment?

LO 11-2 How are we able to perceive the world in three dimensions when our retinas are capable of sensing only two-dimensional images?

LO 11-3 What clues do visual illusions give us about our understanding of general perceptual mechanisms?

gestalt laws of organization A series of principles that describe how we organize bits and pieces of information into meaningful wholes.

Consider the vase shown in Figure 1a for a moment. Or is it a vase? Take another look, and instead you may see the profiles of two people.

Now that an alternative interpretation has been pointed out, you will probably shift back and forth between the two interpretations. Similarly, if you examine the shapes in Figure 1b long enough, you will probably experience a shift in what you're seeing. The reason for these reversals is this: Because each figure is two-dimensional, the usual means we employ for distinguishing the figure (the object being perceived) from the *ground* (the background or spaces within the object) do not work.

The fact that we can look at the same figure in more than one way illustrates an important point. We do not just passively respond to visual stimuli that happen to fall on our retinas. Rather, we actively try to organize and make sense of what we see.

We turn now from a focus on the initial response to a stimulus (sensation) to what our minds make of that stimulus—perception. Perception is a constructive process by which we go beyond the stimuli that are presented to us and attempt to construct a meaningful situation.

The Gestalt Laws of Organization

Some of the most basic perceptual processes can be described by a series of principles that focus on the ways we organize bits and pieces of information into meaningful wholes. Known as **gestalt laws of organization,** these principles were set forth in the early 1900s by a group of German psychologists who studied patterns, or *gestalts* (Wertheimer, 1923). Those psychologists discovered a number of important principles that are valid for visual (as well as auditory) stimuli, illustrated in Figure 2: closure, proximity, similarity, and simplicity.

Figure 2a illustrates *closure*: We usually group elements to form enclosed or complete figures rather than open ones. We tend to ignore the breaks in Figure 2a and

FIGURE 1 When the usual cues we use to distinguish figure from ground are absent, we may shift back and forth between different views of the same figure. In (a), you can see either a vase or the profiles of two people. In (b), the shaded portion of the figure, called a Necker cube, can appear to be either the front or the back of the cube.

(a)

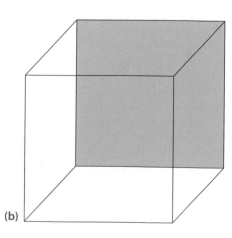

(b)

(a) Closure **(b)** Proximity **(c)** Similarity **(d)** Simplicity

FIGURE 2 Organizing these various bits and pieces of information into meaningful wholes constitutes some of the most basic processes of perception, which are summed up in the gestalt laws of organization. How might we determine if any other species share this organizational tendency?

concentrate on the overall form. Figure 2b demonstrates the principle of *proximity*: We perceive elements that are closer together as grouped together. As a result, we tend to see pairs of dots rather than a row of single dots in Figure 2b.

Elements that are *similar* in appearance we perceive as grouped together. We see, then, horizontal rows of circles and squares in Figure 2c rather than vertical mixed columns. Finally, in a general sense, the overriding gestalt principle is *simplicity*: When we observe a pattern, we perceive it in the most basic, straightforward manner that we can. For example, most of us see Figure 2d as a square with lines on two sides, rather than as the block letter *W* on top of the letter *M*. If we have a choice of interpretations, we generally opt for the simpler one.

Although gestalt psychology no longer plays a prominent role in contemporary psychology, its legacy endures. One fundamental gestalt principle that remains influential is that two objects considered together form a whole that is different from the simple combination of the objects. Gestalt psychologists argued that the perception of stimuli in our environment goes well beyond the individual elements that we sense. Instead, it represents an active, constructive process carried out within the brain (Humphreys & Müller, 2000; Lehar, 2003; van der Helm, 2006; Klapp & Jagacinski, 2011) (see Figure 3).

"I'm turning into my mother."

Understanding this cartoon involves the separation of the figure and ground. If you're having trouble appreciating the humor, stare at the woman on the right, who eventually will be transformed.

Top-Down and Bottom-Up Processing

Study Alert

The gestalt laws of organization are classic principles in the field of psychology. Figure 2 can help you remember them.

Ca- yo- re-d t-is -en-en-e, w-ic- ha- ev-ry -hi-d l-tt-r m-ss-ng? It probably won't take you too long to figure out that it says, "Can you read this sentence, which has every third letter missing?"

If perception were based primarily on breaking down a stimulus into its most basic elements, understanding the sentence, as well as other ambiguous stimuli, would not be possible. The fact that you were probably able to recognize such an imprecise stimulus illustrates that perception proceeds along two different avenues, called top-down processing and bottom-up processing.

In **top-down processing,** perception is guided by higher-level knowledge, experience, expectations, and motivations. You were able to figure out the meaning of the sentence with the missing letters because of your prior reading experience and because written English contains redundancies. Not every letter of each word is

top-down processing Perception that is guided by higher-level knowledge, experience, expectations, and motivations.

FIGURE 3 Although at first it is difficult to distinguish anything in this drawing, keep looking, and eventually you may see the figure of a dog. The dog represents a gestalt, or perceptual, whole, which is something greater than the sum or the individual elements.

necessary to decode its meaning. Moreover, your expectations played a role in your being able to read the sentence. You were probably expecting a statement that had *something* to do with psychology, not the lyrics to a Lady Gaga song.

Top-down processing is illustrated by the importance of context in determining how we perceive objects. Look, for example, at Figure 4. Most of us perceive that the first row consists of the letters *A* through *F*, while the second contains the numbers 9 through 14. But take a more careful look and you'll see that the "B" and the "13" are identical. Clearly, our perception is affected by our expectations about the two sequences—even though the two stimuli are exactly the same.

However, top-down processing cannot occur on its own. Even though top-down processing allows us to fill in the gaps in ambiguous and out-of-context stimuli, we would be unable to perceive the meaning of such stimuli without bottom-up processing. **Bottom-up processing** consists of the progression of recognizing and processing information from individual components of a stimuli and moving to the perception of the whole. We would make no headway in our recognition of the sentence without being able to perceive the individual shapes that make up the letters. Some perception, then, occurs at the level of the patterns and features of each of the separate letters.

Top-down and bottom-up processing occur simultaneously, and interact with each other, in our perception of the world around us. Bottom-up processing permits us to process the fundamental characteristics of stimuli, whereas top-down processing allows us to bring our experience to bear on perception. As we learn more about the complex processes involved in perception, we are developing a better understanding of how

bottom-up processing Perception that consists of the progression of recognizing and processing information from individual components of a stimuli and moving to the perception of the whole.

A B C D E F
9 10 11 12 13 14

FIGURE 4 The power of context is shown in this figure. Note how the B and the 13 are identical. (Adapted from Coren & Ward, 1989.)

the brain continually interprets information from the senses and permits us to make responses appropriate to the environment (Sobel et al., 2007; Folk & Remington, 2008; Westerhausen et al., 2009).

Depth Perception: Translating 2-D to 3-D

As sophisticated as the retina is, the images projected onto it are flat and two-dimensional. Yet the world around us is three-dimensional, and we perceive it that way. How do we make the transformation from 2-D to 3-D?

The ability to view the world in three dimensions and to perceive distance—a skill known as **depth perception**—is due largely to the fact that we have two eyes. Because there is a certain distance between the eyes, a slightly different image reaches each retina. The brain integrates the two images into one view, but it also recognizes the difference in images and uses this difference to estimate the distance of an object from us. The difference in the images seen by the left eye and the right eye is known as *binocular disparity* (Hibbard, 2007; Kara & Boyd, 2009; Gillam, Palmisano, & Govan, 2011).

To get a sense of binocular disparity, hold a pencil at arm's length and look at it first with one eye and then with the other. There is little difference between the two views relative to the background. Now bring the pencil just 6 inches away from your face, and try the same thing. This time you will perceive a greater difference between the two views.

The fact that the discrepancy between the images in the two eyes varies according to the distance of objects that we view provides us with a means of determining distance. If we view two objects and one is considerably closer to us than the other is, the retinal disparity will be relatively large and we will have a greater sense of depth between the two. However, if the two objects are a similar distance from us, the retinal disparity will be minor, and we will perceive them as being a similar distance from us.

depth perception The ability to view the world in three dimensions and to perceive distance.

Railroad tracks that seem to join together in the distance are an example of linear perception.

When the moon is near the horizon, we do not see it by itself, and perceptual constancy leads us to take into account a misleading sense of distance.

In some cases, certain cues permit us to obtain a sense of depth and distance with just one eye. These cues are known as *monocular cues*. One monocular cue— *motion parallax*—is the change in position of an object on the retina caused by movement of your body relative to the object. For example, suppose you are a passenger in a moving car, and you focus your eye on a stable object such as a tree. Objects that are closer than the tree will appear to move backward, and the nearer the object is, the more quickly it will appear to move. In contrast, objects beyond the tree will seem to move at a slower speed, but in the same direction as you are. Your brain is able to use these cues to calculate the relative distances of the tree and other objects.

Similarly, experience has taught us that if two objects are the same size, the one that makes a smaller image on the retina is farther away than is the one that provides a larger image—an example of the monocular cue of *relative size*. But it's not just size of an object that provides information about distance; the quality of the image on the retina helps us judge distance. The monocular cue of *texture gradient* provides information about distance, because the details of things that are far away are less distinct (Proffitt, 2006).

Finally, anyone who has ever seen railroad tracks that seem to come together in the distance knows that distant objects appear to be closer together than are nearer ones, a phenomenon called linear perspective. People use *linear perspective* as a monocular cue in estimating distance, allowing the two-dimensional image on the retina to record the three-dimensional world (Dobbins et al., 1998; Shimono & Wade, 2002; Bruggeman, Yonas, & Konczak, 2007).

Perceptual Constancy

perceptual constancy The phenomenon in which physical objects are perceived as unvarying and consistent despite changes in their appearance or in the physical environment.

Consider what happens as you finish a conversation with a friend and he begins to walk away from you. As you watch him walk down the street, the image on your retina becomes smaller and smaller. Do you wonder why he is shrinking?

Of course not. Despite the very real change in the size of the retinal image, because of perceptual constancy you factor into your thinking the knowledge that your friend is moving farther away from you. **Perceptual constancy** is a phenomenon in which physical objects are perceived as unvarying and consistent despite changes in their appearance or in the physical environment. Perceptual constancy leads us to view objects as having an unvarying size, shape, color, and brightness, even if the image on our retina varies. For example, despite the varying images on the retina as an airplane approaches, flies overhead, and disappears, we do not perceive the airplane as changing shape (Redding, 2002; Wickelgren, 2004; Garrigan & Kellman, 2008).

In some cases, though, our application of perceptual constancy can mislead us. One good example of this involves the rising moon. When the moon first appears at night, close to the horizon, it seems to be huge—much larger than when it is high in the sky later in the evening. You may have thought that the apparent change in the size of the moon was caused by the moon's being physically closer to the earth when it first appears. In fact, though, this is not the case at all: the actual image of the moon on our retina is the same, whether it is low or high in the sky.

There are several explanations for the moon illusion. One suggests that the moon appears to be larger when it is close to the horizon primarily because of perceptual constancy. When the moon is near the horizon, the perceptual cues of intervening terrain and objects such as trees on the horizon produce a misleading sense of distance, leading us to misperceive the moon as relatively large.

In contrast, when the moon is high in the sky, we see it by itself, and we don't try to compensate for its distance from us. In this case, then, perceptual constancy leads us to perceive it as relatively small. To experience perceptual constancy, try looking at the moon when it is relatively low on the horizon through a paper-towel tube; the moon suddenly will appear to "shrink" back to normal size (Coren, 1992; Ross & Plug, 2002; Imamura & Nakamizo, 2006; Kaufman, Johnson, & Liu, 2008).

Perceptual constancy is not the only explanation for the moon illusion, and it remains a puzzle to psychologists. It may be that several different perceptual processes are involved in the illusion (Gregory, 2008; Kim, 2008).

Motion Perception: As the World Turns

When a batter tries to hit a pitched ball, the most important factor is the motion of the ball. How is a batter able to judge the speed and location of a target that is moving at some 90 miles per hour?

The answer rests in part on several cues that provide us with relevant information about the perception of motion. For one thing, the movement of an object across the retina is typically perceived relative to some stable, unmoving background. Moreover, if the stimulus is heading toward us, the image on the retina expands in size, filling more and more of the visual field. In such cases, we assume that the stimulus is approaching—not that it is an expanding stimulus viewed at a constant distance.

It is not, however, just the movement of images across the retina that brings about the perception of motion. If it were, we would perceive the world as moving every time we moved our heads. Instead, one of the critical things we learn about perception is to factor information about our own head and eye movements along with information about changes in the retinal image.

Sometimes we perceive motion when it doesn't occur. Have you ever been on a stationary train that feels as if it is moving, because a train on an adjacent track begins to slowly move past? Or have you been in an IMAX movie theater, in which you feel as if you were falling as a huge image of a plane moves across the screen? In both cases, the experience of motion is convincing. *Apparent movement* is the

Do People Have an Internal Sense of Direction?

Do you have a good sense of direction? When you get lost in an unfamiliar part of town, are you able to navigate your way back to where you started? If you exit a building on your college campus through an unfamiliar door, do you have a sense of which way you should walk to get to your destination? Can you readily point out which direction is north?

If so, you're not alone—many people have this ability to retrace their steps, figure out where they are in relation to familiar locations, or even intuitively know which way is north. Researchers are discovering that this sense may not just be a matter of learning—it may, in fact, be inborn.

Scientists are learning that certain regions of the brain in and around the hippocampus aid our directional sense. Cells in the hippocampus, called *place cells,* become active only when we visit a specific part of the environment. Other cells, called *grid cells*, help to define a grid that enables us to know where we are in relation to our environment. Working together with other cells, called *head-direction* cells, these brain regions give us an internal sense of how we are moving through space—a sort of internal map of

Humans have a remarkable inborn sense of direction, more sophisticated in some ways than GPS technology.

where we are and where we have been (O'Keefe & Dostrovsky, 1971; Fyhn et al., 2007; Langston et al., 2010).

Do these cells provide the sense of direction that helps us navigate? Not necessarily. The ability to understand direction and the ability to find where we want to go are related, but not the same. People with a good sense of direction can visualize their location in space and point out where things are, such as neighboring towns or compass directions. But even people who don't have such a good sense of direction can still figure out where they want to go, if less efficiently (Hager, 2010).

This directional sense, therefore, works a bit like a GPS, telling us where we are relative to other locations so that we can find the most direct path between two points. But if your own "internal GPS" isn't the most accurate, don't despair—although some people have a better sense of where they should go than others do, we all usually manage to get there eventually. Some of us just take a bit longer than others.

RETHINK

- What are some of the benefits of having an internal sense of direction?
- Why do you think some people have a better internal sense of direction than others do?

perception that a stationary object is moving. It occurs when different areas of the retina are quickly stimulated, leading us to interpret motion (Ekroll & Scherzer, 2009; Lindemann & Bekkering, 2009; Brandon & Saffran, 2011). (Also see *Applying Psychology in the 21st Century.*)

Perceptual Illusions: The Deceptions of Perceptions

If you look carefully at the Parthenon, one of the most famous buildings of ancient Greece, still standing at the top of an Athens hill, you'll see that it was built with a bulge on one side. If it didn't have that bulge—and quite a few other architectural "tricks" like it, such as columns that incline inward—it would look as if it were crooked and about to fall down. Instead, it appears to stand completely straight, at right angles to the ground.

The fact that the Parthenon appears to be completely upright is the result of a series of visual illusions. **Visual illusions** are physical stimuli that consistently

visual illusions Physical stimuli that consistently produce errors in perception.

(a)

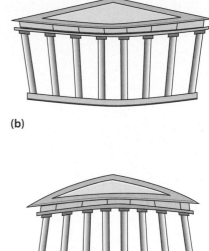

(b)

(c)

FIGURE 5 (a) In building the Parthenon, the Greeks constructed an architectural wonder that looks perfectly straight, with right angles at every corner. (b) However, if it had been built with completely true right angles, it would have looked as it does here. (c) To compensate for this illusion, the Parthenon was designed to have a slight upward curvature, as shown here. (Source: (b) and (c) from Lukiesh, 1921, p. 500.)

produce errors in perception. In the case of the Parthenon, the building appears to be completely square, as illustrated in Figure 5a. However, if it had been built that way, it would look to us as it does in Figure 5b. The reason for this is an illusion that makes right angles placed above a line appear as if they were bent. To offset the illusion, the Parthenon was constructed as in Figure 5c, with a slight upward curvature.

The *Müller-Lyer illusion* (illustrated in Figure 6 on page 124) has fascinated psychologists for decades. Although the two lines are the same length, the one with the arrow tips pointing outward, away from the vertical line (Figure 6a, left) appears to be shorter than the one with the arrow tips pointing inward (Figure 6a, right).

Although all kinds of explanations for visual illusions have been suggested, most concentrate either on the physical operation of the eye or on our misinterpretation of the visual stimulus. For example, one explanation for the Müller-Lyer illusion is that eye movements are greater when the arrow tips point inward, making us perceive the line as longer than it is when the arrow tips face outward. In contrast, a different explanation for the illusion suggests that we unconsciously attribute particular significance to each of the lines (Gregory, 1978; Redding & Hawley, 1993). When we see the left line in Figure 6a we tend to perceive it as if it were the relatively close outside corner of a rectangular object, such as the outside corner of the room illustrated in Figure 6b. In contrast, when we view the line on the right in Figure 6a, we perceive it as the relatively more distant inside corner of a rectangular object, such as the inside room corner in Figure 6c. Because previous experience leads us to assume that the outside corner is closer than the inside corner, we make the further assumption that the inside corner must therefore be longer.

Despite the complexity of the latter explanation, a good deal of evidence supports it. For instance, cross-cultural studies show that people raised in areas where there are few right angles—such as the Zulu in Africa—are much less susceptible to the illusion than are people who grow up where most structures are built using right angles and rectangles (Segall, Campbell, & Herskovits, 1966).

Study Alert

The explanation for the Müller-Lyer illusion is complicated. Figure 6 will help you master it.

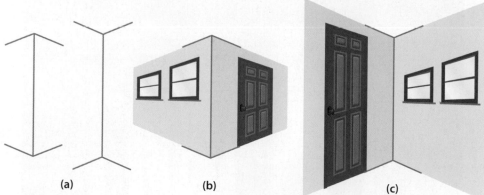

(a)   (b)   (c)

FIGURE 6 In the Müller-Lyer illusion (a), the vertical line on the left appears shorter than the one on the right, even though they are identical in length. One explanation for the Müller-Lyer illusion suggests that the line on the left (with arrow points directed outward) is perceived as the relatively close corner of a rectangular object, such as the building corner in (b), and the line on the right (with the arrow points directed inward) is interpreted as the inside corner of a rectangular object, such as the room extending away from us (c). Our previous experience with distance cues leads us to assume that the outside corner is closer than the inside corner and, consequently, the inside corner must be longer.

Exploring DIVERSITY

Culture and Perception

As the example of the Zulu indicates, the culture in which we are raised has clear consequences for how we perceive the world. Consider the drawing in Figure 7. Sometimes called the "devil's tuning fork," it is likely to produce a mind-boggling effect, as the center tine of the fork alternates between appearing and disappearing.

Now try to reproduce the drawing on a piece of paper. Chances are that the task is nearly impossible for you—unless you are a member of an African tribe with little exposure to Western cultures. For such individuals, the task is simple; they have no trouble reproducing the figure. The reason is that Westerners automatically interpret the drawing as something that cannot exist in three dimensions, and they therefore are inhibited from reproducing it. The African tribal members, in contrast, do not make the assumption that the figure is "impossible" and instead view it in two dimensions, a perception that enables them to copy the figure with ease (Deregowski, 1973).

Cultural differences are also reflected in depth perception. A Western viewer of Figure 8 would interpret the hunter in the drawing as aiming for the antelope in the foreground, while an elephant stands under the tree in the background. A member of an isolated African tribe, however, interprets the scene very differently by assuming that the hunter is aiming at the elephant. Westerners use the difference in sizes between the two animals as a cue that the elephant is farther away than the antelope (Hudson, 1960).

Does this mean that basic perceptual processes differ among people of different cultures? No. Variations in learning and experience produce cross-cultural differences in perception, and the underlying psychological processes involved in perception are similar (McCauley & Henrich, 2006).

Although visual illusions may seem like mere psychological curiosities, they actually illustrate something fundamental about perception. There is a basic connection between our prior knowledge, needs, motivations, and expectations about how the world is put together and the way we perceive it. Our view of the world is very much an outcome, then, of fundamental psychological factors. Furthermore, each person perceives the environment in a way that is unique and special (Knoblich & Sebanz, 2006; Repp & Knoblich, 2007).

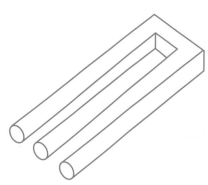

FIGURE 7 The "devil's tuning fork" has three prongs . . . or does it have two?

FIGURE 8 Is the man aiming for the elephant or the antelope? Westerners assume that the difference in size between the two animals indicates that the elephant is farther away, and therefore the man is aiming for the antelope. In contrast, members of some African tribes, not used to depth cues in two-dimensional drawings, assume that the man is aiming for the elephant. (The drawing is based on Hudson, 1960.) Do you think people who view the picture in three dimensions could explain what they see to someone who views the scene in two dimensions and eventually get that person to view it in three dimensions?

SUBLIMINAL PERCEPTION

Can stimuli that we're not consciously aware of change our behavior? In some ways, yes.

Subliminal perception refers to the perception of messages about which we have no awareness. The stimulus could be a written word, a sound, or even a smell that activates the sensory system but that is not intense enough for a person to report having experienced it. For example, in some studies people are exposed to a descriptive label—called a *prime*—about a person (such as the word *smart* or *happy*) so briefly that they cannot report seeing the label. Later, however, they form impressions that are influenced by the content of the prime. Somehow, they have been influenced by the prime that they say they couldn't see, providing some evidence for subliminal perception (Greenwald, Draine, & Abrams, 1996; Key, 2003).

Although subliminal messages (which social psychologists refer to as *priming*) can influence behavior in subtle ways, there's little evidence that it can lead to *major* changes in attitudes or behavior. Most research suggests that they cannot. For example, people who are subliminally exposed to an image of a Coke can and the word "thirst" do later rate themselves as thirstier, and they actually do drink more when given the opportunity. However, they don't particularly care if they drink Coke or some other liquid to quench their thirst (Dijksterhuis, Chartrand, & Aarts, 2007).

In short, although we are able to perceive at least some kinds of information of which we are unaware, there's little evidence that subliminal messages can change our attitudes or behavior in substantial ways. At the same time, subliminal perception does have at least some consequences. If our motivation to carry out a behavior is already high and the appropriate stimuli are presented subliminally, subliminal perception may have at least some effect on our behavior (Abrams, Klinger, & Greenwald, 2002; Pratkanis, Epley, & Savitsky, 2007; Randolph-Seng & Nielsen, 2009).

EXTRASENSORY PERCEPTION (ESP)

Given the lack of evidence that subliminal perception can alter our behavior in substantial ways, psychologists are particularly skeptical of reports of *extrasensory perception*, or ESP—perception that does not involve our known senses. Although half of the general population of the United States believes it exists, most psychologists reject the existence of ESP, asserting that there is no sound documentation of the phenomenon (Gallup Poll, 2001).

However, a debate in one of the most prestigious psychology journals, *Psychological Bulletin*, heightened interest in ESP. According to proponents of ESP, reliable evidence exists for an "anomalous process of information transfer," or *psi*. These researchers, who painstakingly reviewed considerable evidence, argue that a cumulative body of research shows reliable support for the existence of psi (Bem & Honorton, 1994; Storm & Ertel, 2001; Parra & Argibay, 2007).

Their conclusion has been challenged on several counts. For example, critics suggest that the research methodology was inadequate and that the experiments supporting psi are flawed (Milton & Wiseman, 1999; Kennedy, 2004).

Because of questions about the quality of the research, as well as a lack of any credible theoretical explanation for how extrasensory perception might take place, the vast majority of psychologists continue to believe that there is no reliable scientific support for ESP (Rose & Blackmore, 2002; Wiseman & Greening, 2002). Still, the exchanges in *Psychological Bulletin* are likely to heighten the debate. More important, the renewed interest in ESP among psychologists is likely to inspire more research, which is the only way the issue can be resolved.

RECAP/EVALUATE/RETHINK

RECAP

LO 11-1 What principles underlie our organization of the visual world and allow us to make sense of our environment?

- Perception is a constructive process in which people go beyond the stimuli that are physically present and try to construct a meaningful interpretation. (p. 116)
- The gestalt laws of organization are used to describe the way in which we organize bits and pieces of information into meaningful wholes, known as gestalts, through closure, proximity, similarity, and simplicity. (p. 116)
- In top-down processing, perception is guided by higher-level knowledge, experience, expectations, and motivations. In bottom-up processing, perception consists of the progression of recognizing and processing information from individual components of a stimuli and moving to the perception of the whole. (pp. 117, 118)

LO 11-2 How are we able to perceive the world in three dimensions when our retinas are capable of sensing only two-dimensional images?

- Depth perception is the ability to perceive distance and view the world in three dimensions even though the images projected on our retinas are two-dimensional. We are able to judge depth and distance as a result of binocular disparity and monocular cues, such as motion parallax, the relative size of images on the retina, and linear perspective. (pp. 119, 120)
- Perceptual constancy permits us to perceive stimuli as unvarying in size, shape, and color despite changes in the environment or the appearance of the objects being perceived. (p. 120)

- Motion perception depends on cues such as the perceived movement of an object across the retina and information about how the head and eyes are moving. (p. 121)

LO 11-3 What clues do visual illusions give us about our understanding of general perceptual mechanisms?

- Visual illusions are physical stimuli that consistently produce errors in perception, causing judgments that do not reflect the physical reality of a stimulus accurately. One of the best-known illusions is the Müller-Lyer illusion. (p. 123)
- Visual illusions are usually the result of errors in the brain's interpretation of visual stimuli. Furthermore, culture clearly affects how we perceive the world. (p. 124)
- Subliminal perception refers to the perception of messages about which we have no awareness. The reality of the phenomenon, as well as of ESP, is open to question and debate. (p. 125)

EVALUATE

1. Match each of the following organizational laws with its meaning:

    a. closure
    b. proximity
    c. similarity
    d. simplicity

    1. Elements close together are grouped together.
    2. Patterns are perceived in the most basic, direct manner possible.
    3. Groupings are made in terms of complete figures.
    4. Elements similar in appearance are grouped together.

2. _____ analysis deals with the way in which we break an object down into its component pieces in order to understand it.

3. Processing that involves higher functions such as expectations and motivations is known as _____, whereas processing that recognizes the individual components of a stimulus is known as _____.

4. When a car passes you on the road and appears to shrink as it gets farther away, the phenomenon of _____ _____ permits you to realize that the car is not in fact getting smaller.

5. _____ _____ is the ability to view the world in three dimensions instead of two.

6. The brain makes use of a phenomenon known as _____ _____, or the difference in the images the two eyes see, to give three dimensions to sight.

RETHINK

1. In what ways do painters represent three-dimensional scenes in two dimensions on a canvas? Do you think artists in non-Western cultures use the same or different principles to represent three-dimensionality? Why?

2. *From the perspective of a corporate executive:* What arguments might you make if a member of your staff proposed a subliminal advertising campaign? Do you think your explanation would be enough to convince them? Why?

Answers to Evaluate Questions

1. a-3, b-1, c-4, d-2; 2. Feature; 3. top-down, bottom-up; 4. perceptual constancy; 5. Depth perception; 6. binocular disparity

KEY TERMS

gestalt laws of
  organization p. 116

top-down processing p. 117
bottom-up processing p. 118

depth perception p. 119
perceptual constancy p. 120

visual illusions p. 122

Looking Back

Epilogue

We have noted the important distinction between sensation and perception, and we have examined the processes that underlie both of them. We've seen how external stimuli evoke sensory responses and how our different senses process the information contained in those responses. We also have focused on the physical structure and internal workings of the individual senses, including vision, hearing, balance, smell, taste, and the skin senses, and we've explored how our brains organize and process sensory information to construct a consistent, integrated picture of the world around us.

To complete our investigation of sensation and perception, let's reconsider the case of TN who is able to "see" even though he is blind. Using your knowledge of sensation and perception, answer these questions:

1. Would you say that TN's blindness is caused more by a problem with sensation or a problem with perception? Why do you think so?
2. Do you think that even sighted people benefit from the visual pathways that give blindsighted people the ability to respond to visual information? Have you ever, for example, reacted to something that you "saw" without being consciously aware that you saw it?
3. Would the phenomenon of blindsight count as an example of extrasensory perception? Why or why not?
4. How is blindsight similar to subliminal perception?

VISUAL SUMMARY 3 Sensation and Perception

MODULE 8 Sensing the World

Absolute thresholds

Difference thresholds

- • Just noticeable difference

- • Weber's law

Sensory Adaptation

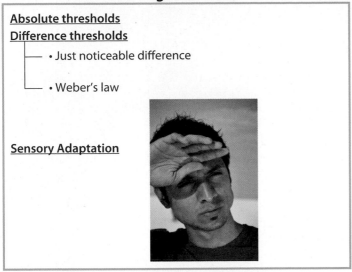

MODULE 9 Vision

Eye Structure

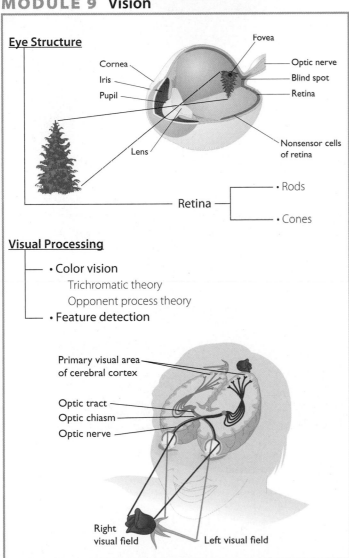

- Cornea
- Iris
- Pupil
- Lens
- Fovea
- Optic nerve
- Blind spot
- Retina
- Nonsensor cells of retina

Retina — • Rods

Retina — • Cones

Visual Processing

- • Color vision
  - Trichromatic theory
  - Opponent process theory
- • Feature detection

- Primary visual area of cerebral cortex
- Optic tract
- Optic chiasm
- Optic nerve
- Right visual field
- Left visual field

MODULE 10 Hearing and Other Senses

Ear Structure

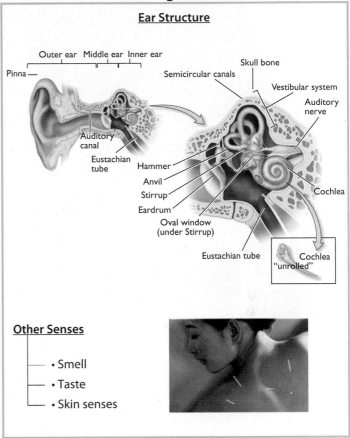

- Outer ear Middle ear Inner ear
- Pinna
- Auditory canal
- Eustachian tube
- Skull bone
- Semicircular canals
- Vestibular system
- Auditory nerve
- Hammer
- Anvil
- Stirrup
- Eardrum
- Oval window (under Stirrup)
- Cochlea
- Eustachian tube
- Cochlea "unrolled"

Other Senses

- • Smell
- • Taste
- • Skin senses

MODULE 11 Perception

Gestalt Laws of Organization

(a) Closure   **(b)** Proximity   **(c)** Similarity   **(d)** Simplicity

Top-down and Bottom-up Processing

A B C D E F

9 10 11 12 13 14

Perceptual Constancy

Perceptual Illusions

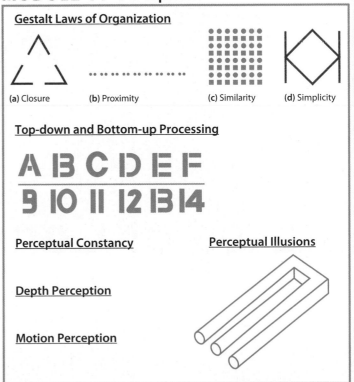

Depth Perception

Motion Perception

4

States of Consciousness

Learning Outcomes for Chapter 4

MODULE 12

LO 12-1 What are the different states of consciousness?

LO 12-2 What happens when we sleep, and what are the meaning and function of dreams?

LO 12-3 What are the major sleep disorders, and how can they be treated?

LO 12-4 How much do we daydream?

Sleep and Dreams

The Stages of Sleep

REM Sleep: The Paradox of Sleep

Why Do We Sleep, and How Much Sleep Is Necessary?

Neuroscience in Your Life: Why Are You Cranky? Your Brain Is Too Awake

The Function and Meaning of Dreaming

Applying Psychology in the 21st Century: Dreams of Failure

Sleep Disturbances: Slumbering Problems

PsychWork: Sleep Technologist

Circadian Rhythms: Life Cycles

Daydreams: Dreams Without Sleep

Becoming an Informed Consumer of Psychology: Sleeping Better

MODULE 13

LO 13-1 What is hypnosis, and are hypnotized people in a different state of consciousness?

LO 13-2 What are the effects of meditation?

Hypnosis and Meditation

Hypnosis: A Trance-Forming Experience?

Meditation: Regulating Our Own State of Consciousness

Exploring Diversity: Cross-Cultural Routes to Altered States of Consciousness

MODULE 14

LO 14-1 What are the major classifications of drugs, and what are their effects?

Drug Use: The Highs and Lows of Consciousness

Stimulants: Drug Highs

Depressants: Drug Lows

Narcotics: Relieving Pain and Anxiety

Hallucinogens: Psychedelic Drugs

Becoming an Informed Consumer of Psychology: Identifying Drug and Alcohol Problems

Lynn Blakes, 39, a language test developer, has had three bouts of depression and says meditation helps prevent a relapse.

"I first suffered depression 13 years ago following the death of my mother and it returned seven years ago when I was working as a teacher. It was a stressful job and I wasn't looking after myself. On both occasions I was prescribed antidepressants, which were effective, but I don't want to rely on drugs.

"I've always been interested in meditation and have used it to help me relax so I enrolled in a course in mindfulness meditation. I learned how to focus on my breathing and to spend time thinking about everyday things such as the sound of birds. You can even focus on brushing your teeth to help switch off. It soon becomes second nature" (Lee, 2010, p. 33).

Looking Ahead

Lynn Blakes discovered that meditation, a technique for focusing attention, helped her relieve her daily life stress enough to prevent a relapse of her depression. Meditation is one of a number of methods people can use to alter their state of consciousness. It is an experience that many people find relaxing and pleasurable. Why this is so, what conscious experience is, and how and why we can alter it are some of the questions we address as we turn our attention to the study of consciousness.

Consciousness is the awareness of the sensations, thoughts, and feelings we experience at a given moment. Consciousness is our subjective understanding of both the environment around us and our private internal world, unobservable to outsiders.

In *waking consciousness*, we are awake and aware of our thoughts, emotions, and perceptions. All other states of consciousness are considered *altered states of consciousness*. Among these, sleeping and dreaming occur naturally; drug use and hypnosis, in contrast, are methods of deliberately altering one's state of consciousness.

In the past, because consciousness is so personal a phenomenon, psychologists were sometimes reluctant to study it. After all, who can say that your consciousness is similar to or, for that matter, different from anyone else's? Although the earliest psychologists, including William James (1890), saw the study of consciousness as central to the field, later psychologists suggested that it was out of bounds for the discipline. They argued that consciousness could be understood only by relying "unscientifically" on what experimental participants said they were experiencing. In this view, it was philosophers—not psychologists—who should speculate on such knotty issues as whether consciousness is separate from the physical body, how people know they exist, and how the body and mind are related to each other (Gennaro, 2004; Barresi, 2007).

Contemporary psychologists reject the view that the study of consciousness is unsuitable for the field of psychology. Instead, they argue that several approaches permit the scientific study of consciousness. For example, behavioral neuroscientists can measure brain-wave patterns under conditions of consciousness ranging from sleep to waking to hypnotic trances. And new understanding of the chemistry of drugs such as marijuana and alcohol has provided insights into the way they produce their pleasurable—as well as adverse—effects (Mosher & Akins, 2007; Baars & Seth, 2009; Wells, Phillips, & McCarthy, 2011).

Yet how humans experience consciousness remains an open question. Some psychologists believe that the experience of consciousness is produced by a quantitative increase in neuronal activity that occurs throughout the brain. For example, an alarm clock moves us from sleep to waking consciousness by its loud ringing, which stimulates neurons throughout the brain as a whole (Greenfield, 2002; Koch & Greenfield, 2007; Ward, 2011).

In contrast, others believe that states of consciousness are produced by particular sets of neurons and neuronal pathways that are activated in specific ways. In this view, an alarm clock wakes us from sleep into consciousness, because specific neurons related to the auditory nerve are activated; the auditory nerve then sends a message to other neurons to release particular neurotransmitters that produce awareness of the alarm (Tononi & Koch, 2008).

Although we don't know yet which of these views is correct, it is clear that whatever state of consciousness we are in—be it waking, sleeping, hypnotic, or drug-induced—the complexities of consciousness are profound.

consciousness The awareness of the sensations, thoughts, and feelings being experienced at a given moment.

Sleep and Dreams

Mike Trevino, 29, slept 9 hours in 9 days in his quest to win a 3,000-mile, cross-country bike race. For the first 38 hrs. and 646 miles, he skipped sleep entirely. Later he napped—with no dreams he can remember—for no more than 90 minutes a night. Soon he began to imagine that his support crew was part of a bomb plot. "It was almost like riding in a movie. I thought it was a complex dream, even though I was conscious," says Trevino, who finished second (Springen, 2004, p. 47).

Trevino's case is unusual—in part because he was able to function with so little sleep for so long—and it raises a host of questions about sleep and dreams. Can we live without sleep? What is the meaning of dreams? More generally, what is sleep?

Although sleeping is a state that we all experience, there are still many unanswered questions about sleep that remain, along with a considerable number of myths. Test your knowledge of sleep and dreams by answering the questionnaire in Figure 1.

Learning Outcomes

LO 12-1 What are the different states of consciousness?

LO 12-2 What happens when we sleep, and what are the meaning and function of dreams?

LO 12-3 What are the major sleep disorders, and how can they be treated?

LO 12-4 How much do we daydream?

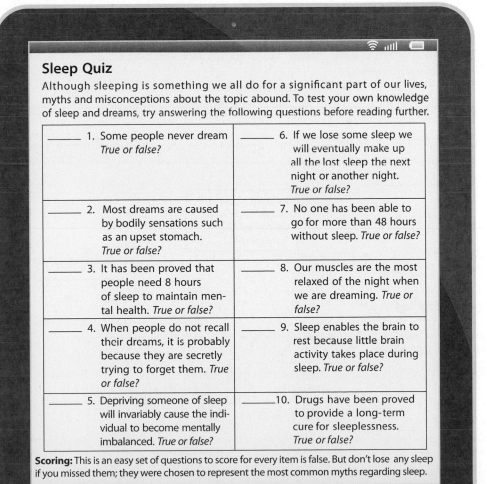

Sleep Quiz

Although sleeping is something we all do for a significant part of our lives, myths and misconceptions about the topic abound. To test your own knowledge of sleep and dreams, try answering the following questions before reading further.

_____ 1. Some people never dream *True or false?*

_____ 2. Most dreams are caused by bodily sensations such as an upset stomach. *True or false?*

_____ 3. It has been proved that people need 8 hours of sleep to maintain mental health. *True or false?*

_____ 4. When people do not recall their dreams, it is probably because they are secretly trying to forget them. *True or false?*

_____ 5. Depriving someone of sleep will invariably cause the individual to become mentally imbalanced. *True or false?*

_____ 6. If we lose some sleep we will eventually make up all the lost sleep the next night or another night. *True or false?*

_____ 7. No one has been able to go for more than 48 hours without sleep. *True or false?*

_____ 8. Our muscles are the most relaxed of the night when we are dreaming. *True or false?*

_____ 9. Sleep enables the brain to rest because little brain activity takes place during sleep. *True or false?*

_____ 10. Drugs have been proved to provide a long-term cure for sleeplessness. *True or false?*

Scoring: This is an easy set of questions to score for every item is false. But don't lose any sleep if you missed them; they were chosen to represent the most common myths regarding sleep.

FIGURE 1 There are many unanswered questions about sleep. Taking this quiz can help you clear up some of the myths. (Source: Palladino & Carducci, 1984.)

The Stages of Sleep

Most of us consider sleep a time of tranquility when we set aside the tensions of the day and spend the night in uneventful slumber. However, a closer look at sleep shows that a good deal of activity occurs throughout the night.

Measures of electrical activity in the brain show that the brain is quite active during the night. It produces electrical discharges with systematic, wavelike patterns that change in height (or amplitude) and speed (or frequency) in regular sequences. There is also significant physical activity in muscle and eye movements.

People progress through a series of distinct stages of sleep during a night's rest—known as *stage 1* through *stage 4* and *REM sleep*—moving through the stages in cycles lasting about 90 minutes. Each of these sleep stages is associated with a unique pattern of brain waves, which you can see in Figure 2.

When people first go to sleep, they move from a waking state in which they are relaxed with their eyes closed into **stage 1 sleep,** which is characterized by relatively rapid, low-amplitude brain waves. This is actually a stage of transition between wakefulness and sleep and lasts only a few minutes. During stage 1, images sometimes appear, as if we were viewing still photos, although this is not true dreaming, which occurs later in the night.

As sleep becomes deeper, people enter **stage 2 sleep,** which makes up about half of the total sleep of those in their early 20s and is characterized by a slower, more regular wave pattern. However, there are also momentary interruptions of sharply pointed, spiky waves that are called, because of their configuration, *sleep spindles*. It becomes increasingly difficult to awaken a person from sleep as stage 2 progresses.

As people drift into **stage 3 sleep,** the brain waves become slower, with higher peaks and lower valleys in the wave pattern. By the time sleepers arrive at **stage 4 sleep,** the pattern is even slower and more regular, and people are least responsive to outside stimulation.

As you can see in Figure 3, stage 4 sleep is most likely to occur during the early part of the night. In the first half of the night, sleep is dominated by stages 3 and 4. The second half is characterized by stages 1 and 2—as well as a fifth stage during which dreams occur.

stage 1 sleep The state of transition between wakefulness and sleep, characterized by relatively rapid, low-amplitude brain waves.

stage 2 sleep A sleep deeper than that of stage 1, characterized by a slower, more regular wave pattern, along with momentary interruptions of "sleep spindles."

stage 3 sleep A sleep characterized by slow brain waves, with greater peaks and valleys in the wave pattern than in stage 2 sleep.

stage 4 sleep The deepest stage of sleep, during which we are least responsive to outside stimulation.

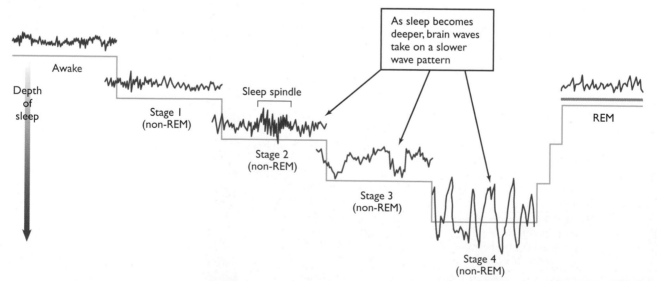

FIGURE 2 Brain-wave patterns (measured by an EEG apparatus) vary significantly during the different stages of sleep (Hobson, 1989). As sleep moves from stage 1 through stage 4, brain waves become slower. During REM sleep, however, the fast wave patterns are similar to relaxed wakefulness.

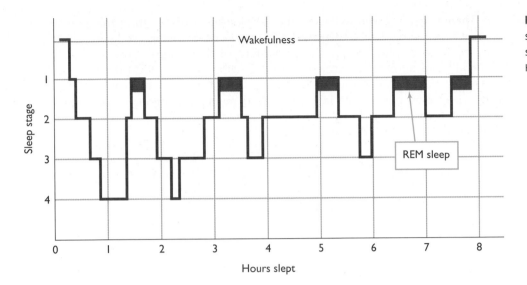

FIGURE 3 During the night, the typical sleeper passes through all four stages of sleep and several REM periods. (Source: Hartmann, 1967.)

REM Sleep: The Paradox of Sleep

Several times a night, when sleepers have cycled back to a shallower state of sleep, something curious happens. Their heart rate increases and becomes irregular, their blood pressure rises, and their breathing rate increases. Most characteristic of this period is the back-and-forth movement of their eyes, as if they were watching an action-filled movie. This period of sleep is called **rapid eye movement,** or **REM sleep,** and it contrasts with stages 1 through 4, which are collectively labeled *non-REM* (or *NREM*) sleep. REM sleep occupies a little more than 20% of adults' total sleeping time.

Paradoxically, while all this activity is occurring, the major muscles of the body appear to be paralyzed. In addition, and most important, REM sleep is usually accompanied by dreams, which—whether or not people remember them—are experienced by *everyone* during some part of their night's sleep. Although some dreaming occurs in non-REM stages of sleep, dreams are most likely to occur in the REM period, where they are the most vivid and easily remembered (Titone, 2002; Conduit, Crewther, & Coleman, 2004; Lu et al., 2006; Leclair-Visonneau et al., 2011).

rapid eye movement (REM) sleep Sleep occupying 20% of an adult's sleeping time, characterized by increased heart rate, blood pressure, and breathing rate; erections; eye movements; and the experience of dreaming.

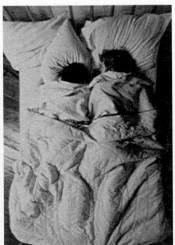

People progress through four distinct stages of sleep during a night's rest spread over cycles lasting about 90 minutes. REM sleep, which occupies only 20% of adults' sleeping time, occurs in stage 1 sleep. These photos, taken at different times of night, show the synchronized patterns of a couple accustomed to sleeping in the same bed.

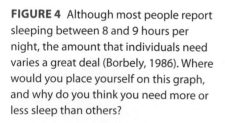

Study Alert

Differentiate the five stages of sleep (stage 1, stage 2, stage 3, stage 4, and REM sleep), which produce different brain-wave patterns.

There is good reason to believe that REM sleep plays a critical role in everyday human functioning. People deprived of REM sleep—by being awakened every time they begin to display the physiological signs of that stage—show a *rebound effect* when allowed to rest undisturbed. With this rebound effect, REM-deprived sleepers spend significantly more time in REM sleep than they normally would. In addition, REM sleep may play a role in learning and memory, allowing us to rethink and restore information and emotional experiences that we've had during the day (Nishida et al., 2009; Walker & van der Helm, 2009).

Why Do We Sleep, and How Much Sleep Is Necessary?

Sleep is a requirement for normal human functioning, although, surprisingly, we don't know exactly why. It is reasonable to expect that our bodies would require a tranquil "rest and relaxation" period to revitalize themselves, and experiments with rats show that total sleep deprivation results in death. But why?

One explanation, based on an evolutionary perspective, suggests that sleep permitted our ancestors to conserve energy at night, a time when food was relatively hard to come by. Consequently, they were better able to forage for food when the sun was up.

A second explanation for why we sleep is that sleep restores and replenishes our brains and bodies. For instance, the reduced activity of the brain during non-REM sleep may give neurons in the brain a chance to repair themselves. Furthermore, the onset of REM sleep stops the release of neurotransmitters called *monoamines* and so permits receptor cells to get some necessary rest and to increase their sensitivity during periods of wakefulness (McNamara, 2004; Steiger, 2007; Bub, Buckhalt, & El-Sheikh, 2011).

Finally, sleep may be essential, because it assists physical growth and brain development in children. For example, the release of growth hormones is associated with deep sleep (Peterfi et al., 2010).

Still, these explanations remain speculative, and there is no definitive answer as to why sleep is essential. Furthermore, scientists have been unable to establish just how much sleep is absolutely required. Most people today sleep between 7 and 8 hours each night, which is 3 hours a night *less* than people slept a hundred years ago. In addition, there is wide variability among individuals, with some people needing as little as 3 hours of sleep (see Figure 4).

Men and women sleep differently. Women typically fall asleep more quickly, sleep for longer periods and more deeply than men, and they get up fewer times in

FIGURE 4 Although most people report sleeping between 8 and 9 hours per night, the amount that individuals need varies a great deal (Borbely, 1986). Where would you place yourself on this graph, and why do you think you need more or less sleep than others?

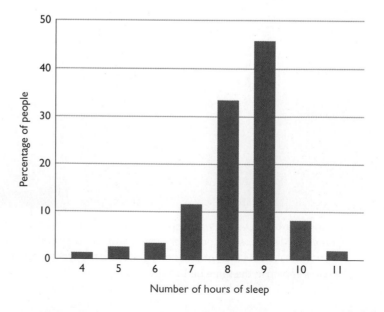

Number of hours of sleep

Neuroscience in Your Life: Why Are You Cranky? Your Brain Is Too Awake

FIGURE 5 One explanation about why we need sleep is that we need to restore and repair various systems in our brains. One such system is the one that regulates our emotions. In the MRI scan, the amygdala, which helps process emotions, shows less activation (seen in reds and oranges) when viewing emotional pictures when participants had enough sleep compared to when they were sleep deprived, suggesting that participants responded more emotionally when they had less sleep. (Source: Walker & van der Helm 2009.)

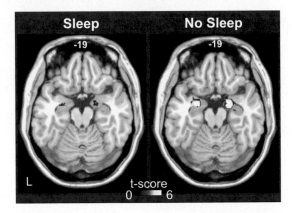

the night. On the other hand, men have fewer concerns about the amount of sleep they get than women, even though they get less sleep. Furthermore, sleep requirements vary over the course of a lifetime: As they age, people generally need less and less sleep (Monk et al., 2011; Petersen, 2011).

People who participate in sleep deprivation experiments, in which they are kept awake for stretches as long as 200 hours, show no lasting effects. It's no fun—they feel weary and irritable, can't concentrate, and show a loss of creativity, even after only minor deprivation. They also show a decline in logical reasoning ability. However, after being allowed to sleep normally, they bounce back quickly and are able to perform at predeprivation levels after just a few days (Babson et al., 2009; Mograss et al., 2009).

In short, as far as we know, most people suffer no permanent consequences of such temporary sleep deprivation. But—and this is an important but—a lack of sleep can make us feel edgy, slow our reaction time, and lower our performance on academic and physical tasks. In addition, we put ourselves, and others, at risk when we carry out routine activities, such as driving, when we're very sleepy (Philip et al., 2005; Anderson & Home, 2006; Morad et al., 2009). (Also see Figure 5 *Neuroscience in Your Life.*)

The Function and Meaning of Dreaming

I was being chased, and I couldn't get away. My attacker, wearing a mask, was carrying a long knife. He was gaining ground on me. I felt it was hopeless; I knew I was about to be killed.

If you have had a similar dream, you know how utterly convincing are the panic and fear that the events in the dream can bring about. *Nightmares*, unusually frightening dreams, occur fairly often. In one survey, almost half of a group of college

Dreams of Failure

It's the last day of final exams. You're packing up your dorm room and getting ready to head home for break when you suddenly remember that one last class that you haven't attended all semester long—the final exam is today! You frantically run through the halls of your college searching for the exam room, and when you finally find it, you slump into a seat and get handed an exam that looks as if it were printed in a foreign language. You don't know any of this stuff! A sinking feeling of dread rises from the pit of your stomach as it dawns on you that you're going to fail.

Then you wake up. Your heart is still beating frantically as you joyfully realize it was just a dream—a very common dream, in fact. Many of your classmates will report having a similar recurring dream about failing an exam. Even people who haven't picked up a #2 pencil in decades find that they occasionally return to a classroom in a similar state of panic during slumber. Why is this dream so pervasive, and what does it tell us about the function of dreams in general (Hoover, 2011)?

According to some experts, many of us share this kind of dream because test-taking is an anxiety-provoking event in our lives that starts at an early age and occurs regularly throughout our early life. Each occurrence challenges our confidence: Even the academically talented harbor a secret insecurity that perhaps success thus far had more to do with luck than ability and that one day that luck just might run out. With each exam we wonder, perhaps subconsciously, whether this will be that

The dreaded feeling of taking a test and not knowing any of the answers is one of the most common dreams related to anxiety.

day. These powerful experiences of uncertainty and fear become imprinted in our memories during a sensitive time and can linger for many years afterward (Barrett, 2007; Hoover, 2011).

Exam dreams may therefore represent a basic anxiety having to do with evaluation. This fear of evaluation becomes symbolically represented based on our earliest experiences with tests. Why should we dream about anxiety-provoking events? One explanation is that such dreams help us to cope with fears that we can't quite express consciously. In fact, some evidence suggests that dreaming of a traumatic event can help us to overcome the trauma. With exam dreams, the real fear usually isn't so much the exam itself as the possibility that we sabotaged ourselves by failing to prepare. So, ultimately, we are reminded of an important lesson: Don't neglect your responsibilities. Far better for us to learn that lesson in a dream than in real life (Barrett & Behbehani, 2003; Barrett, 2002, 2007)!

RETHINK

- Would people who don't particularly value academic performance be likely to have the exam dream? Why or why not?
- Do you think that people who make academia their career—people such as your professors—would be more or less likely than others to have the exam dream? Why do you think so?

students who kept records of their dreams over a 2-week period reported having at least one nightmare. This works out to some 24 nightmares per person each year, on average (Levin & Nielsen, 2009; Schredl et al., 2009; Schredl & Reinhard, 2011). (Also see *Applying Psychology in the 21st Century*.)

However, most of the 150,000 dreams the average person experiences by the age of 70 are much less dramatic. They typically encompass everyday events such as going to the supermarket, working at the office, and preparing a meal. Students dream about going to class; professors dream about lecturing. Dental patients dream of getting their teeth drilled; dentists dream of drilling the wrong tooth. The English have tea with the queen in their dreams; in the United States, people go to a bar with the president (Domhoff, 1996; Schredl & Piel, 2005; Taylor & Bryant, 2007). Figure 6 shows the most common themes found in people's dreams.

Thematic Event	Percentage of Dreams Reporting at Least One Event	
	Males	Females
Aggression	47%	44%
Friendliness	38	42
Sexuality	12	04
Misfortune	36	33
Success	15	08
Failure	15	10

FIGURE 6 Although dreams tend to be subjective to the person having them, common elements frequently occur in everyone's dreams. Why do you think so many common dreams are unpleasant and so few are pleasant? Do you think this tells us anything about the function of dreams? (Source: Domhoff & Schneider, 1998.)

But what, if anything, do all these dreams mean? Whether dreams have a specific significance and function is a question that scientists have considered for many years, and they have developed the three alternative theories we discuss below (and summarized in Figure 7).

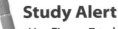

Study Alert

Use Figure 7 to learn the differences between the three main explanations of dreaming.

PSYCHOANALYTIC EXPLANATIONS OF DREAMS: DO DREAMS REPRESENT UNCONSCIOUS WISH FULFILLMENT?

Using psychoanalytic theory, Sigmund Freud viewed dreams as a guide to the unconscious (Freud, 1900). In his **unconscious wish fulfillment theory,** he proposed that dreams represent unconscious wishes that dreamers desire to see fulfilled. However, because these wishes are threatening to the dreamer's conscious awareness, the actual wishes—called the **latent content of dreams**—are disguised. The true subject and meaning of a dream, then, may have little to do with its apparent story line, which Freud called the **manifest content of dreams.**

To Freud, it was important to pierce the armor of a dream's manifest content to understand its true meaning. To do this, Freud tried to get people to discuss their dreams, associating symbols in the dreams with events in the past. He also suggested that certain common symbols with universal meanings appear in dreams. For example, to Freud, dreams in which a person is flying symbolize a wish for sexual intercourse. (See Figure 8 on page 140 for other common symbols.)

Many psychologists reject Freud's view that dreams typically represent unconscious wishes and that particular objects and events in a dream are symbolic. Rather,

unconscious wish fulfillment theory Sigmund Freud's theory that dreams represent unconscious wishes that dreamers desire to see fulfilled.

latent content of dreams According to Freud, the "disguised" meanings of dreams, hidden by more obvious subjects.

manifest content of dreams According to Freud, the apparent story line of dreams.

Theory	Basic Explanation	Meaning of Dreams	Is Meaning of Dream Disguised?
Unconscious wish fulfillment theory (Freud)	Psychoanalytical explanation where dreams represent unconscious wishes the dreamer wants to fulfill	Latent content reveals unconscious wishes	Yes, by manifest content of dreams
Dreams-for-survival theory	Evolutionary explanation where information relevant to daily survival is reconsidered and reprocessed	Clues to everyday concerns about survival	Not necessarily
Activation-synthesis theory	Neuroscience explanation where dreams are the result of random activation of various memories, which are tied together in a logical story line	Dream scenario that is constructed is related to dreamer's concerns	Not necessarily

FIGURE 7 Three theories of dreams. As researchers have yet to agree on the fundamental meaning of dreams, several theories about dreaming have emerged.

Symbol (Manifest Content of Dream)	Interpretation (Latent Content)
Climbing up a stairway, crossing a bridge, riding an elevator, flying in an airplane, walking down a long hallway, entering a room, train traveling through a tunnel	Sexual intercourse
Apples, peaches grapefruits	Breasts
Bullets, fire, snakes, sticks, umbrellas, guns, hoses, knives	Male sex organs
Ovens, boxes, tunnels, closets, caves, bottles, ship	Female sex organs

FIGURE 8 According to Freud, dreams contain common symbols with universal meanings.

they believe that the direct, overt action of a dream is the focal point of its meaning. For example, a dream in which we are walking down a long hallway to take an exam for which we haven't studied does not relate to unconscious, unacceptable wishes. Instead, it simply may mean that we are concerned about an impending test. Even more complex dreams can often be interpreted in terms of everyday concerns and stress (Picchioni et al., 2002; Cartwright, Agargum, & Kirkby, 2006).

Moreover, some dreams reflect events occurring in the dreamer's environment as he or she is sleeping. For example, sleeping participants in one experiment were sprayed with water while they were dreaming. Those unlucky volunteers reported more dreams involving water than did a comparison group of participants who were left to sleep undisturbed (Dement & Wolpert, 1958). Similarly, it is not unusual to wake up to find that the doorbell that was heard ringing in a dream is actually an alarm clock telling us it is time to get up.

However, PET brain scan research does lend a degree of support for the wish fulfillment view. For instance, the limbic and paralimbic regions of the brain, which are associated with emotion and motivation, are particularly active during REM sleep. At the same time, the association areas of the prefrontal cortex, which control logical analysis and attention, are inactive during REM sleep. The high activation of emotional and motivational centers of the brain during dreaming makes it more plausible that dreams may reflect unconscious wishes and instinctual needs, as Freud suggested (Braun et al., 1998; Occhionero, 2004; Wehrle et al., 2007).

EVOLUTIONARY EXPLANATIONS OF DREAMS: DREAMS-FOR-SURVIVAL THEORY

dreams-for-survival theory The theory suggesting that dreams permit information that is critical for our daily survival to be reconsidered and reprocessed during sleep.

According to the **dreams-for-survival theory**, which is based in the evolutionary perspective, dreams permit us to reconsider and reprocess during sleep information that is critical for our daily survival. Dreaming is considered an inheritance from our animal ancestors, whose small brains were unable to sift sufficient information during waking hours. Consequently, dreaming provided a mechanism that permitted the processing of information 24 hours a day.

In the dreams-for-survival theory, dreams represent concerns about our daily lives, illustrating our uncertainties, indecisions, ideas, and desires. Dreams are seen, then, as consistent with everyday living. Rather than being disguised wishes, as Freud suggested, they represent key concerns growing out of our daily experiences (Winson, 1990; Ross, 2006; Horton, 2011).

Research supports the dreams-for-survival theory, suggesting that certain dreams permit people to focus on and to consolidate memories, particularly dreams that pertain to "how-to-do-it" memories related to motor skills. For example, rats seem to dream about mazes that they learned to run through during the day, at least according to the patterns of brain activity that appear while they are sleeping (Stickgold et al., 2001; Kuriyama, Stickgold, & Walker, 2004; Smith, 2006).

A similar phenomenon appears to work in humans. For instance, in one experiment, participants learned a visual memory task late in the day. They were then sent to bed, but awakened at certain times during the night. When they were awakened at times that did not interrupt dreaming, their performance on the memory task typically improved the next day. But when they were awakened during rapid eye movement (REM) sleep—the stage of sleep when people dream—their performance declined. The implication is that dreaming, at least when it is uninterrupted, can play a role in helping us remember material to which we have been previously exposed (Karni et al., 1994; Marshall & Born, 2007; Nishida et al., 2009).

NEUROSCIENCE EXPLANATIONS OF DREAMS: ACTIVATION-SYNTHESIS THEORY

Using the neuroscience perspective, psychiatrist J. Allan Hobson has proposed the activation-synthesis theory of dreams. The **activation-synthesis theory** focuses on the random electrical energy that the brain produces during REM sleep, possibly as a result of changes in the production of particular neurotransmitters. This electrical energy randomly stimulates memories stored in the brain. Because we have a need to make sense of our world even while asleep, the brain takes these chaotic memories and weaves them into a logical story line, filling in the gaps to produce a rational scenario (Porte & Hobson, 1996; Hobson, 2005; Hangya et al., 2011).

Activation-synthesis theory has been refined by the *activation information modulation (AIM)* theory. According to AIM, dreams are initiated in the brain's pons, which sends random signals to the cortex. Areas of the cortex that are involved in particular waking behaviors are related to the content of dreams. For example, areas of the brain related to vision are involved in the visual aspects of the dream, while areas of the brain related to movement are involved in aspects of the dream related to motion (Hobson, 2007).

Activation-synthesis and AIM theories do not entirely reject the view that dreams reflect unconscious wishes. They suggest that the particular scenario a dreamer produces is not random but instead is a clue to the dreamer's fears, emotions, and concerns. Hence, what starts out as a random process culminates in something meaningful.

activation-synthesis theory Hobson's theory that the brain produces random electrical energy during REM sleep that stimulates memories stored in the brain.

Sleep Disturbances: Slumbering Problems

At one time or another, almost all of us have difficulty sleeping—a condition known as insomnia. It could be due to a particular situation, such as the breakup of a relationship, concern about a test score, or the loss of a job. Some cases of insomnia, however, have no obvious cause. Some people are simply unable to fall asleep easily, or they go to sleep readily but wake up frequently during the night. Insomnia is a problem that afflicts as many as one-third of all people. Women and older adults are more likely to suffer from insomnia, as well as people who are unusually thin or are depressed (Bains, 2006; Cooke & Ancoli-Israel, 2006; Henry et al., 2008).

Some people who *think* they have sleeping problems actually are mistaken. For example, researchers in sleep laboratories have found that some people who report being up all night actually fall asleep in 30 minutes and stay asleep all night. Furthermore, some people with insomnia accurately recall sounds that they heard while they were asleep, which gives them the impression that they were awake during the night (Semler & Harvey, 2005; Yapko, 2006). (Also see *PsychWork*.)

PsychTech
Surveys show that use of laptops, tablets, texting, or other technologies in the hour prior to going to bed is associated with sleeping problems.

PsychWork
SLEEP TECHNOLOGIST

Name: Brandon Liebig

Position: Sleep Technologist, Central Sleep Diagnostics, Northbrook, IL

Education: BFA, Studio Art, University of Nebraska at Omaha; Graduate of Accredited Sleep Technology Education Program, University of Massachusetts Memorial Hospital Sleep Center, Worcester, MA; Certified by the Board of Registered Polysomnographic Technologists

Although each of us spends the majority of our time sleeping, sleep—or rather a lack of it—is a state that is problematic for many people. For those seeking treatment for sleep disorders, sleep technologist Brandon Liebig is on the front lines, assisting in clinical assessments, helping to monitor and test patients, and participating in the development of treatment procedures.

As Liebig notes, "Patients seen in the sleep lab often have complicated medical backgrounds and health needs, and some may have cognitive limitations/disabilities or coexisting psychological conditions in addition to their sleep symptoms."

"Sleep technologists must recognize the particular needs of a patient and adjust their style of providing care to best suit the patient and promote the best possible outcomes, both for the patient's experience in the sleep lab and the data collected in research studies."

Liebig continues, "Often, patients may find it stressful, unfamiliar, and sometimes uncomfortable to sleep in a lab setting with the sensors and other equipment attached to their bodies. Sleep technologists use their knowledge of psychology to provide the patient with understanding, reassurance, respect, and patience."

Other sleep problems are less common than insomnia, although they are still widespread. For instance, some 20 million people suffer from sleep apnea. *Sleep apnea* is a condition in which a person has difficulty breathing while sleeping. The result is disturbed, fitful sleep, and a significant loss of REM sleep, as the person is constantly reawakened when the lack of oxygen becomes great enough to trigger a waking response. Some people with apnea wake as many as 500 times during the course of a night, although they may not even be aware that they have wakened. Not surprisingly, such disturbed sleep results in extreme fatigue the next day. Sleep apnea also may play a role in *sudden infant death syndrome (SIDS)*, a mysterious killer of seemingly normal infants who die while sleeping (Gami et al., 2005; Aloia, Smith, & Arnedt, 2007; Tippin, Sparks, & Rizzo, 2009; Arimoto et al., 2011).

Sleepwalking and sleeptalking are more common in children than adults, and they both occur during stage 4 of sleep.

Night terrors are sudden awakenings from non-REM sleep that are accompanied by extreme fear, panic, and strong physiological arousal. Usually occurring in stage 4 sleep, night terrors may be so frightening that a sleeper awakens with a shriek. Although night terrors initially produce great agitation, victims usually can get back to sleep fairly quickly. They are far less frequent than nightmares, and, unlike nightmares, they typically occur during slow-wave, non-REM sleep. They occur most frequently in children between the ages of 3 and 8 (Lowe, Humphreys, & Williams, 2007).

Narcolepsy is uncontrollable sleeping that occurs for short periods while a person is awake. No matter what the activity—holding a heated conversation, exercising, or driving—a narcoleptic will suddenly fall asleep. People with narcolepsy go directly from wakefulness to REM sleep, skipping the other stages. The causes of narcolepsy are not known, although there could be a genetic component, because narcolepsy runs in families (Mahmood & Black, 2005; Ervik, Abdelnoor, & Heier, 2006; Nishino, 2007; Billiard, 2008).

We know relatively little about sleeptalking and sleepwalking, two sleep disturbances that are usually harmless. Both occur during stage 4 sleep and are more common in children than in adults. Sleeptalkers and sleepwalkers usually have a vague consciousness of the world around them, and a sleepwalker may be able to walk with agility around obstructions in a crowded room. Unless a sleepwalker wanders into a dangerous environment, sleepwalking typically poses little risk. And the common idea that it's dangerous to wake a sleepwalker? It's just superstition (Baruss, 2003; Guilleminault et al., 2005; Lee-Chiong, 2006; Licis et al., 2011).

Circadian Rhythms: Life Cycles

The fact that we cycle back and forth between wakefulness and sleep is one example of the body's circadian rhythms. **Circadian rhythms** (from the Latin *circa diem*, or "about a day") are biological processes that occur regularly on approximately a 24-hour cycle. Sleeping and waking, for instance, occur naturally to the beat of an internal pacemaker that works on a cycle of about 24 hours. Several other bodily functions, such as body temperature, hormone production, and blood pressure, also follow circadian rhythms (Saper et al., 2005; Beersma & Gordijn, 2007; Blatter & Cajochen, 2007).

Circadian cycles are complex, and they involve a variety of behaviors. For instance, sleepiness occurs not just in the evening but throughout the day in regular patterns, with most of us getting drowsy in mid-afternoon—regardless of whether we have eaten a heavy lunch. By making an afternoon siesta part of their everyday habit, people in several cultures take advantage of the body's natural inclination to sleep at this time (Wright, 2002; Takahashi et al., 2004; Reilly & Waterhouse, 2007).

The brain's *suprachiasmatic nucleus (SCN)* controls circadian rhythms. However, the relative amount of light and darkness, which varies with the seasons of the year, also plays a role in regulating circadian rhythms. In fact, some people experience *seasonal affective disorder*, a form of severe depression in which feelings of despair and hopelessness increase during the winter and lift during the rest of the year. The disorder appears to be a result of the brevity and gloom of winter days. Daily exposure to bright lights is sometimes sufficient to improve the mood of those with this disorder (Golden et al., 2005; Rohan, Roecklein, & Tierney Lindsey, 2007; Kasof, 2009; Monteleone, Martiadis, & Maj, 2011).

People's moods also seem to follow regular patterns. By examining more than 500 million tweets using publically available Twitter records, a team of psychologists found that words with positive associations (fantastic, super) and negative associations (afraid, mad) followed regular patterns. Across the globe and among different cultures, people were happier in the morning, less so during the day, with a rebound in the evening. Moods are also happier on certain days of the week: we're happier on weekends and holidays. Finally, positive emotions increase from late December to late June as the days get longer, and negative emotions increase as days get shorter (Golder & Macy, 2011; see Figure 9).

Bright lights may counter some of the symptoms of seasonal affective disorder, which occurs during the winter.

circadian rhythms Biological processes that occur regularly on approximately a 24-hour cycle.

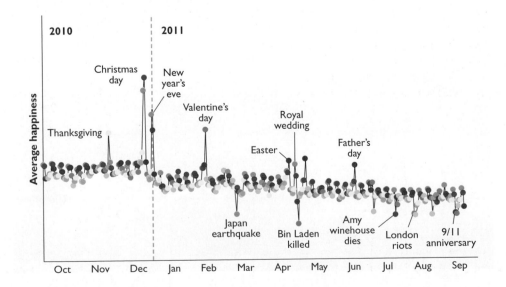

FIGURE 9 A year of tweets shows that Fridays (orange dots), Saturdays (red dots), and Sundays (dark blue dots) are happier than weekdays. The happiest days are holidays, and the unhappiest days are associated with bad news. (Source: Adapted from Peter Sheridan Dodds and Christopher M. Danforth/ University of Vermont, from article: Miller, G. (2011, September 30). Social Scientists Wade into the Tweet Stream, *Science, 333*, 1814–1815.)

Daydreams: Dreams Without Sleep

It is the stuff of magic: Our past mistakes can be wiped out and the future filled with noteworthy accomplishments. Fame, happiness, and wealth can be ours. In the next moment, though, the most horrible tragedies can occur, leaving us devastated, alone, and penniless.

daydreams Fantasies that people construct while awake.

The source of these scenarios is **daydreams,** fantasies that people construct while awake. Unlike dreaming that occurs during sleep, daydreams are more under people's control. Therefore, their content is often more closely related to immediate events in the environment than is the content of the dreams that occur during sleep. Although they may include sexual content, daydreams also pertain to other activities or events that are relevant to a person's life.

Daydreams are a typical part of waking consciousness, even though our awareness of the environment around us declines while we are daydreaming. People vary considerably in the amount of daydreaming they do. For example, around 2% to 4% of the population spend at least half their free time fantasizing. Although most people daydream much less frequently, almost everyone fantasizes to some degree. Studies that ask people to identify what they are doing at random times during the day have shown that they are daydreaming about 10% of the time (Lynn et al., 1996; Holler, 2006; Singer, 2006).

The brain is surprisingly active during daydreaming. For example, several areas of the brain that are associated with complex problem solving become activated during daydreaming. In fact, daydreaming may be the only time these areas are activated simultaneously, suggesting that daydreaming may lead to insights about problems that we are grappling with (Fleck et al., 2008; Kounios et al., 2008).

Furthermore, some scientists see a link between daydreaming and dreams during sleep. The content of daydreams and dreams show many parallels, and the brain areas and processes involved in daydreaming and dreams during sleep are related (Domhoff, 2011).

Daydreams are fantasies that people construct while they are awake. What are the similarities and differences between daydreams and night dreams?

BECOMING AN INFORMED CONSUMER of Psychology

Sleeping Better

Do you have trouble sleeping? You're not alone—70 million people in the United States have sleep problems. For those of us who spend hours tossing and turning in bed, psychologists studying sleep disturbances have a number of suggestions for overcoming insomnia. Here are some ideas (Benca, 2005; Finley & Cowley, 2005; Buysse et al., 2011):

- *Exercise during the day (at least 6 hours before bedtime) and avoid naps.* Not surprisingly, it helps to be tired before going to sleep! Moreover, learning systematic relaxation techniques and biofeedback can help you unwind from the day's stresses and tensions.
- *Choose a regular bedtime and stick to it.* Adhering to a habitual schedule helps your internal timing mechanisms regulate your body more effectively.
- *Avoid drinks with caffeine after lunch.* The effects of beverages such as coffee, tea, and some soft drinks can linger for as long as 8 to 12 hours after they are consumed.
- *Drink a glass of warm milk at bedtime.* Your grandparents were right when they dispensed this advice: Milk contains the chemical tryptophan, which helps people fall asleep.
- *Avoid sleeping pills.* Even though 25% of U.S. adults report having taken medication for sleep in the previous year, in the long run sleep medications can do more harm than good, because they disrupt the normal sleep cycle.
- *Try* not *to sleep.* This approach works because people often have difficulty falling asleep because they are trying so hard. A better strategy is to go to bed only when you feel tired. If you don't get to sleep within 10 minutes, leave the bedroom and do something else, returning to bed only when you feel sleepy. Continue this process all night if necessary. But get up at your usual hour in the morning, and don't take any naps during the day. After three or four weeks, most people become conditioned to associate their beds with sleep—and fall asleep rapidly at night (Sloan et al., 1993; Ubell, 1993; Smith, 2001).

For long-term problems with sleep, you might consider visiting a sleep disorders center. For information on accredited clinics, consult the American Academy of Sleep Medicine at www.aasmnet.org.

RECAP/EVALUATE/RETHINK

RECAP

LO 12-1 What are the different states of consciousness?

- Consciousness is a person's awareness of the sensations, thoughts, and feelings at a given moment. Waking consciousness can vary from more active to more passive states. (p. 132)
- Altered states of consciousness include naturally occurring sleep and dreaming, as well as hypnotic and drug-induced states. (p. 132)

LO 12-2 What happens when we sleep, and what are the meaning and function of dreams?

- The brain is active throughout the night, and sleep proceeds through a series of stages identified by unique patterns of brain waves. (p. 133)

- REM (rapid eye movement) sleep is characterized by an increase in heart rate, a rise in blood pressure, an increase in the rate of breathing, and, in males, erections. Dreams most often occur during this stage. (p. 135)
- According to Freud's psychoanalytic approach, dreams have both a manifest content (an apparent story line) and a latent content (a true meaning). He suggested that the latent content provides a guide to a dreamer's unconscious, revealing unfulfilled wishes or desires. (p. 139)
- The dreams-for-survival theory, grounded in an evolutionary perspective, suggests that information relevant to daily survival is reconsidered and reprocessed in dreams. Taking a neuroscience approach, the activation-synthesis theory proposes that dreams are a result of random electrical energy that stimulates different memories, which then are woven into a coherent story line. (p. 140)

LO 14-3 What are the major sleep disorders, and how can they be treated?

- Insomnia is a sleep disorder characterized by difficulty sleeping. Sleep apnea is a condition in which people have difficulty sleeping and breathing at the same time. People with narcolepsy have an uncontrollable urge to sleep. Sleepwalking and sleeptalking are relatively harmless. (pp. 141, 142)

LO 14-4 How much do we daydream?

- Wide individual differences exist in the amount of time devoted to daydreaming. Almost everyone daydreams or fantasizes to some degree. (p. 144)

EVALUATE

1. _____ is the term used to describe our understanding of the world external to us, as well as our own internal world.
2. A great deal of neural activity goes on during sleep. True or false?
3. Dreams most often occur in _____ sleep.
4. _____ _____ are internal bodily processes that occur on a daily cycle.
5. Freud's theory of unconscious _____ _____ states that the actual wishes an individual expresses in dreams are disguised, because they are threatening to the person's conscious awareness.

6. Match the theory of dreaming with its definition.
   1. activation-synthesis theory
   2. dreams-for-survival theory
   3. dreams as wish fulfillment
   a. Dreams permit important information to be reprocessed during sleep.
   b. The manifest content of dreams disguises the latent content of the dreams.
   c. Electrical energy stimulates random memories, which are woven together to produce dreams.

RETHINK

1. Suppose that a new "miracle pill" allows a person to function with only 1 hour of sleep per night. However, because a night's sleep is so short, a person who takes the pill will never dream again. Knowing what you do about the functions of sleep and dreaming, what would be some advantages and drawbacks of such a pill from a personal standpoint? Would you take such a pill?
2. *From the perspective of an educator:* How might you use the findings in sleep research to maximize student learning?

Answers to Evaluate Questions

1. Consciousness; 2. true; 3. REM; 4. Circadian rhythms; 5. wish fulfillment; 6. 1-c, 2-a, 3-b

KEY TERMS

consciousness p. 132
stage 1 sleep p. 133
stage 2 sleep p. 133
stage 3 sleep p. 133
stage 4 sleep p. 133

rapid eye movement (REM) sleep p. 135
unconscious wish fulfillment theory p. 139
latent content of dreams p. 139

manifest content of dreams p. 139
dreams-for-survival theory p. 140

activation-synthesis theory p. 141
circadian rhythms p. 143
daydreams p. 144

Drug Use: The Highs and Lows of Consciousness

Learning Outcome

LO 14-1 What are the major classifications of drugs, and what are their effects?

John Brodhead began to drink heavily when he was in 6th grade.

psychoactive drugs Drugs that influence a person's emotions, perceptions, and behavior.

addictive drugs Drugs that produce a biological or psychological dependence in the user so that withdrawal from them leads to a craving for the drug that, in some cases, may be nearly irresistible.

John Brodhead's bio reads like a script for an episode of VH1's *Behind the Music*. A young rebel from the New Jersey suburbs falls in with a fast crowd, gets hooked on parties and booze, and, with intensive counseling and a bit of tough love, manages to get his life back together. What makes his story different? Just one thing: his age. John is 13 (Rogers, 2002).

John Brodhead was lucky. Now in recovery, John had begun to drink when he was in the 6th grade. He is not alone: The number of teens who start drinking by the 8th grade has increased by almost a third since the 1970s, even though alcohol consumption overall has stayed fairly steady among the general population.

Drugs of one sort or another are a part of almost everyone's life. From infancy on, most people take vitamins, aspirin, cold-relief medicine, and the like, and surveys find that 80% of adults in the United States have taken an over-the-counter pain reliever in the last 6 months. However, these drugs rarely produce an altered state of consciousness (Dortch, 1996).

In contrast, some substances, known as psychoactive drugs, lead to an altered state of consciousness. **Psychoactive drugs** influence a person's emotions, perceptions, and behavior. Yet even this category of drugs is common in most of our lives. If you have ever had a cup of coffee or sipped a beer, you have taken a psychoactive drug. A large number of individuals have used more potent—and more dangerous—psychoactive drugs than coffee and beer (see Figure 1); for instance, surveys find that 41% of high school seniors have used an illegal drug in the last year. In addition, 30% report having been drunk on alcohol. The figures for the adult population are even higher (Johnston et al., 2010).

Of course, drugs vary widely in the effects they have on users, in part because they affect the nervous system in very different ways. Some drugs alter the limbic system, and others affect the operation of specific neurotransmitters across the synapses of neurons. For example, some drugs block or enhance the release of neurotransmitters, others block the receipt or the removal of a neurotransmitter, and still others mimic the effects of a particular neurotransmitter (see Figure 2.)

Addictive drugs produce a physiological or psychological dependence (or both) in the user, and withdrawal from them leads to a craving for the drug that, in some cases, may be nearly irresistible. In *physiological dependence*, the body becomes so accustomed to functioning in the presence of a drug that it cannot function without it. In *psychological dependence*, people believe that they need the drug to respond to the stresses of daily living. Although we generally associate addiction with drugs such as heroin, everyday sorts of drugs, such as caffeine (found in coffee) and nicotine (found in cigarettes), have addictive aspects as well (Li, Volkow, & Baler, 2007).

We know surprisingly little about the underlying causes of addiction. One of the problems in identifying those causes is that different drugs (such as alcohol and cocaine) affect the brain in very different ways—yet they may be equally addicting. Furthermore, it takes longer to become addicted to some drugs than to others, even though the ultimate consequences of addiction may be equally grave (Crombag & Robinson, 2004; Nestler & Malenka, 2004; Smart, 2007).

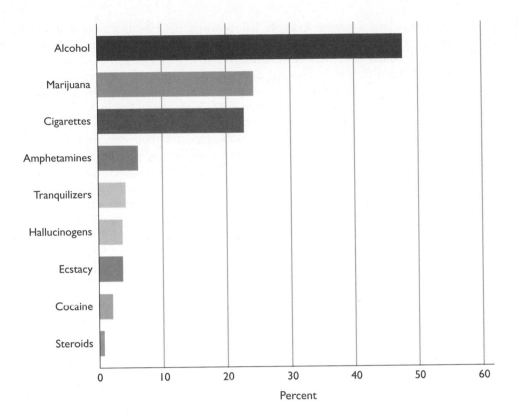

FIGURE 1 How many teenagers use drugs? The results of the most recent comprehensive survey of 14,000 high school seniors across the United States show the percentage of respondents who have used various substances for nonmedical purposes at least once. Can you think of any reasons why teenagers—as opposed to older people—might be particularly likely to use drugs? (Source: Johnston et al., 2011.)

Why do people take drugs in the first place? There are many reasons, ranging from the perceived pleasure of the experience itself, to the escape that a drug-induced high affords from the everyday pressures of life, to an attempt to achieve a religious or spiritual state. However, other factors having little to do with the nature of the experience itself also lead people to try drugs (McDowell & Spitz, 1999; Korcha et al., 2011).

For instance, the highly publicized drug use of role models such as movie stars and professional athletes, the easy availability of some illegal drugs, and peer pressure all play a role in the decision to use drugs. In some cases, the motive is simply the thrill of trying something new. Finally, genetic factors may predispose some people to be more susceptible to drugs and to become addicted to them. Regardless

PsychTech

Drugs are not the only source of addiction. Increasing evidence suggests that people can develop psychological dependence to the use of technologies, such as social networking sites like Facebook or e-mail.

FIGURE 2 Different drugs affect different parts of the nervous system and brain, and each drug functions in one of these specific ways.

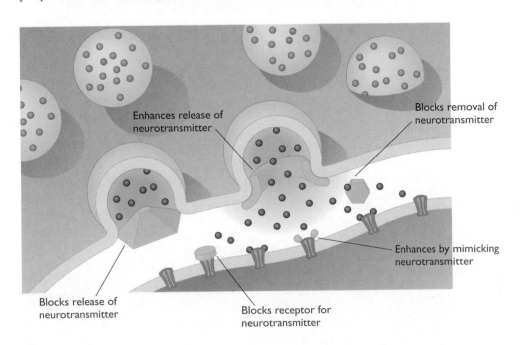

Enhances release of neurotransmitter

Blocks removal of neurotransmitter

Enhances by mimicking neurotransmitter

Blocks release of neurotransmitter

Blocks receptor for neurotransmitter

Study Alert

Use Figure 2 to learn the different ways that drugs produce their effects on a neurological level.

of the forces that lead a person to begin using drugs, drug addiction is among the most difficult of all behaviors to modify, even with extensive treatment (Lemonick, 2000; Mosher & Akins, 2007; Ray & Hutchison, 2007).

Because of the difficulty in treating drug problems, there is little disagreement that the best hope for dealing with the overall societal problem of substance abuse is to prevent people from becoming involved with drugs in the first place. However, there is little accord on how to accomplish this goal.

Even drug reduction programs widely publicized for their effectiveness—such as D.A.R.E. (Drug Abuse Resistance Education)—are of questionable effectiveness. Used in more than 80% of school districts in the United States, D.A.R.E. consists of a series of 17 lessons on the dangers of drugs, alcohol, and gangs taught to 5th- and 6th-graders by a police officer. The program is highly popular with school officials, parents, and politicians. The problem? Repeated careful evaluations have been unable to demonstrate that the D.A.R.E. program is effective in reducing drug use over the long term. In fact, one study even showed that D.A.R.E. graduates were more likely to use marijuana than was a comparison group of nongraduates (West & O'Neal, 2004; Des Jarlais et al., 2006; Lucas, 2008; Vincus et al., 2010).

Stimulants: Drug Highs

It's 1:00 a.m., and you still haven't finished reading the last chapter of the text on which you will be tested later in the morning. Feeling exhausted, you turn to the one thing that may help you stay awake for the next 2 hours: a cup of strong black coffee.

If you have ever found yourself in such a position, you have resorted to a major *stimulant*, caffeine, to stay awake. *Caffeine* is one of a number of **stimulants**, drugs whose effect on the central nervous system causes a rise in heart rate, blood pressure, and muscular tension. Caffeine is present not only in coffee; it is an important ingredient in tea, soft drinks, and chocolate as well (see Figure 3).

stimulants Drugs that have an arousal effect on the central nervous system, causing a rise in heart rate, blood pressure, and muscular tension.

FIGURE 3 How much caffeine do you consume? This chart shows the range of caffeine found in common foods, drinks, and legal drugs. (Source: Center for Science in the Public Interest, 2007.)

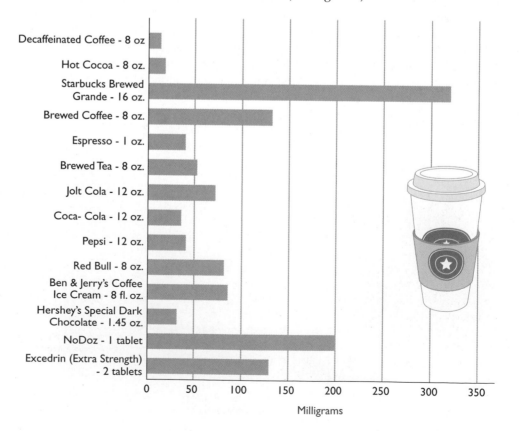

Caffeine produces several reactions. The major behavioral effects are an increase in attentiveness and a decrease in reaction time. Caffeine can also bring about an improvement in mood, most likely by mimicking the effects of a natural brain chemical, adenosine. Too much caffeine, however, can result in nervousness and insomnia. People can build up a biological dependence on the drug. Regular users who suddenly stop drinking coffee may experience headaches or depression. Many people who drink large amounts of coffee on weekdays have headaches on weekends because of the sudden drop in the amount of caffeine they are consuming (Kendler, Myers, & Gardner, 2006; Hammond & Gold, 2008; Clayton & Lundberg-Love, 2009; Kennedy & Haskell, 2011).

Nicotine, found in cigarettes, is another common stimulant. The soothing effects of nicotine help explain why cigarette smoking is addictive. Smokers develop a dependence on nicotine, and those who suddenly stop smoking develop a strong craving for the drug. This is not surprising: Nicotine activates neural mechanisms similar to those activated by cocaine, which, as we see below, is also highly addictive (Haberstick et al., 2007; Ray et al., 2008).

AMPHETAMINES

Amphetamines such as dexedrine and benzedrine, popularly known as speed, are strong stimulants. In small quantities, amphetamines—which stimulate the central nervous system—bring about a sense of energy and alertness, talkativeness, heightened confidence, and a mood "high." They increase concentration and reduce fatigue. Amphetamines also cause a loss of appetite, increased anxiety, and irritability. When taken over long periods of time, amphetamines can cause feelings of being persecuted by others, as well as a general sense of suspiciousness. People taking amphetamines may lose interest in sex. If taken in too large a quantity, amphetamines overstimulate the central nervous system to such an extent that convulsions and death can occur (Carhart-Harris, 2007).

Methamphetamine is a white, crystalline drug that U.S. police now say is the most dangerous street drug. "Meth" is highly addictive and relatively cheap, and it produces a strong, lingering high. It has made addicts of people across the social spectrum, ranging from soccer moms to urban professionals to poverty-stricken inner-city residents. After becoming addicted, users take it more and more frequently and in increasing doses. Long-term use of the drug can lead to brain damage (Sharma, Sjoquist, & Ali, 2007; Halkitis, 2009; Kish et al., 2009).

More than 1.5 million people in the United States are regular methamphetamine users. Because it can be made from nonprescription cold pills, retailers such as Walmart and Target have removed these medications from their shelves. Illicit labs devoted to the manufacture of methamphetamine have sprung up in many locations around the United States (Jefferson, 2005). Figure 4 on page 156 provides a summary of the effects of amphetamines and other illegal drugs.

COCAINE

Although its use has declined over the last decade, the stimulant cocaine and its derivative, crack, still represent a serious concern. Cocaine is inhaled or "snorted" through the nose, smoked, or injected directly into the bloodstream. It is rapidly absorbed into the body and takes effect almost immediately.

When used in relatively small quantities, cocaine produces feelings of profound psychological well-being, increased confidence, and alertness. Cocaine produces this "high" through the neurotransmitter dopamine. Dopamine is one of the chemicals that transmit between neurons messages that are related to ordinary feelings of pleasure. Normally when dopamine is released, excess amounts of the

Drugs	Street Name	Effects	Withdrawal Symptoms	Adverse/Overdose Reactions
Stimulants				
Amphetamines		Increased confidence, mood elevation, sense of energy and alertness, decreased appetite, anxiety, irritability, insomnia, transient drowsiness, delayed orgasm	Apathy, general fatigue, prolonged sleep, depression, disorientation, suicidal thoughts, agitated motor activity, irritability, bizarre dreams	Elevated blood pressure, increase in body temperature, face picking, suspiciousness, bizarre and repetitious behavior, vivid hallucinations, convulsions, possible death
Benzedrine	Speed			
Dexedrine	Speed			
Cocaine	Coke, blow, snow, lady, crack			
Depressants				
Alcohol	Booze	Anxiety reduction, impulsiveness, dramatic mood swings, bizarre thoughts, suicidal behavior, slurred speech, disorientation, slowed mental and physical functioning, limited attention span	Weakness, restlessness, nausea and vomiting, headaches, nightmares, irritability, depression, acute anxiety, hallucinations, seizures, possible death	Confusion, decreased response to pain, shallow respiration, dilated pupils, weak and rapid pulse, coma, possible death
Barbiturates				
Nembutal	Yellowjackets			
Seconal	Reds			
Phenobarbital				
Rohypnol	Roofies, rope, "date-rape drug"	Muscle relaxation, amnesia, sleep	Seizures	Seizures, coma, incapacitation, inability to resist sexual assault
Narcotics				
Heroin	H, hombre, junk, smack, dope, crap, horse	Anxiety and pain reduction, apathy, difficulty in concentration, slowed speech, decreased physical activity, drooling, itching, euphoria, nausea	Anxiety, vomiting, sneezing, diarrhea, lower back pain, watery eyes, runny nose, yawning, irritability, tremors, panic, chills and sweating, cramps	Depressed levels of consciousness, low blood pressure, rapid heart rate, shallow breathing, convulsions, coma, possible death
Morphine	Drugstore dope, cube, first line, mud			

FIGURE 4 Drugs and their effects. A comprehensive breakdown of effects of the most commonly used drugs.

Study Alert

Figure 4, which summarizes the different categories of drugs (stimulants, depressants, narcotics, and hallucinogens), will help you learn the effects of particular drugs.

neurotransmitter are reabsorbed by the releasing neuron. However, when cocaine enters the brain, it blocks reabsorption of leftover dopamine. As a result, the brain is flooded with dopamine-produced pleasurable sensations (Redish, 2004; Jarlais, Arasteh, & Perlis, 2007).

However, there is a steep price to be paid for the pleasurable effects of cocaine. The brain may become permanently rewired, triggering a psychological and physical addiction in which users grow obsessed with obtaining the drug. Over time, users deteriorate mentally and physically. In extreme cases, cocaine can cause hallucinations—a common one is of insects crawling over one's body. Ultimately, an overdose of cocaine can lead to death (George & Moselhy, 2005; Paulozzi, 2006; Little et al., 2009).

Almost 2.5 million people in the United States are occasional cocaine users, and as many as 1.8 million people use the drug regularly. Given the strength of cocaine, withdrawal from the drug is difficult. Although the use of cocaine among high school students has declined in recent years, the drug still represents a major problem (Johnston et al., 2009).

Drugs	Street Name	Effects	Withdrawal Symptoms	Adverse/Overdose Reactions
Oxycodone	Oxy, OC, Percs	Pain reduction, shallow breathing, slow heartbeat, seizure (convulsions); cold, clammy skin; confusion	Sweating, chills, abdominal cramps, insomnia, vomiting, diarrhea	Extreme drowsiness, muscle weakness, confusion, cold and clammy skin, pinpoint pupils, shallow breathing, slow heart rate, fainting, or coma
Hallucinogens				

Cannabis
  Marijuana
  Hashish
  Hash oil
	Bhang, kif, ganja, dope, grass, pot, hemp, joint, weed, bone, Mary Jane, reefer	Euphoria, relaxed inhibitions, increased appetite, disoriented behavior	Hyperactivity, insomnia, decreased appetite, anxiety	Severe reactions rare but include panic, paranoia, fatigue, bizarre and dangerous behavior, decreased testosterone over long-term; immune-system effects

MDMA	Ecstasy	Heightened sense of oneself and insight, feelings of peace, empathy, energy	Depression, anxiety, sleeplessness	Increase in body temperature, memory difficulties
LSD	Acid, quasey, microdot, white lightning	Heightened aesthetic responses; vision and depth distortion; heightened sensitivity to faces and gestures; magnified feelings; paranoia, panic, euphoria	Not reported	Nausea and chills; increased pulse, temperature, and blood pressure; slow, deep breathing; loss of appetite; insomnia; bizarre, dangerous behavior
Steroids				
	Rhoids, juice	Aggression, depression, acne, mood swings, masculine traits in women and feminine traits in men	Symptoms can mimic other medical problems and include weakness, fatigue, decreased appetite, weight loss; women may note menstrual changes	Long-term, high-dose effects of steroid use are largely unknown, but can lead to swelling and weight gain

Depressants: Drug Lows

In contrast to the initial effect of stimulants, which is an increase in arousal of the central nervous system, the effect of **depressants** is to impede the nervous system by causing neurons to fire more slowly. Small doses result in at least temporary feelings of *intoxication*—drunkenness—along with a sense of euphoria and joy. When large amounts are taken, however, speech becomes slurred and muscle control becomes disjointed, making motion difficult. Ultimately, heavy users may lose consciousness entirely.

depressants Drugs that slow down the nervous system.

ALCOHOL

The most common depressant is alcohol, which is used by more people than is any other drug. Based on liquor sales, the average person over the age of 14 drinks 2½ gallons of pure alcohol over the course of a year. This works out to more than

FIGURE 5 Drinking habits of college students (Wechsler et al., 2003). For men, binge drinking was defined as consuming five or more drinks in one sitting; for women, the total was four or more.

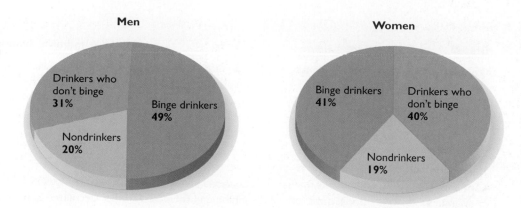

200 drinks per person. Although alcohol consumption has declined steadily over the last decade, surveys show that more than three-fourths of college students indicate that they have had a drink within the last 30 days (Jung, 2002; Midanik, Tam, & Weisner, 2007).

One of the more disturbing trends is the high frequency of binge drinking among college students. For men, *binge drinking* is defined as having five or more drinks in one sitting; for women, who generally weigh less than men and whose bodies absorb alcohol less efficiently, binge drinking is defined as having four or more drinks at one sitting (Mokdad, Brewer, & Naimi, 2007; Rooke & Hine, 2011).

Around 50% of male college students and 40% of female college students say they engaged in binge drinking at least once within the previous 2 weeks (see Figure 5). Some 17% of female students and 31% of male students admitted drinking on 10 or more occasions during the previous 30 days. Furthermore, even light drinkers were affected by the high rate of alcohol use: Two-thirds of lighter drinkers said that they had had their studying or sleep disturbed by drunk students, and a quarter of the women said they had been the target of an unwanted sexual advance by a drunk class-mate (Wechsler et al., 2000, 2002; Read et al., 2008; Grucza, Norberg, & Bierut, 2009).

Women are typically somewhat lighter drinkers than men—although the gap between the sexes is narrowing for older women and has closed completely for teenagers. Women are more susceptible to the effects of alcohol, and alcohol abuse may harm the brains of women more than men (Wuethrich, 2001; Mann et al., 2005; Mancinelli, Binetti, & Ceccanti, 2007; Chavez et al., 2011).

There are also cultural and ethnic differences in alcohol consumption. For example, teenagers in Europe drink more than teenagers in the United States do. Furthermore, people of East Asian backgrounds who live in the United States tend to drink

The effects of alcohol vary significantly, depending on who is drinking it and the setting in which people drink. If alcohol were a newly discovered drug, do you think its sale would be legal?

significantly less than do Caucasians and African Americans, and their incidence of alcohol-related problems is lower. It may be that physical reactions to drinking, which may include sweating, a quickened heartbeat, and flushing, are more unpleasant for East Asians than for other groups (Garcia-Andrade, Wall, & Ehlers, 1997; Garlow, Purselle, & Heninger, 2007; Kantrowitz & Underwood, 2007).

Although alcohol is a depressant, most people claim that it increases their sense of sociability and well-being. The discrepancy between the actual and the perceived effects of alcohol lies in the initial effects it produces in the majority of individuals who use it: release of tension and stress, feelings of happiness, and loss of inhibitions.

As the dose of alcohol increases, however, the depressive effects become more pronounced (see Figure 6). People may feel emotionally and physically unstable. They also show poor judgment and may act aggressively. Moreover, memory is impaired, brain processing of spatial information is diminished, and speech becomes slurred and incoherent. Eventually they may fall into a stupor and pass out. If they drink enough alcohol in a short time, they may die of alcohol poisoning (Zeigler et al., 2005; Thatcher & Clark, 2006).

Number of drinks consumed in 2 hours		Alcohol in blood (percentage)	Typical effects
	2	0.05	Judgment, thought, and restraint weakened; tension released, giving carefree sensation
	3	0.08	Tensions and inhibitions of everyday life lessened; cheerfulness
	4	0.10	Voluntary motor action affected, making hand and arm movements, walk, and speech clumsy
	7	0.20	Severe impairment—staggering, loud, incoherent, emotionally unstable, 100 times greater traffic risk; exuberance and aggressive inclinations magnified
	9	0.30	Deeper areas of brain affected, with stimulus-response and understanding confused; stuporous; blurred vision
	12	0.40	Incapable of voluntary action; sleepy, difficult to arouse; equivalent of surgical anesthesia
	15	0.50	Comatose; centers controlling breathing and heartbeat anesthetized; death increasingly probable

FIGURE 6 The effects of alcohol. The quantities represent only rough benchmarks; the effects vary significantly depending on an individual's weight, height, recent food intake, genetic factors, and even psychological state.

Note: A drink refers to a typical 12-ounce bottle of beer, a 1.5-ounce shot of hard liquor, or a 5-ounce glass of wine.

Even legal drugs, when used improperly, lead to addiction.

Although most people fall into the category of casual users, 14 million people in the United States—1 in every 13 adults—have a drinking problem. *Alcoholics*, people with alcohol-abuse problems, come to rely on alcohol and continue to drink even though it causes serious difficulties. In addition, they become increasingly immune to the effects of alcohol. Consequently, alcoholics must drink progressively more to experience the initial positive feelings that alcohol produces.

In some cases of alcoholism, people must drink constantly in order to feel well enough to function in their daily lives. In other cases, though, people drink inconsistently but occasionally go on binges in which they consume large quantities of alcohol.

It is not clear why certain people become alcoholics and develop a tolerance for alcohol, whereas others do not. There may be a genetic cause, although the question of whether there is a specific inherited gene that produces alcoholism is controversial. What is clear is that the chances of becoming an alcoholic are considerably higher if alcoholics are present in earlier generations of a person's family. However, not all alcoholics have close relatives who are alcoholics. In these cases, environmental stressors are suspected of playing a larger role (Nurnberger & Bierut, 2007; Zimmermann, Blomeyer, & Laucht, 2007; Gizer et al., 2011).

BARBITURATES

Barbiturates, which include drugs such as Nembutal, Seconal, and phenobarbital, are another form of depressant. Frequently prescribed by physicians to induce sleep or reduce stress, barbiturates produce a sense of relaxation. Yet they, too, are psychologically and physically addictive and, when combined with alcohol, can be deadly, since such a combination relaxes the muscles of the diaphragm to such an extent that the user stops breathing.

ROHYPNOL

Rohypnol is sometimes called the "date rape drug," because, when it is mixed with alcohol, it can prevent victims from resisting sexual assault. Sometimes people who are unknowingly given the drug are so incapacitated that they have no memory of the assault.

Narcotics: Relieving Pain and Anxiety

narcotics Drugs that increase relaxation and relieve pain and anxiety.

Narcotics are drugs that increase relaxation and relieve pain and anxiety. Two of the most powerful narcotics, *morphine* and *heroin*, are derived from the poppy seed pod. Although morphine is used medically to control severe pain, heroin is illegal in the United States. This status has not prevented its widespread use.

Heroin users usually inject the drug directly into their veins with a hypodermic needle. The immediate effect has been described as a "rush" of positive feeling, similar in some respects to a sexual orgasm—and just as difficult to describe. After the rush, a heroin user experiences a sense of well-being and peacefulness that lasts 3 to 5 hours. When the effects of the drug wear off, however, the user feels extreme anxiety and a desperate desire to repeat the experience. Moreover, larger amounts of heroin are needed each time to produce the same pleasurable effect. These last two properties are all the ingredients necessary for physiological and psychological dependence: The user is constantly either shooting up or attempting to obtain ever-increasing amounts of the drug. Eventually, the life of the addict revolves around heroin.

Because of the powerful positive feelings the drug produces, heroin addiction is particularly difficult to cure. One treatment that has shown some success is the use of methadone. *Methadone* is a synthetic chemical that satisfies a heroin user's physiological cravings for the drug without providing the "high" that accompanies heroin. When heroin users are placed on regular doses of methadone, they may be able to function relatively normally. The use of methadone has one substantial drawback, however: Although it removes the psychological dependence on heroin, it replaces the physiological dependence on heroin with a physiological dependence on methadone. Researchers are attempting to identify nonaddictive chemical substitutes for heroin as well as substitutes for other addictive drugs that do not replace one addiction with another (Amato et al., 2005; Verdejo, Toribio, & Orozco, 2005; Joe, Flynn, & Broome, 2007; Oviedo-Joekes et al., 2009).

Oxycodone (sold as the prescription drug *OxyContin*) is a type of pain reliever that has led to a significant amount of abuse. Many well-known people (including Courtney Love and Rush Limbaugh) have become dependent on it.

Hallucinogens: Psychedelic Drugs

What do mushrooms, jimsonweed, and morning glories have in common? Besides being fairly common plants, each can be a source of a powerful hallucinogen, a drug that is capable of producing **hallucinations,** or changes in the perceptual process.

MARIJUANA

The most common hallucinogen in widespread use today is *marijuana*, whose active ingredient—tetrahydrocannabinol (THC)—is found in a common weed, cannabis. Marijuana is typically smoked in cigarettes or pipes, although it can be cooked and eaten. Just over 32% of high school seniors and 11% of 8th-graders report having used marijuana in the last year (Johnston et al., 2011; see Figure 7).

The effects of marijuana vary from person to person, but they typically consist of feelings of euphoria and general well-being. Sensory experiences seem more vivid and intense, and a person's sense of self-importance seems to grow. Memory may be impaired, causing users to feel pleasantly "spaced out." However, the effects are not universally positive. Individuals who use marijuana when they feel depressed can end up even more depressed, because the drug tends to magnify both good and bad feelings.

There are clear risks associated with long-term, heavy marijuana use. Although marijuana does not seem to produce addiction by itself, some evidence suggests that there are similarities in the way marijuana and drugs such as cocaine and heroin affect the brain. Furthermore, there is some evidence that heavy use at least temporarily decreases the production of the male sex hormone testosterone, potentially affecting sexual activity and sperm count (Lane, Cherek, & Tcheremissine, 2007; Rossato, Pagano, & Vettor, 2008).

In addition, marijuana smoked during pregnancy may have lasting effects on children who are exposed prenatally, although the results are inconsistent. Heavy use also affects the ability of the immune system to fight off germs and increases stress on the heart, although it is unclear how strong these effects are. There is one unquestionably negative consequence of smoking marijuana: The smoke damages the lungs much the way cigarette smoke does, producing an increased likelihood of developing cancer and other lung diseases (Cornelius et al., 1995; Julien, 2001; Reid, Macleod, & Robertson, 2010).

Despite the possible dangers of marijuana use, there is little scientific evidence for the popular belief that users "graduate" from marijuana to more dangerous drugs. Furthermore, the use of marijuana is routine in certain cultures. For instance, some people in Jamaica habitually drink a marijuana-based tea related to religious practices. In addition, marijuana has several medical uses; it can be used to prevent nausea from chemotherapy, treat some AIDS symptoms, and relieve muscle spasms for people with spinal cord injuries, and it may be helpful in the treatment of Alzheimer's disease. In a controversial move, 13 states have made the use of the drug legal if it is prescribed by a physician—although

hallucinogen A drug that is capable of producing hallucinations, or changes in the perceptual process.

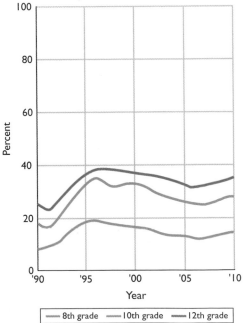

FIGURE 7 Although the level of marijuana use has declined slightly in recent years, overall the absolute number of teenagers who have used the drug in the last year remains relatively high. (Source: Johnston et al., 2011.)

This drawing, made by someone taking LSD, suggests the effects of hallucinogens on thinking.

it remains illegal under U.S. federal law (Chapkis & Webb, 2008; Cohen, 2009; Krishman, Cairns, & Howard, 2009; Baumrucker et al., 2011).

MDMA (ECSTASY) AND LSD

MDMA ("Ecstasy") and *lysergic acid diethylamide (LSD, or "acid")* fall into the category of hallucinogens. Both drugs affect the operation of the neurotransmitter serotonin in the brain, causing an alteration in brain-cell activity and perception (Cloud, 2000; Buchert et al., 2004).

Ecstasy users report a sense of peacefulness and calm. People on the drug report experiencing increased empathy and connection with others, as well as feeling more relaxed, yet energetic. Although the data are not conclusive, some researchers have found declines in memory and performance on intellectual tasks, and such findings suggest that there may be long-term changes in serotonin receptors in the brain (Montgomery et al., 2005; El-Mallakh & Abraham, 2007; Jones et al., 2008).

LSD, which is structurally similar to serotonin, produces vivid hallucinations. Perceptions of colors, sounds, and shapes are altered so much that even the most mundane experience—such as looking at the knots in a wooden table—can seem moving and exciting. Time perception is distorted, and objects and people may be viewed in a new way, with some users reporting that LSD increases their understanding of the world. For others, however, the experience brought on by LSD can be terrifying, particularly if users have had emotional difficulties in the past. Furthermore, people occasionally experience flashbacks, in which they hallucinate long after they initially used the drug (Baruss, 2003; Wu, Schlenger, & Galvin, 2006).

 BECOMING AN INFORMED CONSUMER of Psychology

Identifying Drug and Alcohol Problems

In a society bombarded with commercials for drugs that are guaranteed to do everything from curing restless leg syndrome to erectile dysfunction, it is no wonder that drug-related problems are a major social issue. Yet many people with drug and alcohol problems deny that they have them, and even close friends and family members may fail to realize when occasional social use of drugs or alcohol has turned into abuse.

Certain signs, however, indicate when use becomes abuse (National Institute on Drug Abuse, 2000). Among them are the following:

- Always getting high to have a good time.
- Being high more often than not.
- Getting high to get oneself going.
- Going to work or class while high.
- Missing or being unprepared for class or work because you were high.
- Feeling badly later about something you said or did while high.
- Driving a car while high.
- Coming in conflict with the law because of drugs.
- Doing something while high that you wouldn't do otherwise.
- Being high in nonsocial, solitary situations.
- Being unable to stop getting high.
- Feeling a need for a drink or a drug to get through the day.
- Becoming physically unhealthy.
- Failing at school or on the job.
- Thinking about liquor or drugs all the time.
- Avoiding family or friends while using liquor or drugs.

Any combination of these symptoms should be sufficient to alert you to the potential of a serious drug problem. Because drug and alcohol dependence are almost impossible to cure on one's own, people who suspect that they have a problem should seek immediate attention from a psychologist, physician, or counselor.

You can also get help from national hotlines. For alcohol difficulties, call the National Council on Alcoholism at (800) 622-2255. For drug problems, call the National Institute on Drug Abuse at (800) 662-4357. You can also check your telephone book for a local listing of Alcoholics Anonymous or Narcotics Anonymous. Finally, check out the websites of the National Institute on Alcohol Abuse and Alcoholism (www.niaaa.nih.gov) and the National Institute on Drug Abuse (www.nida.nih.gov).

RECAP/EVALUATE/RETHINK

RECAP

LO 14-1 What are the major classifications of drugs, and what are their effects?

- Drugs can produce an altered state of consciousness. However, they vary in how dangerous they are and in whether they are addictive. (p. 152)
- Stimulants cause arousal in the central nervous system. Two common stimulants are caffeine and nicotine. More dangerous are cocaine and amphetamines, which in large quantities can lead to convulsions and death. (p. 154)
- Depressants decrease arousal in the central nervous system. They can cause intoxication along with feelings of euphoria. The most common depressants are alcohol and barbiturates. (p. 157)
- Alcohol is the most frequently used depressant. Its initial effects of released tension and positive feelings yield to depressive effects as the dose of alcohol increases. Both heredity and environmental stressors can lead to alcoholism. (pp. 157–159)
- Morphine and heroin are narcotics, drugs that produce relaxation and relieve pain and anxiety. Because of their addictive qualities, morphine and heroin are particularly dangerous. (p. 160)
- Hallucinogens are drugs that produce hallucinations or other changes in perception. The most frequently used hallucinogen is marijuana, which has several long-term risks. Two other hallucinogens are LSD and Ecstasy. (p. 161)
- A number of signals indicate when drug use becomes drug abuse. A person who suspects that he or she has a drug problem should get professional help. People are almost never capable of solving drug problems on their own. (p. 162)

EVALUATE

1. Drugs that affect a person's consciousness are referred to as _____.
2. Match the type of drug to an example of that type.
   1. narcotic—a pain reliever
   2. amphetamine—a strong stimulant
   3. hallucinogen—capable of producing hallucinations
   a. LSD
   b. heroin
   c. dexedrine, or speed
3. Classify each drug listed as a stimulant (S), depressant (D), hallucinogen (H), or narcotic (N).
   1. nicotine
   2. cocaine
   3. alcohol
   4. morphine
   5. marijuana
4. The effects of LSD can recur long after the drug has been taken. True or false?
5. _____ is a drug that has been used to treat people with heroin addiction.

RETHINK

1. Why have drug education campaigns largely been ineffective in stemming the use of illegal drugs? Should the use of certain now-illegal drugs be made legal? Would it be more effective to stress reduction of drug use rather than a complete prohibition of drug use?
2. *From the perspective of a substance abuse counselor:* How would you explain why people start using drugs to the family members of someone who was addicted? What types of drug prevention programs would you advocate?

Answers to Evaluate Questions

1. psychoactive; 2. 1-b, 2-c, 3-a; 3. 1-S, 2-S, 3-D, 4-N, 5-H; 4. true; 5. Methadone

KEY TERMS

psychoactive drugs p. 152
addictive drugs p. 152

stimulants p. 154
depressants p. 157

narcotics p. 160
hallucinogen p. 161

Looking Back

Epilogue

Our examination of states of consciousness has ranged widely. It focuses both on natural factors such as sleep, dreaming, and daydreaming and on more intentional modes of altering consciousness, including hypnosis, meditation, and drugs. As we consider why people seek to alter their consciousness, we need to reflect on the uses and abuses of the various consciousness-altering strategies in which people engage.

Return briefly to the case of Lynn Blakes. Consider the following questions in light of your understanding of addictive drugs:

1. Lynn Blakes used meditation to treat her depression in place of antidepressant drugs. Why might both approaches produce similar results?
2. Why do you think Lynn Blakes was able to prevent a recurrence of depression by meditating regularly?
3. In what ways are meditation and hypnosis similar? In what ways are they different?
4. If meditation is simple to do and produces psychological benefits, why do you think more people aren't doing it? How would you explain the benefits of meditation to a friend?

VISUAL SUMMARY 4 States of Consciousness

MODULE 12 Sleep and Dreams

Stages of Sleep: Four stages of sleep, plus REM sleep

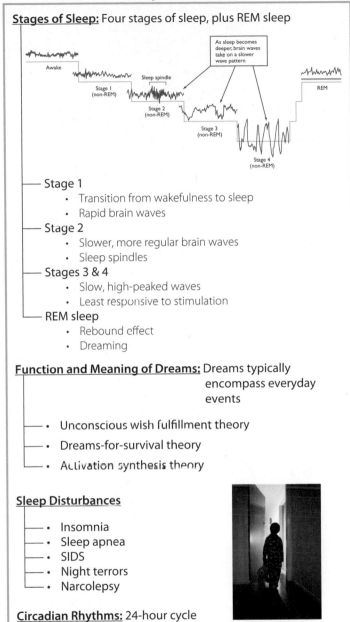

As sleep becomes deeper, brain waves take on a slower wave pattern

Awake
Stage 1 (non-REM)
Sleep spindle
Stage 2 (non-REM)
Stage 3 (non-REM)
Stage 4 (non-REM)
REM

- Stage 1
  - Transition from wakefulness to sleep
  - Rapid brain waves
- Stage 2
  - Slower, more regular brain waves
  - Sleep spindles
- Stages 3 & 4
  - Slow, high-peaked waves
  - Least responsive to stimulation
- REM sleep
  - Rebound effect
  - Dreaming

Function and Meaning of Dreams: Dreams typically encompass everyday events

- Unconscious wish fulfillment theory
- Dreams-for-survival theory
- Activation synthesis theory

Sleep Disturbances

- Insomnia
- Sleep apnea
- SIDS
- Night terrors
- Narcolepsy

Circadian Rhythms: 24-hour cycle

MODULE 13 Hypnosis and Meditation

Hypnosis: A trancelike state of heightened suggestibility

Meditation: Learned technique for refocusing attention

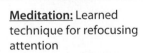

MODULE 14 Drug Use

Stimulants: Increase arousal in the nervous system

- Caffeine
- Cocaine
- Amphetamines

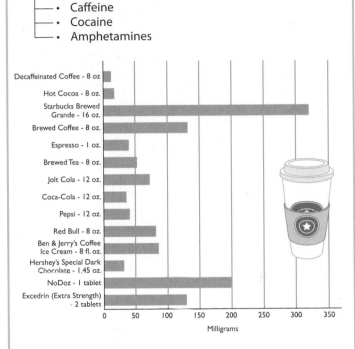

Decaffeinated Coffee - 8 oz
Hot Cocoa - 8 oz.
Starbucks Brewed Grande - 16 oz.
Brewed Coffee - 8 oz.
Espresso - 1 oz.
Brewed Tea - 8 oz.
Jolt Cola - 12 oz.
Coca-Cola - 12 oz.
Pepsi - 12 oz.
Red Bull - 8 oz.
Ben & Jerry's Coffee Ice Cream - 8 fl. oz.
Hershey's Special Dark Chocolate - 1.45 oz.
NoDoz - 1 tablet
Excedrin (Extra Strength) - 2 tablets

0 50 100 150 200 250 300 350
Milligrams

Depressants: Impede the nervous system

- Alcohol
- Barbiturates
- Rohypnol: "Date-rape" drug

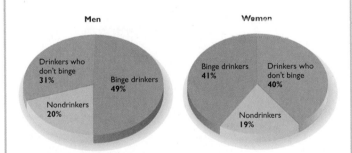

Men
- Drinkers who don't binge 31%
- Binge drinkers 49%
- Nondrinkers 20%

Women
- Binge drinkers 41%
- Drinkers who don't binge 40%
- Nondrinkers 19%

Narcotics: Reduce pain and anxiety

- Heroin
- Morphine

Hallucinogens: Produce changes in perceptual processes

- Marijuana
- MDMA
- LSD

5

Learning

Learning Outcomes for Chapter 5

MODULE 15

LO 15-1 What is learning?

LO 15-2 How do we learn to form associations between stimuli and responses?

Classical Conditioning

The Basics of Classical Conditioning

Applying Conditioning Principles to Human Behavior

Extinction

Generalization and Discrimination

Beyond Traditional Classical Conditioning: Challenging Basic Assumptions

MODULE 16

LO 16-1 What is the role of reward and punishment in learning?

LO 16-2 What are some practical methods for bringing about behavior change, both in ourselves and in others?

Operant Conditioning

Thorndike's Law of Effect

The Basics of Operant Conditioning

Applying Psychology in the 21st Century: Using Operant Conditioning Principles to Save Lives

PsychWork: Seeing Eye Guide Dog Trainer

Becoming an Informed Consumer of Psychology: Using Behavior Analysis and Behavior Modification

MODULE 17

LO 17-1 What is the role of cognition and thought in learning?

Cognitive Approaches to Learning

Latent Learning

Observational Learning: Learning Through Imitation

Neuroscience in Your Life: Learning Through Imitation

Exploring Diversity: Does Culture Influence How We Learn?

Progressive Insurance has a deal for you: If you drive better, you are going to be rewarded. But it's not going to take your word for how careful a driver you are. Instead, it will install a tiny device called Snapshot under your car's dashboard. Snapshot will monitor how fast you drive, how many miles you travel, and if you make any sudden stops. The data are transmitted to the insurance company, and the better you drive, the more you'll save on your insurance (Schultz, 2011).

Looking Ahead

The strategy this insurance company is using to encourage its clients to become safer drivers is not unique to that industry. Some power companies use a similar type of device to provide customers with real-time feedback on their moment-to-moment energy use, allowing them to see how certain behaviors, such as turning on an air conditioner or turning off unneeded lights, directly affect their electric bill.

Offering rewards for desired behavior takes advantage of some fundamental principles of learning—the same processes that allow us to learn to read a book, drive a car, play poker, study for a test, or perform any of the numerous activities that make up our daily routine. Each of us must acquire and then refine our skills and abilities through learning.

Learning is a fundamental topic for psychologists and plays a central role in almost every specialty area of psychology. For example, a psychologist studying perception might ask, "How do we learn that people who look small from a distance are far away and not simply tiny?" A developmental psychologist might inquire, "How do babies learn to distinguish their mothers from other people?" A clinical psychologist might wonder, "Why do some people learn to be afraid when they see a spider?" A social psychologist might ask, "How do we learn to believe that we've fallen in love?"

Each of these questions, although drawn from very different branches of psychology, can be answered only through an understanding of basic learning processes. In each case, a skill or a behavior is acquired, altered, or refined through experience.

Psychologists have approached the study of learning from several angles. Among the most fundamental are studies of the type of learning that is illustrated in responses ranging from a dog salivating when it hears its owner opening a can of dog food to the emotions we feel when our national anthem is played. Other theories consider how learning is a consequence of rewarding circumstances. Finally, several other approaches focus on the cognitive aspects of learning, or the thought processes that underlie learning.

Classical Conditioning

Does the mere sight of the golden arches in front of McDonald's make you feel pangs of hunger and think about hamburgers? If it does, you are displaying an elementary form of learning called classical conditioning. *Classical conditioning* helps explain such diverse phenomena as crying at the sight of a bride walking down the aisle, fearing the dark, and falling in love.

Classical conditioning is one of a number of different types of learning that psychologists have identified, but a general definition encompasses them all: **Learning** is a relatively permanent change in behavior that is brought about by experience.

How do we know when a behavior has been influenced by learning—or even is a result of learning? Part of the answer relates to the nature-nurture question, one of the fundamental issues underlying the field of psychology. In the acquisition of behaviors, experience—which is essential to the definition of learning—is the "nurture" part of the nature-nurture question.

However, it's not always easy to identify whether a change in behavior is due to nature or nurture, because some changes in behavior or performance come about through maturation alone and don't involve experience. For instance, children become better tennis players as they grow older partly because their strength increases with their size—a maturational phenomenon. To understand when learning has occurred, we must differentiate maturational changes from improvements resulting from practice, which indicate that learning actually has occurred.

Similarly, short-term changes in behavior that are due to factors other than learning, such as declines in performance resulting from fatigue or lack of effort, are different from performance changes that are due to actual learning. If Serena Williams has a bad day on the tennis court because of tension or fatigue, this does not mean that she has not learned to play correctly or has "unlearned" how to play well. Because there is not always a one-to-one correspondence between learning and performance, understanding when true learning has occurred is difficult.

It is clear that we are primed for learning from the beginning of life. Infants exhibit a simple type of learning called habituation. *Habituation* is the decrease in response to a stimulus that occurs after repeated presentations of the same stimulus. For example, young infants may initially show interest in a novel stimulus, such as a brightly colored toy, but they will soon lose interest if they see the same toy over and over. (Adults exhibit habituation, too: Newlyweds soon stop noticing that they are wearing a wedding ring.) Habituation permits us to ignore things that have stopped providing new information.

Most learning is considerably more complex than habituation, and the study of learning has been at the core of the field of psychology. Although philosophers since the time of Aristotle have speculated on the foundations of learning, the first systematic research on learning was done at the beginning of the 20th century, when Ivan Pavlov (does the name ring a bell?) developed the framework for learning called classical conditioning.

Learning Outcomes

LO 15-1 What is learning?

LO 15-2 How do we learn to form associations between stimuli and responses?

learning A relatively permanent change in behavior brought about by experience.

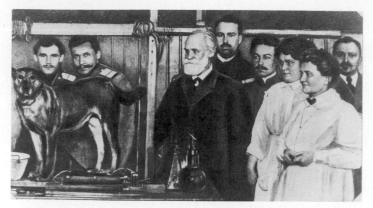

Ivan Pavlov (center) developed the principles of classical conditioning.

The Basics of Classical Conditioning

Ivan Pavlov, a Russian physiologist, never intended to do psychological research. In 1904 he won the Nobel Prize for his work on digestion, testimony to his contribution to that field. Yet Pavlov is remembered not for his physiological research but for his experiments on basic learning processes—work that he began quite accidentally (Marks, 2004; Samoilov & Zayas, 2007; Grant & Wingate, 2011).

Pavlov had been studying the secretion of stomach acids and salivation in dogs in response to the ingestion of varying amounts and kinds of food. While doing that, he observed a curious phenomenon: Sometimes stomach secretions and salivation would begin in the dogs when they had not yet eaten any food. The mere sight of the experimenter who normally brought the food, or even the sound of the experimenter's footsteps, was enough to produce salivation in the dogs. Pavlov's genius lay in his ability to recognize the implications of this discovery. He saw that the dogs were responding not only on the basis of a biological need (hunger) but also as a result of learning—or, as it came to be called, classical conditioning. **Classical conditioning** is a type of learning in which a neutral stimulus (such as the experimenter's footsteps) comes to elicit a response after being paired with a stimulus (such as food) that naturally brings about that response.

To demonstrate classical conditioning, Pavlov (1927) attached a tube to the salivary gland of a dog, allowing him to measure precisely the dog's salivation. He then rang a bell and, just a few seconds later, presented the dog with meat. This pairing occurred repeatedly and was carefully planned so that, each time, exactly the same amount of time elapsed between the presentation of the bell and the meat. At first the dog would salivate only when the meat was presented, but soon it began to salivate at the sound of the bell. In fact, even when Pavlov stopped presenting the meat, the dog still salivated after hearing the sound. The dog had been classically conditioned to salivate to the bell.

As you can see in Figure 1, the basic processes of classical conditioning that underlie Pavlov's discovery are straightforward, although the terminology he chose is not simple. First, consider the diagram in Figure 1a. Before conditioning, there are two unrelated stimuli: the ringing of a bell and meat. We know that normally the ringing of a bell does not lead to salivation but to some irrelevant response, such as pricking up the ears or perhaps a startle reaction. The bell is therefore called the **neutral stimulus,** because it is a stimulus that, before conditioning, does not naturally bring about the response in which we are interested. We also have meat, which naturally causes a dog to salivate—the response we are interested in conditioning. The meat is considered an **unconditioned stimulus (UCS)** because food placed in a dog's mouth automatically causes salivation to occur. The response that the meat elicits (salivation) is called an **unconditioned response (UCR)**—a natural, innate, reflexive response that is not associated with previous learning. Unconditioned responses are always brought about by the presence of unconditioned stimuli.

Figure 1b illustrates what happens during conditioning. The bell is rung just before each presentation of the meat. The goal of conditioning is for the dog to associate the bell with the unconditioned stimulus (meat) and therefore to bring about the same sort of response as the unconditioned stimulus.

After a number of pairings of the bell and meat, the bell alone causes the dog to salivate (as in Figure 1c). When conditioning is complete, the bell has evolved from a neutral stimulus to a **conditioned stimulus (CS).** At this time, salivation that

classical conditioning A type of learning in which a neutral stimulus comes to bring about a response after it is paired with a stimulus that naturally brings about that response.

neutral stimulus A stimulus that, before conditioning, does not naturally bring about the response of interest.

unconditioned stimulus (UCS) A stimulus that naturally brings about a particular response without having been learned.

unconditioned response (UCR) A response that is natural and needs no training (e.g., salivation at the smell of food).

conditioned stimulus (CS) A once-neutral stimulus that has been paired with an unconditioned stimulus to bring about a response formerly caused only by the unconditioned stimulus.

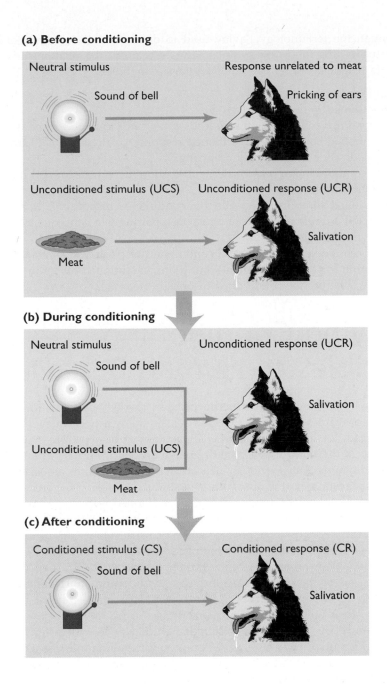

(a) Before conditioning

Neutral stimulus

Sound of bell

Response unrelated to meat

Pricking of ears

Unconditioned stimulus (UCS)   Unconditioned response (UCR)

Meat

Salivation

(b) During conditioning

Neutral stimulus

Sound of bell

Unconditioned response (UCR)

Salivation

Unconditioned stimulus (UCS)

Meat

(c) After conditioning

Conditioned stimulus (CS)

Sound of bell

Conditioned response (CR)

Salivation

FIGURE 1 The basic process of classical conditioning. (a) Before conditioning, the ringing of a bell does not bring about salivation—making the bell a neutral stimulus. In contrast, meat naturally brings about salivation, making the meat an unconditioned stimulus (UCS) and salivation an unconditioned response (UCR). (b) During conditioning, the bell is rung just before the presentation of the meat. (c) Eventually, the ringing of the bell alone brings about salivation. We now can say that conditioning has been accomplished: The previously neutral stimulus of the bell is now considered a conditioned stimulus (CS) that brings about the conditioned response of salivation (CR).

Study Alert

Figure 1 can help you to learn and understand the process (and terminology) of classical conditioning, which can be confusing.

occurs as a response to the conditioned stimulus (bell) is considered a **conditioned response (CR).** After conditioning, then, the conditioned stimulus evokes the conditioned response.

The sequence and timing of the presentation of the unconditioned stimulus and the conditioned stimulus are particularly important. Like a malfunctioning warning light at a railroad crossing that goes on after the train has passed by, a neutral stimulus that *follows* an unconditioned stimulus has little chance of becoming a conditioned stimulus. However, just as a warning light works best if it goes on right before a train passes, a neutral stimulus that is presented *just before* the unconditioned stimulus is most apt to result in successful conditioning. Research has shown that conditioning is most effective if the neutral stimulus (which will become a conditioned stimulus) precedes the unconditioned stimulus by between a half second and several seconds, depending on what kind of response is being conditioned (Wasserman & Miller, 1997; Bitterman, 2006).

conditioned response (CR) A response that, after conditioning, follows a previously neutral stimulus (e.g., salivation at the ringing of a bell).

Although the terminology Pavlov used to describe classical conditioning may seem confusing, the following summary can help make the relationships between stimuli and responses easier to understand and remember:

- Conditioned = learned.
- Unconditioned = not learned.
- An *un*conditioned stimulus (UCS) leads to an *un*conditioned response (UCR).
- *Un*conditioned stimulus–*un*conditioned response pairings are *not* learned and *not* trained: They are naturally occurring.
- During conditioning, a previously neutral stimulus is transformed into the conditioned stimulus.
- A conditioned stimulus (CS) leads to a conditioned response (CR), and a conditioned stimulus–conditioned response pairing is a consequence of learning and training.
- An unconditioned response and a conditioned response are similar (such as salivation in Pavlov's experiment), but the unconditioned response occurs naturally, whereas the conditioned response is learned.

Applying Conditioning Principles to Human Behavior

Although the initial conditioning experiments were carried out with animals, classical conditioning principles were soon found to explain many aspects of everyday human behavior. Recall, for instance, the earlier illustration of how people may experience hunger pangs at the sight of McDonald's golden arches. The cause of this reaction is classical conditioning: The previously neutral arches have become associated with the food inside the restaurant (the unconditioned stimulus), causing the arches to become a conditioned stimulus that brings about the conditioned response of hunger.

Emotional responses are especially likely to be learned through classical conditioning processes. For instance, how do some of us develop fears of mice, spiders, and other creatures that are typically harmless? In a now infamous case study, psychologist John B. Watson and colleague Rosalie Rayner (1920) showed that classical conditioning was at the root of such fears by conditioning an 11-month-old infant named Albert to be afraid of rats. "Little Albert," like most infants, initially was frightened by loud noises but had no fear of rats.

In the study, the experimenters sounded a loud noise whenever Little Albert touched a white, furry rat. The noise (the unconditioned stimulus) evoked fear (the unconditioned response). After just a few pairings of noise and rat, Albert began to show fear of the rat by itself, bursting into tears when he saw it. The rat, then, had become a CS that brought about the CR, fear. Furthermore, the effects of the conditioning lingered: five days later, Albert reacted with some degree of fear not only when shown a rat, but when shown objects that looked similar to the white, furry rat, including a white rabbit, a white seal-skin coat, and even a white Santa Claus mask. (By the way, although we don't know for certain what happened to the unfortunate Little Albert, it appears he was a sickly child who died at the age of 5. In any case, Watson, the experimenter, has been condemned for using ethically questionable procedures that could never be conducted today; Beck, Levinson, & Irons, 2009; Powell, 2011.)

Learning by means of classical conditioning also occurs during adulthood. For example, you may not go to a dentist as often as you should because of previous associations of dentists with pain. In more extreme cases, classical conditioning can lead to the development of *phobias*, which are intense, irrational fears that we will consider later in the book. For example, an insect phobia might develop in someone who is stung by a bee. The insect phobia might be so severe that the person refrains from leaving home.

Posttraumatic stress disorder (PTSD), suffered by some war veterans and others who have had traumatic experiences, can also be produced by classical conditioning.

Even years after their battlefield experiences, veterans may feel a rush of fear and anxiety at a stimulus such as a loud noise (Kaštelan et al., 2007; Roberts, Moore, & Beckham, 2007; Schreurs, Smith-Bell, & Burhans, 2011).

On the other hand, classical conditioning also relates to pleasant experiences. For instance, you may have a particular fondness for the smell of a certain perfume or aftershave lotion because thoughts of an early love come rushing back whenever you encounter it. Or hearing a certain song can bring back happy or bittersweet emotions due to associations that you have developed in the past.

Classical conditioning also explains why drug addictions are so difficult to treat. Drug addicts learn to associate certain stimuli—such as drug paraphernalia like a syringe or a room where they use drugs—with the pleasant feelings produced by the drugs. So simply seeing a syringe or entering a room can produce reactions associated with the drug and continued cravings for it (James et al., 2011).

Extinction

What do you think would happen if a dog that had become classically conditioned to salivate at the ringing of a bell never again received food when the bell was rung? The answer lies in one of the basic phenomena of learning: extinction. **Extinction** occurs when a previously conditioned response decreases in frequency and eventually disappears.

To produce extinction, one needs to end the association between conditioned stimuli and unconditioned stimuli. For instance, if we had trained a dog to salivate (the conditioned response) at the ringing of a bell (the conditioned stimulus), we could produce extinction by repeatedly ringing the bell but *not* providing meat (the unconditioned stimulus). At first the dog would continue to salivate when it heard the bell, but after a few such instances, the amount of salivation would probably decline, and the dog would eventually stop responding to the bell altogether. At that point, we could say that the response had been extinguished. In sum, extinction occurs when the conditioned stimulus is presented repeatedly without the unconditioned stimulus (see Figure 2).

We should keep in mind that extinction can be a helpful phenomenon. Consider, for instance, what it would be like if the fear you experienced while watching the shower murder scene in the classic movie *Psycho* never was extinguished. You might well tremble with fright every time you took a shower.

Once a conditioned response has been extinguished, has it vanished forever? Not necessarily. Pavlov discovered this phenomenon when he returned to his dog a few

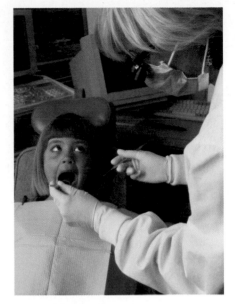

Because of a previous unpleasant experience, a person may expect a similar occurrence when faced with a comparable situation in the future, a process known as stimulus generalization. Can you think of ways that this process occurs in everyday life?

extinction A basic phenomenon of learning that occurs when a previously conditioned response decreases in frequency and eventually disappears.

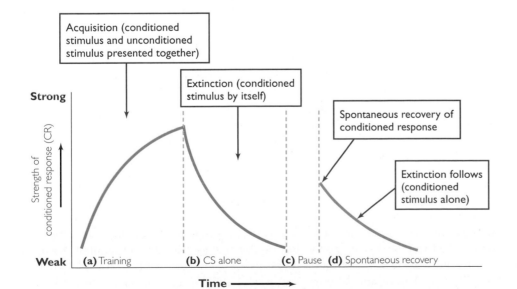

FIGURE 2 Acquisition, extinction, and spontaneous recovery of a classically conditioned response. (a) A conditioned response (CR) gradually increases in strength during training. (b) However, if the conditioned stimulus (CS) is presented by itself enough times, the conditioned response gradually fades, and extinction occurs. (c) After a pause (d) in which the conditioned stimulus is not presented, spontaneous recovery can occur. However, extinction typically reoccurs soon after.

spontaneous recovery The reemergence of an extinguished conditioned response after a period of rest and with no further conditioning.

days after the conditioned behavior had seemingly been extinguished. If he rang a bell, the dog once again salivated—an effect known as **spontaneous recovery,** or the reemergence of an extinguished conditioned response after a period of time and with no further conditioning.

Spontaneous recovery also helps explain why it is so hard to overcome drug addictions. For example, cocaine addicts who are thought to be "cured" can experience an irresistible impulse to use the drug again if they are subsequently confronted by a stimulus with strong connections to the drug, such as a white powder (Rodd et al., 2004; Plowright, Simonds, & Butler, 2006; Díaz & De la Casa, 2011).

Study Alert
Remember that stimulus generalization relates to stimuli that are similar to one another, while stimulus discrimination relates to stimuli that are different from one another.

stimulus generalization A process in which, after a stimulus has been conditioned to produce a particular response, stimuli that are similar to the original stimulus produce the same response.

Generalization and Discrimination

Despite differences in color and shape, to most of us a rose is a rose is a rose. The pleasure we experience at the beauty, smell, and grace of the flower is similar for different types of roses. Pavlov noticed a similar phenomenon. His dogs often salivated not only at the ringing of the bell that was used during their original conditioning but at the sound of a buzzer as well.

Such behavior is the result of stimulus generalization. **Stimulus generalization** is a process in which, after a stimulus has been conditioned to produce a particular response, stimuli that are similar to the original stimulus produce the same response. The greater the similarity between two stimuli, the greater the likelihood of stimulus generalization. Little Albert, who, as we mentioned earlier, was conditioned to be fearful of white rats, grew afraid of other furry white things as well. However, according to the principle of stimulus generalization, it is unlikely that he would have been afraid of a black dog, because its color would have differentiated it sufficiently from the original fear-evoking stimulus.

The conditioned response elicited by the new stimulus is usually not as intense as the original conditioned response, although the more similar the new stimulus is to the old one, the more similar the new response will be. It is unlikely, then, that Little Albert's fear of the Santa Claus mask was as great as his learned fear of a rat. Still, stimulus generalization permits us to know, for example, that we ought to brake at all red lights, even if there are minor variations in size, shape, and shade.

stimulus discrimination The process that occurs if two stimuli are sufficiently distinct from one another that one evokes a conditioned response but the other does not; the ability to differentiate between stimuli.

Stimulus discrimination, in contrast, occurs if two stimuli are sufficiently distinct from each other that one evokes a conditioned response but the other does not. Stimulus discrimination provides the ability to differentiate between stimuli. For example, my dog Cleo comes running into the kitchen when she hears the sound of the electric can opener, which she has learned is used to open her dog food when her dinner is about to be served. She does not bound into the kitchen at the sound of the food processor, although it sounds similar. In other words, she discriminates between the stimuli of can opener and food processor. Similarly, our ability to discriminate between the behavior of a growling dog and that of one whose tail is wagging can lead to adaptive behavior—avoiding the growling dog and petting the friendly one.

Beyond Traditional Classical Conditioning: Challenging Basic Assumptions

Although Pavlov hypothesized that all learning is nothing more than long strings of conditioned responses, this notion has not been supported by subsequent research. It turns out that classical conditioning provides us with only a partial explanation of how people and animals learn; indeed, Pavlov was wrong in some of his basic assumptions (Hollis, 1997).

For example, according to Pavlov, the process of linking stimuli and responses occurs in a mechanistic, unthinking way. In contrast to this perspective, learning theorists influenced by cognitive psychology have argued that learners actively develop an understanding and expectancy about which particular unconditioned stimuli are matched with specific conditioned stimuli. A ringing bell, for instance, gives a dog something to think about: the impending arrival of food (Rescorla, 1988; Kirsch et al., 2004).

Traditional explanations of how classical conditioning operates have also been challenged by John Garcia, a learning psychologist. He found that some organisms—including humans—were *biologically prepared* to quickly learn to avoid foods that smelled or tasted like something that made them sick. For instance, a dog quickly learns to avoid rotting food that in the past made it sick. Similarly, if every time you ate peanuts you had an upset stomach several hours later, eventually you would learn to avoid peanuts. In fact, you might develop a learned *taste aversion,*when the taste of a particular food is associated with unpleasant symptoms such as nausea or vomiting. If you developed a taste aversion to peanuts, merely tasting (or even smelling or in more extreme cases seeing a peanut) could produce such disagreeable symptoms (Garcia, 1990, 2003).

The surprising part of Garcia's discovery was his demonstration that conditioning could occur even when the interval between exposure to the conditioned stimulus of tainted food and the response of sickness was as long as eight hours. Furthermore, the conditioning persisted over very long periods and sometimes occurred after just one exposure.

These findings have had important practical implications. For example, to keep crows from stealing eggs, dairy farmers may lace an egg with a chemical and leave it in a place where crows will find it. The drug temporarily makes the crows ill, but it does not harm them permanently. After exposure to a chemical-laden egg, crows no longer find them appetizing (Cox et al., 2004; Baker, Johnson, & Slater, 2007; Bouton et al., 2011).

RECAP/EVALUATE/RETHINK

RECAP

LO15-1 What is learning?

- Learning is a relatively permanent change in behavior resulting from experience. (p. 169)

LO15-2 How do we learn to form associations between stimuli and responses?

- One major form of learning is classical conditioning, which occurs when a neutral stimulus—one that normally brings about no relevant response—is repeatedly paired with a stimulus (called an unconditioned stimulus) that brings about a natural, untrained response. (p. 170)
- Conditioning occurs when the neutral stimulus is repeatedly presented just before the unconditioned stimulus. After repeated pairings, the neutral stimulus elicits the same response that the unconditioned stimulus brings about. When this occurs, the neutral stimulus has become a conditioned stimulus, and the response a conditioned response. (pp. 170, 171)

- Learning is not always permanent. Extinction occurs when a previously learned response decreases in frequency and eventually disappears. (p. 173)
- Stimulus generalization is the tendency for a conditioned response to follow a stimulus that is similar to, but not the same as, the original conditioned stimulus. The converse phenomenon, stimulus discrimination, occurs when an organism learns to distinguish between stimuli. (p. 174)

EVALUATE

1. _____ involves changes brought about by experience, whereas maturation describes changes resulting from biological development.
2. _____ is the name of the scientist responsible for discovering the learning phenomenon known as _____ conditioning, whereby an organism learns a response to a stimulus to which it normally would not respond.

Refer to the passage below to answer questions 3 through 5:

The last three times little Theresa visited Dr. Lopez for checkups, he administered a painful preventive immunization shot that left her in tears. Today, when her mother takes her for another checkup, Theresa begins to sob as soon as she comes face to face with Dr. Lopez, even before he has had a chance to say hello.

3. The painful shot that Theresa received during each visit was a(n) _____ _____ that elicited the _____ _____, her tears.

4. Dr. Lopez is upset because his presence has become a _____ _____ for Theresa's crying.

5. Fortunately, Dr. Lopez gave Theresa no more shots for quite some time. Over that period she gradually stopped crying and even came to like him. _____ had occurred.

1. How likely is it that Little Albert, Watson's experimental subject, might has gone through life afraid of Santa Claus? Describe what could have happened to prevent his continual dread of Santa.

2. *From the perspective of an advertising executive:* How might knowledge of classical conditioning be useful in creating an advertising campaign? What, if any, ethical issues arise from this use?

Answers to Evaluate Questions

1. Learning; 2. Pavlov, classical; 3. unconditioned stimulus, unconditioned response; 4. conditioned stimulus; 5. Extinction

KEY TERMS

learning p. 169
classical
   conditioning p. 170
neutral stimulus p. 170
unconditioned stimulus
   (UCS) p. 170

unconditioned response
   (UCR) p. 170
conditioned stimulus
   (CS) p. 170

conditioned response
   (CR) p. 171
extinction p. 173
spontaneous recovery p. 174

stimulus
   generalization p. 174
stimulus
   discrimination p. 174

Operant Conditioning

Very good . . . What a clever idea . . . Fantastic . . . I agree . . . Thank you . . . Excellent . . . Super . . . Right on . . . This is the best paper you've ever written; you get an A . . . You are really getting the hang of it . . . I'm impressed . . . You're getting a raise . . . Have a cookie . . . You look great . . . I love you . . .

Few of us mind being the recipient of any of these comments. But what is especially noteworthy about them is that each of these simple statements can be used, through a process known as operant conditioning, to bring about powerful changes in behavior and to teach the most complex tasks. Operant conditioning is the basis for many of the most important kinds of human, and animal, learning.

Operant conditioning is learning in which a voluntary response is strengthened or weakened, depending on its favorable or unfavorable consequences. When we say that a response has been strengthened or weakened, we mean that it has been made more or less likely to recur regularly.

Unlike classical conditioning, in which the original behaviors are the natural, biological responses to the presence of a stimulus such as food, water, or pain, operant conditioning applies to voluntary responses, which an organism performs deliberately to produce a desirable outcome. The term *operant* emphasizes this point: The organism *operates* on its environment to produce a desirable result. Operant conditioning is at work when we learn that toiling industriously can bring about a raise or that studying hard results in good grades.

As with classical conditioning, the basis for understanding operant conditioning was laid by work with animals. We turn now to some of that early research, which began with a simple inquiry into the behavior of cats.

Thorndike's Law of Effect

If you placed a hungry cat in a cage and then put a small piece of food outside the cage, just beyond the cat's reach, chances are that the cat would eagerly search for a way out of the cage. The cat might first claw at the sides or push against an opening. Suppose, though, you had rigged things so that the cat could escape by stepping on a small paddle that released the latch to the door of the cage (see Figure 1 on page 178). Eventually, as it moved around the cage, the cat would happen to step on the paddle, the door would open, and the cat would eat the food.

What would happen if you then returned the cat to the box? The next time, it would probably take a little less time for the cat to step on the paddle and escape. After a few trials, the cat would deliberately step on the paddle as soon as it was placed in the cage. What would have occurred, according to Edward L. Thorndike (1932), who studied this situation extensively, was that the cat would have learned that pressing the paddle was associated with the desirable consequence of getting food. Thorndike summarized that relationship by formulating the *law of effect:* Responses that lead to satisfying consequences are more likely to be repeated.

Thorndike believed that the law of effect operates as automatically as leaves fall off a tree in autumn. It was not necessary for an organism to understand that there

Learning Outcomes

LO 16-1 What is the role of reward and punishment in learning?

LO 16-2 What are some practical methods for bringing about behavior change, both in ourselves and in others?

operant conditioning Learning in which a voluntary response is strengthened or weakened, depending on its favorable or unfavorable consequences.

FIGURE 1 Edward L. Thorndike devised this puzzle box to study the process by which a cat learns to press a paddle to escape from the box and receive food. Do you think Thorndike's work has relevance to the question of why people voluntarily work on puzzles and play games, such as sudoku, Angry Birds, and jigsaw puzzles? Do they receive any rewards?

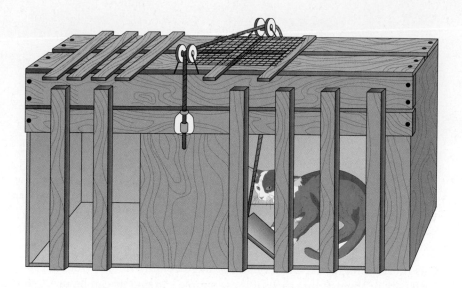

was a link between a response and a reward. Instead, Thorndike believed, over time and through experience the organism would make a direct connection between the stimulus and the response without any awareness that the connection existed.

The Basics of Operant Conditioning

Thorndike's early research served as the foundation for the work of one of the 20th century's most influential psychologists, B. F. Skinner (1904–1990). You may have heard of the Skinner box (shown in Figure 2), a chamber with a highly controlled environment that was used to study operant conditioning processes with laboratory animals. Whereas Thorndike's goal was to get his cats to learn to obtain food by leaving the box, animals in a Skinner box learn to obtain food by operating on their environment within the box. Skinner became interested in specifying how behavior varies as a result of alterations in the environment.

Skinner, whose work went far beyond perfecting Thorndike's earlier apparatus, is considered the inspiration for a whole generation of psychologists studying operant conditioning. To illustrate Skinner's contribution, let's consider what happens to a rat in the typical Skinner box (Pascual & Rodríguez, 2006; Soorya, Carpenter, & Romanczyk, 2011).

Suppose you want to teach a hungry rat to press a lever that is in its box. At first the rat will wander around the box, exploring the environment in a relatively random fashion. At some point, however, it will probably press the lever by chance, and when it does, it will receive a food pellet. The first time this happens, the rat will not learn the connection between pressing a lever and receiving food and will continue to explore the box. Sooner or later the rat will press the lever again and receive a pellet, and in time the frequency of the pressing response will increase. Eventually, the rat will press the lever continually until it satisfies its hunger, thereby demonstrating that it has learned that the receipt of food is contingent on pressing the lever.

REINFORCEMENT: THE CENTRAL CONCEPT OF OPERANT CONDITIONING

reinforcement The process by which a stimulus increases the probability that a preceding behavior will be repeated.

Skinner called the process that leads the rat to continue pressing the key "reinforcement." **Reinforcement** is the process by which a stimulus increases the probability that a preceding behavior will be repeated. In other words, pressing the lever is more likely to occur again because of the stimulus of food.

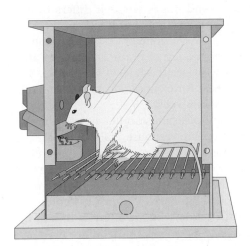

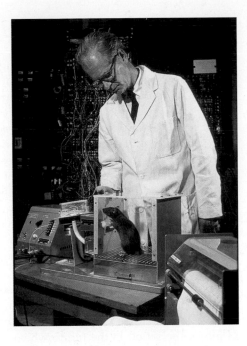

FIGURE 2 B. F. Skinner with a Skinner box used to study operant conditioning. Laboratory rats learn to press the lever in order to obtain food, which is delivered in the tray.

In a situation such as this one, the food is called a reinforcer. A **reinforcer** is any stimulus that increases the probability that a preceding behavior will occur again. Hence, food is a reinforcer, because it increases the probability that the behavior of pressing (formally referred to as the *response* of pressing) will take place.

What kind of stimuli can act as reinforcers? Bonuses, toys, and good grades can serve as reinforcers—if they strengthen the probability of the response that occurred before their introduction. What makes something a reinforcer depends on individual preferences. Although a Hershey's bar can act as a reinforcer for one person, an individual who dislikes chocolate may find one dollar more desirable. The only way we can know if a stimulus is a reinforcer for a particular organism is to observe whether the frequency of a previously occurring behavior increases after the presentation of the stimulus.

Of course, we are not born knowing that one dollar can buy us a candy bar. Rather, through experience we learn that money is a valuable commodity because of its association with stimuli, such as food and drink, that are naturally reinforcing. This fact suggests a distinction between primary reinforcers and secondary reinforcers. A *primary reinforcer* satisfies some biological need and works naturally, regardless of a person's previous experience. Food for a hungry person, warmth for a cold person, and relief for a person in pain all would be classified as primary reinforcers.

In contrast, a *secondary reinforcer* is a stimulus that becomes reinforcing because of its association with a primary reinforcer. For instance, we know that money is valuable, because we have learned that it allows us to obtain other desirable objects, including primary reinforcers such as food and shelter. Money thus becomes a secondary reinforcer (Moher et al., 2008).

Secondary reinforcers make up the heart of *token systems* sometimes used in the treatment of some psychological disorders for those who are in institutions. In a token system, a patient is rewarded for showing desired behavior with a token such as a poker chip. The token—an example of a secondary reinforcer—can then be redeemed for something desirable, such as snacks, games, or real money.

Neuroscientists are beginning to explore the biological underpinnings of reinforcers. For example, we now know that the neurotransmitter *dopamine* (discussed in the "Neuroscience and Behavior" chapter) plays a key role in the reinforcement of behavior. When we are exposed to certain kinds of stimuli, a flood of dopamine cascades through parts of the brain, leading to feelings of pleasure that are reinforcing (Nargeot & Simmers, 2011; Trujillo-Pisanty et al., 2011).

reinforcer Any stimulus that increases the probability that a preceding behavior will occur again.

Study Alert

Remember that primary reinforcers satisfy a biological need; secondary reinforcers are effective due to previous association with a primary reinforcer.

POSITIVE REINFORCERS, NEGATIVE REINFORCERS, AND PUNISHMENT

In many respects, reinforcers can be thought of in terms of rewards; both a reinforcer and a reward increase the probability that a preceding response will occur again. But the term *reward* is limited to *positive* occurrences, and this is where it differs from a reinforcer—for it turns out that reinforcers can be positive or negative.

positive reinforcer A stimulus added to the environment that brings about an increase in a preceding response.

A **positive reinforcer** is a stimulus *added* to the environment that brings about an increase in a preceding response. If food, water, money, or praise is provided after a response, it is more likely that that response will occur again in the future. The paychecks that workers get at the end of the week, for example, increase the likelihood that they will return to their jobs the following week.

negative reinforcer An unpleasant stimulus whose removal leads to an increase in the probability that a preceding response will be repeated in the future.

In contrast, a **negative reinforcer** refers to an unpleasant stimulus whose removal leads to an increase in the probability that a preceding response will be repeated in the future. For example, if you have an itchy rash (an unpleasant stimulus) that is relieved when you apply a certain brand of ointment, you are more likely to use that ointment the next time you have an itchy rash. Using the ointment, then, is negatively reinforcing, because it removes the unpleasant itch. Similarly, if your iPod volume is so loud that it hurts your ears when you first turn it on, you are likely to reduce the volume level. Lowering the volume is negatively reinforcing, and you are more apt to repeat the action in the future when you first turn it on. Negative reinforcement, then, teaches the individual that taking an action removes a negative condition that exists in the environment. Like positive reinforcers, negative reinforcers increase the likelihood that preceding behaviors will be repeated (Magoon & Critchfield, 2008).

punishment A stimulus that decreases the probability that a previous behavior will occur again.

Note that negative reinforcement is not the same as punishment. **Punishment** refers to a stimulus that *decreases* the probability that a prior behavior will occur again. Unlike negative reinforcement, which produces an *increase* in behavior, punishment reduces the likelihood of a prior response. If we receive a shock that is meant to decrease a certain behavior, then we are receiving punishment, but if we are already receiving a shock and do something to stop that shock, the behavior that stops the shock is considered to be negatively reinforced. In the first case, the specific behavior is apt to decrease because of the punishment; in the second, it is likely to increase because of the negative reinforcement.

There are two types of punishment: positive punishment and negative punishment, just as there are positive reinforcement and negative reinforcement. (In both cases, "positive" means adding something, and "negative" means removing something.) *Positive punishment* weakens a response through the application of an unpleasant stimulus. For instance, spanking a child for misbehaving or spending 10 years in jail for committing a crime is positive punishment. In contrast, *negative punishment* consists of the removal of something pleasant. For instance, when a teenager is told she is "grounded" and will no longer be able to use the family car because of her poor grades, or when an employee is informed that he has been demoted with a cut in pay because of a poor job evaluation, negative punishment is being administered. Both positive and negative punishment result in a decrease in the likelihood that a prior behavior will be repeated.

The following rules (and the summary in Figure 3) can help you distinguish these concepts from one another:

- Reinforcement *increases* the frequency of the behavior preceding it; punishment *decreases* the frequency of the behavior preceding it.
- The *application* of a *positive* stimulus brings about an increase in the frequency of behavior and is referred to as positive reinforcement; the *application* of a *negative* stimulus decreases or reduces the frequency of behavior and is called punishment.
- The *removal* of a *negative* stimulus that results in an increase in the frequency of behavior is negative reinforcement; the *removal* of a *positive* stimulus that decreases the frequency of behavior is negative punishment.

Study Alert

The differences between positive reinforcement, negative reinforcement, positive punishment, and negative punishment are tricky, so pay special attention to Figure 3 and the definitions in the text.

Intended Result	When stimulus is added, the result is ...	When stimulus is removed or terminated, the result is ...
Increase in behavior (reinforcement)	**Positive reinforcement** Example: Giving a raise for good performance Result: *Increase* in response of good performance 	**Negative reinforcement** Example: Applying ointment to relieve an itchy rash leads to a higher future likelihood of applying the ointment Result: *Increase* in response of using ointment 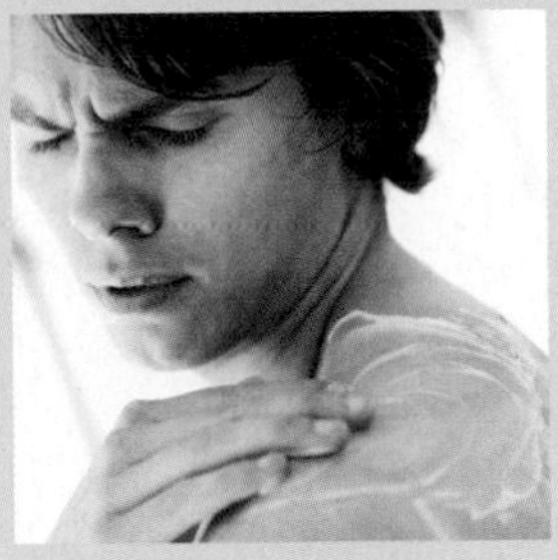
Decrease in behavior (punishment)	**Positive punishment** Example: Yelling at a teenager when she steals a bracelet Result: *Decrease* in frequency of response of stealing 	**Negative punishment** Example: Restricting teenager's access to car due to breaking curfew Result: *Decrease* in response of breaking curfew 

FIGURE 3 Types of reinforcement and punishment.

THE PROS AND CONS OF PUNISHMENT: WHY REINFORCEMENT BEATS PUNISHMENT

Is punishment an effective way to modify behavior? Punishment often presents the quickest route to changing behavior that, if allowed to continue, might be dangerous to an individual. For instance, a parent may not have a second chance to warn a child not to run into a busy street, and so punishing the first incidence of this behavior may prove to be wise. Moreover, the use of punishment to suppress behavior, even temporarily, provides an opportunity to reinforce a person for subsequently behaving in a more desirable way.

There are some rare instances in which punishment can be the most humane approach to treating certain severe disorders. For example, some children suffer from *autism*, a psychological disorder that can lead them to abuse themselves by tearing at their skin or banging their heads against the wall, injuring themselves severely in the process. In such cases—and when all other treatments have failed—punishment in the form of a quick but intense electric shock has been used to prevent self-injurious behavior. Such punishment, however, is used only to keep the child safe and to buy time until positive reinforcement procedures can be initiated (Ducharme, Sanjuan, & Drain, 2007; Matson & LoVullo, 2008; Humphreys & Lee, 2011).

Punishment has several disadvantages that make its routine questionable. For one thing, punishment is frequently ineffective, particularly if it is not delivered shortly after the undesired behavior or if the individual is able to leave the setting in which the punishment is being given. An employee who is reprimanded by the boss may quit; a teenager who loses the use of the family car may borrow a friend's car instead. In such instances, the initial behavior that is being punished may be replaced by one that is even less desirable.

Even worse, physical punishment can convey to the recipient the idea that physical aggression is permissible and perhaps even desirable. A father who yells at and hits his son for misbehaving teaches the son that aggression is an appropriate, adult response. The son soon may copy his father's behavior by acting aggressively toward others. In addition, physical punishment is often administered by people who are themselves angry or enraged. It is unlikely that individuals in such an emotional state will be able to think through what they are doing or control carefully the degree of punishment they are inflicting. Ultimately, those who resort to physical punishment run the risk that they will grow to be feared. Punishment can also reduce the self-esteem of recipients unless they can understand the reasons for it (Leary et al., 2008; Zolotor et al., 2008; Miller-Perrin, Perrin, & Kocur, 2009; Smith, Springer, & Barrett, 2011).

Finally, punishment does not convey any information about what an alternative, more appropriate behavior might be. To be useful in bringing about more desirable behavior in the future, punishment must be accompanied by specific information about the behavior that is being punished, along with specific suggestions concerning a more desirable behavior. Punishing a child for staring out the window in school could merely lead her to stare at the floor instead. Unless we teach her appropriate ways to respond, we have merely managed to substitute one undesirable behavior for another. If punishment is not followed up with reinforcement for subsequent behavior that is more appropriate, little will be accomplished.

In short, reinforcing desired behavior is a more appropriate technique for modifying behavior than using punishment. Both in and out of the scientific arena, then, reinforcement usually beats punishment (Pogarsky & Piquero, 2003; Hiby, Rooney, & Bradshaw, 2004; Sidman, 2006; Hall et al., 2011).

SCHEDULES OF REINFORCEMENT: TIMING LIFE'S REWARDS

The world would be a different place if poker players never played cards again after the first losing hand, fishermen returned to shore as soon as they missed a catch, or telemarketers never made another phone call after their first hang-up. The fact that such unreinforced behaviors continue, often with great frequency and persistence, illustrates that reinforcement need not be received continually for behavior to be learned and maintained. In fact, behavior that is reinforced only occasionally can ultimately be learned better than can behavior that is always reinforced.

schedules of reinforcement Different patterns of frequency and timing of reinforcement following desired behavior.

continuous reinforcement schedule Reinforcing of a behavior every time it occurs.

partial (or intermittent) reinforcement schedule Reinforcing of a behavior some but not all of the time.

When we refer to the frequency and timing of reinforcement that follows desired behavior, we are talking about **schedules of reinforcement.** Behavior that is reinforced every time it occurs is said to be on a **continuous reinforcement schedule;** if it is reinforced some but not all of the time, it is on a **partial (or intermittent) reinforcement schedule.** Although learning occurs more rapidly under a continuous reinforcement schedule, behavior lasts longer after reinforcement stops when it is learned under a partial reinforcement schedule (Staddon & Cerutti, 2003; Gottlieb, 2004; Casey, Cooper-Brown, & Wacher, 2006; Reed, 2007).

Why should intermittent reinforcement result in stronger, longer-lasting learning than continuous reinforcement? We can answer the question by examining how we might behave when using a candy vending machine compared with a Las Vegas slot machine. When we use a vending machine, previous experience has taught us that every time we put in the appropriate amount of money, the reinforcement, a candy bar, ought to be delivered. In other words, the schedule of reinforcement is continuous. In comparison, a slot machine offers intermittent reinforcement. We have learned that after putting in our cash, most of the time we will not receive anything in return. At the same time, though, we know that we will occasionally win something.

Now suppose that, unknown to us, both the candy vending machine and the slot machine are broken, and so neither one is able to dispense anything. It would not be very long before we stopped depositing coins into the broken candy machine. Probably at most we would try only two or three times before leaving the machine in disgust.

But the story would be quite different with the broken slot machine. Here, we would drop in money for a considerably longer time, even though there would be no payoff.

In formal terms, we can see the difference between the two reinforcement schedules: Partial reinforcement schedules (such as those provided by slot machines) maintain performance longer than do continuous reinforcement schedules (such as those established in candy vending machines) before *extinction*—the disappearance of the conditioned response—occurs.

Certain kinds of partial reinforcement schedules produce stronger and lengthier responding before extinction than do others. Although many different partial reinforcement schedules have been examined, they can most readily be put into two categories: schedules that consider the *number of responses* made before reinforcement is given, called fixed-ratio and variable-ratio schedules, and those that consider the *amount of time* that elapses before reinforcement is provided, called fixed-interval and variable-interval schedules (Svartdal, 2003; Pellegrini et al., 2004; Gottlieb, 2006; Reed & Morgan, 2008; Miguez, Witnauer, & Miller, 2011).

Fixed- and Variable-Ratio Schedules. In a **fixed-ratio schedule,** reinforcement is given only after a specific number of responses. For instance, a rat might receive a food pellet every 10th time it pressed a lever; here, the ratio would be 1:10. Similarly, garment workers are generally paid on fixed-ratio schedules: They receive a specific number of dollars for every blouse they sew. Because a greater rate of production means more reinforcement, people on fixed-ratio schedules are apt to work as quickly as possible (see Figure 4).

In a **variable-ratio schedule,** reinforcement occurs after a varying number of responses rather than after a fixed number. Although the specific number of responses

fixed-ratio schedule A schedule by which reinforcement is given only after a specific number of responses are made.

variable-ratio schedule A schedule by which reinforcement occurs after a varying number of responses rather than after a fixed number.

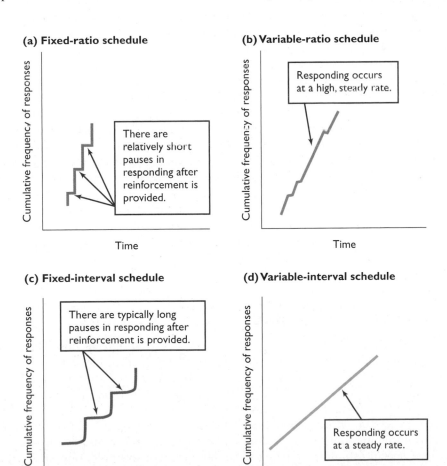

(a) Fixed-ratio schedule

Cumulative frequency of responses

There are relatively short pauses in responding after reinforcement is provided.

Time

(b) Variable-ratio schedule

Cumulative frequency of responses

Responding occurs at a high, steady rate.

Time

(c) Fixed-interval schedule

Cumulative frequency of responses

There are typically long pauses in responding after reinforcement is provided.

Time

(d) Variable-interval schedule

Cumulative frequency of responses

Responding occurs at a steady rate.

Time

FIGURE 4 Typical outcomes of different reinforcement schedules. (a) In a fixed-ratio schedule, reinforcement is provided after a specific number of responses are made. Because the more responses, the more reinforcement, fixed-ratio schedules produce a high rate of responding. (b) In a variable-ratio schedule, responding also occurs at a high rate. (c) A fixed-interval schedule produces lower rates of responding, especially just after reinforcement has been presented, because the organism learns that a specified time period must elapse between reinforcements. (d) A variable-interval schedule produces a fairly steady stream of responses.

fixed-interval schedule A schedule that provides reinforcement for a response only if a fixed time period has elapsed, making overall rates of response relatively low.

variable-interval schedule A schedule by which the time between reinforcements varies around some average rather than being fixed.

necessary to receive reinforcement varies, the number of responses usually hovers around a specific average. A good example of a variable-ratio schedule is a telephone salesperson's job. He might make a sale during the 3rd, 8th, 9th, and 20th calls without being successful during any call in between. Although the number of responses he must make before making a sale varies, it averages out to a 20% success rate. Under these circumstances, you might expect that the salesperson would try to make as many calls as possible in as short a time as possible. This is the case with all variable-ratio schedules, which lead to a high rate of response and resistance to extinction.

Fixed- and Variable-Interval Schedules: The Passage of Time. In contrast to fixed and variable-ratio schedules, in which the crucial factor is the number of responses, fixed-*interval* and variable-*interval* schedules focus on the amount of time that has elapsed since a person or animal was rewarded. One example of a fixed-interval schedule is a weekly paycheck. For people who receive regular, weekly paychecks, it typically makes relatively little difference exactly how much they produce in a given week.

Because a **fixed-interval schedule** provides reinforcement for a response only if a fixed time period has elapsed, overall rates of response are relatively low. This is especially true in the period just after reinforcement, when the time before another reinforcement is relatively great. Students' study habits often exemplify this reality. If the periods between exams are relatively long (meaning that the opportunity for reinforcement for good performance is given fairly infrequently), students often study minimally or not at all until the day of the exam draws near. Just before the exam, however, students begin to cram for it, signaling a rapid increase in the rate of their studying response. As you might expect, immediately after the exam there is a rapid decline in the rate of responding, with few people opening a book the day after a test. Fixed-interval schedules produce the kind of "scalloping effect" shown in Figure 4 on page 183 (Saville, 2009).

One way to decrease the delay in responding that occurs just after reinforcement, and to maintain the desired behavior more consistently throughout an interval, is to use a variable-interval schedule. In a **variable-interval schedule,** the time between reinforcements varies around some average rather than being fixed. For example, a professor who gives surprise quizzes that vary from one every 3 days to one every 3 weeks, averaging one every 2 weeks, is using a variable-interval schedule. Compared to the study habits we observed with a fixed-interval schedule, students' study habits under such a variable-interval schedule would most likely be very different. Students would be apt to study more regularly because they would never know when the next surprise quiz was coming. Variable-interval schedules, in general, are more likely to produce relatively steady rates of responding than are fixed-interval schedules, with responses that take longer to extinguish after reinforcement ends. (Also see *Applying Psychology in the 21st Century*.)

DISCRIMINATION AND GENERALIZATION IN OPERANT CONDITIONING

It does not take a child long to learn that a red light at an intersection means stop and a green light indicates that it is permissible to continue, in the same way that a pigeon can learn to peck a key when a green light goes on but not when a red light appears. Just as in classical conditioning, then, operant learning involves the phenomena of discrimination and generalization.

The process by which people learn to discriminate stimuli is known as stimulus control training. In *stimulus control training,* a behavior is reinforced in the presence of a specific stimulus, but not in its absence. For example, one of the most difficult discriminations many people face is determining when someone's friendliness is not mere friendliness, but a signal of romantic interest. People learn to

Using Operant Conditioning Principles to Save Lives

"This workplace has gone 279 days without an accident."

Signs such as this displayed in work environments are intended to remind employees about safety concerns and to motivate them to engage in good safety habits. But the unspoken message is that safety is measured not in terms of positive behaviors, such as following checklists, reporting close calls, or identifying hazards promptly, but rather in terms of failures—the occurrence of actual, and perhaps preventable, accidents.

The problem with focusing on the accidents is that it's a reactive strategy—the accident you want to prevent actually has to happen, and only then does someone investigate its cause and possibly its prevention. This very act of investigating and determining a cause implies that someone is looking to place blame. This act also assumes that there is an identifiable cause. This approach tends to create a punitive atmosphere that instills fear, stifles conversations about safety practices, and discourages reporting of problems (Geller, 2001, 2011).

A better approach is to implement a procedure called *behavior-based safety*. First, employees gather in discussion groups to list the various tasks of their work. They define safe and unsafe behaviors that pertain to

Instead of focusing on failures in a workplace to promote safety, new studies find that applying a behavior-based safety approach, emphasizing prevention, works better.

each task. These discussions, then, result in a checklist of desirable and undesirable safety behaviors. For instance, if one work task involves lifting a heavy object, safe behaviors might include wearing a back brace and lifting with your legs; unsafe behaviors might be lifting with your back and not using a back brace. Employees can use these checklists to monitor each other's behavior and provide feedback on their safe work habits. Managers can identify tasks where risky behavior is most problematic and take corrective steps, one of which might be to focus employees more on using the checklists (Geller, 2001, 2011).

These checklists, then, identify and help to correct risks *before* an accident happens. There is no individual blame or punishment—instead employees work together to make the workplace safer for everyone. Instead of reacting to failure, employees proactively strive to do better. And very importantly, employees have a sense of personal control over their own safety. They feel a sense of individual responsibility as well as empowerment to make positive changes. In such an environment, safety isn't just a vague value—it's an everyday concern shared by every single employee working together not just to prevent accidents, but to work smarter (Deci & Ryan, 1995; Geller, 2011).

RETHINK

- Why do you think it's important to use checklists that identify positive safety behaviors as well as risky behaviors?
- Why is it important for employees to feel a sense of personal control over the safety of their workplace?

make the discrimination by observing the presence of certain nonverbal cues—such as increased eye contact and touching—that indicate romantic interest. When such cues are absent, people learn that no romantic interest is indicated. In this case, the nonverbal cue acts as a discriminative stimulus, one to which an organism learns to respond during stimulus control training. A *discriminative stimulus* signals the likelihood that reinforcement will follow a response. For example, if you wait until your roommate is in a good mood before you ask to borrow her favorite CD, your behavior can be said to be under stimulus control because you can discriminate between her moods.

Just as in classical conditioning, the phenomenon of stimulus generalization, in which an organism learns a response to one stimulus and then exhibits the same response to slightly different stimuli, occurs in operant conditioning. If you have learned that being polite helps you to get your way in a certain situation (reinforcing your politeness), you are likely to generalize your response to other situations. Sometimes, though, generalization can have unfortunate consequences, as when people behave negatively toward all members of a racial group because they have had an unpleasant experience with one member of that group.

SHAPING: REINFORCING WHAT DOESN'T COME NATURALLY

Consider the difficulty of using operant conditioning to teach people to repair an automobile transmission. If you had to wait until they chanced to fix a transmission perfectly before you provided them with reinforcement, the Model T Ford might be back in style long before they mastered the repair process.

There are many complex behaviors, ranging from auto repair to zoo management, that we would not expect to occur naturally as part of anyone's spontaneous behavior. For such behaviors, for which there might otherwise be no opportunity to provide reinforcement (because the behavior would never occur in the first place), a procedure known as shaping is used. **Shaping** is the process of teaching a complex behavior by rewarding closer and closer approximations of the desired behavior. In shaping, you start by reinforcing any behavior that is at all similar to the behavior you want the person to learn. Later, you reinforce only responses that are closer to the behavior you ultimately want to teach. Finally, you reinforce only the desired response. Each step in shaping, then, moves only slightly beyond the previously learned behavior, permitting the person to link the new step to the behavior learned earlier (Krueger & Dayan, 2009).

Shaping allows even lower animals to learn complex responses that would never occur naturally, ranging from lions jumping through hoops, dolphins rescuing divers lost at sea, or rodents finding hidden land mines. Shaping also underlies the learning of many complex human skills. For instance, the organization of most textbooks is based on the principles of shaping. Typically, information is presented so that new material builds on previously learned concepts or skills. Thus, the concept of shaping could not be presented until we had discussed the more basic principles of operant learning (Meyer & Ladewig, 2008). (Also see *PsychWork*.)

shaping The process of teaching a complex behavior by rewarding closer and closer approximations of the desired behavior.

PsychTech

Computer-based *adaptive learning* techniques—based on the principles of shaping—present students with new material and then quiz them on it online. Presentation of subsequent material is based on students' previous performance on the quiz, so that the level and difficulty of new material is personalized, leading to great student success.

PsychWork

SEEING EYE GUIDE DOG TRAINER

Name: Lea Johnson

Position: Seeing Eye Guide Dog Trainer

Education: BS, Geography, Dartmouth College, Hanover, NH

For decades, guide dogs have provided a set of eyes to the visually impaired, expanding the opportunities open to them and increasing their independence. But it takes a great deal of training to make a dog an effective seeing eye guide dog, according to Lea Johnson, who works with The Seeing Eye agency in Morristown, New Jersey. Johnson teaches apprentice instructors to carry out the demanding, but rewarding, process of training dogs.

"We hire college graduates, and while we don't require a specific major, a background in psychology or animal science allows employees to more easily connect with different aspects of the job," she said.

An apprentice instructor needs to have self-motivation in order to complete all aspects of the dog's training. In addition, they need to be able to work in a team setting, according to Johnson. But that's only part of it.

"The process of training the dogs is complex," says Johnson. "For example, the dog must be obedient and respond to their visually-impaired owner. But they also get praised for sometimes refusing their owner's commands, if it would put their owner in danger."

Once a dog learns the skills it needs, the trainer must then teach a visually-impaired person how to work with the dog.

"After training dogs for four months, the trainers must be able to teach blind people the skills to care for and travel with their Seeing Eye dog safely," Johnson said. Not only must trainers relate well to dogs, but they also must interact well with blind people. She adds, "The training of people is intense and emotionally challenging in a very different way from the dog training portion. Without a good heart to start with, trainers would never be successful."

BIOLOGICAL CONSTRAINTS ON LEARNING: YOU CAN'T TEACH AN OLD DOG JUST ANY TRICK

Not all behaviors can be trained in all species equally well. Instead, there are *biological constraints,* built-in limitations in the ability of animals to learn particular behaviors. In some cases, an organism has a special predisposition that will aid in its learning a behavior (such as pecking behaviors in pigeons). In other cases, biological constraints act to prevent or inhibit an organism from learning a behavior. For example, it's impossible to train pigs to pick up a disk, because they are biologically programmed to push objects like it along the ground. Similarly, although a raccoon can be conditioned to drop a single coin into a piggy bank, it will do so only after rubbing the coin against the outside of the bank. The reason? After catching a fish, raccoons instinctually rub them against the ground to remove their outer covering (Breland & Breland, 1966; Stevens & Pashler, 2002).

Biological constraints make it nearly impossible for animals to learn certain behaviors. Here, psychologist Marian Breland attempts to overcome the natural limitations that inhibit the success of conditioning this rooster.

The existence of biological constraints is consistent with evolutionary explanations of behavior. Clearly, there are adaptive benefits that promote survival for organisms that quickly learn—or avoid—certain behaviors. For example, our ability to rapidly learn to avoid touching hot surfaces increases our chances of survival. Additional support for the evolutionary interpretation of biological constraints lies in the fact the associations that animals learn most readily involve stimuli that are most relevant to the specific environment in which they live (Cosmides & Tooby, 2004; Davis, 2007; Behrendt, 2011).

Furthermore, psychologists taking an evolutionary perspective have suggested that we may be genetically predisposed to be fearful of certain stimuli, such as snakes or even threatening faces. For example, people in experiments learn associations relatively quickly between photos of faces with threatening expressions and neutral stimuli (such as an umbrella). In contrast, they are slower to learn associations between faces that have pleasant expressions and neutral stimuli. Stimuli that pose potential threats, like snakes or people with hostile facial expressions, posed a potential danger to early humans, and there may be an evolved "fear module" in the brain that is sensitized to such threats (Endres & Fendt, 2007; DeLoache & LoBue, 2009; Gerdes, Uhl, & Alpers, 2009).

COMPARING CLASSICAL AND OPERANT CONDITIONING

We've considered classical conditioning and operant conditioning as two completely different processes. And, as summarized in Figure 5 on page 188, there are a number of key distinctions between the two forms of learning. For example, the key concept in classical conditioning is the association between stimuli, whereas in operant conditioning it is reinforcement. Furthermore, classical conditioning involves an involuntary, natural, innate behavior, but operant conditioning is based on voluntary responses made by an organism.

Some researchers are asking if, in fact, the two types of learning are so different after all. Some learning psychologists have suggested that classical and operant conditioning might share some underlying processes. Arguing from an evolutionary viewpoint, they contend that it is unlikely that two completely separate basic processes would evolve. Instead, one process—albeit with considerable complexity in the way it operates—might better explain behavior. Although it's too early to know if this point of view will be supported, it is clear that there are a number of processes that operate both in classical and operant conditioning, including extinction, stimulus generalization, and stimulus discrimination (Donahoe, 2003; Donahoe & Vegas, 2004; Silva, Gonçalves, & Garcia-Mijares, 2007).

Concept	Classical Conditioning	Operant Conditioning
Basic principle	Building associations between a conditioned stimulus and conditioned response.	Reinforcement *increases* the frequency of the behavior preceding it; punishment *decreases* the frequency of the behavior preceding it.
Nature of behavior	Based on involuntary, natural, innate behavior. Behavior is elicited by the unconditioned or conditioned stimulus.	Organism voluntarily operates on its environment to produce a desirable result. After behavior occurs, the likelihood of the behavior occurring again is increased or decreased by the behavior's consequences.
Order of events	Before conditioning, an unconditioned stimulus leads to an unconditioned response. After conditioning, a conditioned stimulus leads to a conditioned response.	Reinforcement leads to an increase in behavior; punishment leads to a decrease in behavior.
Example	After a physician gives a child a series of painful injections (an unconditioned stimulus) that produce an emotional reaction (an unconditioned response), the child develops an emotional reaction (a conditioned response) whenever he sees the physician (the conditioned stimulus).	A student who, after studying hard for a test, earns an A (the positive reinforcer), is more likely to study hard in the future. A student who, after going out drinking the night before a test, fails the test (punishment) is less likely to go out drinking the night before the next test.

FIGURE 5 Comparing key concepts in classical conditioning and operant conditioning.

BECOMING AN INFORMED CONSUMER of Psychology

Using Behavior Analysis and Behavior Modification

A couple who had been living together for 3 years began to fight frequently. The issues of disagreement ranged from who was going to do the dishes to the quality of their love life.

Disturbed, the couple went to a *behavior analyst,* a psychologist who specialized in behavior-modification techniques. He asked them to keep a detailed written record of their interactions over the next 2 weeks.

When they returned with the data, he carefully reviewed the records with them. In doing so, he noticed a pattern: Each of their arguments had occurred just after one or the other had left a household chore undone, such as leaving dirty dishes in the sink or draping clothes on the only chair in the bedroom.

Using the data the couple had collected, the behavior analyst asked them to list all the chores that could possibly arise and assign each one a point value depending on how long it took to complete. Then he had them divide the chores equally and agree in a written contract to fulfill the ones assigned to them. If either failed to carry out one of the assigned chores, he or she would have to place $1 per point in a fund for the other to spend. They also agreed to a program of verbal praise, promising to reward each other verbally for completing a chore.

The couple agreed to try it for a month and to keep careful records of the number of arguments they had during that period. To their surprise, the number declined rapidly.

The case just presented provides an illustration of **behavior modification,** a formalized technique for promoting the frequency of desirable behaviors and decreasing the incidence of unwanted ones. Using the basic principles of learning theory, behavior-modification techniques have proved to be helpful in a variety of situations. People with severe mental retardation have, for the first time in their lives, started dressing and feeding themselves. Behavior modification has also helped people lose weight, give up smoking, and behave more safely (Delinsky, Latner, & Wilson, 2006; Ntinas, 2007; Carels et al., 2011).

The techniques used by behavior analysts are as varied as the list of processes that modify behavior. They include reinforcement scheduling, shaping, generalization training, discrimination training, and extinction. Participants in a behavior-change program do, however, typically follow a series of similar basic steps that include the following:

- *Identifying goals and target behaviors.* The first step is to define *desired behavior.* Is it an increase in time spent studying? A decrease in weight? An increase in the use of language? A reduction in the amount of aggression displayed by a child? The goals must be stated in observable terms and must lead to specific targets. For instance, a goal might be "to increase study time," whereas the target behavior would be "to study at least 2 hours per day on weekdays and an hour on Saturdays."
- *Designing a data-recording system and recording preliminary data.* To determine whether behavior has changed, it is necessary to collect data before any changes are made in the situation. This information provides a baseline against which future changes can be measured.
- *Selecting a behavior-change strategy.* The crucial step is to select an appropriate strategy. Because all the principles of learning can be employed to bring about behavior change, a "package" of treatments is normally used. This might include the systematic use of positive reinforcement for desired behavior (verbal praise or something more tangible, such as food), as well as a program of extinction for undesirable behavior (ignoring a child who throws a tantrum). Selecting the right reinforcers is critical, and it may be necessary to experiment a bit to find out what is important to a particular individual.
- *Implementing the program.* Probably the most important aspect of program implementation is consistency. It is also important to reinforce the intended behavior. For example, suppose a mother wants her son to spend more time on his homework, but as soon as he sits down to study, he asks for a snack. If the mother gets a snack for him, she is likely to be reinforcing her son's delaying tactic, not his studying.
- *Keeping careful records after the program is implemented.* Another crucial task is record keeping. If the target behaviors are not monitored, there is no way of knowing whether the program has actually been successful.
- *Evaluating and altering the ongoing program.* Finally, the results of the program should be compared with baseline, pre-implementation data to determine its effectiveness. If the program has been successful, the procedures employed can be phased out gradually. For instance, if the program called for reinforcing every instance of picking up one's clothes from the bedroom floor, the reinforcement schedule could be modified to a fixed-ratio schedule in which every third instance was reinforced. However, if the program has not been successful in bringing about the desired behavior change, consideration of other approaches might be advisable.

Behavior-change techniques based on these general principles have enjoyed wide success and have proved to be one of the most powerful means of modifying behavior. Clearly, it is possible to employ the basic notions of learning theory to improve our lives.

behavior modification A formalized technique for promoting the frequency of desirable behaviors and decreasing the incidence of unwanted ones.

RECAP/EVALUATE/RETHINK

RECAP

LO 16-1 What is the role of reward and punishment in learning?

- Operant conditioning is a form of learning in which a voluntary behavior is strengthened or weakened. According to B. F. Skinner, the major mechanism underlying learning is reinforcement, the process by which a stimulus increases the probability that a preceding behavior will be repeated. (pp. 177, 178)
- Primary reinforcers are rewards that are naturally effective without previous experience, because they satisfy a biological need. Secondary reinforcers begin to act as if they were primary reinforcers through association with a primary reinforcer. (p. 179)
- Positive reinforcers are stimuli that are added to the environment and lead to an increase in a preceding response. Negative reinforcers are stimuli that remove something unpleasant from the environment, also leading to an increase in the preceding response. (p. 180)
- Punishment decreases the probability that a prior behavior will occur. Positive punishment weakens a response through the application of an unpleasant stimulus, whereas negative punishment weakens a response by the removal of something positive. In contrast to reinforcement, in which the goal is to increase the incidence of behavior, punishment is meant to decrease or suppress behavior. (p. 181)
- Schedules and patterns of reinforcement affect the strength and duration of learning. Generally, partial reinforcement schedules—in which reinforcers are not delivered on every trial—produce stronger and longer-lasting learning than do continuous reinforcement schedules. (p. 182)
- Among the major categories of reinforcement schedules are fixed- and variable-ratio schedules, which are based on the number of responses made, and fixed- and variable-interval schedules, which are based on the time interval that elapses before reinforcement is provided. (pp. 183, 184)
- Stimulus control training (similar to stimulus discrimination in classical conditioning) is reinforcement of a behavior in the presence of a specific stimulus but not in its absence. In stimulus generalization, an organism learns a response to one stimulus and then exhibits the same response to slightly different stimuli. (pp. 184, 185)
- Shaping is a process for teaching complex behaviors by rewarding closer and closer approximations of the desired final behavior. (p. 186)
- There are biological constraints, or built-in limitations, on the ability of an organism to learn: Certain behaviors will be relatively easy for individuals of a species to learn, whereas other behaviors will be either difficult or impossible for them to learn. (p. 187)

LO 16-2 What are some practical methods for bringing about behavior change, both in ourselves and in others?

- Behavior modification is a method for formally using the principles of learning theory to promote the frequency of desired behaviors and to decrease or eliminate unwanted ones. (p. 189)

EVALUATE

1. _____ conditioning describes learning that occurs as a result of reinforcement.
2. Match the type of operant learning with its definition:
   1. An unpleasant stimulus is presented to decrease behavior.
   2. An unpleasant stimulus is removed to increase behavior.
   3. A pleasant stimulus is presented to increase behavior.
   4. A pleasant stimulus is removed to decrease behavior.

   a. positive reinforcement
   b. negative reinforcement
   c. positive punishment
   d. negative punishment

3. Sandy had had a rough day, and his son's noisemaking was not helping him relax. Not wanting to resort to scolding, Sandy told his son in a serious manner that he was very tired and would like the boy to play quietly for an hour. This approach worked. For Sandy, the change in his son's behavior was
   a. positively reinforcing.
   b. negatively reinforcing.
4. In a _____ reinforcement schedule, behavior is reinforced some of the time, whereas in a _____ reinforcement schedule, behavior is reinforced all the time.
5. Match the type of reinforcement schedule with its definition.
   1. Reinforcement occurs after a set time period.
   2. Reinforcement occurs after a set number of responses.
   3. Reinforcement occurs after a varying time period.
   4. Reinforcement occurs after a varying number of responses.

   a. fixed-ratio
   b. variable-interval
   c. fixed-interval
   d. variable-ratio

RETHINK

1. Using the scientific literature as a guide, what would you tell parents who wish to know if the routine use of physical punishment is a necessary and acceptable form of child rearing?
2. *From the perspective of an educator:* How would you use your knowledge of operant conditioning in the classroom to set up a program to increase the likelihood that children will complete their homework more frequently?

Answers to Evaluate Questions

1. Operant; 2. 1-c, 2-b, 3-a, 4-d; 3. b; 4. partial (or intermittent), continuous; 5. 1-c, 2-a, 3-b, 4-d

KEY TERMS

operant
  conditioning p. 177
reinforcement p. 178
reinforcer p. 179
positive
  reinforcer p. 180

negative reinforcer p. 180
punishment p. 180
schedules of
  reinforcement p. 182
continuous reinforcement
  schedule p. 182

partial (or intermittent)
  reinforcement
  schedule p. 182
fixed-ratio schedule p. 183
variable-ratio
  schedule p. 183

fixed-interval schedule p. 184
variable-interval
  schedule p. 184
shaping p. 186
behavior
  modification p. 189

Cognitive Approaches to Learning

Learning Outcome

LO 17-1 What is the role of cognition and thought in learning?

cognitive learning theory An approach to the study of learning that focuses on the thought processes that underlie learning.

Study Alert

Remember that the cognitive learning approach focuses on the *internal* thoughts and expectations of learners, whereas classical and operant conditioning approaches focus on *external* stimuli, responses, and reinforcement.

Consider what happens when people learn to drive a car. They don't just get behind the wheel and stumble around until they randomly put the key into the ignition and, later, after many false starts, accidentally manage to get the car to move forward, thereby receiving positive reinforcement. Rather, they already know the basic elements of driving from previous experience as passengers, when they more than likely noticed how the key was inserted into the ignition, the car was put in drive, and the gas pedal was pressed to make the car go forward.

Clearly, not all learning is due to operant and classical conditioning. In fact, such activities as learning to drive a car imply that some kinds of learning must involve higher-order processes in which people's thoughts and memories and the way they process information account for their responses. Such situations argue against regarding learning as the unthinking, mechanical, and automatic acquisition of associations between stimuli and responses, as in classical conditioning, or the presentation of reinforcement, as in operant conditioning.

Some psychologists view learning in terms of the thought processes, or cognitions, that underlie it—an approach known as **cognitive learning theory.** Although psychologists working from the cognitive learning perspective do not deny the importance of classical and operant conditioning, they have developed approaches that focus on the unseen mental processes that occur during learning, rather than concentrating solely on external stimuli, responses, and reinforcements.

In its most basic formulation, cognitive learning theory suggests that it is not enough to say that people make responses because there is an assumed link between a stimulus and a response—a link that is the result of a past history of reinforcement for a response. Instead, according to this point of view, people, and even lower animals, develop an *expectation* that they will receive a reinforcer after making a response. Two types of learning in which no obvious prior reinforcement is present are latent learning and observational learning.

Latent Learning

latent learning Learning in which a new behavior is acquired but is not demonstrated until some incentive is provided for displaying it.

Evidence for the importance of cognitive processes comes from a series of animal experiments that revealed a type of cognitive learning called latent learning. In **latent learning,** a new behavior is learned but not demonstrated until some incentive is provided for displaying it (Tolman & Honzik, 1930). In short, latent learning occurs without reinforcement.

In the studies demonstrating latent learning, psychologists examined the behavior of rats in a maze such as the one shown in Figure 1a. In one experiment, a group of rats was allowed to wander around the maze once a day for 17 days without ever receiving a reward (called the unrewarded group). Understandably, those rats made many errors and spent a relatively long time reaching the end of the maze. A second group, however, was always given food at the end of the maze (the rewarded group). Not surprisingly, those rats learned to run quickly and directly to the food box, making few errors.

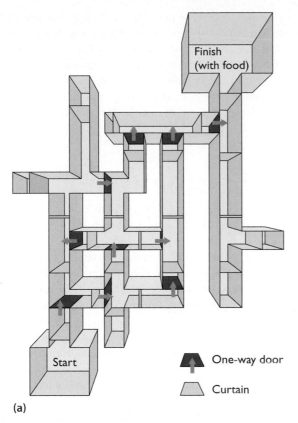

(a)

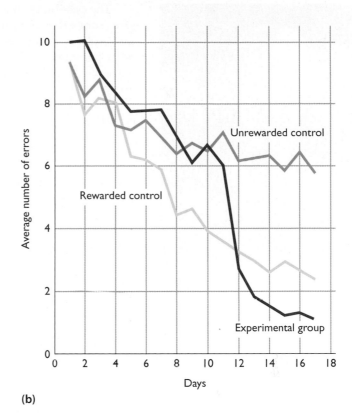

(b)

FIGURE 1 Latent learning. (a) Rats were allowed to roam through a maze of this sort once a day for 17 days. (b) The rats that were never rewarded (the unrewarded control condition) consistently made the most errors, whereas those that received food at the finish every day (the rewarded control condition) consistently made far fewer errors. But the results also showed latent learning: Rats that were rewarded only after the 10th day (the experimental group) showed an immediate reduction in errors and soon became similar in error rate to the rats that had been rewarded consistently. According to cognitive learning theorists, the reduction in errors indicates that the rats had developed a cognitive map—a mental representation—of the maze. Can you think of other examples of latent learning?

A third group of rats (the experimental group) started out in the same situation as the unrewarded rats, but only for the first 10 days. On the 11th day, a critical experimental manipulation was introduced: From that point on, the rats in this group were given food for completing the maze. The results of this manipulation were dramatic, as you can see from the graph in Figure 1b. The previously unrewarded rats, which had earlier seemed to wander about aimlessly, showed such reductions in running time and declines in error rates that their performance almost immediately matched that of the group that had received rewards from the start.

To cognitive theorists, it seemed clear that the unrewarded rats had learned the layout of the maze early in their explorations; they just never displayed their latent learning until the reinforcement was offered. Instead, those rats seemed to develop a *cognitive map* of the maze—a mental representation of spatial locations and directions.

People, too, develop cognitive maps of their surroundings. For example, latent learning may permit you to know the location of a kitchenware store at a local mall you've frequently visited, even though you've never entered the store and don't even like to cook.

Albert Bandura examined the principles of observational learning.

observational learning Learning by observing the behavior of another person, or model.

This boy is displaying observational learning based on previous observation of his father. How does observational learning contribute to learning gender roles?

The possibility that we develop our cognitive maps through latent learning presents something of a problem for strict operant conditioning theorists. If we consider the results of the maze-learning experiment, for instance, it is unclear what reinforcement permitted the rats that initially received no reward to learn the layout of the maze, because there was no obvious reinforcer present. Instead, the results support a cognitive view of learning, in which changes occurred in unobservable mental processes (Frensch & Rünger, 2003; Stouffer & White, 2006; Iaria et al., 2009; Lin et al., 2011).

Observational Learning: Learning Through Imitation

Let's return for a moment to the case of a person learning to drive. How can we account for instances in which an individual with no direct experience in carrying out a particular behavior learns the behavior and then performs it? To answer this question, psychologists have focused on another aspect of cognitive learning: observational learning.

According to psychologist Albert Bandura and colleagues, a major part of human learning consists of **observational learning,** which is learning by watching the behavior of another person, or *model*. Because of its reliance on observation of others—a social phenomenon—the perspective taken by Bandura is often referred to as a *social cognitive* approach to learning (Bandura, 2004, 2009).

Bandura dramatically demonstrated the ability of models to stimulate learning in a classic experiment. In the study, young children saw a film of an adult wildly hitting a 5-feet-tall inflatable punching toy called a Bobo doll (Bandura, Ross, & Ross, 1963a, 1963b). Later the children were given the opportunity to play with the Bobo doll themselves, and, sure enough, most displayed the same kind of behavior, in some cases mimicking the aggressive behavior almost identically.

Not only negative behaviors are acquired through observational learning. In one experiment, for example, children who were afraid of dogs were exposed to a model—dubbed the Fearless Peer—playing with a dog (Bandura, Grusec, & Menlove, 1967). After exposure, observers were considerably more likely to approach a strange dog than were children who had not viewed the Fearless Peer.

Observational learning is particularly important in acquiring skills in which the operant conditioning technique of shaping is inappropriate. Piloting an airplane and performing brain surgery, for example, are behaviors that could hardly be learned by using trial-and-error methods without grave cost—literally—to those involved in the learning process.

Observational learning may have a genetic basis. For example, we find observational learning at work with mother animals teaching their young such activities as hunting. In addition, the discovery of *mirror neurons* that fire when we observe another person carrying out a behavior (discussed in the "Neuroscience and Behavior" chapter) suggests that the capacity to imitate others may be innate (Lepage & Theoret, 2007; Schulte-Ruther et al., 2007; Huesmann, Dubow, & Boxer, 2011) (see Figure 2 *Neuroscience in Your Life*).

Not all behavior that we witness is learned or carried out, of course. One crucial factor that determines whether we later imitate a model is whether the model is rewarded for his or her behavior. If we observe a friend being rewarded for putting more time into his studies by receiving higher grades, we are more likely to imitate his behavior than we would if his behavior resulted only in being stressed and tired. Models who are rewarded for behaving in a particular way are more apt to be mimicked than are models who receive punishment. Observing the punishment of a

Neuroscience in Your Life:
Learning Through Imitation

FIGURE 2 Both children and adults learn, in part, by imitating others. How this learning occurs in the brain, however, is only beginning to be understood. While many recent studies have focused on the role of mirror neurons, researchers have begun to examine how this process also may occur through a process called *mentalizing*, which involves understanding someone's mental state. In these scans, areas of the prefrontal cortex appear to be associated with mentalizing. These areas are engaged when participants are asked to look at pictures of someone completing an action and then asked to imagine answers to the questions of how the person is performing the action, what action is being performed, and why the person is doing it. With each level of question ("how" being the lowest, "why" being the highest) there is increasing activation in the mentalizing areas of the brain as highlighted in the scan. (Source: Spunt, Satpute, & Lieberman, 2011.)

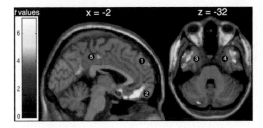

model, however, does not necessarily stop observers from learning the behavior. Observers can still describe the model's behavior—they are just less apt to perform it (Bandura, 1977, 1986, 1994).

Observational learning is central to a number of important issues relating to the extent to which people learn simply by watching the behavior of others. For instance, the degree to which observation of media aggression produces subsequent aggression on the part of viewers is a crucial—and controversial—question, as we discuss next.

VIOLENCE IN TELEVISION AND VIDEO GAMES: DOES THE MEDIA'S MESSAGE MATTER?

In an episode of *The Sopranos*, a former television series, fictional mobster Tony Soprano murdered one of his associates. To make identification of the victim's body difficult, Soprano and one of his henchmen dismembered the body and dumped the body parts.

A few months later, in real life, two half brothers in Riverside, California, strangled their mother and then cut her head and hands from her body. Victor Bautista, 20, and Matthew Montejo, 15, were caught by police after a security guard noticed that the bundle they were attempting to throw in a Dumpster had a foot sticking out of it. They told police that the plan to dismember their mother was inspired by the *Sopranos* episode (Martelle, Hanley, & Yoshino, 2003).

Like other "media copycat" killings, the brothers' cold-blooded brutality raises a critical issue: Does observing violent, antisocial acts in the media lead viewers to behave in similar ways? Because research on modeling shows that people frequently learn and imitate the aggression that they observe, this question is among the most important issues being addressed by psychologists.

Study Alert

A key point of observational learning approaches: Behavior of models who are rewarded for a given behavior is more likely to be imitated than that of models who are punished for the behavior.

Certainly, the amount of violence in the mass media is enormous. By the time of elementary school graduation, the average child in the United States will have viewed more than 8,000 murders and more than 800,000 violent acts on network television (Huston et al., 1992; Mifflin, 1998).

Most psychologists agree that watching high levels of media violence makes viewers more susceptible to acting aggressively. For example, one survey showed that one-fourth of violent young male offenders incarcerated in Florida had attempted to commit a media-inspired copycat crime. A significant proportion of those teenage offenders noted that they paid close attention to the media (Surette, 2002; Savage & Yancey, 2008; Boxer et al., 2009).

Violent video games have also been linked with actual aggression. In one of a series of studies by psychologist Craig Anderson and his colleagues, college students who frequently played violent video games, such as *Postal* or *Doom,* were more likely to have been involved in delinquent behavior and aggression. Frequent players also had lower academic achievement. Some researchers believe that violent video games may produce certain positive results—such as a rise in social networking (Ferguson, 2010, 2011). But most agree the preponderance of evidence suggests that they produce negative outcomes (Anderson & Carnagey, 2009; Anderson et al., 2010; Bailey, West, & Anderson, 2011).

Several aspects of media violence may contribute to real-life aggressive behavior. For one thing, experiencing violent media content seems to lower inhibitions against carrying out aggression—watching television portrayals of violence or using violence to win a video game makes aggression seem a legitimate response to particular situations. Exposure to media violence also may distort our understanding of the meaning of others' behavior, predisposing us to view even nonaggressive acts by others as aggressive. Finally, a continuous diet of aggression may leave us desensitized to violence, and what previously would have repelled us now produces little emotional response. Our sense of the pain and suffering brought about by aggression may be diminished (Bartholow, Bushman, & Sestir, 2006; Weber, Ritterfeld, & Kostygina, 2006; Carnagey, Anderson, & Bushman, 2007).

What about real-life exposure to *actual* violence? Does it also lead to increases in aggression? The answer is yes. Exposure to actual firearm violence (being shot or being shot at) doubles the probability that an adolescent will commit serious violence over the next 2 years. Whether the violence is real or fictionalized, then, observing violent behavior leads to increases in aggressive behavior (Bingenheimer, Brennan, & Earls, 2005; Allwood, 2007).

PsychTech
Video gaming can also have positive consequences: Playing video games with positive, prosocial themes increases empathy and thoughts about helping others.

Illustrating observational learning, this infant observes an adult on television and then is able to imitate his behavior. Learning has obviously occurred through the mere observation of the television model.

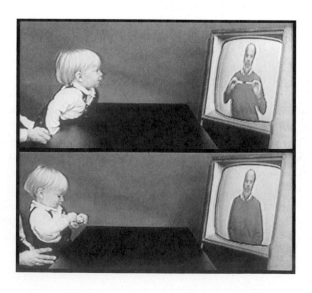

Exploring DIVERSITY

Does Culture Influence How We Learn?

When a member of the Chilcotin Indian tribe teaches her daughter to prepare salmon, at first she allows the daughter only to observe the entire process. A little later, she permits her child to try out some basic parts of the task. Her response to questions is noteworthy. For example, when the daughter asks about how to do "the backbone part," the mother's response is to repeat the entire process with another salmon. The reason? The mother feels that one cannot learn the individual parts of the task apart from the context of preparing the whole fish (Tharp, 1989).

It should not be surprising that children raised in the Chilcotin tradition, which stresses instruction that starts by communicating the entire task, may have difficulty with traditional Western schooling. In the approach to teaching most characteristic of Western culture, tasks are broken down into their component parts. Only after each small step is learned is it thought possible to master the complete task.

Do the differences in teaching approaches between cultures affect how people learn? Some psychologists, taking a cognitive perspective on learning, suggest that people develop particular *learning styles,* characteristic ways of approaching material, based on their cultural background and unique pattern of abilities (Barmeyer, 2004; Wilkinson & Olliver-Gray, 2006; Sternberg, 2011).

Learning styles differ along several dimensions. For example, one central dimension is relational versus analytical approaches to learning. As illustrated in Figure 3, people with a *relational learning style* master material best through exposure to a full unit or phenomenon. Parts of the unit are comprehended only when their relationship to the whole is understood. In contrast, those with an *analytical learning style* do best when they can carry

Relational Style	Analytical Style
● Perceive information as part of total picture	● Focus on detail
● Show intuitive thinking	● Show sequential and structured thinking
● More easily learn materials that have a human, social content	● More easily learn materials that are impersonal
● Have a good memory for verbally presented ideas and information	● Have a good memory for abstract ideas
● Are influenced by others' opinion	● Are not greatly affected by the opinions of others
● Style conflicts with the traditional school environment	● Style matches traditional school environments

FIGURE 3 A comparison of relational versus analytical approaches to learning offers one example of how learning styles differ along several dimensions.

out an initial analysis of the principles and components underlying a phenomenon or situation. By developing an understanding of the fundamental principles and components, they are best able to understand the full picture.

According to James Anderson and Maurianne Adams, particular minority groups in Western societies display characteristic learning styles. For instance, they argue that Caucasian females and African-American, Native-American, and Hispanic-American males and females are more apt to use a relational style of learning than are Caucasian and Asian-American males, who are more likely to employ an analytical style (Anderson & Adams, 1992; Adams et al., 2000; Adams, Bell, & Griffin, 2007).

The conclusion that members of particular ethnic and gender groups have similar learning styles is controversial. Because there is so much diversity within each particular racial and ethnic group, critics argue that generalizations about learning styles cannot be used to predict the style of any single individual, regardless of group membership.

Still, it is clear that values about learning, which are communicated through a person's family and cultural background, have an impact on how successful students are in school. One theory suggests that members of minority groups who were voluntary immigrants are more apt to be successful in school than those who were brought into a majority culture against their will. For example, Korean children in the United States—the sons and daughters of voluntary immigrants—perform quite well, as a group, in school. In contrast, Korean children in Japan, who were often the sons and daughters of people who were forced to immigrate during World War II, essentially as forced laborers, do less well in school. The theory suggests that the motivation to succeed is lower for children in forced immigration groups (Ogbu, 1992, 2003; Foster, 2005).

RECAP/EVALUATE/RETHINK

RECAP

LO 17-1 What is the role of cognition and thought in learning?

- Cognitive approaches to learning consider learning in terms of thought processes, or cognition. Phenomena such as latent learning—in which a new behavior is learned but not performed until some incentive is provided for its performance—and the apparent development of cognitive maps support cognitive approaches. (p. 192)
- Learning also occurs from observing the behavior of others. The major factor that determines whether an observed behavior will actually be performed is the nature of the reinforcement or punishment a model receives. (p. 194)
- Observation of violence is linked to a greater likelihood of subsequently acting aggressively. (p. 195)
- Learning styles are characteristic ways of approaching learning, based on a person's cultural background and unique pattern of abilities. Whether an individual has an analytical or a relational style of learning, for example, may reflect family background or culture. (p. 197)

EVALUATE

1. Cognitive learning theorists are concerned only with overt behavior, not with its internal causes. True or false?

2. In cognitive learning theory, it is assumed that people develop a(n) _____ about receiving a reinforcer when they behave a certain way.
3. In _____ learning, a new behavior is learned but is not shown until appropriate reinforcement is presented.
4. Bandura's _____ theory of learning states that people learn through watching a(n) _____ (another person displaying the behavior of interest).

RETHINK

1. The relational style of learning sometimes conflicts with the traditional school environment. Could a school be created that takes advantage of the characteristics of the relational style? How? Are there types of learning for which the analytical style is clearly superior?
2. *From the perspective of a social worker:* What advice would you give to families about children's exposure to violent media and video games?

Answers to Evaluate Questions

1. False; cognitive learning theorists are primarily concerned with mental processes; 2. expectation; 3. latent; 4. observational, model

KEY TERMS

cognitive learning theory p. 192
latent learning p. 192
observational learning p. 194

Looking Back

Epilogue

Here we have discussed several kinds of learning, ranging from classical conditioning, which depends on the existence of natural stimulus–response pairings, to operant conditioning, in which reinforcement is used to increase desired behavior. These approaches to learning focus on outward, behavioral learning processes. Cognitive approaches to learning focus on mental processes that enable learning.

We have also noted that learning is affected by culture and individual differences, with individual learning styles potentially affecting the ways in which people learn most effectively. And we saw some ways in which our learning about learning can be put to practical use, through such means as behavior-modification programs designed to decrease negative behaviors and increase positive ones.

Return to the prologue of this set of modules and consider the following questions about the use of behavior modification to change driving habits:

1. Does the Snapshot device make use of classical conditioning or operant conditioning principles? What are your reasons for your answer?
2. For users of the Snapshot device, what is the reinforcement?
3. Why would a device that provides real-time feedback on energy use (and cost) be a more effective conditioning tool than the electric bill that customers ordinarily get each month?
4. If you were in charge of implementing the Snapshot device program, what additional program features could you implement to take advantage of cognitive learning principles?

VISUAL SUMMARY 5 Learning

MODULE 15 Classical Conditioning

<u>Ivan Pavlov:</u> Basic principles of classical conditioning

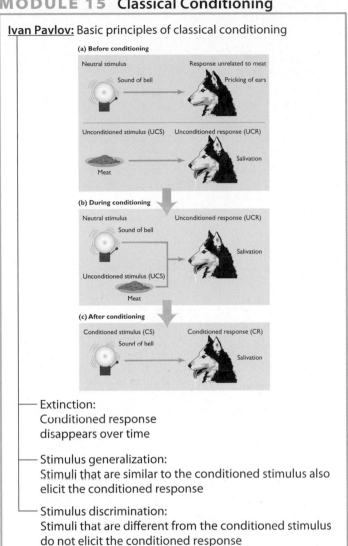

— Extinction:
Conditioned response
disappears over time

— Stimulus generalization:
Stimuli that are similar to the conditioned stimulus also
elicit the conditioned response

— Stimulus discrimination:
Stimuli that are different from the conditioned stimulus
do not elicit the conditioned response

MODULE 16 Operant Conditioning

<u>Basic Principle:</u> Behavior changes in frequency according
to its consequences
— Reinforcement: A stimulus that increases the
probability that a preceding behavior will be repeated

— Positive reinforcement:
A pleasant stimulus is presented

— Negative reinforcement:
An unpleasant stimulus is withdrawn

<u>Basic Principle:</u> Behavior changes in frequency according
to its consequences (continued)

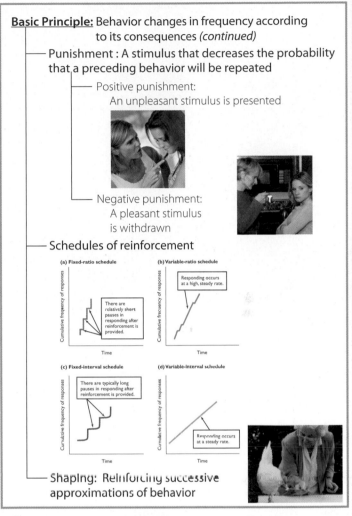

— Punishment : A stimulus that decreases the probability
that a preceding behavior will be repeated

— Positive punishment:
An unpleasant stimulus is presented

— Negative punishment:
A pleasant stimulus
is withdrawn

— Schedules of reinforcement

— Shaping: Reinforcing successive
approximations of behavior

MODULE 17 Cognitive Approaches to Learning

<u>Cognitive Learning Theory:</u> Focuses on the internal
thoughts and expectations

— Latent learning: A new behavior is learned but is not
demonstrated until it is reinforced

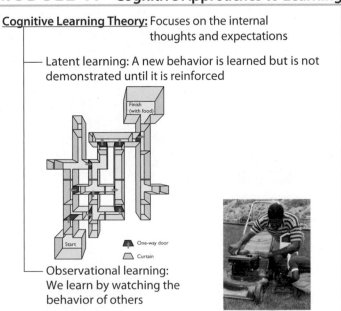

— Observational learning:
We learn by watching the
behavior of others

6

Memory

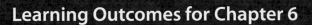

MODULE 18

LO 18-1 What is memory?

LO 18-2 Are there different kinds of memory?

LO 18-3 What are the biological bases of memory?

The Foundations of Memory

Sensory Memory

Short-Term Memory

Working Memory

Long-Term Memory

Neuroscience in Your Life: Experience, Memory, and the Brain

Applying Psychology in the 21st Century: Memory from a Bottle

MODULE 19

LO 19-1 What causes difficulties and failures in remembering?

Recalling Long-Term Memories

Retrieval Cues

Levels of Processing

Explicit and Implicit Memory

Flashbulb Memories

Constructive Processes in Memory: Rebuilding the Past

Exploring Diversity: Are There Cross-Cultural Differences in Memory?

MODULE 20

LO 20-1 Why do we forget information?

LO 20-2 What are the major memory impairments?

Forgetting: When Memory Fails

Why We Forget

Proactive and Retroactive Interference: The Before and After of Forgetting

Memory Dysfunctions: Afflictions of Forgetting

Neuroscience in Your Life: Alzheimer's Disease and Brain Deterioration

Becoming an Informed Consumer of Psychology: Improving Your Memory

Prologue *Remembering It All*

Louise Owen looks much like the typical 37-year-old. A professional violinist, she lives in New York City.

But Louise is far from typical. She can remember every day of her life since the age of 11.

Ask her what she was doing 5, 10, even 20, years ago, and she knows *exactly* what she was doing on a given day.

For example, asked what she was doing on January 2nd, 1990, and she replies, "Right now, I'm remembering the jogging class that I started that morning . . . I can remember the coach saying 'keep going.'"

How does she do it? It's a bit of a mystery even to her. When queried about another date, picked totally at random—April 21st, 1991—she says, "1991, okay. April 21st. So, in the moment between 'April 21st' and '1991,' I have scrolled through 25 April 21sts, thinking, 'Which one is it going to be? Which one is it going to be?' Okay, 1991, which was a Sunday. And I was in Los Angeles, and I had a concert with the American Youth Symphony" (Stahl, 2010).

Looking Ahead

Louise Owen owes her remarkable memory to a rare condition called *hyperthymestic syndrome*, which affects the part of her memory that stores experiences related to life events. She has perfect, vivid memories of virtually every day of her life. By the way, if you are wondering if people like Owen are recalling accurately, they seem to be: every time they say something that can be corroborated by evidence (like the weather on a given date, using weather records), they have been proven to be accurate.

Owen's condition illustrates the complexity and the mystery of the phenomenon we call memory. Memory allows us to retrieve a vast amount of information. We are able to remember the name of a friend we haven't talked with for years and recall the details of a picture that hung in our bedroom as a child. At the same time, though, memory failures are common. We forget where we left the keys to the car and fail to answer an exam question about material we studied only a few hours earlier. Why?

We turn now to the nature of memory, considering the ways in which information is stored and retrieved. We examine the problems of retrieving information from memory, the accuracy of memories, and the reasons information is sometimes forgotten. We also consider the biological foundations of memory and discuss some practical means of increasing memory capacity.

The Foundations of Memory

You are playing a game of Trivial Pursuit, and winning the game comes down to one question: On what body of water is Mumbai located? As you rack your brain for the answer, several fundamental processes relating to memory come into play. You may never, for instance, have been exposed to information regarding Mumbai's location. Or if you have been exposed to it, it may simply not have registered in a meaningful way. In other words, the information might not have been recorded properly in your memory. The initial process of recording information in a form usable to memory, a process called *encoding,* is the first stage in remembering something.

Even if you had been exposed to the information and originally knew the name of the body of water, you may still be unable to recall it during the game because of a failure to retain it. Memory specialists speak of *storage,* the maintenance of material saved in memory. If the material is not stored adequately, it cannot be recalled later.

Memory also depends on one last process—*retrieval*: Material in memory storage has to be located and brought into awareness to be useful. Your failure to recall Mumbai's location, then, may rest on your inability to retrieve information that you learned earlier.

In sum, psychologists consider **memory** to be the process by which we encode, store, and retrieve information (see Figure 1). Each of the three parts of this definition—encoding, storage, and retrieval—represents a different process. You can think of these processes as being analogous to a computer's keyboard (encoding), hard drive (storage), and software that accesses the information for display on the screen (retrieval). Only if all three processes have operated will you experience success and be able to recall the body of water on which Mumbai is located: the Arabian Sea.

Recognizing that memory involves encoding, storage, and retrieval gives us a start in understanding the concept. But how does memory actually function? How do we explain what information is initially encoded, what gets stored, and how it is retrieved?

According to the *three-system approach to memory* that dominated memory research for several decades, there are different memory storage systems or stages through which information must travel if it is to be remembered (Atkinson & Shiffrin, 1968, 1971). Historically, the approach has been extremely influential in

Learning Outcomes

LO 18-1 What is memory?

LO 18-2 Are there different kinds of memory?

LO 18-3 What are the biological bases of memory?

memory The process by which we encode, store, and retrieve information.

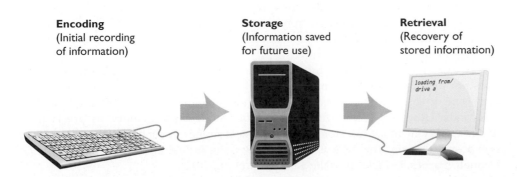

Encoding
(Initial recording of information)

Storage
(Information saved for future use)

Retrieval
(Recovery of stored information)

loading from/ drive a

FIGURE 1 Memory is built on three basic processes—encoding, storage, and retrieval—that are analogous to a computer's keyboard, hard drive, and software to access the information for display on the screen. The analogy is not perfect, however, because human memory is less precise than a computer. How might you modify the analogy to make it more accurate?

205

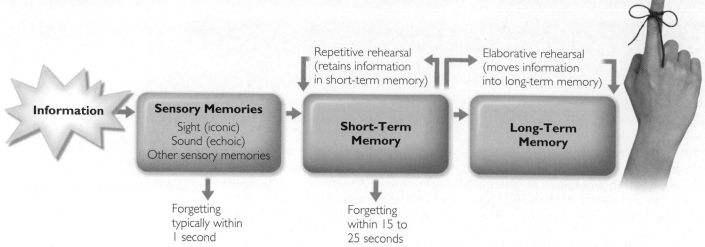

FIGURE 2 In this three-stage model of memory, information initially recorded by the person's sensory system enters sensory memory, which momentarily holds the information. The information then moves to short-term memory, which stores it for 15 to 25 seconds. Finally, the information can move into long-term memory, which is relatively permanent. Whether the information moves from short-term to long-term memory depends on the kind and amount of rehearsal of the material that is performed. (Source: Atkinson & Shifrin, 1968.)

the development of our understanding of memory, and—although new theories have augmented it—it still provides a useful framework for understanding how information is recalled.

The three-system memory theory proposes the existence of the three separate memory stores shown in Figure 2. **Sensory memory** refers to the initial, momentary storage of information that lasts only an instant. Here an exact replica of the stimulus recorded by a person's sensory system is stored very briefly. In a second stage, **short-term memory** holds information for 15 to 25 seconds and stores it according to its meaning rather than as mere sensory stimulation. The third type of storage system is **long-term memory.** Information is stored in long-term memory on a relatively permanent basis, although it may be difficult to retrieve.

sensory memory The initial, momentary storage of information, lasting only an instant.

short-term memory Memory that holds information for 15 to 25 seconds.

long-term memory Memory that stores information on a relatively permanent basis, although it may be difficult to retrieve.

Sensory Memory

A momentary flash of lightning, the sound of a twig snapping, and the sting of a pin-prick all represent stimulation of exceedingly brief duration, but they may nonetheless provide important information that can require a response. Such stimuli are initially—and fleetingly—stored in sensory memory, the first repository of the information the world presents to us. Actually, there are several types of sensory memories, each related to a different source of sensory information. For instance, *iconic memory* reflects information from the visual system. *Echoic memory* stores auditory information coming from the ears. In addition, there are corresponding memories for each of the other senses.

Sensory memory can store information for only a very short time. If information does not pass into short-term memory, it is lost for good. For instance, iconic memory seems to last less than a second, and echoic memory typically fades within 2 or 3 seconds. However, despite the brief duration of sensory memory, its precision is high: Sensory memory can store an almost exact replica of each stimulus to which it is exposed (Darwin, Turvey, & Crowder, 1972; Long & Beaton, 1982; Sams et al., 1993; Deouell, Parnes, & Pickard, 2006; Saneyoshi et al., 2011).

Study Alert

Although the three types of memory are discussed as separate memory stores, these are not mini-warehouses located in specific areas of the brain. Instead, they represent three different types of memory systems with different characteristics.

Psychologist George Sperling (1960) demonstrated the existence of sensory memory in a series of clever and now-classic studies. He briefly exposed people to a series of 12 letters arranged in the following pattern:

$$\begin{array}{cccc} F & T & Y & C \\ K & D & N & L \\ Y & W & B & M \end{array}$$

When exposed to this pattern of letters for just one twentieth of a second, most people could recall only four or five of the letters accurately. Although they knew that they had seen more, the memory of those letters had faded by the time they reported the first few letters. It was possible, then, that the information had initially been accurately stored in sensory memory. But during the time it took to verbalize the first four or five letters, the memory of the other letters faded.

To test that possibility, Sperling conducted an experiment in which a high, medium, or low tone sounded just after a person had been exposed to the full pattern of letters. People were told to report the letters in the highest line if a high tone was sounded, the middle line if the medium tone occurred, or the lowest line at the sound of the low tone. Because the tone occurred after the exposure, people had to rely on their memories to report the correct row.

The results of the study clearly showed that people had been storing the complete pattern in memory. They accurately recalled the letters in the line that had been indicated by the tone regardless of whether it was the top, middle, or bottom line. Obviously, *all* the lines they had seen had been stored in sensory memory. Despite its rapid loss, then, the information in sensory memory was an accurate representation of what people had seen.

By gradually lengthening the time between the presentation of the visual pattern and the tone, Sperling was able to determine with some accuracy the length of time that information was stored in sensory memory. The ability to recall a particular row of the pattern when a tone was sounded declined progressively as the period between the visual exposure and the tone increased. This decline continued until the period reached about 1 second in duration, at which point the row could not be recalled accurately at all. Sperling concluded that the entire visual image was stored in sensory memory for less than a second.

In sum, sensory memory operates as a kind of snapshot that stores information—which may be of a visual, auditory, or other sensory nature—for a brief moment in time. But it is as if each snapshot, immediately after being taken, is destroyed and replaced with a new one. Unless the information in the snapshot is transferred to some other type of memory, it is lost.

A momentary flash of lightning leaves a sensory visual memory, a fleeting but exact replica of the stimulus that fades away.

Short-Term Memory

Because the information that is stored briefly in sensory memory consists of representations of raw sensory stimuli, it is not meaningful to us. If we are to make sense of it and possibly retain it, the information must be transferred to the next stage of memory: short-term memory. Short-term memory is the memory store in which information first has meaning, although the maximum length of retention there is relatively short (Hamilton & Martin, 2007).

The specific process by which sensory memories are transformed into short-term memories is not clear. Some theorists suggest that the information is first translated into graphical representations or images, and others hypothesize that the transfer occurs when the sensory stimuli are changed to words (Baddeley & Wilson, 1985). What is clear, however, is that unlike sensory memory, which holds a relatively full and detailed—if short-lived—representation of the world, short-term memory has incomplete representational capabilities.

FIGURE 3 Examine the chessboard on the left for about 5 seconds. Then cover up the board and draw the position of the pieces on the blank chessboard. (You could also use your own chessboard and place the pieces in the same positions.) Unless you are an experienced chess player, you are likely to have great difficulty carrying out such a task. Yet chess masters—those who win tournaments—do this quite well (deGroot, 1966). They are able to reproduce correctly 90% of the pieces on the board. In comparison, inexperienced chess players are typically able to reproduce only 40% of the board properly. The chess masters do not have superior memories in other respects; they generally test normally on other measures of memory. What they can do better than others is see the board in terms of chunks or meaningful units and reproduce the position of the chess pieces by using those units.

chunk A grouping of information that can be stored in short-term memory.

In fact, the specific amount of information that can be held in short-term memory has been identified as seven items, or "chunks," of information, with variations up to plus or minus two chunks. A **chunk** is a grouping of information that can be stored in short-term memory. For example, a chunk can be a group of seven individual letters or numbers, permitting us to hold a seven-digit phone number (such as 226-4610) in short-term memory.

But a chunk also may consist of larger categories, such as words or other meaningful units. For example, consider the following list of 21 letters:

P B S F O X C N N A B C C B S M T V N B C

Because the list of individual letters exceeds seven items, it is difficult to recall the letters after one exposure. But suppose they were presented as follows:

PBS FOX CNN ABC CBS MTV NBC

In this case, even though there are still 21 letters, you'd be able to store them in short-term memory since they represent only seven chunks.

Chunks can vary in size from single letters or numbers to categories that are far more complicated. The specific nature of what constitutes a chunk varies according to one's past experience. You can see this for yourself by trying an experiment that was first carried out as a comparison between expert and inexperienced chess players and is illustrated in Figure 3 (deGroot, 1978; Oberauer, 2007; Gilchrist, Cowan, & Naveh-Benjamin, 2009).

Although it is possible to remember seven or so relatively complicated sets of information entering short-term memory, the information cannot be held there very long. Just how brief is short-term memory? If you've ever looked up a telephone number in a phone directory, repeated the number to yourself, put away the directory, and then forgotten the number after you've tapped the first three numbers into your phone, you know that information does not remain in short-term memory very long. Most psychologists believe that information in short-term memory is lost after 15 to 25 seconds—unless it is transferred to long-term memory.

REHEARSAL

The transfer of material from short- to long-term memory proceeds largely on the basis of **rehearsal,** the repetition of information that has entered short-term memory. Rehearsal accomplishes two things. First, as long as the information is repeated, it is maintained in short-term memory. More important, however, rehearsal allows us to transfer the information into long-term memory (Kvavilashvili & Fisher, 2007; Jarrold & Tam, 2011).

Whether the transfer is made from short- to long-term memory seems to depend largely on the kind of rehearsal that is carried out. If the information is simply repeated over and over again—as we might do with a telephone number while we rush from the phone book to the phone—it is kept current in short-term memory, but it will not necessarily be placed in long-term memory. Instead, as soon as we stop punching in the phone numbers, the number is likely to be replaced by other information and will be completely forgotten.

rehearsal The repetition of information that has entered short-term memory.

In contrast, if the information in short-term memory is rehearsed using a process called elaborative rehearsal, it is much more likely to be transferred into long-term memory. *Elaborative rehearsal* occurs when the information is considered and organized in some fashion. The organization might include expanding the information to make it fit into a logical framework, linking it to another memory, turning it into an image, or transforming it in some other way. For example, a list of vegetables to be purchased at a store could be woven together in memory as items being used to prepare an elaborate salad, could be linked to the items bought on an earlier shopping trip, or could be thought of in terms of the image of a farm with rows of each item.

By using organizational strategies such as these—called *mnemonics*—we can vastly improve our retention of information. Mnemonics (pronounced "neh MON ix") are formal techniques for organizing information in a way that makes it more likely to be remembered. For instance, when a beginning musician learns that the spaces on the music staff spell the word *FACE,* or when we learn the rhyme "Thirty days hath September, April, June, and November . . . ," we are using mnemonics (Carney & Levin, 2003; Sprenger, 2007; Worthen & Hunt, 2011).

Working Memory

Rather than seeing short-term memory as an independent way station into which memories arrive, either to fade or to be passed on to long-term memory, most contemporary memory theorists conceive of short-term memory as far more active. In this view, short-term memory is like an information-processing system that manages

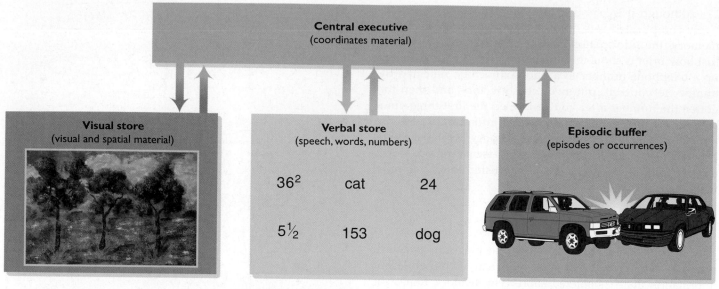

FIGURE 4 Working memory is an active "workspace" in which information is retrieved and manipulated and in which information is held through rehearsal. (Source: Adapted from Baddeley, Chincotta, & Adlam, 2001.)

working memory A set of active, temporary memory stores that actively manipulate and rehearse information.

both new material gathered from sensory memory and older material that has been pulled from long-term storage. In this increasingly influential view, short-term memory is referred to as **working memory** and defined as a set of temporary memory stores that actively manipulate and rehearse information (Bayliss et al., 2005a, 2005b; Unsworth & Engle, 2005; Vandierendonck & Szmalec, 2011).

Working memory is thought to contain a *central executive* processor that is involved in reasoning and decision making. The central executive coordinates three distinct storage-and-rehearsal systems: the *visual store,* the *verbal store,* and the *episodic buffer.* The visual store specializes in visual and spatial information, whereas the verbal store holds and manipulates material relating to speech, words, and numbers. The episodic buffer contains information that represents episodes or events (Rudner & Rönnberg, 2008; Baddeley, Allen, & Hitch, 2011; see Figure 4).

Working memory permits us to keep information in an active state briefly so that we can do something with the information. For instance, we use working memory when we're doing a multistep arithmetic problem in our heads, storing the result of one calculation while getting ready to move to the next stage. (I make use of my working memory when I figure a 20% tip in a restaurant by first calculating 10% of the total bill and then doubling it.)

Although working memory aids in the recall of information, it uses a significant amount of cognitive resources during its operation. In turn, this can make us less aware of our surroundings—something that has implications for why it's unsafe to use cell telephones while driving. If a phone conversation requires thinking, it will burden working memory and leave drivers less aware of their surroundings, an obviously dangerous state of affairs (Sifrit, 2006; Strayer & Drews, 2007).

Furthermore, stress can reduce the effectiveness of working memory by reducing its capacity. In fact, one study found that students with the highest working memory capacity and greatest math ability were the ones who were most vulnerable to pressure to perform well. Those who should have performed best, then, were the ones most apt to choke on the test because their working memory capacities were reduced by the stress (Carey, 2004; Beilock & Carr, 2005; Schweizer & Dalgleish, 2011).

Long-Term Memory

Material that makes its way from short-term memory to long-term memory enters a storehouse of almost unlimited capacity. Like a new file we save on a hard drive, the information in long-term memory is filed and coded so that we can retrieve it when we need it.

Evidence of the existence of long-term memory, as distinct from short-term memory, comes from a number of sources. For example, people with certain kinds of brain damage have no lasting recall of new information received after the damage occurred, although people and events stored in memory before the injury remain intact (Milner, 1966). Because information that was encoded and stored before the injury can be recalled and because short-term memory after the injury appears to be operational—new material can be recalled for a very brief period—we can infer that there are two distinct types of memory: one for short-term and one for long-term storage.

Results from laboratory experiments are also consistent with the notion of separate short-term and long-term memory. For example, in one set of studies, people were asked to recall a relatively small amount of information (such as a set of three letters). Then, to prevent practice of the initial information, participants were required to recite some extraneous material aloud, such as counting backward by threes (Brown, 1958; Peterson & Peterson, 1959). By varying the amount of time between the presentation of the initial material and the need for its recall, investigators found that recall was quite good when the interval was very short but declined rapidly thereafter. After 15 seconds had gone by, recall hovered at around 10% of the material initially presented.

Apparently, the distraction of counting backward prevented almost all the initial material from reaching long-term memory. Initial recall was good because it was coming from short-term memory, but those memories were lost at a rapid rate. Eventually, all that could be recalled was the small amount of material that had made its way into long-term storage despite the distraction of counting backward.

The distinction between short- and long-term memory is also supported by the *serial position effect*, in which the ability to recall information in a list depends on where in the list an item appears. For instance, often a *primacy effect* occurs, in which items presented early in a list are remembered better. There is also a *recency effect*, in which items presented late in a list are remembered best (Bonanni et al., 2007; Tan & Ward, 2008; Tydgat & Grainger, 2009).

LONG-TERM MEMORY MODULES

Just as short-term memory is often conceptualized in terms of working memory, many contemporary researchers now regard long-term memory as having several different components, or *memory modules*. Each of these modules represents a separate memory system in the brain.

One major distinction within long-term memory is that between declarative memory and procedural memory. **Declarative memory** is memory for factual information: names, faces, dates, and facts, such as "a bike has two wheels." In contrast, **procedural memory** (or *nondeclarative memory*) refers to memory for skills and habits, such as how to ride a bike or hit a baseball. Information about *things* is stored in declarative memory; information about *how to do things* is stored in procedural memory (Brown & Robertson, 2007; Bauer, 2008; Freedberg, 2011).

Declarative memory can be subdivided into semantic memory and episodic memory. **Semantic memory** is memory for general knowledge and facts about the world, as well as memory for the rules of logic that are used to deduce other facts. Because of semantic memory, we remember that the ZIP code for Beverly Hills is 90210, that Mumbai is on the Arabian Sea, and that *memoree* is the incorrect spelling of *memory*. Thus, semantic memory is somewhat like a mental almanac of facts (Nyberg & Tulving, 1996; Tulving, 2002).

PsychTech
Research shows that when we are faced with complicated questions and material, we are primed to think of computers and search engines like Google. In what is called the *Google effect*, we are then less likely to store the information in short-term memory and be less likely to recall it—but have a better memory for where we can find it on the web (Sparrow, Liu, & Wegner, 2011).

declarative memory Memory for factual information: names, faces, dates, and the like.

procedural memory Memory for skills and habits, such as riding a bike or hitting a baseball; sometimes referred to as *nondeclarative memory*.

semantic memory Memory for general knowledge and facts about the world, as well as memory for the rules of logic that are used to deduce other facts.

FIGURE 5 Long-term memory can be subdivided into several different types. What type of long-term memory is involved in your recollection of the moment you first arrived on your campus at the start of college? What type of long-term memory is involved in remembering the lyrics to a song, compared with the tune of a song?

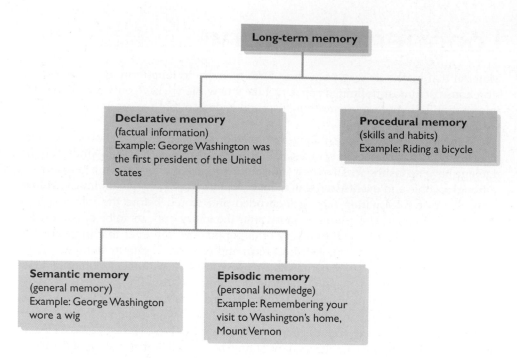

Study Alert

Use Figure 5 to help clarify the distinctions between the different types of long-term memory.

episodic memory Memory for events that occur in a particular time, place, or context.

In contrast, **episodic memory** is memory for events that occur in a particular time, place, or context. For example, recall of learning to hit a baseball, our first kiss, or arranging a surprise 21st birthday party for our brother is based on episodic memories. Episodic memories relate to particular contexts. For example, remembering *when* and *how* we learned that $2 \times 2 = 4$ would be an episodic memory; the fact itself (that $2 \times 2 = 4$) is a semantic memory. (Also see Figure 5.)

Episodic memories can be surprisingly detailed. Consider, for instance, how you'd respond if you were asked to identify what you were doing on a specific day 2 years ago. Impossible? You may think otherwise as you read the following exchange between a researcher and a participant in a study who was asked, in a memory experiment, what he was doing "on Monday afternoon in the third week of September two years ago."

PARTICIPANT: Come on. How should I know?

EXPERIMENTER: Just try it anyhow.

PARTICIPANT: OK. Let's see: Two years ago . . . I would be in high school in Pittsburgh. . . . That would be my senior year. Third week in September—that's just after summer—that would be the fall term. . . . Let me see. I think I had chemistry lab on Mondays. I don't know. I was probably in chemistry lab. Wait a minute—that would be the second week of school. I remember he started off with the atomic table—a big fancy chart. I thought he was crazy trying to make us memorize that thing. You know, I think I can remember sitting . . . (Lindsay & Norman, 1977).

Episodic memory, then, can provide information about events that happened long in the past. But semantic memory is no less impressive, permitting us to dredge up tens of thousands of facts ranging from the date of our birthday to the knowledge that $1 is less than $5.

SEMANTIC NETWORKS

Try to recall, for a moment, as many things as you can think of that are the color red. Now pull from your memory the names of as many fruits as you can recall.

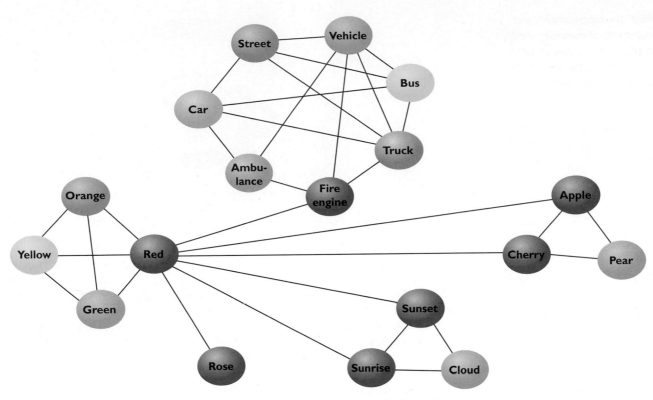

FIGURE 6 Semantic networks in memory consist of relationships between pieces of information, such as those relating to the concept of a fire engine. The lines suggest the connections that indicate how the information is organized within memory. The closer together two concepts are, the greater the strength of the association. (Source: Collins & Loftus, 1975.)

Did the same item appear when you did both tasks? For many people, an apple comes to mind in both cases since it fits equally well in each category. And the fact that you might have thought of an apple when doing the first task makes it even more likely that you'll think of it when doing the second task.

It's actually quite amazing that we're able to retrieve specific material from the vast store of information in our long-term memories. According to some memory researchers, one key organizational tool that allows us to recall detailed information from long-term memory is the associations that we build between different pieces of information. In this view, knowledge is stored in **semantic networks,** mental representations of clusters of interconnected information (Collins & Quillian, 1969; Collins & Loftus, 1975; Cummings, Ceponiene, & Koyama, 2006).

Consider, for example, Figure 6, which shows some of the relationships in memory relating to fire engines, the color red, and a variety of other semantic concepts. Thinking about a particular concept leads to recall of related concepts. For example, seeing a fire engine may activate our recollections of other kinds of emergency vehicles, such as an ambulance, which in turn may activate recall of the related concept of a vehicle. And thinking of a vehicle may lead us to think about a bus that we've seen in the past. Activating one memory triggers the activation of related memories in a process known as *spreading activation* (Foster et al., 2008; Kreher et al., 2008).

semantic networks Mental representations of clusters of interconnected information.

THE NEUROSCIENCE OF MEMORY

Can we pinpoint a location in the brain where long-term memories reside? Is there a single site that corresponds to a particular memory, or is memory distributed in

FIGURE 7 The hippocampus and amygdala, parts of the brain's limbic system, play a central role in the consolidation of memories.
(Source: Van De Graaff, 2000.)

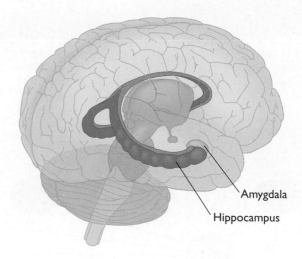

different regions across the brain? Do memories leave an actual physical trace that scientists can view?

The search for the *engram*, the term for the physical memory trace in the brain that corresponds to a memory, has proved to be a major puzzle to psychologists and other neuroscientists interested in memory. Using advanced brain scanning procedures in their efforts to determine the neuroscientific basis of memory formation, investigators have learned that certain areas and structures of the brain specialize in different types of memory-related activities. The *hippocampus*, a part of the brain's limbic system (see Figure 7), plays a central role in the consolidation of memories. Located within the brain's *medial temporal lobes* just behind the eyes, the hippocampus aids in the initial encoding of information, acting as a kind of neurological e-mail system. That information is subsequently passed along to the cerebral cortex of the brain, where it is actually stored (J. Peters et al., 2007; Lavenex & Lavenex, 2009; Dudai, 2011).

The significance of the hippocampus is exemplified by studies of individuals who have particularly good, yet specialized, types of memories. For instance, taxi drivers in London, England, must have accurate, complete recall of the location of the maze of streets and alleys within a 6-mile radius of the center of the city. It takes years of study to memorize the material. MRI brain scans of taxi drivers show that, relative to non–taxi drivers with fewer navigational skills, the back of the hippocampus is larger while the front is smaller. The findings are consistent with the idea that particular areas of the hippocampus are involved in the consolidation of spatial memories (see Figure 8 *Neuroscience in Your Life*; Maguire, Woollett, & Spiers, 2006; Spiers & Maguire, 2007; Woollett & Maguire, 2009).

The *amygdala*, another part of the limbic system, also plays an important role in memory. The amygdala is especially involved with memories involving emotion. For example, if you are frightened by a large Doberman, you're likely to remember the event vividly—an outcome related to the functioning of the amygdala. Encountering the Doberman or any large dog in the future is likely to reactivate the amygdala and bring back the unpleasant memory (Hamann, 2001; Buchanan & Adolphs, 2004; Talmi et al., 2008).

Memory at the Level of Neurons. Although it is clear that the hippocampus and amygdala play a central role in memory formation, how is the transformation of information into a memory reflected at the level of neurons?

One answer is *long-term potentiation*, which shows that certain neural pathways become easily excited while a new response is being learned. At the same time, the number of synapses between neurons increase as the dendrites branch out to receive

Neuroscience in Your Life: Experience, Memory, and the Brain

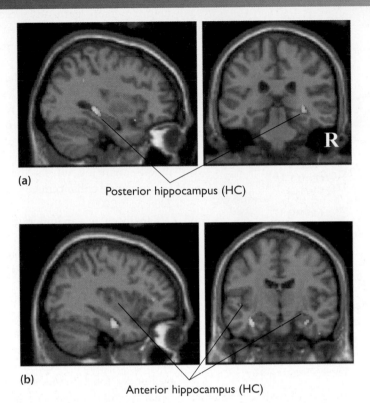

(a)

Posterior hippocampus (HC)

(b)

Anterior hippocampus (HC)

FIGURE 8 Illustrating how experience can shape how our brain processes memories, these fMRI scans show how the number of years spent driving a taxi relates to the size of particular areas of the hippocampus as participants become spatial and navigational memory experts. In (a) we see areas of the posterior (back) hippocampus that increase in activity (in yellow) with the number of years spent driving a taxi. In contrast, in (b) we see areas of the anterior (front) hippocampus that show reduced activity (also in yellow) after many years of driving a taxi and the relationship portrayed graphically. The changes in the areas activated during memory tasks show how practice can shape the brain and how this allows us to develop specialized skills such as memory for spatial locations. (Source: Maguire et al., 2006.)

messages. These changes reflect a process called *consolidation,* in which memories become fixed and stable in long-term memory. Long-term memories take some time to stabilize; this explains why events and other stimuli are not suddenly fixed in memory. Instead, consolidation may continue for days and even years (McGaugh, 2003; Meeter & Murre, 2004; Kawashima, Izaki, & Grace, 2006).

Because a stimulus may contain different sensory aspects, visual, auditory, and other areas of the brain may be simultaneously processing information about that stimulus. Information storage appears to be linked to the sites where this processing occurs, and it is therefore located in the particular areas that initially processed the information in terms of its visual, auditory, and other sensory stimuli. For this reason, memory traces are distributed throughout the brain. For example, when you recall a beautiful beach sunset, your recollection draws on memory stores located in visual areas of the brain (the view of the sunset), auditory areas (the sounds of the ocean), and tactile areas (the feel of the wind) (Brewer et al., 1998; Squire, Clark, & Bayley, 2004).

In short, the physical stuff of memory—the engram—is produced by a complex of biochemical and neural processes. Scientists are just beginning to understand how the brain compiles the individual neural components into a single, coherent memory. It may be that the same neurons that fire when we are initially exposed to material are reactivated during efforts to recall that information. Still, although memory researchers have made considerable strides in understanding the neuroscience behind memory, more remains to be learned—and remembered (Gelbard-Sagiv et al., 2008). (For more on the biological basis of memory, see *Applying Psychology in the 21st Century.*)

Memory from a Bottle

If you could take a pill that would enhance your mental functioning, would you? Perhaps if you had to pull an all-nighter to study for a difficult exam the next day and just needed a little help staying focused? Then again, would that be fair to other students who didn't use artificial enhancement to prepare? And what might be the side effects and long-term consequences of using such a drug? These are tricky questions, and ones that medical ethicists grapple with, too.

The idea of getting a cognitive boost from a "smart drug" is certainly a very popular one, and medicines are available that treat the mental impairment that is associated with certain neurological disorders. For example, *methylphenidate* (also known as Ritalin) helps children with attention-deficit hyperactivity disorder to regain some focus, *modafinil* improves the alertness of people with excessive sleepiness, and *donepezil* is used to help people with Alzheimer's disease improve their memory (Stix, 2009; Sahakian & Morein-Zamir, 2011).

But there are many concerns about using these drugs. Not everyone reacts the same way, and in some people these medications can actually produce the opposite of the intended effect. What is worse, they come with side effects; these can include addiction, cardiovascular complications, seizures, and skin rashes (Greely et al., 2008).

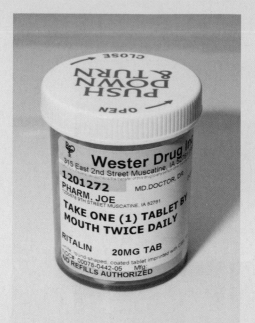

Some students are using certain prescription medications to enhance mental ability, but their use may come at a price due to complications from side effects and the potential for addiction.

And then there's the question of whether these drugs really do what people think they do. It's one thing to bring back some alertness to a person who is chronically fatigued and must perform boring repetitive tasks on the job, but it's another to help a person learn advanced calculus. The medications are intended to correct for impairments, not provide enhancements to fully functioning people. And even among impaired people, the effects of these medications may be less dramatic than is commonly thought; for example, amphetamines used to improve focus make patients feel as though they are performing better, but that may be due more to their mood-enhancing effects than to actual performance enhancements (Rasmussen, 2008; Stix, 2009).

Finally, there's an important question of what these drugs are doing in the brain. In some cases, scientists just don't know for sure. For example, methylphenidate and modafinil act on the neurotransmitter dopamine, but it's unclear what the exact mechanism is that produces their effect. Altering the brain's neurochemistry, then, especially when both the short-term and long-term effects of "smart drugs" are not well understood, doesn't seem to be a particularly smart move. For now, the best ways to enhance one's mental acuity remain the traditional ones: study, practice, and get enough rest.

RETHINK

- How would you explain the drawbacks of using drugs that alter brain chemistry for performance enhancement to a friend who wants to try them?
- Do you agree that the risks of using neurological drugs for performance enhancement in healthy people are not worth the potential benefits? Why do you think so?

RECAP/EVALUATE/RETHINK

RECAP

LO 18-1 What is memory?

- Memory is the process by which we encode, store, and retrieve information. (p. 205)

LO 18-2 Are there different kinds of memory?

- Sensory memory, corresponding to each of the sensory systems, is the first place where information is saved. Sensory memories are very brief, but they are precise, storing a nearly exact replica of a stimulus. (p. 206)
- Roughly seven (plus or minus two) chunks of information can be transferred and held in short-term memory. Information in short-term memory is held from 15 to 25 seconds and, if not transferred to long-term memory, is lost. (p. 207)
- Memories are transferred into long-term storage through rehearsal. If memories are transferred into long-term memory, they become relatively permanent. (p. 209)
- Some theorists view short-term memory as a working memory in which information is retrieved and manipulated and held through rehearsal. In this view, it is a central executive processor involved in reasoning and decision making; it coordinates a visual store, a verbal store, and an episodic buffer. (pp. 209, 210)
- Long-term memory can be viewed in terms of memory modules, each of which is related to separate memory systems in the brain. For instance, we can distinguish between declarative memory and procedural memory. Declarative memory is further divided into episodic memory and semantic memory. (p. 211)
- Semantic networks suggest that knowledge is stored in long-term memory as mental representations of clusters of interconnected information. (pp. 212, 213)

LO 18-3 What are the biological bases of memory?

- The hippocampus and amygdala are especially important in the establishment of memory. (p. 214)

- Memories are distributed across the brain, relating to the different sensory information-processing systems involved during the initial exposure to a stimulus. (p. 215)

EVALUATE

1. Match the type of memory with its definition:
   1. long-term memory
   2. short-term memory
   3. sensory memory

   a. holds information 15 to 25 seconds
   b. stores information on a relatively permanent basis
   c. direct representation of a stimulus

2. A(n) _____ is a meaningful group of stimuli that can be stored together in short-term memory.
3. There appear to be two types of declarative memory: _____ memory for knowledge and facts and _____ memory for personal experiences.
4. Some memory researchers believe that long-term memory is stored as associations between pieces of information in _____ networks.

RETHINK

1. It is a truism that "you never forget how to ride a bicycle." Why might this be so? In what type of memory is information about bicycle riding stored?
2. *From a marketing specialist's perspective:* How might advertisers and others use ways of enhancing memory to promote their products? What ethical principles are involved? Can you think of a way to protect yourself from unethical advertising?

Answers to Evaluate Questions

1. 1-b, 2-a, 3-c; 2. chunk; 3. semantic, episodic; 4. semantic

KEY TERMS

memory p. 205
sensory memory p. 206
short-term memory p. 206

long-term memory p. 206
chunk p. 208
rehearsal p. 209

working memory p. 210
declarative memory p. 211
procedural memory p. 211

semantic memory p. 211
episodic memory p. 212
semantic networks p. 213

Recalling Long-Term Memories

Learning Outcome

LO 19-1 What causes difficulties and failures in remembering?

An hour after his job interview, Ricardo was sitting in a coffee shop, telling his friend Laura how well it had gone, when the woman who had interviewed him walked in. "Well, hello, Ricardo. How are you doing?" Trying to make a good impression, Ricardo began to make introductions, but suddenly realized he could not remember the interviewer's name. Stammering, he desperately searched his memory but to no avail. "I *know* her name," he thought to himself, "but here I am, looking like a fool. I can kiss this job good-bye."

Have you ever tried to remember someone's name, convinced that you knew it but unable to recall it no matter how hard you tried? This common occurrence—known as the **tip-of-the-tongue phenomenon**—exemplifies how difficult it can be to retrieve information stored in long-term memory (Brennen, Vikan, & Dybdahl, 2007; Schwartz, 2002, 2008; Schwartz & Metcalfe, 2011).

tip-of-the-tongue phenomenon The inability to recall information that one realizes one knows—a result of the difficulty of retrieving information from long-term memory.

Retrieval Cues

Perhaps recall of names and other memories is not perfect because there is so much information stored in long-term memory. Because the material that makes its way to long-term memory is relatively permanent, the capacity of long-term memory is vast. For instance, if you are like the average college student, your vocabulary includes some 50,000 words, you know hundreds of mathematical "facts," and you are able to conjure up images—such as the way your childhood home looked—with no trouble at all. In fact, simply cataloging all your memories would probably take years of work.

How do we sort through this vast array of material and retrieve specific information at the appropriate time? One way is through retrieval cues. A *retrieval cue* is a stimulus that allows us to recall more easily information that is in long-term memory. It may be a word, an emotion, or a sound; whatever the specific cue, a memory will suddenly come to mind when the retrieval cue is present. For example, the smell of roasting turkey may evoke memories of Thanksgiving or family gatherings.

recall Memory task in which specific information must be retrieved.

recognition Memory task in which individuals are presented with a stimulus and asked whether they have been exposed to it in the past or to identify it from a list of alternatives.

Retrieval cues guide people through the information stored in long-term memory in much the same way that a search engine such as Google guides people through the Internet. They are particularly important when we are making an effort to *recall* information, as opposed to being asked to *recognize* material stored in memory. In **recall**, a specific piece of information must be retrieved—such as that needed to answer a fill-in-the-blank question or to write an essay on a test. In contrast, **recognition** occurs when people are presented with a stimulus and asked whether they have been exposed to it previously or are asked to identify it from a list of alternatives.

As you might guess, recognition is generally a much easier task than recall (see Figures 1 and 2). Recall is more difficult because it

FIGURE 1 Try to recall the names of these characters. Because this is a recall task, it is relatively difficult.

Answer this recognition question:
Which of the following are the names of the seven dwarfs in the Disney movie
Snow White and the Seven Dwarfs?

Goofy	Bashful
Sleepy	Meanie
Smarty	Doc
Scaredy	Happy
Dopey	Angry
Grumpy	Sneezy
Wheezy	Crazy

(The correct answers are Bashful, Doc, Dopey, Grumpy, Happy, Sleepy, and Sneezy.)

FIGURE 2 Naming the characters in Figure 1 (a recall task) is more difficult than solving the recognition problem posed in this list.

consists of a series of processes: a search through memory, retrieval of potentially relevant information, and then a decision regarding whether the information you have found is accurate. If the information appears to be correct, the search is over, but if it is not, the search must continue. In contrast, recognition is simpler because it involves fewer steps (Miserando, 1991; Leigh, Zinkhan, & Swaminathan, 2006).

Levels of Processing

One determinant of how well memories are recalled is the way in which material is first perceived, processed, and understood. The **levels-of-processing theory** emphasizes the degree to which new material is mentally analyzed. It suggests that the amount of information processing that occurs when material is initially encountered is central in determining how much of the information is ultimately remembered. According to this approach, the depth of information processing during exposure to material—meaning the degree to which it is analyzed and considered—is critical; the greater the intensity of its initial processing, the more likely we are to remember it (Craik & Lockhart, 2008; Mungan, Peynircioğlu, & Halpern, 2011).

Because we do not pay close attention to much of the information to which we are exposed, very little mental processing typically takes place, and we forget new material almost immediately. However, information to which we pay greater attention is processed more thoroughly. Therefore, it enters memory at a deeper level—and is less apt to be forgotten than is information processed at shallower levels.

The theory goes on to suggest that there are considerable differences in the ways in which information is processed at various levels of memory. At shallow levels, information is processed merely in terms of its physical and sensory aspects. For example, we may pay attention only to the shapes that make up the letters in the word *dog*. At an intermediate level of processing, the shapes are translated into meaningful units—in this case, letters of the alphabet. Those letters are considered in the context of words, and specific phonetic sounds may be attached to the letters.

At the deepest level of processing, information is analyzed in terms of its meaning. We may see it in a wider context and draw associations between the meaning of the information and broader networks of knowledge. For instance, we may think of dogs not merely as animals with four legs and a tail, but also in terms of their relationship to cats and other mammals. We may form an image of our own dog, thereby relating the concept to our own lives. According to the levels-of-processing approach, the deeper the initial level of processing of specific information, the longer the information will be retained.

There are considerable practical implications to the notion that recall depends on the degree to which information is initially processed. For example, the depth of information processing is critical when learning and studying course material. Rote

Study Alert

Remember the distinction between recall (in which specific information must be retrieved) and recognition (in which information is presented and must be identified or distinguished from other material).

levels-of-processing theory The theory of memory that emphasizes the degree to which new material is mentally analyzed.

memorization of a list of key terms for a test is unlikely to produce long-term recollection of information because processing occurs at a shallow level. In contrast, thinking about the meaning of the terms and reflecting on how they relate to information that one currently knows results in far more effective long-term retention (Conway, 2002; Wenzel, Zetocha, & Ferraro, 2007).

Explicit and Implicit Memory

If you've ever had surgery, you probably hoped that the surgeons were focused completely on the surgery and gave you their undivided attention while slicing into your body. The reality in most operating rooms is quite different, though. Surgeons may be chatting with nurses about a new restaurant as soon as they sew you up.

If you are like most patients, you are left with no recollection of the conversation that occurred while you were under anesthesia. However, it is very possible that although you had no conscious memories of the discussions on the merits of the restaurant, on some level you probably did recall at least some information. In fact, careful studies have found that people who are anesthetized during surgery can sometimes recall snippets of conversations they heard during surgery—even though they have no conscious recollection of the information (Kihlstrom et al., 1990; Sebel, Bonke, & Winograd, 1993).

The discovery that people have memories about which they are unaware has been an important one. It has led to speculation that two forms of memory, explicit and implicit, may exist side by side. **Explicit memory** refers to intentional or conscious recollection of information. When we try to remember a name or date we have encountered or learned about previously, we are searching our explicit memory.

In contrast, **implicit memory** refers to memories of which people are not consciously aware but that can affect subsequent performance and behavior. Skills that operate automatically and without thinking, such as jumping out of the path of an automobile coming toward us as we walk down the side of a road, are stored in implicit memory. Similarly, a feeling of vague dislike for an acquaintance, without knowing why we have that feeling, may be a reflection of implicit memories. Perhaps the person reminds us of someone else in our past that we didn't like, even though we are not aware of the memory of that other individual (Coates, Butler, & Berry, 2006; Voss & Paller, 2008; Gopie, Craik, & Hasher, 2011).

Implicit memory is closely related to the prejudice and discrimination people exhibit toward members of minority groups. As we first discussed in the module on conducting psychological research, even though people may say and even believe they harbor no prejudice, assessment of their implicit memories may reveal that they have negative associations about members of minority groups. Such associations can influence people's behavior without their being aware of their underlying beliefs (Greenwald, Nosek, & Banaji, 2003; Greenwald, Nosek, & Sriram, 2006; Hofmann et al., 2008).

One way that memory specialists study implicit memory is through experiments that use priming. **Priming** is a phenomenon in which exposure to a word or concept (called a *prime*) later makes it easier to recall related information. Priming effects occur even when people have no conscious memory of the original word or concept (Toth & Daniels, 2002; Schacter, Dobbins, & Schnyer, 2004; Geyer, Gokce, & Müller, 2011).

The typical experiment designed to illustrate priming helps clarify the phenomenon. In priming experiments, participants are rapidly exposed to a stimulus such as a word, an object, or perhaps a drawing of a face. The second phase of the experiment is done after an interval ranging from several seconds to several months. At that point, participants are exposed to incomplete perceptual information that is related to the first stimulus, and they are asked whether they recognize it. For example, the new material may consist of the first letter of a word that had been presented

explicit memory Intentional or conscious recollection of information.

implicit memory Memories of which people are not consciously aware but that can affect subsequent performance and behavior.

priming A phenomenon in which exposure to a word or concept (called a prime) later makes it easier to recall related information, even when there is no conscious memory of the word or concept.

earlier or a part of a face that had been shown earlier. If participants are able to identify the stimulus more readily than they identify stimuli that have not been presented earlier, priming has taken place. Clearly, the earlier stimulus has been remembered—although the material resides in implicit memory, not explicit memory.

The same thing happens to us in our everyday lives. Suppose several months ago you watched a documentary on the planets, and the narrator described the moons of Mars, focusing on its moon named Phobos. You promptly forget the name of the moon, at least consciously. Then, several months later, you're completing a crossword puzzle that you have partially filled in, and it includes the letters *obos*. As soon as you look at the set of letters, you think of Phobos, and suddenly you recall for the first time since your initial exposure to the information that it is one of the moons of Mars. The sudden recollection occurred because your memory was primed by the letters *obos*.

In short, when information that we are unable to consciously recall affects our behavior, implicit memory is at work. Our behavior may be influenced by experiences of which we are unaware—an example of what has been called "retention without remembering" (Horton et al., 2005).

Flashbulb Memories

Do you remember where you were on September 11, 2001?

You may recall your location and a variety of other details that occurred when you heard about the terrorist attacks on the United States, even though the incident happened more than a dozen years ago. Your ability to remember details about this fatal event illustrates a phenomenon known as flashbulb memory. **Flashbulb memories** are memories related to a specific, important, or surprising event that are recalled easily and with vivid imagery.

Several types of flashbulb memories are common among college students. For example, involvement in a car accident, meeting one's roommate for the first time, and the night of high school graduation are all typical flashbulb memories (Romeu, 2006; Bohn & Berntsen, 2007; Talarico, 2009; see Figure 3 on page 222).

Of course, flashbulb memories do not contain every detail of an original scene. I remember vividly that more than four decades ago I was sitting in Mr. Sharp's 10th-grade geometry class when I heard that President John Kennedy had been shot. However, although I recall where I was sitting and how my classmates reacted to the news, I do not recollect what I was wearing or what I had for lunch that day.

Furthermore, the details recalled in flashbulb memories are often inaccurate, particularly when they involve highly emotional events. For example, those old enough to remember the day when the World Trade Center in New York was attacked by terrorists typically remember watching television that morning and seeing images of the first plane, and then the second plane, striking the towers. However, that recollection is wrong: In fact, television broadcasts showed images only of the second plane on September 11. No video of the first plane was available until early the following morning, September 12, when it was shown on television (Begley, 2002; Schaefer, Halldorson, & Dizon-Reynante, 2011).

Flashbulb memories illustrate a more general phenomenon about memory: Memories that are exceptional are more easily retrieved (although not necessarily accurately) than are those relating to events that are commonplace. The more distinctive a stimulus is, and the more personal relevance the event has, the more likely we are to recall it later (Shapiro, 2006; Talarico & Rubin, 2007; Schaefer et al., 2011).

Even with a distinctive stimulus, however, we may not remember where the information came from. *Source amnesia* occurs when an individual has a memory for some material but cannot recall where he or she encountered it. For example, source

flashbulb memories Memories related to a specific, important, or surprising event that are recalled easily and with vivid imagery.

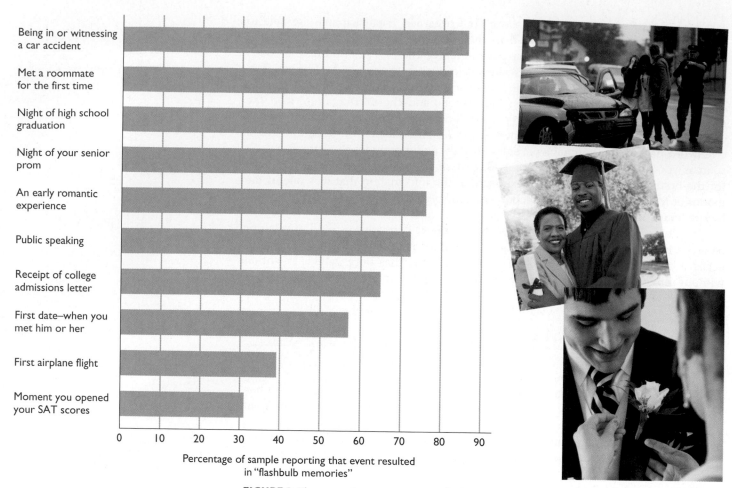

Being in or witnessing
a car accident

Met a roommate
for the first time

Night of high school
graduation

Night of your senior
prom

An early romantic
experience

Public speaking

Receipt of college
admissions letter

First date—when you
met him or her

First airplane flight

Moment you opened
your SAT scores

0   10   20   30   40   50   60   70   80   90

Percentage of sample reporting that event resulted
in "flashbulb memories"

FIGURE 3 These are the most common flashbulb memory events, based on a survey of college students. What are some of your flashbulb memories? (Source: From David C. Rubin, "The Subtle Deceiver: Recalling Our Past," *Psychology Today*, September 1985, pp. 39–46. Reprinted with permission from *Psychology Today* magazine. Copyright © 1985 Sussex Publishers, LLC.)

amnesia can explain situations in which you meet someone you know but can't remember where you'd met that person initially.

Similarly, our motivation to remember material when we are exposed to it initially affects how well we can later recall it. If we know we are going to need to recall material later, we are going to be more attentive to it. In contrast, if we don't expect to need to recall material later, then we are less likely to remember it (Naveh-Benjamin et al., 2000; Kassam et al., 2009).

Constructive Processes in Memory: Rebuilding the Past

constructive processes Processes in which memories are influenced by the meaning we give to events.

As we have seen, although it is clear that we can have detailed recollections of significant and distinctive events, it is difficult to gauge the accuracy of such memories. In fact, it is apparent that our memories reflect, at least in part, **constructive processes,** processes in which memories are influenced by the meaning we give to events. When we retrieve information, then, the memory that is produced is affected not just by the direct prior experience we have had with the stimulus, but also by our guesses and inferences about its meaning.

The notion that memory is based on constructive processes was first put forward by Frederic Bartlett, a British psychologist. He suggested that people tend to remember information in terms of **schemas,** organized bodies of information stored in memory that bias the way new information is interpreted, stored, and recalled (Bartlett, 1932). Because we use schemas to organize information, our memories often consist of a reconstruction of previous experience. Consequently, our schemas are based not only on the actual material to which people are exposed, but also on their understanding of the situation, their expectations about the situation, and their awareness of the motivations underlying the behavior of others.

One of the earliest demonstrations of schemas came from a classic study that involved a procedure similar to the children's game of "telephone," in which information from memory is passed sequentially from one person to another. In the study, a participant viewed a drawing in which there were a variety of people of differing racial and ethnic backgrounds on a subway car, one of whom—a white person—was shown with a razor in his hand (Allport & Postman, 1958). The first participant was asked to describe the drawing to someone else without looking back at it. Then that person was asked to describe it to another person (without looking at the drawing), and then the process was repeated with still one more participant.

The report of the last person differed in significant, yet systematic, ways from the initial drawing. Specifically, many people described the drawing as depicting an African American with a knife—an incorrect recollection, given that the drawing showed a razor in the hand of a Caucasian person. The transformation of the Caucasian's razor into an African American's knife clearly indicates that the participants held a schema that included the unwarranted prejudice that African Americans are more violent than Caucasians and thus more apt to be holding a knife. In short, our expectations and knowledge—and prejudices—affect the reliability of our memories (McDonald & Hirt, 1997; Newby-Clark & Ross, 2003).

Although the constructive nature of memory can result in memories that are partially or completely false, they also may be beneficial in some ways. For example, false memories may allow us to keep hold of positive self-images. In addition, they may help us maintain positive relationships with others as we construct overly positive views of others (Howe, 2011).

Similarly, memory is affected by the emotional meaning of experiences. For example, in one experiment, researchers asked devoted Yankee or Red Sox fans about details of two decisive baseball championship games between the teams, one won by the Yankees and the other won by the Red Sox. Fans recalled details of the game their team won significantly more accurately than the game their team lost (see Figure 4; Breslin & Safer, 2011).

MEMORY IN THE COURTROOM: THE EYEWITNESS ON TRIAL

For Calvin Willis, the inadequate memories of two people cost him more than two decades of his life. Willis was the victim of mistaken identity when a young rape victim picked out his photo as the perpetrator of the rape. On that basis, he was tried, convicted, and sentenced to life in prison. Twenty-one years later, DNA testing showed that Willis was innocent, and the victim's identification wrong (Corsello, 2005).

Unfortunately, Willis is not the only victim to whom apologies have had to be made; many cases of mistaken identity have led to unjustified legal actions. Research on eyewitness identification of suspects, as well as on memory for other details of crimes, has shown that eyewitnesses are apt to make significant errors when they try to recall details of criminal activity—even if they are highly confident about their recollections (Thompson, 2000; Zaragoza, Belli, & Payment, 2007; Paterson, Kemp, & Ng, 2011).

One reason is the impact of the weapons used in crimes. When a criminal perpetrator displays a gun or knife, it acts like a perceptual magnet, attracting the eyes of the witnesses. As a consequence, witnesses pay less attention to other details of the crime and are less able to recall what actually occurred (Steblay et al., 2003; Zaitsu, 2007; Pickel, 2009).

schemas Organized bodies of information stored in memory that bias the way new information is interpreted, stored, and recalled.

Study Alert

A key fact about memory is that it is a constructive process in which memories are influenced by the meaning given to what is being recalled.

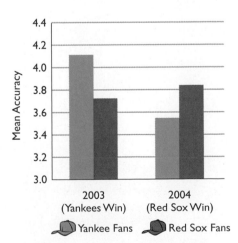

FIGURE 4 Yankee and Red Sox fans were more accurate recalling details of a championship game their team won than they were of a championship game that their team lost. (Source: Breslin & Safer, 2011.)

FIGURE 5 After viewing an accident involving two cars, the participants in a study were asked to estimate the speed of the two cars involved in the collision. Estimates varied substantially, depending on the way the question was worded. (Source: Loftus & Palmer, 1974.)

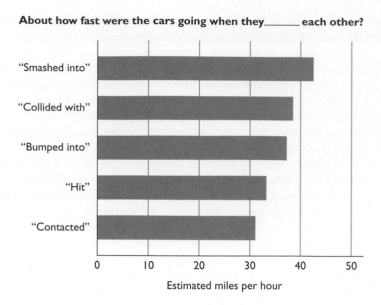

About how fast were the cars going when they_____ each other?

Estimated miles per hour

One reason eyewitnesses are prone to memory-related errors is that the specific wording of questions posed to them by police officers or attorneys can affect the way they recall information, as a number of experiments illustrate. For example, in one experiment the participants were shown a film of two cars crashing into each other. Some were then asked the question, "About how fast were the cars going when they *smashed* into each other?" On average, they estimated the speed to be 40.8 miles per hour. In contrast, when another group of participants was asked, "About how fast were the cars going when they *contacted* each other?" the average estimated speed was only 31.8 miles per hour (Loftus & Palmer, 1974; see Figure 5).

Children's Reliability. The problem of memory reliability becomes even more acute when children are witnesses because increasing evidence suggests that children's memories are highly vulnerable to the influence of others (Loftus, 1993; Douglas, Goldstein, & Bjorklund, 2000). For instance, in one experiment, 5- to 7-year-old girls who had just had a routine physical examination were shown an anatomically explicit doll. The girls were shown the doll's genital area and asked, "Did the doctor touch you here?" Three of the girls who did not have a vaginal or anal exam said that the doctor had in fact touched them in the genital area, and one of those three made up the detail "The doctor did it with a stick" (Saywitz & Goodman, 1990).

Children's memories are especially susceptible to influence when the situation is highly emotional or stressful. For example, in trials in which there is significant pretrial publicity or in which alleged victims are questioned repeatedly, often by untrained interviewers, the memories of the alleged victims may be influenced by the types of questions they are asked (Scullin, Kanaya, & Ceci, 2002; Lamb & Garretson, 2003; Quas, Malloy, & Melinder, 2007; Goodman & Quas, 2008).

Repressed and False Memories: Separating Truth from Fiction. Consider the case of George Franklin Sr., a man charged with murdering his daughter's playmate. The entire case was based on memories of Franklin's daughter, who claimed that she had repressed them until she began to have flashbacks of the event two decades later. Gradually, the memories became clearer until she recalled her father lifting a rock over his head and then seeing her friend covered with blood. On the basis of her memories, her father was convicted—but later was cleared of the crime after an appeal of the conviction.

There is good reason to question the validity of *repressed memories,* recollections of events that are initially so shocking that the mind responds by pushing them into the unconscious. Supporters of the notion of repressed memory (based on Freud's psychoanalytic theory) suggest that such memories may remain hidden, possibly

Six years after being convicted of murder based on a so-called repressed memory of his daughter, George Franklin Sr.'s conviction was overturned.

throughout a person's lifetime, unless they are triggered by some current circumstance, such as the probing that occurs during psychological therapy.

However, memory researcher Elizabeth Loftus maintains that so-called repressed memories may well be inaccurate or even wholly false—representing *false memory*. For example, false memories develop when people are unable to recall the source of a memory of a particular event about which they have only vague recollections. When the source of the memory becomes unclear or ambiguous, people may become confused about whether they actually experienced the event or whether it was imagined. Ultimately, people come to believe that the event actually occurred (Loftus, 2004; Wade, Sharman, & Garry, 2007; Bernstein & Loftus, 2009a).

There is great controversy regarding the legitimacy of repressed memories. Many therapists give great weight to authenticity of repressed memories, and their views are supported by research showing that there are specific regions of the brain that help keep unwanted memories out of awareness. On the other side of the issue are researchers who maintain that there is insufficient scientific support for the existence of such memories. There is also a middle ground: memory researchers who suggest that false memories are a result of normal information processing. The challenge for those on all sides of the issue is to distinguish truth from fiction (Brown & Pope, 1996; Strange, Clifasefi, & Garry, 2007; Bernstein & Loftus, 2009b).

AUTOBIOGRAPHICAL MEMORY: WHERE PAST MEETS PRESENT

Your memory of experiences in your own past may well be a fiction—or at least a distortion of what actually occurred. The same constructive processes that make us inaccurately recall the behavior of others also reduce the accuracy of autobiographical memories. **Autobiographical memories** are our recollections of circumstances and episodes from our own lives. Autobiographical memories encompass the episodic memories we hold about ourselves (Rubin, 1999; Sutin & Robins, 2007; Nalbantian, 2011).

For example, we tend to forget information about our past that is incompatible with the way in which we currently see ourselves. One study found that adults who were well adjusted but who had been treated for emotional problems during the early years of their lives tended to forget important but troubling childhood events, such as being in foster care. College students misremember their bad grades—but remember their good ones (see Figure 6; Walker, Skowronski, & Thompson, 2003; Kemps & Tiggemann, 2007).

Similarly, when a group of 48-year-olds were asked to recall how they had responded on a questionnaire they had completed when they were high school freshman, their accuracy was no better than chance. For example, although 61% of the questionnaire respondents said that playing sports and other physical activities was their favorite pastime, only 23% of the adults recalled it accurately (Offer et al., 2000).

It is not just certain kinds of events that are distorted; particular periods of life are remembered more easily than others. For example, when people reach late adulthood, they remember periods of life in which they experienced major transitions, such as attending college and working at their first job, better than they remember their middle-age years. Similarly, although most adults' earliest memories of their own lives are of events that occurred when they were toddlers, toddlers show evidence of recall of events that occurred when they were as young as 6 months old (Simcock & Hayne, 2002; Wang, 2003; Cordnoldi, De Beni, & Helstrup, 2007).

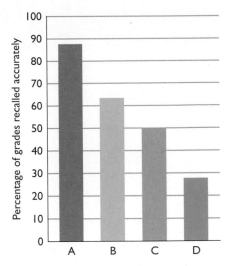

FIGURE 6 We tend to distort memories of unpleasant events. For example, college students are much more likely to accurately recall their good grades while inaccurately recalling their poor ones (Bahrick, Hall, & Berger, 1996). Now that you know this, how well do you think you can recall your high school grades?

autobiographical memories Our recollections of circumstances and episodes from our own lives.

Exploring DIVERSITY

Are There Cross-Cultural Differences in Memory?

Travelers who have visited areas of the world in which there is no written language often have returned with tales of people with phenomenal memories. For instance, storytellers in some preliterate cultures can recount long chronicles that recall the names and activities of people over many generations. Those feats led experts to argue initially that people in preliterate societies develop a different, and perhaps better, type of memory than do those in cultures that employ a written language. They suggested that in a society that lacks writing, people are motivated to recall information with accuracy, especially information relating to tribal histories and traditions that would be lost if they were not passed down orally from one generation to another (Daftary & Meri, 2002; Berntsen & Rubin, 2004).

Today, memory researchers dismiss that view. For one thing, preliterate peoples don't have an exclusive claim to amazing memory feats. Some Hebrew scholars memorize thousands of pages of text and can recall the locations of particular words on the page. Similarly, poetry singers in the Balkans can recall thousands of lines of poetry. Even in cultures in which written language exists, then, astounding feats of memory are possible (Strathern & Stewart, 2003; Rubin et al., 2007).

Memory researchers now suggest that there are both similarities and differences in memory across cultures. Basic memory processes such as short-term memory capacity and the structure of long-term memory—the "hardware" of memory—are universal and operate similarly in people in all cultures. In contrast, cultural differences can be seen in the way information is acquired and rehearsed—the "software" of memory. Culture determines how people frame information initially, how much they practice learning and recalling it, and the strategies they use to try to recall it (Mack, 2003; Wang & Conway, 2006; Rubin et al., 2007).

Storytellers in many cultures can recount hundreds of years of history in vivid detail. Research has found that this amazing ability is due less to basic memory processes than to the ways in which they acquire and retain information.

RECAP/EVALUATE/RETHINK

RECAP

LO 19-1 What causes difficulties and failures in remembering?

- The tip-of-the-tongue phenomenon is the temporary inability to remember information that one is certain one knows. Retrieval cues are a major strategy for recalling information successfully. (p. 218)
- The levels-of-processing approach to memory suggests that the way in which information is initially perceived and analyzed determines the success with which it is recalled. The deeper the initial processing, the greater the recall. (p. 219)
- Explicit memory refers to intentional or conscious recollection of information. In contrast, implicit memory refers to memories of which people are not consciously aware but that can affect subsequent performance and behavior. (p. 220)
- Flashbulb memories are memories centered on a specific, important event. The more distinctive a memory is, the more easily it can be retrieved. (p. 221)
- Memory is a constructive process: We relate memories to the meaning, guesses, and expectations we give to events. Specific information is recalled in terms of schemas, organized bodies of information stored in memory that bias the way new information is interpreted, stored, and recalled. (p. 222)
- Eyewitnesses are apt to make substantial errors when they try to recall the details of crimes. The problem of memory reliability becomes even more acute when the witnesses are children. (p. 223)
- Autobiographical memory is influenced by constructive processes. (p. 225)

EVALUATE

1. While with a group of friends at a dance, Eva bumps into a man she dated last month. But when she tries to introduce him to her friends, she cannot remember his name. What is the term for this occurrence?
2. _____ is the process of retrieving a specific item from memory.
3. A friend tells you, "I know exactly where I was and what I was doing when I heard that Michael Jackson died." What is this type of memory phenomenon called?
4. _____ _____ _____ theory states that the more a person analyzes a statement, the more likely he or she is to remember it later.

RETHINK

1. Research shows that an eyewitness's memory for details of crimes can contain significant errors. How might a lawyer use this information when evaluating an eyewitness's testimony? Should eyewitness accounts be permissible in a court of law?
2. *From a social worker's perspective:* Should a child victim of sexual abuse be allowed to testify in court, based on what you've learned about children's memories under stress?

Answers to Evaluate Questions

1. tip-of-the-tongue phenomenon; 2. Recall; 3. flashbulb memory; 4. Levels-of-processing

KEY TERMS

tip-of-the-tongue phenomenon p. 218
recall p. 218
recognition p. 218

levels-of-processing theory p. 219
explicit memory p. 220
implicit memory p. 220

priming p. 220
flashbulb memories p. 221
constructive processes p. 222

schemas p. 223
autobiographical memories p. 225

Forgetting: When Memory Fails

Learning Outcomes

LO 20-1 Why do we forget information?

LO 20-2 What are the major memory impairments?

Known in the scientific literature by the alias of H.M., he could remember, quite literally, nothing—nothing, that is, that had happened since the loss of his brain's temporal lobes and hippocampus during experimental surgery to reduce epileptic seizures. Until that time, H.M.'s memory had been quite normal. But after the operation he was unable to recall anything for more than a few minutes, and then the memory was seemingly lost forever. He did not remember his address, or the name of the person to whom he was talking. H.M. would read the same magazine over and over again. According to his own description, his life was like waking from a dream and being unable to know where he was or how he got there (Milner, 1966, 2005).

As the case of H.M. illustrates, a person without a normal memory faces severe difficulties. All of us who have experienced even routine instances of forgetting—such as not remembering an acquaintance's name or a fact on a test—understand the very real consequences of memory failure.

Of course, memory failure is also essential to remembering important information. The ability to forget inconsequential details about experiences, people, and objects helps us avoid being burdened and distracted by trivial stores of meaningless data. Forgetting helps keep unwanted and unnecessary information from interfering with retrieving information that is wanted and necessary (Schooler & Hertwig, 2011).

Forgetting also permits us to form general impressions and recollections. For example, the reason our friends consistently look familiar to us is because we're able to forget their clothing, facial blemishes, and other transient features that change from one occasion to the next. Instead, our memories are based on a summary of various critical features—a far more economical use of our memory capabilities.

The first attempts to study forgetting were made by German psychologist Hermann Ebbinghaus about 100 years ago. Using himself as the only participant in his study, Ebbinghaus memorized lists of three-letter nonsense syllables—meaningless sets of two consonants with a vowel in between, such as FIW and BOZ. By measuring how easy it was to relearn a given list of words after varying periods of time had passed since the initial learning, he found that forgetting occurred systematically, as shown in Figure 1. As the figure indicates, the most rapid forgetting occurs in the first 9 hours, particularly in the first hour. After 9 hours, the rate of forgetting slows and declines little, even after the passage of many days.

Despite his primitive methods, Ebbinghaus's study had an important influence on subsequent research, and his basic conclusions have been upheld. There is almost always a strong initial decline in memory, followed by a more gradual drop over time. Furthermore, relearning of previously mastered material is almost always faster than starting from scratch, whether the material is academic information or a motor skill such as serving a tennis ball (Wixted & Carpenter, 2007).

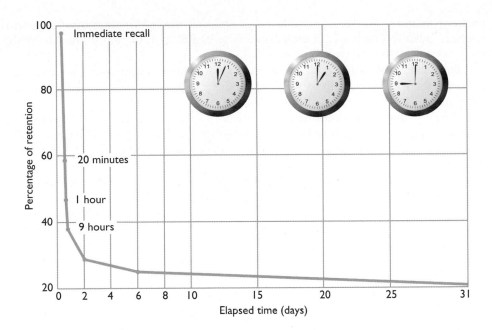

FIGURE 1 In his classic work, Ebbinghaus found that the most rapid forgetting occurs in the first 9 hours after exposure to new material. However, the rate of forgetting then slows down and declines very little even after many days have passed (Ebbinghaus, 1885, 1913). Check your own memory: What were you doing exactly 2 hours ago? What were you doing last Tuesday at 5 p.m.? Which information is easier to retrieve?

Why We Forget

Why do we forget? One reason is that we may not have paid attention to the material in the first place—a failure of *encoding*. For example, if you live in the United States, you probably have been exposed to thousands of pennies during your life. Despite this experience, you probably don't have a clear sense of the details of the coin. (See this for yourself by looking at Figure 2.) Consequently, the reason for your

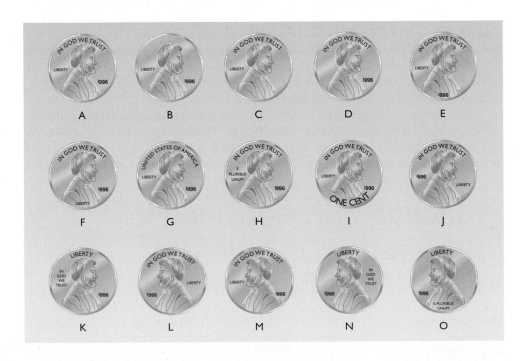

FIGURE 2 One of these pennies is the real thing. Can you find it? Why is this task harder than it seems at first?
(Source: Nickerson & Adams, 1979.)

If you don't have a penny handy, the correct answer is "A."

memory failure is that you probably never encoded the information into long-term memory initially. Obviously, if information was not placed in memory to start with, there is no way the information can be recalled.

But what about material that has been encoded into memory and that can't later be remembered? Several processes account for memory failures, including decay, interference, and cue-dependent forgetting.

Decay is the loss of information in memory through nonuse. This explanation for forgetting assumes that *memory traces,* the physical changes that take place in the brain when new material is learned, simply fade away or disintegrate over time (Grann, 2007).

decay The loss of information in memory through its nonuse.

Although there is evidence that decay does occur, this does not seem to be the complete explanation for forgetting. Often there is no relationship between how long ago a person was exposed to information and how well that information is recalled. If decay explained all forgetting, we would expect that the more time that has elapsed between the initial learning of information and our attempt to recall it, the harder it would be to remember it because there would be more time for the memory trace to decay. Yet people who take several consecutive tests on the same material often recall more of the initial information when taking later tests than they did on earlier tests. If decay were operating, we would expect the opposite to occur (Payne, 1986).

Because decay does not fully account for forgetting, memory specialists have proposed an additional mechanism: interference. In **interference,** information stored in memory disrupts the recall of other information stored in memory. For example, if I'm trying to recall my college classmate Jake's name and all I can remember is the name of another classmate, James, interference may be at work (Naveh-Benjamin, Guez, & Sorek, 2007; Pilotti, Chodorow, & Shono, 2009; Solesio-Jofre et al., 2011).

interference The phenomenon by which information in memory disrupts the recall of other information.

To distinguish between decay and interference, think of the two processes in terms of a row of books on a library shelf. In decay, the old books are constantly crumbling and rotting away, leaving room for new arrivals. Interference processes suggest that new books knock the old ones off the shelf, where they become hard to find or even totally inaccessible.

Finally, forgetting may occur because of **cue-dependent forgetting,** forgetting that occurs when there are insufficient retrieval cues to rekindle information that is in memory (Tulving & Thompson, 1983). For example, you may not be able to remember where you lost a set of keys until you mentally walk through your day, thinking of each place you visited. When you think of the place where you lost the keys—say, the library—the retrieval cue of the library may be sufficient to help you recall that you left them on the desk in the library. Without that retrieval cue, you may be unable to recall the location of the keys.

cue-dependent forgetting Forgetting that occurs when there are insufficient retrieval cues to rekindle information that is in memory.

Most research suggests that interference and cue-dependent forgetting are key processes in forgetting (Mel'nikov, 1993; Bower, Thompson, & Tulving, 1994). We forget things mainly because new memories interfere with the retrieval of old ones or because appropriate retrieval cues are unavailable, not because the memory trace has decayed.

Study Alert

Memory loss through decay comes from nonuse of the memory; memory loss through interference is due to the presence of other information in memory.

Proactive and Retroactive Interference: The Before and After of Forgetting

There are actually two sorts of interference that influence forgetting. One is proactive interference, and the other is retroactive interference (Bunting, 2006; Jacoby et al., 2007).

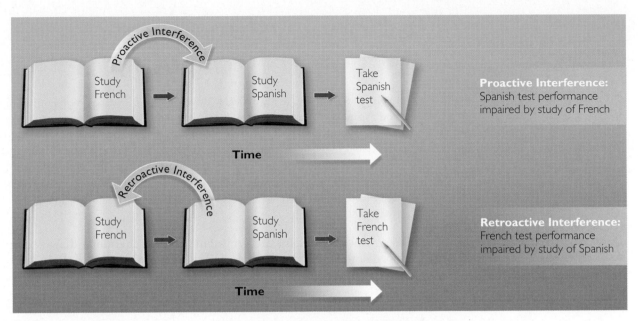

FIGURE 3 Proactive interference occurs when material learned earlier interferes with the recall of newer material. In this example, studying French before studying Spanish interferes with performance on a Spanish test. In contrast, retroactive interference exists when material learned after initial exposure to other material interferes with the recall of the first material. In this case, retroactive interference occurs when recall of French is impaired because of later exposure to Spanish.

In **proactive interference,** information learned earlier disrupts the recall of newer material. Suppose, as a student of foreign languages, you first learned French in the 10th grade, and then in the 11th grade you took Spanish. When in the 12th grade you take a college subject achievement test in Spanish, you may find you have difficulty recalling the Spanish translation of a word because all you can think of is its French equivalent.

In contrast, **retroactive interference** occurs when material that was learned later disrupts the retrieval of information that was learned earlier. If, for example, you have difficulty on a French subject achievement test because of your more recent exposure to Spanish, retroactive interference is the culprit (see Figure 3). Similarly, retroactive interference can account for the lack of accuracy of eyewitness memories, as newer information about a crime obtained from newspaper accounts may disrupt the initial memory of the observation of the crime.

One way to remember the difference between proactive and retroactive interference is to keep in mind that *pro*active interference progresses in time—the past interferes with the present. In contrast, *retro*active interference retrogresses in time, working backward as the present interferes with the past.

Although the concepts of proactive and retroactive interference illustrate how material may be forgotten, they still do not explain whether forgetting is caused by the actual loss or modification of information or by problems in the retrieval of information. Most research suggests that material that has apparently been lost because of interference can eventually be recalled if appropriate stimuli are presented (Tulving & Psotka, 1971; Anderson, 1981), but the question has not been fully answered.

proactive interference Interference in which information learned earlier disrupts the recall of material learned later.

retroactive interference Interference in which material that was learned later disrupts the retrieval of information that was learned earlier.

PsychTech

Having trouble remembering something on your computer screen? According to research by Connor Diemand-Yauman and colleagues, changing the font into something *harder* to read may make it easier to remember. The explanation is that the unusual font forces us to concentrate more intently on the information, making it more memorable.

Memory Dysfunctions: Afflictions of Forgetting

First you notice that you're always misplacing things or that common nouns are evading you as stubbornly as the names of new acquaintances. Pretty soon you're forgetting appointments and getting flustered when you drive in traffic. On bad days you find you can't hold numbers in your mind long enough to dial the phone. You try valiantly to conceal your lapses, but they become ever more glaring. You crash your car. You spend whole mornings struggling to dress yourself properly. And even as you lose the ability to read or play the piano, you're painfully aware of what's happening to you (Cowley, 2000, p. 46).

Alzheimer's disease A progressive brain disorder that heads to a gradual and irreversible decline in cognitive abilities.

These memory problems are symptomatic of **Alzheimer's disease,** A progressive brain disorder that heads to a gradual and irreversible decline in cognitive abilities. Alzheimer's is the fourth leading cause of death among adults in the United States, affecting an estimated 5 million people.

In the beginning, Alzheimer's symptoms appear as simple forgetfulness of things such as appointments and birthdays. As the disease progresses, memory loss becomes more profound, and even the simplest tasks—such as using a telephone—are forgotten. Ultimately, victims may lose their ability to speak or comprehend language, and physical deterioration sets in, leading to death.

The causes of Alzheimer's disease are not fully understood. Increasing evidence suggests that Alzheimer's results from an inherited susceptibility to a defect in the production of the protein beta amyloid, which is necessary for the maintenance of nerve cell connections. When the synthesis of beta amyloid goes awry, large clumps of cells form, triggering inflammation and the deterioration of nerve cells in the brain (Horínek, Varjassyová, & Hort, 2007; Selkoe, 2008; Hyman, 2011; also see Figure 4 *Neuroscience in Your Life*).

amnesia Memory loss that occurs without other mental difficulties.

Alzheimer's disease is one of a number of memory dysfunctions. Another is **amnesia,** memory loss that occurs without other mental difficulties. The type of amnesia immortalized in countless Hollywood films involves a victim who receives a blow to the head and is unable to remember anything from his or her past. In reality, amnesia of this type, known as retrograde amnesia, is quite rare. In **retrograde amnesia,** memory is lost for occurrences prior to a certain event, but not for new events. Usually, lost memories gradually reappear, although full restoration may take as long as several years. In certain cases, some memories are lost forever. But even in cases of severe memory loss, the loss is generally selective. For example, although people suffering from retrograde amnesia may be unable to recall friends and family members, they still may be able to play complicated card games or knit a sweater quite well (Verfaellie & Keane, 2002; Bright, Buckman, & Fradera, 2006).

retrograde amnesia Amnesia in which memory is lost for occurrences prior to a certain event, but not for new events.

A second type of amnesia is exemplified by people who remember nothing of their current activities. In **anterograde amnesia** loss of memory occurs for events that follow an injury. Information cannot be transferred from short-term to long-term memory, resulting in the inability to remember anything other than what was in long-term storage before the accident (Gilboa, Winocur, & Rosenbaum, 2006).

anterograde amnesia Amnesia in which memory is lost for events that follow an injury.

Korsakoff's syndrome A disease that afflicts long-term alcoholics, leaving some abilities intact but including hallucinations and a tendency to repeat the same story.

Amnesia is also a result of **Korsakoff's syndrome,** a disease that afflicts long-term alcoholics. Although many of their intellectual abilities may be intact, Korsakoff's sufferers display a strange array of symptoms, including hallucinations and a tendency to repeat the same story over and over (van Oort & Kessels, 2009).

Fortunately, most of us have intact memory, and the occasional failures we suffer may actually be preferable to having a perfect memory. Consider, for instance, the case of a man who had total recall. After reading passages of Dante's *The Divine*

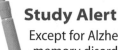

Study Alert

Except for Alzheimer's disease, memory disorders are relatively rare.

Neuroscience in Your Life: Alzheimer's Disease and Brain Deterioration

FIGURE 4 Alzheimer's disease, the fourth leading cause of death among adults in the United State, is characterized by significant memory declines. While most previous neuroscience research has focused on the loss of function and brain tissue, more recent research has begun to look at changes in how the brain communicates internally. In particular, research using *Diffusion Tensor Imaging*, a technique that shows connections between neurons in the brain, shows that connections between areas of the brain involved in memory become altered as Alzheimer's progresses. These images illustrate the differences in communication pathways in healthy older adults (OA) compared with those with Alzheimer's Disease (AD). The pathway examined here is highlighted in blue. (Source: Salat et al., 2010.)

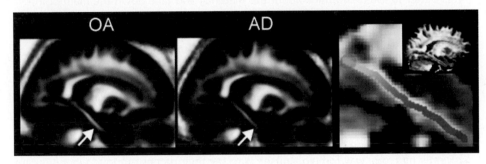

Comedy in Italian—a language he did not speak—he was able to repeat them from memory some 15 years later. He could memorize lists of 50 unrelated words and recall them at will more than a decade later. He could even repeat the same list of words backward, if asked (Luria, 1968).

Such a skill at first may seem to be enviable, but it actually presented quite a problem. The man's memory became a jumble of lists of words, numbers, and names; when he tried to relax, his mind was filled with images. Even reading was difficult since every word evoked a flood of thoughts from the past that interfered with his ability to understand the meaning of what he was reading. Partially as a consequence of the man's unusual memory, psychologist A. R. Luria, who studied his case, found him to be a "disorganized and rather dull-witted person" (Luria, 1968, p. 65). We might be grateful, then, that forgetfulness plays a role in our lives.

BECOMING AN INFORMED CONSUMER of Psychology

Improving Your Memory

Apart from the advantages of forgetting, say, a bad date, most of us would like to find ways to improve our memories. Among the effective strategies for studying and remembering course material:

- *Use the keyword technique.* If you are studying a foreign language, try the *keyword technique* of pairing a foreign word with a common English word that has a similar sound. This English word is known as the *keyword*. For example, to learn the Spanish word for duck (*pato,* pronounced *pot-o*), you might choose the keyword *pot*; for the Spanish word for horse (*caballo*, pronounced *cob-eye-yo*), the keyword might be *eye*. Once you have thought of a keyword, imagine the Spanish word "interacting" with the English keyword. You might envision a duck taking a bath in a pot to remember the word *pato* or a horse with a large, bulging eye in the center of its head to recall *caballo* (Carney & Levin, 1998; Wyra, Lawson, & Hungi, 2007).

- *Rely on organization cues.* Recall material you read in textbooks by organizing the material in memory the first time you read it. Organize your reading on the basis of any advance information you have about the content and about its arrangement. You will then be able to make connections and see relationships among the various facts and process the material at a deeper level, which in turn will later aid recall.

- *Take effective notes.* "Less is more" is perhaps the best advice for taking lecture notes that facilitate recall. Rather than trying to jot down every detail of a lecture, it is better to listen and think about the material, and take down the main points. In effective note taking, thinking about the material when you first hear it is more important than writing it down. This is one reason that borrowing someone else's notes is a bad idea; you will have no framework in memory that you can use to understand them (Feldman, 2010).

- *Practice and rehearse.* Although practice does not necessarily make perfect, it helps. By studying and rehearsing material past initial mastery—a process called *overlearning*—people are able to show better long-term recall than they show if they stop practicing after their initial learning of the material.

- *Talk to yourself.* If you have trouble remembering names of people who you have recently met, one way to help yourself is to say their names out loud when you are first introduced. It will make it easier to retrieve the information later because the information is stored in additional ways in your brain.

- *Don't believe claims about drugs that improve memory.* Advertisements for One-a-Day vitamins with ginkgo biloba or Quanterra Mental Sharpness Product would have you believe that taking a drug or supplement can improve your memory. Not so, according to the results of numerous studies. No research has shown that commercial memory enhancers are effective (Gold, Cahill, & Wenk, 2002; McDaniel, Maier, & Einstein, 2002; Burns, Bryan, & Nettelbeck, 2006).

RECAP/EVALUATE/RETHINK

RECAP

LO 20-1 Why do we forget information?

- Several processes account for memory failure, including decay, interference (both proactive and retroactive), and cue-dependent forgetting. (p. 230)

LO 20-2 What are the major memory impairments?

- Among the memory dysfunctions are Alzheimer's disease, which leads to a progressive loss of memory, and amnesia, a memory loss that occurs without other mental difficulties and can take the forms of retrograde amnesia and anterograde amnesia. Korsakoff's syndrome is a disease that afflicts long-term alcoholics, resulting in memory impairment. (p. 232)

- Techniques for improving memory include the keyword technique to memorize foreign language vocabulary; using the encoding specificity phenomenon;

organizing text material and lecture notes; talking to yourself; and practice and rehearsal, leading to overlearning. (pp. 233, 234)

EVALUATE

1. If, after learning the history of the Middle East for a class 2 years ago, you now find yourself unable to recall what you learned, you are experiencing memory _____, caused by nonuse.

2. Difficulty in accessing a memory because of the presence of other information is known as _____.

3. _____ interference occurs when material is difficult to retrieve because of subsequent exposure to other material; _____ interference refers to difficulty in retrieving material as a result of the interference of previously learned material.

4. Match the following memory disorders with the correct information:
   1. Affects alcoholics; may result in hallucinations.
   2. Memory loss occurring without other mental problems.
   3. Beta amyloid defect; progressive forgetting and physical deterioration.

   a. Alzheimer's disease
   b. Korsakoff's syndrome
   c. Amnesia

RETHINK

1. What are the implications of proactive and retroactive interference for learning multiple foreign languages? Would earlier language training in a different language help or hinder learning a new language?
2. *From a health-care provider's perspective:* Alzheimer's disease and amnesia are two of the most pervasive memory dysfunctions that threaten many individuals. What sorts of activities might health-care providers offer their patients to help them combat their memory loss?

Answers to Evaluate Questions

1. decay; 2. interference; 3. Retroactive, proactive; 4. 1-b, 2-c, 3-a

KEY TERMS

decay p. 230
interference p. 230
cue-dependent forgetting p. 230

proactive interference p. 231
retroactive interference p. 231

Alzheimer's disease p. 232
amnesia p. 232
retrograde amnesia p. 232

anterograde amnesia p. 232
Korsakoff's syndrome p. 232

Looking Back

Epilogue

Our examination of memory has highlighted the processes of encoding, storage, and retrieval, and theories about how these processes occur. We also encountered several phenomena relating to memory, including the tip-of-the-tongue phenomenon and flashbulb memories. Above all, we observed that memory is a constructive process by which interpretations, expectations, and guesses contribute to the nature of our memories.

Before moving on to the next chapter, return to the prologue on Louise Owen's perfect memory for events in her life. Consider the following questions in light of what you now know about memory.

1. What part of Louise Owen's memory is affected by her condition?
2. Do you think that Louise Owen's memory ability is more of a blessing or a curse? Why do you think so?
3. Would you expect Louise Owen to have perfect recall for *all* the facts and information she has encountered in her life, such as textbooks she has read? Why or why not?
4. From a researcher's perspective, how might you determine whether Louise Owen's memory is truly accurate?

VISUAL SUMMARY 6 Memory

MODULE 18 The Foundations of Memory

Memory: Encoding, storing, and retrieving information

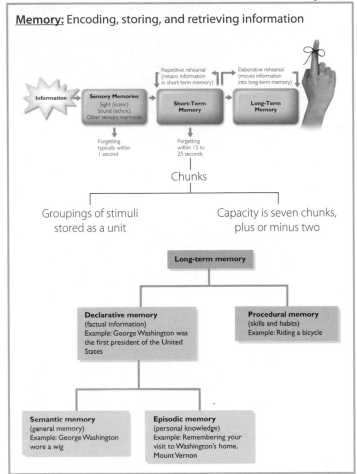

Chunks

Groupings of stimuli stored as a unit

Capacity is seven chunks, plus or minus two

Long-term memory

Declarative memory (factual information) Example: George Washington was the first president of the United States

Procedural memory (skills and habits) Example: Riding a bicycle

Semantic memory (general memory) Example: George Washington wore a wig

Episodic memory (personal knowledge) Example: Remembering your visit to Washington's home, Mount Vernon

MODULE 19 Recalling Long-Term Memories

Retrieval Cues: Stimuli that allow recall of information stored in long-term memory
- Recall: Remembering specific information
- Recognition: Knowing whether one has been previously exposed to given information

Levels of Processing Theory: Recall depends on how much the information was processed when it was first encountered

Explicit Memories: Conscious recall of information

Implicit Memories: Memories of which people are not consciously aware

Flashbulb Memories: Memories related to specific important events

Constructive Processes: Processes in which memories are influenced by the meaning we give to events

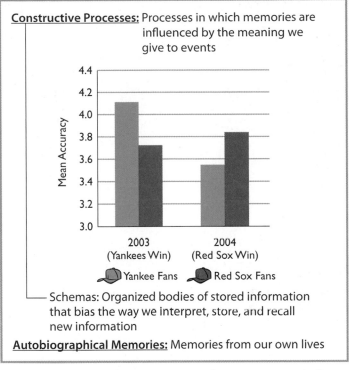

Schemas: Organized bodies of stored information that bias the way we interpret, store, and recall new information

Autobiographical Memories: Memories from our own lives

MODULE 20 Forgetting: When Memory Fails

Decay: Loss of information through nonuse

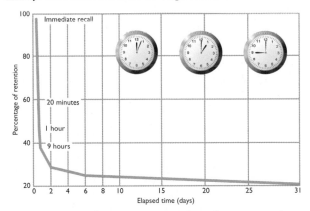

Cue-dependent forgetting: Forgetting that occurs when insufficient retrieval cues are available

Interference: Information in memory disrupts the recall of other information

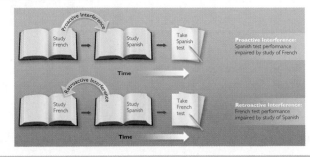

7

Thinking, Language, and Intelligence

Learning Outcomes for Chapter 7

MODULE 21

LO 21-1 What is thinking?

LO 21-2 What processes underlie reasoning and decision making?

LO 21-3 How do people approach and solve problems?

LO 21-4 What are the major obstacles to problem solving?

Thinking and Reasoning

Mental Images: Examining the Mind's Eye

Concepts: Categorizing the World

Algorithms and Heuristics

Applying Psychology in the 21st Century: I'll take "Artificial Intelligence" for $1,000, Alex.

Solving Problems

Creativity and Problem Solving

Becoming an Informed Consumer of Psychology: Thinking Critically and Creatively

MODULE 22

LO 22-1 How do people use language?

LO 22-2 How does language develop?

Language

Grammar: Language's Language

Language Development: Developing a Way with Words

Understanding Language Acquisition: Identifying the Roots of Language

The Influence of Language on Thinking: Do Eskimos Have More Words for Snow Than Texans Do?

Do Animals Use Language?

Exploring Diversity: Teaching with Linguistic Variety: Bilingual Education

Neuroscience in Your Life: Bilingualism and the Brain

MODULE 23

LO 23-1 What are the different definitions and conceptions of intelligence?

LO 23-2 What are the major approaches to measuring intelligence, and what do intelligence tests measure?

LO 23-3 How can the extremes of intelligence be characterized?

LO 23-4 Are traditional IQ tests culturally biased?

LO 23-5 To what degree is intelligence influenced by the environment and to what degree by heredity?

Intelligence

Theories of Intelligence: Are There Different Kinds of Intelligence?

Assessing Intelligence

Variations in Intellectual Ability

PsychWork: Director of Special Education

Group Differences in Intelligence: Genetic and Environmental Determinants

Exploring Diversity: The Relative Influence of Genetics and Environment: Nature, Nurture, and IQ

Prologue *Eureka!*

One day in the fall of their sophomore year, Matthew Fernandez and Akash Krishnan were at Akash's house in Portland, Oregon, trying to come up with an idea for their school's science fair. Temporarily defeated, they popped in a DVD of *I, Robot*.

There's a scene in the movie when Will Smith, who plays a robot-hating cop, visits Bridget Moynahan, the impossibly gorgeous scientist, and they begin to argue. She gets angry.

Her personal robot immediately walks into the room and asks: "Is everything all right, ma'am? I detected elevated stress patterns in your voice." It's a minor exchange—a computer recognizing emotion in a human voice—in a movie full of futuristic robots wreaking havoc, but it was an "aha" moment for a desperate research team. Their reaction, as Matt describes it, was: " 'Hey, that's really cool. I wonder if there's any science there' " (Lichtenstein, 2011, p. 44).

Looking Ahead

Matt and Akash proceeded to work on the problem of developing a computer program that would recognize emotional speech inflections. They had their work cut out for them; it's one thing to program a computer to recognize speech, but it turns out to be quite another thing to program it to recognize emotional subtleties. Even though we can readily identify emotions such as happiness or anxiety in another person's voice, Matt and Akash discovered that it's very difficult to specify exactly what it is we're picking up on to reach such conclusions. But they managed to do it quite well: Their problem-solving skills and creativity ultimately won them the Siemens Competition, one of the major science competitions in the United States, and $100,000 in scholarship funds.

Emotional recognition is just one of many tasks that our amazing human computer—the brain—can accomplish in the course of our daily lives, even though we may have little or no idea how it does so. The mystery of how the brain processes language and all its nuances—as well as how it uses information to solve problems and make decisions—is the subject to which we now turn.

Answers to these questions come from **cognitive psychology,** the branch of psychology that focuses on the study of higher mental processes, including thinking, language, memory, problem solving, knowing, reasoning, judging, and decision making. Clearly, the realm of cognitive psychology is broad.

We begin by considering concepts, the building blocks of thinking. We examine different strategies for approaching problems, means of generating solutions, and ways of making judgments about the usefulness and accuracy of solutions.

Next we turn to the way we communicate with others: Language. We consider how language is developed and acquired, its basic characteristics, and the relationship between language and thought.

Finally, we examine intelligence. We consider the challenges involved in defining and measuring intelligence, and then examine the two groups displaying extremes of intelligence: people with mental retardation and the gifted. We explore what are probably the two most controversial issues surrounding intelligence: the degree to which intelligence is influenced by heredity and by the environment and whether traditional tests of intelligence are biased toward the dominant cultural groups in society—a difficult issue that has both psychological and social significance.

cognitive psychology The branch of psychology that focuses on the study of higher mental processes, including thinking, language, memory, problem solving, knowing, reasoning, and judging.

Thinking and Reasoning

What are you thinking about at this moment?

The mere ability to pose such a question underscores the distinctive nature of the human ability to think. No other species contemplates, analyzes, recollects, or plans the way humans do. Understanding what thinking is, however, goes beyond knowing that we think. Philosophers, for example, have argued for generations about the meaning of thinking, with some placing it at the core of human beings' understanding of their own existence.

Psychologists define **thinking** as the manipulation of mental representations of information. A representation may take the form of a word, a visual image, a sound, or data in any other sensory modality that is stored in memory. Thinking transforms a particular representation of information into new and different forms, allowing us to answer questions, solve problems, or reach goals.

Although a clear sense of what specifically occurs when we think remains elusive, our understanding of the nature of the fundamental elements involved in thinking is growing. We begin by considering our use of mental images and concepts, the building blocks of thought.

Learning Outcomes

LO 21-1 What is thinking?

LO 21-2 What processes underlie reasoning and decision making?

LO 21-3 How do people approach and solve problems?

LO 21-4 What are the major obstacles to problem solving?

thinking The manipulation of mental representations of information.

Mental Images: Examining the Mind's Eye

Think of your best friend.

Chances are that you "see" some kind of visual image when asked to think of her or him, or any other person or object for that matter. To some cognitive psychologists, such mental images constitute a major part of thinking.

Mental images are representations in the mind of an object or event. They are not just visual representations; our ability to "hear" a tune in our heads also relies on a mental image. In fact, every sensory modality may produce corresponding mental images (De Beni, Pazzaglia, & Gardini, 2007; Gardini et al., 2009; Koçak et al., 2011).

Research has found that our mental images have many of the properties of the actual stimuli they represent. For example, it takes the mind longer to scan mental images of large objects than small ones, just as the eye takes longer to scan an actual large object than an actual small one. Similarly, we are able to manipulate and rotate mental images of objects, just as we are able to manipulate and rotate them in the real world (Mast & Kosslyn, 2002; Iachini & Giusberti, 2004; Zacks, 2008; see Figure 1).

Some experts see the production of mental images as a way to improve various skills. For instance, many athletes use mental imagery in their training. Basketball players may try to produce vivid and detailed images of the court, the basket, the ball, and the noisy crowd. They may visualize themselves taking a

mental images Representations in the mind of an object or event.

PsychTech

Researcher Adam Wilson has developed a method of tweeting by thinking. The process involves being outfitted with electrodes that react to changes in brain activity. It's slow going, though: the fastest tweeters are able to create tweets at only 8 characters per minute.

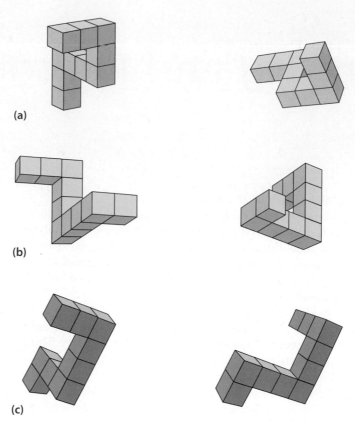

(a)

(b)

(c)

FIGURE 1 Try to mentally rotate one of each pair of patterns to see if it is the same as the other member of that pair. It's likely that the farther you have to mentally rotate a pattern, the longer it will take to decide if the patterns match one another. Does this mean that it will take you longer to visualize a map of the world than a map of the United States? Why or why not? (Source: From Shepard, R. N., & Metzler, J. (1971). Mental rotation of three-dimensional objects. *Science,* 171, no. 3972, 701–703 [Figure 1, p. 702]. Reprinted with permission from AAAS. http://www.sciencemag.org/content/171/3972/701.full)

foul shot, watching the ball, and hearing the swish as it goes through the net. And it works: The use of mental imagery can lead to improved performance in sports (Fournier, Deremaux, & Bernier, 2008; Moran, 2009; Velentzas, Heinen, & Schack, 2011).

Concepts: Categorizing the World

If someone asks you what is in your kitchen cabinet, you might answer with a detailed list of items (a jar of peanut butter, three boxes of macaroni and cheese, six unmatched dinner plates, and so forth). More likely, though, you would respond by naming some broader categories, such as "food" and "dishes."

Using such categories reflects the operation of concepts. **Concepts** are mental groupings of similar objects, events, or people. Concepts enable us to organize complex phenomena into simpler, and therefore more easily usable, cognitive categories (Murphy, 2005; Connolly, 2007; Kreppner et al., 2011).

Concepts help us classify newly encountered objects on the basis of our past experience. For example, we can surmise that someone tapping a handheld screen is probably using some kind of computer or PDA, even if we have never encountered that specific model before. Ultimately, concepts influence behavior. We would assume, for instance, that it might be appropriate to pet an animal after determining that it is a dog, whereas we would behave differently after classifying the animal as a wolf.

Athletes use mental imagery to focus on a task, a process they call "getting in the zone." What other occupations might require the use of strong mental imagery?

concepts A mental grouping of similar objects, events, or people.

When cognitive psychologists first studied concepts, they focused on those that were clearly defined by a unique set of properties or features. For example, an equilateral triangle is a closed shape that has three sides of equal length. If an object has these characteristics, it is an equilateral triangle; if it does not, it is not an equilateral triangle.

Other concepts—often those with the most relevance to our everyday lives—are more ambiguous and difficult to define. For instance, broader concepts such as "table" and "bird" have a set of general, relatively loose characteristic features, rather than unique, clearly defined properties that distinguish an example of the concept from a nonexample. When we consider these more ambiguous concepts, we usually think in terms of examples called **prototypes.** Prototypes are typical, highly representative examples of a concept that correspond to our mental image or best example of the concept. For instance, although a robin and an ostrich are both examples of birds, the robin is an example that comes to most people's minds far more readily. Consequently, robin is a prototype of the concept "bird." Similarly, when we think of the concept of a table, we're likely to think of a coffee table before we think of a drafting table, making a coffee table closer to our prototype of a table.

prototypes Typical, highly representative examples of a concept.

Relatively high agreement exists among people in a particular culture about which examples of a concept are prototypes as well as which examples are not. For instance, most people in Western cultures consider cars and trucks good examples of vehicles, whereas elevators and wheelbarrows are not considered very good examples. Consequently, cars and trucks are prototypes of the concept of a vehicle.

Concepts enable us to think about and understand more readily the complex world in which we live. For example, the suppositions we make about the reasons for other people's behavior are based on the ways in which we classify behavior. Hence, our conclusion about a person who washes her hands 20 times a day could vary, depending on whether we place her behavior within the conceptual framework of a health-care worker or a mental patient. Similarly, physicians make diagnoses by drawing on concepts and prototypes of symptoms that they learned about in medical school. Finally, concepts and prototypes facilitate our efforts to draw suitable conclusions through the cognitive process we turn to next: reasoning.

Algorithms and Heuristics

When faced with making a decision, we often turn to various kinds of cognitive shortcuts, known as algorithms and heuristics, to help us. An **algorithm** is a rule that, if applied appropriately, guarantees a solution to a problem. We can use an algorithm even if we cannot understand why it works. For example, you may know that you can find the length of the third side of a right triangle by using the formula $a^2 + b^2 = c^2$, although you may not have the foggiest notion of the mathematical principles behind the formula.

algorithm A rule that, if applied appropriately, guarantees a solution to a problem.

For many problems and decisions, however, no algorithm is available. In those instances, we may be able to use heuristics to help us. A **heuristic** is a thinking strategy that may lead us to a solution to a problem or decision, but—unlike algorithms—may sometimes lead to errors. Heuristics increase the likelihood of success in coming to a solution, but, unlike algorithms, they cannot ensure it. For example, when I play tic-tac-toe, I follow the heuristic of placing an X in the center square when I start the game. This tactic doesn't guarantee that I will win, but experience has taught me that it will increase my chances of success. Similarly, some students follow the heuristic of preparing for a test by ignoring the assigned textbook reading and only studying their lecture notes—a strategy that may or may not pay off.

heuristic A thinking strategy that may lead us to a solution to a problem or decision, but—unlike algorithms—may sometimes lead to errors.

Although heuristics often help people solve problems and make decisions, certain kinds of heuristics may lead to inaccurate conclusions. For example, we sometimes use the *representativeness heuristic,* a rule we apply when we judge people by the degree to which they represent a certain category or group of people. Suppose, for instance, you are the owner of a fast-food store that has been robbed many times

Study Alert

Remember that algorithms are rules that *always* provide a solution, whereas heuristics are shortcuts that *may* provide a solution.

I'll take "Artificial Intelligence" for $1,000, Alex.

"This facial wear made Israel's Moshe Dayan instantly recognizable worldwide."

Such was the $1,600 clue in the category "The eyes have it" of a mock round of the popular television game show, *Jeopardy*.

The contestants had mere moments to think about the question that appeared in writing in front of them—as long as it took the host to read the words aloud. As soon as he was done, it was time for the contestants to compete to be the first to buzz in and give an answer.

The three contestants quickly performed these mental gymnastics to come up with the correct answer, but only one hit the buzzer first. "What is an eye patch?" he correctly replied, adding $1,600 to his pot and handily beating his opponents—opponents who happened to be former *Jeopardy* champions. But this competitor was special in his own right: he wasn't even human. He was a computer named Watson, and he was winning (Baker, 2011).

This wasn't the first time human intelligence was pitted against artificial intelligence and lost. More than a decade earlier another computer named Deep Blue had beaten the reigning world champion of chess at a chess match. But while Deep Blue's accomplishment was impressive, it was limited in key ways—it didn't have to understand language, recognize subtle clues, or search through giant information databases to ferret out relevant facts and put them together to make a solution. But Watson did.

Nevertheless, even though Watson was able to handily beat human *Jeopardy* champions, its "brain power" still isn't a match for the human brain. Whereas a human contestant familiar with Moshe Dayan

While Watson was able to easily defeat its human opponents, artificial intelligence still has a long way to go before matching the complexity of the human brain.

would immediately make the appropriate connections, conjure up Dayan's face, and understand that the eye patch was the object of interest, Watson worked very differently. It instead combed through its massive database for every conceivable bit of trivia pertinent to Dayan. It had to repeatedly check facts that a human competitor would just know—such as whether Dayan was indeed a person—to determine a probability that each bit of trivia was relevant to the question (Detterman, 2011).

Watson's success shows that problem solving and decision making are logical processes—complicated processes, certainly, but ones that can be broken down into individual steps and rules. But whereas Watson needed a room full of computer processors, fans to cool them, and engineers to run them, our brains solve problems all day, every day—while also making long-term plans, controlling our bodies, keeping us alive, and doing all the other things that make us uniquely human beings (Baker, 2011).

RETHINK

- In what ways is Watson "thinking" like a human being, and in what ways is it not?
- Some people fear that artificial intelligence machines such as Watson might one day displace workers from jobs or even be entrusted with sensitive decisions, such as diagnosing diseases in medical facilities. Do these fears seem realistic to you? Might there be benefits to using machines in these ways?

by teenagers. The representativeness heuristic would lead you to raise your guard each time someone of this age group enters your store (even though, statistically, it is unlikely that any given teenager will rob the store) (Nilsson, Juslin, & Olsson, 2008; Read & Grushka-Cockayne, 2011).

The *availability heuristic* involves judging the probability of an event on the basis of how easily the event can be recalled from memory. According to this heuristic, we assume that events we remember easily are likely to have occurred more frequently in the past—and are more likely to occur in the future—than events that are harder to remember.

For instance, the availability heuristic makes us more afraid of dying in a plane crash than in an auto accident, despite statistics clearly showing that airplane travel is much safer than auto travel. Similarly, although 10 times as many people die from falling out of bed than from lightning strikes, we're more afraid of being hit by lightning. The reason is that plane crashes and lightning strikes receive far more publicity, and they are therefore more easily remembered (Oppenheimer, 2004; Fox, 2006; Kluger, 2006; Caruso, 2008).

We also make use of a *familiarity heuristic,* in which familiar items are seen as superior to those that are unfamiliar. For example, suppose each time you went to a supermarket you had to ponder every type of yogurt to decide which you wanted—as well as every other item on your grocery list. Instead, you see the brand of yogurt you usually buy and settle for it. Usually it's a good rule of thumb because it saves a lot of time.

On the other hand, it's not so good if you are an emergency room physician susceptible to the familiarity heuristic. If you simply settle on the first, most obvious diagnosis for a patient presenting particular symptoms (the ones that are most familiar to you), you may miss making a more accurate diagnosis (Herbert, 2011).

Algorithms and heuristics may be characteristic of human thinking, but scientists are now programming computers to mimic human thinking and problem solving. In fact, they are making significant inroads with computers in terms of the ability to solve problems and carry out some forms of intellectual activities. According to experts who study *artificial intelligence,* the field that examines how to use technology to imitate the outcome of human thinking, problem solving, and creative activities, computers can show rudiments of humanlike thinking because of their knowledge of where to look—and where not to look—for an answer to a problem. They suggest that the capacity of computer programs (such as those that play chess) to evaluate potential moves and to ignore unimportant possibilities gives them thinking ability—as we consider in the *Applying Psychology in the 21st Century* (Sabater & Sierra, 2005; Prasad, 2006; Copeland & Proudfoot, 2007).

Solving Problems

According to an old legend, a group of Vietnamese monks guard three towers on which sit 64 golden rings. The monks believe that if they succeed in moving the rings from the first tower to the third according to a series of rigid rules, the world as we know it will come to an end. (Should you prefer that the world remain in its present state, there's no need for immediate concern: The puzzle is so complex that it will take the monks about a trillion years to solve it.)

In the Tower of Hanoi puzzle, a simpler version of the task facing the monks, three disks are placed on three posts in the order shown in Figure 2. The goal of the

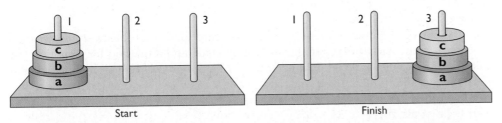

Start   Finish

FIGURE 2 The goal of the Tower of Hanoi puzzle is to move all three disks from the first post to the third and still preserve the original order of the disks, using the fewest number of moves possible while following the rules that only one disk at a time can be moved and no disk can cover a smaller one during a move. Try it yourself before you look at the solution, which is listed according to the sequence of moves.

(Solution: Move C to 3, B to 2, C to 2, A to 3, C to 1, B to 3, and C to 3.)

Preparation
Understanding and diagnosing problems

Production
Generating solutions

Judgment
Evaluating solutions

FIGURE 3 Steps in problem solving.

puzzle is to move all three disks to the third post, arranged in the same order, by using as few moves as possible. There are two restrictions: Only one disk can be moved at a time, and no disk can ever cover a smaller one during a move.

Why are cognitive psychologists interested in the Tower of Hanoi problem? Because the way people go about solving such puzzles helps illuminate how people solve complex, real-life problems. Psychologists have found that problem solving typically involves the three steps illustrated in Figure 3: preparing to create solutions, producing solutions, and evaluating the solutions that have been generated.

PREPARATION: UNDERSTANDING AND DIAGNOSING PROBLEMS

When approaching a problem like the Tower of Hanoi, most people begin by trying to understand the problem thoroughly. If the problem is a novel one, they probably will pay particular attention to any restrictions placed on coming up with a solution—such as the rule for moving only one disk at a time in the Tower of Hanoi problem. If, by contrast, the problem is a familiar one, they are apt to spend considerably less time in this preparation stage.

Problems vary from well defined to ill defined. In a *well-defined problem*—such as a mathematical equation or the solution to a jigsaw puzzle—both the nature of the problem itself and the information needed to solve it are available and clear. Thus, we can make straightforward judgments about whether a potential solution is appropriate. With an *ill-defined problem,* such as how to increase morale on an assembly line or to bring peace to the Middle East, not only may the specific nature of the problem be unclear, the information required to solve the problem may be even less obvious (Vartanian, 2009; Newman, Willoughby, & Pruce, 2011).

Kinds of Problems. Typically, a problem falls into one of the three categories shown in Figure 4: arrangement, inducing structure, and transformation. Solving each type requires somewhat different kinds of psychological skills and knowledge.

Arrangement problems require the problem solver to rearrange or recombine elements in a way that will satisfy a certain criterion. Usually, several different arrangements can be made, but only one or a few of the arrangements will produce a solution. Anagram problems and jigsaw puzzles are examples of arrangement problems (Coventry et al., 2003).

In *problems of inducing structure,* a person must identify the existing relationships among the elements presented and then construct a new relationship among them. In such a problem, the problem solver must determine not only the relationships among the elements but also the structure and size of the elements involved. In the example shown in Figure 4b, a person must first determine that the solution requires the numbers to be considered in pairs (14-24-34-44-54-64). Only after identifying that part of the problem can a person determine the solution rule (the first number of each pair increases by one, whereas the second number remains the same).

The Tower of Hanoi puzzle represents the third kind of problem—*transformation problems*—that consist of an initial state, a goal state, and a method for changing the initial state into the goal state. In the Tower of Hanoi problem, the initial state is the original configuration, the goal state is to have the three disks on the third peg, and the method is the rules for moving the disks (Emick & Welsh, 2005; Majeres, 2007; Van Belle et al., 2011).

Whether the problem is one of arrangement, inducing structure, or transformation, the preparation stage of understanding and diagnosing is critical in problem solving because it allows us to develop our own cognitive representation of the problem and to place it within a personal framework. We may divide the problem into subparts or ignore some information as we try to simplify the task. Winnowing out nonessential information is often a critical step in the preparation stage of problem solving.

a. Arrangement problems

1. Anagrams: Rearrange the letters in each set to make an English word:

2. Two strings hang from a ceiling but are too far apart to allow a person to hold one and walk to the other. On the floor are a book of matches, a screwdriver, and a few pieces of cotton. How could the strings be tied together?

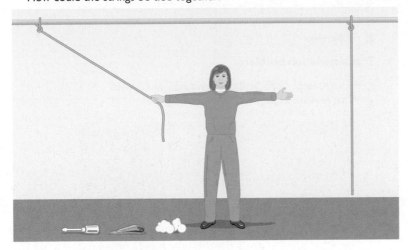

b. Problems of inducing structure

1. What number comes next in the series?

   1 4 2 4 3 4 4 4 5 4 6 4

2. Complete these analogies:

   baseball is to bat as tennis is to_____

   merchant is to sell as customer is to_____

c. Transformation problems

1. Water jars: A person has three jars with the following capacities:

   Jar A:
   28 ounces

   Jar B:
   7 ounces

   Jar C:
   5 ounces

   How can the person measure exactly 11 ounces of water?

2. Ten coins are arranged in the following way. By moving only *two* of the coins, make two rows that each contains six coins.

FIGURE 4 The three major categories of problems: (a) arrangement, (b) inducing structure, and (c) transformation. Solutions appear in Figure 5 on p. 248. (Source: Bourne, L. E., & Dominowski, R. L., *Cognitive Processes,* 2nd ed., p. 233, © 1986. Printed and electronically reproduced by permission of Pearson Education, Inc., Upper Saddle River, New Jersey.

FIGURE 5 Solutions to the problems in Figure 4 on page 247. (Source: Bourne, L. E., & Dominowski, R. L., *Cognitive Processes,* 2nd ed., p. 268, © 1986. Printed and electronically reproduced by permission of Pearson Education, Inc., Upper Saddle River, New Jersey.

a. **Arrangement problems**

1. FACET, DOUBT, THICK, NAIVE, ANVIL

2. The screwdriver is tied to one of the strings. This makes a pendulum that can be swung to reach the other string.

b. **Problems of inducing structure**

1. 7

2. racket; buy

c. **Transformation problems**

1. Fill jar A; empty into jar B once and into jar C twice. What remains in jar A is 11 ounces

2.

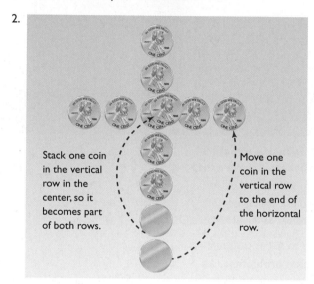

Our ability to represent a problem—and the kind of solution we eventually come to—depends on the way a problem is phrased, or framed. Consider, for example, if you were a cancer patient having to choose between surgery and radiation and were given the two sets of treatment options shown in Figure 6 (Tversky & Kahneman, 1987; Chandran & Menon, 2004). When the options are framed in terms of the likelihood of survival, only 18% of participants in a study chose radiation over surgery. However, when the choice was framed in terms of the likelihood of dying, 44% chose radiation over surgery—even though the outcomes are identical in both sets of framing conditions.

PRODUCTION: GENERATING SOLUTIONS

After preparation, the next stage in problem solving is the production of possible solutions. If a problem is relatively simple, we may already have a direct solution stored in long-term memory, and all we need to do is retrieve the appropriate information. If we cannot retrieve or do not know the solution, we must generate possible solutions and compare them with information in long- and short-term memory.

At the most basic level, we can solve problems through trial and error. Thomas Edison invented the lightbulb only because he tried thousands of different kinds of materials for a filament before he found one that worked (carbon). The difficulty with trial and error, of course, is that some problems are so complicated that it would take a lifetime to try out every possibility. For example, according to some estimates, there are some 10^{120} possible sequences of chess moves (Fine & Fine, 2003).

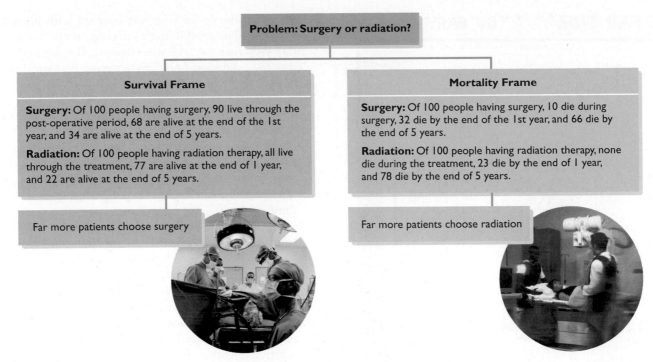

FIGURE 6 A decision often is affected by the way a problem is framed. In this case, most would choose radiation over surgery, despite similar results.

In place of trial and error, complex problem solving often involves the use of heuristics, cognitive shortcuts that can generate solutions. Probably the most frequently applied heuristic in problem solving is a **means-ends analysis,** which involves repeated tests for differences between the desired outcome and what currently exists. Consider this simple example (Huber, Beckmann, & Herrmann, 2004; Chrysikou, 2006; Bosse, Gerritsen, & Treur, 2011):

> I want to take my son to preschool. What's the difference between what I have and what I want? One of distance. What changes distance? My automobile. My automobile won't work. What is needed to make it work? A new battery. What has new batteries? An auto repair shop. . . .

In a means-end analysis, each step brings the problem solver closer to a resolution. Although this approach is often effective, if the problem requires indirect steps that temporarily *increase* the discrepancy between a current state and the solution, means-ends analysis can be counterproductive. For example, sometimes the fastest route to the summit of a mountain requires a mountain climber to backtrack temporarily; a means-end approach—that implies that the mountain climber should always forge ahead and upward—will be ineffective in such instances.

For other problems, the best approach is to work backward by focusing on the goal, rather than the starting point, of the problem. Consider, for example, the water lily problem:

> Water lilies are growing on Blue Lake. The water lilies grow rapidly, so that the amount of water surface covered by lilies doubles every 24 hours. On the first day of summer, there was just one water lily. On the 90th day of the summer, the lake was entirely covered. On what day was the lake half covered? (Reisberg, 1997)

If you start searching for a solution to the problem by thinking about the initial state on day 1 (one water lily) and move forward from there, you're facing a daunting task of trial-and-error estimation. But try taking a different approach: Start with day

means-ends analysis Involves repeated tests for differences between the desired outcome and what currently exists.

PsychTech

Research comparing people working together to solve problems face-to-face versus communicating via e-mail finds that those using e-mail are more satisfied with the process and believe they find better solutions.

insight A sudden awareness of the relationships among various elements that had previously appeared to be independent of one another.

90, when the entire lake was covered with lilies. Given that the lilies double their coverage daily, on the prior day only half the lake was covered. The answer, then, is day 89, a solution found by working backward (Bourne et al., 1986; Hunt, 1994).

Forming Subgoals: Dividing Problems into Their Parts. Another heuristic commonly used to generate solutions is to divide a problem into intermediate steps, or *subgoals*, and solve each of those steps. For instance, in our modified Tower of Hanoi problem, we could choose several obvious subgoals, such as moving the largest disk to the third post.

If solving a subgoal is a step toward the ultimate solution to a problem, identifying subgoals is an appropriate strategy. In some cases, however, forming subgoals is not all that helpful and may actually increase the time needed to find a solution. For example, some problems cannot be subdivided. Others—like some complicated mathematical problems—are so complex that it takes longer to identify the appropriate subdivisions than to solve the problem by other means (Reed, 1996; Kaller et al., 2004; Fishbach, Dhar, & Zhang, 2006).

Insight: Sudden Awareness. Some approaches to generating possible solutions focus less on step-by-step heuristics than on the sudden bursts of comprehension that one may experience during efforts to solve a problem. In a classic study the German psychologist Wolfgang Köhler examined learning and problem-solving processes in chimpanzees (Köhler, 1927). In his studies, Köhler exposed chimps to challenging situations in which the elements of the solution were all present; all the chimps needed to do was put them together.

In one of Köhler's studies, chimps were kept in a cage in which boxes and sticks were strewn about, and a bunch of tantalizing bananas hung from the ceiling, out of reach. Initially, the chimps made trial-and-error attempts to get to the bananas: They would throw the sticks at the bananas, jump from one of the boxes, or leap wildly from the ground. Frequently, they would seem to give up in frustration, leaving the bananas dangling temptingly overhead. But then, in what seemed like a sudden revelation, they would stop whatever they were doing and stand on a box to reach the bananas with a stick (Figure 7). Köhler called the cognitive process underlying the chimps' new behavior **insight,** a sudden awareness of the relationships among various elements that had previously appeared to be unrelated.

Although Köhler emphasized the apparent suddenness of insightful solutions, subsequent research has shown that prior experience and trial-and-error practice in problem solving must precede "insight." Consequently, the chimps' behavior may simply represent the chaining together of previously learned responses, no different from the way a pigeon learns, by trial and error, to peck a key (Windholz & Lamal, 2002; Fields, 2011).

JUDGMENT: EVALUATING SOLUTIONS

The final stage in problem solving is judging the adequacy of a solution. Often this is a simple matter: If the solution is clear—as in the Tower of Hanoi problem—we will know immediately whether we have been successful (Varma, 2007).

(a)   (b)   (c)

FIGURE 7 (a) In an impressive display of insight, Sultan, one of the chimpanzees in Köhler's experiments in problem solving, sees a bunch of bananas that is out of reach. (b) He then carries over several crates, stacks them, and (c) stands on them to reach the bananas.

If the solution is less concrete or if there is no single correct solution, evaluating solutions becomes more difficult. In such instances, we must decide which alternative solution is best. Unfortunately, we often quite inaccurately estimate the quality of our own ideas. For instance, a team of drug researchers working for a particular company may consider their remedy for an illness to be superior to all others, over-estimating the likelihood of their success and downplaying the approaches of competing drug companies (Eizenberg & Zaslavsky, 2004).

Theoretically, if we rely on appropriate heuristics and valid information to make decisions, we can make accurate choices among alternative solutions. However, as we see next, several kinds of obstacles to and biases in problem solving affect the quality of the decisions and judgments we make.

IMPEDIMENTS TO SOLUTIONS: WHY IS PROBLEM SOLVING SUCH A PROBLEM?

Consider the following problem-solving test illustrated in Figure 8 (Duncker, 1945):

> You are given a set of tacks, candles, and matches, each in a small box, and told your goal is to place three candles at eye level on a nearby door so that wax will not drip on the floor as the candles burn. How would you approach this challenge?

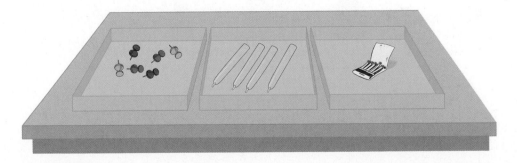

FIGURE 8 The problem here is to place three candles at eye level on a nearby door so that the wax will not drip on the floor as the candles burn—using only material in the figure. For a solution, turn to Figure 10 on p. 253.

If you have difficulty solving the problem, you are not alone. Most people cannot solve it when it is presented in the manner illustrated in the figure, in which the objects are *inside* the boxes. However, if the objects were presented *beside* the boxes, just resting on the table, chances are that you would solve the problem much more readily—which, in case you are wondering, requires tacking the boxes to the door and then placing the candles inside them (see Figure 10 on page 253).

The difficulty you probably encountered in solving this problem stems from its presentation, which misled you at the initial preparation stage. Actually, significant obstacles to problem solving can exist at each of the three major stages. Although cognitive approaches to problem solving suggest that thinking proceeds along fairly rational, logical lines as a person confronts a problem and considers various solutions, several factors can hinder the development of creative, appropriate, and accurate solutions.

functional fixedness The tendency to think of an object only in terms of its typical use.

Functional Fixedness and Mental Set. The difficulty most people experience with the candle problem is caused by **functional fixedness,** the tendency to think of an object only in terms of its typical use. For instance, functional fixedness probably leads you to think of this book as something to read instead of its potential use as a doorstop or as kindling for a fire. In the candle problem, because the objects are first presented inside the boxes, functional fixedness leads most people to see the boxes simply as containers for the objects they hold rather than as a potential part of the solution. They cannot envision another function for the boxes.

mental set The tendency for old patterns of problem solving to persist.

Functional fixedness is an example of a broader phenomenon known as **mental set,** the tendency for old patterns of problem solving to persist. A classic experiment (Luchins, 1946) demonstrated this phenomenon. As you can see in Figure 9, the object of the task is to use the jars in each row to measure out the designated amount of liquid. (Try it yourself to get a sense of the power of mental set before moving on.)

If you have tried to solve the problem, you know that the first five rows are all solved in the same way: First fill the largest jar (B) and then from it fill the middle-size jar (A) once and the smallest jar (C) two times. What is left in B is the designated amount. (Stated as a formula, the designated amount is B–A–2C.) The demonstration of mental set comes in the sixth row of the problem, a point at which you probably encountered some difficulty. If you are like most people, you tried the formula and were perplexed when it failed. Chances are, in fact, that you missed the simple (but different) solution to the problem, which involves merely subtracting C from A. Interestingly, people who were given the problem in row 6 *first* had no difficulty with it at all.

Inaccurate Evaluation of Solutions. When the United States invaded Iraq in 2003, it did so because governmental leaders believed that Saddam Hussein possessed weapons of mass destruction that posed a threat to the security of the Middle East. The belief proved false, and a bipartisan U.S. Senate committee later found that the

FIGURE 9 Try this classic demonstration, which illustrates the importance of mental set in problem solving. The object is to use the jars in each row to obtain the designated amount of liquid.

Given jars with these capacities (in ounces):

	A	B	C	Obtain:
1.	21	127	3	100
2.	14	163	25	99
3.	18	43	10	5
4.	9	42	6	21
5.	20	59	4	31
6.	28	76	3	25

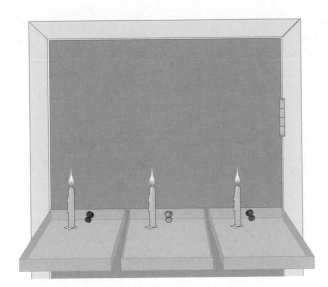

FIGURE 10 A solution to the problem in Figure 8 involves tacking the boxes to the door and placing the candles in the boxes.

belief was based on a flawed interpretation of intelligence information. According to the Senate committee, government leaders had made up their minds early on about the presence of weapons of mass destruction, and they ignored contradictory evidence and focused more on information that supported their view (U.S. Senate Select Committee on Intelligence, 2004).

The mistake made by governmental leaders exemplifies **confirmation bias** in which problem solvers prefer their first hypothesis and ignore contradictory information that supports alternative hypotheses or solutions. Even when we find evidence that contradicts a solution we have chosen, we are apt to stick with our original hypothesis.

Confirmation bias occurs for several reasons. For one thing, because rethinking a problem that appears to be solved already takes extra cognitive effort, we are apt to stick with our first solution. For another, we give greater weight to subsequent information that supports our initial position than to information that is not supportive of it (Parmley, 2007; Rassin, 2008; Allen, 2011).

confirmation bias The tendency to seek out and weight more heavily information that supports one's initial hypothesis and to ignore contradictory information that supports alternative hypotheses or solutions.

Creativity and Problem Solving

Despite obstacles to problem solving, many people adeptly discover creative solutions to problems. One enduring question that cognitive psychologists have sought to answer is what factors underlie **creativity**, the ability to generate original ideas or solve problems in novel ways.

Although identifying the stages of problem solving helps us understand how people approach and solve problems, it does little to explain why some people come up with better solutions than others do. For instance, even the possible solutions to a simple problem often show wide discrepancies. Consider, for example, how you might respond to the question "How many uses can you think of for a newspaper?"

Now compare your solution with this one proposed by a 10-year-old boy:

creativity The ability to generate original ideas or solve problems in novel ways.

You can read it, write on it, lay it down and paint a picture on it . . . You could put it in your door for decoration, put it in the garbage can, put it on a chair if the chair is messy. If you have a puppy, you put newspaper in its box or put it in your backyard for the dog to play with. When you build something and you don't want anyone to see it, put newspaper around it. Put newspaper on the floor if you have no mattress, use it to pick up something hot, use it to stop bleeding, or to catch the drips from drying clothes. You can use a newspaper for curtains, put it in your shoe to cover what is hurting your foot, make a kite out of it, shade a light that is too bright. You can wrap fish in it, wipe windows, or wrap money in it . . . You put washed shoes in newspaper, wipe eyeglasses with it, put it under a dripping sink, put a plant on it, make a paper bowl out of it, use it for a hat if it is raining, tie it on your feet for slippers. You can put it on the sand if you had no towel, use it for bases in baseball, make paper airplanes with it, use it as a dustpan when you sweep, ball it up for the cat to play with, wrap your hands in it if it is cold. (Ward, Kogan, & Pankove, 1972)

This list shows extraordinary creativity. Unfortunately, it is much easier to identify *examples* of creativity than to determine its causes. Similarly, it's not clear that the kind of creativity shown by highly creative people in the arts, such as Pablo Picasso, is the same kind of creativity shown by highly creative people in the sciences, such as Albert Einstein (Simonton, 2009).

However, we do know that several characteristics are associated with creativity. For one thing, highly creative individuals show **divergent thinking,** thinking that generates unusual, yet appropriate, responses to problems or questions. This type of thinking contrasts with **convergent thinking,** which is thinking in which a problem is viewed as having a single answer and which produces responses that are based primarily on knowledge and logic. For instance, someone relying on convergent thinking would answer "You read it" to the query "What can you do with a newspaper?" In contrast, "You use it as a dustpan" is a more divergent—and creative—response (Cropley, 2006; Schepers & van den Berg, 2007; Zeng, Proctor, & Salvendy, 2011).

Another aspect of creativity is its *cognitive complexity,* or preference for elaborate, intricate, and complex stimuli and thinking patterns. For instance, creative people often have a wider range of interests and are more independent and more interested in philosophical or abstract problems than are less creative individuals (Barron, 1990; Richards, 2006; Kaufman & Plucker, 2011).

One factor that is *not* closely related to creativity is intelligence. Traditional intelligence tests, which ask focused questions that have only one acceptable answer, tap convergent thinking skills. Highly creative people may therefore find that such tests penalize their divergent thinking. This may explain why researchers consistently find that creativity is only slightly related to school grades and intelligence when intelligence is measured using traditional intelligence tests (Sternberg & O'Hara, 2000; Heilman, 2005).

divergent thinking Thinking that generates unusual, yet nonetheless apropriate, responses to problems or questions.

convergent thinking Thinking in which a problem is viewed as having a single answer and which produces responses that are based primarily on knowledge and logic.

Study Alert

Remember *d*ivergent thinking produces *d*ifferent and *d*iverse kinds of responses, whereas convergent thinking produces more *common*-sense kinds of responses.

Pablo Picasso is considered one of the greatest artists of the 20th century. Do you think he relied more on convergent or divergent thinking in his art?

BECOMING AN INFORMED CONSUMER of Psychology

Thinking Critically and Creatively

Can we learn to be better and more creative thinkers?

Cognitive researchers have found that people can learn the abstract rules of logic and reasoning and that such knowledge can improve our reasoning about the underlying causes of everyday events in our lives. Research suggests that critical and creative thinkers are made, not born. Consider, for instance, the following suggestions for increasing critical thinking and creativity (Burbach, Matkin, & Fritz, 2004; Kaufman & Baer, 2006).

- *Redefine problems.* We can modify boundaries and assumptions by rephrasing a problem at either a more abstract or a more concrete level.
- *Use subgoals.* By developing subgoals, we can divide a problem into intermediate steps. This process, known as *fractionation,* allows us to examine each part for new possibilities and approaches, leading to a novel solution for the problem as a whole.
- *Adopt a critical perspective.* Rather than passively accepting assumptions or arguments, we can evaluate material critically, consider its implications, and think about possible exceptions and contradictions.
- *Consider the opposite.* By considering the opposite of a concept we're seeking to understand, we can sometimes make progress. For example, to define "good mental health," it may be useful to consider what "bad mental health" means.
- *Use analogies.* Analogies provide alternative frameworks for the interpretation of facts and help us uncover new understanding. One particularly effective means of coming up with analogies is to look for examples in the animal world. For instance, architects discovered how to construct the earliest skyscrapers by noting how lily pads on a pond could support the weight of a person (Getner & Holyoak, 1997; Bearman, Ball, & Ormerod, 2007; Cho, Holyoak, & Cannon, 2007).
- *Think divergently.* Instead of the most logical or common use for an object, consider how you might use the object if you were forbidden to use it in the usual way.
- *Think convergently.* Although it sounds counter-intuitive, researchers have found that a combination of divergent *and* convergent thinking can lead to greater creativity. Programs that attempt to teach children to be more creative train participants to alternate periods of divergent thinking with intense convergent thinking (Beghetto & Kaufman, 2010).
- *Use heuristics.* Heuristics are cognitive shortcuts that can help bring about a solution to a problem. If the problem has a single correct answer and you can use or construct a heuristic, you can often find the solution more rapidly and effectively.
- *Experiment with various solutions.* Don't be afraid to use different routes to find solutions for problems (verbal, mathematical, graphic, even dramatic). For instance, try to come up with every conceivable idea you can, no matter how wild or bizarre it may seem at first. After you've come up with a list of solutions, review each one and try to think of ways to make what at first appeared impractical seem more feasible.

"I'll be happy to give you innovative thinking. What are the guidelines?"

© Leo Cullum/The New Yorker Collection/www.cartoonbank.com

RECAP/EVALUATE/RETHINK

RECAP

LO 21-1 What is thinking?

- Cognitive psychology encompasses the higher mental processes, including the way people know and understand the world, process information, make decisions and judgments, and describe their knowledge and understanding to others. (p. 240)
- Thinking is the manipulation of mental representations of information. Thinking transforms such representations into novel and different forms, permitting people to answer questions, solve problems, and reach goals. (p. 241)
- Mental images are representations in the mind of an object or event. (p. 241)
- Concepts are categorizations of objects, events, or people that share common properties. (p. 242)

LO 21-2 What processes underlie reasoning and decision making?

- Decisions sometimes (but not always) may be improved through the use of algorithms and heuristics. An algorithm is a rule that, if applied appropriately, guarantees a solution; a heuristic is a cognitive shortcut that may lead to a solution but is not guaranteed to do so. (p. 243)

LO 21-3 How do people approach and solve problems?

- Problem solving typically involves three major stages: preparation, production of solutions, and evaluation of solutions that have been generated. (p. 246)
- Preparation involves placing the problem in one of three categories. In arrangement problems, a group of elements must be rearranged or recombined in a way that will satisfy a certain criterion. In problems of inducing structure, a person first must identify the existing relationships among the elements presented and then construct a new relationship among them. Finally, transformation problems consist of an initial state, a goal state, and a method for changing the initial state into the goal state. (p. 247)
- In the production stage, people try to generate solutions. They may find solutions to some problems in long-term memory. Alternatively, they may solve some problems through simple trial and error and use algorithms and heuristics to solve more complex problems. (p. 248)
- Using the heuristic of a means-ends analysis, a person will repeatedly test for differences between the desired outcome and what currently exists, trying each time to come closer to the goal. (p. 249)

- Köhler's research with chimpanzees illustrates insight, a sudden awareness of the relationships among elements that had previously seemed unrelated. (p. 250)

LO 21-4 What are the major obstacles to problem solving?

- Several factors hinder effective problem solving. Mental set, of which functional fixedness is an example, is the tendency for old patterns of problem solving to persist. Inappropriate use of algorithms and heuristics can also act as an obstacle to the production of solutions. Confirmation bias, in which initial hypotheses are favored, can hinder the accurate evaluation of solutions to problems. (p. 252)
- Creativity is the ability to combine responses or ideas in novel ways. Creativity is related to divergent thinking (the ability to generate unusual, but still appropriate, responses to problems or questions) and cognitive complexity. (p. 253)

EVALUATE

1. _____ are representations in the mind of an object or event.
2. _____ are categorizations of objects that share common properties.
3. Solving a problem by trying to reduce the difference between the current state and the goal state is known as a _____.
4. _____ is the term used to describe the sudden "flash" of revelation that often accompanies the solution to a problem.
5. Thinking of an object only in terms of its typical use is known as _____ _____. A broader, related tendency for old problem-solving patterns to persist is known as a _____ _____.
6. Generating unusual but appropriate approaches to a question is known as _____.

RETHINK

1. How might the availability heuristic contribute to prejudices based on race, age, and gender? Can awareness of this heuristic prevent this from happening?
2. *From the perspective of a manufacturer:* How might you encourage your employees to develop creative ways to improve the products that you produce?

Answers to Evaluate Questions

1. Mental images; 2. Concepts; 3. means-end analysis; 4. Insight; 5. functional fixedness, mental set; 6. divergent thinking

KEY TERMS

cognitive psychology p. 240
thinking p. 241
mental images p. 241
concepts p. 242

prototypes p. 243
algorithm p. 243
heuristic p. 243
means-ends analysis p. 249

insight p. 250
functional fixedness p. 252
mental set p. 252
confirmation bias p. 253

creativity p. 253
divergent thinking p. 254
convergent
        thinking p. 254

Language

'Twas brillig, and the slithy toves
Did gyre and gimble in the wabe:
All mimsy were the borogoves,
And the mome raths outgrabe.

Although few of us have ever come face to face with a tove, we have little difficulty in discerning that in Lewis Carroll's (1872) poem "Jabberwocky," the expression *slithy toves* contains an adjective, *slithy,* and the noun it modifies, *toves.*

Our ability to make sense out of nonsense, if the nonsense follows typical rules of language, illustrates the complexity of both human language and the cognitive processes that underlie its development and use. The use of **language**—the communication of information through symbols arranged according to systematic rules—is a central cognitive ability, one that is indispensable for us to communicate with one another. Not only is language central to communication, it is also closely tied to the very way in which we think about and understand the world. Without language, our ability to transmit information, acquire knowledge, and cooperate with others would be tremendously hindered. No wonder psychologists have devoted considerable attention to studying language (Stapel & Semin, 2007; Hoff, 2008; Reisberg, 2009).

language The communication of information through symbols arranged according to systematic rules.

Grammar: Language's Language

To understand how language develops and relates to thought, we first need to review some of the formal elements of language. The basic structure of language rests on **grammar,** the system of rules that determine how our thoughts can be expressed.

Grammar deals with three major components of language: phonology, syntax, and semantics. **Phonology** is the study of **phonemes,** the smallest basic units of speech that affect meaning, and of the way we use those sounds to form words and produce meaning. For instance, the *a* sound in *fat* and the *a* sound in *fate* represent two different phonemes in English (Hardison, 2006; Creel & Bregman, 2011).

Linguists have identified more than 800 different phonemes among all the world's languages. Although English speakers use just 52 phonemes to produce words, other languages use as few as 15 to as many as 141. Differences in phonemes are one reason people have difficulty learning other languages. For example, to a Japanese speaker, whose native language does not have an *r* phoneme, pronouncing such English words as *roar* presents some difficulty (Gibbs, 2002; Iverson et al., 2003).

Syntax refers to the rules that indicate how words and phrases can be combined to form sentences. Every language has intricate rules that guide the order in which words may be strung together to communicate meaning. English speakers have no difficulty recognizing that "TV down the turn" is not a meaningful sequence, whereas "Turn down the TV" is. To understand the effect of syntax in English, consider the changes in meaning caused by the different word orders in the following three utterances: "John kidnapped the boy," "John, the kidnapped boy," and "The boy kidnapped John" (Eberhard, Cutting, & Bock, 2005; Robert, 2006).

grammar The system of rules that determine how our thoughts can be expressed.

phonology The study of the smallest units of speech, called phonemes.

phonemes The smallest units of speech.

syntax Ways in which words and phrases can be combined to form sentences.

semantics The rules governing the meaning of words and sentences.

The third major component of language is **semantics,** the meanings of words and sentences. Semantic rules allow us to use words to convey the subtle nuances in meaning. For instance, we are able to make the distinction between "The truck hit Laura" (which we might say if we had just seen a truck crashing into Laura) versus "Laura was hit by a truck" (which we might say to explain why Laura didn't show up for a party) (Richgels, 2004; Pietarinen, 2006).

Despite the complexities of language, most of us acquire the basics of grammar without even being aware that we have learned its rules. Moreover, even though we may have difficulty explicitly stating the rules of grammar, our linguistic abilities are so sophisticated that we can utter an infinite number of different statements. How do we acquire such abilities?

Language Development: Developing a Way with Words

To parents, the sounds of their infant babbling and cooing are music to their ears (except, perhaps, at three o'clock in the morning). These sounds also serve an important function. They mark the first step on the road to the development of language.

BABBLING

babble Meaningless speech-like sounds made by children from around the age of 3 months through 1 year.

Children **babble**—make speech-like but meaningless sounds—from around the age of 3 months through 1 year. While babbling, they may produce, at one time or another, any of the sounds found in all languages, not just the one to which they are exposed. Even deaf children display their own form of babbling, for infants who are unable to hear yet who are exposed to sign language from birth "babble" with their hands (Petitto, 1993; Locke, 2006; Majorano & D'Odorico, 2011).

An infant's babbling increasingly reflects the specific language being spoken in the infant's environment, initially in terms of pitch and tone and eventually in terms of specific sounds. Young infants can distinguish among all 869 phonemes that have been identified across the world's languages. However, after the age of 6 to 8 months, that ability begins to decline. Infants begin to "specialize" in the language to which they are exposed as neurons in their brains reorganize to respond to the particular phonemes infants routinely hear.

Some theorists argue that a *critical period* exists for language development early in life in which a child is particularly sensitive to language cues and most easily acquires language. In fact, if children are not exposed to language during this critical period, later they will have great difficulty overcoming this deficit (Bates, 2005; Shafer & Garrido-Nag, 2007).

Cases in which abused children have been isolated from contact with others support the theory of such critical periods. In one case, for example, a girl named Genie was exposed to virtually no language from the age of 20 months until she was rescued at age 13. She was unable to speak at all. Despite intensive instruction, she learned only some words and was never able to master the complexities of language (Rymer, 1994; Veltman & Browne, 2001).

PRODUCTION OF LANGUAGE

By the time children are approximately 1 year old, they stop producing sounds that are not in the language to which they have been exposed. It is then a short step to the production of actual words. In English, these are typically short words that start with a consonant sound such as *b, d, m, p,* and *t*—this helps explain why *mama* and *dada* are so often among babies' first words. Of course, even before they produce their first words, children can understand a fair amount of the language they hear. Language comprehension precedes language production.

A syllable in signed language, similar to the ones seen in the manual babbling of deaf infants and in the spoken babbling of hearing infants. The similarities in language structure suggest that language has biological roots.

After the age of 1 year, children begin to learn more complicated forms of language. They produce two-word combinations, the building blocks of sentences, and sharply increase the number of different words they are able to use. By age 2, the average child has a vocabulary of more than 50 words. Just 6 months later, that vocabulary has grown to several hundred words. At that time, children can produce short sentences, although they use **telegraphic speech**—sentences that sound as if they were part of a telegram, in which words not critical to the message are left out. Rather than saying, "I showed you the book," a child using telegraphic speech may say, "I show book," and "I am drawing a dog" may become "Drawing dog." As children get older, of course, they use less telegraphic speech and produce increasingly complex sentences (Volterra et al., 2003; Pérez-Leroux, Pirvulescu, & Roberge, 2011).

By age 3, children learn to make plurals by adding *s* to nouns and to form the past tense by adding *-ed* to verbs. This skill also leads to errors, since children tend to apply rules inflexibly. In such **overgeneralization,** children employ rules even when doing so results in an error. Thus, although it is correct to say "he walked" for the past tense of *walk*, the *-ed* rule doesn't work quite so well when children say "he runned" for the past tense of *run* (Howe, 2002; Rice et al., 2004; Gershkoff-Stowe, Connell, & Smith, 2006; Kidd & Lum, 2008).

By age 5, children have acquired the basic rules of language. However, they do not attain a full vocabulary and the ability to comprehend and use subtle grammatical rules until later. For example, a 5-year-old boy who sees a blindfolded doll and is asked, "Is the doll easy or hard to see?" would have great trouble answering the question. In fact, if he were asked to make the doll easier to see, he would probably try to remove the doll's blindfold. By the time they are 8 years old, however, children have little difficulty understanding this question because they realize that the doll's blindfold has nothing to do with an observer's ability to see the doll (Chomsky, 1968; Hoff, 2003).

telegraphic speech Sentences in which words not critical to the message are left out.

overgeneralization The phenomenon by which children apply language rules even when the application results in an error.

Understanding Language Acquisition: Identifying the Roots of Language

Anyone who spends even a little time with children will notice the enormous strides that they make in language development throughout childhood. However, the reasons for this rapid growth are far from obvious. Psychologists have offered three major explanations: one based on learning theory, one based on innate processes, and one that involves something of a combination of the two.

Learning Theory Approaches: Language as a Learned Skill. The **learning-theory approach** suggests that language acquisition follows the principles of reinforcement and conditioning discovered by psychologists who study learning. For example, a child who says "mama" receives hugs and praise from her mother, which reinforce the behavior of saying "mama" and make its repetition more likely. This view suggests that children first learn to speak by being rewarded for making sounds that approximate speech. Ultimately, through a process of shaping, language becomes more and more like adult speech (Skinner, 1957; Ornat & Gallo, 2004).

In support of the learning-theory approach to language acquisition, the more that parents speak to their young children, the more proficient the children become in language use. In addition, by the time they are 3 years old, children who hear higher levels of linguistic sophistication in their parents' speech show a greater rate of vocabulary growth, vocabulary use, and even general intellectual achievement than do children whose parents' speech is more simple (Hart & Risley, 1997).

learning-theory approach (to language development) The theory that language acquisition follows the principles of reinforcement and conditioning.

The learning-theory approach is less successful in explaining how children acquire language rules. Children are reinforced not only when they use language correctly, but also when they use it incorrectly. For example, parents answer a child's query of "Why the dog won't eat?" as readily as they do the correctly phrased question, "Why won't the dog eat?" Listeners understand both sentences equally well. Learning theory, then, has difficulty fully explaining language acquisition.

NATIVIST APPROACHES: LANGUAGE AS AN INNATE SKILL

nativist approach (to language development) The theory that a genetically determined, innate mechanism directs language development.

Pointing to such problems with learning-theory approaches to language acquisition, linguist Noam Chomsky (1968, 1978, 1991) provided a groundbreaking alternative. Chomsky argued that humans are born with an innate linguistic capability that emerges primarily as a function of maturation. According to his **nativist approach** to language, all the world's languages share a common underlying structure that is pre-wired, biologically determined, and universal. Chomsky suggested that the human brain has an inherited neural system that lets us understand the structure language provides—a kind of *universal grammar*. These inborn capabilities give us strategies and techniques for learning the unique characteristics of our own native language (McGilvray, 2004; Lidz & Gleitman, 2004; White, 2007).

Supporting Chomsky's view is evidence collected by neuroscientists that suggests that the ability to use language, which was a significant evolutionary advance in human beings, is tied to specific neurological developments. For example, scientists have discovered a gene related to the development of language abilities that may have emerged as recently—in evolutionary terms—as 100,000 years ago. Furthermore, it is clear that there are specific sites within the brain that are closely tied to language and that the shape of the human mouth and throat are tailored to the production of speech. And there is evidence that features of specific types of languages are tied to particular genes, such as in "tonal" languages in which pitch is used to convey meaning (Sahin, Pinker, & Halgren, 2006; Gontier, 2008; Grigorenko, 2009; Perovic & Radenovic, 2011).

Still, Chomsky's view has its critics. For instance, learning theorists contend that the apparent ability of certain animals, such as chimpanzees, to learn the fundamentals of human language (as we discuss later in this module) contradicts the innate linguistic capability view.

Noam Chomsky argues that all languages share a universal grammar.

INTERACTIONIST APPROACHES

To reconcile the differing views, many theorists take an **interactionist approach** to language development. The interactionist approach suggests that language development is produced through a combination of genetically determined predispositions and environmental circumstances that help teach language.

Specifically, proponents of the interactionist approach suggest that the brain is hardwired for our acquisition of language, in essence providing the "hardware" that allows us to develop language. However, it is the exposure to language in our environment that allows us to develop the appropriate "software" to understand and produce language.

The interactionist approach has many proponents. Still, the issue of how language is acquired remains hotly contested (Pinker & Jackendoff, 2005; Hoff, 2008; Waxman, 2009).

The Influence of Language on Thinking: Do Eskimos Have More Words for Snow Than Texans Do?

Do Eskimos living in the frigid Arctic have a more expansive vocabulary for discussing snow than people living in warmer climates?

It makes sense, and arguments that the Eskimo language has many more words than English for snow have been made since the early 1900s. At that time, linguist Benjamin Lee Whorf contended that because snow is so relevant to Eskimos' lives, their language provides a particularly rich vocabulary to describe it—considerably larger than what we find in other languages, such as English (Martin & Pullum, 1991; Pinker, 1994).

The contention that the Eskimo language is especially abundant in snow-related terms led to the **linguistic-relativity hypothesis,** the notion that language shapes and, in fact, may determine the way people in a specific culture perceive and understand the world. According to this view, language provides us with categories that we use to construct our view of people and events in the world around us. Consequently, language shapes and produces thought (Whorf, 1956; Casasanto, 2008; Tan et al., 2008).

Let's consider another possibility, however. Suppose that instead of language being the *cause* of certain ways of thinking, thought *produces* language. The only reason to expect that Eskimo language might have more words for snow than English does is that snow is considerably more relevant to Eskimos than it is to people in other cultures.

Which view is correct? Most recent research refutes the linguistic-relativity hypothesis and suggests, instead, that thinking produces language. In fact, new analyses of the Eskimo language suggest that Eskimos have no more words for snow than English speakers. If one examines the English language closely, one sees that it is hardly impoverished when it comes to describing snow (consider, for example, *sleet, slush, blizzard, dusting,* and *avalanche*).

Still, the linguistic-relativity hypothesis has not been entirely discarded. A newer version of the hypothesis suggests that speech patterns may influence certain aspects of thinking. For example, in some languages, such as English, speakers distinguish between nouns that can be counted (such as "five chairs") and nouns that require a measurement unit to be quantified (such as "a liter of water"). In some other languages, such as the Mayan language called Yucatec, however, all nouns require a measurement unit. In such cultures, people appear to think more closely about what things are made of than do people in cultures in which languages such as English are spoken (Gentner, Goldin, & Goldin-Meadow, 2003; Tsukasaki & Ishii, 2004).

interactionist approach (to language development) The view that language development is produced through a combination of genetically determined predispositions and environmental circumstances that help teach language.

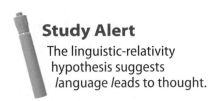

Study Alert
It's important to be able to compare and contrast the major approaches to language development: learning theory, nativist, and interactionist approaches.

linguistic-relativity hypothesis The notion that language shapes and may determine the way people in a particular culture perceive and understand the world.

Study Alert
The linguistic-relativity hypothesis suggests *language leads* to thought.

Similarly, Russian speakers have more words for light and dark blues and are better able to discriminate shades of blue visually. Furthermore, some tribes say north, south, east, and west instead of left and right, and they have better spatial orientation. Finally, the Piraha language uses terms like few and many rather than specific numbers, and speakers are unable to keep track of exact quantities (Boroditsky, 2010; Fuhrman et al., 2011).

In short, although research does not support the linguistic-relativity hypothesis that language *causes* thought, it is clear that language influences how we think. And, of course, it certainly is the case that thought influences language, suggesting that language and thinking interact in complex ways (Ross, 2004; Thorkildsen, 2006; Proudfoot, 2009).

Do Animals Use Language?

One question that has long puzzled psychologists is whether language is uniquely human or if other animals are able to acquire it as well. Many animals communicate with one another in rudimentary forms. For instance, fiddler crabs wave their claws to signal, bees dance to indicate the direction in which food will be found, and certain birds call *"zick, zick"* during courtship and *"kia"* when they are about to fly away. However, researchers have yet to demonstrate conclusively that these animals use true language, which is characterized in part by the ability to produce and communicate new and unique meanings by following a formal grammar.

Psychologists, however, have been able to teach chimps to communicate at surprisingly high levels. For instance, after 4 years of training, a chimp named Washoe learned to make signs for 132 words and combine those signs into simple sentences. Even more impressively, Kanzi, a pygmy chimpanzee, has linguistic skills that some psychologists claim are close to those of a 2-year-old human being. Kanzi's trainers suggest that he can create grammatically sophisticated sentences and can even invent new rules of syntax (Savage-Rumbaugh, Toth, & Schick, 2007; Slocombe, Waller, & Liebal, 2011).

Despite the skills primates such as Kanzi display, critics contend that the language such animals use still lacks the grammar and the complex and novel constructions of human language. Instead, they maintain that the chimps are displaying a skill no different

Sue Savage-Rumbaugh with a primate friend, Panbanisha. Does the use of sign language by primates indicate true mastery of language?

from that of a dog that learns to lie down on command to get a reward. Furthermore, we lack firm evidence that animals can recognize and respond to the mental states of others of their species, an important aspect of human communication. Consequently, the issue of whether other animals can use language in a way that humans do remains controversial (Aboitiz, Garcia, & Brunetti, 2006; Hillix, 2007; Liszkowski et al., 2009).

Exploring DIVERSITY

Teaching with Linguistic Variety: Bilingual Education

In New York City, 1 in 6 of the city's 1.1 million students is enrolled in some form of bilingual or English as a Second Language instruction. And New York City is far from the only school district with a significant population of nonnative English speakers. From the biggest cities to the most rural areas, the face—and voice—of education in the United States is changing. More and more schoolchildren today have last names like Kim, Valdez, and Karachnicoff. In seven states, including Texas and Colorado, more than one-quarter of the students are not native English speakers. For some 47 million Americans, English is their second language (Holloway, 2000; see Figure 1).

How to appropriately and effectively teach the increasing number of children who do not speak English is not always clear. Many educators maintain that *bilingual education* is best. With a bilingual approach, students learn some subjects in their native language while simultaneously learning English. Proponents of bilingualism believe that students must develop a sound footing in basic subject areas and that, initially at least, teaching those subjects in their native language is the only way to provide them with that foundation. During the same period, they learn English, with the eventual goal of shifting all instruction into English.

In contrast, other educators insist that all instruction ought to be in English from the moment students, including those who speak no English at all, enroll in school. In *immersion programs,* students are immediately plunged into English instruction in all subjects. The reasoning—endorsed by voters in California in a referendum designed to end bilingual

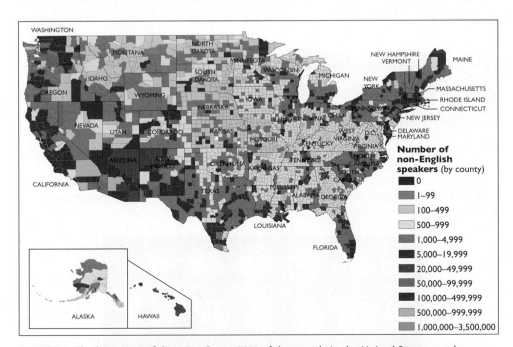

Number of non-English speakers (by county)

- 0
- 1–99
- 100–499
- 500–999
- 1,000–4,999
- 5,000–19,999
- 20,000–49,999
- 50,000–99,999
- 100,000–499,999
- 500,000–999,999
- 1,000,000–3,500,000

FIGURE 1 The language of diversity. Some 22% of the people in the United States speak a language other than English at home. Most of them speak Spanish; the rest speak an astounding variety of different languages. Where are the largest clusters of non-English speakers in the United States, and what do you think explains these concentrations? (Source: MLA Language Map, 2005, based on 2000 Census.)

education—is that teaching students in a language other than English simply hinders nonnative English speakers' integration into society and ultimately does them a disservice. Proponents of English immersion programs point as evidence to improvements in standardized test scores that followed the end of bilingual education programs (Wildavsky, 2000).

Although the controversial issue of bilingual education versus immersion has strong political undercurrents, evidence shows that the ability to speak two languages provides significant cognitive benefits over speaking only one language. For example, bilingual speakers show more cognitive flexibility and may understand concepts more easily than those who speak only one language. They have more linguistic tools for thinking because of their multiple-language abilities. In turn, this makes them more creative and flexible in solving problems (Heyman & Diesendruck, 2002; Bialystok & Martin, 2004; Kuo, 2007).

In addition, the advantages of bilingualism start early: by the time bilingual children are 3 or 4 years old, their cognitive development is superior to that of children who speak only one language. It's an advantage that lasts into old age. In fact, bilingualism provides protection from the cognitive declines that are typical in late adulthood (Bialystok & Craik, 2010; Bialystok et al., 2010; Bialystok, 2011).

Furthermore, speaking several languages changes the organization of the brain. For example, bilingual speakers who learn their second language as adults show different areas of brain activation compared with those who learn their second language in childhood. In addition, brain scans show that people who speak multiple languages have distinct patterns of brain activity according to the language that they are using, and bilingualism affects brain processing in several ways (see Figure 2 *Neuroscience in Your Life*) (Kovelman, Baker, & Petitto, 2008; Kovacs & Mehler, 2009; Luk et al., 2010).

Related to questions about bilingual education is the matter of *biculturalism*—that is, being a member of two cultures and its psychological impact. Some psychologists argue that society should promote an *alternation model* of bicultural competence. Such a model supports members of a culture in their efforts to maintain their original cultural identity as well as in their integration into the adopted culture. In this view, a person can belong to two cultures and have two cultural identities without having to choose between them. Whether society will adopt the alternation model remains to be seen (Carter, 2003; Benet-Martínez, Lee, & Leu, 2006; Tadmor, 2007).

Neuroscience in Your Life:
Bilingualism and the Brain

FIGURE 2 Bilingualism affects brain processing in several ways, including—as these scans show—inhibition (the ability to ignore irrelevant information). When asked to do a task that involves ignoring images that are either congruent (similar) or incongruent (contradictory) to an initial image, monolinguals and bilinguals use different areas of the brain to suppress the irrelevant information, as indicated in blue and red (Luk et al., 2010).

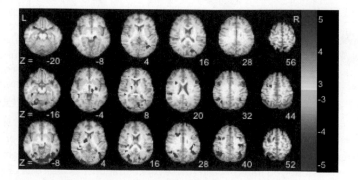

RECAP/EVALUATE/RETHINK

RECAP

LO 22-1 How do people use language?

- Language is the communication of information through symbols arranged according to systematic rules. All languages have a grammar—a system of rules that determines how thoughts can be expressed—that encompasses the three major components of language: phonology, syntax, and semantics. (p. 257)

LO 22-2 How does language develop?

- Language production, which follows language comprehension, develops out of babbling, which then leads to the production of actual words. After 1 year of age, children use two-word combinations, increase their vocabulary, and use telegraphic speech, which drops words not critical to the message. By age 5, acquisition of language rules is relatively complete. (p. 258)
- Learning theorists suggest that language is acquired through reinforcement and conditioning. In contrast, the nativist approach suggests that an innate language-acquisition device guides the development of language. The interactionist approach argues that language development is produced through a combination of genetically determined predispositions and environmental circumstances that help teach language. (p. 259)
- The linguistic-relativity hypothesis suggests that language shapes and may determine the way people think about the world. Most evidence suggests that although language does not determine thought, it does affect the way people store information in memory and how well they can retrieve it. (p. 261)
- The degree to which language is a uniquely human skill remains an open question. Some psychologists contend that even though certain primates communicate at a high level, those animals do not use language. Other psychologists suggest that those primates truly understand and produce language in much the same way as humans. (p. 262)

- People who speak more than one language may have a cognitive advantage over those who speak only one. (pp. 263, 264)

EVALUATE

1. Match the component of grammar with its definition:
   1. Syntax
   2. Phonology
   3. Semantics

   a. Rules showing how words can be combined into sentences.
   b. Rules governing the meaning of words and sentences.
   c. The study of the sound units that affect speech.

2. Language production and language comprehension develop in infants about the same time. True or false?
3. _____ _____ refers to the phenomenon in which young children omit nonessential portions of sentences.
4. A child knows that adding -ed to certain words puts them in the past tense. As a result, instead of saying "He came," the child says "He comed." This is an example of _____.
5. _____ theory assumes that language acquisition is based on principles of operant conditioning and shaping.
6. In his theory of language acquisition, Chomsky argues that language acquisition is an innate ability tied to the structure of the brain. True or false?

RETHINK

1. Do people who use two languages, one at home and one at school, automatically have two cultures? Why might people who speak two languages have cognitive advantages over those who speak only one?
2. *From the perspective of a child-care provider:* How would you encourage children's language abilities at the different stages of development?

Answers to Evaluate Questions

1. 1-a, 2-c, 3-b; 2. false; language comprehension precedes language; 3. Telegraphic speech; 4. overgeneralization; 5. Learning; 6. true

KEY TERMS

language p. 257
grammar p. 257
phonology p. 257
phonemes p. 257
syntax p. 257
semantics p. 258

babble p. 258
telegraphic speech p. 259
overgeneralization p. 259
learning-theory approach (to language development) p. 259

nativist approach (to language development) p. 260
interactionist approach (to language development) p. 261

linguistic-relativity hypothesis p. 261

MODULE 23

Intelligence

Learning Outcomes

LO 23-1 What are the different definitions and conceptions of intelligence?

LO 23-2 What are the major approaches to measuring intelligence, and what do intelligence tests measure?

LO 23-3 How can the extremes of intelligence be characterized?

LO 23-4 Are traditional IQ tests culturally biased?

LO 23-5 To what degree is intelligence influenced by the environment and to what degree by heredity?

Members of the Trukese tribe in the South Pacific often sail a hundred miles in open ocean waters. Although their destination may be just a small dot of land less than a mile wide, the Trukese are able to navigate precisely toward it without the aid of a compass, chronometer, sextant, or any of the other sailing tools that are used by Western navigators. They are able to sail accurately even when the winds do not allow a direct approach to the island and they must take a zigzag course (Gladwin, 1964; Mytinger, 2001).

How are the Trukese able to navigate so effectively? If you asked them, they could not explain it. They might tell you that they use a process that takes into account the rising and setting of the stars and the appearance, sound, and feel of the waves against the side of the boat. But at any given moment as they are sailing along, they could not identify their position or say why they are doing what they are doing. Nor could they explain the navigational theory underlying their sailing technique.

Some people might say that the inability of the Trukese to explain in Western terms how their sailing technique works is a sign of primitive or even unintelligent behavior. In fact, if we gave Trukese sailors a Western standardized test of navigational knowledge and theory or, for that matter, a traditional test of intelligence, they might do poorly on it. Yet, as a practical matter, it is not possible to accuse the Trukese of being unintelligent: Despite their inability to explain how they do it, they are able to navigate successfully through the open ocean waters.

Trukese navigation points out the difficulty in coming to grips with what is meant by intelligence. To a Westerner, traveling in a straight line along the most direct and quickest route by using a sextant and other navigational tools is likely to represent the most "intelligent" kind of behavior; in contrast, a zigzag course, based on the "feel" of the waves, would not seem very reasonable. To the Trukese, who are used to their own system of navigation, however, the use of complicated navigational tools might seem so overly complex and unnecessary that they might think of Western navigators as lacking in intelligence.

It is clear from this example that the term *intelligence* can take on many different meanings. If, for instance, you lived in a remote part of the Australian outback, the way you would differentiate between more intelligent and less intelligent people might have to do with successfully mastering hunting skills, whereas to someone living in the heart of urban Miami, intelligence might be exemplified by being "streetwise" or by achieving success in business.

Each of these conceptions of intelligence is reasonable. Each represents an instance in which more intelligent people are better able to use the resources of their environment than are less intelligent people, a distinction that is presumably basic to any definition of intelligence. Yet it is also clear that these conceptions represent very different views of intelligence.

What does the Trukese people's method of navigation—which is done without maps or instruments—tell us about the nature of intelligence?

That two such different sets of behavior can exemplify the same psychological concept has long posed a challenge to psychologists. For years they have grappled with the issue of devising a general definition of intelligence. Ironically, laypersons have fairly clear ideas of what intelligence is, although the nature of their ideas is related to their culture. Westerners view intelligence as the ability to establish categories and debate rationally. In contrast, people in Eastern cultures and some African communities view intelligence more in terms of understanding and relating to one another (Nisbett, 2003; Brislin, Worthley, & MacNab, 2006; Sternberg, 2005, 2007; Niu & Brass, 2011).

The definition of intelligence that psychologists employ contains some of the same elements found in the layperson's conception. To psychologists, **intelligence** is the capacity to understand the world, think rationally, and use resources effectively when faced with challenges.

This definition does not lay to rest a key question asked by psychologists: Is intelligence a unitary attribute, or are there different kinds of intelligence? We turn now to various theories of intelligence that address the issue.

intelligence The capacity to understand the world, think rationally, and use resources effectively when faced with challenges.

Theories of Intelligence: Are There Different Kinds of Intelligence?

Perhaps you see yourself as a good writer but as someone who lacks ability in math. Or maybe you view yourself as a "science" person who easily masters physics but has few strengths in interpreting literature. Perhaps you view yourself as generally fairly smart with intelligence that permits you to excel across domains.

The different ways in which people view their own talents mirror a question that psychologists have grappled with. Is intelligence a single, general ability, or is it multifaceted and related to specific abilities? Early psychologists interested in intelligence assumed that there was a single, general factor for mental ability, which they called *g*, or the ***g*-factor.** This assumption was based on the fact that different types of measures of intelligence, whether they focused on, say, mathematical expertise, verbal competency, or spatial visualization skills, all ranked test-takers in roughly the same order. People who were good on one test generally were good on others; those who did poorly on one test tended to do poorly on others.

Given that there was a correlation between performance on the different types of tests, the assumption was that there was a general, global intellectual ability underlying performance on the various measures—the *g-factor*. This general intelligence factor was thought to underlie performance in every aspect of intelligence, and it was the *g*-factor that was presumably being measured on tests of intelligence (Spearman, 1927; Colom, Jung, & Haier, 2006; Haier et al., 2009; Major, Johnson, & Bouchard, 2011).

More recent theories explain intelligence in a different light. Rather than viewing intelligence as a unitary entity, some psychologists consider it to be a multidimensional concept that includes different types of intelligence (Tenopyr, 2002; Stankov, 2003; Sternberg & Pretz, 2005).

g or *g*-factor The single, general factor for mental ability assumed to underlie intelligence in some early theories of intelligence.

FLUID AND CRYSTALLIZED INTELLIGENCE

Some psychologists suggest that there are two different kinds of intelligence: fluid intelligence and crystallized intelligence. **Fluid intelligence** is the ability to reason abstractly. It reflects information-processing capabilities and reasoning. If we were asked to solve an analogy or group a series of letters according to some principle,

fluid intelligence Intelligence that reflects the ability to reason abstractly.

Piloting a helicopter requires the use of both fluid intelligence and crystallized intelligence. Which of the two kinds of intelligence do you believe is more important for such a task?

we would be using fluid intelligence. We use fluid intelligence when we're trying to rapidly solve a puzzle (Kane & Engle, 2002; Saggino, Perfetti, & Spitoni, 2006; Di Fabio & Palazzeschi, 2009).

In contrast, **crystallized intelligence** is the accumulation of information, skills, and strategies that people have learned through experience. It reflects our ability to call up information from long-term memory. We would be likely to rely on crystallized intelligence, for instance, if we were asked to participate in a discussion about the solution to the causes of poverty, a task that allows us to draw on our own past experiences and knowledge of the world. In contrast to fluid intelligence, which reflects a more general kind of intelligence, crystallized intelligence is more a reflection of the culture in which a person is raised. The differences between fluid intelligence and crystallized intelligence become especially evident in late adulthood, when people show declines in fluid, but not crystallized, intelligence (Buehner, Krumm, & Ziegler, 2006; Tranter & Koutstaal, 2008; Ackerman, 2011).

crystallized intelligence The accumulation of information, skills, and strategies that are learned through experience and can be applied in problem-solving situations.

theory of multiple intelligences Gardner's intelligence theory that proposes that there are eight distinct spheres of intelligence.

GARDNER'S MULTIPLE INTELLIGENCES: THE MANY WAYS OF SHOWING INTELLIGENCE

Psychologist Howard Gardner has taken an approach very different from traditional thinking about intelligence. Gardner argues that rather than asking "How smart are you?" we should be asking a different question: "How are you smart?" In answering the latter question, Gardner has developed a **theory of multiple intelligences** that has become quite influential (Gardner, 2000).

Gardner argues that we have a minimum eight different forms of intelligence, each relatively independent of the others: musical, bodily kinesthetic, logical-mathematical, linguistic, spatial, interpersonal, intrapersonal, and naturalist. (Figure 1 describes the eight types of intelligence, with some of Gardner's examples of people who excel in each type.) In Gardner's view, each of the multiple intelligences is linked to an independent system in the brain. Furthermore, he suggests that there may be even more types of intelligence, such as *existential intelligence*, which involves identifying and thinking about the fundamental questions of human existence. For example, the Dalai Lama might exemplify this type of intelligence (Gardner, 1999, 2000).

Although Gardner illustrates his conception of the specific types of intelligence with descriptions of well-known people, each person has the same eight kinds of intelligence—in different degrees. Moreover, although the eight basic types of intelligence are presented individually, Gardner suggests that these separate intelligences do not operate in isolation. Normally, any activity encompasses several kinds of intelligence working together.

The concept of multiple intelligences has led to the development of intelligence tests that include questions in which more than one answer can be correct; these provide an opportunity for test-takers to demonstrate creative thinking. In addition, many educators, embracing the concept of multiple intelligences, have designed classroom curricula that are meant to draw on different aspects of intelligence (Douglas, Burton, & Reese-Durham, 2008; Tirri & Nokelainen, 2008; Davis et al., 2011).

Study Alert

Remember, Gardner's theory suggests that each individual has every kind of intelligence but in different degrees.

IS INFORMATION PROCESSING INTELLIGENCE?

One of the newer contributions to understanding intelligence comes from the work of cognitive psychologists who take an *information-processing approach*. They assert that the way people store information in memory and use that information to solve

1. Musical intelligence (skills in tasks involving music). Case example:

When he was 3, Yehudi Menuhin was smuggled into San Francisco Orchestra concerts by his parents. By the time he was 10 years old, Menuhin was an international performer.

2. Bodily kinesthetic intelligence (skills in using the whole body or various portions of it in the solution of problems or in the construction of products or displays, exemplified by dancers, athletes, actors, and surgeons). Case example:

Fifteen-year-old Babe Ruth played third base. During one game, his team's pitcher was doing very poorly and Babe loudly criticized him from third base. Brother Matthias, the coach, called out, "Ruth, if you know so much about it, *you* pitch!" Ruth said later that at the very moment he took the pitcher's mound, he *knew* he was supposed to be a pitcher.

3. Logical-mathematical intelligence (skills in problem solving and scientific thinking). Case example:

Barbara McClintock, who won the Nobel Prize in medicine, describes one of her breakthroughs, which came after thinking about a problem for half an hour . . . : "Suddenly I jumped and ran back to the (corn) field. At the top of the field (the others were still at the bottom) I shouted, 'Eureka, I have it!'"

4. Linguistic intelligence (skills involved in the production and use of language). Case example:

At the age of 10, T. S. Eliot created a magazine called *Fireside*, to which he was the sole contributor.

5. Spatial intelligence (skills involving spatial configurations, such as those used by artists and architects). Case example:

Natives of the Truk Islands navigate at sea without instruments. During the actual trip, the navigator must envision mentally a reference island as it passes under a particular star and from that he computes the number of segments completed, the proportion of the trip remaining, and any corrections in heading.

6. Interpersonal intelligence (skills in interacting with others, such as sensitivity to the moods, temperaments, motivations, and intentions of others). Case example:

When Anne Sullivan began instructing the deaf and blind Helen Keller, her task was one that had eluded others for years. Yet, just 2 weeks after beginning her work with Keller, Sullivan achieved great success.

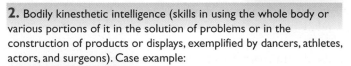

7. Intrapersonal intelligence (knowledge of the internal aspects of oneself; access to one's own feelings and emotions). Case example:

In her essay "A Sketch of the Past," Virginia Woolf displays deep insight into her own inner life through these lines, describing her reaction to several specific memories from her childhood that still, in adulthood, shock her: "Though I still have the peculiarity that I receive these sudden shocks, they are now always welcome; after the first surprise, I always feel instantly that they are particularly valuable. And so I go on to suppose that the shock-receiving capacity is what makes me a writer."

8. Naturalist intelligence (ability to identify and classify patterns in nature). Case example:

During prehistoric times, hunter/gatherers would rely on naturalist intelligence to identify what flora and fauna were edible. People who are adept at distinguishing nuances between large numbers of similar objects may be expressing naturalist intelligence abilities.

FIGURE 1 Howard Gardner believes that there are eight major kinds of intelligences, corresponding to abilities in different domains. In what area does your greatest intelligence reside, and why do you think you have particular strengths in that area? (Source: Adapted from Gardner, 2000.)

intellectual tasks provides the most accurate measure of intelligence. Consequently, rather than focusing on the structure of intelligence or its underlying content or dimensions, information-processing approaches examine the *processes* involved in producing intelligent behavior (Hunt, 2005; Neubauer & Fink, 2005; Pressley & Harris, 2006).

For example, research shows that people with high scores on tests of intelligence spend more time on the initial encoding stages of problems, identifying the parts of a problem and retrieving relevant information from long-term memory, than do people with lower scores. This initial emphasis on recalling relevant information pays off in the end; those who use this approach are more successful in finding solutions than are those who spend relatively less time on the initial stages (Sternberg, 1990; Deary & Der, 2005; Hunt, 2005).

Other information-processing approaches examine the sheer speed of processing. For example, research shows that the speed with which people are able to receive information from memory is related to verbal intelligence. In general, people with high scores on measures of intelligence react more quickly on a variety of information-processing tasks ranging from reactions to flashing lights to distinguishing between letters. The speed of information processing, then, may underlie differences in intelligence (Jensen, 2005; Gontkovsky & Beatty, 2006; Helmbold, Troche, & Rammsayer, 2007; Sheppard & Vernon, 2008).

PRACTICAL AND EMOTIONAL INTELLIGENCE: TOWARD A MORE INTELLIGENT VIEW OF INTELLIGENCE

Consider the following situation:

> An employee who reports to one of your subordinates has asked to talk with you about waste, poor management practices, and possible violations of both company policy and the law on the part of your subordinate. You have been in your present position only a year, but in that time you have had no indications of trouble about the subordinate in question. Neither you nor your company has an "open door" policy, so it is expected that employees should take their concerns to their immediate supervisors before bringing a matter to the attention of anyone else. The employee who wishes to meet with you has not discussed this matter with her supervisors because of its delicate nature. (Sternberg, 1998, p. 17)

Your response to this situation has a lot to do with your future success in a business career, according to psychologist Robert Sternberg. The question is one of a series designed to help give an indication of your intelligence. However, it is not traditional intelligence that the question is designed to tap but rather intelligence of a specific kind: practical intelligence. **Practical intelligence** is intelligence related to overall success in living (Sternberg, 2000, 2002; Muammar, 2007; Wagner, 2002, 2011).

Noting that traditional tests were designed to relate to academic success, Sternberg points to evidence showing that most traditional measures of intelligence do not relate especially well to *career* success (McClelland, 1993). Specifically, although successful business executives usually score at least moderately well on intelligence tests, the rate at which they advance and their ultimate business achievements are only minimally associated with traditional measures of their intelligence.

Sternberg argues that career success requires a very different type of intelligence from that required for academic success. Whereas academic success is based on knowledge of a specific information base obtained from reading and listening, practical intelligence is learned mainly through observation of others' behavior. People who are high in practical intelligence are able to learn general norms and principles and apply them appropriately. Consequently, practical intelligence tests, like the one shown in Figure 2, measure the ability to employ broad principles in solving everyday problems (Sternberg & Pretz, 2005; Stemler & Sternberg, 2006; Stemler et al., 2009).

practical intelligence According to Sternberg, intelligence related to overall success in living.

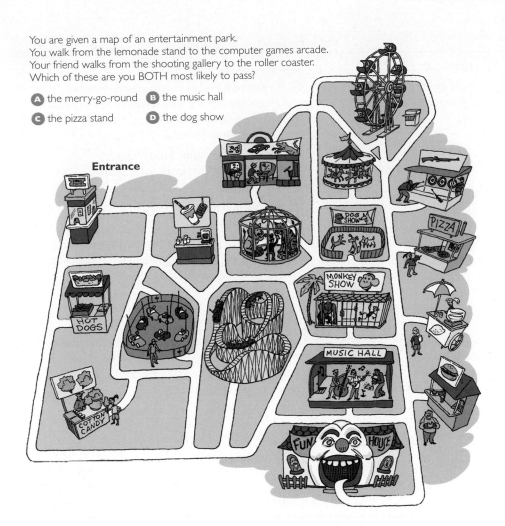

You are given a map of an entertainment park.
You walk from the lemonade stand to the computer games arcade.
Your friend walks from the shooting gallery to the roller coaster.
Which of these are you BOTH most likely to pass?

Ⓐ the merry-go-round   Ⓑ the music hall
Ⓒ the pizza stand   Ⓓ the dog show

Entrance

FIGURE 2 Most standard tests of intelligence primarily measure analytical skills; more comprehensive tests measure creative and practical abilities as well. (Source: Adapted from Sternberg, R. J. (2000). The Holy Grail of general intelligence. *Science, 289,* no. 5478, 399–401.)

In addition to practical intelligence, Sternberg argues there are two other basic, interrelated types of intelligence related to life success: analytical and creative. Analytical intelligence focuses on abstract but traditional types of problems measured on IQ tests, whereas creative intelligence involves the generation of novel ideas and products (Benderly, 2004; Sternberg, Kaufman, & Pretz, 2004; Sternberg, Grigorenko, & Kidd, 2005).

Some psychologists broaden the concept of intelligence even further beyond the intellectual realm to include emotions. **Emotional intelligence** is the set of skills that underlie the accurate assessment, evaluation, expression, and regulation of emotions (Mayer, Salovey, & Caruso, 2004; Humphrey, Curran, & Morris, 2007; Mayer, Salovey, & Caruso, 2008).

Emotional intelligence is the basis of empathy for others, self-awareness, and social skills. It encompasses the ability to get along well with others. It provides us with an understanding of what other people are feeling and experiencing, which permits us to respond appropriately to others' needs. These abilities may help explain why people with only modest scores on traditional intelligence tests can be quite successful: the basis of their success may be a high emotional intelligence, which allows them to respond appropriately and quickly to others' feelings.

Although the notion of emotional intelligence makes sense, it has yet to be quantified in a rigorous manner. Furthermore, the view that emotional intelligence is so important that skills related to it should be taught in school has raised concerns among some educators. They suggest that the nurturance of emotional intelligence is best left to students' families, especially because there is no well-specified set of criteria for what constitutes emotional intelligence (Sleek, 1997; Becker, 2003).

emotional intelligence The set of skills that underlie the accurate assessment, evaluation, expression, and regulation of emotions.

Study Alert

Traditional intelligence relates to academic performance; practical intelligence relates to success in life; emotional intelligence relates to emotional skills.

FIGURE 3 Just as there are many views of the nature of intelligence, there are also numerous ways to demonstrate intelligent behavior. This summary provides an overview of the various approaches used by psychologists.

Major Approaches to Intelligence	
Approach	**Characteristics**
Fluid and crystallized intelligence	Fluid intelligence relates to reasoning, memory, and information-processing capabilities; crystallized intelligence relates to information, skills, and strategies learned through experience
Gardner's multiple intelligences	Eight independent forms of intelligence
Information-processing approaches	Intelligence is reflected in the ways people store and use material to solve intellectual tasks
Practical intelligence	Intelligence in terms of nonacademic, career, and personal success
Emotional intelligence	Intelligence that provides an understanding of what other people are feeling and experiencing and permits us to respond appropriately to others' needs

Still, the notion of emotional intelligence reminds us that there are many ways to demonstrate intelligent behavior—just as there are multiple views of the nature of intelligence (Fox & Spector, 2000; Barrett & Salovey, 2002). Figure 3 presents a summary of the different approaches used by psychologists.

Assessing Intelligence

intelligence tests Tests devised to quantify a person's level of intelligence.

Given the variety of approaches to the components of intelligence, it is not surprising that measuring intelligence has proved challenging. Psychologists who study intelligence have focused much of their attention on the development of **intelligence tests** and have relied on such tests to quantify a person's level of intelligence. These tests have proved to be of great benefit in identifying students in need of special attention in school, diagnosing cognitive difficulties, and helping people make optimal educational and vocational choices. At the same time, their use has proved controversial, raising important social and educational issues.

Historically, the first effort at intelligence testing was based on an uncomplicated but completely wrong assumption: that the size and shape of a person's head could be used as an objective measure of intelligence. The idea was put forward by Sir Francis Galton (1822–1911), an eminent English scientist whose ideas in other domains proved to be considerably better than his notions about intelligence.

Galton's motivation to identify people of high intelligence stemmed from personal prejudices. He sought to demonstrate the natural superiority of people of high social class (including himself) by showing that intelligence is inherited. He hypothesized that head configuration, which is genetically determined, is related to brain size and therefore is related to intelligence.

Galton's theories were proved wrong on virtually every count. Head size and shape are not related to intellectual performance, and subsequent research has found little relationship between brain size and intelligence. However, Galton's work did have at least one desirable result: He was the first person to suggest that intelligence could be quantified and measured in an objective manner (Jensen, 2002).

BINET AND THE DEVELOPMENT OF IQ TESTS

The first real intelligence tests were developed by the French psychologist Alfred Binet (1857–1911). His tests followed from a simple premise: If performance on certain tasks or test items improved with *chronological*, or physical, age, performance

Alfred Binet.

could be used to distinguish more intelligent people from less intelligent ones within a particular age group. On the basis of this principle, Binet devised the first formal intelligence test, which was designed to identify the "dullest" students in the Paris school system in order to provide them with remedial aid.

Binet began by presenting tasks to same-age students who had been labeled "bright" or "dull" by their teachers. If a task could be completed by the bright students but not by the dull ones, he retained that task as a proper test item; otherwise it was discarded. In the end he came up with a test that distinguished between the bright and dull groups, and—with further work—one that distinguished among children in different age groups (Binet & Simon, 1916; Sternberg & Jarvin, 2003).

On the basis of the Binet test, children were assigned a score relating to their **mental age,** the age for which a given level of performance is average or typical. For example, if the average 8-year-old answered, say, 45 items correctly on a test, anyone who answered 45 items correctly would be assigned a mental age of 8 years. Consequently, whether the person taking the test was 20 years old or 5 years old, he or she would have the same mental age of 8 years (Cornell, 2006).

Assigning a mental age to students provided an indication of their general level of performance. However, it did not allow for adequate comparisons among people of different chronological ages. By using mental age alone, for instance, we might assume that an 18-year-old responding at a 20-year-old's level would be demonstrating the same degree of intelligence as a 5-year-old answering at a 7-year-old's level, when actually the 5-year-old would be displaying a much greater *relative* degree of intelligence.

A solution to the problem came in the form of the **intelligence quotient (IQ),** a measure of intelligence that takes into account an individual's mental *and* chronological (physical) age. Historically, the first IQ scores employed the following formula in which *MA* stands for mental age and *CA* for chronological age:

$$\text{IQ score} = \frac{\text{MA}}{\text{CA}} \times 100$$

Using this formula, we can return to the earlier example of an 18-year-old performing at a mental age of 20 and calculate an IQ score of $(20/18) \times 100 = 111$. In contrast, the 5-year-old performing at a mental age of 7 comes out with a considerably higher IQ score: $(7/5) \times 100 = 140$.

As a bit of trial and error with the formula will show you, anyone who has a mental age equal to his or her chronological age will have an IQ equal to 100. Moreover, people with a mental age that is lower than their chronological age will have IQs that exceed 100.

Although the basic principles behind the calculation of an IQ score still hold, today IQ scores are determined in a different manner and are known as *deviation IQ scores.* First, the average test score for everyone of the same age who takes the test is determined, and that average score is assigned an IQ of 100. Then, with the aid of statistical techniques that calculate the differences (or "deviations") between each score and the average, IQ scores are assigned.

As you can see in Figure 4, when IQ scores from large numbers of people are plotted on a graph, they form a *bell-shaped distribution* (called "bell-shaped" because it looks like a bell when plotted). Approximately two-thirds of all individuals fall within 15 IQ points of the average score of 100. As scores increase or fall beyond that range, the percentage of people in a category falls considerably.

CONTEMPORARY IQ TESTS: GAUGING INTELLIGENCE

Remnants of Binet's original intelligence test are still with us, although the test has been revised in significant ways. Now in its fifth edition and called the *Stanford-Binet Intelligence Scale,* the test consists of a series of items that vary according to the age of the person being tested (Roid, Nellis, & McClellan, 2003). For example, young children are asked to copy figures or answer questions about everyday activities.

mental age The age for which a given level of performance is average or typical.

intelligence quotient (IQ) A measure of intelligence that takes into account an individual's mental and chronological ages.

Study Alert

It's important to know the traditional formula for IQ scores in which IQ is the ratio of mental age divided by chronological age, multiplied by 100. Remember, though, that today, the actual calculator of IQ scores is done in a more sophisticated manner.

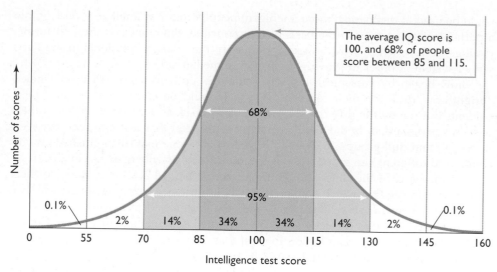

The average IQ score is 100, and 68% of people score between 85 and 115.

FIGURE 4 The average and most common IQ score is 100, and 68% of all people are within a 30-point range centered on 100. Some 95% of the population have scores that are within 30 points above or below 100, and 99.8% have scores that are between 55 and 145.

Older people are asked to solve analogies, explain proverbs, and describe similarities that underlie sets of words.

The test is administered orally and includes both verbal and nonverbal assessments. An examiner begins by finding a mental age level at which a person is able to answer all the questions correctly and then moves on to successively more difficult problems. When a mental age level is reached at which no items can be answered,

Now in its fifth edition, the Stanford-Binet test consists of a series of items that vary in nature according to the age of the person being tested. What can we learn about a person from a test of this type?

Types of Items on WAIS-IV

Name	Goal of Item	Example
Information	Assess general information	Who wrote *Tom Sawyer?*
Comprehension	Assess understanding and evaluation of social norms and past experience	Why is copper often used for electrical wires?
Arithmetic	Assess math reasoning through verbal problems	Three women divided 18 golf balls equally among themselves. How many golf balls did each person receive?
Similarities	Test understanding of how objects or concepts are alike, tapping abstract reasoning	In what way are a circle and a triangle alike?
Figure weights	Test Perceptual Reasoning	Problems require test-taker to determine which possibility balances the final scale.
Matrix reasoning	Test spatial reasoning	Test-taker must decide which of the five possibilities replaces the question mark and completes the sequence.
Block design item	Test understanding of relationship of parts to whole	Problems require test-takers to reproduce a design in fixed amount of time.

FIGURE 5 Typical kinds of items found on the Wechsler Adult Intelligence Scales (WAIS-IV). (Simulated items similar to those in the *Wechsler Adult Intelligence Scale, Fourth Edition (WAIS-IV)*. Copyright © 2008 NCS Pearson, Inc. Reproduced with permission. All rights reserved. "Wechsler Adult Intelligence Scale," "WAIS," and "Wechsler" are trademarks, in the US and/or other countries, of Pearson Education, Inc. or its affiliates.)

the test is over. By studying the pattern of correct and incorrect responses, the examiner is able to compute an IQ score for the person being tested. In addition, the Stanford-Binet test yields separate subscores that provide clues to a test-taker's particular strengths and weaknesses.

The IQ tests most frequently used in the United States were devised by psychologist David Wechsler and are known as the *Wechsler Adult Intelligence Scale–IV*, or, more commonly, the *WAIS-IV* (for adults) and a children's version, the *Wechsler Intelligence Scale for Children–IV*, or *WISC-IV*. Both the WAIS-IV and the WISC-IV measure verbal comprehension, perceptual reasoning, working memory, and processing speed (see sample WAIS-IV items in Figure 5).

Because the Stanford-Binet, WAIS-IV, and WISC-IV all require individualized, one-on-one administration, they are relatively difficult to administer and score on a large-scale basis. Consequently, there are now a number of IQ tests that allow group administration. Rather than having one examiner ask one person at a time to respond to individual items, group IQ tests are strictly paper-and-pencil tests. The primary advantage of group tests is their ease of administration (Anastasi & Urbina, 1997; Danner et al., 2011).

However, sacrifices are made in group testing that, in some cases, may outweigh the benefits. For instance, group tests generally offer fewer kinds of questions than do tests administered individually. Furthermore, people may be more motivated to perform at their highest ability level when working on a one-to-one basis with a test administrator than they are in a group. Finally, in some cases, it is simply impossible to employ group tests, particularly with young children or people with unusually low IQs (Aiken, 1996).

RELIABILITY AND VALIDITY: TAKING THE MEASURE OF TESTS

When we use a ruler, we expect to find that it measures an inch in the same way it did the last time we used it. When we weigh ourselves on the bathroom scale, we hope that the variations we see on the scale are due to changes in our weight and not to errors on the part of the scale (unless the change in weight is in an unwanted direction!).

reliability The property by which tests measure consistently what they are trying to measure.

In the same way, we hope that psychological tests have **reliability**—that they measure consistently what they are trying to measure. We need to be sure that each time we administer the test, a test-taker will achieve the same results—assuming that nothing about the person has changed relevant to what is being measured.

Suppose, for instance, that when you first took the SAT exams, you scored 400 on the verbal section of the test. Then, after taking the test again a few months later, you scored 700. Upon receiving your new score, you might well stop celebrating for a moment to question whether the test is reliable for it is unlikely that your abilities could have changed enough to raise your score by 300 points (T. R. Coyle, 2006).

But suppose your score changed hardly at all, and both times you received a score of about 400. You couldn't complain about a lack of reliability. However, if you knew your verbal skills were above average, you might be concerned that the test did not adequately measure what it was supposed to measure. In sum, the question has now become one of validity rather than reliability. A test has **validity** when it actually measures what it is supposed to measure.

validity The property by which tests actually measure what they are supposed to measure.

Knowing that a test is reliable is no guarantee that it is also valid. For instance, Sir Francis Galton assumed that skull size is related to intelligence, and he was able to measure skull size with great reliability. However, the measure of skull size was not valid—it had nothing to do with intelligence. In this case, then, we have reliability without validity.

However, if a test is unreliable, it cannot be valid. Assuming that all other factors—motivation to score well, knowledge of the material, health, and so forth—are similar, if a person scores high the first time he or she takes a specific test and low the second time, the test cannot be measuring what it is supposed to measure. Therefore, the test is both unreliable and not valid.

Test validity and reliability are prerequisites for accurate assessment of intelligence—as well as for any other measurement task carried out by psychologists. Consequently, the measures of personality carried out by personality psychologists, clinical psychologists' assessments of psychological disorders, and social psychologists' measures of attitudes must meet the tests of validity and reliability for the results to be meaningful (Feldt, 2005; Phelps, 2005; Yao, Zhour, & Jiang, 2006).

Assuming that a test is both valid and reliable, one further step is necessary in order to interpret the meaning of a particular test-taker's score: the establishment of norms. **Norms** are standards of test performance that permit the comparison of one person's score on a test to the scores of others who have taken the same test. For example, a norm permits test-takers to know that they have scored, say, in the top 15% of those who have taken the test previously. Tests for which norms have been developed are known as *standardized tests.*

Test designers develop norms by calculating the average score achieved by a specific group of people for whom the test has been designed. Then the test designers can determine the extent to which each person's score differs from the scores of the other individuals who have taken the test in the past and provide future test-takers with a qualitative sense of their performance.

Obviously, the samples of test-takers who are employed in the establishment of norms are critical to the norming process. The people used to determine norms must be representative of the individuals to whom the test is directed.

ADAPTIVE TESTING: USING COMPUTERS TO ASSESS PERFORMANCE

Ensuring that tests are reliable, valid, and based on appropriate norms has become more critical with computer-administered testing. In computerized versions of tests such as the Graduate Record Exam, a test used to determine entrance to graduate school, not only are test questions viewed and answered on a computer, but the test itself is individualized. With *adaptive testing,* every test-taker does not receive identical sets of test questions. Instead, the computer first presents a randomly selected question of moderate difficulty. If the test-taker answers it correctly, the computer then presents a randomly chosen item of slightly greater difficulty. If the test-taker answers it incorrectly, the computer presents a slightly easier item. Each question becomes slightly harder or easier than the question preceding it, depending on whether the previous response is correct. Ultimately, the greater the number of difficult questions answered correctly, the higher the score (Marszalek, 2007; Belov & Armstrong, 2009; Barrada, Abad, & Olea, 2011).

Variations in Intellectual Ability

More than 7 million people in the United States, including around 11 per 1,000 children, have been identified as far enough below average in intelligence that they can be regarded as having a serious deficit. Individuals with low IQs (people with mental retardation or intellectual disabilities) as well as those with unusually high IQs (the intellectually gifted) require special attention if they are to reach their full potential.

INTELLECTUAL DISABILITIES (MENTAL RETARDATION)

Although sometimes thought of as a rare phenomenon, intellectual disability (or mental retardation as it was more traditionally called) occurs in 1%–3% of the population. There is wide variation among those labeled intellectually disabled, in large part because of the inclusiveness of the definition developed by the American Association on Intellectual and Developmental Disabilities. The association suggests that **intellectual disability** (or **mental retardation**) is a disability characterized by significant limitations both in intellectual functioning and in conceptual, social, and practical adaptive skills (American Association of Mental Retardation, 2002).

Although below-average intellectual functioning can be measured in a relatively straightforward manner—using standard IQ tests—it is more difficult to determine how to gauge limitations in adaptive behavior. Consequently, there is a lack of uniformity in how experts apply the labels *intellectual disabilities* and *mental*

norms Standards of test performance that permit the comparison of one person's score on a test with the scores of other individuals who have taken the same test.

intellectual disability (or mental retardation) A condition characterized by significant limitations both in intellectual functioning and in conceptual, social, and practical adaptive skills.

retardation. People labeled intellectually disabled vary from those who can be taught to work and function with little special attention to those who cannot be trained and are institutionalized throughout their lives (Detterman, Gabriel, & Ruthsatz, 2000; Greenspan, 2006).

Most people with intellectual disabilities have relatively minor deficits and are classified as having *mild retardation.* These individuals, who have IQ scores ranging from 55 to 69, constitute some 90% of all people with intellectual disabilities. Although their development is typically slower than that of their peers, they can function quite independently by adulthood and are able to hold jobs and have families of their own (Bates et al., 2001; Smith, 2006; van Nieuwenhuijzen et al., 2011).

With greater degrees of intellectual deficit— *moderate retardation* (IQs of 40 to 54), *severe retardation* (IQs of 25 to 39), and *profound retardation* (IQs below 25)—the difficulties are more pronounced. For people with moderate retardation, deficits are obvious early, with language and motor skills lagging behind those of peers. Although these individuals can hold simple jobs, they need to have a moderate degree of supervision throughout their lives. Individuals with severe and profound mental retardation are generally unable to function independently and typically require care for their entire lives (Garwick, 2007).

Identifying the Roots of Intellectual Disabilities. What produces intellectual disabilities? In nearly one-third of the cases there is an identifiable cause related to biological or environmental factors. The most common preventable cause of intellectual disabilities is **fetal alcohol syndrome,** produced by a mother's use of alcohol while pregnant. Increasing evidence shows that even small amounts of alcohol intake can produce intellectual deficits. One in every 750 infants is born with fetal alcohol syndrome in the United States (Manning & Hoyme, 2007; Murthy et al., 2009; Jacobson et al., 2011).

Down syndrome represents another major cause of intellectual disabilities. *Down syndrome* results when a person is born with 47 chromosomes instead of the usual 46. In most cases, there is an extra copy of the 21st chromosome, which leads to problems in how the brain and body develop (Sherman et al., 2007).

In other cases of intellectual disabilities, an abnormality occurs in the structure of particular chromosomes. Birth complications, such as a temporary lack of oxygen, may also cause retardation. In some cases, intellectual disabilities begin after birth following a head injury, a stroke, or infections such as meningitis (Plomin, 2005; Bittles, Bower, & Hussain, 2007).

However, the majority of cases of intellectual disabilities are classified as **familial retardation,** in which no apparent biological defect exists but there is a history of retardation in the family. Whether the family background of intellectual disabilities is caused by environmental factors, such as extreme continuous poverty leading to malnutrition, or by some underlying genetic factor is usually impossible to determine (Zigler et al., 2002; Franklin & Mansuy, 2011).

Integrating Individuals with Intellectual Disabilities. Important advances in the care and treatment of those with intellectual disabilities have been made since the Education for All Handicapped Children Act (Public Law 94-142) was passed by Congress in the mid-1970s. In this federal law, Congress stipulated that people with intellectual disabilities are entitled to a full education and that they must be educated and trained in the least restrictive environment. The law increased the educational opportunities for individuals with intellectual disabilities, facilitating their integration into regular classrooms as much as possible—a process known as *mainstreaming* (Katsiyannis, Zhang, & Woodruff, 2005; Aussilloux & Bagdadli, 2006; Gibb et al., 2007).

The philosophy behind mainstreaming suggests that the interaction of students with and without intellectual disabilities in regular classrooms will improve educational opportunities for those with intellectual disabilities, increase their social acceptance, and

fetal alcohol syndrome The most common cause of intellectual disability in newborns, occurring when the mother uses alcohol during pregnancy.

familial retardation Intellectual disability in which no apparent biological defect exists but there is a history of it in the family.

facilitate their integration into society as a whole. Of course, special education classes still exist; some individuals with intellectual disabilities function at too low of a level to benefit from placement in regular classrooms. Moreover, children with intellectual disabilities who are mainstreamed into regular classes typically attend special classes for at least part of the day (Hastings & Oakford, 2003; Williamson, McLeskey, & Hoppey, 2006; also see *PsychWork*).

PsychWork
DIRECTOR OF SPECIAL EDUCATION

For Shannon Lynch, Director of Special Education at The Willow Creek Charter School in Prescott, Arizona, being a special education teacher means providing ways for every student to achieve success. Each child presents different needs, and Lynch approaches her teaching accordingly.

Name: Shannon Lynch

Education: BA, Liberal Studies, Northern Arizona University, Flagstaff, Arizona; MA, Special Education, Northern Arizona University, Flagstaff, Arizona; State of Arizona Teaching Certificate in Elementary and Special Education

"For children with specific learning disabilities, I have found it is helpful to utilize repetition, hands-on activities, music, movements with information, and rhymes to get the information to stick," she explained.

"Children on the autism spectrum have challenges with social skills. Great programs exist that provide models and scripts of appropriate social interactions," Lynch said. Emotional disabilities require a very different approach and involve providing counseling to cope with the difficult emotions students face.

"The biggest factor for students with special needs is providing ways for them to achieve success. They have spent much of their academic career feeling incapable and inadequate, so just giving them small opportunities for success can make a huge difference in their confidence," Lynch noted.

THE INTELLECTUALLY GIFTED

Another group of people—the intellectually gifted—differ from those with average intelligence as much as individuals with mental retardation although in a different manner. Accounting for 2%–4% of the population, the **intellectually gifted** have IQ scores greater than 130.

Although the stereotype associated with the gifted suggests that they are awkward, shy social misfits who are unable to get along well with peers, most research indicates that just the opposite is true. The intellectually gifted are most often outgoing, well-adjusted, healthy, popular people who are able to do most things better than the average person can (Guldemond et al., 2007; Mueller, 2009; Sternberg, Jarvin, & Grigorenko, 2011).

For example, in a famous study by psychologist Lewis Terman that started in the early 1920s, 1,500 children who had IQ scores above 140 were followed for the rest of their lives. From the start, the members of this group were more physically, academically, and socially capable than their nongifted peers. In addition to doing better in school, they also showed better social adjustment than average. All these advantages paid off in terms of career success: As a group, the gifted received more awards and distinctions, earned higher incomes, and made more contributions in art and literature than typical individuals. Perhaps most important, they reported greater satisfaction in life than the nongifted (Hegarty, 2007).

Of course, not every member of the group Terman studied was successful. Furthermore, high intelligence is not a homogeneous quality; a person with a high overall IQ is not necessarily gifted in every academic subject but may excel in just one or two. A high IQ is not a universal guarantee of success (Shurkin, 1992; Winner, 2003; Clemons, 2006).

Study Alert
Remember that in most cases of intellectual disability, there is no apparent biological deficiency, but a history of mental retardation exists in the family.

intellectually gifted The 2%–4% segment of the population who have IQ scores greater than 130.

Group Differences in Intelligence: Genetic and Environmental Determinants

Kwang is often washed with a pleck tied to a:
- (a) rundel
- (b) flink
- (c) pove
- (d) quirj

If you found this kind of item on an intelligence test, you would probably complain that the test was totally absurd and had nothing to do with your intelligence or anyone else's—and rightly so. How could anyone be expected to respond to items presented in a language that was so unfamiliar?

Yet to some people, even more reasonable questions may appear just as nonsensical. Consider the example of a child raised in a city who is asked about procedures for milking cows, or someone raised in a rural area who is asked about subway ticketing procedures. Obviously, the previous experience of the test-takers would affect their ability to answer correctly. And if such types of questions were included on an IQ test, a critic could rightly contend that the test had more to do with prior experience than with intelligence.

Although IQ tests do not include questions that are so clearly dependent on prior knowledge as questions about cows and subways, the background and experiences of test-takers do have the potential to affect results. In fact, the issue of devising fair intelligence tests that measure knowledge unrelated to culture and family background and experience is central to explaining an important and persistent finding: Members of certain racial and cultural groups consistently score lower on traditional intelligence tests than do members of other groups. For example, as a group, blacks tend to average 10 to 15 IQ points lower than whites. Does this variation reflect a true difference in intelligence, or are the questions biased with regard to the kinds of knowledge they test? Clearly, if whites perform better because of their greater familiarity with the kind of information that is being tested, their higher IQ scores are not an indication that they are more intelligent than members of other groups (Fagan & Holland, 2007; Morgan, Marsiske, & Whitfield, 2008; Suzuki, Short, & Lee, 2011).

There is good reason to believe that some standardized IQ tests contain elements that discriminate against minority-group members whose experiences differ from those of the white majority. Consider the question "What should you do if another child grabbed your hat and ran off with it?" Most white middle-class children answer that they would tell an adult, and this response is scored as correct. However, a reasonable response might be to chase the person and fight to get the hat back, the answer that is chosen by many urban black children—but one that is scored as incorrect (Miller-Jones, 1991; Aiken, 1997; Reynolds & Ramsay, 2003).

 Exploring DIVERSITY

The Relative Influence of Genetics and Environment: Nature, Nurture, and IQ

culture-fair IQ test A test that does not discriminate against the members of any minority group.

In an attempt to produce a **culture-fair IQ test,** one that does not discriminate against the members of any minority group, psychologists have tried to devise test items that assess experiences common to all cultures or emphasize questions that do not require language usage. However, test makers have found this difficult to do because past experiences, attitudes, and values almost always have an impact on respondents' answers (Fagan & Holland, 2009).

For example, children raised in Western cultures group things on the basis of what they are (such as putting *dog* and *fish* into the category of *animal*). In contrast, members of the Kpelle tribe in Africa see intelligence demonstrated by grouping things according to what they *do* (grouping *fish* with *swim*). Similarly, children in the United States asked to memorize the position of objects on a chessboard perform better than African children living in remote villages if household objects familiar to the U.S. children are used. But if rocks are used instead of household objects, the African children do better. In short, it is difficult to produce a truly culture-fair test (Sandoval et al., 1998; Serpell, 2000; Valencia & Suzuki, 2003; Barnett et al., 2011).

The efforts of psychologists to produce culture-fair measures of intelligence relate to a lingering controversy over differences in intelligence between members of different racial and ethnic groups. In attempting to identify whether there are differences between such groups, psychologists have had to confront the broader issue of determining the relative contribution to intelligence of genetic factors (heredity) and experience (environment)—the nature-nurture issue that is one of the basic issues of psychology.

Richard Herrnstein, a psychologist, and Charles Murray, a sociologist, fanned the flames of the debate with the publication of their book *The Bell Curve* in the mid-1990s (Herrnstein & Murray, 1994). They argued that an analysis of IQ differences between whites and blacks demonstrated that although environmental factors played a role, there were also basic genetic differences between the two races. They based their argument on a number of findings. For instance, on average, whites score 15 points higher than blacks on traditional IQ tests even when socioeconomic status (SES) is taken into account. According to Herrnstein and Murray, middle- and upper-SES blacks score lower than middle- and upper-SES whites, just as lower-SES blacks score lower on average than lower-SES whites. Intelligence differences between blacks and whites, they concluded, could not be attributed to environmental differences alone. However, this was a conclusion, as we shall see, that was soon refuted.

IQ AND HERITABILITY

There is no doubt that intelligence in general shows a high degree of **heritability,** the degree to which a characteristic can be attributed to genetic, inherited factors (e.g., Miller & Penke, 2007; Plomin, 2009; van Soelen et al., 2011). As can be seen in Figure 6, the closer the genetic link between two related people, the greater the

heritability A measure of the degree to which a characteristic is related to genetic, inherited factors.

Relationship	Genetic overlap	Rearing	Correlation
Monozygotic (identical) twins	100%	Together	.86
Dizygotic (fraternal) twins	50%	Together	.62
Siblings	50%	Together	.41
Siblings	50%	Apart	.24
Parent-child	50%	Together	.35
Parent-child	50%	Apart	.31
Adoptive parent-child	0%	Together	.16
Unrelated children	0%	Together	.25
Spouses	0%	Apart	.29

The difference between these two correlations shows the impact of the environment

The relatively low correlation for unrelated children raised together shows the importance of genetic factors

FIGURE 6 The relationship between IQ and closeness of genetic relationship. In general, the more similar the genetic and environmental background of two people, the greater the correlation is. Note, for example, that the correlation for spouses, who are genetically unrelated and have been reared apart, is relatively low, whereas the correlation for identical twins reared together is substantial. (Source: Adapted from Henderson, 1982.)

correspondence of IQ scores. Using data such as these, Herrnstein and Murray argued that differences between races in IQ scores were largely caused by genetically based differences in intelligence.

However, many psychologists reacted strongly to the arguments laid out in *The Bell Curve*, refuting several of the book's basic conclusions. One criticism is that even when attempts are made to hold socioeconomic conditions constant, wide variations remain among individual households. Furthermore, no one can convincingly assert that the living conditions of blacks and whites are identical even when their socioeconomic status is similar. In addition, as we discussed earlier, there is reason to believe that traditional IQ tests may discriminate against lower-SES urban blacks by asking for information pertaining to experience they are unlikely to have had (American Psychological Association Task Force on Intelligence, 1996; Nisbett, 2007; Levine, 2011).

Moreover, blacks who are raised in economically enriched environments have IQ scores similar to whites in comparable environments. For example, in a study of black children who had been adopted at an early age by white middle-class families of above-average intelligence, the IQ scores of those children averaged 106—about 15 points above the average IQ scores of unadopted black children in the study. Other research shows that the racial gap in IQ narrows considerably after a college education, and cross-cultural data demonstrate that when racial gaps exist in other cultures, the economically disadvantaged groups typically have lower scores. In short, the evidence that genetic factors play the major role in determining racial differences in IQ is not compelling (Scarr & Weinberg, 1976; Sternberg, Grigorenko, & Kidd, 2005; Fagan & Holland, 2007; Nisbett, 2009).

Furthermore, drawing comparisons between different races on any dimension, including IQ scores, is an imprecise, potentially misleading, and often fruitless venture. By far, the greatest discrepancies in IQ scores occur when comparing *individuals*, not when comparing mean IQ scores of different *groups*. There are blacks who score high on IQ tests and whites who score low, just as there are whites who score high and blacks who score low. For the concept of intelligence to aid in the betterment of society, we must examine how *individuals* perform and not the groups to which they belong (Fagan & Holland, 2002, 2007).

The more critical question to ask, then, is not whether hereditary or environmental factors primarily underlie intelligence, but whether there is anything we can do to maximize the intellectual development of each individual. If we can find ways to do this, we will be able to make changes in the environment—which may take the form of enriched home and school environments—that can lead each person to reach his or her potential.

> **Study Alert**
>
> Remember that the differences in IQ scores are much greater when comparing individuals than when comparing groups.

RECAP/EVALUATE/RETHINK

RECAP

LO 23-1 What are the different definitions and conceptions of intelligence?

- Because intelligence can take many forms, defining it is challenging. One commonly accepted view is that intelligence is the capacity to understand the world, think rationally, and use resources effectively when faced with challenges. (p. 267)
- The earliest psychologists assumed that there is a general factor for mental ability called *g*. However,

later psychologists disputed the view that intelligence is uni-dimensional. (p. 267)

- Some researchers suggest that intelligence can be broken down into fluid intelligence and crystallized intelligence. Gardner's theory of multiple intelligences proposes that there are eight spheres of intelligence. (p. 268)
- Information-processing approaches examine the processes underlying intelligent behavior rather than focusing on the structure of intelligence. (p. 268)
- Practical intelligence is intelligence related to overall success in living; emotional intelligence is the

set of skills that underlie the accurate assessment, evaluation, expression, and regulation of emotions. (p. 270)

LO 23-2 What are the major approaches to measuring intelligence, and what do intelligence tests measure?

- Intelligence tests have traditionally compared a person's mental age and chronological age to yield an IQ, or intelligence quotient, score. (p. 272)
- Specific tests of intelligence include the Stanford-Binet test, the Wechsler Adult Intelligence Scale–IV (WAIS-IV), and the Wechsler Intelligence Scale for Children–IV (WISC-IV). (p. 275)
- Tests are expected to be both reliable and valid. Reliability refers to the consistency with which a test measures what it is trying to measure. A test has validity when it actually measures what it is supposed to measure. (p. 276)

LO 23-3 How can the extremes of intelligence be characterized?

- The levels of intellectual disability (or mental retardation) include mild, moderate, severe, and profound retardation. (p. 277)
- About one-third of the cases of retardation have a known biological cause; fetal alcohol syndrome is the most common. Most cases, however, are classified as familial retardation, for which there is no known biological cause. (p. 278)
- The intellectually gifted are people with IQ scores greater than 130. Intellectually gifted people tend to be healthier and more successful than the nongifted. (p. 279)

LO 23-4 Are traditional IQ tests culturally biased?

- Traditional intelligence tests have frequently been criticized for being biased in favor of the white middle-class population. This controversy has led to attempts to devise culture-fair tests, IQ measures that avoid questions that depend on a particular cultural background. (p. 280)

LO 23-5 To what degree is intelligence influenced by the environment and to what degree by heredity?

- Attempting to distinguish environmental from hereditary factors in intelligence is probably futile and certainly misguided. Because individual IQ scores vary far more than group IQ scores, it is more critical to ask what can be done to maximize the intellectual development of each individual. (p. 281)

EVALUATE

1. _____ is a measure of intelligence that takes into account a person's chronological and mental ages.
2. Some psychologists make the distinction between _____ intelligence, which reflects reasoning, memory, and information-processing capabilities, and _____ intelligence, which is the information, skills, and strategies that people have learned through experience.
3. _____ _____ _____ is the most common biological cause of mental retardation.
4. People with high intelligence are generally shy and socially withdrawn. True or false?
5. A(n) _____ test tries to use only questions appropriate to all the people taking the test.

RETHINK

1. What is the role of emotional intelligence in the classroom? How might emotional intelligence be tested? Should emotional intelligence be a factor in determining academic promotion to the next grade?
2. *From the human resource specialist's perspective:* Job interviews are really a kind of test, but they rely on interviewers' judgments and have no formal validity or reliability. Do you think job interviews can be made to have greater validity and reliability?

Answers to Evaluate Questions

1. IQ; 2. fluid, crystallized; 3. Fetal alcohol syndrome; 4. false; the gifted are generally more socially adept than those with lower IQs; 5. culture-fair

KEY TERMS

intelligence p. 267
g or g-factor p. 267
fluid intelligence p. 267
crystallized
   intelligence p. 268
theory of multiple
   intelligences p. 268

practical intelligence p. 270
emotional intelligence p. 271
intelligence tests p. 272
mental age p. 273
intelligence
   quotient (IQ) p. 273
reliability p. 276

validity p. 276
norms p. 277
intellectual disability
   (or mental
   retardation) p. 277
fetal alcohol
   syndrome p. 278

familial retardation p. 278
intellectually gifted p. 279
culture-fair IQ test p. 280
heritability p. 281

Looking Back

Epilogue

The topics in this chapter occupy a central place in the field of psychology, encompassing a variety of areas—including thinking, problem solving, decision making, creativity, language, memory, and intelligence. We first examined thinking and problem solving, focusing on the importance of mental images and concepts and identifying the steps commonly involved in solving problems. We discussed language, describing the components of grammar and tracing language development in children. Finally, we considered intelligence. Some of the most heated discussions in all of psychology focus on this topic, engaging educators, policymakers, politicians, and psychologists alike. The issues include the very meaning of intelligence, its measurement, individual extremes of intelligence, and finally, the heredity/environment question.

Before proceeding, turn back to the prologue about Matthew Fernandez and Akash Krishnan's science project. Answer the following questions in light of what you have learned about reasoning, problem solving, and creativity:

1. Why do you think it's difficult to program a computer to recognize emotional inflections in a speaker's voice?
2. Describe the process that Matt and Akash are likely to use to solve the problem of developing a computer program for their school's science fair.
3. How do you think insight is involved in Matt and Akash's "aha" moment?
4. In what ways do you think divergent and convergent thinking are involved in the processes of invention? Do they play different roles during the various stages of the act of invention, including identifying the need for an invention, devising possible solutions, and creating a practical invention?

VISUAL SUMMARY 7 Thinking, Language, and Intelligence

MODULE 21 Thinking and Reasoning

Mental images: Representations in the mind of an object or event

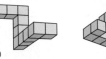

(a)

Concepts:
Categorizations of objects, events, or people that share common properties

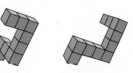
(b)

Prototypes: Typical examples of a concept

(c)

Algorithms: Rules that may guarantee a correct solution

Heuristics: Cognitive shortcuts that may lead to a solution

Solving Problems:
Well-defined and ill-defined problems

Preparation
Understanding and diagnosing problems

Production
Generating solutions

Judgment
Evaluating solutions

Impediments to problem solving
— Functional fixedness

— Mental set

MODULE 22 Language

Language Development
— Babbling: Speech-like sounds that are meaningless
— Telegraphic speech: Leaving out words that are not critical to the message
— Overgeneralization: Using rules of language even when doing so results in an error

Approaches to Learning Language
— Learning theory approach
— Nativist approach
— Interactionist approach

Linguistic-Relativity Hypothesis: Language shapes the way people in a specific culture perceive and understand the world

MODULE 23 Intelligence

Theories of Intelligence
— *g*-factor: Single factor underlying mental ability
— Fluid intelligence: information-processing capabilities, reasoning, and memory

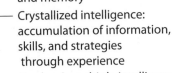

— Crystallized intelligence: accumulation of information, skills, and strategies through experience
— Gardner's multiple intelligences

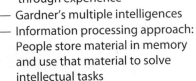

— Information processing approach: People store material in memory and use that material to solve intellectual tasks
— Practical intelligence: Intelligence related to overall success in living
— Emotional intelligence: Skills that underlie the accurate assessment, evaluation, expression, and regulation of emotions

Assessing Intelligence: Intelligence tests
— Binet developed IQ tests
  - Mental age: the average age of individuals who achieve a particular level of performance on a test
  - IQ: a score based on an individual's mental and chronological ages

$$\text{IQ score} = \frac{\text{MA}}{\text{CA}} \times 100$$

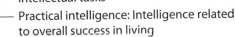

The average IQ score is 100, and 68% of people score between 85 and 115.

68%
95%
0.1%   0.1%
0   55   70   85   100   115   130   145   160

Number of scores

Intelligence test score

— Contemporary IQ tests
  - Wechsler Adult Intelligence Scale–IV
  - Wechsler Intelligence Scale for Children–IV

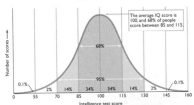

Variations in Intellectual Ability
— Intellectual Disability
  - A disability characterized by significant limitations both in intellectual functioning and in conceptual, social, and practical adaptive skills
  - Fetal alcohol syndrome and familial retardation
— Intellectually Gifted
  - IQ scores greater than 130
  - Most often outgoing, well adjusted, healthy, popular

8
Motivation and Emotion

Learning Outcomes for Chapter 8

LO 24-1 How does motivation direct and energize behavior?

Explaining Motivation

Instinct Approaches: Born to Be Motivated

Drive-Reduction Approaches: Satisfying Our Needs

Arousal Approaches: Beyond Drive Reduction

Incentive Approaches: Motivation's Pull

Cognitive Approaches: The Thoughts Behind Motivation

Maslow's Hierarchy: Ordering Motivational Needs

Applying the Different Approaches to Motivation

LO 25-1 What biological and social factors underlie hunger?

LO 25-2 What are the varieties of sexual behavior?

LO 25-3 How are needs relating to achievement, affiliation, and power motivation exhibited?

Human Needs and Motivation: Eat, Drink, and Be Daring

The Motivation Behind Hunger and Eating

Applying Psychology in the 21st Century: The Rising Stigma of Obesity

PsychWork: Nutritionist

Neuroscience in Your Life: When Regulation of Eating Behavior Goes Wrong—Bulimia

Becoming an Informed Consumer of Psychology: Dieting and Losing Weight Successfully

Sexual Motivation

The Needs for Achievement, Affiliation, and Power

LO 26-1 What are emotions, and how do we experience them?

LO 26-2 What are the functions of emotions?

LO 26-3 What are the explanations for emotions?

LO 26-4 How does nonverbal behavior relate to the expression of emotions?

Understanding Emotional Experiences

The Functions of Emotions

Determining the Range of Emotions: Labeling Our Feelings

The Roots of Emotions

Exploring Diversity: Do People in All Cultures Express Emotion Similarly?

Prologue *Striving to Please*

When an assistant coach asked rookie basketball star John Wall to do him a favor, Wall was happy to comply. No matter that the request was for Wall to do the "Dougie," a popular dance, in front of an enormous crowd of spectators at an all-star rookie game. In fact, Wall—who won the most valuable player award for the game—did the Dougie not once, but three times.

In some ways, Wall's willingness to comply was the perfect example of what defined Wall during his first year as a professional basketball player: his willingness to entertain and help others, striving to make them happy.

In fact, Wall's coach described him as a "pleaser." In his coach's words, "He wants to be great and he wants to please everyone" (Lee, 2011, p. D-1).

Looking Ahead

What explains John Wall's early success as a professional basketball player? Is he driven by the urge to compete and win? Or does the sense of personal accomplishment keep him going? Is it the incentive of a potentially lucrative career, or possibly of winning awards and accolades? And what compels Wall to be a "pleaser," as his coach puts it—are his reasons for striving to please people the same as his reasons for training hard to play basketball, or are they different?

These questions and many others are addressed by psychologists who study the topics of motivation and emotion. Psychologists who study motivation seek to discover the particular desired goals—the motives—that underlie behavior. Behaviors as basic as drinking to satisfy thirst and as inconsequential as taking a stroll to get exercise exemplify motives. Psychologists specializing in the study of motivation assume that such underlying motives steer our choices of activities.

While motivation concerns the forces that direct future behavior, emotion pertains to the feelings we experience throughout our lives. The study of emotions focuses on our internal experiences at any given moment. All of us feel a variety of emotions: happiness at succeeding at a difficult task, sadness over the death of a loved one, anger at being treated unfairly. Because emotions not only play a role in motivating our behavior but also act as a reflection of our underlying motivation, they play an important role in our lives.

We begin this set of modules by focusing on the major conceptions of motivation, discussing how different motives and needs jointly affect behavior. We consider motives that are biologically based and universal in the animal kingdom, such as hunger, as well as motives that are unique to humans, such as the need for achievement.

We then turn to emotions. We consider the roles and functions that emotions play in people's lives and discuss several approaches that explain how people understand their emotions. Finally, we look at how nonverbal behavior communicates emotions.

Explaining Motivation

In just a moment, 27-year-old Aron Ralston's life changed. An 800-pound boulder dislodged in a narrow canyon where Ralston was hiking in an isolated Utah canyon, pinning his lower arm to the ground.

For the next five days, Ralston lay in the dense, lonely forest, unable to escape. An experienced climber who had search-and-rescue training, he had ample time to consider his options. He tried unsuccessfully to chip away at the rock, and he rigged up ropes and pulleys around the boulder in a vain effort to move it.

Finally, out of water and nearly dehydrated, Ralston reasoned there was only one option left short of dying. In acts of incredible bravery, Ralston broke two bones in his wrist, applied a tourniquet, and used a dull pen knife to amputate his arm beneath the elbow.

Freed from his entrapment, Ralston climbed down from where he had been pinned and then hiked five miles to safety (Cox, 2003; Lofholm, 2003).

What motivation lay behind Ralston's resolve?

To answer this question, psychologists employ the concept of **motivation,** the factors that direct and energize the behavior of humans and other organisms. Motivation has biological, cognitive, and social aspects, and the complexity of the concept has led psychologists to develop a variety of approaches. All seek to explain the energy that guides people's behavior in specific directions.

Instinct Approaches: Born to Be Motivated

When psychologists first tried to explain motivation, they turned to **instincts,** inborn patterns of behavior that are biologically determined rather than learned. According to instinct approaches to motivation, people and animals are born preprogrammed with sets of behaviors essential to their survival. Those instincts provide the energy that channels behavior in appropriate directions. Hence, sexual behavior may be a response to an instinct to reproduce, and exploratory behavior may be motivated by an instinct to examine one's territory.

This conception presents several difficulties, however. For one thing, psychologists do not agree on what, or even how many, primary instincts exist. One early psychologist, William McDougall (1908), suggested that there are 18 instincts. Other theorists came up with even more—with one sociologist (Bernard, 1924) claiming that there are exactly 5,759 distinct instincts!

Furthermore, explanations based on the concept of instincts do not go very far toward explaining why one specific pattern of behavior, and not others, has appeared in a given species. In addition, although it is clear that much animal behavior is based on instincts, much of the variety and complexity of human behavior is learned and thus cannot be seen as instinctual.

As a result of these shortcomings, newer explanations have replaced conceptions of motivation based on instincts. However, instinct approaches still play a role in

Learning Outcome

LO 24-1 How does motivation direct and energize behavior?

Aron Ralston today.

motivation The factors that direct and energize the behavior of humans and other organisms.

instincts Inborn patterns of behavior that are biologically determined rather than learned.

certain theories, especially those based on evolutionary approaches that focus on our genetic inheritance. Furthermore, Freud's work suggests that instinctual drives of sex and aggression motivate behavior (Katz, 2001).

Drive-Reduction Approaches: Satisfying Our Needs

drive-reduction approaches to motivation Theories suggesting that a lack of some basic biological need produces a drive to push an organism to satisfy that need.

drive Motivational tension, or arousal, that energizes behavior to fulfill a need.

After rejecting instinct theory, psychologists first proposed simple drive-reduction theories of motivation to take its place (Hull, 1943). **Drive-reduction approaches to motivation** suggest that a lack of some basic biological need (such as a lack of water) produces a drive to push an organism to satisfy that need (in this case, seeking water).

To understand this approach, we begin with the concept of drive. A **drive** is motivational tension, or arousal, that energizes behavior to fulfill a need. Many basic drives, such as hunger, thirst, sleep, and sex, are related to biological needs of the body or of the species as a whole. These are called *primary drives*. Primary drives contrast with secondary drives in which behavior fulfills no obvious biological need. In *secondary drives,* prior experience and learning bring about needs. For instance, some people have strong needs to achieve academically and professionally. We can say that their achievement need is reflected in a secondary drive that motivates their behavior (McKinley et al., 2004; Seli, 2007).

We usually try to satisfy a primary drive by reducing the need underlying it. For example, we become hungry after not eating for a few hours and may raid the refrigerator, especially if the next scheduled meal is not imminent. If the weather turns cold, we put on extra clothing or raise the setting on the thermostat to keep warm. If our bodies need liquids to function properly, we experience thirst and seek out water.

HOMEOSTASIS

homeostasis The body's tendency to maintain a steady internal state.

Homeostasis, the body's tendency to maintain a steady internal state, underlies primary drives. Using feedback loops, homeostasis brings deviations in body functioning back to an optimal state, similar to the way a thermostat and a furnace work in a home heating system to maintain a steady temperature. Receptor cells throughout the body constantly monitor factors such as temperature and nutrient levels. When deviations from the ideal state occur, the body adjusts in an effort to return to an optimal state. Many fundamental needs, including the needs for food, water, stable body temperature, and sleep, operate via homeostasis (Shin, Zheng, & Berthoud, 2009; Vassalli & Dijk, 2009; Porkka-Heiskanen & Kalinchuk, 2011).

Although drive-reduction theories provide a good explanation of how primary drives motivate behavior, they cannot fully explain a behavior in which the goal is not to reduce a drive but rather to maintain or even increase the level of excitement or arousal. For instance, some behaviors seem to be motivated by nothing more than curiosity, such as rushing to check e-mail messages. Similarly, many people pursue thrilling activities such as riding a roller coaster or steering a raft down the rapids of a river. Such behaviors certainly don't suggest that people seek to reduce all drives as drive-reduction approaches would indicate (Begg & Langley, 2001; Rosenbloom & Wolf, 2002).

Both curiosity and thrill-seeking behavior, then, shed doubt on drive-reduction approaches as a complete explanation for motivation. In both cases, rather than seeking to reduce an underlying drive, people and animals appear to be motivated to increase their overall level of stimulation and activity. To explain this phenomenon, psychologists have devised an alternative: arousal approaches to motivation.

Study Alert

To remember the concept of homeostasis, keep in mind the analogy of a thermostat that regulates the temperature in a house.

Arousal Approaches: Beyond Drive Reduction

Arousal approaches seek to explain behavior in which the goal is to maintain or increase excitement. According to **arousal approaches to motivation,** each person tries to maintain a certain level of stimulation and activity. As with the drive-reduction model, this approach suggests that if our stimulation and activity levels become too high, we try to reduce them. But, in contrast to the drive-reduction perspective, the arousal approach also suggests that if levels of stimulation and activity are too low, we will try to increase them by seeking stimulation.

People vary widely in the optimal level of arousal they seek out, with some people looking for especially high levels of arousal. For example, people who participate in daredevil sports, high-stakes gamblers, and criminals who pull off high-risk robberies may be exhibiting a particularly high need for arousal (see Figure 1 on page 292; Zuckerman, 2002; Cavenett & Nixon, 2006; Roets & Van Hiel, 2011).

arousal approaches to motivation The belief that we try to maintain certain levels of stimulation and activity.

Incentive Approaches: Motivation's Pull

When a luscious dessert appears on the table after a filling meal, its appeal has little or nothing to do with internal drives or the maintenance of arousal. Rather, if we choose to eat the dessert, such behavior is motivated by the external stimulus of the dessert itself, which acts as an anticipated reward. This reward, in motivational terms, is an *incentive*.

Incentive approaches to motivation suggest that motivation stems from the desire to obtain valued external goals, or incentives. In this view, the desirable properties of external stimuli—whether grades, money, affection, food, or sex—account for a person's motivation (Festinger et al., 2009).

Although the theory explains why we may succumb to an incentive (such as a mouth-watering dessert) even though we lack internal cues (such as hunger), it does not provide a complete explanation of motivation because organisms sometimes seek to fulfill needs even when incentives are not apparent. Consequently, many psychologists believe that the internal drives proposed by drive-reduction theory work in tandem with the external incentives of incentive theory to "push" and "pull" behavior, respectively. Thus, at the same time that we seek to satisfy our underlying hunger needs (the push of drive-reduction theory), we are drawn to food that appears very appetizing (the pull of incentive theory). Rather than contradicting each other, then, drives and incentives may work together in motivating behavior (Pinel, Assanand, & Lehman, 2000; Lowery, Fillingim, & Wright, 2003; Berridge, 2004).

incentive approaches to motivation Theories suggesting that motivation stems from the desire to obtain valued external goals, or incentives.

Cognitive Approaches: The Thoughts Behind Motivation

Cognitive approaches to motivation suggest that motivation is a product of people's thoughts, expectations, and goals—their cognitions. For instance, the degree to which people are motivated to study for a test is based on their expectation of how well studying will pay off in terms of a good grade.

Cognitive theories of motivation draw a key distinction between intrinsic and extrinsic motivation. *Intrinsic motivation* causes us to participate in an activity for our

cognitive approaches to motivation Theories suggesting that motivation is a product of people's thoughts, expectations, and goals—their cognitions.

FIGURE 1 Some people seek high levels of arousal, whereas others are more easygoing. You can get a sense of your own preferred level of stimulation by completing this questionnaire. (Source: "Do You Seek Out Sensation?" questionnaire from Marvin Zuckerman, "The Search for High Sensation," *Psychology Today*, February 1978, pp. 30–46. Reprinted with permission from *Psychology Today* magazine, Copyright © 1978 Sussex Publishers, LLC.)

Do You Seek Out Sensation?

How much stimulation do you crave in your everyday life? You will have an idea after you complete the following questionnaire, which lists some items from a scale designed to assess your sensation-seeking tendencies. Circle either A or B in each pair or statements.

1. A I would like a job that requires a lot of traveling.
   B I would prefer a job in one location.
2. A I am invigorated by a brisk, cold day.
   B I can't wait to get indoors on a cold day.
3. A I get bored seeing the same old faces.
   B I like the comfortable familiarity of everyday friends.
4. A I would prefer living in an ideal society in which everyone was safe, secure, and happy.
   B I would have preferred living in the unsettled days of our history.
5. A I sometimes like to do things that are a little frightening.
   B A sensible person avoids activities that are dangerous.
6. A I would not like to be hypnotized.
   B I would like to have the experience of being hypnotized.
7. A The most important goal of life is to live it to the fullest and to experience as much as possible.
   B The most important goal life is to live it to the fullest and to experience as much as possible.
8. A I would like to try parachute jumping.
   B I would never want to try jumping out of a plane, with or without a parachute.
9. A I enter cold water gradually, giving myself time to get used to it.
   B I like to dive or jump right into the ocean or a cold pool.
10. A When I go on a vacation, I prefer the comfort of a good room and bed.
    B When I go on a vacation, I prefer the change of camping out.
11. A I prefer people who are emotionally expressive, even if they are a bit unstable.
    B I prefer people who are calm and even-tempered.
12. A A good painting should shock or jolt the senses.
    B A good painting should give one a feeling of peace and security.
13. A People who ride motorcycles must have some kind of unconscious need to hurt themselves.
    B I would like to drive or ride a motorcycle.

Scoring: Give yourself one point for each of the following responses: 1A, 2A, 3A, 4B, 5A, 6B, 7A, 8A, 9B, 10B, 11A, 12A, 13B. Find your total score by adding up the number of points and then use the following scoring key.

0–3 very low sensation seeking
4–5 low
6–9 average
10–11 high
12–13 very high

Keep in mind, of course, that this short questionnaire, for which the scoring is based on the results of college students who have taken it, provides only a rough estimate of your sensation-seeking tendencies. Moreover, as people get older, their sensation-seeking scores tend to decrease. Still, the questionnaire will at least give you an indication of how your sensation-seeking tendencies compare with those of others.

own enjoyment rather than for any concrete, tangible reward that it will bring us. In contrast, *extrinsic motivation* causes us to do something for money, a grade, or some other concrete, tangible reward. For example, when a physician works long hours because she loves medicine, intrinsic motivation is prompting her; if she works hard to make a lot of money, extrinsic motivation underlies her efforts (Lepper, Corpus, & Iyengar, 2005; Shaikholeslami & Khayyer, 2006; Finkelstein, 2009).

We are more apt to persevere, work harder, and produce work of higher quality when motivation for a task is intrinsic rather than extrinsic. In fact, in some cases providing rewards for desirable behavior (thereby increasing extrinsic motivation) actually may decrease intrinsic motivation (James, 2005; Grant, 2008; Nishimura, Kawamura, & Sakurai, 2011).

Maslow's Hierarchy: Ordering Motivational Needs

What do Eleanor Roosevelt, Abraham Lincoln, and Albert Einstein have in common? The common thread, according to a model of motivation devised by psychologist Abraham Maslow, is that each of them fulfilled the highest levels of motivational needs underlying human behavior.

Maslow's model places motivational needs in a hierarchy and suggests that before more sophisticated, higher-order needs can be met, certain primary needs must be satisfied (Maslow, 1970, 1987). A pyramid can represent the model with the more basic needs at the bottom and the higher-level needs at the top (see Figure 2). To activate a specific higher-order need, thereby guiding behavior, a person must first fulfill the more basic needs in the hierarchy.

The basic needs are primary drives: needs for water, food, sleep, sex, and the like. To move up the hierarchy, a person must first meet these basic physiological needs. Safety needs come next in the hierarchy; Maslow suggests that people need a safe, secure environment in order to function effectively. Physiological and safety needs compose the lower-order needs.

Only after meeting the basic lower-order needs can a person consider fulfilling higher-order needs, such as the needs for love and a sense of belonging, esteem, and self-actualization. Love and belongingness needs include the needs to obtain and give affection and to be a contributing member of some group or society. After fulfilling these needs, a person strives for esteem. In Maslow's thinking, esteem relates to the need to develop a sense of self-worth by recognizing that others know and value one's competence.

Once these four sets of needs are fulfilled—no easy task—a person is able to strive for the highest-level need, self-actualization. **Self-actualization** is a state of self-fulfillment in which people realize their highest potentials in their own unique way. Although Maslow first suggested that self-actualization occurred in only a few famous individuals, he later expanded the concept to encompass everyday people. For example, a parent with excellent nurturing skills who raises a family, a teacher who year after year creates an environment that maximizes students' opportunities for success, and an artist who realizes his creative potential all may be self-actualized. The important thing is that people feel at ease with themselves and satisfied that they are using their talents to the fullest. In a sense, achieving self-actualization reduces the striving and yearning for greater fulfillment that mark most people's lives and instead provides a sense of satisfaction with the current state of affairs (Reiss & Havercamp, 2005; Laas, 2006; Bauer, Schwab, & McAdams, 2011).

Although research has been unable to validate the specific ordering of Maslow's stages, and it is difficult to measure self-actualization objectively, Maslow's hierarchy of needs is important for two reasons: It

self-actualization A state of self-fulfillment in which people realize their highest potential in their own unique way.

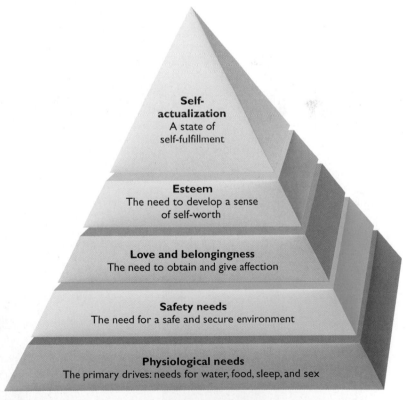

FIGURE 2 Maslow's hierarchy shows how our motivation progresses up the pyramid from the broadest, most fundamental biological needs to higher-order ones. Do you agree that lower-order needs must be satisfied before higher-order needs? Do hermits and monks who attempt to fulfill spiritual needs while denying basic physical needs contradict Maslow's hierarchy? (After Maslow, 1970.)

highlights the complexity of human needs, and it emphasizes the idea that until more basic biological needs are met, people will be relatively unconcerned with higher-order needs. For example, if people are hungry, their first interest will be in obtaining food; they will not be concerned with needs such as love and self-esteem (Hanley & Abell, 2002; Samantaray, Srivastava, & Mishra, 2002; Ojha & Pramanick, 2009).

Maslow's hierarchy of needs has also spawned other approaches to motivation. For example, Edward Deci and Richard Ryan (2008) have considered human needs in terms of psychological well-being. They suggest in their *self-determination theory* that people have the three basic needs of competence, autonomy, and relatedness. Competence is the need to produce desired outcomes, while autonomy is the perception that we have control over our own lives. Finally, relatedness is the need to be involved in close, warm relationships with others. In the view of self-determination theory, these three psychological needs are innate and universal across cultures, and they are essential as basic biological needs (Jang et al., 2009; Ryan & Deci, 2011).

Study Alert

Review the distinctions among the different explanations for motivation (instinct, drive reduction, arousal, incentive, cognitive, and Maslow's hierarchy of needs).

Applying the Different Approaches to Motivation

The various theories of motivation (summarized in Figure 3) give several different perspectives on it. Which provides the fullest account of motivation? Actually, many of the approaches are complementary rather than contradictory. In fact, employing more than one approach can help us understand motivation in a particular instance.

Instinct
People and animals are born with preprogrammed sets of behaviors essential to their survival.

Drive reduction
When some basic biological requirement is lacking, a drive is produced.

Arousal
People seek an optimal level of stimulation. If the level of stimulation is too high, they act to reduce it; if it is too low, they act to increase it.

Incentive
External stimuli direct and energize behavior.

Cognitive
Thoughts, expectations, and understanding of the world direct motivation.

Hierarchy of needs
Needs form a hierarchy; before higher-order needs are met, lower-order needs must be fulfilled.

FIGURE 3 The major approaches to motivation.

Consider, for example, Aron Ralston's accident while hiking (described earlier). His interest in climbing in an isolated and potentially dangerous area may be explained by arousal approaches to motivation. From the perspective of instinct approaches, we realize that Aron had an overwhelming instinct to preserve his life at all costs. From a cognitive perspective, we see his careful consideration of various strategies to extricate himself from the boulder.

In short, applying multiple approaches to motivation in a given situation provides a broader understanding than we might obtain by employing only a single approach. We'll see this again when we consider specific motives—such as the needs for food, achievement, affiliation, and power—and draw on several of the theories for the fullest account of what motivates our behavior.

RECAP/EVALUATE/RETHINK

RECAP

LO 24-1 How does motivation direct and energize behavior?

- Motivation relates to the factors that direct and energize behavior. (p. 289)
- Drive is the motivational tension that energizes behavior to fulfill a need. (p. 290)
- Homeostasis, the maintenance of a steady internal state, often underlies motivational drives. (p. 290)
- Arousal approaches suggest that we try to maintain a particular level of stimulation and activity. (p. 291)
- Incentive approaches focus on the positive aspects of the environment that direct and energize behavior. (p. 291)
- Cognitive approaches focus on the role of thoughts, expectations, and understanding of the world in producing motivation. (p. 291)
- Maslow's hierarchy suggests that there are five basic needs: physiological, safety, love and belongingness, esteem, and self-actualization. Only after the more basic needs are fulfilled can a person move toward meeting higher-order needs. (p. 293)

EVALUATE

1. _____ are forces that guide a person's behavior in a certain direction.
2. Biologically determined, inborn patterns of behavior are known as _____.
3. Your psychology professor tells you, "Explaining behavior is easy! When we lack something, we are motivated to get it." Which approach to motivation does your professor subscribe to?
4. By drinking water after running a marathon, a runner tries to keep his or her body at an optimal level of functioning. This process is called _____.
5. I help an elderly person cross the street because doing a good deed makes me feel good. What type of motivation is at work here? What type of motivation would be at work if I were to help an elderly man across the street because he paid me $20?
6. According to Maslow, a person with no job, no home, and no friends can become self-actualized. True or false?

RETHINK

1. Which approaches to motivation are more commonly used in the workplace? How might each approach be used to design employment policies that can sustain or increase motivation?
2. *From the perspective of an educator:* Do you think that giving students grades serves as an external reward that would decrease intrinsic motivation for the subject matter? Why or why not?

Answers to Evaluate Questions

1. Motives; 2. instincts; 3. drive reduction; 4. homeostasis; 5. intrinsic, extrinsic; 6. false; lower-order needs must be fulfilled before self-actualization can occur

KEY TERMS

motivation p. 289
instincts p. 289
drive-reduction approaches to motivation p. 290
drive p. 290
homeostasis p. 290

arousal approaches to motivation p. 291
incentive approaches to motivation p. 291
cognitive approaches to motivation p. 291
self-actualization p. 293

Human Needs and Motivation: Eat, Drink, and Be Daring

Learning Outcomes

LO 25-1 What biological and social factors underlie hunger?

LO 25-2 What are the varieties of sexual behavior?

LO 25-3 How are needs relating to achievement, affiliation, and power motivation exhibited?

As a sophomore at the University of California, Santa Cruz, Lisa Arndt followed a menu of her own making: For breakfast she ate cereal or fruit with 10 diet pills and 50 chocolate-flavored laxatives. Lunch was a salad or sandwich; dinner: chicken and rice. But it was the feast that followed that Arndt relished most. Almost every night at about 9 p.m., she would retreat to her room and eat an entire small pizza and a whole batch of cookies. Then she'd wait for the day's laxatives to take effect. "It was extremely painful," says Arndt of those days. . . . "But I was that desperate to make up for my binging. I was terrified of fat the way other people are afraid of lions or guns." (Hubbard, O'Neill, & Cheakalos, 1999, p. 55).

Lisa was one of the 10 million women (and 1 million men) who are estimated to suffer from an eating disorder. These disorders, which usually appear during adolescence, can bring about extraordinary weight loss and other forms of physical deterioration. Extremely dangerous, they sometimes result in death.

Why are Lisa and others like her subject to such disordered eating, which revolves around the motivation to avoid weight gain at all costs? And why do so many other people engage in overeating, which leads to obesity?

To answer these questions, we must consider some of the specific needs that underlie behavior. In this module, we examine several of the most important human needs. We begin with hunger, the primary drive that has received the most attention from researchers, and then we turn to secondary drives—those uniquely human endeavors based on learned needs and past experience that help explain why people strive to achieve, to affiliate with others, and to seek power over others.

The Motivation Behind Hunger and Eating

obesity Body weight that is more than 20% above the average weight for a person of a particular height.

Two hundred million people in the United States—some two-thirds of the population—are overweight. Almost a quarter are so heavy that they have **obesity,** body weight that is more than 20% above the average weight for a person of a particular height. And the rest of the world is not far behind: A billion people around the globe are overweight or obese. The World Health Organization has said that worldwide obesity has reached epidemic proportions, producing increases in heart disease, diabetes, cancer, and premature deaths. Projections are that by 2018, 40% of U.S. residents may be obese (Stephenson & Banet-Weiser, 2007; Thorpe, 2009; Shugart, 2011).

The most widely used measure of obesity is *body mass index (BMI)*, which is based on a ratio of weight to height. People with a BMI greater than 30 are considered obese, whereas those with a BMI between 25 and 30 are overweight. (Use the formulas in Figure 1 to determine your own BMI.)

Although the definition of obesity is clear from a scientific point of view, people's perceptions of what an ideal body looks like vary significantly across different cultures and, within Western cultures, from one time period to another. For instance, many contemporary Western cultures stress the importance of slimness in women—a

FIGURE 1 Use this procedure to find your body mass index.

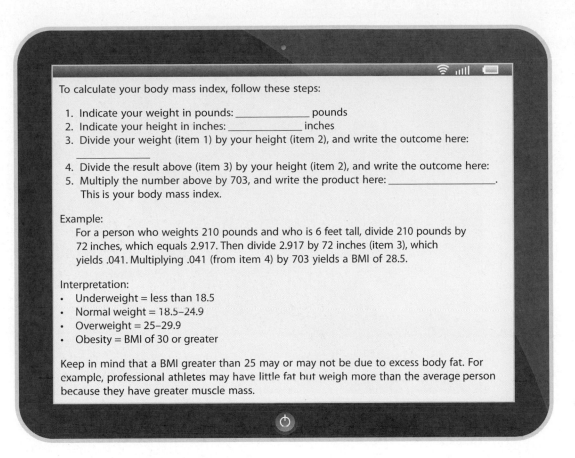

To calculate your body mass index, follow these steps:

1. Indicate your weight in pounds: _____ pounds
2. Indicate your height in inches: _____ inches
3. Divide your weight (item 1) by your height (item 2), and write the outcome here:
   _____
4. Divide the result above (item 3) by your height (item 2), and write the outcome here: _____
5. Multiply the number above by 703, and write the product here: _____.
   This is your body mass index.

Example:
   For a person who weights 210 pounds and who is 6 feet tall, divide 210 pounds by 72 inches, which equals 2.917. Then divide 2.917 by 72 inches (item 3), which yields .041. Multiplying .041 (from item 4) by 703 yields a BMI of 28.5.

Interpretation:
- Underweight = less than 18.5
- Normal weight = 18.5–24.9
- Overweight = 25–29.9
- Obesity = BMI of 30 or greater

Keep in mind that a BMI greater than 25 may or may not be due to excess body fat. For example, professional athletes may have little fat but weigh more than the average person because they have greater muscle mass.

relatively recent view. In 19th-century Hawaii, the most attractive women were those who were the heaviest. Furthermore, for most of the 20th century—except for periods in the 1920s and the most recent decades—the ideal female figure was relatively full. Even today, weight standards differ among different cultural groups. For instance, in some traditional Arab cultures, obese women are so prized as wives that parents force-feed their female children to make them more desirable (Blixen, Singh, & Xu, 2006; Marsh, Hau, & Sung, 2007; Franko & Roehrig, 2011).

Regardless of cultural standards for appearance and weight, no one doubts that being overweight represents a major health risk. However, controlling weight is complicated because eating behavior involves a variety of mechanisms (also see *Applying Psychology in the 21st Century*). In our discussion of what motivates people to eat, we'll start with the biological aspects of eating.

BIOLOGICAL FACTORS IN THE REGULATION OF HUNGER

In contrast to human beings, other species are unlikely to become obese. Internal mechanisms regulate not only the quantity of food they take in, but also the kind of food they desire. For example, rats that have been deprived of particular foods seek out alternatives that contain the specific nutrients their diet is lacking, and many species, given the choice of a wide variety of foods, select a well-balanced diet (Woods et al., 2000; Jones & Corp, 2003).

Complex biological mechanisms tell organisms whether they require food or should stop eating. It's not just a matter of an empty stomach causing hunger pangs and a full one

"Gee, I had no idea you were married to a supermodel."

The Rising Stigma of Obesity

With great publicity, the U.S. government launched a national campaign against the rising problem of childhood obesity, including specific recommendations for addressing the problem and an ambitious goal of reducing the childhood obesity rate by 75% within 20 years. Concern over obesity has reached a high point, with books such as *Fast Food Nation* and films such as *Supersize Me* criticizing the fast-food industry, schools banning the sale of soft drinks and snack foods, and watchdog groups monitoring how food is marketed to children. While these are all welcome developments that help to raise awareness of the dangers of obesity, especially in children, there also has been an unintended consequence: stigma toward the obese (Benac, 2010).

Researcher Alexandra Brewis and her colleagues at Arizona State University surveyed people in 10 different locales around the world, asking them whether they agreed with a number of statements that expressed a variety of positive and negative beliefs about overweight people, such as "people are overweight because they are lazy" or "a big woman is a beautiful woman." The cultures where people were surveyed included body-conscious ones such as the United States, England, New Zealand, and Argentina, as well as ones that have historically held heavier people in high esteem, such as Puerto Rico and American Samoa (Brewis et al., 2011).

Brewis confirmed strong negative attitudes toward overweight people in the nations where she expected to find it. But she also found high levels of this fat stigma in the other locales as well, including nations that once favored big bodies. Not only does it seem that people had become less tolerant of obesity, but also they were

Even in cultures in which obesity has traditionally been seen as desirable, such as in Samoa in the South Pacific, attitudes have recently become more negative, consistent with views of Westerners.

more inclined to see obese others as being to blame for their condition. It seems that public health messages intended to encourage people to take control of their weight may be inadvertently implying that obesity is caused by the individual's lack of self-control, downplaying important social and environmental factors that contribute to the problem.

There is no evidence that blaming people for their obesity and exposing them to shame and stigma is helpful in reducing weight. In fact, it likely complicates the issue by contributing to negative social and occupational outcomes, such as discrimination in the workplace or difficulty making meaningful social ties. While more research is needed to confirm that increased stigma towards the obese is being expressed in these harmful ways, it's clearly a problem that needs to be addressed (Parker-Pope, 2011).

RETHINK

- What do you think is driving the changes in cultural acceptance of overweight people?
- Do you think it's possible to combat obesity without stigmatizing obese people? Why or why not?

alleviating those pangs. (Even individuals who have had their stomachs removed still experience the sensation of hunger.) One important factor is changes in the chemical composition of the blood. For instance, changes in levels of glucose, a kind of sugar, regulate feelings of hunger. In addition, the hormone *insulin* leads the body to store excess sugar in the blood as fats and carbohydrates. Finally, the hormone *ghrelin* communicates to the brain feelings of hunger. The production of ghrelin increases according to meal schedules as well as the sight or smell of food, producing the feeling that tells us we're hungry and should eat (Wren & Bloom, 2007; Kojima & Kangawa, 2008; Langlois et al., 2011).

The brain's *hypothalamus* monitors glucose levels. Increasing evidence suggests that the hypothalamus carries the primary responsibility for monitoring food intake. Injury to the hypothalamus has radical consequences for eating behavior, depending on the site of the injury. For example, rats whose *lateral hypothalamus* is damaged may literally starve to death. They refuse food when it is offered; unless they are force-fed, they eventually die. Rats with an injury to the *ventromedial hypothalamus* display the opposite problem: extreme overeating. Rats with this injury can increase in weight by as much as 400%. Similar phenomena occur in humans who have tumors of the hypothalamus (Seymour, 2006; Fedeli et al., 2009; Barson, Morganstern, & Leibowitz, 2011).

Although the important role the hypothalamus plays in regulating food intake is clear, the exact way this organ operates is still unclear. One hypothesis suggests that injury to the hypothalamus affects the **weight set point,** or the particular level of weight that the body strives to maintain, which in turn regulates food intake. Acting as a kind of internal weight thermostat, the hypothalamus calls for either greater or less food intake (Woods et al., 2000; Berthoud, 2002; Cornier, 2011).

In most cases, the hypothalamus does a good job. Even people who are not deliberately monitoring their weight show only minor weight fluctuations in spite of substantial day-to-day variations in how much they eat and exercise. However, injury to the hypothalamus can alter the weight set point, and a person then struggles to meet the internal goal by increasing or decreasing food consumption. Even temporary exposure to certain drugs can alter the weight set point (Cabanac & Frankham, 2002; Hallschmid et al., 2004; Khazaal et al., 2008).

Genetic factors determine the weight set point, at least in part. People seem destined, through heredity, to have a particular **metabolism,** the rate at which food is converted to energy and expended by the body. People with a high metabolic rate can eat virtually as much as they want without gaining weight, whereas others with low metabolism may eat literally half as much yet gain weight readily (Jequier, 2002; Westerterp, 2006).

weight set point The particular level of weight that the body strives to maintain.

metabolism The rate at which food is converted to energy and expended by the body.

SOCIAL FACTORS IN EATING

You've just finished a full meal and feel completely stuffed. Suddenly your host announced with great fanfare that he will be serving his "house specialty" dessert, bananas flambé, and that he has spent the better part of the afternoon preparing it. Even though you are full and don't even like bananas, you accept a serving of his dessert and eat it all.

Clearly, internal biological factors do not fully explain our eating behavior. External social factors, based on societal rules and on what we have learned about appropriate eating behavior, also play an important role. Take, for example, the simple fact that people customarily eat breakfast, lunch, and dinner at approximately the same times every day. Because we tend to eat on schedule every day, we feel hungry as the usual hour approaches, sometimes quite independently of what our internal cues are telling us.

Similarly, we put roughly the same amount of food on our plates every day, even though the amount of exercise we may have had (and consequently our need for energy replenishment) varies from day to day. We also tend to prefer particular foods over others. Rats and dogs may be a delicacy in certain Asian cultures, but few people in Western cultures find them appealing despite their potentially high nutritional value. Even the amount of food we eat varies according to cultural norms. For instance, people in the United States eat bigger portions than people in France. In sum, cultural influences and our individual habits play important roles in determining when, what, and how much we eat (Miller & Pumariega, 2001; Rozin et al., 2003; Leeman, Fischler, & Rozin, 2011).

Other social factors relate to our eating behavior as well. Some of us head toward the refrigerator after a difficult day seeking solace in a pint of Heath Bar Crunch ice

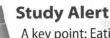

Study Alert

A key point: Eating and hunger are influenced both by biological and social factors.

cream. Why? Perhaps when we were children, our parents gave us food when we were upset. Eventually, we may have learned through the basic mechanisms of classical and operant conditioning to associate food with comfort and consolation. Similarly, we may learn that eating, which focuses our attention on immediate pleasures, provides an escape from unpleasant thoughts. Consequently, we may eat when we feel distressed (O'Connor & O'Connor, 2004; Elfhag, Tynelius, & Rasmussen, 2007; also see *PsychWork*).

PsychWork
NUTRITIONIST

Name: Gail K. Rupert

Education: University of Pennsylvania, West Chester, Pennsylvania; BS in Nutrition and Dietetics

Obesity has become a serious health issue for many Americans, who struggle to maintain a healthy diet and weight. For Gail Rupert, a nutritionist with The Weight Loss Clinic in Harrisburg, PA, motivation is a key ingredient in losing weight.

In her approach to getting people motivated, Rupert says, "It's important to empathize with the patient so they don't feel like they are on their own with no support. I tell them I understand that the weight-loss process can be frustrating and emotional, and it may take a lot of persistence and consistency before seeing any reduction in weight.

"Each client is different. Some patients have absolutely no knowledge of nutrition, while others have at least some familiarity," she explained. "For those with little knowledge, I have to break down more difficult concepts to help them better understand the procedure.

"For all patients, I make sure to give a reason why I'm suggesting a change. Most patients wouldn't change eating or exercise habits if I didn't explain the positive consequences of their actions. For example, exercising three times per week will improve their metabolism and increase their weight loss," she added.

THE ROOTS OF OBESITY

Given that both biological and social factors influence eating behavior, determining the causes of obesity has proved to be a challenging task. Researchers have followed several paths.

Some psychologists suggest that oversensitivity to external eating cues based on social factors, coupled with insensitivity to internal hunger cues, produce obesity. Others argue that overweight people have higher weight set points than other people do. Because their set points are unusually high, their attempts to lose weight by eating less may make them especially sensitive to external, food-related cues and therefore more apt to overeat and perpetuate their obesity (West, Harvey-Berino, & Raczynski, 2004; Tremblay, 2004; Kanoski et al., 2011).

But why may some people's weight set points be higher than those of others? One biological explanation is that obese individuals have a higher level of the hormone *leptin*, which appears to be designed, from an evolutionary standpoint, to "protect" the body against weight loss. The body's weight-regulation system thus appears to be designed more to protect against losing weight than to protect against gaining it. Therefore, it's easier to gain weight than to lose it (Ahiima & Osei, 2004; Zhang et al., 2005; Levin, 2006).

Another biologically based explanation for obesity relates to fat cells in the body. Starting at birth, the body stores fat either by increasing the number of fat cells or by increasing the size of existing fat cells. Furthermore, any loss of weight past infancy does not decrease the number of fat cells; it only affects their size. Consequently, people are stuck with the number of fat cells they inherit from an early age, and the rate of weight gain during the first 4 months of life is related to being overweight during later childhood (Stettler et al., 2005).

Although obesity is reaching epidemic proportions in the United States, its exact causes remain unclear.

According to the weight-set-point hypothesis, the presence of too many fat cells from earlier weight gain may result in the set point's becoming "stuck" at a higher level than desirable. In such circumstances, losing weight becomes a difficult proposition because one is constantly at odds with one's own internal set point when dieting (Freedman, 1995; Leibel, Rosenbaum, & Hirsch, 1995).

Not everyone agrees with the set-point explanation for obesity. Pointing to the rapid rise in obesity over the last several decades in the United States, some researchers suggest that the body does not try to maintain a fixed weight set point. Instead, they suggest, the body has a *settling point*, determined by a combination of our genetic heritage and the nature of the environment in which we live. If high-fat foods are prevalent in our environment and we are genetically predisposed to obesity, we settle into an equilibrium that maintains relatively high weight. In contrast, if our environment is nutritionally healthier, a genetic predisposition to obesity will not be triggered, and we will settle into an equilibrium in which our weight is lower (Comuzzie & Allison, 1998; Pi-Sunyer, 2003).

EATING DISORDERS

Eating disorders are among the 10 most frequent causes of disability in young women. One devastating weight-related disorder is **anorexia nervosa.** In this severe eating disorder, people may refuse to eat while denying that their behavior and appearance—which can become skeleton-like—are unusual. Some 10% of people with anorexia literally starve themselves to death (Striegel-Moore & Bulik, 2007; Arcelus et al., 2011).

Anorexia nervosa mainly afflicts females between the ages of 12 and 40, although both men and women of any age may develop it. People with the disorder are often successful, attractive, and relatively affluent. The disorder often begins after serious dieting, which somehow gets out of control. Life begins to revolve around food: Although people with the disorder eat little, they may cook for others, go shopping for food frequently, or collect cookbooks (Polivy, Herman, & Boivin, 2005; Myers, 2007; Jacobs et al., 2009).

A related problem, **bulimia,** from which Lisa Arndt (described earlier) suffered, is a disorder in which people binge on large quantities of food. For instance, they

anorexia nervosa A severe eating disorder in which people may refuse to eat while denying that their behavior and appearance—which can become skeleton-like—are unusual.

bulimia A disorder in which a person binges on large quantities of food, followed by efforts to purge the food through vomiting or other means.

Despite looking skeleton-like to others, people with the eating disorder anorexia nervosa see themselves as overweight.

may consume an entire gallon of ice cream and a whole pie in a single sitting. After such a binge, sufferers feel guilt and depression and often induce vomiting or take laxatives to rid themselves of the food—behavior known as purging. Constant binging-and-purging cycles and the use of drugs to induce vomiting or diarrhea can lead to heart failure. Often, though, the weight of a person with bulimia remains normal (Mora-Giral et al., 2004; Couturier & Lock, 2006; Lampard et al., 2011).

Eating disorders represent a growing problem: Estimates show that between 1% and 4% of high school–age and college-age women have either anorexia nervosa or bulimia. As many as 10% of women suffer from bulimia at some point in their lives. Furthermore, an increasing amount of research shows that almost as many men suffer from binge eating as women (Swain, 2006; Park, 2007; Striegel et al., 2011).

What are the causes of anorexia nervosa and bulimia? Some researchers suspect a biological cause such as a chemical imbalance in the hypothalamus or pituitary gland, perhaps brought on by genetic factors. Furthermore, brain scans of people with eating disorders show that they process information about food differently from healthy individuals (see Figure 2 *Neuroscience in Your Life*; Polivy & Herman, 2002; Santel et al., 2006; Klump & Culbert, 2007).

Others believe that the cause has roots in society's valuation of slenderness and the parallel notion that obesity is undesirable. These researchers maintain that people with anorexia nervosa and bulimia become preoccupied with their weight and take to heart the cliché that one can never be too thin. This may explain why eating disorders increase as countries become more developed and Westernized and dieting becomes more popular. Finally, some psychologists suggest that the disorders result from overly demanding parents or other family problems (Grilo et al., 2003; Couturier & Lock, 2006; Kluck, 2008).

The complete explanations for anorexia nervosa and bulimia remain elusive. These disorders most likely stem from both biological and social causes, and

Neuroscience in Your Life: When Regulation of Eating Behavior Goes Wrong—Bulimia

FIGURE 2 Recent research suggests that self-regulation among people with bulimia may be impaired. As seen in these fMRI images, when required to inhibit a response on a task in an experiment, participants without bulimia, labeled as "healthy control," more strongly activated areas of the brain associated with self-regulation (indicated in red) than those participants with bulimia, suggesting deficits in self-regulation among people with bulimia. (Source: Marsh et al., 2009.)

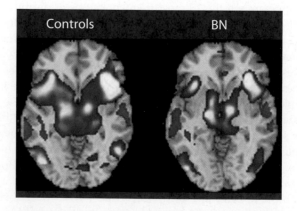

successful treatment probably encompasses several strategies, including therapy and dietary changes (O'Brien & LeBow, 2007; Wilson, Grilo, & Vitousek, 2007; Cooper & Shafran, 2008).

If you or a family member needs advice or help with an eating problem, contact the American Anorexia Bulimia Association at www.aabainc.org or call (212) 575-6200. You can get more information at www.nlm.nih.gov/medlineplus/eatingdisorders.html.

BECOMING AN INFORMED CONSUMER of Psychology

Dieting and Losing Weight Successfully

Although 60% of the people in the United States say they want to lose weight, it's a losing battle for most of them. Most people who diet eventually regain the weight they lost, so they try again and get caught in a seemingly endless cycle of weight loss and gain (Newport & Carroll, 2002; Parker-Pope, 2003; Cachelin & Regan, 2006).

You should keep several things in mind when trying to lose weight (Gatchel & Oordt, 2003; Heshka et al., 2003; Freedman, 2011):

- *There is no easy route to weight control.* You will have to make permanent changes in your life to lose weight without gaining it back. The most obvious strategy—cutting down on the amount of food you eat—is just the first step toward a lifetime commitment to changing your eating habits.
- *Keep track of what you eat and what you weigh.* Unless you keep careful records, you won't really know how much you are eating and whether any diet is working.
- *Eat "big" foods.* Eat fiber and foods that are bulky and heavy but low in calories, such as grapes and soup. Such foods trick your body into thinking you've eaten more and thus decrease hunger.
- *Cut out television.* One reason for the epidemic of obesity is the number of hours people in the United States spend viewing television. Not only does watching television preclude other activities that burn calories (even walking around the house is helpful), people often gorge on junk food while watching TV (Hu et al., 2003).
- *Exercise.* Exercise at least 30 consecutive minutes three times each week. When you exercise, you use up fat stored in your body as fuel for muscles, which is measured in calories. As you use up this fat, you will probably lose weight. Almost any activity helps burn calories.
- *Decrease the influence of external social stimuli on your eating behavior.* Serve yourself smaller portions of food, and leave the table before you see what is being served for dessert. Don't even buy snack foods such as nachos and potato chips; if they're not readily available in the kitchen cupboard, you're not apt to eat them. Wrap refrigerated foods in aluminum foil so that you cannot see the contents and be tempted every time you open the refrigerator.
- *Avoid fad diets.* No matter how popular they are at a particular time, extreme diets, including liquid diets, usually don't work in the long run and can be dangerous to your health.
- *Avoid taking any of the numerous diet pills advertised on television that promise quick and easy results.* They don't work.
- *Lose weight with others by joining a support group.* Being part of a group that is working to lose weight will encourage you to keep to your diet.
- *Maintain good eating habits.* When you have reached your desired weight, maintain the new habits you learned while dieting to avoid gaining back the weight you have lost.
- *Set reasonable goals.* Know how much weight you want to lose before you start to diet. Don't try to lose too much weight too quickly, or you may doom yourself to failure. Even small changes in behavior—such as walking 15 minutes a day or eating a few less bites at each meal—can prevent weight gain (Kirk et al., 2003; Freedman, 2011).

PsychTech

Wireless monitoring systems that track what dieters eat and how much they exercise help them to increase self-monitoring, one of the keys to effective weight loss.

Sexual Motivation

Anyone who has seen two dogs mating knows that sexual behavior has a biological basis. Their sexual behavior appears to occur naturally without much prompting on the part of others. A number of genetically controlled factors influence the sexual behavior of nonhuman animals. For instance, animal behavior is affected by the presence of certain hormones in the blood. Moreover, female animals are receptive to sexual advances only during certain relatively limited periods of the year.

Human sexual behavior, by comparison, is more complicated, although the underlying biology is not all that different from that of related species. In males, for example, the *testes* begin to secrete **androgens,** male sex hormones, at puberty. (See Figure 3 for the basic anatomy of the male and female **genitals,** or sex organs.) Not only do androgens produce secondary sex characteristics, such as the growth of body hair and a deepening of the voice, they also increase the sex drive. Because the level of androgen production by the testes is fairly constant, men are capable of (and interested in) sexual activities without any regard to biological cycles. Given the proper stimuli leading to arousal, male sexual behavior can occur at any time (Goldstein, 2000).

androgens Male sex hormones secreted by the testes.

genitals The male and female sex organs.

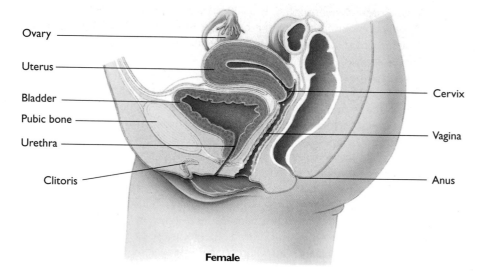

Female

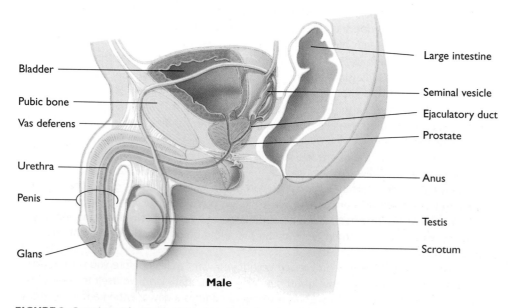

Male

FIGURE 3 Cutaway side views of the female and male sex organs.

Women show a different pattern. When they reach maturity at puberty, the two *ovaries* begin to produce **estrogens** and **progesterone,** female sex hormones. However, those hormones are not produced consistently; instead, their production follows a cyclical pattern. The greatest output occurs during **ovulation,** when an egg is released from the ovaries, making the chances of fertilization by a sperm cell highest. While in nonhumans the period around ovulation is the only time the female is receptive to sex, people are different. Although there are variations in reported sex drive, women are receptive to sex throughout their cycles (Leiblum & Chivers, 2007).

In addition, some evidence suggests that males have a stronger sex drive than females, although the difference may be the result of society's discouragement of female sexuality rather than of innate differences between men and women. It is clear that men think about sex more than women: while 54% of men report thinking about sex every day, only 19% of women report thinking about it on a daily basis (Mendelsohn, 2003; Gangestad et al., 2004; Baumeister & Stillman, 2006; Carvalho & Nobre, 2011).

Though biological factors "prime" people for sex, it takes more than hormones to motivate and produce sexual behavior. In animals the presence of a partner who provides arousing stimuli leads to sexual activity. Humans are considerably more versatile; not only other people but nearly any object, sight, smell, sound, or other stimulus can lead to sexual excitement. Because of prior associations, then, people may be turned on sexually by the smell of perfume or the sound of a favorite song hummed softly in their ears. The reaction to a specific, potentially arousing stimulus, as we shall see, is highly individual—what turns one person on may do just the opposite for another (Benson, 2003).

estrogens Class of female sex hormones.

progesterone A female sex hormone secreted by the ovaries.

ovulation The point at which an egg is released from the ovaries.

MASTURBATION: SOLITARY SEX

If you listened to physicians 75 years ago, you would have been told that **masturbation,** sexual self-stimulation often using the hand to rub the genitals, would lead to a wide variety of physical and mental disorders, ranging from hairy palms to insanity. If those physicians had been correct, however, most of us would be wearing gloves to hide the sight of our hair-covered palms because masturbation is one of the most frequently practiced sexual activities. Some 94% of all males and 63% of all females have masturbated at least once; among college students, the frequency ranges from "never" to "several times a day" (Hunt, 1974; Michael et al., 1994; Polonsky, 2006; Buerkle, 2011).

Men and women typically begin to masturbate for the first time at different ages. Furthermore, men masturbate considerably more often than women, although there are differences in frequency according to age. Male masturbation is most common in the early teens and then declines; females both begin and reach a maximum frequency later. There are also some racial differences: African-American men and women masturbate less than whites do (Oliver & Hyde, 1993; Pinkerton et al., 2002; Das, Parish, & Laumann, 2009).

Although masturbation is often considered an activity to engage in only if no other sexual outlets are available, this view bears little relationship to reality. Close to three-fourths of married men (age 20 to 40) report masturbating an average of 24 times a year, and 68% of the married women in the same age group masturbate an average of 10 times a year (Hunt, 1974; Michael et al., 1994; Das, 2007).

Despite the high incidence of masturbation, attitudes toward it still reflect some of the negative views of yesteryear. For instance, one survey found that around 10% of people who masturbated experienced feelings of guilt; 5% of the males and 1% of the females considered their behavior perverted (Arafat & Cotton, 1974). Despite these negative attitudes, however, most experts on sex view masturbation as a healthy and legitimate—and harmless—sexual activity. In addition, masturbation is seen as providing a means of learning about one's own sexuality and a way of discovering changes in one's body such as the emergence of precancerous lumps (Coleman, 2002; Levin, 2007; Herbenick et al., 2009).

masturbation Sexual self-stimulation.

heterosexuality Sexual attraction and behavior directed to the other sex.

HETEROSEXUALITY

People often believe that the first time they have sexual intercourse they have achieved one of life's major milestones. However, **heterosexuality,** sexual attraction and behavior directed to the other sex, consists of far more than male-female intercourse. Kissing, petting, caressing, massaging, and other forms of sex play are all components of heterosexual behavior. Still, sex researchers' focus has been on the act of intercourse, especially in terms of its first occurrence and its frequency.

PREMARITAL SEX

double standard The view that premarital sex is permissible for males but not for females.

Until fairly recently, premarital sexual intercourse, at least for women, was considered one of the major taboos in our society. Traditionally, women have been warned by society that "nice girls don't do it"; men have been told that premarital sex is okay for them, but they should marry virgins. This view that premarital sex is permissible for males but not for females is called the **double standard** (Liang, 2007; Lyons et al., 2011).

As recently as the 1960s, the majority of adult Americans believed that premarital sex was always wrong. But there has been a dramatic change in public opinion since then. For example, the percentage of middle-age people who say sex before marriage is "not wrong at all" has increased considerably, and overall 60% of Americans say premarital sex is okay. More than half say that living together before marriage is morally acceptable (Thornton & Young-DeMarco, 2001; Harding & Jencks, 2003).

Changes in attitudes toward premarital sex were matched by changes in actual rates of premarital sexual activity. For instance, more than one-half of women between the ages of 15 and 19 have had premarital sexual intercourse. These figures are close to double the number of women in the same age range who reported having intercourse in 1970. Clearly, the trend over the last several decades has been toward more women engaging in premarital sexual activity (Jones, Darroch, & Singh, 2005).

Males, too, have shown an increase in the incidence of premarital sexual intercourse, although the increase has not been as dramatic as it has been for females—probably because the rates for males were higher to begin with. For instance, the first surveys of premarital intercourse carried out in the 1940s showed an incidence of 84% across males of all ages; recent figures are closer to 95%. Moreover, the average age of males' first sexual experience has been declining steadily. Almost half of males have had sexual intercourse by the age of 18; by the time they reach age 20, 88% have had intercourse. For both men and women, 70% of teens have had intercourse by their 19th birthday (Arena, 1984; Hyde, Mezulis, & Abramson, 2008; Allen Guttmacher Institute, 2011).

MARITAL SEX

To judge by the number of articles about sex in heterosexual marriages, one would think that sexual behavior was the number one standard by which marital bliss is measured. Married couples are often concerned that they are having too little sex, too much sex, or the wrong kind of sex (Harvey, Wenzel, & Sprecher, 2005).

Although there are many different dimensions along which sex in marriage is measured, one is certainly the frequency of sexual intercourse. What is typical? As with most other types of sexual activities, there is no easy answer to the question because there are such wide variations in patterns between individuals. We do know that 43% of married couples have sexual intercourse a few times a month and 36% of couples have it two or three times a week. With increasing age and length of marriage, the frequency of intercourse declines. Still, sex continues into late adulthood with almost half of people reporting that they engage in high-quality sexual activity at least once a month (Michael et al., 1994; Powell, 2006).

Although early research found **extramarital sex** to be widespread, the current reality appears to be otherwise. According to surveys, 85% of married women and more than 75% of married men are faithful to their spouses. Furthermore, the median number of sex partners inside and outside of marriage since the age of 18 was six for men and two for women. Accompanying these numbers is a high, consistent degree of disapproval of extramarital sex, with nine of ten people saying that it is "always" or "almost always" wrong (Michael et al., 1994; Daines, 2006; Whisman & Snyder, 2007).

HOMOSEXUALITY AND BISEXUALITY

Homosexuals are sexually attracted to members of their own sex, whereas **bisexuals** are sexually attracted to people of the same sex and the other sex. Many male homosexuals prefer the term *gay* and female homosexuals prefer the term *lesbian* because they refer to a broader array of attitudes and lifestyles than the term *homosexual*, which focuses on the sexual act.

The number of people who choose same-sex sexual partners at one time or another is considerable. Estimates suggest that around 20–25% of males and about 15% of females have had at least one gay or lesbian experience during adulthood. The exact number of people who identify themselves as exclusively homosexual has proved difficult to gauge; some estimates are as low as 1.1% and some as high as 10%. Most experts suggest that 5–10% of both men and women are exclusively gay or lesbian during extended periods of their lives (Hunt, 1974; Sells, 1994; Firestein, 1996).

Although people often view homosexuality and heterosexuality as two completely distinct sexual orientations, the issue is not that simple. Pioneering sex researcher Alfred Kinsey acknowledged this when he considered sexual orientation along a scale or continuum with "exclusively homosexual" at one end and "exclusively heterosexual" at the other. In the middle were people who showed both homosexual and heterosexual behavior. Kinsey's approach suggests that sexual orientation is dependent on a person's sexual feelings and behaviors and romantic feelings (Weinberg, Williams, & Pryor, 1991).

What determines whether people become homosexual or heterosexual? Although there are a number of theories, none has proved completely satisfactory.

Some explanations for sexual orientation are biological, suggesting that there are genetic causes. Evidence for a genetic origin of sexual orientation comes from studies of identical twins. The studies found that when one twin identified himself or herself as homosexual, the occurrence of homosexuality in the other twin was higher than it was in the general population. Such results occur even for twins who have been separated early in life and who therefore are not necessarily raised in similar social environments (Kirk, Bailey, & Martin, 2000; Gooren, 2006; LeVay, 2011).

Hormones also may play a role in determining sexual orientation. For example, research shows that women exposed before birth to DES (diethylstilbestrol—a drug their mothers took to avoid miscarriage) were more likely to be homosexual or bisexual (Meyer-Bahlburg, 1997).

Some evidence suggests that differences in brain structures may be related to sexual orientation. For instance, the structure of the anterior hypothalamus, an area of the brain that governs sexual behavior, differs in male homosexuals and heterosexuals. Similarly, other research shows that, compared with heterosexual men or women, gay men have a larger anterior commissure, which is a bundle of neurons connecting the right and left hemispheres of the brain (LeVay, 1993; Byne, 1996; Witelson et al., 2008).

However, research suggesting that biological causes are at the root of homosexuality is not conclusive because most findings are based on only small samples of individuals. Still, the possibility is real that some inherited or biological factor exists that predisposes people toward homosexuality if certain environmental conditions are met (Veniegas, 2000; Teodorov et al., 2002; Rahman, Kumari, & Wilson, 2003).

extramarital sex Sexual activity between a married person and someone who is not his or her spouse.

homosexuals Persons who are sexually attracted to members of their own sex.

bisexuals Persons who are sexually attracted to people of the same sex and the other sex.

Little evidence suggests that sexual orientation is brought about by child-rearing practices or family dynamics. Although proponents of psychoanalytic theories once argued that the nature of the parent-child relationship can produce homosexuality (e.g., Freud, 1922/1959), research evidence does not support such explanations (Isay, 1994; Roughton, 2002).

Another explanation for sexual orientation rests on learning theory (Masters & Johnson, 1979). According to this view, sexual orientation is learned through rewards and punishments in much the same way that we may learn to prefer swimming over tennis. For example, a young adolescent who had an unpleasant heterosexual experience might develop disagreeable associations with the other sex. If the same person had a rewarding, pleasant gay or lesbian experience, homosexuality might be incorporated into his or her sexual fantasies. If such fantasies are used during later sexual activities—such as masturbation—they may be positively reinforced through orgasm, and the association of homosexual behavior and sexual pleasure eventually may cause homosexuality to become the preferred form of sexual behavior.

Although the learning-theory explanation is plausible, several difficulties rule it out as a definitive explanation. Because our society has traditionally held homosexuality in low esteem, one ought to expect that the negative treatment of homosexual behavior would outweigh the rewards attached to it. Furthermore, children growing up with a gay or lesbian parent are statistically unlikely to become homosexual, which thus contradicts the notion that homosexual behavior may be learned from others (Golombok et al., 1995; Victor & Fish, 1995; Tasker, 2005).

Because of the difficulty in finding a consistent explanation for sexual orientation, we can't definitively answer the question of what determines it. It seems unlikely that any single factor orients a person toward homosexuality or heterosexuality. Instead, it seems reasonable to assume that a combination of biological and environmental factors is involved (Bem, 1996; Hyde, Mezulis, & Abramson, 2008).

Although we don't know at this point exactly why people develop a certain sexual orientation, one thing is clear: There is no relationship between sexual orientation and psychological adjustment. Gays, lesbians, and bisexuals generally enjoy the same quality of mental and physical health that heterosexuals do, although the discrimination they experience may produce higher rates of some disorders, such as depression (Poteat & Espelage, 2007).

Bisexuals and homosexuals also hold equivalent ranges and types of attitudes about themselves that are independent of sexual orientation. For such reasons, the

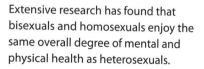

Extensive research has found that bisexuals and homosexuals enjoy the same overall degree of mental and physical health as heterosexuals.

American Psychological Association and other major mental health organizations have endorsed efforts to eliminate discrimination against gays and lesbians. (Cochran, 2000; Perez, DeBord, & Bieschke, 2000; Morris, Waldo, & Rothblum, 2001).

Furthermore, attitudes toward homosexuality have changed dramatically in the last two decades, with younger generations in particular becoming more positive. For example, 64% of those under 30 support same-sex marriage. Overall, tolerance for gays and lesbians has grown substantially in the United States (NORC/University of Chicago, 2011).

TRANSSEXUALISM

Transsexuals are people who believe they were born with the body of the other gender. In fundamental ways, transsexualism represents less of a sexual difficulty than a gender issue involving one's sexual identity (Meyerowitz, 2004; Heath, 2006).

Transsexuals sometimes seek sex-change operations in which their existing genitals are surgically removed and the genitals of the desired sex are fashioned. Several steps, including intensive counseling, hormone injections, and living as a member of the desired sex for several years, precede surgery, which is, not surprisingly, highly complicated. The outcome, though, can be quite positive (O'Keefe & Fox, 2003; Stegerwald & Janson, 2003; Lobato, Koff, & Manenti, 2006; Richards, 2011).

Transsexualism is part of a broader category known as transgenderism. The term *transgenderism* encompasses not only transsexuals, but also people who view themselves as a third gender, transvestites (who dress in the clothes of the other gender), or others who believe that traditional male-female gender classifications inadequately characterize them (Prince, 2005; Hyde, Mezulis, & Abramson, 2008).

Transsexuals are distinct from individuals who are known as *intersex* or by the older term *hermaphrodite*. An intersex person is born with an atypical combination of sexual organs or chromosomal or gene patterns. In some cases, they are born with both male and female sexual organs, or the organs are ambiguous. It is an extremely rare condition found in one in 4,500 births. Intersexism involves a complex mix of physiological and psychological issues (Lehrman, 2007; Diamond, 2009).

transsexuals People who believe they were born with the body of the other gender.

The Needs for Achievement, Affiliation, and Power

Although hunger may be one of the more potent primary drives in our day-to-day lives, powerful secondary drives that have no clear biological basis also motivate us. Among the more prominent of these are the needs for achievement, affiliation, and power.

THE NEED FOR ACHIEVEMENT: STRIVING FOR EXCELLENCE

The **need for achievement** is a stable, learned characteristic in which a person obtains satisfaction by striving for and achieving challenging goals (McClelland et al., 1953). People with a high need for achievement seek out situations in which they can compete against some objective standard—such as grades, money, or winning a game—and prove themselves successful.

But people who have a high need for achievement are selective when it comes to picking their challenges: They tend to avoid situations in which success will come too easily (which would be unchallenging) or situations in which success is highly unlikely. Instead, people high in achievement motivation generally choose tasks that are of intermediate difficulty (Speirs-Neumeister & Finch, 2006; Mills, 2011).

need for achievement A stable, learned characteristic in which a person obtains satisfaction by striving for and achieving challenging goals.

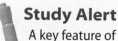

Study Alert

A key feature of people with a high need for achievement is that they prefer tasks of *moderate* difficulty.

FIGURE 4 This ambiguous picture is similar to those used in the Thematic Apperception Test to determine people's underlying motivation. What do you see? Do you think your response is related to your motivation? (Source: © 1943 by the President and Fellows of Harvard College; 1971 by Henry A. Murray.)

need for affiliation An interest in establishing and maintaining relationships with other people.

need for power A tendency to seek impact, control, or influence over others and to be seen as a powerful individual.

In contrast, people with low achievement motivation tend to be motivated primarily by a desire to avoid failure. As a result, they seek out easy tasks so they are sure to avoid failure, or they seek out very difficult tasks for which failure has no negative implications because almost anyone would fail at them. People with a high fear of failure will stay away from tasks of intermediate difficulty because they may fail where others have been successful (Martin & Marsh, 2002; Puca, 2005; Morrone & Pintrich, 2006).

A high need for achievement generally produces positive outcomes, at least in a success-oriented culture such as Western society. For instance, people motivated by a high need for achievement are more likely to attend college than their low-achievement counterparts; once they are in college, they tend to receive higher grades in classes that are related to their future careers. Furthermore, high achievement motivation indicates future economic and occupational success (McClelland, 1985; Thrash & Elliot, 2002).

How can we measure a person's need for achievement? The measuring instrument used most frequently is the *Thematic Apperception Test (TAT)*. Using the TAT, an examiner shows a series of ambiguous pictures, such as the one in Figure 4. The examiner tells participants to write a story that describes what is happening, who the people are, what led to the situation, what the people are thinking or wanting, and what will happen next. Researchers then use a standard scoring system to determine the amount of achievement imagery in people's stories. For example, someone who writes a story in which the main character strives to beat an opponent, studies in order to do well at some task, or works hard in order to get a promotion shows clear signs of an achievement orientation. The inclusion of such achievement-related imagery in the participants' stories is assumed to indicate an unusually high degree of concern with—and therefore a relatively strong need for—achievement (Tuerlinckx, DeBoeck, & Lens, 2002; Verdon, 2011).

THE NEED FOR AFFILIATION: STRIVING FOR FRIENDSHIP

Few of us choose to lead our lives as hermits. Why?

One main reason is that most people have a **need for affiliation,** an interest in establishing and maintaining relationships with other people. Individuals with a high need for affiliation write TAT stories that emphasize the desire to maintain or reinstate friendships and show concern over being rejected by friends.

People who have higher affiliation needs are particularly sensitive to relationships with others. They desire to be with their friends more of the time and alone less often, compared with people who are lower in the need for affiliation. However, gender is a greater determinant of how much time is actually spent with friends: Regardless of their affiliative orientation, female students spend significantly more time with their friends and less time alone than male students do (Cantwell & Andrews, 2002; Johnson, 2004; Semykina & Linz, 2007).

THE NEED FOR POWER: STRIVING FOR IMPACT ON OTHERS

If your fantasies include becoming president of the United States or running Microsoft, your dreams may reflect a high need for power. The **need for power,** a tendency to seek impact, control, or influence over others and to be seen as a powerful individual, is an additional type of motivation (Winter, 2007; Zians, 2007; Pratto et al., 2011).

As you might expect, people with strong needs for power are more apt to belong to organizations and seek office than are those low in the need for power. They also tend to work in professions in which their power needs may be fulfilled, such as business management and—you may or may not be surprised—teaching (Jenkins, 1994). In addition, they seek to display the trappings of power. Even in college, they are more likely to collect prestigious possessions, such as electronic equipment and sports cars.

Some significant gender differences exist in the display of need for power. Men with high power needs tend to show unusually high levels of aggression, drink heavily, act in a sexually exploitative manner, and participate more frequently in competitive sports—behaviors that collectively represent somewhat extravagant, flamboyant behavior. In contrast, women display their power needs with more restraint; this is congruent with traditional societal constraints on women's behavior. Women with high power needs are more apt than men to channel those needs in a socially responsible manner, such as by showing concern for others or displaying highly nurturing behavior (Winter, 1995, 2007; Schubert & Koole, 2009).

RECAP/EVALUATE/RETHINK

RECAP

LO 25-1 What biological and social factors underlie hunger?

- Eating behavior is subject to homeostasis, as most people's weight stays within a relatively stable range. The hypothalamus in the brain is central to the regulation of food intake. (p. 299)
- Social factors, such as mealtimes, cultural food preferences, and other learned habits, also play a role in the regulation of eating by determining when, what, and how much one eats. An oversensitivity to social cues and an insensitivity to internal cues may also be related to obesity. In addition, obesity may be caused by an unusually high weight set point—the weight the body attempts to maintain—and genetic factors. (p. 299)

LO 25-2 What are the varieties of sexual behavior?

- Although biological factors, such as the presence of androgens (male sex hormones) and estrogens and progesterone (female sex hormones), prime people for sex, almost any kind of stimulus can produce sexual arousal depending on a person's prior sexual experience. (p. 304)
- The frequency of masturbation is high, particularly for males. Although attitudes toward masturbation are increasingly liberal, they have traditionally been negative even though no negative consequences have been detected. (p. 305)
- Heterosexuality, or sexual attraction to members of the other sex, is the most common sexual orientation. (p. 306)
- The double standard by which premarital sex is thought to be more permissible for men than for women has declined, particularly among young people. For many people, the double standard has been replaced by endorsement of "permissiveness with affection," the view that premarital intercourse is permissible if it occurs in the context of a loving and committed relationship. (p. 306)

- Homosexuals are sexually attracted to members of their own sex; bisexuals are sexually attracted to people of the same sex and the other sex. No explanation for why people become homosexual has been confirmed; among the possibilities are genetic or biological factors, childhood and family influences, and prior learning experiences and conditioning. However, no relationship exists between sexual orientation and psychological adjustment. (p. 307)

LO 25-3 How are needs relating to achievement, affiliation, and power motivation exhibited?

- Need for achievement refers to the stable, learned characteristic in which a person strives to attain a level of excellence. Need for achievement is usually measured through the Thematic Apperception Test (TAT), a series of pictures about which a person writes a story. (p. 309)
- The need for affiliation is a concern with establishing and maintaining relationships with others, whereas the need for power is a tendency to seek to exert an impact on others. (p. 310)

EVALUATE

1. Match the following terms with their definitions:
   1. Hypothalamus
   2. Lateral hypothalamic damage
   3. Ventromedial hypothalamic damage

   a. Leads to refusal of food and starvation
   b. Responsible for monitoring food intake
   c. Causes extreme overeating

2. The _____ _____ _____ is the specific level of weight the body strives to maintain.
3. _____ is the rate at which the body produces and expends energy.
4. Although the incidence of masturbation among young adults is high, once men and women become involved in intimate relationships, they typically cease masturbating. True or false?

5. The increase in premarital sex in recent years has been greater for women than for men. True or false?

6. Julio is the type of person who constantly strives for excellence. He feels intense satisfaction when he is able to master a new task. Julio most likely has a high need for _____.

7. Debbie's Thematic Apperception Test (TAT) story depicts a young girl who is rejected by one of her peers and seeks to regain her friendship. What major type of motivation is Debbie displaying in her story?
   a. Need for achievement
   b. Need for motivation
   c. Need for affiliation
   d. Need for power

RETHINK

1. In what ways do societal expectations, expressed by television shows and commercials, contribute to both obesity and excessive concern about weight loss? How could television contribute to better eating habits and attitudes toward weight? Should it be required to do so?

2. *From the perspective of a human resources specialist:* How might you use characteristics such as need for achievement, need for power, and need for affiliation to select workers for jobs? What additional criteria would you have to consider?

Answers to Evaluate Questions

1. 1-b, 2-a, 3-c; 2. weight set point; 3. Metabolism; 4. false; 5. true; 6. achievement; 7. c.

KEY TERMS

obesity p. 296
weight set point p. 299
metabolism p. 299
anorexia nervosa p. 301
bulimia p. 301

androgens p. 304
genitals p. 304
estrogens p. 305
progesterone p. 305
ovulation p. 305

masturbation p. 305
heterosexuality p. 306
double standard p. 306
extramarital sex p. 307
homosexuals p. 307

bisexuals p. 307
transsexuals p. 309
need for achievement p. 309
need for affiliation p. 310
need for power p. 310

Understanding Emotional Experiences

Karl Andrews held in his hands the envelope he had been waiting for. It could be the ticket to his future: an offer of admission to his first-choice college. But what was it going to say? He knew it could go either way. His grades were pretty good, and he had been involved in some extracurricular activities, but his SAT scores had not been terrific. He felt so nervous that his hands shook as he opened the thin envelope (not a good sign, he thought). Here it comes. "Dear Mr. Andrews," it read. "The Trustees of the University are pleased to admit you. . . ." That was all he needed to see. With a whoop of excitement, Karl found himself jumping up and down gleefully. A rush of emotion overcame him as it sank in that he had, in fact, been accepted. He was on his way.

At one time or another, all of us have experienced the strong feelings that accompany both very pleasant and very negative experiences. Perhaps we have felt the thrill of getting a sought-after job, the joy of being in love, the sorrow over someone's death, or the anguish of inadvertently hurting someone. Moreover, we experience such reactions on a less intense level throughout our daily lives with such things as the pleasure of a friendship, the enjoyment of a movie, and the embarrassment of breaking a borrowed item.

Despite the varied nature of these feelings, they all represent emotions. Although everyone has an idea of what an emotion is, formally defining the concept has proved to be an elusive task. Here, we'll use a general definition: **Emotions** are feelings that generally have both physiological and cognitive elements and that influence behavior.

Think, for example, about how it feels to be happy. First, we obviously experience a feeling that we can differentiate from other emotions. It is likely that we also experience some identifiable physical changes in our bodies: Perhaps the heart rate increases, or—as in the example of Karl Andrews—we find ourselves "jumping for joy." Finally, the emotion probably encompasses cognitive elements: Our understanding and evaluation of the meaning of what is happening prompts our feelings of happiness.

It is also possible, however, to experience an emotion without the presence of cognitive elements. For instance, we may react with fear to an unusual or novel situation (such as coming into contact with an erratic, unpredictable individual), or we may experience pleasure over sexual excitation without having cognitive awareness or understanding of just what makes the situation exciting.

Some psychologists argue that entirely separate systems govern cognitive responses and emotional responses. A current controversy focuses on whether the emotional response predominates over the cognitive response or vice versa. Some theorists suggest that we first respond to a situation with an emotional reaction and later try to understand it. For example, we may enjoy a complex modern symphony without at first understanding it or knowing why we like it. In contrast, other theorists propose that people first develop cognitions about a situation and then react emotionally. This school of thought suggests that we must think about and understand a stimulus or situation, relating it to what we already know, before we can react on an emotional level (Murphy & Zajonc, 1993; Lazarus, 1995; Oatley, Keltner, & Jenkins, 2006; Martin & Kerns, 2011).

Learning Outcomes

LO 26-1 What are emotions, and how do we experience them?

LO 26-2 What are the functions of emotions?

LO 26-3 What are the explanations for emotions?

LO 26-4 How does nonverbal behavior relate to the expression of emotions?

emotions Feelings that generally have both physiological and cognitive elements and that influence behavior.

Because proponents of both sides of this debate can cite research to support their viewpoints, the question is far from resolved. Perhaps the sequence varies from situation to situation with emotions predominating in some instances and cognitive processes occurring first in others. Both sides agree that we can experience emotions that involve little or no conscious thought. We may not know why we're afraid of mice because we understand objectively that they represent no danger, but we may still be frightened when we see them. Neuroimaging studies of the brain may help resolve this debate as well as others about the nature of emotions (Barrett & Wager, 2006; Niedenthal, 2007; Karaszewski, 2008).

The Functions of Emotions

Imagine what it would be like if we didn't experience emotion. We would have no depths of despair, no depression, and no remorse, but at the same time we would also have no happiness, joy, or love. Obviously, life would be considerably less satisfying and even dull if we lacked the capacity to sense and express emotion.

But do emotions serve any purpose beyond making life interesting? Indeed they do. Psychologists have identified several important functions that emotions play in our daily lives (Frederickson & Branigan, 2005; Frijda, 2005; Gross, 2006; Siemer, Mauss, & Gross, 2007; Rolls, 2011). Among the most important of those functions are the following:

- *Preparing us for action.* Emotions act as a link between events in our environment and our responses. For example, if you saw an angry dog charging toward you, your emotional reaction (fear) would be associated with physiological arousal of the sympathetic division of the autonomic nervous system, the activation of the "fight-or-flight" response.
- *Shaping our future behavior.* Emotions promote learning that will help us make appropriate responses in the future. For instance, your emotional response to unpleasant events teaches you to avoid similar circumstances in the future.
- *Helping us interact more effectively with others.* We often communicate the emotions we experience through our verbal and nonverbal behaviors, making our emotions obvious to observers. These behaviors can act as a signal to observers, allowing them to understand better what we are experiencing and to help them predict our future behavior.

Determining the Range of Emotions: Labeling Our Feelings

If we were to list the words in the English language that have been used to describe emotions, we would end up with at least 500 examples (Averill, 1975). The list would range from such obvious emotions as *happiness* and *fear* to less common ones, such as *adventurousness* and *pensiveness*.

One challenge for psychologists has been to sort through this list to identify the most important, fundamental emotions. Theorists have hotly contested the issue of cataloging emotions and have come up with different lists, depending on how they define the concept of emotion. In fact, some reject the question entirely, saying that *no* set of emotions should be singled out as most basic and that emotions are best understood by breaking them down into their component parts. Other researchers argue for looking at emotions in terms of a hierarchy, dividing them into positive and negative categories and then organizing them into increasingly narrower subcategories (see Figure 1; Manstead, Frijda, & Fischer, 2003; Dillard & Shen, 2007; Livingstone et al., 2011).

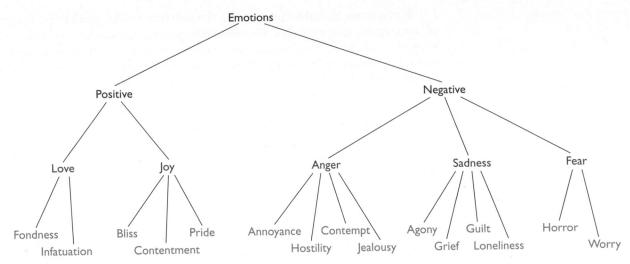

FIGURE 1 One approach to organizing emotions is to use a hierarchy, which divides emotions into increasingly narrow subcategories. (Source: Adapted from Fischer, Shaver, & Carnochan, 1990.)

Still, most researchers suggest that a list of basic emotions would include, at a minimum, happiness, anger, fear, sadness, and disgust. Other lists are broader, including emotions such as surprise, contempt, guilt, and joy (Ekman, 1994a; Shweder, 1994; Tracy & Robins, 2004).

One difficulty in defining a basic set of emotions is that substantial differences exist in descriptions of emotions among various cultures. For instance, Germans report experiencing *schadenfreude*, a feeling of pleasure over another person's difficulties, and the Japanese experience *hagaii*, a mood of vulnerable heartache colored by frustration. In Tahiti, people experience *musu*, a feeling of reluctance to yield to unreasonable demands made by one's parents.

Finding *schadenfreude*, *hagaii*, or *musu* in a particular culture doesn't mean that the members of other cultures are incapable of experiencing such emotions, of course. It suggests, though, that fitting a particular emotion into a linguistic category to describe that emotion may make it easier to discuss, contemplate, and perhaps experience (Russell & Sato, 1995; Li, Kuppens, et al., 2006; van Dijk et al., 2011).

The Roots of Emotions

I've never been so angry before; I feel my heart pounding, and I'm trembling all over. . . . I don't know how I'll get through the performance. I feel like my stomach is filled with butterflies. . . . That was quite a mistake I made! My face must be incredibly red. . . . When I heard the footsteps in the night, I was so frightened that I couldn't catch my breath.

If you examine our language, you will find that there are literally dozens of ways to describe how we feel when we experience an emotion and that the language we use to describe emotions is, for the most part, based on the physical symptoms that are associated with a particular emotional experience (Kobayashi, Schallert, & Ogren, 2003; Manstead & Wagner, 2004; Spackman, Fujiki, & Brinton, 2006).

Consider, for instance, the experience of fear. Pretend that it is late on New Year's Eve. You are walking down a dark road, and you hear a stranger approaching behind you. It is clear that he is not trying to hurry by but is coming directly toward you. You think about what you will do if the stranger attempts to rob you or, worse, hurt you in some way.

While these thoughts are running through your head, something dramatic will be happening to your body. The most likely reactions, which are associated with activation of the autonomic nervous system, include an increase in your rate of breathing, an acceleration of your heart rate, a widening of your pupils (to increase visual sensitivity), and a dryness in your mouth as the functioning of your salivary glands and in fact of your entire digestive system ceases. At the same time, though, your sweat glands probably will increase their activity because increased sweating will help you rid yourself of the excess heat developed by any emergency activity in which you engage.

Of course, all these physiological changes are likely to occur without your awareness. At the same time, though, the emotional experience accompanying them will be obvious to you: You most surely would report being fearful.

Although it is easy to describe the general physical reactions that accompany emotions, defining the specific role that those physiological responses play in the experience of emotions has proved to be a major puzzle for psychologists. As we shall see, some theorists suggest that specific bodily reactions *cause* us to experience a particular emotion—we experience fear, for instance, *because* the heart is pounding and we are breathing deeply. In contrast, other theorists suggest that the physiological reaction results from the experience of an emotion. In this view, we experience fear, and as a result the heart pounds and our breathing deepens.

THE JAMES-LANGE THEORY: DO GUT REACTIONS EQUAL EMOTIONS?

To William James and Carl Lange, who were among the first researchers to explore the nature of emotions, emotional experience is, very simply, a reaction to instinctive bodily events that occur as a response to some situation or event in the environment. This view is summarized in James's statement, "We feel sorry because we cry, angry because we strike, afraid because we tremble" (James, 1890).

James and Lange took the view that the instinctive response of crying at a loss leads us to feel sorrow, that striking out at someone who frustrates us results in our feeling anger, that trembling at a menacing threat causes us to feel fear. They suggested that for every major emotion there is an accompanying physiological or "gut" reaction of internal organs—called a *visceral experience*. It is this specific pattern of visceral response that leads us to label the emotional experience.

In sum, James and Lange proposed that we experience emotions as a result of physiological changes that produce specific sensations. The brain interprets these sensations as specific kinds of emotional experiences (see the first part of Figure 2). This view has come to be called the **James-Lange theory of emotion** (Laird & Bresler, 1990; Cobos et al., 2002).

The James-Lange theory has some serious drawbacks, however. For the theory to be valid, visceral changes would have to occur relatively quickly because we experience some emotions—such as fear upon hearing a stranger rapidly approaching on a dark night—almost instantaneously. Yet emotional experiences frequently occur even before there is time for certain physiological changes to be set into motion. Because of the slowness with which some visceral changes take place, it is hard to see how they could be the source of immediate emotional experience.

The James-Lange theory poses another difficulty: Physiological arousal does not invariably produce emotional experience. For example, a person who is jogging has an increased heartbeat and respiration rate as well as many of the other physiological changes associated with certain emotions. Yet joggers typically do not think of such changes in terms of emotion. There cannot be a one-to-one correspondence, then, between visceral changes and emotional experience. Visceral changes by themselves may not be sufficient to produce emotion.

Finally, our internal organs produce a relatively limited range of sensations. Although some types of physiological changes are associated with specific emotional

James-Lange theory of emotion The belief that emotional experience is a reaction to bodily events occurring as a result of an external situation ("I feel sad because I am crying").

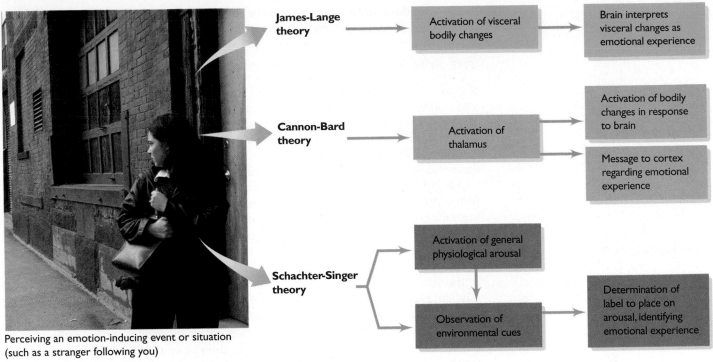

Perceiving an emotion-inducing event or situation (such as a stranger following you)

FIGURE 2 A comparison of three models of emotion.

experiences, it is difficult to imagine how each of the myriad emotions that people are capable of experiencing could be the result of a unique visceral change. Many emotions actually are associated with relatively similar sorts of visceral changes, a fact that contradicts the James-Lange theory (Davidson et al., 1994; Cameron, 2002; Rinaman, Banihashemi, & Koehnle, 2011).

THE CANNON-BARD THEORY: PHYSIOLOGICAL REACTIONS AS THE RESULT OF EMOTIONS

In response to the difficulties inherent in the James-Lange theory, Walter Cannon and later Philip Bard suggested an alternative view. In what has come to be known as the **Cannon-Bard theory of emotion,** they proposed the model illustrated in the second part of Figure 2 (Cannon, 1929). This theory rejects the view that physiological arousal alone leads to the perception of emotion. Instead, the theory assumes that both physiological arousal *and* the emotional experience are produced simultaneously by the same nerve stimulus, which Cannon and Bard suggested emanates from the thalamus in the brain.

The theory states that after we perceive an emotion-producing stimulus, the thalamus is the initial site of the emotional response. Next, the thalamus sends a signal to the autonomic nervous system, thereby producing a visceral response. At the same time, the thalamus also communicates a message to the cerebral cortex regarding the nature of the emotion being experienced. Hence, it is not necessary for different emotions to have unique physiological patterns associated with them—as long as the message sent to the cerebral cortex differs according to the specific emotion.

The Cannon-Bard theory seems to have been accurate in rejecting the view that physiological arousal alone accounts for emotions. However, more recent research has led to some important modifications of the theory. For one thing, we now understand that the hypothalamus and the limbic system, not the thalamus, play a major role in emotional experience. In addition, the simultaneous occurrence of the physiological and emotional responses, which is a fundamental assumption

Cannon-Bard theory of emotion The belief that both physiological arousal and emotional experience are produced simultaneously by the same nerve stimulus.

Study Alert

Use Figure 2 to distinguish the three classic theories of emotion (James-Lange, Cannon-Bard, and Schachter-Singer).

of the Cannon-Bard theory, has yet to be demonstrated conclusively. This ambiguity has allowed room for yet another theory of emotions: the Schachter-Singer theory.

THE SCHACHTER-SINGER THEORY: EMOTIONS AS LABELS

Schachter-Singer theory of emotion
The belief that emotions are determined jointly by a nonspecific kind of physiological arousal and its interpretation, based on environmental cues.

Suppose that as you are being followed down that dark street on New Year's Eve, you notice a man being followed by another shady figure on the other side of the street. Now assume that instead of reacting with fear, the man begins to laugh and act gleeful. Would the reactions of this other individual be sufficient to lay your fears to rest? Might you, in fact, decide there is nothing to fear and get into the spirit of the evening by beginning to feel happiness and glee yourself?

According to an explanation that focuses on the role of cognition, the **Schachter-Singer theory of emotion,** this might very well happen. This approach to explaining emotions emphasizes that we identify the emotion we are experiencing by observing our environment and comparing ourselves with others (Schachter & Singer, 1962).

Schachter and Singer's classic experiment found evidence for this hypothesis. In the study, participants were told that they would receive an injection of a vitamin. In reality, they were given epinephrine, a drug that causes responses that typically occur during strong emotional reactions, such as an increase in physiological arousal, including higher heart and respiration rates and a reddening of the face. The members of both groups were then placed individually in a situation where a confederate of the experimenter acted in one of two ways. In one condition he acted angry and hostile; in the other condition he behaved as if he were exuberantly happy.

The purpose of the experiment was to determine how the participants would react emotionally to the confederate's behavior. When they were asked to describe their own emotional state at the end of the experiment, the participants exposed to the angry confederate reported that they felt angry, whereas those exposed to the happy confederate reported feeling happy. In sum, the results suggest that participants turned to the environment and the behavior of others for an explanation of the physiological arousal they were experiencing.

The results of the Schachter-Singer experiment, then, supported a cognitive view of emotions in which emotions are determined jointly by a relatively nonspecific kind of physiological arousal *and* the labeling of that arousal on the basis of cues from the environment (refer to the third part of Figure 2). Although later research has found that arousal is more specific than Schachter and Singer believed, they were right in assuming that when the source of physiological arousal is unclear, we may look to our surroundings to determine what we are experiencing.

CONTEMPORARY PERSPECTIVES ON THE NEUROSCIENCE OF EMOTIONS

When Schachter and Singer carried out their groundbreaking experiment in the early 1960s, the ways in which they could evaluate the physiology that accompanies emotion were relatively limited. However, advances in the measurement of the nervous system and other parts of the body have allowed researchers to examine more closely the biological responses involved in emotion. As a result, contemporary research on emotion points to a revision of earlier views that physiological responses associated with emotions are undifferentiated. Instead, evidence is growing that specific patterns of biological arousal are associated with individual emotions (Vaitl, Schienle, & Stark, 2005; Woodson, 2006; Stifter, Dollar, & Cipriano, 2011).

For instance, researchers have found that specific emotions produce activation of very different portions of the brain. In one study, participants undergoing positron emission tomography (PET) brain scans were asked to recall events that made them sad, such as deaths and funerals, or events that made them feel happy, such as

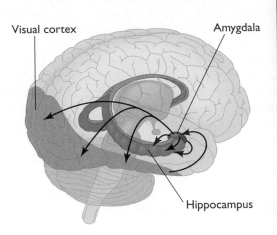

Visual cortex

Amygdala

Hippocampus

FIGURE 3 Connections from the amygdala, seen here in red, allow it to mediate many of the autonomic expressions of emotional states through the hippocampus (purple) and visual cortex (tan). (Source: From Dolan, R. J. (2002). Emotion, cognition, and behavior. *Science, 298*, no. 5596, 1191–1194 (Figure 1, p. 1192). Drawing of brain reprinted with permission from AAAS. http://www.sciencemag.org/content/298/5596/1191.full)

weddings and births. They also looked at photos of faces that appeared to be happy or sad. The results of the PET scans were clear: Happiness was related to a decrease in activity in certain areas of the cerebral cortex, whereas sadness was associated with increases in activity in particular portions of the cortex (George et al., 1995; Hamann et al., 2002; Prohovnik et al., 2004).

In addition, the *amygdala,* in the brain's temporal lobe, is important in the experience of emotions for it provides a link between the perception of an emotion-producing stimulus and the recall of that stimulus later. For example, if we've once been attacked by a vicious pit bull, the amygdala processes that information and leads us to react with fear when we see a pit bull later—an example of a classically conditioned fear response (Miller et al., 2005; Berntson et al., 2007; Kensinger, 2007; LaBar, 2007; Pessoa, 2011).

Because neural pathways connect the amygdala, the visual cortex, and the *hippocampus* (which plays an important role in the consolidation of memories), some scientists speculate that emotion-related stimuli can be processed and responded to almost instantaneously (see Figure 3). This immediate response occurs so rapidly that higher-order, more rational thinking, which takes more time, seems not to be involved initially. In a slower but more thoughtful response to emotion-evoking stimuli, emotion-related sensory information is first evaluated and then sent on to the amygdala. It appears that the quicker system offers an immediate response to emotion-evoking stimuli, whereas the slower system helps confirm a threat and prepare a more thoughtful response (Dolan, 2002).

MAKING SENSE OF THE MULTIPLE PERSPECTIVES ON EMOTION

As new approaches to emotion continue to develop, it is reasonable to ask why so many theories of emotion exist and, perhaps more important, which one provides the most complete explanation. Actually, we have only scratched the surface. There are almost as many explanatory theories of emotion as there are individual emotions (e.g., Manstead, Frijda, & Fischer, 2003; Frijda, 2005; Prinz, 2007; Herzberg, 2009).

Why are theories of emotion so plentiful? For one thing, emotions are not a simple phenomenon but are intertwined closely with motivation, cognition, neuroscience, and a host of related branches of psychology. For example, evidence from brain imaging studies shows that even when people come to supposedly rational, nonemotional decisions—such as making moral, philosophical judgments—emotions come into play (Greene et al., 2001).

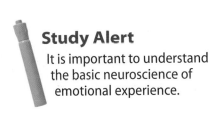

Study Alert

It is important to understand the basic neuroscience of emotional experience.

In short, emotions are such complex phenomena, encompassing both biological and cognitive aspects, that no single theory has been able to explain fully all the facets of emotional experience. Furthermore, contradictory evidence of one sort or another challenges each approach, and therefore no theory has proved invariably accurate in its predictions.

This abundance of perspectives on emotion is not a cause for despair—or unhappiness, fear, or any other negative emotion. It simply reflects the fact that psychology is an evolving, developing science. As we gather more evidence, the specific answers to questions about the nature of emotions will become clearer.

Exploring DIVERSITY

Do People in All Cultures Express Emotion Similarly?

Consider, for a moment, the six photos displayed in Figure 4. Can you identify the emotions being expressed by the person in each of the photos?

If you are a good judge of facial expressions, you will conclude that these expressions display six of the basic emotions: happiness, anger, sadness, surprise, disgust, and fear. Hundreds of studies of nonverbal behavior show that these emotions are consistently distinct and identifiable even by untrained observers (Ekman, 2007).

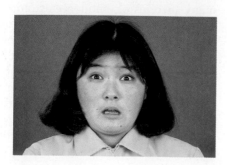

FIGURE 4 These photos demonstrate six of the primary emotions: happiness, anger, sadness, surprise, disgust, and fear.

Interestingly, these six emotions are not unique to members of Western cultures; rather, they constitute the basic emotions expressed universally by members of the human race, regardless of where individuals have been raised and what learning experiences they have had. Psychologist Paul Ekman convincingly demonstrated this point when he studied members of an isolated New Guinea jungle tribe who had had almost no contact with Westerners (Ekman, 1972). The people of the tribe did not speak or understand English, had never seen a movie, and had very limited experience with Caucasians before Ekman's arrival. Yet their nonverbal responses to emotion-evoking stories, as well as their ability to identify basic emotions, were quite similar to those of Westerners.

Being so isolated, the New Guineans could not have learned from Westerners to recognize or produce similar facial expressions. Instead, their similar abilities and manner of responding emotionally appear to have been present innately. Although one could argue that similar experiences in both cultures led the members of each one to learn similar types of nonverbal behavior, this appears unlikely because the two cultures are so very different. The expression of basic emotions, thus, seems to be universal (Ekman, 1994b; Izard, 1994; Matsumoto, 2002).

Why do people across cultures express emotions similarly? A hypothesis known as the **facial-affect program** gives one explanation. The facial-affect program—which is assumed to be universally present at birth—is analogous to a computer program that is turned on when a particular emotion is experienced. When set in motion, the "program" activates a set of nerve impulses that make the face display an appropriate expression. Each primary emotion produces a unique set of muscular movements, forming the kinds of expressions shown in Figure 4. For example, the emotion of happiness is universally displayed by movement of the zygomatic major, a muscle that raises the corners of the mouth and form what we would call a smile (Ekman, 2003; Kendler et al., 2008; Krumhuber & Scherer, 2011).

The importance of facial expressions is illustrated by an intriguing notion known as the **facial-feedback hypothesis.** According to this hypothesis, facial expressions not only *reflect* emotional experience, but they also help *determine* how people experience and label emotions. Basically put, "wearing" an emotional expression provides muscular feedback to the brain that helps produce an emotion congruent with that expression (Izard, 1990; Davis, Senghas, & Ochsner, 2009).

facial-affect program Activation of a set of nerve impulses that make the face display the appropriate expression.

facial-feedback hypothesis The hypothesis that facial expressions not only reflect emotional experience but also help determine how people experience and label emotions.

"And just exactly what is that expression intended to convey?"

© Gahan Wilson/The New Yorker Collection/www.cartoonbank.com

PsychTech

Because human facial expressions of emotions involve using dozens of muscles, it is only recently that researchers, such as Rana el-Kaliouby at M.I.T. Media Lab, have been able to develop software to read them reasonably accurately.

For instance, the muscles activated when we smile may send a message to the brain indicating the experience of happiness—even if there is nothing in the environment that would produce that particular emotion. Some theoreticians have gone further by suggesting that facial expressions are *necessary* for an emotion to be experienced (Rinn, 1984, 1991). In this view, if no facial expression is present, the emotion cannot be felt.

Support for this facial-feedback hypothesis comes from a classic experiment carried out by psychologist Paul Ekman and colleagues (Ekman, Levenson, & Friesen, 1983). In the study, professional actors were asked to follow very explicit instructions regarding the movements of muscles in their faces. You might try this example yourself:

- Raise your brows and pull them together.
- Raise your upper eyelids.
- Now stretch your lips horizontally back toward your ears.

After carrying out these directions—which, as you may have guessed, are meant to produce an expression of fear—the actors' heart rates rose and their body temperatures declined, physiological reactions that characterize fear. Overall, facial expressions representing the primary emotions produced physiological effects similar to those accompanying the genuine emotions in other circumstances (Keillor et al., 2002; Soussignan, 2002).

RECAP/EVALUATE/RETHINK

RECAP

LO 26-1 What are emotions, and how do we experience them?

- Emotions are broadly defined as feelings that may affect behavior and generally have both a physiological component and a cognitive component. Debate continues over whether separate systems govern cognitive and emotional responses and whether one has primacy over the other. (p. 313)

LO 26-2 What are the functions of emotions?

- Emotions prepare us for action, shape future behavior through learning, and help us interact more effectively with others. (p. 314)

LO 26-3 What are the explanations for emotions?

- Several theories explain emotions. The James-Lange theory suggests that emotional experience is a reaction to bodily, or visceral, changes that occur as a response to an environmental event and are interpreted as an emotional response. (p. 316)
- In contrast, the Cannon-Bard theory contends that both physiological arousal and an emotional experience are produced simultaneously by the same nerve stimulus and that the visceral experience does not necessarily differ among differing emotions. (p. 317)
- The Schachter-Singer theory suggests that emotions are determined jointly by a relatively nonspecific physiological arousal and the subsequent labeling of that arousal, using cues from the environment to determine how others are behaving in the same situation. (p. 318)

- The most recent approaches to emotions focus on their biological origins. For instance, it now seems that specific patterns of biological arousal are associated with individual emotions. Furthermore, new scanning techniques have identified the specific parts of the brain that are activated during the experience of particular emotions. (p. 318)

LO 26-4 How does nonverbal behavior relate to the expression of emotions?

- A person's facial expressions can reveal emotions. In fact, members of different cultures understand others' emotional expressions in similar ways. One explanation for this similarity is that an innate facial-affect program activates a set of muscle movements representing the emotion being experienced. (p. 321)
- The facial-feedback hypothesis suggests that facial expressions not only reflect, but also produce, emotional experiences. (p. 321)

EVALUATE

1. Emotions are always accompanied by a cognitive response. True or false?
2. The _____ - _____ theory of emotion states that emotions are a response to instinctive bodily events.
3. According to the _____ - _____ theory of emotion, both an emotional response and physiological arousal are produced simultaneously by the same nerve stimulus.

4. Your friend—a psychology major—tells you, "I was at a party last night. During the course of the evening, my general level of arousal increased. Since I was at a party where people were enjoying themselves, I assume I must have felt happy." What theory of emotion does your friend subscribe to?

5. What are the six primary emotions that can be identified from facial expressions?

RETHINK

1. If researchers learned how to control emotional responses so that targeted emotions could be caused or prevented, what ethical concerns might arise? Under what circumstances, if any, should such techniques be used?

2. *From the perspective of an advertising executive:* How might you use Schachter and Singer's findings on the labeling of arousal to create interest in a product? Can you think of other examples whereby people's arousal could be manipulated, which would lead to different emotional responses?

Answers to Evaluate Questions

1. false; emotions may occur without a cognitive response; 2. James-Lange; 3. Cannon-Bard; 4. Schachter-Singer; 5. surprise, sadness, happiness, anger, disgust, and fear.

KEY TERMS

emotions p. 313
James-Lange theory of emotion p. 316

Cannon-Bard theory of emotion p. 317

Schachter-Singer theory of emotion p. 318
facial-affect program p. 321

facial-feedback hypothesis p. 321

Looking Back

Epilogue

Motivation and emotions are two interrelated aspects of psychology. In these modules, we first considered the topic of motivation, which has spawned a great deal of theory and research examining primary and secondary drives. We then turned to a discussion of emotions, beginning with their functions and proceeding to a review of three major theories that seek to explain what emotions are and how they, and their associated physiological symptoms, emerge in the individual. Finally, we looked at cultural differences in the expression and display of emotions and discussed the facial-affect program, which seems to be innate and to regulate the nonverbal expression of the basic emotions.

Return to the opening scenario of this group of modules, which describes basketball player John Wall and his desire to succeed. Using your knowledge of motivation and emotion, consider the following questions:

1. How could Wall's determination to succeed at basketball be explained by each of the different approaches to motivation?
2. What indications are there that Wall has a high need for achievement? What about a high need for affiliation?
3. How might emotion play a role in whether Wall plays a good game or not?
4. How would you explain Wall's seemingly contradictory desires to please others and to compete against others?

VISUAL SUMMARY 8 Motivation and Emotion

MODULE 24 Explaining Motivation

<u>Motivation:</u> The factors that direct and energize the behavior of humans and other organisms

└── The major approaches to motivation

Instinct
People and animals are born with preprogrammed sets of behaviors essential to their survival.

Drive reduction
When some basic biological requirement is lacking, a drive is produced.

Arousal
People seek an optimal level of stimulation. If the level of stimulation is too high, they act to reduce it; if it is too low, they act to increase it.

Incentive
External stimuli direct and energize behavior.

Cognitive
Thoughts, expectations, and understanding of the world direct motivation.

Hierarchy of needs
Needs form a hierarchy; before higher-order needs are met, lower-order needs must be fulfilled.

MODULE 25 Human Needs and Motivation

<u>Motivation Behind Hunger and Eating</u>
Obesity has reached epidemic proportions

└── Factors that affect eating
  ├── • Biological factors
  ├── • Social factors and learned eating behaviors
└── Eating disorders
  ├── • Anorexia nervosa
  └── • Bulimia

<u>Sexual Motivation</u>

├── Puberty: Hormone secretion begins
├── Men and women differ in hormone production
├── Masturbation: high incidence
├── Heterosexuality: sexual attraction to the other sex
├── Premarital sex: decline in double standard
├── Homosexuality: sexual attraction to one's own sex
├── Bisexuality: sexual attraction to both sexes
└── Transsexualism: people who feel they were born with the other gender's body

Female / **Male**

<u>Needs for Achievement, Affiliation, and Power:</u>
Striving for excellence
Maintaining relationships
Influencing others

MODULE 26 Understanding Emotional Experiences

<u>Functions of Emotions</u>

├── Prepare us for action

├── Shape our future behavior

└── Help us to interact more effectively with others

<u>Roots of Emotions</u>

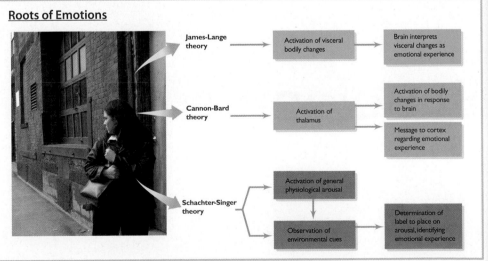

James-Lange theory → Activation of visceral bodily changes → Brain interprets visceral changes as emotional experience

Cannon-Bard theory → Activation of thalamus → Activation of bodily changes in response to brain / Message to cortex regarding emotional experience

Schachter-Singer theory → Activation of general physiological arousal / Observation of environmental cues → Determination of label to place on arousal, identifying emotional experience

325

9
Development

Learning Outcomes for Chapter 9

MODULE 27

LO 27-1 How do psychologists study the degree to which development is an interaction of hereditary and environmental factors?

LO 27-2 What is the nature of development before birth?

LO 27-3 What factors affect a child during the mother's pregnancy?

Nature and Nurture: The Enduring Developmental Issue

Determining the Relative Influence of Nature and Nurture

Developmental Research Techniques

Prenatal Development: Conception to Birth

Applying Psychology in the 21st Century: Gene Therapy and the Coming Medical Revolution

MODULE 28

LO 28-1 What are the major competencies of newborns?

LO 28-2 What are the milestones of physical and social development during childhood?

LO 28-3 How does cognitive development proceed during childhood?

Infancy and Childhood

The Extraordinary Newborn

Neuroscience in Your Life: Emotion Recognition in Infancy

The Growing Child: Infancy Through Middle Childhood

PsychWork: Child Protection Caseworker

MODULE 29

LO 29-1 What major physical, social, and cognitive transitions characterize adolescence?

Adolescence: Becoming an Adult

Physical Development: The Changing Adolescent

Moral and Cognitive Development: Distinguishing Right from Wrong

Social Development: Finding One's Self in a Social World

Exploring Diversity: Rites of Passage: Coming of Age Around the World

MODULE 30

LO 30-1 What are the principal kinds of physical, social, and intellectual changes that occur in early and middle adulthood, and what are their causes?

LO 30-2 How does the reality of late adulthood differ from the stereotypes about that period?

LO 30-3 How can we adjust to death?

Adulthood

Physical Development: The Peak of Health

Social Development: Working at Life

Marriage, Children, and Divorce: Family Ties

Later Years of Life: Growing Old

Becoming an Informed Consumer of Psychology: Adjusting to Death

Prologue *Hitting a Milestone*

"I had never dreaded a birthday before. Turning 30, 40 and then 50 had not exactly breezed by me—but I had seen these ages as milestones of achievement, coupled with a sense of excitement for what was on the other side of the zero," said Rosie Boycott, a British journalist and former editor of *Esquire* magazine.

"But, as the day of my 60th birthday approached just over a week ago, I wanted to bury my head in the sand. Sixty felt terrifying, an end, not a beginning. Or at least, it might be a beginning—but not of anything I wanted to be on the starting line for. Sixty felt like it only represented my invisibility in a fast-paced world which was gradually shutting me out as an irrelevance." (Boycott, 2011, p. 19)

Looking Ahead

Many people dread growing older, just as Rosie Boycott did. They imagine themselves slowing down, withdrawing from their careers and social worlds, becoming less productive and less useful, and perhaps ultimately losing their health and memory as their years advance. But as Rosie soon discovered, one's later adulthood can be filled with new activities and challenges—and age brings with it the benefits of a lifetime of accumulated memories and wisdom.

Rosie's reflections on how her life unfolded and where it was going get to the heart of one of the broadest and most important areas of psychology: developmental psychology.

Developmental psychology is the branch of psychology that studies the patterns of growth and change that occur throughout life. It deals with issues ranging from new ways of conceiving children, to learning how to raise children most sensibly, to understanding the milestones of life that we all face.

Developmental psychologists study the interaction between the unfolding of biologically predetermined patterns of behavior and a constantly changing, dynamic environment. They ask how our genetic background affects our behavior throughout our lives and whether heredity limits our potential. Similarly, they seek to understand the way in which the environment works with—or against—our genetic capabilities, how the world we live in affects our development, and how we can be encouraged to reach our full potential.

We begin by examining the approaches psychologists use to study development change across the life span. Then we consider the very start of development, beginning with conception and the nine months of life before birth. We look at both genetic and environmental influences on the unborn individual and the way they can affect behavior throughout the remainder of the life cycle.

Next, we examine development that occurs after birth: the enormous and rapid growth that takes place during the early stages of life and the physical, social, and cognitive change throughout infancy, toddlerhood, and middle childhood. We then move on to development from adolescence through adulthood. We end with a discussion of the ways in which people prepare themselves for death.

Nature and Nurture: The Enduring Developmental Issue

How many bald, six-foot-six, 250-pound volunteer firefighters in New Jersey wear droopy mustaches, aviator-style eyeglasses, and a key ring on the right side of the belt? The answer is two: Gerald Levey and Mark Newman. They are twins who were separated at birth. Each twin did not even know the other existed until they were reunited—in a fire station—by a fellow firefighter who knew Newman and was startled to see his double, Levey, at a firefighters' convention.

The lives of the twins, although separate, took remarkably similar paths. Levey went to college and studied forestry; Newman planned to study forestry in college but instead took a job trimming trees. Both had jobs in supermarkets. One had a job installing sprinkler systems; the other installed fire alarms.

Both men are unmarried and find the same kind of woman—"tall, slender, long hair"—attractive. They share similar hobbies and enjoy hunting, fishing, going to the beach, and watching old John Wayne movies and professional wrestling. Both like Chinese food and drink the same brand of beer. Their mannerisms are also similar—for example, each one throws his head back when he laughs. And, of course, there is one more thing: They share a passion for fighting fires.

The similarities we see in twins Gerald Levey and Mark Newman vividly raise one of the fundamental questions posed by **developmental psychology,** the study of the patterns of growth and change that occur throughout life. The question is this: How can we distinguish between the *environmental* causes of behavior (the influence of parents, siblings, family, friends, schooling, nutrition, and all the other experiences to which a child is exposed) and *hereditary* causes (those based on an individual's genetic makeup that influence growth and development throughout life)? This question embodies the **nature–nurture issue.** In this context, nature refers to hereditary factors, and nurture refers to environmental influences.

Although the question was first posed as a nature-*versus-*nurture issue, developmental psychologists today agree that *both* nature and nurture interact to produce specific developmental patterns and outcomes. Consequently, the question has evolved into this: *How and to what degree* do environment and heredity both produce their effects? No one develops free of environmental influences or without being affected by his or her inherited *genetic makeup.* However, the debate over the comparative influence of the two factors remains active; different approaches and different theories of development emphasize the environment or heredity to a greater or lesser degree (Rutter, 2006; Belsky & Pluess, 2009; Perovic & Radenovic, 2011).

For example, some developmental theories rely on basic psychological principles of learning and stress the role learning plays in producing changes in a developing child's behavior. Such theories emphasize the role of the environment in development. In contrast, other developmental theories emphasize

Learning Outcomes

LO 27-1 How do psychologists study the degree to which development is an interaction of hereditary and environmental factors?

LO 27-2 What is the nature of development before birth?

LO 27-3 What factors affect a child during the mother's pregnancy?

developmental psychology The branch of psychology that studies the patterns of growth and change that occur throughout life.

nature–nurture issue The issue of the degree to which environment and heredity influence behavior.

Gerald Levey and Mark Newman.

the influence of one's physiological makeup and functioning on development. Such theories stress the role of heredity and *maturation*—the unfolding of biologically predetermined patterns of behavior—in producing developmental change. Maturation can be seen, for instance, in the development of sex characteristics (such as breasts and body hair) that occurs at the start of adolescence.

Furthermore, the work of *behavioral geneticists*, who study the effects of heredity on behavior, and the theories of evolutionary psychologists, who identify behavior patterns that result from our genetic inheritance, have influenced developmental psychologists. Behavioral geneticists are finding increasing evidence that cognitive abilities, personality traits, sexual orientation, and psychological disorders are determined to some extent by genetic factors (Livesley & Jang, 2008; Vernon et al., 2008; Schermer et al., 2011).

Behavioral genetics lies at the heart of the nature–nurture question. Although no one would argue that our behavior is determined *solely* by inherited factors, evidence collected by behavioral geneticists does suggest that our genetic inheritance predisposes us to respond in particular ways to our environment, and even to seek out particular kinds of environments (Ball et al., 2008; Davis, Haworth, & Plomin, 2009; Lakhan & Vieira, 2009; Bienvenu, Davydow, & Kendler, 2011).

Despite their differences over theory, developmental psychologists concur on some points. They agree that genetic factors not only provide the potential for specific behaviors or traits to emerge, but also place limitations on the emergence of such behavior or traits. For instance, heredity defines people's general level of intelligence and sets an upper limit that—regardless of the quality of the environment—people cannot exceed. Heredity also places limits on physical abilities; humans simply cannot run at a speed of 60 miles an hour or grow as tall as 10 feet, no matter the quality of their environment (Dodge, 2004; Pinker, 2004).

Figure 1 lists some of the characteristics most affected by heredity. As you consider these items, it is important to keep in mind that these characteristics are not *entirely* determined by heredity, for environmental factors also play a role.

Developmental psychologists also agree that in most instances environmental factors play a critical role in enabling people to reach the potential capabilities that their genetic background makes possible. If Albert Einstein had received no intellectual stimulation as a child and had not been sent to school, it is unlikely that he would have reached his genetic potential. Similarly, a great athlete such as baseball star Derek Jeter would have been unlikely to display much physical skill if he had not been raised in an environment that nurtured his innate talent and gave him the opportunity to train and perfect his natural abilities.

Study Alert

The nature–nurture issue is a key question that is pervasive throughout the field of psychology. It explores how and to what degree environment and heredity produce their joint effects.

FIGURE 1 Characteristics influenced significantly by genetic factors. Although these characteristics have strong genetic components, they are also affected by environmental factors.

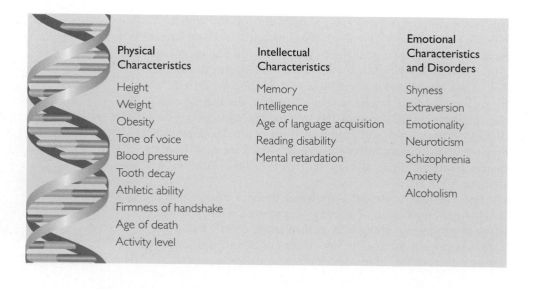

Physical Characteristics	Intellectual Characteristics	Emotional Characteristics and Disorders
Height	Memory	Shyness
Weight	Intelligence	Extraversion
Obesity	Age of language acquisition	Emotionality
Tone of voice	Reading disability	Neuroticism
Blood pressure	Mental retardation	Schizophrenia
Tooth decay		Anxiety
Athletic ability		Alcoholism
Firmness of handshake		
Age of death		
Activity level		

Clearly, the relationship between heredity and environment is complex. Therefore, developmental psychologists typically take an *interactionist* position on the nature–nurture issue by suggesting that a combination of hereditary and environmental factors influences development. Developmental psychologists face the challenge of identifying the relative strength of each of these influences on the individual as well as that of identifying the specific changes that occur over the course of development (McGregor & Capone, 2004; Moffitt, Caspi, & Rutter, 2006).

Determining the Relative Influence of Nature and Nurture

Developmental psychologists use several approaches to determine the relative influence of genetic and environmental factors on behavior. In one approach, researchers can experimentally control the genetic makeup of laboratory animals by carefully breeding them for specific traits. For instance, by observing animals with identical genetic backgrounds placed in varied environments, researchers can learn the effects of specific kinds of environmental stimulation. Although researchers must be careful when generalizing the findings of nonhuman research to a human population, findings from animal research provide important information that cannot be obtained for ethical reasons by using human participants.

Human twins serve as another important source of information about the relative effects of genetic and environmental factors. If **identical twins** (those who are genetically identical) display different patterns of development, those differences have to be attributed to variations in the environment in which the twins were raised. The most useful data come from identical twins (such as Gerald Levey and Mark Newman) who are adopted at birth by different sets of adoptive parents and raised apart in differing environments. Studies of nontwin siblings who are raised in totally different environments also shed some light on the issue. Because they have relatively similar genetic backgrounds, siblings who show similarities as adults provide strong evidence for the importance of heredity (Vitaro, Brendgen, & Arseneault, 2009; Sternberg, 2002, 2011).

Researchers can also take the opposite tack. Instead of concentrating on people with similar genetic backgrounds who are raised in different environments, they may consider people raised in similar environments who have totally dissimilar genetic backgrounds. For example, if they find similar courses of development in two adopted children who have different genetic backgrounds and have been raised in the same family, they have evidence for the importance of environmental influences on development. Moreover, psychologists can carry out research involving animals with dissimilar genetic backgrounds; by experimentally varying the environment in which they are raised, they can determine the influence of environmental factors (independent of heredity) on development (Petrill & Deater-Deckard, 2004).

identical twins Twins who are genetically identical.

Developmental Research Techniques

Because of the demands of measuring behavioral change across different ages, developmental researchers use several unique methods. The most frequently used, **cross-sectional research,** compares people of different ages at the same point in time. Cross-sectional studies provide information about differences in development between different age groups (Creasey, 2005; Huijie, 2006).

cross-sectional research A research method that compares people of different ages at the same point in time.

Suppose, for instance, we were interested in the development of intellectual ability in adulthood. To carry out a cross-sectional study, we might compare a sample of 25-, 45-, and 65-year-olds who all take the same IQ test. We then can determine whether average IQ test scores differ in each age group.

Cross-sectional research has limitations, however. For instance, we cannot be sure that the differences in IQ scores we might find in our example are due to age differences alone. Instead, the scores may reflect differences in the educational attainment of the cohorts represented. A *cohort* is a group of people who grow up at similar times, in similar places, and in similar conditions. In the case of IQ differences, any age differences we find in a cross-sectional study may reflect educational differences among the cohorts studied: People in the older age group may belong to a cohort that was less likely to attend college than were the people in the younger groups.

A longitudinal study, the second major research strategy developmental psychologists use, provides one way around this problem. **Longitudinal research** traces the behavior of one or more participants as the participants age. Longitudinal studies assess *change* in behavior over time, whereas cross-sectional studies assess *differences* among groups of people.

For instance, consider how we might investigate intellectual development during adulthood by using a longitudinal research strategy. First, we might give an IQ test to a group of 25-year-olds. We'd then come back to the same people 20 years later and retest them at age 45. Finally, we'd return to them once more when they were 65 years old and test them again.

By examining changes at several points in time, we can clearly see how individuals develop. Unfortunately, longitudinal research requires an enormous expenditure of time as the researcher waits for the participants to get older. Participants who begin a study at an early age may drop out, move away, or even die as the research continues. Moreover, participants who take the same test at several points in time may become "test-wise" and perform better each time they take it because they have become more familiar with the test.

To make up for the limitations in both cross-sectional and longitudinal research, investigators have devised an alternative strategy. In **sequential research,** researchers combine cross-sectional and longitudinal approaches by examining a number of different age groups at several points in time. For example, investigators might examine a group of 3-, 5-, and 7-year-olds every 6 months for a period of 5 years. This technique allows developmental psychologists to tease out the specific effects of age changes from other possible influential factors.

longitudinal research A research method that investigates behavior as participants age.

Study Alert

Be sure to be able to distinguish the three different types of developmental research—cross-sectional (comparing people of different ages at the same time); longitudinal (studying participants as they age); and sequential (a combination of cross-sectional and longitudinal).

sequential research A research method that combines cross-sectional and longitudinal research by considering a number of different age groups and examining them at several points in time.

Prenatal Development: Conception to Birth

When the Morrisons were expecting their second child, the young couple faced an anguishing dilemma.

Their first child had a condition known as congenital adrenal hyperplasia, or CAH, which can sometimes result in male-like genitals in female newborns. So when Mrs. Morrison became pregnant again, the couple was well aware the baby had a 1-in-8 chance of being born with the same disorder.

There were choices. They could treat the fetus with a powerful steroid that would most likely avert the possibility of the genitals becoming malformed. But the couple worried about doing this. There was little research on the long-term effects of treating a fetus with steroids, and statistically, there was a much greater chance that the baby wouldn't have the genital problem at all. . . .

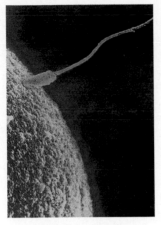
(a) Conception

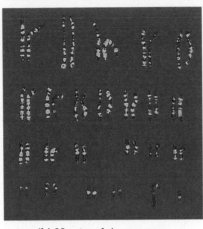
(b) 23 pairs of chromosomes

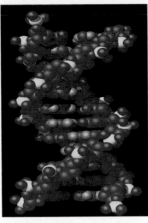
(c) DNA sequence

(d) Genes

FIGURE 2 Every individual's characteristics are determined by the individual's specific genetic information. (a) At the moment of conception, (b) humans receive 23 pairs of chromosomes, half from the mother and half from the father. (c) These chromosomes are made up of coils of DNA. (d) Each chromosome contains thousands of genes that "program" the future development of the body.

The couple decided to forgo the steroid treatment. "It was touch-and-go, but in the end I couldn't expose the baby to the drugs," says Mrs. Morrison. When the baby arrived, it was a girl and, like her older sister, was born with swollen genitalia (Naik, 2009, p. D1).

The Morrisons will never know if they made the right choice. But their case shows the difficult choices that parents may encounter due to our increasing understanding of life spent inside a mother's womb.

Yet, our knowledge of the biology of *conception*—when a male's sperm cell penetrates a female's egg cell—and its aftermath makes the start of life no less of a miracle. Let's consider how an individual is created by looking first at the genetic endowment that a child receives at the moment of conception.

THE BASICS OF GENETICS

The one-cell entity established at conception contains 23 pairs of **chromosomes,** rod-shaped structures that contain all basic hereditary information. One member of each pair is from the mother, and the other is from the father.

Each chromosome contains thousands of **genes**—smaller units through which genetic information is transmitted. Either individually or in combination, genes produce each person's particular characteristics. Composed of sequences of *DNA (deoxyribonucleic acid)* molecules, genes are the biological equivalent of "software" that programs the future development of all parts of the body's hardware. Humans have some 25,000 different genes (see Figure 2).

Some genes control the development of systems common to all members of the human species—the heart, circulatory system, brain, lungs, and so forth; others shape the characteristics that make each human unique, such as facial configuration, height, and eye color. The child's sex is also determined by a particular combination of genes. Specifically, a child inherits an X chromosome from its mother and either an X or a Y chromosome from its father. When it receives an XX combination, it is a female; with an XY combination, it develops as a male. Male development is triggered by a single gene on the Y chromosome; without the presence of that specific gene, the individual will develop as a female.

chromosomes Rod-shaped structures that contain all basic hereditary information.

genes The parts of the chromosomes through which genetic information is transmitted.

Study Alert

It's important to understand the basic building blocks of genetics: chromosomes, which contain genes, which in turn are composed of sequences of DNA.

Gene Therapy and the Coming Medical Revolution

A pediatrician rubs a cotton swab across Meghan Johannsen's inside cheek to get a DNA sample of the month-old girl and hands it to a technician. In several hours, he has a printout of a complete DNA analysis on his desk. He calls Meghan's parents and gives them the good news: By and large, Meghan is quite healthy. However, there are some potential problems—a mild allergy to peanuts, and, more seriously, the likelihood that she will develop high blood pressure in middle age. The pediatrician advises the parents to consider inserting a gene that prevents her blood pressure from rising to dangerous levels and becoming a major problem.

This futuristic view of a visit to a pediatrician's office is no longer the stuff of science fiction. In the not-so-distant future, advances in our understanding of genetics are likely to lead not only to the identification of risk factors in children, but also to the development of new treatments for psychological disorders and physical diseases.

For example, in *gene therapy*, health-care providers inject genes directly into a patient's bloodstream to correct particular diseases. The genes lead the patient's body

In gene therapy, defective genes are replaced to correct health problems.

to produce chemicals that can alleviate the danger. In other cases, additional genes are inserted that replace missing or defective cells. In time, it may even be possible to "harvest" defective cells from a fetus in a process called *germline therapy*. The defective cells could be treated by gene therapy and reintroduced into the unborn child to repair the defect (Sato, Shimamura, & Takeuchi, 2007; Naldini, 2009; Tani, Faustine, & Sufian, 2011).

Although the promise of gene therapy is real, the number of diseases that can be treated today is fairly limited. Furthermore, the long-term success of gene therapy remains unknown. In fact, after they initially seem to be cured, some recipients of gene therapy have relapsed, and some have suffered from unpleasant side effects (Rossi, June, & Kohn, 2007; Miller et al., 2008; Kumar et al., 2011).

Still, the potential uses of gene therapy are considerable. In fact, it could lead to cloning. For example, if both a husband and wife were infertile, they might consider cloning one or the other of themselves to have at least one child who was genetically identical to one of them. The ethical and moral issues of such a procedure, of course, are profound. Most Americans oppose cloning of human embryos, and laws limiting human cloning have already been enacted (Levick, 2004; Greene et al., 2005; Aschheim, 2011).

RETHINK

- Would you choose to be genetically tested so that you could know your susceptibility to genetic diseases?
- Would you want to be tested if you might learn that you had a genetic disorder that was likely to shorten your life? Why or why not?

As behavioral geneticists have discovered, genes are also at least partially responsible for a wide variety of personal characteristics, including cognitive abilities, personality traits, and psychological disorders. Of course, few of these characteristics are determined by a single gene. Instead, most traits result from a combination of multiple genes that operate together with environmental influences (Haberstick et al., 2005; Ramus, 2006; Armbruster et al., 2011).

THE HUMAN GENOME PROJECT

Our understanding of genetics took a giant leap forward in 2001, when scientists were able to map the specific location and sequence of every human gene as part of the massive *Human Genome Project*. The accomplishment was one of the most important in the history of biology (International Human Genome Sequencing Consortium, 2003).

The success of the Human Genome Project started a revolution in health care because scientists can identify the particular genes responsible for genetically caused disorders. It is already leading not only to the identification of risk factors in children, but also to the development of new treatments for physical and psychological disorders, as we consider in *Applying Psychology in the 21st Century*.

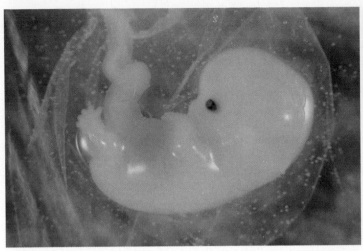 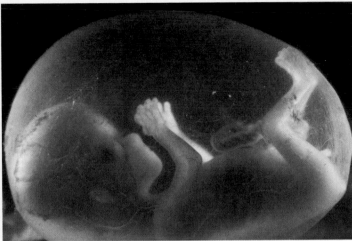

These remarkable photos of live fetuses display the degree of physical development at prenatal ages 4 and 15 weeks.

THE EARLIEST DEVELOPMENT

When an egg becomes fertilized by the sperm, the resulting one-celled entity, called a **zygote,** immediately begins to develop. The zygote starts out as a microscopic speck. Three days after fertilization, though, the zygote increases to around 32 cells; within a week it has grown to 100–150 cells. These first two weeks are known as the *germinal period.*

Two weeks after conception, the developing individual enters the *embryonic period,* which lasts from week 2 through week 8; he or she is now called an **embryo.** As an embryo develops through an intricate, preprogrammed process of cell division, it grows 10,000 times larger by 4 weeks of age and attains a length of about one-fifth of an inch. At this point it has developed a rudimentary beating heart, a brain, an intestinal tract, and a number of other organs. Although all these organs are at a primitive stage of development, they are clearly recognizable. Moreover, by week 8, the embryo is about an inch long and has discernible arms, legs, and a face.

From week 8 and continuing until birth, the developing individual enters the *fetal period* and is called a **fetus.** At the start of this period, it begins to respond to touch; it bends its fingers when touched on the hand. At 16 to 18 weeks, its movements become strong enough for the mother to sense them. At the same time, hair may begin to grow on its head, and the facial features become similar to those the child will display at birth. The major organs begin functioning, although the fetus could not be kept alive outside the mother. In addition, a lifetime's worth of brain neurons are produced—although it is unclear whether the brain is capable of thinking at this early stage.

Within the womb the fetus continues to develop before birth. It begins to grow fatty deposits under the skin, and it gains weight. The fetus reaches the **age of viability,** the point at which it can survive if born prematurely, at about prenatal age 22 weeks. By week 24, a fetus has many of the characteristics it will display as a newborn. In fact, when an infant is born prematurely at this age, it can open and close its eyes; suck; cry; look up, down, and around; and even grasp objects placed in its hands.

At prenatal age 28 weeks, the fetus weighs less than 3 pounds and is about 16 inches long. It may be capable of learning: One study found that the infants of mothers who had repeatedly read aloud *The Cat in the Hat* by Dr. Seuss before the infants' birth preferred the sound of that particular story to other stories after they were born (Spence & DeCasper, 1982; Schenone et al., 2010; Del Giudice, 2011).

zygote The new cell formed by the union of an egg and sperm.

embryo A developed zygote that has a heart, a brain, and other organs.

fetus A developing individual from 8 weeks after conception until birth.

age of viability The point at which a fetus can survive if born prematurely.

Before birth, a fetus passes through several *sensitive periods*. A sensitive period is the time when organisms are particularly susceptible to certain kinds of stimuli. For example, fetuses are especially affected by their mothers' use of drugs during certain sensitive periods before birth. If they are exposed to a particular drug before or after the sensitive period, it may have relatively little impact; if exposure comes during a sensitive period, the impact will be significant (Konig, 2005; Werker & Tees, 2005; Uylings, 2006).

Sensitive periods can also occur after birth. Some language specialists suggest, for instance, that there is a period in which children are particularly receptive to developing language. If children are not exposed to appropriate linguistic stimuli, their language development may be impaired (Sohr-Preston & Scaramella, 2006; Innocenti, 2007).

In the final weeks of pregnancy, the fetus continues to gain weight and grow. At the end of the normal 38 weeks of pregnancy, the fetus typically weighs 7 pounds and is about 20 inches in length. However, the story is different for *preterm infants,* who are born before week 38. Because they have not been able to develop fully, they are at higher risk for illness, future problems, and even death. For infants who have been in the womb for more than 30 weeks, the prospects are relatively good. However, for those born before week 30, the story is often less positive. Such newborns, who may weigh as little as 2 pounds at birth, are in grave danger because they have immature organs; they have less than a 50-50 chance of survival. If they do survive—and it takes extraordinarily heroic (and expensive) medical intervention to assure this—they may later experience significant developmental delays.

GENETIC INFLUENCES ON THE FETUS

The process of fetal growth that we have just described reflects normal development, which occurs in 95–98% of all pregnancies. Some individuals are less fortunate; in the remaining 2–5% of cases, children are born with serious birth defects. A major cause of such defects is faulty genes or chromosomes. Here are some of the more common genetic and chromosomal difficulties.

- *Phenylketonuria (PKU).* A child born with the inherited disease phenylketonuria cannot produce an enzyme that is required for normal development. This deficiency results in an accumulation of poisons that eventually cause profound intellectual disability. The disease is treatable, however, if it is caught early. Most infants today are routinely tested for PKU, and children with the disorder can be placed on a special diet that allows them to develop normally (Ievers-Landis et al., 2005; Christ, Steiner, & Grange, 2006; Widaman, 2009).
- *Sickle-cell anemia.* About 10% of the African-American population has the possibility of passing on sickle-cell anemia, a disease that gets its name from the abnormally shaped red blood cells it causes. Children with the disease may have episodes of pain, yellowish eyes, stunted growth, and vision problems (Taras & Potts-Datema, 2005; Selove, 2007).
- *Tay-Sachs disease.* Children born with Tay-Sachs disease, a disorder most often found in Jews of Eastern European ancestry, usually die by age 3 or 4 because of the body's inability to break down fat. If both parents carry the genetic defect that produces the fatal illness, their child has a 1 in 4 chance of being born with the disease (Leib et al., 2005; Weinstein, 2007).
- *Down syndrome.* Down syndrome, one of the causes of intellectual disability, occurs when the zygote receives an extra chromosome at the moment of conception. Down syndrome is often related to the mother's age; mothers over 35 and younger than 18 stand a higher risk than other women of having a child with the syndrome (Roizen & Patterson, 2003; Sherman et al., 2007).

PRENATAL ENVIRONMENTAL INFLUENCES

Genetic factors are not the only causes of difficulties in fetal development. Environmental influences—the *nurture* part of the nature–nurture equation—also affect the fetus. Some of the more profound consequences are brought about by **teratogens,** environmental agents such as a drug, chemical, virus, or other factor that produce a birth defect. Among the major prenatal environmental influences on the fetus are the following:

teratogens Environmental agents such as a drug, chemical, virus, or other factor that produce a birth defect.

- *Mother's nutrition.* What a mother eats during her pregnancy can have important implications for the health of her baby. Seriously undernourished mothers cannot provide adequate nutrition to a growing fetus, and they are likely to give birth to underweight babies. Poorly nourished babies are also more susceptible to disease, and a lack of nourishment may have an adverse impact on their mental development (Zigler, Finn-Stevenson, & Hall, 2002; Najman et al., 2004; Everette, 2008).

- *Mother's illness.* Several diseases that have a relatively minor effect on the health of a mother can have devastating consequences for a developing fetus if they are contracted during the early part of a pregnancy. For example, rubella (German measles), syphilis, diabetes, and high blood pressure may each produce a permanent effect on the fetus. The virus that causes AIDS can also be passed from mother to child before birth and through breast-feeding after birth (Nesheim et al., 2004; Magoni et al., 2005).

- *Mother's emotional state.* A mother's emotional state affects her baby. Mothers who are anxious and tense during the last months of their pregnancies are more apt to have irritable infants who sleep and eat poorly. The reason? The autonomic nervous system of the fetus becomes especially sensitive as a result of chemical changes produced by the mother's emotional state (Relier, 2001; Hollins, 2007).

- *Mother's use of drugs.* Mothers who take illegal, physically addictive drugs such as cocaine run the risk of giving birth to babies who are similarly addicted. Their newborns suffer painful withdrawal symptoms and sometimes show permanent physical and mental impairment. Even legal drugs taken by a pregnant woman (who may not know that she has become pregnant) can have a tragic effect (Ikonomidou et al., 2000; Schechter, Finkelstein, & Koren, 2005; Singer & Richardson, 2011).

- *Alcohol.* Alcohol is extremely dangerous to fetal development. For example, 1 out of every 750 infants is born with *fetal alcohol syndrome* (*FAS*), a condition resulting in below-average intelligence, growth delays, and facial deformities. FAS is now the primary preventable cause of intellectual disability. Even mothers who use small amounts of alcohol during pregnancy place their child at risk. *Fetal alcohol effects* (*FAE*) is a condition in which children display some although not all of the problems of FAS due to their mother's consumption of alcohol during pregnancy (Henderson, Kesmodel, & Gray, 2007; Niccols, 2007; Murthy et al., 2009).

- *Nicotine use.* Pregnant mothers who smoke put their children at considerable risk. Smoking while pregnant can lead to miscarriage and infant death. For children who do survive, the negative consequences of mother's tobacco use can last a lifetime (Haslam & Lawrence, 2004; Shea & Steiner, 2008; Rogers, 2009).

Several other environmental factors have an impact on the child before and during birth (see Figure 3 on the next page). Keep in mind, however, that although we have been discussing the influences of genetics and environment separately, neither factor works alone. Furthermore, despite the emphasis here on some of the ways in which development can go wrong, the vast majority of births occur without difficulty. And in most instances, subsequent development also proceeds normally.

Environmental Factor	Possible Effect on Prenatal Development
Rubella (German measles)	Blindness, deafness, heart abnormalities, stillbirth
Syphilis	Mental retardation, physical deformities, maternal miscarriage
Addictive drugs	Low birth weight, addiction of infant to drug, with possible death after birth from withdrawal
Nicotine	Premature birth, low birth weight and length
Alcohol	Mental retardation, lower-than-average birth weight, small head, limb deformities
Radiation from X-rays	Physical deformities, mental retardation
Inadequate diet	Reduction in growth of brain, smaller-than-average weight and length at birth
Mother's age—younger than 18 at birth of child	Premature birth, increased incidence of Down syndrome
Mother's age—older than 35 at birth of child	Increased incidence of Down syndrome
DES (diethylstilbestrol)	Reproductive difficulties and increased incidence of genital cancer in children of mothers who were given DES during pregnancy to prevent miscarriage
AIDS	Possible spread of AIDS virus to infant; facial deformities; growth failure
Accutane	Mental retardation and physical deformities

FIGURE 3 A variety of environmental factors can play a role in prenatal development.

RECAP/EVALUATE/RETHINK

RECAP

LO 27-1 How do psychologists study the degree to which development is an interaction of hereditary and environmental factors?

- Developmental psychology studies growth and change throughout life. One fundamental question is how much developmental change is due to heredity and how much is due to environment—the nature–nurture issue. Heredity seems to define the upper limits of our growth and change, whereas the environment affects the degree to which the upper limits are reached. (p. 328)
- Cross-sectional research compares people of different ages with one another at the same point in time. In contrast, longitudinal research traces the behavior of one or more participants as the participants become older. Finally, sequential research combines the two methods by examining several different age groups at several points in time. (p. 331)

LO 27-2 What is the nature of development before birth?

- At the moment of conception, a male's sperm cell and a female's egg cell unite; each contributes to the new individual's genetic makeup. The union of sperm and egg produces a zygote, which contains 23 pairs of chromosomes; one member of each pair comes from the father and the other comes from the mother. (pp. 332, 333)
- Each chromosome contains genes through which genetic information is transmitted. Genes, which are composed of DNA sequences, are the "software" that programs the future development of the body's hardware. (p. 333)
- Genes affect not only physical attributes, but also a wide array of personal characteristics such as cognitive abilities, personality traits, and psychological disorders. (p. 334)
- After two weeks the zygote becomes an embryo. By week 8, the embryo is called a fetus and is responsive to touch and other stimulation. At about week 22 it reaches the age of viability, which means it may survive if born

prematurely. A fetus is normally born after 38 weeks of pregnancy; it weighs around 7 pounds and measures about 20 inches. (p. 335)

LO 27-3 What factors can affect a child during the mother's pregnancy?

- Genetic abnormalities produce birth defects such as phenylketonuria (PKU), sickle-cell anemia, Tay-Sachs disease, and Down syndrome. (p. 336)
- Among the environmental influences on fetal growth are the mother's nutrition, illnesses, and drug intake. (p. 337)

EVALUATE

1. Developmental psychologists are interested in the effects of both _____ and _____ on development.
2. Environment and heredity both influence development with genetic potentials generally establishing limits on environmental influences. True or false?
3. By observing genetically similar animals in differing environments, we can increase our understanding of the influences of hereditary and environmental factors in humans. True or false?
4. _____ research studies the same individuals over a period of time, whereas _____ _____ research studies people of different ages at the same time.

5. Match each of the following terms with its definition:
   1. Zygote
   2. Gene
   3. Chromosome
   a. Smallest unit through which genetic information is passed
   b. Fertilized egg
   c. Rod-shaped structure containing genetic information
6. Specific kinds of growth must take place during a _____ period if the embryo is to develop normally.

RETHINK

1. When researchers find similarities in development between very different cultures, what implications might such findings have for the nature–nurture issue?
2. *From the perspective of a child-care provider:* Consider what factors might determine why a child is not learning to walk at the same pace as his peers. What kinds of environmental influences might be involved? What kinds of genetic influences might be involved? What recommendations might you make to the child's parents about the situation?

Answers to Evaluate Questions

1. heredity (or nature), environment (or nurture); 2. true; 3. true; 4. Longitudinal, cross-sectional; 5. 1-b, 2-a, 3-c; 6. sensitive (or critical)

KEY TERMS

developmental psychology p. 329
nature–nurture issue p. 329
identical twins p. 331

cross-sectional research p. 331
longitudinal research p. 332

sequential research p. 332
chromosomes p. 333
genes p. 333
zygote p. 335

embryo p. 335
fetus p. 335
age of viability p. 335
teratogens p. 337

Infancy and Childhood

Learning Outcomes

LO 28-1 What are the major competencies of newborns?

LO 28-2 What are the milestones of physical and social development during childhood?

LO 28-3 How does cognitive development proceed during childhood?

neonate A newborn child.

His head was molded into a long melon shape and came to a point at the back. . . . He was covered with a thick greasy white material known as "vernix," which made him slippery to hold and also allowed him to slip easily through the birth canal. In addition to a shock of black hair on his head, his body was covered with dark, fine hair known as "lanugo." His ears, his back, his shoulders, and even his cheeks were furry. . . . His skin was wrinkled and quite loose, ready to scale in creased places such as his feet and hands. . . . His ears were pressed to his head in unusual positions—one ear was matted firmly forward on his cheek. His nose was flattened and pushed to one side by the squeeze as he came through the pelvis. (Brazelton, 1969, p. 3)

What kind of creature is this? Although the description hardly fits that of the adorable babies seen in advertisements for baby food, we are in fact talking about a normal, completely developed child just after the moment of birth. Called a **neonate**, a newborn arrives in the world in a form that hardly meets the standards of beauty against which we typically measure babies. Yet ask any parents: Nothing is more beautiful or exciting than the first glimpse of their newborn.

The Extraordinary Newborn

reflexes Unlearned, involuntary responses that occur automatically in the presence of certain stimuli.

Several factors cause a neonate's strange appearance. The trip through the mother's birth canal may have squeezed the incompletely formed bones of the skull together and squashed the nose into the head. The skin secretes *vernix,* a white greasy covering, for protection before birth, and the baby may have *lanugo,* a soft fuzz, over the entire body for a similar purpose. The infant's eyelids may be puffy with an accumulation of fluids because of the upside-down position during birth.

All these features change during the first 2 weeks of life as the neonate takes on a more familiar appearance. Even more impressive are the capabilities a neonate begins to display from the moment of birth—capabilities that grow at an astounding rate over the ensuing months.

REFLEXES

A neonate is born with a number of **reflexes**—unlearned, involuntary responses that occur automatically in the presence of certain stimuli. Critical for survival, many of those reflexes unfold naturally as part of an infant's ongoing maturation. The *rooting reflex,* for instance, causes neonates to turn their heads toward things that touch their cheeks—such as the mother's nipple or a bottle. Similarly, a *sucking reflex* prompts infants to suck at things that touch their lips. Among other reflexes are a *gag reflex* (to clear the throat), the *startle reflex* (a series of movements in which an infant flings

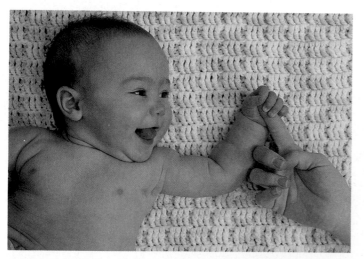

Many of the reflexes that a neonate is born with are critical for survival and unfold naturally as a part of the infant's ongoing maturation. Do you think humans have more or fewer reflexes than other animals?

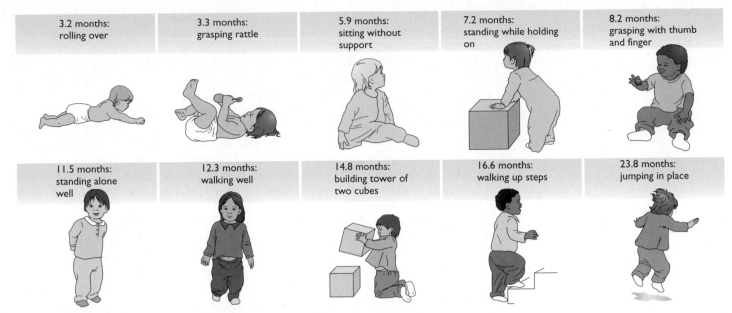

FIGURE 1 Although at birth a neonate can make only jerky, limited voluntary movements, during the first year of life the ability to move independently grows enormously. The ages indicate the time when 50% of children are able to perform each skill. Remember, however, that the time when each skill appears can vary considerably. For example, 25% of children are able to walk well at age 11 months; by 15 months 90% of children are walking well. (Source: Frankenburg et al., 1992.)

out the arms, fans the fingers, and arches the back in response to a sudden noise), and the *Babinski reflex* (a baby's toes fan out when the outer edge of the sole of the foot is stroked).

Infants lose these primitive reflexes after the first few months of life and replace them with more complex and organized behaviors. Although at birth a neonate is capable of only jerky, limited voluntary movements, the ability to move independently grows enormously during the first year of life. The typical baby rolls over by the age of about 3 months, sits without support at about 6 months, stands alone at about 11 months, and walks at just over a year old. Not only does the ability to make large-scale movements improve during this time, but fine-muscle movements also become increasingly sophisticated (see Figure 1).

DEVELOPMENT OF THE SENSES: TAKING IN THE WORLD

When proud parents peer into the eyes of their neonate, is the child able to return their gaze? Although it was thought for some time that newborns can see only a hazy blur, most current findings indicate that neonates' capabilities are far more impressive. Although their eyes have a limited capacity to focus on objects that are not within a 7- to 8-inch distance from the face, neonates can follow objects moving within their field of vision. They also show the beginnings of depth perception as they react by raising their hands when an object appears to be moving rapidly toward the face (Maurer et al., 1999; Craighero et al., 2011).

You might think that it would be hard to figure out just how well neonates can see because their lack of both language and reading ability clearly prevents them from saying what direction the E on a vision chart is facing. However, researchers have devised a number of ingenious methods that rely on the newborn's biological responses and innate reflexes to test perceptual skills.

For instance, infants who see a novel stimulus typically pay close attention to it; as a consequence, their heart rates increase. But if they repeatedly see the same

Study Alert

The basic reflexes—unlearned, involuntary responses—include the rooting reflex, the sucking reflex, the gag reflex, the startle reflex, and the Babinski reflex.

habituation The decrease in the response to a stimulus that occurs after repeated presentations of the same stimulus.

stimulus, their attention to it decreases, as indicated by a return to a slower heart rate. This phenomenon is known as **habituation,** the decrease in the response to a stimulus that occurs after repeated presentations of the same stimulus. By studying habituation, developmental psychologists can tell when a child who is too young to speak can detect and discriminate a stimulus (Grunwald et al., 2003; Hannon & Johnson, 2005; del Rosal, Alonso, & Moreno, 2006).

Researchers have developed many other methods for measuring neonate and infant perception. One technique, for instance, involves babies sucking on a nipple attached to a computer. A change in the rate and vigor with which the babies suck helps researchers infer that babies can perceive variations in stimuli. Other approaches include examining babies' eye movements and observing which way babies move their heads in response to a visual stimulus (Franklin, Pilling, & Davies, 2005; Bulf, Johnson, & Valenza, 2011).

Through the use of such research techniques, we now know that infants' visual perception is remarkably sophisticated from the start of life. At birth, babies prefer patterns with contours and edges over less distinct patterns, indicating that they can respond to the configuration of stimuli. Furthermore, even newborns are aware of size constancy because they are apparently sensitive to the phenomenon by which objects stay the same size even though the image on the retina may change size as the distance between the object and the retina varies (Norcia et al., 2005; Moore, Goodwin, & George, 2007).

In fact, neonates can discriminate facial expressions—and even imitate them. As you can see in Figure 2, newborns can produce a good imitation of an adult's expressions. Even very young infants, then, can respond to the emotions and moods that their caregivers' facial expressions reveal. This capability provides the foundation for social interaction skills in children (Meltzoff, 1996; Lavelli & Fogel, 2005; Grossmann, Striano, & Friederici, 2007).

FIGURE 2 This newborn infant is clearly imitating the expressions of the adult model in these amazing photos. How does this ability contribute to social development? (Source: Courtesy of Dr. Tiffany Field.)

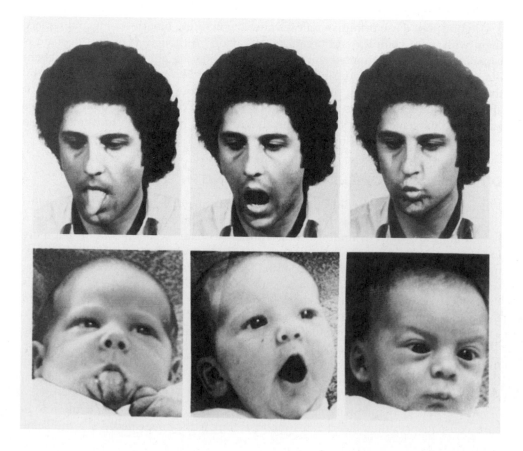

Neuroscience in Your Life:
Emotion Recognition in Infancy

FIGURE 3 To consider how infants process information related to facial expressions, researchers measured of cerebral blood flow while they viewed happy and sad faces. When 6- to 7-month-old infants viewed happy faces, they showed greater activity, which tended to persist after the faces disappeared (the difference between the upper and lower lines on each graph). In contrast, when viewing angry faces, they showed greater activity when the face was shown, but this activity quickly disappeared. The results suggest that infants process positive and negative emotions differently. (Source: Nakato et al., 2011.)

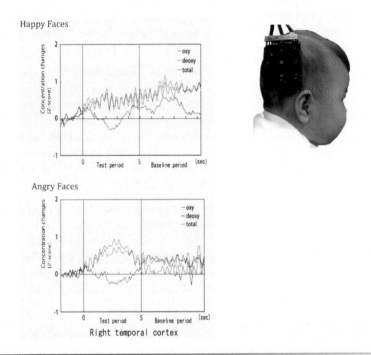

Other visual abilities grow rapidly after birth. By the end of their first month, babies can distinguish some colors from others; after 4 months they can focus on near or far objects. By the age of 4 or 5 months, they are able to recognize two- and three-dimensional objects, and they can perceive the gestalt organizing principles discovered by psychologists who study perception. By the age of 7 months, neural systems related to the processing of information about facial expressions are highly sophisticated and cause babies to respond differently to specific facial expressions (see Figure 3 *Neuroscience in Your Life*). Overall, their perceptual abilities rapidly improve: Sensitivity to visual stimuli, for instance, becomes three to four times greater at 1 year of age than it was at birth (Johnson, 2004; Striano & Vaish, 2006; Leppanen et al., 2007).

In addition to vision, infants display other impressive sensory capabilities. Newborns can distinguish different sounds to the point of being able to recognize their own mothers' voices at the age of 3 days. They can also make the subtle perceptual distinctions that underlie language abilities. For example, at 2 days of age, infants can distinguish between their native tongue and foreign languages, and they can discriminate between such closely related sounds as *ba* and *pa* when they are 4 days old. By 6 months of age, they can discriminate virtually any difference in sound that is relevant to the production of language. Moreover, they can recognize different tastes and smells at a very early age. There even seems to be something of a built-in sweet tooth: Neonates prefer liquids that have been sweetened with sugar over their unsweetened counterparts (Cohen & Cashon, 2003; Rivera-Gaxiola et al., 2005).

The Growing Child: Infancy Through Middle Childhood

It was during the windy days of March that the problem in the day-care center first arose. Its source: 10-month-old Russell Ruud. Otherwise a model of decorum, Russell had somehow learned how to unzip the Velcro chin strap to his winter hat. He would remove the hat whenever he got the urge, seemingly oblivious to the potential health problems that might follow.

But that was just the start of the real difficulty. To the chagrin of the teachers in the day-care center, not to speak of the children's parents, soon other children were following his lead, removing their own caps at will. Russell's mother, made aware of the anarchy at the day-care center—and the other parents' distress over Russell's behavior—pleaded innocent. "I never showed Russell how to unzip the Velcro," claimed his mother, Judith Ruud, an economist with the Congressional Budget Office in Washington, DC. "He learned by trial and error, and the other kids saw him do it one day when they were getting dressed for an outing." (Goleman, 1993, C10)

At the age of 10 months, Russell asserted his personality, illustrating the tremendous growth that occurs in a variety of domains during the first year of life. Throughout the remainder of childhood, moving from infancy into middle childhood and the start of adolescence around age 11 or 12, children develop physically, socially, and cognitively in extraordinary ways. In the remainder of this module, we'll consider this development.

PHYSICAL DEVELOPMENT

Children's physical growth provides the most obvious sign of development. During the first year of life, children typically triple their birthweight, and their height increases by about half. This rapid growth slows down as the child gets older—think how gigantic adults would be if that rate of growth was constant. From age 3 to the beginning of adolescence at around age 13, growth averages a gain of about 5 pounds and 3 inches a year (see Figure 4).

The physical changes that occur as children develop are not just a matter of increasing growth; the relationship of the size of the various body parts to one another changes dramatically as children age. As you can see in Figure 5, the head of a fetus (and a newborn) is disproportionately large. However, the head soon becomes more proportional in size to the rest of the body as growth occurs mainly in the trunk and legs (Berger, 2011).

DEVELOPMENT OF SOCIAL BEHAVIOR: TAKING ON THE WORLD

As anyone who has seen infants smiling at the sight of their mothers can guess, at the same time that infants grow physically and hone their perceptual abilities, they also develop socially. The nature of a child's early social development provides the foundation for social relationships that will last a lifetime.

Attachment, the positive emotional bond that develops between a child and a particular individual, is the most important form of social development that occurs during infancy. The earliest studies of attachment were carried out by animal

attachment The positive emotional bond that develops between a child and a particular individual.

ethologist Konrad Lorenz (1966). Lorenz focused on newborn goslings, which under normal circumstances instinctively follow their mother, the first moving object they perceive after birth. Lorenz found that goslings whose eggs were raised in an incubator and that viewed him immediately after hatching would follow his every movement as if he were their mother. He labeled this process *imprinting*, behavior that

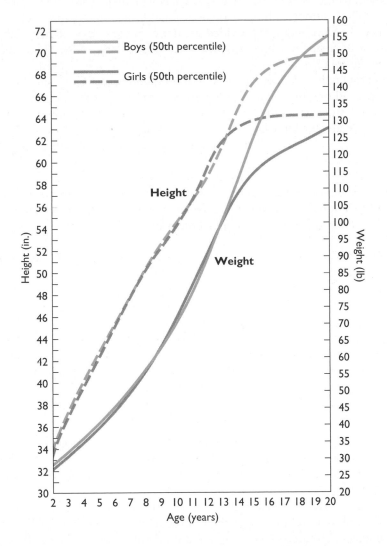

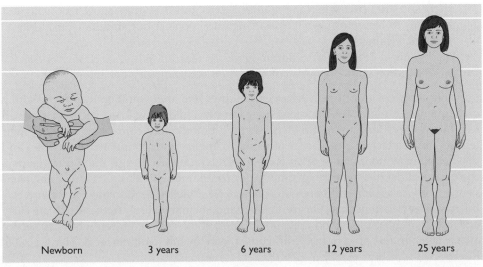

FIGURE 4 The average heights and weights of males and females in the United States from birth through age 20. At what ages are girls typically heavier and taller than boys? (Source: National Center for Health Statistics, 2000.)

FIGURE 5 As development progresses, the size of the head relative to the rest of the body decreases until the individual reaches adulthood. Why do you think the head starts out so large? (Source: Adapted from Figure 5 from W. J. Robbins, *Growth.* New Haven, CT: Yale University Press, 1928.)

FIGURE 6 Although the wire "mother" dispensed milk to the hungry infant monkey, the infant preferred the soft, terry-cloth "mother." Do you think human babies would react the same way? What does this experiment tell us about attachment? (Source: Harry Harlow Primate Laboratory/University of Wisconsin.)

Study Alert

Attachment—the positive emotional bond that develops between a child and a particular individual—is a key concept in understanding the social development of children.

takes place during a critical period and involves attachment to the first moving object that is observed.

Our understanding of attachment progressed when psychologist Harry Harlow, in a classic study, gave infant monkeys the choice of cuddling a wire "monkey" that provided milk or a soft, terry-cloth "monkey" that was warm but did not provide milk. Their choice was clear: They spent most of their time clinging to the warm cloth "monkey," although they made occasional forays to the wire monkey to nurse. Obviously, the cloth monkey provided greater comfort to the infants; milk alone was insufficient to create attachment (Harlow & Zimmerman, 1959; Blum, 2002; Levine, 2011; see Figure 6).

Building on this pioneering work with nonhumans, developmental psychologists have suggested that human attachment grows through the responsiveness of infants' caregivers to the signals the babies provide, such as crying, smiling, reaching, and clinging. The greater the caregiver's responsiveness to the child's signals, the more likely it is that the child will become securely attached. Full attachment eventually develops as a result of the complex series of interactions between caregiver and child. In the course of these interactions, the infant plays as critical and active of a role as the caregiver in the formation of the bond. Infants who respond positively to a caregiver produce more positive behavior on the caregiver's part, which, in turn, produces an even stronger degree of attachment in the child.

Assessing Attachment. Developmental psychologists have devised a quick and direct way to measure attachment. Developed by Mary Ainsworth, the *Ainsworth strange situation* consists of a sequence of events involving a child and (typically) his or her mother. Initially, the mother and baby enter an unfamiliar room, and the mother permits the baby to explore while she sits down. An adult stranger then enters the room; after this the mother leaves. The mother returns, and the stranger leaves. The mother once again leaves the baby alone, and the stranger returns. Finally, the stranger leaves, and the mother returns (Ainsworth et al., 1978; Combrink-Graham & McKenna, 2006; Behrens, Parker, & Haltigan, 2011).

Babies' reactions to the experimental situation vary drastically, depending, according to Ainsworth, on their degree of attachment to the mother:

- Securely attached children. Children who are *securely attached* employ the mother as a kind of home base; they explore independently but return to her occasionally. When she leaves, they exhibit distress, and they go to her when she returns.
- Avoidant children. *Avoidant* children do not cry when the mother leaves, and they seem to avoid her when she returns as if indifferent to her.
- Ambivalent children. *Ambivalent* children display anxiety before they are separated and are upset when the mother leaves, but they may show ambivalent reactions to her return, such as seeking close contact but simultaneously hitting and kicking her.
- Disorganized-disoriented children. A fourth reaction is *disorganized-disoriented*; these children show inconsistent and often contradictory behavior.

The nature of attachment between children and their mothers has far-reaching consequences for later development. For example, children who are securely attached to their mothers tend to be more socially and emotionally competent than are their less securely attached peers, and others find them more cooperative, capable, and playful. Furthermore, children who are securely attached at age 1 show fewer psychological difficulties when they grow older compared with avoidant and ambivalent youngsters. As adults, children who are securely attached tend to have more successful romantic relationships. On the other hand, being securely attached at an early age does not guarantee good adjustment later; conversely, children who lack secure attachment do not always have difficulties later in life (Mikulincer & Shaver, 2005; Roisman et al., 2005; Hardy, 2007).

The Father's Role. Although early developmental research focused largely on the mother-child relationship, more recent research has highlighted the father's role in parenting—and with good reason: The number of fathers who are primary caregivers for their children has grown significantly, and fathers play an increasingly important role in their children's lives. For example, in almost 13% of families with children, the father is the parent who stays at home to care for preschoolers (Parke, 2004; Day & Lamb, 2004; Halford, 2006).

When fathers interact with their children, their play often differs from mothers' play. Fathers engage in more physical, rough-and-tumble sorts of activities, whereas mothers play more verbal and traditional games, such as peekaboo. Despite such behavioral differences, the nature of attachment between fathers and children compared with that between mothers and children can be similar. In fact, children can form multiple attachments simultaneously (Borisenko, 2007; Pellis & Pellis, 2007; Diener et al., 2008).

Social Relationships with Peers. By the time they are 2 years old, children become less dependent on their parents, more self-reliant, and increasingly prefer to play with friends. Initially, play is relatively independent: Even though they may be sitting side by side, 2-year-olds pay more attention to toys than to one another when playing. Later, however, children actively interact, modify one another's behavior, and exchange roles during play (Lindsey & Colwell, 2003; Colwell & Lindsey, 2005; Whitney & Green, 2011).

Cultural factors also affect children's styles of play. For example, Korean-American children engage in less pretend play than their Anglo-American counterparts (Bai, 2005; Drewes, 2005; Suizzo & Bornstein, 2006).

As children reach school age, their social interactions begin to follow set patterns and become more frequent. They may engage in elaborate games involving teams and rigid rules. This play serves purposes other than mere enjoyment. It allows children to become increasingly competent in their social interactions with others. Through play they learn to take the perspective of other people and to infer others' thoughts and feelings, even when those thoughts and feelings are not directly expressed (Royzman, Cassidy, & Baron, 2003).

In short, social interaction helps children interpret the meaning of others' behavior and develop the capacity to respond appropriately. Furthermore, children learn physical and emotional self-control: They learn to avoid hitting a playmate who beats them at a game. They learn to be polite and to control their emotional displays and facial expressions (e.g., smiling even when receiving a disappointing gift). Situations that provide children with opportunities for social interaction, then, may enhance their social development (Feldman, 1993; Talukdar & Shastri, 2006; Whitebread et al., 2009).

The Consequences of Child Care Outside the Home. Research on the importance of social interaction is corroborated by work that examines the benefits of child care out of the home, which is an important part of an increasing number of children's lives. For instance, almost 30% of preschool children whose mothers work outside the home spend their days in child-care centers. By the age of 6 months, almost two-thirds of infants are cared for by people other than their mothers for part of the day. Most of these infants begin child care before the age of 4 months and are cared for by people other than their mothers almost 30 hours per week (National Research Council, 2001; NICHD Early Child Care Research Network, 2006; see Figure 7 on the next page).

Do child-care arrangements outside the home benefit children's development? If the programs are of high quality, they can. According to the results of a large study supported by the U.S. National Institute of Child Health and Development, children who attend high-quality child-care centers may not only do as well as children who stay at home with their parents, but in some respects they may actually do better. Children in child care are generally more considerate and sociable than other children, and they interact more positively with teachers. They may also be more

FIGURE 7 According to a study by the National Institute of Child Health and Human Development, children were more likely to spend time in some kind of child care outside the home or family as they got older. (Source: NICHD, 2006.)

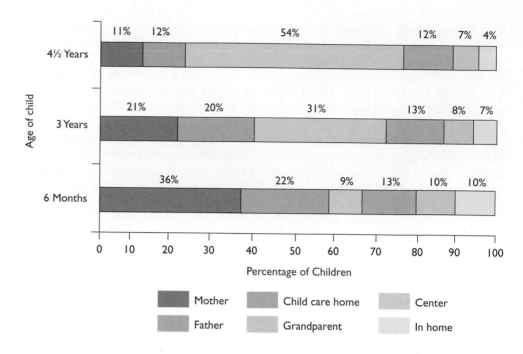

authoritarian parents Parents who are rigid and punitive and value unquestioning obedience from their children.

permissive parents Parents who give their children relaxed or inconsistent direction and, although they are warm, require little of them.

compliant and regulate their own behavior more effectively (NICHD Early Child Care Research Network, 1999, 2001).

In addition, especially for children from poor or disadvantaged homes, child care in specially enriched environments—those with many toys, books, a variety of children, and high-quality providers—may be more intellectually stimulating than the home environment. Such child care can lead to increased intellectual achievement, demonstrated in higher IQ scores, and better language development. In fact, children in care centers sometimes are found to score higher on tests of cognitive abilities than those who are cared for by their mothers or by sitters or home day-care providers—effects that last into adulthood (Wilgoren, 1999; Burchinal, Roberts, & Riggins, 2000; Dearing, McCartney, & Taylor, 2009).

However, child care outside the home does not have universally positive outcomes. Children may feel insecure after placement in low-quality child care or in multiple child-care settings. Furthermore, some research suggests that infants who are involved in outside care more than 20 hours a week in the first year show less secure attachment to their mothers than do those who have not been in child care outside the home. Finally, children who spent long hours in child care as infants and preschoolers may have a reduced ability to work independently and to manage their time effectively when they reach elementary school (NICHD Early Child Care Research Network, 2001; Vandell et al., 2005; Pluess & Belsky, 2009).

The key to the success of nonparental child care is its quality. High-quality child care produces benefits; low-quality child care provides little or no gain and may even hinder children's development. In short, significant benefits result from the social interaction and intellectual stimulation provided by high-quality child-care centers—especially for children from impoverished environments (NICHD Early Child Care Research Network, 2000, 2002; National Association for the Education of Young Children, 2005; Zaslow, Halle, & Martin, 2006).

Parenting Styles and Social Development. Parents' child-rearing practices are critical in shaping their children's social competence. According to classic research by developmental psychologist Diana Baumrind, four main categories describe different parenting styles (Figure 8). Rigid and punitive, **authoritarian parents** value unquestioning obedience from their children. They have strict standards and discourage expressions of disagreement. **Permissive parents** give their children relaxed or

Parenting Style	Parent Behavior	Type of Behavior Produced in Child
Authoritarian	Rigid, punitive, strict standards (example: "If you don't clean your room, I'm going to take away your iPod for good and ground you.")	Unsociable, unfriendly, withdrawn
Permissive	Lax, inconsistent, undemanding (example: "It might be good to clean your room, but I guess it can wait.")	Immature, moody, dependent, low self-control
Authoritative	Firm, sets limits and goals, uses reasoning, encourages independence (example: "You'll need to clean your room before we can go out to the restaurant. As soon as you finish, we'll leave.")	Good social skills, likable, self-reliant, independent
Uninvolved	Detached emotionally, sees role only as providing food, clothing, and shelter (example: "I couldn't care less if your room is a pigsty.")	Indifferent, rejecting behavior

FIGURE 8 According to developmental psychologist Diana Baumrind (1971), four main parenting styles characterize child rearing.

inconsistent direction and, although they are warm, require little of them. In contrast, **authoritative parents** are firm and set limits for their children. As the children get older, these parents try to reason and explain things to them. They also set clear goals and encourage their children's independence. Finally, **uninvolved parents** show little interest in their children. Emotionally detached, they view parenting as nothing more than providing food, clothing, and shelter for children. At their most extreme, uninvolved parents are guilty of neglect, a form of child abuse (Baumrind, 2005; Lagacé-Séguin & d'Entremont, 2006; Lewis & Lamb, 2011).

As you might expect, the four kinds of child-rearing styles seem to produce very different kinds of behavior in children (with many exceptions, of course). Children of authoritarian parents tend to be unsociable, unfriendly, and relatively withdrawn. In contrast, permissive parents' children show immaturity, moodiness, dependence, and low self-control. The children of authoritative parents fare best: With high social skills, they are likable, self-reliant, independent, and cooperative. Worst off are the children of uninvolved parents; they feel unloved and emotionally detached, and their physical development and cognitive development are impeded (Saarni, 1999; Berk, 2005; Snyder, Cramer, & Afrank, 2005).

Before we rush to congratulate authoritative parents and condemn authoritarian, permissive, and uninvolved ones, it is important to note that in many cases non-authoritative parents also produce perfectly well-adjusted children. Moreover, children are born with a particular **temperament**—a basic, inborn characteristic way of responding and behavioral style. Some children are naturally easygoing and cheerful, whereas others are irritable and fussy or pensive and quiet. The kind of temperament a baby is born with may in part bring about specific kinds of parental child-rearing styles (Miner & Clarke-Stewart, 2008; Coplan, Reichel, & Rowan, 2009; Costa & Figueiredo, 2011).

In addition, children vary considerably in their degree of *resilience*, the ability to overcome circumstances that place them at high risk for psychological or even physical harm. Highly resilient children have temperaments that evoke positive responses from caregivers. Such children display unusual social skills: outgoingness, intelligence, and a feeling that they have control over their lives. In a sense, resilient children try to shape their own environment rather than being victimized by it (Luthar, Cicchetti, & Becker, 2000; Deater-Deckard, Ivy, & Smith, 2005; Vellacott, 2007). (Also see *PsychWork*.)

authoritative parents Parents who are firm, set clear limits, reason with their children, and explain things to them.

uninvolved parents Parents who show little interest in their children and are emotionally detached.

Study Alert
Know the four major types of child-rearing practices—authoritarian, permissive, authoritative, and uninvolved—and their effects.

temperament A basic, inborn characteristic way of responding and behavioral style.

PsychWork
CHILD PROTECTION CASEWORKER

Name: Jason Larson

Education: BS in Human Services, Montana State University

Children are among the most vulnerable members of society. When they face abuse or neglect, a child protective services agency intervenes, and a caseworker is assigned to advocate for the child.

Jason Larson, a child protection caseworker with the Child and Family Services Division of the Montana Department of Public Health and Human Services, notes that every case is unique. "The age of the children, the physical condition of the parents or caretakers, the physical condition of the home, whether the alleged perpetrator is living in the home or has access to the child are all factors to be considered," he said. "In addition, whether or not I can corroborate the information quickly enough to gauge whether or not a child can stay in the home or needs to be removed is important as well," he added.

Larson, who has been a caseworker for the past 15 years, works in a remote area of Montana, which provides its own set of challenges. "Living and serving the rural part of Montana I have to be very creative with the services we have, as we are very limited in a lot of small towns across Montana," Larson noted. "As a result, we use many different approaches to protect children."

One of those approaches, according to Larson, is a process called Family Group Decision Making, meetings in which the parents and all the service providers are at one table discussing the children and the family's situation.

"Everyone goes around the room and explains their concerns, and once this is complete, a plan is made for them to follow," he notes. "These meetings are very effective in assisting the family as a whole so that we can apply all the resources available."

We also need to keep in mind that these findings regarding child-rearing styles apply primarily to U.S. society, which highly values children's growing independence and diminishing reliance on their parents. In contrast, Japanese parents encourage dependence to promote the values of cooperation and community life. These differences in cultural values result in very different philosophies of child rearing. For example, Japanese mothers believe it is a punishment to make a young child sleep alone; thus, many children sleep next to their mothers throughout infancy and toddlerhood (Kawasaki et al., 1994; Dennis et al., 2002; Jones, 2007).

In sum, a child's upbringing results from the child-rearing philosophy parents hold, the specific practices they use, and the nature of their own and their child's personalities. As is the case with other aspects of development, then, behavior is a function of a complex interaction of environmental and genetic factors.

Erikson's Theory of Psychosocial Development. In tracing the course of social development, some theorists have considered how the challenges of society and culture change as an individual matures. Following this path, psychoanalyst Erik Erikson developed one of the more comprehensive theories of social development. Erikson (1963) viewed the developmental changes that occur throughout life as a series of eight stages of psychosocial development; of these, four occur during childhood. **Psychosocial development** involves changes in our interactions and understanding of one another as well as in our knowledge and understanding of ourselves as members of society.

Erikson suggests that passage through each of the stages necessitates the resolution of a crisis or conflict. Accordingly, Erikson represents each stage as a pairing of the most positive and most negative aspects of the crisis of that period. Although each crisis is never resolved entirely—life becomes increasingly complicated as we grow older—it has to be resolved sufficiently to equip us to deal with demands made during the following stage of development.

psychosocial development Development of individuals' interactions and understanding of each other and of their knowledge and understanding of themselves as members of society.

In the first stage of psychosocial development, the **trust-versus-mistrust stage** (ages birth to 1½ years), infants develop feelings of trust if their physical requirements and psychological needs for attachment are consistently met and their interactions with the world are generally positive. In contrast, inconsistent care and unpleasant interactions with others can lead to mistrust and leave an infant unable to meet the challenges required in the next stage of development.

In the second stage, the **autonomy-versus-shame-and-doubt stage** (ages 1½ to 3 years), toddlers develop independence and autonomy if exploration and freedom are encouraged, or they experience shame, self-doubt, and unhappiness if they are overly restricted and protected. According to Erikson, the key to the development of autonomy during this period is that the child's caregivers provide the appropriate amount of control. If parents provide too much control, children cannot assert themselves and develop their own sense of control over their environment; if parents provide too little control, the children become overly demanding and controlling.

Next, children face the crises of the **initiative-versus-guilt stage** (ages 3 to 6). In this stage, children's desire to act independently conflicts with the guilt that comes from the unintended and unexpected consequences of such behavior. Children in this period come to understand that they are persons in their own right, and they begin to make decisions about their behavior. If parents react positively to children's attempts at independence, they will help their children resolve the initiative-versus-guilt crisis positively.

The fourth and last stage of childhood is the **industry-versus-inferiority stage** (ages 6 to 12). During this period, increasing competency in all areas, whether social interactions or academic skills, characterizes successful psychosocial development. In contrast, difficulties in this stage lead to feelings of failure and inadequacy.

Erikson's theory suggests that psychosocial development continues throughout life, and he proposes four more crises that are faced after childhood (described in the next module). Although his theory has been criticized on several grounds—such as the imprecision of the concepts he employs and his greater emphasis on male development than female development—it remains influential and is one of the few theories that encompass the entire life span.

COGNITIVE DEVELOPMENT: CHILDREN'S THINKING ABOUT THE WORLD

Suppose you had two drinking glasses of different shapes—one short and broad and one tall and thin. Now imagine that you filled the short, broad one with soda about halfway and then poured the liquid from that glass into the tall one. The soda would appear to fill about three-quarters of the second glass. If someone asked you whether there was more soda in the second glass than there had been in the first, what would you say?

You might think that such a simple question hardly deserves an answer; of course, there is no difference in the amount of soda in the two glasses. However, most 4-year-olds would be likely to say that there is more soda in the second glass. If you then poured the soda back into the short glass, they would say there is now less soda than there was in the taller glass.

Why are young children confused by this problem? The reason is not immediately obvious. Anyone who has observed preschoolers must be impressed by how far they have progressed from the early stages of development. They speak with ease, know the alphabet, count, play complex games, use computers, tell stories, and communicate ably. Yet despite this seeming sophistication, there are deep gaps in children's understanding of the world. Some theorists have suggested that children cannot understand certain ideas and concepts until they reach a particular stage of **cognitive development**—the process by which a child's understanding of the world changes as a function of age and experience. In contrast to the theories of physical and social development discussed earlier (such as those of Erikson), theories of

trust-versus-mistrust stage According to Erikson, the first stage of psychosocial development, occurring from birth to age 1½ years, during which time infants develop feelings of trust or lack of trust.

autonomy-versus-shame-and-doubt stage The period during which, according to Erikson, toddlers (ages 1½ to 3 years) develop independence and autonomy if exploration and freedom are encouraged or shame and self-doubt if they are restricted and overprotected.

initiative-versus-guilt stage According to Erikson, the period during which children ages 3 to 6 years experience conflict between independence of action and the sometimes negative results of that action.

industry-versus-inferiority stage According to Erikson, the last stage of childhood, during which children age 6 to 12 years may develop positive social interactions with others or may feel inadequate and become less sociable.

Study Alert

Four of Erikson's stages of psychosocial development occur during childhood: trust-versus-mistrust, autonomy-versus-shame-and-doubt, initiative-versus-guilt, and industry-versus inferiority.

cognitive development The process by which a child's understanding of the world changes as a function of age and experience.

Cognitive Stage	Approximate Age Range	Major Characteristics
Sensorimotor	Birth–2 years	Development of object permanence, development of motor skills, little or no capacity for symbolic representation
Preoperational	2–7 years	Development of language and symbolic thinking, egocentric thinking
Concrete operational	7–12 years	Development of conservation, mastery of concept of reversibility
Formal operational	12 years–adulthood	Development of logical and abstract thinking

FIGURE 9 According to Piaget, all children pass through four stages of cognitive development.

cognitive development seek to explain the quantitative and qualitative intellectual advances that occur during development.

Piaget's Theory of Cognitive Development. No theory of cognitive development has had more impact than that of Swiss psychologist Jean Piaget. Piaget (1970) suggested that children around the world proceed through a series of four stages in a fixed order. He maintained that these stages differ not only in the *quantity* of information acquired at each stage but in the *quality* of knowledge and understanding as well. Taking an interactionist point of view, he suggested that movement from one stage to the next occurs when a child reaches an appropriate level of maturation *and* is exposed to relevant types of experiences. Piaget assumed that, without having such experiences, children cannot reach their highest level of cognitive growth.

Piaget proposed four stages: the sensorimotor, preoperational, concrete operational, and formal operational (see Figure 9). Let's examine each of them and the approximate ages that they span.

Sensorimotor Stage: Birth to 2 Years. During the **sensorimotor stage,** children base their understanding of the world primarily on touching, sucking, chewing, shaking, and manipulating objects. In the initial part of the stage, children have relatively little competence in representing the environment by using images, language, or other kinds of symbols. Consequently, infants lack what Piaget calls **object permanence,** the awareness that objects—and people—continue to exist even if they are out of sight.

How can we know that children lack object permanence? Although we cannot ask infants, we can observe their reactions when a toy they are playing with is hidden under a blanket. Until the age of about 9 months, children will make no attempt to locate the hidden toy. However, soon after that age they will begin an active search for the missing object, indicating that they have developed a mental representation of the toy. Object permanence, then, is a critical development during the sensorimotor stage.

Preoperational Stage: 2 to 7 Years. The most important development during the **preoperational stage** is the use of language. Children develop internal representational systems that allow them to describe people, events, and feelings. They even use symbols in play, pretending, for example, that a book pushed across the floor is a car.

Although children use more advanced thinking in this stage than they did in the earlier sensorimotor stage, their thinking is still qualitatively inferior to that of adults. We see this when we observe a preoperational child using **egocentric thought,** a way of thinking in which the child views the world entirely from his or her own perspective. Preoperational children think that everyone shares their perspective and knowledge. Thus, children's stories and explanations to adults can be maddeningly uninformative because they are delivered without any context. For example, a

sensorimotor stage According to Piaget, the stage from birth to 2 years, during which a child has little competence in representing the environment by using images, language, or other symbols.

object permanence The awareness that objects—and people—continue to exist even if they are out of sight.

preoperational stage According to Piaget, the period from 2 to 7 years of age that is characterized by language development.

egocentric thought A way of thinking in which a child views the world entirely from his or her own perspective.

preoperational child may start a story with, "He wouldn't let me go," neglecting to mention who "he" is or where the storyteller wanted to go. We also see egocentric thinking when children at the preoperational stage play hiding games. For instance, 3-year-olds frequently hide with their faces against a wall and covering their eyes—although they are still in plain view. It seems to them that if *they* cannot see, then no one else will be able to see them because they assume that others share their view.

In addition, preoperational children have not yet developed the ability to understand the **principle of conservation,** which is the knowledge that quantity is unrelated to the arrangement and physical appearance of objects. Children who understand the principle of conservation have the awareness that important attributes of objects (such as the amount or volume) do not change despite superficial changes. In contrast, children who have not mastered this concept do not know that the overall amount or volume of an object does not change when its shape or configuration changes.

The question about the two glasses—one short and broad, and the other tall and thin—with which we began our discussion of cognitive development illustrates this point clearly. Children who do not understand the principle of conservation invariably state that the amount of liquid changes as it is poured back and forth between glasses of different sizes. They cannot comprehend that a transformation in appearance does not imply a transformation in amount. Instead, it seems as reasonable to the child that there is a change in quantity as it does to the adult that there is no change.

In a number of other ways, some quite startling, the failure to understand the principle of conservation affects children's responses. Research demonstrates that children during the preoperational period may completely misunderstand principles that are obvious to and unquestioned by adults and that children do not grasp the concept of conservation until the next stage of cognitive development (see Figure 10).

Concrete Operational Stage: 7 to 12 Years. Mastery of the principle of conservation marks the beginning of the **concrete operational stage.** However, children do not fully understand some aspects of conservation—such as conservation of weight and volume—for a number of years.

During the concrete operational stage, children develop the ability to think in a more logical manner and begin to overcome some of the egocentrism characteristic of the preoperational period. One of the major principles children learn during this stage is reversibility, the idea that some changes can be undone by reversing an earlier action. For example, they can understand that when someone rolls a ball of clay into a long sausage shape, that person can recreate the original ball by reversing the action. Children can even conceptualize this principle in their heads without having to see the action performed before them.

Although children make important advances in their logical capabilities during the concrete operational stage, their thinking still displays one major limitation: They are largely bound to the concrete, physical reality of the world. For the most part, they have difficulty understanding questions of an abstract or hypothetical nature.

Formal Operational Stage: 12 Years to Adulthood. The **formal operational stage** produces a new kind of thinking that is abstract, formal, and logical. Thinking is no longer tied to events that individuals observe in the environment but makes use of logical techniques to resolve problems.

The way in which children approach the "pendulum problem" devised by Piaget (Piaget & Inhelder, 1958) illustrates the emergence of formal operational thinking. The problem solver is asked to figure out what determines how fast a pendulum swings. Is it the length of the string, the weight of the pendulum, or the force with which the pendulum is pushed? (For the record, the answer is the length of the string.)

Children in the concrete operational stage approach the problem haphazardly without a logical or rational plan of action. For example, they may simultaneously change the length of the string, the weight on the string, and the force with which they push the pendulum. Because they are varying all the factors at once, they cannot tell which factor is the critical one. In contrast, people in the formal operational stage approach the problem systematically. Acting as if they were scientists conducting

Children who have not mastered the principle of conservation assume that the volume of liquid increases when it is poured from a short, wide container to a tall, thin one. What other tasks might a child under age 7 have difficulty comprehending?

principle of conservation The knowledge that quantity is unrelated to the arrangement and physical appearance of objects.

concrete operational stage According to Piaget, the period from 7 to 12 years of age that is characterized by logical thought and a loss of egocentrism.

formal operational stage According to Piaget, the period from age 12 to adulthood that is characterized by abstract thought.

FIGURE 10 These tests are frequently used to assess whether children have learned the principle of conservation across a variety of dimensions. Do you think children in the preoperational stage can be taught to avoid conservation mistakes before the typical age of mastery? (Source: Schickedanz, Judith A., Schickedanz, David I., Forsyth, Peggy D., and Forsyth, G. Alfred, *Understanding Children and Adolescents* (4th Ed.), p. 440, Figure 13.1, © 2001. Reprinted by permission of Pearson Education, Inc., Upper Saddle River, NJ.)

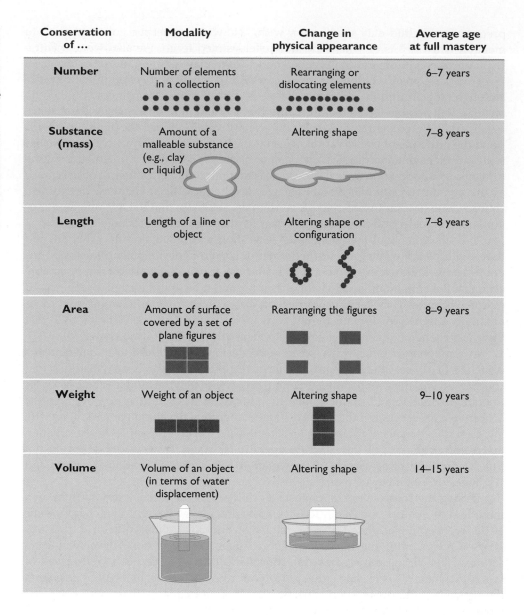

Conservation of ...	Modality	Change in physical appearance	Average age at full mastery
Number	Number of elements in a collection	Rearranging or dislocating elements	6–7 years
Substance (mass)	Amount of a malleable substance (e.g., clay or liquid)	Altering shape	7–8 years
Length	Length of a line or object	Altering shape or configuration	7–8 years
Area	Amount of surface covered by a set of plane figures	Rearranging the figures	8–9 years
Weight	Weight of an object	Altering shape	9–10 years
Volume	Volume of an object (in terms of water displacement)	Altering shape	14–15 years

an experiment, they examine the effects of changes in one variable at a time. This ability to rule out competing possibilities characterizes formal operational thought.

Although formal operational thought emerges during the teenage years, some individuals use this type of thinking only infrequently. Moreover, it appears that many individuals never reach this stage at all; most studies show that only 40–60% of college students and adults fully reach it, with some estimates running as low as 25% of the general population. In addition, in certain cultures—particularly those that are less technically oriented than Western societies—almost no one reaches the formal operational stage (Keating & Clark, 1980; Super, 1980; Genovese, 2006).

Stages Versus Continuous Development: Is Piaget Right? No other theorist has given us as comprehensive a theory of cognitive development as Piaget. Still, many contemporary theorists suggest that a better explanation of how children develop cognitively can be provided by theories that do not involve a stage approach. For instance, children are not always consistent in their performance of tasks that—if Piaget's theory is accurate—ought to be performed equally well at a particular stage (Feldman, 2003, 2004).

Furthermore, some developmental psychologists suggest that cognitive development proceeds in a more continuous fashion than Piaget's stage theory implies. They propose that cognitive development is primarily quantitative rather than qualitative. They argue that although there are differences in when, how, and to what extent a child can use specific cognitive abilities—reflecting quantitative changes, the underlying cognitive processes change relatively little with age (Gelman & Baillargeon, 1983; Case & Okamoto, 1996).

Piaget also underestimated the age at which infants and children can understand specific concepts and principles; in fact, they seem to be more sophisticated in their cognitive abilities than Piaget believed. For instance, some evidence suggests that infants as young as 5 months have rudimentary mathematical skills (Wynn, Bloom, & Chiang, 2002; McCrink & Wynn, 2007; van Marle & Wynn, 2009).

Despite such criticisms, most developmental psychologists agree that although the processes that underlie changes in cognitive abilities may not unfold in the manner Piaget's theory suggests, he has generally provided us with an accurate account of age-related changes in cognitive development. Moreover, his theory has had an enormous influence in education. For example, Piaget suggests that individuals cannot increase their cognitive performance unless both cognitive readiness brought about by maturation and appropriate environmental stimulation are present. This view has inspired the nature and structure of educational curricula and teaching methods. Researchers have also used Piaget's theory and methods to investigate issues surrounding animal cognition, such as whether primates show object permanence (they seem to; Hauser, 2000; Egan, 2005; Cunningham, 2006).

Information-Processing Approaches: Charting Children's Mental Programs. If cognitive development does not proceed as a series of stages as Piaget suggested, what does underlie the enormous growth in children's cognitive abilities that even the most untutored eye can observe? To many developmental psychologists, changes in **information processing,** the way in which people take in, use, and store information, account for cognitive development (Cashon & Cohen, 2004; Munakata, 2006; Casasola, 2011).

information processing The way in which people take in, use, and store information.

According to this approach, quantitative changes occur in children's ability to organize and manipulate information. From this perspective, children become increasingly adept at information processing, much as a computer program may become more sophisticated as a programmer modifies it on the basis of experience. Information-processing approaches consider the kinds of "mental programs" that children invoke when approaching problems.

Several significant changes occur in children's information-processing capabilities. For one thing, speed of processing increases with age as some abilities become more automatic. The speed at which children can scan, recognize, and compare stimuli increases with age. As they grow older, children can pay attention to stimuli longer and discriminate between different stimuli more readily, and they are less easily distracted (Van den Wildenberg & Van der Molen, 2004; Diaz & Bell, 2011).

metacognition An awareness and understanding of one's own cognitive processes.

Memory also improves dramatically with age. Preschoolers can hold only two or three chunks of information in short-term memory, 5-year-olds can hold four, and 7-year-olds can hold five. (Adults are able to keep seven, plus or minus two, chunks in short-term memory.) The size of the chunks also grows with age, as does the sophistication and organization of knowledge stored in memory (see Figure 11). Still, memory capabilities are impressive at a very early age: Even before they can speak, infants can remember for months events in which they actively participated (Cowan et al., 2003; Bayliss et al., 2005a).

Finally improvement in information processing relates to advances in **metacognition,** an awareness and understanding of one's own cognitive processes. Metacognition involves the planning, monitoring, and revising of cognitive strategies. Younger children, who lack an awareness of their own cognitive processes, often do not realize their incapabilities. Thus, when they misunderstand others, they may fail to recognize their own errors. It is only later, when

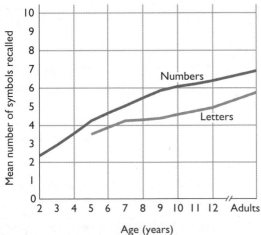

FIGURE 11 Memory span increases with age for both numbers and letters.
(Source: Adapted from Dempster, 1981.)

PsychTech

A quarter of parents with children between the ages of 0 to 5 report that their children use the Internet.

metacognitive abilities become more sophisticated, that children are able to know when they *don't* understand. Such increasing sophistication reflects a change in children's *theory of mind*, their knowledge and beliefs about the way the mind operates (Matthews & Funke, 2006; Lockl & Schneider, 2007; Sodian, 2011).

Vygotsky's View of Cognitive Development: Considering Culture. According to Russian developmental psychologist Lev Vygotsky, the culture in which we are raised significantly affects our cognitive development. In an increasingly influential view, Vygotsky suggests that the focus on individual performance of both Piagetian and information-processing approaches is misplaced. Instead, he holds that we cannot understand cognitive development without taking into account the social aspects of learning (Vygotsky, 1926/1997; Maynard & Martini, 2005; Rieber & Robinson, 2006).

Vygotsky argues that cognitive development occurs as a consequence of social interactions in which children work with others to jointly solve problems. Through such interactions, children's cognitive skills increase, and they gain the ability to function intellectually on their own. More specifically, he suggests that children's cognitive abilities increase when they encounter information that falls within their zone of proximal development. The **zone of proximal development (ZPD)** is the gap between what children already are able to accomplish on their own and what they are not quite ready to do by themselves. When children receive information that falls within the ZPD, they can increase their understanding or master a new task. In contrast, if the information lies outside children's ZPD, they will not be able to master it.

zone of proximal development (ZPD)
According to Vygotsky, the gap between what children already are able to accomplish on their own and what they are not quite ready to do by themselves.

In short, cognitive development occurs when parents, teachers, or skilled peers assist a child by presenting information that is both new and within the ZPD. This type of assistance, called *scaffolding,* provides support for learning and problem solving that encourages independence and growth. Vygotsky claims that scaffolding not only promotes the solution of specific problems, but also aids in the development of overall cognitive abilities (Schaller & Crandall, 2004).

More than other approaches to cognitive development, Vygotsky's theory considers how an individual's specific cultural and social context affects intellectual growth. The way in which children understand the world grows out of interactions with parents, peers, and other members of a specific culture (John-Steiner & Mahn, 2003; Kozulin et al., 2003).

RECAP/EVALUATE/RETHINK

RECAP

LO 28-1 What are the major competencies of newborns?

- Newborns, or neonates, have reflexes—unlearned, involuntary responses that occur automatically in the presence of certain stimuli. (p. 340)
- Sensory abilities also develop rapidly; infants can distinguish color, depth, sound, tastes, and smells relatively soon after birth. (p. 341)
- After birth, physical development is rapid; children typically triple their birthweight in a year. (p. 344)

LO 28-2 What are the milestones of physical and social development during childhood?

- Attachment—the positive emotional bond between a child and a particular individual—marks social

development in infancy. Measured in the laboratory by means of the Ainsworth stranger situation, attachment relates to later social and emotional adjustment. (p. 344)
- As children become older, the nature of their social interactions with peers changes. Initially play occurs relatively independently, but it becomes increasingly cooperative. (p. 347)
- The different child-rearing styles include authoritarian, permissive, authoritative, and uninvolved. (p. 348)
- According to Erikson, eight stages of psychosocial development involve people's changing interactions and understanding of themselves and others. During childhood, the four stages are trust-versus-mistrust (birth to 1½ years), autonomy-versus-shame-and-doubt (1½ to 3 years), initiative-versus-guilt (3 to 6 years), and industry-versus-inferiority (6 to 12 years). (p. 350)

LO 28-3 How does cognitive development proceed during childhood?

- Piaget's theory suggests that cognitive development proceeds through four stages in which qualitative changes occur in thinking: the sensorimotor stage (birth to 2 years), the preoperational stage (2 to 7 years), the concrete operational stage (7 to 12 years), and the formal operational stage (12 years to adulthood). (p. 352)
- Information-processing approaches suggest that quantitative changes occur in children's ability to organize and manipulate information about the world, such as significant increases in speed of processing, attention span, and memory. In addition, children advance in metacognition, the awareness and understanding of one's own cognitive processes. (p. 355)
- Vygotsky argued that children's cognitive development occurs as a consequence of social interactions in which children and others work together to solve problems. (p. 356)

EVALUATE

1. Researchers studying newborns use _____, or the decrease in the response to a stimulus that occurs after repeated presentations of the same stimulus, as an indicator of a baby's interest.
2. The emotional bond that develops between a child and its caregiver is known as _____.
3. Match the parenting style with its definition:
   1. Permissive
   2. Authoritative
   3. Authoritarian
   4. Uninvolved
   a. Rigid; highly punitive; demanding obedience
   b. Gives little direction; lax on obedience
   c. Firm but fair; tries to explain parental decisions
   d. Emotionally detached and unloving

4. Erikson's theory of _____ development involves a series of eight stages, each of which must be resolved for a person to develop optimally.
5. Match the stage of development with the thinking style characteristic of that stage:
   1. Egocentric thought
   2. Object permanence
   3. Abstract reasoning
   4. Conservation
   a. Sensorimotor
   b. Formal operational
   c. Preoperational
   d. Concrete operational reversibility
6. _____-_____ theories of development suggest that the way in which a child handles information is critical to his or her development.
7. According to Vygotsky, information that is within a child's _____ _____ _____ _____ is most likely to result in cognitive development.

RETHINK

1. Do you think the widespread use of IQ testing in the United States contributes to parents' views that their children's academic success is due largely to the children's innate intelligence? Why? Would it be possible (or desirable) to change this view?
2. *From the perspective of a child-care provider:* If a parent was not sure whether to enroll his or her child in your program, what advice would you give about the possible positive and negative consequences about day care?

Answers to Evaluate Questions

1. habituation; 2. attachment; 3. 1-b, 2-c, 3-a, 4-d; 4. psychosocial; 5. 1-c, 2-a, 3-b, 4-d; 6. Information-processing; 7. zone of proximal development

KEY TERMS

neonate p. 340
reflexes p. 340
habituation p. 342
attachment p. 344
authoritarian parents p. 348
permissive parents p. 348
authoritative parents p. 349
uninvolved parents p. 349
temperament p. 349

psychosocial development p. 350
trust-versus-mistrust stage p. 351
autonomy-versus-shame-and-doubt stage p. 351
initiative-versus-guilt stage p. 351
industry-versus-inferiority stage p. 351

cognitive development p. 351
sensorimotor stage p. 352
object permanence p. 352
preoperational stage p. 352
egocentric thought p. 352
principle of conservation p. 353
concrete operational stage p. 353

formal operational stage p. 353
information processing p. 355
metacognition p. 355
zone of proximal development (ZPD) p. 356

Adolescence: Becoming an Adult

LO 29-1 What major physical, social, and cognitive transitions characterize adolescence?

Joseph Charles, Age 13: Being 13 is very hard at school. I have to be bad in order to be considered cool. I sometimes do things that aren't good. I have talked back to my teachers and been disrespectful to them. I do want to be good, but it's just too hard. (Gibbs, 2005, p. 51)

Trevor Kelson, Age 15: "Keep the Hell Out of my Room!" says a sign on Trevor's bedroom wall, just above an unmade bed, a desk littered with dirty T-shirts and candy wrappers, and a floor covered with clothes. Is there a carpet? "Somewhere," he says with a grin. "I think it's gold." (Fields-Meyer, 1995, p. 53)

Lauren Barry, Age 18: "I went to a National Honor Society induction. The parents were just staring at me. I think they couldn't believe someone with pink hair could be smart. I want to be a high-school teacher, but I'm afraid that, based on my appearance, they won't hire me." (Gordon et al., 1999, p. 47)

Although Joseph, Trevor, and Lauren have never met, they share anxieties that are common to adolescence—concerns about friends, parents, appearance, independence, and their futures.

adolescence The developmental stage between childhood and adulthood.

Adolescence, the developmental stage between childhood and adulthood, is a crucial period. It is a time of profound changes and, occasionally, turmoil. Considerable biological change occurs as adolescents attain sexual and physical maturity. At the same time and rivaling these physiological changes, important social, emotional, and cognitive changes occur as adolescents strive for independence and move toward adulthood.

Because many years of schooling precede most people's entry into the workforce in Western societies, the stage of adolescence is fairly long; it begins just before the teenage years and ends just after them. Adolescents are no longer children, yet society doesn't quite consider them adults. They face a period of rapid physical, cognitive, and social change that affects them for the rest of their lives.

Dramatic changes in society also affect adolescents' development. More than half of all children in the United States will spend all or some of their childhood and adolescence in single-parent families. Furthermore, adolescents spend considerably less time with their parents and more with their peers than they did several decades ago. Finally, the ethnic and cultural diversity of adolescents as a group is increasing dramatically. A third of all adolescents today are of non-European descent; by the year 2050 the number of adolescents of Hispanic, African-American, Native-American, and Asian origin collectively will surpass that of whites (National Adolescent Health Information Center, 2003).

Physical Development: The Changing Adolescent

If you think back to the start of your own adolescence, the most dramatic changes you probably remember are physical. A spurt in height, the growth of breasts in girls, deepening voices in boys, the development of body hair, and intense sexual feelings

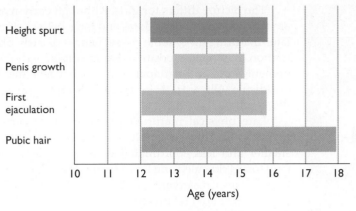

Average male

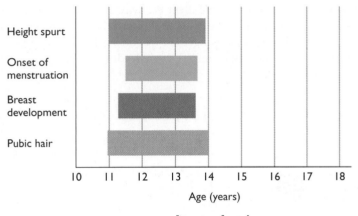

Average female

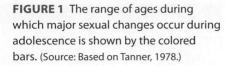

FIGURE 1 The range of ages during which major sexual changes occur during adolescence is shown by the colored bars. (Source: Based on Tanner, 1978.)

cause curiosity, interest, and sometimes embarrassment for individuals entering adolescence.

The physical changes that occur at the start of adolescence result largely from the secretion of various hormones, and they affect virtually every aspect of an adolescent's life. Not since infancy has development been so dramatic. Weight and height increase rapidly because of a growth spurt that typically begins around age 10 for girls and age 12 for boys. Adolescents may grow as much as 5 inches in one year.

Puberty, the period at which maturation of the sexual organs occurs, begins at about age 11 or 12 for girls, when menstruation starts. However, there are wide variations (see Figure 1). For example, some girls begin to menstruate as early as age 8 or 9 or as late as age 16. Furthermore, in Western cultures, the average age at which adolescents reach sexual maturity has been steadily decreasing over the last century most likely as a result of improved nutrition and medical care. Sexual *attraction* to others begins even before the maturation of the sexual organs at around age 10 (see Figure 1; Tanner, 1990; Finlay, Jones, & Coleman, 2002).

For boys, the onset of puberty is marked by their first ejaculation, known as *spermarche*. Spermarche usually occurs around the age of 13 (see Figure 1). At first, relatively few sperm are produced during an ejaculation, but the amount increases significantly within a few years.

The age at which puberty begins has implications for the way adolescents feel about themselves—as well as the way others treat them. Early-maturing boys have a distinct advantage over later-maturing boys. They do better in athletics, are generally more popular with peers, and have more positive self-concepts (Ge et al., 2003; Becker & Luthar, 2007).

puberty The period at which maturation of the sexual organs occurs, beginning at about age 11 or 12 for girls and 13 or 14 for boys.

Although puberty begins around 11 or 12 for girls and 13 or 14 for boys, there are wide variations. What are some of the advantages and disadvantages of early puberty?

The picture differs for girls. Although early-maturing girls are more sought after as dates and have better self-esteem than later-maturing girls, some consequences of early physical maturation may be less positive. For example, early breast development may set them apart from their peers and be a source of ridicule (Olivardia & Pope, 2002; Nadeem & Graham, 2005; Blumenthal et al., 2011).

Late physical maturation may produce certain psychological difficulties for both boys and girls. Boys who are smaller and less coordinated than their more mature peers tend to feel ridiculed and less attractive. Similarly, late-maturing girls are at a disadvantage in middle school and early high school. They hold relatively low social status and may be overlooked in dating (Lanza & Collins, 2002).

Clearly, the rate at which physical changes occur during adolescence can affect the way in which people are viewed by others and the way they view themselves. Just as important as physical changes, however, are the psychological and social changes that unfold during adolescence.

Moral and Cognitive Development: Distinguishing Right from Wrong

In a European country, a woman is near death from a special kind of cancer. The one drug that the doctors think might save her is a medicine that a medical researcher has recently discovered. The drug is expensive to make, and the researcher is charging ten times the cost, or $5,000, for a small dose. The sick woman's husband, Henry, approaches everyone he knows in hope of borrowing money, but he can get together only about $2,500. He tells the researcher that his wife is dying and asks him to lower the price of the drug or let him pay later. The researcher says, "No, I discovered the drug, and I'm going to make money from it." Henry is desperate and considers stealing the drug for his wife.

What would you tell Henry to do?

KOHLBERG'S THEORY OF MORAL DEVELOPMENT

In the view of psychologist Lawrence Kohlberg, the advice you give Henry reflects your level of moral development. According to Kohlberg, people pass through a series of stages in the evolution of their sense of justice and in the kind of reasoning they use to make moral judgments (Kohlberg, 1984). Largely because of the various cognitive limitations that Piaget described, preadolescent children tend to think either in terms of concrete, unvarying rules ("It is always wrong to steal" or "I'll be punished if I steal") or in terms of the rules of society ("Good people don't steal" or "What if everyone stole?").

Adolescents, however, have typically reached Piaget's formal operational stage of cognitive development and can reason on a higher plane. Because they are able to comprehend broad moral principles, they can understand that morality is not always black and white and that conflict can exist between two sets of socially accepted standards.

Kohlberg (1984) suggests that the changes in moral reasoning can be understood best as a three-level sequence (see Figure 2). His theory assumes that people move

	Sample Moral Reasoning of Subjects	
Level	**In Favor of Stealing the Drug**	**Against Stealing the Drug**
Level 1 Preconventional morality: At this level, the concrete interests of the individual are considered in terms of rewards and punishments.	"If you let your wife die, you will get in trouble. You'll be blamed for not spending the money to save her, and there'll be an investigation of you and the druggist for your wife's death."	"You shouldn't steal the drug because you'll be caught and sent to jail if you do. If you do get away, your conscience will bother you thinking how the police will catch up with you at any minute."
Level 2 Conventional morality: At this level, people approach moral problems as members of society. They are interested in pleasing others by acting as good members of society.	"If you let your wife die, you'll never be able to look anybody in the face again."	"After you steal the drug, you'll feel bad thinking how you've brought dishonor on your family and yourself; you won't be able to face anyone again."
Level 3 Postconventional morality: At this level, people use moral principles that are seen as broader than those of any particular society.	"If you don't steal the drug, and if you let your wife die, you'll always condemn yourself for it afterward. You won't be blamed and you'll have lived up to the outside rule of the law, but you won't have lived up to your own conscience and standards of honesty."	"If you steal the drug, you won't be blamed by other people, but you'll condemn yourself because you won't have lived up to your own conscience and standards of honesty."

FIGURE 2 Developmental psychologist Lawrence Kohlberg theorized that people move through a three-level sequence of moral reasoning in a fixed order. However, he contended that few people ever reach the highest level of moral reasoning.

through the levels in a fixed order and that they cannot reach the highest level until about age 13—primarily because of limitations in cognitive development before that age. However, many people never reach the highest level of moral reasoning. In fact, Kohlberg found that only a relatively small percentage of adults rise above the second level of his model (Kohlberg & Ryncarz, 1990; Powers, 2006; Moshman, 2011).

Although Kohlberg's theory has had a substantial influence on our understanding of moral development, the research support is mixed. One difficulty with the theory is that it pertains to moral *judgments*, not moral *behavior*. Knowing right from wrong does not mean that we will always act in accordance with our judgments. In addition, the theory applies primarily to Western society and its moral code; cross-cultural research conducted in cultures with different moral systems suggests that Kohlberg's theory is not necessarily applicable (Coles, 1997; Damon, 1999; Nucci, 2002; Barandiaran, Pascual, & Samaniego, 2006).

MORAL DEVELOPMENT IN WOMEN

One glaring shortcoming of Kohlberg's research is that he primarily used male participants. Furthermore, psychologist Carol Gilligan (1996) argues that because of men's and women's distinctive socialization experiences, a fundamental difference exists in the way each gender views moral behavior. According to Gilligan, men view morality primarily in terms of broad principles, such as justice and fairness. In contrast, women see it in terms of responsibility toward individuals and willingness to make sacrifices to help a specific individual within the context of a particular relationship. Compassion for individuals is a more salient factor in moral behavior for women than it is for men.

Because Kohlberg's model defines moral behavior largely in terms of abstract principles such as justice, Gilligan finds that it inadequately describes females' moral development. She suggests that women's morality centers on individual well-being and social relationships—a morality of *caring*. In her view, compassionate concern for the welfare of others represents the highest level of morality.

The fact that Gilligan's conception of morality differs greatly from Kohlberg's suggests that gender plays an important role in determining what a person sees as moral. Although the research evidence is not definitive, it seems plausible that their differing conceptions of what constitutes moral behavior may lead men and women to regard the morality of a specific behavior in different ways (Jorgensen, 2006; Sherblom, 2008; Walker & Frimer, 2009).

Social Development: Finding One's Self in a Social World

"Who am I?" "How do I fit into the world?" "What is life all about?"

Questions such as these assume special significance during the teenage years, as adolescents seek to find their place in the broader social world. As we will see, this quest takes adolescents along several routes.

ERIKSON'S THEORY OF PSYCHOSOCIAL DEVELOPMENT: THE SEARCH FOR IDENTITY

identity-versus-role-confusion stage According to Erikson, a time in adolescence of major testing to determine one's unique qualities.

identity The distinguishing character of the individual: who each of us is, what our roles are, and what we are capable of.

Erikson's theory of psychosocial development emphasizes the search for identity during the adolescent years. As noted earlier, psychosocial development encompasses the way people's understanding of themselves, one another, and the world around them changes during the course of development (Erikson, 1963).

The fifth stage of Erikson's theory (summarized, with the other stages, in Figure 3), the **identity-versus-role-confusion stage,** encompasses adolescence. During this stage, a time of major testing, people try to determine what is unique about themselves. They attempt to discover who they are, what their strengths are, and what kinds of roles they are best suited to play for the rest of their lives—in short, their **identity.** A person confused about the most appropriate role to play in life may lack a stable identity,

Stage	Approximate Age	Positive Outcomes	Negative Outcomes
1. Trust-vs.-mistrust	Birth–1½ years	Feelings of trust from environmental support	Fear and concern regarding others
2. Autonomy-vs.-shame-and-doubt	1½–3 years	Self-sufficiency if exploration is encouraged	Doubts about self, lack of independence
3. Initiative-vs.-guilt	3–6 years	Discovery of ways to initiate actions	Guilt from actions and thoughts
4. Industry-vs.-inferiority	6–12 years	Development of sense of competence	Feelings of inferiority, no sense of mastery
5. Identity-vs.-role-confusion	Adolescence	Awareness of uniqueness of self, knowledge of role to be followed	Inability to identify appropriate roles in life
6. Intimacy-vs.-isolation	Early adulthood	Development of loving, sexual relationships and close friendships	Fear of relationships with others
7. Generativity-vs.-stagnation	Middle adulthood	Sense of contribution to continuity of life	Trivialization of one's activities
8. Ego-integrity-vs.-despair	Late adulthood	Sense of unity in life's accomplishments	Regret over lost opportunities of life

FIGURE 3 Erikson's stages of psychosocial development. According to Erikson, people proceed through eight stages of psychosocial development across their lives. He suggested that each stage requires the resolution of a crisis or conflict and may produce both positive and negative outcomes.

adopt an unacceptable role such as that of a social deviant, or have difficulty maintaining close personal relationships later in life (Updegraff et al., 2004; Vleioras & Bosma, 2005; Goldstein, 2006).

During the identity-versus-role-confusion period, an adolescent feels pressure to identify what to do with his or her life. Because these pressures come at a time of major physical changes as well as important changes in what society expects of them, adolescents can find the period an especially difficult one. The identity-versus-role-confusion stage has another important characteristic: declining reliance on adults for information with a shift toward using the peer group as a source of social judgments. The peer group becomes increasingly important, enabling adolescents to form close, adult-like relationships and helping them clarify their personal identities. According to Erikson, the identity-versus-role-confusion stage marks a pivotal point in psychosocial development, paving the way for continued growth and the future development of personal relationships.

During early adulthood, people enter the **intimacy-versus-isolation stage.** Spanning the period of early adulthood (from post-adolescence to the early 30s), this stage focuses on developing close relationships with others. Difficulties during this stage result in feelings of loneliness and a fear of such relationships; successful resolution of the crises of this stage results in the possibility of forming relationships that are intimate on a physical, intellectual, and emotional level.

Development continues during middle adulthood as people enter the **generativity-versus-stagnation stage.** Generativity is the ability to contribute to one's family, community, work, and society and to assist the development of the younger generation. Success in this stage results in a person's feeling positive about the continuity of life; difficulties in this stage lead a person to feel that his or her activities are trivial or stagnant and have done nothing for upcoming generations. In fact, if a person has not successfully resolved the identity crisis of adolescence, he or she may still be foundering, for example, in identifying an appropriate career.

Finally, the last stage of psychosocial development, the **ego-integrity-versus-despair stage,** spans later adulthood and continues until death. Now a sense of accomplishment signifies success in resolving the difficulties presented by this stage of life; failure to resolve the difficulties results in regret over what might have been achieved but was not.

Notably, Erikson's theory suggests that development does not stop at adolescence but continues throughout adulthood. A substantial amount of research now confirms this view. For instance, a 22-year study by psychologist Susan Whitbourne found considerable support for the fundamentals of Erikson's theory; the study determined that psychosocial development continues through adolescence and adulthood. In sum, adolescence is not an end point but rather a way station on the path of psychosocial development (Whitbourne et al., 1992; McAdams et al., 1997).

Although Erikson's theory provides a broad outline of identity development, critics have pointed out that his approach is anchored in male-oriented concepts of individuality and competitiveness. In an alternative conception, psychologist Carol Gilligan suggests that women may develop identity through the establishment of relationships. In her view, a primary component of women's identity is the construction of caring networks among themselves and others (Gilligan, 2004).

THE WORLD'S FIRST GENETICALLY ENGINEERED HUMAN HITS ADOLESCENCE

intimacy-versus-isolation stage
According to Erikson, a period during early adulthood that focuses on developing close relationships.

generativity-versus-stagnation stage
According to Erikson, a period in middle adulthood during which we take stock of our contributions to family and society.

ego-integrity-versus-despair stage
According to Erikson, a period from late adulthood until death during which we review life's accomplishments and failures.

STORMY ADOLESCENCE: MYTH OR REALITY?

Does puberty invariably foreshadow a stormy, rebellious period of adolescence?

At one time, psychologists thought that most children entering adolescence were beginning a period fraught with stress and unhappiness. However, research now shows that this characterization is largely a myth, that most young people pass

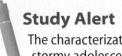

Study Alert
The characterization of a stormy adolescence is a myth for most adolescents.

through adolescence without appreciable turmoil in their lives, and that parents speak easily—and fairly often—with their children about a variety of topics (van Wel, Linssen, & Abma, 2000; Granic, Hollenstein, & Dishion, 2003).

Not that adolescence is completely calm! In most families with adolescents, the amount of arguing and bickering clearly rises. Most young teenagers, as part of their search for identity, experience tension between their attempts to become independent from their parents and their actual dependence on them. They may experiment with a range of behaviors and flirt with a variety of activities that their parents, and even society as a whole, find objectionable. Happily, though, for most families such tensions stabilize during middle adolescence—around age 15 or 16—and eventually decline around age 18 (Smetana, Daddis, & Chuang, 2003; Smetana, 2005).

One reason for the increase in discord during adolescence appears to be the protracted period in which children stay at home with their parents. In prior historical periods—and in some non-Western cultures today—children leave home immediately after puberty and are considered adults. Today, however, sexually mature adolescents may spend as many as 7 or 8 years with their parents. Current social trends even hint at an extension of the conflicts of adolescence beyond the teenage years because a significant number of young adults—known as *boomerang children*—return to live with their parents, typically for economic reasons, after leaving home for some period. Although some parents welcome the return of their children, others are less sympathetic, which opens the way to conflict (Bianchi & Casper, 2000; Lewin, 2003).

Another source of strife with parents lies in the way adolescents think. Adolescence fosters *adolescent egocentrism,* a state of self-absorption in which a teenager views the world from his or her own point of view. Egocentrism leads adolescents to be highly critical of authority figures, unwilling to accept criticism, and quick to fault others. It also makes them believe that they are the center of everyone else's attention, which leads to self-consciousness. Furthermore, they develop *personal fables*, the belief that their experience is unique, exceptional, and shared by no one else. Such personal fables may make adolescents feel vulnerable to the risks that threaten others (Alberts, Elkind, & Ginsberg, 2007; Schwartz, Maynard, & Uzelac, 2008; Boeve-de Pauw, Donche, & Van Petegem, 2011).

Finally, parent-adolescent discord occurs because adolescents are much more apt to engage in risky behavior than later in life. In large part, their riskiness is due to the immaturity of brain systems that regulate impulse control, some of which do not fully develop until people are in their 20s (Steinberg, 2007).

ADOLESCENT SUICIDE

Although the vast majority of teenagers pass through adolescence without major psychological difficulties, some experience unusually severe psychological problems. Sometimes those problems become so extreme that adolescents take their own lives. Suicide is the third leading cause of death for adolescents (after accidents and homicide) in the United States. More teenagers and young adults die from suicide than from cancer, heart disease, AIDS, birth defects, stroke, pneumonia and influenza, and chronic lung disease combined (CDC, 2004b).

A teenager commits suicide every 90 minutes. Furthermore, the reported rate of suicide may actually be understated because medical personnel hesitate to report suicide as a cause of death. Instead, they frequently label a death as an accident in an effort to protect the survivors. Overall, as many as 200 adolescents may attempt suicide for every one who actually takes his or her own life (CDC, 2000; Brausch & Gutierrez, 2009).

Male adolescents are five times more likely to commit suicide than females, although females *attempt* suicide more often than males. The rate of adolescent suicide is significantly greater among whites than among nonwhites. However, the suicide rate of

These students are kneeling by a friend's tombstone. The rate of suicide among teenagers has risen significantly over the last few decades. Can you think of any reasons for this phenomenon?

African-American males has increased much more rapidly than that of white males over the last two decades. Native Americans have the highest suicide rate of any ethnic group in the United States, and Asian Americans have the lowest rate (CDC, 2004b; Boden, Fergusson, & Horwood, 2007; Bossarte & Swahn, 2011).

As the rate of suicide has slowly declined, the rates are still higher for adolescents than any other age group except for the elderly. Some psychologists suggest that the sharp rise in stress that teenagers experience—in terms of academic and social pressure, alcoholism, drug abuse, and family difficulties—provokes the most troubled adolescents to take their own lives. However, that is not the whole story, because the suicide rate for other age groups has remained fairly stable in the last few decades. It is unlikely that stress has increased only for adolescents and not for the rest of the population (Lubell et al., 2004).

Although the question of why adolescent suicide rates are so high remains unanswered, several factors put adolescents at risk. One factor is depression, characterized by unhappiness, extreme fatigue, and—a variable that seems especially important—a profound sense of hopelessness. In other cases, adolescents who commit suicide are perfectionists who are inhibited socially and prone to extreme anxiety when they face any social or academic challenge (see Figure 4; CDC, 2004b; Richardson et al., 2005; Caelian, 2006).

Family background and adjustment difficulties are also related to suicide. A long-standing history of conflicts between parents and children may lead to adolescent behavior problems, such as delinquency, dropping out of school, and aggressive tendencies. In addition, teenage alcoholics and abusers of other drugs have a relatively high rate of suicide (Winstead & Sanchez, 2005; Bagge & Sher, 2008; Hardt et al., 2008).

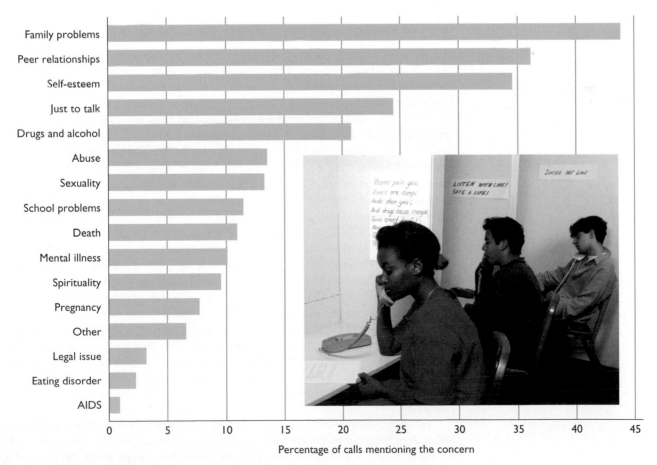

FIGURE 4 According to a review of phone calls to one telephone help line, adolescents who were considering suicide most often mentioned family, peer relationships, and self-esteem problems. (Source: Boehm & Campbell, 1995.)

Several warning signs indicate when a teenager's problems may be severe enough to warrant concern about the possibility of a suicide attempt. They include the following:

- School problems, such as missing classes, truancy, and a sudden change in grades
- Frequent incidents of self-destructive behavior, such as careless accidents
- Loss of appetite or excessive eating
- Withdrawal from friends and peers
- Sleeping problems
- Signs of depression, tearfulness, or overt indications of psychological difficulties, such as hallucinations
- A preoccupation with death, an afterlife, or what would happen "if I died"
- Putting affairs in order, such as giving away prized possessions or making arrangements for the care of a pet
- An explicit announcement of thoughts of suicide

If you know someone who shows signs that he or she is suicidal, urge that person to seek professional help. You may need to take assertive action, such as enlisting the assistance of family members or friends. Talk of suicide is a serious signal for help and not a confidence to be kept.

For immediate help with a suicide-related problem, call (800) 273-8255, a national hotline staffed with trained counselors, or access www.suicidepreventionlifeline.org.

 # Exploring DIVERSITY

Rites of Passage: Coming of Age Around the World

It is not easy for male members of the Awa tribe in New Guinea to make the transition from childhood to adulthood. First come whippings with sticks and prickly branches both for the boys' own past misdeeds and in honor of those tribesmen who were killed in warfare. In the next phase of the ritual, adults jab sharpened sticks into the boys' nostrils. Then they force a five-foot length of vine into the boys' throats until they gag and vomit. Finally, tribesmen cut the boys' genitals, causing severe bleeding.

Although the rites that mark the coming of age of boys in the Awa tribe sound horrifying to Westerners, they are comparable to those in other cultures. In some, youths must kneel on hot coals without displaying pain. In others, girls must toss wads of burning cotton from hand to hand and allow themselves to be bitten by hundreds of ants (Selsky, 1997).

Other cultures have less fearsome although no less important ceremonies that mark the passage from childhood to adulthood. For instance, when a girl first menstruates in traditional Apache tribes, the event is marked by dawn-to-dusk chanting. Western religions, too, have several types of celebrations, including bar mitzvahs and bat mitzvahs at age 13 for Jewish boys and girls, respectively, and confirmation ceremonies for children in many Christian denominations (Magida, 2006).

In most societies, males are the focus of coming-of-age ceremonies. The renowned anthropologist Margaret Mead remarked, only partly in jest, that the preponderance of male ceremonies might reflect the fact that "the worry that boys will not grow up to be men is much more widespread than that girls will not grow up to be women" (1949, p. 195). Said another way, it may be that in most cultures men traditionally have higher status than women, and therefore those cultures regard boys' transition into adulthood as more important.

However, another fact may explain why most cultures place greater emphasis on male rather than female rites. For females, the transition from childhood is marked by a definite biological event: menstruation. For males, in contrast, no single event can be used to pinpoint entry into adulthood. Thus, men are forced to rely on culturally determined rituals to acknowledge their arrival into adulthood.

RECAP/EVALUATE/RETHINK

RECAP

LO 29-1 What major physical, social, and cognitive transitions characterize adolescence?

- Adolescence, the developmental stage between childhood and adulthood, is marked by the onset of puberty, the point at which sexual maturity occurs. The age at which puberty begins has implications for the way people view themselves and the way others see them. (p. 358)
- Moral judgments during adolescence increase in sophistication, according to Kohlberg's three-level model. Although Kohlberg's levels provide an adequate description of males' moral judgments, Gilligan suggests that women view morality in terms of caring for individuals rather than in terms of broad general principles of justice. (p. 360)
- According to Erikson's model of psychosocial development, adolescence may be accompanied by an identity crisis. Adolescence is followed by three more stages of psychosocial development that cover the remainder of the life span. (p. 362)
- Suicide is the third leading cause of death in adolescents. (p. 364)

EVALUATE

1. _____ is the period during which the sexual organs begin to mature.

2. Delayed maturation typically provides both males and females with a social advantage. True or false?
3. _____ proposed a set of three levels of moral development ranging from reasoning based on rewards and punishments to abstract thinking involving concepts of justice.
4. Erikson believed that during adolescence, people must search for _____, whereas during the early adulthood, the major task is _____.

RETHINK

1. In what ways do school cultures help or hurt teenage students who are going through adolescence? What school policies might benefit early-maturing girls and late-maturing boys? Explain how same-sex schools could help students going through adolescence, as some have argued.
2. *From the perspective of a social worker:* How might you determine if an adolescent is at risk for suicide? What strategies would you use to prevent the teen from committing suicide? Would you use different strategies depending on the teenager's gender?

Answers to Evaluate Questions

1. Puberty; 2. false; both male and female adolescents suffer if they mature late; 3. Kohlberg; 4. identity, intimacy

KEY TERMS

adolescence p. 358
puberty p. 359
identity-versus-role-
  confusion stage p. 362

identity p. 362
intimacy-versus-isolation
  stage p. 363

generativity-versus-
  stagnation stage p. 363

ego-integrity-versus-despair
  stage p. 363

Adulthood

Learning Outcomes

LO 30-1 What are the principal kinds of physical, social, and intellectual changes that occur in early and middle adulthood, and what are their causes?

LO 30-2 How does the reality of late adulthood differ from the stereotypes about that period?

LO 30-3 How can we adjust to death?

emerging adulthood The period beginning in the late teenage years and extending into the mid-20s.

I thought I got better as I got older. I found out that wasn't the case in a real hurry last year. After going twelve years in professional football and twelve years before that in amateur football without ever having surgery performed on me, the last two seasons of my career I went under the knife three times. It happened very quickly and without warning, and I began to ask myself, "Is this age? Is this what's happening?" Because up until that moment, I'd never realized that I was getting older. (Brian Sipes, quoted in Kotre & Hall, 1990, pp. 257, 259–260)

As a former professional football player, Brian Sipes intensely felt the changes in his body brought about by aging. But the challenges he experienced are part of a normal process that affects all people as they move through adulthood.

Psychologists generally agree that early adulthood begins around age 20 and lasts until about age 40 to 45 when middle adulthood begins and continues until around age 65. Despite the enormous importance of these periods of life in terms of both the accomplishments that occur in them and their overall length (together they span some 44 years), they have been studied less than has any other stage. For one reason, the physical changes that occur during these periods are less apparent and more gradual than those at other times during the life span. In addition, the diverse social changes that arise during this period defy simple categorization.

The variety of changes that occur in early adulthood have led many developmental psychologists to view the start of the period as a transitional phase called emerging adulthood. **Emerging adulthood** is the period beginning in the late teenage years and extending into the mid-20s. During emerging adulthood, people are no longer adolescents, but they haven't fully taken on the responsibilities of adulthood. Instead, they are still engaged in determining who they are and what their life and career paths should be (Schwartz, Côté, & Arnett, 2005; Bukobza, 2009; Lamborn & Groh, 2009).

The view that adulthood is preceded by an extended period of emerging adulthood reflects the reality that the economies of industrialized countries have shifted away from manufacturing to an economy that focuses on technology and information and thus requires increases in time spent in educational training. Furthermore, the age at which most people marry and have children has risen significantly (Arnett, 2007, 2011).

There's also an increasing ambivalence about reaching adulthood. When people in their late teens and early 20s are asked if they feel they have reached adulthood, most say "yes and no" (see Figure 1). In short, emerging adulthood is an age of identity exploration in which individuals are more self-focused and uncertain than they will be later in early adulthood (Arnett, 2000, 2006).

As we discuss the changes that occur through emerging adulthood, early adulthood, middle adulthood, and ultimately late adulthood, keep in mind the demarcations between the periods are fuzzy. However, the changes are certainly no less profound than they were in earlier periods of development.

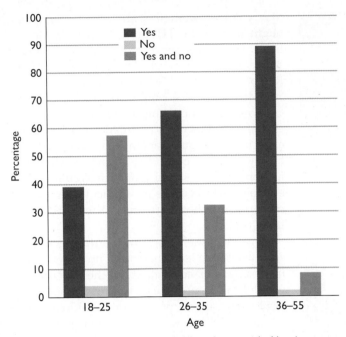

FIGURE 1 Evidence of a period of emerging adulthood is provided by the responses to a questionnaire asking, "Do you feel that you have reached adulthood?" Most people between the ages of 18 and 25 were ambivalent, responding "yes and no." Later, this ambivalence disappeared, with most people 26–35 saying "yes." (Source: Arnett, 2000.)

Physical Development: The Peak of Health

For most people, early adulthood marks the peak of physical health. From about 18 to 25 years of age, people's strength is greatest, their reflexes are quickest, and their chances of dying from disease are quite slim. Moreover, reproductive capabilities are at their highest level.

Around age 25, the body becomes slightly less efficient and more susceptible to disease. Overall, however, ill health remains the exception; most people stay remarkably healthy during early adulthood. (Can you think of any machine other than the body that can operate without pause for so long a period?)

During middle adulthood, people gradually become aware of changes in their bodies. They often experience weight gain (although they can avoid such increases through diet and exercise). Furthermore, the sense organs gradually become less sensitive, and reactions to stimuli are slower. But generally, the physical declines that occur during middle adulthood are minor and often unnoticeable (DiGiovanna, 1994). The major biological change that does occur during middle adulthood pertains to reproductive capabilities. On average, during their late 40s or early 50s, women begin **menopause,** during which they stop menstruating and are no longer fertile. Because menopause is accompanied by a significant reduction in the production of estrogen, a female hormone, women sometimes experience symptoms such as hot flashes, sudden sensations of heat. Many symptoms can be treated through *hormone therapy (HT)* in which menopausal women take the hormones estrogen and progesterone.

However, hormone therapy poses several dangers, such as an increase in the risk of breast cancer, blood clots, and coronary heart disease. These uncertainties make the routine use of HT controversial. Currently, the medical consensus seems to be

menopause The period during which women stop menstruating and are no longer fertile.

Women's reactions to menopause vary significantly across cultures. According to one study, the more a society values old age, the less difficulty its women have during menopause. Why do you think this would be the case?

that younger women with severe menopausal symptoms ought to consider HT on a short-term basis. On the other hand, HT is less appropriate for older women after menopause (Lindh-Astrand, Brynhildsen, & Hoffmann, 2007; Rossouw et al., 2007; MacLennan, 2009).

Menopause was once blamed for a variety of psychological symptoms, including depression and memory loss. However, if such difficulties occur, they may be caused by women's expectations about reaching an "old" age in a society that highly values youth. For example, women's reactions to menopause vary significantly across cultures. The more a society values old age, the less difficulty its women have during menopause (Elliot, Berman, & Kim, 2002; Beyene, Gilliss, & Lee, 2007).

For men, the aging process during middle adulthood is somewhat subtler. There are no physiological signals of increasing age equivalent to the end of menstruation in women; that is, no male menopause exists. In fact, men remain fertile and capable of fathering children until well into late adulthood. However, some gradual physical decline occurs. Sperm production decreases, and the frequency of orgasm tends to decline. Once again, though, any psychological difficulties associated with these changes are usually brought about by an aging individual's inability to meet the exaggerated standards of youthfulness and not by the person's physical deterioration.

Social Development: Working at Life

Whereas physical changes during adulthood reflect development of a quantitative nature, social developmental transitions are qualitative and more profound. During this period, people typically launch themselves into careers, marriage, and families.

The entry into early adulthood is usually marked by leaving one's childhood home and entering the world of work. People envision life goals and make career choices. Their lives often center on their careers, which form an important part of their identity (Vaillant & Vaillant, 1990; Levinson, 1990, 1992).

In their early 40s, however, people may begin to question their lives as they enter a period called the *midlife transition*. The idea that life will end at some point can become more influential in their thinking, which leads them to question their past accomplishments (Gould, 1978).

Although some psychologists—and popular opinion—suggest that physical aging and dissatisfaction with one's life mark a so-called "midlife crisis," there is little evidence for such a "crisis." In fact, the passage into middle age is relatively calm for most people. Most 40-year-olds view their lives and accomplishments positively enough to proceed relatively smoothly through midlife, and the 40s and 50s are often a particularly rewarding period. Rather than looking to the future, people concentrate on the present; their involvement with their families, friends, and other social groups takes on new importance. A major developmental thrust of this period is coming to terms with one's circumstances (Whitbourne, 2000, 2010; Dare, 2011).

Finally, during the last stages of adulthood, people become more accepting of others and of their own lives and are less concerned about issues or problems that once bothered them. They come to accept the fact that death is inevitable, and they try to understand their accomplishments in terms of the broader meaning of life. Although people may begin for the first time to label themselves as "old," many also develop a sense of wisdom and feel freer to enjoy life (Baltes & Kunzmann, 2003; Miner-Rubino, Winter, & Stewart, 2004; Ward-Baker, 2007).

Marriage, Children, and Divorce: Family Ties

In the typical fairy tale, a dashing young man and a beautiful young woman marry, have children, and live happily ever after. However, that scenario does not match the realities of love and marriage in the 21st century. Today, it is just as likely that the man and woman would first live together, then get married and have children, but ultimately get divorced.

The percentage of U.S. households made up of unmarried couples has increased dramatically over the last two decades. At the same time, the average age at which marriage takes place is higher than at any time since the turn of the last century. These changes have been dramatic, and they suggest that the institution of marriage has changed considerably from earlier historical periods.

When people do marry, the probability of divorce is high, especially for younger couples. Even though divorce rates have been declining since they peaked in 1981, about half of all first marriages end in divorce. Before they are 18 years old, two-fifths of children will experience the breakup of their parents' marriages. Moreover, the rise in divorce is not just a U.S. phenomenon: The divorce rate has accelerated over the last several decades in most industrialized countries. In some countries, the increase has been enormous. In South Korea, for example, the divorce rate quadrupled from 11% to 47% in the 12-year period ending in 2002 (Schaefer, 2000; Lankov, 2004; Olson & DeFrain, 2005).

Changes in marriage and divorce trends have doubled the number of single-parent households in the United States over the last two decades. Almost 25% of all family households are now headed by one parent compared with 13% in 1970.

Single-parent families have doubled within the past decade, with the mother usually as head of the household. What are some of the challenges facing children in single-parent families?

If present trends continue, almost three-fourths of American children will spend some portion of their lives in a single-parent family before they turn 18. For children in minority households, the numbers are even higher. Almost 60% of all black children and more than a third of all Hispanic children live in homes with only one parent. Furthermore, in most single-parent families, the children live with the mother rather than the father—a phenomenon that is consistent across racial and ethnic groups throughout the industrialized world (U.S. Bureau of the Census, 2000; Sarsour et al., 2011).

What are the economic and emotional consequences for children living in homes with only one parent? Single-parent families are often economically less well off, and this economic disadvantage has an impact on children's opportunities. More than a third of single-mother families with children have incomes below the poverty line. In addition, good child care at an affordable price is often hard to find. Furthermore, for children of divorce, the parents' separation is often a painful experience that may result in obstacles to establishing close relationships later in life. Children may blame themselves for the breakup or feel pressure to take sides (U.S. Bureau of the Census, 2000; Wallerstein et al., 2000; Liu, He, & Wu, 2007).

Most evidence suggests, however, that children from single-parent families are no less well adjusted than those from two-parent families. In fact, children may be more successful growing up in a harmonious single-parent family than in a two-parent family that engages in continuous conflict (Harold et al., 1997; Clarke-Stewart et al., 2000; Kelly, 2000; Olson & DeFrain, 2005).

CHANGING ROLES OF MEN AND WOMEN

One of the major changes in family life in the last two decades has been the evolution of men's and women's roles. More women than ever before act simultaneously as wives, mothers, and wage earners—in contrast to women in traditional marriages in which the husband is the sole wage earner and the wife assumes primary responsibility for care of the home and children.

Close to 75% of all married women with school-age children are now employed outside the home, and 55% of mothers with children under age 6 are working. In the mid-1960s, only 17% of mothers of 1-year-olds worked full-time; now, more than half are in the labor force (U.S. Bureau of the Census, 2001; Halpern, 2005).

Most married working women are not free of household responsibilities. Even in marriages in which the spouses hold jobs that have similar status and require similar hours, the distribution of household tasks between husbands and wives has not changed substantially. Working wives are still more likely than husbands to feel responsible for traditional homemaking tasks such as cooking and cleaning. In contrast, husbands still view themselves as responsible primarily for household tasks such as repairing broken appliances and doing yardwork (Ganong & Coleman, 1999; Juster, Ono, & Stafford, 2002; Damaske, 2011).

WOMEN'S "SECOND SHIFT"

Working mothers can put in a staggering number of hours. One survey, for instance, found that if we add the number of hours worked on the job and in the home, employed mothers of children under 3 years of age put in an average of 90 hours per week! The additional work women perform is sometimes called the "second shift." National surveys show women who are both employed and mothers put in an extra month of 24-hour days during the course of a year. Researchers see similar patterns in many developing societies throughout the world, with women working at full-time jobs and also having primary responsibilities for child care (Hochschild, 2001; Jacobs & Gerson, 2004; Bureau of Labor Statistics, 2007).

Consequently, rather than careers being a substitute for what women do at home, they are often an addition to the role of homemaker. It is not surprising that some wives feel resentment toward husbands who spend less time on child care and housework than the wives had expected before the birth of their children (Kiecolt, 2003; Gerstel, 2005; Fagan & Press, 2008).

Later Years of Life: Growing Old

I've always enjoyed doing things in the mountains—hiking or, more recently, active cliff-climbing. The more difficult the climb, the more absorbing it is. The climbs I really remember are the ones I had to work on. Maybe a particular section where it took two or three tries before I found the right combination of moves that got me up easily—and, preferably, elegantly. It's a wonderful exhilaration to get to the top and sit down and perhaps have lunch and look out over the landscape and be so grateful that it's still possible for me to do that sort of thing. (Lyman Spitzer, age 74, quoted in Kotre & Hall, 1990, pp. 358–359)

If you can't quite picture a 74-year-old rock-climbing, some rethinking of your view of late adulthood may be in order. In spite of the societal stereotype of "old age" as a time of inactivity and physical and mental decline, gerontologists, specialists who study aging, are beginning to paint a very different portrait of late adulthood.

By focusing on the period of life that starts at around age 65, gerontologists are making important contributions to clarifying the capabilities of older adults. Their work is demonstrating that significant developmental processes continue even during old age. And as life expectancy increases, the number of people who reach older adulthood will continue to grow substantially. Consequently, developing an understanding of late adulthood has become a critical priority for psychologists (Moody, 2000, Schaie, 2005b; Jia, Zack, & Thompson, 2011).

PHYSICAL CHANGES IN LATE ADULTHOOD: THE AGING BODY

Napping, eating, walking, conversing. It probably doesn't surprise you that these relatively nonstrenuous activities represent the typical pastimes of late adulthood. But it is striking that these activities are identical to the most common leisure activities reported in a survey of college students (Harper, 1978). Although the students cited more active pursuits—such as sailing and playing basketball—as their favorite activities, in actuality they engaged in such sports relatively infrequently and spent most of their free time napping, eating, walking, and conversing.

Although the leisure activities in which older adults engage may not differ all that much from the ones that younger people pursue, many physical changes are, of course, brought about by the aging process. The most obvious are those of appearance—hair thinning and turning gray, skin wrinkling and folding, and sometimes a slight loss of height as the thickness of the disks between vertebrae in the spine decreases. But subtler changes also occur in the body's biological functioning. For example, sensory capabilities decrease as a result of aging: Vision, hearing, smell, and taste become less sensitive. Reaction time slows, and physical stamina changes (Stenklev & Laukli, 2004; Schieber, 2006; Madden, 2007).

What are the reasons for these physical declines? **Genetic preprogramming theories of aging** suggest that human cells have a built-in time limit to their reproduction. These theories suggest that after a certain time cells stop dividing or become harmful to the body—as if a kind of automatic self-destruct button had been pushed. In contrast, **wear-and-tear theories of aging** suggest that the mechanical functions of the body simply work less efficiently as people age. Waste byproducts of energy production eventually accumulate, and mistakes are made when cells divide. Eventually the body in effect wears out like an old automobile (Ly et al., 2000; Miquel, 2006; Hayflick, 2007).

genetic preprogramming theories of aging Theories that suggest that human cells have a built-in time limit to their reproduction and that they are no longer able to divide after a certain time.

wear-and-tear theories of aging Theories that suggest that the mechanical functions of the body simply stop working efficiently.

Study Alert

Two major theories of aging—the genetic preprogramming and the wear-and-tear views—explain some of the physical changes that take place in older adults.

Evidence supports both the genetic preprogramming and the wear-and-tear views, and it may be that both processes contribute to natural aging. It is clear, however, that physical aging is not a disease but a natural biological process. Many physical functions do not decline with age. For example, sex remains pleasurable well into old age (although the frequency of sexual activity decreases), and some people report that the pleasure they derive from sex increases during late adulthood (Gelfand, 2000; DeLamater & Sill, 2005; Wilkin & Haddock, 2011).

COGNITIVE CHANGES: THINKING ABOUT—AND DURING—LATE ADULTHOOD

At one time, many gerontologists would have agreed with the popular view that older adults are forgetful and confused. Today, however, most research indicates that this assessment is far from an accurate one of older people's capabilities.

One reason for the change in view is that more sophisticated research techniques exist for studying the cognitive changes that occur in late adulthood. For example, if we were to give a group of older adults an IQ test, we might find that the average score was lower than the score achieved by a group of younger people. We might conclude that this signifies a decline in intelligence. Yet, if we looked a little more closely at the specific test, we might find that the conclusion was unwarranted. For instance, many IQ tests include portions based on physical performance (such as arranging a group of blocks) or on speed. In such cases, poorer performance on the IQ test may be due to gradual decreases in reaction time—a physical decline that accompanies late adulthood and has little or nothing to do with older adults' intellectual capabilities.

Other difficulties hamper research into cognitive functioning during late adulthood. For example, older people are often less healthy than younger ones; when only *healthy* older adults are compared to healthy younger adults, intellectual differences are far less evident. Furthermore, the average number of years in school is often lower in older adults (for historical reasons) than in younger ones, and older adults may be less motivated to perform well on intelligence tests than younger people. Finally, traditional IQ tests may be inappropriate measures of intelligence in late adulthood. Older adults sometimes perform better on tests of practical intelligence than younger individuals do (Willis & Schaie, 1994; Dixon & Cohen, 2003; Johnson & Deary, 2011).

Still, some declines in intellectual functioning during late adulthood do occur, although the pattern of age differences is not uniform for different types of cognitive abilities (see Figure 2). In general, skills relating to *fluid intelligence* (which involves information-processing skills such as memory, calculations, and analogy solving) show declines in late adulthood. In contrast, skills relating to *crystallized intelligence* (intelligence based on the accumulation of information, skills, and strategies learned through experience) remain steady and in some cases actually improve (Rozencwajg et al., 2005; van Hooren, Valentijn, & Bosma, 2007; Kaufman, Johnson, & Liu, 2008).

Even when changes in intellectual functioning occur during later adulthood, people often are able to compensate for any decline. They can still learn what they want to learn; it may just take more time. Furthermore, teaching older adults strategies for dealing with new problems can prevent declines in performance (Saczynski, Willis, & Schaie, 2002; Cavallini, Pagnin, & Vecchi, 2003; Peters et al., 2007).

Although there are declines in fluid intelligence in late adulthood, skills relating to crystallized intelligence remain steady and may actually improve.

MEMORY CHANGES IN LATE ADULTHOOD: ARE OLDER ADULTS FORGETFUL?

One of the characteristics most frequently attributed to late adulthood is forgetfulness. How accurate is this assumption?

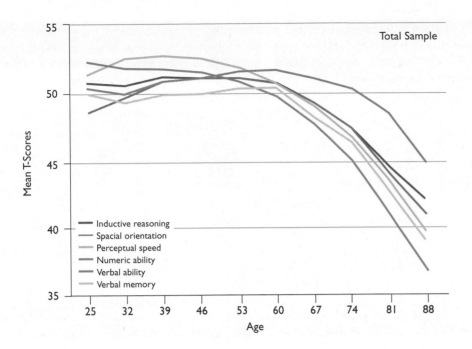

FIGURE 2 Age-related changes in intellectual skills vary according to the specific cognitive ability in question. (Source: Schaie, K. W. (2005a). Longitudinal studies. In *Developmental influences on adult intelligence: The Seattle Longitudinal Study,* Figure 5.7a (p. 127). Copyright © 2005 by Oxford University Press, Inc. By permission of Oxford University Press, Inc. www.oup.com.)

Most evidence suggests that memory change is not an inevitable part of the aging process. For instance, research shows that older people in cultures in which older adults are held in high esteem, such as mainland China, are less likely to show memory losses than those living in cultures in which the expectation is that memory will decline. Similarly, when older people in Western societies are reminded of the advantages of age (for example, "age brings wisdom"), they tend to do better on tests of memory (Levy, 1996; Hess, Hinson, & Statham, 2004; Dixon, Rust, & Feltmate, 2007).

Even when people show memory declines during late adulthood, their deficits are limited to certain types of memory. For instance, losses tend to be limited to episodic memories that relate to specific experiences in people's lives. Other types of memories, such as semantic memories (that refer to general knowledge and facts) and implicit memories (memories of which we are not consciously aware) are largely unaffected by age (Fleischman et al., 2004; Mitchell & Schmitt, 2006; St. Jacques & Levine, 2007).

Declines in episodic memories can often be traced to changes in older adults' lives. For instance, it is not surprising that a retired person, who may no longer face the same kind of consistent intellectual challenges encountered on the job, may have less practice in using memory or even be less motivated to remember things, which leads to an apparent decline in memory. Even in cases in which long-term memory declines, older adults can profit from training that targets memory skills (Fritsch et al., 2007; West, Bagwell, & Dark-Freudeman, 2007; Morcom & Friston, 2011).

In the past, older adults with severe cases of memory decline accompanied by other cognitive difficulties were said to suffer from senility. *Senility* is a broad, imprecise term typically applied to older adults who experience progressive deterioration of mental abilities, including memory loss, disorientation to time and place, and general confusion. Once thought to be an inevitable state that accompanies aging, senility is now viewed by most gerontologists as a label that has outlived its usefulness. Rather than senility being the cause of certain symptoms, the symptoms are deemed to be caused by some other factor.

Some cases of memory loss, however, are produced by actual disease. For instance, **Alzheimer's disease** is a progressive brain disorder that leads to a gradual and irreversible decline in cognitive abilities. More than 5 million Americans have the disease, and one in eight people age 65 and older are afflicted. Unless a cure is found, some 14 million people will experience Alzheimer's by 2050 (Feinberg, 2002; Hurt et al., 2005; Rogers, 2007; Alzheimer's Association, 2009).

Alzheimer's disease A progressive brain disorder that leads to a gradual and irreversible decline in cognitive abilities.

Maintaining interests and activities one had during middle age can contribute to a more successful late adulthood, according to the activity theory of aging.

Alzheimer's occurs when production of the *beta amyloid precursor protein* goes awry, producing large clumps of cells that trigger inflammation and deterioration of nerve cells. The brain shrinks, neurons die, and several areas of the hippocampus and frontal and temporal lobes deteriorate. So far, there is no effective treatment (Wolfe, 2006; Medeiros et al., 2007; Behrens, Lendon, & Roe, 2009).

In other cases, cognitive declines may be caused by temporary anxiety and depression, which can be treated successfully, or may even be due to overmedication. The danger is that people with such symptoms may be left untreated, thereby continuing their decline (Selkoe, 1997; Sachs-Ericsson et al., 2005).

In sum, declines in cognitive functioning in late adulthood are, for the most part, not inevitable. The key to maintaining cognitive skills may lie in intellectual stimulation. Like the rest of us, older adults need a stimulating environment in order to hone and maintain their skills (Bosma et al., 2003; Glisky, 2007; Hertzog et al., 2008).

THE SOCIAL WORLD OF LATE ADULTHOOD: OLD BUT NOT ALONE

Just as the view that old age predictably means mental decline has proved to be wrong, so has the view that late adulthood inevitably brings loneliness. People in late adulthood most often see themselves as functioning members of society; only a small number of them report that loneliness is a serious problem (Binstock & George, 1996; Jylha, 2004; Berkman, Ertel, & Glymour, 2011).

Certainly, late adulthood brings significant challenges. People who have spent their adult lives working and then enter retirement bring about a major shift in the role they play. Moreover, many people must face the death of their spouse. Especially if the marriage has been a long and good one, the death of a partner means the loss of a companion, confidante, and lover. It can also bring about changes in economic well-being.

There is no single way to age successfully. According to the **disengagement theory of aging,** aging produces a gradual withdrawal from the world on physical, psychological, and social levels. However, such disengagement serves an important purpose of providing an opportunity for increased reflectiveness and decreased emotional investment in others at a time of life when social relationships will inevitably be ended by death (Adams, 2004; Wrosch, Bauer, & Scheier, 2005).

disengagement theory of aging A theory that suggests that aging produces a gradual withdrawal from the world on physical, psychological, and social levels.

People in late adulthood usually see themselves as functioning, well-integrated members of society, and many maintain activities in which they participated earlier in life.

Because little research supports disengagement theory, alternative theories have been suggested. According to the **activity theory of aging,** people who age most successfully are those who maintain the interests, activities, and level of social interaction they experienced during middle adulthood. Activity theory argues that late adulthood should reflect a continuation, as much as possible, of the activities in which people participated during the earlier part of their lives (Crosnoe & Elder, 2002; Nimrod & Kleiber, 2007).

Although most research supports activity theory, not all people in late adulthood need a life filled with activities and social interaction to be happy; as in every stage of life, some older adults are just as satisfied leading a relatively inactive, solitary existence. What may be more important is how people view the aging process: Evidence shows that positive self-perceptions of aging are associated with increased longevity (Levy et al., 2002; Levy & Myers, 2004).

Regardless of how people age, most engage in a process of **life review** in which they examine and evaluate their lives. Remembering and reconsidering what has occurred in the past, people in late adulthood often come to a better understanding of themselves. They sometimes resolve lingering problems and conflicts and face their lives with greater wisdom and serenity.

Clearly, people in late adulthood are not just marking time until death. Rather, old age is a time of continued growth and development as important as any other period of life.

activity theory of aging A theory that suggests that the elderly who are most successful while aging are those who maintain the interests and activities they had during middle age.

life review The process by which people examine and evaluate their lives.

BECOMING AN INFORMED CONSUMER of Psychology

Adjusting to Death

At some time in our lives, we all face death—certainly our own as well as the deaths of friends, loved ones, and even strangers. Although there is nothing more inevitable in life, death remains a frightening, emotion-laden topic. Certainly, little is more stressful than the death of a loved one or the contemplation of our own imminent death, and preparing for death is one of our most crucial developmental tasks (Aiken, 2000).

A few generations ago, talk of death was taboo. The topic was never mentioned to dying people, and gerontologists had little to say about it. That changed, however, with the pioneering work of Elisabeth Kübler-Ross (1969), who brought the subject of death

into the open with her observation that those facing impending death tend to move through five broad stages:

- *Denial.* In this stage, people resist the idea that they are dying. Even if told that their chances for survival are small, they refuse to admit that they are facing death.
- *Anger.* After moving beyond the denial stage, dying people become angry—angry at people around them who are in good health, angry at medical professionals for being ineffective, angry at God.
- *Bargaining.* Anger leads to bargaining in which the dying try to think of ways to postpone death. They may decide to dedicate their lives to religion if God saves them. They may say, "If only I can live to see my son married, I will accept death then."
- *Depression.* When dying people come to feel that bargaining is no use, they move to the next stage: depression. They realize that their lives really are coming to an end, which leads to what Kübler-Ross calls "preparatory grief" for their own deaths.
- *Acceptance.* In this stage, people accept impending death. Usually they are unemotional and uncommunicative; it is as if they have made peace with themselves and are expecting death with no bitterness.

It is important to keep in mind that not everyone experiences each of these stages in the same way. In fact, Kübler-Ross's stages pertain only to people who are fully aware that they are dying and have the time to evaluate their impending death. Furthermore, vast differences occur in the way individuals react to impending death. The specific cause and duration of dying, as well as the person's sex, age, personality, and the type of support received from family and friends, all have an impact on how people respond to death (Carver & Scheier, 2002; Coyle, 2006).

Few of us enjoy the contemplation of death. Yet awareness of its psychological aspects and consequences can make its inevitable arrival less anxiety producing and perhaps more understandable.

RECAP/EVALUATE/RETHINK

RECAP

LO 30-1 What are the principal kinds of physical, social, and intellectual changes that occur in early and middle adulthood, and what are their causes?

- Early adulthood marks the peak of physical health. Physical changes occur relatively gradually in men and women during adulthood. (p. 368)
- One major physical change occurs at the end of middle adulthood for women: They begin menopause after which they are no longer fertile. (p. 369)
- During middle adulthood, people typically experience a midlife transition in which the notion that life will end becomes more important. In some cases this may lead to a midlife crisis, although the passage into middle age is typically relatively calm. (p. 370)
- As aging continues during middle adulthood, people realize in their 50s that their lives and accomplishments are fairly well set, and they try to come to terms with them. (p. 370)
- Among the important developmental milestones during adulthood are marriage, family changes, and divorce. Another important determinant of adult development is work. (p. 371)

LO 30-2 How does the reality of late adulthood differ from the stereotypes about that period?

- Old age may bring marked physical declines caused by genetic preprogramming or physical wear and tear. Although the activities of people in late adulthood are not all that different from those of younger people, older adults experience declines in reaction time, sensory abilities, and physical stamina. (p. 373)
- Intellectual declines are not an inevitable part of aging. Fluid intelligence does decline with age, and long-term memory abilities are sometimes impaired. In contrast, crystallized intelligence shows slight increases with age, and short-term memory remains at about the same level. (p. 374)
- Although disengagement theory sees successful aging as a process of gradual withdrawal from the physical, psychological, and social worlds, there is little research supporting this view. Instead, activity theory, which suggests that the maintenance of interests and activities from earlier years leads to successful aging, is a more accurate explanation. (p. 376)

LO 30-3 How can we adjust to death?

- According to Kübler-Ross, dying people move through five stages as they face death: denial, anger, bargaining, depression, and acceptance. (pp. 377, 378)

EVALUATE

1. Rob recently turned 40 and surveyed his goals and accomplishments to date. Although he has accomplished a lot, he realized that many of his goals will not be met in his lifetime. This stage is called a _____ _____.
2. In households where both partners have similar jobs, the division of labor that generally occurs is the same as in "traditional" households where the husband works and the wife stays at home. True or false?
3. _____ _____ theories suggest that there is a maximum time span in which cells are able to reproduce. This time limit explains the eventual breakdown of the body.
4. Lower IQ test scores during late adulthood do not necessarily mean a decrease in intelligence. True or false?
5. During old age, a person's _____ intelligence continues to increase, whereas _____ intelligence may decline.
6. In Kübler-Ross's _____ stage, people resist the idea of death. In the _____ stage, they attempt to make deals to avoid death, and in the _____ stage, they passively await death.

RETHINK

1. Is the possibility that life may be extended for several decades a mixed blessing? What societal consequences might an extended life span bring about?
2. *From the perspective of a health-care provider:* What sorts of recommendations would you make to your older patients about how to deal with aging? How would you handle someone who believed that getting older had only negative consequences?

Answers to Evaluate Questions

1. midlife transition; 2. true; 3. Genetic preprogramming; 4. true; 5. crystallized, fluid; 6. denial, bargaining, acceptance

KEY TERMS

emerging adulthood p. 368
menopause p. 369
genetic preprogramming
  theories of aging p. 373

wear-and-tear theories of
  aging p. 373
Alzheimer's
  disease p. 375

disengagement theory of
  aging p. 376
activity theory of
  aging p. 377

life review p. 377

Looking Back

Epilogue

We have traced major events in the development of physical, social, and cognitive growth throughout the life span. Clearly, people change throughout their lives.

As we explored each area of development, we encountered anew the nature–nurture issue, concluding in every significant instance that both nature and nurture contribute to a person's development of skills, personality, and interactions. Specifically, our genetic inheritance—nature—lays down general boundaries within which we can advance and grow; our environment—nurture—helps determine the extent to which we take advantage of our potential.

Before proceeding to the next set of modules, turn once again to the prologue at the beginning of this chapter that discussed Rosie Boycott's anxiety about turning 60. Using your knowledge of human development, consider the following questions.

1. What might have been some of the developmental milestones that Rosie Boycott mentioned experiencing during earlier decades of her life?
2. Did Rosie have a realistic perspective on entering old age? If you were Rosie's best friend, what might you tell her to help her become more optimistic about turning 60?
3. Was Rosie right to think that she was on the cusp of becoming irrelevant? Why or why not?
4. What strategies might Rosie use to remain healthy, vigorous, and cognitively sharp during her golden years?

VISUAL SUMMARY 9 Development

MODULE 27
Nature and Nurture: The Enduring Developmental Issue

Developmental Research Techniques
- Cross-sectional, longitudinal, sequential

Basics of Genetics: Chromosomes and genes

Earliest Development

- Zygote: a fertilized egg
- Embryo: between 2 and 8 weeks old after conception

- Fetus: between 8 weeks and birth
- Age of viability: about 22 weeks from conception

Nature and Nurture
- Nature: Refers to hereditary factors
- Nurture: Refers to environmental influences

MODULE 28   Infancy and Childhood

The Extraordinary Newborn
- Reflexes: Rooting, sucking, gag, Babinski
- Development of the senses

Infancy Through Middle Childhood, About age 12
- Physical development: rapid growth
- Social development
  - Attachment: positive emotional bond between child and caregiver
  - Ainsworth strange situation
  - Social relationships with peers
- Child care outside the home
- Four parenting styles
- Erikson's theory of psychosocial development
  - Trust-versus-mistrust stage: birth to age 1 ½
  - Autonomy-versus-shame-and-doubt stage: ages 1 ½ to 3
  - Initiative-versus-guilt stage: ages 3 to 6
  - Industry-versus-inferiority stage: ages 6 to 12
- Cognitive development
  - Piaget's theory of cognitive development

Cognitive Stage	Approximate Age Range	Major Characteristics
Sensorimotor	Birth–2 years	Development of object permanence, development of motor skills, little or no capacity for symbolic representation
Preoperational	2–7 years	Development of language and symbolic thinking, egocentric thinking
Concrete operational	7–12 years	Development of conservation, mastery of concept of reversibility
Formal operational	12 years–adulthood	Development of logical and abstract thinking

- Information processing approaches

MODULE 29   Adolescence: Becoming an Adult

Physical Development: Rapid weight and height gains; onset of puberty

Moral Development: Changes in moral reasoning

	Sample Moral Reasoning of Subjects	
Level	In Favor of Stealing the Drug	Against Stealing the Drug
Level 1 Preconventional morality: At this level, the concrete interests of the individual are considered in terms of rewards and punishments.	"If you let your wife die, you will get in trouble. You'll be blamed for not spending the money to save her, and there'll be an investigation of you and the druggist for your wife's death."	"You shouldn't steal the drug because you'll be caught and sent to jail if you do. If you do get away, your conscience will bother you thinking how the police will catch up with you at any minute."
Level 2 Conventional morality: At this level, people approach moral problems as members of society. They are interested in pleasing others by acting as good members of society.	"If you let your wife die, you'll never be able to look anybody in the face again."	"After you steal the drug, you'll feel bad thinking how you've brought dishonor on your family and yourself; you won't be able to face anyone again."
Level 3 Postconventional morality: At this level, people use moral principles that are seen as broader than those of any particular society.	"If you don't steal the drug, and if you let your wife die, you'll always condemn yourself for it afterward. You won't be blamed and you'll have lived up to the outside rule of the law, but you won't have lived up to your own conscience and standards of honesty."	"If you steal the drug, you won't be blamed by other people, but you'll condemn yourself because you won't have lived up to your own conscience and standards of honesty."

Social Development: Erikson's theory of psychosocial development

Stage	Approximate Age	Positive Outcomes	Negative Outcomes
1. Trust-vs.-mistrust	Birth–1½ years	Feelings of trust from environmental support	Fear and concern regarding others
2. Autonomy-vs.-shame-and-doubt	1½–3 years	Self-sufficiency if exploration is encouraged	Doubts about self, lack of independence
3. Initiative-vs.-guilt	3–6 years	Discovery of ways to initiate actions	Guilt from actions and thoughts
4. Industry-vs.-inferiority	6–12 years competence	Development of sense of no sense of mastery	Feelings of inferiority
5. Identity-vs.-role-confusion	Adolescence	Awareness of uniqueness of self, knowledge of role to be followed	Inability to identify appropriate roles in life
6. Intimacy-vs.-isolation	Early adulthood	Development of loving, sexual relationships and close friendships	Fear of relationships with others
7. Generativity-vs.-stagnation	Middle adulthood	Sense of contribution to continuity of life	Trivialization of one's activities
8. Ego-integrity-vs.-despair	Late adulthood	Sense of unity in life's accomplishments	Regret over lost opportunities of life

MODULE 30   Adulthood

Physical Development

- Early adulthood: peak of health
- Middle adulthood: menopause for women

Social Development
- Early adulthood: Focus on career, marriage, family
- Midlife transition: Relatively calm, come to terms with one's circumstances
- Late adulthood: Acceptance of others and one's circumstances

Marriage, Children, and Divorce
- People marry later in life than ever before; about half of all first marriages end in divorce
- Many single-parent households

Growing Old: Late adulthood
- Physical changes
  - Genetic preprogramming aging theory
  - Wear-and-tear aging theory
- Cognitive changes
  - Fluid intelligence declines; crystallized intelligence remains steady
  - Memory change not inevitable
    - Alzheimer's disease: Gradual, irreversible brain disorder that leads to a decline in cognitive abilities
- Social world

  - Disengagement theory of aging
  - Activity theory of aging

10 Personality

Learning Outcomes for Chapter 10

LO 31-1 How do psychologists define and use the concept of personality?

LO 31-2 What do the theories of Freud and his successors tell us about the structure and development of personality?

Psychodynamic Approaches to Personality

Freud's Psychoanalytic Theory: Mapping the Unconscious Mind

The Neo-Freudian Psychoanalysts: Building on Freud

LO 32-1 What are the major aspects of trait, learning, biological and evolutionary, and humanistic approaches to psychology?

Trait, Learning, Biological and Evolutionary, and Humanistic Approaches to Personality

Trait Approaches: Placing Labels on Personality

Applying Psychology in the 21st Century: The Self-Obsessed Generation?

Learning Approaches: We Are What We've Learned

Biological and Evolutionary Approaches: Are We Born with Personality?

Neuroscience in Your Life: Wired to Take Risks—The Biological Underpinnings of Personality

Humanistic Approaches: The Uniqueness of You

Comparing Approaches to Personality

LO 33-1 How can we most accurately assess personality?

LO 33-2 What are the major types of personality measures?

Assessing Personality: Determining What Makes Us Distinctive

Exploring Diversity: Should Race and Ethnicity Be Used to Establish Norms?

Self-Report Measures of Personality

Projective Methods

Behavioral Assessment

PsychWork: Human Resources Manager

Becoming an Informed Consumer of Psychology: Assessing Personality Assessments

Prologue *Who Is the Real Lori Berenson?*

From Schoolyard to Jail Yard: The Odyssey of Lori Berenson

To her parents, Lori Berenson was a sweet and caring person, always looking out for the downtrodden. Even as a child, she defended classmates who had been treated unfairly in her public schools. As she grew older, she worked in New York City soup kitchens and in blood banks, always helping people who were in need. She was an excellent student, majoring in anthropology at a prestigious college. When she decided to study in South America, and later to drop out of college to live and work in Peru, it did not seem out of character: Her parents saw it as a continuation of her interest in helping the downtrodden.

To the government of Peru, however, Berenson was a violent terrorist, a member of the Túpac Amaru rebel group. Arrested for gathering information for the group, Berenson was brought to trial, where prosecutors displayed evidence that she had provided the rebels with a floor plan of the Peruvian Congress. Her handwriting was said to indicate specific locations of where legislators were seated and of security guards. She was also accused of providing money to purchase a vehicle to transport weapons and of having indoctrinated rebels.

Prior to being sentenced, Berenson yelled defiantly, "I have been condemned because of my concern for the hunger and misery that exists here." To her parents, that made sense. To the judge, it was simply an indication that she was a violent revolutionary, involved in a web of terrorism. He sentenced her to life in prison (Egan, 2011).

Looking Ahead

Was Lori Berenson simply an innocent do-gooder, acting legally to help the needy, or was she—as the Peruvian government insists—a member of a violent terrorist group?

Many people, like Berenson, have different sides to their personalities, appearing one way to some and quite differently to others. Determining who a person truly is falls to a branch of psychology that seeks to understand the characteristic ways people behave—personality psychology.

Personality is the pattern of enduring characteristics that produce consistency and individuality in a given person. Personality encompasses the behaviors that make each of us unique and that differentiate us from others. Personality also leads us to act consistently in different situations and over extended periods of time.

We will consider a number of approaches to personality. For historical reasons, we begin with psychodynamic theories of personality, which emphasize the importance of the unconscious. Next, we consider approaches that concentrate on identifying the most fundamental personality traits; theories that view personality as a set of learned behaviors; biological and evolutionary perspectives on personality; and approaches, known as humanistic theories, that highlight the uniquely human aspects of personality. We end our discussion by focusing on how personality is measured and how personality tests can be used.

personality The pattern of enduring characteristics that produce consistency and individuality in a given person.

Psychodynamic Approaches to Personality

The college student was intent on making a good first impression on an attractive woman he had spotted across a crowded room at a party. As he walked toward her, he mulled over a line he had heard in an old movie the night before: "I don't believe we've been properly introduced yet." To his horror, what came out was a bit different. After threading his way through the crowded room, he finally reached the woman and blurted out, "I don't believe we've been properly seduced yet."

Although this student's error may seem to be merely an embarrassing slip of the tongue, according to some personality theorists such a mistake is not an error at all (Motley, 1987). Instead, *psychodynamic personality theorists* might argue that the error illustrates one way in which behavior is triggered by inner forces that are beyond our awareness. These hidden drives, shaped by childhood experiences, play an important role in energizing and directing everyday behavior.

Psychodynamic approaches to personality are based on the idea that personality is motivated by inner forces and conflicts about which people have little awareness and over which they have no control. The most important pioneer of the psychodynamic approach was Sigmund Freud. A number of Freud's followers, including Carl Jung, Karen Horney, and Alfred Adler, refined Freud's theory and developed their own psychodynamic approaches.

Learning Outcomes

LO 31-1 How do psychologists define and use the concept of personality?

LO 31-2 What do the theories of Freud and his successors tell us about the structure and development of personality?

psychodynamic approaches to personality Approaches that assume that personality is motivated by inner forces and conflicts about which people have little awareness and over which they have no control.

Freud's Psychoanalytic Theory: Mapping the Unconscious Mind

Sigmund Freud, an Austrian physician, developed **psychoanalytic theory** in the early 1900s. According to Freud's theory, conscious experience is only a small part of our psychological makeup and experience. He argued that much of our behavior is motivated by the **unconscious,** a part of the personality that contains the memories, knowledge, beliefs, feelings, urges, drives, and instincts of which the individual is not aware.

Like the unseen mass of a floating iceberg, the contents of the unconscious far surpass in quantity the information in our conscious awareness. Freud maintained that to understand personality, it is necessary to expose what is in the unconscious. But because the unconscious disguises the meaning of the material it holds, the content of the unconscious cannot be observed directly. It is therefore necessary to interpret clues to the unconscious—slips of the tongue, fantasies, and dreams—to understand the unconscious processes that direct behavior. A slip of the tongue such as the one quoted earlier (sometimes termed a *Freudian slip*) may be interpreted as revealing the speaker's unconscious sexual desires.

To Freud, much of our personality is determined by our unconscious. Some of the unconscious is made up of the *preconscious*, which contains material that is not threatening and is easily brought to mind, such as the knowledge that $2 + 2 = 4$. But deeper in the unconscious are instinctual drives—the wishes, desires, demands,

psychoanalytic theory Freud's theory that unconscious forces act as determinants of personality.

unconscious A part of the personality that contains the memories, knowledge, beliefs, feelings, urges, drives, and instincts of which the individual is not aware.

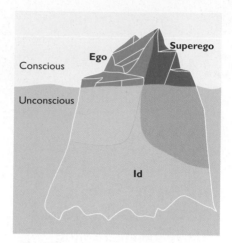

FIGURE 1 In Freud's personality model, there are three major components: the id, the ego, and the superego. As the iceberg analogy shows, only a small portion of personality is conscious. Why do you think that only the ego and superego have conscious components?

Study Alert

Remember that the three parts of personality in Freud's theory—the id, the ego, and the superego— are abstract conceptions that don't exist as physical structures in the brain.

id The raw, unorganized, inborn part of personality whose sole purpose is to reduce tension created by primitive drives related to hunger, sex, aggression, and irrational impulses.

ego The part of the personality that provides a buffer between the id and the outside world.

and needs that are hidden from conscious awareness because of the conflicts and pain they would cause if they were part of our everyday lives. The unconscious provides a "safe haven" for our recollections of threatening events.

STRUCTURING PERSONALITY: ID, EGO, AND SUPEREGO

To describe the structure of personality, Freud developed a comprehensive theory that held that personality consists of three separate but interacting components: the id, the ego, and the superego. Freud suggested that the three structures can be diagrammed to show how they relate to the conscious and the unconscious (see Figure 1).

Although the three components of personality Freud described may appear to be actual physical structures in the nervous system, they are not. Instead, they represent abstract conceptions of a general *model* of personality that describes the interaction of forces that motivate behavior.

If personality consisted only of primitive, instinctual cravings and longings, it would have just one component: the id. The **id** is the raw, unorganized, inborn part of personality. From the time of birth, the id attempts to reduce tension created by primitive drives related to hunger, sex, aggression, and irrational impulses. Those drives are fueled by "psychic energy," which we can think of as a limitless energy source constantly putting pressure on the various parts of the personality.

The id operates according to the *pleasure principle* in which the goal is the immediate reduction of tension and the maximization of satisfaction. However, in most cases, reality prevents the fulfillment of the demands of the pleasure principle: We cannot always eat when we are hungry, and we can discharge our sexual drives only when the time and place are appropriate. To account for this fact of life, Freud suggested a second component of personality, which he called the ego.

The **ego,** which begins to develop soon after birth, strives to balance the desires of the id and the realities of the objective, outside world. In contrast to the pleasure-seeking id, the ego operates according to the *reality principle* in which instinctual energy is restrained to maintain the individual's safety and to help integrate the person into society. In a sense, then, the ego is the "executive" of personality: It makes

Freud suggests that the superego, the part of the personality that represents the rights and wrongs of society, develops from direct teaching from parents, teachers, and other significant individuals.

decisions, controls actions, and allows thinking and problem solving of a higher order than the id's capabilities permit.

The **superego,** the final personality structure to develop in childhood, represents the rights and wrongs of society as taught and modeled by a person's parents, teachers, and other significant individuals. The superego includes the *conscience,* which prevents us from behaving in a morally improper way by making us feel guilty if we do wrong. The superego helps us control impulses coming from the id, making our behavior less selfish and more virtuous.

Both the superego and the id are unrealistic in that they do not consider the practical realities imposed by society. The superego, if left to operate without restraint, would create perfectionists unable to make the compromises that life requires. An unrestrained id would create a primitive, pleasure-seeking, thoughtless individual seeking to fulfill every desire without delay. As a result, the ego must mediate between the demands of the superego and the demands of the id.

DEVELOPING PERSONALITY: PSYCHOSEXUAL STAGES

Freud also provided us with a view of how personality develops through a series of five **psychosexual stages** during which children encounter conflicts between the demands of society and their own sexual urges (in which sexuality is more about experiencing pleasure and less about lust). According to Freud, failure to resolve the conflicts at a particular stage can result in **fixations,** conflicts or concerns that persist beyond the developmental period in which they first occur. Such conflicts may be due to having needs ignored or (conversely) being overindulged during the earlier period.

The sequence Freud proposed is noteworthy because it explains how experiences and difficulties during a particular childhood stage may predict specific characteristics in the adult personality. This theory is also unique in associating each stage with a major biological function, which Freud assumed to be the focus of pleasure in a given period. (See Figure 2 for a summary of the stages.)

In the first psychosexual stage of development, called the **oral stage,** the baby's mouth is the focal point of pleasure. During the first 12 to 18 months of life, children suck, eat, mouth, and bite anything they can put into their mouths. To Freud, this behavior suggested that the mouth is the primary site of a kind of sexual pleasure and that weaning (withdrawing the breast or bottle) represents the main conflict during the oral stage. If infants are either overindulged (perhaps by being fed every time they cry) or frustrated in their search for oral gratification, they may become

superego According to Freud, the final personality structure to develop; it represents the rights and wrongs of society as handed down by a person's parents, teachers, and other important figures.

psychosexual stages Developmental periods that children pass through during which they encounter conflicts between the demands of society and their own sexual urges.

fixations Conflicts or concerns that persist beyond the developmental period in which they first occur.

Study Alert

The five psychosexual stages of personality development in Freud's theory—oral, anal, phallic, latency, and genital—indicate how personality develops as people age.

oral stage According to Freud, a stage from birth to age 12 to 18 months, in which an infant's center of pleasure is the mouth.

Stage	Age	Major Characteristics
Oral	Birth to 12–18 months	Interest in oral gratification from sucking, eating, mouthing, biting
Anal	12–18 months to 3 years	Gratification from expelling and withholding feces; coming to terms with society's controls relating to toilet training
Phallic	3 to 5–6 years	Interest in the genitals; coming to terms with Oedipal conflict leading to identification with same-sex parent
Latency	5–6 years to adolescence	Sexual concerns largely unimportant
Genital	Adolescence to adulthood	Reemergence of sexual interests and establishment of mature sexual relationships

FIGURE 2 Freud's theory of personality development suggests that there are several distinct stages.

According to Freud, a child goes through the anal stage from age 12 months to 18 months until 3 years of age. Toilet training is a crucial event at this stage—one that psychoanalytic theory claims directly influences the formation of an individual's personality.

anal stage According to Freud, a stage from age 12 to 18 months to 3 years of age, in which a child's pleasure is centered on the anus.

phallic stage According to Freud, a period beginning around age 3 during which a child's pleasure focuses on the genitals.

Oedipal conflict A child's sexual interest in his or her opposite-sex parent, typically resolved through identification with the same-sex parent.

identification The process of wanting to be like another person as much as possible, imitating that person's behavior and adopting similar beliefs and values.

latency period According to Freud, the period between the phallic stage and puberty during which children's sexual concerns are temporarily put aside.

genital stage According to Freud, the period from puberty until death, marked by mature sexual behavior (that is, sexual intercourse).

fixated at this stage. For example, fixation might occur if an infant's oral needs were constantly gratified immediately at the first sign of hunger rather than if the infant learned that feeding takes place on a schedule because eating whenever an infant wants to eat is not always realistic. Fixation at the oral stage might produce an adult who was unusually interested in oral activities—eating, talking, smoking—or who showed symbolic sorts of oral interests such as being "bitingly" sarcastic or very gullible ("swallowing" anything).

From around age 12 to 18 months until 3 years of age—a period when the emphasis in Western cultures is on toilet training—a child enters the **anal stage.** At this point, the major source of pleasure changes from the mouth to the anal region, and children obtain considerable pleasure from both retention and expulsion of feces. If toilet training is particularly demanding, fixation might occur. Fixation during the anal stage might result in unusual rigidity, orderliness, punctuality—or extreme disorderliness or sloppiness—in adulthood.

At about age 3, the **phallic stage** begins. At this point there is another major shift in the child's primary source of pleasure. Now interest focuses on the genitals and the pleasures derived from fondling them. During this stage the child must also negotiate one of the most important hurdles of personality development: the **Oedipal conflict.** According to Freudian theory, as children focus attention on their genitals, the differences between male and female anatomy become more salient. Furthermore, according to Freud, at this time the male unconsciously begins to develop a sexual interest in his mother, starts to see his father as a rival, and harbors a wish to kill his father—as Oedipus did in the ancient Greek tragedy. But because he views his father as too powerful, he develops a fear that his father may retaliate drastically by removing the source of the threat: the son's penis. The fear of losing one's penis leads to *castration anxiety,* which ultimately becomes so powerful that the child represses his desires for his mother and identifies with his father. **Identification** is the process of wanting to be like another person as much as possible, imitating that person's behavior and adopting similar beliefs and values. By identifying with his father, a son seeks to obtain a woman like his unattainable mother.

For girls, the process is different. Freud reasoned that girls begin to experience sexual arousal toward their fathers and begin to experience penis envy. They wish they had the anatomical part that, at least to Freud, seemed most clearly "missing" in girls. Blaming their mothers for their lack of a penis, girls come to believe that their mothers are responsible for their "castration." (This aspect of Freud's theory later provoked accusations that he considered women to be inferior to men.) Like males, though, they find that they can resolve such unacceptable feelings by identifying with the same-sex parent, behaving like her, and adopting her attitudes and values. In this way, a girl's identification with her mother is completed.

At this point, the Oedipal conflict is said to be resolved, and Freudian theory assumes that both males and females move on to the next stage of development. If difficulties arise during this period, however, all sorts of problems are thought to occur, including improper sex-role behavior and the failure to develop a conscience.

After the resolution of the Oedipal conflict, typically around age 5 or 6, children move into the **latency period,** which lasts until puberty. During this period, sexual interests become dormant, even in the unconscious. Then, during adolescence, sexual feelings re-emerge, which marks the start of the final period, the **genital stage,** which extends until death. The focus during the genital stage is on mature, adult sexuality, which Freud defined as sexual intercourse.

DEFENSE MECHANISMS

Freud's efforts to describe and theorize about the underlying dynamics of personality and its development were motivated by very practical problems that his patients faced in dealing with *anxiety,* an intense, negative emotional experience.

According to Freud, anxiety is a danger signal to the ego. Although anxiety can arise from realistic fears—such as seeing a poisonous snake about to strike—it can also occur in the form of *neurotic anxiety* in which irrational impulses emanating from the id threaten to burst through and become uncontrollable.

Because anxiety is obviously unpleasant, Freud believed that people develop a range of defense mechanisms to deal with it. **Defense mechanisms** are unconscious strategies that people use to reduce anxiety by distorting reality and concealing the source of the anxiety from themselves.

The primary defense mechanism is **repression** in which unacceptable or unpleasant id impulses are pushed back into the unconscious. Repression is the most direct method of dealing with anxiety; instead of handling an anxiety-producing impulse on a conscious level, we simply ignore it. For example, a college student who feels hatred for his mother may repress those personally and socially unacceptable feelings. The feelings remain lodged within the unconscious because acknowledging them would provoke anxiety. Similarly, memories of childhood abuse may be repressed. Although such memories may not be consciously recalled, according to Freud they can affect later behavior, and they may be revealed through dreams or slips of the tongue or symbolically in some other fashion.

If repression is ineffective in keeping anxiety at bay, we might use other defense mechanisms. Freud and later his daughter Anna Freud (who became a well-known psychoanalyst) formulated an extensive list of potential defense mechanisms. The major defense mechanisms are summarized in Figure 3 (Hentschel et al., 2004; Cramer, 2007; Olson et al., 2011).

defense mechanisms In Freudian theory, unconscious strategies that people use to reduce anxiety by distorting reality and concealing the source of the anxiety from themselves.

repression The primary defense mechanism in which unacceptable or unpleasant id impulses are pushed back into the unconscious.

Study Alert

Use Figure 3 to remember the most common defense mechanisms (unconscious strategies used to reduce anxiety by concealing its source from ourselves and others).

Freud's Defense Mechanisms		
Defense Mechanism	**Explanation**	**Example**
Repression	Unacceptable or unpleasant impulses are pushed back into the unconscious.	A woman is unable to recall that she was raped.
Regression	People behave as if they were at an earlier stage of development.	A boss has a temper tantrum when an employee makes a mistake.
Displacement	The expression of an unwanted feeling or thought is redirected from a more threatening powerful person to a weaker one.	A brother yells at his younger sister after a teacher gives him a bad grade.
Rationalization	People provide self-justifying explanations in place of the actual, but threatening, reason for their behavior.	A student who goes out drinking the night before a big test rationalizes his behavior by saying the test isn't all that important.
Denial	People refuse to accept or acknowledge an anxiety-producing piece of information.	A student refuses to believe that he has flunked a course.
Projection	People attribute unwanted impulses and feelings to someone else.	A man who is unfaithful to his wife and feels guilty suspects that his wife is unfaithful.
Sublimation	People divert unwanted impulses into socially approved thoughts, feelings, or behaviors.	A person with strong feelings of aggression becomes a soldier.
Reaction formation	Unconscious impulses are expressed as their opposite in consciousness.	A mother who unconsciously resents her child acts in an overly loving way toward the child.

FIGURE 3 According to Freud, people are able to use a wide range of defense mechanisms to cope with anxieties.

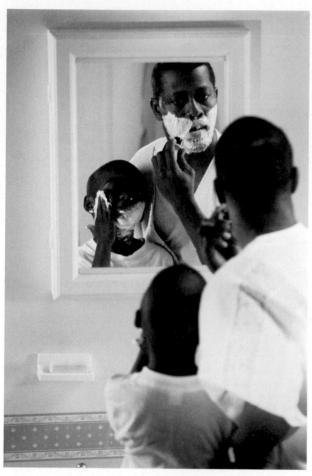

Imitating a person's behavior and adopting similar beliefs and values are part of Freud's concept of identification. How can this concept be applied to the definition of gender roles? Is identification similar in all cultures?

All of us employ defense mechanisms to some degree, according to Freudian theory, and they can serve a useful purpose by protecting us from unpleasant information. Yet some people fall prey to them to such an extent that they must constantly direct a large amount of psychic energy toward hiding and rechanneling unacceptable impulses. When this occurs, everyday living becomes difficult. In such cases, the result is a mental disorder produced by anxiety—what Freud called "neurosis." (Psychologists rarely use this term today, although it endures in everyday conversation.)

EVALUATING FREUD'S LEGACY

Freud's theory has had a significant impact on the field of psychology—and even more broadly on Western philosophy and literature. Many people have accepted the ideas of the unconscious, defense mechanisms, and childhood roots of adult psychological difficulties.

However, many contemporary personality psychologists have leveled significant criticisms against psychoanalytic theory. Among the most important is the lack of compelling scientific data to support it. Although individual case studies *seem* supportive, we lack conclusive evidence that shows the personality is structured and operates along the lines Freud laid out. The lack of evidence is due, in part, to the fact that Freud's conception of personality is built on unobservable abstract concepts. Moreover, it is not clear that the stages of personality Freud laid out provide an accurate description of personality development. We also know now that important changes in personality can occur in adolescence and adulthood—something that Freud did not believe happened. Instead, he argued that personality largely is set by adolescence.

The vague nature of Freud's theory also makes it difficult to predict how an adult will display certain developmental difficulties. For instance, if a person is fixated at the anal stage, according to Freud, he or she may be unusually messy—or unusually neat. Freud's theory offers no way to predict how the difficulty will be exhibited (Crews, 1996; Macmillan, 1996). Furthermore, Freud can be faulted for seeming to view women as inferior to men because he argued that women have weaker superegos than men and in some ways unconsciously yearn to be men (the concept of penis envy).

Finally, Freud made his observations and derived his theory from a limited population. His theory was based almost entirely on upper-class Austrian women living in the strict, puritanical era of the early 1900s, who had come to him seeking treatment for psychological and physical problems. How far one can generalize beyond this population is a matter of considerable debate. For instance, in some Pacific Island societies, the mother's oldest brother and not the father plays the role of disciplinarian. In such a culture, it is unreasonable to argue that the Oedipal conflict will progress in the same way that it did in Austrian society in which the father typically was the major disciplinarian. In short, a cross-cultural perspective raises questions about the universality of Freud's view of personality development (Doi, 1990; Spielberger, 2006; Zepf & Zepf, 2011).

Still, Freud generated an important method of treating psychological disturbances called *psychoanalysis*. As we will see when we discuss treatment approaches to psychological disorders, psychoanalysis remains in use today (Heller, 2005; Riolo, 2007; Frosch, 2011).

Moreover, Freud's emphasis on the unconscious has been partially supported by current research on dreams and implicit memory. As we first noted when we discussed dreaming, advances in neuroscience are consistent with some of Freud's arguments. For example, the fact that some behavior is motivated by occurrences that apparently have been forgotten, as well as the discovery of neural pathways relating to emotional memories, supports the notion of repression. Furthermore, cognitive and social psychologists have found increasing evidence that unconscious processes help us think about and evaluate our world, set goals, and choose a course of action. The degree to which future neuroscientific advances will support the criticisms leveled against Freud's psychoanalytic theory remains to be seen (Derryberry, 2006; Litowitz, 2007; Turnbull & Solms, 2007).

The Neo-Freudian Psychoanalysts: Building on Freud

Freud laid the foundation for important work done by a series of successors who were trained in traditional Freudian theory but later rejected some of its major points. These theorists are known as **neo-Freudian psychoanalysts.**

The neo-Freudians placed greater emphasis than Freud on the functions of the ego by suggesting that it has more control than the id over day-to-day activities. They focused more on the social environment and minimized the importance of sex as a driving force in people's lives. They also paid greater attention to the effects of society and culture on personality development.

neo-Freudian psychoanalysts Psychoanalysts who were trained in traditional Freudian theory but who later rejected some of its major points.

JUNG'S COLLECTIVE UNCONSCIOUS

Carl Jung (pronounced "yoong"), one of the most influential neo-Freudians, rejected Freud's view of the primary importance of unconscious sexual urges. Instead, he looked at the primitive urges of the unconscious more positively and argued that they represented a more general and positive life force that encompasses an inborn drive motivating creativity and more positive resolution of conflict (Lothane, 2005; Cassells, 2007; Wilde, 2011).

Jung suggested that we have a universal **collective unconscious,** a common set of ideas, feelings, images, and symbols that we inherit from our relatives, the whole human race, and even nonhuman animal ancestors from the distant past. This collective unconscious is shared by everyone and is displayed in behavior that is common across diverse cultures—such as love of mother, belief in a supreme being, and even behavior as specific as fear of snakes (Drob, 2005; Hauke, 2006; Finn, 2011).

Jung went on to propose that the collective unconscious contains **archetypes,** universal symbolic representations of a particular person, object, or experience. For instance, a mother archetype, which contains reflections of our ancestors' relationships with mother figures, is suggested by the prevalence of mothers in art, religion, literature, and mythology. (Think of the Virgin Mary, Earth Mother, wicked stepmothers in fairy tales, Mother's Day, and so forth!) Jung also suggested that men possess an unconscious feminine archetype that affects how they behave, whereas women have an unconscious male archetype that colors their behavior (Jung, 1961; Bair, 2003; Smetana, 2007).

collective unconscious According to Jung, a common set of ideas, feelings, images, and symbols that we inherit from our ancestors, the whole human race, and even animal ancestors from the distant past.

archetypes According to Jung, universal symbolic representations of a particular person, object, or experience (such as good and evil).

In terms of Jung's theory, Harry Potter and Voldemort represent the archetypes, or universally recognizable symbols, of good and evil.

To Jung, archetypes play an important role in determining our day-to-day reactions, attitudes, and values. For example, Jung might explain the popularity of the Harry Potter books and movies as being due to their use of broad archetypes of good (Harry Potter) and evil (Voldemort).

Although no reliable research evidence confirms the existence of the collective unconscious—and even Jung acknowledged that such evidence would be difficult to produce—Jung's theory has had significant influence in areas beyond psychology. For example, personality types derived from Jung's personality approach form the basis for the Myers-Briggs personality test, which is widely used in business and industry to provide insights into how employees make decisions and perform on the job (Bayne, 2005; Furnham & Crump, 2005; Wilde, 2011).

Karen Horney was one of the earliest proponents of women's issues.

HORNEY'S NEO-FREUDIAN PERSPECTIVE

Karen Horney (pronounced "HORN-eye") was one of the earliest psychologists to champion women's issues and is sometimes called the first feminist psychologist. Horney suggested that personality develops in the context of social relationships and depends particularly on the relationship between parents and child and how well the child's needs are met. She rejected Freud's suggestion that women have penis envy; she asserted that what women envy most in men is not their anatomy but the independence, success, and freedom women often are denied (Horney, 1937; Smith, 2007; Coolidge et al., 2011).

Horney was also one of the first to stress the importance of cultural factors in the determination of personality. For example, she suggested that society's rigid gender roles for women lead them to experience ambivalence about success because they fear they will make enemies if they are too successful. Her conceptualizations, developed in the 1930s and 1940s, laid the groundwork for many of the central ideas of feminism that emerged decades later (Eckardt, 2005; Jones, 2006).

ADLER AND THE OTHER NEO-FREUDIANS

Alfred Adler, another important neo-Freudian psychoanalyst, also considered Freudian theory's emphasis on sexual needs misplaced. Instead, Adler proposed that the primary human motivation is a striving for superiority, not in terms of superiority over others but in a quest for self-improvement and perfection.

Adler used the term *inferiority complex* to describe adults who have not been able to overcome the feelings of inferiority they developed as children. Early social relationships with parents have an important effect on children's ability to outgrow feelings of personal inferiority and instead to orient themselves toward attaining more socially useful goals, such as improving society.

Other neo-Freudians included Erik Erikson, whose theory of psychosocial development we discussed in earlier modules, and Freud's daughter, Anna Freud. Like Adler and Horney, they focused less than Freud on inborn sexual and aggressive drives and more on the social and cultural factors behind personality.

RECAP/EVALUATE/RETHINK

RECAP

LO 31-1 How do psychologists define and use the concept of personality?

- Personality is the pattern of enduring characteristics that produce consistency and individuality in a given person. (p. 384)

LO 31-2 What do the theories of Freud and his successors tell us about the structure and development of personality?

- According to psychodynamic approaches to personality, much behavior is caused by parts of personality that are found in the unconscious and of which we are unaware. (p. 385)
- Freud's psychoanalytic theory, one of the psychodynamic approaches, suggests that personality is composed of the id, the ego, and the superego. The id is the unorganized, inborn part of personality whose purpose is to immediately reduce tensions relating to hunger, sex, aggression, and other primitive impulses. The ego restrains instinctual energy to maintain the individual's safety and to help the person be a member of society. The superego represents society's rights and wrongs and includes the conscience. (pp. 386, 387)
- Freud's psychoanalytic theory suggests that personality develops through a series of psychosexual stages (oral, anal, phallic, latency, and genital), each of which is associated with a primary biological function. (pp. 387, 388)
- Defense mechanisms, according to Freudian theory, are unconscious strategies that people use to reduce anxiety by distorting reality and concealing the true source of the anxiety from themselves. (pp. 388, 389)
- Freud's psychoanalytic theory has provoked a number of criticisms, including a lack of supportive scientific data, the theory's inadequacy in making predictions, and its reliance on a highly restricted population. On the other hand, recent neuroscience research has offered some support for the concept of the unconscious. (pp. 389, 390)

- Neo-Freudian psychoanalytic theorists built on Freud's work, although they placed greater emphasis on the role of the ego and paid more attention to the role of social factors in determining behavior. (p. 391)

EVALUATE

1. _____ approaches state that behavior is motivated primarily by unconscious forces.
2. Match each section of the personality (according to Freud) with its description:
   1. Ego
   2. Id
   3. Superego

   a. Determines right from wrong on the basis of cultural standards.
   b. Operates according to the "reality principle"; energy is redirected to integrate the person into society.
   c. Seeks to reduce tension brought on by primitive drives.
3. Which of the following represents the proper order of personality development, according to Freud?
   a. Oral, phallic, latency, anal, genital
   b. Anal, oral, phallic, genital, latency
   c. Oral, anal, phallic, latency, genital
   d. Latency, phallic, anal, genital, oral
4. _____ _____ is the term Freud used to describe unconscious strategies used to reduce anxiety by distorting reality and concealing the source of the anxiety from themselves.

RETHINK

1. Can you think of ways in which Freud's theories of unconscious motivations are commonly used in popular culture? How accurately do you think such popular uses of Freudian theories reflect Freud's ideas?
2. *From the perspective of an advertising executive:* How might you use Jung's concept of archetypes in designing your advertisements? Which of the archetypes would you use?

Answers to Evaluate Questions

1. Psychodynamic; 2. 1-b, 2-c, 3-a; 3. c; 4. Defense mechanisms

KEY TERMS

personality p. 384
psychodynamic approaches
   to personality p. 385
psychoanalytic
   theory p. 385
unconscious p. 385
id p. 386

ego p. 386
superego p. 387
psychosexual
   stages p. 387
fixations p. 387
oral stage p. 387
anal stage p. 388

phallic stage p. 388
Oedipal conflict p. 388
identification p. 388
latency
   period p. 388
genital stage p. 388
defense mechanisms p. 389

repression p. 389
neo-Freudian
   psychoanalysts p. 391
collective
   unconscious p. 391
archetypes p. 391

Trait, Learning, Biological and Evolutionary, and Humanistic Approaches to Personality

"Tell me about Nelson," said Johnetta.

"Oh, he's just terrific. He's the friendliest guy I know—goes out of his way to be nice to everyone. He hardly ever gets mad. He's just so even-tempered, no matter what's happening. And he's really smart, too. About the only thing I don't like is that he's always in such a hurry to get things done. He seems to have boundless energy, much more than I have."

"He sounds great to me, especially in comparison to Rico," replied Johnetta. "He is so self-centered and arrogant that it drives me crazy. I sometimes wonder why I ever started going out with him."

Friendly. Even-tempered. Smart. Energetic. Self-centered. Arrogant.

The above exchange is made up of a series of trait characterizations of the speakers' friends. In fact, much of our own understanding of others' behavior is based on the premise that people possess certain traits that are consistent across different situations. For example, we generally assume that if someone is outgoing and sociable in one situation, he or she is outgoing and sociable in other situations (Gilbert et al., 1992; Gilbert, Miller, & Ross, 1998; Mischel, 2004).

Dissatisfaction with the emphasis in psychoanalytic theory on unconscious—and difficult to demonstrate—processes in explaining a person's behavior led to the development of alternative approaches to personality, including a number of trait-based approaches. Other theories reflect established psychological perspectives, such as learning theory, biological and evolutionary approaches, and the humanistic approach.

Learning Outcome

LO 32-1 What are the major aspects of trait, learning, biological and evolutionary, and humanistic approaches to personality?

Trait Approaches: Placing Labels on Personality

If someone asked you to characterize another person, like Johnetta and her friend, you probably would come up with a list of that individual's personal qualities as you see them. But how would you know which of those qualities are most important to an understanding of that person's behavior?

Personality psychologists have asked similar questions. To answer them, they have developed a model of personality known as trait theory. **Trait theory** seeks to explain in a straightforward way the consistencies in individuals' behavior. **Traits** are consistent personality characteristics and behaviors displayed in different situations.

Trait theorists do not assume that some people have a trait and others do not; rather, they propose that all people possess certain traits but the degree to which a particular trait applies to a specific person varies and can be quantified. For instance,

trait theory A model of personality that seeks to identify the basic traits necessary to describe personality.

traits Consistent personality characteristics and behaviors displayed in different situations.

you may be relatively friendly, whereas I may be relatively unfriendly. But we both have a "friendliness" trait, although your degree of "friendliness" is higher than mine. The major challenge for trait theorists taking this approach has been to identify the specific primary traits necessary to describe personality. As we shall see, different theorists have come up with surprisingly different sets of traits.

ALLPORT'S TRAIT THEORY: IDENTIFYING BASIC CHARACTERISTICS

When personality psychologist Gordon Allport systematically pored over an unabridged dictionary in the 1930s, he came up with some 18,000 separate terms that could be used to describe personality. Although he was able to pare down the list to a mere 4,500 descriptors after eliminating words with the same meaning, he was left with a problem crucial to all trait approaches: Which of those traits were the most basic?

Allport eventually answered this question by suggesting that there are three fundamental categories of traits: cardinal, central, and secondary (Allport, 1961, 1966). A *cardinal trait* is a single characteristic that directs most of a person's activities. For example, a totally selfless woman may direct all her energy toward humanitarian activities; an intensely power-hungry person may be driven by an all-consuming need for control.

Most people, however, do not develop a single, comprehensive cardinal trait. Instead, they possess a handful of central traits that make up the core of personality. *Central traits,* such as honesty and sociability, are an individual's major characteristics; they usually number from five to ten in any one person. Finally, *secondary traits* are characteristics that affect behavior in fewer situations and are less influential than central or cardinal traits. For instance, a reluctance to eat meat and a love of modern art would be considered secondary traits (Glicksohn & Nahari, 2007; Smrtnik-Vitulić, & Zupančič, 2011).

Extraversion
• Sociable
• Lively
• Active
• Assertive
• Sensation-seeking

Neuroticism
• Anxious
• Depressed
• Guilt feelings
• Low self-esteem
• Tense

Psychoticism
• Aggressive
• Cold
• Egocentric
• Impersonal
• Impulsive

FIGURE 1 Eysenck described personality in terms of three major dimensions: extraversion, neuroticism, and psychoticism. Using these dimensions, he could predict people's behavior in many types of situations. (Source: Eysenck, 1990.)

CATTELL AND EYSENCK: FACTORING OUT PERSONALITY

Later attempts to identify primary personality traits have centered on a statistical technique known as factor analysis. *Factor analysis* is a statistical method of identifying associations among a large number of variables to reveal more general patterns. For example, a personality researcher might administer a questionnaire to many participants that asks them to describe themselves by referring to an extensive list of traits. By statistically combining responses and computing which traits are associated with one another in the same person, a researcher can identify the most fundamental patterns or combinations of traits—called *factors*—that underlie participants' responses.

Using factor analysis, personality psychologist Raymond Cattell (1965) suggested that 16 pairs of *source traits* represent the basic dimensions of personality. Using those source traits, he developed the Sixteen Personality Factor Questionnaire, or 16 PF, a measure that provides scores for each of the 16 source traits (Cattell, Cattell, & Cattell, 1993, 2000; Djapo et al., 2011).

Another trait theorist, psychologist Hans Eysenck (1995), also used factor analysis to identify patterns of traits, but he came to a very different conclusion about the nature of personality. He found that personality could best be described in terms of just three major dimensions: extraversion, neuroticism, and psychoticism. The *extraversion* dimension relates to the degree of sociability, whereas the *neuroticism* dimension encompasses emotional stability. Finally, *psychoticism* refers to the degree to which reality is distorted. By evaluating people along these three dimensions, Eysenck was able to predict behavior accurately in a variety of situations. Figure 1 lists specific traits associated with each of the dimensions.

The Big Five Personality Factors and Dimensions of Sample Traits

Openness to experience
Independent—Conforming
Imaginative—Practical
Preference for variety—Preference for routine

Conscientiousness
Careful—Careless
Disciplined—Impulsive
Organized—Disorganized

Extraversion
Talkative—Quiet
Fun-loving—Sober
Sociable—Retiring

Agreeableness
Sympathetic—Fault-finding
Kind—Cold
Appreciative—Unfriendly

Neuroticism (Emotional Stability)
Stable—Tense
Calm—Anxious
Secure—Insecure

FIGURE 2 Five broad trait factors, referred to as the "Big Five," are considered to be the core of personality. (Source: Adapted from Pervin, 1990, Chapter 3, and McCrae & Costa, 1986, p. 1002.)

THE BIG FIVE PERSONALITY TRAITS

For the last two decades, the most influential trait approach contends that five traits or factors—called the "Big Five"—lie at the core of personality. Using factor analytic statistical techniques, a host of researchers have identified a similar set of five factors that underlie personality. The five factors, described in Figure 2, are *openness to experience, conscientiousness, extraversion, agreeableness,* and *neuroticism* (emotional stability).

The Big Five emerge consistently across a number of domains. For example, factor analyses of major personality inventories, self-report measures made by observers of others' personality traits, and checklists of self-descriptions yield similar factors. In addition, the Big Five emerge consistently in different populations of individuals, including children, college students, older adults, and speakers of different languages. Cross-cultural research conducted in areas ranging from Europe to the Middle East to Africa also has been supportive. Finally, studies of brain functioning show that Big Five personality traits are related to the way the brain processes information (Schmitt, Allik, & McCrae, 2007; Schmitt et al., 2008; Vecchione et al., 2011).

In short, a growing consensus exists that the Big Five represent the best description of personality traits we have today. Still, the debate over the specific number and kinds of traits—and even the usefulness of trait approaches in general—remains a lively one.

EVALUATING TRAIT APPROACHES TO PERSONALITY

Trait approaches have several virtues. They provide a clear, straightforward explanation of people's behavioral consistencies. Furthermore, traits allow us to readily compare one person with another. Because of these advantages, trait approaches to personality have had an important influence on the development of several useful personality measures (Funder, 1991; Wiggins, 2003; Larsen & Buss, 2006; also see *Applying Psychology in the 21st Century* on page 398).

However, trait approaches also have some drawbacks. For example, we have seen that various trait theories describing personality come to very different conclusions about which traits are the most fundamental and descriptive. The difficulty in determining which of the theories is the most accurate has led some personality psychologists to question the validity of trait conceptions of personality in general.

Actually, there is an even more fundamental difficulty with trait approaches. Even if we are able to identify a set of primary traits, we are left with little more than a label or description of personality—rather than an explanation of behavior. If we say that someone who donates money to charity has the trait of generosity, we still do not know *why* that person became generous in the first place or the reasons for displaying generosity in a specific situation. In the view of some critics, then, traits do not provide explanations for behavior; they merely describe it.

Study Alert

You can remember the "Big Five" set of personality traits by using the acronym OCEAN (*o*penness to experience, *c*onscientiousness, *e*xtraversion, *a*greeableness, and *n*euroticism).

The Self-Obsessed Generation?

In Greek mythology, Narcissus was a handsome hunter who fell in love with the image of his own reflection in a pool of water. People with narcissistic personality traits are similarly self-obsessed—they have an inflated sense of their own importance and expect to be treated as special people. And according to some researchers, that is exactly what young Americans increasingly look like.

Over the last three decades, thousands of college students participating in a wide variety of psychological research studies were asked to take the Narcissism Personality Inventory (NPI), a test of narcissistic tendencies. A summary of over 100 such studies conducted between 1982 and 2008 showed a significant increase in participants' NPI scores over that time period (Twenge & Foster, 2010; Dingfelder, 2011).

Another study used face-to-face interviews with over 34,000 participants. They were asked to recall whether they exhibited the symptoms of narcissistic personality disorder at any point in their lives. More than 9% of participants in their 20s had, compared to only about 3% of those over 65—a startlingly large difference (Stinson et al., 2008).

What might produce the increase in narcissism in young Americans? One researcher points to social networking media. In recent years, it has become typical for young people to self-promote in carefully edited online profiles. The most mundane aspects of their daily lives are viewed as worthy of broadcasting to the world, whether in Twitter tweets, Facebook, or YouTube videos. Another explanation is that parents may increasingly be inflating their children's sense of self-importance by shielding them from situations in which they might fail (Twenge & Foster, 2010; Dingfelder, 2011).

According to one researcher, social networking media such as Twitter and Facebook have been linked to an increase in narcissism among the young.

A tweet of something quite mundane that most people would not care about but that someone thought important to send. The point is to show that some people are quite self-obsessed. Something along this line: "Watching TV right now." Or "Doing my laundry."

On the other hand, some researchers are skeptical of the conclusion that young Americans are becoming more self-obsessed. They point out that there could be many reasons why college students are answering the NPI differently over time, including that the kinds of people who go to college may be changing. Or older people might simply be less likely to recall their self-important young adult years than young people are. Until more definitive research is done, the jury is still out on whether Americans are truly becoming more narcissistic (Dingfelder, 2011).

RETHINK

- Why is it assumed to be undesirable for young people to think very highly of themselves?
- What other cultural influences besides the Internet might be encouraging young people to become obsessively focused on themselves?

Learning Approaches:
We Are What We've Learned

The psychodynamic and trait approaches we've discussed concentrate on the "inner" person—the fury of an unobservable but powerful id, or a hypothetical but critical set of traits. In contrast, learning approaches to personality focus on the external environment and how that determines personality. To a strict learning theorist, personality is simply the sum of learned responses to the external environment. Internal events such as thoughts, feelings, and motivations are ignored. Although the existence of personality is not denied, learning theorists say that it is best understood by looking at features of a person's environment.

SKINNER'S BEHAVIORIST APPROACH

According to the most influential learning theorist, B. F. Skinner (who carried out pioneering work on operant conditioning), personality is a collection of learned behavior patterns (Skinner, 1975). Similarities in responses across different situations are caused by similar patterns of reinforcement that have been received in such situations in the past. If I am sociable both at parties and at meetings, it is because I have been reinforced for displaying social behaviors—not because I am fulfilling an unconscious wish based on experiences during my childhood or because I have an internal trait of sociability.

Strict learning theorists such as Skinner are less interested in the consistencies in behavior across situations than in ways of modifying behavior. Their view is that humans are infinitely changeable through the process of learning new behavior patterns. If we are able to control and modify the patterns of reinforcers in a situation, behavior that other theorists would view as stable and unyielding can be changed and ultimately improved. Learning theorists are optimistic in their attitudes about the potential for resolving personal and societal problems through treatment strategies based on learning theory.

SOCIAL COGNITIVE APPROACHES TO PERSONALITY

Not all learning theories of personality take such a strict view in rejecting the importance of what is "inside" a person by focusing solely on the "outside." Unlike other learning approaches to personality, **social cognitive approaches to personality** emphasize the influence of cognition—thoughts, feelings, expectations, and values—as well as observation of others' behavior, on personality. According to Albert Bandura, one of the main proponents of this point of view, people can foresee the possible outcomes of certain behaviors in a specific setting without actually having to carry them out. This understanding comes primarily through *observational learning*—viewing the actions of others and observing the consequences (Bandura, 1986, 1999).

For instance, children who view a model behaving in, say, an aggressive manner tend to copy the behavior if the consequences of the model's behavior are seen as positive. If, in contrast, the model's aggressive behavior has resulted in no consequences or negative consequences, children are considerably less likely to act aggressively. According to social cognitive approaches, then, personality develops through repeated observation of others' behavior.

Self-Efficacy. Bandura places particular emphasis on the role played by **self-efficacy,** the belief that we have the personal capabilities to master a situation and produce positive outcomes. Self-efficacy underlies people's faith in their ability to carry out a specific task or produce a desired result. People with high self-efficacy have higher aspirations and greater persistence in working to attain goals and ultimately achieve greater success than those with lower self-efficacy (Bandura & Locke, 2003; Betz, 2007; Dunlop, Beatty, & Beauchamp, 2011).

How do we develop self-efficacy? One way is by paying close attention to our prior successes and failures. If we try snowboarding and experience little success, we'll be less likely to try it again. However, if our initial efforts appear promising, we'll be more likely to attempt it again. Direct reinforcement and encouragement from others also play a role in developing self-efficacy (Devonport & Lane, 2006; Buchanan & Selmon, 2008).

social cognitive approaches to personality Theories that emphasize the influence of a person's cognitions—thoughts, feelings, expectations, and values—as well as observation of others' behavior, in determining personality.

self-efficacy The belief that we have the personal capabilities to master a situation and produce positive outcomes.

PsychTech

Researchers have been investigating differences in self-efficacy between people in their use of technology. One difference is age, in which younger adults appear to have more confidence in their technological expertise than older adults.

Compared with other learning theories of personality, social cognitive approaches are distinctive in their emphasis on the reciprocity between individuals and their environment. Not only is the environment assumed to affect personality, but people's behavior and personalities are also assumed to "feed back" and modify the environment (Bandura, 1999, 2000).

HOW MUCH CONSISTENCY EXISTS IN PERSONALITY?

Another social cognitive theorist, Walter Mischel, takes a different approach to personality from that of Albert Bandura. He rejects the view that personality consists of broad traits that lead to substantial consistencies in behavior across different situations. Instead, he sees personality as considerably more variable from one situation to another (Mischel, 2009).

In this view, particular situations give rise to particular kinds of behavior. Some situations are especially influential (think of a movie theater, where everyone displays pretty much the same behavior by sitting quietly and watching the film). Other situations permit much variability in behavior (think of a party, for example, where some people may be dancing, while others are eating and drinking).

Self-efficacy, the belief in one's own capabilities, leads to higher aspirations and greater persistence.

From this perspective, personality cannot be considered without taking the particular context of the situation into account—a view known as *situationism*. In his *cognitive-affective processing system (CAPS)* theory, Mischel argues that people's thoughts and emotions about themselves and the world determine how they view, and then react, in particular situations. Personality is thus seen as a reflection of how people's prior experiences in different situations affect their behavior (Shoda & Mischel, 2006; Mischel & Shoda, 2008; McCrae et al., 2011).

SELF-ESTEEM

self-esteem The component of personality that encompasses our positive and negative self-evaluations.

Our behavior also reflects the view we have of ourselves and the way we value the various parts of our personalities. **Self-esteem** is the component of personality that encompasses our positive and negative self-evaluations. Unlike self-efficacy, which focuses on our views of whether we are able to carry out a task, self-esteem relates to how we feel about ourselves.

Although people have a general level of self-esteem, it is not unidimensional. We may see ourselves positively in one domain but negatively in others. For example, a good student may have high self-esteem in academic domains but lower self-esteem in sports (Salmela-Aro & Nurmi, 2007; Gentile et al., 2009; Gadbois & Sturgeon, 2011).

Self-esteem is strongly affected by culture. For example, in Asian cultures, having high *relationship harmony*—a sense of success in forming close bonds with other people—is more important to self-esteem than it is in more individualistic Western societies (Spencer-Rodgers et al., 2004; Lun & Bond, 2006; Cheng & Kwan, 2008).

Although almost everyone goes through periods of low self-esteem (for instance, after an undeniable failure), some people are chronically low in self-esteem. For them, failure seems to be an inevitable part of life. In fact, low self-esteem may lead to a cycle of failure in which past failure breeds future failure.

For example, consider students with low self-esteem who are studying for a test. Because of their low self-esteem, they expect to do poorly on the test. In turn, this belief raises their anxiety level, which makes it increasingly difficult to study and perhaps even leading them not to work as hard. Because of these attitudes, they do, in fact, ultimately perform badly on the test. Ultimately, the failure reinforces their low self-esteem, and the cycle is perpetuated as illustrated in Figure 3. In short, low self-esteem can lead to a self-destructive cycle of failure.

EVALUATING LEARNING APPROACHES TO PERSONALITY

Because they ignore the internal processes that are uniquely human, traditional learning theorists such as Skinner have been accused of oversimplifying personality to such an extent that the concept becomes meaningless. Their critics think that reducing

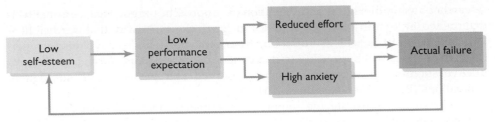

FIGURE 3 The cycle of low self-esteem begins with an individual already having low self-esteem. As a consequence, the person will have low performance expectations and expect to fail a test, thereby producing anxiety and reduced effort. As a result, the person will actually fail, and failure in turn reinforces low self-esteem.

behavior to a series of stimuli and responses and excluding thoughts and feelings from the realm of personality leaves behaviorists practicing an unrealistic and inadequate form of science.

Of course, some of these criticisms are blunted by social cognitive approaches, which explicitly consider the role of cognitive processes in personality. Still, learning approaches tend to share a highly *deterministic* view of human behavior, which maintains that behavior is shaped primarily by forces beyond the individual's control. As in psychoanalytic theory (which suggests that personality is determined by the unconscious forces) and trait approaches (which views personality in part as a mixture of genetically determined traits), learning theory's reliance on deterministic principles de-emphasizes people's ability to pilot their own course through life.

Nonetheless, learning approaches have had a major impact on the study of personality. For one thing, they have helped make personality psychology an objective, scientific venture by focusing on observable behavior and the effects of their environments. In addition, they have produced important, successful means of treating a variety of psychological disorders. The degree of success of these treatments is a testimony to the merits of learning theory approaches to personality.

Biological and Evolutionary Approaches: Are We Born with Personality?

Approaching the question of what determines personality from a different direction, **biological and evolutionary approaches to personality** suggest that important components of personality are inherited. Building on the work of behavioral geneticists,

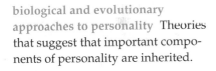

biological and evolutionary approaches to personality Theories that suggest that important components of personality are inherited.

Biological and evolutionary approaches to personality seek to explain the consistencies in personality that are found in some families.

researchers using biological and evolutionary approaches argue that personality is determined at least in part by our genes in much the same way that our height is largely a result of genetic contributions from our ancestors. The evolutionary perspective assumes that personality traits that led to our ancestors' survival and reproductive success are more likely to be preserved and passed on to subsequent generations (Buss, 2001, 2009; Buss, 2011).

Twin studies illustrate the importance of genetic factors in personality. For instance, personality psychologists Auke Tellegen and colleagues at the University of Minnesota examined the personality traits of pairs of twins who were genetically identical but were raised apart from each other (Tellegen et al., 1988; Bouchard et al., 2004). In the study, each twin was given a battery of personality tests, including one that measured 11 key personality characteristics.

The results of the personality tests indicated that in major respects the twins were quite similar in personality, despite having separated at an early age. Moreover, certain traits were more heavily influenced by heredity than others. For example, social potency (the degree to which a person assumes mastery and leadership roles in social situations) and traditionalism (the tendency to follow authority) had particularly strong genetic components, whereas achievement and social closeness had relatively weak genetic components (see Figure 4).

Furthermore, it is increasingly clear that the roots of adult personality emerge in the earliest periods of life. Infants are born with a specific **temperament,** an inborn behavioral style and characteristic way of responding. Temperament encompasses several dimensions, including general activity level and mood. For instance,

temperament An inborn behavioral style and characteristic way of responding that emerges early in life.

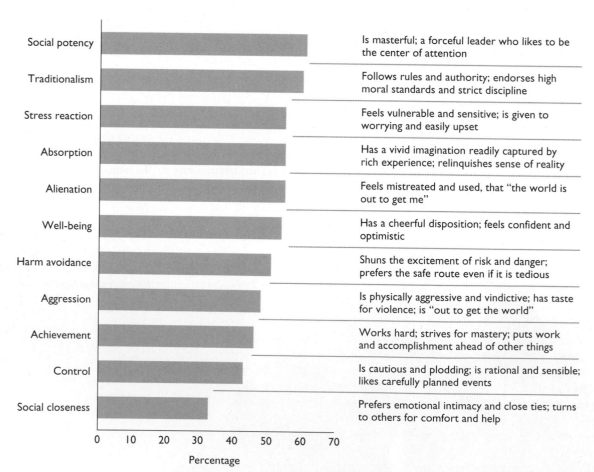

FIGURE 4 The inherited roots of personality. The percentages indicate the degree to which 11 personality characteristics reflect the influence of heredity. (Source: Tellegen et al., 1988.)

Infants are born with particular temperaments—dispositions that are consistent throughout childhood.

some individuals are quite active, while others are relatively calm. Similarly, some are relatively easygoing, while others are irritable, easily upset, and difficult to soothe. Temperament is quite consistent, with significant stability from infancy well into adolescence (Wachs et al., 2004; Kagan et al., 2007; Evans & Rothbart, 2007, 2009; Hori et al., 2011).

Some researchers contend that specific genes are related to personality. For example, people with a longer dopamine-4 receptor gene are more likely to be thrill-seekers than those without such a gene. These thrill-seekers tend to be extroverted, impulsive, quick-tempered, and always in search of excitement and novel situations. Furthermore, the structure of their brains may reflect their thrill-seeking tendencies (see Figure 5 *Neuroscience in Your Life;* Robins, 2005; Golimbet et al., 2007; Ray et al., 2009).

Does the identification of specific genes linked to personality, coupled with the existence of temperaments from the time of birth, mean that we are destined to have certain types of personalities? Hardly. First, it is unlikely that any single gene is linked to a specific trait. For instance, the dopamine-4 receptor accounts for only around 10% of the variation in novelty seeking between different individuals. The rest of the variation is attributable to other genes and environmental factors (Keltikangas-Järvinen et al., 2004; Lahti et al., 2005).

More important, genes interact with the environment. As we see in discussions of the heritability of intelligence and the nature–nurture issue, it is impossible to completely divorce genetic factors from environmental factors. Although studies of identical twins raised in different environments are helpful, they are not definitive because it is impossible to assess and control environmental factors fully. Furthermore, estimates of the influence of genetics are just that—estimates—and apply to groups, not individuals. Consequently, findings such as those shown in Figure 4 must be regarded as approximations.

Finally, even if more genes are found to be linked to specific personality characteristics, genes still cannot be viewed as the sole cause of personality. For one thing, genetically determined characteristics may not be expressed if they are not "turned on" by particular environmental experiences. Furthermore, behaviors produced by genes may help to create a specific environment. For instance, a cheerful, smiley

Neuroscience in Your Life: Wired to Take Risks—The Biological Underpinnings of Personality

FIGURE 5 Many of us like to gamble every once in a while, whether it's playing the lottery or taking the risk that a professor won't notice an absence from class. When and why we take risk, however, is based on both the situation and aspects of our personality, such as how likely we are to give in to strong impulses. In research looking at risk-taking behavior, participants were asked to make a decision that involved the risk of winning or losing money. This fMRI shows that individuals who score higher on risk-taking had increased activation in the area of the brain associated with feelings of urgency as indicated in red-orange. (Source: Xue et al., 2010.)

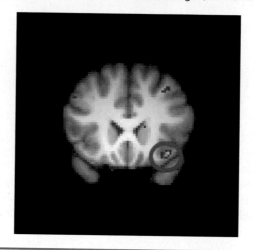

baby may lead the parents to smile more and be more responsive, thereby creating a supportive, pleasant environment. In contrast, the parents of a cranky, fussy baby may be less inclined to smile at the child; in turn, the environment in which that child is raised will be less supportive and pleasant. In a sense, then, genes not only influence a person's behavior—they also help produce the environment in which a person develops (Scarr, 1998; Plomin & Caspi, 1999; Kim-Cohen, Caspi, & Moffitt, 2003; Kim-Cohen et al., 2005).

Although an increasing number of personality theorists are taking biological and evolutionary factors into account, no comprehensive, unified theory that considers biological and evolutionary factors is widely accepted. Still, it is clear that certain personality traits have substantial genetic components and that heredity and environment interact to determine personality (Ebstein, Benjamin, & Belmaker, 2003; Bouchard, 2004; South & Krueger, 2008).

Humanistic Approaches: The Uniqueness of You

In all the approaches to personality that we have discussed, where is an explanation for the saintliness of a Mother Teresa, the creativity of a Michelangelo, and the brilliance and perseverance of an Einstein? An understanding of such unique individuals—as well as more ordinary sorts of people who have some of the same attributes—comes from humanistic theory.

According to humanistic theorists, all the approaches to personality we have discussed share a fundamental misperception in their views of human nature. Instead of seeing people as controlled by unconscious, unseen forces (psychodynamic approaches), a set of stable traits (trait approaches), situational reinforcements and punishments (learning theory), or inherited factors (biological and evolutionary approaches), **humanistic approaches to personality** emphasize people's inherent goodness and their tendency to move toward higher levels of functioning. It is this conscious, self-motivated ability to change and improve, along with people's unique creative impulses, that humanistic theorists argue make up the core of personality.

"So, while extortion, racketeering, and murder may be bad acts, they don't make you a bad person."

ROGERS AND THE NEED FOR SELF-ACTUALIZATION

The major proponent of the humanistic point of view is Carl Rogers (1971). Along with other humanistic theorists, such as Abraham Maslow, Rogers maintains that all people have a fundamental need for **self-actualization,** a state of self-fulfillment in which people realize their highest potential, each in a unique way. He further suggests that people develop a need for positive regard that reflects the desire to be loved and respected. Because others provide this positive regard, we grow dependent on them. We begin to see and judge ourselves through the eyes of other people, relying on their values and being preoccupied with what they think of us.

According to Rogers, one outgrowth of placing importance on others' opinions is that a conflict may grow between people's experiences and their *self-concepts*, the set of beliefs they hold about what they are like as individuals. If the discrepancies are minor, so are the consequences. But if the discrepancies are great, they will lead to psychological disturbances in daily functioning, such as the experience of frequent anxiety.

Rogers suggests that one way of overcoming the discrepancy between experience and self-concept is through the receipt of unconditional positive regard from another person—a friend, a spouse, or a therapist. **Unconditional positive regard** refers to an attitude of acceptance and respect on the observer's part, no matter what a person says or does. This acceptance, says Rogers, gives people the opportunity to evolve and grow both cognitively and emotionally and to develop more realistic self-concepts. You may have experienced the power of unconditional positive regard when you confided in someone, revealing embarrassing secrets because you knew the listener would still love and respect you even after hearing the worst about you (Snyder, 2002; Marshall, 2007).

In contrast, *conditional positive regard* depends on your behavior. In such cases, others withdraw their love and acceptance if you do something of which they don't approve. The result is a discrepancy between your true self and what others wish you would be, which leads to anxiety and frustration (see Figure 6).

humanistic approaches to personality Theories that emphasize people's innate goodness and desire to achieve higher levels of functioning.

self-actualization A state of self-fulfillment in which people realize their highest potential, each in a unique way.

unconditional positive regard An attitude of acceptance and respect on the part of an observer, no matter what a person says or does.

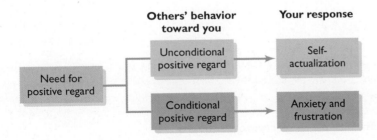

FIGURE 6 According to the humanistic view of Carl Rogers, people have a basic need to be loved and respected. If you receive unconditional positive regard from others, you will develop a more realistic self-concept; but if the response is conditional, it may lead to anxiety and frustration.

EVALUATING HUMANISTIC APPROACHES

Although humanistic theories suggest the value of providing unconditional positive regard toward people, unconditional positive regard toward humanistic theories has been less forthcoming. The criticisms have centered on the difficulty of verifying the basic assumptions of the approach as well as on the question of whether unconditional positive regard does, in fact, lead to greater personality adjustment.

Humanistic approaches have also been criticized for making the assumption that people are basically "good"—a notion that is unverifiable—and, equally important, for using nonscientific values to build supposedly scientific theories. Still, humanistic theories have been important in highlighting the uniqueness of human beings and guiding the development of a significant form of therapy designed to alleviate psychological difficulties (Cain, 2002; Bauman & Kopp, 2006; Elkins, 2009; Kogstad, Ekeland, & Hummelvoll, 2011).

Comparing Approaches to Personality

In light of the multiple approaches we have discussed, you may be wondering which of the theories provides the most accurate description of personality. That question cannot be answered precisely. Each theory is built on different assumptions and focuses on somewhat different aspects of personality (see Figure 7). Furthermore, there is no clear way to scientifically test the various approaches and their assumptions against one another. Given the complexity of every individual, it seems reasonable that personality can be viewed from a number of perspectives simultaneously (Pervin, 2003).

Theoretical Approach and Major Theorists	Conscious Versus Unconscious Determinants of Personality	Nature (Hereditary Factors) Versus Nurture (Environmental Factors)	Free Will Versus Determinism	Stability Versus Modifiability
Psychodynamic (Freud, Jung, Horney, Adler)	Emphasizes the unconscious	Stresses innate, inherited structure of personality while emphasizing importance of childhood experience	Stresses determinism, the view that behavior is directed and caused by factors outside one's control	Emphasizes the stability of characteristics throughout a person's life
Trait (Allport, Cattell, Eysenck)	Disregards both conscious and unconscious	Approaches vary	Stresses determinism, the view that behavior is directed and caused by factors outside one's control	Emphasizes the stability of characteristics throughout a person's life
Learning (Skinner, Bandura)	Disregards both conscious and unconscious	Focuses on the environment	Stresses determinism, the view that behavior is directed and caused by factors outside one's control	Stresses that personality remains flexible and resilient throughout one's life
Biological and Evolutionary (Tellegen)	Disregards both conscious and unconscious	Stresses the innate, inherited determinants of personality	Stresses determinism, the view that behavior is directed and caused by factors outside one's control	Emphasizes the stability of characteristics throughout a person's life
Humanistic (Rogers, Maslow)	Stresses the conscious more than unconscious	Stresses the interaction between both nature and nurture	Stresses the freedom of individuals to make their own choices	Stresses that personality remains flexible and resilient throughout one's life

FIGURE 7 The multiple perspectives of personality.

RECAP/EVALUATE/RETHINK

RECAP

LO 32-1 What are the major aspects of trait, learning, biological and evolutionary, and humanistic approaches to personality?

- Trait approaches have been used to identify relatively enduring dimensions along which people differ from one another—dimensions known as traits. (p. 395)
- Learning approaches to personality concentrate on observable behavior. To a strict learning theorist, personality is the sum of learned responses to the external environment. (pp. 398, 399)
- Social cognitive approaches concentrate on the role of cognition in determining personality. Those approaches pay particular attention to self-efficacy and self-esteem in determining behavior. (p. 399)
- Biological and evolutionary approaches to personality focus on the way in which personality characteristics are inherited. (p. 401)
- Humanistic approaches emphasize people's inherent goodness. They consider the core of personality in terms of a person's ability to change and improve. (p. 404)
- The major personality approaches differ substantially from one another; the differences may reflect both their focus on different aspects of personality and the overall complexity of personality. (p. 406)

EVALUATE

1. Carl's determination to succeed is the dominant force in all his activities and relationships. According to Gordon Allport's theory, this is an example of a _____ trait. In contrast, Cindy's fondness for old western movies is an example of a _____ trait.

2. Eysenck might describe a person who enjoys activities such as parties and hang-gliding as high on what trait?

3. Proponents of which approach to personality would be most likely to agree with the statement, "Personality can be thought of as learned responses to a person's upbringing and environment"?
   a. Humanistic
   b. Biological and evolutionary
   c. Learning
   d. Trait

4. Bandura would rate a person who would make the statement, "I know I can't do it" as low on _____ _____.

5. Which approach to personality emphasizes the innate goodness of people and their desire to grow?
   a. Humanistic
   b. Psychodynamic
   c. Learning
   d. Biological and evolutionary

RETHINK

1. If personality traits are merely descriptive and not explanatory, what use are they? Can assigning a trait to a person be harmful—or helpful? Why or why not?

2. *From the perspective of an educator:* How might you encourage your students' development of self-esteem and self-efficacy? What steps would you take to ensure that their self-esteem did not become over-inflated?

Answers to Evaluate Questions

1. cardinal, secondary; 2. extraversion; 3. c; 4. self-efficacy; 5. a

KEY TERMS

trait theory p. 395
traits p. 395
social cognitive
  approaches to
  personality p. 399

self-efficacy p. 399
self-esteem p. 400
biological and evolutionary
  approaches to
  personality p. 401

temperament p. 403
humanistic approaches to
  personality p. 405

self-actualization p. 405
unconditional positive
  regard p. 405

Assessing Personality: Determining What Makes Us Distinctive

Learning Outcomes

LO 33-1 How can we most accurately assess personality?

LO 33-2 What are the major types of personality measures?

You have a need for other people to like and admire you.

You have a tendency to be critical of yourself.

You have a great deal of unused potential that you have not turned to your advantage.

Although you have some personality weaknesses, you generally are able to compensate for them.

Relating to members of the opposite sex has presented problems for you.

Although you appear to be disciplined and self-controlled to others, you tend to be anxious and insecure inside.

At times you have serious doubts about whether you have made the right decision or done the right thing.

You prefer a certain amount of change and variety and become dissatisfied when hemmed in by restrictions and limitations.

You do not accept others' statements without satisfactory proof.

You have found it unwise to be too frank in revealing yourself to others.

If you think these statements provide a surprisingly accurate account of your personality, you are not alone: Most college students think that these descriptions are tailored just to them. In fact, the statements were designed intentionally to be so vague that they apply to just about anyone (Forer, 1949; Russo, 1981).

The ease with which we can agree with such imprecise statements underscores the difficulty in coming up with accurate and meaningful assessments of people's personalities. Psychologists interested in assessing personality must be able to define the most meaningful ways of discriminating between one person's personality and another's. To do this, they use **psychological tests,** standard measures devised to assess behavior objectively. With the results of such tests, psychologists can help people better understand themselves and make decisions about their lives. Researchers interested in the causes and consequences of personality also employ psychological tests (Hambleton, 2006; Miller, McIntire, & Lovler, 2011).

Like the assessments that seek to measure intelligence, all psychological tests must have reliability and validity. *Reliability* refers to a test's measurement consistency. If a test is reliable, it yields the same result each time it is administered to a specific person or group. In contrast, unreliable tests give different results each time they are administered.

For meaningful conclusions to be drawn, tests also must be valid. Tests have *validity* when they actually measure what they are designed to measure. If a test is constructed to measure sociability, for instance, we need to know that it actually measures sociability and not some other trait.

psychological tests Standard measures devised to assess behavior objectively; used by psychologists to help people make decisions about their lives and understand more about themselves.

Study Alert

The distinction between reliability and validity is important. For instance, a test that measures trustfulness is reliable if it yields the same results each time it is administered, while it would be valid if it measures trustfulness accurately.

Finally, psychological tests are based on *norms*, standards of test performance that permit the comparison of one person's score on a test with the scores of others who have taken the same test. For example, a norm permits test-takers who have received a certain score on a test to know that they have scored in the top 10% of all those who have taken the test.

Norms are established by administering a specific test to a large number of people and determining the typical scores. It is then possible to compare a single person's score with the scores of the group, which provides a comparative measure of test performance against the performance of others who have taken the test.

The establishment of appropriate norms is not a simple endeavor. For instance, the specific group that is employed to determine norms for a test has a profound effect on the way an individual's performance is evaluated. In fact, as we discuss next, the process of establishing norms can take on political overtones.

Exploring DIVERSITY

Should Race and Ethnicity Be Used to Establish Norms?

The passions of politics may confront the objectivity of science when test norms are established, at least in the realm of standardized tests that are meant to predict future job performance. In fact, a national controversy has developed around the question of whether different norms should be established for members of various racial and ethnic groups (Manly, 2005, 2006; Manly & Echemendia, 2007; Pedraza & Mungas, 2008).

The test that sparked the controversy was the U.S. government's General Aptitude Test Battery, a test that measures a broad range of abilities from eye-hand coordination to reading proficiency. The problem was that African Americans and Hispanics tend to score lower on the test, on average, than members of other groups. The lower scores often are due to a lack of prior relevant experience and job opportunities, which in turn has been due to prejudice and discrimination.

To promote the employment of minority racial groups, the government developed a separate set of norms for African Americans and Hispanics. Rather than using the pool of all people who took the tests, the scores of African-American and Hispanic applicants were compared only with the scores of other African Americans and Hispanics. Consequently, a Hispanic who scored in the top 20% of the Hispanics taking the test was considered to have performed equivalently to a white job applicant who scored in the top 20% of the whites who took the test, even though the absolute score of the Hispanic might be lower than that of the white.

Critics of the adjusted norming system suggested that such a procedure discriminates in favor of certain racial and ethnic groups at the expense of others, thereby fanning the flames of racial bigotry. The practice was challenged legally; with the passage of the Civil Rights Act in 1991, race norming on the General Aptitude Test Battery was discontinued (Galef, 2001).

However, proponents of race norming continue to argue that norming procedures that take race into account are an affirmative action tool that simply permits minority job-seekers to be placed on an equal footing with white job-seekers. Furthermore, a panel of the National Academy of Sciences supported the practice of adjusting test norms. It suggested that the unadjusted test norms are not very useful in predicting job performance and that they would tend to screen out otherwise qualified minority group members (Fleming, 2000).

Job testing is not the only area in which issues arise regarding norms and the meaning of test scores. The issue of how to treat racial differences in IQ scores is also controversial and divisive. Clearly, race norming raises profound and intense feelings that may come into conflict with scientific objectivity (Leiter & Leiter, 2003; Rushton & Jensen, 2006; Davis, 2009).

The issue of establishing norms for tests is further complicated by the existence of a wide array of personality measures and approaches to assessment. We next consider some of these measures.

Self-Report Measures of Personality

If someone wanted to assess your personality, one possible approach would be to carry out an extensive interview with you to determine the most important events in your childhood, your social relationships, and your successes and failures. Obviously, though, such a technique would take extraordinary time and effort.

It is also unnecessary. Just as physicians draw only a small sample of your blood to test it, psychologists can utilize **self-report measures** that ask people about a relatively small sample of their behavior. This sampling of self-report data is then used to infer the presence of particular personality characteristics. For example, a researcher who was interested in assessing a person's orientation to life might administer the questionnaire shown in Figure 1. Although the questionnaire consists of only a few questions, the answers can be used to generalize about personality characteristics. (Try it yourself!)

One of the best examples of a self-report measure, and one of the most frequently used personality tests, is the **Minnesota Multiphasic Personality Inventory-2 (MMPI-2).** Although the original purpose of this measure was to identify people with

self-report measures A method of gathering data about people by asking them questions about a sample of their behavior.

Minnesota Multiphasic Personality Inventory-2 (MMPI-2) A widely used self-report test that identifies people with psychological difficulties and is employed to predict some everyday behaviors.

FIGURE 1 The Life Orientation Test–Revised. Complete this test by indicating the degree to which you agree with each of the 10 statements using the scale from 0 to 4 for each item. Try to be as accurate as possible. There are no right or wrong answers. (Copyright © 1994 by the American Psychological Association. Adapted with permission from Table 6 [p. 1073] from Scheier, M. F., Carver, C. S., & Bridges, M. W. [1994]. Distinguishing optimism from neuroticism [and trait anxiety, self-mastery, and self-esteem]: A reevaluation of the Life Orientation Test. *Journal of Personality and Social Psychology*, 67, 1063–1078. No further reproduction or distribution is permitted without written permission from the American Psychological Association.)

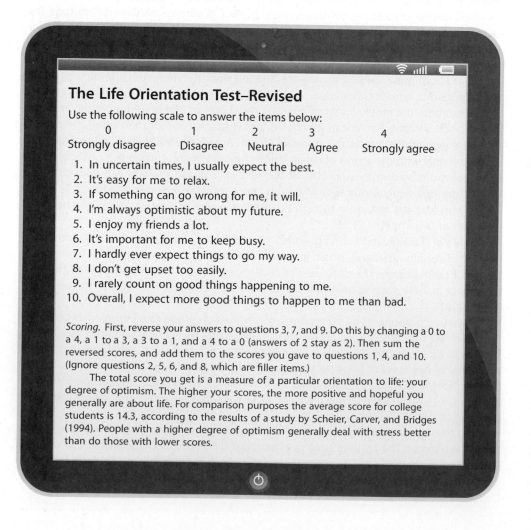

The Life Orientation Test–Revised

Use the following scale to answer the items below:

0	1	2	3	4
Strongly disagree	Disagree	Neutral	Agree	Strongly agree

1. In uncertain times, I usually expect the best.
2. It's easy for me to relax.
3. If something can go wrong for me, it will.
4. I'm always optimistic about my future.
5. I enjoy my friends a lot.
6. It's important for me to keep busy.
7. I hardly ever expect things to go my way.
8. I don't get upset too easily.
9. I rarely count on good things happening to me.
10. Overall, I expect more good things to happen to me than bad.

Scoring. First, reverse your answers to questions 3, 7, and 9. Do this by changing a 0 to a 4, a 1 to a 3, a 3 to a 1, and a 4 to a 0 (answers of 2 stay as 2). Then sum the reversed scores, and add them to the scores you gave to questions 1, 4, and 10. (Ignore questions 2, 5, 6, and 8, which are filler items.)

The total score you get is a measure of a particular orientation to life: your degree of optimism. The higher your scores, the more positive and hopeful you generally are about life. For comparison purposes the average score for college students is 14.3, according to the results of a study by Scheier, Carver, and Bridges (1994). People with a higher degree of optimism generally deal with stress better than do those with lower scores.

specific sorts of psychological difficulties, it has been found to predict a variety of other behaviors. For instance, MMPI-2 scores have been shown to be good predictors of whether college students will marry within 10 years of graduating and whether they will get an advanced degree. Police departments use the test to measure whether police officers are likely to use their weapons. Psychologists in Russia administer a modified form of the MMPI to their astronauts and Olympic athletes (Butcher, 2005; Sellbom & Ben-Porath, 2006; Sellbom, Fischler, & Ben-Porath, 2007; Butcher, 2011).

The test consists of a series of 567 items to which a person responds "true," "false," or "cannot say." The questions cover a variety of issues ranging from mood ("I feel useless at times") to opinions ("People should try to understand their dreams") to physical and psychological health ("I am bothered by an upset stomach several times a week" and "I have strange and peculiar thoughts").

There are no right or wrong answers. Instead, interpretation of the results rests on the pattern of responses. The test yields scores on 10 separate scales, plus three scales meant to measure the validity of the respondent's answers. For example, there is a "lie scale" that indicates when people are falsifying their responses in order to present themselves more favorably (through items such as, "I can't remember ever having a bad night's sleep") (Butcher, 2005; Stein & Graham, 2005; Bacchiochi, 2006).

How did the authors of the MMPI-2 determine what specific patterns of responses indicate? The procedure they used is typical of personality test construction—a process known as **test standardization.** To create the test, the test authors asked groups of psychiatric patients with a specific diagnosis, such as depression or schizophrenia, to complete a large number of items. They then determined which items best differentiated members of those groups from a comparison group of normal participants and included those specific items in the final version of the test. By systematically carrying out this procedure on groups with different diagnoses, the test authors were able to devise a number of subscales that identified different forms of abnormal behavior (see Figure 2).

test standardization A technique used to validate questions in personality tests by studying the responses of people with known diagnoses.

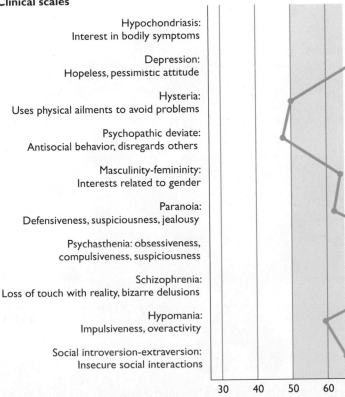

Clinical scales

FIGURE 2 A MMPI-2 profile of a person who suffers from obsessional anxiety, social withdrawal, and delusional thinking.

When the MMPI-2 is used for the purpose for which it was devised—identification of personality disorders—it does a good job. However, like other personality tests, it presents an opportunity for abuse. For instance, employers who use it as a screening tool for job applicants may interpret the results improperly by relying too heavily on the results of individual scales instead of taking into account the overall patterns of results, which require skilled interpretation. Furthermore, critics point out that the individual scales overlap, which makes their interpretation difficult. In sum, although the MMPI-2 remains the most widely used personality test and has been translated into more than 100 different languages, it must be used with caution (Forbey & Ben-Porath, 2007; Ben-Porath & Archer, 2008; Williams & Butcher, 2011).

Projective Methods

If you were shown the shape presented in Figure 3 and asked what it represented to you, you might not think that your impressions would mean very much. But to a psychodynamic theoretician, your responses to such an ambiguous figure would provide valuable clues to the state of your unconscious and ultimately to your general personality characteristics.

The shape in the figure is representative of inkblots used in **projective personality tests,** in which a person is shown an ambiguous stimulus and asked to describe it or tell a story about it. The responses are considered to be "projections" of the individual's personality.

Study Alert

In projective tests such as the Rorschach, researchers present an ambiguous stimulus and ask a person to describe or tell a story about it. They then use the responses to make inferences about personality.

projective personality test A test in which a person is shown an ambiguous stimulus and asked to describe it or tell a story about it.

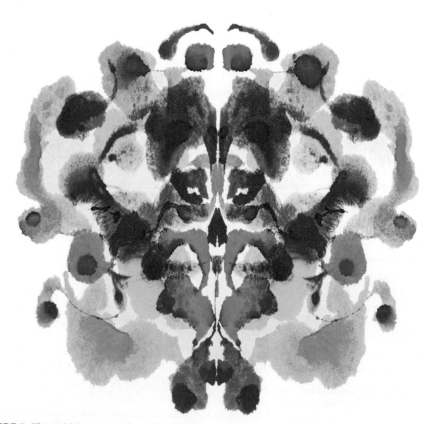

FIGURE 3 This inkblot is similar to the type used in the Rorschach personality test. What do you see in it? (Source: Alloy, Jacobson, & Acocella, 1999.)

The best-known projective test is the **Rorschach test.** Devised by Swiss psychiatrist Hermann Rorschach (1924), the test involves showing a series of symmetrical stimuli similar to the one in Figure 3 to people who are then asked what the figures represent to them. Their responses are recorded, and people are classified by their personality type through a complex set of clinical judgments on the part of the examiner. For instance, respondents who see a bear in one inkblot are thought to have a strong degree of emotional control, according to the scoring guidelines Rorschach developed (Weiner, 2004b; Silverstein, 2007).

The **Thematic Apperception Test (TAT)** is another well-known projective test. The TAT consists of a series of pictures about which a person is asked to write a story. The stories are then used to draw inferences about the writer's personality characteristics (Weiner, 2004a; Langan-Fox & Grant, 2006).

Tests with stimuli as ambiguous as those used in the Rorschach and TAT require particular skill and care in their interpretation—too much skill and care in many critics' estimation. The Rorschach in particular has been criticized for requiring too much inference on the part of the examiner, and attempts to standardize scoring have frequently failed. Furthermore, many critics complain that the Rorschach does not provide much valid information about underlying personality traits. Despite such problems, both the Rorschach and the TAT are widely used, especially in clinical settings, and their proponents suggest that their reliability and validity are great enough to provide useful inferences about personality (Garb et al., 2005; Society for Personality Assessment, 2005; Campos, 2011).

"RORSCHACH! WHAT'S TO BECOME OF YOU?"

Sidney Harris/ScienceCartoonsPlus.com

Rorschach test A test that involves showing a series of symmetrical visual stimuli to people who then are asked what the figures represent to them.

Thematic Apperception Test (TAT) A test consisting of a series of pictures about which a person is asked to write a story.

Behavioral Assessment

If you were a psychologist subscribing to a learning approach to personality, you would be likely to object to the indirect nature of projective tests. Instead, you would be more apt to use **behavioral assessment**—direct measures of an individual's behavior designed to describe characteristics indicative of personality. As with observational research, behavioral assessment may be carried out naturalistically by observing people in their own settings: in the workplace, at home, or in school. In other cases, behavioral assessment occurs in the laboratory under controlled conditions in which a psychologist sets up a situation and observes an individual's behavior (Ramsay, Reynolds, & Kamphaus, 2002; Gladwell, 2004; Miller & Leffard, 2007).

Regardless of the setting in which behavior is observed, an effort is made to ensure that behavioral assessment is carried out objectively and quantifies behavior as much as possible. For example, an observer may record the number of social contacts a person initiates, the number of questions asked, or the number of aggressive acts. Another method is to measure the duration of events: the duration of a child's temper tantrum, the length of a conversation, the amount of time spent working, or the time spent in cooperative behavior.

Behavioral assessment is particularly appropriate for observing—and eventually remedying—specific behavioral difficulties, such as shyness in children. It provides a means of assessing the specific nature and incidence of a problem and subsequently allows psychologists to determine whether intervention techniques have been successful.

Behavioral assessment techniques based on learning theories of personality have also made important contributions to the treatment of certain kinds of psychological difficulties. In addition, they are also used to make hiring and personnel decision in the workplace. (Also see *PsychWork*.)

behavioral assessment Direct measures of an individual's behavior used to describe personality characteristics.

PsychWork
HUMAN RESOURCES MANAGER

Name: John P. Murray

Education: BS in Business Administration; Indiana University–Purdue University, Indianapolis, Indiana

At some point, everyone goes looking for a job, and in many cases the first stop in the process will be with a human resources officer. John Murray, Human Resources Administration Manager of Employment and Compensation Services at Indiana University–Purdue University, is one of those people job applicants meet with initially.

"We try to influence hiring departments to consider diverse applicants during the recruitment process," Murray explained. "We train on and stress the value of behavioral-based interviews, and we try to help hiring managers see patterns of behavior that may not be seen if they only focus on apparent unrelated facts."

The interviewing process depends on the position being advertised, according to Murray. "Interviewing does vary depending on the position but also varies based on organizational needs that may be situational, such as makeup of current staff, anticipated changes in organization, move toward automation, and so forth.

"When I interview for openings that I have or committees that I serve on, I try to quickly get to whether the applicant has the skills to do the job so I can spend more time gaining information to assess motivation, communication styles, and fit," he added.

"For example, when hiring for an employment consultant, technical knowledge of hiring processes is less important to me than consulting skills," Murray explained. "A technical expert in employment law might not be as effective as an individual who can demonstrate communication, analytical, conceptualization, conflict resolution, and other soft skills that are more difficult to develop."

BECOMING AN INFORMED CONSUMER of Psychology

Assessing Personality Assessments

Many companies ranging from General Motors to Microsoft employ personality tests to help determine who gets hired. For example, potential Microsoft employees have been asked brainteasers like, "If you had to remove one of the 50 U.S. states, which would it be?" (Hint: First define "remove." If you mean the death of everyone in the state, suggest a low-population state. If you mean quitting the country, then go for an outlying state like Alaska or Hawaii.) Other employers ask questions that are even more vague ("Describe November"). With such questions, it's not always clear that the tests are reliable or valid (McGinn, 2003).

Before relying too heavily on the results of such personality testing in the role of potential employee, employer, or consumer of testing services, you should keep several points in mind:

- *Understand what the test claims to measure.* Standard personality measures are accompanied by information that discusses how the test was developed, to whom it is most applicable, and how the results should be interpreted. Read any explanations of the test; they will help you understand the results.

- *Do not base a decision only on the results of any one test.* Test results should be interpreted in the context of other information, such as academic records, social interests, and home and community activities.

- *Remember that test results are not always accurate.* The results may be in error; the test may be unreliable or invalid. For example, you may have had a "bad day" when you took the test, or the person scoring and interpreting the test may have made a mistake. You should not place too much significance on the results of a single administration of any test.

In sum, it is important to keep in mind the complexity of human behavior—particularly your own. No single test can provide an understanding of the intricacies of someone's personality without considering a good deal more information than can be provided in a single testing session (Gladwell, 2004; Paul, 2004; Hogan, Davies, & Hogan, 2007).

RECAP/EVALUATE/RETHINK

RECAP

LO 33-1 How can we most accurately assess personality?

- Psychological tests such as the MMPI-2 are standard assessment tools that measure behavior objectively. They must be reliable (measuring what they are trying to measure consistently) and valid (measuring what they are supposed to measure). (p. 410)

LO 33-2 What are the major types of personality measures?

- Self-report measures ask people about a sample range of their behaviors. These reports are used to infer the presence of particular personality characteristics. (p. 476)
- Projective personality tests (such as the Rorschach and the TAT) present an ambiguous stimulus; the test administrator infers information about the test-taker from his or her responses. (p. 413)
- Behavioral assessment is based on the principles of learning theory. It employs direct measurement of an individual's behavior to determine characteristics related to personality. (p. 413)

EVALUATE

1. _____ is the consistency of a personality test; _____ is the ability of a test to actually measure what it is designed to measure.
2. _____ are standards used to compare scores of different people taking the same test.

3. Tests such as the MMPI-2, in which a small sample of behavior is assessed to determine larger patterns, are examples of
   a. Cross-sectional tests
   b. Projective tests
   c. Achievement tests
   d. Self-report tests
4. A person shown a picture and asked to make up a story about it would be taking a _____ personality test.

RETHINK

1. Should personality tests be used for personnel decisions? Should they be used for other social purposes, such as identifying individuals at risk for certain types of personality disorders?
2. *From the perspective of a politician:* Imagine that you had to vote on a law that would require institutions and organizations to perform race norming procedures on standardized performance tests. Would you support such a law? Why or why not? In addition to race, should norming procedures take other factors into account? Which ones and why?

Answers to Evaluate Questions

1. Reliability, validity; 2. Norms; 3. d; 4. projective

KEY TERMS

psychological tests p. 408
self-report measures p. 410
Minnesota Multiphasic Personality
   Inventory-2 (MMPI-2) p. 410

test standardization p. 411
projective personality test p. 412
Rorschach test p. 413

Thematic Apperception Test (TAT) p. 413
behavioral assessment p. 413

Looking Back

Epilogue

We have discussed the different ways in which psychologists have interpreted the development and structure of personality. The perspectives we examined ranged from Freud's analysis of personality based primarily on internal, unconscious factors to the externally based view championed by learning theorists of personality as a learned set of traits and actions. We also noted that there are many ways to interpret personality; by no means does a consensus exist on what the key traits are that are central to personality.

Return to the prologue and consider the case of of Lori Berenson. Use your understanding of personality to consider the following questions.

1. How typical do you think it is for people to have different sides to their personalities, as Berenson apparently does?
2. How could you explain Berenson's personality from a psychodynamic approach? From a learning approach?
3. How do you think Berenson might score on a test of agreeableness? On a test of conscientiousness?
4. Might it be possible for a personality test to discern whether Berenson was really guilty of terrorism or not? Why or why not?

VISUAL SUMMARY 10 Personality

MODULE 31 Psychodynamic Approaches

Freud's Psychoanalytic Theory

- Conscious experience: only part of our psychological experience
- Unconscious: part of the personality of which we are not aware
- Structure of personality
  - Id: Represents the raw, unorganized, inborn part of personality
  - Ego: Strives to balance desires of the id and realities of the outside world
  - Superego: Represents rights and wrongs of society as taught and modeled by significant individuals

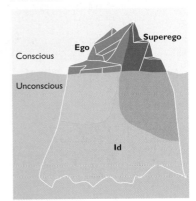

- Psychosexual stages

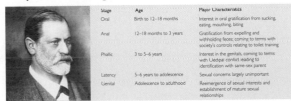

Stage	Age	Major Characteristics
Oral	Birth to 12–18 months	Interest in oral gratification from sucking, eating, mouthing, biting
Anal	12–18 months to 3 years	Gratification from expelling and withholding feces; coming to terms with society's controls relating to toilet training
Phallic	3 to 5–6 years	Interest in the genitals; coming to terms with Oedipal conflict leading to identification with same-sex parent
Latency	5–6 years to adolescence	Sexual concerns largely unimportant
Genital	Adolescence to adulthood	Reemergence of sexual interests and establishment of mature sexual relationships

- Defense mechanisms: Unconscious strategies people use to reduce anxiety

Neo-Freudian Psychoanalysts: Emphasize the ego more than Freud: Carl Jung, Karen Horney, Alfred Adler

MODULE 32 Trait, Learning, Biological and Evolutionary, and Humanistic Approaches

Trait Approaches: Emphasize consistent personality characteristics and behaviors called traits
- Eysenck: Extraversion, neuroticism, and psychoticism
- The big five personality traits: Openness to experience, conscientiousness, extraversion, agreeableness, neuroticism

Learning Approaches: Emphasize that personality is the sum of learned responses to the external environment

- B. F. Skinner: Personality is a collection of learned behavior patterns and are a result of reinforcement

Learning Approaches (continued)

- Social cognitive approaches: Emphasize the influence of cognition as well as observation of others' behavior on personality
- Self-efficacy and self-esteem

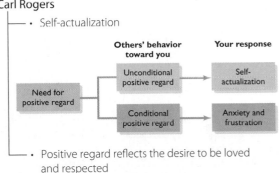

Biological and Evolutionary Approaches: Suggest that important components of personality are inherited, such an temperament

Humanistic Approaches: Emphasize people's inherent goodness and their tendency to move toward higher levels of functioning

- Carl Rogers
  - Self-actualization
  - Positive regard reflects the desire to be loved and respected

MODULE 33 Assessing Personality

Psychological Tests: Standard measures that assess behavior objectively
- Reliability
- Validity
- Norms

Self-report Measures: People answer questions about themselves to determine personality characteristics

Projective Methods: People are shown an ambiguous stimulus and asked to describe it or tell a story about it
- Rorschach test
- Thematic Apperception Test (TAT)

Behavioral Assessment: Measures of a person's behavior designed to describe characteristics indicative of personality

11

Health Psychology: Stress, Coping, and Well-Being

Learning Outcomes for Chapter 11

MODULE 34

LO 34-1 How is health psychology a union between medicine and psychology?

LO 34-2 What is stress, how does it affect us, and how can we best cope with it?

Stress and Coping
Stress: Reacting to Threat and Challenge
The High Cost of Stress
Coping with Stress
Applying Psychology in the 21st Century: What Doesn't Kill You Really Does Make You Stronger
Neuroscience in Your Life: Stress and Social Support
Becoming an Informed Consumer of Psychology: Effective Coping Strategies

MODULE 35

LO 35-1 How do psychological factors affect health-related problems such as coronary heart disease, cancer, and smoking?

Psychological Aspects of Illness and Well-Being
The As, Bs, and Ds of Coronary Heart Disease
Psychological Aspects of Cancer
Smoking
Neuroscience in Your Life: The Addictive Pull of Smoking
Exploring Diversity: Hucksters of Death: Promoting Smoking Throughout the World

MODULE 36

LO 36-1 How do our interactions with physicians affect our health and compliance with medical treatment?

LO 36-2 How does a sense of well-being develop?

Promoting Health and Wellness
Following Medical Advice
Well-Being and Happiness

Prologue *At Wit's End*

It has been a long time since "flight attendant" was a glamorous job title. The hours are long. Passengers with feelings of entitlement bump up against new no-frills policies. Babies scream. Security precautions grate but must be enforced. Airlines demand lightning-quick turnarounds, so attendants herd passengers and collect trash with the grim speed of an Indy pit crew. Everyone, it seems, is in a bad mood. . . .

A JetBlue attendant named Steven Slater decided he had had enough. . . . After a dispute with a passenger who stood to fetch luggage too soon on a full flight just in from Pittsburgh, Mr. Slater, 38 and a career flight attendant, got on the public-address intercom and let loose a string of [curses].

Then, the authorities said, he pulled the lever that activates the emergency-evacuation chute and slid down, making a dramatic exit not only from the plane but, ultimately, from his airline career (Newman & Rivera, 2010, p. A1).

Looking Ahead

While Steven Slater's response was an extreme one, we can all sympathize with the stress he was feeling—so much so that when Slater's story hit the news, many people admitted that his dramatic way of giving the boot to a stressful job represented a fantasy of their own.

Stress and how we cope with it have long been central topics of interest for psychologists. However, in recent years the focus has broadened as psychology has come to view stress in the broader context of one of psychology's newer subfields: health psychology. **Health psychology** investigates the psychological factors related to wellness and illness, including the prevention, diagnosis, and treatment of medical problems. Health psychologists investigate the effects of psychological factors such as stress on illness. They examine the psychological principles underlying treatments for disease and illness. They also study prevention: how healthier behavior can help people avoid and reduce health problems such as stress and heart disease.

Health psychologists take a decisive stand on the enduring mind–body issue that philosophers, and later psychologists, have debated since the time of the ancient Greeks. In their view, the mind and the body are clearly linked rather than representing two distinct systems (Sternberg, 2000; Dalal & Misra, 2006).

Health psychologists recognize that good health and the ability to cope with illness are affected by psychological factors such as thoughts, emotions, and the ability to manage stress. They have paid particular attention to the *immune system,* the complex system of organs, glands, and cells that constitute our bodies' natural line of defense in fighting disease.

In fact, health psychologists are among the primary investigators in a growing field called **psychoneuroimmunology,** or **PNI,** the study of the relationship among psychological factors, the immune system, and the brain. PNI has led to discoveries such as the existence of an association between a person's emotional state and the success of the immune system in fighting

disease (Kemeny, 2007; Byrne-Davis & Vedhara, 2008; Mathews & Janusek, 2011).

In sum, health psychologists view the mind and the body as two parts of a whole human being that cannot be considered independently. This more recent view marks a sharp departure from earlier thinking. Previously, disease was seen as a purely biological phenomenon, and psychological factors were of little interest to most health-care workers. In the early 20th century, the primary causes of death were short-term infections from which one either rapidly recovered—or died. Now, however, the major causes of death, such as heart disease, cancer, and diabetes, are chronic illnesses that pose significant psychological issues because they often cannot be cured and may linger for years (Bishop, 2005; Rotan & Ospina-Kammerer, 2007).

Advances in health psychology have had an impact across a variety of disciplines and professions. For instance, health-care professionals such as physicians and nurses, social workers, dieticians, pharmacists, occupational therapists, and even clergy are increasingly likely to receive training in health psychology.

In the three modules that follow, we discuss the ways in which psychological factors affect health. We first focus on the causes and consequences of stress as well as on the means of coping with it. Next, we explore the psychological aspects of several major health problems, including heart disease, cancer, and ailments resulting from smoking. Finally, we examine the ways in which patient-physician interactions influence our health and offer suggestions for increasing people's compliance with recommendations about behavior that will improve their well-being.

health psychology The branch of psychology that investigates the psychological factors related to wellness and illness, including the prevention, diagnosis, and treatment of medical problems.

psychoneuroimmunology (PNI) The study of the relationship among psychological factors, the immune system, and the brain.

Stress and Coping

Anthony Lepre started feeling awful almost as soon as Tom Ridge [U.S. Homeland Security Secretary] put the nation on high alert for a terrorist attack. . . . He awoke in the middle of the night short of breath, his heart pounding. And the sound of his telephone seemed a sure sign of bad news. By midweek, he was rushing off to Costco to stock up on fruit juice, bottled water, peanut butter, canned tuna, "and extra food for my cats Monster, Monkey and Spike." He also picked up a first-aid kit, six rolls of duct tape, and a bulk package of plastic wrap to seal his windows. "The biggest problem was that I felt helpless," he says, "completely powerless over the situation." (Cowley, 2003, pp. 43–44)

Stress: Reacting to Threat and Challenge

Most of us need little introduction to the phenomenon of **stress,** people's response to events that threaten or challenge them. Whether it is a paper or an exam deadline, a family problem, or even the ongoing threat of a terrorist attack, life is full of circumstances and events known as *stressors* that produce threats to our well-being. Even pleasant events—such as planning a party or beginning a sought-after job—can produce stress, although negative events result in greater detrimental consequences than positive ones.

All of us face stress in our lives. Some health psychologists believe that daily life actually involves a series of repeated sequences of perceiving a threat, considering ways to cope with it, and ultimately adapting to the threat with greater or lesser success. Although adaptation is often minor and occurs without our awareness, adaptation requires a major effort when stress is more severe or long lasting. Ultimately, our attempts to overcome stress may produce biological and psychological responses that result in health problems (Dolbier, Smith, & Steinhardt, 2007; Finan, Zautra, & Wershba, 2011).

THE NATURE OF STRESSORS: MY STRESS IS YOUR PLEASURE

Stress is a very personal thing. Although certain kinds of events, such as the death of a loved one or participation in military combat, are universally stressful, other situations may or may not be stressful to a specific person.

Consider, for instance, bungee jumping. Some people would find jumping off a bridge while attached to a slender rubber tether extremely stressful. However, there are individuals who see such an activity as challenging and fun filled. Whether bungee jumping is stressful depends in part, then, on a person's perception of the activity.

For people to consider an event stressful, they must perceive it as threatening or challenging and must lack all the resources to deal with it effectively. Consequently, the same event may at some times be stressful and at other times provoke no stressful reaction at all. A young man experience stress when he is turned down for a date—if he attributes the refusal to his unattractiveness or unworthiness. But if he

Learning Outcomes

LO 34-1 How is health psychology a union between medicine and psychology?

LO 34-2 What is stress, how does it affect us, and how can we best cope with it?

stress A person's response to events that are threatening or challenging.

Study Alert

Remember the distinction between stressors and stress, which can be tricky: stressors (like an exam) *cause* stress (the physiological and psychological reaction that comes from the exam).

Even positive events can produce significant stress.

cataclysmic events Strong stressors that occur suddenly and typically affect many people at once (e.g., natural disasters).

personal stressors Major life events, such as the death of a family member, that have immediate negative consequences that generally fade with time.

posttraumatic stress disorder (PTSD) A phenomenon in which victims of major catastrophes or strong personal stressors feel long-lasting effects that may include re-experiencing the event in vivid flashbacks or dreams.

attributes it to some factor unrelated to his self-esteem, such as a previous commitment of the woman he asked, the experience of being refused may create no stress at all. Hence, a person's interpretation of events plays an important role in the determination of what is stressful (Folkman & Moskowitz, 2000; Giacobbi Jr., et al., 2004; Friborg et al., 2006).

CATEGORIZING STRESSORS

What kinds of events tend to be seen as stressful? There are three general types of stressors: cataclysmic events, personal stressors, and background stressors.

Cataclysmic events are strong stressors that occur suddenly and typically affect many people simultaneously. Disasters such as tornadoes and plane crashes as well as terrorist attacks are examples of cataclysmic events that can affect hundreds or thousands of people simultaneously.

Although it might seem that cataclysmic events would produce potent, lingering stress, in many cases they do not. In fact, cataclysmic events involving natural disasters may produce less stress in the long run than events that initially are not as devastating. One reason is that natural disasters have a clear resolution. Once they are over, people can look to the future knowing that the worst is behind them. Moreover, others who also experienced the disaster share the stress induced by cataclysmic events. Such sharing permits people to offer one another social support and a firsthand understanding of the difficulties others are going through (Hobfoll et al., 1996; Benight, 2004; Yesilyaprak, Kisac, & Sanlier, 2007).

In contrast, terrorist attacks like the one on the World Trade Center in 2001 are cataclysmic events that produce considerable stress. Terrorist attacks are deliberate, and victims (and observers) know that future attacks are likely. Government warnings in the form of heightened terror alerts may further increase the stress (Murphy, Wismar, & Freeman, 2003; Laugharne, Janca, & Widiger, 2007; Watson, Brymer, & Bonanno, 2011).

The second major category of stressor is the personal stressor. **Personal stressors** include major life events such as the death of a parent or spouse, the loss of one's job, a major personal failure, or even something positive such as getting married. Typically, personal stressors produce an immediate major reaction that soon tapers off. For example, stress arising from the death of a loved one tends to be greatest just after the time of death, but people begin to feel less stress and are better able to cope with the loss after the passage of time.

Some victims of major catastrophes and severe personal stressors experience **posttraumatic stress disorder,** or **PTSD,** in which a person has experienced a significantly stressful event that has long-lasting effects that may include re-experiencing the event in vivid flashbacks or dreams. An episode of PTSD may be triggered by an otherwise innocent stimulus, such as the sound of a honking horn, that leads a person to re-experience a past event that produced considerable stress.

Symptoms of posttraumatic stress disorder also include emotional numbing, sleep difficulties, interpersonal problems, alcohol and drug abuse, and in some cases suicide. For instance, the suicide rate for military veterans, many of whom participated in the Iraq and Afghanistan wars, is twice as high

■ Posttraumatic stress disorder (PTSD) in 20 percent of residents south of Canal Street, close to World Trade Center.

■ PTSD in 7.5 percent of residents north of Canal Street and south of 110th Street, the northernmost point surveyed.

FIGURE 1 The closer people lived to the site of the World Trade Center terrorist attack, the greater the rate of posttraumatic stress disorder. (Source: Susser, Herman, & Aaron, 2002.)

as for nonveterans (Pole, 2007; Kaplan et al., 2007; Magruder & Yeager, 2009).

Around 16% of soldiers returning from Iraq show symptoms of PTSD. Furthermore, those who have experienced child abuse or rape, rescue workers facing overwhelming situations, and victims of sudden natural disasters or accidents that produce feelings of helplessness and shock may suffer from the same disorder. Even witnessing aggression between two people may trigger PTSD (Friedman, 2006; Marmar, 2009; Horesh et al., 2011).

Terrorist attacks produce high incidences of PTSD. For example, 11% of people in New York City had some form of PTSD in the months after the September 11 terrorist attacks. But the responses varied significantly with a resident's proximity to the attacks, as illustrated in Figure 1; the closer someone lived to the World Trade Center, the greater the likelihood of PTSD. Furthermore, for many people, the effects of PTSD were still evident a decade after the attacks (Lee, Isaac, & Janca, 2007; Marshall et al., 2007; Neria, DiGrande, & Adams, 2011).

Everyone confronts daily hassles, or background stressors, at some point. At what point do daily hassles become more than mere irritants?

Background stressors, or more informally, *daily hassles,* are the third major category of stressors. Exemplified by standing in a long line at a bank and getting stuck in a traffic jam, daily hassles are the minor irritations of life that we all face time and time again. Another type of background stressor is a long-term, chronic problem, such as experiencing dissatisfaction with school or a job, being in an unhappy relationship, or living in crowded quarters without privacy (Weinstein et al., 2004; McIntyre, Korn, & Matsuo, 2008; Barke, 2011).

By themselves, daily hassles do not require much coping or even a response on the individual's part, although they certainly produce unpleasant emotions and moods. Yet, daily hassles add up—and ultimately they may take as great of a toll as a single, more stressful incident. In fact, the *number* of daily hassles people face is associated with psychological symptoms and health problems such as flu, sore throat, and backaches.

The flip side of hassles is *uplifts,* the minor positive events that make us feel good—even if only temporarily. As indicated in Figure 2 on page 424, uplifts range from relating well to a companion to finding one's surroundings pleasing. What is especially intriguing about uplifts is that they are associated with people's psychological health in just the opposite way that hassles are: The greater the number of uplifts we experience, the fewer the psychological symptoms we report later (Chamberlain & Zika, 1990; Ravindran et al., 2002; Jain, Mills, & Von Känel, 2007).

background stressors ("daily hassles") Everyday annoyances, such as being stuck in traffic, that cause minor irritations and may have long-term ill effects if they continue or are compounded by other stressful events.

PsychTech

An analysis of the emotional content of words sent in text messages during the hours following the 9/11 terrorist attack showed that, over the course of the day, sadness and anxiety-related words remained steady but anger-related words increased steadily.

The High Cost of Stress

Stress can produce both biological and psychological consequences. Often the most immediate reaction to stress is biological. Exposure to stressors generates a rise in hormone secretions by the adrenal glands, an increase in heart rate and blood pressure, and changes in how well the skin conducts electrical impulses. On a short-term basis, these responses may be adaptive because they produce an "emergency

FIGURE 2 The most common everyday hassles and uplifts. How many of these are part of your life, and how do you cope with them? (Source: Hassles—Chamberlain & Zika, 1990; Uplifts—Kanner et al., 1981.)

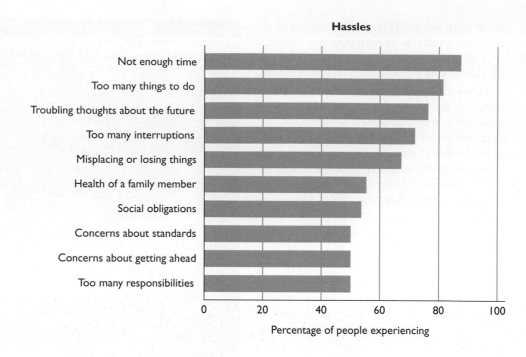

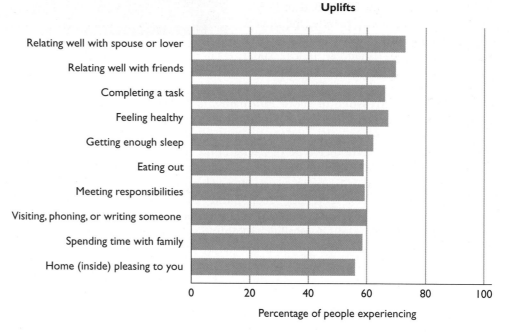

Study Alert

Remember the three categories of stressors—cataclysmic events, personal stressors, and background stressors—and that they produce different levels of stress.

reaction" in which the body prepares to defend itself through activation of the sympathetic nervous system. Those responses may allow more effective coping with the stressful situation (Akil & Morano, 1996; McEwen, 1998).

However, continued exposure to stress results in a decline in the body's overall level of biological functioning because of the constant secretion of stress-related hormones. Over time, stressful reactions can promote deterioration of body tissues such as blood vessels and the heart. Ultimately, we become more susceptible to disease as our ability to fight off infection is lowered (Dean-Borenstein, 2007; Ellins et al., 2008; Miller, Chen, & Parker, 2011).

Furthermore, stress can produce or worsen physical problems. Specifically, **psychophysiological disorders** are medical problems that are influenced by an

psychophysiological disorders
Medical problems influenced by an interaction of psychological, emotional, and physical difficulties.

interaction of psychological, emotional, and physical difficulties. Common psycho-physiological disorders include high blood pressure, headaches, backaches, skin rashes, indigestion, fatigue, and constipation. Stress has even been linked to the common cold (Cohen et al., 2003; Andrasik, 2006).

On a psychological level, high levels of stress prevent people from adequately coping with life. Their view of the environment can become clouded (for example, a minor criticism made by a friend is blown out of proportion). Moreover, at the highest levels of stress, emotional responses may be so extreme that people are unable to act at all. People under a lot of stress also become less able to deal with new stressors.

In short, stress affects us in multiple ways. It may increase the risk that we will become ill, it may directly cause illness, it may make us less able to recover from a disease, and it may reduce our ability to cope with future stress. (See Figure 3 to get a measure of your own level of stress.)

How Stressful Is Your Life?

Test your level of stress by answering these questions, and adding the score from each box. Questions apply to the last month only. A key below will help you determine the extent of your stress.

1. How often have you been upset because of something that happened unexpectedly?
   0=never, 1=almost never, 2=sometimes, 3=fairly often, 4=very often

2. How often have you felt that you were unable to control the important things in your life?
   0=never, 1=almost never, 2=sometimes, 3=fairly often, 4=very often

3. How often have you felt nervous and "stressed"?
   0=never, 1=almost never, 2=sometimes, 3=fairly often, 4=very often

4. How often have you felt confident about your ability to handle your personal problems?
   4=never, 3=almost never, 2=sometimes, 1=fairly often, 0=very often

5. How often have you felt that things were going your way?
   4=never, 3=almost never, 2=sometimes, 1=fairly often, 0=very often

6. How often have you been able to control irritations in your life?
   4=never, 3=almost never, 2=sometimes, 1=fairly often, 0=very often

7. How often have you found that you could not cope with all the things that you had to do?
   0=never, 1=almost never, 2=sometimes, 3=fairly often, 4=very often

8. How often have you felt that you were on top of things?
   4=never, 3=almost never, 2=sometimes, 1=fairly often, 0=very often

9. How often have you been angered because of things that were outside your control?
   0=never, 1=almost never, 2=sometimes, 3=fairly often, 4=very often

10. How often have you felt difficulties were piling up so high that you could not overcome them?
    0=never, 1=almost never, 2=sometimes, 3=fairly often, 4=very often

How You Measure Up

Stress levels vary among individuals—compare your total score to the averages below:

AGE		GENDER	
18–29	14.2	Men	12.1
30–44	13.0	Women	13.7
45–54	12.6		
55–64	11.9		
65 & over	12.0		

MARITAL STATUS

Widowed	12.6
Married or living with a partner	12.4
Single or never wed	14.1
Divorced	14.7
Separated	16.6

FIGURE 3 To get a sense of the level of stress in your life, complete this questionnaire. (Source: Cohen, Kamarck, & Mermelstein, 1983.)

THE GENERAL ADAPTATION SYNDROME MODEL: THE COURSE OF STRESS

general adaptation syndrome (GAS)
A theory developed by Selye that suggests that a person's response to a stressor consists of three stages: alarm and mobilization, resistance, and exhaustion.

The effects of long-term stress are illustrated in a series of stages proposed by Hans Selye (pronounced "sell-yay"), a pioneering stress theorist (Selye, 1976, 1993). This model, the **general adaptation syndrome (GAS),** suggests that the physiological response to stress follows the same set pattern regardless of the cause of stress.

As shown in Figure 4, the GAS has three phases. The first stage—*alarm and mobilization*—occurs when people become aware of the presence of a stressor. On a biological level, the sympathetic nervous system becomes energized, which helps a person cope initially with the stressor.

However, if the stressor persists, people move into the second response stage: *resistance*. During this stage, the body is actively fighting the stressor on a biological level. During resistance, people use a variety of means to cope with the stressor—sometimes successfully but at a cost of some degree of physical or psychological well-being. For example, a student who faces the stress of failing several courses might spend long hours studying seeking to cope with the stress.

If resistance is inadequate, people enter the last stage of the GAS: *exhaustion*. During the exhaustion stage, a person's ability to fight the stressor declines to the point where negative consequences of stress appear: physical illness and psychological symptoms in the form of an inability to concentrate, heightened irritability, or, in severe cases, disorientation and a loss of touch with reality. In a sense, people wear out, and their physiological resources to fight the stressor are used up.

How do people move out of the third stage after they have entered it? In some cases, exhaustion allows people to escape a stressor. For example, people who become ill from overwork may be excused from their duties for a time, which gives them a temporary respite from their responsibilities. At least for a time, then, the immediate stress is reduced.

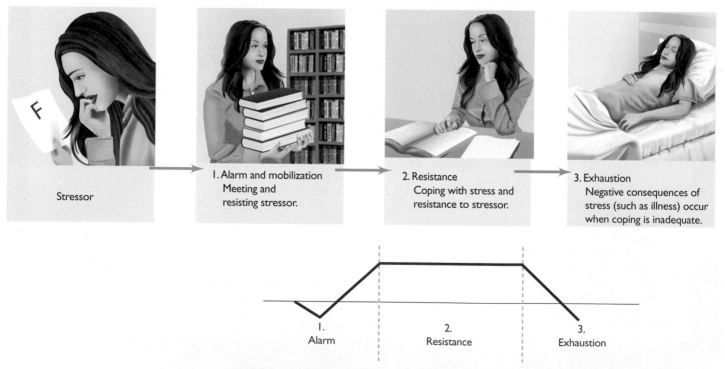

Stressor

1. Alarm and mobilization
Meeting and resisting stressor.

2. Resistance
Coping with stress and resistance to stressor.

3. Exhaustion
Negative consequences of stress (such as illness) occur when coping is inadequate.

1. Alarm   2. Resistance   3. Exhaustion

FIGURE 4 According to the general adaptation syndrome (GAS) model there are three major stages to stress responses: alarm and mobilization; resistance; and exhaustion. The graph below the illustration shows the degree of effort expended to cope with stressors at each of the three stages. (Source: Selye, 1976.)

Although the GAS has had a substantial impact on our understanding of stress, Selye's theory has not gone unchallenged. For example, the theory suggests that the biological reaction is similar regardless of the stressor, but some health psychologists disagree. They believe that people's biological responses are specific to the way they appraise a stressful event. If a stressor is seen as unpleasant but not unusual, then the biological response may be different than if the stressor is seen as unpleasant, out of the ordinary, and unanticipated. This perspective has led to an increased focus on psychoneuroimmunology (Taylor et al., 2000; Gaab et al., 2005; Irwin, 2008).

PSYCHONEUROIMMUNOLOGY AND STRESS

Contemporary health psychologists specializing in PNI have taken a broader approach to stress. Focusing on the outcomes of stress, they have identified three main consequences of it (see Figure 5).

First, stress has direct physiological results, including an increase in blood pressure, an increase in hormonal activity, and an overall decline in the functioning of the immune system. Second, stress leads people to engage in behaviors that are harmful to their health, including increased nicotine, drug, and alcohol use; poor eating habits; and decreased sleep. Finally, stress produces indirect consequences that result in declines in health: a reduction in the likelihood of obtaining health care and decreased compliance with medical advice when it is sought (Sapolsky, 2003; Broman, 2005; Lindblad, Lindahl, & Theorell, 2006).

Why is stress so damaging to the immune system? One reason is that stress may overstimulate it. Rather than fighting invading bacteria, viruses, and other foreign invaders, it may begin to attack the body itself and damage healthy tissue. When that happens, it can lead to disorders such as arthritis and allergic reactions.

Stress can also decrease the immune system response, permitting germs that produce colds to reproduce more easily or allowing cancer cells to spread more rapidly. In normal circumstances, our bodies produce *lymphocytes,* specialized white blood cells that fight disease at an extraordinary rate—some 10 million every few seconds. It is possible that stress can alter this level of production (Segerstrom & Miller, 2004; Dougall & Baum, 2004; Baum, Lorduy, & Jenkins, 2011).

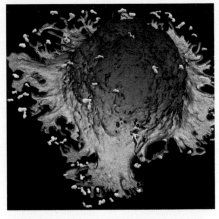

The ability to fight off disease is related to psychological factors. Here a cell from the body's immune system engulfs and destroys disease-producing bacteria.

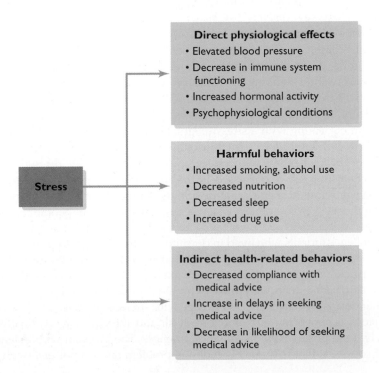

Stress

Direct physiological effects
- Elevated blood pressure
- Decrease in immune system functioning
- Increased hormonal activity
- Psychophysiological conditions

Harmful behaviors
- Increased smoking, alcohol use
- Decreased nutrition
- Decreased sleep
- Increased drug use

Indirect health-related behaviors
- Decreased compliance with medical advice
- Increase in delays in seeking medical advice
- Decrease in likelihood of seeking medical advice

FIGURE 5 Three major types of consequences result from stress: direct physiological effects, harmful behaviors, and indirect health-related behaviors. (Source: Adapted from Baum, 1994.)

Coping with Stress

Stress is a normal part of life—and not necessarily a completely bad part. For example, without stress, we might not be sufficiently motivated to complete the activities we need to accomplish.

However, it is also clear that too much stress can take a toll on physical and psychological health. How do people deal with stress? Is there a way to reduce its negative effects?

coping The efforts to control, reduce, or learn to tolerate the threats that lead to stress.

Efforts to control, reduce, or learn to tolerate the threats that lead to stress are known as **coping.** We habitually use certain coping responses to deal with stress. Most of the time, we're not aware of these responses—just as we may be unaware of the minor stressors of life until they build up to harmful levels (Wrzesniewski & Chylinska, 2007; Chao, 2011).

We also have other, more direct and potentially more positive ways of coping with stress, which fall into two main categories (Folkman & Moskowitz, 2000, 2004; Baker & Berenbaum, 2007):

- **Emotion-focused coping.** In *emotion-focused coping,* people try to manage their emotions in the face of stress by seeking to change the way they feel about or perceive a problem. Examples of emotion-focused coping include strategies such as accepting sympathy from others and looking at the bright side of a situation.
- **Problem-focused coping.** *Problem-focused coping* attempts to modify the stressful problem or source of stress. Problem-focused strategies lead to changes in behavior or to the development of a plan of action to deal with stress. Starting a study group to improve poor classroom performance is an example of problem-focused coping. In addition, one might take a time-out from stress by creating positive events. For example, taking a day off from caring for a relative with a serious, chronic illness to go a health club or spa can bring significant relief from stress.

People often employ several types of coping strategies simultaneously. Furthermore, they use emotion-focused strategies more frequently when they perceive circumstances as being unchangeable and problem-focused strategies more often in situations they see as relatively modifiable (Stanton et al., 2000; Penley, Tomaka, & Wiebe, 2002). (Also see *Applying Psychology in the 21st Century.*)

Some forms of coping are less successful. One of the least effective forms of coping is avoidant coping. In *avoidant coping,* a person may use wishful thinking to reduce stress or use more direct escape routes, such as drug use, alcohol use, and overeating. An example of wishful thinking to avoid a test would be to say to oneself, "Maybe it will snow so hard tomorrow that the test will be canceled." Alternatively, a person might get drunk to avoid a problem. Either way, avoidant coping usually results in a postponement of dealing with a stressful situation, and this often makes the problem even worse (Roesch et al., 2005; Hutchinson, Baldwin, & Oh, 2006; Glass et al., 2009).

Another way of dealing with stress occurs unconsciously through the use of defense mechanisms. As we discussed in the chapter about personality, *defense mechanisms* are unconscious strategies that people use to reduce anxiety by concealing the source from themselves and others. Defense mechanisms permit people to avoid stress by acting as if the stress were not even there. For example, one study examined California college students who lived in dormitories close to a geological fault (Lehman & Taylor, 1988). Those who lived in dorms that were known to be unlikely to withstand an earthquake were significantly *more* likely to doubt experts' predictions of an impending earthquake than were those who lived in safer structures.

Another defense mechanism used to cope with stress is *emotional insulation* in which a person stops experiencing any emotions at all and thereby remains unaffected and unmoved by both positive and negative experiences. The problem with defense mechanisms, of course, is that they merely hide the problem and do not deal with reality.

What Doesn't Kill You Really Does Make You Stronger

Wouldn't it be great never to experience adversity in your life—not to have any loved ones die, never to have a serious illness, or never to experience a natural disaster like an earthquake or fire? You could certainly be forgiven for thinking so, but research suggests that a stress-free life isn't actually as positive as we might expect it to be.

In one study, researchers followed nearly 2,000 adults over several years, monitoring their experience of stressful events with periodic surveys. To begin the study, the participants indicated from a list which stressful life events they had already experienced. They also reported about their overall well-being. Examples of events on the list included divorce, death of a friend, and experiencing a natural disaster. Throughout the course of the study, they reported subsequent adverse events (Seery, Holman, & Silver, 2010).

The researchers immediately noticed something interesting about the participants' initial reports: a small but significant subset of them indicated that they hadn't experienced any of the stressful life events on the list. What kind of person goes through life without experiencing any kind of serious adversity, the researchers wondered. They looked more closely at these participants, digging for some kind of explanation such as youth, excessive cautiousness, or social isolation—and they came up empty handed. But the real surprise was how these participants scored on their sense of well-being: Instead of being the ones with the highest life satisfaction, as one might expect, they scored about the same as participants who experienced a high number of adverse events. The participants with the highest sense of

Research has found that people who are confronted with sudden tragedies become more resilient if given the chance to learn and practice useful coping skills.

well-being were those who experienced a moderate number of life stresses.

Why? The researchers concluded that a moderate level of suffering makes people stronger. When people experience a moderate number of upsetting events, they have a chance to learn and practice useful coping skills. These skills then continue to serve them in life, helping them to deal effectively with subsequent problems. They develop a sense of confidence that when they do encounter a hard time, they will get through it. People who experience very little adversity in their lives, on the other hand, may be less able to cope with significant stressors when they do happen (Seery, Holman, & Silver, 2010).

"Frequency makes a difference, that is the message," said Roxane Cohen Silver, one of the researchers who conducted the study. She goes to say, "Each negative event a person faces leads to an attempt to cope, which forces people to learn about their own capabilities, about their support networks—to learn who their real friends are. That kind of learning we think is extremely valuable for subsequent coping" (Carey, 2011, p. 8).

RETHINK

- If experiencing adversity makes people stronger, why do you think the participants who experienced the most adversity were about as unsatisfied with life as those who experienced the least?
- Based on the findings in this research, how might parents help their young children who experience an unsettling event?

LEARNED HELPLESSNESS

Have you ever faced an intolerable situation that you just couldn't resolve, and you finally simply gave up and accepted things the way they were? This example illustrates one of the possible consequences of being in an environment in which control over a situation is not possible—a state that produces learned helplessness.

learned helplessness A state in which people conclude that unpleasant or aversive stimuli cannot be controlled—a view of the world that becomes so ingrained that they cease trying to remedy the aversive circumstances even if they actually can exert some influence on the situation.

Learned helplessness occurs when people conclude that unpleasant or aversive stimuli cannot be controlled—a view of the world that becomes so ingrained that they cease trying to remedy the aversive circumstances even if they actually can exert some influence on the situation (Seligman, 1975, 2007; Aujoulat, Luminet, & Deccache, 2007).

Victims of learned helplessness have concluded that there is no link between the responses they make and the outcomes that occur. People experience more physical symptoms and depression when they perceive that they have little or no control than they do when they feel a sense of control over a situation (Chou, 2005; Bjornstad, 2006; Figen, 2011).

COPING STYLES: THE HARDY PERSONALITY

Most of us characteristically cope with stress by employing a *coping style* that represents our general tendency to deal with stress in a specific way. For example, you may know people who habitually react to even the smallest amount of stress with hysteria and others who calmly confront even the greatest stress in an unflappable manner. These kinds of people clearly have very different coping styles (Taylor, 2003; Kato & Pedersen, 2005).

hardiness A personality characteristic that is associated with a lower rate of stress-related illness and consists of three components: commitment, challenge, and control.

Among those who cope with stress most successfully are people who are equipped with **hardiness,** a personality characteristic associated with a lower rate of stress-related illness. Hardiness consists of three components (Baumgartner, 2002; Maddi, 2007; Maddi et al., 2011):

- *Commitment.* Commitment is a tendency to throw ourselves into whatever we are doing with a sense that our activities are important and meaningful.
- *Challenge.* Hardy people believe that change rather than stability is the standard condition of life. To them, the anticipation of change serves as an incentive rather than a threat to their security.
- *Control.* Hardiness is marked by a sense of control—the perception that people can influence the events in their lives.

Hardy individuals approach stress optimistically and take direct action to learn about and deal with stressors; they thereby change stressful events into less threatening ones. As a consequence, hardiness acts as a defense against stress-related illness (Andrew et al., 2008; Bartone et al., 2008; Vogt et al., 2008).

For those who confront the most profound difficulties, such as the death of a loved one or a permanent injury such as paralysis after an accident, a key ingredient in their psychological recovery is their degree of resilience. *Resilience* is the ability to withstand, overcome, and actually thrive after profound adversity (Bonanno, 2004; Norlander, Von Schedvin, & Archer, 2005; Jackson, 2006).

Resilient people are generally optimistic, good-natured, and have good social skills. They are usually independent, and they have a sense of control over their own destiny—even if fate has dealt them a devastating blow. In short, they work with what they have and make the best of whatever situation they find themselves in (Spencer et al., 2003; Friborg et al., 2005; Deshields et al., 2006).

Resilience may have its origins in a complex series of biological reactions that occur when people confront devastating situations. These reactions involve the release of the hormone cortisol. Although cortisol is helpful in responding to challenges, too much can produce damage. Other chemicals, however, can moderate the effects of cortisol, and it may be that drugs or therapy can stimulate the production of these moderating chemicals. Furthermore, some people may be genetically predisposed to produce these chemicals, making them more resilient (Cole et al., 2010; Stix, 2011).

"Today, we examined our life style, we evaluated our diet and our exercise program, and we also assessed our behavioral pattern. Then we needed a drink."

SOCIAL SUPPORT: TURNING TO OTHERS

Our relationships with others also help us cope with stress. Researchers have found that **social support,** the knowledge that we are part of a mutual network of caring, interested others, enables us to experience lower levels of stress and better cope with the stress we do undergo (Cohen, 2004; Martin & Brantley, 2004; Bolger & Amarel, 2007).

The social and emotional support people provide each other helps in dealing with stress in several ways. For instance, such support demonstrates that a person is an important and valued member of a social network. Similarly, other people can provide information and advice about appropriate ways of dealing with stress (Day & Livingstone, 2003; Lindorff, 2005).

Finally, people who are part of a social support network can provide actual goods and services to help others in stressful situations. For instance, they can supply temporary living quarters to a person whose house has burned down, or they can offer study help to a student who is experiencing stress because of poor academic performance (Natvig, Albrektsen, & Ovarnstrom, 2003; Takizawa, Kondo, & Sakihara, 2007).

Findings that attendance at religious services (as well as spirituality in general) provides health-related benefits also illustrate the importance of social support. For example, healthy people who regularly attend religious services live longer than those who do not attend regularly (Powell, Shahabi, & Thoresen, 2003; Gilbert, 2007; Hayward & Elliott, 2011).

Recent research is also beginning to identify how social support affects brain processing. For instance, one experiment found that activation of the areas of the brain reflecting stress was reduced when social support—simply being able to hold the hand of another person—was available (see Figure 6 *Neuroscience in Your Life;* Coan, Schaefer, & Davidson, 2006).

social support A mutual network of caring, interested others.

Neuroscience in Your Life:
Stress and Social Support

FIGURE 6 Participants in a study were threatened by being told they would be receiving a shock. When they were provided social support, areas of the brain that become activated during stress showed reduced activation. Specifically, social support in this study was having either a stranger or the participant's spouse hold his or her hand. In the figure, the color green highlights brain areas that showed reductions in activity when a spouse held the participant's hand, and the color blue highlights reductions in activity when either a spouse or a stranger held the participant's hand. (Source: Coan, Schaefer, & Davidson, 2006, Figure 3.)

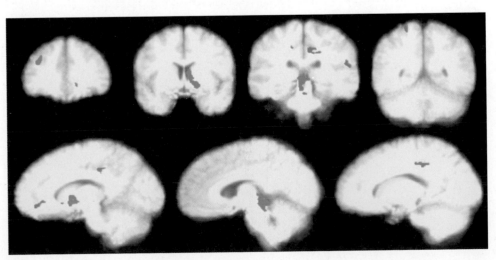

BECOMING AN INFORMED CONSUMER of Psychology

Effective Coping Strategies

How can we deal with the stress in our lives? Although there is no universal solution because effective coping depends on the nature of the stressor and the degree to which it can be controlled, here are some general guidelines (Aspinwall & Taylor, 1997; Folkman & Moskowitz, 2000):

- *Turn a threat into a challenge.* When a stressful situation might be controllable, the best coping strategy is to treat the situation as a challenge and focus on ways to control it. For instance, if you experience stress because your car is always breaking down, you might take a course in auto mechanics and learn to deal directly with the car's problems.

- *Make a threatening situation less threatening.* When a stressful situation seems to be uncontrollable, you need to take a different approach. It is possible to change your appraisal of the situation, view it in a different light, and modify your attitude toward it. Research supports the old truism, "Look for the silver lining in every cloud" (Smith & Lazarus, 2001; Cheng & Cheung, 2005).

- *Change your goals.* If you are faced with an uncontrollable situation, a reasonable strategy is to adopt new goals that are practical in view of the particular situation. For example, a dancer who has been in an automobile accident and has lost full use of her legs may no longer aspire to a career in dance but might modify her goals and try to become a choreographer.

- *Take physical action.* Changing your physiological reaction to stress can help with coping. For example, biofeedback (in which a person learns to control internal physiological processes through conscious thought) can alter basic physiological processes and allow people to reduce blood pressure, heart rate, and other consequences of heightened stress. Exercise can also be effective in reducing stress (Langreth, 2000; Spencer et al., 2003; Hamer, Taylor, & Steptoe, 2006).

- *Prepare for stress before it happens.* A final strategy for coping with stress is *proactive coping,* anticipating and preparing for stress *before* it is encountered. For example, if you're expecting to go through a 1-week period in which you must take a number of major tests, you can try to arrange your schedule so you have more time to study (Aspinwall & Taylor, 1997; Bode et al., 2007).

RECAP/EVALUATE/RETHINK

RECAP

LO 34-1 How is health psychology a union between medicine and psychology?

- The field of health psychology considers how psychology can be applied to the prevention, diagnosis, and treatment of medical problems. (p. 420)

LO 34-2 What is stress, how does it affect us, and how can we best cope with it?

- Stress is a response to threatening or challenging environmental conditions. People encounter stressors—the circumstances that produce stress—of both a positive and a negative nature. (p. 421)
- The way an environmental circumstance is interpreted affects whether it will be considered stressful. Still, there are general classes of events that provoke stress: cataclysmic events, personal stressors, and background stressors (daily hassles). (pp. 422, 423)
- Stress produces immediate physiological reactions. In the short term those reactions may be adaptive, but in the long term they may have negative consequences, including the development of psychophysiological disorders. (pp. 424, 425)
- The consequences of stress can be explained in part by Selye's general adaptation syndrome (GAS), which suggests that there are three stages in stress responses: alarm and mobilization, resistance, and exhaustion. (p. 426)
- Coping with stress can take a number of forms, including the unconscious use of defense mechanisms and the use of emotion-focused or problem-focused coping strategies. (p. 428)
- Stress can be reduced by developing a sense of control over one's circumstances. In some cases, however, people develop a state of learned helplessness. (pp. 429, 430)

EVALUATE

1. _____ is defined as a response to challenging or threatening events.
2. Match each portion of the GAS with its definition.
   1. Alarm and mobilization
   2. Exhaustion
   3. Resistance

   a. Ability to adapt to stress diminishes; symptoms appear.
   b. Activation of sympathetic nervous system.
   c. Various strategies are used to cope with a stressor.
3. Stressors that affect a single person and produce an immediate major reaction are known as
   a. Personal stressors
   b. Psychic stressors
   c. Cataclysmic stressors
   d. Daily stressors
4. People with the personality characteristic of _____ seem to be better able to successfully combat stressors.

RETHINK

1. Why are cataclysmic stressors less stressful in the long run than other types of stressors? Does the reason relate to the coping phenomenon known as social support? How?
2. *From the perspective of a social worker:* How would you help people deal with and avoid stress in their everyday lives? How might you encourage people to create social support networks?

Answers to Evaluate Questions

1. Stress; 2. 1-b, 2-a; 3-c; 3. a; 4. hardiness

KEY TERMS

health psychology p. 420
psychoneuroimmunology (PNI) p. 420
stress p. 421
cataclysmic events p. 422

personal stressors p. 422
posttraumatic stress disorder (PTSD) p. 422
background stressors ("daily hassles") p. 423

psychophysiological disorders p. 424
general adaptation syndrome (GAS) p. 426
coping p. 428

learned helplessness p. 430
hardiness p. 430
social support p. 431

Psychological Aspects of Illness and Well-Being

Learning Outcome

LO 35-1 How do psychological factors affect health-related problems such as coronary heart disease, cancer, and smoking?

I feel that it is absolutely necessary to be my own best advocate, and the best place to learn how to do that is in a group of other well-educated patients and their caregivers. We know what life post-diagnosis is like, and we help each other in ways that no docs, nurses, clergy, well-meaning friends and family possibly can. We laugh, we cry, we bitch, and we push and pull each other! We mourn the losses, celebrate small and large victories, and we educate ourselves and others. But most importantly—we embrace each other and our lives. (Anonymous blogpost, 2010.)

As recently as three decades ago, most psychologists and health-care providers would have scoffed at the notion that a discussion group could improve a cancer patient's chances of survival. Today, however, such methods have gained increasing acceptance.

Growing evidence suggests that psychological factors have a substantial impact both on major health problems that were once seen in purely physiological terms and on our everyday sense of health, well-being, and happiness. We'll consider the psychological components of three major health problems—heart disease, cancer, and smoking—and then consider the nature of people's well-being and happiness.

The As, Bs, and Ds of Coronary Heart Disease

Tim knew it wasn't going to be his day when he got stuck in traffic behind a slow-moving farm truck. How could the driver dawdle like that? Didn't he have anything of any importance to do? Things didn't get any better when Tim arrived on campus and discovered the library didn't have the books he needed. He could almost feel the tension rising.

"I need that material to finish my paper," he thought to himself.

He knew that meant he wouldn't be able to get his paper done early, and that meant he wouldn't have the time he wanted to revise the paper. He wanted it to be a first-class paper. This time Tim wanted to get a better grade than his roommate, Luis. Although Luis didn't know it, Tim felt they were in competition and that Luis was always trying to better him whether academically or just playing cards.

"In fact," Tim mused to himself, "I feel like I'm in competition with everyone, no matter what I'm doing."

Have you, like Tim, ever seethed impatiently at being caught behind a slow-moving vehicle, felt anger and frustration at not finding material you needed at the library, or experienced a sense of competitiveness with your classmates?

Many of us experience these sorts of feelings at one time or another, but for some people they represent a pervasive, characteristic set of personality traits known as the Type A behavior pattern. The **Type A behavior pattern** is a cluster of behaviors involving hostility, competitiveness, time urgency, and feeling driven. In contrast, the

Type A behavior pattern A cluster of behaviors involving hostility, competitiveness, time urgency, and feeling driven.

Type B behavior pattern is characterized by a patient, cooperative, noncompetitive, and nonaggressive manner. It's important to keep in mind that Type A and Type B represent the ends of a continuum, and most people fall somewhere in between the two endpoints. Few people are purely a Type A or a Type B.

The importance of the Type A behavior pattern lies in its links to coronary heart disease. Men who display the Type A pattern develop coronary heart disease twice as often and suffer significantly more fatal heart attacks than those classified as having the Type B pattern. Moreover, the Type A pattern predicts who is going to develop heart disease at least as well as—and independently of—any other single factor, including age, blood pressure, smoking habits, and cholesterol levels in the body (Wielgosz & Nolan, 2000; Beresnevaité, Taylor, & Bagby, 2007; Korotkov et al., 2011).

Hostility is the key component of the Type A behavior pattern that is related to heart disease. Although competition, time urgency, and feelings of being driven may produce stress and potentially other health and emotional problems, they aren't linked to coronary heart disease the way that hostility is (Williams, J. E. et al., 2000; Boyle et al., 2005; Ohira et al., 2007).

Why is hostility so toxic? The key reason is that hostility produces excessive physiological arousal in stressful situations. That arousal, in turn, results in increased production of the hormones epinephrine and norepinephrine as well as increases in heart rate and blood pressure. Such an exaggerated physiological response ultimately produces an increased incidence of coronary heart disease (Demaree & Everhart, 2004; Faker et al., 2004; Myrtek, 2007).

It's important to keep in mind that not everyone who displays Type A behaviors is destined to have coronary heart disease. For one thing, a firm association between Type A behaviors and coronary heart disease has not been established for women; most findings pertain to males partly because until recently most research was done on men. In addition, other types of negative emotions besides the hostility found in Type A behavior appear to be related to heart attacks. For example, psychologist Johan Denollet has found evidence that what he calls *Type D*—for "distressed"—behavior is linked to coronary heart disease. In this view, insecurity, anxiety, and the negative outlook Type Ds display puts them at risk for repeated heart attacks (Schiffer et al., 2005; Spindler et al., 2009; Denollet & Pedersen, 2011).

Type B behavior pattern A cluster of behaviors characterized by a patient, cooperative, noncompetitive, and nonaggressive manner.

Study Alert

It's important to distinguish among Type A (hostility, competitiveness), Type B (patience, cooperativeness), and Type D (distressed) behaviors.

Psychological Aspects of Cancer

Hardly any disease is feared more than cancer. Most people think of cancer in terms of lingering pain, and being diagnosed with the disease is typically viewed as receiving a death sentence.

Although a diagnosis of cancer is not as grim as it once was—several kinds of cancer have a high cure rate if detected early enough—cancer remains the second leading cause of death after coronary heart disease. The precise trigger for the disease is not well understood, but the process by which cancer spreads is straightforward. Certain cells in the body become altered and multiply rapidly in an uncontrolled fashion. As those cells grow, they form tumors; if left unchecked, the tumors suck nutrients from healthy cells and body tissue and ultimately destroy the body's ability to function properly.

Although the processes involved in the spread of cancer are basically physiological, some research suggests that the emotional responses of cancer patients to their disease may affect its course. For example, some findings show that a "fighting spirit" leads to better coping. On the other hand, there is little evidence that long-term survival rates are better than for patients with a less positive attitude (Watson et al., 1999; Rom, Miller, & Peluso, 2009; Heitzmann et al., 2011).

Despite conflicting evidence, health psychologists believe that patients' emotions may at least partially determine the course of their disease. In the case of cancer, it is possible that positive emotional responses may help generate specialized "killer" cells that help control the size and spread of cancerous tumors. Conversely, negative emotions may suppress the ability of those cells to fight tumors (Schedlowski & Tewes, 1999; Noy, 2006).

Is a particular personality type linked to cancer? Some researchers suggest that cancer patients are less emotionally reactive, suppress anger, and lack outlets for emotional release. However, the data are too tentative and inconsistent to suggest firm conclusions about a link between personality characteristics and cancer. Certainly no conclusive evidence suggests that people who develop cancer would not have done so if their personality had been of a different sort or if their attitudes had been more positive (Smith, 1988; Zevon & Corn, 1990; Holland & Lewis, 2001).

What is increasingly clear, however, is that certain types of psychological therapy have the potential for improving quality of life and even extending the lives of cancer patients. For example, the results of one study showed that women with breast cancer who received psychological treatment lived at least a year and a half longer and experienced less anxiety and pain than women who did not participate in therapy. Research on patients with other health problems, such as heart disease, also has found that therapy can be both psychologically and medically beneficial (Spiegel, 1996; Frasure-Smith, Lesperance, & Talajic, 2000; Butler et al., 2009).

Smoking

Would you walk into a convenience store and buy an item with a label warning you that its use could kill you? Although most people would probably answer no, millions make such a purchase everyday: a pack of cigarettes. Furthermore, they do this despite clear, well-publicized evidence that smoking is linked to cancer, heart attacks, strokes, bronchitis, emphysema, and a host of other serious illnesses. Smoking is the greatest preventable cause of death in the United States; one in five U.S. deaths is caused by smoking. Worldwide, close to 5 million people die each year from the effects of smoking (Danaei et al., 2005).

Although smoking is prohibited in an increasing number of places, it remains a substantial social problem.

WHY PEOPLE SMOKE

Why do people smoke despite all the evidence showing that it is bad for their health? It is not that they are somehow unaware of the link between smoking and disease; surveys show that most *smokers* agree with the statement, "Cigarette smoking frequently causes disease and death." And almost three-quarters of the 48 million smokers in the United States say they would like to quit. Still, 700,000 people a year take up the habit (Wetter et al., 1998; Price, 2008).

Heredity seems to determine, in part, whether people will become smokers, how much they will smoke, and how easily they can quit. Genetics also influences how susceptible people are to the harmful effects of smoking. For instance, there is an almost 50% higher rate of lung cancer in African-American smokers than in white smokers. This difference may be due to genetically produced variations in the efficiency with which enzymes are able to reduce the effects of the cancer-causing chemicals in tobacco smoke (Pomerlau, 1995; Li et al., 2003; Li et al., 2008).

However, although genetics plays a role in smoking, most research suggests that environmental factors are the primary cause of the habit. Smoking at first may be seen as "cool" or sophisticated, as a rebellious act, or as facilitating calm performance in stressful situations. Greater exposure to smoking in media such as film also leads to a higher risk of becoming an established smoker. In addition, smoking a cigarette is sometimes viewed as a "rite of passage" for adolescents undertaken at the urging of friends and viewed as a sign of growing up (Sargent et al., 2007; Wills et al., 2008; Heatherton & Sargent, 2009).

Ultimately, smoking becomes a habit. And it's an easy habit to pick up: Smoking even a single cigarette leads to a loss of autonomy, when a smoker finds that not smoking requires an effort or involves discomfort. Subsequently, people begin to label themselves smokers, and smoking becomes part of their self-concept. Moreover, they become dependent physiologically as a result of smoking because nicotine, a primary ingredient of tobacco, is highly addictive. A complex relationship develops among smoking, nicotine levels, and a smoker's emotions in which a certain nicotine level becomes associated with a positive emotional state. As a result, people smoke in an effort to regulate *both* emotional states and nicotine levels in the blood (Kassel et al., 2007; Ursprung, Sanouri, & DiFranza, 2009; Dennis, 2011).

QUITTING SMOKING

Because smoking has both psychological and biological components, few habits are as difficult to break. Long-term successful treatment typically occurs in just 15% of those who try to stop smoking; once smoking becomes a habit, it is as hard to stop as an addiction to cocaine or heroin. In fact, some of the biochemical reactions to nicotine are similar to those to cocaine, amphetamines, and morphine. Furthermore, changes in brain chemistry brought about by smoking may make smokers more resistant to antismoking messages (see also Figure 1 *Neuroscience in Your Life*; Vanasse, Niyonsenga, & Courteau, 2004; Foulds et al., 2006; Dani & Montague, 2007).

Many people try to quit smoking but fail. The average smoker tries to quit 8 to 10 times before being successful, and even then many relapse. Even long-time quitters can fall off the wagon: About 10% relapse after more than year of avoiding cigarettes (Grady & Altman, 2008).

Neuroscience in Your Life: The Addictive Pull of Smoking

FIGURE 1 Smoking is particularly addictive in teenagers, and a recent study helps explain why. When 14-year-olds performed a task that included the possibility of a monetary reward, non-smoking adolescents showed more brain activation in an area associated with responding to reward (A) than smokers (B). The results suggest that adolescents may use smoking to increase activity in reward areas of the brain, making them more susceptible to substance addiction. (Source: Peters et al., 2011.)

Response to Reward Anticipation

A. Comparison Subjects (N=43)

B. Smokers (N=43)

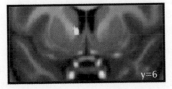

Among the most effective tools for ending the smoking habit are drugs that replace the nicotine found in cigarettes. Whether in the form of gum, patches, nasal sprays, or inhalers, these products provide a dose of nicotine that reduces dependence on cigarettes. Another approach is exemplified by the drugs Zyban and Chantix; rather than replacing nicotine, they reduce the pleasure from smoking and suppress withdrawal symptoms that smokers experience when they try to stop (Shiffman, 2007; Brody, 2008; Dohnke, Weiss-Gerlach, & Spies, 2011).

Behavioral strategies, which view smoking as a learned habit and concentrate on changing the smoking response, can also be effective. Initial "cure" rates of 60% have been reported, and 1 year after treatment more than half of those who quit have not resumed smoking. Individual or group counseling also increases the rate of success in breaking the habit. The best treatment seems to be a combination of nicotine replacement and counseling. What doesn't work? Going it alone: Only 5% of smokers who quit cold-turkey on their own are successful (Rock, 1999; Woodruff, Conway, & Edwards, 2007).

In the long term, the most effective means of reducing smoking may be changes in societal norms and attitudes toward the habit. For instance, many cities and towns have made smoking in public places illegal; legislation based on strong popular sentiment that bans smoking in places such as college classrooms and buildings is being passed with increasing frequency. In addition, smokers are more likely to quit when their friends are quitting, so the social support of others quitting is helpful (Hamilton, Biener, & Brennan, 2008; Christakis & Fowler, 2008).

The long-term effect of the barrage of information regarding the negative consequences of smoking on people's health has been substantial; overall, smoking has declined over the last 2 decades, particularly among males. Still, more than one-fourth of students enrolled in high school are active smokers by the time they graduate, and there is evidence that the decline in smoking is leveling off. Among these students, around 10% become active smokers as early as the 8th grade (see Figure 2; Fichtenberg & Glantz, 2006; Johnston et al., 2011).

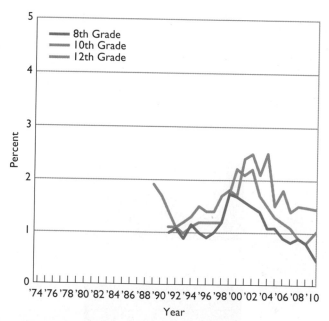

FIGURE 2 Although smoking among teenagers is lower than it was 20 years ago, a significant number still report smoking regularly. What factors might account for the continued high use of tobacco by teenagers despite the increase in antismoking advertising? (Source: Johnston et al., 2010.)

Exploring DIVERSITY

Hucksters of Death: Promoting Smoking Throughout the World

> A Jeep decorated with the Camel logo pulls up to a high school in Buenos Aires. A woman begins handing out free cigarettes to 15- and 16-year-olds during their lunch recess. At a video arcade in Taipei, free American cigarettes are strewn atop each game. At a disco filled with high school students, free packs of Salems are on each table. (Ecenbarger, 1993, p. 50)

Because the number of smokers has steadily declined in the United States, cigarette manufacturers have turned their sights to other parts of the world, where they see a fertile market for their product. Although they must often sell cigarettes more cheaply than they do in the United States, the huge number of potential smokers still makes it financially worthwhile for the tobacco companies. The United States is now the world's largest exporter of cigarettes (Bartecchi, MacKenzie, & Schrier, 1995; Brown, 2001).

Clearly, the push into worldwide markets has been successful. In some Latin American cities, as many as 50% of teenagers smoke. Children as young as age 7 smoke in Hong Kong; 30% of children smoked their first whole cigarette before the age of 10 in India, Ghana, Jamaica, and Poland. The World Health Organization predicts that smoking will prematurely kill some 200 million of the world's children and that ultimately 10% of the world's population will die as a result of smoking. Of everyone alive today, 500 million will eventually die from tobacco use (Mackay & Eriksen, 2002).

One reason for the increase in smoking in developing countries is that their governments make little effort to discourage it. In fact, many governments are in the tobacco business themselves and rely on revenues from tobacco. For example, the world's largest manufacturer of cigarettes is the China National Tobacco Corporation, which is owned by the Chinese government (Marsh, 2008).

In some countries, children as young as 6 smoke regularly.

RECAP/EVALUATE/RETHINK

RECAP

LO 35-1 How do psychological factors affect health-related problems such as coronary heart disease, cancer, and smoking?

- Hostility, a key component of the Type A behavior pattern, is linked to coronary heart disease. The Type A behavior pattern is a cluster of behaviors involving hostility, competitiveness, time urgency, and feeling driven. (p. 434)
- People's attitudes and emotional responses may affect the course of cancer through links to the immune system. (pp. 435, 436)
- Smoking, the leading preventable cause of health problems, has proved to be difficult to quit, even though most smokers are aware of the dangerous consequences of the behavior. (pp. 436, 437)

EVALUATE

1. Type _____ behavior is characterized by cooperativeness and by being easygoing; Type _____ behavior is characterized by hostility and competitiveness.
2. The Type A behavior pattern is known to directly cause heart attacks. True or false?

3. A cancer patient's attitude and emotions may affect that person's _____ system and thus help or hinder the patient's fight against the disease.
4. Smoking is used to regulate both nicotine levels and emotional states in smokers. True or false?

RETHINK

1. Is there a danger of "blaming the victim" when we argue that the course of cancer can be improved if a person with the disease holds positive attitudes or beliefs, particularly when we consider people with cancer who are not recovering? Explain your answer.
2. *From the perspective of a health-care provider:* What type of advice would you give to your patients about the connections between personality and disease? For example, would you encourage Type A people to become "less Type A" in order to decrease their risk of heart disease?

Answers to Evaluate Questions

1. B, A; 2. false; Type A behavior is related to a higher incidence of coronary heart disease but does not necessarily cause it directly; 3. immune; 4. true

KEY TERMS

Type A behavior pattern   p. 434   Type B behavior pattern   p. 435

VISUAL SUMMARY 11 Health Psychology

MODULE 34 Stress and Coping

Stress: People's response to events that threaten or challenge them

— Interpretation of events is important in determining what is stressful

- • Cataclysmic events
- • Personal stressors
- • Background stressors (daily stressors)

— Posttraumatic Stress Disorder (PTSD)

The Cost of Stress

— Psychophysiological disorders: An interaction of psychological, emotional, and physical difficulties

Stress

Direct physiological effects
- • Elevated blood pressure
- • Decrease in immune system functioning
- • Increased hormonal activity
- • Psychophysiological conditions

Harmful behaviors
- • Increased smoking, alcohol use
- • Decreased nutrition
- • Decreased sleep
- • Increased drug use

Indirect health-related behaviors
- • Decreased compliance with medical advice
- • Increase in delays in seeking medical advice
- • Decrease in likelihood of seeking medical advice

— General Adaptation Syndrome (GAS) Model: The physiological response to stress follows the same pattern regardless of the cause of stress

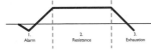

— Psychoneuroimmunology: Relationship among psychological factors, the immune system, and the brain

Coping with Stress: Emotion-focused or problem-focused coping

MODULE 35 Psychological Aspects of Illness and Well-Being

Coronary Heart Disease

— Type A behavior: A cluster of behaviors involving hostility, competitiveness, time urgency, and feeling driven

— Type B behavior: Characterized by a patient, cooperative, noncompetitive and nonaggressive manner

— Type D behavior: Insecure, anxious, and negative outlook

Cancer: Psychological therapy may improve quality of life

Smoking

- • 5 million people die each year from smoking

- • Heredity, in part, determines whether people will become smokers and are susceptible to harmful effects of smoking

- • Few habits are as difficult to break

MODULE 36 Promoting Health and Wellness

Following Medical Advice: Noncompliance with medical advice takes many forms

— Communicating with health-care providers

- • Lack of communication can be a major obstacle
- • Many patients fail to ask questions
- • Gender and cultural factors may hinder communication

— Increasing compliance with medical advice compliance

- • Patients prefer to be well informed even if the news is bad
- • Positively framed messages: most likely to motivate preventive behavior

- • Negatively framed messages: most likely to lead to the detection of a disease

Well-Being and Happiness:

- • Subjective well-being: People's own evaluation of their lives in terms of their thoughts and their emotions
- • Characteristics of happy people: high self-esteem, sense of control, optimism, enjoy being with others
- • Most people are moderately happy most of the time

Faces Scale:"Which face comes closest to expressing how you feel about your life as a whole?"

20%   46%   27%   4%   2%   1%   0%

449

12
Psychological Disorders

Learning Outcomes for Chapter 12

MODULE 37

LO 37-1 How can we distinguish normal from abnormal behavior?

LO 37-2 What are the major perspectives on psychological disorders used by mental health professionals?

LO 37-3 What are the major categories of psychological disorders?

Normal Versus Abnormal: Making the Distinction

Defining Abnormality

Perspectives on Abnormality: From Superstition to Science

Classifying Abnormal Behavior: The ABCs of *DSM*

MODULE 38

LO 38-1 What are the major psychological disorders?

The Major Psychological Disorders

Anxiety Disorders

Neuroscience in Your Life: One Step Closer to Understanding OCD

Somatoform Disorders

Dissociative Disorders

Mood Disorders

Schizophrenia

Neuroscience in Your Life: Brain Changes with Schizophrenia

Personality Disorders

Childhood Disorders

Other Disorders

MODULE 39

LO 39-1 How prevalent are psychological disorders?

LO 39-2 What indicators signal a need for the help of a mental health practitioner?

Psychological Disorders in Perspective

The Social and Cultural Context of Psychological Disorders

Applying Psychology in the 21st Century: Psychological Problems Are Increasing Among College Students

Exploring Diversity: *DSM* and Culture— and the Culture of *DSM*

Becoming an Informed Consumer of Psychology: Deciding When You Need Help

Prologue *Coping with Schizophrenia*

The job was gone, the gun was loaded, and a voice was saying, "You're a waste, give up now, do it now."

It was a command, not a suggestion, and what mattered at that moment—a winter evening in 2000—was not where the voice was coming from, but how assured it was, how persuasive.

Losing his first decent job ever seemed like too much for Joe Holt to live with. It was time.

"All I remember then is a knock on the bedroom door and my wife, Patsy, she sits down on the bed and hugs me, and I'm holding the gun in my left hand, down here, out of sight," said Mr. Holt, 50, a computer consultant and entrepreneur who has a diagnosis of schizophrenia.

"She says, 'Joe, I know you feel like quitting, but what if tomorrow is the day you get what you want?' And walks out. I sat there staring at that gun for an hour at least, and finally decided—never again. It can never be an option. Patsy deserves for me to be trying" (Carey, 2011, p. A1).

Looking **Ahead**

Joe Holt was lucky. With the help of his family and care providers, he has been able to live successfully with schizophrenia, a severe and often debilitating psychological disorder.

Holt's difficulties raise many questions. What triggered his disorder? Were genetic factors involved, or were stressors in his life responsible? Could the disorder have been prevented? And, more generally, how do we distinguish normal from abnormal behavior, and how can Holt's behavior be categorized and classified in such a way as to pinpoint the specific nature of his problem?

We address the issues raised by Holt's case in this chapter. We begin by discussing the difference between normal and abnormal behavior, which can be surprisingly indistinct. We then turn to a consideration of the most significant kinds of psychological disorders. Finally, we'll consider ways of evaluating behavior—one's own and that of others—to determine whether seeking help from a mental health professional is warranted.

Normal Versus Abnormal: Making the Distinction

Universally that person's acumen is esteemed very little perceptive concerning whatsoever matters are being held as most profitable by mortals with sapience endowed to be studied who is ignorant of that which the most in doctrine erudite and certainly by reason of that in them high mind's ornament deserving of veneration constantly maintain when by general consent they affirm that other circumstances being equal by no exterior splendour is the prosperity of a nation . . .

It would be easy to conclude that these words are the musings of a madman. To most people, the passage does not seem to make any sense at all. But literary scholars would disagree. Actually, this passage is from James Joyce's classic *Ulysses,* hailed as one of the major works of 20th-century literature (Joyce, 1934, p. 377).

As this example illustrates, casually examining a person's writing is insufficient to determine the degree to which that person is "normal." But even when we consider more extensive samples of a person's behavior, we will find that there may be only a fine line between behavior that is considered normal and behavior that is considered abnormal.

Learning Outcomes

LO 37-1 How can we distinguish normal from abnormal behavior?

LO 37-2 What are the major perspectives on psychological disorders used by mental health professionals?

LO 37-3 What are the major categories of psychological disorders?

Defining Abnormality

Because of the difficulty in distinguishing normal from abnormal behavior, psychologists have struggled to devise a precise, scientific definition of "abnormal behavior." For instance, consider the following definitions, each of which has advantages and disadvantages:

- *Abnormality as deviation from the average.* To employ this statistically based approach, we simply observe what behaviors are rare or occur infrequently in a specific society or culture and label those deviations from the norm "abnormal."

    The difficulty with this definition is that some statistically rare behaviors clearly do not lend themselves to classification as abnormal. If most people prefer to have cornflakes for breakfast but you prefer raisin bran, this deviation hardly makes your behavior abnormal. Similarly, such a concept of abnormality would unreasonably label a person who has an unusually high IQ as abnormal simply because a high IQ is statistically rare. In short, a definition of abnormality that rests on deviation from the average is insufficient.

- *Abnormality as deviation from the ideal.* An alternative approach considers abnormality in relation to the standard toward which most people are striving—the ideal.

    This sort of definition considers behavior abnormal if it deviates enough from some kind of ideal or cultural standard. However, society has few standards on which people universally agree. (For example, we would be hard pressed to find agreement on whether the New Testament, the Koran, the Talmud, or the Book of Mormon provides the most reasonable

Study Alert

Remember the different definitions of abnormality (deviation from the average, deviation from the ideal, a sense of personal discomfort, inability to function effectively, and abnormality as a legal concept).

Andrea Yates

standards.) Furthermore, standards that do arise change over time and vary across cultures. Thus, the deviation-from-the-ideal approach is also inadequate.

- *Abnormality as a sense of personal discomfort.* A more useful definition concentrates on the psychological consequences of the behavior for the individual. In this approach, behavior is considered abnormal if it produces a sense of personal distress, anxiety, or guilt in an individual—or if it is harmful to others in some way.

  Even a definition that relies on personal discomfort has drawbacks, though, because in some especially severe forms of mental disturbance, people report feeling wonderful even though their behavior seems bizarre to others. In such cases, a personal state of well-being exists, yet most people would consider the behavior abnormal. For example, most of us would think that a woman who says she is hearing uplifting messages from Martians would be displaying abnormal behavior even though she may say that the messages make her feel happy.

- *Abnormality as the inability to function effectively.* Most people are able to feed themselves, hold a job, get along with others, and in general live as productive members of society. Yet there are those who are unable to adjust to the demands of society or function effectively.

  According to this view of abnormality, people who are unable to function effectively and to adapt to the demands of society are considered abnormal. For example, an unemployed, homeless woman living on the street may be considered unable to function effectively. Therefore, her behavior can be viewed as abnormal even if she has chosen to live this way. Her inability to adapt to the requirements of society is what makes her "abnormal," according to this approach.

- *Abnormality as a legal concept.* According to the jury that first heard her case, Andrea Yates, a woman who drowned her five children in a bathtub, was sane. She was sentenced to life in prison for her act.

  Although you might question this view (and a later appeals jury overturned the conviction), the initial verdict reflected the way in which the law defines abnormal behavior. To the judicial system, the distinction between normal and abnormal behavior rests on the definition of insanity, which is a legal but not a psychological term. The definition of insanity varies from one jurisdiction to another. In some states, insanity simply means that defendants cannot understand the difference between right and wrong at the time they commit a criminal act. Other states consider whether defendants are substantially incapable of understanding the criminality of their behavior or unable to control themselves. And in some jurisdictions, pleas of insanity are not allowed at all (Frost & Bonnie, 2001; Sokolove, 2003; Ferguson & Ogloff, 2011).

Clearly, none of the previous definitions is broad enough to cover all instances of abnormal behavior. Consequently, the distinction between normal and abnormal behavior often remains ambiguous even to trained professionals. Furthermore, to a large extent, cultural expectations for "normal" behavior in a particular society influence the understanding of "abnormal behavior" (Scheff, 1998; Sanderson, 2007). Given the difficulties in precisely defining the construct, psychologists typically define **abnormal behavior** broadly as behavior that causes people to experience distress and prevents them from functioning in their daily lives (Nolen-Hoeksema, 2007). Because of the imprecision of this definition, it's best to view abnormal behavior and normal behavior as marking two ends of a continuum rather than as absolute states. Behavior should be evaluated in terms of gradations that range from fully normal functioning to extremely abnormal behavior. Behavior typically falls somewhere between those extremes.

abnormal behavior Behavior that causes people to experience distress and prevents them from functioning in their daily lives.

Perspectives on Abnormality: From Superstition to Science

Throughout much of human history, people linked abnormal behavior to superstition and witchcraft. Individuals who displayed abnormal behavior were accused of being possessed by the devil or some sort of demonic god. Authorities felt justified in "treating" abnormal behavior by attempting to drive out the source of the problem. This typically involved whipping, immersion in hot water, starvation, or other forms of torture in which the cure was often worse than the affliction (Berrios, 1996).

Contemporary approaches take a more enlightened view. Today, six major perspectives are used to understand psychological disorders. These perspectives suggest not only different causes of abnormal behavior but different treatment approaches as well. Furthermore, some perspectives are more applicable to specific disorders than are others. Figure 1 summarizes the perspectives and the way in which they can be applied to the experience of Joe Holt, the person discussed in the chapter prologue.

Study Alert

Use Figure 1 to review the six major perspectives on abnormality and consider how they relate to the major perspectives on the field of psychology that we discussed in Chapter 1.

MEDICAL PERSPECTIVE

When people display the symptoms of tuberculosis, medical professionals can generally find tubercular bacteria in their body tissue. Similarly, the **medical perspective** suggests that when an individual displays symptoms of abnormal behavior, the fundamental cause will be found through a physical examination of the individual, which may reveal a hormonal imbalance, a chemical deficiency, or a brain injury. Indeed, when we speak of mental "illness," "symptoms" of abnormal behavior, and mental "hospitals," we are using terminology associated with the medical perspective.

Because many abnormal behaviors have been linked to biological causes, the medical perspective is a reasonable approach. Yet serious criticisms have been leveled against it. For one thing, many types of abnormal behavior have no apparent biological cause. In addition, some critics have argued that the use of the term *mental*

medical perspective The perspective that suggests that when an individual displays symptoms of abnormal behavior, the root cause will be found in a physical examination of the individual, which may reveal a hormonal imbalance, a chemical deficiency, or a brain injury.

Perspectives on Psychological Disorders		
Perspective	**Description**	**Possible Application of Perspective to Joe's Case**
Medical	Assumes that physiological causes are at the root of psychological disorders	Examine Joe for medical problems, such as brain tumor, chemical imbalance in the brain, or disease
Psychoanalytic	Argues that psychological disorders stem from childhood conflicts	Seek out information about Joe's past, considering possible childhood conflicts
Behavioral	Assumes that abnormal behaviors are learned responses	Concentrate on rewards and punishments for Joe's behavior, and identify environmental stimuli that reinforce his behavior
Cognitive	Assumes that cognitions (people's thoughts and beliefs) are central to psychological disorders	Focus on Joe's perceptions of self and his environment
Humanistic	Emphasizes people's responsibility for their own behavior and the need to self-actualize	Consider Joe's behavior in terms of his choices and efforts to reach his potential
Sociocultural	Assumes that behavior is shaped by family, society, and culture	Focus on how societal demands contributed to Joe's disorder

FIGURE 1 In considering Joe's case discussed in the prologue, we can employ each of the different perspectives on abnormal behavior. Note, however, that because of the nature of his psychological disorder, some of the perspectives are more applicable than others.

illness implies that people who display abnormal behavior have no responsibility for or control over their actions (Laing & Szasz, 2004; Szasz, 1994, 2006).

Still, recent advances in our understanding of the biological bases of behavior underscore the importance of considering physiological factors in abnormal behavior. For instance, some of the more severe forms of psychological disturbance, such as major depression and schizophrenia, are influenced by genetic factors and malfunctions in neurotransmitter signals (Iversen & Iversen, 2007; Howes & Kapur, 2009; Li et al., 2011).

PSYCHOANALYTIC PERSPECTIVE

Whereas the medical perspective suggests that biological causes are at the root of abnormal behavior, the **psychoanalytic perspective** holds that abnormal behavior stems from childhood conflicts over opposing wishes regarding sex and aggression. According to Freud, children pass through a series of stages in which sexual and aggressive impulses take different forms and produce conflicts that require resolution. If these childhood conflicts are not dealt with successfully, they remain unresolved in the unconscious and eventually bring about abnormal behavior during adulthood.

To uncover the roots of people's disordered behavior, the psychoanalytic perspective scrutinizes their early life history. However, because there is no conclusive way to link people's childhood experiences with the abnormal behaviors they display as adults, we can never be sure that the causes suggested by psychoanalytic theory are accurate. Moreover, psychoanalytic theory paints a picture of people as having relatively little control over their behavior because much of it is guided by unconscious impulses. In the eyes of some critics, this perspective suggests that people have little responsibility for their own behavior.

On the other hand, the contributions of psychoanalytic theory have been significant. More than any other approach to abnormal behavior, this perspective highlights the fact that people can have a rich, involved inner life and that prior experiences can have a profound effect on current psychological functioning (Elliott, 2002; Bornstein, 2003; Rangell, 2007).

BEHAVIORAL PERSPECTIVE

Both the medical and psychoanalytic perspectives look at abnormal behaviors as *symptoms* of an underlying problem. In contrast, the **behavioral perspective** views the behavior itself as the problem. Using the basic principles of learning, behavioral theorists see both normal and abnormal behaviors as responses to various stimuli—responses that have been learned through past experience and are guided in the present by stimuli in the individual's environment. To explain why abnormal behavior occurs, we must analyze how an individual has learned it and observe the circumstances in which it is displayed.

The emphasis on observable behavior represents both the greatest strength and the greatest weakness of the behavioral approach to abnormal behavior. This perspective provides the most precise and objective approach for examining behavioral symptoms of specific disorders, such as attention-deficit hyperactivity disorder (ADHD), which we will discuss in a later module. At the same time, though, critics charge that the perspective ignores the rich inner world of thoughts, attitudes, and emotions that may contribute to abnormal behavior.

COGNITIVE PERSPECTIVE

The medical, psychoanalytic, and behavioral perspectives view people's behavior as the result of factors largely beyond their control. To many critics of these views, however, people's thoughts cannot be ignored.

In response to such concerns, some psychologists employ a **cognitive perspective.** Rather than considering only external behavior, as in traditional behavioral approaches, the cognitive approach assumes that *cognitions* (people's thoughts and beliefs) are central to a person's abnormal behavior. A primary goal of treatment using the cognitive perspective is to explicitly teach new, more adaptive ways of thinking.

For instance, suppose that you develop the erroneous belief that "doing well on this exam is crucial to my entire future" whenever you take an exam. Through therapy, you might learn to hold the more realistic and less anxiety-producing thought, "my entire future is not dependent on this one exam." By changing cognitions in this way, psychologists working within a cognitive framework help people free themselves from thoughts and behaviors that are potentially maladaptive (Clark, 2004; Everly & Lating, 2007).

The cognitive perspective is not without critics. For example, it is possible that maladaptive cognitions are the symptoms or consequences of disorders rather than their cause. Furthermore, there are circumstances in which negative beliefs may not be irrational at all but simply reflect accurately the unpleasant circumstances in people's lives. Still, cognitive theorists would argue that one can find a more adaptive way of framing beliefs even in the most negative circumstances.

> **cognitive perspective** The perspective that suggests that people's thoughts and beliefs are a central component of abnormal behavior.

HUMANISTIC PERSPECTIVE

Psychologists who subscribe to the **humanistic perspective** emphasize the responsibility people have for their own behavior even when their behavior is considered abnormal. The humanistic perspective—growing out of the work of Carl Rogers and Abraham Maslow—concentrates on what is uniquely human—that is, it views people as basically rational, oriented toward a social world, and motivated to seek self-actualization (Rogers, 1995).

Humanistic approaches focus on the relationship of the individual to society; it considers the ways in which people view themselves in relation to others and see their place in the world. The humanistic perspective views people as having an awareness of life and of themselves that leads them to search for meaning and self-worth. Rather than assuming that individuals require a "cure," the humanistic perspective suggests that they can, by and large, set their own limits of what is acceptable behavior. As long as they are not hurting others and do not feel personal distress, people should be free to choose the behaviors in which they engage.

Although the humanistic perspective has been criticized for its reliance on unscientific, unverifiable information and its vague, almost philosophical formulations, it offers a distinctive view of abnormal behavior. It stresses the unique aspects of being human and provides a number of important suggestions for helping those with psychological problems.

> **humanistic perspective** The perspective that emphasizes the responsibility people have for their own behavior, even when such behavior is abnormal.

SOCIOCULTURAL PERSPECTIVE

The **sociocultural perspective** assumes that people's behavior—both normal and abnormal—is shaped by the society and culture in which they live. According to this view, societal and cultural factors such as poverty and prejudice may be at the root of abnormal behavior. Specifically, the kinds of stresses and conflicts people experience in their daily lives can promote and maintain abnormal behavior.

This perspective is supported by research showing that some kinds of abnormal behavior are far more prevalent among certain social classes than they are in others. For instance, diagnoses of schizophrenia tend to be higher among members of lower socioeconomic groups than among members of more affluent groups. Proportionally more African-American individuals are hospitalized involuntarily for psychological disorders than are whites. Furthermore, poor economic times seem to be linked to general declines in psychological functioning, and social problems such as

> **sociocultural perspective** The perspective that people's behavior—both normal and abnormal—is shaped by the society and culture in which they live.

homelessness are associated with psychological disorders (Nasir & Hand, 2006; Greenberg & Rosenheck, 2008; Padgett, Stanhope, & Henwood, 2011).

On the other hand, alternative explanations abound for the association between abnormal behavior and social factors. For example, people from lower socioeconomic levels may be less likely than those from higher levels to seek help, gradually reaching a point where their symptoms become severe and warrant a serious diagnosis. Furthermore, sociocultural explanations provide relatively little specific guidance for the treatment of individuals showing mental disturbance because the focus is on broader societal factors (Paniagua, 2000).

Classifying Abnormal Behavior: The ABCs of *DSM*

Crazy. Whacked. Mental. Loony. Insane. Neurotic. Psycho. Strange. Demented. Odd. Possessed.

Society has long placed labels on people who display abnormal behavior. Unfortunately, most of the time these labels have reflected intolerance and have been used with little thought as to what each label signifies.

Providing appropriate and specific names and classifications for abnormal behavior has presented a major challenge to psychologists. It is not hard to understand why, given the difficulties discussed earlier in simply distinguishing normal from abnormal behavior. Yet psychologists and other careproviders need to classify abnormal behavior in order to diagnose it and ultimately treat it.

DSM: DETERMINING DIAGNOSTIC DISTINCTIONS

Diagnostic and Statistical Manual of Mental Disorders, Fourth Edition, Text Revision (*DSM-IV-TR*) and DSM-5 A system, devised by the American Psychiatric Association, used by most professionals to diagnose and classify abnormal behavior.

Over the years, mental health professionals have developed many different classification systems that vary in terms of their utility and the degree to which they have been accepted. However, one standard system, devised by the American Psychiatric Association, has emerged in the United States. Most professionals today use this classification system, known as the *Diagnostic and Statistical Manual of Mental Disorders,* **Fourth Edition, Text Revision (*DSM-IV-TR*)** and the upcoming **DSM-5** to diagnose and classify abnormal behavior.

DSM presents comprehensive and relatively precise definitions for more than 200 disorders divided into 17 major categories. It also includes five types of information, known as axes, which have to be considered in assessing a patient:

- **Axis I: Clinical Disorders.** Disorders that produce distress and impair functioning.
- **Axis II: Personality Disorders and Mental Retardation.** Enduring, rigid behavior patterns.
- **Axis III: General Medical Conditions.** Physical disorders that may be related to psychological disorders.
- **Axis IV: Psychosocial and Environmental Problems.** Problems in a person's life such as stressors or life events that may affect the diagnosis, treatment, and outcome of psychological disorders.
- **Axis V: Global Assessment of Functioning.** Overall level of mental, social, occupational, and leisure functioning.

By following the criteria presented in the *DSM* classification system, diagnosticians can identify the specific problem an individual is experiencing. (Figure 2 provides a brief outline of the major diagnostic categories.)

Categories of Disorders	Examples
Anxiety (problems in which anxiety impedes daily functioning)	Generalized anxiety disorder, panic disorder, phobic disorder, obsessive-compulsive disorder, posttraumatic stress disorder
Somatoform (psychological difficulties displayed through physical problems)	Hypochondriasis, conversion disorder
Dissociative (the splitting apart of crucial parts of personality that are usually integrated)	Dissociative identity disorder (multiple personality), dissociative amnesia, dissociative fugue
Mood (emotions of depression or euphoria that are so strong they intrude on everyday living)	Major depression, bipolar disorder
Schizophrenia and psychotic disorders (declines in functioning, thought and language disturbances, perception disorders, emotional disturbances, and withdrawal from others)	Disorganized, paranoid, catatonic, undifferentiated, residual
Personality (problems that create little personal distress but that lead to an inability to function as a normal member of society)	Antisocial (sociopathic) personality disorder, narcissistic personality disorder
Sexual (problems related to sexual arousal from unusual objects or problems related to functioning)	Paraphilia, sexual dysfunction
Substance-related (problems related to drug dependence and abuse)	Alcohol, cocaine, hallucinogens, marijuana
Dementia, amnesia, and other cognitive disorders	Alzheimer's

FIGURE 2 This list of disorders represents the major categories from the *DSM-IV-TR*. It is only a partial list of the more than 200 disorders included there.

DSM is primarily descriptive and avoids suggesting an underlying cause for an individual's behavior and problems. For instance, the term *neurotic*—a label that is commonly used by people in their everyday descriptions of abnormal behavior— is not listed as a *DSM* category. Because the term *neurosis* refers to problems associated with a specific cause based in Freud's theory of personality, it is not included in *DSM*.

DSM has the advantage, then, of providing a descriptive system that does not specify the cause of or reason for a problem. Rather, it paints a picture of the behavior that is being displayed. Why should this approach be important? For one thing, it allows communication between mental health professionals of diverse backgrounds and theoretical approaches. In addition, precise classification enables researchers to explore the causes of a problem. Without reliable descriptions of abnormal behavior, researchers would be hard pressed to find ways to investigate the disorder. Finally, *DSM* provides a kind of conceptual shorthand through which professionals can describe the behaviors that tend to occur together in an individual (Widiger & Clark, 2000; First, Frances, & Pincus, 2002; Gordon & Heimberg, 2011).

CONNING THE CLASSIFIERS: THE SHORTCOMINGS OF *DSM-IV-TR*

When clinical psychologist David Rosenhan and eight colleagues sought admission to separate mental hospitals across the United States in the 1970s, each stated that he or she was hearing voices—"unclear voices" that said "empty," "hollow," and "thud"—and each was immediately admitted to the hospital. However, the truth was that they actually were conducting a study, and none of them was really hearing voices. Aside from these misrepresentations, *everything* else they did and said represented their true behavior, including the responses they gave during extensive admission interviews and their answers to the battery of tests they were asked to complete. In fact, as soon as they were admitted, they said they no longer heard any voices. In short, each of the pseudo-patients acted in a "normal" way (Rosenhan, 1973).

We might assume that Rosenhan and his colleagues would have been quickly discovered as the impostors they were, but this was not the case. Instead, each of them was diagnosed as severely abnormal on the basis of observed behavior. Mental health professionals labeled most as suffering from schizophrenia and kept them in the hospital 3–52 days, with the average stay of 19 days. Even when they were discharged, most of the "patients" left with the label *schizophrenia—in remission*, implying that the abnormal behavior had only temporarily subsided and could recur at any time. Most disturbing, no one on the hospital staff identified any of the pseudo-patients as impostors—although some of the actual patients figured out the ruse.

The results of Rosenhan's classic study illustrate that placing labels on individuals powerfully influences the way mental health workers perceive and interpret their actions. It also points out that determining who is psychologically disordered is not always a clear-cut or accurate process.

Although *DSM* was developed to provide more accurate and consistent diagnoses of psychological disorders, it has not been entirely successful. For instance, critics charge that it relies too much on the medical perspective. Because it was drawn up by psychiatrists—who are physicians—some condemn it for viewing psychological disorders primarily in terms of the symptoms of an underlying physiological disorder. It also does not fully take into account the advances in behavioral neuroscience that have identified the genetic underpinnings of some psychological disorders. Moreover, critics suggest that *DSM* compartmentalizes people into inflexible, all-or-none categories rather than considering the degree to which a person displays psychologically disordered behavior (Schmidt, Kotov, & Joiner, 2004; Samuel & Widiger, 2006).

Other concerns with *DSM* are more subtle but equally important. For instance, some critics argue that labeling an individual as abnormal provides a dehumanizing, lifelong stigma. (Think, for example, of political contenders whose candidacies have been terminated by the disclosure that they received treatment for severe psychological disorders.) Furthermore, after an initial diagnosis has been made, mental health professionals, who may concentrate on the initial diagnostic category, could overlook other diagnostic possibilities (Quinn, Kahng, & Crocker, 2004; Szasz, 1994; McNally, 2011).

Still, despite the drawbacks inherent in any labeling system, *DSM* has had an important influence on the way in which mental health professionals view psychological disorders. It has increased both the reliability and the validity of diagnostic categorization. In addition, it offers a logical way to organize examination of the major types of mental disturbance.

Study Alert

It is important to understand the advantages and weaknesses of the *DSM* classification system.

RECAP/EVALUATE/RETHINK

RECAP

LO 37-1 How can we distinguish normal from abnormal behavior?

- Definitions of abnormality include deviation from the average, deviation from the ideal, a sense of personal discomfort, the inability to function effectively, and legal conceptions. (pp. 453, 454)
- Although no single definition is adequate, abnormal behavior can be considered to be behavior that causes people to experience distress and prevents them from functioning in their daily lives. Most psychologists believe that abnormal and normal behavior should be considered in terms of a continuum. (p. 454)

LO 37-2 What are the major perspectives on psychological disorders used by mental health professionals?

- The medical perspective views abnormality as a symptom of an underlying disease. (p. 455)
- Psychoanalytic perspectives suggest that abnormal behavior stems from childhood conflicts in the unconscious. (p. 456)
- Behavioral approaches view abnormal behavior not as a symptom of an underlying problem but as the problem itself. (p. 456)
- The cognitive approach suggests that abnormal behavior is the result of faulty cognitions (thoughts and beliefs). In this view, abnormal behavior can be remedied by changing one's flawed thoughts and beliefs. (p. 456)
- Humanistic approaches emphasize the responsibility people have for their own behavior even when such behavior is seen as abnormal. (p. 457)
- Sociocultural approaches view abnormal behavior in terms of difficulties arising from family and other social relationships. (p. 457)

LO 37-3 What are the major categories of psychological disorders?

- The most widely used system for classifying psychological disorders is *DSM-IV-TR—Diagnostic and Statistical Manual of Mental Disorders*, Fourth Edition, Text Revision, and the most recent revision, DSM-5. (p. 458)

EVALUATE

1. One problem in defining abnormal behavior is that
   a. Statistically rare behavior may not be abnormal.
   b. Not all abnormalities are accompanied by feelings of discomfort.
   c. Cultural standards are too general to use as a measuring tool.
   d. All of the above.
2. If abnormality is defined as behavior that causes personal discomfort or harms others, which of the following people is most likely to need treatment?
   a. An executive is afraid to accept a promotion because it would require moving from his ground-floor office to the top floor of a tall office building.
   b. A woman decides to quit her job and chooses to live on the street in order to live a "simpler life."
   c. A man believes that friendly spacemen visit his house every Thursday.
   d. A photographer lives with 19 cats in a small apartment lovingly caring for them.
3. Virginia's mother thinks that her daughter's behavior is clearly abnormal because, despite being offered admission to medical school, Virginia decides to become a waitress. What approach is Virginia's mother using to define abnormal behavior?
4. Which of the following is a strong argument against the medical perspective on abnormality?
   a. Physiological abnormalities are almost always impossible to identify.
   b. There is no conclusive way to link past experience and behavior.
   c. The medical perspective rests too heavily on the effects of nutrition.
   d. Assigning behavior to a physical problem takes responsibility away from the individual for changing his or her behavior.
5. Cheryl is painfully shy. According to the behavioral perspective, the best way to deal with her "abnormal" behavior is to
   a. Treat the underlying physical problem.
   b. Use the principles of learning theory to modify her shy behavior.
   c. Express a great deal of caring.
   d. Uncover her negative past experiences through hypnosis.

RETHINK

1. Do you agree or disagree that *DSM* should be updated every several years? Why? What makes abnormal behavior so variable?

2. *From the perspective of an employer:* Imagine that a well-paid employee was arrested for shoplifting a sweater that costs $15. What sort of explanation for this behavior would the proponents of *each* perspective on abnormality provide:

the medical perspective, the psychoanalytic perspective, the behavioral perspective, the cognitive perspective, the humanistic perspective, and the sociocultural perspective? Based on the potential causes of the shoplifting, would you fire the employee? Why or why not?

Answers to Evaluate Questions

1. d; 2. a; 3. deviation from the ideal; 4. d; 5. b

KEY TERMS

abnormal behavior p. 454
medical perspective p. 455
psychoanalytic perspective p. 456
behavioral perspective p. 456

cognitive perspective p. 457
humanistic perspective p. 457
sociocultural perspective p. 457

Diagnostic and Statistical Manual of Mental Disorders, Fourth Edition, Text Revision *(DSM-IV-TR)* and DSM-5 p. 458

The Major Psychological Disorders

Sally experienced her first panic attack out of the blue, 3 weeks after completing her senior year in college. She had just finished a job interview and was meeting some friends for dinner. In the restaurant, she began to feel dizzy. Within a few seconds, her heart was pounding, and she was feeling breathless, as though she might pass out. Her friends noticed that she did not look well and offered to drive her home. Sally suggested they stop at the hospital emergency room instead. Although she felt better by the time they arrived at the hospital, and tests indicated nothing wrong, Sally experienced a similar episode a week later while at a movie. . . .

Her attacks became more and more frequent. Before long, she was having several attacks per week. In addition, she constantly worried about having attacks. She began to avoid exercise and other activities that produced physical sensations. She also noticed the attacks were worse when she was alone. She began to avoid driving, shopping in large stores, and eating in all restaurants. Some weeks she avoided leaving the house completely. (Antony, Brown, & Barlow, 1992, p. 79)

Sally suffered from panic disorder, one of the specific psychological disorders we'll consider in this module. Keep in mind that although we'll be discussing these disorders objectively, each represents a very human set of difficulties that influence and in some cases considerably disrupt people's lives.

Learning Outcome

LO 38-1 What are the major psychological disorders?

Anxiety Disorders

All of us at one time or another experience *anxiety,* a feeling of apprehension or tension, in reaction to stressful situations. There is nothing "wrong" with such anxiety. It is a normal reaction to stress that often helps rather than hinders our daily functioning. Without some anxiety, for instance, most of us probably would not have much motivation to study hard, undergo physical exams, or spend long hours at our jobs.

But some people experience anxiety in situations in which there is no apparent reason or cause for such distress. **Anxiety disorders** occur when anxiety arises without external justification and begins to affect people's daily functioning. We'll discuss the four major types of anxiety disorders: phobic disorder, panic disorder, generalized anxiety disorder, and obsessive-compulsive disorder.

anxiety disorder The occurrence of anxiety without an obvious external cause that affects daily functioning.

PHOBIC DISORDER

It's not easy moving through the world when you're terrified of electricity. "Donna," 45, a writer, knows that better than most. Get her in the vicinity of an appliance or a light switch or—all but unthinkable—a thunderstorm, and she is overcome by a terror so blinding she can think of nothing but fleeing. That, of course, is not always possible, so over time, Donna has come up with other answers. When she opens the refrigerator door, rubber-sole shoes are a must. If a light bulb blows, she will tolerate the dark until someone else changes it for her. Clothes shopping is done only when necessary, lest static on garments send her running from the store. And swimming at night is absolutely out of the question, lest underwater lights electrocute her. (Kluger, 2001, p. 51)

Phobic Disorder	Description	Example
Agoraphobia	Fear of places, such as unfamiliar or crowded spaces, where help might not be available in case of emergency	Person becomes housebound because any place other than the person's home arouses extreme anxiety symptoms.
Specific phobias	Fear of specific objects, places, or situations	
Animal type	Specific animals or insects	Person has extreme fear of dogs, cats, or spiders.
Natural environment type	Events or situations in the natural environment	Person has extreme fear of storms, heights, or water.
Situational type	Public transportation, tunnels, bridges, elevators, flying, driving	Person becomes extremely claustrophobic in elevators.
Blood injection-injury type	Blood, injury, injections	Person panics when viewing a child's scraped knee.
Social phobia	Fear of being judged or embarrassed by others	Person avoids all social situations and becomes a recluse for fear of encountering others' judgment.

FIGURE 1 Phobic disorders differ from generalized anxiety and panic disorders because a specific stimulus can be identified. Listed here are a number of types of phobias and their triggers. (Source: Adapted from Nolen-Hoeksema, 2007.)

phobias Intense, irrational fears of specific objects or situations.

Donna suffers from a **phobia,** an intense, irrational fear of a specific object or situation. For example, claustrophobia is a fear of enclosed places, acrophobia is a fear of high places, xenophobia is a fear of strangers, social phobia is the fear of being judged or embarrassed by others, and—as in Donna's case—electrophobia is a fear of electricity.

The objective danger posed by an anxiety-producing stimulus (which can be just about anything, as you can see in Figure 1) is typically small or nonexistent. However, to someone suffering from the phobia, the danger is great, and a full-blown panic attack may follow exposure to the stimulus. Phobic disorders differ from generalized anxiety disorders and panic disorders in that there is a specific, identifiable stimulus that sets off the anxiety reaction.

Phobias may have only a minor impact on people's lives if those who suffer from them can avoid the stimuli that trigger fear. For example, a fear of heights may have little impact on people's everyday lives (although it may prevent them from living in a high floor in an apartment)—unless they are firefighters or window-washers. On the other hand, a *social phobia,* or a fear of strangers, presents a more serious problem. In one extreme case, a Washington woman left her home just three times in 30 years—once to visit her family, once for an operation, and once to purchase ice cream for a dying companion (Kimbrel, 2007; Wong, Sarver, & Beidel, 2011).

PANIC DISORDER

panic disorder Anxiety disorder that takes the form of panic attacks lasting from a few seconds to several hours.

In another type of anxiety disorder, **panic disorder,** *panic attacks* occur that last from a few seconds to several hours. Unlike phobias, which are stimulated by specific objects or situations, panic disorders do not have any identifiable stimuli. Instead, during an attack such as those Sally experienced in the case described earlier, anxiety suddenly—and often without warning—rises to a peak, and an individual feels a sense of impending, unavoidable doom. Although the physical symptoms differ from person to person, they may include heart palpitations, shortness of breath, unusual amounts of sweating, faintness and dizziness, gastric sensations, and sometimes a sense of imminent death. After such an attack, it is no wonder that people tend to feel exhausted (Rachman & deSilva, 2004; Laederach-Hofmann & Messerli-Buergy, 2007; Montgomery, 2011).

Panic attacks seemingly come out of nowhere and are unconnected to any specific stimulus. Because they don't know what triggers their feelings of panic, victims of panic attacks may become fearful of going places. In fact, some people with panic disorder develop a complication called *agoraphobia*, the fear of being in a situation in which escape is difficult and in which help for a possible panic attack would not be available. In extreme cases, people with agoraphobia never leave their homes (Herrán, Carrera, & Sierra-Biddle, 2006; Wittchen et al., 2008; McTeague et al., 2011).

Acrophobia, the fear of heights, is not an uncommon phobia. What sort of behavior-modification approaches might be used to deal with acrophobia?

In addition to the physical symptoms, panic disorder affects how the brain processes information. For instance, people with panic disorder have reduced reactions in the anterior cingulate cortex to stimuli (such as viewing a fearful face) that normally produce a strong reaction in those without the disorder. It may be that recurring high levels of emotional arousal that patients with panic disorder experience desensitizes them to emotional stimuli (Pillay et al., 2006; Pillay et al., 2007).

GENERALIZED ANXIETY DISORDER

People with **generalized anxiety disorder** experience long-term, persistent anxiety and uncontrollable worry. Sometimes their concerns are about identifiable issues involving family, money, work, or health. In other cases, though, people with the disorder feel that something dreadful is about to happen but can't identify the reason and thus experience "free-floating" anxiety.

generalized anxiety disorder The experience of long-term, persistent anxiety and worry.

Because of persistent anxiety, people with generalized anxiety disorder cannot concentrate or set their worry and fears aside; their lives become centered on their worry. Furthermore, their anxiety is often accompanied by physiological symptoms such as muscle tension, headaches, dizziness, heart palpitations, or insomnia (Starcevic et al., 2007). Figure 2 on page 466 shows the most common symptoms of generalized anxiety disorder.

OBSESSIVE-COMPULSIVE DISORDER

In **obsessive-compulsive disorder (OCD)**, people are plagued by unwanted thoughts, called obsessions, or feel that they must carry out behaviors, termed compulsions, which they feel driven to perform.

obsessive-compulsive disorder (OCD) A disorder characterized by obsessions or compulsions.

An **obsession** is a persistent, unwanted thought or idea that keeps recurring. For example, a student may be unable to stop thinking that she has neglected to put her name on a test and may think about it constantly for the 2 weeks it takes to get the paper back. A man may go on vacation and wonder the whole time whether he locked his house. A woman may hear the same tune running through her head over and over. In each case, the thought or idea is unwanted and difficult to put out of mind. Of course, many people suffer from mild obsessions from time to time, but usually such thoughts persist only for a short period. For people with serious obsessions, however, the thoughts persist for days or months and may consist of bizarre, troubling images (Lee et al., 2005; Rassin & Muris, 2007; Wenzel, 2011).

obsession A persistent, unwanted thought or idea that keeps recurring.

As part of an obsessive-compulsive disorder, people may also experience **compulsions**, irresistible urges to repeatedly carry out some act that seems strange and unreasonable even to them. Whatever the compulsive behavior is, people experience extreme

compulsion An irresistible urge to repeatedly carry out some act that seems strange and unreasonable.

FIGURE 2 Frequency of symptoms in cases of generalized anxiety disorder. (Source: Adapted from Beck & Emery, 1985, pp. 87–88.)

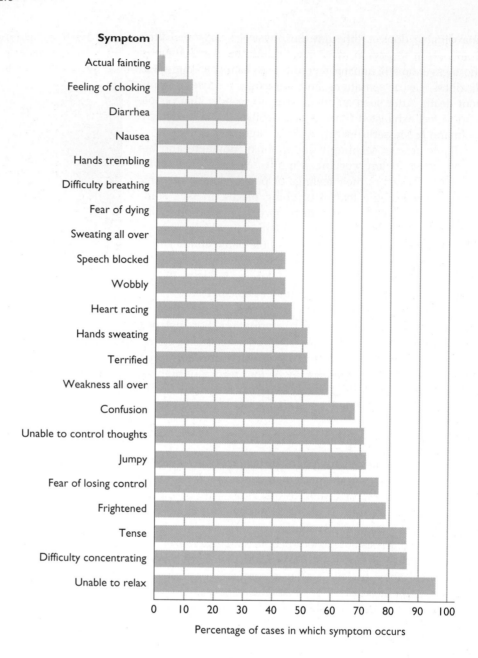

anxiety if they cannot carry it out even if it is something they want to stop. The acts may be relatively trivial, such as repeatedly checking the stove to make sure all the burners are turned off, or more unusual, such as washing one's hands so much that they bleed (Frost & Steketee, 2002; Clark, 2007; Moretz & McKay, 2009).

For example, consider this passage from the autobiography of a person with obsessive-compulsive disorder:

I thought my parents would die if I didn't do everything in exactly the right way. When I took my glasses off at night I'd have to place them on the dresser at a particular angle. Sometimes I'd turn on the light and get out of bed seven times until I felt comfortable with the angle. If the angle wasn't right, I felt that my parents would die. The feeling ate up my insides.

If I didn't grab the molding on the wall just the right way as I entered or exited my room; if I didn't hang a shirt in the closet perfectly; if I didn't read a paragraph a certain way; if my hands and nails weren't perfectly clean, I thought my incorrect behavior would kill my parents. (Summers, 2000, p. 42)

Although carrying out compulsive rituals may lead to some immediate reduction of anxiety, in the long run the anxiety returns. In fact, people with severe cases lead lives filled with unrelenting tension (Goodman, Rudorfer, & Maser, 2000; Penzel, 2000; Dittrich, Johansen, & Fineberg, 2011).

THE CAUSES OF ANXIETY DISORDERS

We've considered the four major types of anxiety disorders, but there are others as well. For instance, *posttraumatic stress disorder* (in which a person re-experiences a stressful event in vivid flashbacks or dreams and which we discussed when we considered stress) is classified as an anxiety disorder.

The variety of anxiety disorders means that no single explanation fits all cases. Genetic factors clearly are part of the picture. For example, if one member of a pair of identical twins has panic disorder, there is a 30% chance that the other twin will have it also. Furthermore, a person's characteristic level of anxiety is related to a specific gene involved in the production of the neurotransmitter serotonin. This is consistent with findings indicating that certain chemical deficiencies in the brain appear to produce some kinds of anxiety disorder (Holmes et al., 2003; Beidel & Turner, 2007; Chamberlain et al., 2008).

Some researchers believe that an overactive autonomic nervous system may be at the root of panic attacks. Specifically, they suggest that poor regulation of the brain's locus ceruleus may lead to panic attacks, which cause the limbic system to become overstimulated. In turn, the overstimulated limbic system produces chronic anxiety, which ultimately leads the locus ceruleus to generate still more panic attacks (Pine et al., 2000; Balaban, 2002; Davies et al., 2008).

There are also biological causes at work in OCD. For example, researchers have found differences in the brains of those with the disorder compared to those without it (see Figure 3 *Neuroscience in Your Life;* Christian et al., 2008).

PsychTech

Although some people seem to use the Internet compulsively, psychologists have yet to agree on whether it represents a true psychological disorder.

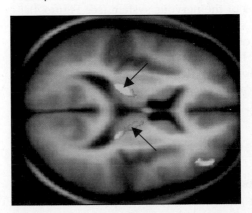

"Spin your partner round and round, then spin your partner round again, spin her round six more times, now touch the light switch near the door."

© Joe Dator/The New Yorker Collection/www.cartoonbank.com

Neuroscience in Your Life: One Step Closer to Understanding OCD

FIGURE 3 People with obsessive-compulsive disorder (OCD) have structural differences in their brains. These images show increased levels of gray matter (i.e., more connections or more neurons) in the thalamus (a) and in the left frontal cortex (b) in people with OCD as compared to people without it. These findings help us to understand the potential causes of OCD and may lead to the development of better treatments for the disorder. (Source: Christian et al., 2008, Figure 1.)

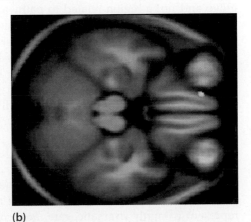

(a)   (b)

Psychologists who employ the behavioral perspective have taken a different approach that emphasizes environmental factors. They consider anxiety to be a learned response to stress. For instance, suppose a dog bites a young girl. When the girl next sees a dog, she is frightened and runs away—a behavior that relieves her anxiety and thereby reinforces her avoidance behavior. After repeated encounters with dogs in which she is reinforced for her avoidance behavior, she may develop a full-fledged phobia regarding dogs.

Finally, the cognitive perspective suggests that anxiety disorders grow out of inappropriate and inaccurate thoughts and beliefs about circumstances in a person's world. For example, people with anxiety disorders may view a friendly puppy as a ferocious and savage pit bull, or they may see an air disaster looming every moment they are in the vicinity of an airplane. According to the cognitive perspective, people's maladaptive thoughts about the world are at the root of an anxiety disorder (Frost & Steketee, 2002; Wang & Clark, 2002; Ouimet, Gawronski, & Dozois, 2009).

Somatoform Disorders

somatoform disorders Psychological difficulties that take on a physical (somatic) form, but for which there is no medical cause.

Somatoform disorders are psychological difficulties that take on a physical (somatic) form but for which there is no medical cause. Even though an individual with a somatoform disorder reports physical symptoms, no biological cause exists, or if there is a medical problem, the person's reaction is greatly exaggerated.

hypochondriasis A disorder in which people have a constant fear of illness and a preoccupation with their health.

One type of somatoform disorder is **hypochondriasis** in which people have a constant fear of illness and a preoccupation with their health. These individuals believe that everyday aches and pains are symptoms of a dread disease. The "symptoms" are not faked; rather, they are misinterpreted as evidence of some serious illness—often in the face of inarguable medical evidence to the contrary (Abramowitz, Olatunji, & Deacon, 2007; Olatunji, 2008; Weck et al., 2011).

conversion disorder A major somatoform disorder that involves an actual physical disturbance, such as the inability to use a sensory organ or the complete or partial inability to move an arm or leg.

Another somatoform disorder is conversion disorder. Unlike hypochondriasis, in which there is no physical problem, **conversion disorders** involve an actual physical disturbance, such as the inability to see or hear or to move an arm or leg. The *cause* of such a physical disturbance is purely psychological; there is no biological reason for the problem. Some of Freud's classic cases involved conversion disorders. For instance, one of Freud's patients suddenly became unable to use her arm without any apparent physiological cause. Later, just as abruptly, the problem disappeared.

Conversion disorders often begin suddenly. Previously normal people wake up one day blind or deaf, or they experience numbness that is restricted to a certain part of the body. A hand, for example, may become entirely numb, while an area above the wrist, controlled by the same nerves, remains sensitive to touch—something that is physiologically implausible. Mental health professionals refer to such a condition as "glove anesthesia" because the numb area is the part of the hand covered by a glove and not a region related to pathways of the nervous system (see Figure 4).

Surprisingly, people who experience conversion disorders frequently remain unconcerned about symptoms that most of us would expect to be highly anxiety producing. For instance, a person in good health who wakes up blind may react in a bland, matter-of-fact way. Considering how most of us would feel if we woke up unable to see, this unemotional reaction (called *la belle indifference*, a French phrase meaning "a beautiful indifference") hardly seems appropriate (Brasic, 2002).

Dissociative Disorders

dissociative disorders Psychological dysfunctions characterized by the separation of different facets of a person's personality that are normally integrated.

The classic movie *The Three Faces of Eve* (about a woman with three wildly different personalities) and the book *Sybil* (about a girl who allegedly had 16 personalities) represent a highly dramatic, rare, and controversial class of disorders: dissociative disorders. **Dissociative disorders** are characterized by the separation (or dissociation)

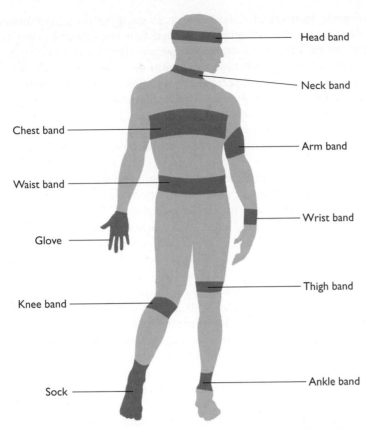

Head band

Neck band

Chest band

Arm band

Waist band

Wrist band

Glove

Thigh band

Knee band

Sock

Ankle band

FIGURE 4 Conversion disorders sometimes produce numbness in specific and isolated areas of the body (indicated by the shaded areas in the figure). For instance, in glove anesthesia, the area of the body covered by a glove feels numb. However, the condition is biologically implausible because of the nerves involved, which suggests that the problem results from a psychological disorder rather than from actual nerve damage.

of different facets of a person's personality that are normally integrated and work together. By dissociating key parts of who they are, people are able to keep disturbing memories or perceptions from reaching conscious awareness and thereby reduce their anxiety (Maldonado & Spiegel, 2003; Houghtalen & Talbot, 2007).

Several dissociative disorders exist, although all of them are rare. A person with a **dissociative identity disorder (DID)** (once called *multiple personality disorder*) displays characteristics of two or more distinct personalities, identities, or personality fragments. Individual personalities often have a unique set of likes and dislikes and their own reactions to situations. Some people with multiple personalities even carry several pairs of glasses because their vision changes with each personality. Moreover, each individual personality can be well adjusted when considered on its own (Ellason & Ross, 2004; Stickley & Nickeas, 2006; Howell, 2011).

The diagnosis of dissociative identity disorder is controversial. It was rarely diagnosed before 1980, when it was added as a category in the third edition of *DSM* for the first time. At that point, the number of cases increased significantly. Some clinicians suggest the increase was due to more precise identification of the disorder, while others suggest the increase was due to an overreadiness to use the classification. In addition, widespread publicity about cases of DID may have influenced patients to report symptoms of more common personality disorders in ways that made it more likely they would receive a diagnosis of DID. There are also significant cross-cultural differences in the incidence of DID (Kihlstrom, 2005a; Xiao et al., 2006).

Dissociative amnesia is another dissociative disorder in which a significant, selective memory loss occurs. Dissociative amnesia is unlike simple amnesia, which involves an actual loss of information from memory and typically results from a physiological

dissociative identity disorder (DID) A disorder in which a person displays characteristics of two or more distinct personalities.

dissociative amnesia A disorder in which a significant, selective memory loss occurs.

cause. In contrast, in cases of dissociative amnesia, the "forgotten" material is still present in memory—it simply cannot be recalled. The term *repressed memories* is sometimes used to describe the lost memories of people with dissociative amnesia.

In the most severe form of dissociative amnesia, individuals cannot recall their names, are unable to recognize parents and other relatives, and do not know their addresses. In other respects, though, they may appear quite normal. Apart from an inability to remember certain facts about themselves, they may be able to recall skills and abilities that they developed earlier. For instance, even though a chef may not remember where he grew up and received training, he may still be able to prepare gourmet meals.

In some cases of dissociative amnesia, the memory loss is profound. For example, in one dramatic case, Raymond Power Jr., an attorney, husband, father of two, and Boy Scout leader, left home to go to work one morning. Two days later he was homeless, living a new life a thousand miles away, and had no memory of who he was or how he got there. He was found 6 months later but still had no recollection of his previous life, including any knowledge of his wife of 30 years or even that he had children (Foderaro, 2006).

dissociative fugue A form of amnesia in which the individual leaves home and sometimes assumes a new identity.

A more unusual form of amnesia is a condition known as **dissociative fugue.** In this state, people take sudden, impulsive trips and sometimes assume a new identity. After a period of time—days, months, or sometimes even years—they suddenly realize that they are in a strange place and completely forget the time they have spent wandering. Their last memories are those from the time just before they entered the fugue state (Hennig-Fast et al., 2008).

The common thread among dissociative disorders is that they allow people to escape from some anxiety-producing situation. Either the person produces a new personality to deal with stress, or the individual forgets or leaves behind the situation that caused the stress as he or she journeys to some new—and perhaps less anxiety-ridden—environment (Putnam, 2000; R. J. Brown, 2006).

Mood Disorders

From the time I woke up in the morning until the time I went to bed at night, I was unbearably miserable and seemingly incapable of any kind of joy or enthusiasm. Everything—every thought, word, movement—was an effort. Everything that once was sparkling now was flat. I seemed to myself to be dull, boring, inadequate, thick brained, unlit, unresponsive, chill skinned, bloodless, and sparrow drab. I doubted, completely, my ability to do anything well. It seemed as though my mind had slowed down and burned out to the point of being virtually useless. (Jamison, 1995, p. 110)

mood disorder A disturbance in emotional experience that is strong enough to intrude on everyday living.

We all experience mood swings. Sometimes we are happy, perhaps even euphoric; at other times we feel upset, saddened, or depressed. Such changes in mood are a normal part of everyday life. In some people, however, moods are so pronounced and lingering—like the feelings described above by writer (and psychiatrist) Kay Jamison—that they interfere with the ability to function effectively. In extreme cases, a mood may become life threatening; in other cases, it may cause the person to lose touch with reality. Situations such as these represent **mood disorders,** disturbances in emotional experience that are strong enough to intrude on everyday living.

MAJOR DEPRESSION

major depression A severe form of depression that interferes with concentration, decision making, and sociability.

President Abraham Lincoln. Queen Victoria. Newscaster Mike Wallace.

The common link among these people? Each suffered from periodic attacks of **major depression,** a severe form of depression that interferes with concentration, decision making, and sociability. Major depression is one of the more common forms of mood disorders. Some 15 million people in the United States suffer from major depression, and at any one time, 6–10% of the U.S. population is clinically depressed. Almost one in five people in the United States experiences major depression at some point in life, and 15% of college students have received a diagnosis of depression. The cost of depression is more than $80 billion a year in lost productivity (Scelfo, 2007; Simon et al., 2008; Edoka, Petrou, & Ramchandani, 2011).

Women are twice as likely to experience major depression as men, with one-fourth of all females apt to encounter it at some point during their lives. Furthermore, although no one is sure why, the rate of depression is going up throughout the world. Results of in-depth interviews conducted in the United States, Puerto Rico, Taiwan, Lebanon, Canada, Italy, Germany, and France indicate that the incidence of depression has increased significantly over previous rates in every area. In fact, in some countries, the likelihood that individuals will have major depression at some point in their lives is three times higher than it was for earlier generations. In addition, people are developing major depression at increasingly younger ages (Kendler et al., 2006a; Staley, Sanacora, & Tagman, 2006; Sado et al., 2011).

When psychologists speak of major depression, they do not mean the sadness that comes from experiencing one of life's disappointments that we all have experienced. Some depression is normal after the breakup of a long-term relationship, the death of a loved one, or the loss of a job. It is normal even after less serious problems, such as doing badly on a test or having a romantic partner forget one's birthday.

People who suffer from major depression experience similar feelings, but the severity tends to be considerably greater. They may feel useless, worthless, and lonely, and they may think the future is hopeless and no one can help them. They may lose their appetite and have no energy. Moreover, they may experience such feelings for months or even years. They may cry uncontrollably, have sleep disturbances, and be at risk for suicide. The depth and duration of such behavior are the hallmarks of major depression. (Figure 5 provides a self-assessment of depression.)

Study Alert

Major depression differs from the normal depression that occasionally occurs during most people's lives; major depression is more intense, lasts longer, and may have no clear trigger.

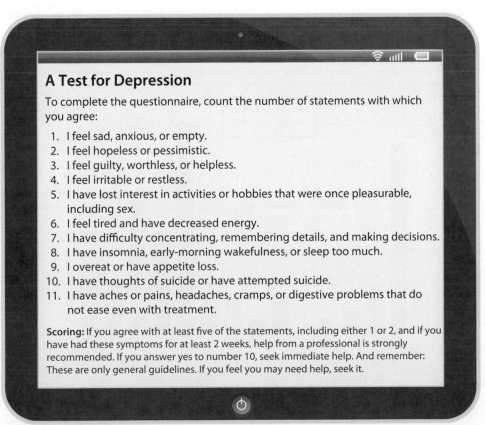

A Test for Depression

To complete the questionnaire, count the number of statements with which you agree:

1. I feel sad, anxious, or empty.
2. I feel hopeless or pessimistic.
3. I feel guilty, worthless, or helpless.
4. I feel irritable or restless.
5. I have lost interest in activities or hobbies that were once pleasurable, including sex.
6. I feel tired and have decreased energy.
7. I have difficulty concentrating, remembering details, and making decisions.
8. I have insomnia, early-morning wakefulness, or sleep too much.
9. I overeat or have appetite loss.
10. I have thoughts of suicide or have attempted suicide.
11. I have aches or pains, headaches, cramps, or digestive problems that do not ease even with treatment.

Scoring: If you agree with at least five of the statements, including either 1 or 2, and if you have had these symptoms for at least 2 weeks, help from a professional is strongly recommended. If you answer yes to number 10, seek immediate help. And remember: These are only general guidelines. If you feel you may need help, seek it.

FIGURE 5 This test is based on the list of signs and symptoms of depression found on the National Institute of Mental Health website at http://www.nimh.nih.gov/health/publications/depression/what-are-the-signs-and-symptoms-of-depression.shtml

MANIA AND BIPOLAR DISORDER

mania An extended state of intense, wild elation.

While depression leads to the depths of despair, mania leads to emotional heights. **Mania** is an extended state of intense, wild elation. People experiencing mania feel intense happiness, power, invulnerability, and energy. Believing they will succeed at anything they attempt, they may become involved in wild schemes. Consider, for example, the following description of an individual who experienced a manic episode:

> Mr. O'Reilly took a leave of absence from his civil service job. He purchased a large number of cuckoo clocks and then an expensive car, which he planned to use as a mobile showroom for his wares, anticipating that he would make a great deal of money. He proceeded to "tear around town" buying and selling clocks and other merchandise, and when he was not out, he was continuously on the phone making "deals." . . . He was $3,000 in debt and had driven his family to exhaustion with his excessive activity and talkativeness. He said, however, that he felt "on top of the world." (Spitzer et al., 1983, p. 115)

bipolar disorder A disorder in which a person alternates between periods of euphoric feelings of mania and periods of depression.

Typically, people sequentially experience periods of mania and depression. This alternation of mania and depression is called **bipolar disorder** (a condition previously known as manic-depressive disorder). The swings between highs and lows may occur a few days apart or may alternate over a period of years. In addition, in bipolar disorder, periods of depression are usually longer than periods of mania.

Ironically, some of society's most creative individuals may have suffered from bipolar disorder. The imagination, drive, excitement, and energy that they display during manic stages allow them to make unusually creative contributions. For instance, historical analysis of the composer Robert Schumann's music shows that he was most prolific during periods of mania. In contrast, his output dropped off drastically during periods of depression (see Figure 6). On the other hand, the high output associated with mania does not necessarily lead to higher quality: Some of Schumann's greatest works were created outside his periods of mania (Ludwig, 1996; Szegedy Maszak, 2003).

Despite the creative fires that may be lit by mania, persons who experience this disorder often show a recklessness that produces emotional and sometimes physical self-injury. They may alienate people with their talkativeness, inflated self-esteem, and indifference to the needs of others.

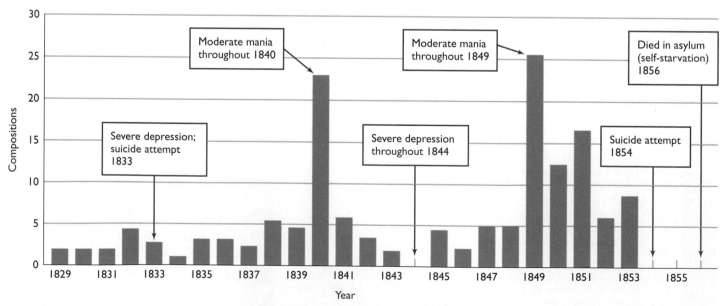

FIGURE 6 The number of pieces written by composer Robert Schumann in a given year is related to his periods of depression and mania (Slater & Meyer, 1959; reprinted in Jamison, 1993). Why do you think mania might be associated with creative productivity in some people?

CAUSES OF MOOD DISORDERS

Because they represent a major mental health problem, mood disorders—and, in particular, depression—have received a good deal of study. Several approaches have been used to explain the disorders.

Some mood disorders clearly have genetic and biochemical roots. In fact, most evidence suggests that bipolar disorders are caused primarily by biological factors. For instance, bipolar disorder (and some forms of major depression) clearly runs in some families, pointing to a genetic cause. Furthermore, researchers have found that several neurotransmitters play a role in depression. For example, alterations in the functioning of serotonin and norepinephrine in the brain are related to the disorder. Finally, research on neuroimaging suggests that a brain structure called area 25 is related to depression: When area 25 is smaller than normal, it is associated with a higher risk of depression (Kato, 2007; Popa et al., 2008; Insel, 2010).

Other explanations for depression have also included a focus on psychological causes. For instance, proponents of psychoanalytic approaches see depression as the result of feelings of loss (real or potential) or of anger directed at oneself. One psychoanalytic approach, for instance, suggests that depression is produced by the loss or threatened loss of a parent early in life (Vanheule et al., 2006).

Behavioral theories of depression argue that the stresses of life produce a reduction in positive reinforcers. As a result, people begin to withdraw, which only reduces positive reinforcers further. In addition, people receive attention for their depressive behavior, which further reinforces the depression (Lewinsohn & Essau, 2002; Lewinsohn et al., 2003).

Some explanations for mood disorders attribute them to cognitive factors. For example, psychologist Martin Seligman suggests that depression is largely a response to learned helplessness. *Learned helplessness* is a learned expectation that events in one's life are uncontrollable and that one cannot escape from the situation. As a consequence, people simply give up fighting aversive events and submit to them, which thereby produces depression. Other theorists go a step further and suggest that depression results from hopelessness, a combination of learned helplessness and an expectation that negative outcomes in one's life are inevitable (Kwon & Laurenceau, 2002; Bjornstad, 2006; Li, B., et al., 2011).

Clinical psychologist Aaron Beck has proposed that faulty cognitions underlie people's depressed feelings. Specifically, his cognitive theory of depression suggests that depressed individuals typically view themselves as life's losers and blame themselves whenever anything goes wrong. By focusing on the negative side of situations, they feel inept and unable to act constructively to change their environment. In sum, their negative cognitions lead to feelings of depression (Newman et al., 2002).

Brain imaging studies suggest that people with depression experience a general blunting of emotional reactions. For example, one study found that the brains of people with depression showed significantly less activation when they viewed photos of human faces displaying strong emotions than did those without the disorder (Gotlib et al., 2004).

Other explanations of depression derive from evolutionary psychology, which considers how our genetic inheritance from our ancestors influences our behavior. In the evolutionary view, depression is an adaptive response to unattainable goals. When people fruitlessly pursue an ever-elusive goal, depression begins, ending pursuit of the goal. Ultimately, when the depression lifts, people can turn to other, more reasonable goals. In this view, depression serves a positive function and in the long run increases the chances of survival for particular individuals, who can then pass the behavior to their offspring. Such reasoning, of course, is highly speculative (Nesse, 2000, Siegert & Ward, 2002; Pfeffer, 2006).

The various theories of depression have not provided a complete answer to an elusive question that has dogged researchers: Why does depression occur in approximately twice as many women as men—a pattern that is similar across a variety of cultures?

One explanation suggests that the stress women experience may be greater than the stress men experience at certain points in their lives—such as when a woman must simultaneously earn a living and be the primary caregiver for her children. In addition, women have a higher risk for physical and sexual abuse, typically earn lower wages than men, report greater unhappiness with their marriages, and generally experience chronic negative circumstances. Furthermore, women and men may respond to stress with different coping mechanisms. For instance, men may abuse drugs, while women respond with depression (Nolen-Hoeksema, 2007; Hyde, Mezulis, & Abramson, 2008; Komarovskaya et al., 2011).

Biological factors may also explain some women's depression. For example, the rate of female depression begins to rise during puberty, so some psychologists believe that hormones make women more vulnerable to the disorder. In addition, 25–50% of women who take oral contraceptives report symptoms of depression, and depression that occurs after the birth of a child is linked to hormonal changes. Finally, structural differences in men's and women's brains that we discussed in the neuroscience and behavior modules may be related to gender differences in depression (Holden, 2005; Graham, Bancroft, & Doll, 2007; Solomon & Herman, 2009).

Ultimately, it is clear that researchers have discovered no definitive solutions to the puzzle of depression, and there are many alternative explanations. Most likely, a complex interaction of several factors causes mood disorders.

Schizophrenia

Things that relate, the town of Antelope, Oregon, Jonestown, Charlie Manson, the Hillside Strangler, the Zodiac Killer, Watergate, King's trial in L.A., and many more. In the last 7 years alone, over 23 Star Wars scientists committed suicide for no apparent reason. The AIDS cover-up, the conference in South America in 87 had over 1,000 doctors claim that insects can transmit it. To be able to read one's thoughts and place thoughts in one's mind without the person knowing it's being done. Realization is a reality of bioelectromagnetic control, which is thought transfer and emotional control, recording individual brainwave frequencies of thought, sensation, and emotions. (Nolen-Hoeksema, 2007, pp. 385–386)

This excerpt illustrates the efforts of a person with schizophrenia, one of the more severe forms of mental disturbance, to communicate. People with schizophrenia account for by far the largest percentage of those hospitalized for psychological disorders. They are also in many respects the least likely to recover from their difficulties.

schizophrenia A class of disorders in which severe distortion of reality occurs.

Schizophrenia refers to a class of disorders in which severe distortion of reality occurs. Thinking, perception, and emotion may deteriorate; the individual may withdraw from social interaction; and the person may display bizarre behavior. Although there are several types of schizophrenia (see Figure 7), the distinctions between them are not always clear. Moreover, the symptoms displayed by persons with schizophrenia may vary considerably over time, and people with schizophrenia show significant differences in the pattern of their symptoms even when they are labeled with the same diagnostic category. Nonetheless, a number of characteristics reliably distinguish schizophrenia from other disorders. They include the following:

- *Decline from a previous level of functioning.* An individual can no longer carry out activities he or she was once able to do.
- *Disturbances of thought and speech.* People with schizophrenia use logic and language in a peculiar way. Their thinking often does not make sense, and their logic is frequently faulty, which is referred to as a *formal thought disorder*. They also do not follow conventional linguistic rules (Penn et al., 1997). Consider, for example, the following response to the question "Why do you think people believe in God?"

Types of Schizophrenia	
Type	**Symptoms**
Disorganized (hebephrenic) schizophrenia	Inappropriate laughter and giggling, silliness, incoherent speech, infantile behavior, strange and sometimes obscene behavior
Paranoid schizophrenia	Delusions and hallucinations of persecution or of greatness, loss of judgment, erratic and unpredictable behavior
Catatonic schizophrenia	Major disturbances in movement; in some phases, loss of all motion, with patient frozen into a single position, remaining that way for hours and sometimes even days; in other phases, hyperactivity and wild, sometimes violent, movement
Undifferentiated schizophrenia	Variable mixture of major symptoms of schizophrenia; classification used for patients who cannot be typed into any of the more specific categories
Residual schizophrenia	Minor signs of schizophrenia after a more serious episode

FIGURE 7 The distinctions among the different types of schizophrenia are not always clear cut, and symptoms may vary considerably over time.

Uh, let's, I don't know why, let's see, balloon travel. He holds it up for you, the balloon. He don't let you fall out, your little legs sticking down through the clouds. He's down to the smokestack, looking through the smoke trying to get the balloon gassed up you know. Way they're flying on top that way, legs sticking out. I don't know, looking down on the ground, heck, that'd make you so dizzy you just stay and sleep you know, hold down and sleep there. I used to be sleep outdoors, you know, sleep outdoors instead of going home. (Chapman & Chapman, 1973, p. 3)

As this selection illustrates, although the basic grammatical structure may be intact, the substance of thinking characteristic of schizophrenia is often illogical, garbled, and lacking in meaningful content (Holden, 2003; Heinrichs, 2005).

- *Delusions.* People with schizophrenia often have delusions, firmly held, unshakable beliefs with no basis in reality. Among the common delusions people with schizophrenia experience are the beliefs that they are being controlled by someone else, they are being persecuted by others, and their thoughts are being broadcast so that others know what they are thinking (Coltheart, Langdon, & McKay, 2007; Startup, Bucci, & Langdon, 2009).

- *Hallucinations and perceptual disorders.* People with schizophrenia do not perceive the world as most other people do. They also may have *hallucinations,* the experience of perceiving things that do not actually exist. Furthermore, they may see, hear, or smell things differently from others (see Figure 8); they do not even have a sense of their bodies in the way that others do and have difficulty determining where their bodies stop and the rest of the world begins (Botvinick, 2004; Thomas et al., 2007; Bauer et al., 2011).

- *Emotional disturbances.* People with schizophrenia sometimes show a lack of emotion in which even the most dramatic events produce little or no emotional response. Conversely, they may display emotion that is inappropriate

FIGURE 8 This unusual art was created by an individual suffering from severe mental disturbance.

to a situation. For example, a person with schizophrenia may laugh uproariously at a funeral or react with anger when being helped by someone.

- *Withdrawal.* People with schizophrenia tend to have little interest in others. They tend not to socialize or hold real conversations with others, although they may talk at another person. In the most extreme cases, they do not even acknowledge the presence of other people and appear to be in their own isolated world.

Usually, the onset of schizophrenia occurs in early adulthood, and the symptoms follow one of two primary courses. In *process schizophrenia,* the symptoms develop slowly and subtly. There may be a gradual withdrawal from the world, excessive daydreaming, and a blunting of emotion until eventually the disorder reaches the point where others cannot overlook it. In other cases, known as *reactive schizophrenia,* the onset of symptoms is sudden and conspicuous. The treatment outlook for reactive schizophrenia is relatively favorable, but process schizophrenia has proved more difficult to treat.

DSM-IV-TR classifies the symptoms of schizophrenia into two types. Positive-symptom schizophrenia is indicated by the presence of disordered behavior such as hallucinations, delusions, and emotional extremes. In contrast, negative-symptom schizophrenia shows an absence or loss of normal functioning, such as social withdrawal or blunted emotions. Schizophrenia researchers sometimes speak of *Type I schizophrenia,* in which positive symptoms are dominant, and *Type II schizophrenia,* in which negative symptoms are more prominent (Buchanan et al., 2007; Levine & Rabinowitz, 2007).

The distinction between Type I and Type II schizophrenia is important because it suggests that two different processes might trigger schizophrenia. Furthermore, it has implications for predicting treatment outcomes.

Study Alert

In Type I schizophrenia, positive symptoms (in which hallucinations, delusions, and emotional extremes are present) are dominant; in Type II schizophrenia, negative symptoms (characterized by an absence or loss of normal functioning) are dominant.

SOLVING THE PUZZLE OF SCHIZOPHRENIA: BIOLOGICAL CAUSES

Although schizophrenic behavior clearly departs radically from normal behavior, its causes are less apparent. It does appear, however, that schizophrenia has both biological and environmental origins (Sawa & Snyder, 2002).

Let's first consider the evidence pointing to a biological cause. Because schizophrenia is more common in some families than in others, genetic factors seem to be involved in producing at least a susceptibility to or readiness for developing schizophrenia. For example, the closer the genetic link between a person with schizophrenia and another individual, the greater the likelihood that the other person will experience the disorder (see Figure 9; Brzustowicz et al., 2000; Plomin & McGuffin, 2003; Gottesman & Hanson, 2005).

However, if genetics alone were responsible for schizophrenia, the chance of both of two identical twins having schizophrenia would be 100% instead of just under 50% because identical twins have the same genetic makeup. Moreover, attempts to find a link between schizophrenia and a particular gene have been only partly successful. Apparently, genetic factors alone do not produce schizophrenia (Franzek & Beckmann, 1996; Lenzenweger & Dworkin, 1998).

One intriguing biological hypothesis to explain schizophrenia is that the brains of people with the disorder may harbor either a biochemical imbalance or a structural abnormality. For example, the *dopamine hypothesis* suggests that schizophrenia occurs when there is excess activity in the areas of the brain that use dopamine as a neurotransmitter. This hypothesis came to light after the discovery that drugs that block dopamine action in brain pathways can be highly effective in reducing the symptoms of schizophrenia. Other research suggests that glutamate, another neurotransmitter, may be a major contributor to the disorder (Stone, Morrison, & Pilowsky, 2007; Howes & Kapur, 2009; Kendler & Schaffner, 2011).

Risk of Developing Schizophrenia, Based on Genetic Relatedness to a Person with Schizophrenia		
Relationship	**Genetic Relatedness, %**	**Risk of Developing Schizophrenia, %**
Identical twin	100	48
Child of two schizophrenic parents	100	46
Fraternal twin	50	17
Offspring of one schizophrenic parent	50	17
Sibling	50	9
Nephew or niece	25	4
Spouse	0	2
Unrelated person	0	1

FIGURE 9 The closer the genetic links between two people, the greater the likelihood that if one experiences schizophrenia, so will the other sometime during his or her lifetime. However, genetics is not the full story; if it were, the risk of identical twins having schizophrenia would be 100% and not the 48% shown in this figure. (Source: Gottesman, 1991.)

Some biological explanations propose that structural abnormalities exist in the brains of people with schizophrenia perhaps as a result of exposure to a virus during prenatal development. For example, individuals with schizophrenia show abnormalities in the neural circuits of the cortex and limbic systems, as well as differences in brain functioning (see Figure 10 *Neuroscience in Your Life*; Bartzokis et al., 2003; Reichenberg & Harvey, 2007; Reichenberg et al., 2009).

Further evidence for the importance of biological factors shows that when people with schizophrenia hear voices during hallucinations, the parts of the brain responsible for hearing and language processing become active. When they have visual

Neuroscience in Your Life:
Brain Changes with Schizophrenia

FIGURE 10 Changes in the brain have been found in people with schizophrenia. In an MRI reconstruction of the brain of a person with schizophrenia (a), the hippocampi (yellow) are shrunken, and the ventricles (gray) are enlarged and fluid-filled. In contrast, an MRI reconstruction of the brain of a person without the disorder (b) is structurally different with larger hippocampi and smaller ventricles. (Source: N.C. Andreasen, University of Iowa.)

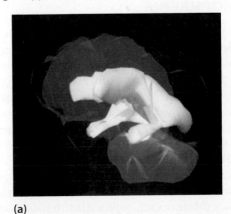
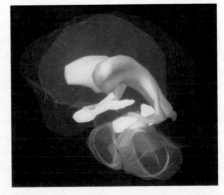

(a)   (b)

hallucinations, the parts of the brain involved in movement and color are active. At the same time, people with schizophrenia often have unusually low activity in the brain's frontal lobes—the parts of the brain involved with emotional regulation, insight, and the evaluation of sensory stimuli (Stern & Silbersweig, 2001).

ENVIRONMENTAL PERSPECTIVES ON SCHIZOPHRENIA

Although biological factors provide important pieces of the puzzle of schizophrenia, we still need to consider past and current experiences in the environments of people who develop the disturbance. For instance, psychoanalytic approaches suggest that schizophrenia is a form of regression to earlier experiences and stages of life. Freud believed that people with schizophrenia lack egos that are strong enough to cope with their unacceptable impulses. They regress to the oral stage—a time when the id and ego are not yet separated. Therefore, individuals with schizophrenia essentially lack an ego and act out impulses without concern for reality.

Although this reasoning is theoretically plausible, little evidence supports psychoanalytic explanations. Somewhat more convincing theories look toward the emotional and communication patterns of the families of people with schizophrenia. For instance, some researchers suggest that schizophrenia is related to a family interaction style known as expressed emotion. *Expressed emotion* is an interaction style characterized by high levels of criticism, hostility, and emotional intrusiveness within a family. Other researchers suggest that faulty communication patterns lie at the heart of schizophrenia (Miklowitz & Thompson, 2003; Lobban, Barrowclough, & Jones, 2006).

Psychologists who take a cognitive perspective on schizophrenia suggest that the problems in thinking that people with the disorder experience point to a cognitive cause. Some suggest that schizophrenia results from *overattention* to stimuli in the environment. Rather than being able to screen out unimportant or inconsequential stimuli and focus on the most important things in the environment, people with schizophrenia may be excessively receptive to virtually everything in their environment. As a consequence, their information-processing capabilities become overloaded and eventually break down. Other cognitive experts argue that schizophrenia results from *underattention* to certain stimuli. According to this explanation, people with schizophrenia fail to focus sufficiently on important stimuli and pay attention to other, less important information in their surroundings (Cadenhead & Braff, 1995).

Although it is plausible that overattention and underattention are related to different forms of schizophrenia, these phenomena do not explain the origins of such information-processing disorders. Consequently, cognitive approaches—like other environmental explanations—do not provide a full explanation of the disorder.

THE MULTIPLE CAUSES OF SCHIZOPHRENIA

The major approach now used to explain the onset of schizophrenia involves both biological and situational factors. The *predisposition model of schizophrenia* suggests that individuals may inherit a predisposition or an inborn sensitivity to schizophrenia. This genetic predisposition, then, makes them particularly vulnerable to stressful factors in the environment, such as social rejection or dysfunctional family communication patterns. The stressors may vary, but if they are strong enough and are coupled with a genetic predisposition, they result in the appearance of schizophrenia. Furthermore, a strong genetic predisposition may lead to the onset of schizophrenia even when the environmental stressors are relatively weak.

In short, the models used today associate schizophrenia with several kinds of biological and environmental factors. It is increasingly clear, then, that no single factor but a combination of interrelated variables produces schizophrenia (Meltzer, 2000; McDonald & Murray, 2004; Opler et al., 2008).

Study Alert

Remember that the multiple causes of schizophrenia include biological and environmental factors.

Personality Disorders

I had always wanted lots of things; as a child I can remember wanting a bullet that a friend of mine had brought in to show the class. I took it and put it into my school bag and when my friend noticed it was missing, I was the one who stayed after school with him and searched the room, and I was the one who sat with him and bitched about the other kids and how one of them took his bullet. I even went home with him to help him break the news to his uncle, who had brought it home from the war for him.

But that was petty compared with the stuff I did later. I wanted a Ph.D. very badly, but I didn't want to work very hard—just enough to get by. I never did the experiments I reported; hell, I was smart enough to make up the results. I knew enough about statistics to make anything look plausible. I got my master's degree without even spending one hour in a laboratory. I mean, the professors believed anything. I'd stay out all night drinking and being with my friends, and the next day I'd get in just before them and tell 'em I'd been in the lab all night. They'd actually feel sorry for me. (Duke & Nowicki, 1979, pp. 309–310)

This excerpt provides a graphic first-person account of a person with a personality disorder. A **personality disorder** is characterized by a set of inflexible, maladaptive behavior patterns that keep a person from functioning appropriately in society. Personality disorders differ from the other problems we have discussed because those affected by them often have little sense of personal distress associated with the psychological maladjustment. In fact, people with personality disorders frequently lead seemingly normal lives. However, just below the surface lies a set of inflexible, maladaptive personality traits that do not permit these individuals to function as members of society (Davis & Millon, 1999; Clarkin & Lenzenweger, 2004; Friedman, Oltmanns, & Turkheimer, 2007).

The best-known type of personality disorder, illustrated by the case above, is the **antisocial personality disorder** (sometimes referred to as a sociopathic personality). Individuals with this disturbance show no regard for the moral and ethical rules of society or the rights of others. Although they can appear quite intelligent and likable (at least at first), upon closer examination they turn out to be manipulative and deceptive. Moreover, they lack any guilt or anxiety about their wrongdoing. When those with antisocial personality disorder behave in a way that injures someone else, they understand intellectually that they have caused harm but feel no remorse (Goodwin & Hamilton, 2003; Hilarski, 2007; Bateman, 2011).

People with antisocial personality disorder are often impulsive and lack the ability to withstand frustration. They can be extremely manipulative. They also may have excellent social skills; they can be charming, engaging, and highly persuasive. Some of the best con artists have antisocial personalities.

What causes such an unusual constellation of problem behaviors? A variety of factors have been suggested ranging from an inability to experience emotions appropriately to problems in family relationships. For example, in many cases of antisocial behavior, the individual has come from a home in which a parent has died or left or one in which there is a lack of affection, a lack of consistency in discipline, or outright rejection. Other explanations concentrate on sociocultural factors because an unusually high proportion of people with antisocial personalities come from lower socioeconomic groups. Still, no one has been able to pinpoint the specific causes of antisocial personalities, and it is likely that some combination of factors is responsible (Rosenstein & Horowitz, 1996; Costa & Widiger, 2002; Chen et al., 2011).

People with **borderline personality disorder** have difficulty developing a secure sense of who they are. As a consequence, they tend to rely on relationships with others to define their identity. The problem with this strategy is that rejections are devastating. Furthermore, people with this disorder distrust others and have difficulty controlling their anger. Their emotional volatility leads to impulsive and self-destructive behavior.

personality disorder A disorder characterized by a set of inflexible, maladaptive behavior patterns that keep a person from functioning appropriately in society.

antisocial personality disorder A disorder in which individuals show no regard for the moral and ethical rules of society or the rights of others.

Study Alert

Unlike most psychological disorders, personality disorders produce little or no personal distress.

borderline personality disorder A disorder in which individuals have difficulty developing a secure sense of who they are.

Individuals with borderline personality disorder often feel empty and alone, and they have difficulty cooperating with others. They may form intense, sudden, one-sided relationships in which they demand the attention of another person and then feel angry when they don't receive it. One reason for this behavior is that they may have a background in which others discounted or criticized their emotional reactions, and they may not have learned to regulate their emotions effectively (Links, Eynan, & Heisel, 2007; King-Casas et al., 2008; Hopwood et al., 2009).

narcissistic personality disorder
A personality disturbance characterized by an exaggerated sense of self-importance.

Another example of a personality disturbance is the **narcissistic personality disorder,** which is characterized by an exaggerated sense of self-importance. Those with the disorder expect special treatment from others while at the same time disregarding others' feelings. In some ways, in fact, the main attribute of the narcissistic personality is an inability to experience empathy for other people.

There are several other categories of personality disorder that range in severity from individuals who may simply be regarded by others as eccentric, obnoxious, or difficult to people who act in a manner that is criminal and dangerous to others. Although they are not out of touch with reality like people with schizophrenia, people with personality disorders lead lives that put them on the fringes of society (Millon, Davis, & Millon, 2000; Trull & Widiger, 2003).

Childhood Disorders

We typically view childhood as a time of innocence and relative freedom from stress. In reality, though, almost 20% of children and 40% of adolescents experience significant emotional or behavioral disorders (Romano et al., 2001; Broidy, Nagin, & Tremblay, 2003; Nolen-Hoeksema, 2007).

For example, although major depression is more prevalent in adults, around 2.5% of children and more than 8% of adolescents suffer from the disorder. In fact, by the time they reach age 20, between 15% and 20% of children and adolescents will experience an episode of major depression (Garber & Horowitz, 2002).

Children do not always display depression the same way adults do. Rather than showing profound sadness or hopelessness, childhood depression may produce the expression of exaggerated fears, clinginess, or avoidance of everyday activities. In older children, the symptoms may be sulking, school problems, and even acts of delinquency (Wenar, 1994; Koplewicz, 2002; Seroczynski, Jacquez, & Cole, 2003).

attention-deficit hyperactivity disorder (ADHD) A disorder marked by inattention, impulsiveness, a low tolerance for frustration, and a great deal of inappropriate activity.

A considerably more common childhood disorder is **attention-deficit hyperactivity disorder,** or **ADHD,** a disorder marked by inattention, impulsiveness, a low tolerance for frustration, and generally a great deal of inappropriate activity. Although all children show such behavior some of the time, it is so common in children diagnosed with ADHD that it interferes with their everyday functioning (Barkley, 2005; Smith, Barkley, & Shapiro, 2006; Barkley, Knouse, & Murphy, 2011).

ADHD is surprisingly widespread with estimates ranging between 3% and 5% of the school-age population—or some 3.5 million children under the age of 18 in the United States. Children diagnosed with the disorder are often exhausting to parents and teachers, and even their peers find them difficult to deal with.

The cause of ADHD is not known, although most experts feel that it is produced by dysfunctions in the nervous system. For example, one theory suggests that unusually low levels of arousal in the central nervous system cause ADHD. To compensate, children with ADHD seek out stimulation to increase arousal. Still, such theories are speculative. Furthermore, because many children occasionally show behaviors characteristic of ADHD, it often is misdiagnosed or in some cases overdiagnosed. Only the frequency and persistence of the symptoms of ADHD allow for a correct diagnosis, which only a trained professional can do (Barkley, 2000; Sciutto & Eisenberg, 2007).

Autism, a severe developmental disability that impairs children's ability to communicate and relate to others, is another childhood disorder that usually appears in the first 3 years and typically continues throughout life. Children with autism have difficulties in both verbal and nonverbal communication, and they may avoid social contact. About one in 110 children are now thought to have the disorder, and its prevalence has risen significantly in the last decade. Whether the increase is the result of an actual rise in the incidence of autism or is due to better reporting is a question of intense debate among researchers (Rice, 2009).

Other Disorders

It's important to keep in mind that the various forms of psychological disorders described in *DSM-IV-TR* cover much more ground than we have been able to discuss in this module. Some relate to topics previously considered in other chapters. For example, *psychoactive substance use disorder* relates to problems that arise from the use and abuse of drugs. Furthermore, *alcohol use disorders* are among the most serious and widespread problems. Both psychoactive substance use disorder and alcohol use disorder co-occur with many other psychological disorders such as mood disorders, posttraumatic stress disorder, and schizophrenia, which complicates treatment considerably (Salgado, Quinlan, & Zlotnick, 2007).

Another widespread problem is *eating disorders*. They include such disorders as *anorexia nervosa* and *bulimia*, which we considered in the chapter on motivation and emotion, as well as *binge-eating disorder*, characterized by binge eating without behaviors designed to prevent weight gain. Finally, *sexual disorders*, in which one's sexual activity is unsatisfactory, are another important class of problems. They include *sexual desire disorders*, *sexual arousal disorders*, and *paraphilias*, atypical sexual activities that may include nonhuman objects or nonconsenting partners.

Another important class of disorders is *organic mental disorders*, some of which we touched on previously. These are problems that have a purely biological basis, such as Alzheimer's disease and some types of mental retardation. Remember, there are other disorders that we have not mentioned at all, and each of the classes we have discussed can be divided into several subcategories (Kopelman & Fleminger, 2002; Pratt et al., 2003; Reijonen et al., 2003).

In the most severe cases of autism, children display self-injurious behavior and must wear protective head gear.

autism A severe developmental disability that impairs children's ability to communicate and relate to others.

RECAP

LO 38-1 What are the major psychological disorders?

- Anxiety disorders are present when a person experiences so much anxiety that it affects daily functioning. Specific types of anxiety disorders include phobic disorder, panic disorder, generalized anxiety disorder, and obsessive-compulsive disorder. (pp. 463, 464)
- Somatoform disorders are psychological difficulties that take on a physical (somatic) form but for which there is no medical cause. Examples are hypochondriasis and conversion disorders. (p. 468)
- Dissociative disorders are marked by the separation, or dissociation, of different facets of a person's personality that are usually integrated. Major kinds of dissociative disorders include dissociative identity disorder, dissociative amnesia, and dissociative fugue. (pp. 468, 469)
- Mood disorders are characterized by emotional states of depression or euphoria so strong that they intrude on everyday living. They include major depression and bipolar disorder. (pp. 470–472)
- Schizophrenia is one of the more severe forms of mental illness. Symptoms of schizophrenia include declines in functioning, thought and language disturbances, perceptual disorders, emotional disturbance, and withdrawal from others. (p. 474)
- Strong evidence links schizophrenia to genetic, biochemical, and environmental factors. According to the predisposition model, an interaction among various factors produces the disorder. (pp. 476–478)

- People with personality disorders experience little or no personal distress, but they do suffer from an inability to function as normal members of society. These disorders include antisocial personality disorder, borderline personality disorder, and narcissistic personality disorder. (pp. 479, 480)
- Childhood disorders include major depression, attention-deficit hyperactivity disorder (ADHD), and autism. (p. 480, 481)

EVALUATE

1. Kathy is terrified of elevators. She could be suffering from a(n)
   a. Obsessive-compulsive disorder
   b. Phobic disorder
   c. Panic disorder
   d. Generalized anxiety disorder
2. Carmen described an incident in which her anxiety suddenly rose to a peak, and she felt a sense of impending doom. Carmen experienced a(n) _____ _____.
3. Troubling thoughts that persist for weeks or months are known as
   a. Obsessions
   b. Compulsions
   c. Rituals
   d. Panic attacks
4. An overpowering urge to carry out a strange ritual is called a(n) _____.

5. The separation of the personality, which provides escape from stressful situations, is the key factor in _____ disorders.
6. States of extreme euphoria and energy paired with severe depression characterize _____ disorder.
7. _____ schizophrenia is characterized by symptoms that are sudden and of easily identifiable onset; _____ schizophrenia develops gradually over a person's life span.
8. The _____ _____ states that schizophrenia may be caused by an excess of certain neurotransmitters in the brain.

RETHINK

1. What cultural factors might contribute to the rate of anxiety disorders found in a culture? How might the experience of anxiety differ among people of different cultures?
2. *From the perspective of a social worker:* Personality disorders are often not apparent to others, and many people with these problems seem to live basically normal lives and are not a threat to others. Because these people often appear from the outside to function well in society, why should they be considered psychologically disordered?

Answers to Evaluate Questions

1. b; 2. panic attack; 3. a; 4. compulsion; 5. dissociative; 6. bipolar; 7. Reactive, process; 8. dopamine hypothesis

KEY TERMS

anxiety disorder p. 463
phobias p. 464
panic disorder p. 464
generalized anxiety
   disorder p. 465
obsessive-compulsive
   disorder (OCD) p. 465
obsession p. 465
compulsion p. 465

somatoform disorders p. 468
hypochondriasis p. 468
conversion disorder p. 468
dissociative disorders p. 468
dissociative identity
   disorder (DID) p. 469
dissociative amnesia p. 469
dissociative fugue p. 470
mood disorder p. 470

major depression p. 470
mania p. 472
bipolar disorder p. 472
schizophrenia p. 474
personality disorder p. 479
antisocial personality
   disorder p. 479
borderline personality
   disorder p. 479

narcissistic personality
   disorder p. 480
attention-deficit
   hyperactivity disorder
   (ADHD) p. 480
autism p. 481

Psychological Disorders in Perspective

How common are the kinds of psychological disorders we've been discussing? Here's one answer: Every second person you meet in the United States is likely to suffer at some point during his or her life from a psychological disorder.

That's the conclusion drawn from a massive study on the prevalence of psychological disorders. In that study, researchers conducted face-to-face interviews with more than 8,000 men and women between the ages of 15 and 54. The sample was designed to be representative of the population of the United States. According to results of the study, 48% of those interviewed had experienced a disorder at some point in their lives. In addition, 30% experienced a disorder in any particular year. Furthermore, a significant number of people experienced simultaneous multiple disorders—a situation known as *comorbidity* (Welkowitz et al., 2000; Merikangas et al., 2007; Kessler & Wang, 2008).

The most common disorder reported in the study was depression; 17% of those surveyed reported at least one major episode. Ten percent had suffered from depression during the current year. The next most common disorder was alcohol dependence, which occurred at a lifetime incidence rate of 14%. In addition, 7% of those interviewed had experienced alcohol dependence in the last year. Other frequently occurring psychological disorders were drug dependence, disorders involving panic (such as an overwhelming fear of talking to strangers and terror of heights), and posttraumatic stress disorder.

Although some researchers think the estimates of severe disorders may be too high (Narrow et al., 2002), the national findings are consistent with studies of college students and their psychological difficulties. For example, in one study of the problems of students who visited a college counseling center, more than 40% of students reported being depressed (see Figure 1 on page 484). These figures include only students who sought help from the counseling center and not those who did not seek treatment. Consequently, the figures are not representative of the entire college population (Benton et al., 2003; also see *Applying Psychology in the 21st Century* on page 486).

The significant level of psychological disorders is a problem not only in the United States; according to the World Health Organization, mental health difficulties are also a global concern. Throughout the world, psychological disorders are widespread. Furthermore, there are economic disparities in treatment; more affluent people with mild disorders receive more and better treatment than poor people who have more severe disorders. In fact, psychological disorders make up 14% of global illness, and 90% of people in developing countries receive no care at all for their disorders (see Figure 2 on page 485; WHO World Mental Health Survey Consortium, 2004; Jacob et al., 2007; Wang et al., 2007).

Also, keep in mind that the incidence of specific disorders varies significantly in other cultures. For instance, cross-cultural surveys show that the incidence of major depression varies significantly from one culture to another. The probability of having at least one episode of depression is only 1.5% in Taiwan and 2.9% in Korea compared with 11.6% in New Zealand and 16.4% in France. Such notable differences underscore the importance of considering the cultural context of psychological disorders (Weissman et al., 1997; Tseng, 2003).

Learning Outcomes

LO 39-1 How prevalent are psychological disorders?

LO 39-2 What indicators signal a need for the help of a mental health practitioner?

Study Alert

Remember that the incidence of various types of psychological disorders in the general population is surprisingly high.

FIGURE 1 The problems reported by students visiting a college counseling center. Would you have predicted this pattern of psychological difficulties? (Source: Benton et al., 2003.)

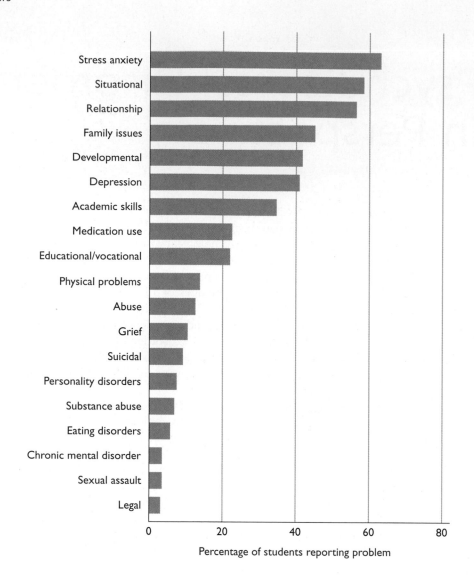

Percentage of students reporting problem

The Social and Cultural Context of Psychological Disorders

In considering the nature of the psychological disorders described in *DSM*, it's important to keep in mind that the specific disorders reflect Western cultures at the turn of the 21st century. The classification system provides a snapshot of how its authors viewed mental disorder when it was published. In fact, the development of the most recent version of the *DSM* was a source of great debate, which in part reflects issues that divide society.

For example, two disorders caused particular controversy during earlier revision. One, known as *self-defeating personality disorder*, was ultimately removed from the appendix, where it had appeared in the previous revision. The term *self-defeating personality disorder* had been applied to cases in which people who were treated unpleasantly or demeaningly in relationships neither left nor took other action. It was typically used to describe people who remained in abusive relationships.

Although some clinicians argued that it was a valid category they observed in clinical practice, the disorder lacked enough research evidence to support its designation as a disorder in *DSM*. Furthermore, some critics complained that use of the label

Study Alert

It is important to understand that the *DSM* is a living document that presents a view of disorders that reflects the culture and historical context of its authors.

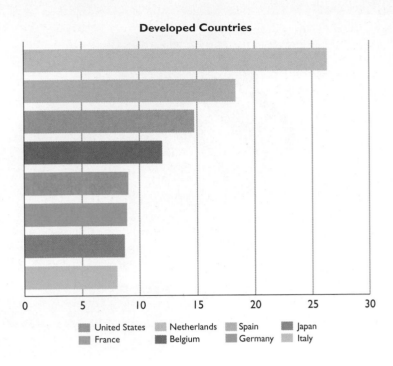

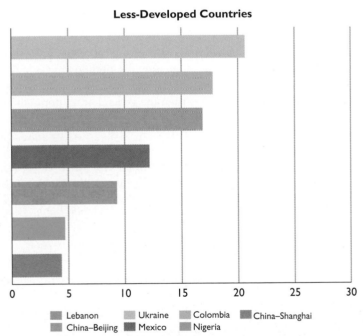

FIGURE 2 According to a global survey conducted by the World Health Organization, the prevalence of psychological disorders is widespread. These figures show the percentage of people who have experienced any psychological disorder within the prior 12-month period. (Source: WHO World Mental Health Survey Consortium, 2004, Table 3.)

had the effect of condemning targets of abuse for their plight—a blame-the-victim phenomenon—and as a result, the category was removed from the manual.

A second and even more controversial category was *premenstrual dysphoric disorder*, which is characterized by severe, incapacitating mood changes or depression related to a woman's menstrual cycle. Some critics argued that the classification simply labels normal female behavior as a disorder. Former U.S. Surgeon General Antonia Novello suggested that what "in women is called PMS [premenstrual syndrome, a

Psychological Problems Are Increasing Among College Students

Does the stress of being in college have you feeling anxious or blue? If so, you're far from alone. New research shows that mental health problems, particularly anxiety, are plaguing more college students today than in the past.

One study examined the responses of many thousands of young people on the Minnesota Multiphasic Personality Inventory (MMPI) between 1938 and 2007 and found that indications of mental health problems increased steadily over those 70 years, with 85% of recent college students scoring higher than the average college student in the 1930s and 1940s on measures of psychological problems. The findings showed elevated levels on a number of MMPI scales, including those measuring indicators of paranoia, schizophrenia, mania, and depression (Twenge et al., 2010).

The researchers noted that the increase in mental disorders coincides with increasing emphasis being placed on extrinsic goals such as attaining wealth and status and decreasing emphasis being placed on intrinsic goals such as creating satisfying interpersonal relationships and a sense of community. They speculated that such emphasis on extrinsic goals might encourage unreasonable expectations for personal achievement, causing two problems: undue stress as people try to achieve unattainable goals and a sense of unfulfillment when they fail to live up to their expectations (Eckersley & Dear, 2002; Jacobs, 2010).

Another comprehensive survey of directors of over 400 college and university counseling centers also showed evidence

Psychological disorders are surprisingly common among college students.

of this increase in psychological problems among college students. Over three-quarters of respondents reported that the number of students with severe psychological problems seen by their staff had increased in the past year. As in past surveys, anxiety and depression were the top two student complaints—but anxiety surpassed depression for the first time since the surveys began in 2006 (Barr et al., 2010).

According to one researcher, Jean Twenge, the findings are a wake-up call. "Students have always had higher anxiety than the general adult population, but the increase over time is startling," she said. "Anxiety is usually a precursor to more serious mental health issues like depression, so it's important to teach young people how to manage their stress now so it doesn't become worse" (Jacobs, 2010).

RETHINK

- What might be some ways that we can teach college students to manage their stress?
- Why might people be putting more emphasis on material goals and less on social ones, even to the detriment of their own psychological health?

similar classification] in men is called healthy aggression and initiative" (Cotton, 1993, p. 270). Advocates for including the disorder prevailed, however, and "premenstrual dysphoric disorder" appears in the appendix of *DSM* (Hartung & Widiger, 1998; Pearlstein & Steiner, 2008).

Such controversies underline the fact that our understanding of abnormal behavior reflects the society and culture in which we live. Future revisions of *DSM* may include a different catalog of disorders. Even now, other cultures might include a list of disorders that are very different from the list that appears in the current *DSM*, as we discuss next.

Exploring DIVERSITY

DSM and Culture—and the Culture of *DSM*

In most people's estimation, a person who hears voices of the recently deceased is probably a victim of a psychological disturbance. Yet some Plains Indians routinely hear the voices of the dead calling to them from the afterlife.

This is only one example of the role of culture in labeling behavior as "abnormal." In fact, among all the major adult disorders included in the *DSM* categorization, a minority are found across all cultures of the world. Most others are prevalent primarily in North America and Western Europe (Kleinman, 1996; Cohen, Slomkowski, & Robins, 1999; López & Guarnaccia, 2000).

For instance, take anorexia nervosa, the disorder in which people become obsessed with their weight and sometimes stop eating, ultimately starving to death in the process. This disorder occurs most frequently in cultures that hold the societal standard that slender female bodies are the most desirable. In most of the world, where such a standard does not exist, anorexia nervosa is rare. Furthermore, the disorder may appear in specific ways in a particular culture. For instance, in Hong Kong, symptoms of one form of anorexia relate to complaints of bloated stomachs, rather than fears of becoming fat (Watters, 2010).

Similarly, dissociative identity (multiple personality) disorder makes sense as a problem only in societies in which a sense of self is fairly concrete. In India, the self is based more on external factors that are relatively independent of the person. There, when an individual displays symptoms of what people in a Western society would call dissociative identity disorder, Indians assume that that person is possessed either by demons (which they view as a malady) or by gods (which does not require treatment).

Furthermore, even though disorders such as schizophrenia are found throughout the world, cultural factors influence the specific symptoms of the disorder. Hence, catatonic schizophrenia in which unmoving patients appear to be frozen in the same position (sometimes for days), is rare in North America and Western Europe. In contrast, in India, 80% of those with schizophrenia are catatonic.

Other cultures have disorders that do not appear in the West. For example, in Malaysia, a behavior called *amok* is characterized by a wild outburst in which a usually quiet and withdrawn person kills or severely injures another. *Koro* is a condition found in Southeast Asian males who develop an intense panic that the penis is about to withdraw into the abdomen. Some West African men develop a disorder when they first attend college that they call "brain fag"; it includes feelings of heaviness or heat in the head as well as depression and anxiety. Finally, *ataque de nervios* is a disorder found most often among Latinos from the Caribbean. It is characterized by trembling, crying, uncontrollable screams, and incidents of verbal or physical aggression (Cohen et al., 1999; López & Guarnaccia, 2000; Adams & Dzokoto, 2007).

Explanations for psychological disorders also differ among cultures. For example, in China, psychological disorders are commonly viewed as a weakness of the heart, a concept that derives from thousands of years of traditional Chinese medicine. Many terms used to describe emotions and symptoms of psychological disorders make direct reference to the heart—but the association isn't simply a metaphorical one. Chinese people are more likely than people in Western cultures to express their emotional anguish in terms of physical symptoms such as heart pain, "heart panic," or "heart vexed." They may also see their emotional pain as merely a side effect of some underlying physical cause or even focus more on the effects that their symptoms are having on their relationships with friends and family members (Miller, 2006; Lee, Kleinman, & Kleinman, 2007; Watters, 2010).

In sum, we should not assume that the *DSM* provides the final word on psychological disorders. The disorders it includes are very much a creation and function of Western cultures at a particular moment in time, and its categories should not be seen as universally applicable (Tseng, 2003).

BECOMING AN INFORMED CONSUMER of Psychology

Deciding When You Need Help

After you've considered the range and variety of psychological disturbances that can afflict people, you may begin to feel that you suffer from one (or more) of the problems we have discussed. In fact, this perception has a name: *medical student's disease*. Although in this case it might more aptly be labeled "psychology student's disease," the basic symptoms are the same: feeling that you suffer from the same sorts of problems you are studying.

Most often, of course, your concerns will be unwarranted. As we have discussed, the differences between normal and abnormal behavior are often so fuzzy that it is easy to jump to the conclusion that you might have the same symptoms that are involved in serious forms of mental disturbance.

Before coming to such a conclusion, though, keep in mind that from time to time we all experience a wide range of emotions, and it is not unusual to feel deeply unhappy, fantasize about bizarre situations, or feel anxiety about life's circumstances. It is the persistence, depth, and consistency of such behavior that set normal reactions apart from abnormal ones. If you have not previously had serious doubts about the normality of your behavior, it is unlikely that reading about others' psychological disorders will prompt you to re-evaluate your earlier conclusion.

On the other hand, many people do have problems that merit concern, and in such cases, it is important to consider the possibility that professional help is warranted. The following list of symptoms can serve as a guideline to help you determine whether outside intervention might be useful (Engler & Goleman, 1992):

- Long-term feelings of distress that interfere with your sense of well-being, competence, and ability to function effectively in daily activities
- Occasions in which you experience overwhelmingly high stress accompanied by feelings of inability to cope with the situation
- Prolonged depression or feelings of hopelessness, especially when they do not have any clear cause (such as the death of someone close)
- Withdrawal from other people
- Thoughts of inflicting harm on oneself or suicide
- A chronic physical problem for which no physical cause can be determined
- A fear or phobia that prevents you from engaging in everyday activities
- Feelings that other people are out to get you or are talking about and plotting against you
- Inability to interact effectively with others, preventing the development of friendships and loving relationships

This list offers a rough set of guidelines for determining when the normal problems of everyday living have escalated beyond your ability to deal with them by yourself. In such situations, the *least* reasonable approach would be to pore over the psychological disorders we have discussed in an attempt at self-diagnosis. A more reasonable strategy is to consider seeking professional help.

RECAP/EVALUATE/RETHINK

RECAP

LO 39-1 How prevalent are psychological disorders?

- About half the people in the United States are likely to experience a psychological disorder at some point in their lives; 30% experience a disorder in any specific year. (p. 483)

LO 39-2 What indicators signal a need for the help of a mental health practitioner?

- The signals that indicate a need for professional help include long-term feelings of psychological distress, feelings of inability to cope with stress, withdrawal from other people, thoughts of inflicting harm on oneself or suicide, prolonged feelings of hopelessness, chronic physical problems with no apparent causes, phobias and compulsions, paranoia, and an inability to interact with others. (p. 488)

EVALUATE

1. The latest version of *DSM* is considered to be the conclusive guideline on defining psychological disorders. True or false?

2. _____ _____ _____ , characterized by severe, incapacitating mood changes or depression related to a woman's menstrual cycle, was eventually added to the appendix of *DSM-IV-TR* despite controversy surrounding its inclusion.

3. Match the disorder with the culture in which it is most common:
   1. amok   a. India
   2. anorexia nervosa   b. Malaysia
   3. brain fag   c. United States
   4. catatonic schizophrenia   d. West Africa

RETHINK

1. Why is inclusion in the *DSM-IV-TR* of "borderline" disorders such as self-defeating personality disorder and premenstrual dysphoric disorder so controversial and political? What disadvantages does inclusion bring? Does inclusion bring any benefits?

2. *From the perspective of a college counselor:* What indicators might be most important in determining whether a college student is experiencing a psychological disorder? Do you believe that all students who show signs of a psychological disorder should seek professional help? How might your responses change if the student were from a different culture (e.g., an African society)?

Answers to Evaluate Questions

1. false; the development of the latest version of *DSM* was a source of great controversy, in part reflecting issues that divide society; 2. Premenstrual dysphoric disorder; 3. 1-b, 2-c, 3-d, 4-a

Looking Back

Epilogue

We've discussed some of the many types of psychological disorders to which people are prone, noted the difficulty psychologists and physicians have in clearly differentiating normal from abnormal behavior, and looked at some of the approaches mental health professionals have taken to explain and treat psychological disorders. We considered today's most commonly used classification scheme, categorized in the *DSM-IV-TR*, and examined some of the more prevalent forms of psychological disorders. To gain a perspective on the topic of psychological disorders, we discussed the surprisingly broad incidence of psychological disorders in U.S. society and the cultural nature of such disorders.

Turn back to the prologue that described the case of Joe Holt. Using the knowledge you've gained about psychological disorders, consider the following questions.

1. Holt was diagnosed as suffering from schizophrenia. What elements of his behavior seem to fit the description of this disorder?
2. How might each of the perspectives on psychological disorders address the causes of his symptoms?
3. Which perspective provides the most useful explanation for Holt's case, in your opinion, and why?

VISUAL SUMMARY 12 Psychological Disorders

MODULE 37 Normal Versus Abnormal: Making the Distinction

Defining Abnormality

- Deviation from the average
- Deviation from the ideal
- Sense of personal discomfort
- Inability to function effectively
- Legal concept

Perspectives on Abnormality

Perspectives on Psychological Disorders

Perspective	Description	Possible Application of Perspective to Joe's Case
Medical	Assumes that physiological causes are at the root of psychological disorders	Examine Joe for medical problems, such as brain tumor, chemical imbalance in the brain, or disease
Psychoanalytic	Argues that psychological disorders stem from childhood conflicts	Seek out information about Joe's past, considering possible childhood conflicts
Behavioral	Assumes that abnormal behaviors are learned responses	Concentrate on rewards and punishments for Joe's behavior, and identify environmental stimuli that reinforce his behavior
Cognitive	Assumes that cognitions (people's thoughts and beliefs) are central to psychological disorders	Focus on Joe's perceptions of self and his environment
Humanistic	Emphasizes people's responsibility for their own behavior and the need to self-actualize	Consider Joe's behavior in terms of his choices and efforts to reach his potential
Sociocultural	Assumes that behavior is shaped by family, society, and culture	Focus on how societal demands contributed to Joe's disorder

Classifying Abnormal Behavior: DSM-IV-TR has shortcomings, but is highly influential.

MODULE 38 Major Psychological Disorders

Anxiety Disorders: Anxiety without external justification

- Phobic disorder
- Panic disorder
- Generalized anxiety disorder
- Obsessive-compulsive disorder
- Causes of anxiety disorders

Somatoform Disorders: Psychological difficulties that take on a physical form with no medical cause

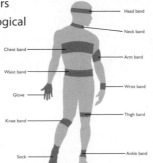

Head band
Neck band
Chest band
Arm band
Waist band
Wrist band
Glove
Thigh band
Knee band
Sock
Ankle band

Dissociative Disorders: Separation of different facets of a person's personality that normally work together

Mood Disorders: Disturbances in emotional experience

- Major depression
- Mania and bipolar disorder
- Causes of mood disorders
  - Genetics
  - Psychological: feelings of loss or anger
  - Behavioral: stress
  - Cognitive: learned helplessness and no hope

Schizophrenia: A class of disorders in which distortion of reality occurs

- Decline from a previous level of functioning
- Disturbances of thought and language
- Delusions
- Hallucinations and perceptual disorders
- Emotional disturbances

Types of Schizophrenia

Type	Symptoms
Disorganized (hebephrenic) schizophrenia	Inappropriate laughter and giggling, silliness, incoherent speech, infantile behavior, strange and sometimes obscene behavior
Paranoid schizophrenia	Delusions and hallucinations of persecution or of greatness, loss of judgment, erratic and unpredictable behavior
Catatonic schizophrenia	Major disturbances in movement; in some phases, loss of all motion, with patient frozen into a single position, remaining that way for hours and sometimes even days; in other phases, hyperactivity and wild, sometimes violent, movement
Undifferentiated schizophrenia	Variable mixture of major symptoms of schizophrenia; classification used for patients who cannot be typed into any of the more specific categories
Residual schizophrenia	Minor signs of schizophrenia after a more serious episode

Personality Disorders: A set of inflexible, maladaptive behavior patterns

- Antisocial personality disorder
- Borderline personality disorder
- Narcissistic personality disorder

Childhood Disorders: Start during childhood or adolescence

- Attention-deficit hyperactivity disorder
- Autism

MODULE 39 Psychological Disorders in Perspective

Social and Cultural Context: Our understanding of abnormal behavior reflects the society and culture in which we live

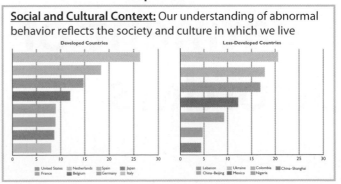

13

Treatment of Psychological Disorders

Learning Outcomes for Chapter 13

MODULE 40

LO 40-1 What are the goals of psychologically based and biologically based treatment approaches?

LO 40-2 What are the psychodynamic, behavioral, and cognitive approaches to treatment?

Psychotherapy: Psychodynamic, Behavioral, and Cognitive Approaches to Treatment

Psychodynamic Approaches to Therapy

Behavioral Approaches to Therapy

Neuroscience in Your Life: How Behavioral Therapy Changes Your Brain

Cognitive Approaches to Therapy

Neuroscience in Your Life: How Cognitive Behavioral Therapy Changes Your Brain

MODULE 41

LO 41-1 What are the humanistic approaches to treatment?

LO 41-2 What is interpersonal therapy?

LO 41-3 How does group therapy differ from individual types of therapy?

LO 41-4 How effective is psychotherapy, and which kind of psychotherapy works best in a given situation?

Psychotherapy: Humanistic, Interpersonal, and Group Approaches to Treatment

Humanistic Therapy

PsychWork: Case Manager and Substance Abuse Counselor

Interpersonal Therapy

Group Therapies

Evaluating Psychotherapy: Does Therapy Work?

Exploring Diversity: Racial and Ethnic Factors in Treatment: Should Therapists Be Color Blind?

MODULE 42

LO 42-1 How are drug, electroconvulsive, and psychosurgical techniques used today in the treatment of psychological disorders?

Biomedical Therapy: Biological Approaches to Treatment

Drug Therapy

Applying Psychology in the 21st Century: Taking the Sting Out of Traumatic Memories

Electroconvulsive Therapy (ECT)

Psychosurgery

Biomedical Therapies in Perspective

Community Psychology: Focus on Prevention

Becoming an Informed Consumer of Psychology: Choosing the Right Therapist

Prologue *Preventing a Tragedy*

Melanie Poorman swiveled in her chair and punched a button on the phone. The caller, an Iraq war veteran in his 30s, had recently broken up with his girlfriend and was watching a movie, "Body of War," that was triggering bad memories. He started to cry.

And he had a 12-gauge shotgun nearby. Could someone please come and take it away, he asked.

Ms. Poorman, 54, gently coaxed the man into unloading the weapon. As a co-worker called the police, she stayed on the line, talking to him about his girlfriend, his work, the war. Suddenly, there were sirens. "I unloaded the gun!" she heard him shout. And then he hung up (Dao, 2010, p. A1).

Looking Ahead

It was a typical night at a suicide prevention hotline run by the Department of Veterans Affairs. Other calls included a drunken man who had hallucinations of people he thought he had murdered; a man with a bipolar disorder having nightmares; and another man who was refusing to take his medications and saying he was going to run into a busy road.

Suicide prevention hotlines are just one way in which trained counselors and therapists assist people suffering from psychological pain. Although treatment can take dozens of forms that range from one-meeting informal counseling sessions to long-term drug therapy, all the approaches have a common objective: the relief of psychological disorders with the ultimate aim of enabling individuals to achieve richer, more meaningful, and more fulfilling lives.

Despite their diversity, approaches to treating psychological disorders fall into two main categories: psychologically based and biologically based therapies. Psychologically based therapy, or **psychotherapy,** is treatment in which a trained professional—a therapist—uses psychological techniques to help someone overcome psychological difficulties and disorders, resolve problems in living, or bring about personal growth. In psychotherapy, the goal is to produce psychological change in a person (called a "client" or "patient") through discussions and interactions with the therapist. In contrast, **biomedical therapy** relies on drugs and medical procedures to improve psychological functioning.

As we describe the various approaches to therapy, keep in mind that although the distinctions may seem clear cut, the classifications and procedures overlap a good deal. In fact, many therapists today take an *eclectic approach* to therapy, which means they use a variety of methods with an individual patient. Assuming that both psychological and biological processes often produce psychological disorders, eclectic therapists may draw from several perspectives simultaneously to address both the psychological and the biological aspects of a person's problems (Goin, 2005; Berman, Jobes, & Silverman, 2006).

psychotherapy Treatment in which a trained professional—a therapist—uses psychological techniques to help a person overcome psychological difficulties and disorders, resolve problems in living, or bring about personal growth.

biomedical therapy Therapy that relies on drugs and other medical procedures to improve psychological functioning.

Psychotherapy: Psychodynamic, Behavioral, and Cognitive Approaches to Treatment

Therapists use some 400 different varieties of psychotherapy, approaches to therapy that focus on psychological factors. Although diverse in many respects, all psychological approaches see treatment as a way of solving psychological problems by modifying people's behavior and helping them gain a better understanding of themselves and their past, present, and future.

In light of the variety of psychological approaches, it is not surprising that the people who provide therapy vary considerably in educational background and training (see Figure 1). Many have doctoral degrees in psychology (that is, they have attended graduate school, learned clinical and research techniques, and held an internship in a facility that treats people with psychological disorders). But therapy is also provided by people in fields allied with psychology, such as psychiatry and social work.

Regardless of their specific training, almost all psychotherapists employ one of four major approaches to therapy: psychodynamic, behavioral, cognitive, and humanistic treatments. These approaches are based on the models of personality and psychological disorders developed by psychologists. Here we'll consider the psychodynamic, behavioral, and cognitive approaches in turn. In the next module, we'll explore the humanistic approach as well as interpersonal psychotherapy and group therapy, and we will evaluate the effectiveness of psychotherapy.

Learning Outcomes

LO 40-1 What are the goals of psychologically based and biologically based treatment approaches?

LO 40-2 What are the psychodynamic, behavioral, and cognitive approaches to treatment?

Getting Help from the Right Person

Clinical Psychologists
Psychologists with a Ph.D. or Psy.D. who have also completed a postgraduate internship. They specialize in assessment and treatment of psychological difficulties, providing psychotherapy and, in some U.S. states, can prescribe drugs.

Counseling Psychologists
Psychologists with a Ph.D. or Ed.D. who typically treat day-to-day adjustment problems, often in a university mental health clinic.

Psychiatrists
M.D.s with postgraduate training in abnormal behavior. Because they can prescribe medication, they often treat the most severe disorders.

Psychoanalysts
Either M.D.s or psychologists who specialize in psychoanalysis, the treatment technique first developed by Freud.

Licensed Professional Counselors or Clinical Mental Health Counselors
Professionals with a master's degree who provide therapy to individuals, couples, and families and who hold a national or state certification.

Clinical or Psychiatric Social Workers
Professionals with a master's degree and specialized training who may provide therapy, usually regarding common family and personal problems.

FIGURE 1 A variety of professionals provide therapy and counseling. Each could be expected to give helpful advice and direction. However, the nature of the problem a person is experiencing may make one or another therapy more appropriate. For example, a person who is suffering from a severe disturbance and who has lost touch with reality will typically require some sort of biologically based drug therapy. In that case, a psychiatrist—who is a physician—would be the professional of choice. In contrast, those suffering from milder disorders, such as difficulty adjusting to the death of a family member, have a broader choice that might include any of the professionals listed in the figure.

Psychodynamic Approaches to Therapy

psychodynamic therapy Therapy that seeks to bring unresolved past conflicts and unacceptable impulses from the unconscious into the conscious, where patients may deal with the problems more effectively.

Psychodynamic therapy seeks to bring unresolved past conflicts and unacceptable impulses from the unconscious into the conscious, where patients may deal with the problems more effectively. Psychodynamic approaches are based on Freud's psychoanalytic approach to personality, which holds that individuals employ *defense mechanisms*, psychological strategies to protect themselves from unacceptable unconscious impulses.

The most common defense mechanism is *repression*, which pushes threatening and unpleasant thoughts and impulses back into the unconscious. However, since unacceptable thoughts and impulses can never be completely buried, some of the anxiety associated with them can produce abnormal behavior in the form of what Freud called *neurotic symptoms*.

How do we rid ourselves of the anxiety produced by unconscious, unwanted impulses and drives? To Freud, the answer was to confront the conflicts and impulses by bringing them out of the unconscious part of the mind and into the conscious part. Freud assumed that this technique would reduce anxiety stemming from past conflicts and that the patient could then participate in his or her daily life more effectively.

A psychodynamic therapist, then, faces the challenge of finding a way to assist patients' attempts to explore and understand the unconscious. The technique that has evolved has a number of components, but basically it consists of guiding patients to consider and discuss their past experiences in explicit detail from the time of their first memories. This process assumes that patients will eventually stumble upon long-hidden crises, traumas, and conflicts that are producing anxiety in their adult lives. They will then be able to "work through"—understand and rectify—those difficulties.

PSYCHOANALYSIS: FREUD'S THERAPY

psychoanalysis Psychotherapy developed by Freud in which the goal is to release hidden unconscious thoughts and feelings in order to reduce their power in controlling behavior.

Classic Freudian psychodynamic therapy, called psychoanalysis, tends to be a lengthy and expensive affair. **Psychoanalysis** is the kind of psychotherapy developed by Freud in which the goal is to release hidden unconscious thoughts and feelings in order to reduce their power in controlling behavior.

In psychoanalysis, patients may meet with a therapist with considerable frequency, sometimes as much as 50 minutes a day, 4 to 5 days a week, for several years. In their sessions, they often use a technique developed by Freud called *free association*. Psychoanalysts using this technique tell patients to say aloud whatever comes to mind, regardless of its apparent irrelevance or senselessness, and the analysts attempt to recognize and label the connections between what a patient says and the patient's unconscious. Therapists also use *dream interpretation*, examining dreams to find clues to unconscious conflicts and problems. Moving beyond the surface description of a dream (called the *manifest content*), therapists seek its underlying meaning (the *latent content*), which thereby reveals the true unconscious meaning of the dream (Auld, Hyman, & Rudzinski, 2005; Bodin, 2006; Blum, 2011).

The processes of free association and dream interpretation do not always move forward easily. The same unconscious forces that initially produced repression may keep past difficulties out of the conscious mind, which produces resistance. *Resistance* is an inability or unwillingness to discuss or reveal particular memories, thoughts, or motivations. Patients can express resistance in many ways. For instance, they may be discussing a childhood memory and suddenly forget what they were saying, or they may change the subject completely. It is the therapist's job to pick

Study Alert

To better understand how psychodynamic therapy works, review Freud's psychoanalytic theory discussed in the chapter on personality.

up instances of resistance and interpret their meaning as well as to ensure that patients return to the subject—which is likely to hold difficult or painful memories for the patients.

Because of the close, almost intimate interaction between patient and psychoanalyst, the relationship between the two often becomes emotionally charged and takes on a complexity unlike most other relationships. Patients may eventually think of the analyst as a symbol of a significant other in their past, perhaps a parent or a lover, and apply some of their feelings for that person to the analyst—a phenomenon known as transference. **Transference** is the transfer of feelings to a psychoanalyst of love or anger that had been originally directed to a patient's parents or other authority figures (Evans, 2007; Steiner, 2008; Høglend et al., 2011).

A therapist can use transference to help a patient recreate past relationships that were psychologically difficult. For instance, if a patient undergoing transference views her therapist as a symbol of her father—with whom she had a difficult relationship—the patient and therapist may "redo" an earlier interaction, this time including more positive aspects. Through this process, the patient may resolve conflicts regarding her real father—something that is beginning to happen in the following therapy session:

The close and intense relationship between therapist and patient may become highly complex.

transference The transfer of feelings to a psychoanalyst of love or anger that had been originally directed to a patient's parents or other authority figures.

> Sandy: My father . . . never took any interest in any of us. . . . It was my mother—rest her soul—who loved us, not our father. He worked her to death. Lord, I miss her. . . . I must sound angry at my father. Don't you think I have a right to be angry?
>
> Therapist: Do you think you have a right to be angry?
>
> Sandy: Of course, I do! Why are you questioning me? You don't believe me, do you?
>
> Therapist: You want me to believe you.
>
> Sandy: I don't care whether you believe me or not. . . . I know what you're thinking—you think I'm crazy—you must be laughing at me—I'll probably be a case in your next book! You're just sitting there—smirking—making me feel like a bad person—thinking I'm wrong for being mad, that I have no right to be mad.
>
> Therapist: Just like your father.
>
> Sandy: Yes, you're just like my father.—Oh my God! Just now—I—I—thought I was talking to him. (Sue, Sue, & Sue, 1990, pp. 514–515)

CONTEMPORARY PSYCHODYNAMIC APPROACHES

Few people have the time, money, or patience to participate in years of traditional psychoanalysis. Moreover, no conclusive evidence shows that psychoanalysis, as originally conceived by Freud in the 19th century, works better than other, more recent forms of psychodynamic therapy.

Today, psychodynamic therapy tends to be of shorter duration and usually lasts no longer than 3 months or 20 sessions. The therapist takes a more active role than Freud would have liked by controlling the course of therapy and prodding and advising the patient with considerable directness. Finally, the therapist puts less emphasis on a patient's past history and childhood and concentrates instead on an individual's current relationships and specific complaints (Charman, 2004; Wolitzky, 2006; Brafman, 2011).

EVALUATING PSYCHODYNAMIC THERAPY

Even with its current modifications, psychodynamic therapy has its critics. In its longer versions, it can be time consuming and expensive,

"And when did you first realize you weren't like other precipitation?"

especially in comparison with other forms of psychotherapy, such as behavioral and cognitive approaches. Furthermore, less articulate patients may not do as well as more articulate ones.

Ultimately, the most important concern about psychodynamic treatment is whether it actually works, and there is no simple answer to this question. Psychodynamic treatment techniques have been controversial since Freud introduced them. Part of the problem is the difficulty in establishing whether patients have improved after psychodynamic therapy. Determining effectiveness depends on reports from the therapist or the patients themselves—reports that are obviously open to bias and subjective interpretation.

Furthermore, critics have questioned the entire theoretical basis of psychodynamic theory; they maintain that constructs such as the unconscious have not been scientifically confirmed. Despite the criticism, though, the psychodynamic treatment approach has remained viable. For some people, it provides solutions to difficult psychological issues, provides effective treatment for psychological disturbance, and also permits the potential development of an unusual degree of insight into one's life (Ablon & Jones, 2005; Bond, 2006; Anestis, Anestis, & Lilienfeld, 2011).

Behavioral Approaches to Therapy

Perhaps, when you were a child, your parents rewarded you with an ice cream cone when you were especially good . . . or sent you to your room if you misbehaved. Sound principles back up such a child-rearing strategy: Good behavior is maintained by reinforcement, and unwanted behavior can be eliminated by punishment.

behavioral treatment approaches
Treatment approaches that make use of the basic processes of learning, such as reinforcement and extinction, and assume that normal and abnormal behavior are both learned.

These principles represent the basic underpinnings of **behavioral treatment approaches.** Building on the basic processes of learning, behavioral treatment approaches make this fundamental assumption: Both abnormal behavior and normal behavior are *learned*. People who act abnormally either have failed to learn the skills they need to cope with the problems of everyday living or have acquired faulty skills and patterns that are being maintained through some form of reinforcement. To modify abnormal behavior, then, proponents of behavioral approaches propose that people must learn new behavior to replace the faulty skills they have developed and unlearn their maladaptive behavior patterns (Krijn et al., 2004; Norton & Price, 2007; Kowalik et al., 2011).

Behavioral psychologists do not need to delve into people's pasts or their psyches. Rather than viewing abnormal behavior as a symptom of an underlying problem, they consider the abnormal behavior as the problem in need of modification. The goal of therapy is to change people's behavior to allow them to function more effectively. In this view, then, there is no problem other than the maladaptive behavior itself; if you can change that behavior, treatment is successful.

Behavioral approaches to treatment would seek to modify the behavior of this couple rather than to focus on the underlying causes of the behavior.

CLASSICAL CONDITIONING TREATMENTS

Suppose you bite into your favorite candy bar and find that not only is it infested with ants, but you've also swallowed a bunch of them. You immediately become sick to your stomach and throw up. Your long-term reaction? You never eat that kind of candy bar again, and it may be months before you eat any type of candy. You have learned through the basic process of classical conditioning to avoid candy so that you will not get sick and throw up.

Aversive Conditioning. This simple example illustrates how a person can be classically conditioned to modify behavior. Behavior therapists use this principle when they employ **aversive conditioning,** a form of therapy that reduces the frequency of undesired behavior by pairing an aversive, unpleasant stimulus with undesired behavior. For example, behavior therapists might use aversive conditioning by pairing alcohol with a drug that causes severe nausea and vomiting. After the two have been paired a few times, the person associates the alcohol alone with vomiting and finds alcohol less appealing.

> **aversive conditioning** A form of therapy that reduces the frequency of undesired behavior by pairing an aversive, unpleasant stimulus with undesired behavior.

Although aversion therapy works reasonably well in inhibiting substance-abuse problems such as alcoholism and certain kinds of sexual disorders, critics question its long-term effectiveness. Also, important ethical concerns surround aversion techniques that employ such potent stimuli as electric shock, which therapists use only in the most extreme cases, such as patient self-mutilation. Clearly, though, aversion therapy offers an important procedure for eliminating maladaptive responses for some period of time—a respite that provides, even if only temporarily, an opportunity to encourage more adaptive behavior patterns (Delgado, Labouliere, & Phelps, 2006; Pautassi et al., 2011).

Systematic Desensitization. Another treatment that grew out of the classical conditioning is systematic desensitization. In **systematic desensitization,** gradual exposure to an anxiety-producing stimulus is paired with relaxation to extinguish the response of anxiety (Choy, Fyer, & Lipsitz, 2007; Dowling, Jackson, & Thomas, 2008; Triscari et al., 2011).

> **systematic desensitization** A behavioral technique in which gradual exposure to an anxiety-producing stimulus is paired with relaxation to extinguish the response of anxiety.

Suppose, for instance, you were extremely afraid of flying. The very thought of being in an airplane would make you begin to sweat and shake, and you couldn't get yourself near enough to an airport to know how you'd react if you actually had to fly somewhere. Using systematic desensitization to treat your problem, you would first be trained in relaxation techniques by a behavior therapist and learn to relax your body fully—a highly pleasant state, as you might imagine (see Figure 2).

Step 1. Pick a focus word or short phrase that's firmly rooted in your personal belief system. For example, a nonreligious individual might choose a neutral word like *one* or *peace* or *love.* A Christian person desiring to use a prayer could pick the opening words of Psalm 23. *The Lord is my shepherd;* a Jewish person could choose *Shalom.*

Step 2. Sit quietly in a comfortable position.

Step 3. Close your eyes.

Step 4. Relax your muscles.

Step 5. Breathe slowly and naturally, repeating your focus word or phrase silently as you exhale.

Step 6. Throughout, assume a passive attitude. Don't worry about how well you're doing. When other thoughts come to mind, simply say to yourself, "Oh, well," and gently return to the repetition.

Step 7. Continue for 10 to 20 minutes. You may open your eyes to check the time, but do not use an alarm. When you finish, sit quietly for a minute or so, at first with your eyes closed and later with your eyes open. Then do not stand for one or 2 minutes.

Step 8. Practice the technique once or twice a day.

FIGURE 2 Following these basic steps will help you achieve a sense of calmness by employing the relaxation response. (Source: Herbert Benson, M.D., Benson-Henry Institute for Mind Body Medicine, Massachusetts General Hospital, Boston.)

The next step would involve constructing a *hierarchy of fears*—a list in order of increasing severity of the things you associate with your fears. For instance, your hierarchy might resemble this one:

1. Watching a plane fly overhead
2. Going to an airport
3. Buying a ticket
4. Stepping into the plane
5. Seeing the plane door close
6. Having the plane taxi down the runway
7. Taking off
8. Being in the air

> **Study Alert**
>
> To help remember the concept of hierarchy of fears, think of something that you are afraid of and construct your own hierarchy of fears.

Once you had developed this hierarchy and learned relaxation techniques, you would learn to associate the two sets of responses. To do this, your therapist might ask you to put yourself into a relaxed state and then imagine yourself in the first situation identified in your hierarchy. Once you could consider that first step while remaining relaxed, you would move on to the next situation. Eventually you would move up the hierarchy in gradual stages until you could imagine yourself being in the air without experiencing anxiety. Ultimately, you would be asked to make a visit to an airport and later to take a flight.

exposure A behavioral treatment for anxiety in which people are confronted either suddenly or gradually with a stimulus that they fear.

Exposure Treatments. Although systematic desensitization has proven to be a successful treatment, today it is often replaced with a less complicated form of therapy called exposure. **Exposure** is a behavioral treatment for anxiety in which people are confronted either suddenly or gradually with a stimulus that they fear. However, unlike systematic desensitization, relaxation training is omitted. Exposure allows the maladaptive response of anxiety or avoidance to extinguish, and research shows that this approach is generally as effective as systematic desensitization (Havermans et al., 2007; Hofmann, 2007; Bush, 2008).

In most cases, therapists use *graded exposure* in which patients are exposed to a feared stimulus in gradual steps. For example, a patient who is afraid of dogs might first view a video of dogs. Gradually the exposure escalates to seeing a live, leashed dog across the room and then actually petting and touching the dog (Berle, 2007; Means & Edinger, 2007).

Exposure has proved to be an effective treatment for a number of problems, including phobias, anxiety disorders, and even impotence and fear of sexual contact. Through this technique, people can learn to enjoy the things they once feared (Franklin, March, & Garcia, 2007; Powers & Emmelkamp, 2008; Tuerk et al., 2011).

OPERANT CONDITIONING TECHNIQUES

Some behavioral approaches make use of the operant conditioning principles that we discussed earlier in the book when considering the topic of learning. These approaches are based on the notion that we should reward people for carrying out desirable behavior and extinguish undesirable behavior by either ignoring it or punishing it.

One example of the systematic application of operant conditioning principles is the *token system,* which rewards a person for desired behavior with a token such as a poker chip or some kind of play money. Although it is most frequently employed in institutional settings for individuals with relatively serious problems and sometimes with children as a classroom management technique, the system resembles what parents do when they give children money for being well behaved—money that the children can later exchange for something they want. The desired behavior may range from simple things such as keeping one's room neat to personal grooming and interacting with other people. In institutions, patients can exchange tokens for some object or activity, such as snacks, new clothes, or, in extreme cases, sleeping in one's own bed rather than in a sleeping bag on the floor.

Contingency contracting, a variant of the token system, has proved quite effective in producing behavior modification. In *contingency contracting,* the therapist and client (or teacher and student or parent and child) draw up a written agreement. The contract states a series of behavioral goals the client hopes to achieve. It also specifies the positive consequences for the client if the client reaches goals—usually an explicit reward such as money or additional privileges. Contracts frequently state negative consequences if the client does not meet the goals. For example, clients who are trying to quit smoking might write out a check to a cause they have no interest in supporting (for instance, the National Rifle Association if they are strong supporters of gun control). If the client smokes on a given day, the therapist will mail the check.

Behavior therapists also use *observational learning,* the process in which the behavior of other people is modeled, to systematically teach people new skills and ways of handling their fears and anxieties. For example, modeling helps when thera-

A "Fearless Peer" who models appropriate and effective behavior can help children overcome their fears.

pists are teaching basic social skills, such as maintaining eye contact during conversation and acting assertively. Similarly, children with dog phobias have been able to overcome their fears by watching another child—called the "Fearless Peer"— repeatedly walk up to a dog, touch it, pet it, and finally play with it. Modeling, then, can play an effective role in resolving some kinds of behavior difficulties, especially if the model receives a reward for his or her behavior (Bandura, Grusec, & Menlove, 1967; Greer, Dudek-Singer, & Gautreaux, 2006; Egliston & Rapee, 2007).

DIALECTICAL BEHAVIOR THERAPY

In **dialectical behavior therapy,** the focus is on getting people to change their behavior and view of themselves by accepting who they are regardless of whether it matches their ideal. Even if their childhood has been dysfunctional or they have ruined relationships with others, that's in the past. What matters is who they wish to become (Lynch et al., 2007; Wagner, Rizvi, & Hamed, 2007; Robins & Rosenthal, 2011).

Like treatment approaches based on the principles of classical and operant conditioning, dialectical behavior therapy is an outgrowth of behavioral approaches, but it also includes components of other perspectives. Therapists using dialectical behavior therapy seek to have patients realize that they basically have two choices: Either they remain unhappy, or they change. Once patients agree that they wish to change, it is up to them to modify their behavior. Patients are taught that even if they experience unhappiness, anger, or any other negative emotion, it doesn't need to rule their behavior. It's their behavior that counts—not their inner life.

Dialectical behavior therapy teaches behavioral skills that help people behave more effectively and keep their emotions in check. Although it is a relatively new form of therapy, increasing evidence supports its effectiveness, particularly with certain personality disorders (Swales & Heard, 2007; Katz, Fotti, & Postl, 2009; Soler et al., 2009).

dialectical behavior therapy A form of treatment in which the focus is on getting people to change their behavior and view of themselves by accepting who they are regardless of whether it matches their ideal.

EVALUATING BEHAVIOR THERAPY

Behavior therapy works especially well for eliminating anxiety disorders, treating phobias and compulsions, establishing control over impulses, and learning complex social skills to replace maladaptive behavior. More than any of the other therapeutic techniques, it provides methods that nonprofessionals can use to change their own behavior. Moreover, it is efficient because it focuses on solving carefully defined problems (Richard & Lauterbach, 2006; Barlow, 2007).

Neuroscience in Your Life:
How Behavioral Therapy Changes Your Brain

FIGURE 3 This figure highlights areas of the brain that show a reduced response to highly emotionally arousing pictures after behavioral therapy in patients with borderline personality disorder. The scans on the left (a) show areas of increased activity (in red, yellow, and orange) in those with borderline personality disorder before behavioral therapy as compared to participants who do not have this disorder. The scans on the right (b) show this same comparison after treatment. The scans on the right (b) contain fewer areas of activation, which suggests that after behavioral therapy, the brains of those with borderline personality disorder react more similarly to the brains of those who do not have the disorder. (Source: Schnell & Herpertz, 2007, Figure 3.)

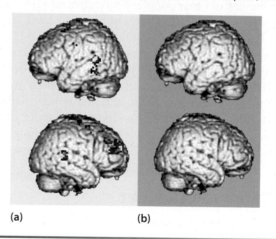

(a)   (b)

Critics of behavior therapy believe that because it emphasizes changing external behavior, people do not necessarily gain insight into thoughts and expectations that may be fostering their maladaptive behavior. On the other hand, neuroscientific evidence shows that behavioral treatments can produce actual changes in brain functioning, which suggests that behavioral treatments can produce changes beyond external behavior.

For example, one experiment looked at the neurological reactions of patients with borderline personality disorder who participated in a 12-week dialectical behavioral therapy program. Compared with a control group composed of people who did not have the disorder, the patients showed significant changes in their reactions to highly arousing emotion-evoking stimuli. Following therapy, the patients' neurological functioning was more similar to those without the disorder than it was prior to therapy (see Figure 3 *Neuroscience in Your Life*).

Cognitive Approaches to Therapy

If you assumed that illogical thoughts and beliefs lie at the heart of psychological disorders, wouldn't the most direct treatment route be to teach people new, more adaptive modes of thinking? The answer is yes, according to psychologists who take a cognitive approach to treatment.

Cognitive treatment approaches teach people to think in more adaptive ways by changing their dysfunctional cognitions about the world and themselves. Unlike behavior therapists, who focus on modifying external behavior, cognitive therapists attempt to change the way people think as well as their behavior. Because they often use basic principles of learning, the methods they employ are sometimes referred to as the **cognitive-behavioral approach** (Beck & Rector, 2005; Friedberg, 2006; Kalodner, 2011).

Although cognitive treatment approaches take many forms, they all share the assumption that anxiety, depression, and negative emotions develop from maladaptive thinking. Accordingly, cognitive treatments seek to change the thought patterns that lead to getting "stuck" in dysfunctional ways of thinking. Therapists systematically teach clients to challenge their assumptions and adopt new approaches to old problems.

Cognitive therapy is relatively short term and usually lasts a maximum of 20 sessions. Therapy tends to be highly structured and focused on concrete problems. Therapists often begin by teaching the theory behind the approach and then continue to take an active role throughout the course of therapy by acting as a combination of teacher, coach, and partner.

One good example of cognitive treatment, **rational-emotive behavior therapy,** attempts to restructure a person's belief system into a more realistic, rational, and logical set of views. According to psychologist Albert Ellis (2002, 2004), many people lead unhappy lives and suffer from psychological disorders because they harbor irrational, unrealistic ideas such as these:

- We need the love or approval of virtually every significant other person for everything we do.
- We should be thoroughly competent, adequate, and successful in all possible respects in order to consider ourselves worthwhile.
- It is horrible when things don't turn out the way we want them to.

Such irrational beliefs trigger negative emotions, which in turn support the irrational beliefs and lead to a self-defeating cycle. Ellis calls it the A-B-C model in which negative activating conditions (A) lead to the activation of an irrational belief system (B), which in turn leads to emotional consequences (C). For example, if a person experiences the breakup of a close relationship (A) and holds the irrational belief (B) that "I'll never be loved again," this triggers negative emotions (C) that in turn feed back into support of the irrational belief (see Figure 4).

Rational-emotive behavior therapy aims to help clients eliminate maladaptive thoughts and beliefs and adopt more effective thinking. To accomplish this goal,

cognitive treatment approaches Treatment approaches that teach people to think in more adaptive ways by changing their dysfunctional cognitions about the world and themselves.

cognitive-behavioral approach A treatment approach that incorporates basic principles of learning to change the way people think.

rational-emotive behavior therapy A form of therapy that attempts to restructure a person's belief system into a more realistic, rational, and logical set of views by challenging dysfunctional beliefs that maintain irrational behavior.

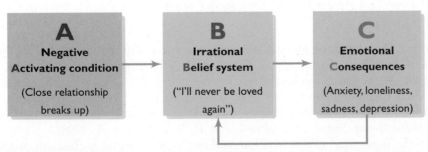

FIGURE 4 In the A-B-C model of rational-emotive behavior therapy, negative activating conditions (A) lead to the activation of an irrational belief system (B), which leads to emotional consequences (C). Those emotional consequences then feed back and support the belief system. At what steps in the model could change occur as a result of rational-emotive behavior therapy?

therapists take an active, directive role during therapy and openly challenge patterns of thought that appear to be dysfunctional. Consider this example:

> Martha: The basic problem is that I'm worried about my family. I'm worried about money. And I never seem to be able to relax.
>
> Therapist: Why are you worried about your family? . . . What's to be concerned about? They have certain demands which you don't want to adhere to.
>
> Martha: I was brought up to think that I mustn't be selfish.
>
> Therapist: Oh, we'll have to knock that out of your head!
>
> Martha: My mother feels that I shouldn't have left home—that my place is with them. There are nagging doubts about what I should—
>
> Therapist: Why are there doubts? Why should you?
>
> Martha: I think it's a feeling I was brought up with that you always have to give of yourself. If you think of yourself, you're wrong.
>
> Therapist: That's a belief. Why do you have to keep believing that—at your age? You believed a lot of superstitions when you were younger. Why do you have to retain them? Your parents indoctrinated you with this nonsense, because that's their belief. . . . Who needs that philosophy? All it's gotten you, so far, is guilt. (Ellis, 1974, pp. 223–286)

By poking holes in Martha's reasoning, the therapist is attempting to help her adopt a more realistic view of herself and her circumstances (Ellis, 2002; Dryden & David, 2008).

Another influential form of therapy that builds on a cognitive perspective is that of Aaron Beck (Beck, 1995, 2004). Like rational-emotive behavior therapy, Beck's cognitive behavior therapy aims to change people's illogical thoughts about themselves and the world.

However, cognitive behavior therapy is considerably less confrontational and challenging than rational-emotive behavior therapy. Instead of the therapist actively arguing with clients about their dysfunctional cognitions, cognitive behavior therapists more often play the role of teacher. Therapists urge clients to obtain information on their own that will lead them to discard their inaccurate thinking through a process of cognitive appraisal. In *cognitive appraisal*, clients are asked to evaluate situations, themselves, and others in terms of their memories, values, beliefs, thoughts, and expectations. During the course of treatment, therapists help clients discover ways of thinking more appropriately about themselves and others (Rosen, 2000; Beck, Freeman, & Davis, 2004; Moorey, 2007; also see Figure 5 *Neuroscience in Your Life*).

EVALUATING COGNITIVE APPROACHES TO THERAPY

Cognitive approaches to therapy have proved successful in dealing with a broad range of disorders, including anxiety disorders, depression, substance abuse, and eating disorders. Furthermore, the willingness of cognitive therapists to incorporate additional treatment approaches (e.g., combining cognitive and behavioral techniques in cognitive behavior therapy) has made this approach a particularly effective form of treatment (Mitte, 2005; Ishikawa et al., 2007; Bhar et al., 2008).

At the same time, critics have pointed out that the focus on helping people to think more rationally ignores the fact that life is in reality sometimes irrational. Changing one's assumptions to make them more reasonable and logical thus may not always be helpful—even assuming it is possible to bring about true cognitive change. Still, the success of cognitive approaches has made it one of the most frequently employed therapies (Leahy, 2003; Beck & Rector, 2005).

PsychTech

Psychologist David Mohr found that an Internet-based treatment for depression in which patients logged into a website and also received e-mail and telephone support was effective in reducing depressive episodes.

Neuroscience in Your Life:
How Cognitive Behavioral Therapy Changes Your Brain

FIGURE 5 Certain psychological disorders, such as generalized anxiety disorder, are often treated with medications such as serotonin reuptake inhibitors (SSRIs). However, similar effects can sometimes be achieved with treatments that focus on changing thought patterns, such as cognitive behavioral therapy (CBT). As seen in this image, adolescents with generalized anxiety disorder show increased activation of the ventrolateral prefrontal cortex (VLPFC) while watching angry faces (thought to provoke anxiety) following both treatment with SSRIs and CBT. The VLPFC is an area of the brain that regulates negative emotions such as anxiety, and increased brain activity is related to reduced severity in generalized anxiety disorder, suggesting that CBT is as effective as drug treatments. (Source: Maslowsky et al., 2010.)

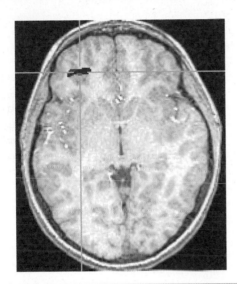

RECAP/EVALUATE/RETHINK

RECAP

LO 40-1 What are the goals of psychologically based and biologically based treatment approaches?

- Psychotherapy (psychologically based therapy) and biomedical therapy (biologically based therapy) share the goal of resolving psychological problems by modifying people's thoughts, feelings, expectations, evaluations, and ultimately behavior. (p. 494)

LO 40-2 What are the psychodynamic, behavioral, and cognitive approaches to treatment?

- Psychoanalytic approaches seek to bring unresolved past conflicts and unacceptable impulses from the unconscious into the conscious, where patients may deal with the problems more effectively. To do this, therapists use techniques such as free association and dream interpretation. (p. 496)

- Behavioral approaches to treatment view abnormal behavior as the problem rather than viewing that behavior as a symptom of some underlying cause. To bring about a "cure," this view suggests that the outward behavior must be changed by using methods such as aversive conditioning, systematic desensitization, observational learning, token systems, contingency contracting, and dialectical behavior therapy. (pp. 498–501)

- Cognitive approaches to treatment consider that the goal of therapy is to help a person restructure his or her faulty belief system into a more realistic, rational, and logical view of the world. Two examples of cognitive treatments are the rational-emotive behavior therapy and cognitive behavior therapy. (p. 503)

EVALUATE

1. Match the following mental health practitioners with the appropriate description.

   1. Psychiatrist
   2. Clinical psychologist
   3. Counseling psychologist
   4. Psychoanalyst

   a. PhD specializing in the treatment of psychological disorders
   b. Professional specializing in Freudian therapy techniques
   c. MD trained in abnormal behavior
   d. PhD specializing in the adjustment of day-to-day problems

2. According to Freud, people use _____ _____ as a means of preventing unwanted impulses from intruding on conscious thought.

3. In dream interpretation, a psychoanalyst must learn to distinguish between the _____ content of a dream, which is what appears on the surface, and the _____ content, its underlying meaning.

4. Which of the following treatments deals with phobias by gradual exposure to the item producing the fear?
   a. Systematic desensitization
   b. Partial reinforcement
   c. Behavioral self-management
   d. Aversion therapy

RETHINK

1. In what ways are psychoanalysis and cognitive therapy similar, and how do they differ?

2. *From the perspective of a child-care provider:* How might you use systematic desensitization to help children overcome their fears?

Answers to Evaluate Questions

1. 1-c, 2-a, 3-d, 4-b; 2. defense mechanisms; 3. manifest, latent; 4. a

KEY TERMS

psychotherapy p. 494
biomedical therapy p. 494
psychodynamic therapy p. 496
psychoanalysis p. 496
transference p. 497

behavioral treatment approaches p. 498
aversive conditioning p. 499
systematic desensitization p. 499

exposure p. 500
dialectical behavior therapy p. 501
cognitive treatment approaches p. 503

cognitive-behavioral approach p. 503
rational-emotive behavior therapy p. 503

Psychotherapy: Humanistic, Interpersonal, and Group Approaches to Treatment

Humanistic Therapy

As you know from your own experience, a student cannot master the material covered in a course without some hard work, no matter how good the teacher and the textbook are. *You must* take the time to study, memorize the vocabulary, and learn the concepts. Nobody else can do it for you. If you choose to put in the effort, you'll succeed; if you don't, you'll fail. The responsibility is primarily yours.

Humanistic therapy draws on this philosophical perspective of self-responsibility in developing treatment techniques. The many different types of therapy that fit into this category have a similar rationale: We have control of our own behavior, we can make choices about the kinds of lives we want to live, and it is up to us to solve the difficulties we encounter in our daily lives.

Humanistic therapists believe that people naturally are motivated to strive for self-actualization. As we discussed in the chapter on motivation, *self-actualization* is the term that clinical psychologist Abraham Maslow used to describe the state of self-fulfillment in which people realize their highest potentials in their own unique way.

Instead of acting in the more directive manner of some psychodynamic and behavioral approaches, humanistic therapists view themselves as guides or facilitators. Therapists using humanistic techniques seek to help people understand themselves and find ways to come closer to the ideal they hold for themselves. In this view, psychological disorders result from the inability to find meaning in life and from feelings of loneliness and a lack of connection to others (Cain, 2002; Watson, Goldman, & Greenberg, 2011).

Humanistic approaches have produced many therapeutic techniques. Among the most important is person-centered therapy.

PERSON-CENTERED THERAPY

Consider the following therapy session excerpt:

Alice: I was thinking about this business of standards. I somehow developed a sort of a knack, I guess, of—well—habit—of trying to make people feel at ease around me, or to make things go along smoothly. . . .

Therapist: In other words, what you did was always in the direction of trying to keep things smooth and to make other people feel better and to smooth the situation.

Alice: Yes. I think that's what it was. Now the reason why I did it probably was—I mean, not that I was a good little Samaritan going around making other people happy, but that was probably the role that felt easiest for me to play. . . .

Therapist: You feel that for a long time you've been playing the role of kind of smoothing out the frictions or differences or what not. . . .

Learning Outcomes

LO 41-1 What are the humanistic approaches to treatment?

LO 41-2 What is interpersonal therapy?

LO 41-3 How does group therapy differ from individual types of therapy?

LO 41-4 How effective is psychotherapy, and which kind of psychotherapy works best in a given situation?

humanistic therapy Therapy in which the underlying rationale is that people have control of their behavior, can make choices about their lives, and are essentially responsible for solving their own problems.

Humanistic therapy focuses on self-responsibility.

Alice: M-hm.

Therapist: Rather than having any opinion or reaction of your own in the situation. Is that it? (Rogers, 1951, pp. 152–153)

The therapist does not interpret or answer the questions the client has raised. Instead, the therapist clarifies or reflects back what the client has said (e.g., "In other words, what you did. . . ."; "You feel that. . . ."; "Is that it?"). This therapeutic technique, known as *nondirective counseling,* is at the heart of person-centered therapy, which was first practiced by Carl Rogers in the mid-20th century (Rogers, 1951, 1980; Raskin & Rogers, 1989).

person-centered therapy Therapy in which the goal is to reach one's potential for self-actualization.

Person-centered therapy (also called *client-centered therapy*) aims to enable people to reach their potential for self-actualization. By providing a warm and accepting environment, therapists hope to motivate clients to air their problems and feelings. In turn, this enables clients to make realistic and constructive choices and decisions about the things that bother them in their current lives (Kirschenbaum, 2004; Bohart, 2006; Cooper & McLeod, 2011).

Instead of directing the choices clients make, therapists provide what Rogers calls *unconditional positive regard*—providing whole-hearted acceptance and understanding, regardless of the feelings and attitudes the client expresses. By doing this, therapists hope to create an atmosphere that enables clients to come to decisions that can improve their lives (Kirschenbaum & Jourdan, 2005; Vieira & Freire, 2006).

Study Alert

To better remember the concept of unconditional positive regard, try offering it to a friend during a conversation by showing your support, acceptance, and understanding no matter what thought or attitude your friend expresses.

Furnishing unconditional positive regard does not mean that therapists must approve of everything their clients say or do. Rather, therapists need to communicate that they are caring, nonjudgmental, and *empathetic*—that is, understanding of a client's emotional experiences (Fearing & Clark, 2000).

Person-centered therapy is rarely used today in its purest form. Contemporary approaches tend to be somewhat more directive with therapists nudging clients toward insights rather than merely reflecting back their statements. However, therapists still view clients' insights as central to the therapeutic process (also see *PsychWork*).

PsychWork

CASE MANAGER AND

SUBSTANCE ABUSE COUNSELOR

Name: Vicki Dickerman

Education: BS in Addiction Studies and Psychology, Park University, Parkville, Missouri; Certified Co-Occurring Disorders Professional

"At the Kansas City Community Center, we help people rebuild their lives."

For Vickie Dickerman, a case manager and substance abuse counselor, this statement is the foundation of her work.

"Treatment is a collaboration between what the client wants from a program and what you, as the professional, see as essential in the treatment planning process. We also assist clients in obtaining their basic needs in order that they may become productive members of society," she said.

Dickerman, who has worked for 20 years in the field of substance abuse with criminal offenders, uses several approaches in helping people rebuild their lives.

"I address 'criminal thinking errors' along with client-centered therapy," she explained. "When clients engage in 'criminal thinking,' they view themselves as victims, focus only their positive attributes, and avoid taking responsibility for their actions." Dickerman seeks to change such thinking and help clients rebuild their self-confidence in their ability to meet their own basic needs.

"Expressing praise to offenders for something that would not appear to be an accomplishment to most of us is of importance since clients' low self-esteem and lack of self-confidence are often the result of lack of reinforcement from family members and their peers," Dickerman added. "Allowing setbacks should be considered a part of the process since individuals with criminal thinking errors experience difficulty with receiving praise and may attempt to sabotage their success."

EVALUATING HUMANISTIC APPROACHES TO THERAPY

The notion that psychological disorders result from restricted growth potential appeals philosophically to many people. Furthermore, when humanistic therapists acknowledge that the freedom we possess can lead to psychological difficulties, clients find an unusually supportive environment for therapy. In turn, this atmosphere can help clients discover solutions to difficult psychological problems (Cooper, 2007).

However, humanistic treatments lack specificity, a problem that has troubled their critics. Humanistic approaches are not very precise and are probably the least scientifically and theoretically developed type of treatment. Moreover, this form of treatment works best for the same type of highly verbal client who profits most from psychoanalytic treatment.

Interpersonal Therapy

Interpersonal therapy (IPT) considers therapy in the context of social relationships. Although its roots stem from psychodynamic approaches, interpersonal therapy concentrates more on the here and now with the goal of improving a client's existing relationships. It typically focuses on interpersonal issues such as conflicts with others, social skills issues, role transitions (such as divorce), or grief (Weissman, Markowitz, & Klerman, 2007; Stangier et al., 2011).

Interpersonal therapy is more active and directive than traditional psychodynamic approaches, and sessions are more structured. The approach makes no assumptions about the underlying causes of psychological disorders but focuses on the interpersonal context in which a disorder is developed and maintained. It also tends to be shorter than traditional psychodynamic approaches and typically lasts only 12–16 weeks. During those sessions, therapists make concrete suggestions on improving relations with others and offer recommendations and advice.

Because interpersonal therapy is short and structured, researchers have been able to demonstrate its effectiveness more readily than longer-term types of therapy. Evaluations of the approach have shown that interpersonal therapy is especially effective in dealing with depression, anxiety, addictions, and eating disorders (Salsman, 2006; Grigoriadis & Ravitz, 2007; Miller et al., 2008).

interpersonal therapy (IPT) Short-term therapy that focuses on the context of current social relationships.

Group Therapies

Although most treatment takes place between a single individual and a therapist, some forms of therapy involve groups of people seeking treatment. In **group therapy**, several unrelated people meet with a therapist to discuss some aspect of their psychological functioning.

People typically discuss with the group their problems, which often center on a common difficulty, such as alcoholism or a lack of social skills. The other members of the group provide emotional support and dispense advice on ways they have coped effectively with similar problems (Scaturo, 2004; Rigby & Waite, 2007; Schachter, 2011).

Groups vary greatly in terms of the particular model they employ; there are psychoanalytic groups, humanistic groups, and groups corresponding to the other therapeutic approaches. Furthermore, groups also differ with regard to the degree of guidance the therapist provides. In some, the therapist is quite directive; in others, the members of the group set their own agenda and determine how the group will proceed (Beck & Lewis, 2000; Stockton, Morran, & Krieger, 2004).

Because several people are treated simultaneously in group therapy, it is a much more economical means of treatment than individual

group therapy Therapy in which people meet in a group with a therapist to discuss problems.

"So, would anyone in the group care to respond to what Clifford has just shared with us?"

© Tom Cheney/The New Yorker Collection/ www.cartoonbank.com

In group therapy, people with psychological difficulties meet with a therapist to discuss their problems.

family therapy An approach that focuses on the family and its dynamics.

psychotherapy. On the other hand, critics argue that group settings lack the individual attention inherent in one-to-one therapy and that especially shy and withdrawn individuals may not receive the attention they need in a group setting.

FAMILY THERAPY

One specialized form of group therapy is family therapy. As the name implies, **family therapy** involves two or more family members, one (or more) of whose problems led to treatment. But rather than focusing simply on the members of the family who present the initial problem, family therapists consider the family as a unit to which each member contributes. By meeting with the entire family simultaneously, family therapists try to understand how the family members interact with one another (Cooklin, 2000; Strong & Tomm, 2007; Bischoff et al., 2011).

Family therapists view the family as a "system" and assume that individuals in the family cannot improve without understanding the conflicts found in interactions among family members. Thus, the therapist expects each member to contribute to the resolution of the problem being addressed.

Many family therapists believe that family members fall into rigid roles or set patterns of behavior with one person acting as the scapegoat, another as a bully, and so forth. In their view, that system of roles perpetuates family disturbances. One goal of this type of therapy, then, is to get the family members to adopt new, more constructive roles and patterns of behavior (Sprenkle & Moon, 1996; Minuchin, 1999; Sori, 2006).

SELF-HELP THERAPY

In many cases, group therapy does not involve a professional therapist. Instead, people with similar problems get together to discuss their shared feelings and experiences. For example, people who have recently experienced the death of a spouse might meet in a *bereavement support group,* or college students may get together to discuss their adjustment to college.

One of the best-known self-help groups is Alcoholics Anonymous (AA), designed to help members deal with alcohol-related problems. AA prescribes 12 steps that alcoholics must pass through on their road to recovery; they begin with an admission that they are alcoholics and powerless over alcohol. AA provides more treatment for alcoholics than any other therapy; AA and other 12-step programs (such as Narcotics Anonymous) can be as successful in treating alcohol and other substance-abuse problems as traditional types of therapy (Bogenschutz, Geppert, & George, 2006; Galanter, 2007; Gossop, Stewart, & Marsden, 2008).

Evaluating Psychotherapy: Does Therapy Work?

Your best friend, Ben, comes to you because he just hasn't been feeling right about things lately. He's upset because he and his girlfriend aren't getting along, but his difficulties go beyond that. He can't concentrate on his studies, has a lot of trouble getting to sleep, and—this is what really bothers him—has begun to think that people are ganging up on him, talking about him behind his back. It seems that no one really cares about or understands him or makes any effort to see why he's become so miserable.

Ben knows that he ought to get *some* kind of help, but he is not sure where to turn. He is fairly skeptical of psychologists and thinks that a lot of what they say is just mumbo-jumbo, but he's willing to put his doubts aside and try anything to feel better. He also knows there are many different types of therapy, and he doesn't have a clue about which would be best for him. He turns to you for advice because he knows you are taking a psychology course. He asks, "Which kind of therapy works best?"

IS THERAPY EFFECTIVE?

This question requires a complex response. In fact, identifying the single most appropriate form of treatment is a controversial and still unresolved task for psychologists specializing in psychological disorders. In fact, even before considering whether one form of therapy works better than another, we need to determine whether therapy in any form effectively alleviates psychological disturbances.

Until the 1950s, most people simply assumed that therapy was effective. But in 1952 psychologist Hans Eysenck published an influential study challenging that assumption. He claimed that people who received psychodynamic treatment and related therapies were no better off at the end of treatment than were people who were placed on a waiting list for treatment but never received it. Eysenck concluded that people would go into **spontaneous remission,** recovery without formal treatment, if they were simply left alone—certainly a cheaper and simpler process.

Although other psychologists quickly challenged Eysenck's conclusions, his review stimulated a continuing stream of better controlled, more carefully crafted studies on the effectiveness of psychotherapy. Today most psychologists agree: Therapy does work. Several comprehensive reviews indicate that therapy brings about greater improvement than no treatment at all, with the rate of spontaneous remission being fairly low. In most cases, then, the symptoms of abnormal behavior do not go away by themselves if left untreated—although the issue continues to be hotly debated (Seligman, 1996; Westen, Novotny, & Thompson-Brenner, 2004; Lutz et al., 2006).

WHICH KIND OF THERAPY WORKS BEST?

Although most psychologists feel confident that psychotherapeutic treatment *in general* is more effective than no treatment at all, the question of whether any specific form of treatment is superior to any other has not been answered definitively (Nathan, Stuart, & Dolan, 2000; Westen, Novotny, & Thompson-Brenner, 2004; Abboud, 2005).

For instance, one classic study comparing the effectiveness of various approaches found that although success rates vary somewhat by treatment form, most treatments show fairly equal success rates. As Figure 1 on page 512 indicates, the rates ranged from about 70–85% greater success for treated compared with untreated individuals. Behavioral and cognitive approaches tended to be slightly more successful, but that result may have been due to differences in the severity of the cases treated (Smith, Glass, & Miller, 1980; Orwin & Condray, 1984).

Other research, which relies on *meta-analysis* in which data from a large number of studies are statistically combined, yields similar general conclusions. Furthermore, a large survey of 186,000 individuals found that respondents felt they had benefited substantially from psychotherapy. However, there was little difference in "consumer satisfaction" on the basis of the specific type of treatment they had received (Seligman, 1995; Malouff, Thorsteinsson, & Schutte, 2007; Cuijpers et al., 2008).

Study Alert

Pay special attention to the discussion of (1) whether therapy is effective in general and (2) what specific types of therapy are effective, because it is a key issue for therapists.

spontaneous remission Recovery without formal treatment.

FIGURE 1 Estimates of the effectiveness of different types of treatment, in comparison to control groups of untreated people. The percentile score shows how much more effective a specific type of treatment is for the average patient rather than is no treatment. For example, people given psychodynamic treatment score, on average, more positively on outcome measures than about three-quarters of untreated people. (Source: Adapted from Smith, Glass, & Miller, 1980.)

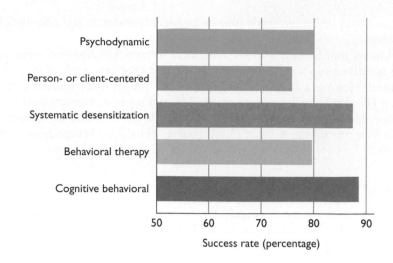

In short, converging evidence allows us to draw several conclusions about the effectiveness of psychotherapy (Strupp & Binder, 1992; Seligman, 1996; Goldfried & Pachankis, 2007):

- *For most people, psychotherapy is effective.* This conclusion holds over different lengths of treatment, specific kinds of psychological disorders, and various types of treatment. Thus, the question, "Does psychotherapy work?" appears to have been answered convincingly: It does (Seligman, 1996; Spiegel, 1999; Westen, Novotny, & Thompson-Brenner, 2004; Payne & Marcus, 2008).

- *On the other hand, psychotherapy doesn't work for everyone.* As many as 10% of people treated show no improvement or actually deteriorated (Boisvert & Faust, 2003; Pretzer & Beck, 2005; Coffman et al., 2007; Lilienfeld, 2007).

- *No single form of therapy works best for every problem, and certain specific types of treatment are better, although not invariably, for specific types of problems.* For example, cognitive therapy works especially well for panic disorders, and exposure therapy relieves specific phobias effectively. However, there are exceptions to these generalizations, and often the differences in success rates for different types of treatment are not substantial (Miller & Magruder, 1999; Westen, et al., 2004).

- *Most therapies share several basic similar elements.* Despite the fact that the specific methods used in different therapies are very different from one another, there are several common themes that lead them to be effective. These elements include the opportunity for a client to develop a positive relationship with a therapist, an explanation or interpretation of a client's symptoms, and confrontation of negative emotions. The fact that these common elements exist in most therapies makes it difficult to compare one treatment against another (Norcross, 2002; Norcross, Beutler, & Levant, 2006).

Consequently, there is no single, definitive answer to the broad question, "Which therapy works best?" because of the complexity in sorting out the various factors that enter into successful therapy. Recently, however, clinicians and researchers have reframed the question by focusing on evidence-based psychotherapy practice. *Evidence-based psychotherapy practice* seeks to use research findings to determine the best practices for treating a specific disorder. To determine best practices, researchers use clinical interviews, client self-reports of improvement in quality of life, reductions in symptoms, observations of behavior, and other outcomes to compare different therapies. By using objective research findings, clinicians are increasingly able to determine the most effective treatment for a specific disorder

PsychTech

Internet-based therapy, in which clients and therapists consult online using teleconferencing software but do not meet in person, is still in the experimental stages, but is being viewed as a way to increase access to treatment for more people.

(American Psychological Association Presidential Task Force, 2006; Brownlee, 2007; Kazdin, 2008).

Because no single type of psychotherapy is invariably effective for every individual, some therapists use an eclectic approach to therapy. In an *eclectic approach to therapy*, therapists use a variety of techniques, thus integrating several perspectives, to treat a person's problems. By employing more than one approach, therapists can choose the appropriate mix of evidence-based treatments to match the individual's specific needs. Furthermore, therapists with certain personal characteristics may work better with particular individuals and types of treatments, and—as we consider next—even racial and ethnic factors may be related to the success of treatment (Cheston, 2000; Chambless et al., 2006; Hays, 2008).

Exploring DIVERSITY

Racial and Ethnic Factors in Treatment: Should Therapists Be Color Blind?

Consider the following case report written by a school counselor about Jimmy Jones, a 12-year-old student who was referred to a counselor because of his lack of interest in schoolwork:

> Jimmy does not pay attention, daydreams often, and frequently falls asleep during class. There is a strong possibility that Jimmy is harboring repressed rage that needs to be ventilated and dealt with. His inability to directly express his anger had led him to adopt passive-aggressive means of expressing hostility, i.e., inattentiveness, daydreaming, falling asleep. It is recommended that Jimmy be seen for intensive counseling to discover the basis of the anger. (Sue & Sue, 1990, p. 44)

The counselor was wrong, however. Rather than suffering from "repressed rage," Jimmy lived in a poverty stricken and disorganized home. Because of overcrowding at his house, he did not get enough sleep and consequently was tired the next day. Frequently, he was also hungry. In short, the stresses arising from his environment and not any deep-seated psychological disturbances caused his problems.

This incident underscores the importance of taking people's environmental and cultural backgrounds into account during treatment for psychological disorders. In particular, members of racial and ethnic minority groups, especially those who are also poor, may behave in ways that help them deal with a society that discriminates against them. As a consequence, behavior that may signal psychological disorder in middle-class and upper-class whites may simply be adaptive in people from other racial and socioeconomic groups. For instance, characteristically suspicious and distrustful people may be displaying a survival strategy to protect themselves from psychological and physical injury rather than suffering from a psychological disturbance (Paniagua, 2000; Tseng, 2003; Pottick et al., 2007).

In fact, therapists must question some basic assumptions of psychotherapy when dealing with racial, ethnic, and cultural minority group members. For example, compared with the dominant culture, Asian and Latino cultures typically place much greater emphasis on the group, family, and society. When an Asian or Latino faces a critical decision, the family helps make it—a cultural practice suggesting that family members should also play a role in psychological treatment. Similarly, the traditional Chinese recommendation for dealing with depression or anxiety is to urge people who experience such problems to avoid thinking about whatever is upsetting them. Consider how this advice contrasts with treatment approaches that emphasize the value of insight (Ponterotto, Gretchen, & Chauhan, 2001; McCarthy, 2005; Leitner, 2007).

Clearly, therapists *cannot* be "color blind." Instead, they must take into account the racial, ethnic, cultural, and social class backgrounds of their clients in determining the nature of a psychological disorder and the course of treatment (Aponte & Wohl, 2000; Pedersen et al., 2002; Hays, 2008).

Therapists' interpretation of their clients' behavior is influenced by racial, ethnic, cultural, and social class backgrounds of the clients.

RECAP/EVALUATE/RETHINK

RECAP

LO 41-1 What are humanistic approaches to treatment?

- Humanistic therapy is based on the premise that people have control of their behavior, that they can make choices about their lives, and that it is up to them to solve their own problems. Humanistic therapies, which take a nondirective approach, include person-centered therapy. (pp. 507, 508)

LO 41-2 What is interpersonal therapy?

- Interpersonal therapy focuses on interpersonal relationships and strives for immediate improvement during short-term therapy. (p. 509)

LO 41-3 How does group therapy differ from individual types of therapy?

- In group therapy, several unrelated people meet with a therapist to discuss some aspect of their psychological functioning and often center on a common problem. (p. 509)

LO 41-4 How effective is psychotherapy, and which kind of psychotherapy works best in a given situation?

- Most research suggests that, in general, therapy is more effective than no therapy, although how much more effective is not known. (p. 511)
- The more difficult question of which therapy works best is harder to answer, but it is clear particular kinds of therapy are more appropriate for some problems than for others. (pp. 511, 512)
- Because no single type of psychotherapy is invariably effective, eclectic approaches in which a therapist uses a variety of techniques and thus integrates several perspectives are sometimes used. (p. 513)

EVALUATE

1. Match each of the following treatment strategies with the statement you might expect to hear from a therapist using that strategy.
   1. Group therapy
   2. Unconditional positive regard
   3. Behavioral therapy
   4. Nondirective counseling

   a. "In other words, you don't get along with your mother because she hates your girlfriend, is that right?"
   b. "I want you all to take turns talking about why you decided to come and what you hope to gain from therapy."
   c. "I can understand why you wanted to wreck your friend's car after she hurt your feelings. Now tell me more about the accident."
   d. "That's not appropriate behavior. Let's work on replacing it with something else."

2. _____ therapies assume that people should take responsibility for their lives and the decisions they make.

3. One of the major criticisms of humanistic therapies is that
   a. They are too imprecise and unstructured.
   b. They treat only the symptom of the problem.
   c. The therapist dominates the patient-therapist interaction.
   d. They work well only on clients of lower socioeconomic status.

4. In a controversial study, Eysenck found that some people go into _____ _____, or recovery without treatment, if they are simply left alone instead of treated.

RETHINK

1. How can people be successfully treated in group therapy when individuals with the "same" problem are so different? What advantages might group therapy offer over individual therapy?

2. *From the perspective of a social worker:* How might the types of therapies you employ vary depending on a client's cultural and socioeconomic background?

Answers to Evaluate Questions

1. 1-b, 2-c, 3-d, 4-a; 2. Humanistic; 3. a; 4. spontaneous remission

KEY TERMS

humanistic therapy p. 507
person-centered therapy p. 508

interpersonal therapy (IPT) p. 509
group therapy p. 509

family therapy p. 510
spontaneous remission p. 511

Biomedical Therapy: Biological Approaches to Treatment

If you get a kidney infection, your doctor gives you an antibiotic; with luck your kidney should be as good as new about a week later. If your appendix becomes inflamed, a surgeon removes it and your body functions normally once more. Could a comparable approach that focuses on the body's physiology be effective for psychological disturbances?

According to biological approaches to treatment, the answer is yes. Therapists routinely use biomedical therapies. This approach suggests that rather than focusing on a patient's psychological conflicts, past traumas, or environmental factors that may produce abnormal behavior, focusing treatment directly on brain chemistry and other neurological factors may be more appropriate. To do this, therapists can provide treatment with drugs, electric shock, or surgery.

Learning Outcome

LO 42-1 How are drug, electroconvulsive, and psychosurgical techniques used today in the treatment of psychological disorders?

Drug Therapy

Drug therapy, the control of psychological disorders through drugs, works by altering the operation of neurotransmitters and neurons in the brain. Some drugs operate by inhibiting neurotransmitters or receptor neurons, which reduces activity at particular synapses, the sites where nerve impulses travel from one neuron to another. Other drugs do just the opposite: They increase the activity of certain neurotransmitters or neurons, which allows particular neurons to fire more frequently (see Figure 1 on page 516).

drug therapy Control of psychological disorders through the use of drugs.

ANTIPSYCHOTIC DRUGS

Probably no greater change has occurred in mental hospitals than the successful introduction in the mid-1950s of **antipsychotic drugs**—drugs used to reduce severe symptoms of disturbance, such as loss of touch with reality and agitation. Previously, the typical mental hospital wasn't very different from the stereotypical 19th-century insane asylum; it gave mainly custodial care to screaming, moaning, clawing patients who displayed bizarre behaviors. However, in just a matter of days after hospital staff members administered antipsychotic drugs, the wards became considerably calmer environments in which professionals could do more than just try to get patients through the day without causing serious harm to themselves or others.

This dramatic change came about through the introduction of the drug *chlorpromazine.* Along with other similar drugs, chlorpromazine rapidly became the most popular and successful treatment for schizophrenia. Today, drug therapy is typically the preferred treatment for most cases of severely abnormal behavior and is used for most patients hospitalized with psychological disorders. The newest generation of anti-psychotics, referred to as *atypical antipsychotics,* have fewer side effects; they include *risperidone, olanzapine,* and *paliperidone* (Lublin, Eberhard, & Levander, 2005; Savas, Yumru, & Kaya, 2007; Nasrallah et al., 2008).

How do antipsychotic drugs work? Most block dopamine receptors at the brain's synapses. Atypical antipsychotics affect both serotonin and dopamine levels in certain parts of the brain, such as those related to planning and goal-directed activity (Sawa & Snyder, 2002; Advokat, 2005; Mizrahi et al., 2011).

antipsychotic drugs Drugs that temporarily reduce psychotic symptoms such as agitation, hallucinations, and delusions.

Drug Treatments			
Class of Drug	**Effects of Drug**	**Primary Action of Drug**	**Examples**
Antipsychotic Drugs, Atypical Antipsychotic Drugs	Reduction in loss of touch with reality, agitation	Block dopamine receptors	Antipsychotic: Chlorpromazine (Thorazine), clozapine (Clozaril), haloperidol (Haldol)
			Atypical Antipsychotic: risperidone, olanzapine
Antidepressant Drugs			
Tricyclic antidepressants	Reduction in depression	Permit rise in neurotransmitters such as norepinepherine	Trazodone (Desyrel), amitriptyline (Elavil), desipramine (Norpamin)
MAO inhibitors	Reduction in depression	Prevent MAO from breaking down neurotransmitters	Phenelzine (Nardil), tranylcypromine (Parnate)
Selective serotonin reuptake inhibitors (SSRIs)	Reduction in depression	Inhibit reuptake of serotonin	Fluoxetine (Prozac), Luvox, Paxil, Celexa, Zoloft, nefazodone (Serzone)
Mood Stabilizers			
Lithium	Mood stabilization	Can alter transmission of impulses within neurons	Lithium (Lithonate), Depakote, Tegretol
Antianxiety Drugs	Reduction in anxiety	Increase activity of neurotransmitter GABA	Benzodiazepines (Valium, Xanax)

FIGURE 1 The major classes of drugs used to treat psychological disorders have different effects on the brain and nervous system.

Despite the effectiveness of antipsychotic drugs, they do not produce a "cure" in the same way that, say, penicillin cures an infection. Most of the time, the symptoms reappear when the drug is withdrawn. Furthermore, such drugs can have long-term side effects, such as dryness of the mouth and throat, dizziness, and sometimes tremors and loss of muscle control, which may continue after drug treatments are stopped (Voruganti et al., 2007).

ANTIDEPRESSANT DRUGS

antidepressant drugs Medications that improve a severely depressed patient's mood and feeling of well-being.

As their name suggests, **antidepressant drugs** are a class of medications used in cases of severe depression to improve a patient's mood and feeling of well-being. They are also sometimes used for other disorders, such as anxiety disorders and bulimia (Walsh et al., 2006; Hedges et al., 2007).

Most antidepressant drugs work by changing the concentration of specific neurotransmitters in the brain. For example, *tricyclic drug* increase the availability of norepinephrine at the synapses of neurons, whereas *MAO inhibitors* prevent the enzyme monoamine oxidase (MAO) from breaking down neurotransmitters. Newer antidepressants—such as Lexapro—are *selective serotonin reuptake inhibitors (SSRIs)*. SSRIs target the neurotransmitter serotonin and permit it to linger at the synapse. Some antidepressants produce a combination of effects. For instance, nefazodone (Serzone) blocks serotonin at some receptor sites but not others, while bupropion (Wellbutrin and Zyban) affects the norepinephrine and dopamine systems (see Figure 2; Lucki & O'Leary, 2004; Robinson, 2007; Dhillon, Yang, & Curran, 2008).

Study Alert

To help organize your study of different drugs used in therapy, review Figure 1, which classifies them according to the categories of antipsychotic, atypical antipsychotic, antidepressant, mood-stabilizing, and antianxiety drugs.

Finally, there are some newer drugs on the horizon. For instance, scientists have found that the anesthetic ketamine blocks the neural receptor NMDA, which affects the neurotransmitter glutamate. Glutamate plays an important role in mood regulation and the ability to experience pleasure, and researchers believe that ketamine

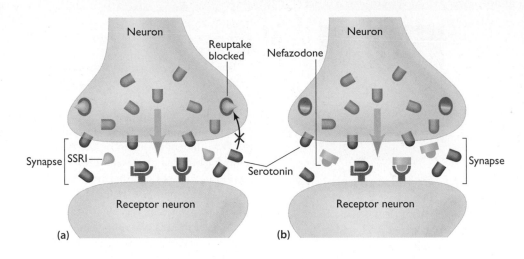

FIGURE 2 In (a), selective serotonin reuptake inhibitors (SSRIs) reduce depression by permitting the neurotransmitter serotonin to remain in the synapse. In (b), a newer antidepressant, Nefazodone (Serzone), operates more selectively to block serotonin at some sites but not others, which helps to reduce the side effects of the drug. (Source: Based on Mischoulon, 2000.)

blockers may prove to be useful in the treatment of depression (Skolnick, Popik, & Trullas, 2009; Schwartzmant & Alexander, 2011).

The overall success rates of antidepressant drugs are good. Unlike antipsychotic drugs, antidepressants can produce lasting, long-term recovery from depression. In many cases, even after patients stop taking the drugs, their depression does not return. On the other hand, antidepressant drugs may produce side effects such as drowsiness and faintness, and there is evidence that SSRI antidepressants can increase the risk of suicide in children and adolescents (Gibbons et al., 2007; Leckman & King, 2007; Olfson & Marcus, 2008).

Consumers spend billions of dollars each year on antidepressant drugs. In particular, the antidepressant *Fluoxetine,* sold under the trade name *Prozac,* has been highlighted on magazine covers and has been the topic of best-selling books.

Does Prozac deserve its acclaim? In some respects, yes. It is effective and has relatively few side effects. Furthermore, many people who do not respond to other types of antidepressants do well on Prozac. On the other hand, 20–30% of users report experiencing nausea and diarrhea, and a smaller number report sexual dysfunctions (Kramer, 1993; Brambilla et al., 2005; Fenter, 2006).

Another substance that has received a great deal of publicity is *St. John's wort,* an herb that some have called a "natural" antidepressant. Although it is widely used in Europe for the treatment of depression, the U.S. Food and Drug Administration considers it a dietary supplement, and therefore the substance is available here without a prescription.

Despite the popularity of St. John's wort, definitive clinical tests have found that the herb is ineffective in the treatment of depression. However, because some research shows that the herb successfully reduces certain psychological symptoms, some proponents argue that using it is reasonable. In any case, people should not use St. John's wort to medicate themselves without consulting a mental health–care professional (Shelton et al., 2002; Thachil, Mohan, & Bhugra, 2007; Rapaport et al., 2011).

MOOD STABILIZERS

Mood stabilizers are used to treat mood disorders. For example, the drug *lithium,* a form of mineral salts, has been used very successfully in patients with bipolar disorders. Although no one knows definitely why, lithium and other mood stabilizers such as divalproex sodium (*Depakote*) and carbamazepine (*Tegretol*) effectively reduce manic episodes. However, they do not effectively treat depressive phases of bipolar disorder, so antidepressants are usually prescribed during those phases (Smith et al., 2007; Salvi et al., 2008; Inoue et al., 2011).

Lithium and similar drugs have a quality that sets them apart from other drug treatments: They can be a *preventive* treatment that blocks future episodes of manic

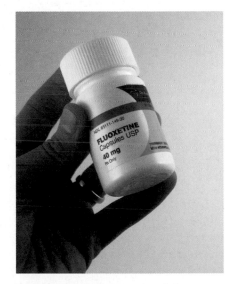

The drug fluoxetine, commonly known as Prozac, is a widely prescribed—but still controversial—antidepressant.

mood stabilizers Drugs used to treat mood disorders that prevent manic episodes of bipolar disorder.

Taking the Sting Out of Traumatic Memories

What can you do when you're haunted by a traumatic memory? Say, for example, that you were chased down and bitten by a neighbor's dog as a child and the experience was so terrifying that you still have an extreme fear of dogs. What could be done to reduce the lingering effects of that experience? In the world of science fiction, you could undergo a procedure that erases the traumatic memory, thereby solving the problem. Even if that were possible, however, erasing individual memories might result in odd gaps in your memory, with disjointed time lines that could prove, at best, disconcerting and, at worst, totally confusing.

But what if there were a way to keep the memory but remove the negative emotions associated with it? This is the reality of a new, emerging therapeutic technique that has potential to offer relief to the many people suffering from anxiety disorders such as posttraumatic stress disorder (Wang, 2010).

The technique works like this: a patient is induced to think about a painful memory

Reliving a traumatic experience may be a thing of the past as new studies combining therapy and medication can potentially help people suffering from post-traumatic stress.

in detail. In the case of a dog bite incident, a patient might be shown a photograph of a similar dog or asked to write a detailed account of exactly what happened that day. Normally this would produce the associated negative emotions of fear and anxiety.

But before the memory is induced, the patient is given the drug propranolol. *Propranolol*, a medication for high blood pressure, inhibits physiological responses to anxiety, such as racing heartbeat and sweating. The patient experiences the traumatic memory, but this time with a reduced fear response. The patient then reconsolidates this modified memory, so that the next time it is retrieved, it has less negative emotion attached to it. This process is then repeated to firmly establish the modified memory.

While this technique is still being researched, early results show promise for it to be a potentially useful therapy for people suffering from posttraumatic stress. Memories remain intact, but the pain associated with them is lost (Brunet et al., 2008; Soeter & Kindt, 2010).

RETHINK

- What do you think are some reasons why it would be undesirable to eliminate a traumatic memory altogether?
- Why do you think traumatic memories don't just lose their emotional impact naturally over time, through repeated reconsolidations?

depression. Often, people who have had episodes of bipolar disorder can take a daily dose of lithium to prevent a recurrence of their symptoms. Most other drugs are useful only when symptoms of psychological disturbance occur.

ANTIANXIETY DRUGS

antianxiety drugs Drugs that reduce the level of anxiety a person experiences essentially by reducing excitability and increasing feelings of well-being.

As the name implies, **antianxiety drugs** reduce the level of anxiety a person experiences and increase feelings of well-being. They are prescribed not only to reduce general tension in people who are experiencing temporary difficulties, but also to aid in the treatment of more serious anxiety disorders (Zito, 1993).

Antianxiety drugs such as Alprazolamand and Valium are among the medications physicians most frequently prescribe. In fact, more than half of all U.S. families have someone who has taken such a drug at one time or another. Furthermore, new approaches are being used for drugs that treat anxiety disorders, as we discuss in *Applying Psychology in the 21st Century.*

Although the popularity of antianxiety drugs suggests that they hold few risks, they can produce a number of potentially serious side effects. For instance, they can cause fatigue, and long-term use can lead to dependence. Moreover, when taken in combination with alcohol, some antianxiety drugs can be lethal. But a more important issue concerns their use to suppress anxiety. Almost every therapeutic approach to psychological disturbance views continuing anxiety as a signal of some other sort of problem. Thus, drugs that mask anxiety may simply be hiding other difficulties. Consequently, rather than confronting their underlying problems, people may be hiding from them through the use of antianxiety drugs.

Electroconvulsive Therapy (ECT)

First introduced in the 1930s, **electroconvulsive therapy (ECT)** is a procedure used in the treatment of severe depression. In the procedure, an electric current of 70–150 volts is briefly administered to a patient's head, which causes a loss of consciousness and often causes seizures. Typically, health-care professionals sedate patients and give them muscle relaxants before administering the current; such preparations help reduce the intensity of muscle contractions produced during ECT. The typical patient receives about 10 ECT treatments in the course of a month, but some patients continue with maintenance treatments for months afterward (Greenberg & Kellner, 2005; Stevens & Harper, 2007).

ECT is a controversial technique. Apart from the obvious distastefulness of a treatment that evokes images of electrocution, side effects occur frequently. For instance, after treatment patients often experience disorientation, confusion, and sometimes memory loss that may remain for months. Furthermore, ECT often does not produce long-term improvement; one study found that without follow-up medication, depression returned in most patients who had undergone ECT treatments. Finally, even when ECT does work, we do not know why, and some critics believe it may cause permanent brain damage (Gardner & O'Connor, 2008; Kato, 2009; Weiner & Falcone, 2011).

In light of the drawbacks to ECT, why do therapists use it at all? Basically, they use it because in many severe cases of depression, it offers the only quickly effective treatment. For instance, it may prevent depressed, suicidal individuals from committing suicide, and it can act more quickly than antidepressive medications.

The use of ECT has risen in the last decade with more than 100,000 people undergoing it each year. Still, ECT tends to be used only when other treatments have proved ineffective, and researchers continue to search for alternative treatments (Fink, 2000; Eranti & McLoughlin, 2003; Pandya, Pozuelo, & Malone, 2007).

One new and promising alternative to ECT is **transcranial magnetic stimulation (TMS).** TMS creates a precise magnetic pulse in a specific area of the brain. By activating particular neurons, TMS has been effective in relieving the symptoms of major depression in a number of controlled experiments. However, the therapy can produce side effects, such as seizures and convulsions, and it is still considered experimental (Leo & Latif, 2007; Kim, Pesiridou, & O'Reardon, 2009; Bentwich et al., 2011).

electroconvulsive therapy (ECT) A procedure used in the treatment of severe depression in which an electric current of 70–150 volts is briefly administered to a patient's head.

transcranial magnetic stimulation (TMS) A depression treatment in which a precise magnetic pulse is directed to a specific area of the brain.

Psychosurgery

If ECT strikes you as a questionable procedure, the use of **psychosurgery**—brain surgery in which the object is to reduce symptoms of mental disorder—probably appears even more dubious. A technique used only rarely today, psychosurgery was introduced as a "treatment of last resort" in the 1930s.

The initial form of psychosurgery, a *prefrontal lobotomy*, consisted of surgically destroying or removing parts of a patient's frontal lobes, which surgeons thought controlled emotionality. In the 1930s and 1940s, surgeons performed the procedure on thousands of patients often with little precision. For example, in one common technique, a surgeon literally would jab an ice pick under a patient's eyeball and swivel it back and forth (El-Hai, 2005; Ogren & Sandlund, 2007).

Psychosurgery often did improve a patient's behavior—but not without drastic side effects. Along with remission of the symptoms of the mental disorder, patients sometimes experienced personality changes and became bland, colorless, and unemotional. In other cases, patients became aggressive and unable to control their impulses. In the worst cases, treatment resulted in the patient's death.

With the introduction of effective drug treatments—and the obvious ethical questions regarding the appropriateness of forever altering someone's personality—psychosurgery became nearly obsolete. However, it is still used in very rare cases when all other

psychosurgery Brain surgery once used to reduce the symptoms of mental disorder but rarely used today.

procedures have failed and the patient's behavior presents a high risk to the patient and others. For example, surgeons sometimes use a more precise form of psychosurgery called a *cingulotomy* in rare cases of obsessive-compulsive disorder in which they destroy tissue in the *anterior cignulate* area of the brain. In another technique, *gamma knife surgery*, beams of radiation are used to destroy areas of the brain related to obsessive-compulsive disorder (Shah et al., 2008; Carey, 2009; Lopes et al., 2009; Wilkinson, 2009).

Occasionally, dying patients with severe, uncontrollable pain also receive psychosurgery. Still, even these cases raise important ethical issues, and psychosurgery remains a highly controversial treatment (Mashour, Walker, & Martuza, 2005; Steele et al., 2007).

Biomedical Therapies in Perspective

In some respects, no greater revolution has occurred in the field of mental health than biological approaches to treatment. As previously violent, uncontrollable patients have been calmed by the use of drugs, mental hospitals have been able to concentrate more on actually helping patients and less on custodial functions. Similarly, patients whose lives have been disrupted by depression or bipolar episodes have been able to function normally, and other forms of drug therapy have also shown remarkable results.

The use of biomedical therapy for everyday problems is rising. For example, one survey of users of a college counseling service found that from 1989 to 2001, the proportion of students receiving treatment who were taking medication for psychological disorders increased from 10% to 25% (Benton et al., 2003).

Furthermore, new forms of biomedical therapy are promising. For example, the newest treatment possibility—which remains experimental at this point—is gene therapy. As we discussed when considering behavioral genetics, specific genes may be introduced to particular regions of the brain. These genes then have the potential to reverse or even prevent biochemical events that give rise to psychological disorders (Sapolsky, 2003; Lymberis et al., 2004; Tuszynski, 2007).

Despite their current usefulness and future promise, biomedical therapies do not represent a cure-all for psychological disorders. For one thing, critics charge that such therapies merely provide relief of the *symptoms* of mental disorder; as soon as the drugs are withdrawn, the symptoms return. Although it is considered a major step in the right direction, biomedical treatment may not solve the underlying problems that led a patient to therapy in the first place. Biomedical therapies also can produce side effects that range from minor to serious physical reactions to the development of *new* symptoms of abnormal behavior. Finally, an overreliance on biomedical therapies may lead therapists to overlook alternative forms of treatment that may be helpful.

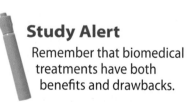

Study Alert

Remember that biomedical treatments have both benefits and drawbacks.

Still, biomedical therapies—sometimes alone and more often in conjunction with psychotherapy—have permitted millions of people to function more effectively. Furthermore, although biomedical therapy and psychotherapy appear distinct, research shows that biomedical therapies ultimately may not be as different from talk therapies as one might imagine, at least in terms of their consequences.

Specifically, measures of brain functioning as a result of drug therapy compared with psychotherapy show little difference in outcomes. For example, one study compared the reactions of patients with major depression who received either an anti-depressant drug or psychotherapy. After 6 weeks of either therapy, activity in the portion of the brain related to the disorder—the basal ganglia—had changed in similar ways, and that area appeared to function more normally. Although such research is not definitive, it does suggest that at least for some disorders, psychotherapy may be just as effective as biomedical interventions— and vice versa. Research also makes it clear that no single treatment is effective universally and that each type of treatment has both advantages and disadvantages (Hollon, Thase, & Markowitz, 2002; DeRubeis, Hollon, & Shelton, 2003; Pinquart, Duberstein, & Lyness, 2006; Greenberg & Goldman, 2009).

"The drug has, however, proved more effective than traditional psychoanalysis."

Community Psychology: Focus on Prevention

Each of the treatments we have reviewed has a common element: It is a "restorative" treatment aimed at alleviating psychological difficulties that already exist. However, an approach known as **community psychology** has a different aim: to prevent or minimize the incidence of psychological disorders.

Community psychology came of age in the 1960s, when mental health professionals developed plans for a nationwide network of community mental health centers. The hope was that those centers would provide low-cost mental health services, including short-term therapy and community educational programs. In another development, the population of mental hospitals has plunged as drug treatments made physical restraint of patients unnecessary.

This transfer of former mental patients out of institutions and into the community—a process known as **deinstitutionalization**—was encouraged by the growth of the community psychology movement (see Figure 3). Proponents of deinstitutionalization wanted to ensure not only that deinstitutionalized patients received proper treatment, but also that their civil rights were maintained (Wolff, 2002; St. Dennis et al., 2006; Henckes, 2011).

Unfortunately, the promise of deinstitutionalization has not been met largely because insufficient resources are provided to deinstitutionalized patients. What started as a worthy attempt to move people out of mental institutions and into the community ended, in many cases, with former patients being dumped into the community without any real support. Many became homeless—between 15% and 35% of all homeless adults are thought to have a major psychological disorder—and some became involved in illegal acts caused by their disorders. In short, many people who need treatment do not get it, and in some cases care for people with psychological disorders has simply shifted from one type of treatment site to another (Shinn et al., 2007; Dumont & Dumont, 2008; Price, 2009).

On the other hand, the community psychology movement has had some positive outcomes. Its emphasis on prevention has led to new approaches to psychological disorders. Furthermore, telephone "hot lines"—of the sort described in the chapter

While deinstitutionalization has had many successes, it has also contributed to the release of mental patients into the community with little or no support. As a result, many have become homeless.

community psychology A branch of psychology that focuses on the prevention and minimization of psychological disorders in the community.

deinstitutionalization The transfer of former mental patients from institutions to the community.

FIGURE 3 As deinstitutionalization has become more prevalent over the last half century, the number of patients being treated in state mental hospitals has declined significantly, while the number of outpatient facilities has increased. (Source: From Rodger Doyle, "Deinstitutionalization," *Scientific American*, December 2002, p. 38. Copyright 2002 Rodger Doyle. Reprinted with permission.)

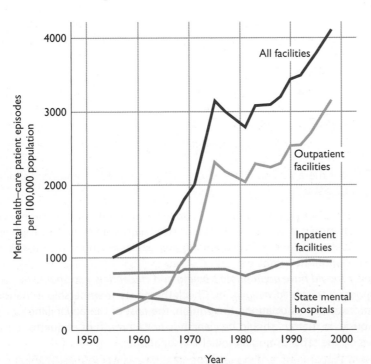

"Looking good!"

Prologue—are now common. At any time of the day or night, people experiencing acute stress can call a trained, sympathetic listener who can provide immediate—although obviously limited—treatment (Reese, Conoley, & Brossart, 2002; Paukert, Stagner, & Hope, 2004; Cauce, 2007).

College and high school crisis centers are another innovation that grew out of the community psychology movement. Modeled after suicide prevention hot-line centers, crisis centers give callers an opportunity to discuss life crises with a sympathetic listener, who is often a volunteer.

BECOMING AN INFORMED CONSUMER of Psychology

Choosing the Right Therapist

If you decide to seek therapy, you're faced with a daunting task. Choosing a therapist is not a simple matter. One place to begin the process of identifying a therapist is at the "Help Center" of the American Psychological Association at http://www.apa.org/helpcenter. And, if you start therapy, several general guidelines can help you determine whether you've made the right choice:

You and your therapist should agree on the goals for treatment. They should be clear, specific, and attainable.

- *You should feel comfortable with your therapist.* You should not be intimidated by or in awe of a therapist. Rather, you should trust the therapist and feel free to discuss the most personal issues without fearing a negative reaction. In sum, the "personal chemistry" should be right.
- *Therapists should have appropriate training and credentials and should be licensed by appropriate state and local agencies.* Check therapists' membership in national and state professional associations. In addition, the cost of therapy, billing practices, and other business matters should be clear. It is not a breach of etiquette to put these matters on the table during an initial consultation.

- *You should feel that you are making progress after therapy has begun, despite occasional setbacks.* If you have no sense of improvement after repeated visits, you and your therapist should discuss this issue frankly. Although there is no set timetable, the most obvious changes resulting from therapy tend to occur relatively early in the course of treatment. For instance, half of patients in psychotherapy improve by the 8th session, and three-fourths by the 26th session. The average number of sessions with college students is just 5 (Crits-Cristoph, 1992; Harvard Mental Health Letter, 1994; Lazarus, 1997).

Be aware that you will have to put in a great deal of effort in therapy. Although our culture promises quick cures for any problem, in reality, solving difficult problems is not easy. You must be committed to making therapy work and should know that it is you, not the therapist, who must do most of the work to resolve your problems. The effort has the potential to pay off handsomely—as you experience a more positive, fulfilling, and meaningful life.

RECAP/EVALUATE/RETHINK

RECAP

LO 42-1 How are drug, electroconvulsive, and psychosurgical techniques used today in the treatment of psychological disorders?

- Biomedical treatment approaches suggest that therapy should focus on the physiological causes of abnormal behavior rather than considering psychological factors. Drug therapy, the best example of biomedical treatments, has brought about dramatic reductions in the symptoms of mental disturbance. (p. 515)
- Antipsychotic drugs such as chlorpromazine very effectively reduce psychotic symptoms. Antidepressant drugs such as Prozac reduce depression so successfully that they are used very widely. Antianxiety drugs, or minor tranquilizers, are among the most frequently prescribed medications of any sort. (pp. 515–518)
- In electroconvulsive therapy (ECT), used in severe cases of depression, a patient receives a brief electric current of 70 to 150 volts. (p. 519)
- Psychosurgery typically consists of surgically destroying or removing certain parts of a patient's brain. (p. 519)
- The community psychology approach encouraged deinstitutionalization in which previously hospitalized mental patients were released into the community. (p. 521)

EVALUATE

1. Antipsychotic drugs have provided effective, long-term, and complete cures for schizophrenia. True or false?

2. One highly effective biomedical treatment for a psychological disorder that is used mainly to arrest and prevent manic-depressive episodes, is
   a. Chlorpromazine
   b. Lithium
   c. Librium
   d. Valium
3. Psychosurgery has grown in popularity as a method of treatment as surgical techniques have become more precise. True or false?
4. The trend toward releasing more patients from mental hospitals and into the community is known as _____.

RETHINK

1. One of the main criticisms of biological therapies is that they treat the symptoms of mental disorder without uncovering and treating the underlying problems from which people are suffering. Do you agree with this criticism? Why?
2. *From the perspective of a politician:* How would you go about regulating the use of electroconvulsive therapy and psychosurgery? Would you restrict their use or make either one completely illegal? Why?

Answers to Evaluate Questions

1. false; schizophrenia can be controlled but not cured by medication; 2. b; 3. false; psychosurgery is now used only as a treatment of last resort; 4. deinstitutionalization

KEY TERMS

drug therapy p. 515
antipsychotic drugs p. 515
antidepressant drugs p. 516
mood stabilizers p. 517

antianxiety drugs p. 518
electroconvulsive therapy
  (ECT) p. 519

transcranial magnetic
  stimulation (TMS) p. 519
psychosurgery p. 519

community psychology
  p. 521
deinstitutionalization p. 521

Looking Back

Epilogue

We have examined how psychological professionals treat people with psychological disorders. We have considered a range of approaches that include both psychologically based and biologically based therapies. Clearly, the field has made substantial progress in recent years both in treating the symptoms of mental disorders and in understanding their underlying causes.

Before we leave the topic of treatment of psychological disorders, turn back to the prologue in which Melanie Poorman offers suicide prevention counseling for military veterans. On the basis of your understanding of the treatment of psychological disorders, consider the following questions.

1. How do suicide prevention hotlines further the goal of community psychology?
2. If Melanie Poorman wanted to encourage a caller to the Department of Veterans Affairs suicide prevention hotline to seek psychotherapy, what could she tell the caller about its effectiveness?
3. If the caller visited a practitioner of psychodynamic therapy, how would his or her treatment differ from another caller who visited a practitioner of person-centered therapy?
4. What kind of remedy is available for people who need fast relief from severe depression because they are at risk of committing suicide?

VISUAL SUMMARY 13 Treatment of Psychological Disorders

MODULE 40 Psychotherapy: Psychodynamic, Behavioral, and Cognitive Approaches

Psychodynamic Therapy

- Psychoanalysis
  - Free association: say aloud whatever comes to mind
  - Dream interpretation: looking for clues to unconscious conflicts and problems in dreams
  - Frequent sessions for a long time
- Contemporary psychodynamic approaches
  - Sessions are of shorter duration
  - Therapist takes more active role: Focus is more in the present

Behavioral Treatment Approaches: Help modify behavior rather than find underlying causes

- Classical conditioning treatments
  - Aversive conditioning
  - Systematic desensitization
  - Exposure treatment
- Operant conditioning techniques
  - Token system
  - Contingency contracting
  - Observational learning
- Dialectical behavior therapy: Helps people to change their behavior and view of themselves by accepting who they are regardless of whether it matches their ideal

Cognitive Approaches: Teach people to think in adaptive ways

- Rational-emotive behavior therapy

A	**B**	**C**
Negative Activating condition	Irrational Belief system	Emotional Consequences
(Close relationship breaks up)	("I'll never be loved again")	(Anxiety, loneliness, sadness, depression)

MODULE 41 Psychotherapy: Humanistic, Interpersonal, and Group Approaches

Humanistic Therapy: Focuses on self-responsibility in treatment techniques

- Person-centered therapy: Helps people to reach their potential for self-actualization using unconditional positive regard

Interpersonal Therapy: Focuses on interpersonal relationships and improvement through short-term therapy

Group Therapy: Several people meet with a therapist to discuss psychological functioning

- Family therapy
- Self-help therapy

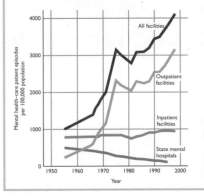

Does Psychotherapy Work?

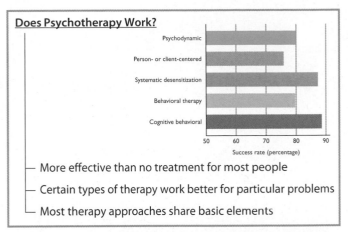

- More effective than no treatment for most people
- Certain types of therapy work better for particular problems
- Most therapy approaches share basic elements

MODULE 42 Biomedical Therapy: Biological Approaches to Treatment

Drug Therapy: Controlling psychological disorders with drugs

Drug Treatments			
Class of Drug	**Effects of Drug**	**Primary Action of Drug**	**Examples**
Antipsychotic Drugs, Atypical Antipsychotic Drugs	Reduction in loss of touch with reality, agitation	Block dopamine receptors	Antipsychotic: Chlorpromazine (Thorazine), clozapine (Clozaril), haloperidol (Haldol)
			Atypical Antipsychotic: risperidone, olanzapine
Antidepressant Drugs			
Tricyclic antidepressants	Reduction in depression	Permit rise in neurotransmitters such as norepinepherine	Trazodone (Desyrel), amitriptyline (Elavil), desipramine (Norpamin)
MAO inhibitors	Reduction in depression	Prevent MAO from breaking down neurotransmitters	Phenelzine (Nardil), tranylcypromine (Parnate)
Selective serotonin reuptake inhibitors (SSRIs)	Reduction in depression	Inhibit reuptake of serotonin	Fluoxetine (Prozac), Luvox, Paxil, Celexa, Zoloft, nefazodone (Serzone)
Mood Stabilizers			
Lithium	Mood stabilization	Can alter transmission of impulses within neurons	Lithium (Lithonate), Depakote, Tegretol
Antianxiety Drugs	Reduction in anxiety	Increase activity of neurotransmitter GABA	Benzodiazepines (Valium, Xanax)

Electroconvulsive Therapy: Used as the only quickly effective treatment for severe depression

Psychosurgery: Brain surgery to reduce symptoms of mental disorders

Community Psychology: Prevention of the incidence of psychological disorders

- Deinstitutionalization: Transfer of mental patients into the community where they may not receive necessary treatment

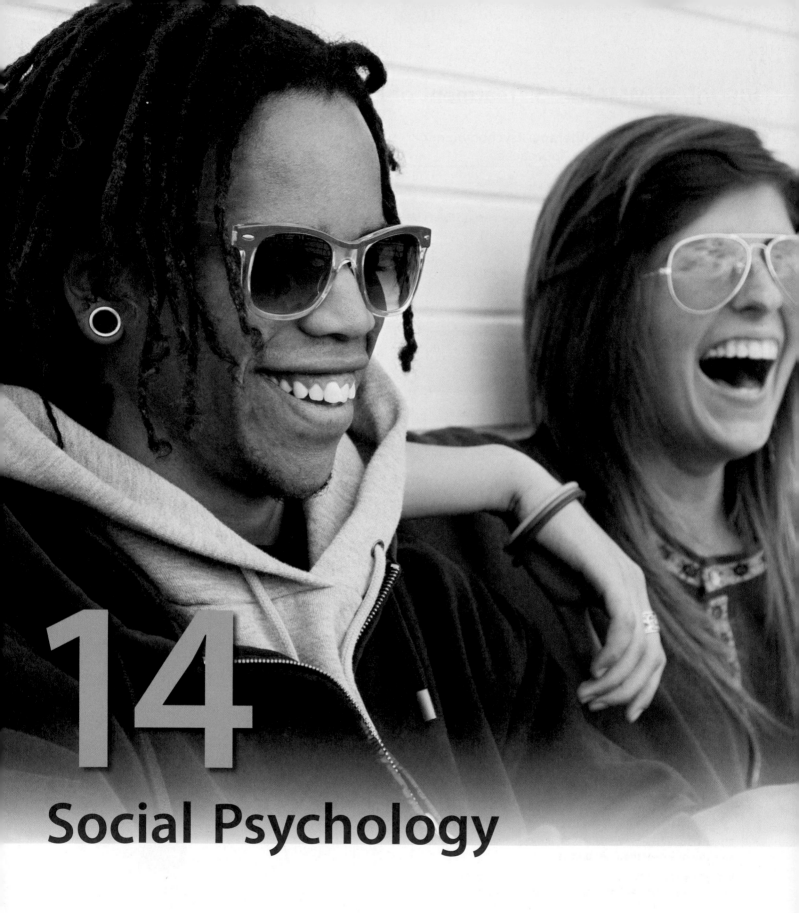

14
Social Psychology

Learning Outcomes for Chapter 14

LO 43-1 What are attitudes, and how are they formed, maintained, and changed?

LO 43-2 How do people form impressions of what others are like and the causes of their behavior?

LO 43-3 What are the biases that influence the ways in which people view others' behavior?

Attitudes and Social Cognition
Persuasion: Changing Attitudes

Applying Psychology in the 21st Century: Advertising in the Information Age: Aiming at Moving Targets

PsychWork: Advertising Agency Creator

Social Cognition: Understanding Others

Exploring Diversity: Attribution Biases in a Cultural Context: How Fundamental Is the Fundamental Attribution Error?

LO 44-1 What are the major sources and tactics of social influence?

Social Influence and Groups
Conformity: Following What Others Do

Compliance: Submitting to Direct Social Pressure

Obedience: Following Direct Orders

LO 45-1 How do stereotypes, prejudice, and discrimination differ?

LO 45-2 How can we reduce prejudice and discrimination?

Prejudice and Discrimination
The Foundations of Prejudice

Neuroscience in Your Life: The Prejudiced Brain

Measuring Prejudice and Discrimination: The Implicit Association Test

Reducing the Consequences of Prejudice and Discrimination

LO 46-1 Why are we attracted to certain people, and what progression do social relationships follow?

LO 46-2 What factors underlie aggression and prosocial behavior?

Positive and Negative Social Behavior
Liking and Loving: Interpersonal Attraction and the Development of Relationships

Neuroscience in Your Life: The Social Brain

Aggression and Prosocial Behavior: Hurting and Helping Others

Helping Others: The Brighter Side of Human Nature

Neuroscience in Your Life: Moral Decisions and the Brain

Becoming an Informed Consumer of Psychology: Dealing Effectively with Anger

Prologue *Helping Hands*

As soon as the news of the disaster at the Perley Farm began to spread—how the fast-rising waters of the White River had washed away nearly 200 bales of hay, flooded the farmhouse, and swept some of the cows down the river to their deaths—neighbors and strangers alike began arriving at the muddy barn in South Royalton, Vermont, to offer help.

Agriculture students from Vermont Technical College showed up with shovels and began digging. A nearby couple brought a wheelbarrow and mucked out the barn and then returned a few days later with homemade lasagna. A couple from New Hampshire brought grain to feed the surviving cows and wood shavings to line the barn.

"My husband and I, we're people that give, you know—we've never had to be on the receiving end," said Penny Severance, ... "We're so grateful" (Cooper, 2011, p. A10).

Looking Ahead

What led the neighbors of Perley Farm to behave so selflessly? Was it simply the circumstances, or were these neighbors especially helpful people? What, in general, drives some people to help others—and conversely, why do other people show no concern for the welfare of others? More broadly, how can we improve social conditions so that people can live together in harmony?

We can fully answer these questions only by taking into account findings from the field of social psychology, the branch of psychology that focuses on the aspects of human behavior that unite—and separate—us from one another. **Social psychology** is the scientific study of how people's thoughts, feelings, and actions are affected by others. Social psychologists consider the kinds and causes of the individual's behavior in social situations. They examine how the nature of situations in which we find ourselves influences our behavior in important ways.

The broad scope of social psychology is conveyed by the kinds of questions social psychologists ask, such as: How can we convince people to change their attitudes or adopt new ideas and values? In what ways do we come to understand what others are like? How are we influenced by what others do and think? Why do some people display so much violence, aggression, and cruelty toward others that people throughout the world live in fear of annihilation at their hands? And why, in comparison, do some people place their own lives at risk to help others? In exploring these and other questions, we also discuss strategies for confronting and solving a variety of problems and issues that all of us face—ranging from achieving a better understanding of persuasive tactics to forming more accurate impressions of others.

We begin with a look at how our attitudes shape our behavior and how we form judgments about others. We'll discuss how we are influenced by others, and we will consider prejudice and discrimination by focusing on their roots and the ways we can reduce them. After examining what social psychologists have learned about the ways people form friendships and relationships, we'll conclude with a look at the determinants of aggression and helping—two opposing sides of human behavior.

social psychology The scientific study of how people's thoughts, feelings, and actions are affected by others.

Attitudes and Social Cognition

What do Rachael Ray and Tom Brady have in common? Both have appeared in advertisements designed to mold or change our attitudes. Such commercials are part of the barrage of messages we receive each day from sources as varied as politicians, sales staff in stores, and celebrities—all of which are meant to influence us.

Persuasion: Changing Attitudes

Persuasion is the process of changing attitudes, one of the central concepts of social psychology. **Attitudes** are evaluations of a person, behavior, belief, or concept. For example, you probably hold attitudes toward the U.S. president (a person), abortion (a behavior), affirmative action (a belief), or architecture (a concept) (Brock & Green, 2005; Hegarty & Massey, 2007; Simon & Hoyt, 2008).

The ease with which we can change our attitudes depends on a number of factors, including:

- *Message source.* The characteristics of a person who delivers a persuasive message, known as an *attitude communicator,* have a major impact on the effectiveness of that message. Communicators who are physically and socially attractive produce greater attitude change than those who are less attractive. Moreover, the communicator's expertise and trustworthiness are related to the impact of a message—except in situations in which the audience believes the communicator has an ulterior motive (Ariyanto, Hornsey, & Gallois, 2006; McClure, Sutton, & Sibley, 2007; Messner, Reinhard, & Sporer, 2008).
- *Characteristics of the message.* It is not just *who* delivers a message but what the message is like that affects attitudes. Generally, two-sided messages—which include both the communicator's position and the one he or she is arguing against—are more effective than one-sided messages, given the assumption that the arguments for the other side can be effectively refuted and the audience is knowledgeable about the topic. In addition, fear-producing messages ("If you don't practice safer sex, you'll get AIDS") are generally effective when they provide the audience with a means for reducing the fear. However, if the fear that is aroused is too strong, messages may evoke people's defense mechanisms and be ignored (Perloff, 2003).
- *Characteristics of the target.* Once a communicator has delivered a message, characteristics of the *target* of the message may determine whether the message will be accepted. For example, intelligent people are more resistant to persuasion than those who are less intelligent. Gender differences in persuasibility also seem to exist. In public settings, women are somewhat more easily persuaded than men, particularly when they have less knowledge about the message's topic. However, they are as likely as men to change their private attitudes. In fact, the magnitude of the differences in resistance to persuasion between men and women is not large (Wood, 2000; Guadagno & Cialdini, 2002; also see *Applying Psychology in the 21st Century*).

Learning Outcomes

LO 43-1 What are attitudes, and how are they formed, maintained, and changed?

LO 43-2 How do people form impressions of what others are like and the causes of their behavior?

LO 43-3 What are the biases that influence the ways in which people view others' behavior?

attitudes Evaluations of a person, behavior, belief, or concept.

Do celebrities such as Patriot quarterback Tom Brady influence attitudes? Advertisers certainly believe this is true, investing millions of dollars in endorsement fees.

Advertising in the Information Age: Aiming at Moving Targets

As a middle-aged man browses a popular sports webpage on his smartphone, more than a dozen cameras monitor his every movement—particularly his eye movements. Other equipment monitors his skin temperature and heart rate, and numerous tiny muscle probes measure every nuance of his changing facial expressions. In a remote room, technicians closely monitor the data his movements produce in real time.

This isn't a scene from a futuristic science-fiction film—it's just an ordinary day at a private research lab owned by the Walt Disney Company. The research technicians are studying the effectiveness of online advertising. While Internet companies have long been investigating the kinds of online ads that successfully entice website users to click through, much less is known about why users *don't* respond. Are the ads failing to capture their attention? If so, what kinds of ads would work better to do that? Is it just a question of creating more vivid visuals, or do users quickly learn to ignore even the most eye-popping banners? Does the structure of the webpage itself make a difference? It's a delicate balance to design online ads that are maximally effective but not so intrusive as

Advertisers are researching how to harness the latest technologies to ensure that they are getting the greatest response for their efforts.

to turn viewers off (Lavrakas, Mane, & Joe, 2010; Hsieh & Chen, 2011).

Advertising companies want to make sure they are getting the most response for their efforts. Rather than leave anything to chance, they are using the latest research methods to ensure that their ads have the intended impact—even going so far as to monitor people's brain activity as they

watch televised ads. "You're seeing science move into the marketing sector in a big way," said David Poltrack, chief research officer for CBS. Artie Bulgrin, ESPN's senior vice president of research, concurs: "We see this as a very powerful research and development tool for the entire Disney company. As ideas arise, we want to research them and have the results in the hands of our sales force as fast as possible," he said (Barnes, 2009, p. 6).

The rapid evolution of Internet technology and the ever-changing ways in which people consume online content have far outpaced researchers' attempts to understand people's usage patterns and the most effective ways of introducing advertising into the mix. Private research labs of major stakeholders such as Disney are working frantically to keep up, but much work is yet to be done. For the most part, advertisers are still relying on methods that worked for older technology until newer media forms are better understood (Li & Leckenby, 2007).

RETHINK

- Why do you think it's so difficult to design effective advertisements for online media?
- Why do you think researchers are keenly interested in users' physical responses as they consume online media?

---

central route processing The type of mental processing that occurs when a persuasive message is evaluated by thoughtful consideration of the issues and arguments used to persuade.

peripheral route processing The type of mental processing that occurs when a persuasive message is evaluated on the basis of irrelevant or extraneous factors.

Study Alert

Central route processing involves the content of the message; peripheral route processing involves how the message is provided.

ROUTES TO PERSUASION

Recipients' receptiveness to persuasive messages relates to the type of information-processing they use. Social psychologists have discovered two primary information-processing routes to persuasion: central route and peripheral route processing. **Central route processing** occurs when the recipient thoughtfully considers the issues and arguments involved in persuasion. In central route processing, people are swayed in their judgments by the logic, merit, and strength of arguments.

In contrast, **peripheral route processing** occurs when people are persuaded on the basis of factors unrelated to the nature or quality of the content of a persuasive message. Instead, factors that are irrelevant or extraneous to the issue, such as who is providing the message, how long the arguments are, or the emotional appeal of the arguments, influence them (Petty et al., 2005; Warden, Wu, & Tsai, 2006; Kao, 2011).

In general, people who are highly involved and motivated use central route processing to comprehend a message. However, if a person is disinterested, unmotivated, bored, or distracted, the characteristics of the message become less important, and peripheral factors become more influential (see Figure 1). Although both central route and peripheral route processing lead to attitude change, central route processing generally leads to stronger, more lasting attitude change.

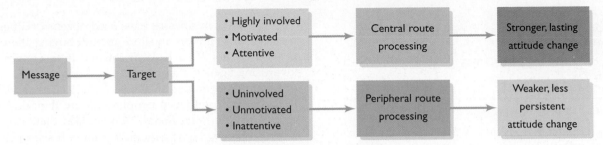

FIGURE 1 Routes to persuasion. Targets who are highly involved, motivated, and attentive use central route processing when they consider a persuasive message, which leads to a more lasting attitude change. In contrast, uninvolved, unmotivated, and inattentive targets are more likely to use peripheral route processing, and attitude change is likely to be less enduring. Can you think of specific advertisements that try to produce central route processing?

Are some people more likely than others to use central route processing rather than peripheral route processing? The answer is yes. People who have a high *need for cognition,* a person's habitual level of thoughtfulness and cognitive activity, are more likely to employ central route processing. Consider the statements shown in Figure 2. People who agree with the first two statements and disagree with the rest have a relatively high need for cognition (Cacioppo et al., 1996; Dai & Wang, 2007).

People who have a high need for cognition enjoy thinking, philosophizing, and reflecting on the world. Consequently, they tend to reflect more on persuasive messages by using central route processing, and they are likely to be persuaded by complex, logical, and detailed messages. In contrast, those who have a low need for cognition become impatient when forced to spend too much time thinking about an issue. Consequently, they usually use peripheral route processing and are persuaded by factors other than the quality and detail of messages (Dollinger, 2003; Van Overwalle & Siebler, 2005). (Also see *PsychWork* on page 532.)

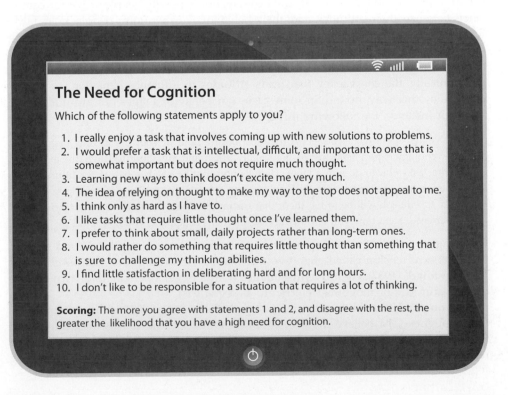

FIGURE 2 This simple questionnaire will give you a general idea of the level of your need for cognition. (Source: Cacioppo, Berntson, & Crites, 1996.)

The Need for Cognition

Which of the following statements apply to you?

1. I really enjoy a task that involves coming up with new solutions to problems.
2. I would prefer a task that is intellectual, difficult, and important to one that is somewhat important but does not require much thought.
3. Learning new ways to think doesn't excite me very much.
4. The idea of relying on thought to make my way to the top does not appeal to me.
5. I think only as hard as I have to.
6. I like tasks that require little thought once I've learned them.
7. I prefer to think about small, daily projects rather than long-term ones.
8. I would rather do something that requires little thought than something that is sure to challenge my thinking abilities.
9. I find little satisfaction in deliberating hard and for long hours.
10. I don't like to be responsible for a situation that requires a lot of thinking.

Scoring: The more you agree with statements 1 and 2, and disagree with the rest, the greater the likelihood that you have a high need for cognition.

PsychWork

ADVERTISING AGENCY
CREATOR

Name: Vlad Kolarov

Education: BA in Law, Sofia University, Sofia, Bulgaria

Over the years, businesses have used dozens of different ways to catch our attention and lure us into buying their products or services. For Vlad Kolarov, owner of the FunnySells.com advertising agency, humor is the best approach.

"Humor is universal. It makes us feel better. Everybody likes a good laugh, even people who say they do not have a sense of humor," he noted. "Companies that use humor in advertising campaigns generally enjoy a boost in the sales of their product and service. The trick, however, is creating a memorable, humorous advertising campaign. Humor and comedy, as a genre, are the toughest to master.

"When done correctly, companies can use it to create and maintain a brand identity; introduce a new product, service, or a change in the existing one; increase the buzz-value of the brand or the company; and increase sales," he added.

Using humor as a promotional tool can be beneficial but tricky as well, according to Kolarov.

"An advertising company needs to determine what the target audience is and determine the best way to present the advertised product or service. When things are not done correctly, they may have a reverse effect," he explained.

Is there anything that can't be promoted with humor?

"I'd like to say no, but the fact is there are products I personally will choose not to advertise with humor. Then again, every rule has an exception. When done cleverly and tastefully, even things we consider impossible can become successful. In this business, as in life, one has to keep an open mind," Kolarov said.

THE LINK BETWEEN ATTITUDES AND BEHAVIOR

Not surprisingly, attitudes influence behavior. The strength of the link between particular attitudes and behavior varies, of course, but generally people strive for consistency between their attitudes and their behavior. Furthermore, people hold fairly consistent attitudes. For instance, you would probably not hold the attitude that eating meat is immoral and still have a positive attitude toward hamburgers (Ajzen, 2002; Conner et al., 2003; Levi, Chan, & Pence, 2006).

Ironically, the consistency that leads attitudes to influence behavior sometimes works the other way around; in some cases our behavior shapes our attitudes. Consider, for instance, the following incident:

> You've just spent what you feel is the most boring hour of your life turning pegs for a psychology experiment. Just as you finally finish and are about to leave, the experimenter asks you to do him a favor. He tells you that he needs a helper for future experimental sessions to introduce subsequent participants to the peg-turning task. Your specific job will be to tell them that turning the pegs is an interesting, fascinating experience. Each time you tell this tale to another participant, you'll be paid $1.

If you agree to help the experimenter, you may be setting yourself up for a state of psychological tension called cognitive dissonance. According to social psychologist Leon Festinger (1957), **cognitive dissonance** occurs when a person holds two contradictory attitudes or thoughts (referred to as *cognitions*).

If you participate in the situation just described, you are left with two contradictory thoughts: (1) I believe the task is boring, but (2) I said it was interesting with little justification ($1). These two thoughts should arouse dissonance. How can you reduce cognitive dissonance? You cannot deny having said that the task is interesting

cognitive dissonance The mental conflict that occurs when a person holds two contradictory attitudes or thoughts (referred to as cognitions).

without breaking with reality. Relatively speaking, it is easier to change your attitude toward the task—and thus the theory predicts that participants will reduce dissonance by adopting more positive attitudes toward the task (Cooper, 2007; Rydell, McConnell, & Mackie, 2008; Dickinson & Oxoby, 2011).

A classic experiment (Festinger & Carlsmith, 1959) confirmed this prediction. The experiment followed essentially the same procedure outlined earlier in which a participant was offered $1 to describe a boring task as interesting. In addition, in a comparison condition, some participants were offered $20 to say that the task was interesting. The reasoning behind this condition was that $20 was so much money that participants in this condition had a good reason to be conveying incorrect information; dissonance would not be aroused, and less attitude change would be expected. The results supported this notion. More of the participants who were paid $1 changed their attitudes (becoming more positive toward the peg-turning task) than participants who were paid $20.

We now know that dissonance explains many everyday events involving attitudes and behavior. For example, smokers who know that smoking leads to lung cancer hold contradictory cognitions: (1) I smoke, and (2) smoking leads to lung cancer. The theory predicts that these two thoughts will lead to a state of cognitive dissonance. More important, it predicts that—assuming they don't change their behavior by quitting smoking—smokers will be motivated to reduce their dissonance by one of the following methods: (1) modifying one or both of the cognitions, (2) changing the perceived importance of one cognition, (3) adding cognitions, or (4) denying that the two cognitions are related to each other. Hence, a smoker may decide that he really doesn't smoke all that much or that he'll quit soon (modifying the cognition), that the evidence linking smoking to cancer is weak (changing the importance of a cognition), that the amount of exercise he gets compensates for the smoking (adding cognitions), or that there is no evidence linking smoking and cancer (denial). Whichever technique the smoker uses results in reduced dissonance (see Figure 3).

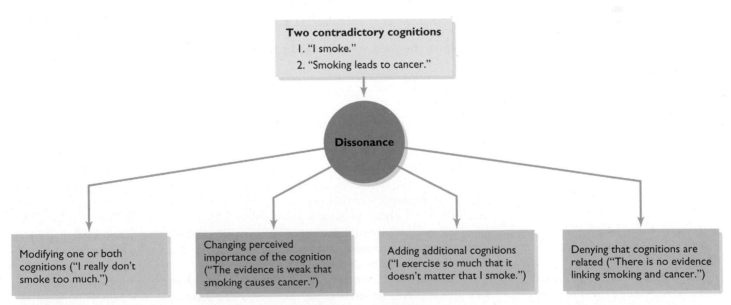

FIGURE 3 Cognitive dissonance. The simultaneous presence of two contradictory cognitions ("I smoke" and "Smoking leads to cancer") produces dissonance, which can be reduced through several methods. What are additional ways in which dissonance can be reduced?

Social Cognition: Understanding Others

Regardless of Bill Clinton's personal transgressions and impeachment trial in the late 1990s, many Americans continued to find him extremely likable throughout his presidency, and even today he is among the most popular U.S. politicians. Cases like this illustrate the power of our impressions and attest to the importance of determining how people develop an understanding of others. One of the dominant areas in social psychology during the last few years has focused on learning how we come to understand what others are like and how we explain the reasons underlying others' behavior.

UNDERSTANDING WHAT OTHERS ARE LIKE

Consider for a moment the enormous amount of information about other people to which we are exposed. How can we decide what is important and what is not and make judgments about the characteristics of others? Social psychologists interested in this question study **social cognition**—the way people understand and make sense of others and themselves. Those psychologists have learned that individuals have highly developed **schemas,** sets of cognitions about people and social experiences. Those schemas organize information stored in memory; represent in our minds the way the social world operates; and give us a framework to recognize, categorize, and recall information relating to social stimuli such as people and groups (Moskowitz, 2004; Smith & Semin, 2007; Amodio & Ratner, 2011).

We typically hold schemas for specific types of people. Our schema for "teacher," for instance, generally consists of a number of characteristics: knowledge of the subject matter he or she is teaching, a desire to impart that knowledge, and an awareness of the student's need to understand what is being said. Or we may hold a schema for "mother" that includes the characteristics of warmth, nurturance, and caring. Regardless of their accuracy, schemas are important because they organize the way in which we recall, recognize, and categorize information about others. Moreover, they help us predict what others are like on the basis of relatively little information because we tend to fit people into schemas even when we do not have much concrete evidence to go on (Bargh & Chartrand, 2000; Ruscher, Fiske, & Schnake, 2000).

IMPRESSION FORMATION

How do we decide that Sayreeta is a flirt, Jacob is obnoxious, or Hector is a really nice guy? The earliest work on social cognition examined *impression formation*, the process by which an individual organizes information about another person to form an overall impression of that person. In a classic study, for instance, students learned that they were about to hear a guest lecturer (Kelley, 1950). Researchers told one group of students that the lecturer was "a rather warm person, industrious, critical, practical, and determined," and told a second group that he was "a rather cold person, industrious, critical, practical, and determined."

The simple substitution of "cold" for "warm" caused drastic differences in the way the students in each group perceived the lecturer even though he gave the same talk in the same style in each condition. Students who had been told he was "warm" rated him considerably more positively than students who had been told he was "cold."

The findings from this experiment led to additional research on impression formation that focused on the way in which people pay particular attention to certain

social cognition The cognitive processes by which people understand and make sense of others and themselves.

schemas Sets of cognitions about people and social experiences.

unusually important traits—known as **central traits**—to help them form an overall impression of others. According to this work, the presence of a central trait alters the meaning of other traits. Hence, the description of the lecturer as "industrious" presumably meant something different when it was associated with the central trait "warm" than it meant when it was associated with "cold" (Widmeyer & Loy, 1988; Glicksohn & Nahari, 2007; McCarthy & Skowronski, 2011).

Other work on impression formation has used information-processing approaches to develop mathematically oriented models of how individual personality traits combine to create an overall impression. Generally, the results of this research suggest that in forming an overall judgment of a person, we use a psychological "average" of the individual traits we see just as we would find the mathematical average of several numbers (Mignon & Mollaret, 2002).

We make such impressions remarkably quickly. In just a few seconds, using what have been called "thin slices of behavior," we are able to make judgments of people that are accurate and that match those of people who make judgments based on longer samples of behavior (Carney, Colvin, & Hall, 2007; Pavitt, 2007; Holleran, Mehl, & Levitt, 2009).

Of course, as we gain more experience with people and see them exhibiting behavior in a variety of situations, our impressions of them become more complex. However, because our knowledge of others usually has gaps, we still tend to fit individuals into personality schemas that represent particular "types" of people. For instance, we may hold a "gregarious person" schema made up of the traits of friendliness, aggressiveness, and openness. The presence of just one or two of those traits may be sufficient to make us assign a person to a particular schema.

However, our schemas are susceptible to error. For example, mood affects how we perceive others. Happy people form more favorable impressions and make more positive judgments than people who are in a bad mood (Forgas & Laham, 2005; Human & Biesanz, 2011).

Even when schemas are not entirely accurate, they serve an important function: They allow us to develop expectations about how others will behave. Those expectations permit us to plan our interactions with others more easily and serve to simplify a complex social world.

> central traits The major traits considered in forming impressions of others.

ATTRIBUTION PROCESSES: UNDERSTANDING THE CAUSES OF BEHAVIOR

When Barbara Washington, a new employee at the Ablex Computer Company, completed a major staffing project 2 weeks early, her boss, Yolanda, was delighted. At the next staff meeting, she announced how pleased she was with Barbara and explained that *this* was an example of the kind of performance she was looking for in her staff. The other staff members looked on resentfully, trying to figure out why Barbara had worked night and day to finish the project not just on time but 2 weeks early. She must be an awfully compulsive person, they decided.

At one time or another, most of us have puzzled over the reasons behind someone's behavior. Perhaps it was in a situation similar to the one above, or it may have been in more formal circumstances, such as being a judge on a student judiciary board in a cheating case. In contrast to theories of social cognition, which describe how people develop an overall impression of others' personality traits, **attribution theory** considers how we decide, on the basis of samples of a person's behavior, what the specific causes of that behavior are.

The general process we use to determine the causes of behavior and other social occurrences proceeds in several steps illustrated in Figure 4. After first noticing that something unusual has happened—for example, tennis star Roger Federer has played a terrible set of tennis—we try to interpret the meaning of the event. This leads us to formulate an initial explanation (maybe Federer stayed up late

> attribution theory The theory that considers how we decide, on the basis of samples of a person's behavior, what the specific causes of that behavior are.

FIGURE 4 Determining why people behave the way they do. The general process we use to determine the causes of others' behavior proceeds in several steps. The kind of explanation we come up with depends on the time available to us, our cognitive resources, and our degree of motivation to come up with an accurate explanation. If time, cognitive resources, and motivation are limited, we'll make use of our first impression, which may be inaccurate. (Source: Adapted from Krull & Anderson, 1997, p. 2.)

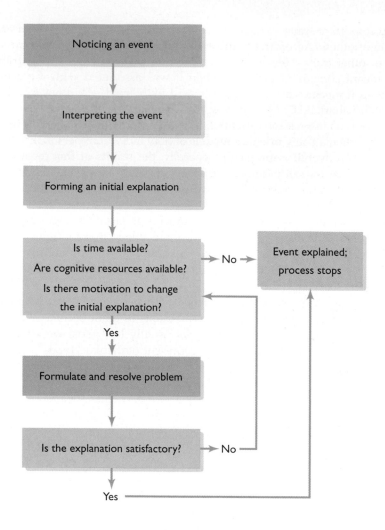

the night before the match). Depending on the time available, the cognitive resources on hand (such as the attention we can give to the matter), and our motivation (determined in part by how important the event is), we may choose to accept our initial explanation or seek to modify it (Federer was sick, perhaps). If we have the time, cognitive resources, and motivation, the event triggers deliberate problem solving as we seek a fuller explanation. During the problem formulation and resolution stage, we may try out several possibilities before we reach a final explanation that seems satisfactory to us (Malle, 2004; Brown, 2006; Martinko, Harvey, & Dasborough, 2011).

In seeking an explanation for behavior, we must answer one central question: Is the cause situational or dispositional? **Situational causes** are those brought about by something in the environment. For instance, someone who knocks over a quart of milk and then cleans it up probably does the cleaning not because he or she is necessarily a neat person but because the *situation* requires it. In contrast, a person who spends hours shining the kitchen floor probably does so because he or she is a neat person. Hence, the behavior has a **dispositional cause**—that is, it is prompted by the person's disposition (his or her internal traits or personality characteristics).

In our example involving Barbara Washington, her fellow employees attributed her behavior to her disposition rather than to the situation. But from a logical standpoint, it is equally plausible that something about the situation caused the behavior. If asked, Barbara might attribute her accomplishment to situational factors and explain that she had so much other work to do she just had to get the project out of

situational causes (of behavior) Perceived causes of behavior that are based on environmental factors.

dispositional causes (of behavior) Perceived causes of behavior that are based on internal traits or personality factors.

the way or the project was not all that difficult and was easy to complete ahead of schedule. To her, then, the reason for her behavior might not be dispositional at all; it could be situational.

ATTRIBUTION BIASES: TO ERR IS HUMAN

If we always processed information in the rational manner that attribution theory suggests, the world might run a lot more smoothly. Unfortunately, although attribution theory generally makes accurate predictions, people do not always process information about others as logically as the theory seems to suggest. In fact, research reveals consistent biases in the ways people make attributions. Typical biases include the following:

- *The halo effect.* Harry is intelligent, kind, and loving. Is he also conscientious? If you were to guess, your most likely response probably would be yes. Your guess reflects the **halo effect,** a phenomenon in which an initial understanding that a person has positive traits is used to infer other uniformly positive characteristics. The opposite would also hold true. Learning that Harry was unsociable and argumentative would probably lead you to assume that he was lazy as well. However, few people have either uniformly positive or uniformly negative traits, so the halo effect leads to misperceptions of others (Goffin, Jelley, & Wagner, 2003; Dennis, 2007; Park, Park, & Dubinsky, 2011).
- *Assumed-similarity bias.* How similar to you—in terms of attitudes, opinions, likes, and dislikes—are your friends and acquaintances? Most people believe that their friends and acquaintances are fairly similar to themselves. But this feeling goes beyond just people we know to a general tendency—known as the **assumed-similarity bias**—to think of people as being similar to oneself even when meeting them for the first time. Given the range of people in the world, this assumption often reduces the accuracy of our judgments (Lemay, Clark, & Feeney, 2007; Lemay & Clark, 2008).
- *The self-serving bias.* When their teams win, coaches usually feel that the success is due to their coaching. But when their teams lose, coaches may think it's due to their players' poor skills. Similarly, if you get an A on a test, you may think it's due to your hard work, but if you get a poor grade, it's due to the professor's inadequacies. The reason is the **self-serving bias,** the tendency to attribute success to personal factors (skill, ability, or effort) and attribute

Study Alert

The central question in making an attribution is whether the cause of behavior is due to situational or dispositional factors.

halo effect A phenomenon in which an initial understanding that a person has positive traits is used to infer other uniformly positive characteristics.

assumed-similarity bias The tendency to think of people as being similar to oneself even when meeting them for the first time.

self-serving bias The tendency to attribute personal success to personal factors (skill, ability, or effort) and to attribute failure to factors outside oneself.

The assumed-similarity bias leads us to believe that others hold similar attitudes, opinions, and likes and dislikes.

fundamental attribution error A tendency to overattribute others' behavior to dispositional causes and minimize the importance of situational causes.

failure to factors outside oneself (Kruscmark, Campbell, & Clementz, 2008; Shepperd, Malone, & Sweeny, 2008).

- *The fundamental attribution error.* One of the more common attribution biases is the tendency to overattribute others' behavior to dispositional causes and the corresponding failure to recognize the importance of situational causes. Known as the **fundamental attribution error,** this tendency is prevalent in Western cultures. We tend to exaggerate the importance of personality characteristics (dispositional causes) in producing others' behavior and minimize the influence of the environment (situational factors). For example, we are more likely to jump to the conclusion that someone who is often late to work is too lazy to take an earlier bus (a dispositional cause) than to assume that the lateness is due to situational factors, such as the bus always running behind schedule.

Why is the fundamental attribution error so common? One reason pertains to the nature of information available to the people making an attribution. When we view another person's behavior in a particular setting, the most conspicuous information is the person's behavior. Because the individual's immediate surroundings remain relatively unchanged and less attention grabbing, we center our attention on the person whose behavior we're considering. Consequently, we are more likely to make attributions based on personal dispositional factors and less likely to make attributions relating to the situation (Follett & Hess, 2002; Langdridge & Butt, 2004; Tal-Or & Papirman, 2007).

Social psychologists' awareness of attribution biases has led, in part, to the development of a new branch of economics called behavioral economics. *Behavioral economics* is concerned with how individuals' biases and irrationally affect economic decisions. Rather than viewing people as rational, thoughtful decision makers who are impartially weighing choices to draw conclusions, behavioral economists focus on the irrationality of judgments (Ariely & Norton, 2009).

 Exploring **DIVERSITY**

Attribution Biases in a Cultural Context: How Fundamental Is the Fundamental Attribution Error?

Attribution biases do not affect all of us in the same way. The culture in which we are raised clearly plays a role in the way we attribute others' behavior.

Take, for example, the fundamental attribution error: the tendency to overestimate the importance of personal, dispositional factors and underattribute situational factors in determining the causes of others' behavior. The error is pervasive in Western cultures and not in Eastern societies. For instance, adults in India were more likely to use situational attributions than dispositional ones in explaining events. These findings are the opposite of those for the United States, and they contradict the fundamental attribution error (Miller, 1984; Lien et al., 2006).

One reason for the difference may lie in the norms and values of Eastern society, which emphasize social responsibility and societal obligations to a greater extent than Western societies. In addition, the language spoken in a culture may lead to different sorts of attributions. For instance, a tardy person using English may say, "I am late"; this suggests a personal, dispositional cause ("I am a tardy person"). In contrast, speakers of Spanish who are late say, "The clock caused me to be late." Clearly, the statement in Spanish implies that the cause is situational (Zebrowitz-McArthur, 1988; Macduff, 2006; Alon & Brett, 2007).

Cultural differences in attributions affect subsequent behavior. For example, parents in Asia tend to attribute good academic performance to effort and hard work (situational factors). In contrast, parents in Western cultures tend to de-emphasize the role of effort and attribute school success to innate ability (a dispositional factor). As a result, Asian students in general may strive harder to achieve and ultimately outperform U.S. students in school (Stevenson, Lee, & Mu, 2000; Lien et al., 2006).

The difference in thinking between people in Asian and Western cultures is a reflection of a broader difference in the way the world is perceived. Asian societies generally have a *collectivistic orientation,* a worldview that promotes the notion of interdependence. People with a collectivistic orientation generally see themselves as parts of a larger, interconnected social network and as responsible to others. In contrast, people in Western cultures are more likely to hold an *individualist orientation* that emphasizes personal identity and the uniqueness of the individual. They focus more on what sets them apart from others and what makes them special (Markus & Kitayama, 2003; Wang, 2004; Markus, 2007).

RECAP/EVALUATE/RETHINK

RECAP

LO 43-1 What are attitudes, and how are they formed, maintained, and changed?

- Social psychology is the scientific study of the ways in which people's thoughts, feelings, and actions are affected by others and the nature and causes of individual behavior in social situations. (p. 528)
- Attitudes are evaluations of a particular person, behavior, belief, or concept. (p. 529)
- Cognitive dissonance occurs when an individual simultaneously holds two cognitions—attitudes or thoughts—that contradict each other. To resolve the contradiction, the person may modify one cognition, change its importance, add a cognition, or deny a link between the two cognitions—thus bringing about a reduction in dissonance. (pp. 532, 533)

LO 43-2 How do people form impressions of what others are like and the causes of their behavior?

- Social cognition involves the way people understand and make sense of others and themselves. People develop schemas that organize information about people and social experiences in memory and allow them to interpret and categorize information about others. (p. 534)
- People form impressions of others in part through the use of central traits—personality characteristics that receive unusually heavy emphasis when we form an impression. (p. 535)
- Information-processing approaches have found that we tend to average together sets of traits to form an overall impression. (p. 535)
- Attribution theory tries to explain how we understand the causes of behavior, particularly with respect to situational or dispositional factors. (p. 535)

LO 43-3 What are the biases that influence the ways in which people view others' behavior?

- Even though logical processes are involved, attribution is prone to error. For instance, people are susceptible to the halo effect, assumed-similarity bias, self-serving bias, and fundamental attribution error (the tendency to over-attribute others' behavior to dispositional causes and the corresponding failure to recognize the importance of situational causes). (pp. 537, 538)

EVALUATE

1. An evaluation of a particular person, behavior, belief, or concept is called a(n) _____.
2. One brand of peanut butter advertises its product by describing its taste and nutritional value. It is hoping to persuade customers through _____ route processing. In ads for a competing brand, a popular actor happily eats the product—but does not describe it. This approach hopes to persuade customers through _____ route processing.
3. Cognitive dissonance theory suggests that we commonly change our behavior to keep it consistent with our attitudes. True or false?
4. Sopan was happy to lend his textbook to a fellow student who seemed bright and friendly. He was surprised when his classmate did not return it. His assumption that the bright and friendly student would also be responsible reflects the _____ effect.

RETHINK

1. Joan sees Annette, a new coworker, act in a way that seems abrupt and curt. Joan concludes that Annette is unkind and unsociable. The next day Joan sees Annette acting kindly toward another worker. Is Joan likely to change her impression of Annette? Why or why not? Finally, Joan sees several friends of hers laughing and joking with Annette, treating her in a very friendly fashion. Is Joan likely to change her impression of Annette? Why or why not?

2. *From the perspective of a marketing specialist:* Suppose you were assigned to develop a full advertising campaign for a product, including television, radio, and print ads. How might theories of persuasion guide your strategy to suit the different media?

Answers to Evaluate Questions

1. attitude; 2. central, peripheral; 3. false; we typically change our attitudes and not our behavior to reduce cognitive dissonance; 4. halo

KEY TERMS

social psychology p. 528
attitudes p. 529
central route
   processing p. 530
peripheral route
   processing p. 530

cognitive dissonance p. 532
social cognition p. 534
schemas p. 534
central traits p. 535
attribution
   theory p. 535

situational causes (of
   behavior) p. 536
dispositional causes
   (of behavior) p. 536
halo effect p. 537

assumed-similarity
   bias p. 537
self-serving bias p. 537
fundamental attribution
   error p. 538

Social Influence and Groups

You have just transferred to a new college and are attending your first class. When the professor enters, your fellow classmates instantly rise, bow to the professor, and then stand quietly with their hands behind their backs. You've never encountered such behavior, and it makes no sense to you. Is it more likely that you will (1) jump up to join the rest of the class or (2) remain seated?

Most people would probably choose the first option. As you undoubtedly know from your own experience, pressures to conform to others' behavior can be painfully strong and can bring about changes in behavior that otherwise never would have occurred.

Conformity pressures are just one type of social influence. **Social influence** is the process by which social groups and individuals exert pressure on an individual, either deliberately or unintentionally.

Social influence is so powerful, in part because groups and other people generally play a central role in our lives. As defined by social psychologists, **groups** consist of two or more people who (1) interact with one another; (2) perceive themselves as part of a group; and (3) are interdependent—that is, the events that affect one group member affect other members, and the behavior of members has significant consequences for the success of the group in meeting its goals.

Groups develop and hold *norms,* expectations regarding behavior appropriate to the group. Furthermore, we understand that not adhering to group norms can result in retaliation from other group members, ranging from being ignored to being overtly derided or even being rejected or excluded by the group. Thus, people conform to meet the expectations of the group (Baumeister, Twenge, & Nuss, 2002; Jetten, Hornsey, & Adarves-Yorno, 2006; Miles, Schaufeli, & van den Bos, 2011).

Groups exert considerable social influence over individuals that ranges from the mundane, such as the decision to wear a certain kind of jeans, to the extreme, such as the cruelty of army guards in the Arab Spring uprisings of 2011. We'll consider three types of social pressure: conformity, compliance, and obedience.

Conformity: Following What Others Do

Conformity is a change in behavior or attitudes brought about by a desire to follow the beliefs or standards of other people. Subtle or even unspoken social pressure results in conformity.

The classic demonstration of pressure to conform comes from a series of studies carried out in the 1950s by Solomon Asch (Asch, 1951). In the experiments, the participants thought they were taking part in a test of perceptual skills with six other people. The experimenter showed the participants one card with three lines of varying length and a second card that had a fourth line that matched one of the first three (see Figure 1 on page 542). The task was seemingly straightforward: Each

Learning Outcome

LO 44-1 What are the major sources and tactics of social influence?

social influence The process by which social groups and individuals exert pressure on an individual, either deliberately or unintentionally.

group Two or more people who interact with one another, perceive themselves as part of a group, and are interdependent.

Study Alert

The distinction between the three types of social pressure—conformity, compliance, and obedience—depends on the nature and strength of the social pressure brought to bear on a person.

conformity A change in behavior or attitudes brought about by a desire to follow the beliefs or standards of other people.

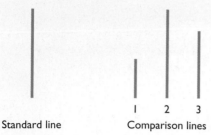

FIGURE 1 Which of the three comparison lines is the same length as the "standard" line?

Standard line · Comparison lines · 1 2 3

of the participants had to announce aloud which of the first three lines was identical in length to the "standard" line on the second card. Because the correct answer was always obvious, the task seemed easy to the participants.

Indeed, because the participants all agreed on the first few trials, the procedure appeared to be simple. But then something odd began to happen. From the perspective of the participant in the group who answered last on each trial, all the answers of the first six participants seemed to be wrong—in fact, unanimously wrong. And this pattern persisted. Over and over again, the first six participants provided answers that contradicted what the last participant believed to be correct. The last participant faced the dilemma of whether to follow his or her own perceptions or follow the group by repeating the answer everyone else was giving.

As you might have guessed, this experiment was more contrived than it appeared. The first six participants were actually confederates (paid employees of the experimenter) who had been instructed to give unanimously erroneous answers in many of the trials. And the study had nothing to do with perceptual skills. Instead, the issue under investigation was conformity.

Asch found that in about one-third of the trials, the participants conformed to the unanimous but erroneous group answer; about 75% of all participants conformed at least once. However, he found strong individual differences. Some participants conformed nearly all the time, whereas others never did.

CONFORMITY CONCLUSIONS

Since Asch's pioneering work, literally hundreds of studies have examined conformity, and we now know a great deal about the phenomenon. Significant findings focus on:

status The social rank held within a group.

- *The characteristics of the group.* The more attractive a group appears to its members, the greater its ability to produce conformity. Furthermore, a person's relative **status,** the social rank held within a group, is critical: The lower a person's status in the group, the greater groups' power over that person's behavior (Hogg & Hains, 2001).
- *The situation in which the individual is responding.* Conformity is considerably higher when people must respond publicly than it is when they can do so privately, as the founders of the United States noted when they authorized secret ballots in voting.
- *The kind of task.* People working on ambiguous tasks and questions (those with no clear answer) are more susceptible to social pressure. When asked to give an opinion on something, such as what type of clothing is fashionable, a person will more likely yield to conformist pressures than he or she will if asked a question of fact. In addition, tasks at which an individual is less competent than others in the group make conformity more likely. For example, a person who is an infrequent computer user may feel pressure to conform to an opinion about computer brands when in a group of experienced computer users.
- *Unanimity of the group.* Groups that unanimously support a position show the most pronounced conformity pressures. But what about the case in which people with dissenting views have an ally in the group, known as a **social supporter,** who agrees with them? Having just one person present who shares the minority point of view is sufficient to reduce conformity pressures (Prislin, Brewer, & Wilson, 2002; Goodwin, Costa, & Adonu, 2004; Levine & Moreland, 2006).

social supporter A group member whose dissenting views make nonconformity to the group easier.

GROUPTHINK: CAVING IN TO CONFORMITY

Although we usually think of conformity in terms of our individual relations with others, in some instances conformity pressures in organizations can lead to disastrous effects with long-term consequences. For instance, consider NASA's determination that the falling foam that hit the space shuttle *Columbia* when it took off in 2003 would

Groupthink may explain the poor decision making of NASA engineers that led to the destruction of the space shuttle *Columbia*.

pose no significant danger when it was time for the *Columbia* to land. Despite some engineers' misgivings, a consensus formed that the foam was not dangerous to the shuttle. Ultimately, that consensus proved wrong: The shuttle came apart as it attempted to land, which killed all the astronauts on board (Schwartz & Wald, 2003).

In hindsight, NASA's decision was clearly wrong. How could such a poor decision have been made?

A phenomenon known as groupthink may provide an explanation. **Groupthink** is a type of thinking in which group members share such a strong motivation to achieve consensus that they lose the ability to critically evaluate alternative points of view. Groupthink is most likely to occur when a popular or powerful leader is surrounded by people of lower status—which is obviously the case with any U.S. president and his advisers but is also true for leaders in a variety of other organizations (Janis, 1997; Kowert, 2002; Baron, 2005; Henningsen, Henningsen, & Eden, 2006).

Groupthink typically leads to poor decisions. Groups limit the list of possible solutions to just a few, and they spend relatively little time considering any alternatives once the leader seems to be leaning toward a particular solution. In addition, groups may fall prey to *entrapment,* a circumstance in which commitments to a failing point of view or course of action are increased to justify investments in time and energy that have already been made (Weiss & Weiss, 2003; Turner, Pratkanis, & Struckman, 2007).

Ultimately, group members may completely ignore information that challenges a developing consensus. Because historical research suggests that many disastrous decisions reflect groupthink, it is important for groups to be on guard (Kowert, 2002; Chapman, 2006; Packer, 2009).

groupthink A type of thinking in which group members share such a strong motivation to achieve consensus that they lose the ability to critically evaluate alternative points of view.

PsychTech

Through the use of Facebook, Twitter, and other social media, social norms can develop and be rapidly communicated to others.

CONFORMITY TO SOCIAL ROLES

Another way in which conformity influences behavior is through social roles. *Social roles* are the behaviors that are associated with people in a given position. For example, the role of "student" comprises behaviors such as studying, listening to an instructor, and attending class. Like a theatrical role, social roles tell us what behavior is associated with a given position.

In some cases, though, social roles influence us so profoundly that we engage in behavior in entirely atypical—and damaging—ways. This fact was brought home in an influential experiment conducted by Philip Zimbardo and colleagues. In the study, the researchers set up a mock prison complete with cells, solitary confinement cubicles, and a small recreation area. The researchers then advertised for participants who were willing to spend 2 weeks in a study of prison life. Once they identified the study participants, a flip of a coin designated who would be a prisoner and who would be a prison guard. Neither prisoners nor guards were told how to fulfill their roles (Zimbardo, Maslach, & Haney, 2000; Zimbardo, 1973, 2007).

After just a few days in this mock prison, the students assigned to be guards became abusive to the prisoners by waking them at odd hours and subjecting them to arbitrary punishment. They withheld food from the prisoners and forced them into hard labor. On the other hand, the students assigned to the prisoner role soon became docile and submissive to the guards. They became extremely demoralized, and one slipped into a depression so severe he was released after just a few days. In fact, after only 6 days of captivity, the remaining prisoners' reactions became so extreme that the study was ended.

The experiment (which, it's important to note, drew criticism on both methodological and ethical grounds) provided a clear lesson: Conforming to a social role can have a powerful consequence on the behavior of even normal, well-adjusted people and induce them to change their behavior in sometimes undesirable ways. This phenomenon may explain how the situation in 2004 in which U.S. Army guards at the Iraqi Abu Ghraib prison found themselves could have led to their abusive behavior toward the prisoners (Zimbardo, 2007; Haney & Zimbardo, 2009; Post, 2011).

Compliance: Submitting to Direct Social Pressure

When we refer to conformity, we usually mean a phenomenon in which the social pressure is subtle or indirect. But in some situations social pressure is much more obvious with direct, explicit pressure to endorse a particular point of view or behave in a certain way. Social psychologists call the type of behavior that occurs in response to direct social pressure **compliance.**

compliance Behavior that occurs in response to direct social pressure.

Several specific techniques represent attempts to gain compliance. Those frequently employed include:

- *Foot-in-the-door technique.* In the *foot-in-the-door technique*, you ask a person to agree to a small request which—because it is small—the likelihood that he or she will comply is fairly high. But later you ask that person to comply with a more important request. It turns out that compliance with the more important request increases significantly when the person first agrees to the smaller favor.

  Researchers first demonstrated the foot-in-the-door phenomenon in a study in which a number of experimenters went door to door asking residents to sign a petition in favor of safe driving (Freedman & Fraser, 1966). Almost everyone complied with that small, benign request. A few weeks later, different experimenters contacted the residents and made a much larger request for the residents to erect a huge sign on their front lawns that read, "Drive Carefully." The results were clear: 55% of those who had signed the petition agreed to the request to put up a sign, whereas only 17% of the people in a control group who had not been asked to sign the petition agreed to put up a sign.

  Why does the foot-in-the-door technique work? For one reason, involvement with the small request leads to an interest in an issue; taking an action—any action—makes the individual more committed to the issue, which thereby increasing the likelihood of future compliance. Another explanation revolves around people's self-perceptions. By complying with the initial request, individuals may come to see themselves as people who provide help when asked. Then, when confronted with the larger request, they agree in order to maintain the kind of consistency in attitudes and behavior that we described earlier. Although we don't know which of these two explanations is more accurate, it is clear that the foot-in-the-door strategy is effective (Burger & Caldwell, 2003; Bloom, McBride, & Pollak, 2006; Guéguen et al., 2008).

- *Door-in-the-face technique.* A fund-raiser asks for a $500 contribution. You laughingly refuse and tell her that the amount is way out of your league. She then asks for a $10 contribution. What do you do? If you are like most people, you'll probably be a lot more compliant than you would be if she hadn't asked for the huge contribution first. In this tactic, called the *door-in-the-face technique,* someone makes a large request, expects it to be refused, and follows it with a smaller one. This strategy, which is the opposite of the foot-in-the-door approach, has also proved to be effective (Turner et al., 2007; Ebster & Neumayr, 2008; Dolinski, 2011).

The persuasive technique identified by social psychologists can be seen in practice at auto dealerships.

In a field experiment that demonstrates the success of this approach, experimenters stopped college students on the street and asked them to agree to a substantial favor—acting as unpaid counselors for juvenile delinquents 2 hours a week for 2 years (Cialdini et al., 1975). Not surprisingly, no one agreed to make such an enormous commitment. But when they were later asked the considerably smaller favor of taking a group of delinquents on a 2-hour trip to the zoo, half the people complied. In comparison, only 17% of a control group of participants who had not first received the larger request agreed.

The use of this technique is widespread. You may have tried it at some point yourself by perhaps by asking your parents for a large increase in your allowance and later settling for less. Similarly, television writers, by sometimes sprinkling their scripts with obscenities that they know network censors will cut out, hope to keep other key phrases intact (Cialdini & Sagarin, 2005).

- *That's-not-all technique.* In this technique, a salesperson offers you a deal at an inflated price. But immediately after the initial offer, the salesperson offers an incentive, discount, or bonus to clinch the deal.

Although it sounds transparent, this practice can be quite effective. In one study, the experimenters set up a booth and sold cupcakes for 75¢ each. In one condition, the experimenters directly told customers that the price was 75¢. In another condition, they told customers that the price was originally $1 but had been reduced to 75¢. As we might predict, more people bought cupcakes at the "reduced" price—even though it was identical to the price in the other experimental condition (Burger, Reed, & DeCesare, 1999; Pratkanis, 2007).

- *Not-so-free* sample. If you ever receive a free sample, keep in mind that it comes with a psychological cost. Although they may not couch it in these terms, salespeople who provide samples to potential customers do so to instigate the norm of reciprocity. The *norm of reciprocity* is the well accepted societal standard dictating that we should treat other people as they treat us. Receiving a *not-so-free sample,* then, suggests the need for reciprocation—in the form of a purchase, of course (Cialdini, 2006; Park & Antonioni, 2007; Burger, 2009).

Companies seeking to sell their products to consumers often use the techniques identified by social psychologists for promoting compliance. But employers also use them to bring about compliance and raise employees' productivity in the workplace. In fact, **industrial-organizational (I/O) psychology,** a close cousin to social psychology,

industrial-organizational (I/O) psychology The branch of psychology focusing on work- and job-related issues, including worker motivation, satisfaction, safety, and productivity.

considers issues such as worker motivation, satisfaction, safety, and productivity. I/O psychologists also focus on the operation and design of organizations; they ask questions such as how decision making can be improved in large organizations and how the fit between workers and their jobs can be maximized.

Obedience: Following Direct Orders

obedience A change in behavior in response to the commands of others.

Compliance techniques are used to gently lead people toward agreement with a request. In some cases, however, requests aim to produce **obedience,** a change in behavior in response to the commands of others. Although obedience is considerably less common than conformity and compliance, it does occur in several specific kinds of relationships. For example, we may show obedience to our bosses, teachers, or parents merely because of the power they hold to reward or punish us.

To acquire an understanding of obedience, consider for a moment how you might respond if a stranger said to you:

I've devised a new way of improving memory. All I need is for you to teach people a list of words and then give them a test. The test procedure requires only that you give learners a shock each time they make a mistake on the test. To administer the shocks, you will use a "shock generator" that gives shocks ranging from 15 to 450 volts. You can see that the switches are labeled from "slight shock" through "danger: severe shock" at the top level, where there are three red Xs. But don't worry; although the shocks may be painful, they will cause no permanent damage.

Presented with this situation, you would be likely to think that neither you nor anyone else would go along with the stranger's unusual request. Clearly, it lies outside the bounds of what we consider good sense.

Or does it? Suppose the stranger asking for your help was a psychologist conducting an experiment. Or suppose the request came from your teacher, your employer, or your military commander—all people in authority with a seemingly legitimate reason for the request.

If you still believe it's unlikely that you would comply—think again. The situation presented above describes a classic experiment conducted by social psychologist Stanley Milgram in the 1960s. In the study, an experimenter told participants to give increasingly stronger shocks to another person as part of a study on learning (see Figure 2). In reality, the experiment had nothing to do with learning; the real issue under consideration was the degree to which participants would comply with the experimenter's requests. In fact, the "learner" supposedly receiving the shocks was a confederate who never really received any punishment (Milgram, 2005).

Most people who hear a description of Milgram's experiment feel it is unlikely that *any* participant would give the maximum level of shock—or, for that matter, any shock at all. Even a group of psychiatrists to whom the situation was described predicted that fewer than 2% of the participants would fully comply and administer the strongest shocks.

However, the actual results contradicted both experts' and nonexperts' predictions. Some 65% of the participants eventually used the highest setting on the shock generator—450 volts—to shock the learner. This obedience occurred even though the learner, who had mentioned at the start of the experiment that he had a heart condition, demanded to be released, screaming, "Let me out of here! Let me out of here! My heart's bothering me. Let me out of here!" Despite the learner's pleas, most participants continued to administer the shocks.

Why did so many individuals comply with the experimenter's demands? The participants, who were extensively interviewed after the experiment, said they

 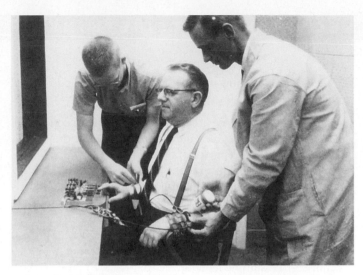

FIGURE 2 This fearsome "shock generator" led participants to believe they were administering electric shocks to another person, who was connected to the generator by electrodes that were attached to the skin. (Source: Copyright 1965 by Stanley Milgram. From the film *Obedience*, distributed by the New York University Film Library and Pennsylvania State University, PCR.)

obeyed primarily because they believed that the experimenter would be responsible for any potential ill effects that befell the learner. The participants accepted the experimenter's orders, then, because they thought that they personally could not be held accountable for their actions—they could always blame the experimenter (Blass, 1996, 2004).

Although most participants in the Milgram experiment said later they felt the knowledge gained from the study outweighed the discomfort they may have felt, the experiment has been criticized for creating an extremely trying set of circumstances for the participants and thereby raised serious ethical concerns. Undoubtedly, the same experiment could not be conducted today because of ethical considerations.

Other critics have suggested that Milgram's methods were ineffective in creating a situation that actually mirrored real-world obedience. For example, how often are people placed in a situation in which someone orders them to continue hurting a victim, while the victim's protests are ignored (Blass, 2000, 2004)?

Despite these concerns, Milgram's research remains the strongest laboratory demonstration of obedience. And partial replications of Milgram's work, conducted in an ethically defensible way, find similar results, which adds credence to the original work (Blass, 2009; Burger, 2009).

Furthermore, we need only consider actual instances of obedience to authority to witness some frightening real-life parallels. For instance, after World War II, the major defense that Nazi officers gave to excuse their participation in atrocities during the war was that they were "only following orders." Milgram's experiment, which was motivated in part by his desire to explain the behavior of everyday Germans during World War II, forces us to ask ourselves this question: Would we be able to withstand the intense power of authority?

Study Alert

Because of its graphic demonstration of obedience to authority, the Milgram experiment is one of the most famous and influential studies in social psychology.

RECAP/EVALUATE/RETHINK

RECAP

LO 44-1 What are the major sources and tactics of social influence?

- Social influence is the area of social psychology concerned with situations in which the actions of an individual or group affect the behavior of others. (p. 541)
- Conformity refers to changes in behavior or attitudes that result from a desire to follow the beliefs or standards of others. (p. 541)
- Compliance is behavior that results from direct social pressure. Among the ways of eliciting compliance are the foot-in-the-door, door-in-the-face, that's-not-all, and not-so-free-sample techniques. (p. 544)
- Obedience is a change in behavior in response to the commands of others. (p. 546)

EVALUATE

1. A _____ _____, or person who agrees with the dissenting viewpoint, is likely to reduce conformity.
2. Who pioneered the study of conformity?
   a. Skinner
   b. Asch
   c. Milgram
   d. Fiala
3. Which of the following techniques asks a person to comply with a small initial request to enhance the likelihood that the person will later comply with a larger request?
   a. Door-in-the-face
   b. Foot-in-the-door
   c. That's-not-all
   d. Not-so-free sample

4. The _____ _____ _____ _____ technique begins with an outrageous request that makes a subsequent, smaller request seem reasonable.
5. _____ is a change in behavior that is due to another person's orders.

RETHINK

1. Why do you think the Milgram experiment is so controversial? What sorts of effects might the experiment have had on participants? Do you think the experiment would have had similar results if it had not been conducted in a laboratory setting but among members of a social group (such as a fraternity or sorority) with strong pressures to conform?
2. *From the perspective of a sales representative:* Imagine that you have been trained to use the various compliance techniques described in this section. Because these compliance techniques are so powerful, should the use of certain such techniques be forbidden? Should consumers be taught defenses against such techniques? Is the use of such techniques ethically and morally defensible? Why?
3. *From the perspective of an educator:* Student obedience in the elementary and secondary classroom is a major issue for many teachers. How might you promote student obedience in the classroom? What are some of the potentially harmful ways that teachers could use their social influence to elicit student obedience?

Answers to Evaluate Questions

1. social supporter; 2. b; 3. b; 4. door-in-the-face; 5. Obedience

KEY TERMS

social influence p. 541
group p. 541
conformity p. 541
status p. 542

social supporter p. 542
groupthink p. 543
compliance p. 544

industrial-organizational
   (I/O) psychology p. 545
obedience p. 546

Prejudice and Discrimination

What do you think when someone says, "He's African American," "She's Chinese," or "That's a woman driver"?

If you're like most people, you'll probably automatically form some sort of impression of what each person is like. Most likely your impression is based on a **stereotype,** a set of generalized beliefs and expectations about a specific group and its members. Stereotypes, which may be negative or positive, grow out of our tendency to categorize and organize the vast amount of information we encounter in our everyday lives. All stereotypes share the common feature of oversimplifying the world: We view individuals not in terms of their unique, personal characteristics, but also in terms of characteristics we attribute to all the members of a particular group.

Stereotypes can lead to **prejudice,** a negative (or positive) evaluation of a group and its members. For instance, racial prejudice occurs when a member of a racial group is evaluated in terms of race and not because of his or her own characteristics or abilities. Although prejudice can be positive ("I love the Irish"), social psychologists have focused on understanding the roots of negative prejudice ("I hate immigrants").

Common stereotypes and forms of prejudice involve race, religion, ethnicity, and gender. Over the years, various groups have been called "lazy" or "shrewd" or "cruel" with varying degrees of regularity by those who are not members of that group. Even today, despite major progress toward reducing legally sanctioned forms of prejudice, such as school segregation, stereotypes remain (Pettigrew, 2004; Hunt, Seifert, & Armenta, 2006; Devos, 2011).

Even people who on the surface appear to be unprejudiced may harbor hidden prejudice. For example, when white participants in experiments are shown faces on a computer screen so rapidly that they cannot consciously perceive the faces, they react more negatively to black than to white faces—an example of what has been called *modern racism* (Dovidio, Gaertner, & Pearson, 2005; Liu & Mills, 2006; Pearson, Dovidio, & Pratto, 2007).

Although usually backed by little or no evidence, stereotypes can have harmful consequences. Acting on negative stereotypes results in **discrimination**—behavior directed toward individuals on the basis of their membership in a particular group. Discrimination can lead to exclusion from jobs, neighborhoods, and educational opportunities, and it may result in lower salaries and benefits for members of specific groups. Discrimination can also result in more favorable treatment to favored groups—for example, when an employer hires a job applicant of his or her own racial group because of the applicant's race (Avery, McKay, & Wilson, 2008; Pager & Shepherd, 2008).

Stereotyping not only leads to overt discrimination, but also can cause members of stereotyped groups to behave in ways that reflect the stereotype through a phenomenon known as the *self-fulfilling prophecy.* Self-fulfilling prophecies are expectations about the occurrence of a future event or behavior that act to increase the likelihood the event or behavior will occur. For example, if people think that members of a specific group lack ambition, they may treat them in a way

Learning Outcomes

LO 45-1 How do stereotypes, prejudice, and discrimination differ?

LO 45-2 How can we reduce prejudice and discrimination?

stereotype A set of generalized beliefs and expectations about a particular group and its members.

prejudice A negative (or positive) evaluation of a particular group and its members.

discrimination Behavior directed toward individuals on the basis of their membership in a particular group.

Study Alert

Remember that *prejudice* relates to *attitudes* about a group and its members, while *discrimination* relates to *behavior* directed to a group and its members.

that actually brings about a lack of ambition (Oskamp, 2000; Seibt & Förster, 2005; Madon, Willard, & Guyll, 2006).

The Foundations of Prejudice

No one has ever been born disliking a specific racial, religious, or ethnic group. People learn to hate in much the same way that they learn the alphabet.

According to *observational learning approaches* to stereotyping and prejudice, the behavior of parents, other adults, and peers shapes children's feelings about members of various groups. For instance, bigoted parents may commend their children for expressing prejudiced attitudes. Likewise, young children learn prejudice by imitating the behavior of adult models. Such learning starts at an early age: Children as young as 6 months judge others according to their skin color, and by 3 years of age they begin to show preferences for members of their own race (Dovidio & Gaertner, 2006; Ponterotto, Utsey, & Pedersen, 2006; Bronson & Merryman, 2009).

The mass media also provide information about stereotypes not just for children but for adults as well. Even today, some television shows and movies portray Italians as Mafia-like mobsters, Jews as greedy bankers, and African Americans as promiscuous or lazy. When such inaccurate portrayals are the primary source of information about minority groups, they can lead to the development and maintenance of unfavorable stereotypes (Coltraine & Messineo, 2000; Ward, 2004; Do, 2006).

Other explanations of prejudice and discrimination focus on how being a member of a specific group helps to magnify one's sense of self-esteem. According to *social identity theory,* we use group membership as a source of pride and self-worth. Social identity theory suggests that people tend to be ethnocentric, viewing the world from their own perspective and judging others in terms of their group membership. Slogans such as "gay pride" and "Black is beautiful" illustrate that the groups to which we belong give us a sense of self-respect (Tajfel & Turner, 2004; Hogg, 2006).

However, the use of group membership to provide social respect produces an unfortunate outcome. In an effort to maximize our sense of self-esteem, we may come to think that our own group (our *ingroup*) is better than groups to which we don't

Like father, like son: Social learning approaches to stereotyping and prejudice suggest that attitudes and behaviors toward members of minority groups are learned through the observation of parents and other individuals. How can this cycle be broken?

belong (our *outgroups*). Consequently, we inflate the positive aspects of our ingroup—and, at the same time, devalue outgroups. Ultimately, we come to view members of outgroups as inferior to members of our ingroup (Tajfel & Turner, 2004). The end result is prejudice toward members of groups of which we are not a part.

Neither the observational learning approach nor the social identity approach provides a full explanation for stereotyping and prejudice. For instance, some psychologists argue that prejudice results when there is perceived competition for scarce societal resources. Thus, when competition exists for jobs or housing, members of majority groups may believe (however unjustly or inaccurately) that minority group members are hindering their efforts to attain their goals; this belief can lead to prejudice. In addition, other explanations for prejudice emphasize human cognitive limitations that lead us to categorize people on the basis of visually conspicuous physical features such as race, sex, and ethnic group. Such categorization can lead to the development of stereotypes and, ultimately, to discriminatory behavior (Mullen & Rice, 2003; Weeks & Lupfer, 2004; Hugenberg & Sacco, 2008).

The most recent approach to understanding prejudice comes from an increasingly important area in social psychology: social neuroscience. **Social neuroscience** seeks to identify the neurological basis of social behavior. It looks at how we can illuminate our understanding of groups, interpersonal relations, and emotions by understanding their neuroscientific underpinnings (Cacioppo, Visser, & Pickett, 2005; Harmon-Jones & Winkielman, 2007; Todorov, Fiske, & Prentice, 2011).

In one example of the value of social neuroscience approaches, researchers examined activation of the *amygdala,* the structure in the brain that relates to emotion-evoking stimuli and situations, while viewing white and black faces. Because the amygdala is especially responsive to threatening, unusual, or highly arousing stimuli, the researchers hypothesized greater activation of the amygdala during exposure to black faces due to negative cultural associations with racial minorities (Lieberman et al., 2005; Lieberman, 2007).

As you can see in Figure 1 *Neuroscience in Your Life,* the hypothesis was confirmed: The amygdala showed more activation when participants saw a black face

social neuroscience The subfield of social psychology that seeks to identify the neurological basis of social behavior.

Neuroscience in Your Life:
The Prejudiced Brain

FIGURE 1 Both white and black participants showed greater activity in the amygdala when viewing black faces as compared to viewing white faces in this composite fMRI scan. The researchers hypothesized that negative cultural messages about blacks lead to higher activation of the amygdala while viewing black faces due to its role in negative emotions. What other explanations might have produced the same findings? (Source: Lieberman et al., 2005, Figure 1b.)

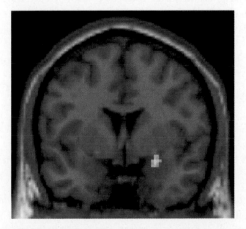

than when they saw a white one. Because both blacks and whites were participants in the study, it is unlikely that the amygdala activation was simply the result of the novelty of viewing members of a racial minority. Instead, the findings suggest that culturally learned societal messages about race led to the brain activation.

Measuring Prejudice and Discrimination: The Implicit Association Test

Could you be prejudiced and not even know it? The answer, according to the researchers who developed the *Implicit Association Test*, is probably yes. People often fool themselves, and they are very careful about revealing their true attitudes about members of various groups, not only to others but to themselves. However, even though they may truly believe that they are unprejudiced, the reality is that they actually routinely differentiate between people on the basis of race, ethnicity, gender, and sexual orientation.

The Implicit Association Test, or IAT, is an ingenious measure of prejudice that permits a more accurate assessment of people's discrimination between members of different groups. It was developed, in part, as a reaction to the difficulty in finding a questionnaire that would reveal prejudice. Direct questions such as, "Would you prefer interacting with a member of Group X rather than Group Y?" typically identify only the most blatant prejudices, because people censor their responses (Schnabel, Asendorpf, & Greenwald, 2008; Greenwald et al., 2009; Aikawa & Fujii, 2011).

In contrast, the IAT makes use of the fact that people's automatic reactions often provide the most valid indicator of what they actually believe. The test asks people a series of questions on a computerized survey that assess the degree to which people associate members of target groups (say, African Americans versus Whites) with positive stimuli (such as a puppy) versus negative stimuli (such as a funeral). The test is based on the fact that growing up in a particular culture teaches us to unconsciously associate members of particular groups with positive or negative qualities, and we tend to absorb associations about those groups that reflect the culture without even being aware of it (Lane et al., 2007). (If you would like to try out a version of the IAT yourself, there is a demonstration website with a sample test at https://implicit.harvard.edu/implicit. You may well be surprised at the results.)

The results of the IAT show that almost 90% of test-takers have an implicit pro-white bias, and more than two-thirds of non-Arab, non-Muslim volunteers display implicit biases against Arab Muslims. Moreover, more than 80% of heterosexuals display an implicit bias against gays and lesbians (Wittenbrink & Schwarz, 2007).

So, of course, having an implicit bias does not mean that people will overtly discriminate, which is a criticism that has been made of the test. Yet it does mean that the cultural lessons to which we are exposed have a considerable unconscious influence on us.

Study Alert

Remember that the IAT allows measurement of attitudes about which people might not be consciously aware as well as attitudes they wish to keep hidden from others.

Reducing the Consequences of Prejudice and Discrimination

How can we diminish the effects of prejudice and discrimination? Psychologists have developed several strategies that have proved effective.

- *Increasing contact between the target of stereotyping and the holder of the stereotype.* Research consistently shows that increasing the amount of interaction between people can reduce negative stereotyping. But only certain kinds of contact are likely to reduce prejudice and discrimination. Situations in which contact is relatively intimate, the individuals are of equal status, or participants must cooperate with one another or are dependent on one another are more likely to reduce stereotyping (Dovidio, Gaertner, & Kawakami, 2003; Tropp & Pettigrew, 2005; Pettigrew & Tropp, 2006).

- *Making values and norms against prejudice more conspicuous.* Sometimes just reminding people about the values they already hold regarding equality and fair treatment of others is enough to reduce discrimination. Similarly, people who hear others making strong, vehement antiracist statements are subsequently more likely to strongly condemn racism (Czopp & Monteith, 2006; Ponterotto, Utsey, & Pedersen, 2006; Tropp & Bianchi, 2006).

- *Providing information about the targets of stereotyping.* Probably the most direct means of changing stereotypical and discriminatory attitudes is education: teaching people to be more aware of the positive characteristics of targets of stereotyping. For instance, when the meaning of puzzling behavior is explained to people who hold stereotypes, they may come to appreciate the actual significance of the behavior (Isbell & Tyler, 2003; Banks, 2006; Nagda, Tropp, & Paluck, 2006).

- *Reducing stereotype threat.* Social psychologist Claude Steele suggests that many African Americans suffer from *stereotype vulnerability,* obstacles to performance that stem from their awareness of society's stereotypes regarding minority group members. He argues that African-American students who receive instruction from teachers who may doubt their abilities and who set up special remedial programs to assist them may come to accept society's stereotypes and believe that they are prone to fail (Aronson & Steele, 2005; Nussbaum & Steele, 2007).

Such beliefs can have devastating effects. When confronted with an academic task, African-American students may fear that their performance will simply confirm society's negative stereotypes. The immediate consequence of this fear is anxiety that hampers performance. But the long-term consequences may be even worse: Doubting their ability to perform successfully in academic environments, African Americans may decide that the risks of failure are so great it is not worth the effort even to attempt to do well. Ultimately, they may "disidentify" with academic success by minimizing the importance of academic endeavors (Steele, 1997; Stone, 2002).

However, Steele's analysis suggests that African Americans may be able to overcome their predicament. Specifically, schools can design intervention programs to train minority group members about their vulnerability to stereotypes and provide them with self-affirmation that reinforces their confidence in their abilities and thereby inoculates them against the fear and doubt triggered by negative stereotypes (Cohen et al., 2006; Wilson, 2006).

- *Increasing the sense of social belonging of ethnic minority students.* Although almost every college student faces feelings of inadequacy and uncertainty about belonging at the start of college, such feelings are especially strong for members of groups who are underrepresented and have been the targets of prejudice and discrimination. However, research shows that a simple intervention in which members of minority groups are made to understand that feelings of inadequacy are not unique to them—and that such feelings usually diminish with time—can help minority students increase their sense of social belonging (Walton & Cohen, 2011).

RECAP/EVALUATE/RETHINK

RECAP

LO 45-1 How do stereotypes, prejudice, and discrimination differ?

- Stereotypes are generalized beliefs and expectations about a specific group and its members. Stereotyping can lead to prejudice and self-fulfilling prophecies. (p. 549)
- Prejudice is the negative (or positive) evaluation of a particular group and its members. (p. 549)
- Stereotyping and prejudice can lead to discrimination, behavior directed toward individuals on the basis of their membership in a particular group. (p. 549)
- According to observational learning approaches, children learn stereotyping and prejudice by observing the behavior of parents, other adults, and peers. Social identity theory suggests that group membership is used as a source of pride and self-worth, and this may lead people to think of their own group as better than others. (p. 550)
- Social neuroscientific approaches to prejudice examine the functioning of the brain and nervous system to understand the basis of prejudice. (p. 551)

LO 45-2 How can we reduce prejudice and discrimination?

- Among the ways of reducing prejudice and discrimination are increasing contact, demonstrating positive values against prejudice, and education. (pp. 552, 553)

EVALUATE

1. Any expectation—positive or negative—about an individual solely on the basis of that person's membership in a group can be a stereotype. True or false?
2. The negative (or positive) evaluation of a group and its members is called
   a. Stereotyping
   b. Prejudice
   c. Self-fulfilling prophecy
   d. Discrimination
3. Paul is a store manager who does not expect women to succeed in business. He therefore offers important, high-profile responsibilities only to men. If the female employees fail to move up in the company, it could be an example of a _____ _____ prophecy.

RETHINK

1. Do you think women can be victims of stereotype vulnerability? In what topical areas might this occur? Can men be victims of stereotype vulnerability? Why?
2. *From the perspective of a corrections officer:* How might overt forms of prejudice and discrimination toward disadvantaged groups (such as African Americans) be reduced in a state or federal prison?

Answers to Evaluate Questions

1. true; 2. b; 3. self-fulfilling

KEY TERMS

stereotype p. 549
prejudice p. 549

discrimination p. 549
social neuroscience p. 551

Positive and Negative Social Behavior

Like philosophers and theologians, social psychologists have pondered the basic nature of humanity. Is it represented mainly by the violence and cruelty we see throughout the world, or does something special about human nature permit loving, considerate, unselfish, and even noble behavior as well?

We turn to two routes that social psychologists have followed in seeking answers to these questions. We first consider what they have learned about the sources of our attraction to others, we end with a look at two opposite sides of human behavior: aggression and helping.

Liking and Loving: Interpersonal Attraction and the Development of Relationships

Nothing is more important in most people's lives than their feelings for others. Consequently, it is not surprising that liking and loving have become a major focus of interest for social psychologists. Known more formally as the study of **interpersonal attraction** or **close relationships,** this area addresses the factors that lead to positive feelings for others.

HOW DO I LIKE THEE? LET ME COUNT THE WAYS

By far the greatest amount of research has focused on liking, probably because it is easier for investigators conducting short-term experiments to produce states of liking in strangers who have just met than to instigate and observe loving relationships over long periods. Consequently, research has given us a good deal of knowledge about the factors that initially attract two people to each other. The important factors social psychologists consider are the following:

- *Proximity.* If you live in a dormitory or an apartment, consider the friends you made when you first moved in. Chances are that you became friendliest with those who lived geographically closest to you. In fact, this is one of the more firmly established findings in the literature on interpersonal attraction: *Proximity* leads to liking (Burgoon et al., 2002; Smith & Weber, 2005).
- *Mere exposure.* Repeated exposure to a person is often sufficient to produce attraction. Interestingly, repeated exposure to *any* stimulus—a person, picture, compact disc, or virtually anything—usually makes us like the stimulus more. Becoming familiar with a person can evoke positive feelings; we then transfer the positive feelings stemming from familiarity to the person him- or herself. There are exceptions, though. In cases of strongly negative initial interactions, repeated exposure is unlikely to cause us to like a person more. Instead, the more we are exposed to him or her, the more we may dislike the individual (Zajonc, 2001; Butler & Berry, 2004).

Learning Outcomes

LO 46-1 Why are we attracted to certain people, and what progression do social relationships follow?

LO 46-2 What factors underlie aggression and prosocial behavior?

interpersonal attraction (or close relationship) Positive feelings for others; liking and loving.

"I'm attracted to you, but then I'm attracted to me, too."

reciprocity-of-liking effect
A tendency to like those who like us.

PsychTech

Research on Facebook and other social media sites indicates that social networking provides a less-intimidating social outlet for students who otherwise have trouble making and keeping friendships, such as those who are introverted or have low self-esteem.

passionate (or romantic) love A state of intense absorption in someone that includes intense physiological arousal, psychological interest, and caring for the needs of another.

companionate love The strong affection we have for those with whom our lives are deeply involved.

- *Similarity.* Folk wisdom tells us that birds of a feather flock together. However, it also maintains that opposites attract. Social psychologists have come up with a clear verdict regarding which of the two statements is correct: We tend to like those who are similar to us. Discovering that others have similar attitudes, values, or traits promotes our liking for them. Furthermore, the more similar others are, the more we like them. One reason similarity increases the likelihood of interpersonal attraction is that we assume people with similar attitudes will evaluate us positively. Because we experience a strong **reciprocity-of-liking effect** (a tendency to like those who like us), knowing that someone evaluates us positively promotes our attraction to that person. In addition, we assume that when we like someone else, that person likes us in return (Bates, 2002; Umphress, Smith-Crowe, & Brief, 2007; Montoya & Insko, 2008).

- *Physical attractiveness.* For most people, the equation *beautiful = good* is quite true. As a result, physically attractive people are more popular than physically unattractive ones, if all other factors are equal. This finding, which contradicts the values that most people say they hold, is apparent even in childhood—with children of nursery school age rating their peers' popularity on the basis of attractiveness—and continues into adulthood. Indeed, physical attractiveness may be the single most important element promoting initial liking in college dating situations, although its influence eventually decreases when people get to know each other better (Zebrowitz & Montepare, 2005; Little, Burt, & Perrett, 2006; Luo & Zhang, 2009).

These factors alone, of course, do not account for liking. For example, in one experiment that examined the desired qualities in a friendship, the top-rated qualities in a same-sex friend included sense of humor, warmth and kindness, expressiveness and openness, an exciting personality, and similarity of interests and leisure activities. In addition, as we see in Figure 1 *Neuroscience in Your Life,* our friendships and social networks may be related to neurological factors (Sprecher & Regan, 2002).

HOW DO I LOVE THEE? LET ME COUNT THE WAYS

Whereas our knowledge of what makes people like one another is extensive, our understanding of love is more limited in scope and recently acquired. For some time, many social psychologists believed that love was too difficult to observe and study in a controlled, scientific way. However, love is such a central issue in most people's lives that eventually social psychologists could not resist its allure.

As a first step, researchers tried to identify the characteristics that distinguish between mere liking and full-blown love. They discovered that love is not simply a greater quantity of liking but a qualitatively different psychological state. For instance, at least in its early stages, love includes relatively intense physiological arousal, an all-encompassing interest in another individual, fantasizing about the other, and relatively rapid swings of emotion. Similarly, love, unlike liking, includes elements of passion, closeness, fascination, exclusiveness, sexual desire, and intense caring. We idealize partners by exaggerating their good qualities and minimizing their imperfections (Murray, Holmes, & Griffin, 2004; Tamini, Bojhd, & Yazdani, 2011).

Other researchers have theorized that there are two main types of love: passionate love and companionate love. **Passionate (or romantic) love** represents a state of intense absorption in someone. It includes intense physiological arousal, psychological interest, and caring for the needs of another. In contrast, **companionate love** is the strong affection we have for those with whom our lives are deeply involved. The love we feel for our parents, other family members, and even some close friends

Neuroscience in Your Life:
The Social Brain

FIGURE 1 Research is beginning to help us understand how cognitive abilities contribute to being social. For example, those with greater skills associated with the ability to understand others' intentions, have more gray matter in certain areas of their brain (in yellow). Moreover, the size of our social networks (i.e., the number of people we voluntarily interact with regularly) also is positively associated with the amount of gray matter volume (in red). Areas that correlate with social network size overlap with areas related to intentionality in the prefrontal cortex (in orange). The correlation of intentionality and social network size with the amount of gray matter in similar areas of the brain suggests understanding others' intentionality is important in the development of social networks and that these may share a related neurological basis. (Source: Lewis & Lamb, 2011.)

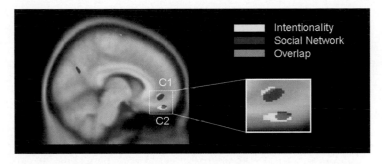

falls into the category of companionate love (Masuda, 2003; Regan, 2006; Loving, Crockett, & Paxson, 2009).

Psychologist Robert Sternberg makes an even finer differentiation between types of love. He proposes that love consists of three parts (See Figure 2):

- *Decision/commitment*, the initial thoughts that one loves someone and the longer-term feelings of commitment to maintain love.
- *Intimacy component*, feelings of closeness and connectedness.
- *Passion component*, the motivational drives relating to sex, physical closeness, and romance.

According to Sternberg, these three components combine to produce the different types of love. He suggests that different combinations of the three components vary

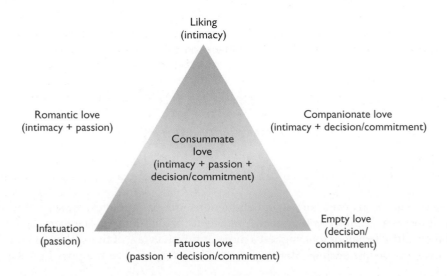

FIGURE 2 According to Sternberg, love has three main components: intimacy, passion, and decision/commitment. Different combinations of these components can create other types of love. Nonlove contains none of the three components.

over the course of relationships. For example, in strong, loving relationships, the level of commitment peaks and then remains stable. Passion, on the other hand, peaks quickly and then declines and levels off relatively early in most relationships. In addition, relationships are happiest in which the strength of the various components are similar between the two partners (Sternberg, Hojjat, & Barnes, 2001; Sternberg, 2004; Sternberg, 2006).

Is love a necessary ingredient in a good marriage? Yes, if you live in the United States. In contrast, it's considerably less important in other cultures. Although mutual attraction and love are the two most important characteristics men and women in the United States desire in a mate, men in China rated good health as most important, and women there rated emotional stability and maturity as most important. Among the Zulu in South Africa, men rated emotional stability first and women rated dependable character first (Buss, Abbott, & Angleitner, 1990; see Figure 3).

Liking and loving clearly show a positive side of human social behavior. Now we turn to behaviors that are just as much a part of social behavior: aggression and helping behavior.

	Rank Ordering of Desired Characteristics in a Mate					
	United States		China		South Africa Zulu	
	Females	Males	Females	Males	Females	Males
Mutual attraction—love	1	1	8	4	5	10
Emotional stability and maturity	2	2	1	5	2	1
Dependable character	3	3	7	6	1	3
Pleasing disposition	4	4	16	13	3	4
Education and intelligence	5	5	4	8	6	6
Good health	9	6	3	1	4	5
Good looks	13	7	15	11	16	14
Sociability	8	8	9	12	8	11
Desire for home and children	7	9	2	2	9	9
Refinement, neatness	12	10	10	7	10	7
Ambition and industriousness	6	11	5	10	7	8
Similar education	10	12	12	15	12	12
Good cook and housekeeper	16	13	11	9	15	2
Favorable social status or rating	14	14	13	14	14	17
Similar religious background	15	15	18	18	11	16
Good financial prospect	11	16	14	16	13	18
Chastity (no prior sexual intercourse)	18	17	6	3	18	13
Similar political background	17	18	17	17	17	15

FIGURE 3 Although love may be an important factor in choosing a marriage partner if you live in the United States, other cultures place less importance on it. (Source: Buss et al., 1990.)

Aggression and Prosocial Behavior: Hurting and Helping Others

Drive-by shootings, carjackings, and abductions are just a few examples of the violence that seems all too common today. Yet we also find examples of generous, unselfish, thoughtful behavior that suggest a more optimistic view of humankind. Consider, for instance, people such as Mother Teresa, who ministered to the poor in India. Or contemplate the simple kindnesses of life: lending a valued compact disc, stopping to help a child who has fallen off a bicycle, or merely sharing a candy bar with a friend. Such instances of helping are no less characteristic of human behavior than the distasteful examples of aggression.

HURTING OTHERS: AGGRESSION

We need look no further than the daily paper or the nightly news to be bombarded with examples of aggression both on a societal level (war, invasion, assassination) and on an individual level (crime, child abuse, and the many petty cruelties humans are capable of inflicting on one another). Is such aggression an inevitable part of the human condition? Or is aggression primarily a product of particular circumstances that, if changed, could lead to its reduction?

The difficulty of answering such knotty questions becomes apparent as soon as we consider how best to define the term *aggression*. Depending on the way we define the word, many examples of inflicted pain or injury may or may not qualify as aggression (see Figure 4). For instance, a rapist is clearly acting with aggression toward his victim. On the other hand, it is less certain that a physician carrying out

FIGURE 4 What is aggression? It depends on how the word is defined and in what context it is used. (Source: Adapted from Benjamin, 1985, p. 41.)

Is This Aggression?

To see for yourself the difficulties involved in defining aggression, consider each of the following acts and determine whether it represents aggressive behavior—according to your own definition of aggression.

1. A spider eats a fly. Yes _____ No _____
2. Two wolves fight for the leadership of the pack. Yes _____ No _____
3. A soldier shoots an enemy at the front line. Yes _____ No _____
4. The warden of a prison executes a convicted criminal. Yes _____ No _____
5. A man viciously kicks a cat. Yes _____ No _____
6. A man, while cleaning a window, knocks over a flower pot, which, in falling, injures a pedestrian. Yes _____ No _____
7. Mr. X, a notorious gossip, speaks disparagingly of many people of his acquaintance. Yes _____ No _____
8. A man mentally rehearses a murder he is about to commit. Yes _____ No _____
9. An angry son purposely fails to write to his mother, who is expecting a letter and will be hurt if none arrives. Yes _____ No_____
10. An enraged boy tries with all his might to inflict injury on his antagonist, a bigger boy, but is not successful in doing so. His efforts simply amuse the bigger boy. Yes _____ No _____
11. A senator does not protest the escalation of bombing to which she is normally opposed. Yes _____ No _____
12. A farmer beheads a chicken and prepares it for supper. Yes _____ No _____
13. A hunter kills an animal and mounts it as a trophy. Yes _____ No _____
14. A physician gives a flu shot to a screaming child. Yes _____ No _____
15. A boxer gives his opponent a bloody nose. Yes _____ No _____
16. A Girl Scout tries to assist an elderly woman but trips her by accident. Yes _____ No _____
17. A bank robber is shot in the back while trying to escape. Yes _____ No _____
18. A tennis player smashes her racket after missing a volley. Yes _____ No _____
19. A person commits suicide. Yes _____ No _____
20. A cat kills a mouse, parades around with it, and then discards it. Yes _____ No _____

aggression The intentional injury of, or harm to, another person.

catharsis The process of discharging built-up aggressive energy.

an emergency medical procedure without an anesthetic, thereby causing incredible pain to the patient, should be considered aggressive.

Most social psychologists define *aggression* in terms of the intent and the purpose behind the behavior. **Aggression** is intentional injury of or harm to another person. By this definition, the rapist is clearly acting aggressively, whereas the physician causing pain during a medical procedure is not (Berkowitz, 2001).

We turn now to several approaches to aggressive behavior developed by social psychologists.

INSTINCT APPROACHES: AGGRESSION AS A RELEASE

If you have ever punched an adversary in the nose, you may have experienced a certain satisfaction despite your better judgment. Instinct theories, which note the prevalence of aggression not only in humans but in animals as well, propose that aggression is primarily the outcome of innate—or inborn—urges.

Sigmund Freud was one of the first to suggest, as part of his theory of personality, that aggression is a primary instinctual drive. Konrad Lorenz, an ethologist (a scientist who studies animal behavior), expanded Freud's notions by arguing that humans, along with members of other species, have a fighting instinct, which in earlier times ensured protection of food supplies and weeded out the weaker of the species (Lorenz, 1966, 1974). Lorenz's instinct approach led to the controversial notion that aggressive energy constantly builds up in an individual until the person finally discharges it in a process called **catharsis.** The longer the energy builds up, says Lorenz, the greater the amount of the aggression displayed when it is discharged.

Lorenz believed that society should offer people acceptable ways of permitting catharsis. For example, he suggested that participation in aggressive sports and games would prevent the discharge of aggression in less socially desirable ways. However, little research has found evidence for the existence of a pent-up reservoir of aggression that needs to be released. In fact, some studies flatly contradict the notion of catharsis, which leads psychologists to look for other explanations for aggression (Bushman, Wang, & Anderson, 2005; Verona & Sullivan, 2008; Richardson & Hammock, 2011).

FRUSTRATION-AGGRESSION APPROACHES: AGGRESSION AS A REACTION TO FRUSTRATION

Suppose you've been working on a paper that is due for a class early the next morning, and your computer printer runs out of ink just before you can print out the paper. You rush to the store to buy more ink only to find the sales clerk locking the door for the day. Even though the clerk can see you gesturing and begging him to open the door, he refuses, shrugs his shoulders, and points to a sign that indicates when the store will open the next day. At that moment, the feelings you experience toward the sales clerk probably place you on the verge of real aggression, and you are undoubtedly seething inside.

Frustration-aggression theory tries to explain aggression in terms of events like this one. It suggests that *frustration* (the reaction to the thwarting or blocking of goals) produces anger, which leads to a readiness to act aggressively. Whether actual aggression occurs depends on the presence of *aggressive cues*, stimuli that have been associated in the past with actual aggression or violence and that will trigger aggression again (Berkowitz, 2001).

What kinds of stimuli act as aggressive cues? They can range from the most explicit, such as the presence of weapons, to more subtle cues, such as the mere mention of the name of an individual who behaved violently in the past. For example, angered participants in experiments behave significantly more aggressively when in the presence of a gun than in a comparable situation in which no guns are present. Similarly, frustrated participants who view a violent movie are more physically aggressive toward a confederate with the same name as the star of the movie than they are toward a confederate with a different name. It appears, then, that frustration does lead to aggression—at least when aggressive cues are present (Marcus-Newhall, Pederson, & Carlson, 2000; Berkowitz, 2001; Jovanović, Stanojević, & Stanojević, 2011).

OBSERVATIONAL LEARNING APPROACHES: LEARNING TO HURT OTHERS

Do we learn to be aggressive? The observational learning (sometimes called social learning) approach to aggression says that we do. Taking an almost opposite view from instinct theories, which focus on innate explanations of aggression, observational learning theory emphasizes that social and environmental conditions can teach individuals to be aggressive. The theory sees aggression not as inevitable, but rather as a learned response that can be understood in terms of rewards and punishments.

Observational learning theory pays particular attention not only to direct rewards and punishments that individuals themselves receive, but also to the rewards and punishments that models—individuals who provide a guide to appropriate behavior—receive for their aggressive behavior. According to observational learning theory, people observe the behavior of models and the subsequent consequences of that behavior. If the consequences are positive, the behavior is likely to be imitated when observers find themselves in a similar situation.

Suppose, for instance, a girl hits her younger brother when he damages one of her new toys. Whereas instinct theory would suggest that the aggression had been pent up and was now being discharged, and frustration-aggression theory would examine the girl's frustration at no longer being able to use her new toy, observational learning theory would look to previous situations in which the girl had viewed others being rewarded for their aggression. For example, perhaps she had watched a friend get to play with a toy after he painfully twisted it out of the hand of another child.

Observational learning theory has received wide research support. For example, children of nursery school age who have watched an adult model behave aggressively and then receive reinforcement for it later display similar behavior themselves if they have been angered, insulted, or frustrated after exposure. Furthermore, a significant amount of research links watching television shows containing violence with subsequent viewer aggression (Winerman, 2005; Greer, Dudek-Singer, & Gautreaux, 2006; Carnagey, Anderson, & Bartholow, 2007).

Helping Others: The Brighter Side of Human Nature

Turning away from aggression, we move now to the opposite—and brighter—side of human nature: helping behavior. Helping behavior, or **prosocial behavior** as it is more formally known, has been considered under many different conditions. However, the question that psychologists have looked at most closely relates to bystander intervention in emergency situations. What are the factors that lead someone to help a person in need?

One critical factor is the number of others present. When more than one person witnesses an emergency situation, a sense of diffusion of responsibility can arise among the bystanders. **Diffusion of responsibility** is the belief that responsibility for intervening is shared, or diffused, among those present. The more people who are present in an emergency, the less personally responsible each individual feels—and therefore the less help he or she provides (Barron & Yechiam, 2002; Blair, Thompson, & Wuensch, 2005; Gray, 2006).

Is road rage a result of frustration? According to frustration-aggression approaches, frustration is a likely cause.

Study Alert

Understand the distinction between the instinctual, frustration-aggression, and observational learning approaches to aggression.

prosocial behavior Helping behavior.

diffusion of responsibility The belief that responsibility for intervening is shared, or diffused, among those present.

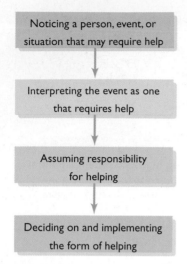

FIGURE 5 The basic steps of helping. (Source: Latané, 1971, pp. 87–91.)

altruism Helping behavior that is beneficial to others but clearly requires self-sacrifice.

For example, think back to the classic case of Kitty Genovese that we described when discussing the topic of research early in the book. Genovese was stabbed multiple times, and—according to some accounts of the event—no one offered help, despite the fact that allegedly close to 40 people who lived in nearby apartments heard her screams for help. The lack of help has been attributed to diffusion of responsibility: The fact that there were so many potential helpers led each individual to feel diminished personal responsibility (Rogers & Eftimiades, 1995; Rosenthal, 2008).

Although most research on helping behavior supports the diffusion-of-responsibility explanation, other factors are clearly involved in helping behavior. According to a model of the helping process, the decision to give aid involves four basic steps (Latané & Darley, 1970; Garcia et al., 2002; see Figure 5):

- *Noticing a person, event, or situation that may require help.*
- *Interpreting the event as one that requires help.* Even if we notice an event, it may be sufficiently ambiguous for us to interpret it as a nonemergency situation. It is here that the presence of others first affects helping behavior. The presence of inactive others may indicate to us that a situation does not require help—a judgment we do not necessarily make if we are alone.
- *Assuming responsibility for helping.* It is at this point that diffusion of responsibility is likely to occur if others are present. Moreover, a bystander's particular expertise is likely to play a role in determining whether he or she helps. For instance, if people with training in medical aid or lifesaving techniques are present, untrained bystanders are less likely to intervene because they feel they have less expertise.
- *Deciding on and implementing the form of helping.* After we assume responsibility for helping, we must decide how to provide assistance. Helping can range from very indirect forms of intervention, such as calling the police, to more direct forms, such as giving first aid or taking the victim to a hospital. Most social psychologists use a rewards–costs approach for helping to predict the nature of the assistance a bystander will choose to provide. The general notion is that the bystander's perceived rewards for helping must outweigh the costs if helping is to occur, and most research tends to support this notion (Koper & Jaasma, 2001; Bartlett & DeSteno, 2006; Lin & Lin, 2007).

After determining the nature of the assistance needed, the actual help must be implemented. A rewards–costs analysis suggests that we are most likely to use the least costly form of implementation. However, this is not always the case: In some situations, people behave altruistically. **Altruism** is helping behavior that is beneficial to others but clearly requires self-sacrifice. For example, people who put themselves at mortal risk to help strangers escape from the burning World Trade Center towers during the 9/11 terrorist attack would be considered altruistic (Batson & Powell, 2003; Manor & Gailliot, 2007; Marshall, 2011).

People who intervene in emergency situations tend to possess certain personality characteristics that differentiate them from nonhelpers. For example, helpers are more self-assured, sympathetic, and emotionally understanding, and they have greater *empathy* (a personality trait in which someone observing another person experiences the emotions of that person) than are nonhelpers (Walker & Frimer, 2007; Stocks, Lishner, & Decker, 2009; Batson, 2011).

Still, most social psychologists agree that no single set of attributes differentiates helpers from nonhelpers. For the most part, temporary situational factors (such as the mood we're in) determine whether we will intervene in a situation requiring aid (Eisenberg, Guthrie, & Cumberland, 2002; Dovidio et al., 2006; Sallquist et al., 2009).

More generally, what leads people to make moral decisions? Clearly, situational factors make a difference. For example, one study asked people to judge the morality of plane crash survivors cannibalizing an injured boy to avoid starvation. Participants in the study were more likely to condemn the behavior if they were

Altruism is often the only bright side of a natural disaster.

placed in an emotional state than if they were less emotional (Schnall et al., 2008; Broeders et al., 2011).

Other psychologists, using a neuroscience perspective, believe that there's a kind of tug-of-war between emotion and rationale thinking in the brain. If the rational side wins out, we're more likely to take a logical view of moral situations (if you're at risk for starving, go ahead and eat the injured boy). On the other hand, if the emotional side prevails, we're more likely to condemn the cannibalism, even if it means we may be harmed. In support of such reasoning, researchers have found that different areas of the brain are involved in moral decisions (Miller, 2008; Greene & Paxton, 2009; see Figure 6 *Neuroscience in Your Life*).

Neuroscience in Your Life: Moral Decisions and the Brain

FIGURE 6 Certain areas of the brain are associated with specific types of moral actions. Specifically, an MRI study shows that taking the perspective of someone who is easing the pain of another person is associated with increased activity in the ventral striatum, while taking the perspective of harming another person results in a decrease in activity in the ventromedial prefrontal cortex and activation in the amygdala. (Source: Decety & Porges, 2011.)

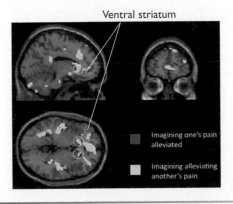

BECOMING AN INFORMED CONSUMER of Psychology

Dealing Effectively with Anger

At one time or another, almost everyone feels angry. The anger may result from a frustrating situation, or it may be due to another individual's behavior. The way we deal with anger may determine the difference between a promotion and a lost job or a broken relationship and one that mends itself.

Social psychologists who have studied the topic suggest several good strategies to deal with anger that maximize the potential for positive consequences (Ellis, 2000; Nelson & Finch, 2000; Bernstein, 2011). Among the most useful strategies are the following:

- *Calm down.* Take a walk or engage in some other physical activity in order to cool down your emotional arousal.
- *Look again at the anger-provoking situation from the perspective of others.* By taking others' points of view, you may be able to understand the situation better, and with increased understanding you may become more tolerant of the apparent shortcomings of others.
- *Minimize the importance of the situation.* Does it really matter that someone is driving too slowly and that you'll be late to an appointment as a result? Reinterpret the situation in a way that is less bothersome.
- *Use language effectively by saying "I," not "you."* Don't say *"You did _____ wrong."* Instead, say *"I felt hurt when you did _____."* When you accuse people of being wrong, they are likely to feel the need to fight back.
- *Fantasize about getting even—but don't act on it.* Fantasy provides a safety valve. In your fantasies, you can yell at that unfair professor all you want and suffer no consequences at all. However, don't spend too much time brooding: Fantasize, but then move on.
- *Relax.* By teaching yourself the relaxation techniques used in systematic desensitization (discussed in the module on treatment of psychological disorders), you can help reduce your reactions to anger. In turn, your anger may dissipate.

No matter which of these strategies you try, above all, don't ignore your anger. People who always try to suppress their anger may experience a variety of consequences, such as self-condemnation, frustration, and even physical illness (Burns, Quartana, & Bruehl, 2007; Quartana & Burns, 2007; Gardner & Moore, 2008).

RECAP/EVALUATE/RETHINK

RECAP

LO 46-1 Why are we attracted to certain people, and what progression do social relationships follow?

- The primary determinants of liking include proximity, exposure, similarity, and physical attractiveness. (pp. 555, 556)
- Loving is distinguished from liking by the presence of intense physiological arousal, an all-encompassing interest in another, fantasies about the other, rapid swings of emotion, fascination, sexual desire, exclusiveness, and strong feelings of caring. (p. 556)
- Love can be categorized as passionate or companionate. In addition, love has several components: intimacy, passion, and decision/commitment. (p. 556)

LO 46-2 What factors underlie aggression and prosocial behavior?

- Aggression is intentional injury of or harm to another person. (pp. 558, 559)
- Explanations of aggression include instinct approaches, frustration-aggression theory, and observational learning. (pp. 560, 561)
- Helping behavior in emergencies is determined in part by the phenomenon of diffusion of responsibility, which results in a lower likelihood of helping when more people are present. (p. 561)
- Deciding to help is the outcome of a four-stage process that consists of noticing a possible need for help, interpreting the situation as requiring aid, assuming responsibility for taking action, and deciding on and implementing a form of assistance. (p. 562)

EVALUATE

1. We tend to like people who are similar to us. True or false?
2. Which of the following sets are the three components of love proposed by Sternberg?
   a. Passion, closeness, sexuality
   b. Attraction, desire, complementarity
   c. Passion, intimacy, decision/commitment
   d. Commitment, caring, sexuality
3. Based on research evidence, which of the following might be the best way to reduce the amount of fighting a young boy does?
   a. Take him to the gym and let him work out on the boxing equipment.
   b. Make him repeatedly watch violent scenes from the film *The Matrix Reloaded* in the hope that it will provide catharsis.
   c. Reward him if he doesn't fight during a certain period.
   d. Ignore it and let it die out naturally.
4. If a person in a crowd does not help in an apparent emergency situation because many other people are present, that person is falling victim to the phenomenon of _____ _____ _____.

RETHINK

1. Can love be studied scientifically? Is there an elusive quality to love that makes it at least partially unknowable? How would you define "falling in love"? How would you study it?
2. *From the perspective of a criminal justice worker:* How would proponents of the three main approaches to the study of aggression—instinct approaches, frustration-aggression approaches, and observational learning approaches—interpret the alleged aggression of James Holmes, accused of killing 12 people at a Colorado movie theater in July of 2012? Do you think any of these approaches fits the Rudolph case more closely than the others?

Answers to Evaluate Questions

1. true; 2. c; 3. c; 4. diffusion of responsibility

KEY TERMS

interpersonal attraction (or close relationship) p. 555
reciprocity-of-liking effect p. 556

passionate (or romantic) love p. 556
companionate love p. 556

aggression p. 560
catharsis p. 560
prosocial behavior p. 561

diffusion of responsibility p. 561
altruism p. 562

Looking Back

Epilogue

We have touched on some of the major ideas, research topics, and experimental findings of social psychology. We examined how people form, maintain, and change attitudes and how they form impressions of others and assign attributions to them. We also saw how groups, through conformity and tactics of compliance, can influence individuals' actions and attitudes. Finally, we discussed interpersonal relationships, including both liking and loving, and looked at aggression and prosocial behavior, the two sides of a coin that represent the extremes of social behavior.

Turn back to the prologue of this set of modules, which describes the neighbors who helped rebuild the Perley Farm. Use your understanding of social psychology to consider the following questions.

1. What factors may have driven the neighbors of Perley Farm to pitch in and help clean up after the flood?
2. Do you believe the Perley Farm neighbors acted because of their personalities or because the situation called for them to be helpful?
3. Why do you think natural disasters such as the hurricane that flooded the Vermont town where Perley Farm was located bring out heroic examples of helping behavior in otherwise ordinary people?
4. What are some ways in which helping behavior can be encouraged in day-to-day life?

VISUAL SUMMARY 14 Social Psychology

MODULE 43 Attitudes and Social Cognition

Persuasion: Attitudes: Evaluations of a particular person, behavior, belief, or concept

- Routes to persuasion

Message → Target →	• Highly involved / • Motivated / • Attentive → Central route processing → **Stronger, lasting attitude change**
	• Uninvolved / • Unmotivated / • Inattentive → Peripheral route processing → Weaker, less persistent attitude change

- Attitude-behavior link

Social Cognition: How people understand what others and themselves are like

- Impression formation: Central traits help us form impressions of others
- Attribution theory: How we decide the specific causes of a person's behavior

  - • Situational causes: a person's behavior brought about by environment
  - • Dispositional causes: a person's inner traits
  - • Attribution biases

[flowchart: Noticing an event → Interpreting the event → Forming an initial explanation → Is time available? Are cognitive resources available? Is there motivation to change the initial explanation? — No → Event explained; process stops; Yes → Formulate and resolve problem → Is the explanation satisfactory? — No; Yes]

MODULE 44 Social Influence and Groups

Conformity: A desire to follow the beliefs or standards of other people

- Groupthink: Group members want to achieve consensus and lose the ability to evaluate alternative points of view
- Social roles: Behaviors associated with people in a given position

Compliance: Social pressure to behave in a certain way

- Foot-in-the-door technique
- Door-in-the-face technique
- That's-not-all technique
- Not-so-free sample

Obedience: Behavior change in response to the commands of others

MODULE 45 Prejudice and Discrimination

Prejudice: A negative or positive evaluation of a group

Discrimination: Behavior directed toward individuals on the basis of their membership in a particular group

Stereotype: Generalized beliefs and expectations about a specific group that arise when we categorize information

Reducing Prejudice and Discrimination

- Increase contact between the target of stereotyping and the holder of the stereotype
- Make values and norms against prejudice more conspicuous
- Provide information about the targets of stereotyping
- Reduce stereotype threat
- Increase a sense of belonging

MODULE 46 Positive and Negative Social Behavior

Liking and Loving

- Determinants of liking
  - • Proximity
  - • Mere exposure
  - • Similarity
  - • Physical attractiveness
- What is love?
  - • Qualitatively different from liking
  - • Three components of love

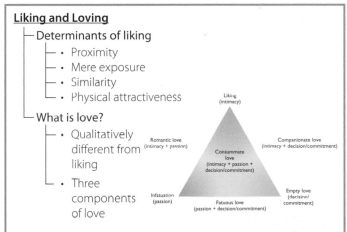

Aggression: Intentional injury of or harm to another person

- Instinct approaches
- Frustration-aggression approach
- Observational learning approaches

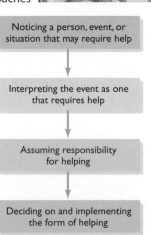

Helping (Prosocial) Behavior: Actions intended to provide aid to others

- Steps for deciding whether to help

[flowchart: Noticing a person, event, or situation that may require help → Interpreting the event as one that requires help → Assuming responsibility for helping → Deciding on and implementing the form of helping]

Glossary

abnormal behavior Behavior that causes people to experience distress and prevents them from functioning in their daily lives. (Module 37)

absolute threshold The smallest intensity of a stimulus that must be present for the stimulus to be detected. (Module 8)

action potential An electric nerve impulse that travels through a neuron's axon when it is set off by a "trigger," changing the neuron's charge from negative to positive. (Module 5)

activation-synthesis theory Hobson's theory that the brain produces random electrical energy during REM sleep that stimulates memories stored in the brain. (Module 12)

activity theory of aging A theory that suggests that the elderly who are most successful while aging are those who maintain the interests and activities they had during middle age. (Module 30)

adaptation An adjustment in sensory capacity after prolonged exposure to unchanging stimuli. (Module 8)

addictive drugs Drugs that produce a biological or psychological dependence in the user so that withdrawal from them leads to a craving for the drug that, in some cases, may be nearly irresistible. (Module 14)

adolescence The developmental stage between childhood and adulthood. (Module 29)

age of viability The point at which a fetus can survive if born prematurely. (Module 27)

aggression The intentional injury of, or harm to, another person. (Module 46)

algorithm A rule that, if applied appropriately, guarantees a solution to a problem. (Module 21)

all-or-none law The rule that neurons are either on or off. (Module 5)

altruism Helping behavior that is beneficial to others but clearly requires self-sacrifice. (Module 46)

Alzheimer's disease A progressive brain disorder that leads to a gradual and irreversible decline in cognitive abilities. (Modules 20, 30)

amnesia Memory loss that occurs without other mental difficulties. (Module 20)

anal stage According to Freud, a stage from age 12 to 18 months to 3 years of age, in which a child's pleasure is centered on the anus. (Module 31)

androgens Male sex hormones secreted by the testes. (Module 25)

anorexia nervosa A severe eating disorder in which people may refuse to eat while denying that their behavior and appearance—which can become skeleton-like—are unusual. (Module 25)

anterograde amnesia Amnesia in which memory is lost for events that follow an injury. (Module 20)

antianxiety drugs Drugs that reduce the level of anxiety a person experiences essentially by reducing excitability and increasing feelings of well-being. (Module 42)

antidepressant drugs Medications that improve a severely depressed patient's mood and feeling of well-being. (Module 42)

antipsychotic drugs Drugs that temporarily reduce psychotic symptoms such as agitation, hallucinations, and delusions. (Module 42)

antisocial personality disorder A disorder in which individuals show no regard for the moral and ethical rules of society or the rights of others. (Module 38)

anxiety disorder The occurrence of anxiety without an obvious external cause that affects daily functioning. (Module 38)

archetypes According to Jung, universal symbolic representations of a particular person, object, or experience (such as good and evil). (Module 31)

archival research Research in which existing data, such as census documents, college records, and newspaper clippings, are examined to test a hypothesis. (Module 3)

arousal approaches to motivation The belief that we try to maintain certain levels of stimulation and activity. (Module 24)

association areas One of the major regions of the cerebral cortex; the site of the higher mental processes, such as thought, language, memory, and speech. (Module 7)

assumed-similarity bias The tendency to think of people as being similar to oneself even when meeting them for the first time. (Module 43)

attachment The positive emotional bond that develops between a child and a particular individual. (Module 28)

attention-deficit hyperactivity disorder (ADHD) A disorder marked by inattention, impulsiveness, a low tolerance for frustration, and a great deal of inappropriate activity. (Module 38)

attitudes Evaluations of a person, behavior, belief, or concept. (Module 43)

attribution theory Considers how we decide, on the basis of samples of a person's behavior, what the specific causes of that behavior are. (Module 43)

authoritarian parents Parents who are rigid and punitive and value unquestioning obedience from their children. (Module 28)

authoritative parents Parents who are firm, set clear limits, reason with their children, and explain things to them. (Module 28)

autism A severe developmental disability that impairs children's ability to communicate and relate to others. (Module 38)

autobiographical memories Our recollections of circumstances and episodes from our own lives. (Module 19)

autonomic division The part of the peripheral nervous system that controls involuntary movement of the heart, glands, lungs, and other organs. (Module 6)

autonomy-versus-shame-and-doubt stage The period during which, according to Erikson, toddlers (ages $1\frac{1}{2}$ to 3 years) develop independence and autonomy if exploration and freedom are encouraged or shame and self-doubt if they are restricted and overprotected. (Module 28)

aversive conditioning A form of therapy that reduces the frequency of undesired behavior by pairing an aversive, unpleasant stimulus with undesired behavior. (Module 40)

axon The part of the neuron that carries messages destined for other neurons. (Module 5)

babble Meaningless speech-like sounds made by children from around the age of 3 months through 1 year. (Module 22)

background stressors ("daily hassles") Everyday annoyances, such as being stuck in traffic, that cause minor irritations and may have long-term ill effects if they continue or are compounded by other stressful events. (Module 34)

basilar membrane A vibrating structure that runs through the center of the cochlea, dividing it into an upper chamber and a lower chamber and containing sense receptors for sound. (Module 10)

behavior modification A formalized technique for promoting the frequency of desirable behaviors and decreasing the incidence of unwanted ones. (Module 16)

behavioral assessment Direct measures of an individual's behavior used to describe personality characteristics. (Module 33)

behavioral genetics The study of the effects of heredity on behavior. (Module 6)

behavioral neuroscientists (or biopsychologists) Psychologists who specialize in considering the ways in which the biological structures and functions of the body affect behavior. (Module 5)

behavioral perspective The approach that suggests that observable, measurable behavior should be the focus of study. (Module 2)

behavioral perspective on psychological disorders The perspective that looks at

the behavior itself as the problem. (Module 37)

behavioral treatment approaches Treatment approaches that make use of the basic processes of learning, such as reinforcement and extinction, and assume that normal and abnormal behavior are both learned. (Module 40)

biofeedback A procedure in which a person learns to control through conscious thought internal physiological processes such as blood pressure, heart and respiration rate, skin temperature, sweating, and the constriction of particular muscles. (Module 7)

biological and evolutionary approaches to personality Theories that suggest that important components of personality are inherited. (Module 32)

biomedical therapy Therapy that relies on drugs and other medical procedures to improve psychological functioning. (Module 40)

bipolar disorder A disorder in which a person alternates between periods of euphoric feelings of mania and periods of depression. (Module 38)

bisexuals Persons who are sexually attracted to people of the same sex and the other sex. (Module 25)

borderline personality disorder A disorder in which individuals have difficulty developing a secure sense of who they are. (Module 38)

bottom-up processing Perception that consists of the progression of recognizing and processing information from individual components of a stimuli and moving to the perception of the whole. (Module 11)

bulimia A disorder in which a person binges on large quantities of food, followed by efforts to purge the food through vomiting or other means. (Module 25)

Cannon-Bard theory of emotion The belief that both physiological arousal and emotional experience are produced simultaneously by the same nerve stimulus. (Module 26)

case study An in-depth, intensive investigation of an individual or small group of people. (Module 3)

cataclysmic events Strong stressors that occur suddenly and typically affect many people at once (e.g., natural disasters). (Module 34)

catharsis The process of discharging built-up aggressive energy. (Module 46)

central core The "old brain," which controls basic functions such as eating and sleeping and is common to all vertebrates. (Module 7)

central nervous system (CNS) The part of the nervous system that includes the brain and spinal cord. (Module 6)

central route processing The type of mental processing that occurs when a persuasive message is evaluated by thoughtful consideration of the issues and arguments used to persuade. (Module 43)

central traits The major traits considered in forming impressions of others. (Module 43)

cerebellum (ser-uh-BELL-um) The part of the brain that controls bodily balance. (Module 7)

cerebral cortex The "new brain," responsible for the most sophisticated information processing in the brain; contains four lobes. (Module 7)

chromosomes Rod-shaped structures that contain all basic hereditary information. (Module 27)

chunk a grouping of information that can be stored in short-term memory. (Module 18)

circadian rhythms Biological processes that occur regularly on approximately a 24-hour cycle.

classical conditioning A type of learning in which a neutral stimulus comes to bring about a response after it is paired with a stimulus that naturally brings about that response. (Module 15)

cochlea (KOKE-lee-uh) A coiled tube in the ear filled with fluid that vibrates in response to sound. (Module 10)

cognitive approaches to motivation Theories suggesting that motivation is a product of people's thoughts, expectations, and goals—their cognitions. (Module 24)

cognitive-behavioral approach A treatment approach that incorporates basic principles of learning to change the way people think. (Module 40)

cognitive development The process by which a child's understanding of the world changes as a function of age and experience. (Module 28)

cognitive dissonance The mental conflict that occurs when a person holds two contradictory attitudes or thoughts (referred to as cognitions). (Module 43)

cognitive learning theory An approach to the study of learning that focuses on the thought processes that underlie learning. (Module 17)

cognitive perspective The approach that focuses on how people think, understand, and know about the world. (Module 2)

cognitive perspective on psychological disorders The perspective that suggests that people's thoughts and beliefs are a central component of abnormal behavior. (Module 37)

cognitive psychology The branch of psychology that focuses on the study of higher mental processes, including thinking, language, memory, problem solving, knowing, reasoning, judging, and decision making. (Module 21)

cognitive treatment approaches Treatment approaches that teach people to think in more adaptive ways by changing their dysfunctional cognitions about the world and themselves. (Module 40)

collective unconscious According to Jung, a common set of ideas, feelings, images, and symbols that we inherit from our ancestors, the whole human race, and even animal ancestors from the distant past. (Module 31)

community psychology A branch of psychology that focuses on the prevention and minimization of psychological disorders in the community. (Module 42)

companionate love The strong affection we have for those with whom our lives are deeply involved. (Module 46)

compliance Behavior that occurs in response to direct social pressure. (Module 44)

compulsion An irresistible urge to repeatedly carry out some act that seems strange and unreasonable. (Module 38)

concepts A mental grouping of similar objects, events, or people. (Module 21)

concrete operational stage According to Piaget, the period from 7 to 12 years of age that is characterized by logical thought and a loss of egocentrism. (Module 28)

conditioned response (CR) A response that, after conditioning, follows a previously neutral stimulus (e.g., salivation at the ringing of a bell). (Module 15)

conditioned stimulus (CS) A once-neutral stimulus that has been paired with an unconditioned stimulus to bring about a

response formerly caused only by the unconditioned stimulus. (Module 15)

cones Cone-shaped, light-sensitive receptor cells in the retina that are responsible for sharp focus and color perception, particularly in bright light. (Module 9)

confirmation bias The tendency to seek out and weight more heavily information that supports one's initial hypothesis and to ignore contradictory information that supports alternative hypotheses or solutions. (Module 21)

conformity A change in behavior or attitudes brought about by a desire to follow the beliefs or standards of other people. (Module 44)

consciousness The awareness of the sensations, thoughts, and feelings being experienced at a given moment. (Module 12)

constructive processes Processes in which memories are influenced by the meaning we give to events. (Module 19)

continuous reinforcement schedule Reinforcing of a behavior every time it occurs. (Module 16)

control group A group participating in an experiment that receives no treatment. (Module 3)

convergent thinking Thinking in which a problem is viewed as having a single answer and which produces responses that are based primarily on knowledge and logic. (Module 21)

conversion disorder A major somatoform disorder that involves an actual physical disturbance, such as the inability to use a sensory organ or the complete or partial inability to move an arm or leg. (Module 38)

coping The efforts to control, reduce, or learn to tolerate the threats that lead to stress. (Module 34)

correlational research Research in which the relationship between two sets of variables is examined to determine whether they are associated, or "correlated." (Module 3)

creativity The ability to generate original ideas or solve problems in novel ways. (Module 21)

cross-sectional research A research method that compares people of different ages at the same point in time. (Module 27)

crystallized intelligence The accumulation of information, skills, and strategies that are learned through experience and can be

applied in problem-solving situations. (Module 23)

cue-dependent forgetting Forgetting that occurs when there are insufficient retrieval cues to rekindle information that is in memory. (Module 20)

culture-fair IQ test A test that does not discriminate against the members of any minority group. (Module 23)

daydreams Fantasies that people construct while awake. (Module 12)

decay The loss of information in memory through its nonuse. (Module 20)

declarative memory Memory for factual information: names, faces, dates, and the like. (Module 18)

defense mechanisms In Freudian theory, unconscious strategies that people use to reduce anxiety by distorting reality and concealing the source of the anxiety from themselves. (Module 31)

deinstitutionalization The transfer of former mental patients from institutions to the community.

dendrite A cluster of fibers at one end of a neuron that receives messages from other neurons.

dependent variable The variable that is measured and is expected to change as a result of changes caused by the experimenter's manipulation of the independent variable. (Module 3)

depressants Drugs that slow down the nervous system. (Module 14)

depth perception The ability to view the world in three dimensions and to perceive distance. (Module 11)

determinism The idea that people's behavior is produced primarily by factors outside of their willful control. (Module 2)

developmental psychology The branch of psychology that studies the patterns of growth and change that occur throughout life. (Module 27)

***Diagnostic and Statistical Manual of Mental Disorders*, Fourth Edition, Text Revision (*DSM-IV-TR*)** A system, devised by the American Psychiatric Association, used by most professionals to diagnose and classify abnormal behavior. (Module 37)

dialectical behavior therapy A form of treatment in which the focus is on getting people to change their behavior and view of themselves by accepting who they are regardless of whether it matches their ideal. (Module 40)

difference threshold (just noticeable difference) The smallest level of added or reduced stimulation required to sense that a change in stimulation has occurred. (Module 8)

diffusion of responsibility The belief that responsibility for intervening is shared, or diffused, among those present. (Module 46)

discrimination Behavior directed toward individuals on the basis of their membership in a particular group. (Module 45)

disengagement theory of aging A theory that suggests that aging produces a gradual withdrawal from the world on physical, psychological, and social levels. (Module 30)

dispositional causes (of behavior) Perceived causes of behavior that are based on internal traits or personality factors. (Module 43)

dissociative amnesia A disorder in which a significant, selective memory loss occurs. (Module 38)

dissociative disorders Psychological dysfunctions characterized by the separation of different facets of a person's personality that are normally integrated. (Module 38)

dissociative fugue A form of amnesia in which the individual leaves home and sometimes assumes a new identity. (Module 38)

dissociative identity disorder (DID) A disorder in which a person displays characteristics of two or more distinct personalities. (Module 38)

divergent thinking Thinking that generates unusual, yet nonetheless appropriate, responses to problems or questions. (Module 21)

double standard The view that premarital sex is permissible for males but not for females. (Module 25)

dreams-for-survival theory The theory suggesting that dreams permit information that is critical for our daily survival to be reconsidered and reprocessed during sleep. (Module 12)

drive Motivational tension, or arousal, that energizes behavior to fulfill a need. (Module 24)

drive-reduction approaches to motivation Theories suggesting that a lack of some basic biological need produces a drive to push an organism to satisfy that need. (Module 24)

drug therapy Control of psychological disorders through the use of drugs. (Module 42)

eardrum The part of the ear that vibrates when sound waves hit it. (Module 10)

ego The part of the personality that provides a buffer between the id and the outside world. (Module 31)

egocentric thought A way of thinking in which a child views the world entirely from his or her own perspective. (Module 28)

ego-integrity-versus-despair stage According to Erikson, a period from late adulthood until death during which we review life's accomplishments and failures. (Module 29)

electroconvulsive therapy (ECT) A procedure used in the treatment of severe depression in which an electric current of 70–150 volts is briefly administered to a patient's head. (Module 42)

embryo A developed zygote that has a heart, a brain, and other organs. (Module 27)

emerging adulthood The period beginning in the late teenage years and extending into the mid-20s. (Module 30)

emotional intelligence The set of skills that underlie the accurate assessment, evaluation, expression, and regulation of emotions. (Module 23)

emotions Feelings that generally have both physiological and cognitive elements and that influence behavior. (Module 26)

endocrine system A chemical communication network that sends messages throughout the body via the bloodstream. (Module 6)

episodic memory Memory for events that occur in a particular time, place, or context. (Module 18)

estrogens Class of female sex hormones. (Module 25)

evolutionary psychology The branch of psychology that seeks to identify behavior patterns that are a result of our genetic inheritance from our ancestors. (Module 6)

excitatory message A chemical message that makes it more likely that a receiving neuron will fire and an action potential will travel down its axon. (Module 5)

experiment The investigation of the relationship between two (or more) variables by deliberately producing a change in one variable in a situation and

observing the effects of that change on other aspects of the situation. (Module 3)

experimental bias Factors that distort how the independent variable affects the dependent variable in an experiment. (Module 4)

experimental group Any group participating in an experiment that receives a treatment. (Module 3)

experimental manipulation The change that an experimenter deliberately produces in a situation. (Module 3)

explicit memory Intentional or conscious recollection of information. (Module 19)

exposure A behavioral treatment for anxiety in which people are confronted either suddenly or gradually with a stimulus that they fear. (Module 40)

extinction A basic phenomenon of learning that occurs when a previously conditioned response decreases in frequency and eventually disappears. (Module 15)

extramarital sex Sexual activity between a married person and someone who is not his or her spouse. (Module 25)

facial-affect program Activation of a set of nerve impulses that make the face display the appropriate expression. (Module 26)

facial-feedback hypothesis The hypothesis that facial expressions not only reflect emotional experience but also help determine how people experience and label emotions. (Module 26)

familial retardation Intellectual disability in which no apparent biological defect exists but there is a history of retardation in the family. (Module 23)

family therapy An approach that focuses on the family and its dynamics. (Module 41)

feature detection The activation of neurons in the cortex by visual stimuli of specific shapes or patterns. (Module 9)

fetal alcohol syndrome The most common cause of intellectual disability in newborns, occurring when the mother uses alcohol during pregnancy. (Module 23)

fetus A developing individual from 8 weeks after conception until birth. (Module 27)

fixations Conflicts or concerns that persist beyond the developmental period in which they first occur. (Module 31)

fixed-interval schedule A schedule that provides reinforcement for a response only if a fixed time period has elapsed, making overall rates of response relatively low. (Module 16)

fixed-ratio schedule A schedule by which reinforcement is given only after a specific number of responses are made. (Module 16)

flashbulb memories Memories related to a specific, important, or surprising event that are recalled easily and with vivid imagery. (Module 19)

fluid intelligence Intelligence that reflects the ability to reason abstractly. (Module 23)

formal operational stage According to Piaget, the period from age 12 to adulthood that is characterized by abstract thought. (Module 28)

free will The idea that behavior is caused primarily by choices that are made freely by the individual. (Module 2)

frequency theory of hearing The theory that the entire basilar membrane acts like a microphone, vibrating as a whole in response to a sound. (Module 10)

functional fixedness The tendency to think of an object only in terms of its typical use. (Module 21)

functionalism An early approach to psychology that concentrated on what the mind does—the functions of mental activity—and the role of behavior in allowing people to adapt to their environments. (Module 2)

fundamental attribution error A tendency to overattribute others' behavior to dispositional causes and minimize the importance of situational causes. (Module 43)

g **or** *g***-factor** The single, general factor for mental ability assumed to underlie intelligence in some early theories of intelligence. (Module 23)

gate-control theory of pain The theory that particular nerve receptors in the spinal cord lead to specific areas of the brain related to pain. (Module 10)

general adaptation syndrome (GAS) A theory developed by Selye that suggests that a person's response to a stressor consists of three stages: alarm and mobilization, resistance, and exhaustion. (Module 34)

generalized anxiety disorder The experience of long-term, persistent anxiety and worry. (Module 38)

generativity-versus-stagnation stage According to Erikson, a period in middle adulthood during which we take stock of our contributions to family and society. (Module 29)

genes The parts of the chromosomes through which genetic information is transmitted. (Module 27)

genetic preprogramming theories of aging Theories that suggest that human cells have a built-in time limit to their reproduction and that they are no longer able to divide after a certain time. (Module 30)

genital stage According to Freud, the period from puberty until death, marked by mature sexual behavior (that is, sexual intercourse). (Module 31)

genitals The male and female sex organs. (Module 25)

gestalt (geh-SHTALLT) laws of organization A series of principles that describe how we organize bits and pieces of information into meaningful wholes. (Module 11)

gestalt psychology An approach to psychology that focuses on the organization of perception and thinking in a "whole" sense rather than on the individual elements of perception. (Module 2)

grammar The system of rules that determine how our thoughts can be expressed. (Module 22)

group Two or more people who interact with one another, perceive themselves as part of a group, and are interdependent. (Module 44)

group therapy Therapy in which people meet in a group with a therapist to discuss problems. (Module 41)

groupthink A type of thinking in which group members share such a strong motivation to achieve consensus that they lose the ability to critically evaluate alternative points of view. (Module 44)

habituation The decrease in the response to a stimulus that occurs after repeated presentations of the same stimulus. (Module 28)

hair cells Tiny cells covering the basilar membrane that, when bent by vibrations entering the cochlea, transmit neural messages to the brain. (Module 10)

hallucinogen A drug that is capable of producing hallucinations, or changes in the perceptual process. (Module 14)

halo effect A phenomenon in which an initial understanding that a person has positive traits is used to infer other uniformly positive characteristics. (Module 43)

hardiness A personality characteristic that is associated with a lower rate of stress-related illness and consists of three

components: commitment, challenge, and control. (Module 34)

health psychology The branch of psychology that investigates the psychological factors related to wellness and illness, including the prevention, diagnosis, and treatment of medical problems. (Module 34)

hemispheres Symmetrical left and right halves of the brain that control the side of the body opposite to their location. (Module 7)

heritability The degree to which a characteristic is related to genetic, inherited factors. (Module 23)

heterosexuality Sexual attraction and behavior directed to the other sex. (Module 25)

heuristic A thinking strategy that may lead us to a solution to a problem or decision, but—unlike algorithms—may sometimes lead to errors. (Module 21)

homeostasis The body's tendency to maintain a steady internal state. (Module 24)

homosexuals Persons who are sexually attracted to members of their own sex. (Module 25)

hormones Chemicals that circulate through the blood and regulate the functioning or growth of the body. (Module 6)

humanistic approaches to personality Theories that emphasize people's innate goodness and desire to achieve higher levels of functioning. (Module 32)

humanistic perspective The approach that suggests that all individuals naturally strive to grow, develop, and be in control of their lives and behavior. (Module 2)

humanistic perspective on psychological disorders The perspective that emphasizes the responsibility people have for their own behavior, even when such behavior is abnormal. (Module 37)

humanistic therapy Therapy in which the underlying rationale is that people have control of their behavior, can make choices about their lives, and are essentially responsible for solving their own problems. (Module 41)

hypnosis A trancelike state of heightened susceptibility to the suggestions of others. (Module 13)

hypochondriasis A disorder in which people have a constant fear of illness and a preoccupation with their health. (Module 38)

hypothalamus A tiny part of the brain, located below the thalamus, that maintains homeostasis and produces and regulates vital behavior, such as eating, drinking, and sexual behavior. (Module 7)

hypothesis A prediction, stemming from a theory, stated in a way that allows it to be tested. (Module 3)

id The raw, unorganized, inborn part of personality whose sole purpose is to reduce tension created by primitive drives related to hunger, sex, aggression, and irrational impulses. (Module 31)

identical twins Twins who are genetically identical. (Module 27)

identification The process of wanting to be like another person as much as possible, imitating that person's behavior and adopting similar beliefs and values. (Module 31)

identity The distinguishing character of the individual: who each of us is, what our roles are, and what we are capable of. (Module 29)

identity-versus-role-confusion stage According to Erikson, a time in adolescence of major testing to determine one's unique qualities. (Module 29)

implicit memory Memories of which people are not consciously aware but that can affect subsequent performance and behavior. (Module 19)

incentive approaches to motivation Theories suggesting that motivation stems from the desire to obtain valued external goals, or incentives. (Module 24)

independent variable The variable that is manipulated by an experimenter. (Module 3)

industrial-organizational (I/O) psychology The branch of psychology focusing on work- and job-related issues, including worker motivation, satisfaction, safety, and productivity. (Module 44)

industry-versus-inferiority stage According to Erikson, the last stage of childhood, during which children age 6 to 12 years may develop positive social interactions with others or may feel inadequate and become less sociable. (Module 28)

information processing The way in which people take in, use, and store information. (Module 28)

informed consent A document signed by participants affirming that they have been told the basic outlines of the study and are aware of what their participation will involve. (Module 4)

inhibitory message A chemical message that prevents or decreases the likelihood that a receiving neuron will fire. (Module 5)

initiative-versus-guilt stage According to Erikson, the period during which children ages 3 to 6 years experience conflict between independence of action and the sometimes negative results of that action. (Module 28)

insight A sudden awareness of the relationships among various elements that had previously appeared to be independent of one another. (Module 21)

instincts Inborn patterns of behavior that are biologically determined rather than learned. (Module 24)

intellectual disability (or mental retardation) A condition characterized by significant limitations both in intellectual functioning and in conceptual, social, and practical adaptive skills. (Module 23)

intellectually gifted The 2%–4% segment of the population who have IQ scores greater than 130. (Module 23)

intelligence The capacity to understand the world, think rationally, and use resources effectively when faced with challenges. (Module 23)

intelligence quotient (IQ) A score that takes into account an individual's mental and chronological ages. (Module 23)

intelligence tests Tests devised to quantify a person's level of intelligence. (Module 23)

interactionist approach (to language development) The view that language development is produced through a combination of genetically determined predispositions and environmental circumstances that help teach language. (Module 22)

interference The phenomenon by which information in memory disrupts the recall of other information. (Module 20)

interneurons Neurons that connect sensory and motor neurons, carrying messages between the two. (Module 6)

interpersonal attraction (or close relationship) Positive feelings for others; liking and loving. (Module 46)

interpersonal therapy (IPT) Short-term therapy that focuses on the context of current social relationships. (Module 41)

intimacy-versus-isolation stage According to Erikson, a period during early adulthood that focuses on developing close relationships. (Module 29)

introspection A procedure used to study the structure of the mind in which subjects are asked to describe in detail what they

are experiencing when they are exposed to a stimulus. (Module 2)

James-Lange theory of emotion The belief that emotional experience is a reaction to bodily events occurring as a result of an external situation ("I feel sad because I am crying"). (Module 26)

Korsakoff's syndrome A disease that afflicts long-term alcoholics, leaving some abilities intact but including hallucinations and a tendency to repeat the same story. (Module 20)

language The communication of information through symbols arranged according to systematic rules. (Module 22)

latency period According to Freud, the period between the phallic stage and puberty during which children's sexual concerns are temporarily put aside. (Module 31)

latent content of dreams According to Freud, the "disguised" meanings of dreams, hidden by more obvious subjects. (Module 12)

latent learning Learning in which a new behavior is acquired but is not demonstrated until some incentive is provided for displaying it. (Module 17)

lateralization The dominance of one hemisphere of the brain in specific functions, such as language. (Module 7)

learned helplessness A state in which people conclude that unpleasant or aversive stimuli cannot be controlled—a view of the world that becomes so ingrained that they cease trying to remedy the aversive circumstances even if they actually can exert some influence on the situation. (Module 34)

learning A relatively permanent change in behavior brought about by experience. (Module 15)

learning-theory approach (to language development) The theory that language acquisition follows the principles of reinforcement and conditioning. (Module 22)

levels-of-processing theory The theory of memory that emphasizes the degree to which new material is mentally analyzed. (Module 19)

life review The process by which people examine and evaluate their lives. (Module 30)

limbic system The part of the brain that controls eating, aggression, and reproduction. (Module 7)

linguistic-relativity hypothesis The notion that language shapes and may determine the way people in a particular culture perceive and understand the world. (Module 22)

lobes The four major sections of the cerebral cortex: frontal, parietal, temporal, and occipital. (Module 7)

longitudinal research A research method that investigates behavior as participants age. (Module 27)

long-term memory Memory that stores information on a relatively permanent basis, although it may be difficult to retrieve. (Module 18)

major depression A severe form of depression that interferes with concentration, decision making, and sociability. (Module 38)

mania An extended state of intense, wild elation. (Module 38)

manifest content of dreams According to Freud, the apparent story line of dreams. (Module 12)

masturbation Sexual self-stimulation. (Module 25)

means-ends analysis Involves repeated tests for differences between the desired outcome and what currently exists. (Module 21)

medical perspective The perspective that suggests that when an individual displays symptoms of abnormal behavior, the root cause will be found in a physical examination of the individual, which may reveal a hormonal imbalance, a chemical deficiency, or a brain injury. (Module 37)

meditation A learned technique for refocusing attention that brings about an altered state of consciousness. (Module 13)

memory The process by which we encode, store, and retrieve information. (Module 18)

menopause The period during which women stop menstruating and are no longer fertile. (Module 30)

mental age The age for which a given level of performance is average or typical. (Module 23)

mental images Representations in the mind of an object or event. (Module 21)

mental set The tendency for old patterns of problem solving to persist. (Module 21)

metabolism The rate at which food is converted to energy and expended by the body. (Module 25)

metacognition An awareness and understanding of one's own cognitive processes. (Module 28)

Minnesota Multiphasic Personality Inventory-2 (MMPI-2) A widely used self-report test that identifies people with psychological difficulties and is employed to predict some everyday behaviors. (Module 33)

mirror neurons Specialized neurons that fire not only when a person enacts a particular behavior, but also when a person simply observes *another* individual carrying out the same behavior. (Module 5)

mood disorder A disturbance in emotional experience that is strong enough to intrude on everyday living. (Module 38)

mood stabilizers Drugs used to treat mood disorders that prevent manic episodes of bipolar disorder. (Module 42)

motivation The factors that direct and energize the behavior of humans and other organisms. (Module 24)

motor area The part of the cortex that is largely responsible for the body's voluntary movement. (Module 7)

motor (efferent) neurons Neurons that communicate information from the nervous system to muscles and glands. (Module 6)

myelin sheath A protective coat of fat and protein that wraps around the axon. (Module 5)

narcissistic personality disorder A personality disturbance characterized by an exaggerated sense of self-importance. (Module 38)

narcotics Drugs that increase relaxation and relieve pain and anxiety. (Module 14)

nativist approach (to language development) The theory that a genetically determined, innate mechanism directs language development. (Module 22)

naturalistic observation Research in which an investigator simply observes some naturally occurring behavior and does not make a change in the situation. (Module 3)

nature–nurture issue The issue of the degree to which environment and heredity influence behavior. (Module 27)

need for achievement A stable, learned characteristic in which a person obtains satisfaction by striving for and achieving challenging goals. (Module 25)

need for affiliation An interest in establishing and maintaining relationships with other people. (Module 25)

need for power A tendency to seek impact, control, or influence over others and to be seen as a powerful individual. (Module 25)

negative reinforcer An unpleasant stimulus whose removal leads to an increase in the probability that a preceding response will be repeated in the future. (Module 16)

neo-Freudian psychoanalysts Psychoanalysts who were trained in traditional Freudian theory but who later rejected some of its major points. (Module 31)

neonate A newborn child. (Module 28)

neurogenesis The creation of new neurons. (Module 7)

neurons Nerve cells, the basic elements of the nervous system. (Module 5)

neuroplasticity Changes in the brain that occur throughout the life span relating to the addition of new neurons, new interconnections between neurons, and the reorganization of information-processing areas. (Module 7)

neuroscience perspective The approach that views behavior from the perspective of the brain, the nervous system, and other biological functions. (Module 2)

neurotransmitters Chemicals that carry messages across the synapse to the dendrite (and sometimes the cell body) of a receiver neuron. (Module 5)

neutral stimulus A stimulus that, before conditioning, does not naturally bring about the response of interest. (Module 15)

norms Standards of test performance that permit the comparison of one person's score on a test with the scores of other individuals who have taken the same test. (Module 23)

obedience A change in behavior in response to the commands of others. (Module 44)

obesity Body weight that is more than 20% above the average weight for a person of a particular height. (Module 25)

object permanence The awareness that objects—and people—continue to exist even if they are out of sight. (Module 28)

observational learning Learning by observing the behavior of another person, or model. (Module 17)

obsession A persistent, unwanted thought or idea that keeps recurring. (Module 38)

obsessive-compulsive disorder (OCD) A disorder characterized by obsessions or compulsions. (Module 38)

Oedipal conflict A child's sexual interest in his or her opposite-sex parent, typically resolved through identification with the same-sex parent. (Module 31)

operant conditioning Learning in which a voluntary response is strengthened or weakened, depending on its favorable or unfavorable consequences. (Module 16)

operational definition The translation of a hypothesis into specific, testable procedures that can be measured and observed. (Module 3)

opponent-process theory of color vision The theory that receptor cells for color are linked in pairs, working in opposition to each other. (Module 9)

optic nerve A bundle of ganglion axons that carry visual information to the brain. (Module 9)

oral stage According to Freud, a stage from birth to age 12 to 18 months, in which an infant's center of pleasure is the mouth. (Module 31)

overgeneralization The phenomenon by which children apply language rules even when the application results in an error. (Module 22)

ovulation The point at which an egg is released from the ovaries. (Module 25)

panic disorder Anxiety disorder that takes the form of panic attacks lasting from a few seconds to several hours. (Module 38)

parasympathetic division The part of the autonomic division of the nervous system that acts to calm the body after an emergency has ended. (Module 6)

partial (or intermittent) reinforcement schedule Reinforcing of a behavior some but not all of the time. (Module 16)

passionate (or romantic) love A state of intense absorption in someone that includes intense physiological arousal, psychological interest, and caring for the needs of another. (Module 46)

perception The sorting out, interpretation, analysis, and integration of stimuli by the sense organs and brain. (Module 8)

perceptual constancy The phenomenon in which physical objects are perceived as unvarying and consistent despite changes in their appearance or in the physical environment. (Module 11)

peripheral nervous system The part of the nervous system that includes the autonomic and somatic subdivisions; made up of neurons with long axons and dendrites, it branches out from the spinal cord and brain and reaches the extremities of the body. (Module 6)

peripheral route processing The type of mental processing that occurs when a persuasive message is evaluated on the basis of irrelevant or extraneous factors. (Module 43)

permissive parents Parents who give their children relaxed or inconsistent direction and, although they are warm, require little of them. (Module 28)

personal stressors Major life events, such as the death of a family member, that have immediate negative consequences that generally fade with time. (Module 34)

personality The pattern of enduring characteristics that produce consistency and individuality in a given person. (Module 31)

personality disorder A disorder characterized by a set of inflexible, maladaptive behavior patterns that keep a person from functioning appropriately in society. (Module 38)

person-centered therapy Therapy in which the goal is to reach one's potential for self-actualization. (Module 41)

phallic stage According to Freud, a period beginning around age 3 during which a child's pleasure focuses on the genitals. (Module 31)

phobias Intense, irrational fears of specific objects or situations. (Module 38)

phonemes The smallest units of speech. (Module 22)

phonology The study of the smallest units of speech, called phonemes. (Module 22)

pituitary gland The major component of the endocrine system, or "master gland," which secretes hormones that control growth and other parts of the endocrine system. (Module 6)

place theory of hearing The theory that different areas of the basilar membrane respond to different frequencies. (Module 10)

placebo A false treatment, such as a pill, "drug," or other substance, without any significant chemical properties or active ingredient. (Module 4)

positive reinforcer A stimulus added to the environment that brings about an increase in a preceding response. (Module 16)

posttraumatic stress disorder (PTSD) A phenomenon in which victims of major catastrophes or strong personal stressors feel long-lasting effects that may include re-experiencing the event in vivid flashbacks or dreams. (Module 34)

practical intelligence According to Sternberg, intelligence related to overall success in living. (Module 23)

prejudice A negative (or positive) evaluation of a particular group and its members. (Module 45)

preoperational stage According to Piaget, the period from 2 to 7 years of age that is characterized by language development. (Module 28)

priming A phenomenon in which exposure to a word or concept (called a prime) later makes it easier to recall related information, even when there is no conscious memory of the word or concept. (Module 19)

principle of conservation The knowledge that quantity is unrelated to the arrangement and physical appearance of objects. (Module 28)

proactive interference Interference in which information learned earlier disrupts the recall of material learned later. (Module 20)

procedural memory Memory for skills and habits, such as riding a bike or hitting a baseball; sometimes referred to as *nondeclarative memory*. (Module 18)

progesterone A female sex hormone secreted by the ovaries. (Module 25)

projective personality test A test in which a person is shown an ambiguous stimulus and asked to describe it or tell a story about it. (Module 33)

prosocial behavior Helping behavior. (Module 46)

prototypes Typical, highly representative examples of a concept. (Module 21)

Prozac A widely prescribed—but still controversial—antidepressant. (Module 42)

psychoactive drugs Drugs that influence a person's emotions, perceptions, and behavior. (Module 14)

psychoanalysis Freudian psychotherapy in which the goal is to release hidden unconscious thoughts and feelings in order to reduce their power in controlling behavior. (Module 40)

psychoanalytic perspective The perspective that suggests that abnormal behavior stems from childhood conflicts over opposing wishes regarding sex and aggression. (Module 37)

psychoanalytic theory Freud's theory that unconscious forces act as determinants of personality. (Module 31)

psychodynamic approaches to personality Approaches that assume that personality is motivated by inner forces and conflicts about which people have little awareness and over which they have no control. (Module 31)

psychodynamic perspective The approach based on the view that behavior is motivated by unconscious inner forces over which the individual has little control. (Module 2)

psychodynamic therapy Therapy that seeks to bring unresolved past conflicts and unacceptable impulses from the unconscious into the conscious, where patients may deal with the problems more effectively. (Module 40)

psychological tests Standard measures devised to assess behavior objectively; used by psychologists to help people make decisions about their lives and understand more about themselves. (Module 33)

psychology The scientific study of behavior and mental processes. (Module 1)

psychoneuroimmunology (PNI) The study of the relationship among psychological factors, the immune system, and the brain. (Module 34)

psychophysics The study of the relationship between the physical aspects of stimuli and our psychological experience of them. (Module 8)

psychophysiological disorders Medical problems influenced by an interaction of psychological, emotional, and physical difficulties. (Module 34)

psychosexual stages Developmental periods that children pass through during which they encounter conflicts between the demands of society and their own sexual urges. (Module 31)

psychosocial development Development of individuals' interactions and understanding of each other and of their knowledge and understanding of themselves as members of society. (Module 28)

psychosurgery Brain surgery once used to reduce the symptoms of mental disorder but rarely used today. (Module 42)

psychotherapy Treatment in which a trained professional—a therapist—uses psychological techniques to help a person overcome psychological difficulties and disorders, resolve problems in living, or bring about personal growth. (Module 40)

puberty The period at which maturation of the sexual organs occurs, beginning at about age 11 or 12 for girls and 13 or 14 for boys. (Module 29)

punishment A stimulus that decreases the probability that a previous behavior will occur again. (Module 16)

random assignment to condition A procedure in which participants are assigned to different experimental groups or "conditions" on the basis of chance and chance alone. (Module 3)

rapid eye movement (REM) sleep Sleep occupying 20% of an adult's sleeping time, characterized by increased heart rate, blood pressure, and breathing rate; erections; eye movements; and the experience of dreaming. (Module 12)

rational-emotive behavior therapy A form of therapy that attempts to restructure a person's belief system into a more realistic, rational, and logical set of views by challenging dysfunctional beliefs that maintain irrational behavior. (Module 40)

recall Memory task in which specific information must be retrieved. (Module 19)

reciprocity-of-liking effect A tendency to like those who like us. (Module 46)

recognition Memory task in which individuals are presented with a stimulus and asked whether they have been exposed to it in the past or to identify it from a list of alternatives. (Module 19)

reflex An automatic, involuntary response to an incoming stimulus. (Module 6)

reflexes Unlearned, involuntary responses that occur automatically in the presence of certain stimuli. (Module 28)

rehearsal The repetition of information that has entered short-term memory. (Module 18)

reinforcement The process by which a stimulus increases the probability that a preceding behavior will be repeated. (Module 16)

reinforcer Any stimulus that increases the probability that a preceding behavior will occur again. (Module 16)

reliability The property by which tests measure consistently what they are trying to measure. (Module 23)

replicated research Research that is repeated, sometimes using other procedures, settings, and groups of participants, to increase confidence in prior findings. (Module 3)

repression The primary defense mechanism in which unacceptable or unpleasant id impulses are pushed back into the unconscious. (Module 31)

resting state The state in which there is a negative electrical charge of about −70 millivolts within a neuron. (Module 5)

reticular formation The part of the brain extending from the medulla through the pons and made up of groups of nerve cells that can immediately activate other parts of the brain to produce general bodily arousal. (Module 7)

retina The part of the eye that converts the electromagnetic energy of light to electrical impulses for transmission to the brain. (Module 9)

retroactive interference Interference in which material that was learned later disrupts the retrieval of information that was learned earlier. (Module 20)

retrograde amnesia Amnesia in which memory is lost for occurrences prior to a certain event, but not for new events. (Module 20)

reuptake The reabsorption of neurotransmitters by a terminal button. (Module 5)

rods Thin, cylindrical receptor cells in the retina that are highly sensitive to light. (Module 9)

Rorschach test A test that involves showing a series of symmetrical visual stimuli to people who then are asked what the figures represent to them. (Module 33)

Schachter-Singer theory of emotion The belief that emotions are determined jointly by a nonspecific kind of physiological arousal and its interpretation, based on environmental cues. (Module 26)

schedules of reinforcement Different patterns of frequency and timing of reinforcement following desired behavior. (Module 16)

schemas Organized bodies of information stored in memory that bias the way new information is interpreted, stored, and recalled. (Module 19)

schemas Sets of cognitions about people and social experiences. (Module 43)

schizophrenia A class of disorders in which severe distortion of reality occurs. (Module 38)

scientific method The approach through which psychologists systematically acquire knowledge and understanding about behavior and other phenomena of interest. (Module 3)

self-actualization A state of self-fulfillment in which people realize their highest potential in their own unique way. (Module 24, 32)

self-efficacy The belief that we have the personal capabilities to master a situation and produce positive outcomes. (Module 32)

self-esteem The component of personality that encompasses our positive and negative self-evaluations. (Module 32)

self-report measures A method of gathering data about people by asking them questions about a sample of their behavior. (Module 33)

self-serving bias The tendency to attribute personal success to personal factors (skill, ability, or effort) and to attribute failure to factors outside oneself. (Module 43)

semantic memory Memory for general knowledge and facts about the world, as well as memory for the rules of logic that are used to deduce other facts. (Module 18)

semantic networks Mental representations of clusters of interconnected information. (Module 18)

semantics The rules governing the meaning of words and sentences. (Module 22)

semicircular canals Three tube-like structures of the inner ear containing fluid that sloshes through them when the head moves, signaling rotational or angular movement to the brain. (Module 10)

sensation The activation of the sense organs by a source of physical energy. (Module 8)

sensorimotor stage According to Piaget, the stage from birth to 2 years, during which a child has little competence in representing the environment by using images, language, or other symbols. (Module 28)

sensory (afferent) neurons Neurons that transmit information from the perimeter of the body to the central nervous system. (Module 6)

sensory area The site in the brain of the tissue that corresponds to each of the senses, with the degree of sensitivity related to the amount of tissue. (Module 7)

sensory memory The initial, momentary storage of information, lasting only an instant. (Module 18)

sequential research A research method that combines cross-sectional and longitudinal research by considering a number of different age groups and examining them at several points in time. (Module 27)

shaping The process of teaching a complex behavior by rewarding closer and closer approximations of the desired behavior. (Module 16)

short-term memory Memory that holds information for 15 to 25 seconds. (Module 18)

significant outcome Meaningful results that make it possible for researchers to feel confident that they have confirmed their hypotheses. (Module 3)

situational causes (of behavior) Perceived causes of behavior that are based on environmental factors. (Module 43)

skin senses The senses of touch, pressure, temperature, and pain. (Module 10)

social cognition The cognitive processes by which people understand and make sense of others and themselves. (Module 43)

social cognitive approaches to personality Theories that emphasize the influence of a person's cognitions—thoughts, feelings, expectations, and values—as well as observation of others' behavior, in determining personality. (Module 32)

social influence The process by which social groups and individuals exert pressure on an individual, either deliberately or unintentionally. (Module 44)

social neuroscience The subfield of social psychology that seeks to identify the neurological basis of social behavior. (Module 45)

social psychology The scientific study of how people's thoughts, feelings, and actions are affected by others. (Module 43)

social support A mutual network of caring, interested others. (Module 34)

social supporter A group member whose dissenting views make non-conformity to the group easier. (Module 44)

sociocultural perspective The perspective that assumes that people's behavior—both normal and abnormal—is shaped by the kind of family group, society, and culture in which they live. (Module 37)

somatic division The part of the peripheral nervous system that specializes in the control of voluntary movements and the communication of information to and from the sense organs. (Module 6)

somatoform disorders Psychological difficulties that take on a physical (somatic) form, but for which there is no medical cause. (Module 38)

sound The movement of air molecules brought about by a source of vibration. (Module 10)

spinal cord A bundle of neurons that leaves the brain and runs down the length of the back and is the main means for transmitting messages between the brain and the body. (Module 6)

spontaneous recovery The reemergence of an extinguished conditioned response after a period of rest and with no further conditioning. (Module 15)

spontaneous remission Recovery without formal treatment. (Module 41)

Stage 1 sleep The state of transition between wakefulness and sleep, characterized by relatively rapid, low-amplitude brain waves. (Module 12)

Stage 2 sleep A sleep deeper than that of stage 1, characterized by a slower, more regular wave pattern, along with momentary interruptions of "sleep spindles." (Module 12)

Stage 3 sleep A sleep characterized by slow brain waves, with greater peaks and valleys in the wave pattern than in stage 2 sleep. (Module 12)

Stage 4 sleep The deepest stage of sleep, during which we are least responsive to outside stimulation. (Module 12)

status The social rank held within a group. (Module 44)

stereotype A set of generalized beliefs and expectations about a particular group and its members. (Module 45)

stimulants Drugs that have an arousal effect on the central nervous system, causing a rise in heart rate, blood pressure, and muscular tension. (Module 14)

stimulus Energy that produces a response in a sense organ. (Module 8)

stimulus discrimination The process that occurs if two stimuli are sufficiently distinct from one another that one evokes a conditioned response but the other does not; the ability to differentiate between stimuli. (Module 15)

stimulus generalization A process in which, after a stimulus has been conditioned to produce a particular response, stimuli that are similar to the original stimulus produce the same response. (Module 15)

stress A person's response to events that are threatening or challenging. (Module 34)

structuralism Wundt's approach, which focuses on uncovering the fundamental mental components of consciousness, thinking, and other kinds of mental states and activities. (Module 2)

subjective well-being People's sense of their happiness and satisfaction with their lives. (Module 36)

superego According to Freud, the final personality structure to develop; it represents the rights and wrongs of society as handed down by a person's parents, teachers, and other important figures. (Module 31)

survey research Research in which people chosen to represent a larger population are asked a series of questions about their behavior, thoughts, or attitudes. (Module 3)

sympathetic division The part of the autonomic division of the nervous system that acts to prepare the body for action in stressful situations, engaging all the organism's resources to respond to a threat. (Module 6)

synapse The space between two neurons where the axon of a sending neuron communicates with the dendrites of a receiving neuron by using chemical messages. (Module 5)

syntax Ways in which words and phrases can be combined to form sentences. (Module 22)

systematic desensitization A behavioral technique in which gradual exposure to an anxiety-producing stimulus is paired with relaxation to extinguish the response of anxiety. (Module 40)

telegraphic speech Sentences in which words not critical to the message are left out. (Module 22)

temperament A basic, inborn characteristic way of responding and behavioral style. (Module 28)

temperament An inborn behavioral style and characteristic way of responding that emerges early in life. (Module 32)

teratogens Environmental agents such as a drug, chemical, virus, or other factor that produce a birth defect. (Module 27)

terminal buttons Small bulges at the end of axons that send messages to other neurons. (Module 5)

test standardization A technique used to validate questions in personality tests by studying the responses of people with known diagnoses. (Module 33)

thalamus The part of the brain located in the middle of the central core that acts primarily to relay information about the senses. (Module 7)

Thematic Apperception Test (TAT) A test consisting of a series of pictures about which a person is asked to write a story. (Module 33)

theories Broad explanations and predictions concerning phenomena of interest. (Module 3)

theory of multiple intelligences Gardner's intelligence theory that proposes that there are eight distinct spheres of intelligence. (Module 23)

thinking The manipulation of mental representations of information. (Module 21)

tip-of-the-tongue phenomenon The inability to recall information that one realizes one knows—a result of the difficulty of retrieving information from long-term memory. (Module 19)

top-down processing Perception that is guided by higher-level knowledge, experience, expectations, and motivations. (Module 11)

traits Consistent personality characteristics and behaviors displayed in different situations. (Module 32)

trait theory A model of personality that seeks to identify the basic traits necessary to describe personality. (Module 32)

transcranial magnetic stimulation (TMS) A depression treatment in which a precise magnetic pulse is directed to a specific area of the brain. (Module 42)

transference The transfer of feelings to a psychoanalyst of love or anger that had been originally directed to a patient's parents or other authority figures. (Module 40)

transsexuals People who believe they were born with the body of the other gender. (Module 25)

treatment The manipulation implemented by the experimenter. (Module 3)

trichromatic theory of color vision The theory that there are three kinds of cones in the retina, each of which responds primarily to a specific range of wavelengths. (Module 9)

trust-versus-mistrust stage According to Erikson, the first stage of psychosocial development, occurring from birth to age $1\frac{1}{2}$ years, during which time infants develop feelings of trust or lack of trust. (Module 28)

Type A behavior pattern A cluster of behaviors involving hostility, competitiveness, time urgency, and feeling driven. (Module 35)

Type B behavior pattern A cluster of behaviors characterized by a patient, cooperative, noncompetitive, and nonaggressive manner. (Module 35)

unconditional positive regard An attitude of acceptance and respect on the part of an observer, no matter what a person says or does. (Module 32)

unconditioned response (UCR) A response that is natural and needs no training (e.g., salivation at the smell of food). (Module 15)

unconditioned stimulus (UCS) A stimulus that naturally brings about a particular response without having been learned. (Module 15)

unconscious A part of the personality that contains the memories, knowledge, beliefs, feelings, urges, drives, and instincts of which the individual is not aware. (Module 31)

unconscious wish fulfillment theory Sigmund Freud's theory that dreams represent unconscious wishes that dreamers desire to see fulfilled. (Module 12)

uninvolved parents Parents who show little interest in their children and are emotionally detached. (Module 28)

validity The property by which tests actually measure what they are supposed to measure. (Module 23)

variable-interval schedule A schedule by which the time between reinforcements varies around some average rather than being fixed. (Module 16)

variable-ratio schedule A schedule by which reinforcement occurs after a varying number of responses rather than after a fixed number. (Module 16)

variables Behaviors, events, or other characteristics that can change, or vary, in some way. (Module 3)

visual illusions Physical stimuli that consistently produce errors in perception. (Module 11)

wear-and-tear theories of aging Theories that suggest that the mechanical functions of the body simply stop working efficiently. (Module 30)

Weber's law A basic law of psychophysics stating that a just noticeable difference is a constant proportion to the intensity of an initial stimulus (rather than a constant amount). (Module 8)

weight set point The particular level of weight that the body strives to maintain. (Module 25)

working memory A set of active, temporary memory stores that actively manipulate and rehearse information. (Module 18)

zone of proximal development (ZPD) According to Vygotsky, the gap between what children already are able to accomplish on their own and what they are not quite ready to do by themselves. (Module 28)

zygote The new cell formed by the union of an egg and sperm. (Module 27)

References

AAUW. *See* American Association of University Women.

Aazh, H., & Moore, B. C. J. (2007). Dead regions in the cochlea at 4 kHz in elderly adults: Relation to absolute threshold, steepness of audiogram, and pure-tone average. *Journal of the American Academy of Audiology, 18,* 97–106.

Abboud, L. (2005, July 27). The next phase in psychiatry. *The Wall Street Journal,* pp. D1, D5.

Ablon, J. S., & Jones, E. E. (2005). On analytic process. *Journal of the American Psychoanalytic Association, 53,* 541–568.

Aboitiz, F., Garcia, R., & Brunetti, E. (2006). The origin of Broca's area and its connections from an ancestral working memory network. In Y. Grodzinsky & K. Amunts (Eds.), *Broca's region.* New York: Oxford University Press.

Abramowitz, J. S., Olatunji, B. O., & Deacon, B. J. (2007). Health anxiety, hypochondriasis, and the anxiety disorders. *Behavior Therapy, 38,* 86–94.

Abrams, R. L., Klinger, M. R., & Greenwald, A. G. (2002). Subliminal words activate semantic categories (not automated responses). *Psychonomic Bulletin & Review, 9,* 100–106.

Accardi, M., & Milling, L. (2009, August). The effectiveness of hypnosis for reducing procedure-related pain in children and adolescents: A comprehensive methodological review. *Journal of Behavioral Medicine, 32,* 328–339.

Ackerman, P. L. (2011). Intelligence and expertise. In R. J. Sternberg & S. Kaufman (Eds.), *The Cambridge handbook of intelligence.* New York: Cambridge University Press.

Adams, G., & Dzokoto, V. A. (2007). Genital-shrinking panic in Ghana: A cultural psychological analysis. *Culture & Psychology, 13,* 83–104.

Adams, K. B. (2004). Changing investment in activities and interests in elders' lives: Theory and measurement. *International Journal of Aging and Human Development, 58,* 87–108.

Adams, M., Bell, L. A., & Griffin, P. (2007). *Teaching for diversity and social justice* (2nd ed.). New York: Routledge/Taylor & Francis Group.

Adams, M., Zuniga, X., Hackman, H. W., Castaneda, C. R., & Blumenfeld, W. J. (2000). *Readings for diversity and social justice: An anthology on racism, sexism, anti-Semitism, heterosexism, classism, and ableism.* New York: Routledge.

Addus, A. A., Chen, D., & Khan, A. S. (2007). Academic performance and advisement of university students: A case study. *College Student Journal, 41,* 316–326.

Advokat, C. (2005). Differential effects of clozapine versus other antipsychotics on clinical outcome and dopamine release in the brain. *Essential Psychopharmacology, 6,* 73–90.

Aftanas, L., & Golosheykin, S. (2005). Impact of regular meditation practice on EEG activity at rest and during evoked negative emotions. *International Journal of Neuroscience, 115,* 893–909.

Ahiima, R. S., & Osei, S. Y. (2004). Leptin signaling. *Physiology and Behavior, 81,* 223–241.

Aikawa, A., & Fujii, T. (2011). Using the Implicit Association Test (IAT) to measure implicit shyness. *Japanese Journal of Psychology, 82,* 41–48.

Aiken, L. (2000). *Dying, death, and bereavement* (4th ed.). Mahwah, NJ: Erlbaum.

Aiken, L. R. (1996). *Assessment of intellectual functioning* (2nd ed.). New York: Plenum.

Aiken, L. R. (1997). *Psychological testing and assessment* (9th ed.). Needham Heights, MA: Allyn & Bacon.

Ajzen, I. (2002). Residual effects of past on later behavior: Habituation and reasoned action perspectives. *Personality and Social Psychology Review, 6,* 107–122.

Akil, H., & Morano, M. I. (1996). The biology of stress: From periphery to brain. In S. J. Watson (Ed.), *Biology of schizophrenia and affective disease.* Washington, DC: American Psychiatric Press.

Alberts, A., Elkind, D., & Ginsberg, S. (2007). The personal fable and risk-taking in early adolescence. *Journal of Youth and Adolescence, 36,* 71–76.

Alexandersen, P., Karsdal, M. A., & Christiansen, C. (2009). Long-term prevention with hormone-replacement therapy after the menopause: Which women should be targeted? *Women's Health, 5,* 637–647.

Alho, K., Vorobyev, V. A., Medvedev, S. V., Pakhomov, S. V., Starchenko, M. G., Terganiemi, M., & Näätänen, R. (2006). Selective attention to human voice enhances brain activity bilaterally in the superior temporal sulcus. *Brain Research, 1075,* 142–150.

Allen, H., Hyworon, Z., & Colombi, A. (2010). Using self-reports of symptom severity to measure and manage workplace depression. *Journal of Occupational and Environmental Medicine, 52(4),* 363–374.

Allen, M. (2011). Theory-led confirmation bias and experimental persona. *Research in Science & Technological Education, 29,* 107–127.

Alloy, L. B., Jacobson, N. S., & Acocella, J. (1999). *Abnormal psychology* (8th ed.). New York: McGraw-Hill.

Allport, G. W. (1961). *Pattern and growth in personality.* New York: Holt, Rinehart and Winston.

Allport, G. W. (1966). Traits revisited. *American Psychologist, 21,* 1–10.

Allport, G. W., & Postman, L. J. (1958). The basic psychology of rumor. In E. D. Maccoby, T. M. Newcomb, & E. L. Hartley (Eds.), *Readings in social psychology* (3rd ed.). New York: Holt, Rinehart and Winston.

Allwood, M. A. (2007). The relations of violence exposure, trauma symptoms and aggressive cognitions to youth violent behavior. *Dissertation Abstracts International: Section B: The Sciences and Engineering, 67,* 5387.

Aloia, M. S., Smith, K., & Arnedt, J. T. (2007). Brief behavioral therapies reduce early positive airway pressure discontinuation rates in sleep apnea syndrome: Preliminary findings *Behavioral Sleep Medicine, 5,* 89–104.

Alon, I., & Brett, J. M. (2007). Perceptions of time and their impact on negotiations in the Arabic-speaking Islamic world. *Negotiation Journal, 23,* 55–73.

Alzheimer's Association. (2009). *Alzheimer's Disease Facts and Figures.* Chicago: Alzheimer's Association.

Amato, L., Davoili, M., Perucci, C. A., Ferri, M., Faggiano, F., & Mattick R. P. (2005). An overview of systematic reviews of the effectiveness of opiate maintenance therapies: Available evidence to inform clinical practice and research. *Journal of Substance Abuse Treatment, 28,* 321–329.

American Association of University Women (AAUW). (1992). *How schools shortchange women: The A.A.U.W. Report.* Washington, DC: AAUW Educational Foundation. American Association of University Women.

American Association of University Women (AAUW). (2001). *Hostile hallways: Bullying, teasing, and sexual harassment in school.* Washington, DC: American Association of University Women.

American Psychological Association (APA). (2000). *Psychology careers for the twenty-first century.* Washington, DC: American Psychological Association.

American Psychological Association (APA). (2002, August 21). *APA ethics code, 2002.* Washington, DC: American Psychological Association.

American Psychological Association (APA). (2007). *Where psychologists work.* Washington, DC: American Psychological Association.

American Psychological Association Presidential Task Force on Evidence-Based Practice. (2006). *Evidence-based practice in psychology, 61,* 271–285.

American Psychological Association Task Force on Intelligence. (1996). *Intelligence: Knowns and unknowns.* Washington, DC: American Psychological Association.

Amid, P. K., & Chen, D. C. (2011). Surgical treatment of chronic groin and testicular pain after laparoscopic and open preperitoneal inguinal hernia repair. *Journal of the American College of Sturgeons, 213*, 531–536.

Amodio, D. M., & Ratner, K. G. (2011). A memory systems model of implicit social cognition. *Current Directions in Psychological Science, 20*, 143–148.

Anastasi, A., & Urbina, S. (1997). *Psychological testing* (7th ed.). Englewood Cliffs, NJ: Prentice Hall.

Anderson, B. F. (1980). *The complete thinker: A handbook of techniques for creative and critical problem solving*. Englewood Cliffs, NJ: Prentice Hall.

Anderson, C. A., Shibuya, A., Ihori, N., Swing, E. L., Bushman, B. J., Sakamoto, A., et al. (2010). Violent video game effects on aggression, empathy, and prosocial behavior in eastern and western countries: A meta-analytic review. *Psychological Bulletin, 136*, 151–173.

Anderson, C., & Carnagey, N. (2009). Causal effects of violent sports video games on aggression: Is it competitiveness or violent content? *Journal of Experimental Social Psychology, 45*, 731–739.

Anderson, C., & Home, J. A. (2006). Sleepiness enhances distraction during monotonous task. *Sleep: Journal of Sleep and Sleep Disorders Research, 29*, 573–576.

Anderson, J. A., & Adams, M. (1992). Acknowledging the learning styles of diverse student populations: Implications for instructional design. *New Directions for Teaching and Learning, 49*, 19–33.

Anderson, J. R. (1981). Interference: The relationship between response latency and response accuracy. *Journal of Experimental Psychology: Human Learning and Memory, 7*, 311–325.

Andrasik, F. (2006). Psychophysiological disorders: Headache as a case in point. In F. Andrasik (Ed.), *Comprehensive handbook of personality and psychopathology, Vol. 2: Adult psycho-pathology*. Hoboken, NJ: John Wiley & Sons.

Andrasik, F. (2007). What does the evidence show? Efficacy of behavioural treatments for recurrent headaches in adults. *Neurological Science, 28, Supplement*, S70–S77.

Andreasen, N. C. (2005). *Research advances in genetics and genomics: Implications for psychiatry*. Washington, DC: American Psychiatric Publishing.

Andrew, M., McCanlies, E., Burchfiel, C., Charles, L., Hartley, T., Fekedulegn, D., et al. (2008). Hardiness and psychological distress in a cohort of police officers. *International Journal of Emergency Mental Health, 10*, 137–148.

Anestis, M. D., Anestis, J. C., & Lilienfeld, S. O. (2011). When it comes to evaluating psychodynamic therapy, the devil is in the details. *American Psychologist, 66*, 149–151.

Angier, N., & Chang, K. (2005, January 24). Gray matter and the sexes: Still a scientific gray area. *The New York Times*, pp. A1, A15.

Anker, A. E., & Feeley, T. (2011). Are nonparticipants in prosocial behavior merely innocent bystanders? *Health Communication, 26*, 13–24.

Ansaldo, A. I., Arguin, M., & Roch-Locours, L. A. (2002). The contribution of the right cerebral hemisphere to the recovery from aphasia: A single longitudinal case study. *Brain Languages, 82*, 206–222.

Antonini, A., & Barone, P. (2008, December). Dopamine agonist-based strategies in the treatment of Parkinson's disease. *Neurological Sciences, 29*, S371–SS374.

Antony, M. M., Brown, T. A., & Barlow, D. H. (1992). Current perspectives on panic and panic disorder. *Current Directions in Psychological Science, 1*, 79–82.

Apanovich, A. M., McCarthy, D., & Salovey, P. (2003). Using message framing to motivate HIV testing among low-income, ethnic minority women. *Health Psychology, 22*, 88–94.

Aponte, J. F., & Wohl, J. (2000). *Psychological intervention and cultural diversity*. Needham Heights, MA: Allyn & Bacon.

Arafat, I., & Cotton, W. L. (1974). Masturbation practices of males and females. *Journal of Sex Research, 10*, 293–307.

Arbuthnott, A., & Sharpe, D. (2009). The effect of physician-patient collaboration on patient adherence in non-psychiatric medicine. *Patient Education and Counseling, 77*, 60–67.

Arcelus, J., Mitchell, A. J., Wales, J., & Nielsen, S. (2011). Mortality rates in patients with anorexia nervosa and other eating disorders: A meta-analysis of 36 studies. *Archives of General Psychiatry, 68*, 724–731.

Arena, J. M. (1984, April). A look at the opposite sex. *Newsweek on Campus*, p. 21.

Ariely, D., & Norton, M. I. (2009). Conceptual consumption. *Annual Review of Psychology, 60*, 475–499.

Ariyanto, A., Hornsey, M. J., & Gallois, C. (2006). Group-directed criticism in Indonesia: Role of message source and audience. *Asian Journal of Social Psychology, 9*, 96–102.

Armbruster, D., Mueller, A., Strobel, A., Lesch, K., Kirschbaum, C., & Brocke, B. (2011). Variation in genes involved in dopamine clearance influence the startle response in older adults. *Journal of Neural Transmission, 118*, 1281–1292.

Arnett, J. (2008). The neglected 95%: Why American psychology needs to become less American. *American Psychologist, 63*, 602–614.

Arnett, J. (2011). Emerging adulthood(s): The cultural psychology of a new life stage. In L. Jensen & L. Jensen (Eds.), *Bridging cultural and developmental approaches to psychology: New syntheses in theory, research, and policy*. New York: Oxford University Press.

Arnett, J. J. (2000). Emerging adulthood. *American Psychologist, 55*, 469–480.

Arnett, J. J. (2006). *Emerging adulthood: The winding road from the late teens through the twenties*. New York: Oxford University Press.

Arnett, J. J. (2007). Afterword: Aging out of care—Toward realizing the possibilities of emerging adulthood. *New Directions for Youth Development, 113*, 151–161.

Aronson, J., & Steele, C. M. (2005). Stereotypes and the fragility of academic competence, motivation, and self-concept. In A. J. Elliot & C. S. Dweck (Eds.), *Handbook of competence and motivation*. New York, Guilford Publications.

Asch, S. E. (1951). Effects of group pressure upon the modification and distortion of judgments. In H. Guetzkow (Ed.), *Groups, leadership, and men*. Pittsburgh: Carnegie Press.

Aschheim, K. (2011). Toward human therapeutic cloning. *Nature Biotechnology, 29*, 986–989.

Aspinwall, L. G., & Taylor, S. E. (1997). A stitch in time: Self-regulation and proactive coping. *Psychological Bulletin, 121*, 417–436.

Atkinson, H. (Ed.). (1997, January 21). Understanding your diagnosis. *HealthNews*, p. 3.

Atkinson, H. G. (2003, August). Are you a "good" patient? *HealthNews*, p. 5.

Atkinson, R. C., & Shiffrin, R. M. (1968). Human memory: A proposed system and its control processes. In K. W. Spence & J. T. Spence (Eds.), *The psychology of learning and motivation: Advances in research and theory* (Vol. 2). New York: Academic Press.

Atkinson, R. C., & Shiffrin, R. M. (1971). The control of short-term memory. *Scientific American, 225*, 82–90.

Aujoulat, I., Luminet, O., & Deccache, A. (2007). The perspective of patients on their experience of powerlessness. *Quality Health Research, 17*, 772–785.

Auld, F., Hyman, M., & Rudzinski, D. (2005). Theory and strategy of dream interpretation. In F. Auld & M. Hyman (Eds.), *Resolution of inner conflict: An introduction to psychoanalytic therapy* (2nd ed.). Washington, DC: American Psychological Association.

Aussilloux, C., & Bagdadli, A. (2006). Handicap mental et société: Soigner, éduquer, intégrer. Mental handicap and society. *Neuropsychiatrie de l'Enfance et de l'Adolescence, 54*, 336–340.

Avery, D., McKay, P., & Wilson, D. (2008). What are the odds? How demographic similarity affects the prevalence of perceived employment discrimination. *Journal of Applied Psychology, 93*, 235–249.

Baars, B., & Seth, A. K. (2009). Consciousness: Theories and models. In W. Banks. (Eds.), *Encyclopedia of consciousness*. New York: Elsevier.

Babson, K., Feldner, M., Trainor, C., & Smith, R. (2009, September). An experimental investigation of the effects of acute sleep deprivation on panic-relevant biological challenge responding. *Behavior Therapy, 40*, 239–250.

Bacchiochi, J. R. (2006). Development and validation of the Malingering Discriminant Function Index (M-DFI) for the Minnesota Multiphasic Personality Inventory-2 (MMPI-2). *Dissertation Abstracts International: Section B: The Sciences and Engineering, 66*(10-B), 5673.

Baddeley, A., Chincotta, D., & Adlam, A. (2001). Working memory and the control of action: Evidence from task switching. *Journal of Experimental Psychology: General, 130*, 641–657.

Baddeley, A., & Wilson, B. (1985). Phonological coding and short-term memory in patients without speech. *Journal of Memory and Language, 24*, 490–502.

Baddeley, A. D., Allen, R. J., & Hitch, G. J. (2011). Binding in visual working memory: The role of the episodic buffer. *Neuropsychologia, 49*, 1393–1400.

Badke, M. B., Sherman, J., Boyne, P., Page, S. & Dunning, K. (2011). Tongue-based biofeedback for balance in stroke: Results of an 8-week pilot study. *Archives of Physical and Medical Rehabilitation, 92*, 1364–1370.

Bagge, C., & Sher, K. (2008). Adolescent alcohol involvement and suicide attempts: Toward the development of a conceptual framework. *Clinical Psychology Review, 28*, 1283–1296.

Bagnall, D. (2010). The use of spinal cord stimulation and intrathecal drug delivery in the treatment of low back-related pain. *Physical Medicine & Rehabilitation Clinics of North America, 21*, 851–858.

Bahrick, H. P., Hall, L. K., & Berger, S. A. (1996). Accuracy and distortion in memory for high school grades. *Psychological Science, 7,* 265–269.

Bai, L. (2005). Children at play: A childhood beyond the Confucian shadow. *Childhood: A Global Journal of Child Research, 12,* 9–32.

Bailey, K., West, R., & Anderson, C. A. (2011). The association between chronic exposure to video game violence and affective picture processing: An ERP study. *Cognitive, Affective, and Behavioral Neuroscience, 11,* 259–276.

Bains, O. S. (2006). Insomnia: Difficulty falling and staying asleep. In N. F. Watson, & B. V. Bradley (Eds.), *Clinician's guide to sleep disorders.* Philadelphia: Taylor & Francis.

Baker, J., & Berenbaum, H. (2007). Emotional approach and problem-focused coping: A comparison of potentially adaptive strategies. *Cognition and Emotion, 21,* 95–118.

Baker, S. (2011). *Final Jeopardy: Man vs. machine and the quest to know everything.* New York: Houghton Mifflin Harcourt.

Baker, S. E., Johnson, P. J., & Slater, D. (2007). Learned food aversion with and without an odour cue for protecting untreated baits from wild mammal foraging [Special issue: Conservation, enrichment, and animal behavior]. *Applied Animal Behaviour Science, 102,* 410–428.

Balaban, C. D. (2002). Neural substrates linking balance control and anxiety [Special issue: The Pittsburgh special issue]. *Physiology and Behavior, 77,* 469–475.

Balaban, C. D., McBurney, D. H., & Affeltranger, M. A. (2005). Three distinct categories of time course of pain produced by oral capsaicin. *The Journal of Pain, 6,* 315–322.

Ball, D. (2004). Genetic approaches to alcohol dependence. *British Journal of Psychiatry, 185,* 449–451.

Ball, H., Arseneault, L., Taylor, A., Maughan, B., Caspi, A., & Moffitt, T. (2008, January). Genetic and environmental influences on victims, bullies and bully-victims in childhood. *Journal of Child Psychology and Psychiatry, 49,* 104–112.

Baltes, P. B., & Kunzmann, U. (2003). Wisdom. *Psychologist, 16,* 131–133.

Bandura, A. (1977). *Social learning theory.* Englewood Cliffs, NJ: Prentice Hall.

Bandura, A. (1986). *Social foundations of thought and action: A social cognitive theory.* Englewood Cliffs, NJ: Prentice Hall.

Bandura, A. (1994). Social cognitive theory of mass communication. In J. Bryant & D. Zillmann (Eds.), *Media effects: Advances in theory and research: LEA's communication series.* Hillsdale, NJ: Erlbaum.

Bandura, A. (1999). Social cognitive theory of personality. In D. Cervone & Y. Shod (Eds.), *The coherence of personality.* New York: Guilford.

Bandura, A. (2000). Self-efficacy: The foundation of agency. In W. J. Perrig & A. Grob (Eds.), *Control of human behavior, mental processes, and consciousness: Essays in honor of the 60th birthday of August Flammer.* Mahwah, NJ: Erlbaum.

Bandura, A. (2004). Swimming against the mainstream: The early years from chilly tributary to transformative mainstream. *Behavior Research and Therapy, 42,* 613–630.

Bandura, A. (2009). Social cognitive theory goes global. *The Psychologist, 22,* 504–506.

Bandura, A., Grusec, J. E., & Menlove, F. L. (1967). Vicarious extinction of avoidance

behavior. *Journal of Personality and Social Psychology, 5,* 16–23.

Bandura, A., & Locke, E. A. (2003). Negative self-efficacy and goal effects revisited. *Journal of Applied Psychology, 88,* 87–99.

Bandura, A., Ross, D., & Ross, S. (1963a). Imitation of film-mediated aggressive models. *Journal of Abnormal and Social Psychology, 66,* 3–11.

Bandura, A., Ross, D., & Ross, S. (1963b). Vicarious reinforcement and imitative learning. *Journal of Abnormal and Social Psychology, 67,* 601–607.

Banich, T., & Heller, W. (1998). Evolving perspectives on lateralization of function. *Current Directions in Psychological Science, 7,* 1–2.

Banks, J. A. (2006). Improving race relations in schools: From theory and research to practice. *Journal of Social Issues, 62,* 607–614.

Baraas, R. C., Foster, D. H., & Amano, K. (2006). Anomalous trichromats' judgments of surface color in natural scenes under different daylights. *Neuroscience, 23,* 629–635.

Barandiaran, A. A., Pascual, A. C., & Samaniego, C. M. (2006). A criticism of the Kohlberg theory: The moral development in adults and educative implications. *Revista de Psicología General y Aplicada, 59,* 165–182.

Bargh, J. A., & Chartrand, T. L. (2000). The mind in the middle: A practical guide to priming and automaticity research. In H. T. Reis & C. M. Judd (Eds.), *Handbook of research methods in social and personality psychology.* New York: Cambridge University Press.

Barke, D. B. (2011). Self-selection for stressful experiences. *Stress and Health: Journal of the International Society for the Investigation of Stress, 27,* 194–205.

Barker, J., & Jones, M. (2008, June). The effects of hypnosis on self-efficacy, affect, and soccer performance: A case study. *Journal of Clinical Sport Psychology, 2,* 127–147.

Barkley, R. (2000). *Taking charge of ADHD* (rev. ed.). New York: Guilford Press.

Barkley, R. (2005). *ADHD and the nature of self-control.* New York: Guilford.

Barkley, R. A., Knouse, L. E., & Murphy, K. R. (2011). Correspondence and disparity in the self- and other ratings of current and childhood ADHD symptoms and impairment in adults with ADHD. *Psychological Assessment, 23,* 437–446.

Barlow, D. H. (2007). *Clinical handbook of psychological disorders: A step-by-step treatment manual* (4th ed.). New York: Guilford Press.

Barmeyer, C. I. (2004). Learning styles and their impact on cross-cultural training: An international comparison in France, Germany and Quebec. *International Journal of Intercultural Relations, 28,* 577–594.

Barnes, B. (2009, July 27). Watching you watching ads. *The New York Times,* B1.

Barnes, T., & Eardley, I. (2007). Premature ejaculation: The scope of the problem. *Journal of Sex & Marital Therapy, 33,* 151–170.

Barnes, V. A., Davis, H. C., Murzynowski, J., & Treiber, F. A. (2004). Impact of meditation on resting and ambulatory blood pressure and heart rate in youth. *Medicine, 66,* 909–914.

Barnett, J. E., Wise, E. H., & Johnson-Greene, D. (2007). Informed consent: Too much of a good thing or not enough? *Professional Psychology: Research and Practice, 38,* 179–186.

Barnett, S. M., Rindermann, H., Williams, W. M., & Ceci, S. J. (2011). Society and intelligence. In R. J. Sternberg & S. Kaufman (Eds.), *The*

Cambridge handbook of intelligence. New York: Cambridge University Press.

Baron, R. S. (2005). So right it's wrong: Groupthink and the ubiquitous nature of polarized group decision making. In M. P. Zanna (Ed.), *Advances in experimental social psychology* (Vol. 37). San Diego, CA: Elsevier Academic Press.

Barrada, J., Abad, F., & Olea, J. (2011). Varying the valuating function and the presentable bank in computerized adaptive testing. *The Spanish Journal of Psychology, 14,* 500–508.

Barresi, J. (2007). Consciousness and intentionality. *Journal of Consciousness Studies, 14, Special issue: Concepts of Consciousness: Integrating an Emerging Science,* 77–93.

Barrett, D. (2002). The 'royal road' becomes a shrewd shortcut: The use of dreams in focused treatment. *Journal of Cognitive Psychotherapy, 16,* 55–64.

Barrett, D. (2007). An evolutionary theory of dreams and problem-solving. In D. Barrett & P. McNamara (Eds.), *The new science of dreaming: Volume 3. Cultural and theoretical perspectives.* Westport, CT: Praeger Publishers/Greenwood Publishing Group.

Barrett, D., & Behbehani, J. (2003). Post-traumatic nightmares in Kuwait following the Iraqi invasion. In S. Krippner & T. M. McIntyre (Eds.), *The psychological impact of war trauma on civilians: An international perspective.* Westport, CT: Praeger Publishers/Greenwood Publishing Group.

Barrett, L. (2011). *Beyond the brain: How body and environment shape animal and human minds.* Princeton, NJ: Princeton University Press.

Barrett, L. F., & Salovey, P. (Eds.). (2002). *The wisdom in feeling: Psychological processes in emotional intelligence.* New York: Guilford Press.

Barrett, L. F., & Wager, T. D. (2006). The structure of emotion: Evidence from neuroimaging studies. *Current Directions in Psychological Science, 15,* 79–83.

Barron, F. (1990). *Creativity and psychological health: Origins of personal vitality and creative freedom.* Buffalo, NY: Creative Education Foundation.

Barron, G., & Yechiam, E. (2002). Private e-mail requests and the diffusion of responsibility. *Computers in Human Behavior, 18,* 507–520.

Barson, J. R., Morganstern, I., & Leibowitz, S. F. (2011). Similarities in hypothalamic and mesocorticolimbic circuits regulating the overconsumption of food and alcohol. *Physiology & Behavior, 104,* 128–137.

Bartecchi, C. E., MacKenzie, T. D., & Schrier, R. W. (1995, May). The global tobacco epidemic. *Scientific American,* pp. 44–51.

Bartholow, B. D., Bushman, B. J., & Sestir, M. A. (2006). Chronic violent video game exposure and desensitization to violence: Behavioral and event-related brain potential data. *Journal of Experimental Social Psychology, 42,* 532–539.

Bartlett, M. Y., & DeSteno, D. (2006). Gratitude and prosocial behavior: Helping when it costs you. *Psychological Science, 17,* 319–325.

Bartocci, G. (2004). Transcendence techniques and psychobiological mechanisms underlying religious experience. *Mental Health, Religion and Culture, 7,* 171–181.

Bartone, P., Roland, R., Picano, J., & Williams, T. (2008). Psychological hardiness predicts success in U.S. Army Special Forces candidates.

International Journal of Selection and Assessment, 16, 78–81.

Bartoshuk, L. (2000, July/August). The bitter with the sweet. *APS Observer, 11*, 33.

Bartoshuk, L., & Lucchina, L. (1997, January 13). Are you a supertaster? *U.S. News & World Report*, pp. 58–59.

Bartzokis, G., Nuechterlein, K. H., Lu, P. H., Gitlin, M., Rogers, S., & Mintz, J. (2003). Dysregulated brain development in adult men with schizophrenia: A magnetic resonance imaging study. *Biological Psychiatry, 53*, 412–421.

Baruss, I. (2003). *Alterations of consciousness: An empirical analysis for social scientists.* Washington, DC: American Psychological Association.

Bassotti, G., Villanacci, V., Fisogni, S., Rossi, E., Baronio, P., Clerici, C., et al. (2007). Enteric glial cells and their role in gastrointestinal motor abnormalities: Introducing the neuro-gliopathies. *World Journal of Gastroenterology, 14*, 4035–4041.

Bassotti, G., & Villanacci, V. (2011). Can 'functional' constipation be considered as a form of enteric neuro-gliopathy? *Glia, 59*, 345–350.

Bateman, A. W. (2011). Commentary on 'Minding the difficult patient': Mentalizing and the use of formulation in patients with borderline personality disorder comorbid with antisocial personality disorder. *Personality and Mental Health, 5*, 85–90.

Bates, E. (2005). Plasticity, localization, and language development. In S. T. Parker & J. Langer (Eds.), *Biology and knowledge revisited: From neurogenesis to psychogenesis.* Mahwah, NJ: Lawrence Erlbaum Associates.

Bates, P. E., Cuvo, T., Miner, C. A., & Korabek, C. A. (2001). Simulated and community-based instruction involving persons with mild and moderate mental retardation. *Research in Developmental Disabilities, 22*, 95–115.

Bates, R. (2002). Liking and similarity as predictors of multi-source ratings. *Personnel Review, 31*, 540–552.

Batson, C. (2011). *Altruism in humans.* New York: Oxford University Press.

Batson, C. D., & Powell, A. A. (2003). Altruism and prosocial behavior. In T. Millon & M. J. Lerner (Eds.), *Handbook of psychology: Personality and social psychology* (Vol. 5). New York: Wiley.

Bauer, J. J., Schwab, J. R., & McAdams, D. P. (2011). Self-actualizing: Where ego development finally feels good? *The Humanistic Psychologist, 39*, 121–136.

Bauer, P. (2008). Toward a neuro-developmental account of the development of declarative memory. *Developmental Psychobiology, 50*, 19–31.

Bauer, S. M., Schanda, H., Karakula, H., Olajossy-Hilkesberger, L., Rudaleviciene, P., Okribelashvili, N., et al. (2011). Culture and the prevalence of hallucinations in schizophrenia. *Comprehensive Psychiatry, 52*, 319–325.

Baum, A. (1994). Behavioral, biological, and environmental interactions in disease processes. In S. Blumenthal, K. Matthews, & S. Weiss (Eds.), *New research frontiers in behavioral medicine: Proceedings of the National Conference.* Washington, DC: NIH Publications.

Baum, A., Lorduy, K., & Jenkins, F. J. (2011). The molecular biology of stress: Cellular defense, immune response, and aging. In R. J. Contrada & A. Baum (Eds.), *The handbook of stress science: Biology, psychology, and health.* New York: Springer Publishing Co.

Bauman, S., & Kopp, T. G. (2006). Integrating a humanistic approach in outpatient sex offender groups. *Journal for Specialists in Group Work, 31*, 247–261.

Baumeister, R. F., & Stillman, T. (2006). Erotic plasticity: Nature, culture, gender, and sexuality. In R. D. McAnulty & M. M. Burnette (Eds.), *Sex and sexuality, Vol. 1: Sexuality today: Trends and controversies.* Westport, CT: Praeger Publishers/Greenwood Publishing.

Baumeister, R. F., Twenge, J. M., & Nuss, C. K. (2002). Effects of social exclusion on cognitive processes: Anticipated aloneness reduces intelligent thought. *Journal of Personality and Social Psychology, 83*, 817–827.

Baumgartner, F. (2002). The effect of hardiness in the choice of coping strategies in stressful situations. *Studia Psychologica, 44*, 69–75.

Baumrind, D. (1971). Current patterns of parental authority. *Developmental Psychology, 4*, 1–104.

Baumrind, D. (2005). Patterns of parental authority and adolescent autonomy. *New Directions for Child and Adolescent Development, 108*, 61–69.

Baumrucker, S., Mingle, P., Harrington, D., Stolick, M., Carter, G. T., & Oertli, K. A. (2011). Medical marijuana and organ transplantation: Drug of abuse, or medical necessity? *American Journal of Hospice & Palliative Medicine, 28*, 130–134.

Bayliss, D. M., Jarrold, C., Baddeley, A. D., & Gunn, D. M. (2005a). The relationship between short-term memory and working memory: Complex span made simple? *Memory, 13*, 414–421.

Bayliss, D. M., Jarrold, C., Baddeley, A. D., Gunn, D. M., & Leigh, E. (2005b). Mapping the developmental constraints on working memory span performance. *Developmental Psychology, 41*, 579–597.

Bayne, R. (2005). *Ideas and evidence: Critical reflections on MBTI® theory and practice.* Gainesville, FL: Center for Applications of Psychological Type, CAPT.

Bazalakova, M. H., Wright, J., Schneble, E. J., McDonald, M. P., Heilman, C. J., Levey, A. I., & Blakely, R. D. (2007). Deficits in acetylcholine homeostasis, receptors and behaviors in choline transporter heterozygous mice. *Genes, Brain & Behavior, 6*, 411–424.

Bearman, C. R., Ball, L. J., & Ormerod, T. C. (2007). The structure and function of spontaneous analogising in domain-based problem solving. *Thinking & Reasoning, 13*, 273–294.

Beatty, J. (2000). *The human brain: Essentials of behavioral neuroscience.* Thousand Oaks, CA: Sage.

Bechara, A., Damasio, A. R., Damasio, H., & Anderson, S. (1994). Insensitivity to future consequences following damage to human prefrontal cortex. *Cognition, 50*, 7–15.

Beck, A. P., & Lewis, C. M. (Eds.). (2000). *The process of group psychotherapy: Systems for analyzing change.* Washington, DC: American Psychological Association.

Beck, A. T. (1995). Cognitive therapy: Past, present, and future. In M. J. Mahoney (Ed.), *Cognitive and constructive psychotherapies: Theory, research, and practice.* New York: Springer.

Beck, A. T. (2004). Cognitive therapy, behavior therapy, psychoanalysis, and pharmacotherapy: A cognitive continuum. In A. Freeman, M. J. Mahoney, P. Devito, & D. Martin (Eds.), *Cognition and Psychotherapy* (2nd ed.). New York: Springer Publishing Co.

Beck, A. T., & Emery, G., with Greenberg, R. L. (1985). *Anxiety disorders and phobias: A cognitive perspective.* New York: Basic Books.

Beck, A. T., Freeman, A., & Davis, D. D. (2004). *Cognitive therapy of personality disorders* (2nd ed.). New York: Guilford Press.

Beck, A. T., & Rector, N. A. (2005). Cognitive approaches to schizophrenia: Theory and therapy. *Annual Review of Clinical Psychology, 1*, 577–606.

Beck, H. P., Levinson, S., & Irons, G. (2009). Finding little Albert: A journey to John B. Watson's infant laboratory. *American Psychologist, 64*, 605–614.

Becker, B. E., & Luthar, S. S. (2007). Peer-perceived admiration and social preference: Contextual correlates of positive peer regard among suburban and urban adolescents. *Journal of Research on Adolescence, 17*, 117–144.

Becker, T. (2003). Is emotional intelligence a viable concept? *Academy of Management Review, 28*, 192–195.

Bedard, W. W., & Persinger, M. A. (1995). Prednisolone blocks extreme intermale social aggression in seizure-induced, braindamaged rats: Implications for the amygdaloid central nucleus, corticotrophin-releasing factor, and electrical seizures. *Psychological Reports, 77*, 3–9.

Beersma, D. G. M., & Gordijn, M. C. M. (2007). Circadian control of the sleep-wake cycle. *Physiology & Behavior, 90*.

Begg, D., & Langley, J. (2001). Changes in risky driving behavior from age 21 to 26 years. *Journal of Safety Research, 32*, 491–499.

Beghetto, R. A., & Kaufman, J. C. (Eds.) (2010). *Nurturing creativity in the classroom.* New York: Cambridge University Press.

Begley, S. (2002, September 13). The memory of September 11 is seared in your mind; but is it really true? *The Wall Street Journal*, p. B1.

Behrendt, R. (2011). *Neuroanatomy of social behaviour: An evolutionary and psychoanalytic perspective.* London England: Karnac Books.

Behrens, M., Lendon, C., & Roe, C. (2009). A common biological mechanism in cancer and Alzheimer's disease? *Current Alzheimer Research, 6*, 196–204.

Beidel, D. C., & Turner, S. M. (2007). Etiology of social anxiety disorder. In D. C. Beidel & S. M. Turner (Eds.), *Shy children, phobic adults: Nature and treatment of social anxiety disorders* (2nd ed.). Washington, DC: American Psychological Association.

Beilock, S. L., & Carr, T. H. (2005). When high-powered people fail: Working memory and "choking under pressure" in math. *Psychological Science, 16*, 101–105.

Belar, C. (2008, April). Clinical health psychology: A health care specialty in professional psychology. *Professional Psychology: Research and Practice, 39*, 229–233.

Belov, D. I., & Armstrong, R. D. (2009). Direct and inverse problems of item pool design for computerized adaptive testing. *Educational and Psychological Measurement, 69*, 533–547.

Belsky, J., & Pluess, M. (2009). The nature (and nurture?) of plasticity in early human development. *Perspectives on Psychological Science, 4*, 345–351.

Bem, D. J. (1996). Exotic becomes erotic: A developmental theory of sexual orientation. *Psychological Review, 103*, 320–335.

Bem, D. J., & Honorton, C. (1994). Does psi exist? Replicable evidence for an anomalous process of information transfer. *Psychological Bulletin, 115,* 4–18.

Benac, N. (2010). United states shifts focus to food marketing in battle to reduce childhood obesity. *Canadian Medical Association Journal, 182,* E459–E460.

Benca, R. M. 2005. Diagnosis and treatment of chronic insomnia: A review. *Psychiatric Services, 56:* 332–343.

Benderly, B. L. (2004). Looking beyond the SAT. *American Psychological Society, 17,* 12–18.

Benet-Martinez, V., Lee, F., & Leu, J. (2006). Biculturalism and cognitive complexity: Expertise in cultural representations. *Journal of Cross-Cultural Psychology, 37,* 386–407.

Benham, G., Woody, E. Z., & Wilson, K. S. (2006). Expect the unexpected: Ability, attitude, and responsiveness to hypnosis. *Journal of Personality and Social Psychology, 91,* 342–350.

Benight, C. C. (2004). Collective efficacy following a series of natural disasters. *Stress and Coping: An International Journal, 17,* 401–420.

Benjamin, L. T., Jr. (1985, February). Defining aggression: An exercise for classroom discussion. *Teaching of Psychology, 12*(1), 40–42.

Ben-Porath, Y., & Archer, R. (2008). The MMPI-2 and MMPI-A. *Personality assessment.* New York: Routledge/Taylor & Francis Group.

Benson, E. (2003, April). The science of sexual arousal. *Monitor on Psychology,* 50–56.

Benson, H., Kornhaber, A., Kornhaber, C., LeChanu, M. N., et al. (1994). Increases in positive psychological characteristics with a new relaxation-response curriculum in high school students. *Journal of Research and Development in Education, 27,* 226–231.

Benton, S. A., Robertson, J. M., Tseng, W. C., Newton, F. B., & Benton, S. L. (2003). Changes in counseling center client problems across 13 years. *Professional Psychology: Research and Practice, 34,* 66–72.

Bentwich, J., Dobronevsky, E., Aichenbaum, S., Shorer, R., Peretz, R., Khaigrekht, M., et al. (2011). Beneficial effect of repetitive transcranial magnetic stimulation combined with cognitive training for the treatment of Alzheimer's disease: A proof of concept study. *Journal of Neural Transmission, 118,* 463–471.

Beresnevaité, M., Taylor, G. J., & Bagby, R. M. (2007). Assessing alexithymia and type A behavior in coronary heart disease patients: A multimethod approach. *Psychotherapy and Psychosomatics, 76,* 186–192.

Bergman, S. M., Fearrington, M. E., Davenport, S. W., & Bergman, J. Z. (2011). Millennials, narcissism, and social networking: What narcissists do on social networking sites and why. *Personality and Individual Differences, 50,* 706–711.

Berk, L. E. (2005). Why parenting matters. In S. Olfman (Ed.), *Childhood lost: How American culture is failing our kids.* Westport, CT: Praeger Publishers/Greenwood Publishing Group.

Berkman, L. F., Ertel, K. A., & Glymour, M. M. (2011). Aging and social intervention: Life course perspectives. In R. H. Binstock & L. K. George (Eds.), *Handbook of aging and the social sciences* (7th ed.). San Diego, CA: Elsevier Academic Press.

Berkowitz, L. (2001). On the formation and regulation of anger and aggression: A cognitive-neoassociationistic analysis. In W. G. Parrott (Ed.), *Emotions in social psychology: Essential readings.* New York: Psychology Press.

Berle, D. (2007). Graded exposure therapy for long-standing disgust-related cockroach avoidance in an older male. *Clinical Case Studies, 6,* 339–347.

Berman, A. L., Jobes, D. A., & Silverman, M. M. (2006). An integrative-eclectic approach to treatment. In A. L. Berman, D. A. Jobes, & M. M. Silverman (Eds.), *Adolescent suicide: Assessment and intervention* (2nd ed.). Washington, DC: American Psychological Association.

Bernal, G., Trimble, J. E., Burlew, A. K., & Leong, F. T. (Eds.). (2002). *Handbook of racial and ethnic minority psychology.* Thousand Oaks, CA: Sage.

Bernard, L. L. (1924). *Instinct: A study in social psychology.* New York: Holt.

Bernstein, D., & Loftus, E. (2009a). How to tell if a particular memory is true or false. *Perspectives on Psychological Science, 4,* 370–374.

Bernstein, D., & Loftus, E. (2009b). The consequences of false memories for food preferences and choices. *Perspectives on Psychological Science, 4,* 135–139.

Bernstein, E. (2011, April 19). Friendly fight: A smarter way to say 'I'm angry.' *Wall Street Journal,* pp. D1, D4.

Berntsen, D., & Rubin, D. C. (2004). Cultural life scripts structure recall from autobiographical memory. *Memory and Cognition, 32,* 427–442.

Berntson, G. G., Bechara, A., Damasio, H., Tranel, D., & Cacioppo, J. T. (2007). Amygdala contribution to selective dimensions of emotion. *Social Cognitive and Affective Neuroscience, 2,* 123–129.

Berridge, K. C. (2004). Motivation concepts in behavioral neuroscience. *Physiology and Behavior, 81,* 179–209.

Berrios, G. E. (1996). *The history of mental symptoms: Descriptive psychopathology since the 19th century.* Cambridge: Cambridge University Press.

Bertakis, K. (2009). The influence of gender on the doctor-patient interaction. *Patient Education and Counseling, 76,* 356–360.

Bertakis, K., Franks, P., & Epstein, R. (2009). Patient-centered communication in primary care: Physician and patient gender and gender concordance. *Journal of Women's Health, 18,* 539–545.

Berthoud, H. R. (2002). Multiple neural systems controlling food intake and body weight. *Neuroscience and Biobehavioral Reviews, 26,* 393–428.

Betz, N. (2007). Career self-efficacy: Exemplary recent research and emerging directions. *Journal of Career Assessment, 15,* 403–422.

Beyene, Y., Gilliss, C., & Lee, K. (2007). "I take the good with the bad, and I moisturize": Defying middle age in the new millennium. *Menopause, 14,* 734–741.

Bhar, S., Gelfand, L., Schmid, S., Gallop, R., DeRubeis, R., Hollon, S., et al. (2008). Sequence of improvement in depressive symptoms across cognitive therapy and pharmacotherapy. *Journal of Affective Disorders, 110,* 161–166.

Bialystok, E. (2011). Reshaping the mind: The benefits of bilingualism. *Canadian Journal of Experimental Psychology 65*(4), 229–235.

Bialystok, E., Barac, R., Blaye, A., & Poulin-Dubois, D. (2010). Word mapping and executive functioning in young monolingual and bilingual children. *Journal of Cognition and Development, 11,* 485–508.

Bialystok, E., & Craik, F. I. M. (2010). Cognitive and linguistic processing in the bilingual mind. *Current Directions in Psychological Science, 19,* 19–23.

Bialystok, E., & Martin, M. M. (2004). Attention and inhibition in bilingual children: Evidence from the dimensional change card sort task. *Developmental Science, 7,* 325–339.

Bianchi, S. M., & Casper, L. M. (2000). American families. *Population Bulletin, 55*(4).

Bienvenu, O. J., Davydow, D. S., & Kendler, K. S. (2011). Psychiatric 'diseases' versus behavioral disorders and degree of genetic influence. *Psychological Medicine: A Journal of Research in Psychiatry and the Allied Sciences, 41,* 33–40.

Billiard, M. (2008). Narcolepsy: Current treatment options and future approaches. *Neuropsychiatric Disease and Treatment, 4,* 557–566.

Bindemann, M., Burton, A., Leuthold, H., & Schweinberger, S. (2008, July). Brain potential correlates of face recognition: Geometric distortions and the N250r brain response to stimulus repetitions. *Psychophysiology, 45,* 535–544.

Binet, A., & Simon, T. (1916). *The development of intelligence in children (The Binet-Simon Scale).* Baltimore: Williams & Wilkins.

Bingenheimer, J. B., Brennan, R. T., & Earls, E J. (2005, May 27). Firearm violence exposure and serious violent behavior. *Science, 308,* 1323–1327.

Bischoff, R. J., Springer, P. R., Felix, D. S., & Hollist, C. S. (2011). Finding the heart of medical family therapy: A content analysis of medical family therapy casebook articles. *Families, Systems, & Health, 29,* 184–196.

Bishop, M. (2005). Quality of life and psychosocial adaptation to chronic illness and disability: Preliminary analysis of a conceptual and theoretical synthesis. *Rehabilitation Counseling Bulletin, 48,* 219–231.

Bitterman, M. E. (2006). Classical conditioning since Pavlov. *Review of General Psychology, 10,* 365–376.

Bittles, A. H., Bower, C., & Hussain, R. (2007). The four ages of Down syndrome. *European Journal of Public Health, 17,* 121–225.

Bizley, J., Walker, K., Silverman, B., King, A., & Schnupp, J. (2009, February). Interdependent encoding of pitch, timbre, and spatial location in auditory cortex. *Journal of Neuroscience, 29,* 2064–2075.

Bjorklund, D. F., & Ellis, B. J. (2005). *Evolutionary psychology and child development: An emerging synthesis.* New York: Guilford Press.

Bjornstad, R. (2006). Learned helplessness, discouraged workers, and multiple unemployment equilibria. *The Journal of Socio-Economics, 35,* 458–475.

Black, A. L., & McCafferty, D. (1998, July 3–5). The age of contentment. *USA Weekend,* pp. 4–6.

Blair, C. A., Thompson, L. F., & Wuensch, K. L. (2005). Electronic helping behavior: The virtual presence of others makes a difference. *Basic and Applied Social Psychology, 27,* 171–178.

Blakeslee, S. (1992, August 11). Finding a new messenger for the brain's signals to the body. *The New York Times,* p. C3.

Blass, T. (1996). Attribution of responsibility and trust in the Milgram obedience experiment. *Journal of Applied Social Psychology, 26,* 1529–1535.

Blass, T. (2004). *The man who shocked the world: The life and legacy of Stanley Milgram.* New York: Basic Books.

Blass, T. (2009). From New Haven to Santa Clara: A historical perspective on the Milgram obedience experiments. *American Psychologist, 64,* 37–45.

Blass, T. (Ed.). (2000). *Obedience to authority: Current perspectives on the Milgram Paradigm.* Mahwah, NJ: Erlbaum.

Blatter, K., & Cajochen, C. (2007). Circadian rhythms in cognitive performance: Methodological constraints, protocols, theoretical underpinnings. *Physiology & Behavior, 90,* 196–208.

Blixen, C. E., Singh, A., & Xu, M. (2006). What women want: Understanding obesity and preferences for primary care weight reduction interventions among African-American and Caucasian women. *Journal of the National Medical Association, 98,* 1160–1170.

Bloom, F., Nelson, C. A., & Lazerson, A. (2001). *Brain, mind, and behavior,* (3rd ed.). New York: Worth Publishers.

Bloom, P. N., McBride, C. M., & Pollak, K. I. (2006). Recruiting teen smokers in shopping malls to a smoking-cessation program using the foot-in-the-door technique. *Journal of Applied Social Psychology, 36,* 1129–1144.

Blum, D. (2002). *Love at goon park: Harry Harlow and the science of affection.* Cambridge, MA: Perseus.

Blum, H. P. (2011). To what extent do you privilege dream interpretation in relation to other forms of mental representations? *The International Journal of Psychoanalysis, 92,* 275–277.

Blumenthal, H., Leen-Feldner, E. W., Babson, K. A., Gahr, J. L., Trainor, C. D., & Frala, J. L. (2011). Elevated social anxiety among early maturing girls. *Developmental Psychology, 47,* 1133–1140.

Boahen, K. (2005, May). Neuromorphic microchips. *Scientific American,* pp. 56–64.

Boake, C. (2008, April). Clinical neuropsychology. *Professional Psychology: Research and Practice, 39,* 234–239.

Bode, C., de Ridder, D. T., Kuijer, R. G., & Bensing, J. M. (2007). Effects of an intervention promoting proactive coping competencies in middle and late adulthood. *Gerontologist, 47,* 42–51.

Boden, J. M., Fergusson, D. M., & Horwood, L. J. (2007). Anxiety disorders and suicidal behaviours in adolescence and young adulthood: Findings from a longitudinal study. *Psychological Medicine, 37,* 431–440.

Bodin, G. (2006). Review of harvesting free association. *Psychoanalytic Quarterly, 75,* 629–632.

Boehm, K. E., & Campbell, N. B. (1995). Suicide: A review of calls to an adolescent peer listening phone service. *Child Psychiatry and Human Development, 26,* 61–66.

Boeve-de Pauw, J., Donche, V., & Van Petegem, P. (2011). Adolescents' environmental worldview and personality: An explorative study. *Journal of Environmental Psychology, 31,* 109–117.

Bogart, R. K., McDaniel, R. J., Dunn, W. J., Hunter, C., Peterson, A. L., & Write, E. E. (2007). Efficacy of group cognitive behavior therapy for the treatment of masticatory myofascial pain. *Military Medicine, 172,* 169–174.

Bogenschutz, M. P., Geppert, C. M., & George, J. (2006). The role of twelve-step approaches in dual diagnosis treatment and recovery. *American Journal of Addiction, 15,* 50–60.

Bohart, A. C. (2006). Understanding person-centered therapy: A review of Paul Wilkins' person-centered therapy in focus. *Person-Centered and Experiential Psychotherapies, 5,* 138–143.

Bohn, A., & Berntsen, D. (2007). Pleasantness bias in flashbulb memories: Positive and negative flashbulb memories of the fall of the Berlin Wall among East and West Germans. *Memory and Cognition, 35,* 565–577.

Boisvert, C. M., & Faust, D. (2003). Leading researchers' consensus on psychotherapy research findings: Implications for the teaching and conduct of psychotherapy. *Professional Psychology: Research and Practice, 34,* 508–513.

Boles, D. B. (2005). A large-sample study of sex differences in functional cerebral lateralization. *Journal of Clinical and Experimental Neuropsychology, 27,* 759–768.

Bolger, N., & Amarel, D. (2007). Effects of social support visibility on adjustment to stress: Experimental evidence. *Journal of Personality and Social Psychology, 92,* 458–475.

Boller, F. (2004). Rational basis of rehabilitation following cerebral lesions: A review of the concept of cerebral plasticity. *Functional Neurology: New Trends in Adaptive and Behavioral Disorders, 19,* 65–72.

Bonanni, R., Pasqualetti, P., Caltagirone, C., & Carlesimo, G. (2007). Primacy and recency effects in immediate free recall of sequences of spatial positions. *Perceptual and Motor Skills, 105,* 483–500.

Bonanno, G.A. (2004). Loss, trauma, and human resilience: Have we underestimated the human capacity to thrive after extremely aversive events? *American Psychologist, 59,* 20–28.

Bond, M. (2006). Psychodynamic psychotherapy in the treatment of mood disorders. *Current Opinion in Psychiatry, 19,* 40–43.

Bonezzi, A., Brendl, C., & De Angelis, M. (2011). Stuck in the middle: The psychophysics of goal pursuit. *Psychological Science, 22,* 607–612.

Bonnardel, V. (2006). Color naming and categorization in inherited color vision deficiencies. *Visual Neuroscience, 23,* 637–643.

Borbély, A. (1986). *Secrets of sleep* (p. 43, graph). New York: Basic Books.

Borisenko, J. (2007). Fatherhood as a personality development factor in men. *The Spanish Journal of Psychology, 10,* 82–90.

Bornstein, R. F. (2003). Psychodynamic models of personality. In T. Millon & M. J. Lerner (Eds.), *Handbook of psychology: Personality and social psychology* (Vol. 5). New York: Wiley.

Boroditsky, L. (2010, July 24-25). Lost in translation. *Wall Street Journal,* p. W3.

Bosma, H., van Boxtel, M. P. J., Ponds, R. W. H. M., Houx, P. J. H., & Jolles, J. (2003). Education and age-related cognitive decline: The contribution of mental workload. *Educational Gerontology, 29,* 165–173.

Bossarte, R. M., & Swahn, M. H. (2011). The associations between early alcohol use and suicide attempts among adolescents with a history of major depression. *Addictive Behaviors, 36.*

Bosse, T., Gerritsen, C. & Treur, J. (2011). Combining rational and biological factors in virtual agent decision making. *Applied Intelligence, 34,* 87–101.

Botvinick, M. (2004, August 6). Probing the neural basis of body ownership. *Science, 305,* 782–783.

Bouchard, T. J., Jr. (2004). Genetic influence on human psychological traits: A survey. *Current Directions in Psychological Science, 13,* 148–151.

Bouchard, T. J., Jr., Segal, N. L., Tellegen, A., McGue, M., Keyes, M., & Krueger, R. (2004). Genetic influence on social attitudes: Another challenge to psychology from behavior genetics. In L. F. DiLalla (Ed.), *Behavior genetics principles: Perspectives in development, personality, and psychopathology.* Washington, DC: American Psychological Association.

Bourne, L. E., Dominowski, R. L., Loftus, E. F., & Healy, A. F. (1986). *Cognitive processes* (2nd ed.). Englewood Cliffs, NJ: Prentice Hall.

Bouton, M. E., Todd, T. P., Vurbic, D., & Winterbauer, N. E. (2011). Renewal after the extinction of free operant behavior. *Learning & Behavior, 39,* 57–67.

Bower, G. H., Thompson, S. S., & Tulving, E. (1994). Reducing retroactive interference: An interference analysis. *Journal of Experimental Psychology Learning, Memory, and Cognition, 20,* 51–66.

Boxer, P., Huesmann, L., Bushman, B., O'Brien, M., & Moceri, D. (2009). The role of violent media preference in cumulative developmental risk for violence and general aggression. *Journal of Youth and Adolescence, 38,* 417–428.

Boycott, R. (2011, May 25). I didn't think I'd feel like this at 60. *The Daily Telegraph (London),* 19.

Boyd-Wilson, B. M., McClure, J., & Walkey, E H. (2004). Are well-being and illusory perceptions linked? The answer may be yes, but. . . . *Australian Journal of Psychology, 56,* 1–9.

Boyle, G. J., Goldman, R., Svoboda, J. S., & Fernandez, E. (2002). Male circumcision: Pain, trauma and psychosexual sequelae. *Journal of Health Psychology, 7,* 329–343.

Boyle, S. H., Williams, R. B., Mark, D. B., Brummett, B. H., Siegler, I. C., & Barefoot, J. C. (2005). Hostility, age, and mortality in a sample of cardiac patients. *American Journal of Cardiology, 96,* 64–72.

Brafman, A. H. (2011). *Fostering independence: Helping and caring in psychodynamic therapies.* London: Karnac Books.

Brambilla, P., Cipriani, A., Hotopf, M., & Barbui, C. (2005). Side-effect profile of fluoxetine in comparison with other SSRIs, tricyclic and newer antidepressants: A meta-analysis of clinical trial data. *Pharmacopsychiatry, 38,* 69–77.

Brandon, M., & Saffran, J. R. (2011). Apparent motion enhances visual rhythm discrimination in infancy. *Attention, Perception, & Psychophysics, 73,* 1016–1020.

Brang, D., Rouw, R., Ramachandran, V. S., & Coulson, S. (2011). Similarly shaped letters evoke similar colors in grapheme–color synesthesia. *Neuropsychologia, 49,* 1355–1358.

Brasic, J. R. (2002). Conversion disorder in childhood. *German Journal of Psychiatry, 5,* 54–61.

Braun, A. R., Balkin, T. J., Wesensten, N. J., Gwadry, F., Carson, R. E., Varga, M., et al. (1998). Dissociated pattern of activity in visual cortices and their projections during human rapid eye movement sleep. *Science, 279,* 91–95.

Brausch, A. M., & Gutierrez, P. M. (2009). Differences in non-suicidal self-injury and suicide attempts in adolescents. *Journal of Youth and Adolescence, 21,* 46–51.

Brazelton, T. B. (1969). *Infants and mothers: Differences in development.* New York: Dell.

Breland, K., & Breland, M. (1966). *Animal behavior.* New York: Macmillan.

Brennan, P. (2011). Pheromones: Fact or fantasy? *Ethology, 117,* 265–266.

Brennen, T., Vikan, A., & Dybdahl, R. (2007). Are tip-of-the-tongue states universal? Evidence from the speakers of an unwritten language. *Memory, 15,* 167–176.

Breslin, C. W., & Safer, M. A. (2011). Effects of event valence on long-term memory for two baseball championship games. *Psychological Science, 20,* 1–5.

Brewer, J. B., Zhao, Z., Desmond, J. E., Glover, G. H., & Gabrieli, J. D. E. (1998, August 21). Making memories: Brain activity that predicts how well visual experience will be remembered. *Science, 281,* 1185–1187.

Brewis, A. Wutich, A., Falletta-Cowden, A. and Rodriguez-Soto, I. (2011). Body norms and fat stigma in global perspective. *Current Anthropology 52,* 2.

Bright, P., Buckman, J., & Fradera, A. (2006). Retrograde amnesia in patients with hippocampal, medial temporal, temporal lobe, or frontal pathology. *Learning & Memory, 13,* 545–557.

Brislin, R., Worthley, R., & MacNab, B. (2006). Cultural intelligence: Understanding behaviors that serve people's goals. *Group & Organization Management, 31,* 40–55.

Brock, T. C., & Green, M. C. (Eds.). (2005). *Persuasion: Psychological insights and perspectives* (2nd ed.). Thousand Oaks, CA: Sage Publications.

Brody, J. (2008, May 20). Trying to break nicotine's grip. *The New York Times,* p. E9.

Broeders, R., van den Bos, K., Müller, P. A., & Ham, J. (2011). Should I save or should I not kill? How people solve moral dilemmas depends on which rule is most accessible. *Journal of Experimental Social Psychology, 47,* 923–934.

Broidy, L. M., Nagin, D. S., & Tremblay, R. E. (2003). Developmental trajectories of childhood disruptive behaviors and adolescent delinquency: A six-site, cross-national study. *Developmental Psychology, 39,* 222–245.

Broman, C. L. (2005). Stress, race and substance use in college. *College Student Journal, 39,* 340–352.

Bronson, P., & Merryman, A. (2009). *NurtureShock.* New York: Twelve.

Brooker, R. J., Widmaier, E. P., Graham, L., & Stiling, P. (2008). *Biology.* New York: McGraw-Hill.

Brown, E. (2001, September 17). The World Health Organization takes on big tobacco (but don't hold your breath): Anti-smoking advocates are mounting a global campaign: It's going to be a long, hard fight. *Forbes,* pp. 37–41.

Brown, J. (2006). Attribution: Theories, affect and evolution. *Dissertation Abstracts International: Section B: The Sciences and Engineering, 67*(2-B), 1201.

Brown, L. S., & Pope, K. S. (1996). *Recovered memories of abuse: Assessment, therapy, forensics.* Washington, DC: American Psychological Association.

Brown, P. K., & Wald, G. (1964). Visual pigments in single rod and cones of the human retina. *Science, 144,* 45–52.

Brown, R., & Robertson, E. (2007). Off-line processing: Reciprocal interactions between declarative and procedural memories. *The Journal of Neuroscience, 27*(39), 10468–10475.

Brown, R. J. (2006). Different types of "dissociation" have different psychological mechanisms. *Journal of Trauma Dissociation, 6,* 7–28.

Brown, S., & Martinez, M. J. (2007). Activation of premotor vocal areas during musical discrimination. *Brain and Cognition, 63,* 9–69.

Brown, S., Martinez, M. J., & Parsons, L. M. (2006). Music and language side by side in the brain: A PET study of the generation of melodies and sentences. *European Journal of Neuroscience, 23,* 2791–2803.

Brownlee, K. (2007). What works for whom? A critical review of psychotherapy research. *Psychiatric Rehabilitation Journal, 30,* 239–240.

Bruce, V., Green, P. R., & Georgeson, M. (1997). *Visual perception: Physiology, psychology and ecology* (3rd ed.). Mahwah, NJ: Erlbaum.

Bruggeman, H., Yonas, A., & Konczak, J. (2007). The processing of linear perspective and binocular information for action and perception. *Neuropsychologia, 45,* 1420–1426.

Brunet, A., Orr, S., Tremblay, J., Robertson, K., Nader, K., & Pitman, R. (2008). Effect of post-retrieval propranolol on psychophysiologic responding during subsequent script-driven traumatic imagery in post-traumatic stress. *Journal of Psychiatric Research, 42,* 503–506.

Bryant, R. M., Coker, A. D., Durodoye, B. A., McCollum, V. J., Pack-Brown, S. P., Constantine, M. G., & O'Bryant, B. J. (2005). Having our say: African American women, diversity, and counseling. *Journal of Counseling and Development, 83,* 313–319.

Brzustowicz, L. M., Hodgkinson, K. A., Chow, E. W. C., Honer, W. G., & Bassett, A. S. (2000, April 28). Location of major susceptibility locus for familial schizophrenia on chromosome 1q21-q22. *Science, 288,* 678–682.

Buchanan, R. W., Javitt, D. C., Marder, S. R., Schooler, N. R., Gold, J. M., McMahon, R. P., et al. (2007). The Cognitive and Negative Symptoms in Schizophrenia Trial (CONSIST): The efficacy of glutamatergic agents for negative symptoms and cognitive impairments. *American Journal of Psychiatry, 164,* 1593–1602.

Buchanan, T., & Selmon, N. (2008). Race and gender differences in self-efficacy: Assessing the role of gender role attitudes and family background. *Sex Roles, 58,* 822–836.

Buchanan, T. W., & Adolphs, R. (2004). The neuroanatomy of emotional memory in humans. In D. Reisberg & P. Hertel (Eds.), *Memory and emotion.* London: Oxford University Press.

Buchert, R., Thomasius, R., Wilke, F., Petersen, K., Nebeling, B., Obrocki, J., Schulze, O., Schmidt, U., & Clausen, M. (2004). A voxel-based PET investigation of the long-term effects of "ecstasy" consumption on brain serotonin transporters. *American Journal of Psychiatry, 161,* 1181–1189.

Buehner, M., Krumm, S., & Ziegler, M. (2006). Cognitive abilities and their interplay: Reasoning, crystallized intelligence, working memory components, and sustained attention. *Journal of Individual Differences, 27,* 57–72.

Buerkle, C. (2011). Masters of their domain: Seinfeld and the discipline of mediated men's sexual economy. In E. Watson & M. E. Shaw (Eds.), *Performing American masculinities: The 21st-century man in popular culture.* Bloomington, IN: Indiana University Press.

Bukobza, G. (2009). Relations between rebelliousness, risk-taking behavior, and identity status during emerging adulthood. *Identity, 9,* 159–177.

Bulf, H., Johnson, S. P., & Valenza, E. (2011). Visual statistical learning in the newborn infant. *Cognition, 121,* 127–132.

Bunge, S. A., & Wallis, J. D. (2008). *Neuroscience of rule-guided behavior.* New York: Oxford University Press.

Bunting, M. (2006). Proactive interference and item similarity in working memory. *Journal of Experimental Psychology: Learning, Memory, and Cognition, 32,* 183–196.

Burbach, M. E., Matkin, G. S., & Fritz, S. M. (2004). Teaching critical thinking in an introductory leadership course utilizing active learning strategies: A confirmatory study. *College Student Journal, 38,* 482–493.

Burchinal, M. R., Roberts, J. E., & Riggins, R., Jr. (2000). Relating quality of center-based child care to early cognitive and language development longitudinally. *Child Development, 71,* 338–357.

Bureau of Labor Statistics. (2007). *American time use survey.* Washington, DC: Bureau of Labor Statistics.

Burger, J. M. (2009). Replicating Milgram: Would people still obey today? *American Psychologist, 64,* 1–11.

Burger, J. M., & Caldwell, D. F. (2003). The effects of monetary incentives and labeling on the foot-in-the-door effect: Evidence for a self-perception process. *Basic and Applied Social Psychology, 25,* 235–241.

Burger, J. M., Reed, M., & DeCesare, K. (1999). The effects of initial request size on compliance: More about the that's-not-all technique. *Basic and Applied Social Psychology, 21,* 243–249.

Burgoon, J. K., & Bacue, A. E. (2003). Nonverbal communication skills. In J. O. Greene & B. R. Burleson (Eds.), *Handbook of communication and social interaction skills.* Mahwah, NJ: Lawrence Erlbaum.

Burgoon, J. K., Bonito, J. A., Ramirez, A. J. R., Dunbar, N. E., Kam, K., & Fischer, J. (2002). Testing the interactivity principle: Effects of mediation, propinquity, and verbal and nonverbal modalities in interpersonal interaction [Special Issue: Research on the relationship between verbal and nonverbal communication: Emerging integrations]. *Journal of Communication, 52,* 657–677.

Burns, J. W., Quartana, P. J., & Bruehl, S. (2007). Anger management style moderates effects of emotion suppression during initial stress on pain and cardiovascular responses during subsequent pain-induction. *Annals of Behavioral Medicine, 34,* 154–165.

Burns, N. R., Bryan, J., & Nettelbeck, T. (2006). Ginkgo biloba: No robust effect on cognitive abilities or mood in healthy young or older adults. *Human Psychopharmacology: Clinical and Experimental, 21,* 27–37.

Busey, T. A., & Loftus, G. R. (2007). Cognitive science and the law. *Trends in Cognitive Science, 11,* 111–117.

Bush, J. (2008). Viability of virtual reality exposure therapy as a treatment alternative. *Computers in Human Behavior, 24,* 1032–1040.

Bushman, B. J., Wang, M. C., & Anderson, C. (2005). Is the curve relating temperature to aggression linear or curvilinear? Assaults and temperature in Minneapolis reexamined. *Journal of Personality and Social Psychology, 89,* 62–66.

Buss, A. H. (2011). *Pathways to individuality: Evolution and development of personality traits.* Washington, DC: American Psychological Association.

Buss, D. (2003). *Evolutionary psychology.* Boston: Allyn & Bacon.

Buss, D. (2009). How can evolutionary psychology successfully explain personality and individual differences? *Perspectives on Psychological Science, 4,* 359–366.

Buss, D. M. (2001). Human nature and culture: An evolutionary psychological perspective. *Journal of Personality, 69,* 955–978.

Buss, D. M. (2004). Sex differences in human mate preferences: Evolutionary hypotheses tested in 37 cultures. In H. T. Reis & C. E. Rusbult (Eds.), *Close relationships: Key readings.* Philadelphia: Taylor & Francis.

Buss, D. M., Abbott, M., & Angleitner, A. (1990). International preferences in selecting mates: A study of 37 cultures. *Journal of Cross-Cultural Psychology, 21,* 5–47.

Butcher, J. N. (2005). *A beginner's guide to the MMPI-2* (2nd ed.). Washington, DC: American Psychological Association.

Butcher, J. N. (2011). *A beginner's guide to the MMPI-2* (3rd ed.). Washington, DC: American Psychological Association.

Butler, L. D., Koopman, C., Neri, E., Giese-Davis, J., Palesh, O., Thorne-Yocam, K. A., et al. (2009). Effects of supportive-expressive group therapy on pain in women with metastatic breast cancer. *Health Psychology, 28,* 579–587.

Butler, L. T., & Berry, D. C. (2004). Understanding the relationship between repetition priming and mere exposure. *British Journal of Psychology, 95,* 467–487.

Buysse, D. J., Germain, A., Moul, D. E., Franzen, P. L., Brar, L. K., Fletcher, M. E., Begley, A., Houck, P. R., Mazumdar, S., Reynolds, C. F., & Monk, T. H. (2011). Efficacy of brief behavioral treatment for chronic insomnia in older adults. *Archives of Internal Medicine, 171,* 887–895.

Byne, W. (1996). Biology and homosexuality: Implications of neuroendocrinological and neuroanatomical studies. In R. P. Cabaj & T. S. Stein (Eds.), *Textbook of homosexuality and mental health.* Washington, DC: American Psychiatric Press.

Byrne-Davis, L., & Vedhara, K. (2008). Psychoneuroimmunology. *Social and Personality Psychology Compass, 2,* 751–764.

Cabanac, M., & Frankham, P. (2002). Evidence that transient nicotine lowers the body weight set point. *Physiology & Behavior, 76,* 539–542.

Cabioglu, M., Ergene, N., & Tan, Ü. (2007, May). Smoking cessation after acupuncture treatment. *International Journal of Neuroscience, 117,* 571–578.

Cacioppo, J. T., Berntson, G. G., & Crites, S. L., Jr. (1996). Social neuroscience: Principles of psychophysiological arousal and response. In E. T. Higgins & A. W. Kruglanski (Eds.), *Social psychology: Handbook of basic principles.* New York: Guilford.

Cacioppo, J. T., & Decety, J. (2009). What are the brain mechanisms on which psychological processes are based? *Perspectives on Psychological Science, 4,* 10–18.

Cacioppo, J. T., Visser, P. S., & Pickett, C. L. (2005). *Social neuroscience: People thinking about thinking people.* Cambridge, MA: MIT Press.

Cadenhead, K., & Braff, D. L. (1995). Neurophysiology of schizophrenia: Attention, information processing, and inhibitory processes in schizophrenia. In J. A. Den Boer., H. G. M. Westenberg & H. M. van Praag (Eds.), *Advances in the neurobiology of schizophrenia.* Oxford, England: John Wiley & Sons.

Caelian, C. F. (2006). The role of perfectionism and stress in the suicidal behaviour of depressed adolescents. *Dissertation Abstracts International: Section B: The Sciences and Engineering, 66(12-B),* 6915.

Cahill, L. (2005, May). His brain, her brain. *Scientific American,* pp. 40–47.

Cain, D. J. (Ed.). (2002). *Humanistic psychotherapies: Handbook of research and practice.*

Washington, DC: American Psychological Association.

Calin-Jageman, R. J., & Fischer, T. M. (2007). Behavioral adaptation of the aplysia siphon-withdrawal response is accompanied by sensory adaptation. *Behavioral Neuroscience, 121,* 200–211.

Cameron, O. G. (2002). *Visceral sensory neuroscience: Interoception.* London: Oxford University Press.

Campos, R. C. (2011). 'It might be what I am': Looking at the use of Rorschach in psychological assessment. *Journal of Projective Psychology & Mental Health, 18,* 28–38.

Cannon, W. B. (1929). Organization for physiological homeostatics. *Physiological Review, 9,* 280–289.

Cantwell, R. H., & Andrews, B. (2002). Cognitive and psychological factors underlying secondary school students' feelings towards group work. *Educational Psychology, 22,* 75–91.

Caplan, D., Waters, G., & Dede, G. (2007). A study of syntactic processing in aphasia I: Behavioral (psycholinguistic) aspects. *Brain and Language, 101,* 103–150.

Carbon, C., & Ditye, T. (2011). Sustained effects of adaptation on the perception of familiar faces. *Journal of Experimental Psychology: Human Perception and Performance, 37,* 615–625.

Carels, R. A., Young, K. M., Koball, A., Gumble, A., Darby, L. A., Oehlhof, M., et al. (2011). Transforming your life: An environmental modification approach to weight loss. *Journal of Health Psychology, 16,* 430–438.

Carey, B. (2004, December 21). When pressure is on, good students suffer. *The New York Times,* p. D7.

Carey, B. (2009, November 27). Surgery for mental ills offers hope and risk. *The New York Times,* p. A1.

Carey, B. (2011, August, 7). Learning to cope with a mind's taunting voices. *The New York Times,* A1.

Carey, B. (2011, January 5). Past resilience hints at future strength. *The International Herald Tribune,* 8.

Carhart-Harris, R. (2007). Speed > Ecstasy > Ritalin: The science of amphetamines. *Journal of Psychopharmacology, 21,* 225.

Carnagey, N., Anderson, C., & Bartholow, B. (2007). Media violence and social neuroscience: New questions and new opportunities. *Current Directions in Psychological Science, 16,* 178–182.

Carnagey, N., Anderson, C. A., & Bushman, B. J. (2007). The effect of video game violence on physiological desensitization to real-life violence. *Journal of Experimental Social Psychology, 43,* 489–496.

Carney, D., Colvin, C., & Hall, J. (2007). A thin slice perspective on the accuracy of first impressions. *Journal of Research in Personality, 41,* 1054–1072.

Carney, R. N., & Levin, J. R. (1998). Coming to terms with the keyword method in introductory psychology: A "neuromnemonic" example. *Teaching of Psychology, 25,* 132–135.

Carney, R. N., & Levin, J. R. (2003). Promoting higher-order learning benefits by building lower-order mnemonic connections. *Applied Cognitive Psychology, 17,* 563–575.

Carpenter, S. (2002, April). What can resolve the paradox of mental health disparities? *APA Monitor, 33,* 18.

Carrillo, M., Ricci, L., Coppersmith, G., & Melloni, R. (2009, August). The effect of increased serotonergic neurotransmission on

aggression: A critical meta-analytical review of preclinical studies. *Psychopharmacology, 205,* 349–368.

Carter, R. T. (2003). Becoming racially and culturally competent: The racial-cultural counseling laboratory. *Journal of Multicultural Counseling and Development, 31,* 20–30.

Cartwright, R. (2006). A neuroscientist looks at how the brain makes up our minds. *PsycCRITIQUES, 51,* 35–41.

Cartwright, R., Agargum, M. Y., & Kirkby, J. (2006). Relation of dreams to waking concerns. *Psychiatry Research, 141,* 261–270.

Caruso, E. (2008). Use of experienced retrieval ease in self and social judgments. *Journal of Experimental Social Psychology, 44,* 148–155.

Carvalho, J., & Nobre, P. (2011). Biopsychosocial determinants of men's sexual desire: Testing an integrative model. *Journal of Sexual Medicine, 8,* 754–763.

Cary, P. (2007). A brief history of the concept of free will: Issues that are and are not germane to legal reasoning. *Behavioral Sciences & the Law, 25, Special issue: Free will,* 165–181.

Casasanto, D. (2008). Who's afraid of the big bad whorf? Crosslinguistic differences in temporal language and thought. *Language Learning, 58,* 63–79.

Casasola, M. (2011). Infant spatial categorization from an information processing approach. In L. M. Oakes, C. H. Cashon, et al. (Eds.), *Infant perception and cognition: Recent advances, emerging theories, and future directions.* New York: Oxford University Press.

Case, R., & Okamoto, Y. (1996). The role of central conceptual structures in the development of children's thought. *Monographs of the Society for Research in Child Development, 61,* v-265.

Casey, S. D., Cooper-Brown, L. J., & Wacher, D. P. (2006). The use of descriptive analysis to identify and manipulate schedules of reinforcement in the treatment of food refusal. *Journal of Behavioral Education, 15,* 41–52.

Cashon, C. H., & Cohen, L. B. (2004). Beyond U-shaped development in infants' processing of faces: An information-processing account. *Journal of Cognition and Development, 5,* 59–80.

Cassells, J. V. S. (2007). The virtuous roles of truth and justice in integral dialogue: Research, theory, and model practice of the evolution of collective consciousness. *Dissertation Abstracts International Section A: Humanities and Social Sciences, 67(10-A),* 4005.

Cattell, R. B., Cattell, A. K., & Catell, H. E. P. (1993). *Sixteen personality factor questionnaire (16PF)* (5th ed.). San Antonio, TX: Harcourt Brace.

Cauce, A. M. (2007). Bringing community psychology home: The leadership, community and values initiative. *American Journal of Community Psychology, 39,* 1–11.

Cavallini, E., Pagnin, A., & Vecchi, T. (2003). Aging and everyday memory: The beneficial effect of memory training. *Archives of Gerontology & Geriatrics, 37,* 241–257.

Cavenett, T., & Nixon, R. D. V. (2006). The effect of arousal on memory for emotionally-relevant information: A study of sky divers. *Behaviour Research and Therapy, 44,* 1461–1469.

Center for Science in the Public Interest. (2007). *Caffeine Content of Food & Drugs.* Washington, DC: Center for Science in the Public Interest.

Centers for Disease Control and Prevention (CDC). (2004b, June 11). Suicide and attempted suicide. *MMWR, 53,* 471.

Centers for Disease Control and Prevention (CDC). (2011). *The National Intimate Partner and Sexual Violence Survey.* Washington, DC: Centers for Disease Control and Prevention.

Chamberlain, K., & Zika, S. (1990). The minor events approach to stress: Support for the use of daily hassles. *British Journal of Psychology, 81,* 469–481.

Chamberlain, S. R., Menzies, L., Hampshire, A., Suckling, J., Fineberg, N. A., del Campo, N., et al. (2008, July 18). Orbitofrontal dysfunction in patients with obsessive-compulsive disorder and their unaffected relatives. *Science, 321,* 421–422.

Chambless, D. L., Crits-Christoph, P., Wampold, B. E., Norcross, J. C., Lambert, M. J., Bohart, A. C., et al. (2006). What should be validated? In J. C. Norcross, L. E. Beutler, et al. (Eds.), *Evidence-based practices in mental health: Debate and dialogue on the fundamental questions.* Washington, DC: American Psychological Association.

Chandler, D. R. (2011). Proactively addressing the shortage of Blacks in psychology: Highlighting the school psychology subfield. *Journal of Black Psychology, 37,* 99–127.

Chandran, S., & Menon, G. (2004). When a day means more than a year: Effects of temporal framing on judgments of health risk. *Journal of Consumer Research, 31,* 375–389.

Chang, J., & Sue, S. (2005). Culturally sensitive research: Where have we gone wrong and what do we need to do now? In M. G. Constantine (Ed.), *Strategies for building multicultural competence in mental health and educational settings.* Hoboken, NJ: John Wiley & Sons.

Chao, R. (2011). Managing stress and maintaining well-being: Social support, problem-focused coping, and avoidant coping. *Journal of Counseling & Development, 89,* 338–348.

Chapkis, W., & Webb, R. (2008). *Dying to get high: Marijuana as medicine.* New York: New York University Press.

Chapman, J. (2006). Anxiety and defective decision making: An elaboration of the groupthink model. *Management Decision, 44,* 1391–1404.

Chapman, L. J., & Chapman, J. P. (1973). *Disordered thought in schizophrenia.* New York: Appleton-Century-Crofts.

Charman, D. P. (2004). *Core processes in brief psychodynamic psychotherapy: Advancing effective practice.* Mahwah, NJ: Lawrence Erlbaum Associates.

Chavez, P. R., Nelson, D. E., Naimi, T. S., & Brewer, R. D. (2011). Impact of a new gender-specific definition for binge drinking on prevalence estimates for women. *American Journal of Preventive Medicine, 40,* 468–471.

Chen, A., Zhou, Y., & Gong, H. (2004). Firing rates and dynamic correlated activities of ganglion cells both contribute to retinal information processing. *Brain Research, 1017,* 13–20.

Chen, Z., Fu, L., Peng, Y., Cai, R., & Zhou, S. (2011). The relationship among childhood abuse, parenting styles, and antisocial personality disorder tendency. *Chinese Journal of Clinical Psychology, 19,* 212–214.

Cheney, C. D. (1996). Medical non adherence: A behavior analysis. In J. R. Cautela & W. Ishaq (Eds.), *Contemporary issues in behavior therapy: Improving the human condition: Applied Clinical Psychology.* New York: Plenum Press.

Cheng, C., & Cheung, M. L. (2005). Cognitive processes underlying coping flexibility: Differentiation and integration. *Journal of Personality, 73,* 859–886.

Cheng, S., & Kwan, K. (2008). Attachment dimensions and contingencies of self-worth: The moderating role of culture. *Personality and Individual Differences, 45,* 509–514.

Cheston, S. E. (2000). A new paradigm for teaching counseling theory and practice. *Counselor Education & Supervision, 39,* 254–269.

Cho, A. (2000, June 16). What's shakin' in the ear? *Science, 288,* 1954–1955.

Cho, S., Holyoak, K. J., & Cannon, T. D. (2007). Analogical reasoning in working memory: Resources shared among relational integration, interference resolution, and maintenance. *Memory & Cognition, 35,* 1445–1455.

Chomsky, N. (1968). *Language and mind.* New York: Harcourt Brace Jovanovich.

Chomsky, N. (1978). On the biological basis of language capacities. In G. A. Miller & E. Lennenberg (Eds.), *Psychology and biology of language and thought.* New York: Academic Press.

Chomsky, N. (1991). Linguistics and cognitive science: Problems and mysteries. In A. Kasher (Ed.), *The Chomskyan turn.* Cambridge, MA: Blackwell.

Chou, K. (2005). Everyday competence and depressive symptoms: Social support and sense of control as mediators or moderators? *Aging and Mental Health, 9,* 177–183.

Choy, Y., Fyer, A. J., & Lipsitz, J. D. (2007). Treatment of specific phobia in adults. *Clinical Psychology Review, 27,* 266–286.

Christ, S. E., Steiner, R. D., & Grange, D. K. (2006). Inhibitory control in children with phenylketonuria. *Developmental Neuropsychology, 30,* 845–864.

Christakis, N. A., & Fowler, J. H. (2008). The collective dynamics of smoking in a large social network. *The New England Journal of Medicine, 358,* 2249–2258.

Christian, C. J., Lencz, T., Robinson, D. G., Burdick, K. E., Ashtari, M., Malhotra, A. K., et al. (2008). Gray matter structural alterations in obsessive-compulsive disorder: Relationship to neuropsychological functions. *Neuroimaging, 164,* 123–131.

Chrysikou, E. G. (2006). When a shoe becomes a hammer: Problem solving as goal-derived, ad hoc categorization. *Dissertation Abstracts International: Section B: The Sciences and Engineering, 67*(1-B), 569.

Cialdini, R. B. (2006). *Influence: The psychology of persuasion.* New York: Collins.

Cialdini, R. B., & Sagarin, B. J. (2005). Principles of interpersonal influence. In T. C. Brock & M. C. Green (Eds.), *Persuasion: Psychological insights and perspectives* (2nd ed.). Thousand Oaks, CA: Sage Publications.

Cialdini, R. B., Schaller, M., Houlihan, D., Arps, K., Fultz, J., & Beaman, A. L. (1975). Reciprocal concessions procedure for inducing compliance: The door-in-the-face technique. *Journal of Personality and Social Psychology, 31,* 206–215.

Clark, D. A. (2004). *Cognitive-behavioral therapy for OCD.* New York: Guilford.

Clark, D. A. (2007). Obsessions and compulsions. In N. Kazantzis & L. L'Abate (Eds.), *Handbook of homework assignments in psychotherapy: Research, practice, prevention.* New York: Springer Science + Business Media.

Clarkin, J. F., & Lenzenweger, M. F. (Eds.). (2004). *Major theories of personality disorders* (2nd ed.). New York: Guilford.

Clayton, K., & Lundberg-Love, P. (2009). Caffeine: Pharmacology and effects of the world's most popular drug. *The Praeger international collection on addictions, Vol. 2: Psychobiological profiles.* Santa Barbara, CA: Praeger/ABC-CLIO.

Clements, A. M., Rimrodt, S. L., & Abel, J. R. (2006). Sex differences in cerebral laterality of language and visuospatial processing. *Brain 8,* 150–158.

Clemons, T. L. (2006). Underachieving gifted students: A social cognitive model. *Dissertation Abstracts International Section A: Humanities and Social Sciences, 66*(9-A), 3208.

Cloud, J. (2000, June 5). The lure of ecstasy. *Time,* pp. 60–68.

Coan, J. A., Schaefer, H. S., & Davidson, R. J. (2006). Lending a hand: Social regulation of the neural response to threat. *Psychological Science, 17*(12), 1032–1039.

Coates, S. L., Butler, L. T., & Berry, D. C. (2006). Implicit memory and consumer choice: The mediating role of brand familiarity. *Applied Cognitive Psychology, 20,* 1101–1116.

Cobos, P., Sanchez, M., Garcia, C., Vera, M. N., et al. (2002). Revisiting the James versus Cannon debate on emotion: Startle and autonomic modulation in patients with spinal cord injuries. *Biological Psychology, 61,* 251–269.

Cochran, S. D. (2000). Emerging issues in research on lesbians' and gay men's mental health: Does sexual orientation really matter? *American Psychologist, 56,* 33–41.

Coderre, T. J. (2011). Complex regional pain syndrome: What's in a name? *The Journal of Pain, 12,* 2–12.

Coffman, S. J., Martell, C. R., Dimidjian, S., Gallop, R., & Holon, S. D. (2007). Extreme non-response in cognitive therapy: Can behavioral activation succeed where cognitive therapy fails? *Journal of Consulting Clinical Psychology, 75,* 531–545.

Cohen, B. H. (2002). *Explaining psychological statistics* (2nd ed.). New York: Wiley.

Cohen, G. L., Garcia, J., Apfel, N., & Master, A. (2006). Reducing the racial achievement gap: A social-psychological intervention. *Science, 313,* 1307–1310.

Cohen, J. (2003). Things I have learned (so far). In A. E. Kazdin (Ed.), *Methodological issues and strategies in clinical research* (3rd ed.). Washington, DC: American Psychological Association.

Cohen, L., & Cashon, C. (2003). Infant perception and cognition. In R. Lerner & M. Easterbrooks (Eds.), *Handbook of psychology: Developmental psychology* (Vol. 6). New York: Wiley.

Cohen, P. (2009). Medical marijuana: The conflict between scientific evidence and political ideology. Part one of two. *Journal of Pain & Palliative Care Pharmacotherapy, 23,* 4–25.

Cohen, P., Slomkowski, C., & Robins, L. N. (Eds.). (1999). *Historical and geographical influences on psychopathology.* Mahwah, NJ: Erlbaum.

Cohen, S. (2004, November). Social relationships and health. *American Psychologist,* 676–684.

Cohen, S., Doyle, W. J., Turner, R., Alper, C. M., & Skoner, D. P. (2003). Sociability and susceptibility to the common cold. *Psychological Science, 14,* 389–395.

Cohen, S., Kamarck, T., & Mermelstein, R. (1983). A global measure of perceived stress. *Journal of Health and Social Behavior, 24,* 385–396.

Coleman, E. (2002). Masturbation as a means of achieving sexual health. *Journal of Psychology and Human Sexuality, 14,* 5–16.

Cole, S. W., Arevalo, J. M., Takahashi, R., Sloan, E. K., Lutgendorf, S. L., Sood, A. K., et al. (2010). Computational identification of Gene-Social Environment interaction at the human IL6 locus. *Proceedings of the National Academy of Sciences of the USA, 107,* 5681–5686.

Coles, R. (1997). *The moral intelligence of children.* New York: Random House.

Coles, R., & Stokes, G. (1985). *Sex and the American teenager.* New York: Harper & Row.

Colland, V. T., Van Essen-Zandvliet, L. E. M., Lans, C., Denteneer, A., Westers, P., & Brackel, H. J. L. (2004). Poor adherence to self-medication instructions in children with asthma and their parents. *Patient Education and Counseling, 55,* 416–421.

Collins, A. M., & Loftus, E. E. (1975). A spreading-activation theory of semantic processing. *Psychological Review, 82,* 407–428.

Collins, A. M., & Quillian, M. R. (1969). Retrieval times from semantic memory. *Journal of Verbal Learning and Verbal Behavior, 8,* 240–247.

Colom, R., Jung, R. E., & Haier, R. J. (2006). Finding the g-factor in brain structure using the method of correlated vectors. *Intelligence, 34,* 561–570.

Coltheart, M., Langdon, R., & McKay, R. (2007). Schizophrenia and monothematic delusions. *Schizophrenia Bulletin, 33,* 642–647.

Coltraine, S., & Messineo, M. (2000). The perpetuation of subtle prejudice: Race and gender imagery in 1990s television advertising. *Sex Roles, 42,* 363–389.

Colwell, M. J., & Lindsey, E. W. (2005). Preschool children's pretend and physical play and sex of play partner: Connections to peer competence. *Sex Roles, 52,* 497–509.

Compagni, A., & Manderscheid, R. W. (2006). A neuroscientist-consumer alliance to transform mental health care. *Journal of Behavioral Health Services & Research, 33,* 265–274.

Comuzzie, A. G., & Allison, D. B. (1998, May 29). The search for human obesity genes. *Science, 280,* 1374–1377.

Conduit, R., Crewther, S. G., & Coleman, G. (2004). Spontaneous eyelid movements (ELMS) during sleep are related to dream recall on awakening. *Journal of Sleep Research, 13,* 137–144.

Conner, M., Povey, R., Sparks, P., James, R., & Shepherd, R. (2003). Moderating role of attitudinal ambivalence within the theory of planned behaviour. *British Journal of Social Psychology, 42,* 75–94.

Connolly, A. C. (2007). Concepts and their features: Can cognitive science make good on the promises of concept empiricism? *Dissertation Abstracts International: Section B: The Sciences and Engineering, 67*(7-B), 4125.

Conway, M. A. (Ed.). (2002). *Levels of processing 30 years on special issue of memory.* Hove, UK: Psychology Press.

Cooke, J. R., & Ancoli-Israel, S. (2006). Sleep and its disorders in older adults. *Psychiatric Clinics of North America, 29,* 1077–1093.

Cooklin, A. (2000). Therapy, the family and others. In H. Maxwell (Ed.), *Clinical psychotherapy for health professionals.* Philadelphia: Whurr Publishers.

Coolidge, F. L., Segal, D. L., Estey, A. J., & Neuzil, P. J. (2011). Preliminary psychometric properties of a measure of Karen Horney's Tridimensional Theory in children and adolescents. *Journal of Clinical Psychology, 67,* 383–390.

Cooper, H., & Patall, E. (2009, June). The relative benefits of meta-analysis conducted with individual participant data versus aggregated data. *Psychological Methods, 14,* 165–176.

Cooper, J. (2007). *Cognitive dissonance: Fifty years of a classic theory.* Thousand Oaks, CA: Sage Publications.

Cooper, M. (2011, September 4). Vermont turns out for its dairies as they take stock and dig out. *The New York Times,* A10.

Cooper, M., & McLeod, J. (2011). Person-centered therapy: A pluralistic perspective. *Person-Centered and Experiential Psychotherapies, 10,* 210–223.

Cooper, Z., & Shafran, R. (2008). Cognitive behaviour therapy for eating disorders. *Behavioural and Cognitive Psychotherapy, 36,* 713–722.

Copeland, J. B., & Proudfoot, D. (2007). Artificial intelligence: History, foundations, and philosophical issues. In P. Thagard (Ed.), *Philosophy of psychology and cognitive science.* Amsterdam, Netherlands: North Holland/Elsevier.

Coplan, R., Reichel, M., & Rowan, K. (2009). Exploring the associations between maternal personality, child temperament, and parenting: A focus on emotions. *Personality and Individual Differences, 46,* 241–246.

Cordnoldi, C., De Beni, R., & Helstrup, T. (2007). Memory sensitivity in autobiographical memory. In S. Magnussen, & T. Helstrup (Eds.), *Everyday memory.* New York: Psychology Press.

Coren, S. (1992). The moon illusion: A different view through the legs. *Perceptual and Motor Skills, 75,* 827–831.

Coren, S. (2004). Sensation and perception. In I. B. Weiner (Ed.), *Handbook of Psychology* (Vol. 1). Hoboken, NJ: John Wiley & Sons.

Coren, S., & Ward, L. M. (1989). *Sensation and perception* (3rd ed.). San Diego, CA: Harcourt Brace Jovanovich.

Cornelius, M. D., Taylor, P. M., Geva, D., & Day, N. L. (1995). Prenatal tobacco and marijuana use among adolescents: Effects on offspring gestational age, growth, and morphology. *Pediatrics, 95,* 57–68.

Cornell, C. B. (2006). A graduated scale for determining mental age. *Dissertation Abstracts International: Section B: The Sciences and Engineering, 66*(9-B), 5121.

Cornier, M. (2011). Is your brain to blame for weight regain? *Physiology & Behavior, 104,* 608–612.

Corsello, A. (2005). The wronged man. In *The best American magazine writing, 2005.* New York: Columbia University Press.

Cosmides, L., & Tooby, J. (2004). Social exchange: The evolutionary design of a neurocognitive system. In M. S. Gazzaniga (Ed.), *Cognitive neurosciences* (3rd ed.). Cambridge, MA: MIT.

Costa, P. T., Jr., & Widiger, T. A. (Eds.). (2002). *Personality disorders and the Five-Factor Model of personality* (2nd ed.). Washington, DC: American Psychological Association.

Costa, R., & Figueiredo, B. (2011). Infant's psychophysiological profile and temperament at 3 and 12 months. *Infant Behavior & Development, 34,* 270–279.

Cotton, P. (1993, July 7). Psychiatrists set to approve DSM-IV. *Journal of the American Medical Association, 270,* 13–15.

Couturier, J., & Lock, J. (2006). Eating disorders: Anorexia nervosa, bulimia nervosa, and binge eating disorder. In T. G. Plante (Ed.), *Mental disorders of the new millennium: Biology and function* (Vol. 3). Westport, CT: Praeger Publishers/Greenwood Publishing.

Coventry, K. R., Venn, S. F., Smith, G. D., & Morley, A. M. (2003). Spatial problem solving and functional relations. *European Journal of Cognitive Psychology, 15,* 71–99.

Cowan, N., Towse, J. N., Hamilton, Z., Saults, J. S., Elliott, E. M., Lacey, J. F., et al. (2003). Children's working-memory processes: A response-timing analysis. *Journal of Experimental Psychology: General, 132,* 113–132.

Cowley, G. (2000, January 31). Alzheimer's: Unlocking the mystery. *Time,* pp. 46–54.

Cowley, G. (2003, February 24). Our bodies, our fears. *Newsweek,* pp. 43–44.

Cox, J. (2003, May 6). How far would you go to save your life? *Denver Post,* p. F1.

Cox, R., Baker, S. E., Macdonald, D. W., & Berdoy, M. (2004). Protecting egg prey from carrion crows: The potential of aversive conditioning. *Applied Animal Behaviour Science, 87,* 325–342.

Coyle, N. (2006). The hard work of living in the face of death. *Journal of Pain and Symptom Management, 32,* 266–274.

Coyle, T. R. (2006). Test-retest changes on scholastic aptitude tests are not related to g. *Intelligence, 34,* 15–27.

Craighero, L., Leo, I., Umiltà, C., & Simion, F. (2011). Newborns' preference for goal-directed actions. *Cognition, 120,* 26–32.

Craik, F., & Lockhart, R. (2008). Levels of processing and Zinchenko's approach to memory research. *Journal of Russian & East European Psychology, 46,* 52–60.

Cramer, P. (2007). Longitudinal study of defense mechanisms: Late childhood to late adolescence. *Journal of Personality, 75,* 1–23.

Creasey, G. L. (2005). *Research methods in lifespan development* (6th ed.). Boston: Allyn & Bacon.

Creel, S. C., & Bregman, M. R. (2011). How talker identity relates to language processing. *Language and Linguistics Compass, 5,* 190–204.

Crews, F. (1996). The verdict on Freud. *Psychological Science, 7,* 63–68.

Criswell, H., Ming, Z., Kelm, M., & Breese, G. (2008, August). Brain regional differences in the effect of ethanol on GABA release from presynaptic terminals. *Journal of Pharmacology and Experimental Therapeutics, 326,* 596–603.

Crits-Christoph, P. (1992). The efficacy of brief dynamic psychotherapy: A meta-analysis. *American Journal of Psychiatry, 149,* 151–158.

Crombag, H. S., & Robinson, R. E. (2004). Drugs, environment, brain, and behavior. *Current Directions in Psychological Science, 13,* 107–111.

Cropley, A. (2006). In praise of convergent thinking. *Creativity Research Journal, 18,* 391–404.

Crosnoe, R., & Elder, G. H., Jr. (2002). Successful adaptation in the later years: A life course approach to aging. *Social Psychology Quarterly, 65,* 309–328.

Crum, A. J., & Langer, E. J. (2007). Mind-set matters: Exercise and the placebo effect. *Psychological Science, 18,* 165–171.

Cuijpers, P., van Straten, A., Andersson, G., & van Oppen, P. (2008). Psychotherapy for depression in adults: A meta-analysis of comparative outcome studies. *Journal of Consulting and Clinical Psychology, 76*, 909–922.

Culhane-Pera, K. A., Borkan, J. M., & Patten, S. (2007). Culture and ethnicity. In O. J. Z. Sahler & J. E. Carr (Eds.), *The behavioral sciences and health care* (2nd rev. and updated ed.). Ashland, OH: Hogrefe & Huber Publishers.

Cullinane, C. A., Chu, D. Z. J., & Mamelak, A. N. (2002). Current surgical options in the control of cancer pain. *Cancer Practice, 10*, s21–s26.

Cummings, A., Ceponiene, R., & Koyama, A. (2006). Auditory semantic networks for words and natural sounds. *Brain Research, 1115*, 92–107.

Cunningham, P. (2006). Early years teachers and the influence of Piaget: Evidence from oral history. *Early Years An International Journal of Research and Development, 26*, 5–16.

Cwikel, J., Behar, L., & Rabson-Hare, J. (2000). A comparison of a vote count and a meta-analysis review of intervention research with adult cancer patients. *Research on Social Work Practice, 10*, 139–158.

Cynkar, A. (2007). The changing gender composition of psychology. *Monitor on Psychology, 38*, 46–48.

Czopp, A. M., & Monteith, M. J. (2006). Thinking well of African Americans: Measuring complimentary stereotypes and negative prejudice. *Basic and Applied Social Psychology, 28*, 233–250.

D'Arcy, R., et al. (2007). A site directed fMRI approach for evaluating functional status in the anterolateral temporal lobes. *Neuroscience Research, 57*, 120–128.

Daftary, F., & Meri, J. W. (2002). *Culture and memory in medieval Islam.* London: I. B. Tauris.

Dai, D. Y., & Wang, X. (2007). The role of need for cognition and reader beliefs in text comprehension and interest development. *Contemporary Educational Psychology, 32*, 332–347.

Daines, B. (2006). Violations of agreed and implicit sexual and emotional boundaries in couple relationships—some thoughts arising from Levine's 'A clinical perspective on couple infidelity.' *Sexual and Relationship Therapy, 21*, 45–53.

Dalal, A. K., & Misra, G. (2006). Psychology of health and well-being: Some emerging perspectives [Special issue: Psychology of health and well-being]. *Psychological Studies, 51*, 91–104.

Dale, A. (2006). Quality issues with survey research. *International Journal of Social Research Methodology: Theory & Practice, 9, Special issue: Quality in Social Research*, 143–158.

Daley, E. M., McDermott, R. J., Brown, K. R. M., & Kittleson, M. J. (2003). Conducting Web-based survey research: A lesson in Internet designs. *American Journal of Health Behavior, 27*, 116–124.

Damaske, S. (2011). A "major career woman"?: How women develop early expectations about work. *Gender & Society, 25*, 409–430.

Damon, W. (1999, August). The moral development of children. *Scientific American*, pp. 72–78.

Danaei, G., Vender Hoorn, S., Lopez, A. D., Murray, C. J. L., & Ezzati, M. (2005). Causes of cancer in the world: Comparative risk assessment of nine behavioural and environmental risk factors. Comparative Risk Assessment collaborating group (Cancers). *Lancet, 366*, 1784–1793.

Dani, J. A., & Montague, P. (2007). Disrupting addiction through the loss of drug-associated internal states. *Nature Neuroscience, 10*, 403–404.

Danner, D., Hagemann, D., Schankin, A., Hager, M., & Funke, J. (2011). Beyond IQ: A latent state-trait analysis of general intelligence, dynamic decision making, and implicit learning. *Intelligence, 39*, 323–334.

Dao, J. (2010, July 31). Voice on phone is lifeline for suicidal veterans. *The New York Times*, A1.

Dare, J. S. (2011). Transitions in midlife women's lives: Contemporary experiences. *Health Care for Women International, 32*, 111–133.

Darley, J. M., & Latané, B. (1968). Bystanders' intervention in emergencies: Diffusion of responsibility. *Journal of Personality and Social Psychology, 8*, 377–383.

Darwin, C. J., Turvey, M. T., & Crowder, R. G. (1972). An auditory analogue of the Sperling partial-report procedure: Evidence for brief auditory storage. *Cognitive Psychology, 3*, 255–267.

Das, A. (2007). Masturbation in the United States. *Journal of Sex & Marital Therapy, 33*, 301–317.

Das, A., Parish, W., & Laumann, E. (2009). Masturbation in urban China. *Archives of Sexual Behavior, 38*, 108–120.

Davidson, J. E., Deuser, R., & Sternberg, R. J. (1994). The role of metacognition in problem solving. In J. Metcalfe & A. P. Shimamura (Eds.), *Metacognition: Knowing About knowing.* Cambridge, MA: MIT.

Davies, S., Jackson, P., Lewis, G., Hood, S., Nutt, D., & Potokar, J. (2008). Is the association of hypertension and panic disorder explained by clustering of autonomic panic symptoms in hypertensive patients? *Journal of Affective Disorders, 111*, 344–350.

Davis, J., Senghas, A., & Ochsner, K. (2009). How does facial feedback modulate emotional experience? *Journal of Research in Personality, 43*, 822–829.

Davis, K., Christodoulou, J., Seider, S., & Gardner, H. (2011). The theory of multiple intelligences. In R. J. Sternberg & S. Kaufman (Eds.), *The Cambridge handbook of intelligence.* New York: Cambridge University Press.

Davis, L. J. (2009, June 15). Sotomayor and the New Haven firefighters case: More myths than facts. *The Washington Times*, p. A04.

Davis, O., Haworth, C., & Plomin, R. (2009, January). Learning abilities and disabilities: Generalist genes in early adolescence. *Cognitive Neuropsychiatry, 14*, 312–331.

Davis, R. D., & Millon, T. (1999). Models of personality and its disorders. In T. Millon, P. H. Blaney, & R. D. Davis (Eds.), *Oxford textbook of psychopathology.* New York: Oxford University Press.

Davis, S. R. (2007). The nose knows best. *PsycCRITIQUES, 52*, 22–31.

Day, A. L., & Livingstone, H. A. (2003). Gender differences in perceptions of stressors and utilization of social support among university students. *Canadian Journal of Behavioural Science, 35*, 73–83.

Day, R. D., & Lamb, M. E. (2004). *Conceptualizing and measuring father involvement.* Mahwah, NJ: Lawrence Erlbaum Associates.

De Beni, R., Pazzaglia, F., & Gardini, S. (2007). The generation and maintenance of visual mental images: Evidence from image type and aging. *Brain and Cognition, 63*, 271–278.

De Dreu, C. K. W., Greer, L. L., Van Kleef, G. A., Shalvi, S., & Handgraaf, M. J. (2011). Oxytocin promotes human ethnocentrism. *PNAS Proceedings of the National Academy of Sciences of the United States of America, 108*, 1262–1266.

de Gelder, B. (2000). More to seeing than meets the eye. *Science, 289*, 1148–1149.

de Gelder, B. (2010, April 27). Uncanny sight in the blind. *Scientific American*, 61.

Dean, C., & Dresbach, T. (2006). Neuroligins and neurexins: Linking cell adhesion, synapse formation and cognitive function. *International Journal of Psychiatry in Clinical Practice, 10 (Suppl.)*, 5–11.

Dean-Borenstein, M. T. (2007). The long-term psychosocial effects of trauma on survivors of human-caused extreme stress situations. *Dissertation Abstracts International: Section B: The Sciences and Engineering, 67(11-B)*, 6733.

DeAngelis, D., & Monahan, J. (2008). Professional credentials and professional regulations: Social work professional development. In B. W. White, K. M. Sowers, et al. (Eds.), *Comprehensive handbook of social work and social welfare, Vol. 1: The profession of social work.* Hoboken, NJ: John Wiley & Sons.

Dearing, E., McCartney, K., & Taylor, B. (2009). Does higher quality early child care promote low-income children's math and reading achievement in middle childhood? *Child Development, 80*, 1329–1349.

Deary, I. J., & Der, G. (2005). Reaction time, age, and cognitive ability: Longitudinal findings from age 16 to 63 years in representative population samples. *Aging, Neuropsychology, & Cognition, 12*, 187–215.

Deater-Deckard, K., Ivy, L., & Smith, J. (2005). Resilience in gene-environment transactions. In S. Goldstein & R. B. Brooks (Eds.), *Handbook of resilience in children.* New York: Kluwer Academic/Plenum Publishers.

Deci, E., & Ryan, R. (1995). *Intrinsic motivation and self-determinism in human behavior.* New York: Plenum.

deGroot, A. (1978). *Thought and choice in chess.* Paris: Mouton de Gruyter.

deGroot, A. D. (1966). Perception and memory versus thought: Some old ideas and recent findings. In B. Kleinmuntz (Ed.), *Problem solving: Research, method, and theory.* New York: Wiley.

Del Giudice, M. (2011). Alone in the dark? Modeling the conditions for visual experience in human fetuses. *Developmental Psychobiology, 53*, 214–219.

del Rosal, E., Alonso, L., & Moreno, R. (2006). Simulation of habituation to simple and multiple stimuli. *Behavioural Processes, 73*, 272–277.

DeLamater, J. D., & Sill, M. (2005). Sexual desire in later life. *Journal of Sex Research, 42*, 138–149.

Delgado, M. R., Labouliere, C. D., & Phelps, E. A. (2006). Fear of losing money? Aversive conditioning with secondary reinforcers [Special issue: Genetic, comparative and cognitive studies of social behavior]. *Social Cognitive and Affective Neuroscience, 1*, 250–259.

Delinsky, S. S., Latner, J. D., & Wilson, G. T. (2006). Binge eating and weight loss in a self-help behavior modification program. *Obesity, 14*, 1244–1249.

DeLoache, J., & LoBue, V. (2009). The narrow fellow in the grass: Human infants associate snakes and fear. *Developmental Science, 12*, 201–207.

Demaree, H. A., & Everhart, D. E. (2004). Healthy high-hostiles: Reduced para-sympathetic activity and decreased sympathovagal flexibility during negative emotional processing. *Personality and Individual Differences, 36*, 457–469.

Dement, W. C., & Wolpert, E. A. (1958). The relation of eye movements, body mobility, and external stimuli to dream content. *Journal of Experimental Psychology, 55*, 543–553.

Dempster, F. N. (1981). Memory span: Sources for individual and developmental differences. *Psychological Bulletin, 89*, 63–100.

Denmark, G. L., & Fernandez, L. C. (1993). Historical development of the psychology of women. In F. L. Denmark & M. A. Paludi (Eds.), *A handbook of issues and theories.* Westport, CT: Greenwood Press.

Dennett, D. C. (2003). *Freedom evolves.* New York: Viking.

Dennis, I. (2007). Halo effects in grading student projects. *Journal of Applied Psychology, 92,* 1169–1176.

Dennis, S. (2011). Smoking causes creative responses: On state antismoking policy and resilient habits. *Critical Public Health, 21,* 25–35.

Dennis, T. A., Cole, P. M., Zahn-Waxler, C., & Mizuta, I. (2002). Self in context: Autonomy and relatedness in Japanese and U.S. mother-preschooler dyads. *Child Development, 73,* 1803–1817.

Denollet, J., & Pedersen, S. S. (2011). Type D personality in patients with cardiovascular disorders. In R. Allan & J. Fisher (Eds.), *Heart and mind: The practice of cardiac psychology* (2nd ed.). Washington, DC: American Psychological Association.

Deouell, L. Y., Parnes, A., & Pickard, N. (2006). Spatial location is accurately tracked by human auditory sensory memory: Evidence from the mismatch negativity. *European Journal of Neuroscience, 24,* 1488–1494.

Deregowski, J. B. (1973). Illusion and culture. In R. L. Gregory & G. H. Combrich (Eds.), *Illusion in nature and art.* New York: Scribner.

Derryberry, W. P. (2006). Review of social motivation: Conscious and unconscious processes. *Journal of Moral Education, 35,* 276–278.

DeRubeis, R., Hollon, S., & Shelton, R. (2003, May 23). Presentation, American Psychiatric Association meeting, Philadelphia.

Des Jarlais, D. C., Sloboda, A., Friedman, S. R., Tempakski, B., McKnight, C., & Braine, N. (2006). Diffusion of the *D.A.R.E* and Syringe Exchange Programs. *American Journal of Public Health, 96,* 1354–1357.

Deshields, T., Tibbs, T., Fan, M. Y., & Taylor, M. (2006). Differences in patterns of depression after treatment for breast cancer [Electronic article published August 12, 2005]. *Psycho-Oncology, 15(5),* 398–406.

Dessing, J. C., Peper, C. E., Bullock, D., & Beek, P. J. (2005). How position, velocity, and temporal information combine in the prospective control of catching: Data and model. *Journal of Cognitive Neuroscience, 17,* 668–686.

Detterman, D. K. (2011). A challenge to Watson. *Intelligence, 39(2–3),* 77–78.

Detterman, D. K., Gabriel, L. T., & Ruthsatz, J. M. (2000). Intelligence and mental retardation. In R. J. Sternberg et al. (Eds.), *Handbook of intelligence.* New York: Cambridge University Press.

Devonport, J. J., & Lane, A. M. (2006). Relationships between self-efficacy, coping and student retention. *Social Behavior and Personality, 34,* 127–138.

Devos, T. (2011). The role of race in American politics: Lessons learned from the 2008 presidential election. In G. S. Parks, M. W. Hughey, et al. (Eds.), *The Obamas and a (post)*

racial America? New York: Oxford University Press.

Dhillon, S., Yang, L., & Curran, M. (2008). Spotlight on bupropion in major depressive disorder. *CNS Drugs, 22,* 613–617.

Di Fabio, A., & Palazzeschi, L. (2009). An in-depth look at scholastic success: Fluid intelligence, personality traits or emotional intelligence? *Personality and Individual Differences, 46,* 581–585.

Diamond, M. (2009). Human intersexuality: Difference or disorder? *Archives of Sexual Behavior, 38,* 172.

Dias, A. M., & van Deusen, A. (2011). A new neurofeedback protocol for depression. *Spanish Journal of Psychology, 14,* 374–84.

Diaz, A., & Bell, M. (2011). Information processing efficiency and regulation at five months. *Infant Behavior & Development, 34,* 239–247.

Díaz, E., & De la Casa, L. G. (2011). Extinction, spontaneous recovery and renewal of flavor preferences based on taste–taste learning. *Learning and Motivation, 42,* 64–75.

Dickinson, D. L., & Oxoby, R. J. (2011). Cognitive dissonance, pessimism, and behavioral spill-over effects. *Journal of Economic Psychology, 32,* 295–306.

Diener, E., & Biswas-Diener, R. (2002). Will money increase subjective well-being? *Social Indicators Research, 57,* 119–169.

Diener, E., & Clifton, D. (2002). Life satisfaction and religiosity in broad probability samples. *Psychological Inquiry, 13,* 206–209.

Diener, E., Lucas, R. E., & Scollon, C. N. (2006). Beyond the hedonic treadmill: Revising the adaptation theory of well-being. *American Psychologist, 61,* 305–314.

Diener, E., & Seligman, M. E. P. (2002). Very happy people. *Psychological Science, 18,* 81–84.

Diener, E., & Seligman, M. E. P. (2004). Beyond money: Toward an economy of well-being. *Psychological Science in the Public Interest, 5,* 1–31.

Diener, M., Isabella, R., Behunin, M., & Wong, M. (2008). Attachment to mothers and fathers during middle childhood: Associations with child gender, grade, and competence. *Social Development, 17,* 84–101.

DiGiovanna, A. G. (1994). *Human aging: Biological perspectives.* New York: McGraw-Hill.

Dijksterhuis, A., Chartrand, T. L., & Aarts, H. (2007). Effects of Priming and Perception on Social Behavior and Goal Pursuit. *Frontiers of Social Psychology, 17,* 33–40.

Dillard, J. P., & Shen, L. (2007). Self-report measures of discrete emotions. In R. A. Reynolds, R. Woods, & J. D. Baker (Eds.), *Handbook of research on electronic surveys and measurements.* Hershey, PA: Idea Group Reference/IGI Global, 2007.

Dillon, J. (2008, April). Reclaiming humanistic psychology from modernity: Problems and solutions. *Journal of Humanistic Psychology, 48,* 221–242.

DiLorenzo, P. M., & Youngentob, S. L. (2003). Olfaction and taste. In M. Gallagher & R. J. Nelson (Eds.), *Handbook of psychology: Biological psychology* (Vol. 3). New York: Wiley.

Dingfelder, S. (2011). Reflecting on narcissism. *Monitor on Psychology, 42,* 64–68.

Dittrich, W. H., Johansen, T., & Fineberg, N. A. (2011). Cognitive Assessment Instrument of Obsessions and Compulsions (CAIOV-13)—A new 13-item scale for evaluating functional impairment associated with OCD. *Psychiatry Research, 187,* 283–290.

Dixon, R. A., & Cohen, A. L. (2003). Cognitive development in adulthood. In R. M. Lerner, M. A. Easterbrooks, et al. (Eds.), *Handbook of psychology: Developmental psychology* (Vol. 6). New York: Wiley.

Dixon, R. A., Rust, T. B., & Feltmate, S. E. (2007). Memory and aging: Selected research directions and application issues. *Canadian Psychology Psychologie Canadienne, 48,* 67–76.

Djapo, N., Kolenovic-Djapo, J., Djokic, R., & Fako, I. (2011). Relationship between Cattell's 16PF and fluid and crystallized intelligence. *Personality and Individual Differences, 51,* 63–67.

Do, V. T. (2006). Asian American men and the media: The relationship between ethnic identity, self-esteem, and the endorsement of stereotypes. *Dissertation Abstracts International: Section B: The Sciences and Engineering, 67(6-B),* 3446.

Dobbins, A. C., Jeo, R. M., Fiser, J., & Allman, J. M. (1998, July 24). Distance modulation of neural activity in the visual cortex. *Science, 281,* 552–555.

Dodge, K. A. (2004). The nature-nurture debate and public policy [Special issue: 50th anniversary issue, part 2: The maturing of the human development sciences—Appraising past, present, and prospective agendas]. *Merrill-Palmer Quarterly: Journal of Developmental Psychology, 50,* 418–427.

Dohnke, B., Weiss-Gerlach, E., & Spies, C. D. (2011). Social influences on the motivation to quit smoking: Main and moderating effects of social norms. *Addictive Behaviors, 36,* 286–293.

Doi, T. (1990). The cultural assumptions of psychoanalysis. In J. W. Stigler, R. A. Shweder, & G. Herdt (Eds.), *Cultural psychology: Essays on comparative human development.* New York: Cambridge University Press.

Dolan, P., & White, M. P. (2007). How can measures of subjective well-being be used to inform public policy? *Perspectives on Psychological Science, 2,* 71–85.

Dolan, R. J. (2002, November 8). Emotion, cognition, and behavior. *Science, 298,* 1191–1194.

Dolbier, C. L., Smith, S. E., & Steinhardt, M. A. (2007). Relationships of protective factors to stress and symptoms of illness. *American Journal of Health Behavior, 31,* 423–433.

Dolinski, D. (2011). A rock or a hard place: The foot-in-the-face technique for inducing compliance without pressure. *Journal of Applied Social Psychology, 41,* 1514–1537.

Dollinger, S. J. (2003). Need for uniqueness, need for cognition and creativity. *Journal of Creative Behavior, 37,* 99–116.

Domhoff, G. W. (2011). The neural substrate for dreaming: Is it a subsystem of the default network? *Consciousness and Cognition, 20,* 1163–1174.

Donahoe, J. W. (2003). Selectionism. In K. A. Lattal & P. N. Chase (Eds.), *Behavior theory and philosophy.* New York: Kluwer Academic/Plenum Publishers.

Donahoe, J. W., & Vegas, R. (2004). Pavlovian conditioning: The CSUR relation. *Journal of Experimental Psychology: Animal Behavior Processes, 30,* 17–33.

Dortch, S. (1996, October). Our aching heads. *American Demographics.*

Doty, R. L., Green, P. A., Ram, C., & Yankell, S. L. (1982). Communication of gender from human breath odors: Relationship to perceived intensity and pleasantness. *Hormones and Behavior, 16,* 13–22.

Dougall, A. L., & Baum, A. (2004). Psychoneuro-immunology and trauma. In P. P. Schnurr & B. L. Green (Eds.), *Trauma and health: Physical health consequences of exposure to extreme stress.* Washington, DC: American Psychological Association.

Douglas, O., Burton, K. S., & Reese-Durham, N. (2008). The effects of the multiple intelligence teaching strategy on the academic achievement of eighth grade math students. *Journal of Instructional Psychology, 35,* 182–187.

Douglas Brown, R., Goldstein, E., & Bjorklund, D. F. (2000). The history and zeitgeist of the repressed-false-memory debate: Scientific and sociological perspectives on suggestibility and childhood memory. In D. F. Bjorklund (Ed.), *False-memory creation in children and adults: Theory, research, and implications.* Mahwah, NJ: Lawrence Erlbaum.

Dovidio, J. F., & Gaertner, S. L. (2006). A multilevel perspective on prejudice: Crossing disciplinary boundaries. In P. A. M. Van Lange (Ed.), *Bridging social psychology: Benefits of transdisci-plinary approaches.* Mahwah, NJ: Lawrence Erlbaum Associates.

Dovidio, J. F., Gaertner, S. L., & Kawakami, K. (2003). Intergroup contact: The past, present, and the future. *Group Processes and Intergroup Relations, 6,* 5–20.

Dovidio, J. F., Gaertner, S. L., & Pearson, A. R. (2005). On the nature of prejudice: The psychological foundations of hate. In R. J. Sternberg (Ed.), *Psychology of hate.* Washington, DC: American Psychological Association.

Dovidio, J. F., Piliavin, J. A., Schroeder, D. A., & Penner, L. A. (2006). *The social psychology of prosocial behavior.* Mahwah, NJ: Lawrence Erlbaum Associates.

Dowling, N., Jackson, A., & Thomas, S. (2008). Behavioral interventions in the treatment of pathological gambling: A review of activity scheduling and desensitization. *International Journal of Behavioral Consultation and Therapy, 4,* 172–187.

Doyle, R. (2002, December). Deinstitutionalization. *Scientific American,* 38.

Drewes, A. A. (2005). Play in selected cultures: Diversity and universality. In E. Gil & A. A. Drewes (Eds.), *Cultural issues in play therapy.* New York: Guilford Press.

Drob, S. (2005). The mystical symbol: Some comments on Ankor, Giegerich, Scholem, and Jung. *Journal of Jungian Theory & Practice, 7,* 25–29.

Dryden, W., & David, D. (2008). Rational emotive behavior therapy: Current status. *Journal of Cognitive Psychotherapy, 22,* 195–209.

Ducharme, J. M., Sanjuan, E., & Drain, T. (2007). Errorless compliance training: Success-focused behavioral treatment of children with Asperger syndrome. *Behavior Modification, 31,* 329–344.

Dudai, Y. (2011). The Engram revisited: On the elusive permanence of memory. In S. Nalbantian, P. M. Matthews, J. L. McClelland, S. Nalbantian, P. M. Matthews & J. L. McClelland (Eds.), *The memory process: Neuroscientific and humanistic perspectives.* Cambridge, MA: MIT Press.

Dugas, C. (2010, February 25). Struggle for words frustrates Woodruff; But journalist can work after his brain injury. *USA Today,* p. 10D.

Duke, M., & Nowicki, S., Jr. (1979). *Abnormal psychology: Perspectives on being different.* Monterey, CA: Brooks/Cole.

Dumont, M., & Dumont, D. (2008). Deinstitutionalization in the United States and Italy: A historical survey. *International Journal of Mental Health, 37,* 61–70.

Duncker, K. (1945). On problem solving. *Psychological Monographs, 58* (5, whole no. 270).

Dunlop, W. L., Beatty, D. J., & Beauchamp, M. R. (2011). Examining the influence of other-efficacy and self-efficacy on personal performance. *Journal of Sport & Exercise Psychology, 33,* 586–593.

Eaker, E. D., Sullivan, L. M., Kelly-Hayes, M., D'Agostino, R. B., Sr., & Benjamin, E. J. (2004). Anger and hostility predict the development of atrial fibrillation in men in the Framingham Offspring Study. *Circulation, 109,* 1267–1271.

Ebbinghaus, H. (1885/1913). *Memory: A contribution to experimental psychology* (H. A. Roger & C. E. Bussenius, Trans.). New York: Columbia University Press.

Eberhard, K. M., Cutting, J. C., & Bock, K. (2005). Making syntax of sense: Number agreement in sentence production. *Psychological Review, 112,* 531–559.

Ebstein, R. P., Benjamin, J., & Belmaker, R. H. (2003). Behavioral genetics, genomics, and personality. In R. Plomin & J. C. DeFries (Eds.), *Behavioral genetics in the postgenomic era.* Washington, DC: American Psychological Association.

Ebster, C., & Neumayr, B. (2008). Applying the door-in-the-face compliance technique to retailing. *The International Review of Retail, Distribution and Consumer Research, 18,* 121–128.

Ecenbarger, W. (1993, April 1). America's new merchants of death. *The Reader's Digest,* p. 50.

Eckardt, M. H. (2005). Karen Horney: A portrait: The 120th anniversary, Karen Horney, September 16, 1885. *American Journal of Psychoanalysis, 65,* 95–101.

Eckersley, R., & Dear, K. (2002). Cultural correlates of youth suicide. *Social Science and Medicine, 55,* 1891–1904.

Edoka, I. P., Petrou, S., & Ramchandani, P. G. (2011). Healthcare costs of paternal depression in the postnatal period. *Journal of Affective Disorders, 133,* 356–360.

Egan, J. (2011, March 6). The liberation of Lori Berenson. *New York Times Magazine,* p. 30.

Egan, K. (2005). Students' development in theory and practice: The doubtful role of research. *Harvard Educational Review, 75,* 25–41.

Egliston, K., & Rapee, R. (2007). Inhibition of fear acquisition in toddlers following positive modelling by their mothers. *Behaviour Research and Therapy, 45,* 1871–1882.

Ehrenfeld, T. (2011). Reflections on mirror neurons. *Association for Psychological Science, 24,* 11–13.

Eisch, A., Cameron, H., Encinas, J., Meltzer, L., Ming, G., & Overstreet-Wadiche, L. (2008, November). Adult neurogenesis, mental health, and mental illness: Hope or hype? *Journal of Neuroscience, 28(46),* 1785–1791.

Eisenberg, N., Guthrie, I. K., & Cumberland, A. (2002). Prosocial development in early adulthood: A longitudinal study. *Journal of Personality and Social Psychology, 82,* 993–1006.

Ekman, P. (1972). Universals and cultural differences in facial expressions of emotion. In J. Cole (Ed.), *Darwin and facial expression: A century of research in review.* New York: Academic Press.

Ekman, P. (1994a). All emotions are basic. In P. Ekman & R. J. Davidson (Eds.), *The nature of emotion: Fundamental questions.* New York: Oxford University Press.

Ekman, P. (1994b). Strong evidence for universals in facial expressions: A reply to Russell's mistaken critique. *Psychological Bulletin, 115,* 268–287.

Ekman, P. (2003). *Emotions revealed: Recognizing faces and feelings to improve communication and emotional life.* New York: Times Books.

Ekman, P. (2007). *Emotions revealed* (2nd ed.). New York: Holt.

Ekroll, V., & Scherzer, T. R. (2009). Apparent visual motion of the observer's own limbs. *Perception, 38,* 778–780.

Elfhag, K., Tynelius, P., & Rasmussen, F. (2007). Sugar-sweetened and artificially sweetened soft drinks in association to restrained, external and emotional eating. *Physiology & Behavior, 91,* 191–195.

El-Hai, J. (2005). *The lobotomist: A maverick medical genius and his tragic quest to rid the world of mental illness.* New York: Wiley.

Elkins, D. (2009). Why humanistic psychology lost its power and influence in American psychology: Implications for advancing humanistic psychology. *Journal of Humanistic Psychology, 49,* 267–291.

Elkins, G., Marcus, J., Bates, J., Hasan, R. M., & Cook, T. (2006). Intensive hypnotherapy for smoking cessation: a prospective study. *International Journal of Clinical Experimental Hypnosis, 54,* 303–315.

Ellason, J. W., & Ross, C. A. (2004). SCL-90-R norms for dissociative identity disorder. *Journal of Trauma and Dissociation, 5,* 85–91.

Ellins, E., Halcox, J., Donald, A., Field, B., Brydon, L., Deanfield, J., et al. (2008). Arterial stiffness and inflammatory response to psychophysiological stress. *Brain, Behavior, and Immunity, 22,* 941–948.

Elliott, A. (2002). *Psychoanalytic theory: An introduction* (2nd ed.). Durham, NC: Duke University Press.

Elliott, J., Berman, H., & Kim, S. (2002). Critical ethnography of Korean Canadian women's menopause experience. *Health Care for Women International, 23,* 377–388.

Ellis, A. (1974). *Growth through reason.* Hollywood, CA: Wilshire Books.

Ellis, A. (2000). *How to control your anger before it controls you.* New York: Citadel.

Ellis, A. (2002). *Overcoming resistance: A rational emotive behavior therapy integrated approach* (2nd ed.). New York: Springer.

Ellis, A. (2004). Expanding the ABCs of rational emotive behavior therapy. In A. Freeman, M. J. Mahoney, P. Devito, & D. Martin (Eds.), *Cognition and psychotherapy* (2nd ed.). New York: Springer Publishing Co.

El-Mallakh, R. S., & Abraham, H. D. (2007). MDMA (Ecstasy). *Annals of Clinical Psychiatry, 19,* 45–52.

Emick, J., & Welsh, M. (2005). Association between formal operational thought and executive function as measured by the Tower of Hanoi-Revised. *Learning and Individual Differences, 15,* 177–188.

Endres, T., & Fendt, M. (2007). Conditioned behavioral responses to a context paired with the predator odor trimethylthiazoline. *Behavioral Neuroscience, 121,* 594–601.

Engen, T. (1987). Remembering odors and their names. *American Scientist, 75,* 497–503.

Engler, J., & Goleman, D. (1992). *The consumer's guide to psychotherapy.* New York: Simon & Schuster.

Eranti, S. V., & McLoughlin, D. M. (2003). Electroconvulsive therapy: State of the art. *British Journal of Psychiatry, 182,* 8–9.

Erickson, R. (2008, February). A study of the science of taste: On the origins and influence of the core ideas. *Behavioral and Brain Sciences, 31,* 59–75.

Erikson, E. H. (1963). *Childhood and society.* New York: Norton.

Ervik, S., Abdelnoor, M., & Heier, M. S. (2006). Health-related quality of life in narcolepsy. *Acta Neurologica Scandinavica, 114,* 198–204.

Evans, A. M. (2007). Transference in the nurse patient relationship. *Journal of Psychiatric and Mental Health Nursing, 14,* 189–195.

Evans, D. E., & Rothbart, M. K. (2007). Developing a model for adult temperament. *Journal of Research in Personality, 41,* 868–888.

Evans, D. E., & Rothbart, M. K. (2009). A two-factor model of temperament. *Personality and Individual Differences, 47,* 565–570.

Evcik, D., Kavuncu, V., Cakir, T., Subasi, V., & Yaman, M. (2007). Laser therapy in the treatment of carpal tunnel syndrome: A randomized controlled trial. *Photomedical Laser Surgery, 25,* 34–39.

Everette, M. (2008). Gestational weight and dietary intake during pregnancy: Perspectives of African American women. *Maternal & Child Health Journal, 12,* 718–724.

Everly, G. S., Jr., & Lating, J. M. (2007). Psychotherapy: A cognitive perspective. In A. Monat, R. S. Lazarus, et al. (Eds.), *The Praeger handbook on stress and coping* (Vol. 2). Westport, CT: Praeger Publishers/Greenwood Publishing.

Eysenck, H. J. (1990). Biological dimensions of personality. In L. A. Pervin (Ed.), *Handbook of personality: Theory and research.* New York: Guilford Press.

Eysenck, H. J. (1995). *Eysenck on extraversion.* New York: Wiley.

Fagan, J. F., & Holland, C. R. (2002). Equal opportunity and racial differences in IQ. *Intelligence, 30,* 361–387.

Fagan, J. F., & Holland, C. R. (2007). Racial equality in intelligence: Predictions from a theory of intelligence as processing. *Intelligence, 35,* 319–334.

Fagan, J., & Press, J. (2008). Father influences on employed mothers' work-family balance. *Journal of Family Issues, 29,* 1136–1160.

Fallon, A. (2006). Informed consent in the practice of group psychotherapy. *International Journal of Group Psychotherapy, 56,* 431–453.

Fanselow, M. S., & Poulos, A. M. (2005). The neuroscience of mammalian associative learning. *Annual Review of Psychology, 56,* 207–234.

Fearing, V. G., & Clark, J. (Eds.). (2000). *Individuals in context: A practical guide to client-centered practice.* Chicago: Slack Publishing.

Fedeli, A., Braconi, S., Economidou, D., Cannella, N., Kallupi, M., Guerrini, R., et al. (2009). The paraventricular nucleus of the hypothalamus is a neuroanatomical substrate for the inhibition of palatable food intake by neuropeptide S. *European Journal of Neuroscience, 30,* 1594–1602.

Fee, E., Brown, T. M., Lazarus, J., & Theerman, P. (2002). Exploring acupuncture: Ancient ideas, modern techniques. *American Journal of Public Health, 92,* 1592.

Feinberg, A. W. (2002, April). Homocysteine may raise Alzheimer's risk: A physician's perspective. *HealthNews,* p. 4.

Feldman, D. H. (2003). Cognitive development in childhood. In R. M. Lerner, M. A. Easterbrooks, et al. (Eds.), *Handbook of psychology: Developmental psychology* (Vol. 6.). New York: Wiley.

Feldman, D. H. (2004). Piaget's stages: The unfinished symphony of cognitive development. *New Ideas in Psychology, 22,* 175–231.

Feldman, R. S. (2010). *P.O.W.E.R. Learning: Strategies for Success in College and Life* (5th ed). New York: McGraw-Hill.

Feldt, L. S. (2005). Estimating the reliability of cichotomous or trichotomous scores. *Educational and Psychological Measurement, 65,* 28–41.

Feng, B., Bell, R. A., Jerant, A. F., & Kravitz, R. L. (2011). What do doctors say when prescribing medications? An examination of medical recommendations from a communication perspective. *Health Communication, 26,* 286–296.

Fenter, V. L. (2006). Concerns about Prozac and direct-to-consumer advertising of prescription drugs. *International Journal of Risk & Safety in Medicine, 18,* 1–7.

Ferguson, C. J. (2010). Blazing angels or resident evil? Can violent video games be a force for good? *Review of General Psychology, 14,* 68–81.

Ferguson, C. J. (2011). Video games and youth violence: A prospective analysis in adolescents. *Journal of Youth and Adolescence, 40,* 377–391.

Ferguson, M., & Ogloff, J. P. (2011). Criminal responsibility evaluations: Role of psychologists in assessment. *Psychiatry, Psychology and Law, 18,* 79–94.

Feshbach, S., & Tangney, J. (2008, September). Television viewing and aggression: Some alternative perspectives. *Perspectives on Psychological Science, 3,* 387–389.

Festinger, D., Marlowe, D., Croft, J., Dugosh, K., Arabia, P., & Benasutti, K. (2009). Monetary incentives improve recall of research consent information: It pays to remember. *Experimental and Clinical Psychopharmacology, 17,* 99–104.

Festinger, L. (1957). *A theory of cognitive dissonance.* Stanford, CA: Stanford University Press.

Festinger, L., & Carlsmith, J. M. (1959). Cognitive consequences of forced compliance. *Journal of Abnormal and Social Psychology, 58,* 203–210.

Fichtenberg, C. M., & Glantz, S. A. (2006). Association of the California tobacco control program with declines in cigarette consumption and mortality from heart disease. In K. E. Warner (Ed.), *Tobacco control policy.* San Francisco, CA: Jossey-Bass.

Fields, C. (2011). From "Oh, OK" to "Ah, yes" to "Aha!": Hyper-systemizing and the rewards of insight. *Personality and Individual Differences, 50,* 1159–1167.

Fields, R. D. (2004, April). The other half of the brain. *Scientific American,* pp. 55–61.

Fields-Meyer, T. (1995, September 25). Having their say. *People,* pp. 50–60.

Figen, A. (2011). The relationship between test anxiety and learned helplessness. *Social Behavior and Personality, 39,* 101–112.

Finan, P. H., Zautra, A. J., & Wershba, R. (2011). The dynamics of emotion in adaptation to stress. In R. J. Contrada & A. Baum (Eds.), *The handbook of stress science: Biology, psychology, and health.* New York: Springer Publishing Co.

Fine, R., & Fine, L. (2003). *Basic chess endings.* New York: Random House.

Fingelkurts, A., Fingelkurts, A. A., & Kallio, S. (2007). Hypnosis induces a changed composition of brain oscillations in EEG: A case study. *Contemporary Hypnosis, 24,* 3–18.

Fink, G. (Ed.). (2000). *Encyclopedia of stress.* New York: Academic Press.

Finkelstein, M. (2009). Intrinsic vs. extrinsic motivational orientations and the volunteer process. *Personality and Individual Differences, 46,* 653–658.

Finkler, K. (2004). Traditional healers in Mexico: The effectiveness of spiritual practices. In U. P. Gielen, J. M. Fish, & J. G. Draguns (Eds.), *Handbook of culture, therapy, and healing.* Mahwah, NJ: Lawrence Erlbaum Associates.

Finlay, F. O., Jones, R., & Coleman, J. (2002). Is puberty getting earlier? The views of doctors and teachers. *Child: Care, Health and Development, 28,* 205–209.

Finley, C. L., & Cowley, B. J. (2005). The effects of a consistent sleep schedule on time taken to achieve sleep. *Clinical Case Studies, 4,* 304–311.

Finn, A. (2011). Jungian analytical theory. In D. Capuzzi & D. R. Gross (Eds.), *Counseling and psychotherapy* (5th ed.). Alexandria, VA: American Counseling Association.

Firestein, B. A. (Ed.). (1996). *Bisexuality: The psychology and politics of an invisible minority.* Thousand Oaks, CA: Sage.

First, M. B., Frances, A., & Pincus, H. A. (2002). *DSM-IV-TR handbook of differential diagnosis.* Arlington, VA: American Psychiatric Publishing.

Fischer, K. W., Shaver, P. R., & Carnochan, P. (1990). How emotions develop and how they organize development. *Cognition and Emotion, 4,* 81–127.

Fishbach, A., Dhar, R., & Zhang, Y. (2006). Subgoals as substitutes or complements: The role of goal accessibility. *Journal of Personality and Social Psychology, 91,* 232–242.

Fisher, C. B. (2003). *Decoding the ethics code: A practical guide for psychologists.* Thousand Oaks, CA: Sage.

Fisher, C. B., Hoagwood, K., Boyce, C., Duster, T., Frank, D. A., Grisso, T., et al. (2002). Research ethics for mental health science involving ethnic minority children and youths. *American Psychologist, 57,* 1024–1040.

Fitzgerald, P., & Daskalakis, Z. (2008, January). The use of repetitive transcranial magnetic stimulation and vagal nerve stimulation in the treatment of depression. *Current Opinion in Psychiatry, 21,* 25–29.

Flam, F. (1991, June 14). Queasy riders. *Science, 252,* 1488.

Flavell, S. W., Cowan, C. W., Kim, T., Greer, P. L., Lin, Y., Paradis, S., et al. (2006, February 17). Activity-dependent regulation of MEF2 transcription factors suppresses excitatory synapse number. *Science, 311,* 1008–1010.

Fleck, J. I., Green, D. L., Payne, L., Stevenson, J. L., Bowden, E. M., Jung-Beeman, M., et al. (2008). The transliminal brain at rest: Baseline EEG, unusual experiences, and access to unconscious mental activity. *Cortex, 44,* 1353–1363.

Fleischman, D. A., Wilson, R. S., Gabrieli, J. D. E., Bienias, J. L., & Bennett, D. A. (2004). A longitudinal study of implicit and explicit memory in old persons. *Psychology and Aging, 19,* 617–625.

Fleming, J. (2000). Affirmative action and standardized test scores. *Journal of Negro Education, 69,* 27–37.

Foderaro, L. W. (2006, February 16). Westchester lawyer, his memory lost, is found in Chicago shelter after 6 months. *The New York Times*, p. B3.

Folk, C., & Remington, R. (2008, January). Bottom-up priming of top-down attentional control settings. *Visual Cognition, 16*, 215–231.

Folkman, S., & Moskowitz, J. T. (2000). Stress, positive emotion, and coping. *Current Directions in Psychological Science, 9*, 115–118.

Folkman, S., & Moskowitz, J. T. (2004). Coping: Pitfalls and promise. *Annual Review of Psychology, 55*, 745–774.

Follett, K., & Hess, T. M. (2002). Aging, cognitive complexity, and the fundamental attribution error. *Journal of Gerontology: Series B: Psychological Sciences and Social Sciences, 57B*, P312–P323.

Forbey, J., & Ben-Porath, Y. (2007). Computerized adaptive personality testing: A review and illustration with the MMPI-2 computerized adaptive version. *Psychological Assessment, 19*, 14–24.

Forer, B. (1949). The fallacy of personal validation: A classroom demonstration of gullibility. *Journal of Abnormal and Social Psychology, 44*, 118–123.

Forgas, J. P., & Laham, S. M. (2005). The interaction between affect and motivation in social judgments and behavior. In J. P. Forgas, K. P. Williams, & S. M. Laham (Eds.), *Social motivation: Conscious and unconscious processes*. New York: Cambridge University Press.

Forlenza, M. J., & Baum, M. J. (2004). Psychoneuroimmunology. In T. J. Boll, R. G. Frank, et al. (Eds), *Handbook of clinical health psychology, Vol. 3: Models and perspectives in health psychology*. Washington, DC: American Psychological Association.

Foster, K. M. (2005). Introduction: John Uzo Ogbu (1939-2003): How do you ensure the fair consideration of a complex ancestor? Multiple approaches to assessing the work and legacy of John Uzo Ogbu. *International Journal of Qualitative Studies in Education, 18*, 559–564.

Foster, P., Drago, V., FitzGerald, D., Skoblar, B., Crucian, G., & Heilman, K. (2008). Spreading activation of lexical-semantic networks in Parkinson's disease. *Neuropsychologia, 46*, 1908–1914.

Foulds, J., Gandhi, K. K., Steinberg, M. B., Richardson, D. L., Williams, J. M., Burke, M. V., et al. (2006). Factors associated with quitting smoking at a tobacco dependence treatment clinic. *American Journal of Health Behavior, 30*, 400–412.

Fournier, J., Deremaux, S., & Bernier, M. (2008). Content, characteristics and function of mental images. *Psychology of Sport and Exercise, 9*, 734–748.

Fowler, C. A., & Galantucci, B. (2008). The relation of speech perception and speech production. In D. B. Pisoni & R. E. Remez (Eds.), *The handbook of speech perception*. Malden, MA: Blackwell Publishing.

Fox, S., & Spector, P. E. (2000). Relations of emotional intelligence, practical intelligence, general intelligence, and trait affectivity with interview outcomes: It's not all just "G." *Journal of Organizational Behavior, 21*, 203–220.

Frankenburg, W. K., et al. (1992). *Denver II training manual*. Denver, CO: Denver Developmental Materials.

Franklin, A., Pilling, M., & Davies, I. (2005). The nature of infant color categorization: Evidence from eye movements on a target decision task. *Journal of Experimental Child Psychology, 91*, 227–248.

Franklin, M. E., March, J. S., & Garcia, A. (2007). Treating obsessive-compulsive disorder in children and adolescents. In C. Purdon, M. M. Antony, & L. J. Summerfeldt (Eds.), *Psychological treatment of obsessive-compulsive disorder: Fundamentals and beyond*. Washington, DC: American Psychological Association.

Franklin, T. B., & Mansuy, I. M. (2011). The involvement of epigenetic defects in mental retardation. *Neurobiology of Learning and Memory, 96*, 61–67.

Franko, D. L., & Roehrig, J. P. (2011). African American body images. In T. F. Cash & L. Smolak (Eds.), *Body image: A handbook of science, practice, and prevention* (2nd ed.). New York: Guilford Press.

Franzek, E., & Beckmann, H. (1996). Gene-environment interaction in schizophrenia: Season-of-birth effect reveals etiologically different subgroups. *Psychopathology, 29*, 14–26.

Frasure-Smith, N., Lesperance, F., & Talajic, M. (2000). The prognostic importance of depression, anxiety, anger, and social support following myocardial infarction: Opportunities for improving survival. In P. M. McCabe, N. Schneiderman, T. M. Field, & A. R. Wellens (Eds.), *Stress, coping, and cardiovascular disease*. Mahwah, NJ: Erlbaum.

Frederickson, B. L., & Branigan, C. (2005). Positive emotions broaden the scope of attention and thought-action repertoires. *Cognition and Emotion, 19*, 313–332.

Freedberg, D. (2011). Memory in art: History and the neuroscience of response. In S. Nalbantian, P. M. Matthews, et al. (Eds.), *The memory process: Neuroscientific and humanistic perspectives*. Cambridge, MA: MIT Press.

Freedman, D. S. (1995). The importance of body fat distribution in early life. *American Journal of the Medical Sciences, 310*, S72–S76.

Freedman, J. L., & Fraser, S. C. (1966). Compliance without pressure: The foot-in-the-door technique. *Journal of Personality and Social Psychology, 4*, 195–202.

Frensch, P. A., & Rünger, D. (2003). Implicit learning. *Current Directions in Psychological Science, 12*, 13–18.

Freud, S. (1900). *The interpretation of dreams*. London: Hogarth Press.

Freud, S. (1922/1959). *Group psychology and the analysis of the ego*. London: Hogarth.

Friborg, O., Barlaug, D., Martinussen, M., Rosenvinge, J. H., & Hjemdal, O. (2005). Resilience in relation to personality and intelligence. *International Journal of Methods in Psychiatric Research, 14*, 29–42.

Friborg, O., Hjemdal, O., & Rosenvinge, J. H. (2006). Resilience as a moderator of pain and stress. *Journal of Psychosomatic Research, 61*, 213–219.

Friedberg, R. D. (2006). A cognitive-behavioral approach to family therapy. *Journal of Contemporary Psychotherapy, 36*, 159–165.

Friedman, J. N. W., Oltmanns, T. F., & Turkheimer, E. (2007). Interpersonal perception and personality disorders: Utilization of a thin slice approach. *Journal of Research in Personality, 41*, 667–688.

Friedman, M. J. (2006). Posttraumatic stress disorder among military returnees from Afghanistan and Iraq. *American Journal of Psychiatry, 163*, 586–593.

Frijda, N. H. (2005). Emotion experience. *Cognition and Emotion, 19*, 473–497.

Frincke, J. L., & Pate, W. E., II. (2004, March). *Yesterday, today, and tomorrow. Careers in Psychology 2004, what students need to know*. Paper presented at the Annual Convention of the Southeastern Psychological Association, Atlanta, GA.

Frings, L., Wagner, K., Unterrainer, J., Spreer, J., Halsband, U., & Schulze-Bonhage, A. (2006). Gender-related differences in lateralization of hippocampal activation and cognitive strategy. *Neuroreport, 17*, 417–421.

Fritsch, T., McClendon, M. J., Smyth, K. A., Lerner, A. J., Friedland, R. P., & Larsen, J. D. (2007). Cognitive functioning in healthy aging: The role of reserve and lifestyle factors early in life. *Gerontologist, 47*, 307–322.

Frosch, A. (2011). The effect of frequency and duration on psychoanalytic outcome: A moment in time. *Psychoanalytic Review, 98*, 11–38.

Frost, L. E., & Bonnie, R. J. (Eds.). (2001). *The evolution of mental health law*. Washington, DC: American Psychological Association.

Frost, R. O., & Steketee, G. (Eds.). (2002). *Cognitive approaches to obsessions and compulsions: Theory, assessment, and treatment*. New York: Pergamon Press.

Fuhrman, O., McCormick, K., Chen, E., Jiang, H., Shu, D., Mao, S., & Boroditsky, L. (2011). How linguistic and cultural forces shape conceptions of time: English and Mandarin time in 3D. *Cognitive Science: A Multidisciplinary Journal, 7*, 1305–1328.

Funder, D. C. (1991). Global traits: Aneo-Allportian approach to personality. *Psychological Science, 2*, 31–39.

Furnham, A., & Crump, J. (2005). Personality traits, types, and disorders: An examination of the relationship between three self-report measures. *European Journal of Personality, 19*, 167–184.

Furumoto, L., & Scarborough, E. (2002). Placing women in the history of psychology: The first American women psychologists. In W. E. Pickren (Ed.), *Evolving perspectives on the history of psychology*. Washington, DC: American Psychological Association.

Fusari, A., & Ballesteros, S. (2008, August). Identification of odors of edible and nonedible stimuli as affected by age and gender. *Behavior Research Methods, 40*, 752–759.

Fyhn, M., Hafting, T., Treves, A., Moser, M., & Moser, E. (2007). Hippocampal remapping and grid realignment in entorhinal cortex. *Nature 446*, 190.

Gaab, J., Rohleder, N., Nater, U. M., & Ehlert, U. (2005). Psychological determinants of the cortisol stress response: The role of anticipatory cognitive appraisal. *Psychoneuroendocrinology, 30*, 599–610.

Gadbois, S. A., & Sturgeon, R. D. (2011). Academic self-handicapping: Relationships with learning specific and general self-perceptions and academic performance over time. *British Journal of Educational Psychology, 81*, 207–222.

Galanter, M. (2007). Spirituality and recovery in 12-step programs: An empirical model. *Journal of Substance Abuse Treatment, 33*, 265–272.

Galef, D. (2001, April 27). The information you provide is anonymous, but what was your name again? *The Chronicle of Higher Education, 47,* p. B5.

Gallese, V., Gernsbacher, M. A., Heyes, C., Hickok, G., & Iacoboni, M. (2011). Mirror neuron forum. *Perspectives on Psychological Science, 6,* 369–407.

Gallup Poll. (2001, June 8). *Americans' belief in psychic and paranormal phenomena is up over last decade.* Washington, DC: The Gallup Organization.

Gami, A. S., Howard, D. E., Olson, E. J., & Somers, V. K. (2005). Day-night pattern of sudden death in obstructive sleep apnea. *New England Journal of Medicine, 353,* 1206–1214.

Gangestad, S. W., Simpson, J. A., Cousins, A. J., Garver-Apgar, C. E., & Christensen, P. N. (2004). Women's preferences for male behavioral displays change across the menstrual cycle. *Psychological Science, 15,* 203–207.

Ganong, L. H., & Coleman, M. (1999). *Changing families, changing responsibilities: Family obligations following divorce and remarriage.* Mahwah, NJ: Erlbaum.

Garb, H. N., Wood, J. M., Lilenfeld, S. O., & Nezworski, M. T. (2005). Roots of the Rorschach controversy. *Clinical Psychology Review, 25,* 97–118.

Garber, J., & Horowitz, J. L. (2002). Depression in children. In I. H. Gotlib & C. L. Hammen (Eds.), *Handbook of depression.* New York: Guilford Press.

Garcia, J. (1990). Learning without memory. *Journal of Cognitive Neuroscience, 2,* 287–305.

Garcia, J. (2003). Psychology is not an enclave. In R. J. Sternberg (Ed.), *Psychologists defying the crowd: Stories of those who battled the establishment and won.* Washington, DC: American Psychological Association.

Garcia, S. M., Weaver, K., Moskowitz, G. B., & Darley, J. M. (2002). Crowded minds: The implicit bystander effect. *Journal of Personality and Social Psychology, 83,* 843–853.

Garcia-Andrade, C., Wall, T. L., & Ehlers, C. L. (1997). The firewater myth and response to alcohol in Mission Indians. *Journal of Psychiatry, 154,* 983–988.

Garcia-Palacios, A., Hoffman, H., & Carlin, A. (2002). Virtual reality in the treatment of spider phobia: A controlled study. *Behavior Research & Therapy, 40,* 983–993.

Gardini, S., Cornoldi, C., De Beni, R., & Venneri, A. (2009). Cognitive and neuronal processes involved in sequential generation of general and specific mental images. *Psychological Research/Psychologische Forschung, 73,* 633–643.

Gardner, B., & O'Connor, D. (2008). A review of the cognitive effects of electroconvulsive therapy in older adults. *The Journal of ECT, 24,* 68–80.

Gardner, E. P., & Kandel, E. R. (2000). Touch. In E. R. Kandel, J. H. Schwartz, & T. M. Jessell (Eds.), *Principles of neural science* (4th ed.). New York: McGraw-Hill.

Gardner, F., & Moore, Z. (2008). Understanding clinical anger and violence: The anger avoidance model. *Behavior Modification, 32,* 897–912.

Gardner, H. (1975). *The shattered mind: The person after brain damage.* New York: Knopf.

Gardner, H. (1999). *Intelligence reframed: Multiple intelligences for the 21st century.* New York: Basic Books.

Gardner, H. (2000). The giftedness matrix: A developmental perspective. In R. C. Friedman &

B. M. Shore (Eds.), *Talents unfolding: Cognition and development.* Washington, DC: American Psychological Association.

Gardner, H. (2005). Scientific psychology: Should we bury it or praise it? In R. J. Sternberg (Ed.), *Unity in psychology: Possibility or pipe dream?* Washington, DC: American Psychological Association.

Garlow, S. J., Purselle, D. C., & Heninger, M. (2007). Cocaine and alcohol use preceding suicide in African American and White adolescents. *Journal of Psychiatric Research, 41,* 530–536.

Garrigan, P., & Kellman, P. (2008, February). Perceptual learning depends on perceptual constancy. *PNAS Proceedings of the National Academy of Sciences of the United States of America, 105,* 2248–2253.

Garwick, G. B. (2007). Intelligence-related terms in mental retardation, learning disability, and gifted/talented professional usage, 1983-2001: The 1992 mental retardation redefinition as natural experiment. *Dissertation Abstracts International Section A: Humanities and Social Sciences, 67*(9-A), 3296.

Gass, C. S., Luis, C. A., Meyers, T. L., & Kuljis, R. O. (2000). Familial Creutzfeldt-Jakob disease: A neuro-psychological case study. *Archives of Clinical Neuropsychology, 15,* 165–175.

Gatchel, R. J., & Weisberg, J. N. (2000). *Personality characteristics of patients with pain.* Washington, DC: APA Books.

Gazzaniga, M. S. (1998, July). The split brain revisited. *Scientific American,* pp. 50–55.

Gazzaniga, M. S., Ivry, R. B., & Mangun, G. R. (2002). *Cognitive neuroscience: The biology of the mind* (2nd ed.). New York: W. W. Norton.

Ge, X., Kim, I. J., Brody, G. H., Conger, R. D., Simons, R. L., Gibbons, E X., et al. (2003). It's about timing and change: Pubertal transition effects on symptoms of major depression among African American youths. *Developmental Psychology, 39,* 430–439.

Gegenfurtner, K. R. (2003). Color vision. *Annual Review of Neuroscience, 26,* 181–206.

Gelbard-Sagiv, H., Mukamel, R., Harel, M., Malach, R., & Fried, I. (March 2008). Internally generated reactivation of single neurons in human hippocampus during free recall. *Science, 322,* 96–101.

Gelfand, M. M. (2000). Sexuality among older women. *Journal of Women's Health and Gender Based Medicine, 9*(Suppl. 1), S15–S20.

Geller, E. (2001). *Working safe: How to help people actively care for health and safety* (2nd ed.). New York: Lewis Publishers.

Geller, E. (2011). Psychological science and safety: Large-scale success at preventing occupational injuries and fatalities. *Current Directions in Psychological Science, 20,* 109–114.

Gelman, R., & Baillargeon, R. (1983). A review of some Piagetian concepts. In J. H. Flavell & E. M. Markman (Eds.), *Handbook of child psychology, Vol. 3: Cognitive development* (4th ed.). New York: Wiley.

Gelstein, S., Yeshurun, Y., Rozenkrantz, L., Shusha, S., Frumin, I., Roth, Y., et al. (2011, January 14). Human tears contain a chemosignal. *Science, 331,* 226–230.

Gennaro, R. J. (2004). *Higher-order theories of consciousness: An anthology.* Amsterdam, Netherlands: John Benjamins.

Genovese, J. E. C. (2006). Piaget, pedagogy, and evolutionary psychology. *Evolutionary Psychology, 4,* 2127–2137.

Gentile, B., Grabe, S., Dolan-Pascoe, B., Twenge, J., Wells, B., & Maitino, A. (2009). Gender differences in domain-specific self-esteem: A meta-analysis. *Review of General Psychology, 13,* 34–45.

Gentner, D., Goldin, S., & Goldin-Meadow, S. (Eds.). (2003). *Language in mind: Advances in the study of language and cognition.* Cambridge, MA: MIT.

George, M. S., Wassermann, E. M., Williams, W. A., Callahan, A., et al. (1995). Daily repetitive transcranial magnetic stimulations (rTMS) improves mood in depression. *Neuroreport: An International Journal for the Rapid Communication of Research in Neuroscience, 6,* 1853–1856.

George, S., & Moselhy, H. (2005). Cocaine-induced trichotillomania. *Addiction, 100,* 255–256.

Gerdes, A., Uhl, G., & Alpers, G. (2009). Spiders are special: Fear and disgust evoked by pictures of arthropods. *Evolution and Human Behavior, 30,* 66–73.

Gershkoff-Stowe, L., Connell, B., & Smith, L. (2006). Priming overgeneralizations in two- and four-year-old children. *Journal of Child Language, 33,* 461–486.

Gerstel, N. (2005, April 8). In search of time. *Science, 308,* 204–205.

Getner, D., & Holyoak, K. J. (1997, January). Reasoning and learning by analogy. *American Psychologist, 52,* 32–34.

Geyer, T., Gokce, A., & Müller, H. J. (2011). Reinforcement of inhibitory positional priming by spatial working memory contents. *Acta Psychologica, 137,* 235–242.

Giacobbi, P. R., Jr., Lynn, T. K., Wetherington, J. M., Jenkins, J., Bodendorf, M., & Langley, B. (2004). Stress and coping during the transition to university for first-year female athletes. *Sports Psychologist, 18,* 1–20.

Giacomini, M., Baylis, F., & Robert, J. (2007). Banking on it: Public policy and the ethics of stem cell research and development. *Social Sciences Medicine, 22,* 88–84.

Giannopoulos, V. L., & Vella-Brodrick, D. A. (2011). Effects of positive interventions and orientations to happiness on subjective well-being. *The Journal of Positive Psychology, 6,* 95–105.

Gibb, K., Tunbridge, D., Chua, A., & Frederickson, N. (2007). Pathways to inclusion: Moving from special school to mainstream. *Educational Psychology in Practice, 23,* 109–127.

Gibbons, R. D., Brown, C. H., Hur, K., Marcus, S. M., Bhamik, D. K., Erkens, J. A., et al. (2007). Early evidence on the effects of regulators' suicidal warnings on SSRI prescriptions and suicide in children and adolescents. *American Journal of Psychiatry, 164,* 1356–1363.

Gibbs, N. (2005, August 8). Being 13. *Time,* pp. 41–55.

Gibbs, W. W. (2002, August.) From mouth to mind. *Scientific American,* p. 26.

Giedd, J., Stockman, M., Weddle, C., Liverpool, M., Alexander-Bloch, A., Wallace, G., et al. (2010). Anatomic magnetic resonance imaging of the developing child and adolescent brain and effects of genetic variation. *Neuropsychology Review, 20,* 349–361.

Gilbert, D. T., McNulty, S. E., Guiliano, T. A., & Benson, J. E. (1992). Blurry words and fuzzy deeds: The attribution of obscure behavior. *Journal of Personality and Social Psychology, 62,* 18–25.

Gilbert, D. T., Miller, A. G., & Ross, L. (1998). Speeding with Ned: A personal view of the correspondence bias. In J. M. Darley & J. Cooper (Eds.), *Attribution and social interaction: The legacy of Edward E. Jones.* Washington, DC: American Psychological Association.

Gilboa, A., Winocur, G., & Rosenbaum, R. S. (2006). Hippocampal contributions to recollection in retrograde and anterograde amnesia. *Hippocampus, 16,* 966–980.

Gilchrist, A., Cowan, N., & Naveh-Benjamin, M. (2009). Investigating the childhood development of working memory using sentences: New evidence for the growth of chunk capacity. *Journal of Experimental Child Psychology, 104,* 252–265.

Gillam, B., Palmisano, S. A., & Govan, D. G. (2011). Depth interval estimates from motion parallax and binocular disparity beyond interaction space. *Perception, 40,* 39–49.

Gilligan, C. (1996). The centrality of relationships in psychological development: A puzzle, some evidence, and a theory. In G. G. Noam & K. W. Fischer (Eds.), *Development and vulnerability in close relationships.* Hillsdale, NJ: Erlbaum.

Gilligan, C. (2004). Recovering psyche: Reflections on life-history and history. *Annual of Psychoanalysis, 32,* 131–147.

Gizer, I. R., Ehlers, C. L., Vieten, C., Seaton-Smith, K. L., Feiler, H. S., Lee, J. V., et al. (2011). Linkage scan of alcohol dependence in the UCSF Family Alcoholism Study. *Drug and Alcohol Dependence, 113,* 125–132.

Gladwell, M. (2004, September 20). Annals of psychology: Personality, plus how corporations figure out who you are. *The New Yorker,* 42–45.

Gladwin, T. (1964). Culture and logical process. In N. Goodenough (Ed.), *Explorations in cultural anthropology: Essays in honor of George Peter Murdoch.* New York: McGraw-Hill.

Glass, K., Flory, K., Hankin, B., Kloos, B., & Turecki, G. (2009). Are coping strategies, social support, and hope associated with psychological distress among Hurricane Katrina survivors? *Journal of Social and Clinical Psychology, 28,* 779–795.

Glicksohn, J., & Nahari, G. (2007). Interacting personality traits? Smoking as a test case. *European Journal of Personality, 21,* 225–234.

Glisky, E. L. (2007). Changes in cognitive function in human aging. In D. R. Riddle (Ed.), *Brain aging: Models, methods, and mechanisms.* Boca Raton, FL: CRC Press.

Goffin, R. D., Jelley, R. B., & Wagner, S. H. (2003). Is halo helpful? Effects of inducing halo on performance rating accuracy. *Social Behavior and Personality, 31,* 625–636.

Goin, M. K. (2005). A current perspective on the psychotherapies. *Psychiatric Services, 56,* 255–257.

Gold, P. E., Cahill, L., & Wenk, G. L. (2002). Ginkgo biloba: A cognitive enhancer? *Psychological Science in the Public Interest, 3,* 2–7.

Golden, R. N., Gaynes, B. N., Ekstrom, R. D., Hamer, R. M., Jacobsen, F. M., Suppes, T., et al. (2005). The efficacy of light therapy in the treatment of mood disorders: A review and meta-analysis of the evidence. *The American Journal of Psychiatry, 162,* 656–662.

Golden, W. L. (2006). Hypnotherapy for anxiety, phobias and psychophysiological disorders. In R. A. Chapman (Ed.), *The clinical use of hypnosis in cognitive behavior therapy: A practitioner's casebook.* New York: Springer Publishing.

Golder, S. A., & Macy, M. W. (2011, September 30). Diurnal and seasonal mood vary with work, sleep, and day length across diverse cultures. *Science, 333,* 1878–1881.

Goldfried, M. R., & Pachankis, J. E. (2007). On the next generation of process research. *Clinical Psychology Review, 27,* 760–768.

Goldstein, I. (2000). Female sexual arousal disorder: New insights. *International Journal of Impotence Research, 12*(Suppl. 4), S152–S157.

Goldstein, S. N. (2006). The exploration of spirituality and identity status in adolescence. *Dissertation Abstracts International: Section B: The Sciences and Engineering, 67*(6-B), 3481.

Goleman, D. (1988, January 21). Doctor and patient; physicians may bungle key part of treatment: The medical interview. *The New York Times,* p. B16.

Goleman, D. (1993, July 21). "Expert" babies found to teach others. *The New York Times,* p. C10.

Golimbet, V. E., Alfimova, M. V., Gritsenko, I. K., & Ebstein, R. P. (2007). Relationship between dopamine system genes and extraversion and novelty seeking. *Neuroscience Behavior and Physiology, 37,* 601–606.

Golombok, S., Cook, R., Bish, A., & Murray, C. (1995). Families created by the new reproductive technologies: Quality of parenting and social and emotional development of the children. *Child Development, 66,* 285–298.

Gontier, N. (2008). Genes, brains, and language: An epistemological examination of how genes can underlie human cognitive behavior. *Review of General Psychology, 12,* 170–180.

Gontkovsky, S. T. (2005). Neurobiological bases and neuropsychological correlates of aggression and violence. In J. P. Morgan (Ed.), *Psychology of aggression.* Hauppauge, NY: Nova Science Publishers.

Gontkovsky, S. T., & Beatty, W. W. (2006). Practical methods for the clinical assessment of information processing speed. *International Journal of Neuroscience, 116,* 1317–1325.

Goode, E. (1999, April 13). If things taste bad, "phantoms" may be at work. *The New York Times,* pp. D1–D2.

Goodman, G., & Quas, J. (2008). Repeated interviews and children's memory: It's more than just how many. *Current Directions in Psychological Science, 17,* 386–390.

Goodman, W. K., Rudorfer, M. V., & Maser, J. D. (2000). *Obsessive-compulsive disorder: Contemporary issues in treatment.* Mahwah, NJ: Lawrence Erlbaum Associates.

Goodwin, R., Costa, P., & Adonu, J. (2004). Social support and its consequences: 'Positive' and 'deficiency' values and their implications for support and self-esteem. *British Journal of Social Psychology, 43,* 465–474.

Goodwin, R. D., & Hamilton, S. P. (2003). Lifetime comorbidity of antisocial personality disorder and anxiety disorders among adults in the community. *Psychiatry Research, 117,* 159–166.

Gooren, L. (2006). The biology of human psychosexual differentiation. *Hormones and Behavior, 50,* 589–601.

Gopie, N., Craik, F. M., & Hasher, L. (2011). A double dissociation of implicit and explicit memory in younger and older adults. *Psychological Science, 22,* 634–640.

Gordon, D., & Heimberg, R. G. (2011). Reliability and validity of DSM-IV generalized anxiety disorder features. *Journal of Anxiety Disorders, 25,* 813–821.

Gossop, M., Stewart, D., & Marsden, J. (2008). Attendance at Narcotics Anonymous and Alcoholics Anonymous meetings, frequency of attendance and substance use outcomes after residential treatment for drug dependence: A 5-year follow-up study. *Addiction, 103,* 119–125.

Gotlib, I. H., Krasnoperova, E., Yue, D. N., & Joorman, J. (2004). Attentional biases for negative interpersonal stimuli in clinical depression. *Journal of Abnormal Psychology, 113,* 127–135.

Gottesman, I. I. (1991). *Schizophrenia genesis: The origins of madness.* New York: Freeman.

Gottesman, I. I., & Hanson, D. R. (2005). Human development: Biological and genetic processes. *Annual Review of Psychology, 56,* 263–286.

Gottlieb, D. A. (2004). Acquisition with partial and continuous reinforcement in pigeon autoshaping. *Learning and Behavior, 32,* 321–334.

Gottlieb, D. A. (2006). Effects of partial reinforcement and time between reinforced trials on terminal response rate in pigeon autoshaping. *Behavioural Processes, 72,* 6–13.

Gould, E., Reeves, A. J., Graziano, M. S. A., & Gross, C. G. (1999, October 15). Neurogenesis in the neocortex of adult primates. *Science,* 548–552.

Gould, R. L. (1978). *Transformations.* New York: Simon & Schuster.

Gradinaru, V., Mogri, M., Thompson, K. R., Henderson, J. M., & Deisseroth, K. (2009). Optical deconstruction of Parkinsonian neural circuitry. *Science, 324,* 354–359.

Grady, D., & Altman, L. K. (2008, December 29). Lessons for other smokers in Obama's efforts to quit. *The New York Times,* p. A12.

Graham, C. A., Bancroft, J., & Doll, H. A. (2007). Does oral contraceptive-induced reduction in free testosterone adversely affect the sexuality or mood of women? *Psychoneuroendocrinology, 32,* 246–255.

Grahek, N. (2007). *Feeling pain and being in pain* (2nd ed.). Cambridge, MA: MIT Press.

Granic, I., Hollenstein, T., & Dishion, T. (2003). Longitudinal analysis of flexibility and reorganization in early adolescence: A dynamic systems study of family interactions. *Developmental Psychology, 39,* 606–617.

Grann, J. D. (2007). Confidence in knowledge past: An empirical basis for a differential decay theory of very long-term memory monitoring. *Dissertation Abstracts International Section A: Humanities and Social Sciences, 67,* 2462.

Grant, A. (2008). Does intrinsic motivation fuel the prosocial fire? Motivational synergy in predicting persistence, performance, and productivity. *Journal of Applied Psychology, 93,* 48–58.

Grant, D. M., & Wingate, L. R. (2011). Cognitive-behavioral therapy. In C. Silverstein & C. Silverstein (Eds.), *The initial psychotherapy interview: A gay man seeks treatment.* Amsterdam Netherlands: Elsevier.

Gray, G. C. (2006). The regulation of corporate violations: Punishment, compliance, and the blurring of responsibility. *British Journal of Criminology, 46,* 875–892.

Graziano, M. S., Taylor, C. S., & Moore, T. (2002). Complex movements evoked by microstimulation of precentral cortex. *Neuron, 34,* 841–851.

Greely, H., Sahakian, B., Harris, J., Kessler, R. C., Gazzaniga, M., Campbell, P., & Farah, M. J. (2008). Towards responsible use of cognitive-enhancing drugs by the healthy. *Nature, 456,* 702–705.

Green, B. G., & George, P. (2004). Thermal taste predicts higher responsiveness to chemical taste and flavor. *Chemical Senses, 29,* 617–628.

Green, J., Lynn, S., & Montgomery, G. (2008, January). Gender-related differences in hypnosis-based treatments for smoking: A follow-up meta-analysis. *American Journal of Clinical Hypnosis, 50,* 259–271.

Greenberg, G., & Rosenheck, R. (2008). Jail incarceration, homelessness, and mental health: A national study. *Psychiatric Services, 59,* 170–177.

Greenberg, R., & Goldman, E. (2009). Antidepressants, psychotherapy or their combination: Weighing options for depression treatments. *Journal of Contemporary Psychotherapy, 39,* 83–91.

Greenberg, R. M., & Kellner, C. H. (2005). Electroconvulsive therapy: A selected review. *The American Journal of Geriatric Psychiatry, 13,* 268–281.

Greene, J. D., & Paxton, J. M. (2009). Patterns of neural activity associated with honest and dishonest moral decisions. *PNAS Proceedings of the National Academy of Sciences of the United States of America, 106(30),* 12506–12511.

Greene, J. D., Sommerville, R. B., Nystrom, L. E., Darley, J. M., et al. (2001, September 14). An fMRI investigation of emotional engagement in moral judgment. *Science, 293,* 2105–2108.

Greenfield, S. (2002). Mind, brain and consciousness. *British Journal of Psychiatry, 181,* 91–93.

Greenspan, S. (2006). Functional concepts in mental retardation: Finding the natural essence of an artificial category. *Exceptionality, 14,* 205–224.

Greenwald, A. G., Draine S. C., & Abrams, R. L. (1996, September 20). Three cognitive markers of unconscious semantic activation. *Science, 272,* 1699–1702.

Greenwald, A. G., Nosek, B. A., & Banaji, M. R. (2003). Understanding and using the Implicit Association Test: 1. An improved scoring algorithm. *Journal of Personality and Social Psychology 85,* 197–216.

Greenwald, A. G., Nosek, B. A., & Sriram, N. (2006). Consequential validity of the implicit association test: Comment on Blanton and Jaccard. *American Psychologist, 61,* 56–61.

Greenwald, A. G., Poehlman, T., Uhlmann, E., & Banaji, M. (2009). Understanding and using the Implicit Association Test: III. Meta-analysis of predictive validity. *Journal of Personality and Social Psychology, 97,* 17–41.

Greer, R. D., Dudek-Singer, J., & Gautreaux, G. (2006). Observational learning. *International Journal of Psychology, 41,* 486–499.

Grefkes, C., & Fink, G. R. (2011). Reorganization of cerebral networks after stroke: New insights from neuroimaging with connectivity approaches. *Brain, 134,* 1264–1276.

Gregory, R. L. (1978). *The psychology of seeing* (3rd ed.). New York: McGraw-Hill.

Gregory, R. L. (2008). Emmert's Law and the moon illusion. *Spatial Vision, 21,* 407–720.

Grigorenko, E. (2009). Speaking genes or genes for speaking? Deciphering the genetics of speech and language. *Journal of Child Psychology and Psychiatry, 50,* 116–125.

Grigoriadis, S., & Ravitz, P. (2007). An approach to interpersonal psychotherapy for postpartum depression: Focusing on interpersonal changes. *Canadian Family Physician, 53,* 1469–1475.

Grilo, C. M., Sanislow, C. A., Shea, M., Skodol, A. E., Stout, R. L., Pagano, M. E., & . . . McGlashan, T. H. (2003). The Natural Course of Bulimia Nervosa and Eating Disorder not Otherwise Specified is not Influenced by Personality Disorders. *International Journal of Eating Disorders, 34,* 319–330.

Grimes, T., & Bergen, L. (2008, April). The epistemological argument against a causal relationship between media violence and sociopathic behavior among psychologically well viewers. *American Behavioral Scientist, 51,* 1137–1154.

Grimm, J. W. (2011). Craving. In M. C. Olmstead & M. C. Olmstead (Eds.), *Animal models of drug addiction.* Totowa, NJ: Humana Press.

Gronholm, P., Rinne, J. O., Vorobyev, V., & Laine, M. (2005). Naming of newly learned objects: A PET activation study. *Brain Research and Cognitive Brain Research, 14,* 22–28.

Gross, D. M. (2006). *The secret history of emotion: From Aristotle's rhetoric to modern brain science.* Chicago: University of Chicago Press.

Grossmann, T., Striano, T., & Friederici, A. D. (2007). Developmental changes in infants' processing of happy and angry facial expressions: A neurobehavioral study. *Brain and Cognition, 64,* 30–41.

Groves, R. M., Singer, E., Lepkowski, J. M., Heeringa, S. G., & Alwin, D. F. (2004). In S. J. House, F. T. Juster, et al. (Eds.), *A telescope on society: Survey research and social science at the University of Michigan and beyond.* Ann Arbor, MI: University of Michgan Press.

Grucza, R., Norberg, K., & Bierut, L. (2009). Binge drinking among youths and young adults in the United States: 1979-2006. *Journal of the American Academy of Child & Adolescent Psychiatry, 48,* 692–702.

Grunwald, T., Boutros, N. N., Pezer, N., von Oertzen, J., Fernandez, G., Schaller, C., & Elger, C. E. (2003). Neuronal substrates of sensory gating within the human brain. *Biological Psychiatry, 15,* 511–519.

Guadagno, R. E., & Cialdini, R. B. (2002). Online persuasion: An examination of gender differences in computer-mediated interpersonal influence [Special issue: Groups and Internet]. *Group Dynamics, 6,* 38–51.

Guastella, A., Mitchell, P., & Dadds, M. (2008, January). Oxytocin increases gaze to the eye region of human faces. *Biological Psychiatry, 63,* 3–5.

Guéguen, N., Marchand, M., Pascual, A., & Lourel, M. (2008). Foot-in-the-door technique using a courtship request: A field experiment. *Psychological Reports, 103,* 529–534.

Guerrero, L., La Valley, A., & Farinelli, L. (2008, October). The experience and expression of anger, guilt, and sadness in marriage: An equity theory explanation. *Journal of Social and Personal Relationships, 25,* 699–724.

Guiard, B. P., Chenu, F., Mansari, M., & Blier, P. (2011). Characterization of the electrophysiological properties of triple reuptake inhibitors on monoaminergic neurons. *International Journal of Neuropsychopharmacology, 14,* 211–223.

Guilleminault, C., Kirisoglu, C., Bao, G., Arias, V., Chan, A., & Li, K. K. (2005). Adult chronic sleepwalking and its treatment based on poly-somnography. *Brain, 128* (Pt. 5), 1062–1069.

Guldemond, H., Bosker, R., Kuyper, H., & van der Werf, G. (2007). Do highly gifted students really have problems? [Special issue: Current research on giftedness: International perspectives]. *Educational Research and Evaluation, 13,* 555–568.

Gurin, P. (2006). Informing theory from practice and applied research. *Journal of Social Issues, 62,* 621–628.

Gwynn, M. I., & Spanos, N. P. (1996). Hypnotic responsiveness, nonhypnotic suggestibility, and responsiveness to social influence. In R. G. Kunzendorf, N. P. Spahos, & B. Wallace (Eds.), *Hypnosis and imagination.* Amityville, NY: Baywood.

Haberstick, B. C., Schmitz, S., Young, S. E., & Hewitt, J. K. (2005). Contributions of genes and environments to stability and change in externalizing and internalizing problems during elementary and middle school. *Behavior Genetics, 35,* 381–396.

Hackam, D. G. (2007). Translating animal research into clinical benefit. *British Medical Journal, 334,* 163–164.

Hager, E. (2010, June 18). Bronx is up? Innate sense may tell us. *The New York Times,* A-21.

Haier, R. J. (2011). Biological basis of intelligence. In R. J. Sternberg & S. Kaufman (Eds.), *The Cambridge handbook of intelligence.* New York: Cambridge University Press.

Haier, R. J., Colom, R., Schroeder, D. H., Condon, C. A., Tang, C., Eaves, E., et al. (2009). Gray matter and intelligence factors: Is there a neuro-g? *Intelligence, 37,* 136–144.

Haley, W. E., Clair, J. M., & Saulsberry, K. (1992). Family caregiver satisfaction with medical care of their demented relatives. *Gerontologist, 32,* 219–226.

Halford, S. (2006). Collapsing the boundaries? Fatherhood, organization and home-working. *Gender, Work & Organization, 13,* 383–402.

Halkitis, P. (2009). *Methamphetamine addiction: Biological foundations, psychological factors, and social consequences.* Washington, DC: American Psychological Association.

Hall, P. J., Chong, C., McNaughton, N., & Corr, P. J. (2011). An economic perspective on the reinforcement sensitivity theory of personality. *Personality and Individual Differences, 51,* 242–247.

Hallschmid, M., Benedict, C., Born, J., Fehm, H., & Kern, W. (2004). Manipulating central nervous mechanisms of food intake and body weight regulation by intranasal administration of neuropeptides in man. *Physiology and Behavior, 83,* 55–64.

Halpern, D., & Riggio, H. (2002). *Thinking critically about critical thinking.* Mahwah, NJ: Erlbaum.

Halpern, D. F. (2005). Psychology at the intersection of work and family: Recommendations for employers, working families, and policymakers. *American Psychologist, 60,* 397–409.

Halpern, D. F. (2010, December, 3). How neuromythologies support sex role stereotypes. *Science, 330,* 1320–1322.

Halpert, J. (2003, April 28). What do patients want? *Newsweek,* pp. 63–64.

Hamani, Y., Sciaki-Tamir, Y., Deri-Hasid, R., Miller-Pogrund, T., Milwidsky, A., & Haimov-Kochman, R. (2007). Misconceptions about oral contraception pills among adolescents and physicians. *Human Reproduction, 22,* 3078–3083.

Hamann, S. (2001). Cognitive and neural mechanisms of emotional memory. *Trends in Cognitive Sciences, 5,* 394–400.

Hamann, S. B., Ely, T. D., Hoffman, J. M., & Kilts, C. D. (2002). Ecstasy and agony: Activation of human amygdala in positive and negative emotion. *Psychological Science, 13,* 135–141.

Hambleton, R. K. (2006). Psychometric models, test designs and item types for the next generation of educational and psychological tests. In D. Bartram, & R. K. Hambleton, *Computer-based testing and the Internet: Issues and advances.* New York: John Wiley & Sons.

Hamer, M., Taylor, A., & Steptoe, A. (2006). The effect of acute aerobic exercise on stress related blood pressure responses: A systematic review and meta-analysis. *Bi Psychology, 71,* 183–190.

Hamilton, A. C., & Martin, R. C. (2007). Semantic short-term memory deficits and resolution of interference: A case for inhibition. In D. S. Gorfein & C. M. Macleod (Eds.), *Inhibition in cognition.* Washington, DC: American Psychological Association.

Hamilton, W. L., Biener, L., & Brennan, R. T. (2007). Do local tobacco regulations influence perceived smoking norms? Evidence from adult and youth surveys in Massachusetts. *Health Education Research, 23,* 709–722.

Hammond, C., & Gold, M. (2008). Caffeine dependence, withdrawal, overdose and treatment: A review. *Directions in Psychiatry, 28,* 177–190.

Hammond, D. C. (2007, April). Review of the efficacy of clinical hypnosis with headaches and migraines [Special issue: Evidence-based practice clinical hypnosis—part 1]. *International Journal of Clinical and Experimental Hypnosis 55,* 207–219.

Haney, C., & Zimbardo, P. (2009). Persistent dispositionalism in interactionist clothing: Fundamental attribution error in explaining prison abuse. *Personality and Social Psychology Bulletin, 35,* 807–814.

Hangya, B., Tihanyi, B. T., Entz, L., Fabo, D., Eröss, L., Wittner, L., et al. (2011). Complex propagation patterns characterize human cortical activity during slow-wave sleep. *The Journal of Neuroscience, 31,* 8770–8779.

Hanley, S. J., & Abell, S. C. (2002). Maslow and relatedness: Creating an interpersonal model of self-actualization. *Journal of Humanistic Psychology, 42,* 37–56.

Hannon, E. E., & Johnson, S. P. (2005). Infants use meter to categorize rhythms and melodies: Implications for musical structure learning. *Cognitive Psychology, 50,* 354–377.

Harding, D. J., & Jencks, C. (2003). Changing attitudes toward premarital sex: Cohort, period, and aging effects. *The Public Opinion Quarterly, 67,* 211–226.

Hardison, D. M. (2006). Review of phonetics and phonology in language comprehension and production: Differences and similarities. *Studies in Second Language Acquisition, 28,* 138–140.

Hardt, J., Sidor, A., Nickel, R., Kappis, B., Petrak, P., & Egle, U. (2008). Childhood adversities and suicide attempts: A retrospective study. *Journal of Family Violence, 23,* 713–718.

Hardy, L. T. (2007). Attachment theory and reactive attachment disorder: Theoretical perspectives

and treatment implications. *Journal of Child and Adolescent Psychiatric Nursing, 20,* 27–39.

Harlow, H. F., & Zimmerman, R. R. (1959). Affectional responses in the infant monkey. *Science, 130,* 421–432.

Harlow, J. M. (1869). Recovery from the passage of an iron bar through the head. *Massachusetts Medical Society Publication, 2,* 329–347.

Harmon-Jones, E., & Winkielman, P. (2007). *Social neuroscience: Integrating biological and psychological explanations of social behavior.* New York, Guilford Press.

Harold, G. T., Fincham, F. D., Osborne, L. N., & Conger, R. D. (1997). Mom and dad are at it again: Adolescent perceptions of marital conflict and adolescent psychological distress. *Developmental Psychology, 33,* 333–350.

Harper, T. (1978, November 15). It's not true about people 65 or over. *Green Bay Press-Gazette* (Wisconsin), p. D-1.

Hart, B., & Risley, T. R. (1997). Use of language by three-year-old children. Courtesy of Drs. Betty Hart and Todd Risley, University of Kansas.

Hartmann, E. (1967). *The biology of dreaming.* Springfield, IL: Charles C Thomas Publisher.

Hartung, C. M., & Widiger, T. A. (1998). Gender differences in the diagnosis of mental disorders: Conclusions and controversies of the DSM-IV. *Psychological Bulletin, 123,* 260–278.

Harvard Mental Health Letter (HMHL). (1994, March). Brief psychodynamic therapy—Part I. *Harvard Mental Health Letter,* p. 10.

Harvey, J. H., Wenzel, A., & Sprecher, S. (Eds.). (2004). *The handbook of sexuality in close relationships.* Mahwah, NJ: Lawrence Erlbaum Associates.

Haselton, M. G., & Gildersleeve, K. (2011). Can men detect ovulation? *Current Directions in Psychological Science, 20,* 87–92.

Haslam, C., & Lawrence, W. (2004). Health-related behavior and beliefs of pregnant smokers. *Health Psychology, 23,* 486–491.

Hastings, R. P., & Oakford, S. (2003). Student teachers' attitudes towards the inclusion of children with special needs. *Educational Psychology, 23,* 87–94.

Hatsopoulos, N. G., & Donoghue, J. P. (2009). The Science of Neural Interface Systems. *Annual Review of Neuroscience, 19,* 245–251.

Hauke, C. (2006). The unconscious: Personal and collective. In R. K. Papadopoulos (Ed.), *The handbook of Jungian psychology: Theory, practice and applications.* New York: Routledge.

Hauser, M. D. (2000). The sound and the fury: Primate vocalizations as reflections of emotion and thought. In N. L. Wallin & B. Merker (Eds.), *The origins of music.* Cambridge, MA: MIT.

Havermans, R. C., Mulkens, S., Nederkoorn, C., & Jansen, A. (2007). The efficacy of cue exposure with response prevention in extinguishing drug and alcohol cue reactivity. *Behavioral Interventions, 22,* 121–135.

Haviland-Jones, J., & Chen, D. (1999, April 17). *Human olfactory perception.* Paper presented at the Association for Chemoreception Sciences, Sarasota, Florida.

Haviland-Jones, J. M., & Wilson, P. J. (2008). A 'nose' for emotion: Emotional information and challenges in odors and semiochemicals. In M. Lewis, J. M. Haviland-Jones, & L. G. Barrett (Eds.), *Handbook of emotions* (3rd ed.). New York: Guilford Press.

Hawkes, Christopher H., & Doty, R. L. (2009). *The neurology of olfaction.* Cambridge, UK: Cambridge University Press.

Hayflick, L. (2007). Biological aging is no longer an unsolved problem. *Annals of the New York Academy of Sciences, 1100,* 1–13.

Haynes, P., Nixon, J. C., & West, J. F. (1990). Time perception and consumer behaviour: Some cross-cultural implications. *International Journal of Consumer Studies, 14,* 14–27.

Hays, P. A. (2008). *Addressing cultural complexities in practice: Assessment, diagnosis, and therapy* (2nd ed.). Washington, DC: American Psychological Association.

Hayward, R., & Elliott, M. (2011). Subjective and objective fit in religious congregations: Implications for well-being. *Group Processes & Intergroup Relations, 14,* 127–139.

Health Pages. (2003, March 13). Just what the doctor ordered. Retrieved from http://www.thehealthpages.com/articles/ar-drord.html

Heath, R. A. (2006). *The Praeger handbook of transsexuality: Changing gender to match mindset.* Westport, CT: Praeger Publishers/Greenwood Publishing.

Heatherton, T., & Sargent, J. (2009). Does watching smoking in movies promote teenage smoking? *Current Directions in Psychological Science, 18,* 63–67.

Hecht, J. M. (2007). *The happiness myth: Why what we think is right is wrong. A history of what really makes us happy.* New York: HarperSanFrancisco/HarperCollins.

Hedges, D. W., Brown, B. L., Shwalk, D. A., Godfrey, K., & Larcher, A. M. (2007). The efficacy of selective serotonin reuptake inhibitors in adult social anxiety disorder: A meta-analysis of double-blind, placebo-controlled trials. *Journal of Psychopharmacology, 21,* 102–111.

Hegarty, P. (2007). From genius inverts to gendered intelligence: Lewis Terman and the power of the norm [Special issue: Power matters: Knowledge politics in the history of psychology]. *History of Psychology, 10,* 132–155.

Hegarty, P., & Massey, S. (2007). Anti-homosexual prejudice . . . as opposed to what? Queer theory and the social psychology of anti-homosexual attitudes. *Journal of Homosexuality, 52,* 47–71.

Heilman, K. M. (2005). *Creativity and the brain.* New York: Psychology Press.

Heinrichs, R. W. (2005). The primacy of cognition in schizophrenia. *American Psychologist, 60,* 229–242.

Heitzmann, C. A., Merluzzi, T. V., Jean-Pierre, P., Roscoe, J. A., Kirsh, K. L., & Passik, S. D. (2011). Assessing self-efficacy for coping with cancer: Development and psychometric analysis of the brief version of the Cancer Behavior Inventory (CBI-B). *Psycho-Oncology, 20,* 302–312.

Heller, S. (2005). *Freud A to Z.* New York: Wiley.

Helmbold, N., Troche, S., & Rammsayer, T. (2007). Processing of temporal and nontemporal information as predictors of psychometric intelligence: A structural-equation-modeling approach. *Journal of Personality, 75,* 985–1006.

Helmuth, L. (2000, August 25). Synapses shout to overcome distance. *Science, 289,* 1273.

Henckes, N. (2011). Reforming psychiatric institutions in the mid-twentieth century: A framework for analysis. *History of Psychiatry, 22,* 164–181.

Henderson, J., Kesmodel, U., & Gray, R. (2007). Systematic review of the fetal effects of prenatal binge-drinking. *Journal of Epidemiology and Community Health, 61,* 1069–1073.

Henderson, N. D. (1982). Correlations in IQ for pairs of people with varying degrees of genetic relatedness and shared environment. *Annual Review of Psychology, 33,* 219–243.

Hennig-Fast, K., Meister, F., Frodl, T., Beraldi, A., Padberg, F., Engel, R., et al. (2008). The case of persistent retrograde amnesia following a dissociative fugue: Neuropsychological and neurofunctional underpinnings of loss of autobiographical memory and self-awareness. *Neuropsychologia, 46*(12), 2993–3005.

Henningsen, D. D., Henningsen, M. L., & Eden, J. (2006). Examining the symptoms of group-think and retrospective sensemaking. *Small Group Research, 37,* 36–64.

Henrich, J., Heine, S., & Norenzayan, A. (2010). The weirdest people in the world? *Behavioral and Brain Sciences, 33,* 61–83.

Henry, D., McClellen, D., Rosenthal, L., Dedrick, D., & Gosdin, M. (2008, February). Is sleep really for sissies? Understanding the role of work in insomnia in the US. *Social Science & Medicine, 66,* 715–726.

Hentschel, U., Smith, G., Draguns, J. G., & Elhers, W. (2004). *Defense mechanisms: Theoretical, research and clinical perspectives.* Oxford, England: Elsevier Science.

Herbenick, D., Reece, M., Sanders, S., Dodge, B., Ghassemi, A., & Fortenberry, J. (2009). Prevalence and characteristics of vibrator use by women in the United States: Results from a nationally representative study. *Journal of Sexual Medicine, 6,* 1857–1866.

Herbert, W. (2011). *On second thought: Outsmarting your mind's hard-wired habits.* New York: Broadway.

Herrán, A., Carrera, M., & Sierra-Biddle, D. (2006). Panic disorder and the onset of agoraphobia. *Psychiatry and Clinical Neurosciences, 60,* 395–396.

Herrington, D. M., & Howard, T. D. (2003). From presumed benefit to potential harm—Hormone therapy and heart disease. *New England Journal of Medicine, 349,* 519–521.

Herrnstein, R. J., & Murray, D. (1994). *The bell curve.* New York: Free Press.

Hertzog, C., Kramer, A., Wilson, R., & Lindenberger, U. (2008). Enrichment effects on adult cognitive development: Can the functional capacity of older adults be preserved and enhanced? *Psychological Science in the Public Interest, 9,* 1–65.

Herzberg, L. (2009). Direction, causation, and appraisal theories of emotion. *Philosophical Psychology, 22,* 167–186.

Hess, M. J., Houg, S., & Tammaro, E. (2007). The experience of four individuals with paraplegia enrolled in an outpatient interdisciplinary sexuality program. *Sexuality and Disability, 25,* 189–195.

Hess, T. M., Hinson, J. T., & Statham, J. A. (2004). Explicit and implicit stereotype activation effects on memory: Do age and awareness moderate the impact of priming? *Psychology and Aging, 19,* 495–505.

Heyman, G. D., & Diesendruck, G. (2002). The Spanish *ser/estar* distinction in bilingual children's reasoning about human psychological characteristics. *Developmental Psychology, 38,* 407–417.

Hibbard, P. (2007, February). A statistical model of binocular disparity. *Visual Cognition, 15,* 149–165.

Hiby, E. F., Rooney, N. J., & Bradshaw, J. W. S. (2004). Dog training methods: Their use, effectiveness and interaction with behaviour and welfare. *Animal Welfare, 13,* 63–69.

Hilarski, C. (2007). Antisocial personality disorder. In B. A. Thyer & J. S. Wodarski (Eds.), *Social work in mental health: An evidence-based approach.* Hoboken, NJ: John Wiley & Sons.

Hilgard, E. (1992). Disassociation and theories of hypnosis. In E. Fromm & M. E. Nash (Eds.), *Contemporary hypnosis research.* New York: Guilford.

Hillix, W. A. (2007). The past, present, and possible futures of animal language research. In D. A. Washburn (Ed.), *Primate perspectives on behavior and cognition.* Washington, DC: American Psychological Association.

Hines, M. (2004) *Brain gender.* New York: Oxford University Press.

Hinterberger, T., Schöner, J., & Halsband, U. (2011). Analysis of electrophysiological state patterns and changes during hypnosis induction. *International Journal of Clinical and Experimental Hypnosis, 59,* 165–179.

Hirsh, I. J., & Watson, C. S. (1996). Auditory psychophysics and perception. *Annual Review of Psychology, 47,* 461–484.

Hoare, P., & Machin, M. (2010). The impact of reemployment on access to the latent and manifest benefits of employment and mental health. *Journal of Occupational and Organizational Psychology, 83,* 759–770.

Hobfoll, S. E., Freedy, J. R., Green B. L., & Solomon, S. D. (1996). Coping in reaction to extreme stress: The roles of resource loss and resource availability. In M. Zeidner & N. S. Endler (Eds.), *Handbook of coping: Theory, research, applications.* New York: Wiley.

Hobfoll, S. E., Hall, B. J., & Canetti-Nisim, D. (2007). Refining our understanding of traumatic growth in the face of terrorism: Moving from meaning cognitions to doing what is meaningful. *Applied Psychology: An International Review, 56,* 345–366.

Hobson, J. A. (1989). *Sleep.* New York: W. H. Freeman.

Hobson, J. A. (2005). In bed with Mark Solms? What a nightmare! A reply to Domhoff. *Dreaming, 15,* 21–29.

Hobson, J. A. (2007). States of Conciseness: Normal and abnormal variation. In P. D. Zelazo, M. Moscovitch, et al. (Eds.), *The Cambridge Handbook of Consciousness.* London: Cambridge University Press.

Hobson, K. (2011, March 28). How can you help the medicine go down? *The Wall Street Journal.* R10.

Hochschild, A. (2001, February). A generation without public passion. *Atlantic Monthly,* pp. 33–42.

Hock, H. S., & Ploeger, A. (2006). Linking dynamical perceptual decisions at different levels of description in motion pattern formation: Psychophysics. *Perception & Psychophysics, 68,* 505–514.

Hoff, E. (2003). Language development in childhood. In R. M. Lerner et al. (Eds.), *Handbook of psychology: Developmental psychology* (Vol. 6). New York: Wiley.

Hoff, E. (2008). *Language development.* New York: Wadsworth.

Hoffer, T. B., Selfa, L., Welch, V., Jr., Williams, K., Hess, M., Friedman, J., et al. (2005, March 8). *Doctorate recipients from United States universities: Summary report 2003.* Chicago: NORC at the University of Chicago.

Hofmann, S. G. (2007). Enhancing exposure-based therapy from a translational research perspective. *Behaviour Research and Therapy, 45,* 1987–2001.

Hofmann, W., Gschwendner, T., Castelli, L., & Schmitt, M. (2008). Implicit and explicit attitudes and interracial interaction: The moderating role of situationally available control resources. *Group Processes & Intergroup Relations, 11,* 69–87.

Hogan, J., Davies, S., & Hogan, R. (2007). Generalizing personality-based validity evidence. In S. M. McPhail (Ed.), *Alternative validation strategies: Developing new and leveraging existing validity evidence.* Hoboken, NJ: John Wiley & Sons.

Hogg, M. A. (2006). Social identity theory. In P. J. Burke (Ed.), *Contemporary social psychological theories.* Palo Alto, CA: Stanford University Press.

Hogg, M. A., & Hains, S. C. (2001). Intergroup relations and group solidarity: Effects of group identification and social beliefs on depersonalized attraction. In M. A. Hogg & D. Abrams (Eds.), *Intergroup relations: Essential readings.* New York: Psychology Press.

Høglend, P. P., Dahl, H. S., Hersoug, A. G., Lorentzen, S. S., & Perry, J. C. (2011). Long-term effects of transference interpretation in dynamic psychotherapy of personality disorders. *European Psychiatry, 26,* 419–424.

Holden, C. (2003, January 17). Deconstructing schizophrenia. *Science, 299,* 333–335.

Holden, C. (2007, June 29). Embryonic stem cells. Stem cell science advances as politics stall. *Science, 316,* 1825.

Holden, L. M. (2005). Complex adaptive systems: Holland, J. C., & Lewis, S. (2001). *The human side of cancer: Living with hope, coping with uncertainty.* New York: Quill.

Holler, G. D. (2006). Relations of hypnotic susceptibility, absorption, imagery, sexual fantasy, sexual daydreaming, and social desirability to sexual satisfaction. *Dissertation Abstracts International: Section B: The Sciences and Engineering, 67,* 3453.

Holleran, S., Mehl, M., & Levitt, S. (2009). Eavesdropping on social life: The accuracy of stranger ratings of daily behavior from thin slices of natural conversations. *Journal of Research in Personality, 43,* 660–672.

Hollingworth, H. L. (1943/1990). *Leta Stetter Hollingworth: A biography.* Boston: Anker.

Hollins, K. (2007). Consequences of antenatal mental health problems for child health and development. *Current Opinions on Obstetric Gynecology, 19,* 568–573.

Hollis, K. L. (1997, September). Contemporary research on Pavlovian conditioning: A "new" functional analysis. *American Psychologist, 52,* 956–965.

Hollon, S. D., Thase, M. E., & Markowitz, J. C. (2002). Treatment and prevention of depression. *Psychological Science in the Public Interest, 3,* 39–77.

Holloway, L. (2000, December 16). Chief of New York City schools plans to revamp bilingual study. *The New York Times,* p. A1.

Holmes, A., Yang, R. J., Lesch, K. P., Crawley, J. N., & Murphy, D. L. (2003). Mice lacking the serotonin transporter exhibit 5-HT-sub(1A) receptor-mediated abnormalities in tests for anxiety-like behavior. *Neuropsychopharmacology, 28,* 2077–2088.

Holowka, S., & Petitto, L. A. (2002, August 30). Left hemisphere cerebral specialization for babies while babbling. *Science, 297,* 1515.

Holt, M., & Jahn, R. (2004, March, 26). Synaptic vesicles in the fast lane. *Science, 303,* 1986–1987.

Holtz, J. (2011). *Applied clinical neuropsychology: An introduction.* New York: Springer Publishing Co.

Hongchun, W., & Ming, L. (2006). About the research on suggestibility and false memory. *Psychological Science (China), 29,* 905–908.

Hopkins, W., & Cantalupo, C. (2008, June). Theoretical speculations on the evolutionary origins of hemispheric specialization. *Current Directions in Psychological Science, 17,* 233–237.

Hopwood, C., Newman, D., Donnellan, M., Markowitz, J., Grilo, C., Sanislow, C., et al. (2009). The stability of personality traits in individuals with borderline personality disorder. *Journal of Abnormal Psychology, 118,* 806–815.

Horesh, D., Solomon, Z. Z., Zerach, G. G., & Ein-Dor, T. T. (2011). Delayed-onset PTSD among war veterans: The role of life events throughout the life cycle. *Social Psychiatry and Psychiatric Epidemiology, 46,* 863–870.

Hori, H., Teraishi, T., Sasayama, D., Matsuo, J., Kawamoto, Y., Kinoshita, Y., & Kunugi, H. (2011). Relationships between season of birth, schizotypy, temperament, character and neurocognition in a non-clinical population. *Psychiatry Research, 189,* 388–397.

Horinek, D., Varjassyová, A., & Hort, J. (2007). Magnetic resonance analysis of amygdalar volume in Alzheimer's disease. *Current Opinion in Psychiatry, 20,* 273–277.

Horney, K. (1937). *Neurotic personality of our times.* New York: Norton.

Horton, C. L. (2011). Recall and recognition of dreams and waking events: A diary paradigm. *International Journal of Dream Research, 4,* 8–16.

Horton, K. D., Wilson, D. E., Vonk, J., Kirby, S. L., & Nielsen, T. (2005). Measuring automatic retrieval: A comparison of implicit memory, process dissociation, and speeded response procedures. *Acta Psychologica, 119,* 235–263.

Houghtalen, R. P., & Talbot, N. (2007). Dissociative disorders and cognitive disorders. In O. J. Z. Sahler & J. E. Carr (Eds.), *The behavioral sciences and health care* (2nd rev. and updated ed.). Ashland, OH: Hogrefe & Huber Publishers, 2007.

Howe, C. J. (2002). The countering of overgeneralization. *Journal of Child Language, 29,* 875–895.

Howe, M. L. (2011). The adaptive nature of memory and its illusions. *Psychological Science, 20,* 312–315.

Howell, E. F. (2011). *Understanding and treating dissociative identity disorder: A relational approach.* New York: Routledge/Taylor & Francis Group.

Howes, O., & Kapur, S. (2009). The dopamine hypothesis of schizophrenia: Version III—The final common pathway. *Schizophrenia Bulletin, 35,* 549–562.

Howitt, D., & Cramer, D. (2000). *First steps in research and statistics: A practical workbook for psychology students.* Philadelphia: Psychology Press.

Hsieh, Y., & Chen, K. (2011). How different information types affect viewer's attention on internet advertising. *Computers in Human Behavior, 27*(2), 935–945.

Hubbard, K., O'Neill, A., & Cheakalos, C. (1999, April 12). Out of control. *People,* pp. 52–72.

Hubel, D. H., & Wiesel, T. N. (2004). *Brain and visual perception: The story of a 25-year collaboration.* New York: Oxford University Press.

Huber, F., Beckmann, S. C., & Herrmann, A. (2004). Means-end analysis: Does the affective state influence information processing style? *Psychology and Marketing, 21,* 715–737.

Hudson, W. (1960). Pictorial depth perception in subcultural groups in Africa. *Journal of Social Psychology, 52,* 183–208.

Hudspeth, A. J. (2000). Hearing. In E. R. Kandel, J. H. Schwartz, & T. M. Jessell (Eds.), *Principles of neural science* (4th ed.). New York: McGraw-Hill.

Huesmann, L., Dubow, E. F., & Boxer, P. (2011). The transmission of aggressiveness across generations: Biological, contextual, and social learning processes. In P. R. Shaver, M. Mikulincer, P. R. Shaver & M. Mikulincer (Eds.), *Human aggression and violence: Causes, manifestations, and consequences.* Washington, DC: American Psychological Association.

Hugenberg, K., & Sacco, D. (2008). Social categorization and stereotyping: How social categorization biases person perception and face memory. *Social and Personality Psychology Compass, 2,* 1052–1072.

Huijie, T. (2006). The measurement and assessment of mental health: A longitudinal and cross-sectional research on undergraduates, adults and patients. *Psychological Science (China), 29,* 419–422.

Hull, C. L. (1943). *Principles of behavior.* New York: Appleton-Century-Crofts.

Human, L. J., & Biesanz, J. C. (2011). Through the looking glass clearly: Accuracy and assumed similarity in well-adjusted individuals' first impressions. *Journal of Personality and Social Psychology, 100,* 349–364.

Humphrey, N., Curran, A., & Morris, E. (2007). Emotional intelligence and education: A critical review. *Educational Psychology, 27,* 235–254.

Humphreys, G. W., & Müller, H. (2000). A search asymmetry reversed by figure-ground assignment. *Psychological Science, 11,* 196–200.

Humphreys, K. L., & Lee, S. S. (2011). Risk taking and sensitivity to punishment in children with ADHD, ODD, ADHD+ODD, and controls. *Journal of Psychopathology and Behavioral Assessment, 33,* 299–307.

Hunt, E. (1994). Problem solving. In R. J. Sternberg (Ed.), *Thinking and problem solving: Handbook of perception and cognition* (2nd ed.). San Diego, CA: Academic Press.

Hunt, E. (2005). Information processing and intelligence: Where we are and where we are going. In R. J. Sternberg & J. E. Pretz (Eds.), *Cognition and intelligence: Identifying the mechanisms of the mind.* New York: Cambridge University Press.

Hunt, J. S., Seifert, A. L., & Armenta, B. E. (2006). Stereotypes and prejudice as dynamic constructs: Reminders about the nature of intergroup bias from the hurricane Katrina relief efforts. *Analyses of Social Issues and Public Policy (ASAP), 6,* 237–253.

Hunt, M. (1974). *Sexual behaviors in the 1970s.* New York: Dell.

Hurt, C. S., Ganerjee, S., Tunnard, C., Whitehead, D. L., Tsolaki, M., Mecocci, P., et al. (2005). Insight, cognition and quality of life in Alzheimer's disease. *NeuroMed Consortium,*

Journal of Neurology, Neurosurgery & Psychiatry, 81, 331–336.

Huston, A. C., Donnerstein, E., Fairchild, H. H., Feshback, N. D., Katz, P., Murray, J. P., et al. (1992). *Big world, small screen: The role of television in American society.* Omaha, NE: University of Nebraska Press.

Hutchinson, S. L., Baldwin, C. K., & Oh, S-S. (2006). Adolescent coping: Exploring adolescents' leisure-based responses to stress. *Leisure Sciences, 28,* 115–131.

Hyde, J., Mezulis, A. H., & Abramson, L. Y. (2008). The ABCs of depression: Integrating affective, biological, and cognitive models to explain the emergence of the gender difference in depression. *Psychological Review, 115,* 291–313.

Hyde, K., Peretz, I., & Zatorre, R. (2008, February). Evidence for the role of the right auditory cortex in fine pitch resolution. *Neuropsychologia, 46,* 632–639.

Hyman, B. T. (2011). Amyloid-dependent and amyloid-independent stages of Alzheimer disease. *Archives of Neurology, 68,* 1662–1664.

Iachini, T., & Giusberti, E (2004). Metric properties of spatial images generated from locomotion: The effect of absolute size on mental scanning. *European Journal of Cognitive Psychology, 16,* 573–596.

Iacoboni, M. (2009, January). Imitation, empathy, and mirror neurons. *Annual Review of Psychology, 60,* 653–670.

Iaria, G., Palermo, L., Committeri, G., & Barton, J. (2009). Age differences in the formation and use of cognitive maps. *Behavioural Brain Research, 196,* 187–191.

Ievers-Landis, C. E., Hoff, A. L., Brez, C., Cancilliere, M. K., McConnell, J., & Kerr, D. (2005). Situational analysis of dietary challenges of the treatment regimen for children and adolescents with phenylketonuria and their primary caregivers. *Journal of Developmental and Behavioral Pediatrics, 26,* 186–193.

Iglesias, A. (2005). Awake-alert hypnosis in the treatment of panic disorder: A case report. *American Journal of Clinical Hypnosis, 47,* 249–257.

Igo, S. E. (2006). Review of a telescope on society: Survey research and social science at the University of Michigan and beyond. *Journal of the History of the Behavioral Sciences, 42,* 95–96.

Ihler, E. (2003). Patient-physician communication. *Journal of the American Medical Association, 289,* 92.

Ikonomidou, C., Bittigau, P., Ishimaru, M. J., Wozniak, D. F., Koch, C., Genz, K., et al. (2000, February 11). Ethanol-induced apoptotic neurodegeneration and fetal alcohol syndrome. *Science, 287,* 1056–1060.

Imamura, M., & Nakamizo, S. (2006). An empirical test of formal equivalence between Emmert's Law and the size-distance invariance hypothesis. *The Spanish Journal of Psychology, 9*(2), 295–299.

Innocenti, G. M. (2007). Subcortical regulation of cortical development: Some effects of early, selective deprivations. *Progressive Brain Research, 164,* 23–37.

Inoue, T., Abekawa, T., Nakagawa, S., Suzuki, K., Tanaka, T., Kitaichi, Y., et al. (2011). Long-term naturalistic follow-up of lithium augmentation: Relevance to bipolarity. *Journal of Affective Disorders, 129,* 64–67.

Insel, T. R. (2010, April.) Faulty circuits. *Science,* pp. 44–5 1.

International Human Genome Sequencing Consortium. (2003). *International Consortium completes Human Genome Project.* Bethesda, MD: National Human Genome Research Institute.

Irwin, M. (2008). Human psychoneuroimmunology: 20 years of discovery. *Brain, Behavior, and Immunity, 22,* 129–139.

Irwin, R. R. (2006). Spiritual development in adulthood: Key concepts and models. In C. Hoare (Ed.), *Handbook of adult development and learning.* New York: Oxford University Press.

Isay, R. A. (1994). *Being homosexual: Gay men and their development.* Lanham, MD: Jason Aronson.

Isbell, L. M., & Tyler, J. M. (2003). Teaching students about in-group favoritism and the minimal groups paradigm. *Teaching of Psychology, 30,* 127–130.

Ishikawa, S., Okajima, I., Matsuoka, H., & Sakano, Y. (2007). Cognitive behavioural therapy for anxiety disorders in children and adolescents: A meta-analysis. *Child and Adolescent Mental Health, 12,* 164–172.

Iversen, S., & Iversen, L. (2007). Dopamine: 50 years in perspective. *Trends in Neurosciences, 30,* 188–193.

Iverson, P., Kuhl, P. K., Reiko, A. Y., Diesch, E., Tohkura, Y., Ketterman, A., et al. (2003). A perceptual interference account of acquisition difficulties for non-native phonemes. *Cognition, 87,* B47–B57.

Iwai, Y., Honda, S., Ozeki, H., Hashimoto, M., & Hirase, H. (2011). A simple head-mountable LED device for chronic stimulation of optogenetic molecules in freely moving mice. *Neuroscience Research, 70,* 124–127.

Izard, C. E. (1990). Facial expressions and the regulation of emotions. *Journal of Personality and Social Psychology, 58,* 487–498.

Izard, C. E. (1994). Innate and universal facial expressions: Evidence from developmental and cross-cultural research. *Psychological Bulletin, 115,* 288–299.

Jackson, J. D. (2006). Trauma, attachment, and coping: Pathways to resilience. *Dissertation Abstracts International: Section B: The Sciences and Engineering, 67*(1-B), 547.

Jacob, K. S., Kumar, P. S., Gayathri, K., Abraham, S., & Prince, M. J. (2007). *The diagnosis of dementia in the community* [Special issue: Focus on psychogeriatrics in the developing world]. *International Psychogeriatrics, 19,* 669–678.

Jacobs, G. (2010, January 11). High-strung and stressed students more common. San Diego State University NewsCenter. Retrieved September 6, 2011 from http://newscenter.sdsu.edu/sdsu_newscenter/news.aspx?s=71813

Jacobs, J. A., & Gerson, K. (2004). *The time divide: Work, family, and gender inequality.* Cambridge, MA: Harvard University Press.

Jacobs, M., Roesch, S., Wonderlich, S., Crosby, R., Thornton, L., Wilfley, D., et al. (2009). Anorexia nervosa trios: Behavioral profiles of individuals with anorexia nervosa and their parents. *Psychological Medicine, 39,* 451–461.

Jacobson, S. W., Stanton, M. E., Dodge, N. C., Pienaar, M., Fuller, D. S., Molteno, C. D., et al. (2011). Impaired delay and trace eyeblink conditioning in school-age children with fetal alcohol syndrome. *Alcoholism: Clinical and Experimental Research, 35,* 250–264.

Jacoby, L. L., Bishara, A. J., Hessels, S., & Hughes, A. (2007). Probabilistic retroactive interference: The role of accessibility bias in interference effects. *Journal of Experimental Psychology: General, 136,* 200–216.

Jain, S., Mills, P. J., & Von Känel, R. (2007). Effects of perceived stress and uplifts on inflammation and coagulability. *Psychophysiology, 44,* 154–160.

James, H. S., Jr. (2005). Why did you do that? An economic examination of the effect of extrinsic compensation on intrinsic motivation and performance. *Journal of Economic Psychology, 26,* 549–566.

James, M. H., Charnley, J. L., Flynn, J. R., Smith, D. W., & Dayas, C. V. (2011). Propensity to 'relapse' following exposure to cocaine cues is associated with the recruitment of specific thalamic and epithalamic nuclei. *Neuroscience, 125,* 88–96.

James, W. (1890). *The principles of psychology.* New York: Holt.

Jamieson, G. A. (2007). *Hypnosis and conscious states: The cognitive neuroscience perspective.* New York: Oxford University Press.

Jamison, K. R. (1995). *An unquiet mind: A memoir of moods and madness.* New York: Knopf.

Jang, H., Reeve, J., Ryan, R. M., & Kim, A. (2009, August). Can self-determination theory explain what underlies the productive, satisfying learning experiences of collectivistically oriented Korean students? *Journal of Educational Psychology, 101,* 644–661.

Janis, I. L. (1997). Groupthink. In R. P. Vecchio (Ed.), *Leadership: Understanding the dynamics of power and influence in organizations.* Notre Dame, IN: University of Notre Dame Press.

Jarlais, D. C. D., Arasteh, K., & Perlis, T. (2007). The transition from injection to non-injection drug use: Long-term outcomes among heroin and cocaine users in New York City. *Addiction, 102,* 778–785.

Jarrold, C., & Tam, H. (2011). Rehearsal and the development of working memory. In P. Barrouillet & V. Gaillard (Eds.), *Cognitive development and working memory: A dialogue between neo-Piagetian theories and cognitive approaches.* New York: Psychology Press.

Jefferson, D. J. (2005, August 8). America's most wanted drug. *Newsweek, 146,* 40–48.

Jenkins, A. M., Albee, G. W., Paster, V. S., Sue, S., Baker, D. B., Comas-Diaz, L., et al. (2003). Ethnic minorities. In D. K. Freedheim (Ed.), *Handbook of psychology: History of psychology* (Vol. 1). Hoboken, NJ: John Wiley & Sons.

Jensen, A. R. (2002). Galton's legacy to research on intelligence. *Journal of Biosocial Science, 34,* 145–172.

Jensen, A. R. (2005). Psychometric g and mental chronometry. *Cortex, 41,* 230–231.

Jequier, E. (2002). Pathways to obesity. *International Journal of Obesity and Related Metabolic Disorders, 26,* S12–S17.

Jetten, J., Hornsey, M. J., & Adarves-Yorno, I. (2006). When group members admit to being conformist: The role of relative intragroup status in conformity self-reports. *Personality and Social Psychology Bulletin, 32,* 162–173.

Jia, H., Zack, M. M., & Thompson, W. W. (2011). State quality-adjusted life expectancy for U.S. adults from 1993 to 2008. *Quality of Life Research: An International Journal of Quality of Life Aspects of Treatment, Care & Rehabilitation, 20,* 853–863.

Joe, G. W., Flynn, P. M., & Broome, K. M. (2007). Patterns of drug use and expectations in methadone patients. *Addictive Behaviors, 32,* 1640–1656.

Johnson, G. B. (2000). *The Living World* (p. 600), Boston: McGraw-Hill.

Johnson, H. D. (2004). Gender, grade and relationship differences in emotional closeness within adolescent friendships. *Adolescence, 39,* 243–255.

Johnson, W., & Deary, I. J. (2011). Placing inspection time, reaction time, and perceptual speed in the broader context of cognitive ability: The VPR model in the Lothian Birth Cohort 1936. *Intelligence, 39,* 405–417.

John-Steiner, V., & Mahn, H. (2003). Sociocultural contexts for teaching and learning. In W. M. Reynolds & G. E. Miller (Eds.), *Handbook of psychology: Educational psychology* (Vol. 7). New York: Wiley.

Johnston, L. D., O'Malley, P. M., Bachman, J. G., & Schulenberg, J. E. (2009). *Monitoring the future national results on adolescent drug use; overview of key findings, 2008* (NIH Publication No. 09-7401). Bethesda, MD: National Institute on Drug Abuse.

Johnston, L. D., O'Malley, P. M., Bachman, J. G., & Schulenberg, J. E. (2010). *Monitoring the future national survey results on drug use: 1975–2008. Volume I: Secondary school students* (NIH Publication No. 09-7402). Bethesda, MD: National Institute on Drug Abuse.

Johnston, L. D., O'Malley, P. M., Bachman, J. G., & Schulenberg, J. E. (2011). *Monitoring the future national survey results on drug use: 2010. Volume I: Secondary school students.* Bethesda, MD: National Institute on Drug Abuse.

Johnston, M. V. (2004). Clinical disorders of brain plasticity. *Brain and Development, 26,* 73–80.

Jones, A. L. (2006). The contemporary psychoanalyst: Karen Horney's theory applied in today's culture. *PsycCRITIQUES, 51,* 127–134.

Jones, D. (2010). A WEIRD view of human nature skews psychologists' studies. *Science, 328,* 1627.

Jones, J. E., & Corp, E. S. (2003). Effect of naltrexone on food intake and body weight in Syrian hamsters depends on metabolic status. *Physiology and Behavior, 78,* 67–72.

Jones, J. M. (2007). Exposure to chronic community violence: Resilience in African American children. *Journal of Black Psychology, 33,* 125–149.

Jones, K., Callen, F., Blagrove, M., & Parrott, A. (2008). Sleep, energy and self rated cognition across 7 nights following recreational ecstasy/MDMA use. *Sleep and Hypnosis, 10,* 2–38.

Jones, R. K., Darroch, J. E., & Singh, S. (2005). Religious differentials in the sexual and reproductive behaviors of young women in the United States. *Journal of Adolescent Health, 36,* 279–288.

Jorgensen, G. (2006). Kohlberg and Gilligan: Duet or duel? *Journal of Moral Education, 35,* 179–196.

Jovanovi´c, D., Stanojevi´c, P., & Stanojevi´c, D. (2011). Motives for, and attitudes about, driving-related anger and aggressive driving. *Social Behavior and Personality, 39,* 755–764.

Joyce, J. (1934). *Ulysses.* New York: Random House.

Julien, R. M (2001). *A primer of drug action* (9th ed.). New York: Freeman.

Jung, C. G. (1961). *Freud and psychoanalysis.* New York: Pantheon.

Jung, J. (2002). *Psychology of alcohol and other drugs: A research perspective.* Thousand Oaks, CA: Sage.

Juster, E T., Ono, H., & Stafford, E (2002). *Report on housework and division of labor.* Ann Arbor, MI: Institute for Social Research.

Justman, S. (2011). From medicine to psychotherapy: The placebo effect. *History of the Human Sciences, 24,* 95–107.

Jylha, M. (2004). Old age and loneliness: Cross-sectional and longitudinal analyses in the Tampere longitudinal study on aging. *Canadian Journal on Aging/La Revue Canadienne du Vieillissement, 23,* 157–168.

Kadosh, R., Henik, A., & Walsh, V. (2009, May). Synaesthesia: Learned or lost? *Developmental Science, 12,* 484–491.

Kagan, J., Snidman, N., Kahn, V., & Towsley, S. (2007). The preservation of two infant temperaments into adolescence. *Monographs of the Society for Research in Child Development, 72,* 1–75.

Kahneman, D., Diener, E., & Schwarz, N. (1998). *Well-being: The foundations of hedonic psychology.* New York: Russell Sage Foundation.

Kalb, C. (2003, May 19). Taking a new look at pain. *Newsweek,* pp. 51–52.

Kaller, C. P., Unterrainer, J. M., Rahm, B., & Halsband, U. (2004). The impact of problem structure on planning: Insights from the Tower of London task. *Cognitive Brain Research, 20,* 462–472.

Kallio, S., & Revonsuo, A. (2003). Hypnotic phenomena and altered states of consciousness: A multilevel framework of description and explanation. *Contemporary Hypnosis, 20,* 111–164.

Kalodner, C. R. (2011). Cognitive-behavioral theories. In D. Capuzzi & D. R. Gross (Eds.), *Counseling and psychotherapy* (5th ed.). Alexandria, VA: American Counseling Association.

Kandel, E. R., Schwartz, J. H., & Jessell, T. M. (Eds.). (2000). *Principles of neural science* (4th ed.). New York: McGraw-Hill.

Kane, M. J., & Engle, R. W. (2002). The role of prefrontal cortex in working-memory capacity, executive attention, and general fluid intelligence: An individual-differences perspective. *Psychonomic Bulletin and Review, 9,* 637–671.

Kanner, A. D., Coyne, J. C., Schaefer, C., & Lazarus, R. S. (1981). Comparison of two modes of stress measurement: Daily hassles and uplifts versus major life events. *Journal of Behavioral Medicine, 4,* 14.

Kanoski, S. E., Hayes, M. R., Greenwald, H. S., Fortin, S. M., Gianessi, C. A., Gilbert, J. R., & Grill, H. J. (2011). Hippocampal leptin signaling reduces food intake and modulates food-related memory processing. *Neuro-psychopharmacology, 36,* 1859–1870.

Kantrowitz, B., & Underwood, A. (2007, June 25). The teen drinking dilemma. *Newsweek,* pp. 36–37.

Kao, D. (2011). Message sidedness in advertising: The moderating roles of need for cognition and time pressure in persuasion. *Scandinavian Journal of Psychology, 52,* 329–340.

Kaplan, H. S. (1974). *The new sex therapy.* New York: Brunner-Mazel.

Kaplan, J. R., & Manuck, S. B. (1989). The effect of propranolol on behavioral interactions among adult male cynomolgus monkeys *(Macacafascicularis)* housed in disrupted social groupings. *Psychosomatic Medicine, 51,* 449–462.

Kaplan, M. S., Huguer, N., McFarland, B. H., & Newsom, J. T. (2007). Suicide among male veterans: A prospective population-based study. *Journal of Epidemiological Community Health, 61,* 619–624.

Kara, P., & Boyd, J. (2009, April). A microarchitecture for binocular disparity and ocular dominance in visual cortex. *Nature, 458*(7238), 627–631.

Karaszewski, B. (2008). Sub-neocortical brain: A mechanical tool for creative generation? *Trends in Cognitive Sciences, 12,* 171–172.

Karni, A., Tanne, D., Rubenstein, B. S., Askenasy, J. J. M., & Sagi, D. (1994, July 29). Dependence on REM sleep of overnight improvement of a perceptual skill. *Science, 265,* 679–682.

Kasof, J. (2009, May). Cultural variation in seasonal depression: Cross-national differences in winter versus summer patterns of seasonal affective disorder. *Journal of Affective Disorders, 115,* 79–86.

Kassam, K. S., Gilbert, D. T., Swencionis, J. K., & Wilson, T. D. (2009). Misconceptions of memory: The Scooter Libby effect. *Psychological Science, 20,* 551–552.

Kassel, J. D., Evatt, D. P., Greenstein, J. E., Wardle, M. C., Yates, M. C., & Veilleux, J. C. (2007). The acute effects of nicotine on positive and negative affect in adolescent smokers. *Journal of Abnormal Psychology, 116,* 543–553.

Kassin, S. M. (2005). On the psychology of confessions: Does innocence put innocents at risk? *American Psychologist, 60,* 215–228.

Kaštelan, A., Franciškovic, A., Tanja, M., & Moro, L. (2007). Psychotic symptoms in combat-related post-traumatic stress disorder. *Military Medicine, 172,* 273–277.

Kato, K., & Pedersen, N. L. (2005). Personality and coping: A study of twins reared apart and twins reared together. *Behavior Genetics, 35,* 147–158.

Kato, N. (2009). Neurophysiological mechanisms of electroconvulsive therapy for depression. *Neuroscience Research, 64,* 3–11.

Kato, T. (2007). Molecular genetics of bipolar disorder and depression. *Psychiatry and Clinical Neurosciences, 61,* 3–19.

Katsiyannis, A., Zhang, D., & Woodruff, N. (2005). Transition supports to students with mental retardation: An examination of data from the national longitudinal transition study 2. *Education and Training in Developmental Disabilities, 40,* 109–116.

Katz, L., Fotti, S., & Postl, L. (2009). Cognitive-behavioral therapy and dialectical behavior therapy: Adaptations required to treat adolescents. *Psychiatric Clinics of North America, 32,* 95–109.

Katz, M. (2001). The implications of revising Freud's empiricism for drive theory. *Psychoanalysis and Contemporary Thought, 24,* 253–272.

Kaufman, A., Johnson, C., & Liu, X. (2008). A CHC theory-based analysis of age differences on cognitive abilities and academic skills at ages 22 to 90 years. *Journal of Psychoeducational Assessment, 26,* 350–381.

Kaufman, J. C., & Baer, J. (2006). *Creativity and reason in cognitive development.* New York: Cambridge University Press.

Kaufman, J. C., & Plucker, J. A. (2011). Intelligence and creativity. In R. J. Sternberg & S. Kaufman, (Eds.), *The Cambridge handbook of intelligence.* New York: Cambridge University Press.

Kawasaki, C., Nugent, J. K., Miyashita, H., Miyahara, H., & Brazelton, T. B. (1994). The cultural organization of infants' sleep [Special issue: Environments of birth and infancy]. *Children's Environment, 11,* 135–141.

Kawashima, H., Izaki, Y., & Grace, A. A. (2006). Cooperativity between hippocampal-prefrontal short-term plasticity through associative long-term potentiation. *Brain Research, 1109,* 37–44.

Kazar, D. B. (2006). Forensic psychology: Did we leave anything out? *PsycCRITIQUES, 51,* 88–97.

Kazdin, A. (2008). Evidence-based treatment and practice: New opportunities to bridge clinical research and practice, enhance the knowledge base, and improve patient care. *American Psychologist, 63,* 146–159.

Kearns, K. P. (2005). Broca's aphasia. In L. L. LaPointe (Ed.), *Aphasia and related neurogenic language disorders* (3rd ed.). New York: Thieme New York.

Keating, D. P., & Clark, L. V. (1980). Development of physical and social reasoning in adolescence. *Developmental Psychology, 16,* 23–30.

Keller, J. (2007). Stereotype threat in classroom settings: The interactive effect of domain identification, task difficulty and stereotype threat on female students' math performance. *British Journal of Educational Psychology, 77,* 323–338.

Kelley, H. (1950). The warm-cold variable in first impressions of persons. *Journal of Personality and Social Psychology, 18,* 431–439.

Kelly, J. B. (2000). Children's adjustment in conflicted marriage and divorce: A decade review of research. *Journal of the American Academy of Child & Adolescent Psychiatry, 39,* 963–973.

Keltikangas-Järvinen, L., Räikkönen, K., Ekelund, J., & Peltonen, L. (2004). Nature and nurture in novelty seeking. *Molecular Psychiatry, 9,* 308–311.

Kemeny, M. E. (2007). Psychoneuroimmunology. In H. S. Friedman & R. C. Silver (Eds.), *Foundations of health psychology.* New York: Oxford University Press.

Kempermann, G. (2011). Seven principles in the regulation of adult neurogenesis. *European Journal of Neuroscience, 33,* 1018–1024.

Kempermann, G., & Gage, F. H. (1999, May). New nerve cells for the adult brain. *Scientific American,* pp. 48–53.

Kemps, E., & Tiggemann, M. (2007). Reducing the vividness and emotional impact of distressing autobiographical memories: The importance of modality-specific interference. *Memory, 15,* 412–422.

Kendler, K. S., Gatz, M., & Gardner, C. O. (2006a). Personality and major depression. *Archives of General Psychiatry, 63,* 1113–1120.

Kendler, K., Halberstadt, L., Butera, F., Myers, J., et al. (2008). The similarity of facial expressions in response to emotion-inducing films in reared-apart twins. *Psychological Medicine, 38*(10), 1475–1483.

Kendler, K. S., Myers, J. O., & Gardner, C. (2006b). Caffeine intake, toxicity and dependence and lifetime risk for psychiatric and substance use disorders: An epidemiologic and co-twin control analysis. *Psychological Medicine, 36,* 1717–1725.

Kendler, K. S., & Schaffner, K. F. (2011). The dopamine hypothesis of schizophrenia: An historical and philosophical analysis. *Philosophy, Psychiatry, & Psychology, 18,* 41–63.

Kennedy, C. E., Moore, P. J., Peterson, R. A., Katzman, M. A., Vermani, M., & Charmak, W. D. (2011). What makes people anxious about pain? How personality and perception combine to determine pain anxiety responses in clinical and non-clinical populations.

Anxiety, Stress & Coping: An International Journal, 24, 179–200.

Kennedy, D. O., & Haskell, C. F. (2011). Cerebral blood flow and behavioural effects of caffeine in habitual and non-habitual consumers of caffeine: A near infrared spectroscopy study. *Biological Psychology, 86,* 296–305.

Kennedy, J. E. (2004). A proposal and challenge for proponents and skeptics of psi. *Journal of Parapsychology, 68,* 157–167.

Kennedy, P. (2011, September 18). The cyborg in us all. *New York Times Magazine,* pp. 24–31.

Kennison, S. M., & Bowers, J. (2011). Illustrating brain lateralisation in a naturalistic observation of cell-phone use. *Psychology Learning & Teaching, 10,* 46–51.

Kensinger, E. (2007). Negative emotion enhances memory accuracy: Behavioral and neuro-imaging evidence. *Current Directions in Psychological Science, 16,* 213–218.

Kensinger, E. A., & Schacter, D. L. (2006). Neural processes underlying memory attribution on a reality-monitoring task. *Cerebral Cortex, 16,* 1126–1133.

Kesebir, P., & Diener, E. (2008). In pursuit of happiness: Empirical answers to philosophical questions. *Perspectives on Psychological Science, 3,* 117–125.

Kess, J. F., & Miyamoto, T. (1994). *Japanese psycholinguistics.* Amsterdam, Netherlands: John Benjamins.

Kessler, R. C., & Wang, P. S. (2008). The descriptive epidemiology of commonly occurring mental disorders in the United States. *Annual Review of Public Health, 29,* 115–129.

Kettenmann, H., & Ransom, B. R. (2005). *Neuroglia* (2nd ed.). New York: Oxford University Press.

Key, W. B. (2003). Subliminal sexuality: The fountainhead for America's obsession. In T. Reichert & J. Lambaiase (Eds.), *Sex in advertising: Perspectives on the erotic appeal. LEA's communication series.* Mahwah, NJ: Lawrence Erlbaum.

Khalil, E. L. (2011). The mirror neuron paradox: How far is understanding from mimicking? *Journal of Economic Behavior & Organization, 77,* 86–96.

Khazaal, Y., Chatton, A., Claeys, F., Ribordy, F., Zullino, D., & Cabanac, M. (2008). Antipsychotic drug and body weight set-point. *Physiology & Behavior, 95,* 157–160.

Kidd, E., & Lum, J. (2008). Sex differences in past tense overregularization. *Developmental Science, 11,* 882–889.

Kiecolt, J. K. (2003). Satisfaction with work and family life: No evidence of a cultural reversal. *Journal of Marriage and Family, 65,* 23–35.

Kihlstrom, J. F. (2005a). Dissociative disorders. *Annual Review of Clinical Psychology, 1,* 227–253.

Kihlstrom, J. F. (2005b). Is hypnosis an altered state of consciousness or what? Comment. *Contemporary Hypnosis, 22,* 34–38.

Kihlstrom, J. F., Schacter, D. L., Cork, R. C., Hurt, C. A., & Behr, S. E. (1990). Implicit and explicit memory following surgical anesthesia. *Psychological Science, 1,* 303–306.

Kim, D. R., Pesiridou, A., & O'Reardon, J. P. (2009). Transcranial magnetic stimulation in the treatment of psychiatric disorders. *Current Psychiatry Reports, 11,* 447–52.

Kim, H., Clark, D., & Dionne, R. (2009, July). Genetic contributions to clinical pain and analgesia: Avoiding pitfalls in genetic research. *The Journal of Pain, 10,* 663–693.

Kim, N. (2008). The moon illusion and the size-distance paradox. In S. Cummins-Sebree, M. A. Riley, et al. (Eds.), *Studies in perception and action IX: Fourteenth International Conference on Perception and Action.* Mahwah, NJ: Lawrence Erlbaum Associates.

Kimbrel, N. A. (2007). A model of the development and maintenance of generalized social phobia. *Clinical Psychological Review, 8,* 69–75.

Kim-Cohen, J., Caspi, A., & Moffitt, T. E. (2003). Prior juvenile diagnoses in adults with mental disorder: Developmental follow-back of a prospective-longitudinal cohort. *Archives of General Psychiatry, 60,* 709–717.

Kim-Cohen, J., Moffitt, T. E., Taylor, A., Pawlby, S. J., & Caspi, A. (2005). Maternal depression and children's antisocial behavior: Nature and nurture effects. *Archives of General Psychiatry, 62,* 173–181.

King-Casas, B., Sharp, C., Lomax-Bream, L., Lohrenz, T., Fonagy, P., & Montague, P. R. (2008, August 8). The rupture and repair of cooperation in borderline personality disorder. *Science, 321,* 806–810.

Kirk, K. M., Bailey, J. M., & Martin, N. G. (2000). Etiology of male sexual orientation in an Australian twin sample. *Psychology, Evolution & Gender, 2,* 301–311.

Kirsch, I., & Braffman, W. (2001). Imaginative suggestibility and hypnotizability. *Current Directions in Psychological Science, 10,* 57–61.

Kirsch, I., Lynn, S. J., Vigorito, M., & Miller, R. R. (2004). The role of cognition in classical and operant conditioning. *Journal of Clinical Psychology, 60,* 369–392.

Kirschenbaum, H. (2004). Carl Rogers's life and work: An assessment on the 100th anniversary of his birth. *Journal of Counseling and Development, 82,* 116–124.

Kirschenbaum, H., & Jourdan, A. (2005). The current status of Carl Rogers and the person-centered approach. *Psychotherapy: Theory, Research, Practice, Training, 42,* 37–51.

Kish, S., Fitzmaurice, P., Boileau, I., Schmunk, G., Ang, L., Furukawa, Y., et al. (2009). Brain serotonin transporter in human methamphetamine users. *Psychopharmacology, 202,* 649–661.

Kiss, A. (2004). Does gender have an influence on the patient-physician communication? *Journal of Men's Health and Gender, 1,* 77–82.

Klapp, S. T., & Jagacinski, R. J. (2011). Gestalt principles in the control of motor action. *Psychological Bulletin, 137,* 443–462.

Kleinman, A. (1996). How is culture important for DSM-IV? In J. E Mezzich, A. Kleinman, H. Fabrega, Jr., & D. L. Parron (Eds.), *Culture and psychiatric diagnosis: A DSM-IV perspective.* Washington, DC: American Psychiatric Press.

Klötz, F., Garle, M., & Granath, F. (2006). Criminality among individuals testing positive for the presence of anabolic androgenic steroids. *Archives of General Psychiatry, 63,* 1274–1279.

Kluck, A. (2008). Family factors in the development of disordered eating: Integrating dynamic and behavioral explanations. *Eating Behaviors, 9,* 471–483.

Kluger, J. (2001, April 2). Fear not! *Time,* pp. 51–62.

Kluger, J. (2006, December 4). Why we worry about the things we shouldn't and ignore the things we should. *Time,* pp. 64–71.

Klump, K., & Culbert, K. (2007). Molecular genetic studies of eating disorders: Current status and future directions. *Current Directions in Psychological Science, 16,* 37–41.

Knight, S. C., & Meyer, R. G. (2007). Forensic hypnosis. In A. M. Goldstein (Ed.), *Forensic psychology: Emerging topics and expanding roles.* Hoboken, NJ: John Wiley & Sons.

Knoblich, G., & Sebanz, N. (2006). The social nature of perception and action. *Current Directions in Psychological Science, 15,* 99–111.

Kobayashi, F., Schallert, D. L., & Ogren, H. A. (2003). Japanese and American folk vocabularies for emotions. *Journal of Social Psychology, 143,* 451–478.

Koçak, O., Özpolat, A., Atbaşoğlu, C., & Çiçek, M. (2011). Cognitive control of a simple mental image in patients with obsessive–compulsive disorder. *Brain and Cognition, 76,* 390–399.

Koch, C., & Greenfield, S. (2007, October). How does consciousness happen? *Scientific American,* pp. 76–83.

Kogstad, R. E., Ekeland, T. J., & Hummelvoll, J. K. (2011). In defence of a humanistic approach to mental health care: Recovery processes investigated with the help of clients' narratives on turning points and processes of gradual change. *Journal of Psychiatric and Mental Health Nursing, 18,* 479–486.

Kohlberg, L. (1984). *The psychology of moral development: Essays on moral development* (Vol. 2). San Francisco: Harper & Row.

Kohlberg, L., & Ryncarz, R. A. (1990). Beyond justice reasoning: Moral development and consideration of a seventh stage. In C. N. Alexander & E. J. Langer (Eds.), *Higher stages of human development: Perspectives on adult growth.* New York: Oxford University Press.

Köhler, W. (1927). *The mentality of apes.* London: Routledge & Kegan Paul.

Kojima, M., & Kangawa, K. (2008). Structure and function of ghrelin. *Results & Problems in Cell Differentiation, 46,* 89–115.

Kolata, G. (2002, December 2). With no answers on risks, steroid users still say "yes." *The New York Times,* p. 1A.

Kolb, B., Gibb, R., & Robinson, T. E. (2003). Brain plasticity and behavior. *Current Directions in Psychological Science, 12,* 1–5.

Komarovskaya, I., Loper, A., Warren, J., & Jackson, S. (2011). Exploring gender differences in trauma exposure and the emergence of symptoms of PTSD among incarcerated men and women. *Journal of Forensic Psychiatry & Psychology, 22,* 395–410.

Koocher, G. P., Norcross, J. C., & Hill, S. S. (2005). *Psychologists' desk reference* (2nd ed.). New York: Oxford University Press.

Kopelman, M. D., & Fleminger, S. (2002). Experience and perspectives on the classification of organic mental disorders. *Psychopathology, 35,* 76–81.

Koper, R. J., & Jaasma, M. A. (2001). Interpersonal style: Are human social orientations guided by generalized interpersonal needs? *Communications Reports, 14,* 117–129.

Koplewicz, H. (2002). *More than moody: Recognizing and treating adolescent depression.* New York: Putnam.

Korcha, R. A., Polcin, D. L., Bond, J. C., Lapp, W. M., & Galloway, G. (2011). Substance use and motivation: A longitudinal perspective. *The American Journal of Drug and Alcohol Abuse, 37,* 48–53.

Korotkov, D., Perunovic, M., Claybourn, M., Fraser, I., Houlihan, M., Macdonald, M., & Korotkov, K. (2011). The Type B behavior pattern as a moderating variable of the relationship between stressor chronicity and health behavior. *Journal of Health Psychology, 16*, 397–409.

Kosambi, D. D. (1967). The Vedic "Five Tribes." *American Oriental Society, 14*, 5–12.

Kosslyn, S. M., Cacioppo, J. T., Davidson, R. J., Hugdahl, K., Lovallo, W. R., Spiegel, D., et al. (2002). Bridging psychology and biology. *American Psychologist, 57*, 341–351.

Kotre, J., & Hall, E. (1990). *Seasons of life.* Boston: Little, Brown.

Kounios, J., Fleck, J. I., Green, D. L., Payne, L., Stevenson, J. L., Bowden, E. M., et al. (2008). The origins of insight in resting-state brain activity. *Neuropsychologia, 46*, 281–291.

Kovacs, A. M., & Mehler, J. (2009, July 31). Flexible learning of multiple speech structures in bilingual infants. *Science, 325*, 611–612.

Kovelman, I., Baker, S. A., & Petitto, L. A. (2008). Bilingual and monolingual brains compared: A functional magnetic resonance imaging investigation of syntactic processing and a possible "neural signature" of bilingualism. *Journal of Cognitive Neuroscience, 20*(1), 153–169.

Kowalik, J., Weller, J., Venter, J., & Drachman, D. (2011). Cognitive behavioral therapy for the treatment of pediatric posttraumatic stress disorder: A review and meta-analysis. *Journal of Behavior Therapy and Experimental Psychiatry, 42*, 405–413.

Kowert, P. A. (2002). *Groupthink or deadlock: When do leaders learn from their advisors? SUNY Series on the presidency.* Albany: State University of New York Press.

Kozulin, A., Gindis, B., Ageyev, V. S., & Miller, S. M. (2003). *Vygotsky's educational theory in cultural context.* New York: Cambridge University Press.

Kramer, P. (1993). *Listening to Prozac.* New York: Viking.

Kreher, D., Holcomb, P., Goff, D., & Kuperberg, G. (2008). Neural evidence for faster and further automatic spreading activation in schizophrenic thought disorder. *Schizophrenia Bulletin, 34*, 473–482.

Kreppner, J., Rutter, M., Marvin, R., O'Connor, T., & Sonuga-Barke, E. (2011). Assessing the concept of the 'insecure-other' category in the Cassidy–Marvin scheme: Changes between 4 and 6 years in the English and Romanian adoptee study. *Social Development, 20*, 1–16.

Kreuger, A. (2007). Are we having fun yet? Categorizing and evaluating changes in time allocation. *Brookings Papers on Economic Activity* (Vol. 2), *38*, 193–218.

Krijn, M., Emmelkamp, P. M. G., Olafsson, R. P., & Biemond, R. (2004). Virtual reality exposure therapy of anxiety disorders: A review. *Clinical Psychology Review, 24*, 259–281.

Krishman, S., Cairns, R., & Howard, R. (2009). Cannabinoids for the treatment of dementia. *Cochrane Database of Systematic Reviews.* Downloaded 12/15/11. http://www.ncbi.nlm.nih.gov/pubmed/19370677

Krueger, K., & Dayan, P. (2009). Flexible shaping: How learning in small steps helps. *Cognition, 110*, 380–394.

Krull, D. S., & Anderson, C. A. (1997). The process of explanation. *Current Directions in Psychological Science, 6*, 1–5.

Krumhuber, E. G., & Scherer, K. R. (2011). Affect bursts: Dynamic patterns of facial expression. *Emotion, 11*, 825–841.

Krusemark, E., Campbell, W., & Clementz, B. (2008). Attributions, deception, and event

related potentials: An investigation of the self-serving bias. *Psychophysiology, 45*, 511–515.

Kübler-Ross, E. (1969). *On death and dying.* New York: Macmillan.

Kubovy, M., Epstein, W., & Gepshtein, S. (2003). Foundations of visual perception. In A. F. Healy & R. W. Proctor (Eds.), *Handbook of psychology: Experimental psychology* (Vol. 4). New York: Wiley.

Kumar, S., Ruchi, R., James, S. R., & Chidiac, E. J. (2011). Gene therapy for chronic neuropathic pain: How does it work and where do we stand today? *Pain Medicine, 12*, 808–822.

Kuo, L. J. (2007). Effects of bilingualism on development of facets of phonological competence (China). *Dissertation Abstracts International Section A: Humanities and Social Sciences, 67*(11-A), 4095.

Kuppens, P., Ceulemans, E., Timmerman, M. E., Diener, E., et al. (2006). Universal intracultural and intercultural dimensions of the recalled frequency of emotional experience. *Journal of Cross Cultural Psychology, 37*, 491–515.

Kuriyama, K., Stickgold, R., & Walker, M. P. (2004). Sleep-dependent learning and motor-skill complexity. *Learning and Memory, 11*, 705–713.

Kuther, T. L. (2003). *Your career in psychology: Psychology and the law.* New York: Wadsworth.

Kvavilashvili, L., & Fisher, L. (2007). Is time-based prospective remembering mediated by self-initiated rehearsals? Role of incidental cues, ongoing activity, age, and motivation. *Journal of Experimental Psychology: General, 136*, 112–132.

Kwate, N. O. A. (2001). Intelligence or misorientation? Eurocentrism in the WISC-III. *Journal of Black Psychology, 27*, 221–239.

Kwon, P., & Laurenceau, J. P. (2002). A longitudinal study of the hopelessness theory of depression: Testing the diathesis-stress model within a differential reactivity and exposure framework [Special issue: Reprioritizing the role of science in a realistic version of the scientist-practitioner model]. *Journal of Clinical Psychology, 50*, 1305–1321.

Laas, I. (2006). Self-actualization and society: A new application for an old theory. *Journal of Humanistic Psychology, 46*, 77–91.

LaBar, K. (2007). Beyond fear: Emotional memory mechanisms in the human brain. *Current Directions in Psychological Science, 16*, 173–177.

Laederach-Hofmann, K., & Messerli-Buergy, N. (2007). Chest pain, angina pectoris, panic disorder, and Syndrome X. In J. Jordan, B. Barde, et al. (Eds.), *Contributions toward evidence-based psychocardiology: A systematic review of the literature.* Washington, DC: American Psychological Association.

Lagacé-Séguin, D. G., & d'Entremont, M. L. (2006). The role of child negative affect in the relations between parenting styles and play. *Early Child Development and Care, 176*, 461–477.

Lahti, J., Räikkönen, K., Ekelund, J., Peltonen, L., Raitakari, O. T., & Keltikangas-Järvinen, L. (2005). Novelty seeking: Interaction between parental alcohol use and dopamine D4 receptor gene exon III polymorphism over 17 years. *Psychiatric Genetics, 15*, 133–139.

Laing, R. D., & Szasz, T. (2004). "Knowing what ain't so." *Psychoanalytic Review, 91*, 331–346.

Laird, J. D., & Bresler, C. (1990). William James and the mechanisms of emotional experience. *Personality and Social Psychology Bulletin, 16*, 636–651.

Lakhan, S., & Vieira, K. (2009, May 15). Schizophrenia pathophysiology: Are we any closer to a complete model? *Annals of General Psychiatry, 8.*

Lal, S. (2002). Giving children security: Mamie Phipps Clark and the racialization of child psychology. *American Psychologist, 57*, 20–28.

Lamal, P. A. (1979). College students' common beliefs about psychology. *Teaching of Psychology, 6*, 155–158.

Lamb, M. E., & Garretson, M. E. (2003). The effects of interviewer gender and child gender on the informativeness of alleged child sexual abuse victims in forensic interviews. *Law and Human Behavior, 27*, 157–171.

Lamborn, S. D., & Groh, K. (2009). A four-part model of autonomy during emerging adulthood: Associations with adjustment. *International Journal of Behavioral Development, 33*, 393–401.

Lampard, A. M., Byrne, S. M., McLean, N., & Fursland, A. (2011). An evaluation of the enhanced cognitive-behavioural model of bulimia nervosa. *Behaviour Research and Therapy, 49*, 529–535.

Landro, L. (2010, May 11). New ways to treat pain. *Wall Street Journal*, pp. D1–D2.

Landro, L. (2011, April 26). 'Use only as direct' isn't easy. *Wall Street Journal*, pp. D1–D2.

Lane, K. A., Banaji, M. R., Nosek, B. A., & Greenwald, A. G. (Eds.). (2007). Understanding and using the implicit association test: IV: What we know (so far) about the method. In B. Wittenbrink & N. Schwarz (Eds.), *Implicit measures of attitudes.* New York: Guilford Press.

Lane, S. D., Cherek, D. R., & Tcheremissine, O. V. (2007). Response perseveration and adaptation in heavy marijuana-smoking adolescents. *Addictive Behaviors, 32*, 977–990.

Lang, A. J., Sorrell, J. T., & Rodgers, C. S. (2006). Anxiety sensitivity as a predictor of labor pain. *European Journal of Pain, 10*, 263–270.

Langan-Fox, J., & Grant, S. (2006). The Thematic Apperception Test: Toward a standard measure of the big three motives. *Journal of Personality Assessment, 87*, 277–291.

Langdridge, D., & Butt, T. (2004). The fundamental attribution error: A phenomenological critique. *British Journal of Social Psychology, 43*, 357–369.

Langlois, F., Langlois, M., Carpentier, A. C., Brown, C., Lemieux, S., & Hivert, M. (2011). Ghrelin levels are associated with hunger as measured by the Three-Factor Eating Questionnaire in healthy young adults. *Physiology & Behavior, 104*, 373–377.

Langreth, R. (2000, May 1). Every little bit helps: How even moderate exercise can have a big impact on your health. *The Wall Street Journal*, p. R5.

Langston, R., Ainge, J., Couey, J., Canto, C., Bjerknes, T., Witter, M., et al. (2010). Development of the spatial representation system in the rat. *Science, 328*, 1576–1580.

Lankov, A. (2004). The dawn of modern Korea: Changes for better or worse. *The Korea Times*, p. A1.

Lanza, S. T., & Collins, L. M. (2002). Pubertal timing and the onset of substance use in females during early adolescence. *Prevention Science, 3*, 69–82.

Larsen, R. J., & Buss, D. M. (2006). *Personality psychology: Domains of knowledge about human nature with PowerWeb* (2nd ed.). New York: McGraw-Hill.

Lascaratos, G., Ji, D., & Wood, J. P. (2007). Visible light affects mitochondrial function and induces neuronal death in retinal cell cultures. *Vision Research, 47*, 1191–1201.

Latané, B., & Darley, J. M. (1970). *The unresponsive bystander: Why doesn't he help?* New York: Appleton-Century-Crofts.

Laugharne, J., Janca, A., & Widiger, T. (2007). Posttraumatic stress disorder and terrorism: 5 years after 9/11. *Current Opinion in Psychiatry, 20*, 36–41.

Laumann, E. O., Paik, A., & Rosen, R. C. (1999, February 10). Sexual dysfunction in the United States: Prevalence and predictors. *Journal of the American Medical Association, 281*, 537–544.

Lavelli, M., & Fogel, A. (2005). Developmental changes in the relationship between the infant's attention and emotion during early face-to-face communication. *Developmental Psychology, 41*, 265–280.

Lavenex, P., & Lavenex, P. (2009). Spatial memory and the monkey hippocampus: Not all space is created equal. *Hippocampus, 19*, 8–19.

Lavrakas, P. J., Mane, S., & Joe, L. (2010). 'Does anyone really know if online ad campaigns are working?': An evaluation of methods used to assess the effectiveness of advertising on the internet. *Journal of Advertising Research, 50*(4), 354–373.

Lazarus, A. A. (1997). *Brief but comprehensive psychotherapy: The multimodal way.* New York: Springer.

Lazarus, R. S. (1995). Emotions express a social relationship, but it is an individual mind that creates them. *Psychological Inquiry, 6*, 253–265.

Leahy, R. L. (2003). *Roadblocks in cognitive-behavioral therapy: Transforming challenges into opportunities for change.* New York: Guilford Press.

Leary, C., Kelley, M., Morrow, J., & Mikulka, P. (2008). Parental use of physical punishment as related to family environment, psychological well-being, and personality in undergraduates. *Journal of Family Violence, 23*, 1–7.

Leckman, J. F., & King, R. A. (2007). A developmental perspective on the controversy surrounding the use of SSRIs to treat pediatric depression. *American Journal of Psychiatry, 164*, 1304–1306.

Leclair-Visonneau, L., Oudiette, D., Gaymard, B., Leu-Semenescu, S., & Arnulf, I. (2011). "Do the eyes scan dream images during rapid eye movement sleep? Evidence from the rapid eye movement sleep behaviour disorder model": Corrigendum. *Brain: A Journal of Neurology, 134*, 88–97.

Lee, A., Isaac, M. & Janca, A. (2007). Posttraumatic stress disorder and terrorism. In A. Monat, R. S. Lazarus, et al. (Eds.), *The Praeger handbook on stress and coping* (Vol. 1). Westport, CT: Praeger Publishers/Greenwood Publishing Group.

Lee, A. Y., & Aaker, J. L. (2004). Bringing the frame into focus: The influence of regulatory fit on processing fluency and persuasion. *Journal of Personality and Social Psychology, 86*, 205–218.

Lee, D., Kleinman, J., & Kleinman, A. (2007). Rethinking depression: An ethnographic study of the experiences of depression among Chinese. *Harvard Review of Psychiatry, 15*, 1–8.

Lee, F. H., & Raja, S. N. (2011). Complementary and alternative medicine in chronic pain. *Pain, 152*, 28–30.

Lee, H. J., Kwon, S. M., Kwon, J. S., & Telch, M. J. (2005). Testing the autogenous reactive model of obsessions. *Depress Anxiety, 21*, 118–129.

Lee, M. (2011, April 22). Pleasure and pain. *The Washington Post*, D-1.

Lee-Chiong, T. L. (2006). *Sleep: A comprehensive handbook.* New York: Wiley-Liss.

Leeman, R. F., Fischler, C., & Rozin, P. (2011). Medical doctors' attitudes and beliefs about diet and health are more like those of their lay countrymen (France, Germany, Italy, UK and USA) than those of doctors in other countries. *Appetite, 56*, 558–563.

Lehar, S. (2003). *The world in your head: A gestalt view of the mechanism of conscious experience.* Mahwah, NJ: Lawrence Erlbaum Associates.

Lehman, D. R., & Taylor, S. E. (1988). Date with an earthquake: Coping with a probable, unpredictable disaster. *Personality and Social Psychology Bulletin, 13*, 546–555.

Lehrman, S. (2007). Going beyond X and Y. *Scientific American*, pp. 40–41.

Leib, J. R., Gollust, S. E., Hull, S. C., & Wilfond, B. S. (2005). Carrier screening panels for Ashkenazi Jews: Is more better? *Genetic Medicine, 7*, 185–190.

Leibel, R. L., Rosenbaum, M., & Hirsch, J. (1995, March 9). Changes in energy expenditure resulting from altered body. *New England Journal of Medicine, 332*, 621–628.

Leiblum, S. R., & Chivers, M. L. (2007). Normal and persistent genital arousal in women: New perspectives. *Journal of Sex & Marital Therapy, 33*, 357–373.

Leigh, J. H., Zinkhan, G. M., & Swaminathan, V. (2006). Dimensional relationships of recall and recognition measures with selected cognitive and affective aspects of print ads. *Journal of Advertising, 35*, 105–122.

Leiter, S., & Leiter, W. M. (2003). *Affirmative action in antidiscrimination law and policy: An overview and synthesis. SUNY series in American constitutionalism.* Albany: State University of New York Press.

Leitner, L. M. (2007). Diversity issues, postmodernism, and psychodynamic therapy. *PsycCRITIQUES, 52*, no pagination specified.

Lemay, E., & Clark, M. (2008). How the head liberates the heart: Projection of communal responsiveness guides relationship promotion. *Journal of Personality and Social Psychology, 94*, 647–671.

Lemay, E. P., Jr., Clark, M. S., & Feeney, B. C. (2007). Projection of responsiveness to needs and the construction of satisfying communal relationships. *Journal of Personality and Social Psychology, 92*, 834–853.

Lemonick, M. D. (2000, December 11). Downey's downfall. *Time*, p. 97.

Lenzenweger, M. F., & Dworkin, R. H. (Eds.). (1998). *The origins and development of schizophrenia: Advances in experimental psychopathology.* Washington, DC: American Psychological Association.

Leo, R. J., & Latif, T. (2007). Repetitive transcranial magnetic stimulation (rTMS) in experimentally induced and chronic neuropathic pain: A review. *The Journal of Pain, 8*, 453–459.

Lepage, J. F., & Theoret, H. (2007). The mirror neuron system: Grasping others' actions from birth? *Developmental Science, 10*, 513–523.

Lepper, M. R., Corpus, J. H., & Iyengar, S. S. (2005). Intrinsic and extrinsic motivational orientations in the classroom: Age differences and academic correlates. *Journal of Educational Psychology, 97*, 184–196.

Leuthardt, E. C., Gaona, C., Sharma, M., Szrama, N., Roland, J., Freudenberg, Z., et al. (2011). Using the electrocorticographic speech network to control a brain-computer interface in humans. *Journal of Neural Engineering, 8*, 332–339.

LeVay, S. (1993). *The sexual brain.* Cambridge, MA: MIT.

LeVay, S. (2011). *Gay, straight, and the reason why: The science of sexual orientation.* New York: Oxford University Press.

Levi, A., Chan, K. K., & Pence, D. (2006). Real men do not read labels: The effects of masculinity and involvement on college students' food decisions. *Journal of American College Health, 55*, 91–98.

Levick, S. E. (2004). *Clone being: Exploring the psychological and social dimensions.* Lanham, MD: Rowman & Littlefield.

Levin, B. E. (2006). Metabolic sensing neurons and the control of energy homeostasis. *Physiology & Behavior, 89*, 486–489.

Levin, R., & Nielsen, T. (2009, April). Nightmares, bad dreams, and emotion dysregulation: A review and new neurocognitive model of dreaming. *Current Directions in Psychological Science, 18*, 84–88.

Levin, R. J. (2007). Sexual activity, health and well-being—the beneficial roles of coitus and masturbation. *Sexual and Relationship Therapy, 22*, 135–148.

Levine, J. M., & Moreland, R. L. (2006). Small groups: An overview. In J. M. Levine & R. L. Moreland (Eds.), *Small groups.* New York: Psychology Press.

Levine, S. Z. (2011). Elaboration on the association between IQ and parental SES with subsequent crime. *Personality and Individual Differences, 50*, 1233–1237.

Levine, S. Z., & Rabinowitz, J. (2007). Revisiting the 5 dimensions of the Positive and Negative Syndrome Scale. *Journal of Clinical Psychopharmacology, 27*, 431–436.

Levinson, D. (1992). *The seasons of a woman's life.* New York: Knopf.

Levinson, D. J. (1990). A theory of life structure development in adulthood. In C. N. Alexander & E. J. Langer (Eds.), *Higher stages of human development: Perspectives on adult growth.* New York: Oxford University Press.

Levy, B. (1996). Improving memory in old age through implicit self-stereotyping. *Journal of Personality and Social Psychology, 71*, 1092–1107.

Levy, B. R., & Myers, L. M. (2004). Preventive health behaviors influenced by self-perceptions of aging. *Preventive Medicine: An International Journal Devoted to Practice and Theory, 39*, 625–629.

Levy, B. R., Slade, M. D., Kunkel, S. R., & Kasl, S. V. (2002). Longevity increased by positive self-perceptions of aging. *Journal of Personality & Social Psychology, 83*, 261–270.

Lewin, T. (2003, December 22). For more people in their 20s and 30s, going home is easier because they never left. *The New York Times*, p. A27.

Lewinsohn, P. M., & Essau, C. A. (2002). Depression in adolescents. In I. H. Gotlib & C. L. Hammen (Eds.), *Handbook of depression.* New York: Guilford Press.

Lewinsohn, P. M., Petit, J. W., Joiner, T. E., Jr., & Seeley, J. R. (2003). The symptomatic expression of major depressive disorder in adolescents and young adults. *Journal of Abnormal Psychology, 112*, 244–252.

Lewis, C., & Lamb, M. (2011). The role of parent-child relationships in child development. In M. E. Lamb & M. H. Bornstein, (Eds.), *Social and personality development: An advanced textbook.* New York: Psychology Press.

Li, B., Piriz, J., Mirrione, M., Chung, C., Proulx, C. D., Schulz, D., et al. (2011). Synaptic potentiation onto habenula neurons in learned helplessness model of depression. *Nature, 470*, 535–539.

Li, H., & Leckenby, J. D. (2007). Examining the effectiveness of internet advertising formats. In D. W. Schumann & E. Thorson (Eds.), *Internet advertising theory and research.* Mahwah, NJ: Lawrence Erlbaum Associates.

Li, M. D., Cheng, R., Ma, J. Z., & Swan, G. E. (2003). A meta-analysis of estimated genetic and environmental effects on smoking behavior in male and female adult twins. *Addiction, 98*, 23–31.

Li, M. D., Lou, X., Chen, G., Ma, J. Z., & Elston, R. C. (2008). Gene-gene interactions among CHRNA4, CHRNB2, BDNF, and NTRK2 in nicotine dependence. *Biological Psychiatry, 64*, 951–957.

Li, T-K., Volkow, N. D., & Bal, R. D. (2007). The biological bases of nicotine and alcohol co-addiction. *Biological Psychiatry, 61*, 1–3.

Liang, K. A. (2007). Acculturation, ambivalent sexism, and attitudes toward women who engage in premarital sex among Chinese American young adults. *Dissertation Abstracts International: Section B: The Sciences and Engineering, 67*(10-B), 6065.

Libedinsky, C., & Livingstone, M. (2011). Role of prefrontal cortex in conscious visual perception. *The Journal of Neuroscience, 31*, 64–69.

Lichtenstein, J. (2011, March 27). The seekers. *The New York Times Magazine*, p. 44.

Licis, A. K., Desruisseau, D. M., Yamada, K. A., Duntley, S. P., & Gurnett, C. A. (2011). Novel genetic findings in an extended family pedigree with sleepwalking. *Neurology, 76*, 49–52.

Lidz, J., & Gleitman, L. R. (2004). Argument structure and the child's contribution to language learning. *Trends in Cognitive Sciences, 8*, 157–161.

Lieberman, M. D. (2007). Social cognitive neuroscience: A review of core processes. *Annual Review of Psychology, 58*, 259–289.

Lieberman, M. D., Hariri, A., Jarcho, J. M., Eisenberger, N. I., & Bookheimer, S. Y. (2005). An fMRI investigation of race-related amygdala activity in African-American and Caucasian-American individuals. *Nature Neuroscience, 8*, 720–722.

Liedl, A., Müller, J., Morina, N., Karl, A., Denke, C., & Knaevelsrud, C. (2011). Physical activity within a CBT intervention improves coping with pain in traumatized refugees: Results of a randomized controlled design. *Pain Medicine, 12*, 138–145.

Lien, Y-W., Chu, R-L., Jen, C-H., & Wu, C-H. (2006). Do Chinese commit neither fundamental attribution error nor ultimate attribution error? *Chinese Journal of Psychology, 48*, 163–181.

Lilienfeld, S. O. (2007). Psychological treatments that cause harm. *Perspectives on Psychological Science, 2*, 53–58.

Lin, C-H., & Lin, H-M. (2007). What price do you ask for the 'extra one'? A social value orientation perspective. *Social Behavior and Personality, 35*, 9–18.

Lin, Y., Li, K., Sung, W., Ko, H., Tzeng, O. L., Hung, D. L., et al. (2011). The relationship between development of attention and learning in children: A cognitive neuroscience approach. *Bulletin of Educational Psychology, 42*, 517–542.

Lin, Y. Y., Chen, W. T., Liao, K. K., Yeh, T. C., Wu, Z. Z., & Ho, L. T. (2005). Hemispheric balance in coding speech and non-speech sounds in Chinese participants. *Neuroreport, 16*, 469–473.

Lindblad, F., Lindahl, M., & Theorell, T. (2006). Physiological stress reactions in 6th and 9th graders during test performance. *Stress and Health: Journal of the International Society for the Investigation of Stress, 22*, 189–195.

Lindemann, O., & Bekkering, H. (2009). Object manipulation and motion perception: Evidence of an influence of action planning on visual processing. *Journal of Experimental Psychology: Human Perception and Performance, 35*, 1062–1071.

Lindh-Astrand, L., Brynhildsen, J., & Hoffmann, M. (2007). Attitudes towards the menopause and hormone therapy over the turn of the century. *Maturitas, 56*, 12–20.

Lindley, L. D. (2006). The paradox of self-efficacy: Research with diverse populations. *Journal of Career Assessment, 14*, 143–160.

Lindorff, M. (2005). Determinants of received social support: Who gives what to managers? *Journal of Social and Personal Relationships, 22*, 323–337.

Lindsay, P. H., & Norman, D. A. (1977). *Human information processing* (2nd ed.). New York: Academic Press.

Lindsey, E., & Colwell, M. (2003). Preschoolers' emotional competence: Links to pretend and physical play. *Child Study Journal, 33*, 39–52.

Links, P. S., Eynan, R., & Heisel, M. J. (2007). Affective instability and suicidal ideation and behavior in patients with borderline personality disorder. *Journal of Personality Disorders, 21*, 72–86.

Liszkowski, U., Schäfer, M., Carpenter, M., & Tomasello, M. (2009). Prelinguistic infants, but not chimpanzees, communicate about absent entities. *Psychological Science, 20*, 654–660.

Litowitz, B. E. (2007). Unconscious fantasy: A once and future concept. *Journal of the American Psychoanalytic Association, 55*, 199–228.

Little, A., Burt, D. M., & Perrett, D. I. (2006). What is good is beautiful: Face preference reflects desired personality. *Personality and Individual Differences, 41*, 1107–1118.

Little, K., Ramssen, E., Welchko, R., Volberg, V., Roland, C., & Cassin, B. (2009). Decreased brain dopamine cell numbers in human cocaine users. *Psychiatry Research, 168*, 173–180.

Liu, J. H., & Mills, D. (2006). Modern racism and neo-liberal globalization: The discourses of plausible deniability and their multiple functions. *Journal of Community & Applied Social Psychology, 16*, 83–99.

Liu, L., He, S-Z., & Wu, Y. (2007). An analysis of the characteristics of single parent families with different structures and their children. *Chinese Journal of Clinical Psychology, 15*, 68–70.

Livesley, W., & Jang, K. (2008). The behavioral genetics of personality disorder. *Annual Review of Clinical Psychology, 4*, 247–274.

Livingstone, A. G., Spears, R., Manstead, A. R., Bruder, M., et al. (2011). We feel, therefore we are: Emotion as a basis for self-categorization and social action. *Emotion, 11*, 754–767.

Lobato, M. I., Koff, W. J., & Manenti, C. (2006). Follow-up of sex reassignment surgery in transsexuals: A Brazilian cohort. *Archives of Sexual Behavior, 35*, 711–715.

Lobban, F., Barrowclough, C., & Jones, S. (2006). Does expressed emotion need to be understood within a more systemic framework? An examination of discrepancies in appraisals between patients diagnosed with schizophrenia and their relatives. *Social Psychiatry and Psychiatric Epidemiology, 41*, 50–55.

Lobo, I., & Harris, R. (2008, July). $GABA_a$ receptors and alcohol. *Pharmacology, Biochemistry and Behavior, 90*, 90–94.

Locicero, A., & Sinclair, S. (2008, March). Terrorism and terrorist leaders: Insights from developmental and ecological psychology. *Studies in Conflict & Terrorism, 31*, 227–250.

Locke, J. L. (2006). Parental selection of vocal behavior: Crying, cooking, babbling, and the evolution of language. *Human Nature, 17*, 155–168.

Lockl, K., & Schneider, W. (2007). Knowledge about the mind: Links between theory of mind and later metamemory. *Child Development, 78*, 148–167.

Lofholm, N. (2003, May 6). Climber's kin share relief: Ralston saw 4 options, they say; death wasn't one of them. *Denver Post*, p. A1.

Loftus, E. F. (1993). Psychologists in the eyewitness world. *American Psychologist, 48*, 550–552.

Loftus, E. F. (2004). Memories of things unseen. *Current Directions in Psychological Science, 13*, 145–147.

Loftus, E. F., & Bernstein, D. M. (2005). Rich false memories: The royal road to success. In A. F. Healy (Ed.), *Experimental cognitive psychology and its applications.* Washington, DC: American Psychological Association.

Loftus, E. F., & Palmer, J. C. (1974). Reconstruction of automobile destruction: An example of the interface between language and memory. *Journal of Verbal Learning and Verbal Behavior, 13*, 585–589.

Loitfelder, M. M., Fazekas, F. F., Petrovic, K. K., Fuchs, S. S., Ropele, S. S., Wallner-Blazek, M. M., et al. (2011). Reorganization in cognitive networks with progression of multiple sclerosis: Insights from fMRI. *Neurology, 76*, 526–533.

Long, G. M., & Beaton, R. J. (1982). The case for peripheral persistence: Effects of target and background luminance on a partial-report task. *Journal of Experimental Psychology: Human Perception and Performance, 8*, 383–391.

Lopes, A. C., Greenberg, B. D., Noren, G., Canteras, M. M., Busatto, G. F. de Mathis, et al. (2009). Treatment of resistant obsessive-compulsive disorder with ventral capsular/ventral striatal gamma capsulotomy: A pilot prospective study. *The Journal of Neuropsychiatry and Clinical Neurosciences, 21*, 381–392.

López, S. R., & Guarnaccia, P. J. J. (2000). Cultural psychopathology: Uncovering the social world of mental illness. *Annual Review of Psychology, 51*, 571–598.

Lorenz, K. (1966). *On aggression.* New York: Harcourt Brace Jovanovich.

Lorenz, K. (1974). *Civilized man's eight deadly sins.* New York: Harcourt Brace Jovanovich.

Lothane, Z. (2005). Jung, A biography. *Journal of the American Psychoanalytic Association, 53*, 317–324.

Loving, T., Crockett, E., & Paxson, A. (2009). Passionate love and relationship thinkers:

Experimental evidence for acute cortisol elevations in women. *Psychoneuroendocrinology, 34*, 939–946.

Lowe, P., Humphreys, C., & Williams, S. J. (2007). Night terrors: Women's experiences of (not) sleeping where there is domestic violence. *Violence against Women, 13*, 549–561.

Lowery, D., Fillingim, R. B., & Wright, R. A. (2003). Sex differences and incentive effects on perceptual and cardiovascular responses to cold pressor pain. *Psychosomatic Medicine, 65*, 284–291.

Lu, J., Sherman, D., Devor, M., & Saper, C. B. (2006). A putative flip-flop switch for control of REM sleep. *Nature, 441*, 589–594.

Lubell, K. M., Swahn, M. H., Crosby, A. E., & Kegler, S. R. (2004). Methods of suicide among persons aged 10–19 years—United States, 1992–2001. *MMWR, 53*, 471–473. Retrieved from http://www.cdc.gov/mmwr/PDF/wk/mm5322.pdf.

Lublin, H., Eberhard, J., & Levander, S. (2005). Current therapy issues and unmet clinical needs in the treatment of schizophrenia: A review of the new generation antipsychotics. *International Clinical Psychopharmacology, 20*, 183–198.

Lucas, W. (2008). Parents' perceptions of the Drug Abuse Resistance Education program (DARE). *Journal of Child & Adolescent Substance Abuse, 17*, 99–114.

Luchins, A. S. (1946). Classroom experiments on mental set. *American Journal of Psychology, 59*, 295–298.

Lucki, I., & O'Leary, O. E (2004). Distinguishing roles for norepinephrine and serotonin in the behavioral effects of antidepressant drugs. *Journal of Clinical Psychiatry, 65*, 11–24.

Luckiesh, M. (1921). Visual illusions in the arts. *Scientific American Monthly, 3*, 497–501.

Luders, E., Narr, K. L., Zaidel, E., Thompson, P. M., & Toga, A. W. (2006). Gender effects on callosal thickness in scaled and unscaled space. *Neuroreport, 17*, 1103–1106.

Ludwig, A. M. (1996, March). Mental disturbances and creative achievement. *The Harvard Mental Health Letter*, pp. 4–6.

Luk, G., Anderson, J. A. E., Craik, F. I. M., Grady, C., Bialystok, E. (2010). Distinct neural correlates for two types of inhibition in bilinguals: Response inhibition versus interference suppression. *Brain and Cognition, 74*, 347–357, figure 3a.

Lun, V. M., & Bond, M. H. (2006). Achieving relationship harmony in groups and its consequence for group performance. *Asian Journal of Social Psychology, 9*, 195–202.

Luo, S., & Zhang, G. (2009). What leads to romantic attraction: Similarity, reciprocity, security, or beauty? Evidence from a speed-dating study. *Journal of Personality, 77*, 933–964.

Luria, A. R. (1968). *The mind of a mnemonist*. Cambridge, MA: Basic Books.

Luthar, S. S., Cicchetti, D., & Becker, B. (2000). The construct of resilience: A critical evaluation and guidelines for future work. *Child Development, 71*, 543–562.

Lutz, C. K., & Novak, M. A. (2005). Environmental enrichment for nonhuman primates: Theory and application. *ILAR Journal, 46*, 178–191.

Lutz, W., Lambert, M. J., Harmon, S. C., Tschitsaz, A., Schurch, E., & Stulz, N. (2006). The probability of treatment success, failure and duration—What can be learned from empirical data to support decision making in clinical practice? *Clinical Psychology & Psychotherapy, 13*, 223–232.

Lymberis, S. C., Parhar, P. K., Katsoulakis, E., & Formenti, S. C. (2004). Pharmacogenomics and breast cancer. *Pharmacogenomics, 5*, 31–55.

Lynch, T. R., Trost, W. T., Salsman, N., & Linehan, M. M. (2007). Dialectical behavior therapy for borderline personality disorder. *Annual Review of Clinical Psychology, 3*, 181–205.

Lynn, S. J., Fassler, O., & Knox, J. (2005). Hypnosis and the altered state debate: Something more or nothing more? Comment. *Contemporary Hypnosis, 22*, 39–45.

Lynn, S. J., Kirsch, I., Barabasz, A., Cardena, E., & Patterson, D. (2000). Hypnosis as an empirically supported clinical intervention: The state of the evidence and a look to the future. *International Journal of Clinical and Experimental Hypnosis, 48*, 239–259.

Lynn, S. J., Lock, T., Loftus, E. F., Krackow, E., & Lilienfeld, S. O. (2003). The remembrance of things past: Problematic memory recovery techniques in psychotherapy. In S. O. Lilienfeld, S. J. Lynn, & J. M. Lohr (Eds.), *Science and pseudoscience in clinical psychology*. New York: Guilford Press.

Lynn, S. J., Neufeld, V., Green, J. P., Sandberg, D., et al. (1996). Daydreaming, fantasy, and psycho-pathology. In R. G. Kunzendorf, N. P. Spanos, & B. Wallace (Eds.), *Hypnosis and imagination. Imagery and human development series*. Amityville, NY: Baywood.

Lyons, H., Giordano, P. C., Manning, W. D., & Longmore, M. A. (2011). Identity, peer relationships, and adolescent girls' sexual behavior: An exploration of the contemporary double standard. *Journal of Sex Research, 48*, 437–449.

Ma, Y., Wang, C., & Han, S. (2011). Neural responses to perceived pain in others predict real-life monetary donations in different socioeconomic contexts. *NeuroImage, 57*, 1273–1280.

Macaluso, E., & Driver, J. (2005). Multisensory spatial interactions: A window onto functional integration in the human brain. *Trends in Neurosciences, 28, Issue 5*, 264–271.

Macaluso, E., Frith, C. D., & Driver, J. (2000, August 18). Modulation of human visual cortex by crossmodal spatial attention. *Science, 289*, 1206–1208.

Macduff, I. (2006). Your pace or mine? Culture, time and negotiation. *Negotiation Journal, 22*, 31–45.

Mack, J. (2003). *The museum of the mind*. London: British Museum Publications.

Mackay, J., & Eriksen, M. (2002). *The tobacco atlas*. Geneva, Switzerland: World Health Organization.

MacLean, L., Edwards, N., Garrard, M., Sims-Jones, N., Clinton, K., & Ashley, L. (2009, March). Obesity, stigma and public health planning. *Health Promotion International, 24*, 88–93.

MacLennan, A. (2009). Evidence-based review of therapies at the menopause. *International Journal of Evidence-Based Healthcare, 7*, 112–123.

Macmillan, M. (1996). *Freud evaluated: The completed arc*. Cambridge, MA: MIT.

MacNeilage, P. F., Rogers, L. J., & Vallortigara, G. (2009, July). Origins of the left & right brain. *Scientific American*, pp. 60–67.

Madden, D. J. (2007). Aging and visual attention. *Current Directions in Psychological Science, 16*, 70–74.

Maddi, S. R. (2007). The story of hardiness: Twenty years of theorizing, research, and practice. In A. Monat, R. S. Lazarus, et al. (Eds.), *The Praeger handbook on stress and coping* (Vol. 2). Westport, CT: Praeger Publishers/Greenwood Publishing.

Maddi, S. R., Khoshaba, D. M., Harvey, R. H., Fazel, M., & Resurreccion, N. (2011). The personality construct of hardiness, V: Relationships with the construction of existential meaning in life. *Journal of Humanistic Psychology, 51*, 369–388.

Mader, S. S. (2000). *Biology* (6th ed.). Boston: McGraw-Hill.

Madon, S., Willard, J., & Guyll, M. (2006). Self-fulfilling prophecy effects of mothers' beliefs on children's alcohol use: Accumulation, dissipation, and stability over time. *Journal of Personality and Social Psychology, 90*, 911–926.

Magida, A. J. (2006). *Opening the doors of wonder: Reflections on religious rites of passage*. Berkeley, CA: University of California Press.

Magis, D., & Schoenen, J. (2011). Treatment of migraine: Update on new therapies. *Current Opinions in Neurology, 24*, 203–210.

Magoni, M., Bassani, L., Okong, P., Kituuka, P., Germinario, E. P., Giuliano, M., et al. (2005). Mode of infant feeding and HIV infection in children in a program for prevention of mother-to-child transmission in Uganda. *AIDS, 19*, 433–437.

Magoon, M., & Critchfield, T. (2008). Concurrent schedules of positive and negative reinforcement: Differential-impact and differential-outcomes hypotheses. *Journal of the Experimental Analysis of Behavior, 90*, 1–22.

Magruder, K., & Yeager, D. (2009). The prevalence of PTSD across war eras and the effect of deployment on PTSD: A systematic review and meta-analysis. *Psychiatric Annals, 39*, 778–788.

Maguire, E. A., Woollett, K., & Spiers, H. J. (2006). London taxi drivers and bus drivers: A structural MRI and neuropsychological analysis. *Hippocampus, 16*, 1091–1101.

Mahmood, M., & Black, J. (2005). Narcolepsycataplexy: How does recent understanding help in evaluation and treatment? *Current Treatment Options in Neurology, 7*, 363–371.

Majeres, R. L. (2007). Sex differences in phonological coding: Alphabet transformation speed. *Intelligence, 35*, 335–346.

Major, J. T., Johnson, W., & Bouchard, T. R. (2011). The dependability of the general factor of intelligence: Why small, single-factor models do not adequately represent g. *Intelligence, 39*, 418–433.

Majorano, M., & D'Odorico, L. (2011). The transition into ambient language: A longitudinal study of babbling and first word production of Italian children. *First Language, 31*, 47–66.

Maldonado, J. R., & Spiegel, D. (2003). Dissociative disorders. In R. E. Hales & S. C. Yudofsky (Eds.), *The American Psychiatric Publishing textbook of clinical psychiatry* (4th ed.). Washington, DC: American Psychiatric Publishing.

Malle, B. E (2004). *How the mind explains behavior: Folk explanations, meaning, and social interaction*. Cambridge, MA: MIT.

Malouff, J. M., Thorsteinsson, E. B., & Schutte, N. S. (2007). The efficacy of problem solving therapy in reducing mental and physical health problems: A meta-analysis. *Clinical Psychology Review, 27,* 46–57.

Mancinelli, R., Binetti, R., & Ceccanti, M. (2007). Woman, alcohol and environment: Emerging risks for health. *Neuroscience & Biobehavioral Reviews, 31,* 246–253.

Manly, J., & Echemendia, R. (2007). Race-specific norms: Using the model of hypertension to understand issues of race, culture, and education in neuropsychology. *Archives of Clinical Neuropsychology, 22,* 319–325.

Manly, J. J. (2005). Advantages and disadvantages of separate norms for African Americans. *Clinical Neuropsychologist, 19,* 270–275.

Manly, J. J. (2006). Deconstructing race and ethnicity: Implications for measurement of health outcomes [Special issue: Measurement in a multi-ethnic society]. *Medical Care, 44,* S10–S16.

Mann, K., Ackermann, K., Croissant, B., Mundle, G., Nakovics, H., & Diehl, A. (2005). Neuroimaging of gender differences in alcohol dependence: Are women more vulnerable? *Alcoholism: Clinical & Experimental Research, 29,* 896–901.

Mann, R. E., & Hollin, C. R. (2007). Sexual offenders' explanations for their offending. *Journal of Sexual Aggression, 13,* 3–9.

Manning, M. A., & Hoyme, E. H. (2007). Fetal alcohol spectrum disorders: A practical clinical approach to diagnosis. *Neuroscience & Biobehavioral Reviews, 31,* 230–238.

Manor, J. K., & Gailliot, M. T. (2007). Altruism and egoism: Prosocial motivations for helping

Manstead, A. S. R., Frijda, N., & Fischer, A. H. (Eds.). (2003). *Feelings and emotions: The Amsterdam Symposium.* Cambridge, England: Cambridge University Press.

Manstead, A. S. R., & Wagner, H. L. (2004). *Experience emotion.* Cambridge, England: Cambridge University Press.

Marcus-Newhall, A., Pedersen, W. C., & Carlson, M. (2000). Displaced aggression is alive and well: A meta-analytic review. *Journal of Personality and Social Psychology, 78,* 670–689.

Marks, I. M. (2004). The Nobel prize award in physiology to Ivan Petrovich Pavlov-1904. *Australian and New Zealand Journal of Psychiatry, 38,* 674–677.

Markus, H. R. (2007). Sociocultural psychology: The dynamic interdependence among self systems and social systems. In S. Kitayama & D. Cohen (Eds.), *Handbook of cultural psychology.* New York: Guilford Press.

Markus, H. R., & Kitayama, S. (2003). Models of agency: Sociocultural diversity in the construction of action. In V. Murphy-Berman & J. J. Berman (Eds.), *Cross-cultural differences in perspectives on the self.* Lincoln, NE: University of Nebraska Press.

Marmar, C. (2009). Mental health impact of Afghanistan and Iraq deployment: Meeting the challenge of a new generation of veterans. *Depression and Anxiety, 26,* 493–497.

Marsh, B. (2008, February 24). A growing cloud over the planet. *The New York Times,* p. WK4.

Marsh, H. W., Hau, K. T., & Sung, R. Y. T. (2007). Childhood obesity, gender, actual-ideal body image discrepancies, and physical self-concept in Hong Kong children: Cultural differences in the value of moderation. *Developmental Psychology, 43,* 647–662.

Marsh, R., Steinglass, J. E., Gerber, A. J., O'Leory, K., Wang, 2., Murphy, D., & . . . Peterson, B. S.

(2009). Deficient activity in the neural systems that mediate self-regulatory control in bulimia nervosa. *Archives of General Psychiatry, 66,* 51–63.

Marshall, J. R. (2011). Ultimate causes and the evolution of altruism. *Behavioral Ecology and Sociobiology, 65,* 503–512.

Marshall, K., Laing, D. G., & Jinks, A. L. (2006). The capacity of humans to identify components in complex odor-taste mixtures. *Chemical Senses, 31,* 539–545.

Marshall, L., & Born, J. (2007, October). The contribution of sleep to hippocampus-dependent memory consolidation. *Trends in Cognitive Sciences, 11*(10), 442–450.

Marshall, M. K. (2007). The critical factors of coaching practice leading to successful coaching outcomes. *Dissertation Abstracts International: Section B: The Sciences and Engineering, 67*(7-B), 4092.

Marshall, R. D., Bryant, R. A., & Amsel, L. (2007). The psychology of ongoing threat: Relative risk appraisal, the September 11 attacks, and terrorism-re-lated fears. *American Psychologist, 62,* 304–316.

Marshall, R. D., Bryant, R. A., Amsel, L., Suh, E. J., Cook, J. M., & Neria, Y. (2007). The psychology of ongoing threat: Relative risk appraisal, the September 11 attacks and terrorism-related fears. *American Psychologist, 62,* 304–316.

Marszalek, J. (2007). Computerized adaptive testing and the experience of flow in examinees. *Dissertation Abstracts International Section A: Humanities and Social Sciences, 67*(7-A), 2465.

Martelle, S., Hanley, C., & Yoshino, K. (2003, January 28). "Sopranos" scenario in slaying? *Los Angeles Times,* p. B1.

Martin, A. J., & Marsh, H. W. (2002). Fear of failure: Friend or foe? *Australian Psychologist, 38,* 31–38.

Martin, E. A., & Kerns, J. G. (2011). The influence of positive mood on different aspects of cognitive control. *Cognition and Emotion, 25,* 265–279.

Martin, L., & Pullum, G. K. (1991). *The great Eskimo vocabulary hoax.* Chicago: University of Chicago Press.

Martin, P. D., & Brantley, P. J. (2004). Stress, coping, and social support in health and behavior. In J. M. Raczynski & L. C. Leviton (Eds.), *Handbook of clinical health psychology, Vol. 2: Disorders of behavior and health.* Washington, DC: American Psychological Association.

Martindale, C. (1981). *Cognition and consciousness.* Homewood, IL: Dorsey.

Martinko, M. J., Harvey, P., & Dasborough, M. T. (2011). Attribution theory in the organizational sciences: A case of unrealized potential. *Journal of Organizational Behavior, 32,* 144–149.

Mashour, G. A., Walker, E. E., & Martuza, R. L. (2005). Psychosurgery: Past, present, and future. *Brain Research Reviews, 48,* 409–419.

Maslow, A. H. (1970). *Motivation and personality.* New York: Harper & Row.

Maslow, A. H. (1987). *Motivation and personality* (3rd ed.). New York: Harper & Row.

Maslowsky, J., Mogg, K., Bradley, B. P., McClure-Tone, E., et al. (2010). A Preliminary Investigation of Neural Correlates of Treatment in Adolescents with Generalized Anxiety Disorder. *Journal of Child and Adolescent Psychopharmacology, 20*(2), 105–111.

Massaro, D. W., & Chen, T. H. (2008). The motor theory of speech perception revisited. *Psychonomic Bulletin & Review, 15,* 453–457.

Mast, F. W., & Kosslyn, S. M. (2002). Visual mental images can be ambiguous: Insights from individual differences in spatial transformation abilities. *Cognition, 86,* 57–70.

Masters, W. H., & Johnson, V. E. (1979). *Homosexuality in perspective.* Boston: Little, Brown.

Masuda, M. (2003). Meta-analyses of love scales: Do various love scales measure the same psychological constructs? *Japanese Psychological Research, 45,* 25–37.

Mathews, H. L., & Janusek, L. (2011). Epigenetics and psychoneuroimmunology: Mechanisms and models. *Brain, Behavior, and Immunity, 25,* 25–39.

Maton, K. I., Kohout, J. L., Wicherski, M., Leary, G. E., & Vinokurov, A. (2006). Minority students of color and the psychology graduate pipeline. *American Psychologist, 61,* 117–131.

Matson, J., & LoVullo, S. (2008). A review of behavioral treatments for self-injurious behaviors of persons with autism spectrum disorders. *Behavior Modification, 32,* 61–76.

Matsumoto, D. (2002). Methodological requirements to test a possible in-group advantage in judging emotions across cultures: Comment on Elfenbein and Ambady (2002) and evidence. *Psychological Bulletin, 128,* 236–242.

Matthews, G., & Funke, G. J. (2006). Worry and information-processing. In G. C. L. Davey & A. Wells (Eds.), *Worry and its psychological disorders: Theory, assessment and treatment.* Hoboken, NJ: Wiley Publishing.

Maurer, D., Lewis, T. L., Brent, H. P., & Levin, A. V. (1999, October 1). Rapid improvement in the acuity of infants after visual input. *Science, 286,* 108–110.

Mayer, J. D., Salovey, P., & Caruso, D. R. (2004). Emotional intelligence: Theory, findings, and implications. *Psychological Inquiry, 15,* 197–215.

Mayer, J. D., Salovey, P., & Caruso, D. R. (2008). Emotional intelligence: New ability or eclectic traits? *American Psychologist, 63,* 503–517.

Maynard, A. E., & Martini, M. I. (2005). *Learning in cultural context: Family, peers, and school.* New York: Kluwer Academic/Plenum Publishers.

McAdams, D. P., Diamond, A., de St. Aubin, E., & Mansfield, E. (1997). Stories of commitment: The psychosocial construction of generative lives. *Journal of Personality and Social Psychology, 72,* 678–694.

McCabe, C., & Rolls, E. T. (2007). Umami: A delicious flavor formed by convergence of taste and olfactory pathways in the human brain. *European Journal of Neuroscience, 25,* 1855–1864.

McCarthy, J. (2005). Individualism and collectivism: What do they have to do with counseling? *Journal of Multicultural Counseling and Development, 33,* 108–117.

McCarthy, R. J., & Skowronski, J. J. (2011). You're getting warmer: Level of construal affects the impact of central traits on impression formation. *Journal of Experimental Social Psychology, 47,* 1304–1307.

McCaul, K. D., Johnson, R. J., & Rothman, A. J. (2002). The effects of framing and action instructions on whether older adults obtain flu shots. *Health Psychology, 21,* 624–628.

McCauley, R. N., & Henrich, J. (2006). Susceptibility to the Müller-Lyer illusion, theory-neutral observation, and the diachronic penetrability of the visual input. *Philosophical Psychology, 19,* 79–101.

McClelland, D. C. (1985). How motives, skills, and values determine what people do. *American Psychologist, 40*, 812–825.

McClelland, D. C. (1993). Intelligence is not the best predictor of job performance. *Current Directions in Psychological Research, 2*, 5–8.

McClelland, D. C., Atkinson, J. W., Clark, R. A., & Lowell, E. L. (1953). *The achievement motive.* New York: Appleton-Century-Crofts.

McClure, J., Sutton, R. M., & Sibley, C. G. (2007). Listening to reporters or engineers? How instance-based messages about building design affect earthquake fatalism. *Journal of Applied Social Sciences, 37*, 1956–1973.

McCrae, R. R., & Costa, P. T., Jr. (1986). A five-factor theory of personality. In L. A. Pervin & O. P. John (Eds.), *Handbook of personality: Theory and research* (2nd ed.). New York: Guilford.

McCrae, R. R., Kurtz, J. E., Yamagata, S., & Terracciano, A. (2011). Internal consistency, retest reliability, and their implications for personality scale validity. *Personality and Social Psychology Review, 15*, 28–50.

McCrink, K., & Wynn, K. (2007). Ratio abstraction by 6-month-old infants. *Psychological Science, 18*, 740–745.

McDaniel, M. A., Maier, S. F., & Einstein, G. O. (2002). "Brain specific" nutrients: A memory cure? *Psychological Science in the Public Interest, 3*, 12–18.

McDonald, C., & Murray, R. M. (2004). Can structural magnetic resonance imaging provide an alternative phenotype for genetic studies of schizophrenia? In M. S. Keshavan, J. L. Kennedy, & R. M. Murray (Eds.), *Neurodevelopment and schizophrenia.* New York: Cambridge University Press.

McDonald, H. E., & Hirt, E. R. (1997). When expectancy meets desire: Motivational effects in reconstructive memory. *Journal of Personality and Social Psychology, 72*, 5–23.

McDougall, W. (1908). *Introduction to social psychology.* London: Methuen.

McDowell, D. M., & Spitz, H. I. (1999). *Substance abuse.* New York: Brunner/Mazel.

McEwen, B. S. (1998, January 15). Protective and damaging effects of stress mediators [Review article]. *New England Journal of Medicine, 338*, 171–179.

McGaugh, J. L. (2003). *Memory and emotion: The making of lasting memories.* New York: Columbia University Press.

McGilvray, J. (Ed.). (2004). *The Cambridge companion to Chomsky.* Oxford, England: Cambridge University Press.

McGinn, D. (2003, June 9). Testing, testing: The new job search. *Time*, pp. 36–38.

McGregor, K. K., & Capone, N. C. (2004). Genetic and environmental interactions in determining the early lexicon: Evidence from a set of tri-zygotic quadruplets. *Journal of Child language, 31*, 311–337.

McIntyre, K., Korn, J., & Matsuo, H. (2008). Sweating the small stuff: How different types of hassles result in the experience of *stress*. *Stress and Health: Journal of the International Society for the Investigation of Stress, 24*, 383–392.

McKinley, M. J., Cairns, M. J., Denton, D. A., Egan, G., Mathai, M. L., Uschakov, A., et al. (2004). Physiological and pathophysiological influences on thirst. *Physiology and Behavior, 81*, 795–803.

McMurtray, A. M., Licht, E., Yeo, T., Krisztal, E., Saul, R. E., & Mendez, M. F. (2007). Positron emission tomography facilitates diagnosis of early-onset Alzheimer's disease. *European Neurology, 59*, 31–37.

McNally, R. J. (2011). *What is mental illness?* Cambridge, MA: Harvard University Press.

McNamara, P. (2004). *An evolutionary psychology of sleep and dreams.* Westport, CT: Praeger Publishers/Greenwood Publishing Group.

McTeague, L. M., Lang, P. J., Laplante, M., & Bradley, M. M. (2011). Aversive imagery in panic disorder: Agoraphobia severity, comorbidity, and defensive physiology. *Biological Psychiatry, 70*, 415–424.

Mead, M. (1949). *Male and female.* New York: Morrow.

Means, M. K., & Edinger, J. D. (2007). Graded exposure therapy for addressing claustrophobic reactions to continuous positive airway pressure: A case series report. *Behavioral Sleep Medicine, 5*, 105–116.

Medeiros, R., Prediger, R. D. S., Passos, G. F., Pandolfo, P., et al. (2007). Connecting TNF-α signaling pathways to iNOS expression in a mouse model of Alzheimer's disease: Relevance for the behavioral and synaptic deficits induced by amyloid β protein. *Journal of Neuroscience, 27*, 5394–5404.

Meeter, M., & Murre, J. M. J. (2004). Consolidation of long-term memory: Evidence and alternatives. *Psychological Bulletin, 130*, 843–857.

Mehl-Madrona, L. E. (2004). Hypnosis to facilitate uncomplicated birth. *American Journal of Clinical Hypnosis, 46*, 299–312.

Meinlschmidt, G., & Heim, C. (2007). Sensitivity to intranasal oxytocin in adult men with early parental separation. *Biological Psychiatry, 61*, 1109–1111.

Mel, B. W. (2002, March 8). What the synapse tells the neuron. *Science, 295*, 1845–1846.

Mel'nikov, K. S. (1993, October-December). On some aspects of the mechanistic approach to the study of processes of forgetting. *Vestnik Moskovskogo Universiteta Seriya 14 Psikhologiya*, pp. 64–67.

Meltzer, H. Y. (2000). Genetics and etiology of schizophrenia and bipolar disorder. *Biological Psychiatry, 47*, 171–173.

Meltzoff, A. N. (1996). The human infant as imitative generalist: A 20-year progress report on infant imitation with implications for comparative psychology. In C. M. Heyes & B. G. Galef, Jr. (Eds.), *Social learning in animals: The roots of culture.* San Diego, CA: Academic Press.

Melzack, R., & Katz, J. (2001). The McGill Pain Questionnaire: Appraisal and current status. In D. Turk & R. Melzack (Eds.), *Handbook of pain assessment* (2nd ed.). New York: Guilford Press.

Mendelsohn, J. (2003, November 7–9). What we know about sex. *USA Weekend*, pp. 6–9.

Mercadillo, R. E., Díaz, J., Pasaye, E. H., & Barrios, F. A. (2011). Perception of suffering and compassion experience: Brain gender disparities. *Brain and Cognition, 76*, 5–14.

Merikangas, K. R., Ames, M., Cui, L., Stang, P. E., Ustun, T. B., VonKorff, M., et al. (2007). The impact of comorbidity of mental and physical conditions on role disability in the US adult household population. *Archives of General Psychiatry, 64*, 1180–1188.

Mesoudi, A. (2011). Evolutionary psychology meets cultural psychology. *Journal of Evolutionary Psychology, 9*, 83–87.

Messner, M., Reinhard, M., & Sporer, S. (2008). Compliance through direct persuasive appeals: The moderating role of communicator's attractiveness in interpersonal persuasion. *Social Influence, 3*, 67–83.

Meyer, I. & Ladewig, J. (2008). The relationship between number of training sessions per week and learning in dogs. *Applied Animal Behaviour Science, 111*, 311–320.

Meyer-Bahlburg, H. (1997). The role of prenatal estrogens in sexual orientation. In L. Ellis & L. Ebertz (Eds.), *Sexual orientation: Toward biological understanding.* Westport, CT: Praeger.

Meyerowitz, J. (2004). *How sex changed: A history of transsexuality in the United States.* Cambridge, MA: Harvard University Press.

Michael, R. T., Gagnon, J. H., Laumann, E. O., & Kolata, G. (1994). *Sex in America: A definitive survey.* Boston: Little, Brown.

Micheau, J., & Marighetto, A. (2011). Acetylcholine and memory: A long, complex and chaotic but still living relationship. *Behavioural Brain Research, 221*, 424–429.

Midanik, L. T., Tam, T. W., & Weisner, C. (2007). Concurrent and simultaneous drug and alcohol use: Results of the 2000 national alcohol survey. *Drug and Alcohol Dependence, 90*, 72–80.

Middlebrooks, J. C., Furukawa, S., Stecker, G. C., & Mickey, B. J. (2005). Distributed representation of sound-source location in the auditory cortex. In R. König, P. Heil, E. Budinger, & H. Scheich (Eds.), *Auditory cortex: A synthesis of human and animal research.* Mahwah, NJ: Lawrence Erlbaum Associates.

Miesenbock, G. (2008, October). Lighting up the brain. *Scientific American*, pp. 52–59.

Mifflin, L. (1998, January 14). Study finds a decline in TV network violence. *The New York Times*, p. A14.

Mignon, A., & Mollaret, P. (2002). Applying the affordance conception of traits: A person perception study. *Personality and Social Psychology Bulletin, 28*, 1327–1334.

Miguez, G., Witnauer, J. E., & Miller, R. R. (2011). The role of contextual associations in producing the partial reinforcement acquisition deficit. *Journal of Experimental Psychology: Animal Behavior Processes, 37*, 88–97.

Mika, V. S., Wood, P. R., Weiss, B. D., & Trevino, L. (2007). Ask Me 3: Improving communication in a Hispanic pediatric outpatient practice. *American Journal of Behavioral Health, 31*, S115–S121.

Miklowitz, D. J., & Thompson, M. C. (2003). Family variables and interventions in schizophrenia. In G. Sholevar & G. Pirooz (Eds.), *Textbook of family and couples therapy: Clinical applications.* Washington, DC: American Psychiatric Publishing.

Mikulincer, M., & Shaver, P. R. (2005). Attachment security, compassion, and altruism. *Current Directions in Psychological Science, 14*, 34–38.

Miles, P., Schaufeli, W. B., & van den Bos, K. (2011). When weak groups are strong: How low cohesion groups allow individuals to act according to their personal absence tolerance norms. *Social Justice Research, 24*, 207–230.

Milgram, S. (1965). *Obedience* [film]. New York University Film Library and Pennsylvania State University, PCR.

Milgram, S. (2005). *Obedience to authority.* Pinter & Martin: New York.

Miller, C., & Williams, A. (2011). Ethical guidelines in research. In J. C. Thomas & M. Hersen (Eds.), *Understanding research in clinical and counseling psychology* (2nd ed.). New York: Routledge/Taylor & Francis Group.

Miller, G. (2006). A spoonful of medicine—and a steady diet of normalcy. *Science, 311*, 464–465.

Miller, G. (2008, May 9). The roots of morality. *Science, 320,* 734–737.

Miller, G. (2011, September 30.) Social scientists wade into the Tweet stream. *Science, 333,* 1814–1815.

Miller, G. E., Chen, E., & Parker, K. J. (2011). Psychological stress in childhood and susceptibility to the chronic diseases of aging: Moving toward a model of behavioral and biological mechanisms. *Psychological Bulletin, 137,* 959–997.

Miller, G. F., & Penke, L. (2007). The evolution of human intelligence and the coefficient of additive genetic variance in human brain size. *Intelligence, 35,* 97–114.

Miller, J. A., & Leffard, S. A. (2007). Behavioral assessment. In S. R. Smith & L. Handler (Eds.), *The clinical assessment of children and adolescents: A practitioner's handbook.* Mahwah, NJ: Lawrence Erlbaum Associates.

Miller, J. G. (1984). Culture and the development of everyday social explanation. *Journal of Personality and Social Psychology, 46,* 961–978.

Miller, L. A., Taber, K. H., Gabbard, G. O., & Hurley, R. A. (2005). Neural underpinnings of fear and its modulation: Implications for anxiety disorders. *The Journal of Neuropsychiatry and Clinical Neurosciences, 17,* 1–6.

Miller, L., Gur, M., Shanok, A., & Weissman, M. (2008). Interpersonal psychotherapy with pregnant adolescents: Two pilot studies. *Journal of Child Psychology and Psychiatry, 49,* 733–742.

Miller, L. A., McIntire, S. A., & Lovler, R. L. (2011). *Foundations of psychological testing: A practical problem* (3rd ed.). Thousand Oaks, CA: Sage Publications, Inc.

Miller, M. N., & Pumariega, A. J. (2001). Culture and eating disorders: A historical and cross-cultural review. *Psychiatry: Interpersonal and Biological Processes, 64,* 93–110.

Miller, N. E., & Magruder, K. M. (Eds.). (1999). *Cost-effectiveness of psychotherapy: A guide for practitioners, researchers, and policymakers.* New York: Oxford University Press.

Miller-Jones, D. (1991). Informal reasoning in inner-city children. In J. F. Voss & D. N. Perkins (Eds.), *Informal reasoning and education.* Hillsdale, NJ: Lawrence Erlbaum.

Miller-Perrin, C., Perrin, R., & Kocur, J. (2009). Parental physical and psychological aggression: Psychological symptoms in young adults. *Child Abuse & Neglect, 33,* 1–11.

Millon, T., Davis, R., & Millon, C. (2000). *Personality disorders in modern life.* New York: Wiley.

Mills, M. J. (2011). Associations among achievement measures and their collective prediction of work involvement. *Personality and Individual Differences, 50,* 360–364.

Milner, B. (1966). Amnesia following operation on temporal lobes. In C. W. M. Whitty & P. Zangwill (Eds.), *Amnesia.* London: Butterworth.

Milner, B. (2005). The medial temporallobe amnesic syndrome. *Psychiatric Clinics of North America, 28,* 599–611.

Milton, J., & Wiseman, R. (1999). Does psi exist? Lack of replication of an anomalous process of information transfer. *Psychological Bulletin, 125,* 387–391.

Miner, J., & Clarke-Stewart, K. (2008). Trajectories of externalizing behavior from age 2 to age 9: Relations with gender, temperament, ethnicity, parenting, and rater. *Developmental Psychology, 44,* 771–786.

Miner-Rubino, K., Winter, D. G., & Stewart, A. J. (2004). Gender, social class, and the subjective experience of aging: Self-perceived personality change from early adulthood to late midlife. *Personality and Social Psychology Bulletin, 30,* 1599–1610.

Mintz, A., & Brule, D. (2009). Methodological issues in studying suicide terrorism. *Political Psychology, 30,* 361–367.

Minuchin, S. (1999). Retelling, reimagining, and re-searching: A continuing conversation. *Journal of Marital and Family Therapy, 25,* 9–14.

Miquel, J. (2006). Integración de teorías del envejecimiento (parte I). Integration of theories of ageing. *Revista Espanola de Geriatria y Gerontologia, 41,* 55–63.

Mischel, W. (2004). Toward an integrative science of the person. *Annual Review of Psychology, 55,* 1–22.

Mischel, W. (2009). From Personality and Assessment (1968) to Personality Science, 2009. *Journal of Research in Personality, 43,* 282–290.

Mischel, W., & Shoda, Y. (2008). Toward a unified theory of personality: Integrating dispositions and processing dynamics within the cognitive-affective processing system. In O. P. Oliver, R. W. Robins, et al. (Eds.), *Handbook of personality psychology: Theory and research* (3rd ed.). New York: Guilford Press.

Mischoulon, D. (2000, June). Anti-depressants: Choices and controversy. *HealthNews,* p. 4.

Miserando, M. (1991). Memory and the seven dwarfs. *Teaching of Psychology, 18,* 169–171.

Mitchell, D. B., & Schmitt, F. A. (2006). Short- and long-term implicit memory in aging and Alzheimer's disease. *Neuropsychological Development and Cognition, B, Aging and Neuropsychological Cognition, 13,* 611–635.

Mitte, K. (2005). Meta-analysis of cognitive-behavioral treatments for generalized anxiety disorder: A comparison with pharmacotherapy. *Psychological Bulletin, 131,* 785–795.

Mizrahi, R., Agid, O., Borlido, C., Suridjan, I., Rusjan, P., Houle, S., et al. (2011). Effects of antipsychotics on D3 receptors: A clinical PET study in first episode antipsychotic naive patients with schizophrenia using [11C]-(+)-PHNO. *Schizophrenia Research, 131,* 63–68.

MLA. (2005). MLA Language Map; all languages other than English combined. Retrieved from http://www.mla.org/census_map&source= county (based on 2000 U.S. Census Bureau figures).

Moffitt, T. E., & Caspi, A. (2007). Evidence from behavioral genetics for environmental contributions to antisocial conduct. In J. E. Grusec & P. D. Hastings (Eds.), *Handbook of socialization: Theory and research.* New York: Guilford Press.

Moffitt, T. E., Caspi, A., & Rutter, M. (2006). Measured gene-environment interactions in psychopathology: Concepts, research strategies, and implications for research, intervention, and public understanding of genetics. *Perspectives on Psychological Science, 1,* 5–27.

Mograss, M., Guillem, F., Brazzini-Poisson, V., & Godbout, R. (2009, May). The effects of total sleep deprivation on recognition memory processes: A study of event-related potential. *Neurobiology of Learning and Memory, 91,* 343–352.

Mohan, A., Sharma, R., & Bijlani, R. L. (2011). Effect of meditation on stress-induced changes in cognitive functions. *The Journal of Alternative and Complementary Medicine, 17,* 207–212.

Mohapel, P., Leanza, G., Kokaia, M., & Lindvall, O. (2005). Forebrain acetylcholine regulates adult hippo-campal neurogenesis and learning. *Neurobiology of Aging, 26,* 939–946.

Moher, C., Gould, D., Hegg, E., & Mahoney, A. (2008). Non-generalized and generalized conditioned reinforcers: Establishment and validation. *Behavioral Interventions, 23,* 13–38.

Mokdad, A. H., Brewer, R. D., & Naimi, T. (2007). Binge drinking is a problem that cannot be ignored. *Preventive Medicine: An International Journal Devoted to Practice and Theory, 44,* 303–304.

Møller, A. R. (2011). Anatomy and physiology of the auditory system. In A. R. Møller, B. Langguth, et al. (Eds.), *Textbook of tinnitus.* New York: Springer Science + Business Media.

Monk, T. H., Buysse, D. J., Billy, B. D., Fletcher, M. E., Kennedy, K. S., Schlarb, J. E., et al. (2011). Circadian type and bed-timing regularity in 654 retired seniors: Correlations with subjective sleep measures. *Sleep, 34,* 235–239.

Montcleone, P., Martiadis, V., & Maj, M. (2011). Circadian rhythms and treatment implications in depression. *Progress in Neuro-Psychopharmacology & Biological Psychiatry, 35,* 1569–1574.

Montgomery, K. L. (2011). Living with panic, worry, and fear: Anxiety disorders. In C. Franklin & R. Fong (Eds.), *The church leader's counseling resource book: A guide to mental health and social problems.* New York: Oxford University Press.

Montgomery, S. (2006). Serotonin noradrenaline reuptake inhibitors: Logical evolution of anti-depressant development. *International Journal of Psychiatry in Clinical Practice, 10,* 5–11.

Montgomery, S. A., Nil, R., Dürr-Pal, N., Loft, H., & Boulenger, J. P. (2005). A 24-week randomized, double-blind, placebo-controlled study of escitalopram for the prevention of generalized social anxiety disorder. *Journal of Clinical Psychiatry, 66,* 1270–1278.

Montoya, R., & Insko, C. (2008). Toward a more complete understanding of the reciprocity of liking effect. *European Journal of Social Psychology, 38,* 477–498.

Moody, H. R. (2000). *Aging: Concepts and controversies.* Thousand Oaks, CA: Sage.

Moore, D. G., Goodwin, J. E., & George, R. (2007). Infants perceive human point-light displays as solid forms. *Cognition, 104,* 377–396.

Moore, M. M. (2002). Behavioral observation. In M. W. Wiederman & B. E. Whitley (Eds.), *Handbook for conducting research on human sexuality.* Mahwah, NJ: Lawrence Erlbaum.

Moorey, S. (2007). Cognitive therapy. In W. Dryden (Ed.), *Dryden's handbook of individual therapy* (5th ed.). Thousand Oaks, CA: Sage Publications.

Morad, Y., Barkana, Y., Zadok, D., Hartstein, M., Pras, E., & Bar-Dayan, Y. (2009, July). Ocular parameters as an objective tool for the assessment of truck drivers fatigue. *Accident Analysis and Prevention, 41,* 856–860.

Mora-Giral, M., Raich-Escursell, R. M., Segues, C.V., Torras-Claras, A. J., & Huon, G. (2004). Bulimia symptoms and risk factors in university students. *Eating and Weight Disorders, 9,* 163–169.

Moran, A. (2009). Cognitive psychology in sport: Progress and prospects. *Psychology of Sport and Exercise, 10,* 420–426.

Morcom, A. M., & Friston, K. J. (2011, September 1). Decoding episodic memory in ageing: A bayesian analysis of activity patterns predicting memory. *NeuroimageI, 33,* 88–91.

Moretz, M., & McKay, D. (2009). The role of perfectionism in obsessive-compulsive symptoms: 'Not just right' experiences and checking compulsions. *Journal of Anxiety Disorders, 23*, 640–644.

Morgan, A. A., Marsiske, M., & Whitfield, K. E. (2008). Characterizing and explaining differences in cognitive test performance between African American and European American older adults. *Experimental Aging Research, 34*, 80–100.

Morone, N. E., & Greco, C. M. (2007). Mind-body interventions for chronic pain in older adults: A structured review. *Pain Medicine, 8*, 359–375.

Morris, J. F., Waldo, C. R., & Rothblum, E. D. (2001). A model of predictors and outcomes of outness among lesbian and bisexual women. *American Journal of Orthopsychiatry, 71*, 61–71.

Morrone, A. S., & Pintrich, P. R. (2006). Achievement motivation. In G. G. Bear & K. M. Minke (Eds.), *Children's needs III: Development, prevention, and intervention.* Washington, DC: National Association of School Psychologists.

Morrow, J., & Wolff, R. (1991, May). Wired for a miracle. *Health*, pp. 64–84.

Mosher, C. J., & Akins, S. (2007). *Drugs and drug policy: The control of consciousness alteration.* Thousand Oaks, CA: Sage Publications.

Moshman, D. (2011). *Adolescent rationality and development: Cognition, morality, and identity* (3rd ed.). New York: Psychology Press.

Moskowitz, G. B. (2004). *Social cognition: Understanding self and others.* New York: Guilford Press.

Motley, M. T. (1987, February). What I meant to say. *Psychology Today*, pp. 25–28.

Muammar, O. M. (2007). An integration of two competing models to explain practical intelligence. *Dissertation Abstracts International: Section B: The Sciences and Engineering, 67(7-B)*, 4128.

Mueller, C. E. (2009). Protective factors as barriers to depression in gifted and nongifted adolescents. *Gifted Child Quarterly, 53*, 3–14.

Mullen, B., & Rice, D. R. (2003). Ethnophaulisms and exclusion: The behavioral consequences of cognitive representation of ethnic immigrant groups. *Personality and Social Psychology Bulletin, 29*, 1056–1067.

Munakata, Y. (2006). Information processing approaches to development. In D. Kuhn, R. S. Siegler, et al. (Eds.) *Handbook of child psychology: Vol 2, Cognition, perception, and language* (6th ed.). Hoboken, NJ: John Wiley & Sons.

Mungan, E., Peynircioğlu, Z. F., & Halpern, A. R. (2011). Levels-of-processing effects on 'remember' responses in recognition for familiar and unfamiliar tunes. *American Journal of Psychology, 124*, 37–48.

Munroe, R. L., Hulefeld, R., Rodgers, J. M., Tomeo, D. L., & Yamazaki, S. K. (2000). Aggression among children in four cultures. *Cross-Cultural Research: The Journal of Comparative Social Science, 34*, 3–25.

Murphy, G. J., Glickfield, L. L., Balsen, Z., & Isaacson, J. S. (2004). Sensory neuron signaling to the brain: Properties of transmitter release from olfactory nerve terminals. *Journal of Neuroscience, 24*, 3023–3030.

Murphy, G. L. (2005). The study of concepts inside and outside the laboratory: Medin versus Medin. In W. Ahn, R. L. Goldstone, et al. (Eds.), *Categorization inside and outside the laboratory: Essays in honor of Douglas L. Medin.*

Washington, DC: American Psychological Association.

Murphy, R. T., Wismar, K., & Freeman, K. (2003). Stress symptoms among African-American college students after the September 11, 2001 terrorist attacks. *Journal of Nervous and Mental Disease, 191*, 108–114.

Murphy, S. T., & Zajonc, R. B. (1993). Affect, cognition, and awareness: Affective priming with optimal and suboptimal stimulus exposures. *Journal of Personality and Social Psychology, 64*, 723–739.

Murray, B. (June 2002). Good news for bachelor's grads. *Monitor on Psychology*, pp. 30–32.

Murray, R., Lappin, J., & Di Forti, M. (2008, August). Schizophrenia: From developmental deviance to dopamine dysregulation. *European Neuropsychopharmacology, 18*, S129–SS134.

Murray, S. L., Holmes, J. G., & Griffin, D. W. (2004). The benefits of positive illusions: Idealization and the construction of satisfaction in close relationships. In H. T. Reis & C. E. Rusbult (Eds.), *Close relationships: Key readings.* Philadelphia, PA: Taylor & Francis.

Murthy, P., Kudlur, S., George, S., & Mathew, G. (2009). A clinical overview of fetal alcohol syndrome. *Addictive Disorders & Their Treatment, 8*, 1–12.

Myers, D. G. (2000). The funds, friends, and faith of happy people. *American Psychologist, 55*, 56–67.

Myers, L. L. (2007). Anorexia nervosa, bulimia nervosa, and binge eating disorder. In B. A. Thyer & J. S. Wodarski (Eds.), *Social work in mental health: An evidence-based approach.* Hoboken, NJ: John Wiley & Sons.

Myrtek, M. (2007). Type A behavior and hostility as independent risk factors for coronary heart disease. In J. Jordan, B. Barde, et al. (Eds.), *Contributions toward evidence-based psychocardiology: A systematic review of the literature.* Washington, DC: American Psychological Association.

Mytinger, C. (2001). *Headhunting in the Solomon Islands: Around the Coral Sea.* Santa Barbara, CA: Narrative Press.

Nadeem, E., & Graham, S. (2005). Early puberty, peer victimization, and internalizing symptoms in ethnic minority adolescents. *Journal of Early Adolescence, 25*, 197–222.

Nagai, Y., Goldstein, L. H., Fenwick, P. B. C., & Trimble, M. R. (2004). Clinical efficacy of galvanic skin response biofeedback training in reducing seizures in adult epilepsy: A preliminary randomized controlled study. *Epilepsy and Behavior, 5*, 216–223.

Nagda, B. A., Tropp, L. R., & Paluck, E. L. (2006). Looking back as we look ahead: Integrating research, theory, and practice on intergroup relations. *Journal of Social Research, 62*, 439–451.

Nagy, T. F. (2011). Informed consent. In T. F. Nagy (Ed.), *Essential ethics for psychologists: A primer for understanding and mastering core issues.* Washington, DC: American Psychological Association.

Naik, G. (2009, February 3). Parents agonize over treatment in the womb. *Wall Street Journal*, p. D1.

Najman, J. M., Aird, R., Bor, W., O'Callaghan, M., Williams, G. M., & Shuttlewood, G. J. (2004). The generational transmission of socioeconomic inequalities in child cognitive development and emotional health. *Social Science and Medicine, 58*, 1147–1158.

Nakamura, Y., Goto, T. K., Tokumori, K., Yoshiura, T., Kobayashi, K., Nakamura, Y., et al. (2011). Localization of brain activation by umami taste in humans. *Brain Research, 1390*, 156–163.

Nakato, E., Otsuka, Y., Kanazawa, S., Yamaguchi, M. K., & Kakigi, R. (2011). Distinct differences in the pattern of hemodynamic response to happy and angry facial expressions in infants—A near-infrared spectroscopic study. *NeuroImage, 54*, 1600–1606.

Nalbantian, S. (2011). Autobiographical memory in modernist literature and neuroscience. In S. Nalbantian, P. M. Matthews, et al. (Eds.), *The memory process: Neuroscientific and humanistic perspectives.* Cambridge, MA: MIT Press.

Naldini, L. (2009, November 6). A comeback for gene therapy. *Science, 326*, 805–806.

Nargeot, R., & Simmers, J. (2011). Neural mechanisms of operant conditioning and learning-induced behavioral plasticity in Aplysia. *Cellular and Molecular Life Sciences, 68*, 803–816.

Narrow, W. E., Rae, D. S., Robins, L. N., & Regier, D. A. (2002). Revised prevalence estimates of mental disorders in the United States: Using a clinical significance criterion to reconcile 2 surveys' estimates. *Archives of General Psychiatry, 59*, 115–123.

Nasir, N. S., & Hand, V. (2006). From the court to the classroom: Opportunities for engagement, learning, and identity in basketball and classroom mathematics. *Journal of the Learning Sciences, 17*, 143–179.

Nasrallah, H., Black, D., Goldberg, J., Muzina, D., & Pariser, S. (2008). Issues associated with the use of atypical antipsychotic medications. *Annals of Clinical Psychiatry, 20*, S24–S29.

Nathan, P. E., Stuart, S. P., & Dolan, S. L. (2000). Research on psychotherapy efficacy and effectiveness: Between Scylla and Charybdis? *Psychological Bulletin, 126*, 964–981.

National Adolescent Health Information Center. (2003). *Fact Sheet on Demographics: Adolescents.* San Francisco: University of California, San Francisco.

National Association for the Education of Young Children. (2005). *Position statements of the NAEYC.* Retrieved from http://www.naeyc.org/about/positions.asp#where.

National Center for Health Statistics. (2000). *Health United States, 2000 with adolescent health chartbook.* National Center for Health Statistics, Hyattsville, MD.

National Depression Screening Day. (2003, March 26). Questionnaire on website. Retrieved from http://www.mentalhealthscreening.org/dep/depsample.htm#sampletest

National Institute of Child Health and Human Development (NICHD) Early Child Care Research Network. (1999). Child care and mother-child interaction in the first 3 years of life. *Psychology, 35*, 1399–1413.

National Institute of Child Health and Human Development (NICHD) Early Child Care Research Network. (2000). The relation of child care to cognitive and language development. *Child Development, 71*, 960–980.

National Institute of Child Health and Human Development (NICHD) Early Child Care Research Network. (2001). Child-care and family predictors of preschool attachment and stability from infancy. *Development Psychology, 37*, 847–862.

National Institute of Child Health and Human Development (NICHD) Early Child Care

Research Network. (2002). Child-care structure—process—outcome: Direct and indirect effects of child-care quality on young children's development. *Psychological Science, 13*, 199–206.

National Institute of Child Health and Human Development (NICHD) Early Child Care Research Network. (2006). Child-care effect sizes for the NICHD study of early child care and youth development. *American Psychologist, 61*, 99–116.

National Institute on Drug Abuse. (2000). *Principles of drug addiction treatment: A research-based guide.* Washington, DC: National Institute on Drug Abuse.

National Research Council. (2001). *Eager to learn: Educating our preschoolers.* Washington, DC: National Academy Press.

Natvig, G. K., Albrektsen, G., & Ovarnstrom, U. (2003). Methods of teaching and class participation in relation to perceived social support and stress: Modifiable factors for improving health and well-being among students. *Educational Psychology, 23*, 261–274.

Naveh-Benjamin, M., Craik, F. I. M., Gavrilescu, D., & Anderson, N. D. (2000). Asymmetry between encoding and retrieval processes: Evidence from divided attention and a calibration analysis. *Memory & Cognition, 28*, 965–967.

Naveh-Benjamin, M., Guez, J., & Sorek, S. (2007). The effects of divided attention on encoding processes in memory: Mapping the locus of interference. *Canadian Journal of Experimental Psychology, 61*, 1–12.

Neher, A. (2006). Evolutionary psychology: Its programs, prospects, and pitfalls. *American Journal of Psychology, 119*, 517 566.

Neitz, J., Neitz, M., & Kainz, P. M. (1996, November 1). Visual pigment gene structure and the severity of color vision defects. *Science, 274*, 801–804.

Nelson, W. M., III, & Finch, A. J., Jr. (2000). Managing anger in youth: A cognitive-behavioral intervention approach. In P. C. Kendall (Ed.), *Child & adolescent therapy: Cognitive-behavioral procedures* (2nd ed.). New York: Guilford Press.

Neria, Y., DiGrande, L., U Adams, G. G. (2011). Postraumatic stress disorder following the September 11, 2011, terrorist attacks. *American Psychologist, 66*, 429–446.

Neron, S., & Stephenson, R. (2007). Effectiveness of hypnotherapy with cancer patients' trajectory: Emesis, acute pain, and analgesia and anxiolysis in procedures. *International Journal of Clinical Experimental Hypnosis, 55*, 336–354.

Nesheim, S., Henderson, S., Lindsay, M., Zuberi, J., Grimes, V., Buehler, J., et al. (2004). *Prenatal HIV testing and antiretroviral prophylaxis at an urban hospital—Atlanta, Georgia, 1997–2000.* Atlanta, GA: Centers for Disease Control.

Nesse, R. M. (2000). Is depression an adaptation? *Archives of General Psychiatry, 57*, 14–20.

Nestler, E. J., & Malenka, R. C. (2004, March). The addicted brain. *Scientific American,* pp. 78–83.

Nestoriuc, Y., & Martin, A. (2007, March). Efficacy of biofeedback for migraine: A meta-analysis. *Pain, 128*, 111–127.

Nestoriuc, Y., Martin, A., Rief, W., & Andrasik, F. (2008, September). Biofeedback treatment for headache disorders: A comprehensive efficacy review. *Applied Psychophysiology and Biofeedback, 33*, 125–140.

Neubauer, A. C., & Fink, A. (2005). Basic information processing and the psychophysiology of intelligence. In R. J. Sternberg & J. E. Pretz (Eds.), *Cognition and intelligence: Identifying the mechanisms of the mind.* New York: Cambridge University Press.

Neumann, N., & Birbaumer, N. (2004, December). Thinking out loud. *Scientific American: Mind,* pp. 37–45.

Neumark-Sztainer, D. (2009, March). Preventing obesity and eating disorders in adolescents: What can health care providers do? *Journal of Adolescent Health, 44*, 206–213.

Newby-Clark, I. R., & Ross, M. (2003). Conceiving the past and future. *Personality and Social Psychology Bulletin, 29*, 807–818.

Newman, A., & Rivera, R. (2010, August 10). Fed-up flight attendant lets curses fly, then makes sliding exit. *The New York Times,* A-1.

Newman, C. F., Leahy, R. L., Beck, A. T., Reilly-Harrington, N. A., & Gyulai, L. (2002). *Bipolar disorder: A cognitive therapy approach.* Washington, DC: American Psychological Association.

Newman, M., & Bakay, R. (2008, April). Therapeutic potentials of human embryonic stem cells in Parkinson's disease. *Neurotherapeutics, 5*, 237–251.

Newman, S. D., Willoughby, G., & Pruce, B. (2011). The effect of problem structure on problem-solving: An fmri study of word versus number problems. *Brain Research, 30*, 88–96.

Niccols, A. (2007). Fetal alcohol syndrome and the developing socio-emotional brain. *Brain Cognition, 65*, 135–142.

Nichols, S. (2011, March 18). Experimental philosophy and the problem of free will. *Science, 331*, 1401–1403.

Nickerson, R. S., & Adams, M. J. (1979). *Cognitive Psychology, 11*, 297.

Niedenthal, P. M. (2007, May 18). Embodying emotion. *Science, 316*, 1002–1005.

Nielsen, C., Staud, R., & Price, D. (2009, March). Individual differences in pain sensitivity: Measurement, causation, and consequences. *The Journal of Pain, 10*, 231–237.

Nijboer, T. C. W., te Pas, S. F., & van der Smagt, M. J. (2011). Detecting gradual visual changes in colour and brightness agnosia: A double dissociation. *NeuroReport: For Rapid Communication of Neuroscience Research, 22*, 175–180.

Nilsson, H., Juslin, P., & Olsson, H. (2008). Exemplars in the mist: The cognitive substrate of the representativeness heuristic. *Scandinavian Journal of Psychology, 49*, 201–212.

Nimrod, G., & Kleiber, D. A. (2007). Reconsidering change and continuity in later life: Toward an innovation theory of successful aging. *International Journal of Human Development, 65*, 1–22.

Nisbet, E. K., Zelenski, J. M., & Murphy, S. A. (2011). Happiness is in our nature: Exploring nature relatedness as a contributor to subjective well-being. *Journal of Happiness Studies, 12*, 303–322.

Nisbett, R. (2003). *The geography of thought.* New York: Free Press.

Nisbett, R. E. (2007, December 9). All brains are the same color. *The New York Times,* p. E11.

Nisbett, R. E. (2009, February). All brains are the same color. *Association for Psychological Science Observer, 22*(3), 20–21.

Nishida, M., Pearsall, J., Buckner, R., & Walker, M. (2009, May). REM sleep, prefrontal theta, and the consolidation of human emotional memory. *Cerebral Cortex, 19*, 1158–1166.

Nishimoto, S., Vu, A. T., Naselaris, T., Benjamini, Y., Yu, B., & Gallant, J. L. (2011). Reconstructing visual experiences from brain activity evoked by natural movies. *Current Biology,* doi:10.1016/j.cub.2011.08.031.

Nishimura, T., Kawamura, S., & Sakurai, S. (2011). Autonomous motivation and meta-cognitive strategies as predictors of academic performance: Does intrinsic motivation predict academic performance? *Japanese Journal of Educational Psychology, 59*, 77–87.

Nishino, S. (2007, June). Clinical and neurobiological aspects of narcolepsy. *Sleep Medicine, 8*, 373–399.

Nissle, S., & Bschor, T. (2002). Winning the jackpot and depression: Money cannot buy happiness. *International Journal of Psychiatry in Clinical Practice, 6*, 183–186.

Nittrouer, S., & Lowenstein, J. H. (2007). Children's weighting strategies for word-final stop voicing are not explained by auditory sensitivities. *Journal of Speech, Language, and Hearing Research, 50*, 58–73.

Niu, W., & Brass, J. (2011). Intelligence in worldwide perspective. In R. J. Sternberg & S. Kaufman (Eds.), *The Cambridge handbook of intelligence.* New York: Cambridge University Press.

Nolen-Hoeksema, S. (2007). *Abnormal psychology* (4th ed.). New York: McGraw-Hill.

Norcia, A. M., Pei, F., Bonnch, Y., Hou, C., Sampath, V., & Petter, M. W. (2005). Development of sensitivity to texture and contour information in the human infant. *Journal of Cognitive Neuroscience, 17*, 569–579.

Norcross, J. C. (2002). Empirically supported therapy relationships. In J. C. Norcross (Ed.), *Psychotherapy relationships that work: Therapist contributions and responsiveness to patients.* New York: Oxford University Press.

Norcross, J. C., Beutler, L. E., & Levant, R. F. (2006). *Evidence-based practices in mental health: Debate and dialogue on the fundamental questions.* Washington, DC: American Psychological Association.

Norlander, T., Von Schedvin, H., & Archer, T. (2005). Thriving as a function of affective personality: Relation to personality factors, coping strategies and stress. *Anxiety, Stress & Coping: An International Journal, 18*, 105–116.

Norton, P. J., & Price, E. C. (2007). A meta-analytic review of adult cognitive-behavioral treatment outcome across the anxiety disorders. *Journal of Nervous and Mental Disease, 195*, 521–531.

Noy, V. M. (2006). A psychoneuroimmunology program for Hispanic women with stage I–H breast cancer. *Dissertation Abstracts International: Section B: The Sciences and Engineering, 66*(11-B), 6287.

Ntinas, K. M. (2007). Behavior modification and the principle of normalization: Clash or synthesis? *Behavioral Interventions, 22*, 165–177.

Nucci, L. P. (2002). The development of moral reasoning. In U. Goswami (Ed.), *Blackwell handbook of childhood cognitive development. Blackwell Handbooks of developmental psychology.* Malden, MA: Blackwell.

Nurnberger, J. I., Jr., & Bierut, L. J. (2007, April). Seeking the connections: Alcoholism and our genes. *Scientific American,* pp. 46–53.

Nussbaum, A. D., & Steele, C. M. (2007). Situational disengagement and persistence in the face of adversity. *Journal of Experimental Social Psychology, 43,* 127–134.

Nyberg, L., & Tulving, E. (1996). Classifying human long-term memory: Evidence from converging dissociations. *European Journal of Cognitive Psychology, 8,* 163–183.

O'Brien, K. M., & LeBow, M. D. (2007). Reducing maladaptive weight management practices: Developing a psychoeducational intervention program. *Eating Behaviors, 8,* 195–210.

O'Connor, D. B., & O'Connor, R. C. (2004). Perceived changes in food intake in response to stress: The role of conscientiousness. *Stress and Health: Journal of the International Society for the Investigation of Stress, 20,* 279–291.

O'Keefe, J. & Dostrovsky, J. (1971). The hippocampus as a spatial map. Preliminary evidence from unit activity in the freely-moving rat. *Brain Research 34,* 171.

O'Keefe, T., & Fox, K. (Eds.). (2003). *Finding the real me: True tales of sex and gender diversity.* San Francisco: Jossey-Bass.

Oatley, K., Keltner, D., & Jenkins, J. M. (2006). *Understanding emotions.* Oxford, England: Blackwell.

Oberauer, K. (2007). In search of the magic number. *Experimental Psychology, 54,* 245–246.

Occhionero, M. (2004). Mental processes and the brain during dreams. *Dreaming, 14,* 54–64.

Offer, D., Kaiz, M., Howard, K. I., & Bennett, E. S. (2000). The altering of reported experiences. *Journal of the American Academy of Child & Adolescent Psychiatry, 39,* 735–742.

Ogbu, J. (1992). Understanding cultural diversity and learning. *Educational Researcher, 21,* 5–14.

Ogren, K., & Sandlund, M. (2007). Lobotomy at a state mental hospital in Sweden. A survey of patients operated on during the period 1947–1958. *Nordic Journal of Psychiatry, 61,* 355–362.

Ohira, T., Hozawa, A., Iribarren, C., Daviglus, M. L., Matthews, K. A., Gross, M. D., et al. (2007). Longitudinal association of serum carotenoids and tocopherols with hostility: The CARDIA study. *American Journal of Epidemiology, 18,* 235–241.

Ojha, H., & Pramanick, M. (2009). Effects of age on intensity and priority of life needs. *Journal of the Indian Academy of Applied Psychology, 35,* 131–136.

Olatunji, B. (2008). New directions in research on health anxiety and hypochondriasis: Commentary on a timely special series. *Journal of Cognitive Psychotherapy, 22,* 183–190.

Olds, M. E., & Fobes, J. L. (1981). The central basis of motivation: Intracranial self-stimulation studies. *Annual Review of Psychology, 32,* 123–129.

Olfson, M., & Marcus, S. (2008). A case-control study of antidepressants and attempted suicide during early phase treatment of major depressive episodes. *Journal of Clinical Psychiatry, 69,* 425–432.

Olivardia, R., & Pope, H. (2002). Body image disturbance in childhood and adolescence. In D. Castle & K. Phillips (Eds.), *Disorders of body image.* Petersfield, England: Wrightson Biomedical Publishing.

Oliver, M. B., & Hyde, J. S. (1993). Gender differences in sexuality: A meta-analysis. *Psychological Bulletin, 114,* 29–51.

Olson, D. H., & DeFrain, J. (2005). *Marriages and families: Intimacy, diversity, and strengths with PowerWeb.* New York: McGraw-Hill.

Olson, T. R., Perry, J., Janzen, J. I., Petraglia, J., & Presniak, M. D. (2011). Addressing and interpreting defense mechanisms in psychotherapy: General considerations. *Psychiatry: Interpersonal and Biological Processes, 74,* 142–165.

Opler, M., Perrin, M., Kleinhaus, K., & Malaspina, D. (2008). Factors in the etiology of schizophrenia: Genes, parental age, and environment. *Primary Psychiatry, 15,* 37–45.

Oppenheimer, D. M. (2004). Spontaneous discounting of availability in frequency judgment tasks. *Psychological Science, 15,* 100–105.

Ornat, S. L., & Gallo, P. (2004). Acquisition, learning, or development of language? Skinner's "Verbal behavior" revisited. *Spanish Journal of Psychology, 7,* 161–170.

Orwin, R. G., & Condray, D. S. (1984). Smith and Glass' psychotherapy conclusions need further probing: On Landman and Dawes' re-analysis. *American Psychologist, 39,* 71–72.

Oskamp, S. (Ed.). (2000). *Reducing prejudice and discrimination.* Mahwah, NJ: Erlbaum.

Otake, K., Shimai, S., & Tanaka-Matsumi, J. (2006). Happy people become happier through kindness: A counting kindnesses intervention. *Journal of Happiness Studies, 7,* 361–375.

Ouimet, A., Gawronski, B., & Dozois, D. (2009). Cognitive vulnerability to anxiety: A review and an integrative model. *Clinical Psychology Review, 29,* 459–470.

Oviedo-Joekes, E., et al. (2009). Diacetylmorphine versus methadone for the treatment of opioid addiction. *The New England Journal of Medicine, 361,* 777–786.

Packer, D. (2009). Avoiding groupthink: Whereas weakly identified members remain silent, strongly identified members dissent about collective problems. *Psychological Science, 20,* 546–548.

Padgett, D. K., Stanhope, V., & Henwood, B. F. (2011). Housing-first services for homeless adults with co-occurring disorders: An evidence-based practice. In M. Roberts-DeGennaro & S. J. Fogel (Eds.), *Using evidence to inform practice for community and organizational change.* Chicago: Lyceum Books.

Pager, D., & Shepherd, H. (2008). The sociology of discrimination: Racial discrimination in employment, housing, credit, and consumer markets. *Annual Review of Sociology, 34,* 181–209.

Pagonis, T. A., Angelopoulos, N., & Koukoulis, G. N. (2006). Psychiatric side effects induced by supraphysiological doses of combinations of anabolic steroids correlate to the severity of abuse. *European Psychiatry, 21,* 551–562.

Pallanti, S., & Bernardi, S. (2009, July). Neurobiology of repeated transcranial magnetic stimulation in the treatment of anxiety: A critical review. *International Clinical Psychopharmacology, 24,* 163–173.

Pandya, M., Pozuelo, L., & Malone, D. (2007). Electroconvulsive therapy: What the internist needs to know. *Cleveland Clinic Journal of Medicine, 74,* 679–685.

Paniagua, F. A. (2000). *Diagnosis in a multicultural context: A casebook for mental health professionals.* Thousand Oaks, CA: Sage.

Paquier, P. F., & Mariën, P. (2005). A synthesis of the role of the cerebellum in cognition. *Aphasiology, 19,* 3–19.

Parish, C. L., & Arenas, E. (2007). Stem-cell-based strategies for the treatment of Parkinson's disease. *Neurodegenerative Disease, 4,* 339–347.

Park, H., & Antonioni, D. (2007). Personality, reciprocity, and strength of conflict resolution strategy. *Journal of Research in Personality, 41,* 110–125.

Park, J., Park, K., & Dubinsky, A. J. (2011). Impact of retailer image on private brand attitude: Halo effect and summary construct. *Australian Journal of Psychology, 63,* 173–183.

Parke, R. D. (2004). Development in the family. *Annual Review of Psychology, 55,* 365–399.

Parker-Pope, T. (2011, March 30). Fat stigma is fast spreading around the globe. *The New York Times,* A-1.

Parmley, M. C. (2007). The effects of the confirmation bias on diagnostic decision making. *Dissertation Abstracts International: Section B: The Sciences and Engineering, 67*(8-B), 4719.

Parra, A., & Argibay, J. C. (2007). Comparing psychics and non-psychics through a 'token-object' forced-choice ESP test. *Journal of the Society for Psychical Research, 71,* 80–90.

Paterson, H. M., Kemp, R. I., & Ng, J. R. (2011). Combating co-witness contamination: Attempting to decrease the negative effects of discussion on eyewitness memory. *Applied Cognitive Psychology, 25,* 43–52.

Paukert, A., Stagner, B., & Hope, K. (2004). The assessment of active listening skills in helpline volunteers. *Stress, Trauma, and Crisis: An International Journal, 7,* 61–76.

Paul, A. M. (2004). *Cult of personality: How personality tests are leading us to miseducate our children, mismanage our companies and misunderstand ourselves.* New York: Free Press.

Paulmann, S., Jessen, S., & Kotz, S. A. (2009). Investigating the multimodal nature of human communication: Insights from ERPs. *Journal of Psychophysiology, 23,* 63–76.

Paulozzi, L. J. (2006). Opioid analgesic involvement in drug abuse deaths in American metropolitan areas. *American Journal of Public Health, 96,* 1755–1757.

Pautassi, R., Myers, M., Spear, L., Molina, J., & Spear, N. E. (2011). Ethanol induces second-order aversive conditioning in adolescent and adult rats. *Alcohol, 45,* 45–55.

Pavitt, C. (2007). Impression formation. In B. B. Whaley & W. Samter (Eds.), *Explaining communication: Contemporary theories and exemplars.* Mahwah, NJ: Lawrence Erlbaum Associates.

Pavlov, I. (1927). *Conditional reflexes.* London: Oxford University Press.

Payne, D. G. (1986). Hyperamnesia for pictures and words: Testing the recall level hypothesis. *Journal of Experimental Psychology: Learning, Memory, and Cognition, 12,* 16–29.

Payne, K., & Marcus, D. (2008). The efficacy of group psychotherapy for older adult clients: A meta-analysis. *Group Dynamics: Theory, Research, and Practice, 12,* 268–278.

Pearce, J. M. S. (2007). Synaesthesia. *European Neurology, 57,* 120–124.

Pearce, R. R., & Lin, Z. (2007). Chinese American post-secondary achievement and attainment: A cultural and structural analysis. *Educational Review, 59,* 19–36.

Pearlstein, T., & Steiner, M. (2008). Premenstrual dysphoric disorder: Burden of illness and treatment update. *Journal of Psychiatry & Neuroscience, 33,* 291–301.

Pearson, A. R., Dovidio, J. F., & Pratto, E. (2007). Racial prejudice, intergroup hate, and blatant and subtle bias of whites toward blacks in legal decision making in the United States.

International Journal of Psychology & Psychological Therapy, 7, 125–134.

Pearson, J., & Clifford, C. W. G. (2005). When your brain decides what you see: Grouping across monocular, binocular, and stimulus rivalry. *Psychological Science, 16,* 516–519.

Pedersen, P. B., Draguns, J. G., Lonner, W. J., & Trimble, J. E. (Eds.). (2002). *Counseling across cultures* (5th ed.). Thousand Oaks, CA: Sage.

Pedraza, O., & Mungas, D. (2008). Measurement in cross-cultural neuropsychology. *Neuropsychology Review, 18,* 184–193.

Peiro, J. M., & Lunt, I. (2002). The context for a European framework for psychologists' training. *European Psychologist, 7,* 169–179.

Pell, M. D., Monetta, L., Paulmann, S., & Kotz, S. A. (2009). Recognizing emotions in a foreign language. *Journal of Nonverbal Behavior, 33,* 107–120.

Pellegrini, S., Muzio, R. N., Mustaca, A. E., & Papini, M. R. (2004). Successive negative contrast after partial reinforcement in the consummatory behavior of rats. *Learning and Motivation, 35,* 303–321.

Pelli, D. G., Burns, C. W., & Farell, B. (2006). Feature detection and letter identification. *Vision Research, 46,* 4646–4674.

Pellis, S. M., & Pellis, V. C. (2007). Rough-and-tumble play and the development of the social brain. *Current Directions in Psychological Science, 16,* 95–97.

Penley, J. A., Tomaka, J., & Wiebe, J. S. (2002). The association of coping to physical and psychological health outcomes: A meta-analytic review. *Journal of Behavioral Medicine, 25,* 551–603.

Penn, D. L., Corrigan, P. W., Bentall, R. P., Racenstein, J. M., & Newman, L. (1997). Social cognition in schizophrenia. *Psychological Bulletin, 121,* 114–132.

Penney, J. B., Jr. (2000). Neurochemistry. In B. S. Fogel, et al. (Eds.), *Synopsis of neuropsychiatry.* New York: Lippincott Williams & Wilkins.

Penzel, F. (2000). *Obsessive-compulsive disorders: A complete guide to getting well and staying well.* New York: Oxford University Press.

Perez, R. M., DeBord, K. A., & Bieschke, K. J. (Eds.). (2000). *Handbook of counseling and psychotherapy with lesbian, gay, and bisexual clients.* Washington, DC: American Psychological Association.

Pérez-Leroux, A. T., Pirvulescu, M., & Roberge, Y. (2011). Topicalization and object omission in child language. *First Language, 31,* 280–299.

Perloff, R. M. (2003). *The dynamics of persuasion: Communication and attitudes in the 21st century* (2nd ed.). Mahwah, NJ: Erlbaum.

Perovic, S., & Radenovic, L. (2011). Fine-tuning nativism: The 'nurtured nature' and innate cognitive structures. *Phenomenology and the Cognitive Sciences, 10,* 399–417.

Pert, C. B. (2002). The wisdom of the receptors: Neuropeptides, the emotions, and body-mind. *Advances in Mind-Body Medicine, 18,* 30–35.

Pervin, L. A. (1990). *Handbook of personality: Theory and research.* New York: Guilford Press.

Pervin, L. A. (2003). *The science of personality* (2nd ed.). London: Oxford University Press.

Pesce, N. L. (2011, September 18). Woodruff "stand up" for veterans. *Daily News,* 8.

Pesmen, C. (2006). Health and wealth techniques to help keep chronic pain from taking over. *Money Builder, 35,* 48.

Pessoa, L. (2011). Reprint of: Emotion and cognition and the amygdala: From "what is it?" to "what's to be done?" *Neuropsychologia, 49,* 681–694.

Peterfi, Z., McGinty, D., Sarai, E., & Szymusiak, R. (2010). Growth hormone-releasing hormone activates sleep regulatory neurons of the rat preoptic hypothalamus. *American Journal of Physiology: Regulatory, Integrative and Comparative Physiology, 298,* R147–R156.

Peters, E., Hess, T. M., Västfjäll, D., & Auman, C. (2007). Adult age differences in dual information processes. *Perspectives on Psychological Science, 2,* 1–23.

Peters, J., Suchan, B., Koster, O., & Daum, I. (2007). Domain-specific retrieval of source information in the medial temporal lobe. *European Journal of Neuroscience, 26,* 1333–1343.

Peters, J., et al. (2011). Lower ventral striatal activation during reward anticipation in adolescent smokers. *American Journal of Psychiatry, 168,* 540–549.

Petersen, A. (2011, August 23). A sleep battle of the sexes. *Wall Street Journal,* pp. D1, D4.

Peterson, C. (2000). The future of optimism. *American Psychologist, 55,* 44–55.

Petersson, K. M., Silva, C., Castro-Caldas, A., Ingvar, M., & Reis, A. (2007). Literacy: A cultural influence on functional left-right differences in the inferior parietal cortex. *European Journal of Neuroscience, 26,* 791–799.

Petrill, S. A., & Deater-Deckard, K. (2004). The heritability of general cognitive ability: A within-family adoption design. *Intelligence, 32,* 403–409.

Pettigrew, T. F. (2004). Justice deferred: A half century after *Brown v. Board of Education. American Psychologist, 59,* 521–529.

Pettigrew, T. F., & Tropp, L. R. (2006). A meta-analytic test of intergroup contact theory. *Journal of Personality and Social Psychology, 90,* 751–783.

Petty, R. E., Cacioppo, J. T., Strathman, A. J., & Priester, J. R. (2005). To think or not to think: Exploring two routes to persuasion. In T. C. Brock & M. C. Green (Eds.), *Persuasion: Psychological insights and perspectives* (2nd ed.). Thousand Oaks, CA: Sage Publications.

Pfeffer, C. R. (2006). An evolutionary perspective on childhood depression. In P. S. Jensen, P. Knapp, et al. (Eds.), *Toward a new diagnostic system for child psychopathology: Moving beyond the DSM.* New York: Guilford Press.

Phelps, R. P. (2005). *Defending standardized testing.* Mahwah, NJ: Lawrence Erlbaum Associates.

Philip, P., Sagaspe, P., Moore, N., Taillard, J., Charles, A., Guilleminault, C., et al. (2005). Fatigue, sleep restriction and driving performance. *Accident Analysis and Prevention, 37,* 473–478.

Piaget, J. (1970). Piaget's theory. In P. H. Mussen (Ed.), *Carmichael's manual of child psychology* (3rd ed., Vol. I). New York: Wiley.

Piaget, J., & Inhelder, B. (1958). *The growth of logical thinking from childhood to adolescence* (A. Parsons & S. Seagrin, Trans.). New York: Basic Books.

Picchioni, D., Goeltzenleucher, B., Green, D. N., Convento, M. J., Crittenden, R., Hallgren, M., et al. (2002). Nightmares as a coping mechanism for stress. *Dreaming: Journal of the Association for the Study of Dreams, 12,* 155–169.

Pickel, K. (2009). The weapon focus effect on memory for female versus male perpetrators. *Memory, 17,* 664–678.

Pickering, G. J., & Gordon, R. (2006). Perception of mouth feel sensations elicited by red wine are associated with sensitivity to 6-N-propylthiouracil. *Journal of Sensory Studies, 21,* 249–265.

Pietarinen, A-V. (2006). The evolution of semantics and language-games for meaning. *Interaction Studies: Social Behaviour and Communication in Biological and Artificial Systems, 7,* 79–104.

Pillay, S. S., Gruber, S. A., Rogowska, J., Simpson, N., & Yurgelun-Todd, D. A. (2006). fMRI of fearful facial affect recognition in panic disorder: The cingulate gyrus-amygdala connection. *Journal of Affective Disorders, 94,* 173–181.

Pillay, S. S., Rogowska, J., Gruber, S. A., Simpson, N., & Yurgelun-Todd, D. A. (2007). Recognition of happy facial affect in panic disorder: An fMRI study. *Journal of Anxiety Disorders, 21,* 381–393.

Pilotti, M., Chodorow, M., & Shono, Y. (2009). The benefits and costs of prior exposure: A large-scale study of interference effects in stimulus identification. *American Journal of Psychology, 122,* 191–208.

Pincus, T., & Morley, S. (2001). Cognitive processing bias in chronic pain: A review and integration. *Psychological Bulletin, 127,* 599–617.

Pine, D. S., Klein, R. G., Coplan, J. D., Papp, L. A., Hoven, C. W., Martinez, J., et al. (2000). Differential carbon dioxide sensitivity in childhood anxiety disorders and nonill comparison group. *Archives of General Psychiatry, 57,* 960–967.

Pinel, J. P. J., Assanand, S., & Lehman, D. R. (2000). Hunger, eating and ill health. *American Psychologist, 55,* 1105–1116.

Pinker, S. (1994). *The language instinct.* New York: William Morrow.

Pinker, S. (2004). Clarifying the logical problem of language acquisition. *Journal of Child Language, 31,* 949–953.

Pinker, S., & Jackendoff, R. (2005). The faculty of language: What's special about it? *Cognition, 96,* 201–236.

Pinkerton, S. D., Bogart, L. M., Cecil, H., & Abramson, P. R. (2002). Factors associated with masturbation in a collegiate sample. *Journal of Psychology and Human Sexuality, 14,* 103–121.

Pinquart, M., Duberstein, P. R., & Lyness J. M. (2006). Treatments for later-life depressive conditions: A meta-analytic comparison of pharmacotherapy and psychotherapy. *American Journal of Psychiatry, 163,* 1493–1501.

Pi-Sunyer, X. (2003). A clinical view of the obesity problem. *Science, 299,* 859–860.

Platek, S., & Kemp, S. (2009, February). Is family special to the brain? An event-related fMRI study of familiar, familial, and self-face recognition. *Neuropsychologia, 47,* 849–858.

Plomin, R. (2003). 50 years of DNA: What it has meant to psychological science. *American Psychological Society, 16,* 7–8.

Plomin, R. (2005). Finding genes in child psychology and psychiatry: When are we going to be there? *Journal of Child Psychology and Psychiatry, 46,* 1030–1038.

Plomin, R. (2004). The nature of nurture. In K. McCartney & R. A. Weinberg (Eds.), *Experience and development: A festschrift in honor of Sandra Wood Scarr.* New York: Psychology Press.

Plomin, R., & Caspi, R. (1999). Behavioral genetics and personality. In L. A. Pervin & O. P. John (Eds.), *Handbook of personality: Theory and research* (2nd ed.). New York: Guilford.

Plomin, R., & McGuffin, P. (2003). Psychopathology in the postgenomic era. *Annual Review of Psychology, 54,* 205–228.

Plowright, C. M. S., Simonds, V. M., & Butler, M. A. (2006). How bumblebees first find flowers: Habituation of visual pattern preferences, spontaneous recovery, and dishabituation. *Learning and Motivation, 37*, 66–78.

Pluess, M., & Belsky, J. (2009). Differential susceptibility to rearing experience: The case of childcare. *Journal of Child Psychology and Psychiatry, 50*, 396–404.

Pogarsky, G., & Piquero, A. R. (2003). Can punishment encourage offending? Investigating the 'resetting' effect. *Journal of Research in Crime and Delinquency, 40*, 95–120.

Pole, N. (2007).The psychophysiology of post-traumatic stress disorder: A meta-analysis. *Psychological Bulletin, 133*, 34–45.

Polivy, J., & Herman, C. P. (2002). Causes of eating disorders. *Annual Review of Psychology, 53*, 187–213.

Polivy, J., Herman, C. P., & Boivin, M. (2005). Eating disorders. In J. E. Maddux & B. A. Winstead (Eds.), *Psychopathology: Foundations for a contemporary understanding*. Mahwah, NJ: Lawrence Erlbaum Associates.

Pollack, A. (2006, July 13). Paralyzed man uses thoughts to move a cursor. *The New York Times*, p. B5.

Polonsky, D. C. (2006). Review of the big book of masturbation: From angst to zeal. *Journal of Sex & Marital Therapy, 32*, 75–78.

Pomerlau, O. F. (1995). Individual differences in sensitivity to nicotine: Implications of genetic research on nicotine dependence [Special issue: Genetic, environmental, and situational factors mediating the effects of nicotine]. *Behavior Genetics, 25*, 161–177.

Ponterotto, J. G., Gretchen, D., & Chauhan, R. V. (2001). Cultural identity and multicultural assessment: Quantitative and qualitative tools for the clinician. In L. A. Suzuki & J. G. Ponterotto (Eds.), *Handbook of multicultural assessment: Clinical, psychological, and educational applications* (2nd ed.). San Francisco: Jossey-Bass/Pfeiffer.

Ponterotto, J. G., Utsey, S. O., & Pedersen, P. B. (2006). *Preventing prejudice: A guide for counselors, educators, and parents*. Thousand Oaks, CA: Sage Publications.

Poo, C., & Isaacson, J. S. (2007). An early critical period for long-term plasticity and structural modification of sensory synapses in olfactory cortex. *Journal of Neuroscience, 27*, 7553–7558.

Popa, D., Léna, C., Alexandre, C., & Adrien, J. (2008). Lasting syndrome of depression produced by reduction in serotonin uptake during postnatal development: Evidence from sleep, stress, and behavior. *The Journal of Neuroscience, 28*, 88–97.

Porkka-Heiskanen, T., & Kalinchuk, A. V. (2011). Adenosine, energy metabolism and sleep homeostasis. *Sleep Medicine Reviews, 15*, 123–135.

Porte, H. S., & Hobson, J. A. (1996). Physical motion in dreams: One measure of three theories. *Journal of Abnormal Psychology, 105*, 329–335.

Posner, M. I., & DiGirolamo, G. J. (2000). Cognitive neuroscience: Origins and promise. *Psychological Bulletin, 126*, 873–889.

Post, J., Ali, F., Henderson, S., Shanfield, S., Victoroff, J., & Weine, S. (2009, Spring). The psychology of suicide terrorism. *Psychiatry: Interpersonal and Biological Processes, 72*, 13–31.

Post, J. M. (2011). Crimes of obedience: 'Groupthink' at Abu Ghraib. *International Journal of Group Psychotherapy, 61*, 49–66.

Poteat, V. P., & Espelage, D. L. (2007, May). Predicting psychosocial consequences of homophobic victimization in middle school students. *Journal of Early Adolescence, 27*(2), 175–191.

Pottick, K. J., Kirk, S. A., Hsieh, D. K., & Tian, X. (2007). Judging mental disorder in youths: Effects of client, clinician, and contextual differences. *Journal of Consulting Clinical Psychology, 75*, 1–8.

Powell, L., Richmond, V. P., & Williams, G. C. (2011). Social networking and political campaigns: Perceptions of candidates as interpersonal constructs. *North American Journal of Psychology, 13*, 331–342.

Powell, L. H. (2006). Review of marital and sexual lifestyles in the United States: Attitudes, behaviors, and relationships in social context. *Family Relations, 55*, 149.

Powell, L. H., Shahabi, L., & Thoresen, C. E. (2003). Religion and spirituality: Linkages to physical health. *American Psychology, 58*, 36–52.

Powell, R. A. (2011). Research notes: Little Albert, lost or found: Further difficulties with the Douglas Merritte hypothesis. *History of Psychology, 14*, 106–107.

Powers, K. D. (2006). An analysis of Kohlbergian moral development in relationship to biblical factors of morality in seminary students (Lawrence Kohlberg). *Dissertation Abstracts International: Section B: The Sciences and Engineering, 67*(6-B), 3485.

Powers, M., & Emmelkamp, P. (2008). Virtual reality exposure therapy for anxiety disorders: A meta-analysis. *Journal of Anxiety Disorders, 22*, 561–569.

Prasad, B. (2006). Recent advances in artificial intelligence [Special issue: Recent advances in AI]. *Journal of Experimental & Theoretical Artificial Intelligence, 18*, 433–434.

Pratkanis, A. R. (2007). Social influence analysis: An index of tactics. In A. R. Pratkanis (Ed.), *The science of social influence: Advances and future progress*. New York: Psychology Press.

Pratkanis, A. R., Epley, N., & Savitsky, K. (2007). Issue 12: Is subliminal persuasion a myth? In J. A. Nier (Ed.), *Taking sides: Clashing views in social psychology* (2nd ed.). New York: McGraw-Hill.

Pratt, H. D., Phillips, E. L., Greydanus, D. E., & Patel, D. R. (2003). Eating disorders in the adolescent population: Future directions [Special issue: Eating disorders in adolescents]. *Journal of Adolescent Research, 18*, 297–317.

Pratto, F., Lee, I., Tan, J. Y., & Pitpitan, E. Y. (2011). Power basis theory: A psychoecological approach to power. In D. Dunning, D. Dunning (Eds.), *Social motivation*. New York: Psychology Press.

Pressley, M. P., & Harris., K. R. (2006). Cognitive strategies instruction: From basic research to classroom instruction. In P. A. Alexander & P. H. Winne (Eds.), *Handbook of educational psychology*. Mahwah, NJ: Lawrence Erlbaum Associates.

Pretzer, J. L., & Beck, A. T. (2005). A cognitive theory of personality disorders. In M. F. Lenzenweger & J. F. Clarkin (Eds.), *Major theories of personality disorder* (2nd ed.). New York: Guilford Press.

Price, M. (2008, September). Against doctors' orders. *Monitor on Psychology*, pp. 34–36.

Priester, J. R., & Petty, R. E. (2011). The pot-holed path to happiness, possibly paved with money: A research dialogue. *Journal of Consumer Psychology, 21*, 113–114.

Prince, C. V. (2005). Homosexuality, transvestism and transsexuality: Reflections on their etymology and differentiation. *International Journal of Transgenderism, 8*, 15–18.

Prinz, J. J. (2007). Emotion: Competing theories and philosophical issues. In P. Thagard (Ed.), *Philosophy of psychology and cognitive science*. Amsterdam, Netherlands: North Holland/Elsevier.

Prislin, R., Brewer, M., & Wilson, D. J. (2002). Changing majority and minority positions within a group versus an aggregate. *Personality and Social Psychology Bulletin, 28*, 640–647.

Proffitt, D. R. (2006). Distance perception. *Current Directions in Psychological Science, 15*, 131–139.

Prohovnik, I., Skudlarski, P., Fulbright, R. K., Gore, J. C., et al. (2004). Functional MRI changes before and after onset of reported emotions. *Psychiatry Research: Neuroimaging, 132*, 239–250.

Proudfoot, D. (2009). Meaning and mind: Wittgenstein's relevance for the 'does language shape thought?' debate. *New Ideas in Psychology, 27*, 163–183.

Puca, R. M. (2005). The influence of the achievement motive on probability estimates in pre- and post-decisional action phases. *Journal of Research in Personality, 39*, 245–262.

Puhl, R., & Latner, J. (2007). Stigma, obesity, and the health of the nation's children. *Psychological Bulletin, 133*, 557–580.

Putnam, E. W. (2000). Dissociative disorders. In A. J. Sameroff & M. Lewis (Eds.), *Handbook of developmental psychopathology* (2nd ed.). Dordrecht, Netherlands: Kluwer Academic Publishers.

Quartana, P. J., & Burns, J. W. (2007). Painful consequences of anger suppression. *Emotion, 7*, 400–414.

Quas, J. A., Malloy, L. C., & Melinder, A. (2007). Developmental differences in the effects of repeated interviews and interviewer bias on young children's event memory and false reports. *Developmental Psychology, 43*, 823–837.

Quenot, J. P., Boichot, C., Petit, A., Falcon-Eicher, S., d'Athis, P., Bonnet, C., et al. (2005). Usefulness of MRI in the follow-up of patients with repaired aortic coarctation and bicuspid aortic valve. *International Journal of Cardiology, 103*, 312–316.

Quinn, D. M., Kahng, S. K., & Crocker, J. (2004). Discreditable: Stigma effects of revealing a mental illness history on test performance. *Personality and Social Psychology Bulletin, 30*, 803–815.

Quinn, T. C., & Overbaugh, J. (2005, June 10). HIV/AIDS in women: An expanding epidemic. *Science, 308*, 1582–1583.

Quintana, S. M., Aboud, F. E., & Chao, R. K. (2006). Race, ethnicity, and culture in child development: Contemporary research and future directions. *Child Development, 77*, 1129–1141.

Rabin, J. (2004). Quantification of color vision with cone contrast sensitivity. *Visual Neuroscience, 21*, 483–485.

Rachman, S., & deSilva, P. (2004). *Panic disorders: The facts*. Oxford, England: Oxford University Press.

Rado, J., Dowd, S., & Janicak, P. (2008). The emerging role of transcranial magnetic stimulation (TMS) for treatment of psychiatric disorders. *Directions in Psychiatry, 28,* 315–332.

Rahman, Q., Kumari, V., & Wilson, G. D. (2003). Sexual orientation-related differences in pre-pulse inhibition of the human startle response. *Behavioral Neuroscience, 117,* 1096–1102.

Rajagopal, S. (2006). The placebo effect. *Psychiatric Bulletin, 30,* 185–188.

Rajecki, D. W., & Borden, V. M. H. (2011). Psychology degrees: Employment, wage, and career trajectory consequences. *Perspectives on Psychological Science, 6,* 321–335.

Ramachandra, V. (2009, February). On whether mirror neurons play a significant role in processing affective prosody. *Perceptual and Motor Skills, 108,* 30–36.

Ramachandran, V. S., & Hubbard, E. M. (2001). Synesthesia—a window into perception, thought and language. *Journal of Consciousness Studies, 8,* 3–34.

Ramos, R. T. (2006). Antidepressants and dizziness. *Journal of Psychopharmacology, 20,* 708–713.

Ramsay, M. C., Reynolds, C. R., & Kamphaus, R. W. (2002). *Essentials of behavioral assessment.* New York: Wiley.

Ramus, F. (2006). Genes, brain, and cognition: A roadmap for the cognitive scientist. *Cognition, 101,* 247–269.

Randolph-Seng, B., & Nielsen, M. E. (2009). Opening the doors of perception: Priming altered states of consciousness outside of conscious awareness. *Archiv für Religionspsychologie/Archive for the Psychology of Religions, 31,* 237–260.

Rangell, L. (2007). *The road to unity in psychoanalytic theory.* Lanham, MD: Jason Aronson.

Rapaport, M., Nierenberg, A. A., Howland, R., Dording, C., Schettler, P. J., & Mischoulon, D. (2011). The treatment of minor depression with St. John's wort or citalopram: Failure to show benefit over placebo. *Journal of Psychiatric Research, 45,* 931–941.

Rapport, R. L. (2005). *Nerve endings: The discovery of the synapse.* New York: W. W. Norton.

Raskin, N. J., & Rogers, C. R. (1989). Person-centered therapy. In R. J. Corsini & D. Wedding (Eds.), *Current psychotherapies* (4th ed.). Itasca, IL: F. E. Peacock.

Rasmussen, N. (2008). *On speed: The many lives of amphetamine.* New York: New York University Press.

Rassin, E. (2008). Individual differences in the susceptibility to confirmation bias. *Netherlands Journal of Psychology, 64,* 87–93.

Rassin, E., & Muris, P. (2007). Abnormal and normal obsessions: A reconsideration. *Behaviour Research and Therapy, 45,* 1065–1070.

Ravindran, A. V., Matheson, K., Griffiths, J., Merali, Z., & Anisman, H. (2002). Stress, coping, uplifts, and quality of life in subtypes of depression: A conceptual framework and emerging data. *Journal of Affective Disorders, 71,* 121–130.

Ray, L., Bryan, A., MacKillop, J., McGeary, J., Hesterberg, K., & Hutchison, K. (2009). The dopamine D4 receptor gene exon III polymorphism, problematic alcohol use and novelty seeking: Direct and mediated genetic effects. *Addiction Biology, 14,* 238–244.

Ray, L. A., & Hutchison, K. E. (2007). Effects of naltrexone on alcohol sensitivity and genetic moderators of medication response: A double-blind placebo-controlled study. *Archives of General Psychiatry, 64,* 1069–1077.

Ray, R., et al. (2008). Neuroimaging, genetics and the treatment of nicotine addiction. *Behavioural Brain Research, 193,* 159–169.

Raz, A. (2007). Suggestibility and hypnotizability: Mind the gap. *American Journal of Clinical Hypnosis, 49,* 205–210.

Raznahan, A., Lee, Y., Stidd, R., Long, R., Greenstein, D., Clasen, L., et al. (2010). Longitudinally mapping the influence of sex and androgen signaling on the dynamics of human cortical maturation in adolescence. *Proceedings of the National Academy of Sciences, 107,* 16988–16993.

Read, D., & Grushka-Cockayne, Y. (2011). The similarity heuristic. *Journal of Behavioral Decision Making, 24,* 23–46.

Read, J., Beattie, M., Chamberlain, R., & Merrill, J. (2008). Beyond the 'binge' threshold: Heavy drinking patterns and their association with alcohol involvement indices in college students. *Addictive Behaviors, 33,* 225–234.

Redding, G. M. (2002). A test of size-scaling and relative-size hypotheses for the moon illusion. *Perception and Psychophysics, 64,* 1281–1289.

Redding, G. M., & Hawley, E. (1993). Length illusion in fractional Müller-Lyer stimuli: An object-perception approach. *Perception, 22,* 819–828.

Redish, A. D. (2004). Addiction as a computational process gone awry. *Science, 306,* 1944–1947.

Reece, M., Herbenick, D., Sanders, S., Dodge, B., Ghassemi, A., & Fortenberry, J. (2009, July). Prevalence and characteristics of vibrator use by men in the United States. *Journal of Sexual Medicine, 6,* 1867–1874.

Reed, P. (2007). Response rate and sensitivity to the molar feedback function relating response and reinforcement rate on VI+ schedules of reinforcement. *Journal of Experimental Psychology: Animal Behavior Processes, 33,* 428–439.

Reed, P., & Morgan, T. (2008). Effect on subsequent fixed-interval schedule performance of prior exposure to ratio and interval schedules of reinforcement. *Learning & Behavior, 36,* 82–91.

Reed, S. K. (1996). *Cognition: Theory and applications* (4th ed.). Pacific Grove, CA: Brooks/Cole.

Reese, R. J., Conoley, C. W., & Brossart, D. F. (2002). Effectiveness of telephone counseling: A field-based investigation. *Journal of Counseling Psychology, 49,* 233–242.

Regan, P. C. (2006). Love. In R. D. McAnulty & M. M. Burnette (Eds.), *Sex and sexuality, Vol 2: Sexual function and dysfunction.* Westport, CT: Praeger Publishers/Greenwood Publishing.

Reichenberg, A., & Harvey, P. D. (2007). Neuropsychological impairments in schizophrenia: Integration of performance-based and brain imaging findings. *Psychological Bulletin, 133,* 212–223.

Reichenberg, A., Harvey, P., Bowie, C., Mojtabai, R., Rabinowitz, J., Heaton, R., et al. (2009). Neuropsychological function and dysfunction in schizophrenia and psychotic affective disorders. *Schizophrenia Bulletin, 35,* 1022–1029.

Reid, J. R., MacLeod, J., & Robertson, J. R. (2010). Cannabis and the lung. *Journal of the Royal College of Physicians, 40,* 328–334.

Reijonen, J. H., Pratt, H. D., Patel, D. R., & Greydanus, D. E. (2003). Eating disorders in the adolescent population: An overview [Special issue: Eating disorders in adolescents]. *Journal of Adolescent Research, 18,* 209–222.

Reilly, T., & Waterhouse, J. (2007). Altered sleep-wake cycles and food intake: The Ramadan model. *Physiology & Behavior, 90,* 219–228.

Reiner, R. (2008, March). Integrating a portable biofeedback device into clinical practice for patients with anxiety disorders: Results of a pilot study. *Applied Psychophysiology and Biofeedback, 33,* 55–61.

Reisberg, D. (1997). *Cognition: Exploring the science of the mind.* New York: Norton.

Reisberg, D. (2009). *Cognition: Exploring the science of the mind.* New York: Norton.

Reiss, S., & Havercamp, S. M. (2005). Motivation in developmental context: A new method for studying self-actualization. *Journal of Humanistic Psychology, 45,* 41–53.

Relier, J. P. (2001). Influence of maternal stress on fetal behavior and brain development. *Biology of the Neonate, 79,* 168–171.

Rende, R. (2007). Thinking inside and outside the (black) box: Behavioral genetics and human development. *Human Development, 49,* 343–346.

Renshaw, D. C. (2006). Male and female circumcision today. *The Family Journal, 14,* 283–285.

Repp, B. H., & Knoblich, G. (2007). Action can affect auditory perception. *Psychological Science, 18,* 6–7.

Rescorla, R. A. (1988). Pavlovian conditioning: It's not what you think it is. *American Psychologist, 43,* 151–160.

Reynolds, C. R., & Ramsay, M. C. (2003). Bias in psychological assessment: An empirical review and recommendations. In J. R. Graham & J. A. Naglieri (Eds.), *Handbook of psychology: Assessment psychology* (Vol. 10). New York: Wiley.

Rice, C. (2009, December 18). Prevalence of Autism Spectrum Disorders—Autism and Developmental Disabilities Monitoring Network, United States, 2006. *MMWR, 58*(SS10), 1–20.

Rice, E., Milburn, N. G., & Monro, W. (2011). Social networking technology, social network composition, and reductions in substance use among homeless adolescents. *Prevention Science, 12,* 80–88.

Rice, M. L., Tomblin, J. B., Hoffman, L., Richman, W. A., & Marquis, J. (2004). Grammatical tense deficits in children with SLI and nonspecific language impairment: Relationships with non-verbal IQ over time. *Journal of Speech, Language, and Hearing Research, 47,* 816–834.

Rich, E. L., & Shapiro, M. L. (2007). Prelimbic/infralimbic inactivation impairs memory for multiple task switches, but not flexible selection of familiar tasks. *Journal of Neuroscience, 27,* 4747–4755.

Richard, D. C. S., & Lauterbach, D. (Eds.). (2006). *Handbook of exposure therapies.* New York: Academic Press.

Richards, C. (2011). Transsexualism and existentialism. *Existential Analysis, 22*(2), 272–279.

Richards, R. (2006). Frank Barron and the study of creativity: A voice that lives on. *Journal of Humanistic Psychology, 46,* 352–370.

Richardson, A. S., Bergen, H. A., Martin, G., Roeger, L., & Allison, S. (2005). Perceived academic performance as an indicator of risk of attempted suicide in young adolescents. *Archives of Suicide Research, 9,* 163–176.

Richardson, D., & Hammock, G. S. (2011). Is it aggression?: Perceptions of and motivations for passive and psychological aggression. In J. P. Forgas, A. W. Kruglanski, et al. (Eds.), *The psychology of social conflict and aggression*. New York: Psychology Press.

Richgels, D. J. (2004). Paying attention to language. *Reading Research Quarterly, 39*, 470–477.

Rieber, R. W., & Robinson, D. K. (2006). Review of the essential Vygotsky. *Journal of the History of the Behavioral Sciences, 42*, 178–180.

Riedel, G., Platt, B., & Micheau, J. (2003). Glutamate receptor function in learning and memory. *Behavioural Brain Research, 140*, 1–47.

Rigby, L., & Waite, S. (2007). Group therapy for self-esteem: Using creative approaches and metaphor as clinical tools. *Behavioural and Cognitive Psychotherapy, 35*, 361–364.

Rinaman, L., Banihashemi, L., & Koehnle, T. J. (2011). Early life experience shapes the functional organization of stress-responsive visceral circuits. *Physiology & Behavior, 104*, 632–640.

Riniolo, T. C., Koledin, M., Drakulic, G. M., & Payne, R. A. (2003). An archival study of eyewitness memory of the Titanic's final plunge. *Journal of General Psychology, 130*, 89–95.

Riolo, E (2007). Ricordare, ripetere e rielaborare: Un lascito di Freud alia psicoanalisi futura. Remembering, repeating, and working through: Freud's legacy to the psychoanalysis of the future. *Rivista di Psicoanalisi, 53*, 439–446.

Rivera-Gaxiola, M., Klarman, L., Garcia-Sierra, A., & Kuhl, P. K. (2005). Neural patterns to speech and vocabulary growth in American infants. *Neuroreport: For Rapid Communication of Neuroscience Research, 16*, 495–498.

Robbins, B. (2008). What is the good life? Positive psychology and the renaissance of humanistic psychology. *The Humanistic Psychologist, 36*, 96–112.

Robert, S. (2006). Deictic space in Wolof: Discourse, syntax and the importance of absence. In M. Hickman & S. Robert (Eds.), *Space in languages: Linguistic systems and cognitive categories*. Amsterdam, Netherlands: John Benjamins.

Roberts, M. E., Moore, S. D., & Beckham, J. C. (2007). Post-traumatic stress disorder and substance use disorders. In M. Al'bsi (Ed.), *Stress and addiction: Biological and psychological mechanisms*. San Diego, CA: Elsevier Academic Press.

Robins, C. J., & Rosenthal, M. (2011). Dialectical behavior therapy. In J. D. Herbert & E. M. Forman (Eds.), *Acceptance and mindfulness in cognitive behavior therapy: Understanding and applying the new therapies*. Hoboken, NJ: John Wiley & Sons Inc.

Robins, R. W. (2005, October 7). The nature of personality: Genes, culture, and national character. *Science, 310*, 62–63.

Robinson, D. N. (2007). Theoretical psychology: What is it and who needs it? *Theory & Psychology, 17*, 187–198.

Robinson, N. M. (2003). Two wrongs do not make a right: Sacrificing the needs of gifted students does not solve society's unsolved problems. *Journal for the Education of the Gifted, 26*, 251–273.

Rock, A. (1999, January). Quitting time for smokers. *Money*, pp. 139–141.

Rodd, Z. A., Bell, R. L., Sable, H. J. K., Murphy, J. M., & McBride, W. J. (2004). Recent advances in animal models of alcohol craving and relapse. *Pharmacology, Biochemistry and Behavior, 79*, 439–450.

Roesch, S. C., Adams, L., Hines, A., Palmores, A., Vyas, P., Tran, C., et al. (2005). Coping with prostate cancer: A meta-analytic review. *Journal of Behavioral Medicine, 28*, 281–293.

Roets, A., & Van Hiel, A. (2011). An integrative process approach on judgment and decision making: The impact of arousal, affect, motivation, and cognitive ability. *The Psychological Record, 61*, 497–520.

Rogalsky, C., Love, T., Driscoll, D., Anderson, S. W., & Hickok, G. (2011). Are mirror neurons the basis of speech perception? Evidence from five cases with damage to the purported human mirror system. *Neurocase, 17*, 178–187.

Rogers, C. (1980). *A way of being*. Boston: Houghton Mifflin.

Rogers, C. R. (1951). *Client-centered therapy*. Boston: Houghton-Mifflin.

Rogers, C. R. (1971). A theory of personality. In S. Maddi (Ed.), *Perspectives on personality*. Boston: Little, Brown.

Rogers, C. R. (1995). *A way of being*. Boston: Houghton Mifflin.

Rogers, J. M. (2009). Tobacco and pregnancy: Overview of exposures and effects. *Birth Defects Res. C. Embryo Today, 84*, 152–160.

Rogers, P. (2002, August 2). Too much, too soon. *People*, pp. 79–82.

Rogers, P., & Eftimiades, M. (1995, July 24). Bearing witness. *People Weekly*, pp. 42–43.

Rogers, S. (2007). The underlying mechanisms of semantic memory loss in Alzheimer's disease and semantic dementia. *Dissertation Abstracts International: Section B: The Sciences and Engineering, 67*(10-B), 5591.

Rohan, K. J., Roecklein, K. A., & Tierney Lindsey, K. (2007). A randomized controlled trial of cognitive-behavioral therapy, light therapy, and their combination for seasonal affective disorder. *Journal of Consulting and Clinical Psychology, 75*, 489–500.

Roid, G., Nellis, L., & McLellan, M. (2003). Assessment with the Leiter International Performance Scale—Revised and the S-BIT. In R. S. McCallum & R. Steve (Eds.), *Handbook of nonverbal assessment*. New York: Kluwer Academic/Plenum Publishers.

Roisman, G. I., Collins, W. A., Sroufe, L. A., & Egeland, B. (2005). Predictors of young adults' representations of and behavior in their current romantic relationship: Prospective tests of the prototype hypothesis. *Attachment and Human Development, 7*, 105–121.

Roizen, N. J., & Patterson, D. (2003). Down's syndrome. *Lancet, 361*, 1281–1289.

Rollman, G. B. (2004). *Ethnocultural variations in the experience of pain*. Mahwah, NJ: Lawrence Erlbaum Associates.

Rolls, E. T. (2011). Functions of human emotional memory: The brain and emotion. In S. Nalbantian, P. M. Matthews, J. L. McClelland, S. Nalbantian, et al. (Eds.), *The memory process: Neuroscientific and humanistic perspectives*. Cambridge, MA: MIT Press.

Rom, S. A., Miller, L., & Peluso, J. (2009). Playing the game: Psychological factors in surviving cancer. *International Journal of Emergency Mental Health, 11*, 25–36.

Romano, E., Tremblay, R. E., Vitaro, E., Zoccolillo, M., & Pagani, L. (2001.) Prevalence of psychiatric diagnoses and the role of perceived impairment: Findings from an adolescent community sample. *Journal of Child Psychology and Psychiatry and Allied Disciplines, 42*, 451–461.

Romeu, P. E. (2006). Memories of the terrorist attacks of September 11, 2001: A study of the consistency and phenomenal characteristics of flashbulb memories. *The Spanish Journal of Psychology, 9*, 52–60.

Rooke, S. E., & Hine, D. W. (2011). A dual process account of adolescent and adult binge drinking. *Addictive Behaviors, 36*, 341–346.

Rorschach, H. (1924). *Psychodiagnosis: A diagnostic test based on perception*. New York: Grune & Stratton.

Rosen, H. (2000). The creative evolution of the theoretical foundations for cognitive therapy [Special issue: Creativity in the context of cognitive therapy]. *Journal of Cognitive Psychotherapy, 14*, 123–134.

Rosen, J. (2005, August 28.) The future v. Roberts. *The New York Times Magazine*, pp. 24–29, 44, 50–51.

Rosenbloom, T., & Wolf, Y. (2002). Sensation seeking and detection of risky road signals: A developmental perspective. *Accident Analysis and Prevention, 34*, 569–580.

Rosenhan, D. L. (1973). On being sane in insane places. *Science, 179*, 250–258.

Rosenstein, D. S., & Horowitz, H. A. (1996). Adolescent attachment and psychopathology. *Journal of Consulting and Clinical Psychology, 64*, 244–253.

Rosenthal, A. M. (2008). *Thirty-eight witnesses: The Kitty Genovese case*. Hoboken, NJ: Melville House Publishing.

Rosenthal, N. F. (2003). *The emotional revolution: How the new science of feeling can transform your life*. New York: Citadel.

Rosenthal, R. (2002). Covert communication in classrooms, clinics, courtrooms and cubicles. *American Psychologist, 57*, 838–849.

Rosenthal, R. (2003). Covert communication in laboratories, classrooms, and the truly real world. *Current Directions in Psychological Science, 12*, 151–154.

Ross, H. E., & Plug, C. (2002). *The mystery of the moon illusion: Exploring size perception*. Oxford: University Press.

Ross, J. (2006). Sleep on a problem . . . It works like a dream. *The Psychologist, 19*, 738–740.

Ross, L. A., Molholm, S., Blanco, D., Gomez-Ramirez, M., Saint-Amour, D., & Foxe, J. J. (2011). The development of multisensory speech perception continues into the late childhood years. *European Journal of Neuroscience, 33*, 2329–2337.

Ross, P. E. (2004, April). Draining the language out of color. *Scientific American*, pp. 46–51.

Rossato, M., Pagano, C., & Vettor, R. (2008). The cannabinoid system and male reproductive functions. *Journal of Neuroendocrinology, 20*, 90–93.

Rossi, J. J., June, C. H., & Kohn, D. B. (2007). Genetic therapies against HIV. *Natural Biotechnology, 25*, 1444–1454.

Rossouw, J. E., Prentice, R. L., Manson, J. E., Wu, L., Barad, D., Barnabei, V. M., et al. (2007). Postmenopausal hormone therapy and risk of cardiovascular disease by age and years since menopause. *Journal of the American Medical Association, 297*, 1465–1477.

Rotan, L. W., & Ospina-Kammerer, V. (2007). *Mindbody medicine: Foundations and practical applications*. New York: Routledge/Taylor & Francis Group.

Roter, D. L., Hall, J. A., & Aoki, Y. (2002). Physician gender effects in medical communication: A meta-analytic review. *Journal of* the *American Medical Association, 288,* 756–764.

Roughton, R. E. (2002). Rethinking homosexuality: What it teaches us about psychoanalysis. *Journal of the American Psychoanalytic Association, 50,* 733–763.

Routtenberg, A., & Lindy, J. (1965). Effects of the availability of rewarding septal and hypothalamic stimulation on bar pressing for food under conditions of deprivation. *Journal of Comparative and Physiological Psychology, 60,* 158–161.

Rowe, J. B., Toni, I., Josephs, O., Frackowiak, R. S. J., & Passingham, R. E. (2000, June 2). The pre-frontal cortex: Response selection or maintenance within working memory? *Science, 288,* 1656–1660.

Royzman, E. B., Cassidy, K. W., & Baron, J. (2003). "I know, you know": Epistemic egocentrism in children and adults. *Review of General Psychology, 7,* 38–65.

Rozencwajg, P., Cherfi, M., Ferrandez, A. M., Lautrey, J., Lemoine, C., & Loarer, E. (2005). Age-related differences in the strategies used by middle aged adults to solve a block design task. *International Journal of Aging and Human Development, 60,* 159–182.

Rozin, P., Kabnick, K., Pete, E., Fischler, C., & Shields, C. (2003). The ecology of eating: Smaller portion sizes in France than in the United States help explain the French paradox. *Psychological Science, 14,* 450–454.

Rubichi, S., Ricci, F., Padovani, R., & Scaglietti, L. (2005). Hypnotic susceptibility, baseline attentional functioning, and the Stroop task. *Consciousness and Cognition: An International Journal, 14,* 296–303.

Rubin, B. D., & Katz, L. C. (1999). Optical imaging of odorant representations in the mammalian olfactory bulb. *Neuron 23,* 499–511.

Rubin, D. C. (1985, September). The subtle deceiver: Recalling our past. *Psychology Today,* pp. 39–46.

Rubin, D. C., Schrauf, R. W., Gulgoz, S., & Naka, M. (2007). Cross-cultural variability of component processes in autobiographical remembering: Japan, Turkey, and the USA. *Memory, 15,* 536–547.

Rudner, M., & Rönnberg, J. (2008). The role of the episodic buffer in working memory for language processing. *Cognitive Processing, 9,* 19–28.

Rusche, B. (2003). The 3Rs and animal welfare—conflict or the way forward? *ALTEX, 20, (Suppl. 1),* 63–76.

Ruscher, J. B., Fiske, S. T., & Schnake, S. B. (2000). The motivated tactician's juggling act: Compatible vs. incompatible impression goals. *British Journal of Social Psychology, 39,* 241–256.

Rushton, J. P., & Jensen, A. R. (2006). The totality of available evidence shows the race IQ gap still remains. *Psychological Science, 17,* 921–922.

Russell, J. A., & Sato, K. (1995). Comparing emotion words between languages. *Journal of Cross Cultural Psychology, 26,* 384–391.

Russo, N. (1981). Women in psychology. In L. T. Benjamin, Jr. & K. D. Lowman (Eds.), *Activities handbook for the teaching of psychology.* Washington, DC: American Psychological Association.

Rutherford, B., Rose, S., Sneed, J., & Roose, S. (2009, April). Study design affects participant expectations: A survey. *Journal of Clinical Psychopharmacology, 29,* 179–181.

Rutter, M. (2002). Nature, nurture, and development: From evangelism through science toward policy and practice. *Child Development, 73,* 1–21.

Rutter, M. (2006). *Genes and behavior: Nature-nurture interplay explained.* Malden, MA: Blackwell Publishing.

Ryan, R. M., & Deci, E. L. (2011). A self-determination theory perspective on social, institutional, cultural, and economic supports for autonomy and their importance for well-being. In V. I. Chirkov, R. M. Ryan, et al. (Eds.), *Human autonomy in cross-cultural context: Perspectives on the psychology of agency, freedom, and well-being.* New York: Springer Science + Business Media.

Rydell, R., McConnell, A., & Mackie, D. (2008). Consequences of discrepant explicit and implicit attitudes: Cognitive dissonance and increased information processing. *Journal of Experimental Social Psychology, 44,* 1526–1532.

Rymer, R. (1994). *Genie: A scientific tragedy.* New York: Penguin.

Saarni, C. (1999). *Developing emotional competence.* New York: Guilford.

Sabater, J., & Sierra, C. (2005). Review on computational trust and reputation models. *Artificial Intelligence Review, 24,* 33–60.

Sachs-Ericsson, N., Joiner, T., Plant, E. A., & Blazer, D. G. (2005). The influence of depression on cognitive decline in community-dwelling elderly persons. *American Journal of Geriatric Psychiatry, 13,* 402–408.

Sacks, O. (2003, July 28). The mind's eye. *The New Yorker,* pp. 48–59.

Saczynski, J., Willis, S., & Schaie, K. (2002). Strategy use in reasoning training with older adults. *Aging, Neuropsychology, & Cognition, 9,* 48–60.

Sado, M., Yamauchi, K., Kawakami, N., Ono, Y., Furukawa, T. A., Tsuchiya, M., et al. (2011). Cost of depression among adults in Japan in 2005. *Psychiatry and Clinical Neurosciences, 65,* 442–450.

Saggino, A., Perfetti, B., & Spitoni, G. (2006). Fluid intelligence and executive functions: New perspectives. In L. V. Wesley (Eds.), *Intelligence: New research.* Hauppauge, NY: Nova Science Publishers.

Sahakian, B. J., & Morein-Zamir, S. (2011). Neuroethical issues in cognitive enhancement. *Journal of Psychopharmacology, 25,* 197–204.

Sahin, N. T., Pinker, S., & Halgren, E. (2006). Abstract grammatical processing of nouns and verbs in Broca's area: Evidence from fMRI. *Cortex, 42,* 540–562.

Salat, D. H., Tuch, D. S., van der Kouwe, A. J. W., Greve, D. N., Pappu, V., Lee, S. Y., et al. (2010). White matter pathology isolates the hippocampal formation in Alzheimer's disease. *Neurobiology of Aging, 31* (2000), 244–256.

Salgado, D. M., Quinlian, K. J., & Zlotnick, C. (2007). The relationship of lifetime polysubstance dependence to trauma exposure, symptomatology, and psychosocial functioning in incarcerated women with comorbid PTSD and substance use disorder. *Journal of Trauma Dissociation, 8,* 9–26.

Sallquist, J., Eisenberg, N., Spinrad, T. L., Eggum, N. D., & Gaertner, B. (2009). Assessment of preschoolers' positive empathy: Concurrent and longitudinal relations with positive emotion, social competence, and sympathy. *The Journal of Positive Psychology, 4,* 223–233.

Salmela-Aro, K., & Nurmi, J-E. (2007). Self-esteem during university studies predicts career characteristics 10 years later. *Journal of Vocational Behavior, 70,* 463–477.

Salsman, N. L. (2006). Interpersonal change as an outcome of Time-Limited Interpersonal Therapy. *Dissertation Abstracts International: Section B: The Sciences and Engineering, 66(9-B),* 5103.

Salvi, V., Fagiolini, A., Swartz, H., Maina, G., & Frank, E. (2008). The use of antidepressants in bipolar disorder. *Journal of Clinical Psychiatry, 69,* 1307–1318.

Samantaray, S. K., Srivastava, M., & Mishra, P. K. (2002). Fostering self concept and self actualization as bases for empowering women in national development: A challenge for the new millennium. *Social Science International, 18,* 58–63.

Samoilov, V., & Zayas, V. (2007). Ivan Petrovich Pavlov (1849-1936). *Journal of the History of the Neurosciences, 16,* 74–89.

Sams, M., Hari, R., Rif, J., & Knuutila, J. (1993). The human auditory memory trace persists about 10 sec: Neuromagnetic evidence. *Journal of Cognitive Neuroscience, 5,* 363–370.

Samuel, D. B., & Widiger, T. A. (2006). Differentiating normal and abnormal personality from the perspective of the DSM. In S. Strack (Ed.), *Differentiating normal and abnormal personality* (2nd ed.). New York: Springer Publishing.

Sanderson, M. (2007). Assessment of manic symptoms in different cultures. *British Journal of Psychiatry, 190,* 178.

Sandomir, R. (2007, July 17). W. W. E.'s testing is examined after Bennoit murder-suicide. *The New York Times,* p. S3.

Sandoval, J., Frisby, C. L., Geisinger, K. F., Scheuneman, J. D., & Grenier, J. R. (Eds.). (1998). *Test interpretation and diversity: Achieving equity in assessment.* Washington, DC: American Psychological Association.

Saneyoshi, A., Niimi, R., Suetsugu, T., Kaminaga, T., & Yokosawa, K. (2011). Iconic memory and parietofrontal network: fMRI study using temporal integration. *Neuroreport: For Rapid Communication of Neuroscience Research, 22,* 515–519.

Santel, S., Baving, L., Krauel, K., Munte, T. F., & Rotte, M. (2006, October 9). Hunger and satiety in anorexia nervosa: fMRI during cognitive processing of food pictures. *Brain Research, 1114,* 138–148.

Santelli, J., Carter, M., Orr, M., & Dittus, P. (2009, April). Trends in sexual risk behaviors, by nonsexual risk behavior involvement, U.S. high school students, 1991–2007. *Journal of Adolescent Health, 44,* 372–379.

Saper, C. B., Lu, J., Chou, T. C., & Gooley, J. (2005). The hypothalamic integrator for circadian rhythms. *Trends in Neuroscience, 28,* 152–157.

Sapolsky, R. M. (2003). Gene therapy for psychiatric disorders. *American Journal of Psychiatry, 160,* 208–220.

Sargent, J. D., Stoolmiller, M., Worth, K. A., Cal, C. S., Wills, T. A., Gibbons, F. X., et al. (2007). Exposure to smoking depictions in movies: Its association with established adolescent smoking. *Archives of Pediatric Adolescent Medicine, 161,* 849–856.

Sarsour, K., Sheridan, M., Jutte, D., Nuru-Jeter, A., Hinshaw, S., & Boyce, W. (2011). Family socioeconomic status and child executive functions:

The roles of language, home environment, and single parenthood. *Journal of the International Neuropsychological Society, 17*, 120–132.

Sato, N., Shimamura, M., & Takeuchi, D. (2007). Gene therapy for ischemic brain disease with special reference to vascular dementia. *Geriatrics & Gerontology International, 7*, 1–14.

Saucier, D. A., & Cain, M. E. (2006). The foundations of attitudes about animal research. *Ethics & Behavior, 16*, 117–133.

Savage, J., & Yancey, C. (2008). The effects of media violence exposure on criminal aggression: A meta-analysis. *Criminal Justice and Behavior, 35*, 772–791.

Savage-Rumbaugh, E. S., Toth, N., & Schick, K. (2007). Kanzi learns to knap stone tools. In D. A. Washburn (Ed.), *Primate perspectives on behavior and cognition*. Washington, DC: American Psychological Association.

Savas, H. A., Yumru, M., & Kaya, M. C. (2007). Atypical antipsychotics as 'mood stabilizers': A retrospective chart review. *Progress in Neuro-Psychopharmacology & Biological Psychiatry, 31*, 1064–1067.

Savazzi, S., Fabri, M., Rubboli, G., Paggi, A., Tassinari, C. A., & Marzi, C. A. (2007). Inter-hemispheric transfer following callosotomy in humans: Role of the superior colliculus. *Neuropsychologia, 45*, 2417–2427.

Sawa, A., & Snyder, S. H. (2002, April 26). Schizophrenia: Diverse approaches to a complex disease. *Science, 296*, 692–695.

Saywitz, K., & Goodman, G. (1990). Unpublished study reported in Goleman, D. (1990, November 6). Doubts rise on children as witnesses. *The New York Times*, pp. C1, C6.

Scarr, S. (1998). American child care today. *American Psychologist, 53*, 95–108.

Scarr, S., & Weinberg, R. A. (1976). I.Q. test performance of black children adopted by white families. *American Psychologist, 31*, 726–739.

Scaturo, D. J. (2004). Fundamental clinical dilemmas in contemporary group psychotherapy. *Group Analysis, 37*, 201–217.

Scelfo, J. (2007, February 26). Men & depression: Facing darkness. *Newsweek*, p. 43–50.

Schachter, R. (2011). Using the group in cognitive group therapy. *Group, 35*, 135–149.

Schachter, S., & Singer, J. E. (1962). Cognitive, social, and physiological determinants of emotional state. *Psychological Review, 69*, 379–399.

Schacter, D. L., Dobbins, I. G., & Schnyer, D. M. (2004). Specificity of priming: A cognitive neuroscience perspective. *Nature Reviews Neuroscience, 5*, 853–862.

Schaefer, E. G., Halldorson, M. K., & Dizon-Reynante, C. (2011). TV or not TV? Does the immediacy of viewing images of a momentous news event affect the quality and stability of flashbulb memories? *Memory, 19*, 251–266.

Schaefer, R. T. (2000). *Sociology: A brief introduction* (3rd ed.). Boston: McGraw-Hill.

Schaie, K. W. (2005a). Longitudinal studies. In *Developmental influences on adult intelligence: The Seattle Longitudinal Study*. New York: Oxford University Press.

Schaie, K. W. (2005b). What can we learn from longitudinal studies of adult development? *Research in Human Development, 2*, 133–158.

Schaller, M., & Crandall, C. S. (Eds.). (2004). *The psychological foundations of culture*. Mahwah, NJ: Lawrence Erlbaum Associates.

Schechter, T., Finkelstein, Y., & Koren, G. (2005). Pregnant "DES daughters" and their offspring. *Canadian Family Physician, 51*, 493–494.

Schedlowski, M., & Tewes, U. (Eds.). (1999). *Psychoneuroimmunology: An interdisciplinary introduction*. New York: Plenum.

Scheff, T. J. (1998). Shame in the labeling of mental illness. In P. Gilbert & B. Andrews, (Eds.), *Shame: Interpersonal behavior, psychopathology, and culture*. New York: Oxford University Press.

Scheier, M. F., Carver, C. S., & Bridges, M. W. (1994). Distinguishing optimism from neuroticism (and trait anxiety, self-mastery, and self-esteem): A reevaluation of the Life Orientation Test. *Journal of Personality and Social Psychology, 67*, 1063–1078.

Schenone, M. H., Aquin, E., Li, Y., Lee, C., Kruger, M., & Bahado-Singh, R. O. (2010). Prenatal prediction of neonatal survival at the borderline viability. *Journal of Maternal-Fetal Neonatal Medicine, 12*, 31–38.

Schepers, P., & van den Berg, P. T. (2007). Social factors of work-environment creativity. *Journal of Business and Psychology, 21*, 407–428.

Schermer, J., Johnson, A. M., Vernon, P. A., & Jang, K. L. (2011). The relationship between personality and self-report abilities: A behavior-genetic analysis. *Journal of Individual Differences, 32*, 47–53.

Schieber, E. (2006). Vision and aging. In J. E. Birren & K. W. Schaire (Eds.), *Handbook of the psychology of aging* (6th ed.). Amsterdam, Netherlands: Elsevier.

Schiffer, A. A., Pedersen, S. S., Widdershoven, J. W., Hendriks, E. H., Winter, J. B., & Denollet, J. (2005). The distressed (type D) personality is independently associated with impaired health status and increased depressive symptoms in chronic heart failure. *European Journal of Cardiovascular Prevention and Rehabilitation, 12*, 341–346.

Schillinger, D., Bindman, A., Wang, F., Stewart, A., & Piette, J. (2004). Functional health literacy and the quality of physician-patient communication among diabetes patients. *Patient Education and Counseling, 52*, 315–323.

Schlinger, H. R. (2011). Skinner as missionary and prophet: A review of Burrhus F. Skinner: Shaper of behaviour. *Journal of Applied Behavior Analysis, 44*, 217–225.

Schmidt, J. P. (2006). The discovery of neurotransmitters: A fascinating story and a scientific object lesson. *PsycCRITIQUES, 61*, 101–115.

Schmidt, N. B., Kotov, R., & Joiner, T. E., Jr. (2004). *Taxometrics: Toward a new diagnostic scheme for psychopathology*. Washington, DC: American Psychological Association.

Schmitt, D., Realo, A., Voracek, M., & Allik, J. (2008). Why can't a man be more like a woman? Sex differences in Big Five personality traits across 55 cultures. *Journal of Personality and Social Psychology, 94*, 168–182.

Schmitt, D. P., Allik, J., & McCrae, R. R. (2007). The geographic distribution of Big Five personality traits: Patterns and profiles of human self-description across 56 nations. *Journal of Cross-Cultural Psychology, 38*, 173–212.

Schnabel, K., Asendorpf, J., & Greenwald, A. (2008). Assessment of individual differences in implicit cognition: A review of IAT measures. *European Journal of Psychological Assessment, 24*, 210–217.

Schnall, S., Haidt, J., Clore, G. L., & Jordan, A. H. (2008). Disgust as embodied moral judgment. *Personality and Social Psychology Bulletin, 34*, 1096–1109.

Schnatz, P. F., Murphy, J. L., O'Sullivan, D. M., & Sorosky, J. I. (2007). Patient choice: Comparing criteria for selecting an obstetrician-gynecologist based on image, gender, and professional attributes. *American Journal of Obstetrics and Gynecology, 197*, 548–561.

Schneider, A., & Domhoff, G. W. (2002). *The quantitative study of dreams*. www.dreamresearch.net.

Schnell, K., & Herpertz, S. C. (2007). Effects of dialectic-behavioral-therapy on the neural correlates of affective hyperarousal in borderline personality disorder. *Journal of Psychiatric Research, 41*, 837–847.

Schnupp, J., Nelken, I., & King, A. (2011). *Auditory neuroscience: Making sense of sound*. Cambridge, MA: MIT Press.

Schredl, M., & Piel, E. (2005). Gender differences in dreaming: Are they stable over time? *Personality and Individual Differences, 39*, 309–316.

Schredl, M., & Reinhard, I. (2011). Gender differences in nightmare frequency: A meta-analysis. *Sleep Medicine Reviews, 15*, 115–121.

Schreurs, B. G., Smith-Bell, C. A., & Burhans, L. B. (2011). Classical conditioning and conditioning-specific reflex modification of rabbit heart rate as a function of unconditioned stimulus location. *Behavioral Neuroscience, 125*, 604–612.

Schroers, M., Prigot, J., & Fagen, J. (2007, December). The effect of a salient odor context on memory retrieval in young infants. *Infant Behavior & Development, 30*, 685–689.

Schubert, T., & Koole, S. (2009). The embodied self: Making a fist enhances men's power-related self-conceptions. *Journal of Experimental Social Psychology, 45*, 828–834.

Schulte-Ruther, M., Markowitsch, J. J., Fink, G. R., & Piefke, M. (2007). Mirror neuron and theory of mind mechanisms involved in face-to-face interactions: A functional magnetic resonance imaging approach to empathy. *Journal of Cognitive Neuroscience, 19*, 1354–1372.

Schultz, E. (2011, March 14). Flo thumbs a ride with drivers; In 'game-changer,' Progressive insurance offers device to monitor motoring and reward good habits with discounts. *Advertising Age, 82*, 1.

Schwartz, B. (2008). Working memory load differentially affects tip-of-the-tongue states and feeling-of-knowing judgments. *Memory & Cognition, 36*, 9–19.

Schwartz, B. L. (2002). The phenomenology of naturally-occurring tip-of-the-tongue states: A diary study. In S. P. Shohov (Ed.), *Advances in psychology research* (Vol. 8). Huntington, NY: Nova.

Schwartz, B. L., & Metcalfe, J. (2011). Tip-of-the-tongue (TOT) states: Retrieval, behavior, and experience. *Memory & Cognition, 39*, 737–749.

Schwartz, J., & Wald, M. L. (2003). NASA's curse? "Groupthink" is 30 years old, and still going strong. *The New York Times*, p. C1.

Schwartz, J. M., & Begley, S. (2002). *The mind and the brain: Neuroplasticity and the power of mental force*. New York: Regan Books/Harper Collins.

Schwartz, P., Maynard, A., & Uzelac, S. (2008). Adolescent egocentrism: A contemporary view. *Adolescence, 43*(171), 441–448.

Schwartz, S. J., Côté, J. E., & Arnett, J. J. (2005). Identity and agency in emerging adulthood: Two developmental routes in the individualization process. *Youth & Society, 37*, 201–229.

Schwartzmant, R. J., Alexander, G. M., & Grothusen, J. R. (2011). The use of ketamine in complex regional pain syndrome: Possible mechanisms. *Expert Review of Neurotherapeutics, 11*, 719–734.

Schweizer, S., & Dalgleish, T. (2011). Emotional working memory capacity in posttraumatic stress disorder (PTSD). *Behaviour Research and Therapy, 49*, 498–504.

Sciutto, M., & Eisenberg, M. (2007). Evaluating the evidence for and against the overdiagnosis of ADHD. *Journal of Attention Disorders, 11*, 106–113.

Scullin, M. H., Kanaya, T., & Ceci, S. J. (2002). Measurement of individual differences in children's suggestibility across situations. *Journal of Experimental Psychology: Applied, 8*, 233–246.

Sebastiani, L., Castellani, E., & D'Alessandro, L. (2011). Emotion processing without awareness: Features detection or significance evaluation? *International Journal of Psychophysiology, 80*, 150–156.

Sebel, P. S., Bonke, B., & Winograd, E. (Eds.). (1993). *Memory and awareness in anesthesia.* Englewood Cliffs, NJ: Prentice-Hall.

Seeley, R., Stephens, T., & Tate, P. (2000). *Anatomy & Physiology* (5th ed.). Boston: McGraw-Hill.

Seeman, P. (2011). All roads to schizophrenia lead to dopamine supersensitivity and elevated dopamine D2 receptors. *CNS Neuroscience & Therapeutics, 17*, 118–132.

Seery, M. D., Holman, E., & Silver, R. (2010). Whatever does not kill us: Cumulative lifetime adversity, vulnerability, and resilience. *Journal of Personality and Social Psychology*, 1025–1041.

Sefcek, J. A., Brumbach, B. H., & Vasquez, G. (2007). The evolutionary psychology of human mate choice: How ecology, genes, fertility, and fashion influence mating strategies. *Journal of Psychology & Human Sexuality, 18*, 125–182.

Segall, M. H., Campbell, D. T., & Herskovits, M. J. (1966). *The influence of culture on visual perception.* New York: Bobbs-Merrill.

Segerstrom, S. C., & Miller, G. E. (2004). Psychological stress and the human immune system: A meta-analytic study of 30 years of inquiry. *Psychological Bulletin, 130*, 601–630.

Seibt, B., & Förster, J. (2005). Stereotype threat and performance: How self-stereotypes influence processing by inducing regulatory foci. *Journal of Personality and Social Psychology, 87*, 38–56.

Seli, H. (2007). Self in self-worth protection: The relationship of possible selves to achievement motives and self-worth protective strategies. *Dissertation Abstracts International Section A: Humanities and Social Sciences, 67*(9-A), 3302.

Seligman, M. E. (2007). *What you can change. . . and what you can't: The complete guide to successful self-improvement.* New York: Vintage.

Seligman, M. E. P. (1975). *Helplessness: On depression, development, and death.* San Francisco: Freeman.

Seligman, M. E. P. (1995, December). The effectiveness of psychotherapy: The *Consumer Reports* study. *American Psychologist, 50*, 965–974.

Seligman, M. E. P. (1996, October). Science as an ally of practice. *American Psychologist, 51*, 1072–1079.

Selkoe, D. (2008). Soluble oligomers of the amyloid β-protein impair synaptic plasticity and behavior. *Behavioural Brain Research, 192*, 106–113.

Selkoe, D. J. (1997, January 31). Alzheimer's disease: Genotypes, phenotype, and treatments. *Science, 275*, 630–631.

Sellbom, M., & Ben-Porath, Y. S. (2006). The Minnesota Multiphasic Personality Inventory-2. In R. P. Archer (Ed.), *Forensic uses of clinical assessment instruments.* Mahwah, NJ: Lawrence Erlbaum Associates.

Sellbom, M., Fischler, G., & Ben-Porath, Y. (2007). Identifying MMPI-2 Predictors of police officer integrity and misconduct. *Criminal Justice and Behavior, 34*, 985–1004.

Sells, R. (1994, August). *Homosexuality study.* Paper presented at the annual meeting of the American Statistical Association, Toronto.

Selove, R. (2007). The glass is half full: Current knowledge about pediatric cancer and sickle cell anemia. *PsycCRITIQUES, 52*, 88–99.

Selsky, A. (1997, February 16). African males face circumcision rite. *The Boston Globe*, p. C7.

Selye, H. (1976). *The stress of life.* New York: McGraw-Hill.

Selye, H. (1993). History of the stress concept. In L. Goldberger & S. Breznitz (Eds.), *Handbook of stress: Theoretical and clinical aspects* (2nd ed.). New York: Free Press.

Semler, C. N., & Harvey, A. G. (2005). Misperception of sleep can adversely affect daytime functioning in insomnia. *Behaviour Research and Therapy, 43*, 843–856.

Semykina, A., & Linz, S. J. (2007). Gender differences in personality and earnings: Evidence from Russia. *Journal of Economic Psychology, 28*, 387–410.

Seroczynski, A. D., Jacquez, F. M., & Cole, D. A. (2003). Depression and suicide during adolescence. In G. R. Adams & M. D. Berzonsky (Eds.), *Blackwell handbook of adolescence.* Malden, MA: Blackwell Publishers.

Seymour, B. (2006). Carry on eating: Neural pathways mediating conditioned potentiation of feeding. *Journal of Neuroscience, 26*, 1061–1062.

Shafer, V. L., & Garrido-Nag, K. (2007). The neurodevelopmental bases of language. In E. Hoff & M. Shatz (Eds.), *Blackwell handbook of language development.* Malden, MA: Blackwell Publishing.

Shah, D. B., Pesiridou, A., Baltuch, G. H., Malone, D. A., & O'Reardon, J. P. (2008). Functional neurosurgery in the treatment of severe obsessive compulsive disorder and major depression: Overview of disease circuits and therapeutic targeting for the clinician. *Psychiatry, 5*, 24–33.

Shaikholeslami, R., & Khayyer, M. (2006). Intrinsic motivation, extrinsic motivation, and learning English as a foreign language. *Psychological Reports, 99*, 813–818.

Shankar, G., & Simmons, A. (2009, January). Understanding ethics guidelines using an internet-based expert system. *Journal of Medical Ethics, 35*, 65–68.

Shapiro, L. R. (2006). Remembering September 11th: The role of retention interval and rehearsal on flashbulb and event memory. *Memory, 14*, 129–147.

Sharma, H. S., Sjoquist, P. O., & Ali, S. F. (2007). Drugs of abuse-induced hyperthermia, blood-brain barrier dysfunction and neurotoxicity: Neuroprotective effects of a new antioxidant compound h-290/51. *Current Pharmaceutical Design, 13*, 1903–1923.

Shea, A., & Steiner, M. (2008). Cigarette smoking during pregnancy. *Nicotine & Tobacco Research, 10*, 267–278.

Shelton, R. C., Keller, M. B., Gelenberg, A., Dunner, D. L., Hirschfeld, R. M. A., Thase, M. E., et al. (2002). The effectiveness of St. John's wort in major depression: A multi-center, randomized placebo-controlled trial. *Journal of the American Medical Association, 285*, 1978–1986.

Shepard, R. N., & Metzler, J. (1971). Mental rotation of three-dimensional objects. *Science, 171*(3972), 701–703.

Sheppard, L. D., & Vernon, P. A. (2008). Intelligence and speed of information-processing: A review of 50 years of research. *Personality and Individual Differences, 44*, 535–551.

Shepperd, J., Malone, W., & Sweeny, K. (2008). Exploring causes of the self-serving bias. *Social and Personality Psychology Compass, 2*, 895–908.

Sherblom, S. (2008). The legacy of the 'care challenge': Re-envisioning the outcome of the justice-care debate. *Journal of Moral Education, 37*, 81–98.

Sherman, S. L., Allen, E. G., Bean, L. H., & Freeman, S. B. (2007). Epidemiology of Down syndrome [Special issue: Down syndrome]. *Mental Retardation and Developmental Disabilities Research Reviews, 13*, 221–227.

Shier, D., Butler, J., & Lewis, R. (2000). *Hole's essentials of human anatomy and physiology* (7th ed.). Boston: McGraw-Hill.

Shiffman, S. (2007). Use of more nicotine lozenges leads to better success in quitting smoking. *Addiction, 102*, 809–814.

Shimono, K., & Wade N. J. (2002). Monocular alignment in different depth planes. *Vision Research, 42*, 1127–1135.

Shin, A., Zheng, H., & Berthoud, H. (2009). An expanded view of energy homeostasis: Neural integration of metabolic, cognitive, and emotional drives to eat. *Physiology & Behavior, 97*, 572–580.

Shinn, M., Gottlieb, J., Wett, J. L., Bahl, A., Cohen, A., & Baron, E. D. (2007). Predictors of homelessness among older adults in New York City: Disability, economic, human and social capital and stressful events. *Journal of Health Psychology, 12*, 696–708.

Shirky, C. (2010, June 5). Does the internet make you smarter or dumber? *The Wall Street Journal*, p. W-1.

Shmuel, A., Chaimow, D., Raddatz, G., Ugurbil, K., & Yacoub, E. (2010). Mechanisms underlying decoding at 7 T: Ocular dominance columns, broad structures, and macroscopic blood vessels in V1 convey information on the stimulated eye. *NeuroImage, 49*, 1957–1964.

Shoda, Y., & Mischel, W. (2006). Applying metatheory to achieve generalisability and precision in personality science. *Applied Psychology: An International Review, 55*, 439–452.

Shors, T. J. (2009, March). Saving new brain cells. *Scientific American*, pp. 47–54.

Shugart, H. A. (2011). Shifting the balance: The contemporary narrative of obesity. *Health Communication, 26*, 37–47.

Shurkin, J. N. (1992). *Terman's kids: The groundbreaking study of how the gifted grow up.* Boston: Little, Brown.

Shweder, R. A. (1994). You're not sick, you're just in love: Emotion as an interpretive system. In P. Ekman & R. J. Davidson (Eds.), *The nature of emotion: Fundamental questions.* New York: Oxford.

Sidman, M. (2006). The distinction between positive and negative reinforcement: Some additional considerations. *Behavior Analyst, 29,* 135–139.

Siegel, R. K. (1989). *Intoxication: Life in pursuit of artificial paradise.* New York: E. P. Dutton.

Siegert, R. J., & Ward, T. (2002). Clinical psychology and evolutionary psychology: Toward a dialogue. *Review of General Psychology, 6,* 235–259.

Siemer, M., Mauss I., & Gross, J. J. (2007). Same situation—different emotions: How appraisals shape our emotions. *Emotion, 7,* 592–600.

Sifrit, K. J. (2006). The effects of aging and cognitive decrements on simulated driving performance. *Dissertation abstracts international: Section B: The sciences and engineering, 67,* 2863.

Silva, A. J. (2011). Molecular genetic approaches to memory consolidation. In S. Nalbantian, P. M. Matthews, et al. (Eds.), *The memory process: Neuroscientific and humanistic perspectives.* Cambridge, MA: MIT Press.

Silva, M. T. A., Gonçalves, E. L., & Garcia-Mijares, M. (2007). Neural events in the reinforcement contingency. *Behavior Analyst, 30,* 17–30.

Silverman, K., Roll, J., & Higgins, S. (2008). Introduction to the special issue on the behavior analysis and treatment of drug addiction. *Journal of Applied Behavior Analysis, 41,* 471–480.

Silverstein, M. L. (2007). Rorschach test findings at the beginning of treatment and 2 years later, with a 30-year follow-up. *Journal of Personality Assessment, 88,* 131–143.

Simcock, G., & Hayne, H. (2002). Breaking the barrier? Children fail to translate their preverbal memories into language. *Psychological Science, 13,* 225–231.

Simon, G., Ludman, E., Unützer, J., Operskalski, B., & Bauer, M. (2008). Severity of mood symptoms and work productivity in people treated for bipolar disorder. *Bipolar Disorders, 10,* 718–725.

Simon, S., & Hoyt, C. (2008). Exploring the gender gap in support for a woman for president. *Analyses of Social Issues and Public Policy (ASAP), 8,* 157–181.

Simonton, D. K. (2000). Archival research. In A. E. Kazdin (Ed.), *Encyclopedia of psychology* (Vol. 1). Washington, DC: American Psychological Association.

Simonton, D. K. (2009). Varieties of (scientific) creativity: A hierarchical model of domain-specific disposition, development, and achievement. *Perspectives on Psychological Science, 4,* 441–452.

Singer, J. L. (2006). Why imagery, personal memories, and daydreams matter. In J. L. Singer (Ed.), *Imagery in psychotherapy.* Washington, DC: American Psychological Association.

Singer, L. T., & Richardson, G. A. (2011). Introduction to "understanding developmental consequences of prenatal drug exposure: Biological and environmental effects and their interactions." *Neurotoxicology and Teratology, 33,* 5–8.

Sininger, Y. S., & Cone-Wesson, B. (2004, September 10). Asymmetric cochlear processing mimics hemispheric specialization. *Science, 305,* 1581.

Sininger, Y. S., & Cone-Wesson, B. (2006). Lateral asymmetry in the ABR of neonates: Evidence and mechanisms. *Hearing Research, 212,* 203–211.

Skinner, B. F. (1957). *Verbal behavior.* New York: Appleton-Century-Crofts.

Skinner, B. F. (1975). The steep and thorny road to a science of behavior. *American Psychologist, 30,* 42–49.

Skolnick, P., Popik, P., & Trullas, R. (2009). Glutamate-based antidepressants: 20 years on. *Trends in Pharmacological Science, 30,* 563–569.

Slater, E., & Meyer, A. (1959). Contributions to a pathography of the musicians: Robert Schumann. *Confinia Psychiatrica.* Reprinted in K. R. Jamison, *Touched with fire: Manic-depressive illness and the artistic temperament.* New York: Free Press.

Sleek, S. (1997, June). Can "emotional intelligence" be taught in today's schools? *APA Monitor,* p. 25.

Sloan, E. P., et al. (1993). The nuts and bolts of behavioral therapy for insomnia. *Journal of Psychosomatic Research, 37* (Suppl.), 19–37.

Slocombe, K. E., Waller, B. M., & Liebal, K. (2011). The language void: The need for multimodality in primate communication research. *Animal Behaviour, 81,* 919–924.

Smart, R. G. (2007). Review of introduction to addictive behaviours. *Addiction, 102,* 831.

Smetana, J., Daddis, C., & Chuang, S. (2003). "Clean your room!" A longitudinal investigation of adolescent-parent conflict and conflict resolution in middle-class African American families. *Journal of Adolescent Research, 18,* 631–650.

Smetana, J. B. (2007). Strategies for understanding archetypes and the collective unconscious of an organization. *Dissertation Abstracts International Section A: Humanities and Social Sciences, 67*(12-A), 4714.

Smetana, J. G. (2005). Adolescent-parent conflict: Resistance and subversion as developmental process. In L. Nucci (Ed.), *Conflict, contradiction, and contrarian elements in moral development and education.* Mahwah, NJ: Lawrence Erlbaum Associates.

Smith, B. H., Barkley, R. A., & Shapiro, C. J. (2006). Attention-Deficit/Hyperactivity Disorder. In E. J. Mash & R. A. Barkley (Eds.), *Treatment of childhood disorders* (3rd. ed). New York: Guilford Press.

Smith, C. (2006). Symposium V—Sleep and learning: New developments [Special issue: Methods and learning in functional MRI]. *Brain and Cognition, 60,* 331–332.

Smith, C. A., & Lazarus, R. S. (2001). Appraisal components, core relational themes, and the emotions. In W. G. Parrott (Ed.), *Emotions in social psychology: Essential readings* Philadelphia: Psychology Press.

Smith, C. D., Chebrolu, J., Wekstein, D. R., Schmitt, F. A., & Markesbery, W. R. (2007). Age and gender effects on human brain anatomy: A voxel-based morphometric study in healthy elderly. *Neurobiology of Aging, 28,* 1057–1087.

Smith, D. E., Springer, C. M., & Barrett, S. (2011). Physical discipline and socioemotional adjustment among Jamaican adolescents. *Journal of Family Violence, 26,* 51–61.

Smith, E. (1988, May). Fighting cancerous feelings. *Psychology Today,* pp. 22–23.

Smith, E. R., & Semin, G. R. (2007). Situated social cognition. *Current Directions in Psychological Science, 16,* 132–135.

Smith, L., Cornelius, V., Warnock, A., Bell, A., & Young, A. (2007). Effectiveness of mood stabilizers and antipsychotics in the maintenance phase of bipolar disorder: A systematic review of randomized controlled trials. *Bipolar Disorders, 9,* 394–412.

Smith, M. B. (2003). Moral foundations in research with human participants. In A. E. Kazdin (Ed.), *Methodological issues & strategies in clinical research* (3rd ed.). Washington, DC: American Psychological Association.

Smith, M. L., Glass, G. V., & Miller, T. I. (1980). *The benefits of psychotherapy.* Baltimore: The Johns Hopkins University Press.

Smith, R. A., & Weber, A. L. (2005). Applying social psychology in everyday life. In F. W. Schneider, J. A. Gruman, et al. (Eds.), *Applied social psychology: Understanding and addressing social and practical.* Thousand Oaks, CA: Sage Publications.

Smith, W. B. (2007). Karen Horney and psychotherapy in the 21st century. *Clinical Social Work Journal, 35,* 57–66.

Smrtnik-Vitulič, H., & Zupančič, M. (2011). Personality traits as a predictor of academic achievement in adolescents. *Educational Studies, 37,* 127–140.

Snyder, D. J., Fast, K., & Bartoshuk, L. M. (2004). Valid comparisons of suprathreshold sensations. *Journal of Consciousness Studies, 11,* 96–112.

Snyder, J., Cramer, A., & Afrank, J. (2005). The contributions of ineffective discipline and parental hostile attributions of child misbehavior to the development of conduct problems at home and school. *Developmental Psychology, 41,* 30–41.

Snyder, M. (2002). Applications of Carl Rogers' theory and practice to couple and family therapy: A response to Harlene Anderson and David Bott. *Journal of Family Therapy, 24,* 317–325.

Sobel, K., Gerrie, M., Poole, B., & Kane, M. (2007, October). Individual differences in working memory capacity and visual search: The roles of top-down and bottom-up processing. *Psychonomic Bulletin & Review, 14,* 840–845.

Society for Personality Assessment. (2005). The status of Rorschach in clinical and forensic practice: An official statement by the board of trustees of the Society for Personality Assessment. *Journal of Personality Assessment, 85,* 219–237.

Sodian, B. (2011). Theory of mind in infancy. *Child Development Perspectives, 5,* 39–43.

Soeter, M., & Kindt, M. (2010). Dissociating response systems: Erasing fear from memory. *Neurobiology of Learning and Memory* 30–41.

Sohr-Preston, S. L., & Scaramella, L. V. (2006). Implications of timing of maternal depressive symptoms for early cognitive and language development. *Clinical Child and Family Psychology Review, 9,* 65–83.

Sokolove, M. (2003, November 16). Should John Hinckley go free? *The New York Times Magazine,* pp. 52–54, 92.

Soler, J., Pascual, J., Tiana, T., Cebriã , A., Barrachina, J., Campins, M., et al. (2009). Dialectical behaviour therapy skills training compared to standard group therapy in borderline personality disorder: A 3-month randomised controlled clinical trial. *Behaviour Research and Therapy, 47,* 353–358.

Solesio-Jofre, E., Lorenzo-López, L., Gutiérrez, R., López-Frutos, J., Ruiz-Vargas, J., & Maestú, F. (2011). Age effects on retroactive interference during working memory maintenance. *Biological Psychology, 88,* 72–82.

Solomon, M., & Herman, J. (2009). Sex differences in psychopathology: Of gonads, adrenals and mental illness. *Physiology & Behavior, 97,* 250–258.

Somers, T. J., Moseley, G., Keefe, F. J., & Kothadia, S. M. (2011). Neuroimaging of pain: A psychosocial perspective. In R. A. Cohen & L. H. Sweet, (Eds.), *Brain imaging in behavioral medicine and clinical neuroscience.* New York: Springer Science + Business Media.

Sommer, R., & Sommer, B. (2001). *A practical guide to behavioral research: Tools and techniques* (5th ed.). New York: Oxford University Press.

Soorya, L. V., Carpenter, L., & Romanczyk, R. G. (2011). Applied behavior analysis. In E. Hollander, A. Kolevzon, et al. (Eds.), *Textbook of autism spectrum disorders.* Arlington, VA: American Psychiatric Publishing, Inc.

Sori, C. E. (Ed.). (2006). *Engaging children in family therapy: Creative approaches to integrating theory and research in clinical practice.* New York: Routledge/Taylor & Francis Group.

South, S., & Krueger, R. (2008). An interactionist perspective on genetic and environmental contributions to personality. *Social and Personality Psychology Compass, 2,* 929–948.

Spackman, M. P., Fujiki, M., & Brinton, B. (2006). Understanding emotions in context: The effects of language impairment on children's ability to infer emotional reactions. *International Journal of Language & Communication Disorders, 41,* 173–188.

Spanos, N. P., Barber, T. X., & Lang, G. (2005). Cognition and self-control: Cognitive control of painful sensory input. *Integrative Physiological & Behavioral Science, 40,* 119–128.

Sparrow, B., Liu, J., & Wegner, D. M. (2011, August 5). Google effects on memory: Cognitive consequences of having information at our fingertips. *Science, 333,* 776–778.

Spearman, C. (1927). *The abilities of man.* London: Macmillan.

Spence, M. J., & DeCasper, A. J. (1982, March). *Human fetuses perceive maternal speech.* Paper presented at the meeting of the International Conference on Infant Studies, Austin, TX.

Spence-Cochran, K., & Pearl, C. (2006). Moving toward full inclusion. In P. Wehman (Ed.), *Life beyond the classroom: Transition strategies for young people with disabilities* (4th ed.). Baltimore: Paul H. Brookes Publishing.

Spencer, S. J., Fein, S., Zanna, M. P., & Olson, J. M. (Eds.). (2003). *Motivated social perception: The Ontario Symposium* (Vol. 9). Mahwah, NJ: Erlbaum.

Spencer-Rodgers, J., Peng, K., Wang, L., & Hou, Y. (2004). Dialectical self-esteem and East-West differences in psychological well-being. *Personality and Social Psychology Bulletin, 30,* 1416–1432.

Sperling, G. (1960). The information available in brief visual presentation. *Psychological Monographs, 74,* 29.

Sperry, R. (1982). Some effects of disconnecting the cerebral hemispheres. *Science, 217,* 1223–1226.

Spiegel, D. (1996). Hypnosis. In R. E. Hales & S. C. Yudofsky (Eds.), *The American Psychiatric Press synopsis of psychiatry.* Washington, DC: American Psychiatric Press.

Spiegel, D. (Ed.). (1999). *Efficacy and cost-effectiveness of psychotherapy.* New York: American Psychiatric Press.

Spielberger, C. D. (2006). Cross-cultural assessment of emotional states and personality traits. *European Psychologist, 11,* 297–303.

Spiers, H. J., & Maguire, E. A. (2007). Decoding human brain activity during real-world experiences. *Trends in Cognitive Science, 11,* 356–365.

Spindler, H., Kruse, C., Zwisler, A., & Pedersen, S. (2009). Increased anxiety and depression in Danish cardiac patients with a type D personality: Cross-validation of the Type D Scale (DS14). *International Journal of Behavioral Medicine, 16,* 98–107.

Spinella, M., & Lester, D. (2006). Can money buy happiness? *Psychological Reports, 99,* 992.

Spitzer, R. L., Skodol, A. E., Gibbon, M., & Williams, J. B. W. (1983). *Psychopathology: A case book.* New York: McGraw-Hill.

Sprecher, S., & Regan, P. C. (2002). Liking some things (in some people) more than others: Partner preferences in romantic relationships and friendships. *Journal of Social and Personal Relationships, 19,* 436–481.

Sprenger, M. (2007). *Memory 101 for educators.* Thousand Oaks, CA: Corwin Press.

Sprenkle, D. H., & Moon, S. M. (Eds.). (1996). *Research methods in family therapy.* New York: Guilford Press.

Springen, K. (2004, August 9). Anxiety: Sweet and elusive sleep. *Newsweek,* p. 21.

Spunt, R. P., Satpute, A. B., & Lieberman, M. D. (2011). Identifying the what, why, and how of an observed action: An fMRI study of mentalizing and mechanizing during action observation. *Journal of Cognitive Neuroscience,* 63–74.

Squire, L. R., Clark, R. E., & Bayley, P. J. (2004). Medial temporal lobe function and memory. In M. S. Gazzaniga (Ed.), *Cognitive neurosciences* (3rd ed.). Cambridge, MA: MIT.

St. Dennis, C., Hendryx, M., Henriksen, A. L., Setter, S. M., & Singer, B. (2006). Postdischarge treatment costs following closure of a state gero-psychiatric ward: Comparison of 2 levels of community care. *Primary Care Companion Journal of Clinical Psychiatry, 8,* 279–284.

St. Jacques, P. L., & Levine, B. (2007). Ageing and autobiographical memory for emotional and neutral events. *Memory, 15,* 129–144.

Staddon, J. E. R., & Cerutti, D. T. (2003). Operant conditioning. *Annual Review of Psychology, 54,* 115–144.

Stahl, L. (2010, December 19). *The gift of endless memory.* New York: 60 Minutes.

Staley, J. K., Sanacora, G., & Tamagnan, G. (2006). Sex differences in diencephalon serotonin transporter availability in major depression. *Biological Psychiatry, 59,* 40–47.

Stangier, U., Schramm, E., Heidenreich, T., Berger, M., & Clark, D. M. (2011). Cognitive therapy vs interpersonal psychotherapy in social anxiety disorder: A randomized controlled trial. *Archives of General Psychiatry, 68,* 692–700.

Stankov, L. (2003). Complexity in human intelligence. In R. J. Sternberg, J. Lautrey, et al. (Eds.), *Models of intelligence: International perspectives.* Washington, DC: American Psychological Association.

Stanojevic, S., Mitic, K., & Vujic, V. (2007). Exposure to acute physical and psychological stress alters the response of rat macrophages to corticosterone, neuropeptide Y and beta-endorphin. *International Journal on the Biology of Stress, 10,* 65–73.

Stanton, A. L., Danoff-Burg, S., Cameron, C. L., Bishop, M., Collins, C. A., Kirk, S. B., et al. (2000). Emotionally expressive coping predicts psychological and physical adjustment to breast cancer. *Journal of Consulting and Clinical Psychology, 68,* 875–882.

Stapel, D. A., & Semin, G. R. (2007). The magic spell of language: Linguistic categories and their perceptual consequences. *Journal of Personality and Social Psychology, 93,* 23–33.

Starcevic, V., Berle, D., Milicevic, D., Hannan, A., Pamplugh, C., & Eslick, G. D. (2007). Pathological worry, anxiety disorders and the impact of co-occurrence with depressive and other anxiety disorders. *Journal of Anxiety Disorders, 21,* 1016–1027.

Startup, M., Bucci, S., & Langdon, R. (2009). Delusions of reference: A new theoretical model. *Cognitive Neuropsychiatry, 14,* 110–126.

Staub, A. (2011). Word recognition and syntactic attachment in reading: Evidence for a staged architecture. *Journal of Experimental Psychology: General, 140,* 407–433.

Steblay, N., Dysart, J., Fulero, S., & Lindsay, R. C. L. (2003). Eyewitness accuracy rates in police showup and lineup presentations: A meta-analytic comparison. *Law & Human Behavior, 27,* 523–540.

Steele, C. M. (1997). A threat in the air: How stereotypes shape intellectual identity and performance. *American Psychologist, 52,* 613–629.

Steele, J. D., Christmas, D., Eljamel, M. S., & Matthews, K. (2007). Anterior cingulotomy for major depression: Clinical outcome and relationship to lesion characteristics. *Biological Psychiatry, 12,* 127–134.

Stegerwald, F., & Janson, G. R. (2003). Conversion therapy: Ethical considerations in family counseling. *Family Journal—Counseling and Therapy for Couples and Families, 11,* 55–59.

Steiger, A. (2007). Neurochemical regulation of sleep. *Journal of Psychiatric Research, 41,* 537–552.

Stein, L. A. R., & Graham, J. R. (2005). Ability of substance abusers to escape detection on the Minnesota Multiphasic Personality Inventory-Adolescent (MMPI-A) in a juvenile correctional facility. *Assessment, 12,* 28–39.

Steinberg, L. (2007). Risk taking in adolescence: New perspectives from brain and behavioral science. *Current Directions in Psychological Science, 16,* 55–59.

Steiner, J. (2008). Transference to the analyst as an excluded observer. *The International Journal of Psychoanalysis, 89,* 39–54.

Stemler, S. E., & Sternberg, R. J. (2006). Using situational judgment tests to measure practical intelligence. In J. A. Weekley & R. E. Ployhart (Eds.), *Situational judgment tests: Theory, measurement, and application.* Mahwah, NJ: Lawrence Erlbaum Associates.

Stemler, S. E., Sternberg, R. J., Grigorenko, E. L., Jarvin, L., & Sharpes, K. (2009). Using the theory of successful intelligence as a framework for developing assessments in AP physics. *Contemporary Educational Psychology, 34,* 195–209.

Stenbacka, L., & Vanni, S. (2007). fMRI of peripheral visual field representation. *Clinical Neurophysiology, 108,* 1303–1314.

Stenklev, N. C., & Laukli, E. (2004). Cortical cognitive potentials in elderly persons. *Journal of the American Academy of Audiology, 15,* 401–413.

Stern, E., & Silbersweig, D. A. (2001). Advances in functional neuroimaging methodology for the study of brain systems underlying human neuropsychological function and dysfunction. In D. A. Silbersweig & E. Stern (Eds.), *Neuropsychology and functional neuroimaging: Convergence, advances and new directions.* Amsterdam, Netherlands: Swets and Zeitlinger.

Stern, R. M., & Koch, K. L. (1996). Motion sickness and differential susceptibility. *Current Directions in Psychological Science, 5,* 115–120.

Sternberg, R. J. (1990). *Metaphors of mind: Conceptions of the nature of intelligence.* New York: Cambridge University Press.

Sternberg, R. J. (1998). *Successful intelligence: How practical and creative intelligence determine success in life.* New York: Plume.

Sternberg, R. J. (2000). The Holy Grail of general intelligence. *Science, 289,* no. 5478, 399–401.

Sternberg, R. J. (2002). Individual differences in cognitive development. In U. Goswami (Ed.), *Blackwell handbook of childhood cognitive development. Blackwell handbooks of developmental psychology.* Malden, MA: Blackwell.

Sternberg, R. J. (2004). A triangular theory of love. In H. T. Reis & C. E. Rusbult (Eds.), *Close relationships: Key readings.* Philadelphia, PA: Taylor & Francis.

Sternberg, R. J. (2005). Culture and measurement. *Measurement: Interdisciplinary Research and Perspectives, 3,* 108–113.

Sternberg, R. J. (2006). A duplex theory of love. In R. J. Sternberg (Ed.), *The new psychology of love.* New Haven, CT: Yale University Press.

Sternberg, R. J. (2007). Who are the bright children? The cultural context of being and acting intelligent. *Educational Researcher, 36,* 148–155.

Sternberg, R. J. (2011). Individual differences in cognitive development. In U. Goswami & U. Goswami (Eds.), *The Wiley-Blackwell handbook of childhood cognitive development* (2nd ed.). New York: Wiley-Blackwell.

Sternberg, R. J., & Jarvin, L. (2003). Alfred Binet's contributions as a paradigm for impact in psychology. In R. J. Sternberg (Ed.), *The anatomy of impact: What makes the great works of psychology great.* Washington, DC: American Psychological Association.

Sternberg, R. J., Grigorenko, E. L., & Kidd, K. K. (2005). Intelligence, race, and genetics. *American Psychologist, 60,* 46–59.

Sternberg, R. J., Hojjat, M., & Barnes, M. L. (2001). Empirical aspects of a theory of love as a story. *European Journal of Personality, 15,* 1–20.

Sternberg, R. J., Jarvin, L., & Grigorenko, E. L. (2011). *Explorations in giftedness.* New York: Cambridge University Press.

Sternberg, R. J., Kaufman, J. C., & Pretz, J. E. (2004). A propulsion model of creative leadership [Special issue: Creativity in the workplace]. *Creativity and Innovation Management, 13,* 145–153.

Sternberg, R. J., & O'Hara, L. A. (2000). Intelligence and creativity. In R. Sternberg (Eds.), *Handbook of intelligence.* New York: Cambridge University Press.

Sternberg, R. J., & Pretz, J. E. (2005). *Cognition and intelligence: Identifying the mechanisms of the mind.* New York: Cambridge University Press.

Stettler, N., Stallings, V. A., Troxel, A. B., Zhao, J. Z., Schinnar, R., Nelson, S. E., et al. (2005). Weight gain in the first week of life and overweight in adulthood. *Circulation, 111,* 1897–1903.

Stevens, G., & Gardner, S. (1982). *The women of psychology: Pioneers and innovators* (Vol. 1). Cambridge, MA: Schenkman.

Stevens, M. J., & Gielen, U. P. (Eds.). (2007). *Toward a global psychology: Theory, research, intervention, and pedagogy.* Mahwah, NJ: Lawrence Erlbaum.

Stevens, P., & Harper, D. J. (2007). Professional accounts of electroconvulsive therapy: A discourse analysis. *Social Science & Medicine, 64,* 1475–1486.

Stevens, S. S., & Pashler, H. E. (2002). *Steven's handbook of experimental psychology: Learning, motivation, and emotion.* New York: Wiley.

Stevenson, H. W., Lee, S., & Mu, X. (2000). Successful achievement in mathematics: China and the United States. In C. F. M. van Lieshout & P. G. Heymans (Eds.), *Developing talent across the life span.* New York: Psychology Press.

Stevenson, R. J., & Case, T. I. (2005). Olfactory imagery: A review. *Psychonomic Bulletin and Review, 12,* 244–264.

Stickgold, R., Hobson, J. A., Fosse, R., & Fosse, M. (2001, November 2). Sleep, learning, and dreams: Off-line memory reprocessing. *Science, 294,* 1052–1057.

Stickley, T., & Nickeas, R. (2006). Becoming one person: Living with dissociative identity disorder. *Journal of Psychiatric and Mental Health Nursing, 13,* 180–187.

Stifter, C. A., Dollar, J. M., & Cipriano, E. A. (2011). Temperament and emotion regulation: The role of autonomic nervous system reactivity. *Developmental Psychobiology, 53,* 266–279.

Stinson, F. S., Dawson, D. A., Goldstein, R. B., Chou, S., Huang, B., Smith, S. M., et al. (2008). Prevalence, correlates, disability, and comorbidity of DSM-IV narcissistic personality disorder: Results from the Wave 2 National Epidemiologic Survey on Alcohol and Related Conditions. *Journal of Clinical Psychiatry, 69,* 1033–1045.

Stix, G. (2008, November). Jacking into the brain. *Scientific American,* 56–61.

Stix, G. (2009, October). Turbocharging the brain. *Scientific American,* 46–55.

Stix, G. (2011, March). The neuroscience of true grit. *Scientific American,* 29–33.

Stockdale, M. S., & Sagrestano, L. M. (2011). Resources for targets of sexual harassment. In M. A. Paludi, C. R. Paludi, et al. (Eds.), *Praeger handbook on understanding and preventing workplace discrimination* (Vols. 1 & 2). Santa Barbara, CA: Praeger/ABC-CLIO.

Stocks, E., Lishner, D., & Decker, S. (2009). Altruism or psychological escape: Why does empathy promote prosocial behavior? *European Journal of Social Psychology, 39,* 649–665.

Stockton, R., Morran, D. K., & Krieger, K. (2004). An overview of current research and best practices for training beginning group leaders. In J. L. DeLucia-Waack, D. A. Gerrity, et al. (Eds.), *Handbook of group counseling and psychotherapy.* Thousand Oaks, CA: Sage Publications.

Stone, J. (2002). Battling doubt by avoiding practice: The effects of stereotype threat on self-handicapping in white athletes. *Personality and Social Psychology Bulletin, 28,* 1667–1678.

Stone, J., Morrison, P., & Pilowsky, L. (2007). Glutamate and dopamine dysregulation in schizophrenia—A synthesis and selective review. *Journal of Psychopharmacology, 21,* 440–452.

Storm, L., & Ertel, S. (2001). Does psi exist? Comments on Milton and Wiseman's (1999) meta-analysis of Ganzfeld's research. *Psychological Bulletin, 127,* 424–433.

Stouffer, E. M., & White, N. M. (2006). Neural circuits mediating latent learning and conditioning for salt in the rat. *Neurobiology of Learning and Memory, 86,* 91–99.

Strange, D., Clifasefi, S., & Garry, M. (2007). False memories. In M. Garry & H. Hayne (Eds.), *Do justice and let the sky fall: Elizabeth Loftus and her contributions to science, law, and academic freedom.* Mahwah, NJ: Lawrence Erlbaum Associates.

Strathern, A., & Stewart, P. J. (2003). *Landscape, memory and history: Anthropological perspectives.* London: Pluto Press.

Strauss, E. (1998, May 8). Writing, speech separated in split brain. *Science, 280,* 287.

Strayer, D. L., & Drews, F. A. (2007). Cell-phone-induced driver distraction. *Current Directions in Psychological Science, 16,* 128–131.

Striano, T., & Vaish, A. (2006). Seven- to 9-month-old infants use facial expressions to interpret others' actions. *British Journal of Developmental Psychology, 24,* 753–760.

Striegel, R. H., Bedrosian, R., Wang, C., & Schwartz, S. (2011). Why men should be included in research on binge eating: Results from a comparison of psychosocial impairment in men and women. *International Journal of Eating Disorders,* http://onlinelibrary.wiley.com/doi/10.1002/eat.20962/full

Striegel-Moore, R., & Bulik, C. M. (2007). Risk factors for eating disorders. *American Psychologist, 62,* 181–198.

Stroink, M. (2007). Processes and preconditions underlying terrorism in second-generation immigrants. *Peace and Conflict: Journal of Peace Psychology, 13,* 293–312.

Strong, T., & Tomm, K. (2007). Family therapy as re-coordinating and moving on together. *Journal of Systemic Therapies, 26,* 42–54.

Strupp, H. H., & Binder, J. L. (1992). Current developments in psychotherapy. *The Independent Practitioner, 12,* 119–124.

Sue, D. W., & Sue, D. (1990). *Counseling the culturally different: Theory and practice* (2nd ed.). Oxford, England: John Wiley & Sons.

Sue, D. W., Sue, D., & Sue, S. (1990). *Understanding abnormal behavior* (3rd ed.). Boston: Houghton-Mifflin.

Suh, E. M. (2002). Culture, identity consistency, and subjective well-being. *Journal of Personality & Social Psychology, 83,* 1378–1391.

Suhail, K., & Chaudhry, H. R. (2004). Predictors of subjective well-being in an Eastern Muslim culture. *Journal of Social and Clinical Psychology, 23,* 359–376.

Suizzo, M-A., & Bornstein, M. H. (2006). French and European American child-mother play: Culture and gender considerations. *International Journal of Behavioral Development, 30,* 498–508.

Sullivan, J., Riccio, C., & Reynolds, C. (2008, September). Variations in students' school- and teacher-related attitudes across gender, ethnicity, and age. *Journal of Instructional Psychology, 35,* 296–305.

Summers, M. (2000). *Everything in its place.* New York: Putnam.

Super, C. M. (1980). Cognitive development: Looking across at growing up. In C. M. Super & S. Harakness (Eds.), *New directions for child development: Anthropological perspectives on child development.* San Francisco: Jossey-Bass.

Surette, R. (2002). Self-reported copycat crime among a population of serious and violent juvenile offenders. *Crime & Delinquency, 48,* 46–69.

Susser, E. S., Herman, D. B., & Aaron, B. (2002, August). Combating the terror of terrorism. *Scientific American,* pp. 70–77.

Sutin, A. R., & Robins, R. W. (2007). Phenomenology of autobiographical memories: The Memory Experiences Questionnaire. *Memory, 15,* 390–411.

Suzuki, L. A., Short, E. L., & Lee, C. S. (2011). Racial and ethnic group differences in intelligence in the United States: Multicultural perspectives. In R. J. Sternberg & S. Kaufman, (Eds.), *The Cambridge handbook of intelligence*. New York: Cambridge University Press.

Svarstad, B. (1976). Physician-patient communication and patient conformity with medical advice. In D. Mechanic (Ed.), *The growth of bureaucratic medicine*. New York: Wiley.

Svartdal, F. (2003). Extinction after partial reinforcement: Predicted vs. judged persistence. *Scandinavian Journal of Psychology, 44*, 55–64.

Swain, P. I. (2006). *New developments in eating disorders research*. Hauppauge, NY: Nova Science Publishers.

Swain, R. A., Kerr, A. L., & Thompson, R. F. (2011). The cerebellum: A neural system for the study of reinforcement learning. *Frontiers in Behavioral Neuroscience, (18)*, 89–96.

Swales, M. A., & Heard, H. L. (2007). The therapy relationship in dialectical behaviour therapy. In P. Gilbert & R. L. Leahy (Eds.), *The therapeutic relationship in the cognitive behavioral psycho-therapies*. New York: Routledge/Taylor & Francis.

Szasz, T. (2006). The pretense of psychology as science: The myth of mental illness in statu nascendi. *Current Psychology: Developmental, Learning, Personality, Social, 25*, 42–49.

Szasz, T. S. (1994). *Cruel compassion: Psychiatric control of society's unwanted*. New York: Wiley.

Szegedy Maszak, M. (2003, January 13). The sound of unsound minds. *U.S. News & World Report*, pp. 45–46.

Tadmor, C. T. (2007). Biculturalism: The plus side of leaving home? The effects of second-culture exposure on integrative complexity and its consequences for overseas performance. *Dissertation Abstracts International Section A: Humanities and Social Sciences, 67*(8-A), 3068.

Tajfel, H., & Turner, J. C. (2004). The social identity theory of intergroup behavior. In J. T. Jost & J. Sidanius (Eds.), *Political psychology: Key readings*. New York: Psychology Press.

Takahashi, M., Nakata, A., Haratani, T., Ogawa, Y., & Arito, H. (2004). Post-lunch nap as a worksite intervention to promote alertness on the job. *Ergonomics, 47*, 1003–1013.

Takizawa, T., Kondo, T., & Sakihara, S. (2007). Stress buffering effects of social support on depressive symptoms in middle age: Reciprocity and community mental health: Corrigendum. *Psychiatry and Clinical Neurosciences, 61*, 336–337.

Talarico, J. (2009). Freshman flashbulbs: Memories of unique and first-time events in starting college. *Memory, 17*, 256–265.

Talarico, J., & Rubin, D. (2007). Flashbulb memories are special after all; in phenomenology, not accuracy. *Applied Cognitive Psychology, 21*, 557–578.

Talmi, D., Anderson, A., Riggs, L., Caplan, J., & Moscovitch, M. (2008). Immediate memory consequences of the effect of emotion on attention to pictures. *Learning & Memory, 15*, 172–182.

Tal-Or, N., & Papirman, Y. (2007). The fundamental attribution error in attributing fictional figures' characteristics to the actors. *Media Psychology, 9*, 331–345.

Talukdar, S., & Shastri, J. (2006). Contributory and adverse factors in social development of young children. *Psychological Studies, 51*, 294–303.

Tamini, B., Bojhd, F., & Yazdani, S. (2011). Love types, psychological well-being and self-concept. *Journal of the Indian Academy of Applied Psychology, 37*, 169–178.

Tan, G., Rintala, D. H., Jensen, M. P., Richards, J. S., Holmes, S. A., Parachuri, R., et al. (2011). Efficacy of cranial electrotherapy stimulation for neuropathic pain following spinal cord injury: A multi-site randomized controlled trial with a secondary 6-month open-label phase. *Journal of Spinal Cord Medicine, 34*, 285–296.

Tan, L., & Ward, G. (2008). Rehearsal in immediate serial recall. *Psychonomic Bulletin & Review, 15*, 535–542.

Tan, L., Chan, A., Kay, P., Khong, P., Yip, L., & Luke, K. (2008). Language affects patterns of brain activation associated with perceptual decision. *PNAS Proceedings of the National Academy of Sciences of the United States of America, 105*(10), 4004–4009.

Tani, J., Faustine, L., & Sufian, J. T. (2011). Updates on current advances in gene therapy. *West Indian Medical Journal, 60*, 188–194.

Tanner, J. M. (1978). *Education and physical growth* (2nd ed.). New York: International Universities Press.

Tanner, J. M. (1990). *Foetus into man: Physical growth from conception to maturity* (rev. ed.). Cambridge, MA: Harvard University Press.

Taras, H., & Potts-Datema, W. (2005). Chronic health conditions and student performance at school. *Journal of School Health, 75*, 255–266.

Tasker, F. (2005). Lesbian mothers, gay fathers, and their children: A review. *Journal of Developmental and Behavioral Pediatrics, 26*, 224–240.

Taylor, F., & Bryant, R. A. (2007). The tendency to suppress, inhibiting thoughts, and dream rebound. *Behaviour Research and Therapy, 45*, 163–168.

Taylor, S. (2003). Anxiety sensitivity and its implications for understanding and treating PTSD. *Journal of Cognitive Psychotherapy, 17*, 179–186.

Taylor, S. E. (1995). Quandary at the crossroads: Paternalism versus advocacy surrounding end-of-treatment decisions. *American Journal of Hospital Palliatory Care, 12*, 43–46.

Taylor, S. E., Kemeny, M. E., Reed, G. M., Bower, J. E., & Gruenewald, T. L. (2000). Psychological resources, positive illusions, and health. *American Psychologist, 55*, 99–109.

Tellegen, A., Lykken, D. T., Bouchard, T. J., Jr., Wilcox, K. J., Segal, N. L., & Rich, S. (1988). Personality similarity in twins reared apart and together. *Journal of Personality and Social Psychology, 54*, 1031–1039.

Tenenbaum, H. R., & Ruck, M. D. (2007). Are teachers' expectations different for racial minority than for European American students? A meta-analysis. *Journal of Educational Psychology, 99*, 253–273.

Tenopyr, M. L. (2002). Theory versus reality: Evaluation of 'g' in the workplace. *Human Performance, 15*, 107–122.

Teodorov, E., Salzgerber, S. A., Felicio, L. F., Varolli, F. M. F., & Bernardi, M. M. (2002). Effects of perinatal picrotoxin and sexual experience on heterosexual and homosexual behavior in male rats. *Neurotoxicology and Teratology, 24*, 235–245.

Thachil, A. F., Mohan, R., & Bhugra, D. (2007). The evidence base of complementary and alternative therapies in depression. *Journal of Affective Disorders, 97*, 23–35.

Tharp, R. G. (1989). Psychocultural variables and constants: Effects on teaching and learning in schools [Special issue: Children and their development: Knowledge base, research agenda, and social policy application]. *American Psychologist, 44*, 349–359.

Thatcher, D. L., & Clark, D. B. (2006). Adolescent alcohol abuse and dependence: Development, diagnosis, treatment and outcomes. *Current Psychiatry Reviews, 2*, 159–177.

Thomas, P., Mathur, P., Gottesman, I. I., Nagpal, R., Nimgaonkar, V. L., & Deshpande, S. N. (2007). Correlates of hallucinations in schizophrenia: A cross-cultural evaluation. *Schizophrenia Research, 92*, 41–49.

Thompson, J. (2000, June 18). "I was certain, but I was wrong." *The New York Times*, p. E14.

Thorkildsen, T. A. (2006). An empirical exploration of language and thought. *PsycCRITIQUES, 51*, no pagination specified.

Thorndike, E. L. (1932). *The fundamentals of learning*. New York: Teachers College.

Thornhill, R., Gangestad, S. W., Miller, R., Scheyd, G., McCollough, J. K., & Franklin, M. (2003). Major histocompatibility complex genes, symmetry, and body scent attractiveness in men and women. *Behavioral Ecology, 14*, 668–678.

Thornton, A., & Young-DeMarco, L. (2001). Four decades of trends in attitudes toward family issues in the United States: The 1960s through the 1990s. *Journal of Marriage and the Family, 63*, 1009–1017.

Thorpe, K. (2009). *The future costs of obesity: National and state estimates of the impact of obesity on direct health care expenses*. Washington, DC: United Health Foundation.

Thrash, T. M., & Elliot, A. J. (2002). Implicit and self-attributed achievement motives: Concordance and predictive validity. *Journal of Personality, 70*, 729–755.

Tippin, J., Sparks, J., & Rizzo, M. (2009, August). Visual vigilance in drivers with obstructive sleep apnea. *Journal of Psychosomatic Research, 67*, 143–151.

Tirri, K., & Nokelainen, P. (2008). Identification of multiple intelligences with the Multiple Intelligence Profiling Questionnaire III [Special issue: High-ability assessment]. *Psychology Science, 50*, 206–221.

Titone, D. A. (2002). Memories bound: The neuroscience of dreams. *Trends in Cognitive Science, 6*, 4–5.

Todorov, A., Fiske, S., & Prentice, D. (Eds.). (2011). *Social neuroscience: Toward understanding the underpinnings of the social mind*. New York: Oxford University Press.

Tolman, E. C., & Honzik, C. H. (1930). Introduction and removal of reward and maze performance in rats. *University of California Publications in Psychology, 4*, 257–275.

Tommasi, L. (2009). Mechanisms and functions of brain and behavioural asymmetries. *Philosophical Transactions of the Royal Society B, 364*, 855–859.

Tononi, G., & Koch, C. (2008). The neural correlates of consciousness: An update. In A. Kingstone & M. B. Miller (Eds.), *The year in cognitive neuroscience*. Malden, MA: Blackwell Publishing.

Toth, J. P., & Daniels, K. A. (2002). Effects of prior experience on judgments of normative word frequency: Automatic bias and correction. *Journal of Memory and Language, 46*, 845–874.

Touhara, K. (2007). Molecular biology of peptide pheromone production and reception in mice. *Advanced Genetics, 59*, 147–171.

Tracy, J. L., & Robins, R. W. (2004). Show your pride: Evidence for a discrete emotion expression. *Psychological Science, 15*, 194–197.

Tramontana, J. (2011). *Sports hypnosis in practice: Scripts, strategies and case examples*. Norwalk, CT: Crown House Publishing Limited.

Tranter, L. J., & Koutstaal, W. (2008). Age and flexible thinking: An experimental demonstration of the beneficial effects of increased cognitively stimulating activity on fluid intelligence in healthy older adults. *Neuropsychology and Cognition, 15,* 184–207.

Travis, F. (2006). From I to I: Concepts of self on a object-referral/self-referral continuum. In A. P. Prescott (Ed.), *The concept of self in psychology.* Hauppauge, NY: Nova Science Publishers.

Travis, F., et al. (2009, February). Effects of transcendental meditation practice on brain functioning and stress reactivity in college students. *International Journal of Psychophysiology, 71,* 170–176.

Tremblay, A. (2004). Dietary fat and body weight set point. *Nutrition Review, 62*(7, Pt 2), S75–S77.

Triesch, J., Jasso, H., & Deák, G. O. (2007). Emergence of mirror neurons in a model of gaze following. *Adaptive Behavior, 15,* 149–165.

Triscari, M., Faraci, P., D'Angelo, V., Urso, V., & Catalisano, D. (2011). Two treatments for fear of flying compared: Cognitive behavioral therapy combined with systematic desensitization or eye movement desensitization and reprocessing (EMDR). *Aviation Psychology and Applied Human Factors, 1,* 9–14.

Tropp, L. R., & Bianchi, R. A. (2006). Valuing diversity and interest in intergroup contact. *Journal of Social Issues, 62,* 533–551.

Tropp, L. R., & Pettigrew, T. F. (2005). Differential relationships between intergroup contact and affective and cognitive dimensions of prejudice. *Personality and Social Psychology Bulletin, 31,* 1145–1158.

Trudel, G. (2002). Sexuality and marital life: Results of a survey. *Journal of Sex and Marital Therapy, 28,* 229–249.

Trujillo-Pisanty, I., Hernandez, G., Moreau-Debord, I., Cossette, M. P., Conover, K., Cheer, J. F., et al. (2011). Cannabinoid receptor blockade reduces the opportunity cost at which rats maintain operant performance for rewarding brain stimulation. *Journal of Neuroscience, 31,* 5426–5430.

Trull, T. J., & Widiger, T. A. (2003). Personality disorders. In. G. Stricker, T. A. Widiger, et al. (Eds.), *Handbook of psychology: Clinical psychology* (Vol. 8). New York: Wiley.

Tsai, K. J., Tsai, Y. C., & Shen, C. K. (2007). GCSF rescues the memory impairment of animal models of Alzheimer's disease. *Journal of Experimental Medicine, 11,* 1273–1289.

Tsaousis, I., Nikolaou, I., & Serdaris, N. (2007). Do the core self-evaluations moderate the relationship between subjective well-being and physical and psychological health? *Personality and Individual Differences, 42,* 1441–1452.

Tseng, W. S. (2003). *Clinician's guide to cultural psychiatry.* San Diego, CA: Elsevier Publishing.

Tsukasaki, T., & Ishii, K. (2004). Linguistic-cultural relativity of cognition: Rethinking the Sapir-Whorf hypothesis. *Japanese Psychological Review, 47,* 173–186.

Tsunoda, T. (1985). *The Japanese brain: Uniqueness and universality.* Tokyo: Taishukan Publishing.

Tuerk, P. W., Yoder, M., Grubaugh, A., Myrick, H., Hamner, M., & Acierno, R. (2011). Prolonged exposure therapy for combat-related posttraumatic stress disorder: An examination of treatment effectiveness for veterans of the wars in Afghanistan and Iraq. *Journal of Anxiety Disorders, 25,* 397–403.

Tuerlinckx, F., De Boeck, P., & Lens, W. (2002). Measuring needs with the Thematic Apperception Test: A psychometric study. *Journal of Personality and Social Psychology, 82,* 448–461.

Tugay, N., et al. (2007). Effectiveness of transcutaneous electrical nerve stimulation and interferential current in primary dysmenorrhea. *Pain Medicine, 8,* 295–300.

Tulving, E. (2002). Episodic memory and common sense: How far apart? In A. Baddeley & J. P. Aggleton (Eds.), *Episodic memory: New directions in research.* London: Oxford University Press.

Tulving, E., & Psotka, J. (1971). Retroactive inhibition in free recall: Inaccessibility of information available in the memory store. *Journal of Experimental Psychology, 87,* 1–8.

Tulving, E., & Thompson, D. M. (1983). Encoding specificity and retrieval processes in episodic memory. *Psychological Review, 80,* 352–373.

Turk, D. C. (1994). Perspectives on chronic pain: The role of psychological factors. *Current Directions in Psychological Science, 3,* 45–49.

Turkewitz, G. (1993). The origins of differential hemispheric strategies for information processing in the relationships between voice and face perception. In B. de Boysson-Bardies, S. de Schonen, et al. (Eds.), *Developmental neurocognition: Speech and face processing in the first year of life. NATO ASI series D: Behavioural and social sciences* (Vol. 69). Dordrecht, Netherlands: Kluwer Academic.

Turnbull, O., & Solms, M. (2007). Awareness, desire, and false beliefs: Freud in the light of modern neuropsychology. *Cortex, 43,* 1083–1090.

Turner, M., Tamborini, R., Limon, M., & Zuckerman-Hyman, C. (2007). The moderators and mediators of door-in-the-face requests: Is it a negotiation or a helping experience? *Communication Monographs, 74,* 333–356.

Turner, M. E., Pratkanis, A. R., & Struckman, C. K. (2007). Groupthink as social identity maintenance. In C. K. Struckman (Ed.), *The science of social influence: Advances and future progress.* New York: Psychology Press.

Tuszynski, M. H. (2007). Nerve growth factor gene therapy in Alzheimer's disease. *Alzheimer's Disease and Associated Disorders, 21,* 179–189.

Tversky, A., & Kahneman, D. (1987). Rational choice and the framing of decisions. In R. Hogarth & M. Reder (Eds.), *Rational choice: The contrast between economics and psychology.* Chicago: University of Chicago Press.

Twenge, J., Abebe, E., & Campbell, W. (2010). Fitting in or standing out: Trends in American parents' choices for children's names, 1880–2007. *Social Psychological and Personality Science, 1,* 19–25.

Twenge, J., & Foster, J. (2010). Birth cohort increases in narcissistic personality traits among american college students, 1982–2009. *Social Psychological and Personality Science, 1,* 99–106.

Twenge, J. M., Gentile, B., DeWall, C., Ma, D., Lacefield, K., & Schurtz, D. R. (2010). Birth cohort increases in psychopathology among young Americans, 1938–2007: A cross-temporal meta-analysis of the MMPI. *Clinical Psychology Review, 30,* 145–154.

Tydgat, I., & Grainger, J. (2009). Serial position effects in the identification of letters, digits, and symbols. *Journal of Experimental Psychology: Human Perception and Performance, 35,* 480–498.

U.S. Bureau of the Census. (2000). *Census 2000.* Retrieved from American Fact Finder http://factfinder.census.gov/servlet/BasicFactsServlet

U.S. Bureau of the Census. (2001). *Living arrangements of children.* Washington, DC: Author.

U.S. Senate Select Committee on Intelligence. (2004, July 9). *Report of the U.S. intelligence community's prewar intelligence assessments on Iraq.* Retrieved from http://www.gpoaccess.gov/serialset/creports/iraq.html

Ubell, E. (1993, January 10). Could you use more sleep? *Parade,* pp. 16–18.

Umphress, E. E., Smith-Crowe, K., & Brief, A. P. (2007). When birds of a feather flock together and when they do not: Status composition, social dominance orientation, and organizational attractiveness. *Journal of Applied Psychology, 92,* 396–409.

Underwood, A. (2005, October 3). The good heart. *Newsweek,* p. 49.

Unsworth, N., & Engle, R. W. (2005). Individual differences in working memory capacity and learning: Evidence from the serial reaction time task. *Memory and Cognition, 33,* 213–220.

Updegraff, K. A., Helms, H. M., McHale, S. M., Crouter, A. C., Thayer, S. M., & Sales, L. H. (2004). Who's the boss? Patterns of perceived control in adolescents' friendships. *Journal of Youth & Adolescence, 33,* 403–420.

Ursprung, W. W., Sanouri, A., & DiFranza, J. R. (2009). The loss of autonomy over smoking in relation to lifetime cigarette consumption. *Addictive Behaviors, 22,* 12–19.

Uylings, H. B. M. (2006). Development of the human cortex and the concept of 'critical' or 'sensitive' periods. *Language Learning, 56,* 59–90.

Vaillant, G. E., & Vaillant, C. O. (1990). Natural history of male psychological health: XII. A 46-year study of predictors of successful aging at age 65. *American Journal of Psychiatry, 147,* 31–37.

Vaitl, D., Schienle, A., & Stark, R. (2005). Neurobiology of fear and disgust. *International Journal of Psychophysiology, 57,* 1–4.

Valencia, R. R., & Suzuki, L. A. (2003). *Intelligence testing and minority students: Foundations, performance factors, and assessment issues.* Thousand Oaks, CA: Sage.

Van Belle, V., Pelckmans, K., Suykens, J. A. K., & Van Huffel, S. (2011). Learning transformation models for ranking and survival analysis. *Journal of Machine Learning Research, 12,* 819–862.

Van De Graaff, K. (2000). *Human anatomy* (5th ed.). Boston: McGraw-Hill.

Van den Wildenberg, W. P. M., & Van der Molen, M. W. (2004). Developmental trends in simple and selective inhibition of compatible and incompatible responses. *Journal of Experimental Child Psychology, 87,* 201–220.

van der Helm, P. A. (2006). Review of perceptual dynamics: Theoretical foundations and philosophical implications of gestalt psychology. *Philosophical Psychology, 19,* 274–279.

Van der Zee, E. A., Platt, B. B., & Riedel, G. G. (2011). Acetylcholine: Future research and perspectives. *Behavioural Brain Research, 221,* 583–586.

van Dijk, W. W., Ouwerkerk, J. W., Wesseling, Y. M., & van Koningsbruggen, G. M. (2011). Towards understanding pleasure at the misfortunes of others: The impact of self-evaluation threat on schadenfreude. *Cognition and Emotion, 25,* 360–368.

van Hooren, S. A. H., Valentijn, A. M., & Bosma, H. (2007). Cognitive functioning in healthy older adults aged 64–81: A cohort study into the effects of age, sex, and education. *Aging, Neuropsychology, and Cognition, 14,* 40–54.

van Marle, K., & Wynn, K. (2009). Infants' auditory enumeration: Evidence for analog magnitudes in the small number range. *Cognition, 111,* 302–316.

van Nieuwenhuijzen, M. M., Vriens, A. A., Scheepmaker, M. M., Smit, M. M., & Porton, E. E. (2011). The development of a diagnostic instrument to measure social information processing in children with mild to borderline intellectual disabilities. *Research in Developmental Disabilities, 32,* 358–370.

van Oort, R., & Kessels, R. (2009). Executive dysfunction in Korsakoff's syndrome: Time to revise the DSM criteria for alcohol-induced persisting amnestic disorder? *International Journal of Psychiatry in Clinical Practice, 13,* 78–81.

Van Overwalle, F., & Siebler, F. (2005). A connectionist model of attitude formation and change. *Personality and Social Psychology Review, 9,* 231–274.

van Soelen, I. C., Brouwer, R. M., van Leeuwen, M., Kahn, R. S., Pol, H., & Boomsma, D. I. (2011). Heritability of verbal and performance intelligence in a pediatric longitudinal sample. *Twin Research and Human Genetics, 14,* 119–128.

Vanasse, A., Niyonsenga, T., & Courteau, J. (2004). Smoking cessation within the context of family medicine: Which smokers take action? *Preventive Medicine: An International Journal Devoted to Practice and Theory, 38,* 330–337.

Vandell, D. L., Burchinal, M. R., Belsky, J., Owen, M. T., Friedman, S. L., Clarke-Stewart, et al. (2005). *Early child care and children's development in the primary grades: Follow-up results from the NICHD Study of Early Child Care.* Paper presented at the biennial meeting of the Society for Research in Child Development, Atlanta, GA.

Vandervert, L. R., Schimpf, P. H., & Liu, H. (2007). How working memory and the cerebellum collaborate to produce creativity and innovation. *Creativity Research Journal, 19,* 1–18.

Vandierendonck, A., & Szmalec, A. (Eds.). (2011). *Spatial working memory.* New York: Psychology Press.

Vanheule, S., Desmet, M., Rosseel, Y., & Meganck, R. (2006). Core transference themes in depression. *Journal of Affective Disorders, 91,* 71–75.

Varma, S. (2007). A computational model of Tower of Hanoi problem solving. *Dissertation Abstracts International: Section B: The Sciences and Engineering, 67*(8-B), 4736.

Vartanian, O. (2009). Variable attention facilitates creative problem solving. *Psychology of Aesthetics, Creativity, and the Arts, 3,* 57–59.

Vassalli, A., & Dijk, D. (2009). Sleep function: Current questions and new approaches. *European Journal of Neuroscience, 29,* 1830–1841.

Vecchione, M., Schoen, H., Castro, J., Cieciuch, J., Pavlopoulos, V., & Caprara, G. (2011). Personality correlates of party preference: The Big Five in five big European countries. *Personality and Individual Differences, 51,* 737–742.

Vega, C. P. (2006). The effects of therapeutic components on at-risk middle school children's grades and attendance: An archival study of an after-school prevention program. *Dissertation Abstracts International: Section B: The Sciences and Engineering, 66,* 4504.

Velentzas, K., Heinen, T., & Schack, T. (2011). Routine integration strategies and their effects on volleyball serve performance and players' movement mental representation. *Journal of Applied Sport Psychology, 23,* 209–222.

Vellacott, J. (2007). Resilience: A psychoanalytic exploration. *British Journal of Psychotherapy, 23,* 163–170.

Veltman, M. W. M., & Browne, K. D. (2001). Three decades of child mal-treatment research: Implications for the school years. *Trauma Violence and Abuse, 2,* 215–239.

Veniegas, R. C. (2000). Biological research on women's sexual orientations: Evaluating the scientific evidence. *Journal of Social Issues, 56,* 267–282.

Verdejo, A., Toribio, I., & Orozco, C. (2005). Neuropsychological functioning in methadone maintenance patients versus abstinent heroin abusers. *Drug and Alcohol Dependence, 78,* 283–288.

Verdon, B. (2011). The case of thematic tests adapted to older adults: On the importance of differentiating latent and manifest contents in projective tests. *Rorschachiana, 32,* 46–71.

Verfaellie, M., & Keane, M. M. (2002). Impaired and preserved memory processes in amnesia. In L. R. Squire & D. L. Schacter (Eds.), *Neuropsychology of memory* (3rd ed.). New York: Guilford Press.

Vernon, P., Villani, V., Vickers, L., & Harris, J. (2008, January). Abehavioral genetic investigation of the Dark Triad and the Big 5. *Personality and Individual Differences, 44,* 445–452.

Verona, E., & Sullivan, E. (2008). Emotional catharsis and aggression revisited: Heart rate reduction following aggressive responding. *Emotion, 8,* 331–340.

Victor, S. B., & Fish, M. C. (1995). Lesbian mothers and their children: A review for school psychologists. *School Psychology Review, 24,* 456–479.

Vieira, E. M., & Freire, J. C. (2006). Alteridade e psicologia humanista: Uma leitura ética da abordagem centrada na pessoa. Alterity and humanistic psychology: An ethical reading of the person-centered approach. *Estudos de Psicologia, 23,* 425–432.

Villemure, C., Slotnick, B. M., & Bushnell, M. C. (2003). Effects of odors on pain perception: Deciphering the roles of emotion and attention. *Pain, 106,* 101–108.

Vincus, A. A., Ringwalt, C., Harris, M. S., & Shamblen, S. R. (2010). A short-term, quasi-experimental evaluation of D.A.R.E.'s revised elementary school curriculum. *Journal of Drug Education, 40,* 37–49.

Vitak, J., Zube, P., Smock, A., Carr, C. T., Ellison, N., & Lampe, C. (2011). It's complicated: Facebook users' political participation in the 2008 election. *Cyberpsychology, Behavior, and Social Networking, 14,* 107–114.

Vitaro, F., Brendgen, M., & Arseneault, L. (2009). Methods and measures: The discordant MZ-twin method: One step closer to the holy grail of causality. *International Journal of Behavioral Development, 33,* 376–382.

Vitello, P. (2006, June 12). A ring tone meant to fall on deaf ears. *The New York Times,* A1.

Vitiello, A. L., Bonello, R. P., & Pollard, H. P. (2007). The effectiveness of ENAR® for the treatment of chronic neck pain in Australian adults: A preliminary single-blind, randomised controlled trial. *Chiropractic Osteopathology, 9,* 9.

Vleioras, G., & Bosma, H. A. (2005). Are identity styles important for psychological well-being? *Journal of Adolescence, 28,* 397–409.

Vogt, D., Rizvi, S., Shipherd, J., & Resick, P. (2008). Longitudinal investigation of reciprocal relationship between stress reactions and

hardiness. *Personality and Social Psychology Bulletin, 34,* 61–73.

Volterra, V., Caselli, M. C., Capirci, O., Tonucci, F., & Vicari, S. (2003). Early linguistic abilities of Italian children with Williams syndrome [Special issue: Williams syndrome]. *Developmental Neuropsychology, 23,* 33–58.

Voruganti, L. P., Awad, A. G., Parker, B., Forrest, C., Usmani, Y., Fernando, M. L. D., et al. (2007). Cognition, functioning and quality of life in schizophrenia treatment: Results of a one-year randomized controlled trial of olanzapine and quetiapine. *Schizophrenia Research, 96,* 146–155.

Voss, J., & Paller, K. (2008). Brain substrates of implicit and explicit memory: The importance of concurrently acquired neural signals of both memory types. *Neuropsychologia, 46*(13), 3021–3029.

Vygotsky, L. S. (1926/1997). *Educational psychology.* Delray Beach, FL: St. Lucie Press.

Wachs, T. D., Pollitt, E., Cueto, S., & Jacoby, E. (2004). Structure and cross-contextual stability of neonatal temperament. *Infant Behavior and Development, 27,* 382–396.

Waddell, J., & Shors, T. J. (2008). Neurogenesis, learning and associative strength. *European Journal of Neurosciences, 27,* 3020–3028.

Wade, K. A., Sharman, S. J., & Garry, M. (2007). False claims about false memory research. *Consciousness and Cognition: An International Journal, 16,* 18–28.

Wager, T. D. (2005). The neural bases of placebo effects in pain. *Current Directions in Psychological Science, 14,* 175–180.

Wagner, A. W., Rizvi, S. L., & Hamed, M. S. (2007). Applications of dialectical behavior therapy to the treatment of complex trauma-related problems: When one case formulation does not fit all. *Journal of Trauma Stress, 20,* 391–400.

Wagner, R. K. (2002). Smart people doing dumb things: The case of managerial incompetence. In R. J. Sternberg (Ed.), *Why smart people can be so stupid.* New Haven, CT: Yale University Press.

Wagner, R. K. (2011). Practical intelligence. In R. J. Sternberg & S. Kaufman (Eds.), *The Cambridge handbook of intelligence.* New York: Cambridge University Press.

Wagstaff, G. (2009, January). Is there a future for investigative hypnosis? *Journal of Investigative Psychology and Offender Profiling, 6,* 43–57.

Wagstaff, G. F., Wheatcroft, J. M., & Jones, A. (2011). Are high hypnotizables especially vulnerable to false memory effects? A sociocognitive perspective. *International Journal of Clinical and Experimental Hypnosis, 59,* 310–326.

Wain, H. J., Grammer, G. G., & Stasinos, J. (2006). Psychiatric intervention for medical and surgical patients following traumatic injuries. In E. C. Ritchie, P. J. Watson, et al. (Eds.), *Interventions following mass violence and disasters: Strategies for mental health practice.* New York: Guilford Press.

Walker, L., & Frimer, J. (2009). The song remains the same: Rebuttal to Sherblom's re-envisioning of the legacy of the care challenge. *Journal of Moral Education, 38,* 53–68.

Walker, L. J., & Frimer, J. A. (2007). Moral personality of brave and caring exemplars. *Journal of Personality and Social Psychology, 93,* 845–860.

Walker, M. P., & van der Helm, E. (2009). Overnight therapy? The role of sleep in emotional brain processing. *Psychological Bulletin, 135,* 731–748.

Walker, W. (2008, May). Introducing hypnosis for pain management to your practice. *Australian Journal of Clinical & Experimental Hypnosis, 36,* 23–29.

Walker, W. R., Skowronski, J. J., & Thompson, C. P. (2003). Consolidation of long-term memory: Evidence and alternatives. *Review of General Psychology, 7,* 203–210.

Waller, B., Cray, J., & Burrows, A. (2008, June). Selection for universal facial emotion. *Emotion, 8,* 435–439.

Wallerstein, J. S., Lewis, J., Blakeslee, S., & Lewis, J. (2000). *The unexpected legacy of divorce.* New York: Hyperion.

Walsh, B. T., Kaplan, A. S., Attia, E., Olmstead, M., Parides, M., Carter, J. C., et al. (2006). Fluoxetine after weight restoration in anorexia nervosa: A randomized controlled trial. *JAMA: Journal of the American Medical Association, 295,* 2605–2612.

Walsh, R., & Shapiro, S. L. (2006). The meeting of meditative disciplines and western psychology. *American Psychologist, 61,* 227–239.

Walton, G. M., & Cohen, G. L. (2011, March 18). A brief social-belonging intervention improves academic and health outcomes of minority students. *Science, 331,* 1447–1451.

Wang, A., & Clark, D. A. (2002). Haunting thoughts: The problem of obsessive mental intrusions [Special issue: Intrusions in cognitive behavioral therapy]. *Journal of Cognitive Psychotherapy, 16,* 193–208.

Wang, F. F., Kameda, M. M., Yasuhara, T. T., Tajiri, N. N., Kikuchi, Y. Y., Liang, H. B., et al. (2011). Gdnf-pretreatment enhances the survival of neural stem cells following transplantation in a rat model of Parkinson's disease. *Neuroscience Research, (18),* 202–211.

Wang, O. (2003). Infantile amnesia reconsidered: A cross-cultural analysis. *Memory, 11,* 65–80.

Wang, P. S., Aguilar-Gaxiola, S., Alonso, J., Angermeyer, M. C., Borges, G., Bromet, E. J., et al. (2007, September 8). Use of mental health services for anxiety, mood, and substance disorders in 17 countries in the WHO world mental health surveys. *Lancet, 370,* 841–850.

Wang, Q. (2004). The emergence of cultural self-constructs: Autobiographical memory and self-description in European American and Chinese children. *Developmental Psychology, 40,* 3–15.

Wang, Q., & Conway, M. A. (2006). Autobiographical memory, self, and culture. In L-G. Nilsson & N. Ohta (Eds.), *Memory and society: Psychological perspectives.* New York: Psychology Press.

Wang, S. (2010, March 16). Can you alter your memory? *The Wall Street Journal,* D1.

Wang, X., Lu, T., Snider, R. K., & Liang, L. (2005). Sustained firing in auditory cortex evoked by preferred stimuli. *Nature, 435,* 341–346.

Ward, L. M. (2004). Wading through the stereotypes: Positive and negative associations between media use and Black adolescents' conceptions of self. *Developmental Psychology, 40,* 284–294.

Ward, L. M. (2011). The thalamic dynamic core theory of conscious experience. *Consciousness and Cognition: An International Journal, 20,* 464–486.

Ward, W. C., Kogan, N., & Pankove, E. (1972). Incentive effects in children's creativity. *Child Development, 43,* 669–677.

Ward-Baker, P. D. (2007). The remarkable oldest old: A new vision of aging. *Dissertation Abstracts International Section A: Humanities and Social Sciences, 67*(8-A), 3115.

Warden, C. A., Wu, W-Y., & Tsai, D. (2006). Online shopping interface components: Relative importance as peripheral and central cues. *CyberPsychology & Behavior, 9,* 285–296.

Wark, B., Lundstrom, B., & Fairhall, A. (2007, August). Sensory adaptation. *Current Opinion in Neurobiology, 17,* 423–429.

Wasserman, E. A., & Miller, R. R. (1997). What's elementary about associative learning? *Annual Review of Psychology, 48,* 573–607.

Watson, J. B. (1924). *Behaviorism.* New York: Norton.

Watson, J. C., Goldman, R. N., & Greenberg, L. S. (2011). Humanistic and experiential theories of psychotherapy. In J. C. Norcross, G. R. VandenBos, et al. (Eds.), *History of psychotherapy: Continuity and change* (2nd ed.). Washington, DC: American Psychological Association.

Watson, M., Haviland, J. S., Greer, S., Davidson, J., & Bliss, J. M. (1999). Influence of psychological response on survival in breast cancer: A population-based cohort study. *Lancet, 354,* 1331–1336.

Watson, P. J., Brymer, M. J., & Bonanno, G. A. (2011). Postdisaster psychological intervention since 9/11. *American Psychologist, 66,* 482–494.

Watters, E. (2010, January 10). The Americanization of mental illness. *The New York Times,* p. C2.

Waxman, S. (2009). Learning from infants' first verbs. *Monographs of the Society for Research in Child Development, 74,* 127–132.

Weber, R., Ritterfeld, U., & Kostygina, A. (2006). Aggression and violence as effects of playing violent video games? In P. Vorderer, & J. Bryant (Eds.), *Playing video games: Motives, responses, and consequences.* Mahwah, NJ: Lawrence Erlbaum Associates.

Wechsler, H., Kuo, M., Lee, H., & Dowdall, G. W. (2000). *Environmental correlates of underage alcohol use and related problems of college students.* Cambridge, MA: Harvard School of Public Health.

Wechsler, H., Lee, J. E., Nelson, T. F., & Kuo, M. (2002). Underage college students' drinking behavior, access to alcohol, and the influence of deterrence policies. *Journal of American College Health, 50,* 223–236.

Weck, F., Bleichhardt, G., Witthöft, M., & Hiller, W. (2011). Explicit and implicit anxiety: Differences between patients with hypochondriasis, patients with anxiety disorders, and healthy controls. *Cognitive Therapy and Research, 35,* 317–325.

Weeks, M., & Lupfer, M. B. (2004). Complicating race: The relationship between prejudice, race, and social class categorizations. *Personality and Social Psychology Bulletin, 30,* 972–984.

Wehrle, R., Kaufmann, C., Wetter, T. C., Holsboer, F., Auer, D. P., Pollmacher, T., et al. (2007). Functional microstates within human REM sleep: First evidence from fMRI of a thalamo-cortical network specific for phasic REM periods. *European Journal of Neuroscience, 25,* 863–871.

Weinberg, M. S., Williams, C. J., & Pryor, D. W. (1991, February 27). Personal communication. Indiana University, Bloomington.

Weiner, I. B. (2004a). Monitoring psychotherapy with performance-based measures of personality functioning. *Journal of Personality Assessment, 83,* 323–331.

Weiner, I. B. (2004b). Rorschach Inkblot method. In M. E. Maruish (Ed.), *Use of psychological testing for treatment planning and outcomes assessment, Vol. 3: Instruments for adults* (3rd ed.). Mahwah, NJ: Lawrence Erlbaum Associates.

Weiner, R. D., & Falcone, G. (2011). Electroconvulsive therapy: How effective is it? *Journal of the American Psychiatric Nurses Association, 17,* 217–218.

Weinstein, L. (2007). Selected genetic disorders affecting Ashkenazi Jewish families. *Family & Community Health, 30,* 50–62.

Weinstein, M., Glei, D. A., Yamazaki, A., & Ming-Cheng, C. (2004). The role of intergenerational relations in the association between life stressors and depressive symptoms. *Research on Aging, 26,* 511–530.

Weiss, A., Bates, T., & Luciano, M. (2008). Happiness is a personal(ity) thing: The genetics of personality and well-being in a representative sample. *Psychological Science, 19,* 205–210.

Weiss, W. M., & Weiss, M. R. (2003). Attraction- and entrapment-based commitment among competitive female gymnasts. *Journal of Sport & Exercise Psychology, 25,* 229–247.

Weissman, M., Markowitz, J., & Klerman, G. L. (2007). *Clinician's quick guide to interpersonal psychotherapy.* New York: Oxford University Press.

Weissman, M. M., Bland, R. C., Canino, G. J., Faravelli, C., Greenwald, S., Hwu, H. G., et al. (1997, July 24–31). Cross-national epidemiology of major depression and bipolar disorder. *Journal of the American Medical Association, 276,* 293–299.

Welkowitz, L. A., Struening, E. L., Pittman, J., Guardino, M., & Welkowitz, J. (2000). Obsessive-compulsive disorder and comorbid anxiety problems in a national anxiety screening sample. *Journal of Anxiety Disorders, 14,* 471–482.

Wells, R., Phillips, R. S., & McCarthy, E. P. (2011). Patterns of mind-body therapies in adults with common neurological conditions. *Neuroepidemiology, 36,* 46–51.

Wenar, C. (1994). *Developmental psychopathology: From infancy through adolescence* (3rd ed.). New York: McGraw-Hill.

Wenzel, A. (2011). Obsessions and compulsions. In A. Wenzel &, S. Stuart (Eds.), *Anxiety in childbearing women: Diagnosis and treatment.* Washington, DC: American Psychological Association.

Wenzel, A., Zetocha, K., & Ferraro, R. F. (2007). Depth of processing and recall of threat material in fearful and nonfearful individuals. *Anxiety, Stress & Coping: An International Journal, 20,* 223–237.

Werblin, F., & Roska, B. (2007, April). The movies in our eyes. *Scientific American,* pp. 73–77.

Werker, J. F., & Tees, R. C. (2005). Speech perception as a window for understanding plasticity and commitment in language systems of the brain. *Developmental Psychobiology, 46,* 233–234.

Werner, J. S., Pinna, B., & Spillmann, L. (2007, March). Illusory color and the brain. *Scientific American,* 90–96.

Wertheimer, M. (1923). Untersuchungen zur Lehre von der Gestalt, II. *Psychol. Forsch., 5,* 301–350. In R. Beardsley & M. Wertheimer (Eds.). (1958), *Readings in perception.* New York: Van Nostrand.

West, D. S., Harvey-Berino, J., & Raczynski, J. M. (2004). Behavioral aspects of obesity, dietary intake, & chronic disease. In J. M. Raczynski & L. C. Leviton (Eds.), *Handbook of clinical health psychology: Vol. 2. Disorders of behavior and health.* Washington, DC: American Psychological Association.

West, R. L., Bagwell, D. K., & Dark-Freudeman, A. (2007). Self-efficacy and memory aging: The impact of a memory intervention based on self-efficacy. *Neuropsychological Development and Cognition, B, Aging and Neuropsychological Cognition, 14,* 1–28.

West, S. L., & O'Neal, K. K. (2004). Project D.A.R.E. outcome effectiveness revisited. *American Journal of Public Health, 94,* 1027–1029.

Westen, D., Novotny, C. M., & Thompson-Brenner, H. (2004). The empirical status of empirically supported psychotherapies: Assumptions, findings, and reporting in controlled clinical trials. *Psychological Bulletin, 130,* 631–663.

Westerhausen, R., Moosmann, M., Alho, K., Medvedev, S., Hämäläinen, H., & Hugdahl, K. (2009, January). Top-down and bottom-up interaction: Manipulating the dichotic listening ear advantage. *Brain Research, 1250,* 183–189.

Westerterp, K. R. (2006). Perception, passive overfeeding and energy metabolism. *Physiology & Behavior, 89,* 62–65.

Wetter, D. W., Fiore, M. C., Gritz, E. R., Lando, H. A., Stitzer, M. L., Hasselblad, V., et al. (1998). The Agency for Health Care Policy and Research. Smoking cessation clinical practice guideline: Findings and implications for psychologists. *American Psychologist, 53,* 657–669.

Whaley, B. B. (Ed.). (2000). *Explaining illness: Research, theory, and strategies.* Mahwah, NJ: Erlbaum.

Whisman, M., & Snyder, D. (2007). Sexual infidelity in a national survey of American women: Differences in prevalence and correlates as a function of method of assessment. *Journal of Family Psychology, 21,* 14–154.

Whitbourne, S. (2010). *The search for fulfillment.* New York: Ballantine.

Whitbourne, S. K. (2000). The normal aging process. In S. K. Whitbourne & S. Krauss (Eds.), *Psychopathology in later adulthood.* New York: Wiley.

Whitbourne, S. K., & Wills, K. (1993). Psychological issues in institutional care of the aged. In S. B. Goldsmith (Ed.), *Long-term care.* Gaithersburg, MD: Aspen Press.

Whitbourne, S. K., Zuschlag, M. K., Elliot, L. B., & Waterman, A. S. (1992). Psychosocial development in adulthood: A 22-year sequential study. *Journal of Personality and Social Psychology, 63,* 260–271.

White, L. (2007). Linguistic theory, universal grammar, and second language acquisition. In B. Van Patten & J. Williams (Eds.), *Theories in second language acquisition: An introduction.* Mahwah, NJ: Lawrence Erlbaum Associates.

Whitebread, D., Coltman, P., Jameson, H., & Lander, R. (2009). Play, cognition and self-regulation: What exactly are children learning when they learn through play? *Educational and Child Psychology, 26,* 40–52.

Whitehouse, W. G., Orne, E. C., Dinges, D. F., Bates, B. L., Nadon, R., & Orne, M. T. (2005). The cognitive interview: Does it successfully avoid the dangers of forensic hypnosis? *American Journal of Psychology, 118,* 213–234.

Whitney, P. G., & Green, J. A. (2011). Changes in infants' affect related to the onset of independent locomotion. *Infant Behavior & Development, 34,* 459–466.

WHO World Mental Health Survey Consortium. (2004). Prevalence, severity, and unmet need for treatment of mental disorders in the World Health Organization World Mental Health Surveys. *Journal of the American Medical Association, 291,* 2581–2590.

Whorf, B. L. (1956). *Language, thought, and reality.* New York: Wiley.

Wickelgren, E. A. (2004). Perspective distortion of trajectory forms and perceptual constancy in visual event identification. *Perception and Psychophysics, 66,* 629–641.

Widaman, K. (2009). Phenylketonuria in children and mothers: Genes, environments, behavior. *Current Directions in Psychological Science, 18,* 48–52.

Widiger, T. A., & Clark, L. A. (2000). Toward *DSM-V* and the classification of psychopathology. *Psychological Bulletin, 126,* 946–963.

Widmeyer, W. N., & Loy, J. W. (1988). When you're hot, you're hot! Warm-cold effects in first impressions of persons and teaching effectiveness. *Journal of Educational Psychology, 80,* 118–121.

Wielgosz, A. T., & Nolan, R. P. (2000). Biobehavioral factors in the context of ischemic cardiovascular disease. *Journal of Psychosomatic Research, 48,* 339–345.

Wiggins, J. S. (2003). *Paradigms of personality assessment.* New York: Guilford Press.

Wildavsky, B. (2000, September 4). A blow to bilingual education. *U.S. News & World Report,* pp. 22–28.

Wilde, D. J. (2011). *Jung's personality theory quantified.* New York: Springer-Verlag Publishing.

Wilgoren, J. (1999, October 22). Quality day care, early, is tied to achievements as an adult. *The New York Times,* p. A16.

Wilkin, L., & Haddock, B. (2011). Functional fitness of older adults. *Activities, Adaptation & Aging, 35,* 197–209.

Wilkinson, H. A. (2009). Cingulotomy. *Journal of Neurosurgery, 110,* 607–611.

Wilkinson, L., & Olliver-Gray, Y. (2006). The significance of silence: Differences in meaning, learning styles, and teaching strategies in cross-cultural settings [Special issue: Child language]. *Psychologia: An International Journal of Psychology in the Orient, 49,* 74–88.

Willander, J., & Larsson, M. (2006). Smell your way back to childhood: Autobiographical odor memory. *Psychonomic Bulletin & Review, 13,* 240–244.

Williams, C. L., & Butcher, J. N. (2011). The nuts and bolts: Administering, scoring, and augmenting MMPI-A assessments. In C. L. Williams & J. N. Butcher (Eds.), *A beginner's guide to the MMPI—A.* Washington, DC: American Psychological Association.

Williams, J. E., Paton, C. C., Siegler, I. C., Eigenbrodt, M. L., Nieto, F. J., & Tyroler, H. A. (2000). Anger proneness predicts coronary heart disease risk: Prospective analysis from the Atherosclerosis Risk in Communities (ARIC) Study. *Circulation, 101,* 2034–2039.

Williamson, P., McLeskey, J., & Hoppey, D. (2006). Educating students with mental retardation in general education classrooms. *Exceptional Children, 72,* 347–361.

Willis, G. L. (2005). The therapeutic effects of dopamine replacement therapy and its psychiatric side effects are mediated by pineal function. *Behavioural Brain Research, 160,* 148–160.

Willis, S. L., & Schaie, K. W. (1994). In C. B. Fisher & R. M. Lerner (Eds.), *Applied de-velopmental psychology.* New York: McGraw-Hill.

Wills, T., Sargent, J., Stoolmiller, M., Gibbons, F., & Gerrard, M. (2008). Movie smoking exposure and smoking onset: A longitudinal study of mediation processes in a representative sample of U.S. adolescents. *Psychology of Addictive Behaviors, 22,* 269–277.

Wilson, T. D. (2006, September 1). The power of social psychological interventions. *Science, 313,* 1251–1252.

Wilson, T. G., Grilo, C. M., & Vitousek, K. M. (2007). Psychological treatment of eating disorders [Special issue: Eating disorders]. *American Psychologist, 62,* 199–216.

Windholz, G., & Lamal, P. A. (2002). Koehler's insight revisited. In R. A. Griggs (Ed.), *Handbook for teaching introductory psychology, Vol. 3: With an emphasis on assessment.* Mahwah, NJ: Erlbaum.

Winerman, L. (2005, June). ACTing up. *Monitor on Psychology,* pp. 44–45.

Winner, E. (2003). Creativity and talent. In M. H. Bornstein & L. Davidson (Eds.), *Well-being: Positive development across the life course.* Mahwah, NJ: Lawrence Erlbaum.

Winson, J. (1990, November). The meaning of dreams. *Scientific American,* pp. 86–96.

Winstead, B. A., & Sanchez, A. (2005). Gender and psychopathology. In J. E. Maddux & B. A. Winstead (Eds.), *Psychopathology: Foundations for a contemporary understanding.* Mahwah, NJ: Lawrence Erlbaum Associates.

Winston, J. S., O'Doherty, J., & Kilner, J. M. (2006). Brain systems for assessing facial attractiveness. *Neuropsychologia, 45,* 195–206.

Winter, D. G. (1995). *Personality: Analysis and interpretation of lives.* New York: McGraw-Hill.

Winter, D. G. (2007). The role of motivation, responsibility, and integrative complexity in crisis escalation: Comparative studies of war and peace crises. *Journal of Personality and Social Psychology, 92,* 920–937.

Winters, B. D., & Bussey, T. J. (2005). Glutamate receptors in perirhinal cortex mediate encoding, retrieval, and consolidation of object recognition memory. *Journal of Neuroscience, 25,* 4243–4251.

Wiseman, R., & Greening, E. (2002). The mind machine: A mass participation experiment into the possible existence of extra-sensory perception. *British Journal of Psychology, 93,* 487–499.

Witelson, S., Kigar, D., Scamvougeras, A., Kideckel, D., Buck, B., Stanchev, P., et al. (2008). Corpus callosum anatomy in right-handed homosexual and heterosexual men. *Archives of Sexual Behavior, 37,* 857–863.

Witt, C. M., Jena, S., & Brinkhaus, B. (2006). Acupuncture for patients with chronic neck pain. *Pain, 125,* 98–106.

Wittchen, H., Nocon, A., Beesdo, K., Pine, D., Hofler, M., Lieb, R., et al. (2008). Agoraphobia and panic. *Psychotherapy and Psychosomatics, 77,* 147–157.

Wittenbrink, B., & Schwarz, N. (Eds.). (2007). *Implicit measures of attitudes.* New York: Guilford Press.

Wixted, J. T., & Carpenter, S. K. (2007). The Wickelgren Power Law and the Ebbinghaus Savings Function. *Psychological Science, 18,* 133–134.

Wolfe, M. S. (2006, May). Shutting down Alzheimer's. *Scientific American,* 73–79.

Wolff, N. (2002). Risk, response, and mental health policy: Learning from the experience of the United Kingdom. *Journal of Health Politic and Policy Law, 27,* 801–802.

Wolitzky, D. L. (2006). Psychodynamic theories. In J. C. Thomas & D. L. Segal (Eds.), *Comprehensive handbook of personality and psychopathology, Vol. 1: Personality and everyday functioning.* Hoboken, NJ: John Wiley & Sons.

Wong, N., Sarver, D. E., & Beidel, D. C. (2011). Quality of life impairments among adults with social phobia: The impact of subtype. *Journal of Anxiety Disorders, 14,* 88–95.

Wood, E., Desmarais, S., & Gugula, S. (2002). The impact of parenting experience on gender stereotyped toy play of children. *Sex Roles, 47,* 39–49.

Wood, W. (2000). Attitude change: Persuasion and social influence. *Annual Review of Psychology, 51,* 539–570.

Wood, W., & Eagly, A. H. (2002). A cross-cultural analysis of the behavior of women and men: Implications for the origins of sex differences. *Psychological Bulletin, 128,* 699–727.

Woodruff, S. I., Conway, T. L., & Edwards, C. C. (2007). Sociodemographic and smoking-related psychosocial predictors of smoking behavior change among high school smokers. *Addictive Behaviors, 33,* 354–358.

Woods, S. C., Schwartz, M. W., Baskin, D. G., & Seeley, R. J. (2000). Food intake and the regulation of body weight. *Annual Review of Psychology, 51,* 255–277.

Woodson, S. R. J. (2006). Relationships between sleepiness and emotion experience: An experimental investigation of the role of subjective sleepiness in the generation of positive and negative emotions. *Dissertation Abstracts International: Section B: The Sciences and Engineering, 67*(5-B), 2849.

Woollett, K., & Maguire, E. (2009). Navigational expertise may compromise anterograde associative memory. *Neuropsychologia, 47,* 1088–1095.

Worthen, J. B., & Hunt, R. (2011). *Mnemonology: Mnemonics for the 21st century.* New York: Psychology Press.

Wren, A. M., & Bloom, S. R. (2007). Gut hormones and appetite control. *Gastroenterology, 132,* 2116–2130.

Wright, K. (2002, September). Times of our lives. *Scientific American,* pp. 59–65.

Wrosch, C., Bauer, I., & Scheier, M. (2005, December). Regret and quality of life across the adult life span: The influence of disengagement and available future goals. *Psychology and Aging, 20,* 657–670.

Wrzesniewski, K., & Chylinska, J. (2007). Assessment of coping styles and strategies with school-related stress. *School Psychology International, 28,* 179–194.

Wu, L-T., Schlenger, W. E., & Galvin, D. M. (2006). Concurrent use of methamphetamine, MDMA, LSD, ketamine, GHB, and flunitrazepam among American youths. *Drug and Alcohol Dependence, 84,* 102–113.

Wuethrich, B. (2001, March 16). Does alcohol damage female brains more? *Science, 291,* 2077–2079.

Wurtz, R. H., & Kandel, E. R. (2000). Central visual pathways. In E. R. Kandel, J. H. Schwartz, et al. (Eds.), *Principles of neural science* (4th ed.). New York: McGraw-Hill.

Wynn, K., Bloom, P., & Chiang, W. C. (2002). Enumeration of collective entities by 5-month-old infants. *Cognition, 83,* B55-B62.

Wyra, M., Lawson, M. J., & Hungi, N. (2007). The mnemonic keyword method: The effects of bidirectional retrieval training and of ability to image on foreign language vocabulary recall. *Learning and Instruction, 17,* 360–371.

Xiao, Z., Yan, H., Wang, Z., Zou, Z., Xu, Y., Chen, J., et al. (2006). Trauma and dissociation in China. *American Journal of Psychiatry, 163,* 1388–1391.

Xue, G., Lu, Z., Levin, I. P., & Bechara, A. (2010). The impact of prior risk experiences on subsequent risky decision-making: The role of the insula. *NeuroImage, 50,* 709–716.

Yao, S-Q., Zhour, Y-H., & Jiang, L. (2006). The intelligence scale for Chinese adults: Item

Yapko, M. D. (2006). Utilizing hypnosis in addressing ruminative depression-related insomnia. In M. D. Yapko (Ed.), *Hypnosis and treating depression: Applications in clinical practice.* New York: Routledge/Taylor & Francis Group.

Yardley, L., & Moss-Morris, R. (2009, January). Current issues and new directions in psychology and health: Increasing the quantity and quality of health psychology research. *Psychology & Health, 24,* 1–4.

Yeomans, M. R., Tepper, B. J., & Ritezschel, J. (2007). Human hedonic responses to sweetness: Role of taste genetics and anatomy. *Physiology & Behavior, 91,* 264–273.

Yesilyaprak, B., Kisac, I., & Sanlier, N. (2007). Stress symptoms and nutritional status among survivors of the Marmara region earthquakes in Turkey. *Journal of Loss & Trauma, 12,* 1–8.

Zacks, J. (2008). Neuroimaging studies of mental rotation: A meta-analysis and review. *Journal of Cognitive Neuroscience, 20,* 1–19.

Zaitsu, W. (2007). The effect of fear on eyewitness' retrieval in recognition memory. *Japanese Journal of Psychology, 77,* 504–511.

Zajonc, R. B. (2001). Mere exposure: A gateway to the subliminal. *Current Directions in Psychological Science, 10,* 224–228.

Zaragoza, M. S., Belli, R. F., & Payment, K. E. (2007). Misinformation effects and the suggestibility of eyewitness memory. In M. Garry & H. Hayne (Eds.), *Do justice and let the sky fall: Elizabeth Loftus and her contributions to science, law, and academic freedom.* Mahwah, NJ: Lawrence Erlbaum Associates.

Zarren, J. I., & Eimer, B. N. (2002). *Brief cognitive hypnosis: Facilitating the change of dysfunctional behavior.* New York: Springer.

Zaslow, J. (2003, May 1). Going on after the unthinkable: A rape victim shares her story. *The Wall Street Journal,* p. A2.

Zaslow, M., Halle, T., & Martin, L. (2006). Child outcome measures in the study of child care quality. *Evaluation Review, 30,* 577–610.

Zebrowitz, L. A., & Montepare, J. M. (2005, June 10). Appearance DOES matter. *Science, 308,* 1565–1566.

Zebrowitz-McArthur, L. (1988). Person perception in cross-cultural perspective. In M. H. Bond (Ed.), *The cross-cultural challenge to social psychology.* Newbury Park, CA: Sage.

Zeigler, D. W., et al. (2005). The neurocognitive effects of alcohol on adolescents and college students. *Preventive Medicine: An International Journal Devoted to Practice and Theory, 40,* 23–32.

Zeng, L., Proctor, R. W., & Salvendy, G. (2011). Can traditional divergent thinking tests be trusted in measuring and predicting real-world creativity? *Creativity Research Journal, 23,* 24–37.

Zepf, S., & Zepf, F. D. (2011). 'You are requested to close an eye': Freud's seduction theory and theory of the Oedipus complex revisited. *Psychoanalytic Review, 98,* 287–323.

Zevon, M., & Corn, B. (1990). Paper presented at the annual meeting of the American Psychological Association, Boston, MA.

Zhang, F., Chen, Y., Heiman, M., & Dimarchi, R. (2005). Leptin: Structure, function and biology. *Vitamins and Hormones: Advances in Research and Applications, 71,* 345–372.

Zhou, Z., & Buck, L. B. (2006, March 10). Combinatorial effects of odorant mixes in olfactory cortex. *Science,* 1477–1481.

Zhou, Z., Liu, Q., & Davis, R. L. (2005). Complex regulation of spiral ganglion neuron firing patterns by neurotrophin-3. *Journal of Neuroscience, 25,* 7558–7566.

Zians, J. (2007). A comparison of trait anger and depression on several variables: Attribution style, dominance, submissiveness, need for power, efficacy and dependency. *Dissertation Abstracts International: Section B: The Sciences and Engineering, 67*(7-B), 4124.

Zigler, E. F., Finn-Stevenson, M., & Hall, N. W. (2002). The first three years and beyond: Brain development and social policy. In E. F. Zigler, M. Finn-Stevenson, et al. (Eds.), *Current perspectives in psychology.* New Haven, CT: Yale University Press.

Zigler, E., Bennett-Gates, D., Hodapp, R., & Henrich, C. (2002). Assessing personality traits of individuals with mental retardation. *American Journal on Mental Retardation, 107,* 181–193.

Zimbardo, P. (2007). *The Lucifer effect: Understanding how good people turn evil.* New York: Random House.

Zimbardo, P. G. (1973). On the ethics of intervention in human psychological research: With special reference to the Stanford Prison Experiment. *Cognition, 2,* 243–256.

Zimbardo, P. G. (2004). Does psychology make a significant difference in our lives? *American Psychologist, 59,* 339–351.

Zimbardo, P. G., Maslach, C., & Haney, C. (2000). Reflections on the Stanford Prison Experiment: Genesis, transformations, consequences. In T. Blass (Ed.), *Obedience to authority: Current perspectives on the Milgram Paradigm.* Mahwah, NJ: Lawrence Erlbaum Associates.

Zimmermann, U. S., Blomeyer, D., & Laucht, M. (2007). How gene-stress-behavior interactions can promote adolescent alcohol use: The roles of predrinking allostatic load and childhood behavior disorders [Special issue: Adolescents, drug abuse and mental disorders]. *Pharmacology, Biochemistry and Behavior, 86,* 246–262.

Zito, J. M. (1993). *Psychotherapeutic drug manual* (3rd ed., rev.). New York: Wiley.

Zolotor, A., Theodore, A., Chang, J., Berkoff, M., & Runyan, D. (2008). Speak softly—and forget the stick: Corporal punishment and child physical abuse. *American Journal of Preventive Medicine, 35,* 364–369.

Zuckerman, M. (1978, February). The search for high sensation. *Psychology Today,* pp. 30–46.

Zuckerman, M. (2002). Genetics of sensation seeking. In J. Benjamin, R. P. Ebstein, et al. (Eds.), *Molecular genetics and the human personality.* Washington, DC: American Psychiatric Publishing.

Zuger, A. (2005, November 10). Doctors learn how to say what no one wants to hear. *The New York Times,* p. S1.

Credits

Text and Line Art Credits

Chapter 1 Module 3: Figure 5: From Darley, J. M., & Latané, B. (1968). Bystander intervention in emergencies: Diffusion of responsibility. *Journal of Personality and Social Psychology, 8*, 377–383. Published by The American Psychological Association, adapted with permission.

Chapter 2 Module 5: Figure 1: Line art from Kent Van De Graaff, *Human Anatomy*, updated 5th ed. Copyright © 2000 by The McGraw-Hill Companies, Inc. Reprinted with permission. Figure 3: From Sylvia S. Mader, *Human Biology*, 6th ed., p. 250. Copyright © 2000 by The McGraw-Hill Companies, Inc. Reprinted with permission. Figure 4a: From Sylvia S. Mader, *Human Biology*, 6th ed., p. 250. Copyright © 2000 by The McGraw-Hill Companies, Inc. Reprinted with permission. Figure 4b: From George B. Johnson, *The Living World*, 2nd ed., p. 600. Copyright © 2000 by The McGraw-Hill Companies, Inc. Reprinted with permission. Module 6: Figure 2: From Michael W. Passer and Ronald E. Smith, *Psychology*. Copyright © 2001 by The McGraw-Hill Companies, Inc. Reprinted with permission. Figure 3: From Michael W. Passer and Ronald E. Smith, *Psychology*, p. 91. Copyright © 2001 by The McGraw-Hill Companies, Inc. Reprinted with permission. Figure 4: Adapted from Robert J. Brooker, Eric P. Widmaier, Linda Graham, and Peter Stiling, *Biology*, p. 1062. Copyright © 2008 by The McGraw-Hill Companies, Inc. Reprinted with permission. Module 7: Figure 2: From Rod R. Seeley, Trent D. Stephens, and Philip Tate, *Anatomy & Physiology*, 5th ed., p. 384. Copyright © 2000 by The McGraw-Hill Companies, Inc. Reprinted with permission. Figure 4: Adapted from Allen M. Schneider and Barry Tarshis, *Elements of Physiological Psychology*, p. 87. Copyright © 1995 by The McGraw-Hill Companies, Inc. Reprinted with permission. Figure 8: From Robert J. Brooker, Eric P. Widmaier, Linda Graham, and Peter Stiling, *Biology*, p. 943. Copyright © 2008 by The McGraw-Hill Companies, Inc. Reprinted with permission.

Chapter 3 Module 9: Figure 1: From Camille B. Wortman, Elizabeth F. Loftus, and Charles Weaver, *Psychology*, 5th ed., p. 113. Copyright © 1999 by The McGraw-Hill Companies, Inc. Reprinted with permission. Figure 3: From David Shier, Jackie Butler, and Ricki Lewis, *Hole's Essentials of Human Anatomy and Physiology*, 7th ed., p. 283. Copyright © 2000 by The McGraw-Hill Companies, Inc. Reprinted with permission. Figure 5: From Sylvia S. Mader, *Human Biology*, 6th ed., p. 250. Copyright © 2000 by The McGraw-Hill Companies, Inc. Reprinted with permission. Module 10: Figure 1: From Robert J. Brooker, Eric P. Widmaier, Linda Graham, and Peter Stiling, *Biology*, p. 956. Copyright © 2008 by The McGraw-Hill Companies, Inc. Reprinted with permission. Figure 2: From Rod R. Seeley, Trent D. Stephens, and Philip Tate, *Anatomy & Physiology*, 5th ed., p. 384. Copyright © 2000 by The McGraw-Hill Companies, Inc. Reprinted with permission. Figure 3: New York Times Graphic, Hearing High Tones, from Paul Vitello, "A Ring Tone Meant to Fall on

Deaf Ears." From *The New York Times*, June 12, 2006. © 2006 The New York Times. All rights reserved. Used by permission and protected by the Copyright Laws of the United States. The printing, copying, redistribution, or retransmission of this Content without express written permission is prohibited. www.nytimes.com Figure 4: Adapted from Bartoshuk, L., & Lucchina, L., "Take a taste test" from Brownlee, S., & Watson, T. (1997, January 13). The senses. *U.S. News & World Report*, pp. 51–59. Reprinted by permission of Linda Bartoshuk. Module 11: Figure 8: From Fig. 1 (p. 186) from Hudson, W. (1960). Pictorial depth perception in sub-cultural groups in Africa. *Journal of Social Psychology, 52* (2), 183–208, reprinted by permission of the publisher (Taylor & Francis Ltd, http://www.tandf.co.uk/journals/).

Chapter 4 Module 12: Figure 1: From Palladino, J. J., & Carducci, B. J. (1984). Students' knowledge of sleep and dreams. *Teaching of Psychology*, vol. 11, no. 3, pp. 189–191, copyright © 1984 by Division Two of the American Psychological Association. Reprinted by permission of SAGE Publications, Inc. Figure 2: "Figure of brain-wave patterns" from *Sleep* by J. Allan Hobson. Copyright © 1989 by J. Allan Hobson, M.D. Reprinted by permission of Henry Holt and Company, LLC. Figure 4: From Borbély, A. (1986). *Secrets of Sleep*, Figure 3.4 (p. 43). English translation, Copyright © 1986 by Basic Books. © 1984 by Deutsche Verlags-Anstalt GmbH, Stuttgart. Reprinted by permission of Basic Books, a member of the Perseus Books Group. Figure 6: Domhoff, G. W., & Schneider, A. (1998). New rationales and methods for quantitative dream research outside the laboratory. *Sleep, 21*, 398–404 (from Table 1, p. 401). Copyright 1998. Reproduced with permission of American Academy of Sleep Medicine in the format Textbook via Copyright Clearance Center. Figure 9: From Dodds, P. S., et al. (2011). Temporal patterns of happiness and information in a global social network: Hedonometrics and Twitter. *PLoS ONE, 6*, Figure S2. As appeared in Miller, G. (2011, 30 Sept.). Social scientists wade into the tweet stream. *Science, 333*, 1814–1815, from figure on p. 1814. http://creativecommons.org/licenses/by/3.0/ Module 14: Figure 2: From Sylvia S. Mader, *Human Biology*, 6th ed., p. 250. Copyright © 2000 by The McGraw-Hill Companies, Inc. Reprinted with permission.

Chapter 5 Module 17: Figure 1: From Tolman, E. C., & Honzik, C. H. (1930). Introduction and removal of reward and maze performance in rats. *University of California Publications in Psychology, 4*, 257–275.

Chapter 6 Module 18: Figure 6: From Collins, A. M., & Loftus, E. F. (1975). A spreading-activation theory of semantic processing. *Psychological Review, 82*, 407–428. Published by The American Psychological Association, adapted with permission. Figure 7: From Kent Van De Graaff, *Human Anatomy*, updated 5th ed. Copyright © 2000 by The McGraw-Hill Companies, Inc. Reprinted with permission. Module 19: Figure 4: From Breslin, C. W., & Safer, M. A. (2011). Effects of event valence on long-term memory for two baseball championship games. *Psychological Science, 22* (11), 1408–1412 (Figure 1, p. 1409), copyright © 2011 by

Association for Psychological Science. Reprinted by permission of SAGE Publications. Figure 5: Reprinted from *Journal of Verbal Learning and Verbal Behavior*, vol. 13, Loftus, E. F., & Palmer, J. C., "Reconstruction of automobile destruction: An example of the interface between language and memory," pp. 585–589, Copyright 1974, with permission from Elsevier. http://www.science-direct.com/science/journal/00225371 Figure 6: From Table 2 (p. 266) from Bahrick, H. P., Hall, L. K., & Berger, S. A. (1996). Accuracy and distortion in memory for high school grades. *Psychological Science, 7*, no. 5, 265–269, copyright © 1996 Association for Psychological Science. Reprinted by permission of SAGE Publications. Module 20: Figure 2: Reprinted from *Cognitive Psychology*, vol. 11, Nickerson, R. S., & Adams, M. J., "Long-term memory for a common object," pp. 287–307, Copyright 1979, with permission from Elsevier. http://www.sciencedirect.com/science/journal/00100285

Chapter 7 Module 22: Figure 1: MLA Language Map, 2005. Reprinted by permission of the Modern Language Association. © 2005 Modern Language Association. Module 23: Figure 1: Text from Gardner, H. (2006). *Multiple Intelligences: New Horizons in Theory and Practice*, pp. 8, 9–10, 11, 13, 15, 16. Copyright © 2006 by Howard Gardner. First edition © 1993 by Howard Gardner. Reprinted by permission of Basic Books, a member of the Perseus Books Group. Figure 6: Republished with permission of Annual Reviews, Inc., from Henderson, N. D. (1982). Human behavior genetics. *Annual Review of Psychology*, vol. 33, pp. 403–440 (adapted from Table 1, p. 410). © 1982 by Annual Reviews. Permission conveyed through Copyright Clearance Center, Inc.

Chapter 8 Module 26: Figure 1: Adapted from Figure 1 (p. 1067) from Shaver, P., Schwartz, J., Kirson, D., & O'Connor, C. (1987). Emotion knowledge: Further exploration of a prototype approach. *Journal of Personality and Social Psychology, 52*, 1061–1086. Published by The American Psychological Association, adapted with permission.

Chapter 9 Module 28: Figure 3: Graphs reprinted from *NeuroImage*, vol. 54, Nakato, E., et al., "Distinct differences in the pattern of hemodynamic response to happy and angry facial expressions in infants—A near-infrared spectroscopic study," pp. 1600–1606, Copyright 2011, with permission from Elsevier. http://www.sciencedirect.com/science/journal/10538119 Figure 11: From Dempster, F. N. (1981). Memory span: Sources for individual and developmental differences. *Psychological Bulletin, 89*, 63–100. Published by The American Psychological Association, adapted with permission. Module 29: Figure 2: From Rest, J. (1968). *Developmental Hierarchy in Preference and Comprehension of Moral Judgment*. Unpublished doctoral dissertation, University of Chicago. Appeared in Kohlberg, L. (1969). Stage and sequence: The cognitive-developmental approach to socialization. In D. Goslin (Ed.), *Handbook of Socialization Theory and Research* (pp. 381–382). Chicago: Rand McNally. Figure 4: Graph adapted from Table 2 (p. 64) from Boehm, K. E., & Campbell, N. B. (1995). Suicide: A review of calls to an adolescent peer listening phone service. *Child Psychiatry and Human Development, 26,* 61–66. Copyright © 1995 Springer Netherlands. With kind permission of Springer Science and Business Media. Module 30: Figure 1: Figure 2 (p. 472) from Arnett, J. J. (2000). Emerging adulthood: A theory of development from the late teens through the twenties. *American Psychologist, 55,* 469–480. Published by The American Psychological Association, reprinted with permission.

Chapter 10   Module 32: Figure 1: From Eysenck, H. J. (1990). Biological dimensions of personality. In L. A. Pervin (Ed.), *Handbook of Personality: Theory and Research* (p. 246). New York: Guilford. Reprinted by permission of The Guilford Press. Figure 2: From L. A. Pervin (Ed.), (1990). *Handbook of Personality: Theory and Research* (chapter 3). New York: Guilford. Reprinted by permission of The Guilford Press. Figure 4: From Tellegen, A., Lykken, D. T., Bouchard, T. J., Jr., Wilcox, K. J., Segal, N. L., & Rich, S. (1988). Personality similarity in twins reared apart and together. *Journal of Personality and Social Psychology, 54,* 1031–1039. Published by The American Psychological Association, reprinted with permission. Module 33: Figure 2: From Richard P. Halgin and Susan Krauss Whitbourne, *Abnormal Psychology,* p. 72. Copyright © 1994 by The McGraw-Hill Companies, Inc. Reprinted with permission.

Chapter 11   Module 34: Figure 1: Map by Cleo Vilett, from Susser, E. S., Herman, D. B., & Aaron, B. (2002, August). Combating the terror of terrorism. *Scientific American,* p. 74. Reprinted by permission of Cleo Vilett. Figure 2 (Hassles): From Table 2 (p. 475) from Chamberlain, K., & Zika, S. (1990). The minor events approach to stress: Support for the use of daily hassles. British *Journal of Psychology, 81,* no. 4, 469–481. © The British Psychological Society. Reprinted by permission of John Wiley & Sons, Inc. Figure 2 (Uplifts): Adapted from Table III (p. 14) from Kanner, A. D., Coyne, J. C., Schaefer, C., & Lazarus, R. S. (1981). Comparison of two modes of stress measurement: Daily hassles and uplifts versus major life events. *Journal of Behavioral Medicine, 4,* 1–39. © 1981 Plenum Publishing Corporation. With kind permission of Springer Science and Business Media. Figure 3: "Perceived Stress Scale" (pp. 394–395) adapted from Cohen, S., Kamarck, T., & Mermelstein, R. (1983). A global measure of perceived stress. *Journal of Health and Social Behavior, 24,* 385–396. Reprinted by permission of the American Sociological Association. Figure 4: From Hans Selye, *The Stress of Life.* Copyright © 1976 by The McGraw-Hill Companies, Inc. Reprinted with permission. Module 36: Figure 2: From Andrews, F. M., & Withey, S. B. (1976). *Social Indicators of Well-Being: Americans' Perceptions of Life Quality,* p. 376. © 1976 Plenum Press, New York. With kind permission of Springer Science and Business Media.

Chapter 12   Module 38: Figure 1: Adapted from Susan Nolen-Hoeksema, *Abnormal Psychology,* 4th ed., p. 232. Copyright © 2007 by The McGraw-Hill Companies, Inc. Reprinted with permission. Figure 2: From Beck, A. T., & Emery, G., with Greenberg, R. L. (1985). *Anxiety Disorders and Phobias: A Cognitive Perspective,* pp. 87–88. Copyright © 1985 by Aaron T. Beck, M.D., and Gary Emery, Ph.D. Revised paperback edition published in 2005. Reprinted by permission of Basic Books, a member of the Perseus Books Group. Figure 6: Adapted from Slater, E., & Meyer, A. (1959). Contributions to a pathography of the musicians: Robert

Schumann. *Confinia Psychiatrica, 2,* 65–94, Table II. Reprinted by permission of S. Karger AG, Basel. Figure 9: "Table of genetic links" from *Schizophrenia Genesis: The Origins of Madness* by I. I. Gottesman. Copyright © 1990 by Irving I. Gottesman. Reprinted by permission of Henry Holt and Company, LLC. Module 39: Figure 1: From Benton, S. A., et al. (2003). Changes in counseling center client problems across 13 years. *Professional Psychology: Research and Practice, 34,* 66–72. Published by The American Psychological Association, adapted with permission.

Chapter 13   Module 40: Figure 2: Text reprinted by permission of Herbert Benson, M.D., Benson-Henry Institute for Mind Body Medicine, Massachusetts General Hospital, Boston.

Chapter 14   Module 43: Figure 2: From Cacioppo, J. T., Berntson, G. G., & Crites, S. L., Jr. (1996). Social neuroscience: Principles of psychophysiological arousal and response. In E. T. Higgins & A. W. Kruglanski (Eds.), *Social Psychology: Handbook of Basic Principles.* © 1996 The Guilford Press. Reprinted by permission of the publisher. Figure 4: Adapted from Anderson, C. A., Krull, D. S., & Weiner, B. (1996). Explanations: Processes and consequences. In E. T. Higgins & A. W. Kruglanski (Eds.), *Social Psychology: Handbook of Basic Principles* (p. 274). © 1996 The Guilford Press. Reprinted by permission of the publisher. Module 46: Figure 2: From Sternberg, R. J. (1986). A triangular theory of love. *Psychological Review, 93,* 119–135. Published by The American Psychological Association, adapted with permission. Figure 3: From Buss, D. M., et al. (1990). International preferences in selecting mates: A study of 37 cultures. *Journal of Cross-Cultural Psychology, 21,* no. 1, 5–47, copyright © 1990 by SAGE Publications. Reprinted by permission of SAGE Publications. Figure 4: Excerpts from Table 1 "Aggression Questionnaire" (p. 41) from Benjamin, L. T., Jr. (1985). Defining aggression. An exercise for classroom discussion. *Teaching of Psychology, 12,* no. 1, pp. 40–42, copyright © 1985 Society for the Teaching of Psychology, reprinted by permission of SAGE Publications.

Photo Credits

Front Matter: p. xxxvi: © Comstock/PunchStock RF; p. xxxviii: © Stockbyte/Getty RF; p. xxxix: © Photodisc/PunchStock RF; p. xl: © Digital Vision/Getty RF; p. xli: © Fuse/Getty RF; p. xlii: © Stockbyte/Getty RF; p. xlv: © Stockbyte/PunchStock RF

Chapter 1   Opener: © Erik Dreyer/Getty; CO1.1: © Zigy Kaluzny/Getty RF; CO1.2: © Bettmann/Corbis; CO1.3: © Bill Aron/PhotoEdit; CO1.4 © Douglas Faulkner/Photo Researchers; Prologue p. 4: © Chip Somodevilla/Getty; Looking Ahead p. 4: © Erik Dreyer/Getty; p. 7 (top): © Jeff Greenberg/Photo Researchers; p. 7 (middle): © Chuck Keeler/Getty; p. 7 (bottom): © David Buffington/Getty RF; PsychWork p. 10: © Phanie Agency/Photo Researchers; p. 14: © Bettmann/Corbis; p. 16 Descartes: © SPL/Photo Researchers; p. 16 Locke: © Bettmann/Corbis; p. 16 James © Photo by Paul Thompson/FPG/Getty; p. 16 Calkins © Wellesley College Archives, Photographed by Notman; Pavlov p. 16: © Bettmann/Corbis; p. 17 Watson: © Culver Pictures; p. 17 Maslow © The Granger Collection; p. 17 Piaget: © Bettmann/Corbis; p. 17 Loftus: © Elizabeth Loftus; p. 18 Cognitive: © David Sanger/The Image Bank/Getty; p. 18 Behavioral: © Blend Images RF; p. 18 Humanistic: © White

Packer/The Image Bank/Getty; p. 18 (bottom): © Bettmann Corbis; p. 20: © AP Photo/Idaho Statesman/Darin Oswald; p. 21 Cognitive: © David Sanger/The Image Bank/Getty; p. 21 Behavioral: © Blend Images RF; p. 21 Humanistic: © White Packer/The Image Bank/Getty; p. 23: Attribution: modified from Shinji Nishimoto, An T. Vu, Thomas Naselaris, Yuval Benjamini, Bin Yu & Jack L. Gallant (2011). "Reconstructing dynamic visual experiences from brain activity evoked by natural movies" in *Current Biology;* p. 32: © Bill Aron/PhotoEdit; p. 30: © Robert I. M. Campbell/National Geographic Image Collection; p. 34: © J. Wilson/Woodfin Camp; p. 36 (top): © Bill Aron/PhotoEdit; 36 (bottom): © Marc Steinmetz/VISUM/The Image Works; p. 41: © Thomas Pflaum/Visum/The Image Works; p. 42 (top): Reprinted from *NeuroImage,* (Special Issue: Educational Neurosciences), Vol 57/, Yina Ma, et al., "Neural responses to perceived pain in others predict real-life monetary donations in different socioeconomic contexts", 1273–1280. Copyright 2011, with permission from Elsevier; p. 42 (bottom): © Douglas Faulkner/Photo Researchers; Looking Back p. 46: © Erik Dreyer/Getty; Vs Sum 1.1 p. 47: © Blend Images RF; Vs Sum 1.2 p. 47: © White Packer/The Image Bank/Getty; Vs Sum 1.3 p. 47: © Thomas Pflaum/Visum/The Image Works; Vs Sum 1.4 p. 47: © Douglas Faulkner/Photo Researchers

Chapter 2   Opener: © Lane Oatey/Blue Jean Images/Getty RF; CO2.1 © Dennis Kunkel/Visuals Unlimited; CO2.2 © Passieka/SPL/Photo Researchers; CO2.3 © Martin Rotker/Photo Researchers; p. 50: © Photo by George Napolitano/Film Magic/Getty; Looking Ahead p. 50: © Lane Oatey/Blue Jean Images/Getty RF; p. 52: © Dennis Kunkel/Visuals Unlimited; p. 57: © Michael Buckner/Getty Images for Michael J. Fox Foundation for Parkinson's Research; p. 66: © AP Images/Jeff Roberson; p. 68: © Martin Rotker/Photo Researchers; p. 69a: © SPL/Photo Researchers; p. 69b: © Volker Steger/Peter Arnold/Getty; p. 69c: © Roger Ressmeyer/Corbis; p. 69d: © Bryan Christie Design; p. 71: © Stephane de Sakutin/AFP/Getty; PsychWork p. 75: © AP Photo/Chris O'Meara; p. 76: © Natural History Museum London; p. 78: From Grefkes C., et al., "Cortical connectivity after subcortical stroke assessed with functional magnetic resonance imaging." in *Ann Neurology,* 2008 Feb; 63(2):236–46. Reprinted by permission of John Wiley & Sons; Looking Back p. 84: © Lane Oatey/Blue Jean Images/Getty RF; Vs Sum 2.1 p. 85: © Dennis Kunkel/Visuals Unlimited

Chapter 3   Opener: © ImageBazaar/Getty; CO3.1: © Digital Vision/Getty RF; CO3.2: © Joe Epstein Design ALConceptions; CO3.3: © Digital Vision/Getty RF; Looking Ahead p. 88: © ImageBazaar/Getty; p. 91: © Digital Vision/Getty RF; p. 92: © iStockphoto; p. 95 (left & right): © Biophoto Associates/Photo Researchers; p. 100: Shmuel, A., Chaimow, D., Raddatz, G., Ugerbil, K., Yacoub, E. (2010). "Mechanisms underlying decoding at 7T: Ocular dominance columns, broad structures, and macroscopic blood vessels in V1 convey information on the stimulated eye" in *NeuroImage,* 49, 1957–1964. © 2010 with permission from Elsevier; p. 101a-c: © Joe Epstein/Design Conceptions; p. 108 (top): © StockTrek/Getty RF; p. 108 (bottom): © Prof. P. Motta/Dept. of Anatomy/University "La Sapienza", Rome/SPL/Photo Researchers; p. 109: © Omikron/Photo Researchers; p. 112: © Liu Yang/Redlink/Corbis RF; p. 119: © Jeff Greenberg/Stock Boston; p. 120: © Cary Wolinsky/Stock Boston; p. 122: © Aaron Roeth Photography; p. 123: © John G. Ross/Photo Researchers; Look-

Name Index

Page numbers followed by *f* indicate figures.

A

Aaker, J. L., 444
Aaron, B., 422*f*
Aarts, H., 125
Aazh, H., 90
Abad, F., 277
Abbott, M., 558, 558*f*
Abboud, L., 511
Abdelnoor, M., 142
Abebe, E., 486
Abekawa, T., 517
Abel, J. R., 79
Abell, S. C., 294
Ablon, J. S., 498
Aboitiz, F., 263
Abraham, H. D., 162
Abraham, S., 483
Abramowitz, J. S., 468
Abrams, R. L., 125
Abramson, L. Y., 306, 308, 309, 474
Abramson, P. R., 306
Accardi, M., 113, 149
Acierno, R., 500
Ackerman, P. L., 268
Ackermann, K., 158
Acocella, J., 412*f*
Adams, G. G., 423
Adams, K. B., 376
Adams, L., 428
Adams, M., 198
Adams, M. J., 229*f*
Adarves-Yorno, I., 541
Addington, A., 80
Addus, A. A., 30
Adlam, A., 210*f*
Adler, A., 385, 392–393, 406*f*
Adolphs, R., 214
Adonu, J., 542
Adrien, J., 58, 473
Advokat, C., 515
Affeltranger, M. A., 114
Afrank, J., 349
Aftanas, L., 150
Agargum, M. Y., 140
Agid, O., 515
Aguilar-Gaxiola, S., 483
Ahiima, R. S., 300
Aichenbaum, S., 519
Aikawa, A., 552
Aiken, L. R., 276, 280, 377
Ainge, J., 122
Ainsworth, M., 346
Ajzen, I., 532
Akil, H., 424
Akins, S., 132, 154
Alberts, A., 364
Albrektsen, G., 431
Alexander, G. M., 516–517, 517
Alexander-Bloch, A., 80
Alexandersen, P., 65
Alexandre, C., 58, 473
Alfimova, M. V., 403
Alho, K., 107, 118–119
Ali, S. F., 155
Allen, H., 20
Allen, M., 253
Allen, R. J., 210
Allik, J., 397
Allison, D. B., 301
Allman, J. M., 120
Alloy, L. B., 412*f*
Allport, G. W., 223, 396, 406*f*
Allwood, M. A., 196

Aloia, M. S., 142
Alon, I., 151, 538
Alonso, J., 483
Alonso, L., 342
Alper, C. M., 425
Alpers, G., 187
Altman, L. K., 437
Alzheimer's Association, 375
Amano, K., 102
Amarel, D., 431
Amato, L., 161
American Psychological Association (APA), 9, 10*f*, 11, 40, 522
American Psychological Association Presidential Task Force on Evidence-Based Practice, 512–513
American Psychological Association Task Force on Intelligence, 282
Ames, M., 483
Amid, P. K., 113
Amodio, D. M., 534
Amsel, L., 24
Anastasi, A., 276
Ancoli-Israel, S., 141
Anderson, A., 214
Anderson, C. A., 137, 196, 536*f*, 560, 561
Anderson, J. A., 198
Anderson, J. R., 231
Anderson, N. D., 222
Anderson, S. W., 54, 76
Andersson, G., 511
Andews, B., 310
Andrasik, F., 82, 425
Andreasen, N. C, 477*f*
Andrew, M., 430
Andrews, F. M., 446*f*
Andrews, K., 313
Anestis, J. C., 498
Anestis, M. D., 498
Ang, L., 155
Angelopoulos, N., 66
Angermeyer, M. C., 483
Angleitner, A., 558, 558*f*
Anisman, H., 423
Anker, A. E., 27
Ansaldo, A. I., 79
Antonini, A., 58
Antonioni, D., 545
Antony, M. M., 463
Aoki, Y., 442–443
Apanovich, A. M., 444
Apfel, N., 553
Aponte, J. F., 513
Arafat, I., 305
Arasteh, K., 156
Arbuthnott, A., 443–444
Arcelus, J., 301
Archer, J., 412
Archer, T., 430
Arena, J. M., 306
Arenas, E., 77
Arevalo, J. M., 430
Argibay, J. C., 126
Arguin, M., 79
Arias, V., 142
Ariely, D., 538
Arimoto, M., 142
Aristotle, 169
Arito, H., 143
Ariyanto, A., 529
Armbruster, D., 334
Armenta, B. E., 549
Armstrong, R. D., 277
Arndt, L., 296, 301
Arndt, J. T., 142

Arnett, J. J., 41, 368, 369*f*
Arnulf, I., 135
Aronson, J., 553
Arps, K., 545
Arseneault, L., 331
Asch, S. E., 541
Aschheim, K., 334
Asendorpf, J., 552
Ashtari, M., 467, 467*f*
Askenasy, J. J. M., 141
Aspinwall, L. G., 432
Assanand, S., 291
Atbaşoğlu, C., 250
Atkinson, H. G., 442, 443
Atkinson, R. C., 205–206, 206*f*
Attia, E., 516
Auer, D. P., 140
Aujoulat, I., 430
Auld, F., 496
Aussilloux, C., 278
Avery, D., 549
Awad, A. G., 516

B

Baars, B., 132
Babson, K. A., 137
Bacchiochi, J. R., 411
Bachman, J. G., 152, 153*f*, 156, 161, 161*f*, 438, 438*f*
Baddeley, A., 210*f*
Baddeley, A. D., 207, 210
Badke, M. B., 82
Baer, J., 255
Bagby, R. M., 435
Bagdadli, A., 278
Bagge, C., 365
Bagnall, D., 113
Bagwell, D. K., 375
Bahl, A., 521
Bahrick, H. P., 225*f*
Bai, L., 347
Bailey, J. M., 307
Bailey, K., 196
Baillargeon, R., 355
Bains, O. S., 141
Bakay, R., 77
Baker, J., 428
Baker, S., 244
Baker, S. A., 264
Baker, S. E., 175
Balaban, C. D., 114, 467
Baldwin, C. K., 428
Baler, R. D., 152
Balkin, T. J., 140
Ball, D., 57
Ball, H., 330
Ball, L. J., 255
Ballesteros, S., 109
Balsen, Z., 109
Baltes, P. B., 371
Baltuch, G. H., 520
Banaji, M. R., 220, 552
Bancroft, J., 474
Bandura, A., 194, 194*f*, 195, 399, 400, 406*f*, 501
Banich, T., 79
Banihashemi, L., 317
Banks, J. A., 553
Bao, G., 142
Baraas, R. C., 206
Barabasz, A., 148
Barber, T. X., 113
Barbui, C., 517
Bard, P., 317–318
Barefoot, J. C., 435
Bargh, J. A., 534

Barkana, Y., 137
Barke, D. B., 423
Barker, J., 149
Barkley, R. A., 480
Barlaug, D., 430
Barlow, D. H., 463, 501
Barmeyer, C. I., 197
Barnes, B., 530
Barnes, M. L., 558
Barnes, V. A., 149
Barnett, J. E., 40–41
Barnett, S. M., 281
Baron, E. D., 521
Baron, J., 347
Baron, R. S., 543
Barone, P., 58
Baronio, P., 51
Barr, V., 486
Barrachina, J., 501
Barrada, J., 277
Barresi, J., 132
Barrett, D., 138
Barrett, L., 23
Barrett, L. F., 272, 314
Barrett, S., 182
Barrios, F. A., 80
Barron, F., 254
Barron, G., 561
Barrowclough, C., 478
Barson, J. R., 299
Bartecchi, C. E., 439
Bartholow, B. D., 196, 561
Bartlett, F., 223
Bartlett, M. Y., 562
Bartocci, G., 150
Barton, J., 194
Bartone, P., 430
Bartoshuk, L., 110*f*
Bartoshuk, L. M., 109
Bartzokis, G., 477
Baruss, I., 142, 162
Bassett, A. S., 476
Bassotti, G., 51
Bateman, A. W., 479
Bates, B. L., 149
Bates, J., 149
Bates, P. E., 278
Bates, R., 556
Bates, T., 445–446
Batson, C. D., 562
Bauer, I., 376
Bauer, J. J., 293, 475
Bauer, M., 471
Bauer, P., 211
Baum, A., 427, 427*f*
Baum, M. J., 60
Bauman, S., 406
Baumeister, R. F., 305, 541
Baumgartner, F., 430
Baumrind, D., 348–349, 349*f*
Baumrucker, S. J., 161–162
Bautista, V., 195
Bayley, P. J., 215
Baylis, F., 78
Bayliss, D. M., 210, 355
Bayne, R., 392
Bazalakova, M. H., 57
Beach, S. R., 137
Beaman, A. L., 545
Bearman, C. R., 255
Beaton, R. J., 206
Beattie, M., 158
Beatty, D. J., 399
Beatty, J., 50
Beatty, W. W., 270
Beauchamp, M. R., 399
Bechara, A., 76, 404*f*
Beck, A. P., 509

Beck, A. T., 466, 466*f*, 473, 503, 504, 512
Beck, H. P., 172
Becker, B. E., 349, 358
Becker, T., 271
Beckham, J. C., 173
Beckmann, H., 476
Beckmann, S. C., 249
Bedard, W. W., 73
Beek, P. J., 75
Beersma, D. G. M., 143
Beesdo, K., 465
Begg, D., 290
Beghetto, R. A., 255
Begley, S., 77, 221
Behar, L., 37
Behbehani, J., 138
Behr, S. E., 220
Behrendt, R., 187
Behrens, M., 376
Beidel, D. C., 464, 467
Beilock, S. L., 210
Bekkering, H., 121–122
Belar, C., 8
Bell, L. A., 198
Bell, M., 355
Bell, R. A., 442
Bell, R. L., 174
Belli, R. F., 223
Belmaker, R. H., 404
Belov, D. I., 277
Belsky, J., 329, 348
Bem, D. J., 126, 308
Benac, N., 298
Benca, R. M., 145
Benderly, B. L., 271
Benet-Martinez, V., 264
Benham, G., 147
Benight, C. C., 422
Benjamin, E. J., 435
Benjamin, J., 404
Benjamin, L. T., Jr., 559*f*
Bennett, E. S., 225
Benoit, C., 66
Ben-Porath, Y. S., 411, 412
Bensing, J. M., 432
Benson, E., 305
Benson, H., 150, 499*f*
Benson, J. E., 395
Bentall, R. P., 474
Benton, S. A., 483, 484*f*, 520
Benton, S. L., 483, 484*f*, 520
Bentwich, J., 519
Beraldi, A., 470
Berdoy, M., 175
Berenbaum, H., 428
Berenson, L., 384, 416
Beresnevaité, M., 435
Bergen, L., 32
Berger, M., 509
Berger, S. A., 225*f*
Bergman, J. Z., 20
Bergman, S. M., 20
Berk, L. E., 349
Berkman, L. F., 376
Berkoff, M., 182
Berkowitz, L., 560, 561
Berle, D., 465, 500
Berman, A. L., 494
Berman, H., 370
Bernal, G., 11
Bernard, L. L., 289
Bernardi, S., 70
Bernier, M., 242
Bernstein, D., 225
Bernstein, D. M., 20
Bernstein, E., 564
Bernston, G. G., 319
Berntsen, D., 221, 226

Berntson, G. G., 531, 531f
Berridge, K. C., 291
Berrios, G. E., 455
Berry, D. C., 220, 555
Bertakis, K., 442–443
Berthoud, H. R., 290, 299
Betz, N., 399
Beutler, L. E., 512
Beyene, Y., 370
Bhamik, D. K., 517
Bhar, S., 504
Bhugra, D., 517
Bialystok, E., 264
Bianchi, R. A., 553
Bianchi, S. M., 364
Biemond, R., 498
Biener, L., 438
Bierut, L. J., 158, 160
Biesanz, J. C., 535
Bijlani, R. L., 150
Billiard, M., 142
Billy, B. D., 137
Bindemann, M., 99
Binder, J. L., 512
Bindman, A., 442
Binet, A., 272f, 272–273
Binetti, R., 158
Bingenheimer, J. B., 196
Birbaumer, N., 71
Bischoff, R. J., 510
Bishara, A. J., 230
Bishop, M., 420, 428
Biswas-Diener, R., 445
Bitterman, M. E., 171
Bittles, A. H., 278
Bizley, J., 76
Bjerknes, T., 122
Bjorklund, D. F., 9, 224
Bjornstad, R., 430, 473
Black, A. L., 446
Black, D., 515
Black, J., 142
Blagrove, M., 162
Blair, C. A., 561
Blakely, R. D., 57
Blakes, L., 132, 164
Blakeslee, S., 77
Blanco, D., 107
Blass, T., 547
Blatter, K., 143
Bleichhardt, G., 468
Blier, P., 56
Bliss, J. M., 435
Blixen, C. E., 297
Blomeyer, D., 160
Bloom, F., 72f
Bloom, P., 355
Bloom, P. N., 545
Bloom, S. R., 298–299
Blum, D., 346
Blum, H. P., 496
Blumenfeld, W. J., 198
Blumenthal, H., 360
Boahen, K., 51, 60
Boake, C., 9
Bock, K., 257
Bode, C., 432
Boden, J. M., 365
Bodendorf, M., 422
Bodin, G., 496
Boehm, K. E., 365f
Boeve-de Pauw, J., 364
Bogart, R. K., 113
Bogenschutz, M. P., 510
Bohart, A. C., 508, 513
Bohn, A., 221
Boichot, C., 69
Boileau, I., 155
Boisvert, C. M., 512
Boivin, M., 301
Bojhd, F., 556
Boles, D. B., 79
Bolger, N., 431
Boller, F., 74
Bolster, R. B., 69
Bonanni, R., 211
Bonanno, G. A., 422, 430
Bond, J. C., 153
Bond, M., 498
Bond, M. H., 400

Bonello, R. P., 113
Bonezzi, A., 89
Bonito, J. A., 555
Bonke, B., 220
Bonnardel, V., 100
Bonnet, C., 69
Bonnie, R. J., 454
Bookheimer, S. Y., 551, 551f
Borbély, A., 136f
Borden, V. M. H., 11
Borges, G., 483
Borisenko, J., 347
Borkan, J. M., 443
Borlido, C., 515
Born, J., 141, 423
Bornstein, M. H., 347
Bornstein, R. F., 456
Bosma, H. A., 362–363, 374, 376
Bosse, T., 249
Botvinick, M., 475
Bouchard, T. J., Jr., 402, 402f, 404
Bouchard, T. R., 267
Boulenger, J. P., 162
Bourne, L. E., 247f, 248f, 250
Bouton, M. E., 175
Bowden, E. M., 144
Bower, C., 278
Bower, G. H., 230
Bower, J. E., 427, 445
Bowers, J., 29
Bowie, C., 477
Boxer, P., 194, 196
Boycott, R., 328
Boyd, J., 119
Boyd-Wilson, B. M., 445
Boyle, S. H., 435
Boyne, P., 82
Brackel, H. J. L., 441
Bradley, M. M., 465
Bradshaw, J. W. S., 182
Braff, D. L., 478
Braffman, W., 147
Brafman, A. H., 497
Braine, N., 154
Brambilla, P., 517
Brandon, M., 121–122
Brang, D., 114
Branigan, C., 314
Brantley, P. J., 431
Brasic, J. R., 468
Brass, J., 267
Braun, A. R., 140
Brausch, A. M., 364
Brazelton, T. B., 340
Brazzini-Poisson, V., 137
Breese, G., 57
Bregman, M. R., 257
Breland, K., 187
Breland, M., 187
Brendgen, M., 331
Brendl, C., 89
Brennan, P., 109
Brennan, R. T., 196, 438
Brennen, T., 218
Breshears, J., 71
Bresler, C., 316
Breslin, C. W., 223, 223f
Brett, J. M., 151, 538
Brewer, J. B., 215
Brewer, M., 542
Brewer, R. D., 158
Brewis, A., 298
Bridges, M. W., 410f
Brief, A. P., 556
Bright, P., 232
Brinkhaus, B., 112
Brinton, B., 315
Brislin, R., 267
Brock, T. C., 529
Brodhead, J., 152
Brody, J., 438
Broeders, R., 562–563
Broidy, L. M., 480
Broman, C. L., 427
Bromet, E. J., 483
Bronson, P., 550
Brooker, R. J., 81f, 105f
Broome, K. M., 161
Brossart, D. F., 522

Brown, B. L., 516
Brown, C. H., 517
Brown, E., 439
Brown, J., 536
Brown, L. S., 225
Brown, P. K., 101
Brown, R., 211
Brown, R. J., 470
Brown, S., 74, 76
Brown, T. A., 463
Brown, T. M., 112
Browne, K. D., 258
Brownlee, K., 512–513
Bruce, V., 100
Bruehl, S., 564
Bruggeman, H., 120
Brule, D., 20
Brumbach, B. H., 8–9
Brummett, B. H., 435
Brunet, A., 518
Brunetti, E., 263
Bryan, A., 403
Bryan, J., 234
Bryant, R. A., 24, 138
Bryant, R. M., 11
Brydon, L., 424
Brymer, M. J., 422
Brynhildsen, J., 370
Brzustowicz, L. M., 476
Bschor, T., 445
Bucci, S., 475
Buchanan, R. W., 476
Buchanan, T., 399
Buchanan, T. W., 214
Buchert, R., 162
Buck, L. B., 225
Buckman, J., 232
Buckner, R., 136, 141
Buehner, M., 268
Buerkle, C., 305
Bukobza, G., 368
Bulf, H., 342
Bulgrin, A., 530
Bulik, C. M., 301
Bullock, D., 75
Bunge, S. A., 23
Bunting, M., 230
Burbach, M. E., 255
Burchfiel, C., 430
Burchinal, M. R., 348
Burdick, K. E., 467, 467f
Burger, J. M., 545, 547
Burgoon, J. K., 555
Burhans, L. B., 173
Burke, M. V., 437
Burns, C. W., 99
Burns, J. W., 564
Burns, N. R., 234
Burrows, A., 27
Burt, D. M., 556
Burton, A., 99
Burton, K. S., 268
Busatto, G. F. de Mathis, 520
Busey, T. A., 20
Bush, J., 500
Bushman, B. J., 196, 560
Bushnell, M. C., 112
Buss, D. M., 8–9, 397, 402,
    558, 558f
Bussey, T. J., 57
Butcher, J. N., 411, 412
Butler, J., 97f
Butler, L. D., 436
Butler, L. T., 220, 555
Butler, M. A., 174
Butt, S., 538
Buysse, D. J., 137
Byne, W., 307
Byrne-Davis, L., 420

C

Cabanac, M., 299
Cabioglu, M., 112
Cacioppo, J. T., 23, 50, 79, 530,
    531, 531f, 551
Cadenhead, K., 478
Caelian, C. F., 365
Cahill, L., 80, 234

Cai, R., 479
Cain, D. J., 406, 507
Cain, M. E., 43
Cairns, R., 161–162
Cajochen, C., 143
Cakir, T., 113
Cal, C. S., 436
Caldwell, D. F., 545
Calin-Jageman, R. J., 92
Calkins, M., 15, 16f
Callen, F., 162
Caltagirone, C., 211
Calvalupo, C., 78
Cameron, C. L., 428
Cameron, H., 77
Cameron, O. G., 317
Campbell, D. T., 123
Campbell, N. B., 365f
Campbell, P., 216
Campbell, W., 486, 537–538
Campins, M., 501
Campos, R. C., 413
Canetti-Nisim, D., 24
Cannon, T. D., 82, 255
Cannon, W., 317–318
Cantalupo, C., 78
Canteras, M. M., 520
Canto, C., 122
Cantwell, R. H., 310
Caplan, D., 76–77
Caplan, L., 214
Capone, N. C., 331
Caprara, G., 397
Carbon, C., 92
Cardena, E., 148
Carels, R. A., 189
Carey, B., 210, 429, 452, 520
Carhart-Harris, R., 155
Carlesimo, G., 211
Carlin, A., 37
Carlsmith, J. M., 533
Carlson, M., 561
Carnagey, N., 196, 561
Carney, D., 535
Carney, R. N., 209, 234
Carnochan, P., 315f
Carpenter, L., 178
Carpenter, S., 41
Carpenter, S. K., 228
Carr, T. H., 210
Carrera, M., 465
Carrillo, M., 58
Carroll, L., 257
Carson, R. E., 140
Carter, G. T., 161–162
Carter, J., 516
Carter, R. T., 264
Cartwright, R., 50, 140
Caruso, D. R., 271
Caruso, E., 245
Carvalho, J., 305
Carver, C. S., 410f
Casasanto, D., 261
Casasola, M., 355
Case, R., 355
Case, T. I., 108
Casey, S. D., 182
Cashon, C. H., 344, 355
Casper, L. M., 364
Caspi, A., 9, 331, 404
Caspi, R., 404
Cassells, J. V. S., 391
Cassidy, K. W., 347
Cassin, B., 156
Castaneda, C. R., 198
Castellani, E., 99
Castelli, L., 220
Castro, J., 397
Castro-Caldas, A., 80
Catalisano, D., 499
Catell, H. E. P., 396
Cattell, A. K., 396
Cattell, R. B., 396, 406f
Cauce, A. M., 522
Cavallini, E., 374
Cavenett, T., 291
Cebriã, A., 501
Ceccanti, M., 158
Ceci, S. J., 224
Center for Science in the
    Public Interest, 154f

Centers for Disease Control
    and Prevention (CDC),
    364–365
Ceponiene, R., 213
Cerutti, D. T., 182
Chaimow, D., 100f
Chamberlain, K., 423, 424f
Chamberlain, R., 158
Chamberlain, S. R., 467
Chambless, D. L., 513
Chan, A., 142
Chan, K. K., 532
Chandler, D. R., 11
Chandran, S., 248
Chang, J., 24, 182
Chao, R., 428
Chapkis, W., 161–162
Chapman, J., 543
Chapman, J. P., 475
Chapman, L. J., 475
Charles, A., 137
Charles, L., 430
Charmak, W. D., 112
Charman, D. P., 497
Charnley, J. L., 173
Chartrand, T. L., 125, 534
Chaudhry, H. R., 446
Chauhan, R. V., 513
Chavez, P. R., 158
Cheakalos, C., 296
Chebrolu, J., 80
Cheer, J. F., 179
Chen, D. C., 30, 109, 113
Chen, E., 424
Chen, G., 436
Chen, J., 469
Chen, K., 530
Chen, T. H., 107
Chen, W. T., 80
Chen, Z., 479
Cheney, C. D., 443–444
Cheng, C., 432
Cheng, S., 400
Chenu, F., 56
Cherek, D. R., 161
Cheston, S. E., 513
Cheung, M. L., 432
Chiang, W. C., 355
Chincotta, D., 210f
Chivers, M. L., 305
Cho, A., 105
Cho, S., 82, 255
Chodorow, M., 230
Chomsky, N., 259, 260, 260f
Chong, C., 182
Chou, K., 430
Chou, S., 398
Chou, T. C., 143
Chow, E. W. C., 476
Choy, Y., 499
Christ, S. E., 336
Christakis, N. A., 438
Christian, C. J., 467, 467f
Christiansen, C., 65
Christmas, D., 520
Christodoulou, J., 268
Chrysikou, E. G., 249
Chu, D. Z. J., 113
Chu, R-L., 538, 539
Chuang, S., 364
Chung, C., 456, 473
Chylinska, J., 428
Cialdini, R. B., 529, 545
Cicchetti, D., 349
Çiçek, M., 250
Cieciuch, J., 397
Cipriani, A., 517
Cipriano, E. A., 318
Clair, J. M., 444
Clark, D., 111–112
Clark, D. A., 457, 466, 468
Clark, D. B., 159
Clark, D. M., 509
Clark, J., 508
Clark, L. A., 459
Clark, L. V., 354
Clark, M. P., 15
Clark, M. S., 537
Clark, R. E., 215

Clarke-Stewart, K., 349
Clarkin, J. F., 479
Clasen, L., 80
Clausen, M., 162
Claybourn, M., 435
Clayton, K., 155
Clément-Guillotin, C., 364
Clements, A. M., 79
Clementz, B., 537–538
Clerici, C., 51
Clifasefi, S., 225
Clifford, C. W. G., 98
Clifton, D., 446
Clinton, B., 534
Clore, G. L., 562–563
Cloud, J., 162
Coan, J. A., 431, 431f
Coates, S. L., 220
Cobos, P., 316
Cochran, S. D., 309
Coderre, T. J., 110
Coffman, S. J., 512
Cohen, A., 521
Cohen, A. L., 374
Cohen, B. H., 37
Cohen, G. L., 553
Cohen, J., 38
Cohen, L. B., 344, 355
Cohen, P., 161–162, 487
Cohen, S., 425, 425f, 431
Cole, D. A., 480
Cole, S. W., 430
Coleman, E., 305
Coleman, G., 135
Coleman, J., 359
Coleman, M., 372
Coles, R., 361
Colland, V. T., 441
Collins, A. M., 213, 213f
Collins, C. A., 428
Collins, L. M., 360
Colom, R., 267
Colombi, A., 20
Coltheart, M., 475
Coltraine, S., 550
Colvin, C., 535
Colwell, M. J., 347
Committeri, G., 194
Compagni, A., 50
Comuzzie, A. G., 301
Condray, D. S., 511
Conduit, R., 135
Cone-Wesson, B., 107
Conner, M., 532
Connolly, A. C., 242
Conoley, C. W., 522
Conover, K., 179
Convento, M. J., 140
Conway, M. A., 220, 226
Conway, T. L., 438
Cook, T., 149
Cooke, J. R., 141
Cooklin, A., 510
Coolidge, F. L., 392
Cooper, H., 37
Cooper, J., 509, 533
Cooper, M., 508, 528
Cooper, Z., 302–303
Cooper-Brown, L. J., 182
Copeland, J. B., 245
Coplan, J. D., 467
Coplan, R., 349
Coppersmith, G., 58
Cordnoldi, C., 225
Coren, S., 92, 118f, 121, 123f
Cork, R. C., 220
Corn, B., 436
Cornelius, M. D., 161
Cornell, C. B., 273
Cornier, M., 299
Corp, E. S., 297
Corpus, J. H., 292
Corr, P. J., 182
Corrigan, P. W., 474
Corsello, A., 223
Cosmides, L., 187
Cossette, M. P., 179
Costa, P. T., Jr., 397f, 479, 542
Costa, R., 349
Côté, J. E., 368

Cotton, P., 486
Cotton, W. L., 305
Couey, J., 122
Coulson, S., 114
Courteau, J., 437
Courturier, J., 302
Coventry, K. R., 246
Cowan, C. W., 56
Cowan, N., 208, 355
Cowley, B. J., 145
Cowley, G., 232, 421
Cox, J., 289
Cox, R., 175
Coyle, N., 378
Coyle, T. R., 276
Coyne, J. C., 424f
Craighero, L., 341
Craik, F. I. M., 219, 220, 222, 264
Cramer, A., 349
Cramer, D., 28
Cramer, P., 389
Crandall, C. S., 356
Crawley, J. N., 467
Cray, J., 27
Creasey, G. L., 331
Creel, S. C., 257
Crews, F., 390
Crewther, S. G., 135
Criswell, H., 57
Critchfield, T., 180
Crites, S. L., Jr., 531, 531f
Crits-Christoph, P., 513, 523
Crittenden, R., 140
Crocker, J., 460
Crockett, E., 556–557
Croissant, B., 158
Crombag, H. S., 152
Cropley, A., 254
Crosnoe, R., 377
Crowder, R. G., 206
Crucian, G., 213
Crum, A. J., 44, 58
Crump, J., 392
Cueto, S., 403
Cui, L., 483
Cuijpers, P., 23, 511
Culbert, K., 302
Culhane-Pera, K. A., 443
Cullinane, C. A., 113
Cumberland, A., 562
Cummings, A., 213
Cunningham, P., 355
Curran, A., 271
Curran, M., 516
Cutting, J. C., 257
Cwikel, J., 37
Czajkowski, N., 111–112
Czisch, M., 140
Czopp, A. M., 553

D

Daddis, C., 364
Dadds, M., 64–65
Daftary, F., 226
D'Agostino, R. B., Sr., 435
Dai, D. Y., 531
Daines, B., 307
Dalai Lama, 268
Dalal, A. K., 420
Dale, A., 30
D'Alessandro, L., 99
Daley, E. M., 30
Dalgleish, T., 210
Damasio, A. R., 76
Damasio, H., 76
Damaske, S., 372
Damon, W., 361
Danaei, G., 436
D'Angelo, V., 499
Dani, J. A., 437
Daniels, K. A., 220
Danner, D., 276
Danoff-Burg, S., 428
Dante, 232–233
Dao, J., 494
Darby, L. A., 189
D'Arcy, R. C. N., 69
Dare, J. S., 370

Dark-Freudeman, A., 375
Darley, J. M., 27–29, 33–37, 40, 41, 562
Darling, J., 110
Darroch, J. E., 306
Darwin, C., 8
Darwin, C. J., 206
Das, A., 305
Dasborough, M. T., 536
Daskalakis, Z., 70
Date, I. I., 77
d'Athis, P., 69
Daum, I., 214
David, D., 504
Davidson, J., 435
Davidson, J. E., 317
Davidson, R. J., 50, 79, 431, 431f
Davies, I., 342
Davies, S., 415, 467
Daviglus, M. L., 435
Davis, D. D., 504
Davis, H. C., 149
Davis, J., 321
Davis, K., 268
Davis, L. J., 409
Davis, O., 330
Davis, R. D., 479, 480
Davis, R. L., 105
Davis, S. R, 187
Davoili, M., 161
Davydow, D. S., 330
Dawson, D. A., 398
Day, A. L., 431
Day, N. L., 161
Day, R. D., 347
Dayan, P., 186
Dayas, C. V., 173
Deacon, B. J., 468
Deák, G. O., 54
Dean, C., 55–56
Dean-Borenstein, M. T., 424
Deanfield, J., 424
DeAngelis, D., 9
De Angelis, M., 89
Dear, K., 486
Dearing, E., 348
Deary, I. J., 270, 374
Deater-Deckard, K., 331, 349
De Beni, R., 225, 241
DeBoeck, P., 310
DeBord, K. A., 309
DeCasper, A. J., 335
Deccache, A., 430
DeCesare, K., 545
Decety, J., 23, 563f
Deci, E. L., 185, 294
Decker, S., 562
Dede, G., 76–77
De Dreu, C. W., 64–65
Dedrick, D., 141
DeFrain, J., 371, 372
De Gelder, B., 88, 99
deGroot, A. D., 208f
Deisseroth, K., 70
De la Casa, L. G., 174
DeLamater, J. D., 374
del Campo, N., 467
Delgado, M. R., 499
Del Giudice, M., 335
Delinsky, S. S., 189
DeLoache, J., 187
del Rosal, E., 342
Demaree, H. A., 435
Dement, W. C., 140
DeMichael, T., 81–82
Dempster, F. N., 355f
Denke, C., 113
Denmark, G. L., 15
Dennett, D. C., 23
Dennis, I., 537
Dennis, S., 437
Dennis, T. A., 350
Denollet, J., 435
Denteneer, A., 441
d'Entremont, M. L., 349
Deouell, L. Y., 206
Der, G., 270
Deregowski, J. B., 124
Deremaux, S., 242
de Ridder, D. T., 432

Deri-Hasid, R., 441
Derryberry, W. P., 391
DeRubeis, R., 504, 520
Descartes, R., 14, 16f
Deshields, T., 430
Deshpande, S. N., 475
deSilva, P., 465
Des Jarlais, D. C., 154
Desmet, M., 473
Desmond, J. E., 215
Desruisseau, D. M., 142
Dessing, J. C., 75
DeSteno, D., 562
Detterman, D. K., 244, 277–278
Devonport, J. J., 399
Devor, M., 135
Dewey, J., 15
Dhar, R., 250
Dhillon, S., 516
Diamond, M., 309
Dias, A. M., 82
Diaz, A., 355
Díaz, E., 174
Díaz, J., 80
Dickerman, V., 508
Dickinson, D. L., 533
Diehl, A., 158
Diemand-Yauman, C., 231
Diener, E., 444–446
Diener, M., 347
Diesendruck, G., 264
Di Fabio, A., 268
Di Forti, M., 58
DiFranza, J. R., 437
DiGiovanna, A. G., 369
DiGirolamo, G. J., 50
DiGrande, L., 423
Dijk, D., 290
Dijksterhuis, A., 125
Dillard, J. P., 314
Dillon, J., 19
DiLorenzo, P. M., 109
Dimidjian, S., 512
Dinges, D. F., 149
Dingelder, S., 398
Dinse, H., 75
Dionne, R., 111–112
Dittrich, W. H., 467
Dityē, T., 92
Dixon, R. A., 374, 375
Dizon-Reynante, C., 221
Djapo, N., 396
Djokic, R., 396
Do, V. T., 550
Dobbins, A. C., 120
Dobbins, I. G., 220
Dobronevsky, E., 519
Dodge, K. A., 330
D'Odorico, L., 258
Dohnke, B., 438
Doi, T., 390
Dolan, R. J., 319, 319f
Dolan, S. L., 511
Dolan-Pascoe, B., 400
Dolbier, C. L., 421
Dolinski, D., 545
Doll, H. A., 474
Dollar, J. M., 318
Dollinger, S. J., 531
Domhoff, G. W., 138, 139f, 144
Dominowski, R. L., 247f, 248f
Donahoe, J. W., 187
Donald, A., 424
Donche, V., 364
Donnellan, M., 480
Donnerstein, E., 196
Donoghue, J. P., 71
Dording, C., 517
Dortch, S., 152
Dostrovsky, J., 122
Doty, R. L., 109
Dougall, A. L., 427
Douglas, O., 268
Douglas Brown, R., 224
Dovidio, J. F., 549, 550, 553, 562
Dowd, S., 70
Dowdall, G. W., 158
Dowling, N., 499

Downey, J. E., 15
Doyle, R., 521f
Doyle, W. J., 425
Dozois, D., 468
Drachman, D., 498
Drago, V., 213
Draguns, J. G., 389, 513
Drain, T., 181
Draine, S. C., 125
Dresbach, Tr., 55–56
Drewes, A. A., 347
Drews, F. A., 210
Driscoll, D., 54
Driver, J., 99, 114
Drob, S., 391
Dryden, W., 504
Duberstein, P. R., 520
Dubinsky, A. J., 537
Dubow, E. F., 194
Ducharme, J. M., 181
Dudai, Y., 214
Dudek-Singer, J., 501, 561
Dugas, C., 50
Duke, M., 479
Dumont, D., 521
Dumont, M., 521
Dunbar, N. E., 555
Duncker, K., 251
Dunlop, W. L., 399
Dunn, W. J., 113
Dunner, D. L., 517
Dunning, K., 82
Duntley, S. P., 142
Durán, M., 357
Dürr-Pal, N., 162
Dworkin, R. H., 476
Dybdahl, R., 218
Dysart, J., 223

E

Eaker, E. D., 435
Earls, E. J., 196
Ebbinghaus, H., 15, 228, 229f
Eberhard, J., 515
Eberhard, K. M., 257
Ebstein, R. P., 403, 404
Ebster, C., 545
Ecenbarger, W., 439
Echemendia, R., 409
Eckardt, M. H., 392
Eckersley, R., 486
Eden, J., 543
Edinger, J. D., 500
Edison, T., 248
Edoka, I. P., 471
Edwards, C. C., 438
Eftimiades, M., 562
Egan, J., 384
Egan, K., 355
Eggum, N. D., 562
Egliston, K., 501
Ehlers, C. L., 159, 160
Ehlert, U., 427
Ehrenfeld, T., 55
Ehlert, U., 427
Eimer, B. N., 149
Ein-Dor, T. T., 423
Einstein, A., 254, 330
Einstein, G. O., 234
Eisch, A., 77
Eisenberg, M., 480
Eisenberg, N., 562
Eisenberger, N. I., 551, 551f
Ekeland, T. J., 406
Ekelund, J., 403
Ekman, P., 315, 320–322
Ekroll, V., 121–122
Ekstsrom, R. D., 143
Elder, G. H., Jr., 377
Elfhag, K., 300
El-Hai, J., 519
Elhers, W., 389
Eliot, T. S., 269f
Eljamel, M. S., 520
el-Kaliouby, R., 321
Elkind, D., 364, 406
Elkins, G., 149
Ellason, J. W., 469
Ellins, E., 424

Elliot, A. J., 310
Elliott, A., 456
Elliott, J., 370
Elliott, M., 431
Ellis, A., 503, 504, 564
Ellis, B. J., 9
El-Mallakh, R. S., 162
Elston, R. C., 436
El Tom, S., 75
Emery, G., 466, 466f
Emick, J., 246
Emmelkamp, P. M. G., 498, 500
Encinas, J., 77
Endres, T., 187
Engel, R., 470
Engen, T., 108
Engle, R. W., 210, 268
Engler, J., 488
Entz, L., 141
Enzinger, C. C., 69
Epley, N., 125
Epstein, R., 442–443
Epstein, W., 98
Eranti, S. V., 519
Ergene, N., 112
Erickson, R., 109
Eriksen, M., 439
Erikson, E. H., 350–352, 362f,
    362–363, 393
Erkens, J. A., 517
Eröss, L., 141
Ertel, K. A., 376
Ertel, S., 126
Ervik, S., 142
Eslick, G. D., 465
Espelage, D. L., 308
Essau, C. A., 473
Essén, B., 370
Estey, A. J., 392
Evans, A. M., 497
Evans, D. E., 403
Evatt, D. P., 437
Everette, M., 337
Everhart, D. E., 435
Everly, G. S., Jr., 457
Eynan, R., 480
Eysenck, H. J., 396, 396f,
    406f, 511
Ezzati, M., 436

F

Fabo, D., 141
Fabri, M., 80
Fagan, J., 373
Fagan, J. F., 280, 282
Fagen, J., 108
Faggiano, F., 161
Fagiolini, A., 517
Fairchild, H. H., 196
Fairhall, A., 92
Fako, I., 396
Falcone, G., 519
Falcon-Eicher, S., 69
Fallon, A., 40–41
Fan, M. Y., 430
Fanselow, M. S., 55–56
Faraci, P., 499
Farah, M. J., 216
Farell, B., 99
Farinelli, L., 27
Fast, K., 109
Faust, D., 512
Faustisne, L., 334
Fazekas, F. F., 69
Fazel, M., 430
Fearing, V. G., 508
Fedeli, A., 299
Federer, S., 535–536
Fee, E., 112
Feeley, T., 27
Feeney, B. C., 537
Feiler, H. S., 160
Fein, S., 430, 432
Fekedulegn, D., 430
Feldman, D. H., 102
Feldman, R. S., 234
Feldner, M., 137

Feldt, L. S., 276
Felix, D. S., 510
Feltmate, S. E., 375
Fendt, M., 187
Feng, B., 442
Fenter, V. L., 517
Fenwick, P. B. C., 82
Ferguson, C. J., 196
Ferguson, M., 454
Fergusson, D. M., 365
Fernandez, L. C., 15
Fernandez, M., 240, 284
Fernando, M. L. D., 516
Ferraro, R. F., 220
Ferri, M., 161
Feshback, N. D., 196
Festinger, D., 291
Festinger, L., 17f, 532, 533
Fichtenberg, C. M., 438
Field, B., 424
Field, T., 342f
Fields, C., 250
Fields-Meyer, T., 358
Figen, A., 430
Figueiredo, B., 349
Fillingim, R. B., 291
Finan, P. H., 421
Finch, A. J., Jr., 564
Fine, L., 248
Fine, R., 248
Fineberg, N. A., 467
Fingelkurts, A. A., 148
Fink, A., 270
Fink, G., 519
Fink, G. R., 54, 78f, 194
Finkelstein, M., 292
Finkelstein, Y., 337
Finkler, K., 151
Finlay, F. O., 359
Finley, C. L., 145
Finn, A., 391
Fiore, M. C., 436
Firestein, B. A., 307
First, M. B., 459
Fischer, A. H., 314, 319
Fischer, J., 555
Fischer, K. W., 315f
Fischer, T. M., 92
Fischler, C., 299
Fischler, G., 411
Fiser, J., 120
Fish, M. C., 308
Fishbach, A., 250
Fisher, C. B., 40
Fisher, L., 209
Fiske, S. T., 534, 551
Fisogni, S., 51
FitzGerald, D., 213
Fitzgerald, P., 70
Fitzmaurice, P., 155
Flam, F., 108
Flavell, S. W., 56
Fleck, J. I., 144
Fleischman, D. A., 375
Fleming, J., 409
Fleminger, S., 481
Fletcher, M. E., 137
Flory, K., 428
Flynn, J. R., 173
Flynn, P. M., 161
Fobes, J. L., 73
Foderaro, L. W., 470
Fogel, A., 342
Folk, C., 118–119
Folkman, S., 422, 428, 432
Follett, K., 538
Fonagy, P., 480
Forbey, J., 412
Forer, B., 408
Forgas, J. P., 535
Forlenza, M. J., 60
Formenti, S. C., 520
Forrest, C., 516
Förster, J., 549–550
Fosse, M., 140
Fosse, R., 140
Fossey, D., 30f
Foster, D. H., 102
Foster, J., 398
Foster, K. M., 198

Foster, P., 213
Fotti, S., 501
Foulds, J., 437
Fountas, K. N., 73
Fournier, J., 242
Fowler, C. A., 107
Fowler, J. H., 438
Fox, K., 309
Fox, M. J., 57f, 58
Fox, S., 272
Foxe, J. J., 107
Frackowiak, R. S. J., 76
Fradera, A., 232
Frances, A., 459
Franciskovic, A., 173
Frank, E., 517
Frankenberg, W. K., 341f
Frankham, P., 299
Franklin, A., 342
Franklin, G., Sr., 224f
Franklin, M. E., 500
Franklin, T. B., 278
Franko, D. L., 297
Franks, P., 442–443
Franzek, E., 476
Fraser, I., 435
Fraser, S. C., 544
Frasure-Smith, N., 436
Frederickson, B. L., 314
Freedberg, D., 211
Freedman, D. S., 301
Freedman, J. L., 544
Freedman, M. R., 303
Freedy, J. R., 422
Freeman, A., 504
Freeman, K., 422
Freire, J. C., 508
Frensch, P. A., 194
Freud, A., 15, 389, 393
Freud, S., 15, 16f, 18, 139–140,
    140, 290, 308, 385–391, 406f,
    468, 478, 496, 498, 560
Freudenberg, Z., 71
Fricke-Oerkermann, L., 138
Fried, I., 215
Friedberg, R. D., 503
Friederici, A. D., 342
Friedman, J. N. W., 479
Friedman, M. J., 423
Friedman, S. R., 154
Frijda, N., 314
Frijda, N. H., 314, 319
Frimer, J. A., 362, 562
Frings, L., 80
Friston, K. J., 375
Frith, C. D., 99
Fritsch, T., 375
Fritz, S. M., 255
Frodl, T., 470
Frosch, A., 390
Frost, L. E., 454
Frost, R. O., 466, 468
Frumin, I., 109
Fu, L., 479
Fuchs, S. S., 69
Fujii, T., 552
Fujiki, M., 315
Fulero, S., 223
Fultz, J., 545
Funder, D. C., 114
Funke, G. J., 356
Furnham, A., 392
Furukawa, S., 107
Furukawa, T. A., 471
Furukawa, Y., 155
Furumoto, L., 15
Fusari, A., 109
Fyer, A. J., 499
Fyhn, M., 122

G

Gaab, J., 427
Gabriel, L. T., 277–278
Gabrieli, J. D. E., 215
Gadbois, S. A., 400
Gaertner, B., 562
Gaertner, S. L., 549, 550, 553

Gage, F. H., 79
Gage, P., 76
Galanter, M., 510
Galantucci, B., 107
Galef, D., 409
Gall, F. J., 14, 16f
Gallese, V., 55
Gallo, P., 259
Gallop, R., 504, 512
Galloway, G., 153
Gallup Poll, 125
Galton, F., 272
Galvin, D. M., 162
Gami, A. S., 142
Gandhi, K. K., 437
Gangestad, S. W., 305
Ganong, L. H., 372
Gaona, C., 71
Garb, H. N., 413
Garber, J., 480
Garcia, A., 500
Garcia, J., 175, 553
Garcia, R., 263
Garcia, S. M., 562
Garcia-Andrade, C., 159
Garcia-Mijares, M., 187
Garcia-Palacios, A., 37
Gardini, S., 241
Gardner, B., 519
Gardner, C., 155
Gardner, C. O., 471
Gardner, E. P., 111
Gardner, F., 564
Gardner, H., 76–77, 89, 268, 269f
Gardner, S., 15
Garle, M., 66
Garlow, S. J., 159
Garretson, M. E., 224
Garrigan, P., 121
Garry, M., 225
Garwick, G. B., 278
Gass, C. S., 30
Gatchel, R. J., 112
Gates, B., 446
Gatz, M., 471
Gautreaux, G., 501, 561
Gavrilescu, D., 222
Gawronski, B., 468
Gayathri, K., 483
Gaymard, B., 135
Gaynes, B. N., 143
Gazzaniga, M. S., 50, 80, 216
Ge, X., 359
Gegenfurtner, K. R., 102
Gelbard-Sagiv, H., 215
Gelenberg, A., 517
Gelfand, L., 504
Gelfand, M. M., 374
Geller, E., 185
Gelman, R., 355
Gelstein, S., 109
Gennaro, R. J., 132
Genovese, J. E. C., 354
Genovese, K., 27–28, 562
Gentile, B., 400
Gentner, D., 261
George, J., 510
George, M. S., 319
George, P., 114
George, R., 342
George, S., 156
Georgeson, M., 100
Geppert, C. M., 510
Gepshtein, S., 98
Gerdes, A., 187
Gernsbacher, M. A., 55
Gerrard, M., 436
Gerrie, M., 118–119
Gerritsen, C., 249
Gershkoff-Stowe, L., 259
Gerson, K., 372
Gerstel, N., 373
Getner, D., 255
Geva, D., 161
Geyer, T., 220
Giacobbi, P. R., Jr., 422
Giacomini, M., 78
Giannopoulos, V. L., 444

Gibb, R., 77
Gibbon, M., 472
Gibbons, F. X., 436
Gibbons, R. D., 517
Gibbs, N., 358
Gibbs, W. W., 257
Giedd, J., 80
Gielen, U. P., 10
Giese-Davis, J., 436
Gilbert, D. T., 222, 395
Gilbert, P. D., 431
Gilboa, A., 232
Gilchrist, A., 208
Gillam, B., 119
Gilligan, C., 361–363
Gilliss, C., 370
Ginsberg, S., 364
Gitlin, M., 477
Giusberti, E., 241
Gizer, I. R., 160
Gladwell, M., 413, 415
Gladwin, T., 266
Glantz, S. A., 438
Glass, G. V., 511, 512f
Glass, K., 428
Glei, D. A., 423
Gleitman, L. R., 260
Glickfield, L. L., 109
Glicksohn, J., 396, 535
Glisky, E. L., 376
Glover, G. H., 215
Glymour, M. M., 376
Godbout, R., 137
Godfrey, K., 516
Goeltzenleucher, B., 140
Goff, D., 213
Goffin, R. D., 537
Gogtay, N., 80
Goin, M. K., 494
Gokce, A., 220
Gold, J. M., 476
Gold, M., 155
Gold, P. E., 234
Goldberg, J., 515
Golden, R. N., 143
Golden, W. L., 149
Golder, S. A., 143
Goldfried, M. R., 512
Goldin, S., 261
Goldin-Meadow, S., 261
Goldman, E., 520
Goldman, R. N., 507
Goldstein, E., 224
Goldstein, I., 304
Goldstein, L. H., 82
Goldstein, R. B., 398
Goldstein, S. N., 362–363
Goleman, D., 344, 443f, 488
Golimbet, V. E., 403
Golombok, S., 308
Golosheykin, S., 150
Gomez-Ramirez, M., 107
Gonçalves, E. L., 187
Gong, H., 102
Gontkovsky, S. T., 73, 270
Goode, E., 108
Goodman, G., 224
Goodman, W. K., 467
Goodwin, J. E., 342
Goodwin, R., 542
Goodwin, R. D., 479
Gooley, J., 143
Gooren, L., 307
Gopie, N., 220
Gordijn, M. C. M., 143
Gordon, D., 459
Gordon, R., 109
Gosdin, M., 141
Gossop, M., 510
Gotlib, I. H., 473
Goto, T. K., 119
Gottesman, I. I., 475, 476, 477f
Gottlieb, D. A., 182, 183
Gottlieb, J., 521
Gould, D., 179
Gould, E., 79
Gould, R. L., 370
Govan, D. G., 119
Grabe, S., 400
Grace, A. A., 215

Gradinaru, V., 70
Grady, D., 437
Graham, C. A., 474
Graham, J. R., 411
Graham, L., 81f, 105f
Graham, S., 360
Grahek, N., 112
Grainger, J., 211
Grammer, G. G., 442
Granath, F., 66
Grange, D. K., 336
Granic, I., 363–364
Grann, J. D., 230
Grant, A., 292–293
Grant, B. F., 398
Grant, D. M., 170
Grant, S., 413
Gray, G. C., 561
Gray, R., 337
Graziano, M. S. A., 75, 79
Greco, C. M., 82
Greely, H., 216
Green, B. G., 114
Green, B. L., 422
Green, D. L., 144
Green, D. N., 140
Green, J., 149
Green, J. A., 347
Green, J. P., 144
Green, M. C., 529
Green, P. A., 109
Green, P. R., 100
Greenberg, B. D., 520
Greenberg, G., 457–458
Greenberg, L. S., 507
Greenberg, R., 520
Greenberg, R. L., 466, 466f
Greenberg, R. M., 519
Greene, J. D., 319, 563
Greenfield, S., 132
Greening, F., 126
Greenspan, S., 277–278
Greenstein, D., 80
Greenstein, J. E., 437
Greenwald, A. G., 125, 220, 552
Greer, L. L., 64–65
Greer, P. L., 56
Greer, R. D., 501, 561
Greer, S., 435
Grefkes, C., 78f
Gregory, R. L., 121, 123
Gretchen, D., 513
Greve, D. N., 233
Greydanus, D. E., 481
Griffin, D. W., 556
Griffin, P., 198
Griffiths, J., 423
Grigorenko, E. L., 271, 279, 282
Grigoriadis, S., 509
Grilo, C. M., 302–303, 480
Grimes, T., 32
Grimm, J. W., 73
Grinspoon, S., 441
Gritsenko, I. K., 403
Gritz, E. R., 436
Groh, K., 368
Gronholm, P., 69
Gross, C. G., 79
Gross, D. M., 314
Gross, J. J., 314
Gross, M. D., 435
Grossmann, T., 342
Grothusen, J. R., 516–517, 517
Groves, R. M., 30
Grubaugh, A., 500
Gruber, S. A., 465
Grucza, R., 158
Gruenewald, T. L., 427, 445
Grünert, U., 98
Grunwald, T., 342
Grusec, J. E., 194, 501
Grushka-Cockayne, Y., 244
Gschwendner, T., 220
Guadagno, R. E., 529
Guardino, M., 483
Guarnaccia, P. J. J., 487
Guastella, A., 64–65
Guéguen, N., 545
Guerrero, L., 27
Guez, J., 230

Guiard, B. P., 56
Guiliano, T. A., 395
Guillem, F., 137
Guilleminault, C., 137, 142
Guldemond, H., 279
Gulgoz, S., 226
Gumble, A., 189
Gunn, D. M., 210
Gur, M., 509
Gurin, P., 28
Gurnett, C. A., 142
Guthrie, I. K., 562
Gutierrez, P. M., 364
Gutiérrez, R., 230
Guttmacher Institute, 306
Guyll, M., 549–550
Gwadry, F., 140
Gwynn, M. I., 147
Gyulai, L., 473

H

Haberstick, B. C., 155, 334
Hackam, D. G., 43
Hackman, H. W., 198
Haddock, B., 374
Hafting, T., 122
Hager, E., 122
Haidt, J., 562–563
Haier, R. J., 267
Haimov-Kochman, R., 441
Hains, S. C., 542
Halcox, J., 424
Haley, W. E., 444
Halford, S., 347
Halgren, E., 260
Halkitis, P., 155
Hall, B. J., 24
Hall, E., 368, 373
Hall, J., 535
Hall, J. A., 442–443
Hall, L. K., 225f
Hall, P. J., 182
Halldorson, M. K., 221
Halle, T., 348
Hallgren, M., 140
Hallschmid, M., 299
Halpern, A. R., 219
Halpern, D. F., 372
Halpert, J., 442
Halsband, U., 80, 148
Ham, J., 562–563
Hamani, Y., 441
Hamann, S., 214
Hambleton, R. K., 408
Hamed, M. S., 501
Hamer, M., 432
Hamer, R. M., 143
Hamilton, A. C., 207
Hamilton, S. P., 479
Hamilton, W. L., 438
Hammann, S. B., 319
Hammock, G. S., 560
Hammond, C., 155
Hammond, D. C., 149
Hamner, M., 500
Hampshire, A., 467
Hand, V., 457–458
Handgraaf, M. J., 64–65
Haney, C., 544
Hangya, B., 141
Hankin, B., 428
Hanley, C., 195
Hanley, S. J., 294
Hannan, A., 465
Hannon, E. E., 342
Hanson, D. R., 476
Haratani, T., 143
Harding, D. J., 306
Hardison, D. M., 257
Hardt, J., 365
Hardy, L. T., 346
Harel, M., 215
Hari, R., 206
Hariri, A., 551, 551f
Harlow, H. F., 346
Harlow, J. M., 76
Harmon, S. C., 511

Harmon-Jones, E., 551
Harold, G. T., 372
Harper, D. J., 519
Harper, T., 373
Harrington, D., 161–162
Harris, J., 64, 111–112, 216
Harris, K. R., 270
Harris, M. S., 154
Harris, R., 57
Hart, B., 259
Hartley, T., 430
Hartmann, E., 135f
Hartstein, M., 137
Hartung, C. M., 486
Harvard Mental Health Letter (HMHL), 523
Harvey, A. G., 141
Harvey, J. H., 306
Harvey, P. D., 477, 536
Harvey, R. H., 430
Harvey-Berino, J., 300
Hasan, R. M., 149
Hasher, L., 220
Hashimoto, M., 70
Haskell, C. F., 155
Haslam, C., 337
Hasselblad, V., 436
Hastings, R. P., 279
Hatsopoulos, N. G., 71
Hau, K. T., 297
Hauke, C., 391
Hauser, M. D., 355
Havercamp, S. M., 293
Havermans, R. C., 500
Haviland, J. S., 435
Haviland-Jones, J. M., 109
Hawkes, Christopher H., 109
Hawley, E., 123
Haworth, C., 330
Hayflick, L., 373
Hayne, H., 225
Haynes, P., 151
Hayward, R., 431
He, S-Z., 372
Heard, H. L., 501
Heath, R. A., 309
Heatherton, T., 436
Heaton, R., 477
Hecht, J. M., 446
Hedges, D. W., 516
Hegarty, P., 529
Hegg, É., 179
Heidenreich, T., 509
Heier, M. S., 142
Heilman, C. J., 57
Heilman, K. M., 213, 254
Heim, C., 64–65
Heimberg, R. G., 459
Heine, S., 41
Heinen, T., 242
Heinrichs, R. W., 475
Heisel, M. J., 480
Heitzmann, C. A., 435
Heller, S., 390
Heller, W., 79
Helmbold, N., 270
Helmholz, H. von, 101
Helmuth, L., 56
Helstrup, T., 225
Henckes, N., 521
Henderson, J., 337
Henderson, J. M., 70
Henderson, S., 337
Hendriks, E. H., 435
Hendryx, M., 521
Henik, A., 113
Heninger, M., 159
Hennig-Fast, K., 470
Henningsen, D. D., 543
Henningsen, M. L., 543
Henrich, J., 41, 124
Henriksen, A. L., 521
Henry, D., 141
Hentschel, U., 389
Henwood, B. F., 457–458
Herbenick, D., 305
Herbert, W., 245
Hering, E., 102
Herman, C. P., 301, 302

Herman, D. B., 422f
Herman, J., 474
Hernandez, G., 179
Herpertz, S. C., 502f
Herrán, A., 465
Herrington, D. M., 65
Herrmann, A., 249
Herrnstein, R. J., 281–282
Herskovits, M. J., 123
Hertwig, R., 228
Hertzog, C., 376
Herzberg, L., 319
Hess, M. J., 81–82
Hess, T. M., 375, 538
Hessels, S., 230
Hesterberg, K., 403
Hewitt, J. K., 155
Heyes, C., 55
Heyman, G. D., 264
Hibbard, P., 119
Hiby, E. F., 182
Hickok, G., 54, 55
Higgins, S., 19
Hilarski, M., 70
Hilgard, E., 148
Hill, S. S., 40–41
Hiller, W., 468
Hillix, W. A., 263
Hine, D. W., 158
Hines, A., 428
Hines, M., 79
Hinman, N., 189
Hinson, J. T., 375
Hinterberger, T., 148
Hippocrates, 16f
Hirase, H., 70
Hirsch, J., 301
Hirschfeld, R. M. A., 517
Hirsh, I. J., 107
Hirt, E. R., 223
Hitch, G. J., 210
Hjemdal, O., 422, 430
Ho, L. T., 80
Ho, S. M. Y., 443
Hoare, P., 20
Hobfoll, S. E., 24, 422
Hobson, J. A., 134f, 140, 141
Hobson, K., 441
Hochschild, A., 372
Hock, H. S., 89
Hodgkinson, K. A., 476
Hoff, E., 257, 259, 261
Hoffer, T. B., 11
Hoffman, H., 37
Hoffmann, M., 370
Hofler, M., 465
Hofmann, S. G., 500
Hofmann, W., 220
Hogan, J., 415
Hogan, R., 415
Hogg, M. A., 542, 550
Hojjat, M., 558
Holcomb, P., 213
Holden, C., 78, 475
Holland, C. R., 280, 282
Holland, J. C., 436
Hollenstein, T., 363–364
Holler, G. D., 144
Holleran, S., 535
Hollingworth, H. I., 15
Hollingworth, L. S., 15, 17f
Hollins, K., 337
Hollis, K. L., 174–175
Hollist, C. S., 510
Hollon, S. D., 504, 520
Holman, E., 429
Holmes, A., 467
Holmes, J. G., 556
Holmes, S. A., 113
Holon, S. D., 512
Holowka, S., 79
Holsboer, F., 140
Holt, J., 452, 455, 490
Holt, M., 56
Holtz, J., 9
Holyoak, K. J., 82, 255
Home, J. A., 137
Honda, S., 70
Honer, W. G., 476
Hongchun, W., 148

Honorton, C., 126
Honzik, C. H., 192
Hood, S., 467
Hope, K., 522
Hopkins, W., 78
Hoppey, D., 279
Hopwood, C., 480
Horesh, D., 423
Hori, H., 403
Horínek, D., 232
Horney, K., 15, 385, 392, 392f, 393, 406f
Hornsey, M. J., 529, 541
Horowitz, H. A., 479
Horowitz, J. L., 480
Hort, J., 232
Horton, C. L., 140
Horton, K. D., 221
Horwood, L. J., 365
Hotopf, M., 517
Hou, Y., 400
Houg, S., 81–82
Houghtalen, R. P., 469
Houle, S., 515
Houlihan, D., 545
Houlihan, M., 435
Hoven, C. W., 467
Howard, D. E., 142
Howard, K. I., 225
Howard, R., 161–162
Howard, T. D., 65
Howe, C. J., 259
Howe, M. L., 223
Howell, E. F., 469
Howes, O., 58, 456, 476
Howitt, D., 28
Howland, R., 517
Hoyme, E. H., 278
Hoyt, C., 529
Hozawa, A., 435
Hsieh, D. K., 513
Hsieh, Y., 530
Huang, B., 398
Hubbard, E. M., 113, 114f
Hubbard, K., 296
Hubel, D. H., 17f, 98, 99
Huber, F., 249
Hudson, W., 124, 125f
Hudspeth, A. J., 76, 107
Huesmann, L., 194, 196
Hugdahl, K., 50, 79, 118–119
Hugenberg, K., 551
Hughes, A., 230
Huguer, N., 422–423
Huijie, T., 331
Hull, C. L., 290
Human, L. J., 535
Hummelvoll, J. K., 406
Humphrey, N., 271
Humphreys, C., 142
Humphreys, G. W., 117
Humphreys, K. L., 181
Hung, D. L., 194
Hungi, N., 234
Hunt, E., 250, 270
Hunt, J. S., 549
Hunt, M., 305, 307
Hunt, R., 209
Hunter, C., 113
Hur, K., 517
Hurt, C. A., 220
Hurt, C. S., 375
Hussain, R., 278
Hussein, S., 252–253
Huston, A. C., 196
Hutchinson, S. L., 428
Hutchison, K. E., 154, 403
Hyde, J. S., 306, 308, 309, 474
Hyde, K., 76
Hyman, B. T., 232
Hyman, M., 496
Hyworon, Z., 20

I

Iachini, T., 241
Iacoboni, M., 54, 55
Iaria, G., 194
Ievers-Landis, C. E., 336

Iglesias, A., 149
Igo, S. E., 30
Ihler, E., 442
Ihori, N., 196
Ikonomidou, C., 337
Imamura, M., 121
Inafuku, S., 142
Inagawa, S., 142
Ingvar, M., 80
Inhelder, B., 353
Innocenti, G. M., 336
Inoue, T., 517
Insel, T. R., 473
Insko, C., 556
International Human Genome
    Sequencing Consortium, 334
Iribarren, C., 435
iriz, J., 473
Irons, G., 172
Irwin, M., 427
Irwin, R. R., 150
Isaac, M., 423
Isaacson, J. S., 77, 109
Isay, R. A., 308
Isbell, L. M., 553
Ishii, K., 261
Ishikawa, S., 504
Iversen, L., 58, 456
Iversen, S., 58, 456
Iverson, P., 257
Ivry, R. B., 50
Ivy, L., 349
Iwai, Y., 70
Iyengar, S. S., 292
Izaki, Y., 215
Izard, C. E., 321

J

Jaasma, M. A., 562
Jackendoff, R., 261
Jackson, A., 499
Jackson, J. D., 430
Jackson, P., 467
Jackson, S., 474
Jacob, K. S., 483
Jacobs, G., 486
Jacobs, J. A., 372
Jacobs, M., 301
Jacobsen, F. M., 143
Jacobson, J. L., 278
Jacobson, N. S., 412f
Jacoby, E., 403
Jacoby, L. L., 230
Jacquez, F. M., 480
Jagacinski, R. J., 117
Jahn, R., 56
Jain, S., 423
James, M. H., 173
James, R., 532
James, W., 14, 15, 16f,
    132, 316
Jamieson, G. A., 148
Jamison, K. R., 470, 472f
Janca, A., 422, 423
Jang, H., 294
Jang, K. L., 64, 330
Janicak, P., 70
Janis, I. L., 543
Jansen, A., 500
Janson, G. R., 309
Janusek, L., 420
Janzen, J. I., 389
Jarcho, J. M., 551, 551f
Jarlais, D. C. D., 156
Jarrold, C., 209, 210
Jarvin, L., 279
Jasso, H., 54
Javitt, D. C., 476
Jean-Pierre, P., 435
Jefferson, D. J., 155
Jelley, R. B., 537
Jen, C-H., 538, 539
Jena, S., 112
Jencks, C., 306
Jenkins, A. M., 11
Jenkins, F. J., 427
Jenkins, J., 422
Jenkins, J. M., 313
Jensen, A. R., 270, 272, 409

Jensen, M. P., 113
Jeo, R. M., 120
Jequier, E., 299
Jerant, A. F., 442
Jessell, T. M., 60
Jessen, S., 114
Jeter, D., 51, 330
Jetten, J., 541
Ji, D., 98
Jia, H., 373
Jiang, L., 276
Jinks, A. L., 109
Jobes, D. A., 494
Joe, G. W., 161
Joe, L., 530
Johannsen, M., 334
Johansen, T., 467
Johnson, A. M., 64
Johnson, C., 121, 374
Johnson, G. B., 55f
Johnson, H. D., 79, 310, 343
Johnson, L., 186
Johnson, P. J., 175
Johnson, R. J., 444
Johnson, S. P., 342
Johnson, V. E., 308
Johnson, W., 267, 374
Johnson-Greene, D., 40–41
John-Steiner, V., 356
Johnston, L. D., 152, 153f, 156,
    161, 161f, 438, 438f
Joiner, T. E., Jr., 460, 473
Jones, A., 148
Jones, A. L., 392
Jones, D., 41
Jones, E. E., 498
Jones, J. E., 297
Jones, J. M., 350
Jones, K., 162
Jones, M., 149
Jones, R., 359
Jones, R. K., 306
Jones, S., 478
Joorman, J., 473
Jordan, A. H., 562–563
Jorgensen, G., 362
Josephs, O., 76
Jourdan, A., 508
Jovanović, D., 561
Joyce, J., 453
Juan, C., 194
Julien, R. M, 161
June, C. H., 334
Jung, C. G., 385, 391–392, 406f
Jung, J., 158
Jung, R. E., 267
Jung-Beeman, M., 144
Juslin, P., 244
Juster, E. T., 372
Justman, S., 44
Jusuf, P. R., 98

K

Kadosh, R., 113
Kagan, J., 403
Kahn, V., 403
Kahneman, D., 248, 445–446
Kahng, S. K., 460
Kainz, P. M., 100
Kaiz, M., 225
Kalb, C., 111, 113
Kalinchuk, A. V., 290
Kaller, C. P., 250
Kallio, S., 148
Kalodner, C. R., 503
Kam, K., 555
Kamarck, T., 425, 425f
Kameda, M. M., 77
Kaminaga, T., 206
Kamphaus, R. W., 413
Kanaya, T., 224
Kandel, E. R., 60, 76, 111
Kangawa, K., 298–299
Kanner, A. D., 424f
Kanoski, S. E., 300
Kantrowitz, B., 159
Kao, D., 530
Kaplan, A. S., 516

Kaplan, J. R., 35f
Kaplan, M. S., 422–423
Kapur, S., 58, 456, 476, 515
Kara, P., 119
Karaszewski, B., 314
Karl, A., 113
Karni, A., 141
Karsdale, M. A., 65
Kashima, H., 471
Kasof, J., 143
Kassam, K. S., 222
Kassel, J. D., 437
Kassin, S. M., 20
Kaštelan, A., 173
Kato, K., 430
Kato, N., 519
Kato, T., 473
Katsiyannis, A., 278
Katsoulakis, E., 520
Katz, J., 112
Katz, L., 501
Katz, M., 290
Katz, P., 196
Katzman, M. A., 112
Kaufman, A., 121, 374
Kaufman, J. C., 254, 255, 271
Kaufmann, C., 140
Kavuncu, V., 113
Kawakami, K., 553
Kawakami, N., 471
Kawamoto, Y., 403
Kawamura, S., 292–293
Kawasaki, C., 350
Kawashima, H., 215
Kaya, M. C., 515
Kazar, D. B., 149
Kazdin, A., 512–513
Keane, M. M., 232
Kearns, K. P., 76–77
Keating, D. P., 354
Keefe, F. J., 112
Kelley, H., 534
Kelley, M., 182
Kellman, P., 121
Kellner, C. H., 519
Kelly, J. B., 372
Kelly-Hayes, M., 435
Kelm, M., 57
Keltikangas-Järvinen, L., 403
Keltner, D., 313
Kemeny, M. E., 420, 427, 445
Kemp, R. I., 223
Kemp, S., 99
Kempermann, G., 77, 79
Kemps, E., 225
Kendler, K., 321
Kendler, K. S., 155, 330,
    471, 476
Kennedy, C. E., 112
Kennedy, D. O., 155
Kennedy, J. E., 126
Kennedy, J. F., 221
Kennedy, K. S., 137
Kennedy, P., 71
Kennison, S. M., 29
Kensinger, E., 319
Kerns, J. G., 313
Kerr, A. L., 70
Kesebir, P., 444
Kesmodel, U., 337
Kess, J. F., 80
Kessels, R., 232
Kessler, R. C., 216, 483
Kettenmann, H., 51
Key, W. B., 125
Khaigrekht, M., 519
Khalil, E. L., 54
Khan, A. S., 30
Khayyer, M., 292
Khazaal, Y., 299
Khoshaba, D. M., 430
Kidd, E., 259
Kidd, K. K., 271, 282
Kiecolt, J. K., 373
Kihlstrom, J. F., 148, 220, 469
Kikuchi, Y. Y., 77
Kilner, J. M., 99
Kilm, D. R., 519
Kim, H., 111–112

Kim, N., 121
Kim, S., 370
Kim, T., 56
Kimbrel, N. A., 464
Kim-Cohen, J., 404
Kindt, M., 518
King, A., 76, 104
King, R. A., 517
King-Casas, B., 480
Kinoshita, Y., 403
Kinsey, A. C., 307
Kirby, S. L., 221
Kirisoglu, C., 142
Kirk, K. M., 307
Kirk, S. A., 513
Kirk, S. B., 428
Kirkby, J., 140
Kirsch, I., 147, 148, 175
Kirschenbaum, H., 508
Kirsh, K. L., 435
Kisac, I., 422
Kish, S., 155
Kiss, A., 442–443
Kitaichi, Y., 517
Kitayama, S., 539
Klapp, S. T., 117
Kleiber, D. A., 377
Klein, R. G., 467
Kleinhaus, K., 478
Kleinman, A., 149, 487
Kleinman, J., 149, 487
Klerman, G. L., 483, 509
Klinger, M. R., 125
Kloos, B., 428
Klötz, F., 66
Kluck, A., 302
Kluger, J., 245, 463
Klump, K., 302
Knaevelsrud, C., 113
Knight, S. C., 149
Knoblich, G., 124
Knouse, L. E., 480
Knuutila, J., 206
Ko, H., 194
Koball, A., 189
Kobayashi, F., 315
Kobayashi, K., 109
Koçak, O., 241
Koch, C., 132
Koch, K. L., 108
Kocur, J., 182
Koehnle, T., 317
Koff, W. J., 309
Kogan, N., 253–254
Kogstad, R. E., 406
Kohlberg, L., 360–361, 361f
Köhler, W., 250
Kohn, D. B., 334
Kojima, M., 298–299
Kokaia, M., 57
Kolarov, V., 532
Kolata, G., 58
Kolb, B., 77
Kolenovic-Djapo, J., 396
Komarovskaya, I., 474
Konczak, J., 120
Kondo, T., 431
Konig, R., 336
Koocher, G. P., 40–41
Koole, S., 311
Koopman, C., 436
Kopelman, M. D., 481
Koper, R. J., 562
Koplewicz, H., 480
Kopp, T. G., 406
Korcha, R. A., 153
Koren, G., 337
Korn, J., 423
Kornhaber, A., 150
Kornhaber, C., 150
Korotkov, D., 435
Korotkov, K., 435
Kosambi, D. D., 112
Kosslyn, S. M., 50, 79, 241
Koster, O., 214
Kostygina, A., 196
Kothadia, S. M., 112
Kotov, R., 460
Kotre, J., 368, 373
Kotz, S. A., 107, 114
Koukoulis, G. N., 66

Kounios, J., 144
Koutstaal, W., 268
Kovacs, A. M., 264
Kovelman, I., 264
Kowalik, J., 498
Kowert, P. A., 543
Koyama, A., 213
Koyama, T., 517
Kozulin, A., 356
Kramer, P., 517
Krasnoperova, E., 473
Kravitz, R. L., 442
Kreher, D., 213
Kreppner, J., 242
Kreuger, A., 445
Krieger, K., 509
Krijn, M., 498
Krishman, S., 161–162
Krishnan, A., 240, 284
Krisztal, E., 69
Krueger, K., 186
Krueger, R., 402, 404
Krull, D. S., 536f
Krumhuber, E. G., 321
Krumm, S., 268
Kruse, C., 435
Krusemark, E., 537–538
Krylowicz, B., 486
Kübler-Ross, E., 377–378
Kubovy, M., 98
Kuijer, R. G., 432
Kumar, A., 213
Kumar, P. S., 483
Kumar, S., 334
Kumari, V., 307
Kunugi, H., 403
Kunzmann, U., 371
Kuo, L. J., 264
Kuo, M., 158
Kuperberg, G., 213
Kuppens, P., 315
Kuriyama, K., 140
Kurtz, J. E., 400
Kuther, T. L., 11, 12f
Kvavilashvili, L., 209
Kwan, K., 400
Kwon, J. S., 465
Kwon, P., 473
Kwon, S. M., 465

L

Laas, I., 293
LaBar, K., 319
Labouliere, C. D., 499
Ladewig, J., 186
Laederach-Hofmann, K., 465
Lagacé-Séguin, D. G., 415
Laham, S. M., 535
Lahti, J., 403
Laine, M., 69
Laing, D. G., 109
Laing, R. D., 455–456
Laird, J. D., 316
Lakhan, S., 330
Lal, S., 15
Lalonde, F., 80
Lamal, P. A., 5f, 250
Lamb, M., 557f
Lamb, M. E., 224, 347, 349
Lambert, M. J., 511, 513
Lamborn, S. D., 368
Lampard, A. M., 302
Lando, H. A., 436
Landro, L., 113, 442
Lane, A. M., 399
Lane, K. A., 552
Lane, S. D., 161
Lang, A. J., 112
Lang, G., 113
Lang, P. J., 465
Langan-Fox, J., 413
Langdon, R., 475
Langdridge, D., 538
Lange, C., 316
Langer, E. J., 44, 58
Langley, B., 422
Langley, J., 290
Langlois, F., 298–299
Langreth, R., 432
Langston, R., 122

Lankov, A., 371
Lans, C., 441
Lanza, S. T., 360
Laplante, M., 465
Lapp, W. M., 153
Lappin, J., 58
Larcher, A. M., 516
Larsen, R. J., 397
Larson, J., 350
Larsson, M., 108
Lascaratos, G., 98
Lashgari-Saegh, S., 113
Latané, B., 27–29, 33–37, 35, 40, 41, 49, 562
Latif, T., 519
Lating, J. M., 457
Latner, J. D., 20, 189
Laucht, M., 160
Laugharne, J., 422
Laukli, E., 373
Laumann, E. O., 305
Laurenceau, J. P., 473
Lauterbach, D., 501
La Valley, A., 27
Lavelli, M., 342
Lavenex, P., 214
Lavrakas, P. J., 530
Lawrence, W., 337
Lawson, M. J., 234
Lazarus, A. A., 523
Lazarus, J., 112
Lazarus, R. S., 424f, 432
Lazerson, A., 72f
Leahy, R. L., 473, 504
Leanza, G., 57
Leary, C., 182
LeBow, M. D., 302–303
LeChanu, M. N., 150
Leckenby, J. D., 530
Leckman, J. F., 517
Leclair-Visonneau, L., 135
Lee, A., 423
Lee, A. Y., 444
Lee, C. S., 280
Lee, D., 149, 487
Lee, F., 264
Lee, F. H., 113
Lee, H., 158
Lee, H. J., 465
Lee, J. V., 160
Lee, K., 370
Lee, M., 288
Lee, N., 80
Lee, S., 539
Lee, S. S., 98, 181
Lee, S. Y., 233
Lee, Y., 80
Lee-Chiong, T. L., 142
Leeman, R. F., 299
Leffard, S. A., 413
Lehar, S., 117
Lehman, D. R., 291, 428
Lehmkuhl, G., 138
Lehrman, S., 309
Leib, J. R., 336
Leibel, R. L., 301
Leiblum, S. R., 305
Leibowitz, S. F., 299
Leigh, E., 210
Leigh, J. H., 219
Leiter, S., 409
Leiter, W. M., 409
Leitner, L. M., 513
Lemay, E. P., Jr., 537
Lemonick, M. D., 154
Léna, C., 58, 473
Lencz, T., 467, 467f
Lendon, C., 376
Lenroot, R., 80
Lens, W., 310
Lenzenweger, M. F., 476, 479
Leo, R. J., 519
Lepage, J. F., 54, 194
Lepper, M. R., 292
Lepre, A., 421
Lesch, K. P., 467
Lesperance, F., 436
Lester, D., 445
Leu, J., 264
Leu-Semenescu, S., 135
Leuthardt, E. C., 71

Leuthold, H., 99
Levander, S., 515
Levant, R. F., 512
LeVay, S., 307
Levey, A. I., 57
Levey, G., 329, 331
Levi, A., 532
Levick, S. E., 334
Levin, B. E., 300
Levin, I. P., 404f
Levin, J. R., 209, 234
Levin, R., 138
Levin, R. J., 305
Levine, B., 375
Levine, J. M., 542
Levine, S. Z., 282, 346, 476
Levinson, D. J., 370
Levinson, S., 172
Levitt, S., 535
Levy, B. R., 375, 377
Lewin, T., 364
Lewinsohn, P. M., 473
Lewis, C., 349, 557f
Lewis, C. M., 509
Lewis, G., 467
Lewis, R., 97f
Lewis, S., 436
Li, B., 456, 473
Li, H., 530
Li, K. K., 142, 194
Li, M. D., 436
Li, T-K., 152
Liang, H. B., 77
Liang, K. A., 306
Liang, L., 107
Liao, K. K., 80
Libedinsky, C., 76
Licht, E., 69
Lichtenstein, J., 248
Licis, A. K., 142
Lidz, J., 260
Lieb, R., 465
Liebal, K., 262
Lieberman, M. D., 195f, 551, 551f
Liebig, B., 142
Liedl, A., 113
Lien, Y-W., 538, 539
Lilienfeld, S. O., 413, 498, 512
Limbaugh, R., 161
Limon, M., 545
Lin, C-H., 562
Lin, H-M., 562
Lin, Y. Y., 56, 80, 194
Lincoln, A., 293
Lindahl, M., 427
Lindblad, F., 427
Lindemann, O., 121–122
Lindh-Astrand, L., 370
Lindley, L. D., 41
Lindorff, M., 431
Lindsay, P. H., 212
Lindsay, R. C. L., 223
Lindsey, E. W., 347
Lindvall, O., 57
Lindy, J., 73
Linehan, M. M., 501
Links, P. S., 480
Linz, S., 310
Lipsitz, J. D., 499
Lishner, D., 562
Liszkowski, U., 263
Litowitz, B. E., 391
Little, A., 556
Little, K., 156
Liu, H., 70
Liu, J., 211, 211f
Liu, J. H., 549
Liu, L., 372
Liu, Q., 105
Liu, X., 121, 374
Liverpool, M., 80
Livesley, W., 64, 330
Livingstone, A. G., 314
Livingstone, H. A., 431
Livingstone, M., 76
Lobato, M. I., 309
Lobban, F., 478
Lobo, I., 57
Locicero, A., 20

Lock, J., 302
Locke, E. A., 399
Locke, J., 14, 16f
Locke, J. L., 258
Lockhart, R., 219
Lockl, K., 356
Lofholm, N., 289
Loft, H., 162
Loftus, E. E, 213f
Loftus, E. F., 17f, 20, 213, 224, 224f, 225
Loftus, G. R., 20
Lohrenz, T., 480
Loitfelder, M. M., 69
Lomax-Bream, L., 480
Long, G. M., 206
Long, R., 80
Lonner, W. J., 513
Loper, A., 474
Lopes, A. C., 520
Lopez, A. D., 436
López, S. R., 487
López-Frutos, J., 230
Lorduy, K., 427
Lorenz, K., 344–345, 560
Lorenzo-López, L., 230
Lothane, Z., 391
Lou, X., 436
Lourel, M., 545
Lovallo, W. R., 50, 79
Love, C., 161
Love, T., 54
Loving, T., 556–557
Lovler, R. L., 408
LoVullo, S., 181
Lowe, P., 142
Lowenstein, J. H., 91
Lowery, D., 291
Loy, J. W., 535
Lu, J., 135, 143
Lu, P. H., 477
Lu, T., 107
Lu, Z., 404f
Lubell, K. M., 365
Lublin, H., 515
Lucas, R. E., 445–446
Lucas, W., 154
Lucchina, L., 110f
Luchins, A. S., 252
Luciano, M., 445–446
Lucki, I., 516
Luckiesh, M., 123f
Luders, E., 80
Ludman, E., 471
Ludwig, A. M., 472
Lum, J., 259
Luminet, O., 430
Lun, V. M., 400
Lundberg-Love, P., 155
Lundstrom, B., 92
Lunt, I., 10
Luo, S., 556
Lupfer, M. B., 551
Luria, A. R., 233
Luthar, S. S., 349, 359
Lutz, C. K., 43
Lutz, W., 511
Lykken, D. T., 402, 402f
Lymberis, S. C., 520
Lynch, S., 279
Lynch, T. R., 501
Lyness, J. M., 520
Lynn, S. J., 144, 148, 149, 175
Lynn, T. K., 422
Lyons, H., 306

M

Ma, J. Z., 436
Ma, Y., 42f
Macaluso, E., 99, 114
Macdonald, D. W., 175
Macdonald, M., 435
Macduff, I., 538
Machavoine, J., 443
Machin, M., 20
Mack, J., 226
Mackay, J., 439
MacKenzie, T. D., 439
Mackey, S., 112

Mackie, D., 533
MacKillop, J., 403
MacLean, L., 20
MacLennan, A., 370
MacLeod, J., 161
Macmillan, M., 390
MacNab, B., 267
MacNeilage, P. F., 78
Macy, M. W., 143
Madden, D. J., 373
Maddi, S. R., 430
Mader, S. S., 55f, 99f
Madon, S., 549–550
Maestú, F., 230
Magida, A. J., 366
Magis, D., 82
Magoni, M., 337
Magoon, M., 180
Magruder, K. M., 422–423, 512
Maguire, E. A., 214, 215f
Mahmood, M., 142
Mahn, H., 356
Mahoney, A., 179
Maier, S. F., 234
Maina, G., 517
Maitino, A., 400
Maj, M., 143
Majeres, R. L., 246
Major, J. T., 267
Majorano, M., 258
Malach, R., 215
Maldonado, J. R., 469
Malenka, R. C., 152
Malhotra, A. K., 467, 467f
Malinow, R., 456, 473
Malle, B. F., 536
Malloy, L. C., 224
Malone, D. A., 519, 520
Malone, W., 537–538
Malouff, J. M., 511
Mamelak, A. N., 113
Mancinelli, R., 158
Manderscheid, R. W., 50
Mane, S., 530
Manenti, C., 309
Mangun, G. R., 50
Manly, J. J., 409
Mann, K., 158
Manning, M. A., 278
Mansari, M., 56
Manson, C., 474
Manstead, A. R., 314
Manstead, A. S. R., 315, 319
Mansuy, I. M., 278
Manuck, S. B., 35f
March, J. S., 500
Marchand, M., 545
Marcus, D., 512
Marcus, J., 149
Marcus, S. M., 517
Marcus-Newhall, A., 561
Marder, S. R., 476
Mariën, P., 70
Marighetto, A., 57
Mark, D. B., 435
Markesbery, W. R., 80
Markowitsch, J. J., 54, 194
Markowitz, J. C., 480, 483, 509, 520
Marks, I. M., 170
Markus, H. R., 539
Marmar, C., 423
Marsden, J., 510
Marsh, B., 439
Marsh, H. W., 297, 310
Marsh, R., 302f
Marshall, J. R., 562
Marshall, K., 109
Marshall, L., 141, 423
Marshall, M., 405
Marshall, R. D., 24
Marsiske, M., 280
Marszalek, J., 277
Martell, C. R., 512
Martelle, S., 195
Martiadis, V., 143
Martin, A., 82, 113
Martin, A. J., 310
Martin, E. A., 313
Martin, L., 261, 348

Martin, M. M., 264
Martin, N. G., 307
Martin, P. D., 431
Martin, R. C., 207
Martinez, J., 467
Martinez, M. J., 74, 76
Martini, M. I., 356
Martinko, M. J., 536
Martuza, R. L., 520
Marzi, C. A., 80
Maser, J. D., 467
Mashour, G. A., 520
Maslach, C., 544
Maslow, A. H., 17f, 19, 293f, 293–295, 405, 406f, 457, 507
Massaro, D. W., 107
Massey, S., 529
Mast, F. W., 241
Master, A., 553
Masters, W. H., 308
Masuda, M., 556–557
Matheson, K., 423
Mathews, H. L., 420
Mathur, P., 475
Matkin, G. S., 255
Maton, K. I., 11
Matson, J., 181
Matsumoto, D., 321
Matsuo, H., 423
Matsuo, J., 403
Matsuoka, H., 504
Matthews, G., 356
Matthews, K. A., 435, 520
Mattick, R. P., 161
Maurer, D., 341
Mauss, I., 314
Mayer, J. D., 271
Maynard, A. E., 356, 364
McAdams, D. P., 293, 363, 475
McBride, C. M., 545
McBride, W. J., 174
McBurney, D. H., 114
McCabe, C., 109
McCafferty, D., 446
McCanlies, E., 430
McCarthy, D., 444
McCarthy, E. P., 132
McCarthy, J., 513
McCarthy, R. J., 535
McCartney, K., 348
McCaul, K. D., 444
McCauley, R. N., 124
McClelland, D. C., 270, 309, 310
McClellen, D., 141
McClintock, S., 269f
McClure, J., 445, 529
McConnell, A., 533
McCrae, R. R., 397, 397f, 400
McCrink, K., 355
McDaniel, M. A., 234
McDaniel, R. J., 113
McDonald, C., 478
McDonald, H. E., 223
McDonald, M. P., 57
McDougall, W., 289
McDowell, D. M., 153
McEwen, B. S., 424
McFarland, B. H., 422–423
McGaugh, J. L., 215
McGeary, J., 403
McGilvray, J., 260
McGinn, D., 414
McGinty, D., 136
McGregor, K. K., 331
McGue, M., 402
McGuffin, P., 476
McIntire, S. A., 408
McIntyre, K., 423
McKay, D., 466
McKay, P., 549
McKay, R., 475
McKinley, M. J., 290
McKnight, C., 154
McLellan, M., 273
McLeod, J., 508
McLeskey, J., 279
McLoughlin, D. M., 519
McMahon, R. P., 476
McMurtray, A. M., 69
McNally, R. J., 460

McNamara, P., 136
McNaughton, N., 182
McNulty, S. E., 395
McTeague, L. M., 465
Mead, M., 366
Means, M. K., 500
Medeiros, R., 376
Medvedev, S. V., 107, 118–119
Meeter, M., 215
Meganck, R., 473
Megías, J. L., 357
Mehl, M. R., 535
Mehler, J., 264
Mehl-Madrona, L. E., 149
Meinlschmidt, G., 64–65
Meister, F., 470
Mel, B. W., 56
Melinder, A., 224
Melloni, R., 58
Mel'nikov, K. S., 230
Meltzer, H. Y., 478
Meltzer, L., 77
Meltzoff, A. N., 342
Melzack, R., 112
Mendelsohn, J., 305
Mendez, M. F., 69
Menlove, F. L., 194, 501
Menon, G., 248
Menuhin, Y., 269f
Menzies, L., 467
Merali, Z., 423
Mercadillo, R. E., 80
Meri, J. W., 226
Merikangas, K. R., 483
Merluzzi, T. V., 435
Mermelstein, R., 425, 425f
Merrill, J., 158
Merryman, A., 550
Mesoudi, A., 9
Messerli-Buergy, N., 465
Messineo, M., 550
Messner, M., 529
Metcalfe, J., 218
Metzler, J., 242f
Meyer, A., 472f
Meyer, I., 186
Meyer, R. G., 149
Meyer-Bahlburg, H., 307
Meyerowitz, J., 309
Mezulis, A. H., 306, 308, 309, 474
Michael, R. T., 305, 306, 307
Micheau, J., 57
Mickey, B. J., 107
Midanik, L. T., 158
Middlebrooks, J. C., 107
Miesenbock, G., 70
Mifflin, L., 196
Mignon, A., 535
Miguez, G., 183
Mika, V. S., 442
Miklowitz, D. J., 478
Mikulincer, M., 346
Mikulka, P., 182
Milburn, N. G., 20
Miles, P., 541
Milgram, S., 546–547, 547f
Milicevic, D., 465
Miller, A. G., 395
Miller, C., 43
Miller, G., 143f, 487, 563
Miller, G. E., 424, 427
Miller, G. F., 281
Miller, J. A., 413
Miller, J. G., 538
Miller, L., 334, 435, 509
Miller, L. A., 319, 408
Miller, M. N., 299
Miller, N. E., 512
Miller, R. R., 171, 175, 183
Miller, T. I., 511, 511f
Miller-Jones, D., 280
Miller-Perrin, C., 182
Miller-Pogrund, T., 441
Milling, L., 113, 149
Millon, C., 480
Millon, T., 479, 480
Mills, D., 549
Mills, M. J., 309
Mills, P. J., 423
Milner, B., 73, 211, 228

Milton, J., 126
Milwidsky, A., 441
Miner, J., 349
Miner-Rubino, K., 371
Ming, G., 77
Ming, L., 148
Ming, Z., 57
Ming-Cheng, C., 423
Mingle, P., 161–162
Mintz, A., 20
Mintz, J., 477
Minuchin, S., 510
Miquel, J., 373
Mirrione, M., 456, 473
Mischel, W., 395, 400
Mischoulon, D., 517, 517f
Miserando, M., 219
Mishra, P. K., 293
Misra, G., 420
Mitchell, D. B., 375
Mitchell, P., 64–65
Mitic, K., 58
Mitschke, A., 138
Mitte, K., 504
Miyamoto, T., 80
Mizrahi, R., 515
Moceri, D., 196
Moffitt, T. E., 9, 331, 404
Mograss, M., 137
Mogri, M., 70
Mohan, A., 150
Mohan, R., 517
Mohapel, P., 57
Moher, C., 179
Mohr, D., 504
Mojtabai, R., 477
Mokdad, A. H., 158
Molholm, S., 107
Molina, J., 499
Mollaret, P., 535
Møller, A. R., 105
Monahan, J., 9
Monetta, L., 107
Monk, T. H., 137
Monro, W., 20
Montague, P. R., 437, 480
Monteith, M. J., 553
Montejo, M., 195
Monteleone, P., 143
Montepare, J. M., 556
Montgomery, G., 149
Montgomery, K. L., 465
Montgomery, S., 56
Montgomery, S. A., 162
Montoya, R., 556
Moody, H. R., 373
Moon, S. M., 510
Moore, B. C. J., 90
Moore, D. G., 342
Moore, M. M., 29
Moore, N., 137
Moore, P. J., 112
Moore, S. D., 173
Moore, T., 75
Moore, Z., 564
Moorey, S., 504
Moosmann, M., 118–119
Morad, Y., 137
Mora-Giral, M., 302
Moran, A., 242
Morano, M. I., 424
Morcom, A. M., 375
Moreau-Debord, I., 179
Morein-Zamir, S., 216
Moreland, R. L., 542
Moreno, R., 342
Moretz, M., 466
Morgan, A. A., 280
Morgan, T., 183
Morganstern, I., 299
Morina, N., 113
Morley, S., 112
Moro, L., 173
Morone, N. E., 82
Morran, D. K., 509
Morris, E., 271
Morris, J. F., 309
Morrison, P., 476
Morrone, A. S., 310
Morrow, J., 81–82, 182
Moscovitch, M., 214

Moseley, G., 112
Moselhy, H., 156
Moser, E., 122
Moser, M., 122
Mosher, C. J., 132, 154
Moshman, D., 361
Moskowitz, G. B., 534, 562
Moskowitz, J. T., 422, 428, 432
Moss-Morris, R., 8
Motley, M. T., 385
Moynahan, B., 240
Mu, X., 539
Muammar, O. M., 270
Mueller, C. E., 279
Mukamel, R., 215
Mukens, S., 500
Mullen, B., 551
Müller, H., 117
Müller, H. J., 220
Müller, J., 113
Müller, P. A., 562–563
Munakata, Y., 355
Mundle, G., 158
Mungan, E., 219
Mungas, D., 409
Muris, P., 465
Murphy, D. L., 467
Murphy, G. J., 109
Murphy, G. L., 242
Murphy, J. L., 442–443
Murphy, J. M., 174
Murphy, K. R., 480
Murphy, R. T., 422
Murphy, S. A., 445
Murphy, S. T., 313
Murray, B., 11
Murray, C. J. L., 436
Murray, D., 281–282
Murray, J. P., 196, 414
Murray, R., 58
Murray, R. M., 478
Murray, S. L., 556
Murre, J. M. J., 215
Murthy, P., 278, 337
Murzynowski, J., 149
Mustaca, A. E., 183
Muzina, D., 515
Muzio, R. N., 183
Myers, D. G., 445
Myers, J. O., 155
Myers, L. L., 301
Myers, L. M., 377
Myers, M., 499
Myrick, H., 500
Myrtek, M., 435
Mytinger, C., 266

N

Näätänen, R., 107
Nadeem, E., 360
Nader, K., 518
Nadon, R., 149
Nagai, Y., 82
Nagda, B. A., 553
Nagin, D. S., 480
Nagpal, R., 475
Nagy, T. F., 40–41
Nahari, G., 396, 535
Naimi, T. S., 158
Najman, J. M., 337
Naka, M., 226
Nakagawa, S., 517
Nakamizo, S., 121
Nakamura, Y., 109
Nakata, A., 143
Nakato, E., 343f
Nakovics, H., 158
Nalbantian, S., 225
Naldini, L., 334
Narcissus, 398
Nargeot, R., 179
Narr, K. L., 80
Narrow, W. E., 483
Nasir, N. S., 457–458
Nasrallah, H., 515
Nater, U. M., 427
Nathan, P. E., 511
National Adolescent Health
    Information Center, 358

National Association for the
    Education of Young
    Children, 348
National Center for Health
    Statistics, 345f
National Institute of Child
    Health and Human
    Development (NICHD) Early
    Child Care Research
    Network, 347–348, 348f
National Institute on Drug
    Abuse, 162–163
National Research Council, 347
Natvig, G. K., 431
Naveh-Benjamin, M., 208,
    222, 230
Nebeling, B., 162
Nederkoorn, C., 500
Neher, A., 9
Neitz, J., 100
Neitz, M., 100
Nelken, I., 104
Nellis, L., 273
Nelson, C. A., 72f
Nelson, D. E., 158
Nelson, W. M., III, 564
Neri, E., 436
Neria, Y., 423
Neron, S., 113
Nesheim, S., 337
Nesse, R. M., 473
Nestler, E. J., 152
Nestoriuc, Y., 82, 113
Nettelbeck, T., 234
Neubauer, A. C., 270
Neufeld, V., 144
Neumann, N., 71
Neumark-Sztainer, D., 20
Neumayr, B., 545
Neuzil, P. J., 392
Newby-Clark, I. R., 223
Newman, A., 420
Newman, C. F., 473
Newman, D., 480
Newman, L., 474
Newman, M., 77, 329, 331
Newman, S. D., 246
Newsom, J. T., 422–423
Newton, F. B., 483, 484f, 520
Nezworski, M. T., 413
Ng, J. R., 223
Nguyen, D., 98
Niccols, A., 337
Nichols, 19
Nickeas, R., 469
Nickerson, R. S., 229f
Niedenthal, P. M., 314
Nielsen, C., 111–112
Nielsen, M. E., 125
Nielsen, T., 138, 221
Nierenberg, A. A., 517
Niimi, R., 206
Nijboer, T. C. W., 100
Nikolaou, I., 444
Nil, R., 162
Nilsson, H., 244
Nimgaonkar, V. L., 475
Nimrod, G., 377
Nisbet, E. K., 445
Nisbett, R. E., 267, 282
Nishida, M., 136, 141
Nishimoto, S., 23f
Nishimura, T., 292–293
Nishino, S., 142
Nissle, S., 445
Nittrouer, S., 91
Niu, W., 267
Nixon, J. C., 151
Nixon, R. D. V., 291
Niyonsenga, T., 437
Nobre, P., 305
Nocon, A., 465
Nokelainen, P., 268
Nolan, R. P., 435
Nolen-Hoeksema, S., 454, 464f,
    474, 480
Norberg, K., 158
Norcia, M. A., 342
Norcross, J. C., 512, 513
NORC/University of
    Chicago, 309

Noren, G., 520
Norenzayan, A., 41
Norlander, T., 430
Norman, D. A., 212
Norton, M. I., 538
Norton, P. J., 498
Nosek, B. A., 220, 552
Novak, M. A., 43
Novello, A., 485–486
Novotny, C. M., 511, 512
Nowicki, S., Jr., 479
Noy, V. M., 436
Ntinas, K. M., 189
Nucci, L. P., 361
Nuechterlein, K. H., 477
Nurmi, J-E., 400
Nurnberger, J. I., Jr., 160
Nuss, C. K., 541
Nussbaum, A. D., 553
Nutt, D., 467
Nyberg, L., 211

O

Oakford, S., 279
Oatley, K., 313
Oberauer, K., 208
O'Brien, K. M., 302–303
O'Brien, M., 196
Obrocki, J., 162
Occhionero, M., 140
Ochsner, K., 321
O'Connor, D., 519
O'Connor, D. B., 300
O'Connor, R. C., 300
O'Doherty, J., 99
Oehlhof, M., 189
Oertli, K. A., 161–162
Offer, D., 225
Ogawa, Y., 143
Ogbu, J., 198
Ogloff, J. P., 454
Ogren, H. A., 315
Ogren, K., 519
Oh, S-S., 428
O'Hara, L. A., 254, 420
Ohira, T., 435
Ojha, H., 294
Okajima, I., 504
Okamoto, Y., 355
O'Keefe, J., 122
O'Keefe, T., 309
Olafsson, R. P., 498
Olatunji, B. O., 468
Olds, M. E., 73
Olea, J., 277
O'Leary, O. E, 516
Olfson, M., 517
Olivardia, R., 360
Olliver-Gray, Y., 197
Olmstead, M., 516
Olson, D. H., 371, 372
Olson, E. J., 142
Olson, J. M., 430, 432
Olson, T. R., 389
Olsson, H., 244
Oltmanns, T. F., 479
O'Malley, P. M., 152, 153f, 156,
    161, 161f, 438, 438f
O'Neal, K. K., 154
O'Neill, A., 296
Ono, H., 372
Ono, Y., 471
Operskalski, B., 471
Opler, M., 478
Oppenheimer, D. M., 245
O'Reardon, J. P., 519, 520
Ormerod, T. C., 255
Ornat, S. L., 259
Orne, E. C., 149
Orne, M. T., 149
Orozco, C., 161
Orr, S., 518
Orwin, R. G., 511
Osei, S. Y., 300
Oskamp, S., 549–550
Ospina-Kammerer, V., 420
O'Sullivan, D. M., 442–443
Otake, K., 445
Oudiette, D., 135

Ouimet, A., 468
Ovarnstrom, U., 431
Overstreet-Wadiche, L., 77
Oviedo-Joekes, E., 161
Owen, L., 204
Oxoby, R. J., 533
Ozeki, H., 70
Özpolat, A., 250

P

Pääbo, S., 25
Pachankis, J. E., 512
Packer, D., 543
Padberg, F., 470
Padgett, D. K., 457–458
Padovani, R., 147
Pagani, L., 480
Pagano, C., 161
Page, S., 82
Pager, D., 549
Paggi, A., 80
Pagnin, A., 374
Pagonis, T. A., 66
Pakhomov, S. V., 107
Palazzeschi, L., 268
Palermo, L., 194
Palesh, O., 436
Pallanti, S., 70
Paller, K., 220
Palmer, J. C., 224, 224f
Palmisano, S. A., 119
Palmores, A., 428
Paluck, E. L., 553
Pamplugh, C., 465
Pandya, M., 519
Paniagua, F. A., 458, 513
Pankove, E., 253–254
Papini, M. R., 183
Papirman, Y., 538
Papp, L. A., 467
Pappu, V., 233
Paquier, P. F., 70
Parachuri, R., 113
Paradis, S., 56
Parhar, P. K., 520
Parides, M., 516
Pariser, S., 515
Parish, C. L., 77
Parish, W., 305
Park, H., 545
Park, J., 537
Park, K., 537
Parke, R. D., 347
Parker, B., 516
Parker, K. J., 424
Parker-Pope, T., 298, 303
Parmley, M. C., 253
Parnes, A., 206
Parra, A., 126
Parrott, A., 162
Parsinger, M. A., 73
Parson, L. M., 74
Pasaye, E. H., 80
Pascual, A., 545
Pascual, A. C., 361
Pascual, J., 501
Pashler, H. E., 187
Pasqualetti, P., 211
Passik, S. D., 435
Passingham, R. E., 76
Patall, E., 37
Patel, D. R., 481
Paterson, H. M., 223
Patten, S., 443
Patterson, D., 148, 336
Paukert, A., 522
Paul, A. M., 415
Paulmann, S., 107, 114
Paulozzi, L. J., 156
Pautassi, R., 499
Pavitt, C., 535
Pavlopoulos, V., 397
Pavlov, I., 16f, 169, 170, 172, 174–175
Pawlby, S. J., 404
Paxson, A., 556–557
Paxton, J. M., 563
Payment, K. E., 223
Payne, D. G., 230

Payne, K., 512
Payne, L., 144
Pazzaglia, F., 241
Pearce, J. M. S., 113
Pearlstein, T., 486
Pearsall, J., 136, 141
Pearson, A. R., 549
Pearson, J., 98
Pedersen, N. L., 430
Pedersen, P. B., 513, 550, 553
Pedersen, S. S., 435
Pedersen, W. C., 561
Pedraza, O., 409
Peiro, J. M., 10
Pell, M. D., 107
Pellegrini, S., 183
Pelli, D. G., 99
Pellis, S. M., 347
Pellis, V. C., 347
Peltonen, L., 403
Peluso, J., 435
Pence, D., 532
Peng, K., 400
Peng, Y., 479
Penke, L., 281
Penley, J. A., 428
Penn, D. L., 474
Penner, L. A., 562
Penney, J. B., Jr., 56–57
Penzel, F., 467
Peper, C. E., 75
Peretz, I., 76
Peretz, R., 519
Perez, R. M., 309
Pérez-Leroux, A. T., 259
Perfetti, B., 268
Perlis, T., 156
Perloff, R. M., 529
Perovic, S., 329
Perrett, D. I., 556
Perrin, M., 478
Perrin, R., 182
Perry, J., 389
Perl, C. B., 58
Perucci, C. A., 161
Perunovic, M., 435
Pervin, L. A., 397f, 406
Pesce, N. L., 50
Pesiridou, A., 519, 520
Pesmen, C., 111, 113
Pessoa, L., 319
Peterfi, Z., 136
Peters, E., 374
Peters, J., 214, 437f
Petersen, A., 137
Petersen, K., 162
Peterson, A. L., 113
Peterson, C., 445
Peterson, L. R., 211
Peterson, M. J., 211
Peterson, R. A., 112
Petersson, K. M., 80
Petit, A., 69
Petit, J. W., 473
Petitto, L. A., 264
Petraglia, J., 389
Petrill, S. A., 331
Petrou, S., 471
Petrovic, K. K., 69
Pettigrew, T. F., 549, 553
Pettito, L. A., 79, 258
Petty, R. E., 445, 530
Peynircioğlu, Z. F., 219
Pfeffer, C. R., 473
Phelps, E. A., 499
Phelps, R. P., 276
Philip, P., 137
Phillips, E. L., 481
Phillips, R. S., 132
Piaget, J., 17f, 352f, 352–355
Picano, J., 430
Picasso, P., 254, 254f
Picchioni, D., 140
Pickard, N., 206
Pickel, K., 223
Pickering, G. J., 109
Pickett, C. L., 551
Piefke, M., 54, 194
Piel, E., 138
Pietarinen, A-V., 258
Piette, J., 442

Piliavin, J. A., 562
Pillay, S. S., 465
Pilling, M., 342
Pilotti, M., 230
Pilowsky, L., 476
Pincus, H. A., 459
Pincus, T., 112
Pine, D. S., 465, 467
Pinel, J. P. J., 291
Pinker, S., 260, 261, 330
Pinkerton, S. D., 305
Pinna, B., 99
Pinquart, M., 520
Pintrich, P. R., 310
Piquero, A. R., 182
Piriz, J., 456
Pirvulescu, M., 259
Pi-Sunyer, X., 301
Pitman, R., 518
Pittman, J., 483
Platek, S., 99
Plato, 14
Platt, B. B., 57
Pleger, B., 75
Ploeger, A., 89
Plomin, R., 50, 278, 281, 330, 404, 476
Plowright, C. M. S., 174
Plucker, J. A., 254
Pluess, M., 329, 348
Plug, C., 121
Poehlman, T., 552
Pogarsky, G., 182
Poirier, C., 10
Polcin, D. L., 153
Pole, N., 422–423
Polivy, J., 301, 302
Pollack, A., 71
Pollak, K. I., 545
Pollard, H. P., 113
Pollitt, E., 403
Pollmacher, T., 140
Polonsky, D. C., 305
Poltrack, D., 530
Pomerlau, O. F., 436
Ponterotto, J. G., 513, 550, 553
Poo, C., 77
Poole, B., 118–119
Poorman, M., 494, 524
Popa, D., 58, 473
Pope, H., 360
Pope, K. S., 225
Popik, P., 516–517
Porges, F. C., 563f
Porkka-Heiskanen, T., 290
Porte, H. S., 141
Post, J., 20
Post, J. M., 544
Postl, L., 501
Postman, L. J., 223
Poteat, V. P., 308
Potokar, J., 467
Pottick, K. J., 513
Potts-Datema, W., 336
Poulos, A. M., 55–56
Povey, R., 532
Powell, A. A., 562
Powell, L., 20
Powell, L. H., 306, 431
Powell, R. A., 172
Power, R., Jr., 470
Powers, K. D., 361
Powers, M., 500
Pozuelo, L., 519
Pramanick, M., 294
Pras, E., 137
Prasad, B., 245
Pratkanis, A. R., 125, 543, 545
Pratt, H. D., 481
Pratto, E., 549
Pratto, F., 310
Prentice, D., 551
Presniak, M. D., 389
Press, J., 373
Pressley, M. P., 270
Pretz, J. E., 267, 270, 271
Pretzer, J. L., 512
Price, D., 111–112
Price, E. C., 498
Price, L. R., 113

Price, M., 516
Priester, J. R., 445, 530
Prigot, J., 108
Prince, C. V., 309
Prince, M. J., 483
Prinz, J. J., 319
Prislin, R., 542
Proctor, R. W., 254
Proffitt, D. R., 120
Prohovnik, I., 319
Proudfoot, D., 245, 262
Proulx, C. D., 456, 473
Pruce, B., 246
Pryor, D. W., 307
Psotka, J., 231
Puca, R. M., 310
Puhl, R., 20
Pullum, G. K., 261
Pumariega, A. J., 299
Purselle, D. C., 159
Putnam, F. W., 470

Q

Quartana, P. J., 564
Quas, J. A., 224
Quenot, J. P., 69
Quillian, M. R., 213
Quinlin, K. J., 481
Quinn, D. M., 460
Quintana, S. M., 24

R

Rabey, J. M., 519
Rabin, J., 100
Rabinowitz, J., 476, 477
Rabson-Hare, J., 37
Racenstein, J. M., 474
Rachman, S., 465
Raczynski, J. M., 300
Raddatz, G., 100f
Radenovic, L., 329
Rado, J., 70
Rae, D. S., 483
Ragert, P., 75
Rahman, M., 307
Räikkönen, K., 403
Raitakari, O. T., 403
Raja, S. N., 113
Rajagopal, S., 44, 58
Rajecki, D. W., 11
Ralston, A., 289, 295
Ram, C., 109
Ramachandran, V. S., 54, 113, 114, 114f
Ramchandani, P. G., 471
Ramirez, A. J. R., 555
Rammsayer, T., 270
Ramos, R. T., 56
Ramsay, M. C., 280, 413
Ramssen, E., 156
Ramus, F., 334
Rando, R., 486
Randolph-Seng, B., 125
Rangell, L., 456
Ransom, B. R., 51
Rapaport, M., 517
Rapee, R. A., 501
Rapoport, J., 80
Rapoport-Hubschman, N., 443
Rapport, R. L., 56
Raskin, N. J., 508
Rasmussen, F., 300
Rasmussen, N., 216
Rassin, E., 253, 465
Ratner, K. G., 534
Ravindran, A. V., 423
Ravitz, P., 509
Ray, L., 403
Ray, L. A., 154
Ray, R., 155
Rayner, R., 172
Raz, A., 147
Raznahan, A., 80
Read, D., 244
Read, J., 158
Realo, A., 397
Rector, N. A., 503, 504

Redding, G. M., 121, 123
Redish, A. D., 156
Reece, M., 30
Reed, G. M., 427, 445
Reed, M., 545
Reed, P., 182, 183
Reed, S. K., 250
Reese, R. J., 522
Reese-Durham, N., 268
Reetz, D., 486
Reeves, A. J., 79
Regan, P. C., 556–557
Regier, D. A., 483
Reichel, M., 349
Reichenberg, A., 477
Reid, J. R., 161
Reijonen, J. H., 481
Reilly, T., 143
Reilly-Harrington, N. A., 473
Reiner, R., 82
Reinhard, I., 138
Reinhard, M., 529
Reis, A., 80
Reisberg, D., 249, 257
Reiss, S., 293
Relier, J. P., 337
Remington, R., 118–119
Rende, R., 9
Repp, B. H., 124
Rescorla, R. A., 175
Resick, P., 430
Resurreccion, N., 430
Reynolds, C., 29
Reynolds, C. R., 280, 413
Ricci, F., 147
Ricci, L., 58
Riccio, C., 29
Rice, C., 481
Rice, D. R., 551
Rice, E., 20
Rice, M. L., 259
Rich, E. L., 73
Rich, S., 402, 402f
Richard, D. C. S., 501
Richards, C., 309
Richards, J. S., 113
Richards, R., 254
Richardson, A. S., 365
Richardson, D., 560
Richardson, D. L., 437
Richardson, G. A., 337
Richgels, D. J., 258
Richmond, V. P., 20
Ridge, T., 421
Rieber, R. W., 356
Riedel, G. G., 57
Rief, W., 82
Rif, J., 206
Rigby, L., 509
Riggins, R., Jr., 348
Riggs, L., 214
Rimrodt, S. L., 79
Rinaman, L., 317
Ringwalt, C., 154
Riniolo, T. C., 29
Rinne, J. O., 69
Rintala, D. H., 113
Riolo, E., 390
Risley, T. R., 259
Ritezschel, J., 109
Ritterfeld, U., 196
Rivera, R., 420
Rivera-Gaxiola, M., 344
Rizvi, S. L., 430, 501
Rizzo, M., 142
Robbins, B., 19
Robbins, W. J., 345f
Roberge, Y., 259
Robert, J., 78
Robert, S., 257
Roberts, J. E., 348
Roberts, M. E., 173
Robertson, E., 211
Robertson, J. M., 483, 484f, 520
Robertson, J. R., 161
Robertson, K., 518
Robins, C. J., 501
Robins, L. N., 483, 487
Robins, R. W., 225, 315, 403
Robinson, D. G., 467, 467f
Robinson, D. K., 356

Robinson, D. N., 102, 516
Robinson, R. E., 152
Robinson, T. E., 77
Roch-Locours, L. A., 79
Rock, A., 438
Rodd, Z. A., 174
Rodgers, C. S., 112
Roe, C., 376
Roecklein, K. A., 143
Roehrig, J. P., 297
Roesch, S. C., 428
Roets, A., 291
Rogalsky, C., 54
Rogers, C. R., 17f, 19, 405, 405f, 406f, 457, 507–508
Rogers, J. M., 337
Rogers, L. J., 78
Rogers, P., 152, 562
Rogers, S., 375, 477
Rogowska, J., 465
Rohan, K. J., 143
Rohleder, N., 427
Roid, G., 273
Roisman, G. I., 346
Roizen, N. J., 336
Roland, C., 156
Roland, J., 71
Roland, R., 430
Roll, J., 19
Rollman, G. B., 112
Rolls, E. T., 109, 314
Rom, S. A., 435
Romanczyk, R. G., 178
Romano, E., 480
Romeu, P. E, 221
Rönnberg, J., 210
Rooke, S. E., 158
Rooney, N. J., 182
Roosevelt, E., 293
Ropele, S. S., 69
Rorschach, H., 413
Roscoe, J. A., 435
Rosen, H., 504
Rosen, J., 78
Rosenbaum, M., 301
Rosenbaum, R. S., 232
Rosenbloom, T., 290
Rosenhan, D. L., 460
Rosenheck, R., 457–458
Rosenstein, D. S., 479
Rosenthal, A. M., 562
Rosenthal, L., 141
Rosenthal, M., 501
Rosenthal, N. F., 446
Rosenthal, R., 43
Rosenvinge, J. H., 422, 430
Roska, B., 99
Ross, C. A., 469
Ross, D., 194
Ross, H. E., 121
Ross, J., 140
Ross, L., 395
Ross, L. A., 107
Ross, M., 223
Ross, P. E., 262
Ross, S., 194
Rossato, M., 161
Rosseel, Y., 473
Rossi, E., 51
Rossi, J. J., 334
Rossouw, J. E., 370
Rotan, L. W., 420
Roter, D. L., 442–443
Roth, Y., 109
Rothbart, M. K., 403
Rothblum, E. D., 309
Rothman, A. J., 444
Rothstein, H. R., 196
Roughton, R. E., 308
Routtenberg, A., 73
Rouw, R., 114
Rowan, K., 349
Rowe, J. B., 76
Royzman, E. B., 347
Rozencwajg, P., 374
Rozenkrantz, L., 109
Rozin, P., 299
Rubboli, G., 80
Rubenstein, B. S., 141
Rubichi, S., 147
Rubin, D. C., 221, 222f, 226

Ruck, M. D., 37
Rudner, M., 210
Rudorfer, M. V., 467
Rudzinski, D., 496
Ruiz-Vargas, J., 230
Rünger, D., 194
Runyan, D., 182
Rupert, G. K., 300
Rusche, B., 43
Ruscher, J. B., 534
Rushton, J. P., 409
Rusjan, P., 515
Russell, J. A., 315
Russo, N., 408
Rust, T. B., 375
Ruth, B., 269f
Rutherford, B., 43
Ruthsatz, J. M., 277–278
Rutter, M., 329, 331
Ruud, R., 344
Ryan, B., 185
Ryan, R. M., 294
Rydell, R., 533
Rymer, R., 258
Ryncarz, R. A., 361
Ryner, L., 69

S

Saarni, C., 349
Sabater, J., 245
Sable, H. J. K., 174
Sacco, D., 551
Sachs-Ericsson, N., 376
Sacks, O., 74
Saczynski, J., 374
Sado, M., 471
Safer, M. A., 223, 223f
Saffran, J. R., 121–122
Sagarin, B. J., 545
Sagaspe, P., 137
Saggino, A., 268
Sagi, D., 141
Sahakian, B. J., 216
Sahin, N. T., 260
St. Dennis, C., 521
St. Jacques, P. L., 375
Sakamoto, A., 196
Sakano, Y., 504
Sakihara, S., 431
Sakurai, S., 292–293
Salat, D. H., 233
Saleem, M., 196
Salgado, D. M., 481
Sallquist, J., 562
Salmela-Aro, K., 400
Salovey, P., 271, 272, 444
Salsman, N. L., 501, 509
Saltel, P., 443
Salvendy, G., 254
Salvi, V., 517
Samaniego, C. M., 361
Samantaray, S. K., 294
Samoilov, V., 170
Sams, M., 206
Samuel, D. B., 460
Sanacora, G., 471
Sanchez, A., 365
Sandberg, D., 144
Sanderson, M., 454
Sandlund, M., 519
Sandomir, R., 66
Sandoval, J., 281
Saneyoshi, A., 206
Sanislow, C. A., 480
Sanjuan, E., 181
Sanlier, N., 422
Sanouri, A., 437
Santel, S., 302
Santelli, J., 30
Santhouse, C., 79
Saper, C. B., 135, 143
Sapolsky, R. M., 427, 520
Sarai, E., 136
Sargent, J. D., 436
Sarsour, K., 372
Sarver, D. E., 464
Sasanabe, R., 142
Sasayama, D., 403
Sato, K., 315

Sato, N., 334
Satpute, A. B., 195f
Saucier, D. A., 43
Saul, R. E., 69
Saulsberry, K., 444
Savage, J., 196
Savage-Rumbaugh, E. S., 262, 262f
Savas, H. A., 515
Savazzi, S., 80
Savitsky, K., 125
Sawa, A., 476, 515
Saywitz, K., 224
Scaglietti, L., 147
Scaramella, L. V., 336
Scarborough, E., 15
Scarr, S., 282, 404
Scaturo, D. J., 509
Scelfo, J., 471
Schachter, R., 509
Schachter, S., 318
Schack, T., 242
Schacter, D. L., 220
Schaefer, C., 424f
Schaefer, E. G., 220
Schaefer, H. S., 431, 431f
Schaefer, R. T., 371
Schäfer, M., 277
Schaffner, K. F., 476
Schaie, K. W., 373, 374, 375f
Schalk, G., 71
Schaller, M., 356, 545
Schallert, D. L., 315
Schaufeli, W. B., 541
Schechter, T., 337
Schedlowski, M., 436
Scheff, T. J., 454
Scheier, M. F., 376, 410f
Schenone, M. H., 335
Schepers, P., 254
Scherer, K. R., 321
Schermer, J., 64, 330
Scherzer, T. R., 121–122
Schettler, P. J., 517
Schick, K., 262
Schieber, E., 373
Schienle, A., 318
Schiffer, A. A., 435
Schillinger, D., 442
Schimpf, P. H., 70
Schlarb, J. E., 137
Schlenger, W. E., 162
Schlinger, H. R., 19
Schmid, S., 504
Schmidt, J. P., 56–57
Schmidt, N. B., 460
Schmidt, U., 162
Schmitt, D. P., 397
Schmitt, F. A., 80, 375
Schmitt, M., 220
Schmitz, S., 155
Schmunk, G., 155
Schnabel, K., 552
Schnake, S. B., 534
Schnall, S., 562–563
Schnatz, P. F., 442–443
Schneble, E. J., 57
Schneider, A., 139f
Schneider, W., 356
Schnell, K., 502f
Schnupp, J., 76, 104
Schnyer, D. M., 220
Schoen, H., 397
Schoenen, J., 82
Schöner, J., 148
Schooler, L. J., 228
Schooler, N. R., 476
Schramm, E., 509
Schrauf, R. W., 226
Schredl, M., 138
Schreurs, B. G., 173
Schrier, R. W., 439
Schroeder, D. A., 562
Schroers, M., 108
Schubert, T., 311
Schulenberg, J. E., 152, 153f, 156, 161, 161f, 438, 438f
Schulte-Ruther, M., 54, 194
Schultz, E., 168
Schulz, D., 456, 473
Schulze, O., 162

Schulze-Bonhage, A., 80
Schumann, R., 472
Schurch, E., 511
Schutte, N. S., 511
Schwab, J. R., 293, 475
Schwartz, B. L., 218
Schwartz, J., 543
Schwartz, J. H., 60
Schwartz, J. M., 77
Schwartz, P., 364
Schwartz, S. J., 368
Schwartzmant, R. J., 516–517, 517
Schwarz, N., 445–446, 552
Schweinberger, S., 99
Schweizer, S., 210
Schwenkreis, P., 75
Sciaki-Tamir, Y., 441
Sciutto, M., 480
Scollon, C. N., 445–446
Scullin, M. H., 224
Seaton-Smith, K. L., 160
Sebanz, N., 124
Sebastiani, L., 99
Sebel, P. S., 220
Seeley, J. R., 473
Seeley, R., 70XR, 106f
Seeman, P., 58
Seery, M. D., 429
Sefcek, J. A., 8–9
Segal, D. L., 392
Segal, N., 402, 402f
Segall, M. H., 123
Segerstrom, S. C., 427
Seibt, B., 549–550
Seider, S., 268
Seifert, A. L., 549
Seli, H., 290
Selkoe, D. J., 232, 376
Sellbom, M., 411
Sells, R., 307
Selmon, N., 399
Selove, R., 336
Selsky, A., 366
Selye, H., 426f, 426–427
Semin, G. R., 257, 534
Semler, C. N., 141
Semykina, A., 310
Senghas, A., 321
Serdaris, N., 444
Seroczynski, A. D., 480
Sestir, M. A., 196
Seth, A. K., 132
Setter, S. M., 521
Seuss, Dr., 335
Seymour, B., 299
Shafer, V. L., 258
Shafran, R., 302–303
Shah, D. B., 520
Shahabi, L., 431
Shaikholeslami, R., 292
Shalvi, S., 64–65
Shamblen, S. R., 154
Shankar, G., 43
Shanok, A., 509
Shapiro, C. J., 480
Shapiro, L. R., 221
Shapiro, M. L., 73
Shapiro, S. L., 150
Sharma, H. S., 155
Sharma, M., 71
Sharma, R., 150
Sharman, S. J., 225
Sharp, C., 480
Sharpe, D., 443–444
Shastri, J., 347
Shaver, P. R., 315f, 346
Shea, A., 337
Shelton, R. C., 517, 520
Shen, C. K., 77
Shen, L., 314
Shepard, R. N., 242f
Shepherd, H., 549
Shepherd, R., 532
Sheppard, L. D., 270
Shepperd, J., 537–538
Sher, K., 365
Sherblom, S., 362
Sherman, D., 135

Sherman, J., 82
Sherman, S. L., 278, 336
Shibuya, A., 196
Shier, D., 97f
Shiffman, S., 438
Shiffrin, R. M., 205–206, 206f
Shimai, S., 445
Shimamura, M., 334
Shimono, K., 120
Shin, A., 290
Shinn, M., 521
Shiomi, T., 142
Shipherd, J., 430
Shizgal, P., 179
Shmuel, A., 100f
Shoda, Y., 400
Shono, Y., 230
Shorer, R., 519
Shors, T. J., 77
Short, E. L., 280
Shugart, H. A., 296
Shurkin, J. N., 279
Shusha, S., 109
Shwalk, D. A., 516
Shweder, R. A., 315
Sibley, C. G., 529
Sidman, M., 182
Siebler, F., 531
Siegel, R. K., 151
Siegert, R. J., 473
Siegler, I. C., 435
Sierra, C., 245
Sierra-Biddle, D., 465
Sifrit, K. J., 210
Silbersweig, D. A., 478
Sill, M., 374
Silva, A. J., 109
Silva, C., 80
Silva, M. T. A., 187
Silver, R., 429
Silverman, B., 76
Silverman, K., 19
Silverman, M. M., 494
Silverstein, M. L., 413
Simcock, G., 225
Simmers, J., 179
Simmons, A., 43
Simon, G., 471
Simon, S., 529
Simon, T., 273
Simonds, V. M., 174
Simonton, D. K., 29, 254
Simpson, N., 465
Sinclair, A., 20
Singer, B., 521
Singer, J. E., 318
Singer, J. L., 144
Singer, L. T., 337
Singh, A., 297
Singh, S., 306
Sininger, Y. S., 107
Sipes, B., 368
Sjoquist, P. O., 155
Skinner, B. F., 17f, 19, 178–179, 179f, 259, 399, 406f
Skoblar, B., 213
Skodol, A. E., 472
Skolnick, P., 516–517
Skoner, D. P., 425
Skowronski, J. J., 225, 535
Slater, D., 175
Slater, E., 472f
Slater, S., 420, 448
Sleek, S., 271
Sloan, E. K., 430
Sloan, E. P., 145
Sloboda, A., 154
Slocombe, K. E., 262
Slomkowski, C., 487
Slotnick, B. M., 112
Smart, R. G., 152
Smetana, J. B., 391
Smetana, J. G., 364
Smith, B. H., 278, 480
Smith, C., 140
Smith, C. A., 432
Smith, C. D., 80
Smith, D. E., 182
Smith, D. W., 173
Smith, E., 436
Smith, E. R., 534

Smith, G., 389
Smith, J., 349
Smith, J. R., 73
Smith, K., 142
Smith, M. B., 40
Smith, M. L., 511, 512f
Smith, R., 137
Smith, R. A., 555
Smith, S. E., 421
Smith, S. M., 398
Smith, W. B., 392
Smith-Bell, C. A., 173
Smith-Crowe, K., 556
Smrtnik-Vitulič, H., 396
Snider, R. K., 107
Snidman, N., 403
Snyder, D., 307
Snyder, D. J., 109
Snyder, J., 349
Snyder, M., 405
Snyder, S. H., 476, 515
Sobel, K., 118–119
Sobel, N., 109
Society for Personality
    Assessment, 413
Sodian, B., 356
Soeter, M., 518
Sohr-Preston, S. L., 336
Sokolove, M., 454
Soler, J., 501
Solesio-Jofre, E., 230
Solis, J., 71
Solms, M., 391
Solomon, M., 474
Solomon, S. D., 422
Solomon, Z. Z., 423
Somers, T. J., 112
Somers, V. K., 142
Sommer, B., 30
Sommer, R., 30
Sood, A. K., 430
Soorya, L. V., 178
Sorek, S., 230
Sori, C. E., 510
Sorosky, J. I., 442–443
Sorrell, J. T., 112
South, S., 404
Spackman, M. P., 315
Spanos, N. P., 113, 147
Sparks, J., 142
Sparks, P., 532
Sparrow, B., 211, 211f
Spear, L., 499
Spear, N. E., 499
Spearman, C., 267
Spector, P. E., 272
Spence, M. J., 335
Spencer, S. J., 430, 432
Spencer-Rodgers, J., 400
Sperling, G., 207
Sperry, R., 80
Spiegel, D., 50, 79, 436, 443,
    469, 512
Spielberger, C. D., 390
Spiers, H. J., 214, 215f
Spies, C. D., 438
Spillmann, L., 99
Spindler, H., 435
Spinella, M., 445
Spinrad, T. L., 562
Spitoni, G., 268
Spitz, H. I., 153
Spitzer, L., 373
Spitzer, R. L., 472
Sporer, S., 529
Sprecher, S., 306, 556
Spreer, J., 80
Sprenger, M., 209
Sprenkle, D. H., 510
Springen, K., 133
Springer, C. M., 182
Springer, P. R., 510
Spunt, R. P., 195f
Squire, L. R., 215
Sririam, N., 220
Srivastava, M., 294
Staddon, J. E. R., 182
Stafford, J., 372
Stagner, B., 522
Stahl, L., 204
Staley, J. K., 471

Stang, P. E., 483
Stangier, U., 509
Stanhope, V., 457–458
Stankov, L., 267
Stanojević, D., 561
Stanojević, P., 561
Stanojevic, S., 58
Stanton, A. L., 428
Stapel, D. A., 257
Starcevic, V., 465
Starchenko, M. G., 107
Stark, J., 77
Stark, R., 318
Stark, S., 77
Startup, M., 475
Stasinos, J., 442
Statham, J. A., 375
Staub, A., 32
Staud, R., 111–112
Steblay, N., 223
Stecker, G. C., 107
Steele, C. M., 553
Steele, J. D., 520
Stegerwald, F., 309
Steiger, A., 136
Stein, L. A. R., 411
Steinberg, L., 364
Steinberg, M. B., 437
Steiner, J., 497
Steiner, M., 337, 486
Steiner, R. D., 336
Steinhardt, M. A., 421
Steketee, G., 466, 468
Stemler, S. E., 270
Stenbacka, L., 76
Stenklev, N. C., 373
Stephens, T., 70XR, 106f
Stephenson, R., 113
Steptoe, A., 432
Stern, E., 478
Stern, R. M., 108
Sternberg, R. J., 62, 197, 254,
    267, 270–271, 279, 282, 331,
    420, 557f, 557–558, 558
Stettler, N., 300
Stevens, G., 15
Stevens, M. J., 10
Stevens, P., 519
Stevens, S. S., 187
Stevenson, H. W., 539
Stevenson, J. L., 144
Stevenson, R. J., 108
Stewart, A., 442
Stewart, A. J., 371
Stewart, D., 510
Stewart, P. J., 226
Stickgold, R., 140
Stickley, T., 469
Stidd, R., 80
Stifter, C. A., 318
Stiling, P., 81f, 105f
Stillman, T., 305
Stinson, F. S., 398
Stitzer, M. L., 436
Stix, G., 216, 430
Stockman, M., 80
Stocks, E., 562
Stockton, R., 509
Stolick, M., 161–162
Stone, J., 476, 553
Stoolmiller, M., 436
Storm, L., 126
Stouffer, E. M., 194
Strange, D., 225
Strathern, A., 226
Strathman, A. J., 530
Strauss, E., 80
Strayer, D. L., 210
Striano, T., 342, 343
Striegel-Moore, R., 301, 302
Strong, T., 510
Struckman, C. K., 543
Struening, E. L., 483
Strupp, H. H., 512
Stuart, S. P., 511
Stubhaug, A., 111–112
Stulz, N., 511
Sturgeon, R. D., 400
Subasi, V., 113
Suchan, B., 214
Suckling, J., 467

Sue, D., 497, 513
Sue, D. W., 497, 513
Sue, S., 24, 497
Suetsugu, T., 206
Sufian, J. T., 334
Suh, E. M., 446
Suhail, K., 446
Suizzo, M-A., 347
Sullivan, A., 269f
Sullivan, E., 560
Sullivan, J., 29
Sullivan, L. M., 435
Summers, M., 466
Summers, R., 63
Sung, R. Y. T., 297
Sung, W., 194
Super, C. M., 354
Suppes, T., 143
Surette, R., 196
Suridjan, I., 515
Sutin, A. R., 225
Sutton, R. M., 529
Suzuki, K., 517
Suzuki, L. A., 280, 281
Svarstad, B., 442
Svartdal, F., 183
Swahn, M. H., 365
Swain, P. I., 302
Swain, R. A., 70
Swales, M. A., 501
Swaminathan, V., 219
Swartz, H., 517
Sweeny, K., 537–538
Swencionis, J. K., 222
Swing, E. L., 196
Szasz, T. S., 455–456, 460
Szegedy Maszak, M., 472
Szmalec, A., 210
Szrama, N., 71
Szymusiak, R., 136

T

Tadmor, C. T., 264
Taillard, J., 137
Tajfel, H., 550, 551
Tajiri, N. N., 77
Takahashi, M., 143
Takahashi, R., 430
Takeuchi, D., 334
Takizawa, R., 431
Talajic, M., 436
Talarico, J., 221
Talbot, N., 469
Talmi, D., 214
Tal-Or, N., 538
Talukdar, S., 347
Tam, H., 209
Tam, T. W., 158
Tamagnan, G., 471
Tamborini, R., 545
Tamini, B., 556
Tammaro, E., 81–82
Tan, G., 113
Tan, L., 211, 261
Tan, Ü., 112
Tanaka, T., 517
Tanaka-Matsumi, J., 445
Tani, J., 334
Tanja, M., 173
Tanne, D., 141
Tanner, J. M., 359, 359f
Taras, V., 428
Tasker, F., 308
Tassinari, C. A., 80
Tate, P., 70XR, 106f
Taylor, A., 404, 432
Taylor, B., 348
Taylor, C. S., 75
Taylor, F., 138
Taylor, G. J., 435
Taylor, M., 430
Taylor, N., 161
Taylor, S. E., 427, 428, 430, 432,
    441, 445
Tcheremissine, O. V., 161
Tees, R. C., 336
Tegenthoff, M., 75
Telch, M. J., 465

Tellegen, A., 402, 402f, 406f
Tempakski, B., 154
Tenenbaum, H. R., 37
Tenopyr, M. L., 267
Teodorov, E., 307
te Pas, S. F., 100
Tepper, B. J., 109
Teraishi, T., 403
Terganiemi, M., 107
Terman, L., 279
Terracciano, A., 400
Tewes, U., 436
Thachil, A. F., 517
Tharp, R. G., 197
Thase, M. E., 517, 520
Thatcher, D. L., 159
Theerman, P., 112
Theodore, A., 182
Theorell, T., 427
Theoret, H., 54, 194
Thomas, P., 475
Thomas, S., 499
Thomasius, R., 162
Thompson, C. P., 225
Thompson, D. M., 230
Thompson, J., 223
Thompson, K. R., 70
Thompson, L. F., 561
Thompson, M. C., 478
Thompson, P. M., 80
Thompson, R. F., 70
Thompson, S. S., 230
Thompson, W. W., 373
Thompson-Brenner, H.,
    511, 512
Thoresen, C. E., 431
Thorkildsen, T. A., 262
Thorndike, E. L., 177–178, 178f
Thorne-Yocam, K. A., 436
Thornton, A., 306
Thorpe, K., 296
Thorsteinsson, E. B., 511
Thrash, T. M., 310
Tian, X., 513
Tiana, T., 501
Tibbs, T., 430
Tierney Lindsey, K., 143
Tiggemann, M., 225
Tihanyi, B. T., 141
Tippin, J., 142
Tirri, K., 268
Titone, D. A., 135
Todd, T. P., 175
Todorov, A., 551
Toga, A. W., 80
Tokumori, K., 109
Tolman, E. C., 192
Tomaka, J., 428
Tomm, K., 510
Tommasi, L., 78
Toni, I., 76
Tononi, G., 132
Tooby, J., 187
Toribio, I., 161
Toth, J. P., 220
Toth, N., 262
Touhara, K., 109
Towsley, S., 403
Tracy, J. L., 315
Trainor, C. D., 137
Tramontana, J., 149
Tran, C., 428
Tranter, L. J., 268
Travis, F., 149, 151
Treiber, F. A., 149
Tremaine, M., 75
Tremblay, A., 300
Tremblay, J., 518
Tremblay, R. E., 480
Treur, J., 249
Treves, A., 122
Trevino, L., 442
Triesch, J., 54
Trimble, J. E., 513
Trimble, M. R., 82
Triscari, M., 499
Troche, S., 270
Tropp, L. R., 553
Trost, W. T., 501
Trujillo-Pisanty, I., 179
Trull, T. J., 480

Trullas, R., 516–517
Tsai, D., 530
Tsai, K. J., 77
Tsai, Y. C., 77
Tsaousis, I., 444
Tschitsaz, A., 511
Tseng, W. C., 483, 484f, 520
Tseng, W. S., 483, 487, 513
Tsuchiya, M., 471
Tsukasaki, T., 261
Tsunoda, T., 80
Tuch, D. S., 233
Tuerk, P. W., 500
Tuerlinckx, F., 310
Tugay, N., 113
Tulving, E., 211, 230, 231
Turecki, G., 428
Turk, D. C., 112
Turkewitz, G., 79
Turkheimer, E., 479
Turnbull, O., 391
Turner, J. C., 550, 551
Turner, M. E., 543, 545
Turner, R., 425
Turner, S. M., 467
Turvey, M. T., 206
Tuszynski, M. H., 520
Tversky, A., 248
Twenge, J., 398, 400, 486, 541
Tydgat, I., 211
Tyler, J. M., 553
Tynelius, P., 300
Tzeng, O. L., 194

U

Ubell, E., 145
Ueda, H., 142
Ugurbil, K., 100f
Uhl, G., 187
Uhlmann, E., 552
Ulbert, I., 141
UmiltÀ, C., 407
Umphress, E. E., 556
Underwood, A., 113, 159
U.S. Bureau of the Census, 372
U.S. Senate Select Committee
    on Intelligence, 253
Unsworth, N., 210
Unterrainer, J. M., 80
Unützer, J., 471
Updegraff, K. A., 362–363
Urbina, S., 276
Urso, V., 499
Ursprung, W. W., 437
Usmani, Y., 516
Ustun, T. B., 483
Utsey, S. O., 550, 553
Uylings, H. B. M., 336
Uzelac, S., 364

V

Vaccaro, D., 51
Vaillant, C. O., 370
Vaillant, G. E., 370
Vaish, A., 343
Vaitl, D., 318
Valencia, R. R., 281
Valentijn, A. M., 374
Valenza, E., 342
Vallortigara, G., 78
Vanasse, A., 437
Van Belle, V., 246
Van De Graaff, K., 214f
Vandell, D. L., 348
van den Berg, P. T., 254
van den Bos, K., 541, 562–563
Van den Wildenberg,
    W. P. M., 355
van der Helm, E., 136, 137f
van der Helm, P. A., 117
Van der Kouwe, A. J. W., 233
Van der Molen, M. W., 355
van der Smagt, M. J., 100
Vandervert, L. R., 70
Van der Zee, E. A., 57
van Deusen, A., 82
Vandierendonck, A., 210

Van Dijk, W. W., 315
Van Essen-Zandvliet, L. E. M., 441
Vanheule, S., 473
Van Hiel, A., 291
van Hooren, S. A. H., 374
Van Kleef, G. A., 64–65
van Marle, K., 355
Vanni, S., 76
van Nieuwenhuijzen, M. M., 278
van Oort, R., 232
Van Oppen, P., 511
Van Overwalle, F., 531
Van Petegem, P., 364
van Soelen, I. C., 281
van Straten, A., 511
Varga, M., 140
Varjassyová, A., 232
Vartanian, O., 246
Vasquez, G., 8–9
Vassalli, A., 290
Vassend, O., 111–112
Västfjäll, D., 440
Vecchi, T., 374
Vecchione, M., 397
Vedhara, K., 420
Vega, C. P., 29
Vegas, R., 187
Veilleux, J. C., 437
Velentzas, K., 242
Vella-Brodrick, D. A., 444
Vellacott, J., 349
Veltman, M. W. M., 258
Vender Hoorn, S., 436
Veniegas, R. C., 307
Venter, J., 498
Verdejo, A., 161
Verdon, B., 310
Verfaellie, M., 232
Vermani, M., 112
Vernon, P. A., 64, 270, 330
Verona, E., 560
Vettor, R., 161
Vickers, L., 64
Victor, S. B., 308
Vieira, E. M., 508
Vieira, K., 330
Vieten, C., 160
Vigorito, M., 175
Vikan, A., 218
Villanacci, V., 51
Villani, V., 64
Villemure, C., 112
Vincus, A. A., 154
Visser, P. S., 551
Vitak, J., 30
Vitaro, E., 480
Vitaro, F., 331
Vitello, P., 106, 106f
Vitiello, A. L., 113
Vitousek, K. M., 302–303
Vleioras, G., 362–363
Vogt, D., 430
Volberg, V., 156
Volkow, N. D., 152
Volterra, V., 259
Vonk, J., 221
Von Känel, R., 423
VonKorff, M., 483
Von Schedvin, H., 430
Voracek, M., 397
Vorobyev, V. A., 69, 107
Voruganti, L. P., 516
Voss, J., 220
Vujic, V., 58
Vurbic, D., 175
Vyas, P., 428
Vygotsky, L. S., 356

W

Wacher, D. P., 182
Wachs, T. D., 403
Waddell, J., 77
Wade, K. A., 225
Wade, N. J., 120
Wager, T. D, 58

Wager, T. D., 314
Wagner, A. W., 501
Wagner, H. L., 315
Wagner, K., 80
Wagner, R. K., 270
Wagner, S. H., 537
Wagstaff, G. F., 148
Wain, H. J., 442
Waite, S., 509
Wald, G., 101
Wald, M. L., 543
Waldo, C. R., 309
Walker, E. E., 520
Walker, K., 76
Walker, L. J., 362, 562
Walker, M. P., 136, 137f, 140, 141
Walker, W., 113
Walker, W. R., 225
Walkey, E. H., 445
Wall, J., 288
Wall, T. L., 159
Wallace, G., 80
Waller, B., 27
Waller, B. M., 262
Wallerstein, J. S., 372
Wallis, J. D., 23
Wallner-Blazek, M. M., 69
Walsh, B. T., 516
Walsh, M., 150
Walsh, V., 113
Walton, G. M., 553
Wampold, B. E., 513
Wang, A., 468
Wang, F., 442
Wang, F. F., 77
Wang, L., 400
Wang, M. C., 560
Wang, O., 225
Wang, P. S., 483
Wang, Q., 226, 539
Wang, S., 518
Wang, X., 107, 531
Wang, Z., 469
Ward, G., 211
Ward, L. M., 118f, 123f, 132, 550
Ward, T., 473
Ward, W. C., 253–254
Ward-Baker, P. D., 371
Warden, C. A., 530
Wardle, M. C., 437
Wark, B., 92
Warren, J., 474
Washburn, M. F., 15
Wasserman, E. A., 171
Waterhouse, J., 143
Waters, G., 76–77
Watson, C. S., 107
Watson, J. B., 17f, 18–19, 172
Watson, J. C., 507
Watson, M., 435
Watson, P. J., 422
Watters, E., 487
Waxman, S., 261
Weaver, K., 562
Webb, R., 161–162
Weber, A. L., 555
Weber, R., 196
Wechsler, D., 275
Wechsler, H., 158
Weck, F., 468
Weddle, C., 80
Weeks, M., 551
Wegner, D. M., 211, 211f
Wehrle, R., 140
Weinberg, M. S., 307
Weinberg, R. A., 282
Weiner, I. B., 413
Weiner, R. D., 519
Weinstein, L., 336
Weinstein, M., 423
Weisberg, J. N., 112
Weisner, C., 158
Weiss, A., 445–446
Weiss, B. D., 442
Weiss, M. R., 543
Weiss, W. M., 543
Weiss-Gerlach, E., 438
Weissman, M., 483, 509
Wekstein, D. R., 80

Welchko, R., 156
Welkowitz, J., 483
Welkowitz, L. A., 483
Weller, J., 498
Wells, B., 400
Wells, R., 132
Welsh, M., 246
Wenar, C., 480
Wenk, G. L., 234
Wenzel, A., 220, 306, 465
Werblin, F., 99
Werker, J. F., 336
Werner, J. S., 99
Wershba, R., 421
Wertheimer, M., 15, 116
Wesensten, N. J., 140
West, D. S., 300
West, J. F., 151
West, R., 196
West, R. L., 375
West, S. L., 154
Westen, D., 511, 512
Westerhausen, R., 118–119
Westers, P., 441
Westerterp, K. R., 299
Wetherington, J. M., 422
Wett, J. L., 521
Wetter, D. W., 436
Wetter, T. C., 140
Whaley, B. B., 443
Wheatcroft, J. M., 148
Whisman, M., 307
Whitbourne, S. K., 363, 370, 442
White, L., 260
White, N. M., 194
Whitebread, D., 347
Whitehouse, W. G., 149
Whitfield, K. E., 280
Whitney, P. G., 347
Whorf, B. L., 261
WHO World Mental Health Survey Consortium, 483, 485f
Wiater, A., 138
Wickelgren, E. A., 121
Widaman, K., 336
Widdershoven, J. W., 435
Widiger, T. A., 422, 459, 460, 479, 480, 486
Widmaier, E. P., 81f, 105f
Widmeyer, W. N., 535
Wiebe, J. S., 428
Wielgosz, A. T., 435
Wiesel, T. N., 17f, 98, 99
Wiggins, J. S., 397
Wilcox, K. J., 402, 402f
Wildavsky, B., 264
Wilde, D. J., 391, 392
Wilgoren, J., 348
Wilhelmsen, K. C., 160
Wilke, F., 162
Wilkin, L., 374
Wilkinson, H. A., 520
Wilkinson, L., 197
Willander, J., 108
Willard, J., 549–550
Williams, A., 43
Williams, C. J., 307
Williams, C. L., 412
Williams, G. C., 20
Williams, J. B. W., 472
Williams, J. M., 437
Williams, R. B., 435
Williams, S., 51
Williams, S. J., 142
Williams, T., 430
Williamson, P., 279
Willis, C., 223
Willis, G. L., 6, 58
Willis, S. L., 374
Willoughby, G., 246
Wills, K., 442
Wills, T. A., 436
Wilson, A., 241
Wilson, B., 207
Wilson, D. E., 221
Wilson, D. J., 542
Wilson, G. D., 307
Wilson, G. T., 189

Wilson, K. S., 147
Wilson, P. J., 109
Wilson, T. D., 222, 553
Wilson, T. G., 302–303
Windholz, G., 250
Winerman, L., 561
Winfrey, O., 446
Wingate, L. R., 170
Winkielman, P., 551
Winner, E., 279
Winocur, G., 232
Winograd, E., 220
Winson, J., 140
Winstead, B. A., 365
Winston, J. S., 99
Winter, D. G., 310, 311, 371
Winter, J. B., 435
Winterbauer, N. E., 175
Winters, B. D., 57
Wise, E. H., 40–41
Wiseman, R., 126
Wismar, K., 422
Witelson, S., 307
Withey, S. B., 446f
Witnauer, J. E., 183
Witt, C. M., 112
Wittchen, H., 465
Wittenbrink, B., 552
Witter, M., 122
Witthöft, M., 468
Wittner, L., 141
Wixted, J. T., 228
Wohl, J., 513
Wolf, Y., 290
Wolfe, M. S., 376
Wolff, N., 521
Wolff, R., 81–82
Wolitzky, D. L., 497
Wolpert, E. A., 140
Wong, N., 464
Wood, J. M., 413
Wood, J. P., 98
Wood, P. R., 442
Wood, W., 529
Woodruff, N., 278
Woodruff, R., 50
Woodruff, S. I., 438
Woods, S. C., 297, 299
Woodson, S. R. J., 318
Woody, E. Z., 147
Woolf, V., 269f
Woollett, K., 214, 215f
Worth, K. A., 436
Worthen, J. B., 209
Worthley, R., 267
Wren, A. M., 298–299
Wright, J., 57
Wright, K., 143
Wright, R. A., 291
Write, E. E., 113
Wrosch, C., 376
Wrzesniewski, K., 428
Wu, C-H., 538, 539
Wu, L-T., 162
Wu, W-Y., 530
Wu, Y., 372
Wu, Z. Z., 80
Wuensch, K. L., 561
Wuethrich, B., 158
Wundt, W., 14–15, 16f
Wurtz, R. H., 76
Wynn, K., 355
Wyra, M., 234

X

Xiao, Z., 469
Xu, M., 297
Xu, Y., 469
Xue, G., 404f

Y

Yacoub, E., 100f
Yamada, K. A., 142
Yamagata, S., 400
Yaman, M., 113

Yamauchi, K., 471
Yamazaki, A., 423
Yan, H., 469
Yancey, C., 196
Yang, L., 516
Yang, R. J., 467
Yankell, S. L., 109
Yao, S-Q., 276
Yapko, M. D., 141
Yardley, L., 8
Yasuhara, T. T., 77
Yates, A., 454
Yates, M. C., 437
Yazdani, S., 556
Yeager, D., 422–423
Yechiam, E., 561
Yeh, T. C., 80
Yeo, T., 69
Yeomans, M. R., 109
Yeshurun, Y., 109
Yesilyaprak, B., 422
Yoder, M., 500
Yokosawa, K., 206
Yonas, A., 120
Yoshino, A., 195
Yoshiura, K., 109
Yoshiura, T., 109
Yougentob, S. L., 109
Young, K. M., 189
Young, S. E., 155
Young, T., 101
Young-DeMarco, L., 306
Yue, D. N., 473
Yumru, M., 515
Yurgelun-Todd, D. A., 465

Z

Zack, M. M., 373
Zacks, J., 241
Zadok, D., 137
Zaidel, E., 80
Zaitsu, W., 223
Zajonc, R. B., 313, 555
Zanna, M. P., 430, 432
Zaragoza, M. S., 223
Zarren, J. I., 149
Zatorre, R., 76
Zautra, A. J., 421
Zayas, V., 170
Zebrowitz, L. A., 556
Zeigler, D. W., 159
Zelenski, J. M., 445
Zeng, L., 254
Zepf, F. D., 390
Zepf, S., 390
Zerach, G. G., 423
Zetocha, K., 220
Zevon, M., 436
Zhang, D., 278
Zhang, F., 300
Zhang, G., 556
Zhang, Y., 250
Zhao, Z., 215
Zheng, H., 290
Zhou, S., 479
Zhou, Y., 102
Zhou, Z., 105, 109
Zhour, Y-H., 276
Zians, J., 310
Ziegler, M., 268
Zigler, E., 278
Zika, S., 423, 424f
Zimbardo, P. G., 24, 543–544
Zimmerman, R. R., 346
Zimmerman, U. S., 160
Zinkhan, G. M., 219
Zito, J. M., 518
Zlotnick, C., 481
Zoccolillo, M., 480
Zolotor, A., 182
Zou, Z., 469
Zuckerman, M., 291, 292f
Zuckerman-Hyman, C., 545
Zuger, A., 444
Zuniga, X., 198
Zupančič, M., 396
Zwisler, A., 435

Subject Index

Page numbers followed by *f* indicate figures.

A

Abnormal behavior
  behavioral perspective, 455f, 456
  classifying, 458–460, 487
  cognitive perspective, 455f, 456–457
  defining abnormality, 453–454
  humanistic perspective, 455f, 457
  medical/biological perspective, 455f, 455–456
  psychoanalytic perspective, 455f, 456
  sociocultural perspective, 455f, 457–458
Absolute thresholds, 90–91
Acceptance, in adjusting to death, 378
Accommodation, visual, 96
Accutane, 338f
Acetylcholine (ACh), 57f, 58
Achievement
  measuring achievement motivation, 309–310
  need for, 309–310
Acquired immune deficiency syndrome (AIDS), 338f
Acrophobia, 465f
Action potential, 53, 53f, 54f
Activation information modulation (AIM) theory, 141
Activation-synthesis theory, 139f, 141
Activity theory of aging, 377
Acupuncture, 112
Adaptation
  defined, 92
  sensory, 92
Adaptive learning techniques, 186
Adaptive testing, 277
Addictive drugs, 152–154, 337, 338f, 437f, 437–438
Adenosine, 155
ADHD (attention-deficit hyperactivity disorder), 216, 456, 480
Adolescence, 358–367
  cognitive development, 360–362
  defined, 358
  Erikson's psychosocial stages, 361–362, 362f
  Kohlberg's theory of moral development, 360–361
  moral development, 360–362
  physical development, 358–360
  Piaget's cognitive development stages, 352f, 352–353, 360
  psychological disorders, 364–366, 474, 480–481
  psychosexual stages, 387f, 388
  rites of passage around the world, 366, 436
  smoking in, 436, 437, 437f, 438f

social development, 361f, 362–363
  suicide in, 364–366
Adolescent egocentrism, 364
Adrenal glands, 65f
Adulthood, 368–379
  changing gender roles, 372
  children and parenthood, 371–373
  cognitive changes, 374–376
  death and, 377–378
  divorce, 371–372
  early, 368, 369, 476
  emerging, 368, 369f
  Erikson's psychosocial stages, 352f, 363
  late, 368, 373–378
  marriage. *See* Marriage
  middle, 368, 369
  onset of schizophrenia, 476
  physical development, 369–370, 373–374
  psychosexual stages, 387f, 388
  social development, 370–371, 376–377
Advertising
  advertising agency creator, 532
  of cigarettes in developing countries, 439
  persuasion through, 439, 530
Advertising agency creator, 532
Affiliation, need for, 310
African Americans
  adolescent suicide, 364–365
  in establishing norms, 409
  impact of stereotypes on, 553
  intelligence and, 280–281
  learning styles, 198
  sickle-cell anemia, 336
Afterimages, 101–102
Age
  chronological/mental, 272–276
  of mother at pregnancy, 338f
  of viability, 335
Aggression, 559–561
  The Dark Knight Rises theater shootings, 4
  dealing with anger, 564
  defining, 559–560
  frustration-aggression approaches, 560–561
  instinct approaches, 560
  observational learning and, 195–196, 561
  rape, 156f
  television and, 32, 32f, 195–196
  video games and, 196
  weapons and eyewitness testimony, 223–224
Agoraphobia, 464f, 465
Agreeableness, 397, 397f
AIDS (acquired immune deficiency syndrome), 338f
Ainsworth Strange situation, 350
Alarm and mobilization, 426

Alcohol
  alcoholism, 160
  alcohol use disorder, 481
  binge drinking, 158, 159f
  as depressant, 156f, 157–160
  effects, 159f
  fetal alcohol syndrome, 278, 337
  identifying problems with, 158, 159f, 160, 162–163
  in prenatal development, 278, 337, 338f
Alcoholics Anonymous (AA), 163, 510
Algorithms, 243
All-or-none law, 52
Altered states of consciousness, 132, 147–163
Alternation model of bicultural competence, 264
Altruism, 562
Alzheimer's disease (AD), 57, 77, 216, 232, 375–376
Ambivalent children, 346
American Academy of Sleep Medicine, 145
American Anorexia Bulimia Association, 303
American Association on Intellectual and Developmental Disabilities, 277
American Psychological Association (APA), 15, 20
  on discrimination against gays and lesbians, 308–309
  "Help Center," 522–523
Amnesia
  anterograde, 232
  dissociative, 469–470
  retrograde, 232
  source, 221–222
Amok, 487
Amphetamines, 155, 156f, 216
Amplitude, 106
Amygdala, 72f, 73, 73f, 137, 137f
  emotions and, 319, 319f
  social neuroscience and, 551f, 551–552
Analogies, 255
Anal stage (Freud), 387f, 388
Analytical intelligence, 271–272
Analytical learning style, 197f, 197–198
Androgens, 304
Anemia, sickle-cell, 336
Anger
  in adjusting to death, 378
  in borderline personality disorder, 479–480
  coronary heart disease and, 435
  dealing with, 564
Animal research
  on attachment, 344–346
  on classical conditioning, 170–172, 171f
  on cognitive learning theory, 192–193, 193f
  ethics of, 42–43

impact of propranolol on heart disease, 35f
  on language development, 262–263
  naturalistic observation, 30f
  nature-nurture issue and, 331
  on operant conditioning, 177–187, 178f, 179f, 187f
  on problem solving, 250, 251f
Animal type phobia, 464f
Anorexia nervosa, 301–303, 481, 487
Anterograde amnesia, 232
Antianxiety drugs, 516f, 518
Antidepressant drugs, 56, 132, 516f, 516–517
Antipsychotic drugs, 515–516, 516f
Antisocial personality disorder, 479
Anxiety
  antianxiety drugs, 516f, 518
  defense mechanisms and, 388–390
Anxiety disorders, 463–468
  causes, 467–468
  defined, 463
  generalized anxiety disorder, 465, 466f
  obsessive-compulsive disorder (OCD), 465–467, 467f
  panic disorder, 464–465
  phobic disorder, 463–464, 464f
Apache tribes, rites of passage, 366
Apparent movement, 121–122
Archetypes, 391–392
Archival research, 29, 36f
Arousal approaches to motivation, 291, 294f
Arrangement problems, 246, 247f, 248f
Artificial intelligence (AI), 244, 245
Assessment
  of intelligence. *See* Intelligence tests
  of personality. *See* Psychological tests
  reliability in, 408
  self-report measures. *See* Self-report measures
  test standardization, 411
  validity in, 408
Association areas of cortex, 74, 74f, 76–77
Assumed-similarity bias, 537
Athletic performance, hypnosis in improving, 149
Attachment, 344–347
  animal research on, 344–346
  assessing, 346
  defined, 344
  imprinting, 344–346
  types of, 346
Attention-deficit hyperactivity disorder (ADHD), 216, 456, 480
Attitude communicators, 529
Attitudes
  defined, 529
  link between behavior and, 532–533
  persuasion in changing, 529–533
  toward aging process, 370, 375

Attribution biases, 537–539
  in cultural context, 538–539
  types of, 537–538
Attribution theory, 535–539
  attribution biases, 537–539
  attribution processes, 535–537
Auditory area of cortex, 74f, 76, 107
Authoritarian parents, 348–350, 349f
Authoritative parents, 348–350, 349f
Autism, 481
Autobiographical memories, 225
Autonomic division, 61f, 62
Autonomic nervous system, 62–63, 63f
  in anxiety disorders, 467
  roots of emotions in, 316
Autonomy-versus-shame-and-doubt
  stage (Erikson), 351, 362f
Availability heuristic, 244–245
Aversive conditioning, 499
Avoidant children, 346
Avoidant coping, 428
Awa tribe, rites of passage, 366
Axons, 51, 52, 56

B

Babbling, 258
Babinski reflex, 341
Background stressors, 423
Balance, 107–108
Barbiturates, 156f, 160
Bargaining, in adjusting to death, 378
Basilar membrane, 104–105, 105f, 107
Bedtime, 145
Behavior
  attribution theory and, 535–539
  link between attitudes and, 532–533
Behavioral assessment, 413
Behavioral economics, 538
Behavioral genetics, 7f, 9, 64, 330, 334,
  401–402
Behavioral neuroscience, 6, 7f
Behavioral neuroscientists, 50, 132
Behavioral perspective
  on abnormal behavior, 455f, 456
  on anxiety disorders, 468
  behavioral treatment approaches,
  498–502
  characteristics of, 18f, 18–19
  key issues and controversies, 21f
  learning in, 399
  on mood disorders, 473
  treatment in, 498–502
Behavioral treatment approaches,
  498–502
  classical conditioning techniques,
  498–500
  dialectical behavior therapy, 501
  evaluating, 501–502
  operant conditioning techniques,
  500–501
Behavior analysts, 188–189
Behavior-based safety, 185
Behavior modification, 189
Bell Curve, The (Herrnstein and Murray),
  281–282
Benzadrine, 155, 156f
Bereavement support group, 510
Beta amyloid precursor protein, 378
Bias
  assumed-similarity, 537
  attribution, 537–539
  confirmation, 252–253
  experimental, 43–44
  Implicit Association Test (IAT)
  and, 552
Big Five Personality Traits, 397, 397f
Bilingual education, 263–264

Binge drinking, 158, 159f
Binge eating, 301–303, 481
Binocular disparity, 119
Biofeedback, 81–82
  to improve sleep, 145
  in pain management, 113
Biological constraints, on learning, 187
Biological perspective. *See also* Medical
  perspective; Neuroscience
  perspective
  on abnormal behavior, 455f, 455–456
  on anxiety disorders, 467, 467f
  biological and evolutionary
  approaches to personality,
  401–404, 406f
  on mood disorders, 473, 474
  on schizophrenia, 476–478
Biomedical therapy, 515–520
  defined, 494
  drug therapy, 515–518
  electroconvulsive therapy (ECT), 519
  medical perspective on abnormal
  behavior, 455f, 455–456
  in perspective, 520
  psychosurgery, 519–520
Bipolar cells, 97, 97f
Bipolar disorder, 472–474
Birth complications, 278
Bisexuality, 307–309
Blacks. *See* African Americans
Blindsight, 88
Blind spot, 97–98, 98f
Blood injection-injury type phobia, 464f
Bodily kinesthetic intelligence, 268, 269f
Boomerang children, 364
Borderline personality disorder, 479–480
Bottom-up processing, 118–119
Brain, 61f, 68–83. *See also* Neuroscience
  perspective
  biofeedback and, 81–82, 113, 145
  central core, 70f, 70–72
  cerebral cortex, 73–77
  directing computers with, 71
  human diversity and, 79–80
  limbic system, 72–73
  neuroplasticity and, 77–78, 78f
  processing visual message,
  98–99, 100f
  sending message from eye to, 96–98
  sexual orientation and, 307
  specialization of hemispheres, 78–79,
  80–81
  studying structure and functions,
  68–70, 72f
  types of brain scans, 68–70
Broca's aphasia, 76
Bulimia, 301–303, 481
Bystander behavior
  diffusion of responsibility, 27–29,
  32–38, 561–562
  research on, 27–29, 32–38, 41–42, 46,
  561–562

C

Caffeine, 145
  as stimulant, 154f, 154–155
CAH (congenital adrenal hyperplasia),
  332–333
Cancer, 435–436
Cannabis, 157f, 161–162
Cannon-Bard theory of emotion, 317f,
  317–318
Cardinal traits, 396
Career options, 10–11, 12f. *See also*
  Psychologists
  advertising agency creator, 532
  case manager, 508

child protection caseworker, 350
  director of special education, 279
  human resources manager, 414
  licensed social worker, 10
  nutritionist, 300
  rehabilitation counselor, 75
  seeing eye dog trainer, 186
  sleep technologist, 142
  substance abuse counselor, 508
Caring, 361–362, 363
Case manager, 508
Case studies, 30, 36f
Cataclysmic events, 422
Catatonic schizophrenia, 475f
Catharsis, 560
Central core, 70f, 70–72
Central executive processor, 210
Central nervous system (CNS),
  60–62, 61f
Central route processing, 530–531, 531f
Central traits, 534–535
Cerebellum, 70, 72f
Cerebral cortex, 65f, 70f, 72f, 73–77
  association areas, 74, 74f, 76–77
  motor area, 74, 74f, 75
  sensory areas, 74, 74f, 75–76, 99f, 107
Child-care arrangements, 347–348
Childhood. *See* Infancy and childhood
Child protection caseworker, 350
Children. *See* Infancy and childhood
China
  desired characteristics in a mate,
  558, 558f
  psychological disorders, 487
  smoking in, 439
Chlorpromazine, 515
Chromosomes
  defined, 333
  types of, 333–334
Chronological age, 272–273
Chunking, 208f, 208–209, 355
Cingulotomy, 520
Circadian rhythms, 143
Civil Rights Act of 1991, 409
Classical conditioning, 169–176
  animal research on, 170–172, 171f
  applying to human behavior, 172–173,
  498–500
  aversive conditioning, 499
  basics of, 170–172, 171f
  in behavioral treatment approaches,
  498–500
  challenging basic assumptions,
  174–175
  defined, 170
  discrimination, 174
  exposure treatments, 500
  extinction, 173–174
  generalization, 174
  operant conditioning versus,
  177, 187, 188f
  role of, 169
  systematic desensitization, 499–500
Clinical mental health counselor, 495f
Clinical neuropsychology, 7f, 9
Clinical psychology, 7f, 8, 11,
  168, 495f
Clinical social worker, 495f
Cocaine, 155–156, 156f
Cochlea, 104–105, 105f
Cognitive-affective processing system
  (CAPS), 400
Cognitive appraisal, 504
Cognitive approaches
  to motivation, 291–293, 294f
  treatment, 502–505
Cognitive-behavioral approach,
  503, 505f
Cognitive complexity, 254

Cognitive development
  adolescent period, 360–362
  aging process and, 374–376
  defined, 351
  infancy and childhood periods,
  351–356
  information-processing approaches,
  19, 355–356
  Kohlberg's theory of moral
  development, 360–361, 361f
  memory and, 374–376
  Piaget's theory of cognitive
  development, 352–355
  Vygotsky's view of cognitive
  development, 356
Cognitive dissonance, 532–533, 533f
Cognitive learning theory, 192–199
  cultural impact on learning, 197–198
  defined, 192
  latent learning, 192–194, 193f
  observational learning, 194f,
  194–196, 196f
Cognitive maps, 193–194
Cognitive perspective, 240–265
  on abnormal behavior, 455f, 456–457
  on anxiety disorders, 468
  characteristics of, 18f, 19
  cognitive learning theory, 192–199
  key issues and controversies, 21f
  language in, 257–258
  on mood disorders, 473
  problem solving in, 244, 245–254
  on schizophrenia, 478
  thinking and reasoning in, 241–256
  treatment in, 502–505
Cognitive psychology, 6, 7f, 240
Cognitive restructuring, in pain
  management, 113
Cognitive treatment approaches, 502–505
  cognitive-behavioral approach,
  503, 505f
  evaluating, 504
  rational-emotive therapy, 503–504
Cohorts, 332
Collective unconscious, 391–392
Collectivistic orientation, 539
Color vision/color blindness, 100–102
  explaining color vision, 101–102
  neonate perception of color, 343
  opponent-process theory of color
  vision, 102
  trichromatic theory of color vision,
  101–102
Columbia space shuttle disaster, 542–543
Communication
  environmental perspective on
  schizophrenia, 478
  with health-care providers,
  442–443, 444
Community psychology, 521–522
Comorbidity, 483
Companionate love, 556–558
Compliance, 544–546
  defined, 544
  techniques to gain, 544–546
Compulsions, 465–466
Computers. *See also* Social media
  adaptive learning techniques, 186
  in adaptive testing, 277
  artificial intelligence, 244, 245
  directing with brain, 71
  in problem solving, 244
Conception
  defined, 333, 333f
  development stages following,
  335–336
Concepts, 242–243
Concrete operational stage (Piaget),
  352f, 353

Conditional positive regard, 405
Conditioned response (CR), 170–171, 172, 173–174
Conditioned stimulus (CS), 170–171, 172, 173–174
Cones of retina, 96, 97f, 97–98, 101–102
Confirmation bias, 252–253
Conformity, 541–544
  conclusions, 542
  defined, 541
  groupthink, 542–543
  to social roles, 543–544
Congenital adrenal hyperplasia (CAH), 332–333
Conscience, 386f, 387
Conscientiousness, 397, 397f
Consciousness. See also States of consciousness; Unconscious
  defined, 132
  levels of, 132
Conscious versus unconscious, 21f, 22. See also States of consciousness
Conservation principle, 353, 354f
Consistency
  link between attitudes and behavior, 532
  of personality, 400
Consolidation, 215
Constructive processes, 222–225
  autobiographical memory, 225
  defined, 222
  eyewitness testimony, 223–225
Contingency contracting, 501
Continuous reinforcement, 182–183
Control group, 33
Conventional morality, 361f
Convergent thinking, 254, 255
Conversion disorders, 468, 469f
Coping, 428–432
  defense mechanisms in, 388–390, 428, 430
  defined, 428
  effective strategies, 432
  emotion-focused, 428
  problem-focused, 428
  with schizophrenia, 452, 490
Coronary heart disease, 434–435
Corpus callosum, 72f, 80, 81f
Correlational research, 31–32, 36f
Correlation coefficient, 31
Cortex. See Cerebral cortex
Cortisol, 430
Counseling psychology, 7f, 8, 495f
Creative intelligence, 271–272
Creativity
  critical thinking and, 255
  defined, 253
  in problem solving, 253–254
Critical period, 258
Critical thinking
  creativity and, 255
  psychological research, 44
Cross-cultural psychology, 7f, 8
Cross-sectional research, 331–332
Crystallized intelligence, 268, 272f, 374
Cue-dependent forgetting, 230
Culture
  alcohol use, 158–159
  attitudes toward aging process, 370, 375
  attribution bias in cultural context, 538–539
  brain lateralization, 80
  communication barriers between patients and physicians, 443
  cross-cultural differences in memory, 225–226, 226f

cross-cultural routes to altered consciousness, 150–151
  emotions and, 315, 320–322
  as factor in psychotherapy, 513
  impact of cultural differences learning, 197–198
  intelligence measures and, 281–282
  obesity and, 296–297, 298
  perception and, 124
  play and, 347
  psychological disorders, 483, 484–487
  race and ethnicity in establishing norms, 409–410. See also Ethnicity; Race
  rites of passage, 366, 436
  in Vygotsky's view of cognitive development, 356
Culture-fair IQ test, 280–281

D

Daily hassles, 423, 424f
D.A.R.E. (Drug Abuse Resistance Education), 154
Dark adaptation, 96
The Dark Knight Rises theater shootings, 4
Date rape, 156f
Daydreams, 144, 144f
Death. See also Suicide
  adjusting to, 377–378
  sudden infant death syndrome (SIDS), 142
Decay, 230
Decibels, 106
Declarative memory, 211, 212f
Deep Blue (computer), 244
Defense mechanisms
  coping and, 388–390, 428, 430
  defined, 389
  list of, 389f
Deinstitutionalization, 521–522
Delusions, 475
Dendrites, 51, 52, 56
Denial
  in adjusting to death, 378
  as defense mechanism, 389f
Dependent variable, 33–34
Depressants, 156f, 157–160
Depression
  in adjusting to death, 378
  in adolescence, 364–366, 480
  adulthood and, 370
  antidepressant drugs, 56, 132, 516f, 516–517
  electroconvulsive therapy (ECT), 519
  major. See Major depression
  need for treatment, 488
  prevalence and incidence, 483
  seasonal affective disorder, 143, 143f
Depth perception, 119–120, 124
DES (diethylstilbestrol), 307, 338f
Determinism
  defined, 19, 22
  free will versus, 19, 21f, 22
  in learning approaches to personality, 401
Development, 326–380
  adolescence, 358–367
  adulthood, 362f, 363, 368–379
  cognitive. See Cognitive development
  developmental research techniques, 331–332
  infancy and childhood, 340–357
  milestones in, 328
  nature-nurture issue in, 329–331

physical. See Physical development
  prenatal, 332–335
  social. See Social development
Developmental psychology, 6, 7f, 168, 328, 329
  nature-nurture issue in, 329–331
  research techniques in, 331–332
Dexedrine, 155, 156f
Diabetes, in prenatal development, 337
Diagnostic and Statistical Manual of Mental Disorders Fourth Edition, Text Revision (DSM-IV-TR), 458–460
  culture of, 487
  determining diagnostic distinctions, 458–459
  major categories, 458–459, 459f
  shortcomings, 459–460
Dialectical behavior therapy, 501
Diethylstilbestrol (DES), 307, 338f
Dieting, 303
Difference thresholds, 91–92
Diffusion of responsibility, 27–29, 32–38, 561–562
Diffusion Tensor Imaging, 233
Direction, internal sense of, 122
Director of special education, 279
Discrimination
  in classical conditioning, 174
  defined, 549
  measuring, 552
  in operant conditioning, 184–185
  prejudice and, 549–554
  reducing consequences of, 552–553
Discriminative stimulus, 185
Disengagement theory of aging, 378
Disorganized-disoriented children, 346
Disorganized (hebephrenic) schizophrenia, 475f
Displacement, as defense mechanism, 389f
Dispositional causes, 536–537
Dissociative amnesia, 469–470
Dissociative disorders, 468–470, 487
Dissociative fugue, 470
Dissociative identity disorder (DID), 469, 487
Divergent thinking, 254, 255
Diversity
  bilingual education, 263–264
  brain and, 79–80
  cultural differences in memory, 225–226, 226f
  cultural impact on learning, 197–198
  culture and perception, 124
  intelligence and, 281–282
  language and, 277–278
  among psychologists, 10–11
  race and ethnicity in establishing norms, 409–410
  of sexual behavior, 304–309
  smoking throughout the world, 439
Divided consciousness, 148
Divorce, 371–372
DNA (deoxyribonucleic acid), 333, 334
Donepezil, 216
Door-in-the-face technique, 545
Dopamine (DA), 57f, 58, 155–156, 179
Dopamine hypothesis, 476
Double-blind procedures, 44
Double standard, sexual, 306
Down syndrome, 278, 336
Dream interpretation, 139, 140f, 496–497
Dreams, 132, 135–136, 137–141
  evolutionary explanations, 140–141
  function and meaning of, 137–141
  manifest content of, 139, 140f, 496–497
  number of, 138
  REM (rapid eye movement) sleep and, 134f, 135f, 135–136, 141, 142

themes of, 138–139, 139f
  unconscious wish fulfillment theory, 139f, 139–140
Dreams-for-survival theory, 139f, 140–141
Drive-reduction approaches to motivation, 290, 294f
  drive, defined, 290
  homeostasis in, 290
Drug therapy, 515–518. See also Drug use
  antianxiety drugs, 516f, 518
  antidepressant drugs, 56, 132, 516f, 516–517
  antipsychotic drugs, 515–516, 516f
  defined, 515
  MAO inhibitors, 516, 516f
  mood stabilizers, 516f, 517–518
  selective serotonin reuptake inhibitors (SSRIs), 56, 505f, 516f, 516–517, 517f
Drug use, 132, 152–163. See also Drug therapy
  addictive drugs, 152–154, 337, 338f, 437f, 437–438
  depressants, 156f, 157–160
  extent of, 153f
  hallucinogens, 157f, 161–162
  identifying problems with, 162–163
  to improve memory, 216, 234
  narcotics, 156–157f, 160–161
  in prenatal development, 337, 338f
  psychoactive drugs, 152, 515–518
  sleeping pills, 145
  stimulants, 154–156, 156f
  treating drug addiction, 173

E

Eardrum, 104, 105f
Eating disorders, 296, 301–303, 481, 487
Eclectic approach, 494, 513
Economics, 20
Ecstasy (MDMA), 157f, 162
Educational psychology, 7f
Education for All Handicapped Children Act (Public Law 94-142), 278
EEG (electroencephalogram), 68, 69, 69f, 134f
Ego, 386f, 386–387
Egocentric thought, 352–353, 364
Ego-integrity-versus despair stage (Erikson), 362f, 363
Ejaculation, 359
Electroconvulsive therapy (ECT), 519
Electrocorticographic (ECoG) implant, 71
Electroencephalogram (EEG), 68, 69, 69f, 134f
E-mail, 250
Embryo, 335
Embryonic period, 335
Emerging adulthood, 368, 369f
Emotional disturbances, 475–476
Emotional insulation, 428–429
Emotional intelligence, 272f, 293–294
Emotion-focused coping, 428
Emotions, 313–323
  culture and, 315, 320–322
  defined, 313
  determining range of, 314–315
  facial expressions and, 319, 319f
  functions of, 314
  labeling feelings, 314–315, 315f, 317
  neuroscience perspective on, 318–319
  in prenatal development, 337
  theories on roots of, 315–320
Empathy, 508
Encoding, 205, 205f, 229

Endocrine system, 64–66
  hormones. See Hormones
  location and function of endocrine
    glands, 65f
Endorphins, 57f, 58, 112
Engram, 214, 215
Environment. See also Nature-nurture
    issue
  in prenatal development,
    337–338, 338f
Environmental psychology, 7f
Epilepsy, 71
Epinephrine, coronary heart disease
    and, 435
Episodic memory, 212, 212f, 375
Erikson's theory of psychosocial
    development, 350–351, 362–363
  autonomy-versus-shame-and-doubt
    stage, 351, 362f
  ego-integrity-versus despair stage,
    362f, 363
  generativity-versus-stagnation stage,
    362f, 363
  identity-versus-role-confusion stage,
    362f, 362–363
  industry-versus-inferiority stage,
    351, 362f
  initiative-versus-guilt stage, 351, 362f
  intimacy-versus-isolation stage,
    362f, 363
  trust-versus-mistrust stage, 351, 362f
Eskimo language, 261
ESP (extrasensory perception),
    125–126
Estrogens, 305
Ethics of research, 40–44
  animal research, 42–43
  critical thinking and, 44
  experimental bias, 43–44
  informed consent, 40–41
  representative participants, 41, 42f
Ethnic group. See also names of specific
    ethnic groups
  alcohol use, 158–159
  learning styles and, 197–198
Ethnicity. See also specific ethnicities
  in establishing norms, 409–410
  as factor in psychotherapy, 513
  impact of stereotyping and, 553
  of psychologists, 10–11
  self-rating of happiness, 446
Evidence-based psychotherapy practice,
    512–513
Evolutionary perspective
  dreams in, 140–141
  learning in, 187
Evolutionary psychology, 7f, 8–9,
    63–64, 473
Excitatory messages, 56
Exercise
  habits regarding, 303
  to improve sleep, 145
  weight loss and, 303
Existential intelligence, 268
Expectations
  experimenter, 44
  participant, 43–44
Experiment, defined, 32
Experimental bias, 43–44
Experimental group, 33
Experimental manipulation, 32
Experimental psychology, 6, 7f
Experimental research, 32–38, 36f. See
    also Animal research
  control groups, 33
  dependent variable, 33–34
  experiment, defined, 32
  experimental groups, 33
  experimental manipulation and, 32

independent variable, 33–34
  random assignment of participants,
    34–35
  replication, 37–38
Explicit memory, 220–221
Exposure treatments, 500
Expressed emotion, 478
Extinction, 173–174, 183
Extramarital sex, 307
Extrasensory perception (ESP),
    125–126
Extraversion, 396, 397, 397f
Extrinsic motivation, 321–323
Eyewitness testimony, 20, 223–225
  of children, 224
  false memories, 224–225
  hypnosis in, 149
  repressed memories, 225
  weapons and, 223–224

F

Facebook, 20, 364, 556
Facial-affect program, 321
Facial expression
  emotions and, 319f, 320–322
  neonate discrimination of, 342, 342f,
    343, 343f
Facial-feedback hypothesis, 321–322
Factor analysis, 396–397
Fad diets, 303
False memories, 224–225
Familial retardation, 278
Familiarity heuristic, 245
Family background, in adolescent
    suicide, 365
Family therapy, 510
Fantasy, in dealing with anger, 564
Fathers. See also Males
  attachment and, 347
  parenting styles, 348–350
Fears
  hierarchy of, 500
  phobias, 463–465
Feature detection, 98–99
Females. See also Gender; Gender
    differences; Mothers; Sexual
    behavior; Sexuality; Women in
    psychology
  adolescent suicide, 364–366
  aging process, 369–370
  height and weight by age, 345f
  menopause, 65, 369–370
  menstruation, 359, 366, 485–486
  mood disorders and, 470–471, 473–474
  moral development, 361–362
  obesity and, 296–297, 298
  physical development in adolescence,
    359f, 359–360
  psychosexual development, 388, 391
  rape, 156f
  sex organs, 304f
  in single-parent families, 358, 372
  women in psychology, 10–11, 15,
    16–17f, 361–362, 392, 393
  work outside home, 372–373
Fertilization, 335
Fetal alcohol effects (FAE), 337
Fetal alcohol syndrome (FAS), 278, 337
Fetal period, 335–336, 338f
Fetus
  defined, 335
  environmental influences on, 278,
    337–338, 338f
  genetic influences on, 336
  stages of development, 335–336
Fight-or-flight response, 314
Fixations, 387–388

Fixed-interval schedule of
    reinforcement, 183f, 184
Fixed-ratio schedule of reinforcement,
    183, 183f
Flashbulb memories, 221–222, 222f
Fluid intelligence, 267–268, 272f, 374
fMRI (functional magnetic resonance
    imaging), 23f, 68, 69, 69f, 214, 215f
Foot-in-the-door technique, 544–545
Forebrain, 70
Forensic psychology, 7f
Forgetting, 228–235
  afflictions of, 57, 77, 221–222, 232–233,
    469–470
  eyewitness testimony and, 20, 149,
    223–225
  methods of reducing, 233–234
  proactive interference, 230–231, 231f
  reasons for, 229–230
  retroactive interference, 231
Formal operational stage (Piaget), 352f,
    353–354, 360
Formal thought disorder, 474
Fractionation, 255
Free association, 496–497
Free will
  defined, 19, 22
  determinism versus, 19, 21f, 22
Frequency, 105–106, 106f, 107
Frequency theory of hearing, 107
Freudian slip, 385
Freud's psychoanalytic theory, 385–391
  defense mechanisms, 388–390, 389f
  developing personality, 387–388
  evaluating, 390–391
  neo-Freudian analysts, 391–393, 497
  psychosexual stages, 387f, 387–388
  structuring personality, 386–387
  unconscious, 385–386, 498
Friendship, interpersonal attraction
    and, 555–556
Frontal lobe, 73f, 74, 74f
Frustration-aggression theory, 560–561
Functional fixedness, 252
Functionalism, 15
Functional magnetic resonance imaging
    (fMRI), 23f, 68, 69, 69f, 214, 215f
Fundamental attribution error, 538, 539
Future of psychology, 20, 23f, 23–24

G

GABA (gamma-amino butyric acid),
    57, 57f
Gag reflex, 340
Galaga (video game), 71
Gamma-amino butyric acid (GABA),
    57, 57f
Gamma knife surgery, 520
Ganglion cells, 97, 97f, 98
Gate-control theory of pain, 112
Gay/lesbian, 307–309
Gender. See also Females; Gender
    differences; Gender roles; Males;
    Sexuality
  binge drinking and, 158
  brain lateralization, 80
  brain size, 80
  of health-care providers, 442–443
  hormones and, 65–66
  learning styles and, 198
  sense of smell, 108–109
  verbal abilities, 80
  women in psychology, 10–11, 15,
    16–17f, 361–362, 363, 392, 393
Gender differences
  in changing attitudes, 529
  happiness and, 445

in need for power, 311
  personality and, 390
  sleep and, 136–137
Gender roles
  aging process and, 372
  in Horney's neo-Freudian
    perspective, 392
General adaptation syndrome (GAS),
    426f, 426–427
General Aptitude Test Battery, 409
Generalization
  in classical conditioning, 174
  in operant conditioning, 185
  overgeneralization in language
    development, 259
Generalized anxiety disorder, 465, 466f
Generativity-versus-stagnation stage
    (Erikson), 362f, 363
Genes. See also Nature-nurture issue
  in anxiety disorders, 467
  defined, 333
  in gene therapy, 334
  genetic factors in personality, 401–402
  Human Genome Project and, 334
  influences on fetus, 337–338
  in schizophrenia, 476–477, 477f
Gene therapy, 334
Genetic preprogramming theories of
    aging, 373–374
Genetics. See also Heredity; Nature-
    nurture issue
  behavioral, 7f, 9, 64, 330, 334, 401–402
  in prenatal development, 333–334
  weight set point and, 299
Genitals, 304f, 304–305
Genital stage (Freud), 387f, 388
German measles (rubella), 337, 338f
Germinal period, 335
Germline therapy, 334
Gestalt laws of organization, 116–117
Gestalt psychology, 15, 116–117
G-factor, 267
Ghrelin, 298–299
Giftedness, 279
Glial cells, 51
Glutamate, 57, 57f
Google effect, 211
Graded exposure, 500
Graduate Record Exam (GRE), 277
Grammar, 257–258
  defined, 257
  phonemes, 257, 258
  phonology, 257
  semantics, 258
  syntax, 257
Greece, ancient, 14, 122–123, 123f
Groups, defined, 541
Group therapies, 509–510
  family therapy, 510
  self-help therapy, 163, 510
Groupthink, 542–543
Growth hormones, 136

H

Habituation, 169, 342
Hair cells, 105
Hallucinations, 156, 475, 477–478
Hallucinogens, 157f, 161–162
Halo effect, 537
Happiness, 444–446
  characteristics of happy people, 445
  circadian rhythms, 143
  money and, 445–446
  set point for, 445–446
Hardiness, 430
Hashish, 157f
Hash oil, 157f

Head-direction cells, 122
Health-care providers
  communicating with, 442–443, 444
  following medical advice, 441–444
  increasing compliance with medical advice, 443–444
  noncompliance with medical advice, 441–442
Health psychology, 6–8, 7f, 418–449
  cancer, 435–436
  coronary heart disease, 434–435
  defined, 420
  following medical advice, 441–444
  psychoneuroimmunology (PNI), 420, 427
  smoking, 436–439
  stress and coping with stress, 421–433
  subjective well-being, 444–446
Hearing, 104–108
  auditory area of cortex, 74f, 76
  neonate perception of sound, 343–344
  parts of ear, 104–105, 105f
  physical aspects of sound, 105–108
  sensing sound, 104–108
Heart, 65f
Helping others, 561–563
Hemispherectomy, 79
Hemispheres of brain
  defined, 79
  lateralization, 79–80
  specialization, 78–79
  split-brain patients, 80–81
Heredity, 8. See also Genes; Genetics; Nature-nurture issue
  in determining intelligence, 278, 280–282
  schizophrenia and, 476–477, 477f
Heritability, intelligence and, 281–282
Hermaphrodites, 309
Heroin, 156f, 160–161
Heterosexuality, 306–307
  defined, 306
  extramarital sex, 307
  marital sex, 306
  marriage, 306, 371–373
  premarital sex, 306
  sexual double standard, 306
Heuristics, 243–245, 255
Hierarchy of fears, 500
Hierarchy of needs, 293f, 293–294, 294f, 405
High blood pressure, in prenatal development, 337
Hindbrain, 70
Hippocampus, 73, 73f
  Alzheimer's disease (AD) and, 376
  emotions and, 319
  memory and, 214, 215f
  place cells, 122
Hispanic Americans
  in establishing norms, 409
  learning styles, 198
History of psychology, 14–16
"H.M." case, 228
Homelessness, 521
Homeostasis, 72, 290
Homosexuality, 307–309
Hormone replacement therapy (HRT), 65
Hormones, 64–66
  in adolescent development, 359f, 359–360
  growth, 136
  in human sexual response, 304–305
  in sexual orientation, 307
Hormone therapy (HT), 369–370
Horney's neo-Freudian perspective, 392
Human Genome Project, 334

Humanistic perspective
  on abnormal behavior, 455f, 457
  characteristics of, 18f, 19
  humanistic approaches to personality, 404–406, 406f
  key issues and controversies, 21f
  Rogers and need for self-actualization, 405
  treatment in, 507–509
Humanistic therapy, 507–509
  evaluating, 509
  person-centered therapy, 507–508
Human resources manager, 414
Human sexual response. See also Sexuality
  biology of sexual behavior, 304–309
  physiological aspects, 304–305
Hunger
  biological factors in regulating, 297–299
  hypothalamus in regulating, 299
  social factors in eating, 299–300
Hyperthymestic syndrome, 204
Hypnosis, 132, 147–149
  as different state of consciousness, 148–149
  in pain management, 113, 149
  uses of, 113, 148–149
Hypochondriasis, 468
Hypothalamus, 64, 65f, 72, 72f, 299
Hypotheses
  archival research in testing, 29
  confirmation bias and, 252–253
  defined, 28
  in scientific method, 28

Id, 386, 386f
Identical twins, 329, 329f, 331
Identification, 388
Identity
  adolescent search for, 362–363
  defined, 362
  sexual orientation, 306–309
Identity-versus-role-confusion stage (Erikson), 362f, 362–363
Illusions, 122–123, 123f, 124f
Imitation
  media violence and, 195–196
  in observational learning, 194–196
Immersion programs, 263–264
Immigration
  culture and learning style, 198
  forced, impact of, 198
Implicit Association Test (IAT), 552
Implicit memory, 220–221
Impression formation, 534–535
Imprinting, 344–346
Impulses, 52
Incentive approaches to motivation, 291, 294f
Independent variable, 33–34
Individual differences versus universal principles, 21f, 22
Individualist orientation, 539
Industrial-organizational (I/O) psychology, 7f, 545–546
Industry-versus-inferiority stage (Erikson), 351, 362f
Ineffability, 151
Infancy and childhood, 340–357
  cognitive development, 351–356
  Erikson's psychosocial stages, 351, 362f
  eyewitness testimony of children, 224
  information-processing approaches to development, 355–356
  language development, 258–261

neonate phase, 340–344
obesity in, 298
physical development, 340–344, 341f, 344
Piaget's cognitive development stages, 352f, 352–355
play and, 347
psychological disorders, 480–481
psychosexual stages, 387f, 387–388
smoking by children, 439
social development, 344–351
Vygotsky's view of cognitive development, 356
Inferiority complex, 393
Information processing
  in cognitive perspective, 19, 355–356
  as intelligence, 268–270, 272f
  memory and, 209–210
  mental programs in childhood development, 355–356
Informed consent, 40–41
Ingroups, 550–551
Inhibited sexual desire, 481
Inhibitory messages, 56
Initiative-versus-guilt stage (Erikson), 351, 362f
Inner ear, 104–105, 105f
Insight, 250
Instincts, 289–290
  defined, 289
  instinct approaches to aggression, 560
  motivation and, 289–290, 294f
Insulin, 298–299
Intellectual disability (mental retardation), 277–279
  fetal development issues and, 336–338, 338f
  identifying roots of, 278
  integrating individuals, 278–279
  labeling, 277–279
Intellectually gifted, 279
Intelligence, 266–283. See also Intelligence quotient (IQ)
  analytical, 271–272
  assessing. See Intelligence tests
  creative, 271–272
  creativity versus, 254
  crystallized, 268, 272f, 374
  defined, 267
  emotional, 272f, 293–294
  fluid, 267–268, 272f, 374
  genetic and environmental determinants, 278, 280–282
  multiple intelligences, 268, 269f, 272f
  nature of, 266–267
  practical, 270–271, 272f
  theories of, 267–272
Intelligence quotient (IQ), 272–274. See also Intelligence; Intelligence tests
  aging process and, 374
  Binet and, 272f, 272–274
  giftedness and, 279
  intellectual disabilities (mental retardation), 277–279, 336–338, 338f
  nature-nurture issue and, 278, 280–282
  Wechsler and, 275–276
Intelligence tests, 270, 271f, 272–279. See also Intelligence; Intelligence quotient (IQ)
  adaptive testing, 277
  culture and, 281–282
  defined, 272f
  g-factor, 267
  improving scores on, 277
  mental age, 273–276
  reliability, 276–277
  standardized tests, 277
  validity, 276

Interactionist approaches
  to development, 331
  to language development, 261
  to motivation, 294–295
Interference
  defined, 230
  proactive, 230–231, 231f
  retroactive, 231
Intermittent reinforcement, 182–183
Interneurons, 62
Interpersonal attraction, 555–558
  defined, 555
  factors in liking, 555–556
  factors in loving, 556–558
Interpersonal intelligence, 268, 269f
Interpersonal therapy (IPT), 509
Intersex persons, 309
Intimacy-versus-isolation stage (Erikson), 362f, 363
Intrapersonal intelligence, 268, 269f
Intrinsic motivation, 321–323
Introspection, 14–15
Inventories. See Assessment; Self-report measures
IQ. See Intelligence quotient (IQ)
Iraq, U.S. invasion in 2003, 252–253

J

"Jabberwocky" (Carroll), 257
James-Lange theory of emotion, 316–317, 317f
Japan, child-rearing style, 350
Jeopardy (TV game show), 244
Jews
  rites of passage, 366
  Tay-Sachs disease, 336
Job testing, 409
Judgment, in problem solving, 250–251
Jung's collective unconscious, 391–392
Just noticeable difference, 91–92

K

Kanzi (pygmy chimpanzee), 262–263
Keyword technique, in improving memory, 233–234
Kidneys, 65f
Kohlberg's theory of moral development, 360–361, 361f
Koreans, learning styles, 198
Koro, 487
Korsakoff's syndrome, 232

L

Labeling
  of abnormal behavior, 458–460, 476, 487
  of feelings, 314–315, 315f, 317
  of giftedness, 279
  of intellectual disability (mental retardation), 277–279
Language, 257–265
  animal use of, 262–263
  bilingual education, 263–264
  defined, 257
  grammar, 257–258
  influence on thinking, 261–262
  language development, 258–261, 343–344, 426
  sensitive periods, 336
Lanugo, 340
Late adulthood, 368, 373–378
  Alzheimer's disease (AD), 57, 77, 216, 232, 375–376
  cognitive changes, 374–376

Late adulthood—*Cont.*
 death and, 377–378
 memory and, 374–376
 physical changes, 373–374
 social world in, 376–377
Latency stage (Freud), 387*f*, 388
Latent content of dreams, 139, 140*f*,
  496–497
Latent learning, 192–194, 193*f*
Lateralization, 79–80
Latinos. *See* Hispanic Americans
Law enforcement
 conformity of prison guards, 543–544
 eyewitness testimony in, 20, 149,
  223–225
 hypnosis in, 149
Law of effect, 177–178
Learned helplessness, 429–430, 473
Learning, 166–201
 aggression and, 561
 animal research on, 170–172, 171*f*,
  177–187, 178*f*, 179*f*, 187*f*, 192–193, 193*f*
 behavior-change techniques, 188–189
 biological constraints on, 187
 classical conditioning, 169–176,
  498–500
 cognitive learning theory, 192–199
 cultural impact on, 197–198
 defined, 169
 learning styles and, 197–198
 learning-theory approach to language
  development, 259–260
 operant conditioning, 177–191, 399,
  500–501
 personality and. *See* Learning
  approaches to personality
 sexual orientation and, 308
Learning approaches to personality,
  398–401, 406*f*
 consistency of personality, 400
 evaluating, 400–401
 self-esteem, 400, 401*f*, 445
 Skinner's behaviorist approach, 399
 social cognitive approaches, 399–400
Learning styles, 197*f*, 197–198
Leptin, 300
Lesbian/gay, 307–309
Levels-of-processing theory, 219–220
Licensed professional counselor, 495*f*
Licensed social worker, 10
Life Orientation Test, 410*f*
Light adaptation, 96
Light therapy
 in pain management, 113
 for seasonal affective disorder, 143*f*
Liking, interpersonal attraction and,
  555–556
Limbic system, 72–73
Linear perspective, 120
Linguistic intelligence, 268, 269*f*
Linguistic-relativity hypothesis, 261–262
"Little Albert" experiments, 172, 174
Liver, 65*f*
Lobes, 73*f*, 74, 74*f*
Logical-mathematical intelligence,
  268, 269*f*
Longitudinal research, 332
Long-term memory, 211–215, 218–227
 autobiographical, 225
 constructive processes in rebuilding
  the past, 222–225
 cross-cultural differences in,
  225–226, 226*f*
 defined, 206
 explicit, 220–221
 eyewitness, 20, 149, 223–225
 flashbulb memories, 221–222, 222*f*
 implicit, 220–221
 levels of processing, 219–220

long-term memory modules,
  211–213, 212*f*
 neuroscience of memory, 213–216,
  215*f*, 232, 233*f*
 rehearsal, 209, 234
 retrieval cues, 218–219
 semantic networks, 212–213, 213*f*
 short-term memory versus, 211
 in three-system approach to memory,
  205–206, 206*f*
Long-term potentiation, 214–215
Lou Gehrig's disease, 71
Loving
 interpersonal attraction and,
  556–558
 types of love, 556–558
LSD (lysergic acid diethylamide),
  157*f*, 162
Lymphocytes, stress and, 427

M

Mainstreaming, 278–279
Major depression, 470–471, 473–474
 antidepressant drugs, 56, 132, 516*f*,
  516–517
 electroconvulsive therapy (ECT), 519
Males. *See also* Fathers; Gender; Gender
  differences; Sexual behavior;
  Sexuality
 adolescent suicide, 364–366
 aging process, 370
 ejaculation, 359, 417
 height and weight by age, 345*f*
 mood disorders and, 470–471,
  473–474
 moral development, 360–361
 Oedipal conflict and, 388, 390
 physical development in adolescence,
  359*f*, 359–360
 psychosexual development,
  388, 391
 rape, 156*f*
 sex organs, 304*f*
Mania, 472*f*, 472–474
Manifest content of dreams, 139, 140*f*,
  496–497
Mantra, 149
MAO inhibitors, 516, 516*f*
Marijuana, 157*f*, 161*f*, 161–162
Marital sex, 306
Marriage, 306, 371–373
 desired characteristics in a mate,
  558, 558*f*
 divorce and, 371–372
 extramarital sex, 307
 love and, 558
 marital sex, 306
 premarital sex, 306
 single-parent families, 358, 372
Maslow's hierarchy of needs, 293*f*,
  293–294, 294*f*, 405
Masturbation, 305
Maturation, 330
McDonald's, 169, 172
MDMA (Ecstasy), 157*f*, 162
Means-end analysis, 249–250
Medial temporal lobe, 214
Medical perspective. *See also* Biomedical
  therapy; Drug therapy; Health-care
  providers; Health psychology;
  Neuroscience perspective
 on abnormal behavior, 455*f*, 455–456
 defined, 455
Medical student's disease, 488
Medication. *See* Drug therapy; Drug use
Meditation, 132, 149–150
Medulla, 65*f*, 70, 72*f*

Memory, 202–237
 adulthood and, 370, 374–376
 Alzheimer's disease (AD), 57, 77, 216,
  232, 375–376
 in childhood development, 355
 constructive processes in, 222–225
 cross-cultural differences in,
  225–226, 226*f*
 defined, 205
 dissociative amnesia, 469–470
 explicit, 220–221
 false memories, 224–225
 flashbulb memories, 221–222, 222*f*
 forgetting and, 228–235. *See also*
  Forgetting
 hyperthymestic syndrome, 204
 implicit, 220–221
 improving, 216, 233–234
 levels of processing, 219–220
 long-term, 206, 206*f*, 211–215, 218–227
 medication to improve, 216, 234
 repressed memories, 225, 469–470
 retrieval cues, 205, 205*f*, 218–219
 sensory, 205–207, 206*f*, 207*f*
 short-term, 206, 206*f*, 207–209, 211
 three-system approach to,
  205–206, 206*f*
 traumatic memories, 518
 working, 209–210, 210*f*
Memory modules, 211–213, 212*f*
Menarche, 359, 366
Menopause, 65, 369–370
Menstruation, 359, 366, 485–486
Mental age, 273–276
Mental images, 241–242, 242*f*
Mentalizing, 195
Mental programs, 355–356
Mental retardation. *See* Intellectual
  disability (mental retardation)
Mental set, 252, 252*f*
Mere exposure, interpersonal attraction
  and, 555
Messages
 in changing attitudes, 529
 excitatory/inhibitory, 56
 positively/negatively framed, 444
 processing of visual, 96–99, 100*f*
Message source, in changing
  attitudes, 529
Meta-analysis, 37–38, 511–512
Metabolism, 299
Metacognition, 355–356
Methadone, 161
Methamphetamine, 155, 156*f*
Methylphenidate, 216
Midbrain, 70
Middle ear, 104, 105*f*
Midlife crisis, 370
Midlife transition, 370
Milgram obedience experiments, 546–547
Minnesota Multiphasic Personality
  Inventory-2 (MMPI-2), 410–412,
  411*f*, 486
Mirror neurons, 54–55, 194, 195*f*
Mnemonics, 209
Modafinil, 216
Modern racism, 549
Monocular cues, 120
Mood disorders, 470–474
 bipolar disorder, 472–474
 causes, 473–474
 defined, 470
 major depression, 470–471, 473–474
 mania, 472*f*, 472–474
 mood stabilizers, 516*f*, 517–518
Moral development. *See also* Prosocial
  behavior
 altruism, 562
 nature of, 360–362

Morphine, 156*f*, 160
Mothers. *See also* Females; Pregnancy
 Ainsworth strange situation, 346
 attachment and, 344–346
 Oedipal conflict and, 388, 390
 parenting styles, 348–350
 prenatal development and, 337, 338*f*
Motion perception, 121–122
Motivation, 288–312
 for achievement, 309–310
 for affiliation, 310
 applying different approaches,
  294–295
 arousal approaches to, 291, 294*f*
 cognitive approaches to, 291–293, 294*f*
 defined, 289
 drive-reduction approaches to,
  290, 294*f*
 for hunger and eating, 296–303
 incentive approaches to, 291, 294*f*
 instinct approaches to, 289–290, 294*f*
 Maslow's hierarchy of needs, 293*f*,
  293–294, 294*f*, 405
 for power, 310–311
Motor area of cortex, 74, 74*f*, 75
Motor (efferent) neurons, 62
Müller-Lyer illusion, 123, 124*f*
Multimodal perception, 114
Multiple intelligences, 268, 269*f*, 272*f*
Multiple personality disorder, 469, 487
Musical intelligence, 268, 269*f*
Myelin sheath, 52
Myers-Briggs personality test, 392

N

Narcissism, 398, 480
Narcissism Personality Inventory
  (NPI), 398
Narcissistic personality disorder,
  398, 480
Narcolepsy, 142
Narcotics, 156–157*f*, 160–161
Narcotics Anonymous (NA), 163, 510
National Academy of Sciences, 409
National Institute of Child Health and
  Development (NICHD), research
  on impact of child-care
  arrangements, 347–348, 348*f*
National Institute of Mental Health
  (NIMH), 41
National Science Foundation (NSF), 41
Native Americans
 adolescent suicide, 365
 labeling psychological disorders, 487
 learning styles, 197, 198
 rites of passage, 366
Nativistic approaches, to language
  development, 260
Natural environment type phobia, 464*f*
Naturalistic intelligence, 268, 269*f*
Naturalistic observation, 29–30, 36*f*
Nature-nurture issue, 21*f*, 21–22, 329*f*,
  329–331
 in anxiety disorders, 467
 in determining relative influence of
  nature and nurture, 331
 in fetal development, 336–338
 in homosexuality/bisexuality,
  307–309
 in hunger and obesity, 296–301
 intelligence and, 278, 280–282
 personality and, 403–404
 in schizophrenia, 476–478
Navigational ability, 122, 214, 215*f*, 266,
  266*f*, 269*f*
Need for achievement, 309–310
Need for affiliation, 310

Need for cognition, 531, 531*f*
Need for power, 310–311
Negative correlation, 31
Negatively framed messages, 444
Negative punishment, 180, 181*f*
Negative reinforcers, 180, 181*f*
Nembutal, 156*f*, 160
Neo-Freudian psychoanalysts, 391–393, 497
Neonates, 340–344
    defined, 340
    reflexes, 60, 340–341
    sensory development, 341–344, 342*f*, 343*f*
Nervous system, 60–64
    autonomic, 62–63, 63*f*, 316, 467
    central nervous system (CNS), 60–62, 61*f*
    evolutionary foundations, 63–64
    peripheral nervous system (PNS), 61*f*, 62
Neural receptors, 112
Neurofeedback, 81–82
Neurogenesis, 77
Neurons, 51–59
    action potential, 53, 53*f*, 54*f*
    defined, 51
    firing of, 52–55
    memory and, 214–215
    mirror, 54–55, 194, 195*f*
    motor (efferent), 62
    neurotransmitters, 56–58
    sensory (afferent), 62
    speed of transmission, 53–54
    structure of, 51–52, 52*f*
    synapses, 55*f*, 55–56
Neuroplasticity, 77–78, 78*f*
Neuroscience perspective, 48–85
    on anxiety disorders, 467, 467*f*
    behavioral neuroscience/neuroscientists, 6, 7*f*, 50, 132
    on behavioral treatment approaches, 502*f*
    biofeedback and, 81–82
    brain in, 68–83
    characteristics of, 17–18, 18*f*
    on cognitive treatment approaches, 505*f*
    on emotions, 318–319
    endocrine system in, 64–66
    in future of psychology, 23, 23*f*
    infant processing of facial expression, 343*f*
    key issues and controversies, 21*f*
    on language development, 264, 264*f*
    on memory, 213–216, 215*f*, 232, 233*f*
    on mood disorders, 473
    moral decisions in, 563*f*
    on need for sleep, 137*f*
    nervous system in, 60–64
    neurons in, 51–59
    observational learning in, 194, 195*f*
    on personality, 404*f*
    regulation of eating behavior, 302*f*
    representative participants in research, 42*f*
    on schizophrenia, 477*f*
    smoking as addiction, 437*f*, 437–438
    social neuroscience/neuroscientists and, 23, 551–552
    social skills and, 557*f*
    social support and stress, 431*f*
Neurosis, 496
Neuroticism, 396, 397, 397*f*, 496
Neurotransmitters, 56–58
    defined, 56
    types of, 56*f*, 56–58
Neutral stimulus, 170
Newborns. *See* Neonates

Nicotine, 155
    as addictive, 437–438
    in prenatal development, 337, 338*f*
Nightmares, 137–138
Night terrors, 142
Nondirective counseling, 508
Non-REM (NREM) sleep, 135, 136
Norepinephrine, coronary heart disease and, 435
Norm of reciprocity, 545
Norms, 277
    defined, 409
    race and ethnicity in establishing, 409–410
Note-taking, in improving memory, 234
Not-so-free samples, 545
Nutrition
    dieting and weight loss, 303
    in prenatal development, 337, 338*f*
Nutritionist, 300

O
Obedience, 546–547
    defined, 546
    Milgram experiments, 546–547
Obesity, 20, 296–303
    biological factors in regulation of hunger, 297–299
    culture and, 296–297, 298
    defined, 296–297
    dieting and weight loss, 303
    roots of, 300–301
    social factors in eating, 299–300
    stigma of, 298
    weight set point and, 299, 301
Object permanence, 352
Observable behavior versus internal mental processes, 21*f*, 22
Observation. *See* Naturalistic observation
Observational learning, 194–196, 501, 550
    aggression and, 195–196, 561
    defined, 194
    media violence and, 195–196
    as social cognitive approach, 194–196
Obsession, 465
Obsessive-compulsive disorder (OCD), 465–467, 467*f*
Occipital lobe, 74, 74*f*
Oedipal conflict, 388, 390
Olfactory cells, 108*f*, 109
On the Origin of Species (Darwin), 8
Openness to experience, 397, 397*f*
Operant conditioning, 177–191, 399
    animal research on, 177–187, 178*f*, 179*f*, 187*f*
    basics of, 178–187
    in behavioral treatment approaches, 500–501
    classical conditioning versus, 177, 187, 188*f*
    defined, 177
    discrimination, 184–185
    generalization, 185
    reinforcement, 178–184
    in saving lives, 185
    shaping, 186
    Thorndike's law of effect, 177–178
    token system, 500–501
Operational definition, 28
Opponent-process theory of color vision, 102
Optic chiasm, 98, 99*f*
Optic nerve, 97–98, 99*f*
Optimism, 445
Oral stage (Freud), 387*f*, 387–388

Organic mental disorders, 481
Organizational cues, in improving memory, 234
Otoliths, 107–108
Outgroups, 550–551
Ovaries, 65*f*
Overattention, 478
Overgeneralization, 259
Ovulation, 305
Oxycodone, 157*f*, 161
Oxytocin, 64–65

P
Pain
    gate-control theory of, 112
    managing, 113, 149
    skin senses, 110–112
Pancreas, 65*f*
Panic disorder, 464–465
Paranoid schizophrenia, 475*f*
Paraphilias, 481
Paraplegia, 62
Parasympathetic division, 61*f*, 62, 63*f*
Parathyroids, 65*f*
Parents. *See also* Fathers; Mothers
    parenting styles, 348–350
    single-parent families, 358, 372
Parietal lobe, 74, 74*f*
Parkinson's disease, 58, 77
Partial reinforcement, 182–183
Participants in research
    animals, 35*f*, 42–43. *See also* Animal research
    expectations of, 43–44
    random assignment, 34–35
    representative, 41, 42*f*
Passionate (or romantic) love, 556–558
Peers
    infant and childhood relationships, 347
    liking and interpersonal attraction, 555–556
    types of love, 556–558
Pendulum problem, 353–354
Perception, 116–126
    bottom-up processing, 118–119
    culture and, 124
    defined, 88, 89
    depth, 119–120, 124
    extrasensory (ESP), 125–126
    gestalt laws of organization, 116–117
    internal sense of direction, 122, 214, 215*f*, 266, 266*f*, 269*f*
    motion, 121–122
    multimodal, 114
    perceptual constancy, 120–121
    perceptual illusions, 122–123, 123*f*, 124*f*
    sensation versus, 88, 89, 128
    subliminal, 125
    top-down processing, 117–118
Perceptual constancy, 120–121
Perceptual disorders, 475
Peripheral-nerve stimulation, in pain management, 113
Peripheral nervous system (PNS), 61*f*, 62
Peripheral route processing, 530–531, 531*f*
Peripheral vision, 96
Permissive parents, 348–350, 349*f*
Personal fables, 364
Personality, 382–417
    assessing. *See* Psychological tests
    biological and evolutionary approaches, 401–404, 406*f*
    cancer and, 436
    comparing approaches, 406

coronary heart disease and, 434–435
    defined, 384
    gender differences and, 390
    genetic factors, 401–402
    hardy/resilient, 349, 429, 430
    humanistic approaches, 404–406, 406*f*
    learning approaches, 398–401, 406*f*
    psychodynamic approaches, 385–393, 406*f*
    trait approaches, 395–398, 406*f*
Personality disorders, 479–480
    defined, 479
    types, 479–480
Personality psychology, 6, 7*f*
Personal stressors, 422
Person-centered therapy, 507–508
Perspectives on psychology
    behavioral. *See* Behavioral perspective
    cognitive. *See* Cognitive perspective
    current, 16–19, 20
    future, 20, 23*f*, 23–24
    historical roots, 14–16
    humanistic. *See* Humanistic perspective
    neuroscience. *See* Neuroscience perspective
    psychodynamic. *See* Psychodynamic perspective
Persuasion, 529–533
    through advertising, 439, 530
    central/peripheral route processing in, 530–531
    in changing attitudes, 529–533
    need for cognition and, 531, 531*f*
    routes to, 530–531, 531*f*
PET (positron emission tomography), 68, 69, 69*f*, 77, 140, 318–319
Phallic stage (Freud), 387*f*, 388
PhD (doctor of philosophy) degree, 10*f*, 11
Phenobarbital, 156*f*, 160
Phenylketonuria (PKU), 336
Pheromones, 109
Phobia, 463–465
Phobic disorders, 463–464, 464*f*
Phonemes, 257, 258
Phonology, 257
Physical attractiveness, interpersonal attraction and, 556
Physical development
    adolescent period, 358–360
    adulthood period, 369–370, 373–374
    aging process and, 373–374
    infancy and childhood periods, 340–344, 341*f*, 344
    neonate period, 340–344
    reflexes, 60, 340–341
    sensory development, 341–344
    sexuality, 359*f*, 359–360
Physiological dependence, 152
Piaget's theory of cognitive development, 352–355
    concrete operational stage, 352*f*, 353
    formal operational stage, 352*f*, 353–354, 360
    preoperational stage, 352*f*, 352–353
    sensorimotor stage, 352, 352*f*
    stages versus continuous development, 355
Pineal gland, 65*f*
Pitch, 105–106
Pituitary gland, 64, 65*f*, 72*f*
Placebos, 44, 58
Place cells, 122
Place theory of hearing, 107
Play
    culture factors in, 347
    fathers versus mothers, 347

Pleasure principle, 386, 386f
PMS (premenstrual syndrome), 485–486
Pons, 70
Population, in survey research, 30, 36f
Positive correlation, 31
Positive illusions, 445
Positively framed messages, 444
Positive punishment, 180, 181f
Positive reinforcers, 180, 181f
Positron emission tomography (PET), 68, 69, 69f, 77, 140, 318–319
Postconventional morality, 361f
Posttraumatic stress disorder (PTSD), 172–173, 422–423, 467
Power, need for, 310–311
Practical intelligence, 270–271, 272f
Practice, in improving memory, 234
Preconscious, 385–386
Preconventional morality, 361f
Predisposition model of schizophrenia, 478
Prefrontal lobotomy, 519
Pregnancy. See also Prenatal development
   birth complications, 278
   conception, 333, 335
   fetal development, 335–338
   influences on fetus, 336–338, 338f
Prejudice
   defined, 549
   discrimination and, 549–554
   foundations of, 550–552
   measuring, 552
   reducing consequences of, 552–553
Premarital sex, 306
Premenstrual dysphoric disorder, 485–486
Prenatal development, 332–335
   basics of genetics, 333–334
   environmental influences, 337–338, 338f
   genetic influences, 336
   stages of earliest development, 335–336
Preoperational stage (Piaget), 352f, 352–353
Preterm infants, 336
Primacy effect, 211
Primary drives, 290
Primary reinforcers, 179
Priming, 220–221
Principle of conservation, 353, 354f
Prison guards, conformity to social roles, 543–544
Proactive interference, 230–231, 231f
Problem-focused coping, 428
Problems of inducing structure, 246, 248f
Problem solving, 245–254
   computers and, 244
   creativity and, 253–254
   critical thinking and, 255
   impediments to solutions, 251–253
   judgment, 250–251
   kinds of problems, 246–248, 248f
   preparation, 246–248
   production of solutions, 248–250
   Tower of Hanoi puzzle, 245f, 245–246, 250
Procedural memory, 211, 212f
Process schizophrenia, 476
Production of language, 258–259
Progesterone, 305
Program evaluation, 7f
Progressive Insurance, 168
Projection, as defense mechanism, 389f
Projective personality tests, 412–413

Prosocial behavior
   altruism and, 562
   defined, 561
   diffusion of responsibility and, 27–29, 32–38, 561–562
Prototypes, 243
Proximity, interpersonal attraction and, 555
Prozac, 517, 517f
Psychiatric social worker, 495f
Psychiatry, 495f
Psychoactive drugs, 152, 515–518
Psychoactive substance use disorder, 481
Psychoanalysis, 495f
   Freud and, 390, 391, 496–497
   neo-Freudians and, 391–393, 497
Psychoanalytic perspective
   on abnormal behavior, 455f, 456
   on mood disorders, 473
Psychoanalytic theory, 385–391
Psychodynamic approaches to personality, 385–393, 406f
   Adler and the other neo-Freudians, 392–393
   Freud's psychoanalytic theory, 385–391
   Horney's neo-Freudian perspective, 392
   Jung's collective unconscious, 391–392
   neo-Freudian psychoanalysts, 391–393
Psychodynamic perspective
   characteristics of, 18, 18f
   key issues and controversies, 21f
   treatment in, 496–498
Psychodynamic therapy, 496–498
   contemporary approaches, 497
   evaluating, 497–498
   psychoanalysis, 390–393, 495f, 496–497
Psychological dependence, 152
Psychological disorders, 450–525
   adolescent period, 364–366, 474, 480–481
   anxiety disorders, 463–468
   biomedical therapy in treating, 494, 515–520
   childhood disorders, 480–481
   classifying abnormal behavior, 458–460, 487
   community psychology in prevention, 521–522
   culture and, 483, 484–487
   dissociative disorders, 468–470, 487
   mood disorders, 470–474
   normal versus abnormal behavior, 453–462
   other disorders, 481
   personality disorders, 479–480
   perspectives on abnormality, 455–458
   prevalence and incidence, 483, 484f, 485f, 486
   schizophrenia, 58, 452, 474–478, 487, 490
   social and cultural context of, 484–487
   somatoform disorders, 468, 469f
   therapist selection, 495f, 522–523
   treatment, 149, 488, 492–525
Psychological research, 33–45
   animal research. See Animal research
   archival, 29, 36f
   avoiding experimental bias, 43–44
   case studies, 30, 36f
   correlational research, 31–32, 36f
   critical thinking and, 44
   developmental research techniques, 331–332
   diversity in, 41–42. See also Diversity
   ethics of, 40–44
   experimental research, 32–38, 36f

   naturalistic observation, 29–30, 36f
   scientific method as basis of, 5, 5f, 26–28
   social issues for, 20
   survey research, 30, 36f
Psychological tests, 30, 392, 396–398, 408–415, 552. See also Personality
   behavioral assessment, 413
   defined, 408
   evaluating, 414–415
   norms, 409–410
   projective methods, 412–413
   reliability, 408
   self-report measures, 410–412
   validity, 408
Psychologists, 5–9
   characteristics of, 10–11
   education of, 10f, 11
   PhD or PsyD degrees of, 10f, 11
   subfields, 6–9, 495f
   therapist selection, 495f, 522–523
   types of psychology professionals, 7f, 495f
Psychology
   career options, 10, 11, 12f. See also Career options
   current perspectives on, 16–19, 20
   defined, 5
   future of, 20, 23f, 23–24
   historical roots of, 14–16
   importance of, 20
   key issues and controversies, 21f, 21–22
   scientific method as basis, 5, 5f
   subfields of, 6–9, 495f
   women in, 10–11, 15, 16–17f, 361–362, 392, 393
   working at. See Career options; Psychologists
Psychology of women, 7f
Psychoneuroimmunology (PNI), 420, 427
Psychophysics, 89
Psychophysiological disorders, 424–425
Psychosexual stages, 387f, 387–388
Psychosocial development, 350–351, 362–363
Psychosurgery, 519–520
Psychotherapy, 495–514
   behavioral treatment approaches, 498–502
   choosing a therapist, 495f, 522–523
   cognitive treatment approaches, 502–505
   defined, 494
   eclectic approach, 494, 513
   evaluating, 510–513
   group therapies, 509–510
   humanistic therapy, 507–509
   interpersonal therapy, 509
   professionals offering, 495f
   psychodynamic therapy, 496–498
   racial and ethnic factors, 513
Psychoticism, 396
PsychWork. See Career options
PsyD (doctor of psychology) degree, 10f, 11
PTSD (posttraumatic stress disorder), 172–173, 422–423, 467
Puberty, 359
   depression and, 364–366, 474
Punishment
   negative, 180, 181f
   positive, 180, 181f
   pros and cons of, 181–182
   reinforcement versus, 180, 181f, 181–182
Pupils of eyes, 95f, 95–96
Purging, 301–303

R
Race
   in establishing norms, 409–410
   as factor in psychotherapy, 513
   of psychologists, 10–11
Racism, modern, 549
Random assignment to condition, 34–35
Rape/date rape, 156f
Rational-emotive behavior therapy, 503–504
Rationalization, as defense mechanism, 389f
Reaction formation, as defense mechanism, 389f
Reactive schizophrenia, 476
Reality principle, 386f, 386–387
Reasoning
   algorithms, 243
   heuristics, 243–245, 255
Rebound effect, 136
Recall, 218f, 218–219, 219f, 232–233
Recency effect, 211
Reciprocity-of-liking effect, 556
Recognition, 218–219
Reflexes, 60, 340–341
Reflex sympathetic dystrophy syndrome (RSDS), 110
Refraction, 95
Regression
   as defense mechanism, 389f
   schizophrenia as, 478
Rehabilitation counselor, 75
Rehearsal, 209, 234
Reinforcement, 178–184, 181f, 399
   punishment versus, 180, 181f, 181–182
   schedules of, 182–184
Reinforcers
   defined, 179
   negative, 180, 181f
   positive, 180, 181f
Relational learning style, 197f, 197–198
Relationship harmony, 400
Relaxation techniques
   to improve sleep, 145
   in pain management, 113
Reliability, 276–277, 408
REM (rapid eye movement) sleep, 134f, 135f, 135–136, 141, 142
Replication, 37–38
Representation, in problem solving, 246–248
Representativeness heuristic, 243–244
Repressed memories, 225, 469–470
Repression, as defense mechanism, 389, 389f
Research. See also Psychological research
   defined, 28
Residual schizophrenia, 475f
Resilience, 349, 429, 430
Resistance, 426
Resting state, 52
Retardation. See Intellectual disability (mental retardation)
Reticular formation, 70, 72f
Retina, 96, 97f, 97–98
Retrieval, 205, 205f, 218–219
Retroactive interference, 231
Retrograde amnesia, 232
Reuptake, 56
Risk-taking behavior, 404f
Ritalin, 216
Rites of passage, 366, 436
Rods of retina, 96, 97f, 97–98
Rohypnol, 156f, 160
Rooting reflex, 340
Rorschach test, 412f, 413
Rubella (German measles), 337, 338f
Russian language, 262

S

St. John's wort, 517
Sample, in survey research, 30, 36f
SAT exams, 276
Scalloping effect, 184
Schachter-Singer theory of emotion, 317f, 318
Schedules of reinforcement, 182–184
Schemas, 223, 534
Schizophrenia, 58, 474–478
  causes, 476–478
  characteristics, 474–476, 487
  coping with, 452, 490
  defined, 474
  onset, 476
  types, 475f
School psychology, 7f
Scientific method
  as basis of psychological research, 5, 5f, 26–28
  defined, 26
  hypotheses in, 28
  overview of, 26f
  theories in, 27–28
Seasonal affective disorder, 143, 143f
Seconal, 156f, 160
Secondary drives, 290
Secondary reinforcers, 179
Secondary traits, 396
Securely attached children, 346
Seeing eye dog trainer, 186
Selective serotonin reuptake inhibitors (SSRIs), 56, 505f, 516f, 516–517, 517f
Self-actualization, 293, 405
Self-defeating personality disorder, 484–485
Self-determination theory, 294
Self-efficacy, 399–400
Self-esteem, 445
  defined, 400
  in personality, 400, 401f
Self-fulfilling prophecy, 549–550
Self-help therapy, 163, 510
Self-report measures, 410–412
  defined, 410
  of depression, 471f
  of happiness, 446
  of need for cognition, 531f
  of personality, 396, 410–412, 486
  of prejudice, 552
  of stress, 425f
Self-serving bias, 537–538
Semantic memory, 211, 212f, 375
Semantic networks, 212–213, 213f
Semantics, 258
Semicircular canals, 107–108
Senility, 375–376
Sensation, 89–92
  absolute thresholds, 90–91
  defined, 88, 89
  difference thresholds, 91–92
  early sensory development, 341–344
  perception versus, 88, 89, 128
  sensory adaptation, 92
Sensitive periods, 336
Sensorimotor stage, 352, 352f
Sensory adaptation, 92
Sensory (afferent) neurons, 62
Sensory areas of cortex, 74, 74f, 75–76, 99f, 107
Sensory development, neonate period, 341–344
Sensory memory, 205–207, 206f, 207f
  defined, 206
  in three-system approach to memory, 205–206, 206f
Sequential research, 332
Serial position effect, 211

Serotonin, 57f, 58
Set point
  happiness, 445–446
  weight, 299, 301
Sexual behavior, 304–309
  bisexuality, 307–309
  heterosexuality, 306–307
  homosexuality, 307–309
  masturbation, 305
  sexually transmitted infection (STI), 337, 338f
  sexual problems and disorders, 481
  transsexualism, 309
Sexuality
  in adolescent development, 359f, 359–360
  aging process and, 369–370
  diversity of sexual behavior, 304–309
  human sexual response, 304–309
  psychosexual stages, 387f, 387–388
Sexually transmitted infection (STI), 337, 338f
Sexual orientation, 306–309
Shaping, 186, 314
Short-term memory, 207–209
  chunking, 208f, 208–209
  defined, 206
  long-term memory versus, 211
  rehearsal, 209
  in three-system approach to memory, 205–206, 206f
Sickle-cell anemia, 336
SIDS (sudden infant death syndrome), 142
Siemens Competition, 240
Signed language, 258f
Significant outcomes, 37
Similarity, interpersonal attraction and, 556
Single-parent families, 358, 372
Situational causes, 536–537
Situational type phobia, 464f
Situationism, 400
Sixteen Personality Factor Questionnaire (16PF), 396
Skinner box, 178, 179f
Skin senses, 110–112
  defined, 111
  pain, 110–112
  synesthesia, 113–114
Sleep, 132, 133–146
  amount needed, 136f, 136–137, 137f
  circadian rhythms, 143
  disturbances, 141–142
  dreams, 135–136, 137–141
  impact of sleep deprivation, 137
  improving, 145
  reasons for, 136–137
  REM sleep, 134f, 135f, 135–136, 141, 142
  stages, 134–136, 142
Sleep apnea, 142
Sleeptalking, 142, 142f
Sleep technologist, 142
Sleepwalking, 142, 142f
Slow cortical potentials, 71
Small intestine, 65f
Smart drugs, 216
Smell, 108–109, 113–114
Smoking, 436–439
  by adolescents, 436, 437, 437f, 438f
  by children, 439
  cognitive dissonance in, 533, 533f
  in developing countries, 439
  hypnosis to reduce, 149
  nicotine as stimulant, 155
  in prenatal development, 337, 338f
  quitting, 437–438
  reasons for, 436–437

Social cognitive approach, 194–196, 534–539
  attribution theory, 535–539
  impression formation, 534–535
  personality and, 399–400
  self-efficacy and, 399–400
  social cognition, defined, 534
  understanding what others are like, 534
Social development
  adolescent period, 361f, 362–363
  adolescent suicide, 364–366
  adulthood, 370–371, 376–377
  attachment and, 344–347
  child-care arrangements, 347–348
  Erikson's theory of psychosocial development, 350–351, 362–363
  infancy and childhood periods, 344–351
  parenting styles, 348–350
  peer relationships, 347
  stormy adolescence myth versus reality, 363–364
  in Vygotsky's view of cognitive development, 356
Social identity theory, 550
Social influence
  compliance, 544–546
  conformity, 541–544
  defined, 541
  obedience, 546–547
Social media, 20, 556
  adolescent use of, 364
  media violence and, 196
  narcissistic personality and, 398
Social neuroscience, 23, 551–552
Social phobia, 464f
Social psychology, 7f, 8, 23, 526–567
  aggression and, 559–561, 564
  attitude change in, 529–533
  compliance and, 544–546
  conformity and, 541–544
  defined, 528
  helping others and, 561–563
  interpersonal attraction and, 555–558
  obedience and, 546–547
  persuasion in, 529–533
  prejudice and discrimination and, 549–554
  social cognition in, 534–539
  stereotypes and, 549–550, 552–553
Social roles
  conformity to, 543–544
  mock prison experiments, 543–544
Social support
  coping with stress and, 431
  defined, 431
  in self-help groups, 163, 510
  in weight-loss process, 303
Social supporters, 542
Social workers, licensed, 10
Sociocultural perspective, on abnormal behavior, 455f, 457–458
Socioeconomic status (SES)
  impact of child-care arrangements on children, 348
  intelligence and, 281
  single-parent families and, 358, 372
Sociopathic personality, 479
Somatic division, 61f, 62
Somatoform disorders, 468, 469f
Somatosensory area of cortex, 74, 74f, 76f
Sopranos, The (TV program), 195
Sound
  defined, 104
  neonate perception of, 343–344
  physical aspects of, 105–108
  sensory memory, 206–207

synesthesia, 113–114
  theories of, 106–107
Sound localization, 104
Source amnesia, 221–222
Source traits, 396
South Africa, desired characteristics in a mate, 558, 558f
Spatial intelligence, 268, 269f
Specialization, hemispheric, 78–79
Specific phobias, 464f
Speech inflections, 240
Speech perception, 107
Spermarche, 359
Spinal cord, 60, 61f
Spirituality, coping with stress and, 431
Split-brain patients, 80–81
Spontaneous recovery, 173–174
Spontaneous remission, 511
Sport psychology, 7f
SSRIs (selective serotonin reuptake inhibitors), 56, 505f, 516f, 516–517, 517f
Stage 1 sleep, 134, 134f
Stage 2 sleep, 134, 134f
Stage 3 sleep, 134, 134f
Stage sleep, 134f, 142
Stage 4 sleep, 134
Stage 5/REM sleep, 134f, 135f, 135–136, 141, 142
Stages of sleep, 134f, 134–136
Standardized tests, 277
Stanford-Binet Intelligence Scale, 272f, 273–276
Startle reflex, 340–341
States of consciousness, 130–165
  altered, 132, 147–163
  consciousness, defined, 132
  cross-cultural routes to altered states, 150–151
  daydreams, 144, 144f
  drug use, 132, 152–163
  hypnosis, 113, 132, 147–149
  meditation, 132, 149–150
  sleep and dreams, 132, 133–146
Status
  conformity and, 542
  defined, 542
  socioeconomic. See Socioeconomic status (SES)
Stem cells, 77–78
Stereotypes
  defined, 549
  increased contact in reducing, 552–553
  as self-fulfilling prophecy, 549–550
Stereotype threat, 553
Stereotype vulnerability, 553
Steroids, 65–66, 66f, 157f
Stimulants, 154–156
  amphetamines, 155, 156f, 216
  cocaine, 155–156, 156f
Stimulus, defined, 89
Stimulus control training, 184–185
Stimulus discrimination, 174
Stimulus generalization, 174
Stimulus-response pairings, 170–175
STI (sexually transmitted infection), 337, 338f
Stomach, 65f
Storage, 205, 205f
Storytelling, cultural differences in memory, 225–226, 226f
Stress, 421–433
  categorizing stressors, 422–423
  consequences of, 427f
  coping with, 428–432
  cost of, 423–427
  defined, 421

Stress—*Cont.*
    general adaptation syndrome (GAS)
        model of, 426*f*, 426–427
    hardy/resilient personality, 349,
        429, 430
    learned helplessness and,
        429–430, 473
    nature of stressors, 421–422
    psychoneuroimmunology (PNI) and,
        420, 427
    resilience and, 349, 429, 430
    social support and, 431, 510
Stroke, 78*f*
Structuralism, 14–15
Subfields of psychology, 6–9, 495*f*
    basic questions for, 6–8
    expanding frontiers, 8–9
    lists of, 7*f*, 495*f*
Subgoals, in problem solving, 250, 255
Subjective well-being, 444–446
Sublimation, as defense
        mechanism, 389*f*
Subliminal perception, 125
Substance abuse counselor, 508
Substance P, 111
Sucking reflex, 340, 342
Sudden infant death syndrome
        (SIDS), 142
Suicide
    adolescent, 364–366
    post-traumatic stress disorder (PTSD)
        and, 422–423
    suicide prevention hotlines,
        366, 494
    warning signs, 366
Superego, 386*f*, 387
Supertasters, 109–110
Suprachiasmatic nucleus (SCN), 143
Surgery
    in pain management, 113
    psychosurgery, 519–520
Survey research, 30, 36*f*
Sympathetic division, 61*f*, 62
Synapses, 55*f*, 55–56
Synesthesia, 113–114
Syntax, 257
Syphilis, 337, 338*f*
Systematic desensitization, 499–500

T

Taste, 109, 110*f*, 113–114
Taste aversion, 175
Taste buds, 109, 109*f*
Tay-Sachs disease, 336
Telegraphic speech, 259
Television
    aggression and, 32, 32*f*, 195–196
    media-inspired copycat crimes,
        195–196
    observational learning and,
        195–196, 196*f*
    weight loss and, 303
Temperament, 402–403
    defined, 349
    parenting style and, 349
Temporal lobe, 74, 74*f*, 214
Teratogens, 337–338
Terminal buttons, 51

Terrorism, 20, 221
    stress and, 421–423, 422*f*
    World Trade Center terrorist attacks
        (2001), 421–423, 422*f*
Testes, 65*f*
Testing. *See* Assessment; Intelligence
        tests; Psychological tests; Self-
        report measures
Testosterone, 65–66, 66*f*
Test standardization, 411
Tetrahydrocannabinol (THC), 161–162
Thalamus, 72, 72*f*
That's-not-all technique, 545
Thematic Apperception Test (TAT),
        310, 413
Theories
    defined, 27
    in scientific method, 27–28
Theory of multiple intelligences, 268,
        269*f*, 272*f*
Thinking, 241–243
    concepts, 242–243
    defined, 241
    influence of language on, 261–262
    mental images, 241–242, 242*f*
Thorndike's law of effect, 177–178
Three-system approach to memory,
        205–206, 206*f*
Thresholds
    absolute, 90–91
    difference, 91–92
Thyroid, 65*f*
Tip-of-the-tongue phenomenon, 218
TMS (transcranial magnetic stimulation
        imaging), 68, 69*f*, 69–70, 519
Toilet training, 388
Token system, 500–501
Top-down processing, 117–118
Tower of Hanoi puzzle, 245*f*,
        245–246, 250
Trait theory, 395–398, 406*f*
    of Allport, 396
    Big Five Personality Traits,
        397, 397*f*
    of Cattell, 396
    defined, 395
    evaluating, 397
    of Eysenck, 396*f*
    narcissistic personality, 398, 480
    traits, defined, 395
Transcranial magnetic stimulation
        imaging (TMS), 68, 69*f*, 69–70, 519
Transference, 497
Transformation problems, 246, 248*f*
Transgenderism, 309
Transsexualism, 309
Traumatic memories, 518
Treatment of psychological disorders,
        488, 492–525
    behavioral treatment approaches,
        498–502
    biomedical therapy, 515–520
    cognitive treatment approaches,
        502–505
    drug therapy, 515–518
    in experimental research, 33
    psychodynamic treatment
        approaches, 496–498
Trichromatic theory of color vision,
        101–102

Trukese, navigational abilities, 266,
        266*f*, 269*f*
Trust-versus-mistrust stage (Erikson),
        353, 362*f*
Tryptophan, 145
Twin studies
    genetic factors in personality,
        402, 402*f*
    identical twins, 281*f*, 329, 329*f*, 331
    intelligence and, 281*f*
    nature-nurture issue in, 329, 331
    on sexual orientation, 307
Twitter, 20, 143, 143*f*
Type A behavior pattern, 434–435
Type B behavior pattern, 434–435

U

Ulysses (Joyce), 453
Umami, 109
Unanimity of group, 542–543
Unconditional positive regard, 405, 508
Unconditioned response (UCR),
        170, 172
Unconditioned stimulus (UCS), 170,
        172, 175
Unconscious
    conscious versus, 21*f*, 22
    in Freud's psychoanalytic theory,
        385–386, 498
    in Jung's collective unconscious,
        391–392
Unconscious wish fulfillment theory,
        139*f*, 139–140
Underattention, 478
Undifferentiated schizophrenia, 475*f*
Uninvolved parents, 349*f*, 349–350
Universal grammar, 260
Uplifts, 423, 424*f*

V

Validity, 276, 408
Valium, 57
Variable-interval schedule of
        reinforcement, 183*f*, 184
Variable-ratio schedule of
        reinforcement, 183*f*, 183–184
Variables
    defined, 31
    independent/dependent, 33–34
Vernix, 340
Vestibular system, 107–108
Viability, 335
Video games, observational learning
        and, 196
Violence. *See* Aggression
Virtual lesions, 69–70
Visceral experience, 316–318
Visible spectrum, 94*f*
Vision, 94–103
    blindsight, 88
    blind spot, 97–98, 98*f*
    color vision/color blindness,
        100–102, 343
    culture and perception, 124
    depth perception, 119–120, 124
    gestalt laws of organization, 116–117

    light waves in, 94, 94*f*
    motion perception, 121–122
    neonate development of,
        341–343, 342*f*
    perceptual constancy, 120–121
    processing visual images, 98–99, 100*f*
    retina, 96, 97*f*, 97–98
    seeing eye dog trainer, 186
    sending message from eye to brain,
        96–98
    sensory memory, 206–207, 207*f*
    structure of eye, 95–96
    synesthesia, 113–114
    visual illusions, 122–123, 124*f*
Visual area of cortex, 74*f*, 76, 99*f*
Visual illusions, 122–123, 124*f*
Visual store, 210
Vomeronasal organ, 109
Voodoo death, 62
Vygotsky's view of cognitive
        development, 356

W

Waking consciousness, 132
Walt Disney Company, 530
Washoe (chimpanzee), 262
Water lily problem, 249–250
Wear-and-tear theories of aging,
        373–374
Weber's law, 91–92, 114
Wechsler Adult Intelligence Scale-IV
        (WAIS-IV), 275–276
Wechsler Intelligence Scale for Children-IV
        (WISC-IV), 275–276
Weight set point, 299, 301
Wernicke's aphasia, 76–77
Withdrawal, 476
Women in psychology, 10–11, 15, 16–17*f*,
        361–362, 363, 392, 393
Working memory, 209–210, 210*f*
Workplace
    adult roles and, 372
    child-care arrangements, 348, 348*f*
    psychological testing, 409, 414–415
    single-parent families, 358, 372
    working at psychology, 9–12. *See also*
        Career options; Psychologists
World Health Organization (WHO)
    mental health difficulties, 483, 485*f*
    obesity and, 296
    smoking and, 439

X

X chromosomes, 333–334

Y

Y chromosomes, 333–334

W

Zone of proximal development
        (ZPD), 356
Zygotes, 335